The Basic
Writings
of
Jonathan Swift

THE BASIC
WRITINGS
OF
JONATHAN SWIFT

*Selected and with an
Introduction by Claude Rawson*

Notes by Ian Higgins

THE MODERN LIBRARY
NEW YORK

CONTENTS

Introduction by Claude Rawson   ix

Chonology   xxxi

A Note on the Text   xxxvii

(Dates refer, respectively, to composition and first publication. Question marks
denote indeterminacy. A single date refers to first publication.)

I. A TALE OF A TUB   1

A Tale of a Tub (1704)   3

A Full and True Account of the Battel Fought last Friday, Between
    the Antient and the Modern Books in St. James's Library   115

A Discourse Concerning the Mechanical Operation of the Spirit
    in a Letter to a Friend. A Fragment.   141

II. EARLY WRITINGS ON RELIGION   161

The Sentiments of a Church-of-England Man, with Respect
    to Religion and Government (1708, 1711)   163

An Argument to Prove, That the Abolishing of Christianity
    in England, May, as Things now Stand, be attended with some
    Inconveniencies, and perhaps, not produce those many good
    Effects proposed thereby (1708, 1711)   187

A Project for the Advancement of Religion, and the Reformation
    of Manners (1709)   201

III. ENGLISH POLITICAL WRITINGS   221

From *The Examiner*, November 23, 1710   223

A short Character of his Excellency Thomas Earl of Wharton,
    Lord Lieutenant of Ireland (1710)   229

The Importance of the Guardian Considered, in a Second Letter
    to the Bailiff of Stockbridge (1713)   237

IV. MISCELLANEOUS PROSE WRITINGS 257

Mr. C——ns's Discourse of Free-Thinking, Put into plain English,
by way of Abstract, for the Use of the Poor (1713) 259

Some Thoughts on Free-Thinking (?, 1765) 277

A Letter to a Young Lady, on her Marriage (1723, 1727) 279

V. WRITINGS ON IRELAND 289

The Story of the Injured Lady. Written by Herself. In a Letter
to her Friend, with his Answer. (1707, 1746) 291

A Proposal for the Universal use of Irish Manufacture, in Cloaths
and Furniture of Houses, &c. Utterly Rejecting and
Renouncing Every Thing wearable that comes from England (1720) 299

Causes of the Wretched Condition of Ireland (1715, 1762) 307

From *The Drapier's Letters* 318

    Letter I. A Letter to the Tradesmen, Shop-Keepers, Farmers, and
      Country-People in General, of the Kingdom of Ireland (1724) 318

    Letter IV. To the Whole People of Ireland (1724)

A Short View of the State of Ireland (1728) 338

A Modest Proposal for Preventing the Children of poor People
in Ireland, from being a Burden to their Parents or Country;
and for making them beneficial to the Publick (1729) 345

A Proposal for giving Badges to the Beggars in all the Parishes
of Dublin. By the Dean of St. Patrick's. (1737) 355

VI. GULLIVER'S TRAVELS (1726) 365

VII. PERSONAL WRITINGS 629

Of Mean and Great Figures Made by Several Persons (?, 1765) 631

Family of Swift (?, 1765) 635

On the Death of Mrs. Johnson, [Stella.] (1727, 1765) 643

Thoughts on Various Subjects (1711) 651

Thoughts on Religion (?, 1765) 655

VIII. PARODIES, HOAXES, AND SOTTISIERS, ETC. 659

A Meditation upon a Broom-Stick: According to The Style and
Manner of the Honourable Robert Boyle's Meditations (1703, 1710) 661

From *The Bickerstaff Papers* 665

Predictions for the Year 1708 (1708)   667
The Accomplishment of the First of Mr. Bickerstaff's Predictions.
    Being an Account of the Death of Mr. Partrige, the Almanack-maker,
    upon the 29th Inst. (1708)   675
A Vindication of Isaac Bickerstaff, Esq; Against What is objected to him
    by Mr. Partrige, in his Almanack for the present Year 1709. (1708)   678
A Famous Prediction of Merlin, the British Wizard, Written above
    a thousand Years ago, and relating to the Year 1709. (1709)   683

From A Compleat Collection of genteel and Ingenious Conversation,
    According to the Most polite Mode and Method, now used at court,
    and in the best Companies of England. [Second dialogue] (1738)   687

The Last Speech and Dying Words of Ebenezor Elliston,
    who was Executed the Second Day of May, 1722 (1722)   711

Directions to Servants (1745)   717

IX. POEMS   769

Verses Wrote in a Lady's Ivory Table-Book (1698, 1711)   771
*To Their Excellencies the Lords Justices of Ireland. The Humble Petition
    of Francis Harris, Who must Starve, and Die a Maid if it miscarries*
    (1701, 1711)   772
Baucis and Philemon. Imitated, From the Eighth Book of Ovid (1706, 1709)   774
A Description of the Morning (1709)   779
A Description of a City Shower (1710)   780
Cadenus and Vanessa (1713?, 1726)   782
The Author upon Himself (1714, 1735)   806
Mary the Cook-Maid's Letter to Dr. Sheridan (1718, 1732)   808
On Stella's Birth-day (1719, 1728)   809
Phillis, or The Progress of Love (1719, 1728)   810
The Progress of Beauty (1719, 1728)   813
The Progress of Poetry (1720, 1728)   817
To Stella, Visiting me in my Sickness (1720, 1728)   818
To Stella, Who Collected and Transcribed his Poems (1720?, 1728)   822
Verses to Vanessa (1720, 1814)   826
Stella's Birth-day (1721, 1728)   827
To Stella on her Birth-day (1722, 1766)   829
A Satirical Elegy On the Death of a late Famous General (1722, 1764)   829
The Progress of Marriage (1722, 1765)   830
Stella's Birth-Day. A great Bottle of Wine, long buried, being that Day dug up.
    (1723, 1728)   835
Stella at Wood-Park, A House of Charles Ford, Esq; eight miles from Dublin
    (1723, 1735)   838
*To Stella [Written on the Day of her Birth, but not on the Subject,
    when I was sick in bed.]* (1724, 1765)   841

Prometheus, A Poem (1724)   842

Stella's Birth-day (1725, 1728)   844

On Wood the Iron-monger (1725, 1735)   846

A Receipt to Restore Stella's Youth (1725, 1735)   847

Stella's Birth-day (1727, 1728)   848

Clever Tom Clinch going to be hanged (1726?, 1735)   851

Holyhead. Sept. 25, 1727 (1727, 1882)   852

Irel.ᵈ (1727, 1882)   853

Directions for a Birth-day Song (1729, 1765)   855

A Dialogue between an eminent Lawyer and Dr. Swift Dean of St. Patrick's,
   being an allusion to the first Satire of the second book of Horace (1729, 1755)   862

Traulus (1730)   864

The Lady's Dressing Room (1730, 1732)   869

A Beautiful Young Nymph Going to Bed (1731?, 1734)   873

Strephon and Chloe (1731, 1734)   875

Cassinus and Peter, a Tragical Elegy (1731, 1734)   884

To Mr. Gay on his being Steward to the Duke of Queensberry (1731, 1735)   887

Verses on the Death of Dr. Swift, D.S.P.D. Occasioned By reading a Maxim
   in Rochefoucault (1731, 1733)   892

An Epistle to a Lady (1732?, 1733)   908

On Poetry: A Rapsody (1733?)   916

The Yahoo's Overthrow (1734, 1765)   930

A Character, Panegyric, and Description of the Legion Club (1736)   933

Verses made for Women who cry Apples, &c. (?, 1746)   940

X. SELECTED CORRESPONDENCE   943

From *Journal to Stella*, Letter VI: Swift to Esther Johnson and
   Rebecca Dingley, 10 October 1710   945

From *Journal to Stella*, Letter XXXII: Swift to Esther Johnson and
   Rebecca Dingley, 9 October 1711   950

Swift to Alexander Pope, 29 September 1725   951

Swift to Alexander Pope, 26 November 1725   953

Swift to Charles Wogan, July–2 August 1732   953

Swift to William Pulteney, 12 May 1735   957

Notes   959

Further Reading   1017

Index of Short Titles   1023

Index of First Lines   1027

INTRODUCTION

Claude Rawson

Jonathan Swift was born in Dublin on November 30, 1667, of English parents. His father had recently died. He was educated at Kilkenny School and Trinity College, Dublin. In 1689 he went to live at Moor Park in Surrey, and intermittently served as secretary to its owner, Sir William Temple, a retired diplomat and author, until Temple's death in 1699. Swift felt that his career did not prosper under Temple's patronage. In 1694, he left Temple's household for a time and took orders. He acquired his first parish at Kilroot, near Belfast, Northern Ireland, in 1695, in a largely Presbyterian district, where he was unhappy. He returned to Moor Park, where he wrote most of *A Tale of a Tub*, though it was not published until 1704.

At Moor Park, he formed a deep friendship with Esther Johnson (1681–1728), the daughter of Temple's housekeeper. This friendship is reflected in the playful letters known as the *Journal to Stella* and in the series of poems he later wrote on her birthday and other occasions, the closest Swift ever came to writing love poems. The name "Stella" was taken from Sir Philip Sidney's sonnet sequence *Astrophel and Stella* (c. 1582). The compliments Swift paid to Stella's beauties of body and mind belong to a tradition of love poetry that Swift generally mocked, though Stella gets a gruffly tender version of this. We don't know the exact nature of their friendship, but the night she died, on January 28, 1728, Swift wrote perhaps the most affecting personal statement of his life:

> This day, being Sunday, January 28th, 1727–8, about eight o'clock at night, a servant brought me a note, with an account of the death of the truest,

most virtuous, and valuable friend, that I, or perhaps any other person ever was blessed with. She expired about six in the evening of this day; and, as soon as I am left alone, which is about eleven at night, I resolve, for my own satisfaction, to say something of her life and character.

She was born at Richmond in Surrey on the thirteenth day of March, in the year 1681. Her father was a younger brother of a good family in Nottinghamshire, her mother of a lower degree; and indeed she had little to boast of her birth. I knew her from six years old, and had some share in her education, by directing what books she should read, and perpetually instructing her in the principles of honour and virtue; from which she never swerved in any one action or moment of her life. She was sickly from her childhood until about the age of fifteen: But then grew into perfect health, and was looked upon as one of the most beautiful, graceful, and agreeable young women in London, only a little too fat. Her hair was blacker than a raven, and every feature of her face in perfection....

The friendship with Stella followed a pattern which may also be detected in his friendship with Esther Vanhomrigh (1688–1723), for whom Swift invented the name "Vanessa," which has since become a common personal name. In both, a strong teacher-pupil bond acted as a frame for a relationship whose erotic content was full of mystification and teasing secrecy. Swift taught that qualities of mind, not physical beauty, are the surest foundation of love, and denounced social conventions which treated women alternately as goddesses and decorative idiots. Swift was ahead of his time in insisting that women deserved educating in the same way as men, and were capable (more or less) of the same intellectual achievements.

Swift and Vanessa met in 1707 or 1708. Vanessa fell in love with Swift, whose poem *Cadenus and Vanessa* ("Cadenus" is an anagram of *decanus* or dean) tells the story of an older man disconcerted by the love of a beautiful young woman. Its somewhat self-serving implication is that Vanessa learned from Swift's own lessons to love those qualities of intellect that distinguished both her and him from the shallow lovers sung by the poets or approved by social convention. *Cadenus and Vanessa* was probably written around 1713, but was not published until 1726, a few months before *Gulliver's Travels,* early drafts of which Vanessa had read in manuscript. Their friendship probably ended in 1722, and Vanessa died the following year.

During the years 1699–1710, as a clergyman of the Church of Ireland (i.e. the Anglican Church in Ireland), Swift traveled to England and wrote on religious and ecclesiastical topics. He jealously guarded the interests of the national church. His *Sentiments of a Church-of-England Man, with Respect to Religion and Government* (1708, published 1711) is perhaps the most comprehensive summary of his views on matters of church and state. *An Argument Against Abolishing Christianity* (1708, published 1711) is a brilliant and inventive satirical fantasy. On the other hand, *A Project for the Advancement of Religion* (1709), sometimes wishfully read as ironic, especially for its (not uncommon) view that hypocrisy is preferable to openly vicious behavior, seems a sober hard-line statement, disconcerting to modern readers. He became friendly with the Whig politician-journalists Addison and Steele, and helped the latter to start the *Tatler,* which printed two of Swift's best-known early poems, "A Description of the Morning" (1709) and "A Description of a City-Shower" (1710). Swift was initially aligned with the Whig lords whom he defended in the *Contests and Dissensions in Athens and Rome* (1701; their leader Lord Somers, to whom *A Tale of a Tub* was dedicated, was later to be fiercely attacked in Swift's posthumous *History of the Four Last Years of the Queen*). But he was closer to a Tory view of the prerogatives of the Church, and in the period 1710–14 became identified with the moderate Tory-led government of Robert Harley, created Earl of Oxford in 1711.

In these years Swift was, for the only time in his life, close to the center of political power. He became editor of the *Examiner* in 1710, supporting Harley's ministry. He wrote a series of important pamphlets in the closing years of the War of Spanish Succession defending a policy of peace with France. His writings of this period included the vitriolic *Short Character of Thomas Earl of Wharton* (1710); *The Conduct of the Allies* (1711); two attacks on Steele, *The Importance of the Guardian Considered* (1713) and *The Publick Spirit of the Whigs* (1714), which ended their friendship; and the parody *Mr. Collins's Discourse of Free-Thinking, Put into Plain English, by Way of Abstract, for the Use of the Poor* (1713), which is one of the best of his lesser-known ironic works. In this period, together with a small group of friends, including Alexander Pope (1688–1744) and John Gay (1685–1732), Swift became a founder member of the Scriblerus Club, one of England's most brilliant literary coteries. The group had a relatively short existence, but the Scriblerians remained in personal touch or correspondence, and some of their best works are the aftermath of their intellectual exchanges. *Gulliver's Travels* (1726), Gay's *Beggar's Opera* (1728), and Pope's *Dunciad* (1728–43), which is addressed to Swift, are all products of their reciprocal encouragement and complicity.

Swift's participation in Scriblerian meetings ceased in 1713, when he was made Dean of St. Patrick's Cathedral in Dublin, a promotion he found bitterly disappointing. He had hoped to be made a bishop, and in England rather than Ireland. He felt that this outcome was due to the Queen's hostility, and to the reputation of *A Tale of a Tub* for irreligious tendencies. Queen Anne's death in 1714, moreover, ended the Tory administration to which Swift's political fortunes were tied. From then on, Swift was either outside politics or in political opposition. He lived in Ireland thereafter, occasionally visiting England, as when he came to arrange for the publication of *Gulliver's Travels* in 1726. The long years of what he regarded as exile were those of his greatest achievements, as a writer and a political activist. His main Irish writings belong to the 1720s and 1730s, as do his prose masterpieces other than the *Tale*, and the bulk of his best poetry.

Swift developed the disease now known as Ménière's syndrome, an illness of the inner ear which caused dizziness. He did not understand the symptoms, and mistakenly thought he was going mad. In his seventies, however, he became senile, and was declared of unsound mind in 1742. A lurid mythology of his descent into madness took root, and Samuel Johnson wrote in his *Vanity of Human Wishes* (1749) that Swift expired a driveler and a show. This crude scenario is sometimes associated with a dubious stereotype of titanic misanthropy, and with the reputed "Juvenalian" intensity of Swift's writings. In fact, Swift carefully avoided titanic pretensions, as well as the style of Juvenalian denunciation. The sad disintegration of his later years was a private event. He died on October 19, 1745.

———

A Tale of a Tub, with the *Battle of the Books* and the *Discourse Concerning the Mechanical Operation of the Spirit*, appeared anonymously in 1704. Most of Swift's major prose writings, including the *Drapier's Letters*, *Gulliver's Travels*, and *A Modest Proposal*, appeared anonymously or pseudonymously. He had a strong penchant for mystification. In addition to his temperamental guardedness, he also shared a common feeling that it was ungentlemanly to appear in print. Since many of his works contained elements that seemed politically subversive or personally offensive, there must also have been anxieties of a more practical kind. But the *Tale* was never publicly acknowledged in any way. It did not appear in any authorized lifetime edition of his works—unlike *Gulliver's Travels*, for example, which was republished in the major 1735 edition of his *Works*, in a carefully revised and extended version which nevertheless remained formally or ostensibly pseudonymous.

Swift was extremely proud of the *Tale,* and raged inwardly when he saw it, or parts of it, ascribed to others. He is said later in life to have exclaimed: "Good God! What a genius I had when I wrote that book." Its final form, in which it is now generally read, was not arrived at until the fifth edition of 1710. Its tearaway parody, the elusive virtuosity of its irony, its intimate elaborations of self-mockery and self-consciousness, its jeering mimicry of the self-centeredness of "modern" writing, its plethora of prefatory matter and its soberly signposted digressions, look forward to Sterne's *Tristram Shandy,* to the self-conscious broodings of some Beckettian heroes, and to the posturing of Norman Mailer's *Advertisements for Myself.* None of these books, nor anything resembling them, existed in Swift's time. He picked up an intuitive sense of these forthcoming modes of modern writing from scattered hints in authors he disliked, especially Dryden. But in throwing himself into a future he would have disliked intensely, Swift wrote the first, and one of the best, books in a genre he virtually created by parodying it in advance.

The last thing Swift would have wanted to be was a modern, and it is a tribute to the energy of his imaginative participation in his own rejectionist intuitions that he was used and sometimes celebrated as a model by later writers, from Sterne to Joyce, Beckett, and Nabokov, and from Sade to the Surrealists and the literature of "cruelty." If the *Tale* had not existed, *Finnegans Wake, Watt,* and *Pale Fire* would not exist in their present form. Swift's overt purposes, in the *Tale* and elsewhere, were to arrest the filthy modern tide of which these works would have seemed an example. The book affirms the cultural rule of law represented by the classical tradition, as well as law and order in religion and society, all seen as bulwarks against the dangerous and perverse spirit of innovation. But it was itself an innovative work, sometimes considered dangerous and perverse.

The *Tale,* along with the *Battle of the Books,* was the most brilliant literary achievement of the so-called quarrel of the Ancients and Moderns. It is hard to think of a comparable imaginative contribution to what was mainly a discursive polemic, obsessively pursued for generations all over learned Europe. The history or prehistory of this *querelle* (best known in the French form of the word) can be traced back to the Renaissance. The feeling of intellectual liberation created by the rediscovery of the philosophers and poets of Greece and Rome also engendered a questioning of the value of the classical models which helped make the liberation possible in the first place. Did the new freedom of mind and endeavor mean that the models themselves could be confronted in a critical spirit, or were they to be thought of as unsurpassable masterpieces which modern writers could only hope to imitate from a distance? Were modern achievements capable of excelling them, by accepting the old models and improving on them, or else by striking out in new directions, for example in experimental science.

The *Tale* proceeds on two parallel or alternating tracks. One of these, the story of the brothers, an allegorical history of Christianity, is described as a satire on abuses in religion. The other, mainly in the "digressions," is offered as a satire on modern learning. The religious satire attacks sectarian groups, most specifically the Dissenters. Their chief vice is a self-sufficiency that exalts the individual worshiper or small congregation, their claims to inner light, their emphasis on private conscience, their spontaneous accesses of devotion, unchecked by tradition and institutional authority. Corresponding to them on a secular plane are the journalists, literary hacks, and pedants satirized in the digressions, with their cult of the immediate moment and their wayward and willful affirmations of self. Both groups are seen as surrendering to the flow of irrational feeling, and the usual word for this abandonment of rational control is "enthusiasm" (then mainly a term of abuse). This is the state described in the Digression on Madness, in which the "imagination" overwhelms reason, the senses, and the common forms of conduct and thought. "Enthusiastic" worship is a principal preoccupation of the *Discourse Concerning the Mechanical Operation of the Spirit*, the second or "religious" appendage to the *Tale*. The worshipers are shown as manipulated by unscrupulous preachers, who fan the devotional excitability of their flock into orgiastic states of sexual lewdness, a frequent accusation against the Puritan sects. It is important to recognize that these lewd devotions are not represented as mainly hypocritical. The mechanical operators are self-deceived, of course, but fraught with a hideous sincerity. That, for Swift, is their real danger.

———

Gulliver's Travels (1726) is the work by which Swift is best known throughout the world. It has been translated into most languages, and often, in bowdlerized form, published as a children's book. It is, however, one of the harshest anatomies of the human condition ever written. It is also amusing, with a wit and comic sense that enter into disconcerting interactions with the radical bleakness of the work's general outlook. In the first two books, Gulliver visits symmetrically contrasted societies, the first (Lilliput) consisting of people six inches high, the second (Brobdingnag) of giants who tower over Gulliver in exactly the proportions by which Europeans tower over Lilliputians. Gulliver's contempt for the minuscule Lilliputians, who disgrace themselves by presuming to behave like full-sized people and who share in all human follies and depravities, comes home to roost when he realizes that he is himself a Lilliputian in the eyes of the Brobdingnagians. When Gulliver tells the king of Brobdingnag about European ways, the king, in a famous outburst, concludes "the Bulk of your Natives, to be the most pernicious Race of little odious Vermin that Nature ever suffered to crawl upon the Surface of the Earth."

Lilliput is a society which had once been run on decent principles, and has since degenerated. Brobdingnag was once a troubled and politically contentious land whose institutions have been salvaged by a wise monarchy. Between them they show a sense of the cyclical movement of human societies, except that for Swift, as for Plato, there is an implicit understanding that cycles tend more usually toward deterioration than improvement. *Gulliver's Travels* offers little prospect of improvement or progress in human affairs. The pairing of the two societies, and the arithmetically exact and symmetrical physical proportions of their difference from humans, depend for part of their effect on the discoveries of the microscope and telescope. By drawing attention to unexpected scales of vision, Swift is able to exploit tricks of perspective that are damaging to human self-importance, and to any complacency that may be felt about the human form divine. But the pairing also shows Swift putting humanity, including his readers and himself, in a characteristic bind. The discredit falls on real-life humans whichever society they compare themselves to: bad because like Lilliput, and bad because unlike Brobdingnag.

Book III, which breaks away from this particular schematism, offers a series of societies allegorizing various aspects of social, intellectual, and political viciousness, including a parable of English tyranny over Ireland. It also contains an otherworldly country in which we are shown unillusioned portrayals of the illustrious dead. The climactic episode is a visit to the Struldbruggs, a people who have perpetual life without perpetual youth. The result is a moral and physical degeneration that is a *donnée* of their condition, producing incurable debilities and depravities which they cannot help, but which come over as part of the guilt of being who they are. Although Book III may seem loose and episodic, the Struldbruggs provide a bridge to the more absolute world of Book IV, whose subject is the guilt of being merely human. In all the previous books human depravity is a matter of specific badnesses of character or behavior: pride, greed, lechery, political and military abuses. These appear also in Book IV, but in the humanoid Yahoos of this final part it is made clear that the condition of being a Yahoo is itself culpable, irrespective of particular doings. This incorporates a kind of secular version of original sin, for which the condition of the decaying Struldbruggs gives a partial prefiguration. Thus even good humans, like the Portuguese Captain who rescues Gulliver and treats him well, are nevertheless, definitionally, Yahoos.

Gulliver is gradually trapped into this realization. The Yahoos have "perfect" human bodies, and a Yahoo female lusts after Gulliver, a classic sign of biological kinship. They are originally shown as having the generic features of "all savage Nations," with some emphasis on American Indians, still in some ways the "typical" savages of travel writers, and on the Irish, who were often portrayed as resembling Indians. But everything we read about their behavior enforces the idea that all humanity is implicated in the indictment. It is a habitual trick of Swift's to identify a despised subgroup and then to assimilate humanity to it, in a portrait not intended to be flattering to either side.

The Houyhnhnms, a nation of horse-shaped rational creatures who rule over the Yahoos, are an uncompromisingly severe, but also highly traditional, example of a "good" society, derived in part from the Sparta of Lycurgus, and from Plato's *Republic*, More's *Utopia*, and Montaigne's essay "Of Cannibals." We are not invited to feel affection for the Houyhnhnms, but coerced into acknowledging that their virtues are those of truly rational beings, unattainable to humans. The irony is that humans believe that it is they who, in comparison with other creatures, are the rational animals. The logic treatises studied in universities all over Europe traditionally propounded this definition, often using horses as the type of a highly developed animal which nevertheless fails the test of reason. This contrast of man and horse was thus a textbook commonplace. In Samuel Butler's *Hudibras* (1663–80), a favorite of Swift's, the hero, who "was in *Logick* a great Critick," would

> undertake to prove by force
> Of Argument, a Man's no Horse.

The Houyhnhnms are partly designed to stand this pairing on its head. This is clear from the letter Swift wrote to Pope on September 29, 1725, where he speaks of disproving the definition of man as an *animal rationale*. Swift's point is made by a cunning and poetically effective sleight-of-hand, which consists of sliding over the fact that he is using the words "reason" and "rational" in a different sense from the one implied by the definition. When men are defined as rational animals, the definition implies no more than a basic acknowledgment of the cognitive powers which we believe animals lack. The definition in no way pretends to the high ideal of "rational" living embodied in the Houyhnhnms' nature and institutions. Failure to acknowledge this half-buried but ostentatiously implicit pun, a calculated verbal slippage, has led to extraordinary paper wars in the late Ph.D. era.

The fact that the Yahoos are like "all savage Nations" shows no great admiration for the "primitive" peoples about whom Swift read in the travel books *Gulliver's Travels* mimics, and among whom Swift, like Spenser, Camden, and other English writers, professed to include the "savage" Irish. But there is no corresponding admiration for the European powers who invade, plunder, and kill such peoples in the name of a higher Christian civilization, as the indignant diatribe in the final chapter of Book IV makes clear. The European conqueror is just as Yahoo as the savage he conquers, and sometimes more so. When the Houyhnhnm Assembly periodically debates "Whether the *Yahoos* should be exterminated from the Face of the Earth," Swift is recalling God's announcement before Noah's Flood: "I will destroy man whom I have created from the face of the earth" (Gen. 6:7). Some have seen the Houyhnhnms' proposal as evidence of their Hitlerian instincts, disowned by Swift. By the logic of this view, Swift would have to be thought to have the same opinion of God, whose wording the Houyhnhnms were appropriating. It seems more likely that Swift's point is that the Yahoos, in the Houyhnhnms' eyes, deserved the punishment, much as humanity did in God's.

By the time *Gulliver's Travels* appeared, Swift had been writing on Irish affairs for several years. If the Yahoos of Book IV are in part a portrayal of the savage Irish, Book III strongly denounces English tyranny over its smaller and dependent kingdom. The latter denunciation is part of a consistent stance, which has earned Swift his honored place among the heroes of Ireland's liberation. Swift's standing as an Irish patriot, however, had little to do with his feelings about the "savage" natives, whose cause he did not champion and to whom he did not usually give a good press. This reflects a paradox about Anglo-Irish culture, as well as contradictions inherent in Swift's personal temperament and outlook.

The most eloquent tribute to Swift by a patriot of the Irish Free State was Yeats's poem of 1930, "Swift's Epitaph":

> Swift has sailed into his rest;
> Savage indignation there
> Cannot lacerate his breast.
> Imitate him if you dare,
> World-besotted traveller; he
> Served human liberty.

This tribute, from one great Irishman to another, embodies many of the familiar features by which Swift is traditionally recognized: the "savage indignation" of the merciless satirist, the self-tormenting "conjured spirit," the champion of "human liberty." The portrait is paradoxical and in some ways misleading. "Savage indignation" does not accurately describe his writings, few if any of which adopt the tone of fiercely righteous denunciation implied by the phrase. Swift is indeed traditionally thought of as the English Juvenal, in contrast to his friend Pope, who ostentatiously modeled himself on the more urbane Horace. But it is Swift who wrote in a low key, declaring, in "An Epistle to a Lady," that he declined the "lofty Stile." He preferred, for his harsh ironies, a mode of downbeat ridicule which he himself thought of as Horatian. It is Pope who, even in his *Imitations of Horace,* sometimes adopted accents of exhilarated majesty which, as critics have noticed, sometimes approximate to a Juvenalian loftiness.

Similarly, hardly any, even of his most personal and unpublished writings, show any sign of Swift "lacerating his breast." As to serving human liberty, he was authoritarian and conservative in his social outlook and political convictions. The very style of Yeats's epitaph, with its fervid celebrative glow, was alien to anything we would readily expect from Swift's pen. It is an example of precisely that lofty style in which he said he would make "a Figure scurvy." The lines are splendid, but it would be hard for a reader familiar with Swift's tone and manner not to think that Swift might be embarrassed at being associated with them.

And yet, as is well known, Yeats's poem is almost a word-for-word translation of the Latin epitaph Swift composed for his own grave, possibly with Juvenal in his thoughts, and which can be seen, carved in stone, in St. Patrick's Cathedral in Dublin, of which Swift was dean:

Hic depositum est Corpus
JONATHAN SWIFT ...,
Ubi saeva Indignatio
Ulterius
Cor lacerare nequit.
Abi Viator
Et imitare, si poteris,
Strenuum pro virili
Libertatis Vindicatorem.

Literally translated (though the Latin is eccentric), this says: "Here is laid the Body of JONATHAN SWIFT, ... Where savage indignation can no longer lacerate his heart. Go, traveller, and imitate, if you can, this strong defender, to the utmost of his powers, of liberty."

Yeats has added a few flourishes or variations: "sailed into his rest," "breast" instead of "heart," "dare" instead of "can," "World-besotted." But the main points are after all in the original: savage indignation, the lacerated heart, the champion of liberty. They are evidently what Swift wanted people to think of him, though he studiously avoided showing it in his lifetime. The words were designed to be read after his death, in what Gibbon in another context called "the obscurity of a learned language." Latin had the dignity and permanence of the classical, and epitaphs are a sanctioned place for marmoreal formality, but the "obscurity" would have suited Swift's temperamental shrinking from grand styles, and from the risks of a self-inflation which he disliked but did not wish to deny himself.

There is one place where a similar monument to himself is allowed into one of his published works:

> Fair LIBERTY was all his Cry;
> For her he stood prepar'd to die;
> For her he boldly stood alone;
> For her he oft expos'd his own.
> Two Kingdoms, just as Faction led,
> Had set a Price upon his Head;
> But, not a Traytor cou'd be found,
> To sell him for Six Hundred Pound.

The lines refer to episodes of political courage in the "Two Kingdoms" of England (1713) and Ireland (1724). The second episode was his most spectacular success in the cause of Ireland. Through the *Drapier's Letters*, a series of pamphlets ostensibly by a linen-draper, he foiled an English scheme to force the Irish to adopt a coinage known as Wood's half-pence, which was widely thought to be a danger to the Irish economy. Swift became a hero in Ireland, the darling of the populace, and although his identity as the Drapier was widely known, no one was willing to betray him to the authorities, when "a Reward of Three Hundred Pounds" (a considerable sum in those days) was offered "to any Person who could discover the Author."

His pride in his political courage and effectiveness was justified, but it is interesting that the lines occur in the *Verses on the Death of Dr. Swift*, where they are represented as the words not of Swift himself but of an "impartial" commentator, "quite indiff'rent in the Cause," who is delivering a posthumous and disinterested assessment. The words are those of a funeral oration or an obituary, a kind of extended epitaph, with the formality and the licensed rhetoric of that genre. Their attribution to the impartial speaker has the effect of distancing Swift himself from a celebration that was nevertheless, like the Latin epitaph, entirely scripted by himself. The distancing invites attention, because many poets would not have felt the need for it. Such glowing self-aggrandizement was traditionally permitted, and indeed expected, in poems in which a poet was defending his own character and achievement. Thus Swift's friend Pope had no hesitation when, accused of being "strangely proud" in his satiric aggression, he answered in his own name:

> So proud, I am no Slave:
> So impudent, I own myself no Knave:
> So odd, my Country's Ruin makes me Grave.
> Yes, I am proud; I must be proud to see
> Men not afraid of God, afraid of me.

The same is true of Yeats's celebration of his role, and that of his friends, in the cultural regeneration of Ireland, as he gazes on their portraits in the Municipal Gallery:

> You that would judge me do not judge alone
> This book or that, come to this hallowed place
> Where my friends' portraits hang and look thereon;
> Ireland's history in their lineaments trace;
> Think where man's glory both begins and ends
> And say my glory was I had such friends.

Yeats and Pope write with a proud, elated sweep, often in similar cadences, and in essentially the same metrical form, the five-foot, ten-syllable English heroic line. Yeats loved Swift and disliked Pope, but he shared Pope's haughty mastery, and a similar sense of his own work and that of his associates as central to the cultural integrity of the nation. It is Swift, equally committed, who retreats from the full grandeur of the pretension. Even metrically, the verse announces more modest claims. The meter of the ringing declaration "Fair LIBERTY was all his Cry," a four-foot line, or tetrameter, is also the meter of his "light" verse, of "Strephon and Chloe" and "The Lady's Dressing Room." Indeed, large parts of the *Verses on the Death of Dr. Swift* are themselves written in an idiom of flippant, low-pitched *vers de société* (Swift's poetry was, incidentally, a model for T. S. Eliot's witty society verses). The champion of liberty thus comes over with full honors, but in an ambience that playfully absolves Swift from his own deserved grandeurs and coexists with more familiar and light-hearted accents.

Swift claimed that he himself was "only a Man of Rhimes, and that upon Trifles, never having written serious Couplets in my Life; yet never any without a moral View." This was in a letter of 1732 to Charles Wogan, a Jacobite Catholic officer from an old Irish family who served in the armies of France and Spain. The letter contains the same important discussions of his literary record and aspirations, as well as an unusual statement about Ireland. On the subject of poetry, Swift may be seen, in hindsight, to be expressing a modest defense of serious light verse, in a tradition that runs from Skelton and Butler to Byron, T. S. Eliot, and Auden. He was not conscious of making such a claim. By "serious Couplets," Swift was referring with unquestioning respect to that heroic couplet which Pope convinced the world that he had brought to its finest flowering. Swift deferred to this view, and indeed expressed it in the *Verses on the Death*. As well as being Pope's friend, he thought of him, as many later writers thought of T. S. Eliot, as poetry's authoritative voice for the time. Swift wrote almost as much verse as Pope, if we exclude Pope's translations of Homer, but his poetry is overshadowed by the towering achievement of his prose satires, by his own self-depreciation, and by his shyness of poetry itself as a form of grand statement. Later poets (Byron, Eliot, Auden) have been readier than the critics to recognize his gifts as a poet, and have sometimes taken more from him, and to better effect, than from Pope.

Swift, however, disclaimed poetic pretensions, and the disavowal of "serious Couplets" is bound up with the refusal of the "heroick Stile" which he expounds in "An Epistle to a Lady." But Yeats's version of "Swift's Epitaph" shows how much majesty can be accommodated in traditionally subheroic meters. It even adds its own majestic touches to Swift's original epitaph, as well as to the analogue in the *Verses on the Death*. In spite of the undercutting, the subterfuges, and the gestures of self-distancing, the celebration of the record, both in the *Verses* and the epitaph, mattered to Swift. He desired as well as deserved the praise, but he wanted to be known to deserve it without seeming to desire it. In this, as in other parts of the *Verses,* there is a small but distinct hint of bad faith. If the gestures of disengagement, the device of the impartial commentator, the consciously lowered temperature of the poem's entire atmosphere, compete with or undercut the celebrative grandeur, they also seem to claim credit for doing so. It is Swift who wrote the script, celebration, disengagement, and all.

———

Serving human liberty, making it all his cry, was for Swift, as for Yeats, mainly a matter of Irish interests. Both men were Irish patriots, but of Anglo-Irish or Ascendancy stock. For Yeats and Charles Stewart Parnell, the struggle for Ireland demanded a degree of autonomy wider and more inclusive of the "whole people," including especially its "native" Catholic population. This population was the majority, in modern terms, to which they themselves did not belong. When Swift's Drapier wrote his *Letter to the Whole People of Ireland,* the phrase almost certainly excluded that majority. He was addressing his own group, the Protestant "governing class," mainly of English descent, who formed the political, social, professional and commercial elite. His position was not that of the native oppressed by a conquering power but of the settler who, like the European *colons* of British Kenya or French Algeria, equally despised the natives and resented the rulers from the remote *métropole* of London or Paris.

Swift's idea of "home rule" was the maintenance of an Irish Parliament whose jurisdiction was not subservient to the Parliament of England. His constitutional doctrine was that of William Molyneux's *The Case of Ireland* (1698), that Ireland was not a "depending Kingdom" but a separate kingdom with its own Parliament, ruled by the same monarch as England. The political realities kept eroding any possibility of achieving recognition of this claim. But the aspiration itself was not to national independence in any currently understood sense, least of all for what we would now call the native majority, whose legal status was nil. The Irish Parliament whose rights Swift fought for was an Anglo-Irish institution, no more democratic, in a present-day sense, than the Parliament of England, and with no representation for the natives. Swift fought for the political, commercial, and agricultural interests of this Irish group against English oppression and exploitation, and also denounced the same group for their failure to act to their own advantage in the many spheres in which the English were not in a position to obstruct them. He advocated the use of Irish manufactures in preference to English, for example, and complained of absentee landlords who ruined their estates, and the country's agriculture, by squandering their wealth in London.

This is a theme of his most famous Irish pamphlet, *A Modest Proposal* (1729), which is unusual in being a satire mainly directed not at the English oppressor but at the Irish victim. That victim is mainly a settler class failing to look after its own interest, as is clear from the passage listing "other Expedients." These expedients are the several measures Swift had vainly urged his countrymen to implement. The Proposer argues that since there is no hope that any of them will in fact be implemented, the only alternative is to save the economy through a trade in Irish babies, sold for food. In this trade, the producers of babies will be the Catholic natives, and the consumers will be Swift's own Anglo-Irish population of landowners, administrators, clergymen, and merchants. Far from complaining, as is sometimes supposed, at the exploitation of the underprivileged Irish poor, Swift's joke relies on a traditional imputation that the Irish natives, like American Indians, were cannibals.

The special sting is that since it is the governing group who are doing the eating, they have sunk to the level of the savages from the bush or the bog. The latter are seen as only too happy to produce the goods. Indeed, the prospect of making a profit from their infants is likely to encourage them to feed those infants properly and to refrain from beating their pregnant wives. The portrait of the Irish poor in *A Modest Proposal,* as in the later and unironic *Proposal for Giving Badges to the Beggars* (1737), is that of a subhuman race of idlers, thieves, beggars, wife-beaters, and whores. The Irish natives were one of the prototypes for the wild Yahoos of *Gulliver's Travels.* That the dominant group sinks to the level of the ignoble subgroup does not make the latter look any better.

It is a signature of Swiftian satire that the vices we impute to rejected or pariah groups (savages, the poor, women) are those of the human animal. The Yahoos begin by being similar to beasts and savages and end up representing humankind. It is a curious inversion of what we nowadays call racism or sexism; instead of imputing certain kinds of degradation to selected populations, Swift takes what is commonly said about specific populations and imputes it to everyone else. In *A Modest Proposal* the reach is narrower. It is the ruling group, not humanity as a whole, that is guilty of what is imputed to the savage subgroup it victimizes. But the formula differs from a traditional irony according to which the oppressor is said to be more savage than his savage victim. In *A Modest Proposal,* both groups are equally guilty. They are also both victims, since the settlers are after all themselves oppressed by England, "*a Country, which would be glad to eat up our whole Nation without* [*Salt*]." So, in an incidental sarcasm, the English oppressor is cannibal too.

A Modest Proposal is unusual in being a satire whose main targets are the victims, and (in the case of the native riffraff) the victims' victims. In this, we see a typical Swiftian spiral, in which exposure of the lowest groups eventually encompasses successive layers above it. In *Gulliver's Travels,* the transition is from the Yahoo, as bestial Hibernian humanoid, to the rest of humankind. The fact that the qualities of the despised group extend to other groups, including those who despise them, is not, in Swift, an exculpation. There is no suggestion in *A Modest Proposal* or anywhere else that because the vices of the natives extend to their betters, they are in some way better than their betters. Swift had very few things to say in favor of the native Irish, and the common idea that *A Modest Proposal* was written in their defense and against English oppression flies in the face of the evidence.

"Victims" of colonial or tyrannical oppression are not, in general, a category on whom Swift expends much sympathy. The Yahoos, a composite of "all savage Nations," make this evident. If Swift detested tyrants and conquerors, it is not because he felt much tenderness toward those they oppressed but because of the raw human nastiness they displayed in their own right. This nastiness he often saw as matched by that of their victims. A rare exception, the "harmless People" brutalized by European conquerors in the anticolonial diatribe at the end of *Gulliver's Travels,* are shadowy schematic creatures whose "harmlessness" has little active existence except as a sign of the wickedness of their invaders. The Yahoos, and the murderous natives of New Holland (Australia) who attack Gulliver when he leaves Houyhnhnmland, are compelling examples of what Swift really thought of "savage Nations," whether subjugated or not.

Swift was sometimes willing to attribute the faults of the native Irish to the effects of oppression (by England, as well as by his own settler class). A species of compassion sometimes merges with the anger and contempt. But even that takes on the accents of cruel play, as when, after a stinging reference to the conditions that induce people in Ireland, both Papists and Protestants, to emigrate to America, he adds:

> I confess myself to be touched with a very sensible pleasure, when I hear of a mortality in any country-parish or village, where the wretches are forced to pay for a filthy cabin and two ridges of potatoes treble the worth, brought up to steal or beg, for want of work, to whom death would be the best thing to be wished for, on account both of themselves and the public.

It is perhaps to the Catholic Charles Wogan, the distinguished Jacobite soldier who had written to him from Spain, and whom Swift says he checked out carefully before deciding he deserved a serious reply, that we find his most considered expression of sympathy for the Catholic Irish, both those who, among the better families, deserted to the Jacobite cause and to foreign armies, and also the miserable natives:

> I cannot but highly esteem those Gentlemen of *Ireland,* who, with all the Disadvantages of being Exiles and Strangers, have been able to distinguish themselves by their Valour and Conduct in so many Parts of *Europe,* I think above all other Nations, which ought to make the *English* ashamed of the Reproaches they cast on the Ignorance, the Dulness, and the Want of Courage, in the *Irish* Natives; those Defects, wherever they happen, arising only from the Poverty and Slavery they suffer from their inhuman Neighbours, and the base corrupt Spirits of too many of the chief Gentry, *&c.* By such Events as these, the very *Grecians* are grown slavish, ignorant, and superstitious. I do assert that from several Experiments I have made in travelling over both Kingdoms, I have found the poor Cottagers here, who could speak our Language, to have much better natural Taste for good Sense, Humour, and Raillery, than ever I observed among People of the like Sort in *England.* But the Millions of Oppressions they lye under, the Tyranny of their Landlords, the ridiculous Zeal of their Priests, and the general Misery of the whole Nation, have been enough to damp the best Spirits under the Sun.

It is interesting to set this beside the sarcastic passage in *A Modest Proposal* about the "*helpless Infants;* who, as they grow up, either turn *Thieves* for want of Work; or leave *their dear Native Country, to fight for the Pretender in* Spain, or sell themselves to the *Barbadoes.*" The panegyric to the "poor Cottagers" also seems more designed to please Swift's correspondent than an expression of his usual view. The sniping at Irish priests, elsewhere called couple-beggars, is in Swift's more usual mode. But the final sentence is totally consistent with Swift's frequent statements about the ruinous maladministration of the country, including some grudging compassion for its despised natives.

More often, these beggarly natives are viewed as an unmitigated plague, "fitter to be rooted out off the Face of the Earth, than suffered to levy a vast annual Tax upon the City." Swift, like many of his class, regarded living in Ireland as a form of exile. Though born in Ireland, he described this as "a perfect Accident," considered himself English, and angrily acknowledged that the circumstances of his birth nevertheless made him "a *Teague,* or an *Irishman,* or what People please, although the best Part of my Life was in *England.*" Nevertheless, he did battle for the land he disliked, and found a wry fellow-feeling for it: "if I love Ireland better than I did it is because we are nearer related, for I am deeply allyed to its Poverty." It is an effort: "I must learn to make my Court to that Country and People better than I have done." On a rare occasion, he might even say, "I always left it with Regret." There is no doubting the effectiveness of his political efforts of the 1720s and 1730s to mitigate the effects of English oppression, and to rouse his Anglo-Irish compatriots to a more effective sense of their own self-interest. He was proud of becoming a popular hero, but never surrendered his pitying distaste for Ireland's beggarly hordes. And just as his personal charities and kindnesses were said to be gruff and unflattering, so was his final bequest to the nation, endowing what we now call a mental hospital, which survives to this day. As he said, or made his "impartial" spokesman say, at the end of the *Verses on the Death:*

> He gave the little Wealth he had,
> To build a House for Fools and Mad:
> And shew'd by one satyric Touch,
> No Nation wanted it so much.

———

That Swift remains an Irish hero, in the eyes of the descendants of these natives or the representatives of their interest, is a splendid and honorable fact. On April 25, 1967, Eamon De Valera, at the time president of the Irish Republic and a one-time rebel leader against British rule, made a speech that was reported as follows in the *Irish Times* the next day:

> In his brief opening speech, Mr. De Valera said that ... the famous Dean's name had been part of the folk-history he had experienced as a boy. He first

met Swift's writings at school,... where he remembered remarks that had been made about him in a history of English literature. Over the years he had found out more about Swift, he had discovered no reason to revise the favourable judgment of this book: the Dean had been a great prose-writer and satirist, and a powerful political pamphleteer.

Later, when he became more interested in politics than he had been as a boy, he had learned that Swift had been one of the pioneers of a group of Anglo-Irishmen—"the Irish colonists, I might call them"—who realised that they ought not to permit themselves to be governed by Ministers from England. He was a bit doubtful about Swift, as an Irishman he had preferred to live in England, and, when he came here, did not take very kindly to the Irish people but realised that Swift had set a headline which had been followed not merely in the 18th century but much later.

I was present on that occasion. It was the opening of a celebration of the tercentenary of Swift's birth, and took place at Trinity College, where Swift had studied as an undergraduate. The imposing ceremony included speeches from the heads of Trinity College and its Roman Catholic counterpart, University College, the mayors of various cities, and other dignitaries. Members of the government, including the prime minister, took part in a banquet that evening, or officiated at the openings of academic proceedings and visits to Swiftian sites. The president was a tall, imposing figure, then in his mideighties and blind, with an armed and uniformed officer sitting behind him whom I remember thinking of as a bodyguard, though I think he was also wearing a lot of medals. After the president had spoken, he sat upright for several hours, while the speeches of academic and local dignitaries droned on in the increasingly stuffy hall. It was a swelteringly hot day, and heads were nodding drowsily, not only among the audience but at the long table where all the speakers sat. As the old statesman sat upright, giving every sign of listening to every word with courteous alertness, I noticed that the bodyguard figure behind him had slumped over his weapon and was gently snoring.

De Valera's comportment exemplifies the naturalness with which Swift has been absorbed into the pantheon of Irish heroes, even by those who might be expected to have been affronted by some of his views of Ireland and its people. Something he said, which I cannot reconstruct from memory, gives a revealing glimpse. In the same issue of the *Irish Times,* in a column entitled "Swift, Swift and more Swift," the radio critic reviewed a program whose author, John O'Donovan, had said, "echoing a remark President De Valera made on Tuesday in Trinity—that he 'got my first impressions of Swift from a greasy joxer in a greasy suit ... [who] had become a Swift expert by the process of assimilating tradition rather than by studying his hero's writings and doings.'"

This suggests something more than the impressive but incomplete accommodation of an independent Ireland with its Anglo-Irish Protestant heritage. One is reminded, in contrast to O'Donovan's remarks on the radio, of Yeats's militant admonition to the Irish Senate, in the divorce debate in 1925, not to undervalue that minority heritage:

> We are one of the great stocks of Europe. We are the people of Burke; we are the people of Grattan; we are the people of Swift, the people of Emmet, the people of Parnell. We have created most of the modern literature of this country. We have created the best of its political intelligence.

If this call to attention has its own urgency, denouncing bigotries of exclusion, the testimony of De Valera and O'Donovan suggests a more populist level of acceptance, not overburdened with detailed knowledge but not ignorant of Swift's harsh views, and prepared to assimilate him with an intelligent and unsentimental awareness. This has a direct bearing on the phenomenon of a national government not merely conferring an official blessing on a learned commemoration of Swift but actually participating in it, as several cabinet ministers did, with every sign of having read at least some of Swift's writings. It is not easy to imagine a comparable phenomenon in either the United Kingdom or the United States at that (or any) time.

This awareness, an unforced sense of the obligation or propriety of homage, should also be recognized as related to what Yeats sought to remind the Senate of, with a forcefulness that saw no unforced awareness in that somewhat resistant body. Yeats's message was that, like Yeats himself, whose role in Irish nationalism was a living reality to those he was addressing, Swift and the other Ascendancy figures were vital and determining forces in Ireland's effort to shake off British rule and realize the aspiration to nationhood: examples of that leadership from above, from the governing class or "race," that sometimes provides the impetus for the liberation of the governed. It is interesting that on February 6, 1933, thirty-four years before the Swift celebration and eight years after Yeats's Senate speech, De Valera gave a radio address at the opening of the Athlone Broadcasting station in which he invoked the great Anglo-Irish figures of the eighteenth century, in a list reminiscent of Yeats's roll call of Ascendancy heroes:

Ireland has produced in Dean Swift perhaps the greatest satirist in the English language; in Edmund Burke probably the greatest writer on politics; in William Carleton a novelist of the first rank; in Oliver Goldsmith a poet of rare merit. Henry Grattan was one of the most eloquent orators of his time.... Theobald Wolfe Tone has left us one of the most delightful autobiographies in literature.

The list has a sting in it. It addresses the literary achievements of these heroes rather than their patriotic contribution, and in the case of Swift, and especially Wolfe Tone, the sting seems especially pointed. The freer acknowledgment of Swift's Irish credentials had to wait until 1967, when Ireland's political and cultural standing may have seemed more securely established. Even so, the passage of 1933 seems the more remarkable because not powered by Yeatsian fervors of dynastic exaltation, and because spoken in a context in which the speaker was insisting on what he considered even greater achievements in the Irish language, and on the cruelties of English oppression, and from a sense of perceived menace from Britain at the time of speaking.

———

CLAUDE RAWSON is the Maynard Mack Professor of English at Yale. He has written widely on the literature of the eighteenth and twentieth centuries. Among his books, those dealing with Swift include *Gulliver and the Gentle Reader* (1972, 1991), *Order from Confusion Sprung* (1985, 1992), *Satire and Sentiment 1660–1830* (1994, 2000), and *God, Gulliver, and Genocide: Barbarism and the European Imagination 1492–1945* (2001). He is a Fellow of the American Academy of Arts and Sciences. Both he and Ian Higgins are general editors of the Cambridge Edition of the *Works of Jonathan Swift*, 14 volumes, in preparation.

CHRONOLOGY

1660   Restoration of Charles II

1663–64 Samuel Butler, *Hudibras*, I and II

1667   Birth of Swift in Dublin on 30 November; birth of John Arbuthnot; Milton, *Paradise Lost* (1st edition); Thomas Sprat, *History of the Royal Society*

1670   Birth of William Congreve, (?) Bernard Mandeville

1671   Milton, *Paradise Regained, Samson Agonistes*

1672   Birth of Joseph Addison, Richard Steele; Andrew Marvell, *Rehearsal Transpos'd* (Part II, 1673)

1673–82 Swift at school at Kilkenny

1674   Milton, *Paradise Lost* (2nd edition, in twelve books); death of Milton

1678   John Bunyan, *Pilgrim's Progress*, I; Samuel Butler, *Hudibras*, III; Popish Plot; death of Andrew Marvell

1679   Birth of Thomas Parnell, poet and friend of Swift and Pope, and member of Scriblerus Club

1680   Death of Butler, Rochester, La Rochefoucauld; Sir Robert Filmer, *Patriarcha*; Rochester, *Poems*; Sir William Temple, *Miscellanea*, I

1681   Dryden, *Absalom and Achitophel*

1682–89 Swift attends Trinity College Dublin, B.A. *speciali gratia* 1686. He remains there until the outbreak of war between James II and William of Orange.

1682   Dryden, *The Medall, Religio Laici, Mac Flecknoe, Absalom and Achi-*

tophel, II; Sir William Petty, *Essay Concerning the Multiplication of Mankind; together with an Essay on Political Arithmetick* (see 1690)

1683   Rye House Plot

1684   Bunyan, *Pilgrim's Progress,* II

1685   Death of Charles II, accession of James II; birth of John Gay and George Berkeley

1687   Newton, *Principia;* James II's Declaration of Indulgence

1688   Glorious Revolution: William of Orange invades England and James II flees to France (transfer of the crown to William and Mary in 1689); as civil war breaks out in Ireland, Swift leaves for England (perhaps early the following year); birth of Alexander Pope; death of Bunyan; Shadwell named Poet Laureate in succession to Dryden; Charles Perrault, *Parallèle des Anciens et des Modernes* (completed 1697)

1689   Swift employed in Sir William Temple's household at Moor Park, near Farnham, Surrey; meets Esther Johnson (Stella), then eight years old; accession of William and Mary; John Locke, *First Letter on Toleration*

1690   James II defeated by William III in Ireland (Battle of the Boyne) and flees to France; Swift returns to Ireland in May; Temple, *Miscellanea*, II, includes "An Essay upon the Ancient and Modern Learning," which triggers Phalaris controversy (rev. 1692); Locke, *Two Treatises of Government, Essay Concerning Human Understanding* (enlarged 1694–1700); *Second Letter on Toleration;* Petty, *Political Arithmetick* (see 1682)

1691   Swift, *Ode. To the King on His Irish Expedition;* Swift back in England in August, and returns to Moor Park

1692   Swift obtains M.A., Oxford; publishes *Ode to the Athenian Society;* Locke, *Third Letter on Toleration;* death of Shadwell

1693   Dryden, "Discourse Concerning Satire," prefixed to trs. of Juvenal and Persius; Locke, *Thoughts Concerning Education*

1694   Swift returns to Ireland, takes deacon's orders; William Wotton, *Reflections on Ancient and Modern Learning;* death of Mary II; founding of Bank of England; *Dictionary* of French Academy

1695   Swift ordained priest, becomes prebendary of Kilroot, near Belfast; Charles Boyle, ed., *Epistles of Phalaris;* Locke, *Reasonableness of Christianity, Vindication of the Reasonableness of Christianity* (second *Vindication,* 1697)

1696–99 Swift at Moor Park, at work on *A Tale of a Tub* and related works

1697   Richard Bentley, "Dissertation upon the *Epistles of Phalaris*" (in 2nd edition of Wotton's *Reflections,* see 1694); birth of William Hogarth

1698   Boyle, *Dr. Bentley's Dissertations on the Epistles of Phalaris and the Fables of Aesop Examin'd;* Jeremy Collier, *Short View of the Immorality and Prophaneness of the English Stage* (controversy involving Congreve, Vanbrugh, Dryden, and others continues for several years); William Molyneux, *The Case of Ireland Stated*

1699   Sir William Temple dies. Swift returns to Ireland after Temple's death as chaplain to Earl of Berkeley, Lord Justice of Ireland; Bentley, *Dissertation upon the Epistles of Phalaris, with an Answer to the Honourable Charles Boyle*

1700   Swift appointed Vicar of Laracor, Co. Meath, and prebendary of St. Patrick's Cathedral, Dublin; death of Dryden; Temple, *Letters,* ed. Swift; Congreve, *Way of the World*

1701   Swift goes to England with Lord Berkeley; publishes *Contests and Dissensions in Athens and Rome;* Temple, *Miscellanea,* III, ed. Swift; death of James II; Act of Settlement

1702   Swift becomes D.D., Trinity College, Dublin; Defoe, *Shortest Way with the Dissenters;* death of William III, accession of Queen Anne

1704   Swift, *Tale of a Tub, Battle of the Books,* and *Mechanical Operation of the Spirit;* Defoe, *Review,* started; Battle of Blenheim; death of Locke

1705   Wotton, *Reflections upon Ancient and Modern Learning,* 3rd edition, with a *Defense of the Reflections* including "Observations upon *The Tale of a Tub*"; Mandeville, *The Grumbling Hive*

1706   Birth of Benjamin Franklin

1707   Union of England and Scotland; Swift writes "Story of the Injured Lady"; birth of Henry Fielding

1707–09 Swift in London on Church of Ireland business; meets Addison, Steele, and other authors, writes tracts on political and ecclesiastical issues; begins friendship with Esther Vanhomrigh (Vanessa)

1708   Shaftesbury, *Letter Concerning Enthusiasm*

1708–09 Swift, *Bickerstaff Papers*

1709   Swift, *Project for the Advancement of Religion;* Pope, *Pastorals;* Temple, *Memoirs,* III, ed. Swift; Berkeley, *New Theory of Vision;* Steele starts *Tatler* with Swift's help and Swift's poem "A Description of the Morning" appears in No. 9; birth of Samuel Johnson

1710   Swift comes to London in September on behalf of the Church of

Ireland soliciting for a remission of some financial imposts on the clergy of the Church of Ireland; meets Robert Harley, leader of the new Tory government; appointed editor of the pro-government paper *The Examiner;* friends include Matthew Prior, John Arbuthnot, and others; writes letters known as *Journal to Stella,* 1710–13; "A Description of a City Shower" appears in *Tatler,* No. 238; *Tale of a Tub,* 5th edition; Berkeley, *Principles of Human Knowledge*

1710–14 Swift active as political pamphleteer, writing for Tory government against Marlborough and Whig party; estrangement from Addison and Steele; friendship with Pope, Gay, Congreve, Arbuthnot, Parnell; close friendship with Vanessa

1711 Swift, *Miscellanies in Prose and Verse* (includes *Sentiments of a Church-of-England Man, Argument Against Abolishing Christianity*), *Conduct of the Allies;* Pope, *Essay on Criticism;* Addison and Steele start *Spectator,* to which Swift contributes; Shaftesbury, *Characteristics;* Harley becomes Earl of Oxford

1712 Swift, *Proposal for Correcting the English Tongue;* Pope, *Rape of the Lock* (two-canto version); Arbuthnot, *History of John Bull;* Gay, *The Mohocks*

1713 Swift installed as Dean of St. Patrick's Cathedral, Dublin, and returns to London; founding of Scriblerus Club (including Swift, Pope, Arbuthnot, Gay, Parnell, and Robert Harley, Earl of Oxford); Swift, *Mr. Collins's Discourse of Free-Thinking, Importance of the Guardian Considered;* Pope, *Windsor-Forest;* Gay, *Rural Sports;* Parnell, *Essay on the Different Styles of Poetry;* Addison, *Cato;* Steele, *Guardian, Englishman;* Treaty of Utrecht ends War of Spanish Succession

1714 Swift returns to Ireland after fall of Tory government and death of Queen Anne; Swift, *Publick Spirit of the Whigs;* Pope, *Rape of the Lock* (five-canto version); Gay, *Shepherd's Week;* Mandeville, *Fable of the Bees* (expanded 1723); accession of George I

1715 Jacobite Rebellion; impeachment of Earl of Oxford on charges of Jacobite intrigue; death of Louis XIV of France

1715–20 Pope, trs. of *Iliad,* 6 vols.

1716 Gossip about possible secret marriage to Stella; Gay, *Trivia*

1717 Earl of Oxford released from impeachment on procedural grounds; Pope, *Works;* Gay, Pope, and Arbuthnot, *Three Hours after Marriage;* Parnell, *Homer's Battle of the Frogs and Mice*

1718 Death of Parnell

1719   Defoe, *Robinson Crusoe;* death of Addison

1720   Swift, *Proposal for the Universal Use of Irish Manufacture; Letter to a Young Gentleman, Lately Entered into Holy Orders;* British House of Lords becomes ultimate court of appeal in Irish cases and British Parliament's right to legislate in Ireland asserted (Declaratory Act); South Sea Bubble

1721–42 Walpole emerges as leading Whig minister (1721). Britain's first "prime minister"

1721   Death of Matthew Prior

1722   Parnell, *Poems on Several Occasions,* ed. Pope; Defoe, *Journal of the Plague Year, Moll Flanders, Colonel Jack;* Government discovery of a Jacobite conspiracy, the "Atterbury Plot"

1723   Death of Vanessa

1724   Swift, *Drapier's Letters;* has popular reputation as Hibernian Patriot and government offers reward for "discovery" of Drapier; death of Earl of Oxford

1724–34 Gilbert Burnet, *History of His Own Times*

1725   Pope's edition of Shakespeare (6 vols.)

1725–26 Pope's trs. of *Odyssey* (5 vols.)

1726   Swift visits London for several months, stays with Pope, has unfruitful meeting with Walpole discussing Irish affairs; *Cadenus and Vanessa, Gulliver's Travels;* Lewis Theobald, *Shakespeare Restored; Craftsman* (opposition paper) started

1727   Swift's final visit to London; death of George I, accession of George II

1727–38 Gay, *Fables*

1728   Death of Stella, Swift writes "On the Death of Mrs. Johnson," *Short View of the State of Ireland;* Swift and Thomas Sheridan, *Intelligencer;* Pope, *Dunciad* (three-book version), dedicated to Swift; Gay, *Beggar's Opera*

1728–37 Henry Fielding's career as playwright, over twenty plays acted and published

1729   Swift, *Modest Proposal;* Pope, *Dunciad Variorum;* death of Congreve, Steele

1730   Colley Cibber, Poet Laureate

1731   Swift writes *Verses on the Death of Dr. Swift* (published 1739) and several of the so-called "scatological poems"; Pope, *Epistle to Burlington;* death of Defoe

1732   Pope, *Epistle to Bathurst;* death of Gay

1733   Swift, *On Poetry: A Rhapsody, Epistle to a Lady;* Pope, *Epistle to Cobham;* death of Mandeville

1733–34 Pope, *Essay on Man, First Satire of the Second Book of Horace, Imitated*

1735   Swift, *Works,* Dublin (four volumes; volume 3 includes revised version of *Gulliver's Travels*); Pope, *Epistle to Dr. Arbuthnot, Epistle to a Lady;* death of Arbuthnot

1736   Swift, *The Legion Club,* attacking members of Irish Parliament

1737   Swift, *A Proposal for Giving Badges to the Beggars;* Stage Licensing Act

1738   Swift, *Complete Collection of Genteel and Ingenious Conversation;* Pope, *Epilogue to the Satires;* Samuel Johnson, *London*

1739   Swift, *Verses on the Death of Dr. Swift* published

1740   Richardson, *Pamela;* Colley Cibber, *Apology for his Life;* birth of James Boswell

1741   Arbuthnot, Pope, and others, *Memoirs of Martinus Scriblerus;* Fielding, *Shamela*

1742   Swift declared "of unsound mind and memory"; Pope, *New Dunciad* (Book IV of *Dunciad*); Fielding, *Joseph Andrews;* Walpole resigns all offices, is pensioned and created Earl of Oxford

1743   Pope, *Dunciad* (four-book version, with Cibber replacing Theobald as hero); Fielding, *Miscellanies,* 3 vols. (includes *Jonathan Wild*)

1744   Death of Pope, Theobald

1745   Death of Swift, 19 October; Swift, *Directions to Servants;* death of Walpole; Jacobite Rebellion

A NOTE ON THE TEXT

The texts of this Modern Library Paperback Classics edition of the basic writings of Jonathan Swift derive from four principal sources: *The Prose Works of Jonathan Swift,* edited by Herbert Davis (Oxford: Basil Blackwell, 1939–68); *The Poems of Jonathan Swift,* edited by Harold Williams (Oxford, 2nd edn. Rev., 1958), *The Journal to Stella,* edited by Harold Williams (Oxford, 1948), and *The Correspondence of Jonathan Swift,* edited by Harold Williams (Oxford, 1963–65). Permission credits appear on the copyright page.

I

A TALE OF A TUB

A TALE OF A TUB.

Written for the Univerſal Improvement of Mankind.

Diu multumque deſideratum.

To which is added,

An ACCOUNT of a BATTEL

BETWEEN THE

Antient and Modern BOOKS in St. *James*'s Library.

Baſima eacabaſa eanaa irrauriſta, diarba da caeotaba fobor camelanthi. *Iren. Lib.* I. C. 18.

———— *Juvatque novos decerpere flores,*
Inſignemque meo capiti petere inde coronam,
Unde prius nulli velarunt tempora Muſæ. Lucret.

The Fifth EDITION: With the Author's Apology and Explanatory Notes. By *W. W-tt-n*, B. D. and others.

LONDON: Printed for *John Nutt*, near *Stationers-Hall.* MDCCX.

Treatises wrote by the same Author, most of them mentioned in the following Discourses; which will be speedily published.

A Character of the present Set of Wits *in this Island.*

A Panegyrical Essay upon the Number THREE.

A Dissertation upon the principal Productions of Grub-street.[1]

Lectures upon a Dissection of Human Nature.

A Panegyrick upon the World.

An Analytical Discourse upon Zeal, Histori-theo-physi-logically *considered.*

A general History of Ears.

A Modest Defence of the Proceedings of the Rabble *in all Ages.*

A Description of the Kingdom of Absurdities.

A Voyage into England, *by a Person of Quality in* Terra Australis incognita,[2] *translated from the Original.*

A Critical Essay upon the Art of Canting, *Philosophically, Physically, and Musically considered.*

An Apology

FOR THE, &C.

If good and ill Nature equally operated upon Mankind, I might have saved my self the Trouble of this Apology; for it is manifest by the Reception the following Discourse hath met with, that those who approve it, are a great Majority among the Men of Tast; yet there have been two or three Treatises[3] written expresly against it, besides many others that have flirted at it occasionally, without one Syllable having been ever published in its Defence, or even Quotation to its Advantage, that I can remember, except by the Polite Author of a late Discourse[4] between a Deist and a Socinian.

Therefore, since the Book seems calculated to live at least as long as our Language, and our Tast admit no great Alterations, I am content to convey some Apology along with it.

The greatest Part of that Book was finished above thirteen Years since, 1969, which is eight Years before it was published. The Author was then young, his Invention at the Height, and his Reading fresh in his Head. By the Assistance of some Thinking, and much Conversation, he had endeavour'd to Strip himself of as many real Prejudices as he could; I say real ones, because under the Notion of Prejudices,[5] he knew to what dangerous Heights some Men have proceeded. Thus prepared, he thought the numerous and gross Corruptions in Religion and Learning might furnish Matter for a Satyr, that would be useful and diverting: He resolved to proceed in a manner, that should be altogether new, the World having been already too long nauseated with endless Repetitions upon every Subject. The Abuses in Religion he proposed to set forth in the Allegory of the Coats, and the three Brothers, which was to make up the Body of the Discourse. Those in Learning he chose to introduce by way of Digressions. He was then a young Gentleman much in the World, and wrote to the Tast of those who were like himself; therefore in order to allure them, he gave a

Liberty to his Pen, which might not suit with maturer Years, or graver Characters, and which he could have easily corrected with a very few Blots, had he been Master of his Papers for a Year or two before their Publication.

Not that he would have governed his Judgment by the ill-placed Cavils of the Sour, the Envious, the Stupid, and the Tastless, which he mentions with disdain. He acknowledges there are several youthful Sallies, which from the Grave and the Wise may deserve a Rebuke. But he desires to be answerable no farther than he is guilty, and that his Faults may not be multiply'd by the ignorant, the unnatural, and uncharitable Applications of those who have neither Candor to suppose good Meanings, nor Palate to distinguish true Ones. After which, he will forfeit his Life, if any one Opinion can be fairly deduced from that Book, which is contrary to Religion or Morality.

Why should any Clergyman of our Church be angry to see the Follies of Fanaticism and Superstition exposed, tho' in the most ridiculous Manner? since that is perhaps the most probable way to cure them, or at least to hinder them from farther spreading. Besides, tho' it was not intended for their Perusal; it raillies nothing but what they preach against. It contains nothing to provoke them by the least Scurrillity upon their Persons or their Functions. It Celebrates the Church of England as the most perfect of all others in Discipline and Doctrine, it advances no Opinion they reject, nor condemns any they receive. If the Clergy's Resentments lay upon their Hands, in my humble Opinion, they might have found more proper Objects to employ them on: Nondum tibi defuit Hostis;[6] I mean those heavy, illiterate Scriblers, prostitute in their Reputations, vicious in their Lives, and ruin'd in their Fortunes, who to the shame of good Sense as well as Piety, are greedily read, meerly upon the Strength of bold, false, impious Assertions, mixt with unmannerly Reflections upon the Priesthood, and openly intended against all Religion; in short, full of such Principles as are kindly received, because they are levell'd to remove those Terrors that Religion tells Men will be the Consequence of immoral Lives. Nothing like which is to be met with in this Discourse, tho' some of them are pleased so freely to censure it. And I wish, there were no other Instance of what I have too frequently observed, that many of that Reverend Body are not always very nice in distinguishing between their Enemies and their Friends.

Had the Author's Intentions met with a more candid Interpretation from some whom out of Respect he forbears to name, he might have been encouraged to an Examination of Books written by some of those Authors above-described, whose Errors, Ignorance, Dullness and Villany, he thinks he could have detected and exposed in such a Manner, that the Persons who are most conceived to be infected by them, would soon lay them aside and be ashamed: But he has now given over those Thoughts, since the weightiest Men in the weightiest Stations are pleased to think it a more dan-

gerous Point to laugh at those Corruptions in Religion, which they themselves must disapprove, than to endeavour pulling up those very Foundations, wherein all Christians have agreed.

He thinks it no fair Proceeding, that any Person should offer determinately to fix a name upon the Author of this Discourse, who hath all along concealed himself from most of his nearest Friends: Yet several have gone a farther Letter of *Step, and pronounced another Book to have been the Work of the same* Enthusiasm. [7] *Hand with this; which the Author directly affirms to be a thorough mistake; he having yet never so much as read that Discourse, a plain Instance how little Truth, there often is in general Surmises, or in Conjectures drawn from a Similitude of Style, or way of thinking.*

Had the Author writ a Book to expose the Abuses in Law, or in Physick, he believes the Learned Professors in either Faculty, would have been so far from resenting it, as to have given him Thanks for his Pains, especially if he had made an honourable Reservation for the true Practice of either Science: But Religion they tell us ought not to be ridiculed, and they tell us Truth, yet surely the Corruptions in it may; for we are taught by the tritest Maxim in the World, that Religion being the best of Things, its Corruptions are likely to be the worst.

There is one Thing which the judicious Reader cannot but have observed, that some of those Passages in this Discourse, which appear most liable to Objection are what they call Parodies, where the Author personates the Style and Manner of other Writers, whom he has a mind to expose. I shall produce one Instance, it is in the [39th] *Page.* Dryden, L'Estrange,[8] *and some others I shall not name, are here levelled at, who having spent their Lives in Faction, and Apostacies, and all manner of Vice, pretended to be Sufferers for Loyalty and Religion. So* Dryden *tells us in one of his Prefaces of his Merits and Suffering, thanks God that he* possesses his Soul in Patience:[9] *In other Places he talks at the same Rate, and* L'Estrange *often uses the like Style, and I believe the Reader may find more Persons to give that Passage an Application: But this is enough to direct those who may have over-look'd the Authors Intention.*

There are three or four other Passages which prejudiced or ignorant Readers have drawn by great Force to hint at ill Meanings; as if they glanced at some tenets in Religion, in answer to all which, the Author solemnly protests he is entirely Innocent, and never had it once in his Thoughts that anything he said would in the least be capable of such Interpretations, which he will engage to deduce full as fairly from the most innocent Book in the World. And it will be obvious to every Reader, that this was not any part of his Scheme or Design, the Abuses he notes being such as all Church of England *Men agree in, nor was it proper for his Subject to meddle with other Points, than such as have been perpetually controverted since the Reformation.*

To instance only in that Passage about the three wooden Machines mentioned in the Introduction: In the Original Manuscript there was a description of a Fourth, which those who had the Papers in their Power, blotted out, as having something in it of Satyr, that I suppose they thought was too particular, and therefore they were forced to change it to the Number Three, from whence some have endeavour'd to squeeze out a dangerous Meaning that was never thought on. And indeed the Conceit was half spoiled by changing the Numbers; that of Four being much more Cabalistick, and therefore better exposing the pretended Virtue of Numbers, a Superstition there intended to be ridicul'd.

Another Thing to be observed is, that there generally runs an Irony through the Thread of the whole Book, which the Men of Tast will observe and distinguish, and which will render some Objections that have been made, very weak and insignificant.

This Apology being chiefly intended for the Satisfaction of future Readers, it may be thought unnecessary to take any notice of such Treatises as have been writ against this ensuing Discourse, which are already sunk into waste Paper and Oblivion; after the usual Fate of common Answerers to Books, which are allowed to have any Merit: they are indeed like Annuals that grow about a young Tree, and seem to vye with it for a Summer, but fall and die with the Leaves in Autumn, and are never heard of any more. When Dr. Eachard writ his Book about the Contempt of the Clergy, numbers of those Answerers immediately started up, whose Memory if he had not kept alive by his Replies, it would now be utterly unknown that he were ever answered at all. There is indeed an Exception, when any great Genius thinks it worth his while to expose a foolish Piece; so we still read Marvel's Answer to Parker with Pleasure, tho' the Book it answers be sunk long ago; so the Earl of Orrery's Remarks[10] will be read with Delight, when the Dissertation he exposes will neither be sought nor found; but these are no Enterprises for common Hands, nor to be hoped for above once or twice in an Age. Men would be more cautious of losing their Time in such an Undertaking, if they did but consider, that to answer a Book effectually, requires more Pains and Skill, more Wit, Learning, and Judgment than were employ'd in the Writing it. And the Author assures those Gentlemen who have given themselves that Trouble with him, that his Discourse is the Product of the Study, the Observation, and the Invention of several Years, that he often blotted out much more than he left, and if his Papers had not been a long time out of his Possession, they must have still undergone more severe Corrections; and do they think such a Building is to be battered with Dirt-Pellets however envenom'd the Mouths may be that discharge them. He hath seen the Productions but of two Answerers, One of which[11] first appear'd as from an unknown hand, but since avowed by a Person, who upon some Occasions hath discover'd no ill Vein of Humor. 'Tis a Pity any Occasions should put him under a necessity of being so hasty in his Productions, which otherwise might often be entertaining. But there were other Reasons obvious enough for his Miscarriage in *this; he writ against the Conviction of his Talent, and enter'd upon one of the wrongest Attempts in Nature, to turn into ridicule by a Weeks Labour, a Work which had cost so much time, and met with so much Success in ridiculing others, the manner how he has handled his* Subject, *I have now forgot, having just look'd it over when it first came out, as others did, meerly for the sake of the Title.*

The other Answer[12] is from a Person of a graver Character, and is made up of half Invective, and half Annotation.[13] In the latter of which he hath generally succeeded well enough. And the Project at that time was not amiss, to draw in Readers to his Pamphlet, several having appear'd desirous that there might be some Explication of the more difficult Passages. Neither can he be altogether blamed for offering at the Invective Part, because it is agreed on all hands that the Author had given him sufficient Provocation. The great Objection is against his manner of treating it, very unsuitable to one of his Function. It was determined by a fair Majority, that this Answerer had in a way not to be pardon'd, drawn his Pen against a certain great Man then alive, and universally reverenced for every good Quality that could possibly enter into the Composition of the most accomplish'd Person; it was observed, how he was pleased and affected to have that noble Writer call'd his Adversary, and it was a Point of Satyr well directed, for I have been told, Sir W. T.[14] *was sufficiently mortify'd at the Term. All the Men of Wit and Politeness were immediately up in Arms, through Indignation, which prevailed over their Contempt, by the Consequences they apprehended from such an Example, and it grew to be* Porsenna's *Case;* Idem trecenti juravimus.[15] *In short, things were ripe for a general Insurrection, till my Lord* Orrery *had a little laid the Spirit, and settled the Ferment. But his Lordship being principally engaged with another Antagonist,[16] it was thought necessary in order to quiet the Minds of Men, that this Opposer should receive a Reprimand, which partly occasioned that Discourse of the Battle of the Books, and the Author was farther at the Pains to insert one or two Remarks on him in the Body of the Book.*

This Answerer has been pleased to find Fault with about a dozen Passages, which the Author will not be at the Trouble of defending, farther than by assuring the Reader, that for the greater Part the Reflecter is entirely mistaken, and forces Interpretations which never once entered into the Writer's Head, nor will he is sure into that of any Reader of Tast and Candor; he allows two or three at most there produced to have been deliver'd unwarily, for which he desires to plead the Excuse offered already, of his Youth, and Franckness of Speech, and his Papers being out of his Power at the Time they were published.

But this Answerer insists, and says, what he chiefly dislikes, is the Design; *what that was I have already told, and I believe there is not a Person in* England *who can understand that Book, that ever imagined it to have been any thing else, but to expose the Abuses and Corruptions in Learning and Religion.*

But it would be good to know what Design *this Reflecter was serving, when he* concludes his Pamphlet with a Caution to Readers, to beware of thinking the Authors Wit was entirely his own, surely this must have had some Allay of Personal Animosity, at least mixt with the Design *of serving the Publick by so useful a Discovery;* and it indeed touches the Author in a very tender Point, who insists upon it, that through the whole Book he has not borrowed one single Hint from any Writer in the World; and he thought, of all Criticisms, that would never have been one, He conceived it was never disputed to be an Original, whatever Faults it might have. However this Answerer produces three Instances to prove this Author's Wit is not his own in many Places. *The first is, that the Names of* Peter, Martin *and* Jack *are borrowed from a Letter of the late Duke of* Buckingham. *Whatever Wit is contained in those three Names, the Author is content to give it up, and desires his Readers will substract as much as they placed upon that Account; at the same time protesting solemnly that he never once heard of that Letter, except in this Passage of the Answerer: So that the Names were not borrowed as he affirms, tho' they should happen to be the same; which however is odd enough, and what he hardly believes; that of* Jack, *being not quite so obvious as the other two. The second Instance to shew* the Author's Wit is not his own, *is* Peter*'s* Banter (*as he calls it in his* Alsatia Phrase*)*[17] *upon Transubstantiation, which is taken from the same Duke's Conference with an* Irish *Priest, where a Cork is turned into a Horse. This the Author confesses to have seen, about ten Years after his Book was writ, and a Year or two after it was published. Nay, the Answerer overthrows this himself; for he allows the Tale was writ in 1697; and I think that Pamphlet was not printed in many Years after. It was necessary, that Corruption should have some Allegory as well as the rest; and the Author invented the properest he could, without enquiring what other People had writ, and the commonest Reader will find, there is not the least Resemblance between the two Stories. The third Instance is in these Words:* I have been assured, that the Battle in St. *James's* Library, is *mutatis mutandis,* taken out of a *French* Book, entituled, *Combat des livres,* if I misremember not. *In which Passage there are two Clauses observable:* I have been assured; *and,* if I misremember not. *I desire first to know, whether if that Conjecture proves an utter falshood, those two Clauses will be a sufficient Excuse for this worthy Critick. The Matter is a Trifle; but, would he venture to pronounce at this Rate upon one of greater Moment? I know nothing more contemptible in a Writer than the Character of a Plagiary; which he here fixes at a venture, and this, not for a Passage, but a whole Discourse, taken out from another Book only* mutatis mutandis.[18] *The Author is as much in the dark about this as the Answerer; and will imitate him by an Affirmation at Random; that if there be a word of Truth in this Reflection, he is a paultry, imitating Pedant, and the Answerer is a Person of Wit, Manners and Truth. He takes his Boldness, from never having seen any such Treatise in his Life nor heard of it before; and he is sure* *it is impossible for two Writers of different Times and Countries to agree in their Thoughts after such a Manner, that two continued Discourses shall be the same only* mutatis mutandis. *Neither will he insist upon the mistake of the Title, but let the Answerer and his Friend produce any Book they please, he defies them to shew one single Particular, where the judicious Reader will affirm he has been obliged for the smallest Hint; giving only Allowance for the accidental encountring of a single Thought, which he knows may sometimes happen; tho' he has never yet found it in that Discourse, nor has heard it objected by any body else.*

So that if ever any design was unfortunately executed, it must be that of this Answerer, who when he would have it observed that the Author's Wit is not his own, is able to produce but three Instances, two of them meer Trifles, and all three manifestly false. If this be the way these Gentlemen deal with the World in those Criticisms, where we have not Leisure to defeat them, their Readers had need be cautious how they rely upon their Credit; and whether this Proceeding can be reconciled to Humanity or Truth, let those who think it worth their while, determine.

It is agreed, this Answerer would have succeeded much better, if he had stuck wholly to his Business as a Commentator upon the Tale of a Tub, *wherein it cannot be deny'd that he hath been of some Service to the Publick, and has given very fair Conjectures towards clearing up some difficult Passages; but, it is the frequent Error of those Men (otherwise very commendable for their Labors) to make Excursions beyond their Talent and their Office, by pretending to point out the Beauties and the Faults; which is no part of their Trade, which they always fail in, which the World never expected from them, nor gave them any thanks for endeavouring at. The Part of* Min-ellius, *or* Farnaby[19] *would have fallen in with his Genius, and might have been serviceable to many Readers who cannot enter into the abstruser Parts of that Discourse; but* Optat ephippia bos piger.[20] *The dull, unwieldy, ill-shaped Ox would needs put on the Furniture of a Horse, not considering he was born to Labour, to plow the Ground for the Sake of superior Beings, and that he has neither the Shape, Mettle nor Speed of that nobler Animal he would affect to personate.*

It is another Pattern of this Answerer's fair dealing, to give us Hints that the Author is dead, and yet to lay the Suspicion upon somebody, I know not who, in the Country; to which can be only returned, that he is absolutely mistaken in all his Conjectures; and surely Conjectures are at best too light a Pretence to allow a Man to assign a Name in Publick. He condemns a Book, and consequently the Author, of whom he is utterly ignorant, yet at the same time fixes in Print, what he thinks a disadvantageous Character upon those who never deserved it. A Man who receives a Buffet in the Dark may be allowed to be vexed; but it is an odd kind of Revenge to go to Cuffs in broad day with the first he meets with, and lay the last Nights Injury at his Door. And thus much for this discreet, candid, pious, *and* ingenious *Answerer.*

How the Author came to be without his Papers, is a Story not proper to be told, and of very little use, being a private Fact of which the Reader would believe as little or as much as he thought good. He had however a blotted Copy by him, which he intended to have writ over, with many Alterations, and this the Publishers were well aware of, having put it into the Booksellers Preface, that they apprehended a surreptitious Copy, which was to be altered, &c. This though not regarded by Readers, was a real Truth, only the surreptitious Copy was rather that which was printed, and they made all hast they could, which indeed was needless; the Author not being at all prepared; but he has been told, the Bookseller was in much Pain, having given a good Sum of Money for the Copy.

In the Authors Original Copy there were not so many Chasms as appear in the Book; and why some of them were left he knows not; had the Publication been trusted to him, he should have made several Corrections of Passages against which nothing hath been ever objected. He should likewise have altered a few of those that seem with any Reason to be excepted against, but to deal freely, the greatest Number he should have left untouch'd, as never suspecting it possible any wrong Interpretations could be made of them.

The Author observes, at the End of the Book there is a Discourse called A Fragment; which he more wondered to see in Print than all the rest. Having been a most imperfect Sketch with the Addition of a few loose Hints, which he once lent a Gentleman who had designed a Discourse of somewhat the same Subject; he never thought of it afterwards, and it was a sufficient Surprize to see it pieced up together, wholly out of the Method and Scheme he had intended, for it was the Ground-work of a much larger Discourse, and he was sorry to observe the Materials so foolishly employ'd.

There is one farther Objection made by those who have answered this Book, as well as by some others, that Peter is frequently made to repeat Oaths and Curses. Every Reader observes it was necessary to know that Peter did Swear and Curse. The Oaths are not printed out, but only supposed, and the Idea of an Oath is not immoral, like the Idea of a Prophane or Immodest Speech. A Man may laugh at the Popish Folly of cursing People to Hell, and imagine them swearing, without any crime; but lewd Words, or dangerous Opinions though printed by halves, fill the Readers Mind with ill Idea's; and of these the Author cannot be accused. For the judicious Reader will find that the severest Stroaks of Satyr in his Book are levelled against the modern Custom of Employing Wit upon those Topicks, of which there is a remarkable Instance in the [79th] Page, as well as in several others, tho' perhaps once or twice exprest in too free a manner, excusable only for the Reasons already alledged. Some Overtures have been made by a third Hand to the Bookseller for the Author's altering those Passages which he thought might require it. But it seems the Bookseller will not hear of any such Thing, being apprehensive it might spoil the Sale of the Book.

The Author cannot conclude this Apology, without making this one Reflection; that, as Wit is the noblest and most useful Gift of humane Nature, so Humor is the most agreeable, and where these two enter far into the Composition of any Work, they will render it always acceptable to the World. Now, the great Part of those who have no Share or Tast of either, but by their Pride, Pedantry and Ill Manners, lay themselves bare to the Lashes of Both, think the Blow is weak, because they are insensible, and where Wit hath any mixture of Raillery; 'Tis but calling it Banter, and the work is done. This Polite Word of theirs was first borrowed from the Bullies in White-Fryars, then fell among the Footmen, and at last retired to the Pedants, by whom it is applied as properly to the Productions of Wit, as if I should apply it to Sir Isaac Newton's Mathematicks, but, if this Bantring as they call it, be so despisable a Thing, whence comes it to pass they have such a perpetual Itch towards it themselves? To instance only in the Answerer already mentioned; it is grievous to see him in some of his Writings at every turn going out of his way to be waggish, to tell us of a Cow that prickt up her Tail, and in his answer to this Discourse, he says it is all a Farce and a Ladle; With other Passages equally shining. One may say of these Impedimenta Literarum,[21] that Wit ows them a Shame; and they cannot take wiser Counsel than to keep out of harms way, or at least not to come till they are sure they are called.

To conclude; with those Allowances above-required, this Book should be read, after which the Author conceives, few things will remain which may not be excused in a young Writer. He wrote only to the Men of Wit and Tast, and he thinks he is not mistaken in his Accounts, when he says they have been all of his side, enough to give him the vanity of telling his Name, wherein the World with all its wise Conjectures, is yet very much in the dark, which Circumstance is no disagreeable Amusement either to the Publick or himself.

The Author is informed, that the Bookseller has prevailed on several Gentlemen, to write some explanatory Notes, for the goodness of which he is not to answer, having never seen any of them, nor intends it, till they appear in Print, when it is not unlikely he may have the Pleasure to find twenty Meanings, which never enter'd into his Imagination.

June 3. 1709.

POSTSCRIPT

Since the writing of this which was about a Year ago; a Prostitute Bookseller[22] hath publish'd a foolish Paper, under the Name of Notes on the Tale of a Tub, with some Account of the Author, and with an Insolence which I suppose is punishable by Law, hath presumed to assign certain Names. It will be enough for the Author to assure the *world, that the Writer of that Paper is utterly wrong in all his Conjectures upon that Affair. The Author farther asserts that the whole Work is entirely of one Hand, which every Reader of Judgment will easily discover. The Gentleman who gave the Copy to the Bookseller, being a Friend of the Author, and using no other Liberties besides that of expunging certain Passages where now the Chasms appear under the Name of* Desiderata. *But if any Person will prove his Claim to three Lines in the whole Book, let him step forth and tell his Name and Titles, upon which the Bookseller shall have Orders to prefix them to the next Edition, and the Claimant shall from henceforward be acknowledged the undisputed Author.*

To The Right Honourable,
John Lord Sommers[23]

My LORD,

THO' the Author has written a large Dedication, yet That being address'd to a Prince, whom I am never likely to have the Honor of being known to; A Person, besides, as far as I can observe, not at all regarded, or thought on by any of our present Writers; And, being wholly free from that Slavery, which Booksellers usually lie under, to the Caprices of Authors; I think it a wise Piece of Presumption, to inscribe these Papers to your Lordship, and to implore your Lordship's Protection of them. God and your Lordship know their Faults, and their Merits; for as to my own Particular, I am altogether a Stranger to the Matter; And, tho' every Body else should be equally ignorant, I do not fear the Sale of the Book, at all the worse, upon that Score. Your Lordship's Name on the Front, in Capital Letters, will at any time get off one Edition: Neither would I desire any other Help, to grow an Alderman, than a Patent for the sole Priviledge of Dedicating to your Lordship.

I should now, in right of a Dedicator, give your Lordship a List of your own Virtues, and at the same time, be very unwilling to offend your Modesty; But, chiefly, I should celebrate your Liberality towards Men of great Parts and small Fortunes, and give you broad Hints, that I mean my self. And, I was just going on in the usual Method, to peruse a hundred or two of Dedications, and transcribe an Abstract, to be applied to your Lordship; But, I was diverted by a certain Accident. For, upon the Covers of these Papers, I casually observed written in large Letters, the two following Words, *DETUR DIGNISSIMO;* which, for ought I knew, might contain some important Meaning. But, it unluckily fell out, that none of the Authors I employ, understood *Latin* (tho' I have them often in pay, to translate out of that Language) I was therefore compelled to have recourse to the Curate of our Parish, who Englished it thus, *Let it be given to the Worthiest;* And his Comment was, that the Author meant, his Work should be dedicated to the sublimest Genius of the Age, for Wit, Learning, Judgment, Eloquence and Wisdom. I call'd at a Poet's Chamber (who works for my Shop) in an Alley hard by, shewed him the Translation, and desired his Opinion, who it was that the Author could mean; He told me, after some Consideration, that Vanity was a Thing he abhorr'd; but by the Description, he thought Himself to be the Person aimed at; And, at the same time, he very kindly offer'd his own Assistance *gratis,* towards penning a Dedication to Himself. I desired him, however, to give a second Guess; Why then, said he, It must be I, or my Lord *Sommers.* From thence I went to several other Wits of my Acquaintance, with no small Hazard and Weariness to my Person, from a prodigious Number of dark, winding Stairs; But found them all in the same Story, both of your Lordship and themselves. Now, your Lordship is to understand, that this Proceeding was not of my own Invention; For, I have somewhere heard, it is a Maxim, that those, to whom every Body allows the second Place, have an undoubted Title to the First.

THIS infallibly convinced me, that your Lordship was the Person intended by the Author. But, being very unacquainted in the Style and Form of Dedications, I employ'd those Wits aforesaid, to furnish me with Hints and Materials, towards a Panegyrick upon your Lordship's Virtues.

IN two Days, they brought me ten Sheets of Paper, fill'd up on every Side. They swore to me, that they had ransack'd whatever could be found in the Characters of *Socrates, Aristides, Epaminondas, Cato, Tully, Atticus,* and other hard Names, which I cannot now recollect. However, I have Reason to believe, they imposed upon my Ignorance, because, when I came to read over their Collections, there was not a Syllable there, but what I and every body else knew as well as themselves: Therefore, I grievously suspect a Cheat; and, that these Authors of mine, stole and transcribed every Word, from the universal Report of Mankind. So that I look upon my self, as fifty Shillings out of Pocket, to no manner of Purpose.

IF, by altering the Title, I could make the same Materials serve for another Dedication (as my Betters have done) it would help to make up my Loss: But, I have made several Persons, dip here and there in those Papers, and before they read three Lines, they have all assured me, plainly, that they cannot possibly be applied to any Person besides your Lordship.

I expected, indeed, to have heard of your Lordship's Bravery, at the Head of an Army; Of your undaunted Courage, in mounting a Breach, or scaling a Wall; Or, to have had your Pedigree trac'd in a Lineal Descent from the House of *Austria;* Or, of your wonderful Talent at Dress and Dancing; Or, your Profound Knowledge in *Algebra, Metaphysicks,* and the Oriental Tongues. But to ply the World with an old beaten Story of your Wit, and Eloquence, and Learning, and Wisdom, and Justice, and Politeness, and Candor, and Evenness of Temper in all Scenes of Life; Of that great Discernment in Discovering, and Readiness in Favouring deserving Men; with forty other common Topicks: I confess, I have neither Conscience, nor Countenance to do it. Because, there is no Virtue, either of a Publick or Private Life, which some Circumstances of your own, have not often produced upon the Stage of the World; And those few, which for want of Occasions to exert them, might otherwise have pass'd unseen or unobserved by your *Friends,* your *Enemies* have at length brought to Light.

'TIS true, I should be very loth, the Bright Example of your Lordship's Virtues should be lost to After-Ages, both for their sake and your own; but chiefly, because they will be so very necessary to adorn the History of a *late Reign;*[24] And That is another Reason, why I would forbear to make a Recital of them here; Because, I have been told by Wise Men, that as Dedications have run for some Years past, a good Historian will not be apt to have Recourse thither, in search of Characters.

THERE is one Point, wherein I think we Dedicators would do well to change our Measures; I mean, instead of running on so far, upon the Praise of our Patrons *Liberality,* to spend a Word or two, in admiring their *Patience.* I can put no greater Compliment on your Lordship's, than by giving you so ample an Occasion to exercise it at present. Tho', perhaps, I shall not be apt to reckon much Merit to your Lordship upon that Score, who having been formerly used to tedious Harangues, and sometimes to as little Purpose, will be the readier to pardon this, especially, when it is offered by one, who is with all Respect and Veneration,

My LORD,
Your Lordship's most Obedient,
and most Faithful Servant,
THE BOOKSELLER.

THE BOOKSELLER TO THE READER

It is now Six Years since these Papers came first to my Hands, which seems to have been about a Twelvemonth after they were writ: For, the Author tells us in his Preface to the first Treatise, that he hath calculated it for the Year 1697, and in several Passages of that Discourse, as well as the second, it appears, they were written about that Time.

As to the Author, I can give no manner of Satisfaction; However, I am credibly informed that this Publication is without his Knowledge; for he concludes the Copy is lost, having lent it to a Person, since dead, and being never in Possession of it after: So that, whether the Work received his last Hand, or, whether he intended to fill up the defective Places, is like to remain a Secret.

If I should go about to tell the Reader, by what Accident, I became Master of these Papers, it would, in this unbelieving Age, pass for little more than the Cant, or Jargon of the Trade. I, therefore, gladly spare both him and my self so unnecessary a Trouble. There yet remains a difficult Question, why I publish'd them no sooner. I forbore upon two Accounts: First, because I thought I had better Work upon my Hands; and Secondly, because I was not without some Hope of hearing from the Author, and receiving his Directions. But, I have been lately alarm'd with Intelligence of a surreptitious Copy, which a certain great Wit had new polish'd and refin'd, or as our present Writers express themselves, fitted to the Humor of the Age; as they have already done, with great Felicity, to Don Quixot, Boccalini, la Bruyere *and other Authors. However, I thought it fairer Dealing, to offer the whole Work in its Naturals. If any Gentleman will please to furnish me with a Key, in order to explain the more difficult Parts, I shall very gratefully acknowledge the Favour, and print it by it self.*

The Epistle Dedicatory,
to His Royal Highness
Prince Posterity

Sir,

I here present *Your Highness* with the Fruits of a very few leisure Hours, stollen from the short Intervals of a World of Business, and of an Employment quite alien from such Amusements as this: The poor Production of that Refuse of Time which has lain heavy upon my Hands, during a long Prorogation of Parliament, a great Dearth of Forein News, and a tedious Fit of rainy Weather: For which, and other Reasons, it cannot chuse extreamly to deserve such a Patronage as that of *Your Highness,* whose numberless Virtues in so few Years, make the World look upon You as the future Example to all Princes: For altho' *Your Highness* is hardly got clear of Infancy, yet has the universal learned World already resolv'd upon appealing to Your future Dictates with the lowest and most resigned Submission: Fate having decreed You sole Arbiter of the Productions of human Wit, in this polite and most accomplish'd Age. Methinks, the Number of Appellants were enough to shock and startle any Judge of a Genius less unlimited than Yours: But in order to prevent such glorious Tryals, the *Person* (it seems) to whose Care the Education of *Your Highness* is committed, has resolved (as I am told) to keep you in almost an universal Ignorance of our Studies, which it is Your inherent Birth-right to inspect.

The Citation out of Irenæus *in the* Title-Page, *which seems to be all* Gibberish, *is a Form of Initiation used antiently by the* Marcosian *Hereticks.* W. Wotton.

It is the usual Style of decry'd Writers to appeal to Posterity, *who is here represented as a Prince in his Nonage, and* Time *as his Governour, and the Author begins in a way very frequent with him, by personating other Writers, who sometimes offer such Reasons and Excuses for publishing their Works as they ought chiefly to conceal and be asham'd of.*

IT is amazing to me, that this *Person* should have Assurance in the face of the Sun, to go about persuading *Your Highness,* that our Age is almost wholly illiterate, and has hardly produc'd one Writer upon any Subject. I know very well, that when *Your Highness* shall come to riper Years, and have gone through the Learning of Antiquity, you will be too curious to neglect inquiring into the Authors of the very age before You: And to think that this *Insolent,* in the Account he is preparing for Your View, designs to reduce them to a Number so insignificant as I am asham'd to mention; it moves my Zeal and my Spleen for the Honor and Interest of your vast flourishing Body, as well as of my self, for whom I know by long Experience, he has profess'd, and still continues a peculiar Malice.

'TIS not unlikely, that when *Your Highness* will one day peruse what I am now writing, You may be ready to expostulate with Your *Governour* upon the Credit of what I here affirm, and command Him to shew You some of our Productions. To which he will answer, (for I am well informed of his Designs) by asking *Your Highness,* where they are? and what is become of them? and pretend it a Demonstration that there never were any, because they are not then to be found: Not to be found! Who has mislaid them? Are they sunk in the Abyss of Things? 'Tis certain, that in their own Nature they were *light* enough to swim upon the Surface for all Eternity. Therefore the Fault is in Him, who tied Weights so heavy to their Heels, as to depress them to the Center. Is their very Essence destroyed? Who has annihilated them? Were they drowned by *Purges* or martyred by *Pipes*? Who administred them to the Posteriors of ——? But that it may no longer be a Doubt with *Your Highness,* who is to be the Author of this universal Ruin; I beseech You to observe that large and terrible *Scythe* which your *Governour* affects to bear continually about him. Be pleased to remark the Length and Strength, the Sharpness and Hardness of his *Nails* and *Teeth:* Consider his baneful abominable *Breath,* Enemy to Life and Matter, infectious and corrupting: And then reflect whether it be possible for any mortal Ink and Paper of this Generation to make a suitable Resistance. Oh, that *Your Highness* would one day resolve to disarm this Usurping *Maitre du Palais,** of his furious Engins, and bring Your Empire *hors de Page.*†

IT were endless to recount the several Methods of Tyranny and Destruction, which Your *Governour* is pleased to practise upon this

---

* *Comptroller.*
† *Out of Guardianship.*

Occasion. His inveterate malice is such to the Writings of our Age, that of several Thousands produced yearly from this renowned City, before the next Revolution of the Sun, there is not one to be heard of: Unhappy Infants, many of them barbarously destroyed, before they have so much as learnt their *Mother-Tongue* to beg for Pity. Some he stifles in their Cradles, others he frights into Convulsions, whereof they suddenly die; Some he flays alive, others he tears Limb from Limb: Great Numbers are offered to *Moloch*,[25] and the rest tainted by his Breath, die of a languishing Consumption.

BUT the Concern I have most at Heart, is for our Corporation of *Poets*, from whom I am preparing a Petition to *Your Highness*, to be subscribed with the Names of one hundred thirty six of the first Rate, but whose immortal Productions are never likely to reach your Eyes, tho' each of them is now an humble and an earnest Appellant for the Laurel, and has large comely Volumes ready to shew for a Support to his Pretensions. The *never-dying* Works of these illustrious Persons, Your *Governour*, Sir, has devoted to unavoidable Death, and *Your Highness* is to be made believe, that our Age has never arrived at the Honor to produce one single Poet.

WE confess *Immortality* to be a great and powerful Goddess, but in vain we offer up to her our Devotions and our Sacrifices, if *Your Highness's Governour*, who has usurped the *Priesthood*, must by an unparallel'd Ambition and Avarice, wholly intercept and devour them.

To affirm that our Age is altogether Unlearned, and devoid of Writers in any kind, seems to be an Assertion so bold and so false, that I have been sometime thinking, the contrary may almost be proved by uncontroulable Demonstration. 'Tis true indeed, that altho' their Numbers be vast, and their Productions numerous in proportion, yet are they hurryed so hastily off the Scene, that they escape our Memory, and delude our Sight. When I first thought of this Address, I had prepared a copious List of *Titles* to present *Your Highness* as an undisputed Argument for what I affirm. The Originals were posted fresh upon all Gates and Corners of Streets; but returning in a very few Hours to take a Review, they were all torn down, and fresh ones in their Places: I enquired after them among Readers and Booksellers, but I enquired in vain, the *Memorial of them was lost among Men, their Place was no more to be found*:[26] and I was laughed to scorn, for a *Clown* and a *Pedant*, without all Taste and Refinement, little versed in the Course of *present* Affairs, and that knew nothing of what had pass'd in the best Companies of Court and Town. So that I can only avow in general to *Your Highness*, that we do abound in Learning and Wit; but to fix upon Particulars, is a Task too slippery for my slender Abilities. If I should venture in a windy Day, to affirm to *Your Highness*, that there is a huge Cloud near the *Horizon* in the Form of a *Bear*, another in the *Zenith* with the Head of an *Ass*, a third to the Westward with Claws like a *Dragon*; and *Your Highness* should in a few Minutes think fit to examine the Truth; 'tis certain, they would all be changed in Figure and Position, new ones would arise, and all we could agree upon would be, that Clouds there were, but that I was grosly mistaken in the *Zoography* and *Topography* of them.

BUT Your *Governour*, perhaps, may still insist, and put the Question: what is then become of those immense Bales of Paper, which must need have been employ'd in such Numbers of Books? Can these also be wholly annihilate, and so of a sudden as I pretend? What shall I say in return of so invidious an Objection? It ill befits the Distance between *Your Highness* and Me, to send You for ocular Conviction to a *Jakes*,[27] or an *Oven*; to the Windows of a *Bawdy-house*, or to a sordid *Lanthorn*. Books, like Men their Authors, have no more than one Way of coming into the World, but there are ten Thousand to go out of it, and return no more.

I profess to *Your Highness*, in the Integrity of my Heart, that what I am going to say is literally true this Minute I am writing: What Revolutions may happen before it shall be ready for your Perusal, I can by no means warrant: However I beg You to accept it as a Specimen of our Learning, our Politeness and our Wit. I do therefore affirm upon the Word of a sincere Man, that there is now actually in being, a certain Poet called *John Dryden*, whose Translation of *Virgil* was lately printed in a large Folio, well bound,[28] and if diligent search were made, for ought I know, is yet to be seen. There is another call'd *Nahum Tate*, who is ready to make Oath that he has caused many Rheams of Verse to be published, whereof both himself and his Bookseller (if lawfully required) can still produce authentick Copies, and therefore wonders why the World is pleased to make such a Secret of it. There is a Third, known by the Name of *Tom Durfey*, a Poet of a vast Comprehension, an universal Genius, and most profound Learning. There are also one Mr. *Rymer*, and one Mr. *Dennis*, most profound Criticks. There is a Person styl'd Dr. *Bentley*, who has written near a thousand Pages of immense Erudition, *giving a full and true Account* of a certain *Squable* of wonderful Importance between himself and a Bookseller: He is a Writer of infinite Wit and Humour; no Man raillyes with a better Grace, and in more sprightly Turns. Father, I avow to *Your Highness*, that with these Eyes I have beheld the Person of *William Wotton*, B.D. who has written a good sizeable Volume against a *Friend of Your Governor*[29] (from whom, alas! he must therefore look for little Favour) in a most gentlemanly Style, adorned with utmost Politeness and Civility; replete with Discoveries equally valuable for their Novelty and Use: and embellish'd with *Traits* of Wit so poignant and so apposite, that he is a worthy Yokemate to his fore-mention'd *Friend*.

WHY should I go upon farther Particulars, which might fill a Volume with the just Elogies[30] of my contemporary Brethren? I shall bequeath this Piece of Justice to a larger Work: wherein I intend to write a Character of the present Set of *Wits* in our Nation: Their Persons I shall describe particularly, and at Length, their Genius and Understandings in *Mignature*.[31]

IN the mean time, I do here make bold to present *Your Highness* with a faithful Abstract drawn from the Universal Body of all Arts and Sciences, intended wholly for your Service and Instruction: Nor do I doubt in the least, but *Your Highness* will peruse it as carefully, and make as considerable Improvements, as *other* young *Princes* have already done by the many Volumes of late Years written for a Help to their Studies.

THAT *Your Highness* may advance in Wisdom and Virtue, as well as Years, and at last out-shine all Your Royal Ancestors, shall be the daily Prayer of,

Decemb.
1697.

SIR,
Your Highness's
Most devoted, &c.

THE PREFACE

The Wits of the present Age being so very numerous and penetrating, it seems, the Grandees of *Church* and *State* begin to fall under horrible Apprehensions, lest these Gentlemen, during the intervals of a long Peace, should find leisure to pick Holes in the weak sides of Religion and Government. To prevent which, there has been much Thought employ'd of late upon certain Projects for taking off the Force, and Edge of those formidable Enquirers, from canvasing and reasoning upon such delicate Points. They have at length fixed upon one, which will require some Time as well as Cost, to perfect. Mean while the Danger hourly increasing, by new Levies of Wits all appointed (as there is Reason to fear) with Pen, Ink, and Paper which may at an hours Warning be drawn out into Pamphlets, and other Offensive Weapons, ready for immediate Execution: It was judged of absolute necessity, that some present Expedient be thought on, till the main Design can be brought to Maturity. To this End, at a Grand Committee, some Days ago, this important Discovery was made by a certain curious and refined Observer; That Sea-men have a Custom when they meet a *Whale,* to fling him out an empty *Tub,* by way of Amusement, to divert him from laying violent Hands upon the Ship. This Parable was immediately mythologiz'd: The *Whale* was interpreted to be *Hobbes*'s *Leviathan,* which tosses and plays with all other Schemes of Religion and Government, whereof a great many are hollow, and dry, and empty, and noisy, and wooden, and given to Rotation.[32] This is the *Leviathan* from whence the terrible Wits of our Age are said to borrow their Weapons.[33] The *Ship* in danger, is easily understood to be its old Antitype the *Com-*

monwealth. But, how to analyze the *Tub,* was a Matter of difficulty; when after long Enquiry and Debate, the literal Meaning was preserved: And it was decreed, that in order to prevent these *Leviathans* from tossing and sporting with the *Commonwealth,* (which of it self is too apt to *fluctuate*) they should be diverted from that Game by a *Tale of a Tub.* And my Genius being conceived to lye not unhappily that way, I had the Honor done me to be engaged in the Performance.

THIS is the sole Design in publishing the following Treatise, which I hope will serve for an *Interim* of some Months to employ those unquiet Spirits, till the perfecting of that great Work: into the Secret of which, it is reasonable the courteous Reader should have some little Light.

IT is intended that a large Academy be erected, capable of containing nine thousand seven hundred forty and three Persons; which by modest Computation is reckoned to be pretty near the current Number of *Wits* in this Island. These are to be disposed into the several Schools of this Academy, and there pursue those Studies to which their Genius most inclines them. The Undertaker himself will publish his Proposals with all convenient speed, to which I shall refer the curious Reader for a more particular Account, mentioning at present only a few of the Principal Schools. There is first, a large *Pederastick* School, with *French* and *Italian* Masters. There is also, the *Spelling* School, *a very spacious Building:* the School of *Looking Glasses:* The School of *Swearing:* the School of *Criticks:* the School of *Salivation:* The School of *Hobby-Horses:* The School of *Poetry:** The School of *Tops:* the School of *Spleen:*[34] The School of *Gaming:* with many others too tedious to recount. No Person to be admitted member into any of these Schools, without an Attestation under two sufficient Persons Hands, certifying him to be a *Wit.*

BUT, to return. I am sufficiently instructed in the Principal Duty of a Peface, if my Genius were capable of arriving at it. Thrice have I forced my Imgaintion to make the *Tour* of my Invention, and thrice it has returned empty; the latter having been wholly drained by the following Treatise. Not so, my more successful Brethren the *Moderns,* who will by no means let slip a Preface or Dedication, without some notable distinguishing Stroke, to surprize the Reader at the Entry, and kindle a Wonderful Expectation of what is to ensue. Such was that of a most ingenious Poet,

---

* *This I think the Author should have omitted, it being of the very same Nature with the* School of Hobby-Horses, *if one may venture to censure one who is so severe a Censurer of others, perhaps with too little Distinction.*

who solliciting his Brain for something new, compared himself to the *Hangman*, and his Patron to the *Patient*: This was *Insigne, recens, indictum ore alio.** When I went thro' That necessary and noble† Course of Study, I had the happiness to observe many such egregious Touches, which I shall not injure the Authors by transplanting: Because I have remarked, that nothing is so very tender as a *Modern* Piece of Wit, and which is apt to suffer so much in the Carriage. Some things are extreamly witty *to day*, or *fasting*, or *in this place*, or *at eight a clock*, or *over a Bottle*, or *spoke by Mr.* What d'y'call'm, or *in a Summer's Morning*: Any of which, by the smallest Transposal or Misapplication, is utterly annihilate. Thus, *Wit* has its Walks and Purlieus, out of which it may not stray the breadth of an Hair, upon peril of being lost. The *Moderns* have artfully fixed this *Mercury*, and reduced it to the Circumstances of Time, Place and Person. Such a Jest there is, that will not pass out of *Covent-Garden*; and such a one, that is no where intelligible but at *Hide-Park* Corner. Now, tho' it sometimes tenderly affects me to consider, that all the towardly Passages I shall deliver in the following Treatise, will grow quite out of date and relish with the first shifting of the present Scene: yet I must need subscribe to the Justice of this Proceeding: because, I cannot imagine why we should be at Expence to furnish Wit for succeeding Ages, when the former have made no sort of Provision for ours; wherein I speak the Sentiment of the very newest, and consequently the most Orthodox Refiners, as well as my own. However, being extreamly sollicitous, that every accomplished Person who has got into the Taste of Wit, calculated for this present Month of *August*, 1697, should descend to the very *bottom* of all the *Sublime* throughout this Treatise; I hold fit to lay down this general Maxim. Whatever Reader desires to have a thorow Comprehension of an Author's Thoughts, cannot take a better Method, than by putting himself into the Circumstances and Postures of Life, that the Writer was in, upon every important Passage as it flow'd from his Pen; For this will introduce a Parity and strict Correspondence of Idea's between the Reader and the Author. Now, to assist the diligent Reader in so delicate an Affair, as far as brevity will permit, I have recollected, that the shrewdest Pieces of this Treatise, were conceived in Bed, in a Garret: At other times (for a Reason best known to my self) I thought fit to sharpen my Invention with Hunger; and in general, the whole Work was begun, continued, and ended, under a long Course of Physick, and a great want of Money. Now, I do affirm, it

* Hor.
† Reading Prefaces, &c.

---

* Something extraordinary, new and never hit upon before.

will be absolutely impossible for the candid Peruser to go along with me in a great many bright Passages, unless upon the several Difficulties emergent, he will please to capacitate and prepare himself by these Directions. And this I lay down as my principal *Postulatum*.

BECAUSE I have profess'd to be a most devoted Servant of all *Modern* Forms: I apprehend some curious *Wit* may object against me, for proceeding thus far in a Preface, without declaiming, according to the Custom, against the Multitude of Writers whereof the whole Multitude of Writers most reasonably complains. I am just come from perusing some hundreds of Prefaces, wherein the Authors do at the very beginning address the gentle Reader concerning this enormous Grievance. Of these I have preserved a few Examples, and shall set them down as near as my Memory has been able to retain them.

One begins thus;

For a Man to set up for a Writer, when the Press swarms with, &c.

Another;

The Tax upon Paper does not lessen the Number of Scriblers, who daily pester, &c.

Another;

When every little Would-be-wit takes Pen in hand, 'tis in vain to enter the Lists, &c.

Another;

To observe what Trash the Press swarms with, &c.

Another;

SIR, *It is meerly in Obedience to your Commands that I venture into the Publick; for who upon a less Consideration would be of a Party with such a Rabble of Scriblers,* &c.

Now, I have two Words in my own Defence, against his Objection. First: I am far from granting the Number of Writers, a Nuisance to our Nation, having strenuously maintained the contrary in several Parts of the following Discourse. Secondly: I do not well understand the Justice of this Proceeding, because I observe many of these political Prefaces, to be not only from the same Hand, but from those who are most voluminous in their several Productions. Upon which I shall tell the Reader a short Tale.

A Mountebank in Leicester-Fields, *had drawn a huge Assembly about him. Among the rest, a fat unweildy Fellow, half stifled in the Press, would be every fit crying out, Lord! what a filthy Crowd is here? Pray, good People, give way a little, Bless me! what a Devil has rak'd this Rabble together: Z——ds, what squeezing is this! Honest Friend, remove your Elbow. At last, a* Weaver *that stood next him could hold no longer. A Plague confound you* (said he) *for an over-grown Sloven; and who (in the Devil's Name) I wonder, helps to make up the Crowd half so much as your self? Don't you consider (with a Pox) that you take up more room with that Carkass than any five here? Is not the Place as free for us as for you? Bring your own Guts to a reasonable Compass (and be d——n'd) and then I'll engage we shall have room enough for us all.*

THERE are certain common Privileges of a Writer, the Benefit whereof, I hope, there will be no Reason to doubt; Particularly, that where I am not understood, it shall be concluded, that something very useful and profound is coucht underneath: And again, that whatever word or Sentence is Printed in a different Character, shall be judged to contain something extraordinary either of *Wit* or *Sublime*.

As for the Liberty I have thought fit to take of praising myself, upon some Occasions or none; I am sure it will need no Excuse, if a Multitude of great Examples be allowed sufficient Authority: For it is here to be noted, that *Praise* was originally a Pension paid by the World: but the *Moderns* finding the Trouble and Charge too great in collecting it, have lately bought out the *Fee-Simple;* since which time, the Right of Presentation is wholly in our selves. For this Reason it is, that when an Author makes his own Elogy, he uses a certain form to declare and insist upon his Title, which is commonly in these or the like words, *I speak without Vanity;* which I think plainly shews it to be a Matter of Right and Justice. Now, I do here once for all declare, that in every Encounter of this Nature, thro' the following Treatise, the Form aforesaid is imply'd; which I mention, to save the Trouble of repeating it on so many Occasions.

'TIS a great Ease to my Conscience that I have writ so elaborate and useful a discourse without one grain of Satyr intermixt; which is the sole point wherein I have taken leave to dissent from the famous Originals of our Age and Country. I have observ'd some Satyrists to use the Publick much at the Rate that Pedants do a naughty Boy ready Hors'd for Discipline:[35] First expostulate the Case, then plead the Necessity of the Rod, from great Provocations, and conclude every Period with a Lash. Now, if I know any thing of Mankind, these Gentlemen might very well spare their Reproof and Correction: For there is not, through all Nature, another so callous and insensible a Member as the *World's Posteriors,* whether you apply to it the *Toe* or the *Birch.* Besides, most of our late Satyrists seem to lye under a sort of Mistake, that because *Nettles* have the Prerogative to Sting, therefore all *other Weeds* must do so too. I make not this comparison out of the least Design to detract from these worthy Writers: For it is well known among *Mythologists,* that *Weeds* have the Preeminence over all other Vegetables; and therefore the first *Monarch* of this Island,[36] whose Taste and Judgment were so acute and refined, did very wisely root out the *Roses* from the Collar of the *Order,* and plant the *Thistles*[37] in their stead as the nobler Flower of the two. For which Reason it is conjectured by profounder Antiquaries, that the Satyrical Itch, so prevalent in this part of our Island, was first brought among us from beyond the *Tweed.*[38] Here may it long flourish and abound; May it survive and neglect the Scorn of the World, with as much Ease and Contempt as the World is insensible to the Lashes of it. May their own Dullness, or that of their Party, be no Discouragement for the Authors to proceed; but let them remember, it is with *Wits* as with *Razors,* which are never so apt to *cut* those they are employ'd on, as when they have *lost their Edge.* Besides, those whose Teeth are too rotten to bite, are best of all others, qualified to revenge that Defect with their Breath.

I am not like other Men, to envy or undervalue the Talents I cannot reach; for which Reason I must needs bear a true Honour to this large eminent Sect of our *British* Writers. And I hope, this little Panegyrick will not be offensive to their Ears, since it has the Advantage of being only designed for themselves. Indeed, Nature her self has taken order, that Fame and Honour should be purchased at a better Pennyworth by Satyr, than by any other Productions of the Brain; the World being soonest provoked to *Praise* by *Lashes,* as Men are to *Love.* There is a Problem in an ancient Author, why Dedications, and other Bundles of Flattery run all upon stale musty Topicks, without the smallest Tincture of any thing New; not only to the torment and nauseating of the *Christian* Reader, but (if not suddenly prevented) to the universal spreading of that pestilent Disease, the Lethargy, in this Island: whereas, there is very little Satyr which has not something in it untouch'd before. The Defects of the former are usually imputed to the want of Invention among those who are Dealers in that kind: But, I think, with a great deal of Injustice; the Solution being easy and natural. For, the Materials of Panegyrick being very few in Number, have been long since exhausted: For, as Health is but one Thing, and has been always the same, whereas Diseases are by thousands, besides new and daily Additions; So, all the Virtues that have been ever in Mankind, are to be counted upon a few Fingers, but his Follies and Vices are innumerable, and Time adds hourly to the Heap. Now, the utmost a poor Poet can do is to get by heart a List of the Cardinal Virtues, and deal them with his utmost Liberality to his Hero or his Patron: He may ring the Changes as far as it will go, and vary his Phrase till he has talk'd round; but the Reader quickly finds, it is all *Pork*,*[39] with a little variety of Sawce: For there is no inventing Terms of Art beyond our Idea's; and when Idea's are exhausted, Terms of Art must be so too.   * *Plutarch.*

BUT, tho' the Matter for Panegyrick were as fruitful as the Topicks of Satyr, yet would it not be hard to find out a sufficient Reason, why the latter will be always better received than the first. For, this being bestowed only upon one or a few Persons at a time, is sure to raise Envy, and consequently ill words from the rest, who have no share in the Blessing: But Satyr being levelled at all, is never resented for an offence by any, since every individual Person makes bold to understand it of others, and very wisely removes his particular Part of the Burthen upon the shoulders of the World, which are broad enough, and able to bear it. To this purpose, I have sometimes reflected upon the Difference between *Athens* and *England,* with respect to the Point before us. In the *Attick** Commonwealth,[40] it was the Privilege and Birth-right of every Citizen and Poet, to rail aloud and in publick, or to expose upon the Stage by Name, any Person they pleased, tho' of the greatest Figure, whether a *Creon,* an *Hyperbolus,* an *Alcibiades,* or a *Demosthenes:* But on the other side, the least reflecting word let fall against the *People* in general, was immediately caught up, and revenged upon the Authors, however considerable for their Quality or their Merits. Whereas, in *England* it is just the Reverse of all this. Here, you may securely display your utmost *Rhetorick* against Mankind, in the Face of the World; tell them, *"That all are gone astray; That there is none that doth good, no not one; That we live in the very Dregs of Time; That Knavery and Atheism are Epidemick as the Pox; That Honesty is fled with Astræa"*; with any other Common places *equally* new and eloquent, which are furnished by the *Splendida bilis**.[41] And when you have done, the whole Audience, far from being offended, shall return you thanks as a Deliverer of precious and useful Truths. Nay farther; It is but to venture your Lungs, and you may preach in *Convent-Garden*[42] against Foppery and Fornication, and *something else:* Against Pride, and Dissimulation, and Bribery, at *White Hall:*[43] You may expose Rapine and Injustice in the *Inns* of *Court*[44] Chappel: And in a *City*[45] Pulpit be as fierce as you please, against Avarice, Hypocrisie and Extortion. 'Tis but a *Ball* bandied to and fro, and every Man carries a *Racket* about Him to strike it from himself among the rest of the Company. But on the other side,

    * *Vid. Xenoph.*

    * *Hor.*

* *Spleen.*

whoever should mistake the Nature of things so far, as to drop but a single Hint in publick, How *such a one,* starved half the Fleet, and half-poison'd the rest: How *such a one,* from a true Principle of *Love* and *Honour,* pays no Debts but for *Wenches* and *Play:* How *such a one* has got a Clap and runs out of his Estate: How *Paris* bribed by *Juno* and *Venus,*** loath to offend either Party, slept out the whole Cause on the Bench: Or, how *such an Orator* makes long Speeches in the Senate with much Thought, little Sense, and to no Purpose; whoever, I say, should venture to be thus particular, must expect to be imprisoned for *Scandalum Magnatum:*[46] to have *Challenges* sent him; to be sued for *Defamation;* and to be *brought before the Bar of the House.*[47]

BUT I forget that I am expatiating on a Subject, wherein I have no concern, having neither a Talent nor an Inclination for Satyr; On the other side, I am so entirely satisfied with the whole present Procedure of human Things, that I have been for some Years preparing Materials towards *A Panegyrick upon the World;* to which I intended to add a Second Part, entituled, *A Modet Defence of the Proceedings of the Rabble in all Ages.* Both these I had Thoughts to publish by way of Appendix to the following Treatise; but finding my Common-Place-Book fill much slower than I had reason to expect, I have chosen to defer them to another Occasion. Besides, I have been unhappily prevented in that Design, by a certain Domestick Misfortune, in the Particulars whereof, tho' it would be very seasonable, and much in the *Modern* way, to inform the *gentle Reader,* and would also be of great Assistance towards extending this Preface into the Size now in Vogue, which by Rule ought to be *large* in proportion as the subsequent Volume is *small;* Yet I shall now dismiss our impatient Reader from any farther Attendance at the *Porch;* and having duly prepared his Mind by a preliminary Discourse, shall gladly introduce him to the sublime Mysteries that ensue.

---

* Juno *and* Venus *are Money and a Mistress, very powerful Bribes to a Judge, if Scandal says true. I remember such Reflexions were cast about that time, but I cannot fix the Person intended here.*

A Tale of a Tub, &c.

SECTION I

THE INTRODUCTION

Whoever hath an Ambition to be heard in a Crowd, must press, and squeeze, and thrust, and climb with indefatigable Pains, till he has exalted himself to a certain Degree of Altitude above them. Now, in all Assemblies, tho' you wedge them ever so close, we may observe this peculiar Property; that, over their Heads there is Room enough; but how to reach it, is the difficult Point; It being as hard to get quit of *Number* as of *Hell;*

———*Evadere ad auras,*
*Hoc opus, hic labor est.**

To this End, the Philosopher's Way in all Ages has been by erecting certain *Edifices in the Air;* But, whatever Practice and Reputation these kind of Structures have formerly possessed, or may still continue in, not excepting even that of *Socrates,* when he was suspended in a Basket to help Contemplation;[48] I think, with due Submission, they seem to labour under two Inconveniences. *First,* That the Foundations being laid too high, they have been often out of *Sight,* and ever out of *Hearing. Secondly,* That the Materials, being very transitory, have suffer'd much from Inclemencies of Air, especially in these North-West Regions.

* But to return, and view the cheerful Skies;
  In this the Task and mighty Labour lies.

THEREFORE, towards the just Performance of this great Work, there remain but three Methods that I can think on; Whereof the Wisdom of our Ancestors being highly sensible, has, to encourage all aspiring Adventurers, thought fit to erect three wooden Machines, for the Use of those Orators who desire to talk much without Interruption. These are, the *Pulpit,* the *Ladder,* and the *Stage-Itinerant.* For, as to the *Bar,* tho' it be compounded of the same Matter, and designed for the same Use, it cannot however be well allowed the Honor of a fourth, by reason of its level or inferior Situation, exposing it to perpetual Interruption from Collaterals. Neither can the *Bench* it self, tho raised to a proper Eminency, put in a better Claim, whatever its Advocates insist on. For if they please to look into the original Design of its Erection, and the Circumstances or Adjuncts subservient to that Design, they will soon acknowledge the present Practice exactly correspondent to the Primitive Institution, and both to answer the Etymology of the Name, which in the *Phœnician* Tongue is a Word of great Signification, importing, if literally interpreted, *The Place of Sleep;* but in common Acceptation, *A Seat well bolster'd and cushion'd, for the Repose of old and gouty Limbs: Senes ut in otia tuta recedant.*[49] Fortune being indebted to them this Part of Retaliation, that, as formerly, they have long *Talkt,* whilst others *Slept,* so now they may *Sleep* as long whilst others *Talk.*

BUT if no other Argument could occur to exclude the *Bench* and the *Bar* from the List of Oratorial Machines, it were sufficient, that the Admission of them would overthrow a Number which I was resolved to establish, whatever Argument it might cost me; in imitation of that prudent Method observed by many other Philosophers and great Clerks, whose chief Art in Division has been, to grow fond of some proper mystical Number, which their Imaginations have rendred Sacred, to a Degree, that they force common Reason to find room for it in every part of Nature; reducing, including, and adjusting every *Genus* and *Species* within that Compass, by coupling some against their Wills, and banishing others at any Rate. Now among all the rest, the profound Number *THREE* is that which hath most employ'd my sublimest Speculations, nor ever without wonderful Delight. There is now in the Press, (and will be publish'd next Term) a Panegyrical Essay of mine upon this Number, wherein I have by most convincing Proofs, not only reduced the *Senses* and the *Elements* under its Banner, but brought over several Deserters from its two great Rivals *SEVEN* and *NINE.*

Now, the first of these Oratorial Machines in Place as well as Dignity, is the *Pulpit*. Of *Pulpits* there are in this Island several sorts; but I esteem only That made of Timber from the *Sylva Caledonia*,[50] which agrees very well with our Climate. If it be upon its Decay, 'tis the better, both for Conveyance of Sound, and for other Reasons to be mentioned by and by. The Degree of Perfection in Shape and Size, I take to consist, in being extreamly narrow, with little Ornament, and best of all without a Cover; (for by antient Rule, it ought to be the only uncover'd *Vessel* in every Assembly where it is rightfully used) by which means, from its near Resemblance to a Pillory, it will ever have a mighty Influence on human Ears.[51]

OF *Ladders* I need say nothing: 'Tis observed by Foreigners themselves, to the Honor of our Country, that we excel all Nations in our Practice and Understanding of this Machine. The ascending Orators do not only oblige their Audience in the agreeable Delivery, but the whole World in their *early* Publication of these Speeches; which I look upon as the choicest Treasury of our *British* Eloquence, and whereof I am informed, that worthy Citizen and Bookseller, Mr. *John Dunton,* hath made a faithful and a painful Collection, which he shortly designs to publish in Twelve Volumes in Folio, illustrated with Copper-Plates. A Work highly useful and curious, and altogether worthy of such a Hand.

THE last Engine of Orators, is the *Stage Itinerant,** erected with much Sagacity, *sub Jove pluvio, in triviis & quadriviis.*† It is the great Seminary of the two former, and its Orators are sometimes preferred to the One, and sometimes to the Other, in proportion to their Deservings, there being a strict and perpetual Intercourse between all three.

FROM this accurate Deduction it is manifest, that for obtaining Attention in Publick, there is of necessity required a *superiour Position of Place*. But, altho' this Point be generally granted, yet the Cause is little agreed in; and it seems to me, that very few Philosophers have fallen into a true, natural Solution of this *Phænomenon*. The deepest Account, and the most fairly digested of any I have yet met with, is this, That Air being a heavy Body, and therefore (according to the System of *Lucret. Epicurus**) continually descending, must needs be more, so, Lib. 2. when loaden and press'd down by Words; which are also Bodies of much Weight and Gravity, as it is manifest from those deep *Impressions* they make and leave upon us; and therefore must be delivered from a due

---

* *Is the* Mountebank's Stage, *whose Orators the Author determines either to the* Gallows *or a* Conventicle.

† *In the Open Air, and in Streets where the greatest Resort is.*

Altitude, or else they will neither carry a good Aim, nor fall down with a sufficient Force.

> *Corpoream quoque enim vocem constare fatendum est,*
> *Et sonitum, quoniam possunt impellere Sensus.* Lucr. *Lib. 4.**[52]

AND I am the readier to favour this Conjecture, from a common Observation; that in the several Assemblies of these Orators, Nature it self hath instructed the Hearers, to stand with their Mouths open, and erected parallel to the Horizon, so as they may be intersected by a perpendicular Line from the Zenith to the Center of the Earth. In which Position, if the Audience be well compact, every one carries home a Share, and little or nothing is lost.

I confess, there is something yet more refined in the Contrivance and Structure of our Modern Theatres. For, First; the Pit is sunk below the Stage with due regard to the Institution above-deduced; that whatever *weighty* Matter shall be delivered thence (whether it be *Lead* or *Gold*) may fall plum into the Jaws of certain *Criticks* (as I think they are called) which stand ready open to devour them. Then, the Boxes are built round, and raised to a Level with the Scene, in deference to the Ladies, because, That large Portion of Wit laid out in raising Pruriences and Protuberances, is observ'd to run much upon a Line, and ever in a Circle. The whining Passions and little starved Conceits, are gently wafted up by their own extreme Levity, to the middle Region, and there fix and are frozen by the frigid Understandings of the Inhabitants. Bombast and Buffoonry, by Nature lofty and light, soar highest of all, and would be lost in the Roof, if the prudent Architect had not with much Foresight contrived for them a fourth Place, called *the Twelve-Peny Gallery*, and there planted a suitable Colony, who greedily intercept them in their Passage.

Now this Physico-logical Scheme of Oratorial Receptacles or Machines, contains a great Mystery, being a Type, a Sign, an Emblem, a Shadow, a Symbol, bearing Analogy to the spacious Commonwealth of Writers, and to those Methods by which they must exalt themselves to a certain Eminency above the inferiour World. By the *Pulpit* are adumbrated the Writings of our *Modern Saints* in *Great Britain*, as they have spiritualized and refined them from the Dross and Grossness of *Sense* and *Human Reason*. The Matter, as we have said, is of rotten Wood, and

---

* *'Tis certain then, that* Voice *that thus can wound*
  Is all Material; Body *every* Sound.

that upon two Considerations; Because it is the Quality of rotten Wood to give *Light* in the Dark: And secondly, Because its Cavities are full of Worms: which is a Type with a Pair of Handles, having a Respect to the two principal Qualifications of the Orator, and the two different Fates attending upon his Works.*

THE *Ladder* is an adequate Symbol of *Faction* and of *Poetry,* to both of which so noble a Number of Authors are indebted for their Fame. Of *Faction,*† because * * * * * * * * * * * * * * *

* * * * * * * * * * * * * * * * * * *   *Hiatus in MS.*

* * * * * * * * * * * * * * * * * * *

* * * * * * * * * *   Of *Poetry,* because its Orators do *perorare* with a Song;[53] and because climbing up by slow Degrees, Fate is sure to turn them off before they can reach within many Steps of the Top: And because it is a Preferment attained by transferring of Propriety, and a confounding of *Meum* and *Tuum.*[54]

UNDER the *Stage-Itinerant* are couched those Productions designed for the Pleasure and Delight of Mortal Man; such as, *Six-peny-worth of Wit,* Westminster *Drolleries, Delightful Tales, Compleat Jesters,* and the like; by which the Writers of and for *GRUB-STREET,* have in these latter Ages so nobly triumph'd over *Time;* have clipt his Wings, pared his Nails, filed his Teeth, turn'd back his Hour-Glass, blunted his Scythe, and drawn the Hob-Nails out of his Shoes. It is under this *Classis,* I have presumed to list my present Treatise, being just come from having the Honor conferred upon me, to be adopted a Member of that Illustrious Fraternity.

Now, I am not unaware, how the Productions of the *Grub-street* Brotherhood, have of late Years fallen under many Prejudices, nor how it has been the perpetual Employment of two *Junior* start-up Societies, to ridicule them and their Authors, as unworthy their established Post in the Commonwealth of Wit and Learning. Their own Consciences will easily inform them, whom I mean; Nor has the World been so negligent a Looker on, as not to observe the continual Efforts made by the Societies of *Gresham*[55] and of *Will's*‡ to edify a Name and Reputation upon the Ruin of

* *The Two Principal Qualifications of a Phanatick Preacher are, his Inward Light, and his Head full of Maggots, and the Two different Fates of his Writings are, to be burnt or Worm eaten.*

† *Here is pretended a Defect in the Manuscript, and this is very frequent with our Author, either when he thinks he cannot say any thing worth Reading, or when he has no mind to enter on the Subject, or when it is a Matter of little Moment, or perhaps to amuse his reader (whereof he is frequently very fond) or lastly, with some Satyrical Intention.*

‡ Wills' Coffee-House, *was formerly the Place where the Poets usually met, which tho it be yet fresh in memory, yet in some Years may be forgot, and want this Explanation.*

OURS. And this is yet a more feeling Grief to Us upon the Regards of
Tenderness as well as of Justice, when we reflect on their Proceedings, not
only as unjust, but as ungrateful, undutiful, and unnatural. For, how can it
be forgot by the World or themselves, (to say nothing of our own Records,
which are full and clear in the Point) that they both are Seminaries, not
only of our *Planting,* but our *Watering* too? I am informed, Our two *Rivals*
have lately made an Offer to enter into the Lists with united Forces, and
Challenge us to a Comparison of Books, both as to *Weight* and
Number. In Return to which, (with Licence from our *President*) I   * Viz. *About*
humbly offer two Answers: First, We say, the proposal is like   *moving the*
that which *Archimedes* made upon a *smaller** Affair, including an   *Earth.*
impossiblity in the Practice; For, where can they find Scales of *Capacity*
enough for the first, or an Arithmetician of *Capacity* enough for the Second. Secondly, We are ready to accept the Challenge, but with this Condition, that a third indifferent Person be assigned, to whose impartial
Judgment it shall be left to decide, which Society each Book, Treatise or
Pamphlet do most properly belong to. This Point, God knows, is very far
from being fixed at present; For, We are ready to produce a Catalogue of
some Thousands, which in all common Justice ought to be entitled to Our
Fraternity, but by the revolted and new-fangled Writers, most perfidiously
ascribed to the others. Upon all which, we think it very unbecoming our
Prudence, that the Determination should be remitted to the Authors
themselves; when our Adversaries by Briguing and Caballing,[56] have
caused so universal a Defection from us, that the greatest Part of our Society hath already deserted to them, and our nearest Friends begin to
stand aloof, as if they were half-ashamed to own Us.

THIS is the utmost I am authorized to say upon so ungrateful and melancholy a Subject; because We are extreme unwilling to inflame a Controversy, whose Continuance may be so fatal to the Interests of Us All,
desiring much rather that Things be amicably composed; and We shall so
far advance on our Side, as to be ready to receive the two *Prodigals*[57] with
open Arms, whenever they shall think fit to return from their
Husks and their *Harlots;* which I think from the present* Course   * *Virtuoso*
of their Studies they most properly may be said to be engaged   *Experiments, and*
in; and like an indulgent Parent, continue to them our Affec-   *Modern*
tion and our Blessing.   *Comedies.*

BUT the greatest Maim given to that general Reception, which the
Writings of our Society have formerly received, (next to the transitory
State of all sublunary Things,) hath been a superficial Vein among many
Readers of the present Age, who will by no means be persuaded to inspect

beyond the Surface and the Rind of Things; whereas, *Wisdom* is a *Fox*, who after long hunting, will at last cost you the Pains to dig out: 'Tis a *Cheese*, which by how much the richer, has the thicker, the homelier, and the courser Coat; and whereof to a judicious Palate, the *Maggots* are the best. 'Tis a *Sack-Posset*,[58] wherein the deeper you go, you will find it the sweeter. *Wisdom* is a *Hen*, whose *Cackling* we must value and consider, because it is attended with an *Egg;* But then, lastly, 'tis a *Nut*, which unless you chuse with Judgment, may cost you a Tooth, and pay you with nothing but a *Worm*. In consequence of these momentous Truths, the *Grubæan* Sages have always chosen to convey their Precepts and their Arts, shut up within the Vehicles of Types and Fables, which having been perhaps more careful and curious in adorning, than was altogether necessary, it has fared with these Vehicles after the usual Fate of Coaches over-finely painted and gilt; that the transitory Gazers have so dazzled their Eyes, and fill'd their Imaginations with the outward Lustre, as neither to regard or consider, the Person or the Parts of the Owner within. A Misfortune we undergo with somewhat less Reluctancy, because it has been common to us with *Pythagoras, Æsop, Socrates,* and other of our Predecessors.

However, that neither the World nor our selves may any longer suffer by such misunderstandings, I have been prevailed on, after much importunity from my Friends, to travel in a compleat and laborious Dissertation upon the prime Productions of our Society, which besides their beautiful Externals for the Gratification of superficial Readers, have darkly and deeply couched under them, the most finished and refined Systems of all Sciences and Arts; as I do not doubt to lay open by Untwisting or Unwinding, and either to draw up by Exantlation,[59] or display by Incision.

This great Work was entered upon some Years ago, by one of our most eminent Members: He began with the History of *Reynard* the *Fox*,* but neither lived to publish his Essay, nor to proceed farther in so useful an Attempt which is very much to be lamented, because the Discovery he made, and communicated with his Friends, is now universally received; nor, do I think, any of the Learned will dispute, that famous Treatise to be a compleat Body of Civil Knowledge, and the *Revelation,* or rather the *Apocalyps* of all State-*Arcana.* But the Progress I have made is much greater, having already finished my Annotations upon several Dozens; From some

---

* *The Author seems here to be mistaken, for I have seen a Latin Edition of* Reynard *the Fox, above an hundred Years old, which I take to be the Original; for the rest it has been thought by many People to contain some Satyrical Design in it.*

of which, I shall impart a few Hints to the candid Reader, as far as will be necessary to the Conclusion at which I aim.

THE first Piece I have handled is that of *Tom Thumb*,[60] whose Author was a *Pythagorean* Philosopher. This dark Treatise contains the whole Scheme of the *Metempsychosis,* deducing the Progress of the Soul thro' all her Stages.

THE next is Dr. *Faustus,* penn'd by *Artephius,* an Author *bonæ notæ,* and an *Adeptus;* He published it in the nine hundred eighty fourth Year of his Age;* this Writer proceeds wholly by *Reincrudation,* or in the *via humida:* And the Marriage between *Faustus* and *Helen,* does most conspicuously dilucidate the fermenting of the *Male* and *Female Dragon.* *He lived a thousand.*

WHITTINGTON *and his Cat,* is the Work of that Mysterious *Rabbi, Jehuda Hannasi,* containing a Defence of the *Gemara* of the *Jerusalem Misna,* and its just preference to that of *Babylon,* contrary to the vulgar Opinion.

THE *Hind and Panther.* This is the Master-piece of a famous Writer† now living,[61] intended for a compleat Abstract of sixteen thousand Schoolmen from *Scotus* to *Bellarmin.* † *Viz in the Year 1698.*

TOMMY POTTS.[62] Another Piece supposed by the same Hand, by way of Supplement to the former.

THE *Wise Men of* Goatham, *cum Appendice.* This is a Treatise of immense Erudition, being the great Original and Fountain of those Arguments, bandied about both in *France* and *England,* for a just Defence of the *Modern* Learning and Wit, against the Presumption, the Pride, and the Ignorance of the *Antients.* This unknown Author hath so exhausted the Subject, that a penetrating Reader will easily discover, whatever hath been written since upon that Dispute, to be little more than Repetition. An Abstract‡ of this Treatise hath been lately published by a *worthy Member* of our Society.

THESE Notices may serve to give the Learned Reader an Idea as well as a Taste of what the whole Work is likely to produce: wherein I have now altogether circumscribed my Thoughts and my Studies; and if I can bring it to a Perfection before I die, shall reckon I have well emloy'd the poor Remains of an unfortunate Life.§ This indeed is more than I can justly expect from a Quill worn to the Pith in the Service of the State, in *Pro's* and *Con's*

‡ *This I suppose to be understood of Mr.* Wottons *Discourse of Antient and Modern Learning.*

§ *Here the Author seems to personate* L'estrange, Dryden, *and some others, who after having past their Lives in Vices, Faction and Falshood, have the Impudence to talk of Merit and Innocence and Sufferings.*

upon *Popish Plots*, and *Meal-Tubs*,* and *Exclusion Bills*, and *Passive Obedience*, and *Addresses of Lives and Fortunes;* and *Prerogative*, and *Property*, and *Liberty of Conscience*, and *Letters to a Friend:* From an Understanding and a Conscience, thread-bare and ragged with perpetual turning; From a Head broken in a hundred places, by the Malignants of the opposite Factions, and from a Body spent with Poxes ill cured, by trusting to Bawds and Surgeons, who, (as it afterwards appeared) were profess'd Enemies to Me and the Government, and revenged their Party's Quarrel upon my Nose and Shins. Four-score and eleven Pamphlets have I writ under three Reigns, and for the Service of six and thirty Factions. But finding the State has no farther Occasion for Me and my Ink, I retire willingly to draw it out into Speculations more becoming a Philosopher, having, to my unspeakable Comfort, passed a long Life, with a Conscience void of Offence.

But to return. I am assured from the Reader's Candor, that the brief Specimen I have given, will easily clear all the rest of our Society's Productions from an Aspersion grown, as it is manifest, out of Envy and Ignorance: That they are of little farther Use or Value to Mankind, beyond the common Entertainments of their Wit and their Style: For these I am sure have never yet been disputed by our keenest Adversaries: In both which, as well as the more profound and mystical Part, I have throughout this Treatise closely followed the most applauded Originals. And to render all compleat, I have with much Thought and Application of Mind, so ordered, that the chief Title prefixed to it, (I mean, That under which I design it shall pass in the common Conversations of Court and Town) is modelled exactly after the Manner peculiar to *Our* Society.

† *The Title Page in the Original was so torn, that it was not possible to recover several Titles which the Author here speaks of.*

I confess to have been somewhat liberal in the Business of Titles,† having observed the humor of multiplying them, to bear great Vogue among certain Writers, whom I exceedingly Reverence. And indeed, it seems not unreasonable, that Books, the Children of the Brain, should have the Honor to be Christned with variety of Names, as well as other Infants of Quality. Our famous *Dryden* has ventured to proceed a Point farther, endeavouring to introduce also a Multiplicity of *God-fathers;*‡ which is an Improvement of much more Advantage, upon a very obvious Account. 'Tis a Pity this admirable Invention has not been better cultivated, so as to grow

‡ *See* Virgil *translated*, &c.

* *In King* Charles *the* II. *Time, there was an Account of a* Presbyterian *Plot, found in a Tub, which then made much Noise.*

by this time into general Imitation, when such an Authority serves it for a Precedent. Nor have my Endeavours been wanting to second so useful an Example: But it seems there is an unhappy Expence usually annexed to the Calling of a God-Father, which was clearly out of my Head, as it is very reasonable to believe. Where the Pinch lay, I cannot certainly affirm; but having employ'd a World of Thoughts and Pains, to split my Treatise into forty Sections, and having entreated forty Lords of my Acquaintance, that they would do me the Honor to stand, they all made it a Matter of Conscience, and sent me their Excuses.

SECTION II

Once upon a Time, there was a Man who had Three Sons* by one Wife, and all at a Birth, neither could the Mid-Wife tell certainly which was the Eldest. Their Father died while they were young, and upon his Death-Bed, calling the Lads to him, spoke thus,

SONS; *because I have purchased no Estate, nor was born to any, I have long considered of some good Legacies to bequeath You; And at last, with much Care as well as Expence, have provided each of you* (here they are) *a new Coat.†Now, you are to understand, that these Coats have two Virtues contained in them: One is, that with good wearing they will last you fresh and sound as long as you live: The other is, that they will grow in the same proportion with your Bodies, lengthning and widening of themselves, so as to be always fit. Here, let me see them on you before I die. So, very well, Pray Children, wear them clean, and brush them often. You will find in my Will‡* (here it is) *full Instructions in every particular concerning the Wearing and Management of your Coats; wherein you must be very exact, to avoid the Penalties I have appointed for every Transgression or Neglect, upon which your future Fortunes will entirely depend. I have also commanded in my Will, that you should live together in one House like Brethren and Friends, for then you will be sure to thrive, and not otherwise.*

HERE the Story says, this good Father died, and the three Sons went all together to seek their Fortunes.

* *By these three Sons,* Peter, Martyn *and* Jack; Popery, *the* Church *of* England, *and our Protestant* Dissenters *are designed.* W. Wotton.

† *By his Coats which he gave his Sons, the Garments of the* Israelites. W. Wotton.

An Error (with Submission) of the learned Commentator; for by the Coats are meant the Doctrine and Faith of Christianity, *by the Wisdom of the Divine Founder fitted to all Times, Places and Circumstances.* Lambin.[63]

‡ *The New Testament.*

I shall not trouble you with recounting what Adventures they met for the first seven Years, any farther than by taking notice, that they carefully observed their Father's Will, and kept their Coats in very good Order; That they travelled thro' several Countries, encountered a reasonable Quantity of Gyants and slew certain Dragons.

BEING now arrived at the proper Age for producing themselves, they came up to Town, and fell in love with the Ladies, but espcially three, who about that time were in chief Reputation: The Dutchess *d' Argent, Madame de Grands Titres,* and the Countess *d' Orgueil.*[*] On their first Appeareance, our three Adventurers met with a very bad Reception; and soon with great Sagacity guessing out the Reason, they quickly began to improve in the good Qualities of the Town: They Writ, and Raillyed, and Rhymed, and Sung, and Said, and said Nothing; They Drank, and Fought, and Whor'd, and Slept, and Swore, and took Snuff: They went to new Plays on the first Night, haunted the *Chocolate*-Houses, beat the Watch, lay on Bulks,[64] and got Claps: They bilkt[65] Hackney-Coachmen, ran in Debt with Shop-keepers, and lay with their Wives: They kill'd Bayliffs, kick'd Fidlers down Stairs, eat at *Locket's,* loytered at *Will's:* They talk'd of the Drawing-Room and never came there, Dined with Lords they never saw; Whisper'd a Dutchess, and spoke never a Word; exposed the Scrawls of their Laun-dress for Billets-doux of Quality: came ever just from Court and were never seen in it; attended the Levee *sub dio;*[66] Got a list of Peers by heart in one Company, and with great Familiarity retailed them in another. Above all, they constantly attended those Committees of Senators who are silent in the *House,* and loud in the *Coffee-House,* where they nightly ad-journ to chew the Cud of Politicks, and are encompass'd with a Ring of Disciples, who lye in wait to catch up their Droppings. The three Brothers had acquired forty other Qualifications of the like Stamp, too tedious to recount, and by consequence, were justly reckoned the most accomplish'd Persons in Town: But all would not suffice, and the Ladies aforesaid continued still inflexible: To clear up which difficulty, I must with the Reader's good Leave and Patience, have recourse to some Points of Weight, which the Authors of that Age have not sufficiently illustrated.

FOR, about this Time† it happened a Sect arose, whose Tenents ob-tained and spread very far, especially in the *Grand Monde,* and among

---

* *Their Mistresses are the* Dutchess d'Argent, Madamoiselle de Grands Titres, *and the* Countess d'Orgueil, *i. e.* Covetousness, Ambition *and* Pride, *which were the three great Vices that the ancient Fathers inveighed against as the first Corruptions of Christianity.* W. Wotton.

† *This is an Occasional Satyr upon Dress and Fashion, in order to introduce what follows.*

every Body of good Fashion. They worshipped a sort of *Idol,* who, as their Doctrine delivered, did daily create Men, by a kind of Manufactory Operation. This *Idol** they placed in the highest Parts of the House, on an Altar erected about three Foot: He was shewn in the Posture of a *Persian* Emperor, sitting on a *Superficies,* with his Legs interwoven under him. This God had a *Goose* for his Ensign; whence it is, that some Learned Men pretend to deduce his Original from *Jupiter Cápitolinus.*[67] At his left Hand, beneath the Altar, *Hell* seemed to open, and catch at the Animals the *Idol* was creating; to prevent which, certain of his Priests hourly flung in Pieces of the uninformed Mass, or Substance, and sometimes whole Limbs already enlivened, which that horrid Gulph insatiably swallowed, terrible to behold. The *Goose* was also held a subaltern Divinity, or *Deus minorum Gentium,*[68] before whose Shrine was sacrificed that Creature, whose hourly Food is humane Gore, and who is in so great Renown abroad, for being the Delight and Favourite of the *Ægyptian Cercopithecus.*† Millions of these Animals were cruelly slaughtered every Day, to appease the Hunger of that consuming Deity. The chief *Idol* was also worshipped as the Inventor of the *Yard* and the *Needle,* whether as the God of Seamen, or on Account of certain other mystical Attributes, hath not been sufficiently cleared.

THE Worshippers of this Deity had also a System of their Belief, which seemed to turn upon the following Fundamental. They held the Universe to be a large *Suit of Cloaths,* which *invests* every Thing: That the Earth is *invested* by the Air; The Air is *invested* by the Stars; and the Stars are *invested* by the *Primum Mobile.* Look on this Globe of Earth, you will find it to be a very compleat and fashionable *Dress.* What is that which some call *Land,* but a fine Coat faced with Green? or the Sea, but a Wastcoat of Water-Tabby? Proceed to the particular Works of the Creation, you will find how curious *Journey-man* Nature hath been, to trim up the *vegetable* Beaux: Observe how sparkish a Perewig adorns the Head of a *Beech,* and what a fine Doublet of white Satin is worn by the *Birch.* To conclude from all, what is Man himself but a *Micro-Coat,*‡ or rather a compleat Suit of Cloaths with all its Trimmings? As to his Body, there can be no dispute; but examine even the Acquirements of his Mind, you will find them all contribute in their Order, towards furnishing out an exact Dress: To instance

---

* *By this* Idol *is meant a Taylor.*

† *The* Ægyptians *worship'd a Monkey, which Animal is very fond of eating Lice, styled here Creatures that feed on Human Gore.*

‡ *Alluding to the Word* Microcosm, *or a little World, as Man hath been called by Philosophers.*

no more; Is not Religion a *Cloak,* Honesty a *Pair of Shoes,* worn out in the Dirt, Self-love a *Surtout,* Vanity a *Shirt,* and Conscience a *Pair of Breeches,* which, tho' a Cover for Lewdness as well as Nastiness, is easily slipt down for the Service of both.

THESE *Postulata* being admitted, it will follow in due Course of Reasoning, that those Beings which the World calls improperly *Suits of Cloaths,* are in Reality the most refined Species of Animals, or to proceed higher, that they are Rational Creatures, or Men. For, is it not manifest, that They live, and move, and talk, and perform all other Offices of Human Life? Are not Beauty, and Wit, and Mien, and Breeding, their inseparable Proprieties? In short, we see nothing but them, hear nothing but them. Is it not they who walk the Streets, fill up *Parliament——, Coffee—, Play—, Bawdy-Houses?* 'Tis true indeed, that these Animals, which are vulgarly called *Suits of Cloaths,* or *Dresses,* do according to certain Compositions receive different Appellations. If one of them be trimm'd up with a Gold Chain, and a red Gown, and a white Rod, and a great Horse, it is called a *Lord-Mayor;* If certain Ermins and Furs be placed in a certain Position, we stile them a *Judge,* and so, an apt Conjunction of Lawn and black Sattin, we intitle a *Bishop.*

OTHERS of these Professors, though agreeing in the main System, were yet more refined upon certain Branches of it; and held that Man was an Animal compounded of two *Dresses,* the *Natural* and the *Celestial Suit,* which were the Body and the Soul: That the Soul was the outward, and the Body the inward Cloathing; that the latter was *ex traduce;*[69] but the former of daily Creation and Circumfusion. This last they proved by *Scripture,* because, *in Them we Live, and Move, and have our Being:* As likewise by Philosophy, because they are *All in All, and All in every Part.* Besides, said they, separate these two, and you will find the Body to be only a sensless unsavory Carcass. By all which it is manifest, that the outward Dress must needs be the Soul.

To this System of Religion were tagged several subaltern Doctrines, which were entertained with great Vogue: as particularly, the Faculties of the Mind were deduced by the Learned among them in this manner: *Embroidery,* was *Sheer wit; Gold Fringe* was *agreeable Conversation, Gold Lace* was *Repartee,* a huge long *Periwig* was *Humor,* and a *Coat full of Powder* was very good *Raillery:* All which required abundance of *Finesse* and *Delicatesse* to manage with Advantage, as well as a strict Observance after Times and Fashions.

I have with much Pains and Reading, collected out of antient Authors, this short Summary of a Body of Philosophy and Divinity, which seems to have been composed by a Vein and Race of Thinking, very different from any other Systems, either *Antient* or *Modern*. And it was not meerly to entertain or satisfy the Reader's Curiosity, but rather to give him Light into several Circumstances of the following Story: that knowing the State of Dispositions and Opinions in an Age so remote, he may better comprehend those great Events which were the issue of them. I advise therefore the courteous Reader, to peruse with a world of Application, again and again, whatever I have written upon this Matter. And so leaving these broken Ends, I carefully gather up the chief Thread of my Story, and proceed.

THESE Opinions therefore were so universal, as well as the Practices of them, among the refined Part of Court and Town, that our three Brother-Adventurers, as their Circumstances then stood, were strangely at a loss. For, on the one side, the three Ladies they address'd themselves to, (whom we have named already) were ever at the very Top of the Fashion, and abhorred all that were below it, but the breadth of a Hair. On the other side, their Father's Will was very precise, and it was the main Precept in it, with the greatest Penalties annexed, not to add to, or diminish from their Coats, one Thread, without a positive Command in the Will. Now, the Coats their Father had left them were, 'tis true, of very good Cloth, and besides, so neatly sown, you would swear they were all of a Piece, but at the same time, very plain, and with little or no Ornament; And it happened, that before they were a Month in Town, great *Shoulder-knots** came up; Strait, all the World was *Shoulder-knots;* no approaching the Ladies *Ruelles* without the *Quota* of *shoulder-knots: That Fellow,* cries one, *has no Soul; where is his Shoulder-knot?* Our three Brethren soon discovered their Want by sad Expe-

---

The first part of the Tale *is the History of* Peter; *thereby* Popery *is exposed, every Body knows the* Papists *have made great Additions to Christianity, that indeed is the great Exception which the* Church of England *makes against them, accordingly* Peter *begins his Pranks, with adding a* Shoulder-knot *to his Coat.* W., Wotton.

His Description of the Cloth of which the Coat was made, has a farther meaning than the Words may seem to import, "The Coats their Father had left them, were of very good Cloth, and besides so neatly Sown, you would swear it had been all of a Piece, but at the same time very plain with little or no Ornament." *This is the distinguishing Character of the Christian Religion.* Christiana Religio absoluta & simplex, *was* Ammianus Marcellinus's *Description of it, who was himself a Heathen.* W. Wotton.

* *By this is understood the first introducing of Pageantry, and unnecessary Ornaments in the Church, such as were neither for Convenience nor Edification, as a* Shoulder-knot, *in which there is neither Symmetry nor Use.*

rience, meeting in their Walks with forty Mortifications and Indignities. If they went to the *Play-house,* the Door-keeper shewed them into the Twelve-peny Gallery. If they called a Boat, says a Water-man, *I am first Sculler.* If they stept to the *Rose* to take a Bottle, the Drawer would cry, *Friend, we sell no Ale.* If they went to visit a Lady, a Footman met them at the Door with, *Pray send up your Message.* In this unhappy Case, they went immediately to consult their Father's Will, read it over and over, but not a Word of the *Shoulder-knot.* What should they do? What Temper should they find? Obedience was absolutely necessary, and yet *Shoulder-knots* appeared extreamly requisite. After much Thought, one of the Brothers who happened to be more *Book-learned* than the other two, said he had found an Expedient. *'Tis true,* said he, *there is nothing here in this Will,* totidem verbis,*[70] *making mention of* Shoulder-knots, *but I dare conjecture, we may find them* inclusivè, *or* totidem syllabis.[71] This Distinction was immediately approved by all; and so they fell again to examine the Will. But their evil Star had so directed the Matter, that the first Syllable was not to be found in the whole Writing. Upon which Disappointment, he, who found the former Evasion, took heart, and said, *Brothers, there is yet Hopes; for tho' we cannot find them* totidem verbis, *nor* totidem syllabis, *I dare engage we shall make them out* tertio modo, *or* totidem literis.[72] This Discovery was also highly commended, upon which they fell once more to the Scrutiny, and soon picked out *S, H, O, U, L, D, E, R;* when the same Planet, Enemy to their Repose, had wonderfully contrived, that a *K* was not to be found. Here was a weighty Difficulty! But the distinguishing Brother (for whom we shall hereafter find a Name) now his Hand was in, proved by a very good Argument, that *K* was a modern illegitimate Letter, unknown to the Learned Ages, nor any where to be found in antient Manu-scripts. 'Tis true, said he, the Word *Calendæ* hath in *Q.V.C.*† been sometimes writ with a *K,* but erroneously, for in the best Copies it is ever spelt with a *C.* And by consequence it was a gross Mis-take in our Language to spell *Knot* with a *K,* but that from henceforward, he would take care it should be writ with a *C.* Upon this, all farther Difficulty vanished; *Shoulder-Knots* were made clearly out, to be *Jure Paterno,*[73] and our three Gentlemen swaggered with as large and as flanting ones as the best.

† *Quibusdam Veteribus Codicibus.*

BUT, as human Happiness is of a very short Duration, so in those Days

---

* *When the Papists cannot find any thing which they want in Scripture, they go to* Oral Tradition: *Thus* Peter *is introduced satisfy'd with the Tedious way of looking for all the Letters of any Word, which he has occasion for in the* Will, *when neither the constituent Syllables, nor much less the whole Word, were there* in Terminis. W. Wotton.

† *Some antient Manuscripts.*

were human Fashions, upon which it entirely depends. *Shoulder-Knots* had
their Time, and we must now imagine them in their Decline; for a certain
Lord came just from *Paris*, with fifty Yards of *Gold Lace* upon his Coat, exactly trimm'd after the Court-Fashion of that *Month*. In two Days, all
Mankind appear'd closed up in Bars of *Gold Lace*:* whoever durst peep
abroad without his Complement of *Gold Lace*, was as scandalous as a ———,
and as ill received among the Women. What should our three Knights do
in this momentous Affair? They had sufficiently strained a Point already, in
the Affair of *Shoulder-Knots*: Upon Recourse to the Will, nothing appeared
there but *altum silentium*.[74] That of the *Shoulder-Knots* was a loose, flying, circumstantial Point; but this of *Gold Lace*, seemed too considerable an Alteration without better Warrant; it did *aliquo modo essentiæ adhærere*,[75] and
therefore required a positive Precept. But about this time it fell out, that
the Learned Brother aforesaid, had read *Aristotelis Dialectica*, and especially
that wonderful Piece *de Interpretatione*, which has the Faculty of teaching
its Readers to find out a Meaning in every Thing but it self; like Commentators on the *Revelations*, who proceed Prophets without understanding
a Syllable of the Text. *Brothers*, said he, *You are to be informed,* †*that, of Wills,*
duo sunt genera,[76] *Nuncupatory and scriptory:* ‡ *that in the Scriptory Will here
before us, there is no Precept or Mention about Gold Lace*, conceditur: *But*, si idem
affirmetur de nuncupatorio, negatur,[77] *For Brothers, if you remember, we heard
a Fellow say when we were Boys, that he heard my Father's Man say, that he heard
my Father say, that he would advise his Sons to get* Gold Lace *on their Coats, as
soon as ever they could procure Money to buy it. By G— that is very true*, cries
the other; *I remember it perfectly well*, said the third. And so without more ado
they got the largest *Gold Lace* in the Parish, and walk'd about as fine as
Lords.

A while after, there came up *all in Fashion*, a pretty sort of *flame Coloured
Sattin*§ for Linings, and the *Mercer* brought a Pattern of it immediately to
our three Gentlemen, *An please your Worships* (said he) *My Lord C—, and Sir*

---

* *I cannot tell whether the Author means any new Innovation by this Word, or whether it be only to
introduce the new Methods of forcing and perverting Scripture.*

† *The next Subject of our Author's Wit, is the Glosses and Interpretations of Scripture, very many absurd ones of which are allow'd in the most Authentick Books of the* Church of Rome. W. Wotton.

‡ *By this is meant* Tradition, *allowed to have equal Authority with the Scripture, or rather greater.*

§ *This is Purgatory, whereof he speaks more particularly hereafter, but here only to shew how Scripture was perverted to prove it, which was done by giving equal Authority with the* Canon *to* Apocrypha,
called here a Codicil annex'd.

*It is likely the Author, in every one of these Changes in the Brother's Dresses, refers to some particular
Error in the* Church of Rome; *tho' it is not easy I think to apply them all, but by this of* Flame

J. W.* *had Linings out of this very Piece last Night; it takes wonderfully, and I shall not have a Remnant left, enough to make my Wife a Pin-cushion by to morrow Morning at ten a Clock.* Upon this, they fell again to romage the Will, because the present Case also required a positive Precept, the Lining being held by Orthodox Writers to be of the Essence of the Coat. After long search, they could fix upon nothing to the Matter in hand, except a short Advice of their Fathers in the Will, to take care of *Fire*,† and put out their *Candles* before they went to Sleep. This tho' a good deal for the Purpose, and helping very far towards Self-Conviction, yet not seeming wholly of Force to establish a Command; and being resolved to avoid farther Scruple, as well as future Occasion for Scandal, says He that was the Scholar; *I remember to have read in Wills, of a Codicil annexed, which is indeed a Part of the Will, and what it contains hath equal authority with the rest. Now, I have been considering of this same Will here before us, and I cannot reckon it to be compleat for want of such a Codicil. I will therefore fasten one in its proper Place very dexteriously; I have had it by me some Time, it was written by a Dog-keeper‡ of my Grand-father's, and talks a great deal (as good Luck would have it) of this very flame-colour'd Sattin.* The Project was immediately approved by the other two; an old Parchment Scrowl was tagged on according to Art, in the Form of a *Codicil annext,* and the *Sattin* bought and worn.

NEXT Winter, a *Player,* hired for the Purpose by the Corporation of *Fringe-makers,* acted his Part in a new Comedy, all covered with *Silver Fringe,*§ and according to the laudable Custom gave Rise to that Fashion. Upon which, the Brothers consulting their Father's Will, to their great Astonishment found these Words; Item, I *charge and command my said three Sons, to wear no sort of* Silver Fringe *upon or about their said Coats,* &c. with a Penalty in case of Disobedience, too long here to insert. However, after some Pause the Brother so often mentioned for his Erudition, who was well Skill'd in Criticisms, had found in a certain Author, which he said should be nameless, that the same Word which in the Will is called *Fringe,* does also signifie a *Broom-stick;* and doubtless ought to have the same

---

Colour'd Satin *is manifestly intended* Purgatory; *by* Gold Lace *may perhaps be understood, the lofty Ornaments and Plate in the Churches. The* Shoulder-Knots *and* Silver Fringe, *are not so obvious, at least to me; but the* Indian Figures *of Men, Women and Children plainly relate to the Pictures in the Romish Churches, of God like an old Man, of the Virgin* Mary *and our Saviour as a child.*

* *This shews the Time the Author writ, it being about fourteen Years since those two Persons were reckoned the fine Gentlemen of the Town.*

† *That is, to take care of Hell, and, in order to do that, to subdue and extinguish their Lusts.*

‡ *I believe this refers to that part of the* Apocrypha *where mention is made of* Tobit *and his* Dog.

§ *This is certainly the farther introducing the Pomps of Habit and Ornament.*

Interpretation in this Paragraph. This, another of the Brothers disliked, because of that Epithet, *Silver,* which could not, he humbly conceived, in Propriety of Speech be reasonably applied to a *Broom-stick:* but it was replied upon him, that this Epithet was understood in a *Mythological,* and *Allegorical* Sense. However, he objected again, why their Father should forbid them to wear a *Broom-stick* on their Coats, a Caution that seemed unnatural and impertinent; upon which he was taken up short, as one that spoke irreverently of a *Mystery,* which doubtless was very useful and significant, but ought not to be over-curiously pryed into, or nicely reasoned upon. And in short, their Father's Authority being now considerably sunk, this Expedient was allowed to serve as a lawful Dispensation, for wearing their full Proportion of *Silver Fringe.*

A while after, was rivived an old Fashion, long antiquated, of *Embroidery* with *Indian Figures** of Men, Women and Children. Here they had no Occasion to examine the Will. They remembered but too well, how their Father had always abhorred this Fashion; that he made several Paragraphs on purpose, importing his utter Detestation of it, and bestowing his everlasting Curse to his Sons whenever they should wear it. For all this, in a few Days, they appeared higher in the Fashion than any Body else in the Town. But they solved the Matter by saying, that these Figures were not at all the *same* with those that were formerly worn, and were meant in the Will. Besides, they did not wear them in that Sense, as forbidden by their Father, but as they were a commendable Custom, and of great Use to the Publick. That these rigorous Clauses in the Will did therefore require some *Allowance,* and a favourable Interpretation, and ought to be understood *cum grano Salis.*[78]

BUT, Fashions perpetually altering in that Age, the Scholastick Brother grew weary of searching farther Evasions, and solving everlasting Contradictions. Resolved therefore at all Hazards, to comply with the Modes of the World, they concerted Matters together, and agreed unanimously, to lock up their Father's Will in a *Strong-Box,*† brought out of *Greece* or *Italy,* (I have forgot which) and trouble themselves no farther to examine it, but

---

* *The Images of Saints, the Blessed Virgin, and our Saviour an Infant.*

Ibid. *Images in the* Church of Rome *give him but too fair a Handle.* The Brothers remembred, &c. *The Allegory here is direct.* W. Wotton.

† *The Papists formerly forbad the People the Use of Scripture in a Vulgar Tongue,* Peter *therefore* locks up his Father's Will in a Strong Box, brought out of *Greece* or *Italy. Those Countries are named because the* New Testament *is written in* Greek; *and the* Vulgar Latin, *which is the Authentick Edition of the* Bible *in the Church of* Rome, *is in the Language of old* Italy. W. Wotton.

only refer to its Authority whenever they thought fit. In consequence whereof, a while after, it grew a general Mode to wear an infinite Number of *Points*, most of them *tagg'd with Silver.* Upon which the Scholar pronounced *ex Cathedra*, that *Points* were absolutely *Jure Paterno*, as they might very well remember. *"Tis true indeed, the Fashion prescribed somewhat more than were directly named in the Will; However, that they, as Heirs general of their Father, had power to make and add certain Clauses for publick Emolument, though not deducible, *totidem verbis*, from the Letter of the Will, or else, *Multa absurda sequerentur.*[79] This was understood for *Canonical*, and therefore on the following *Sunday* they came to Church all covered with *Points*.

THE Learned Brother so often mentioned, was reckon'd the best Scholar in all that or the next Street to it; insomuch, as having run something behind-hand with the World, he obtained the Favour from a *certain Lord*,† to receive him into his House, and to teach his Children. A while after, the *Lord* died, and he by long Practice upon his Father's Will, found the way of contriving a *Deed of Conveyance* of that House to Himself and his Heirs: Upon which he took Possession, turned the young Squires out, and received his Brothers in their stead.

SECTION III

A DIGRESSION CONCERNING CRITICKS

Tho' I have been hitherto as cautious as I could, upon all Occasions, most nicely to follow the Rules and Methods of Writing, laid down by the Example of our illustrious *Moderns*; yet has the unhappy shortness of my Memory led me into an Error, from which I must immediately extricate my self, bofore I can decently pursue my Principal Subject. I confess with Shame, it was an unpardonable Omission to proceed so far as I have already done, before I had performed the due Discourses, Expostulatory,

---

* *The* Popes *in their Decretals and Bulls, have given their Sanction to very many gainful Doctrines which are now received in the* Church of Rome *that are not mention'd in Scripture, and are unknown to the Primitive Church.* Peter *accordingly pronounces* ex Cathedra, *That* Points *tagged with Silver were absolutely* Jure Paterno, *and so they wore them in great Numbers.* W. Wotton.

† *This was* Constantine the Great, *from whom the* Popes *pretend a Donation of St.* Peter's *Patrimony, which they have been never able to produce.*

Ibid. *The Bishops of* Rome *enjoyed their Priviledges in* Rome *at first by the favour of Emperors, whom at last they shut out of their own Capital City, and then forged a Donation from* Constantine the Great, *the better to justifie what they did. In Imitation of this,* Peter *having run something behind hand in the World, obtained Leave of a certain Lord, &c.* W. Wotton.

Supplicatory, or Deprecatory with my *good Lords* the *Criticks.* Towards some Atonement for this grievous Neglect, I do here make humbly bold to present them with a short Account of themselves and their *Art,* by looking into the Original and Pedigree of the Word, as it is generally understood among us, and very briefly considering the antient and present State thereof.

BY the Word, *Critick,* at this Day so frequent in all Conversations, there have sometimes been distinguished three very different Species of Mortal Men, according as I have read in *Antient Books and Pamphlets.* For first, by this Term were understood such Persons as invented or drew up Rules for themselves and the World, by observing which, a careful Reader might be able to pronounce upon the productions of the *Learned,* form his Taste to a true Relish of the *Sublime* and the *Admirable,* and divide every Beauty of Matter or of Style from the Corruption that Apes it: In their common perusal of Books, singling out the Errors and Defects, the Nauseous, the Fulsome, the Dull, and the Impertinent, with the Caution of a Man that walks thro' *Edenborough* Streets in a Morning, who is indeed as careful as he can, to watch diligently, and spy out the Filth in his Way, not that he is curious to observe the Colour and Complexion of the Ordure, or take its Dimensions, much less to be padling in, or tasting it: but only with a Design to come out as cleanly as he may. These men seem, tho' very erroneously, to have understood the Appellation of, *Critick* in a literal Sence; That one principal part of his Office was to Praise and Acquit; and, that a *Critick,* who sets up to Read, only for an Occasion of Censure and Reproof, is a Creature as barbarous as a *Judge,* who should take up a Resolution to hang all Men that came before him upon a Tryal.

AGAIN; by the Word *Critick,* have been meant, the Restorers of Antient Learning from the Worms, and Graves, and Dust of Manuscripts.

NOW, the Races of these two have been for some Ages utterly extinct; and besides, to discourse any farther of them would not be at all to my purpose.

THE Third, and Noblest Sort, is that of the *TRUE CRITICK,* whose Original is the most Antient of all. Every *True Critick* is a Hero born, descending in a direct Line from a Celestial Stem, by *Momus* and *Hybris,* who begat *Zoilus,* who begat *Tigellius,*[80] who begat *Etcætera* the Elder, who begat *Bently,* and *Rymer,* and *Wotton,* and *Perrault,* and *Dennis,* who begat *Etcætera* the Younger.

AND these are the *Criticks* from whom the Commonwealth of Learning has in all Ages received such immense benefits, that the Gratitude of their

Admirers placed their Origine in Heaven, among those of *Hercules, Theseus, Perseus,* and other great Deservers of Mankind. But Heroick Virtue it self hath not been exempt from the Obloquy of Evil Tongues. For it hath been objected, that those Antient Heroes, famous for their Combating so many Giants, and Dragons, and Robbers, were in their own Persons a greater Nuisance to Mankind, than any of those Monsters they subdued; and therefore, to render their Obligations more Compleat, when all *other* Vermin were destroy'd, should in Conscience have concluded with the same Justice upon themselves: as *Hercules* most generously did, and hath upon that Score, procured to himself more Temples and Votaries than the best of his Fellows. For these Reasons, I suppose it is, why some have conceived, it would be very expedient for the Publick Good of Learning, that every *True Critick,* as soon as he had finished his Task assigned, should immediately deliver himself up to Ratsbane, or Hemp, or from some convenient *Altitude,* and that no Man's Pretensions to so illustrious a Character, should by any means be received, before That Operation were performed.

Now, from this Heavenly Descent of *Criticism,* and the close Analogy it bears to *Heroick Virtue,* 'tis easie to Assign the proper Employment of a *True Antient Genuine Critick;* which is, to travel thro' this vast World of Writings: to pursue and hunt those Monstrous Faults bred within them: to drag out the lurking Errors like *Cacus* from his Den; to multiply them like *Hydra's* Heads; and rake them together like *Augeas's* Dung. Or else to drive away a sort of *Dangerous Fowl,* who have a perverse Inclination to plunder the best Branches of the *Tree of Knowledge,* like those *Stymphalian* Birds that eat up the Fruit.

These Reasonings will furnish us with an adequate Definition of a *True Critick;* that, He is *a Discoverer and Collector of Writers Faults.* Which may be farther put beyond Dispute by the following Demonstration: That whoever will examine the Writings in all kinds, wherewith this antient Sect has honour'd the World, shall immediately find, from the whole Thread and Tenour of them, that the Idea's of the Authors have been altogether conversant, and taken up with the Faults and Blemishes, and Oversights, and Mistakes of other Writers; and let the Subject treated on be whatever it will, their Imaginations are so entirely possess'd and replete with the Defects of other Pens, that the very Quintessence of what is bad, does of necessity distill into their own: by which means the Whole appears to be nothing else but an *Abstract* of the *Criticisms* themselves have made.

Having thus briefly consider'd the Original and Office of a *Critick,* as the Word is understood in its most noble and universal Acceptation, I proceed to refute the Objections of those who argue from the Silence and Pretermission of Authors; by which they pretend to prove, that the very Art of *Criticism*, as now exercised, and by me explained, is wholly *Modern;* and consequently, that the *Criticks* of *Great Britain* and *France,* have no Title to an Original so Antient and Illustrious as I have deduced. Now, If I can clearly make out on the contrary, that the most Antient Writers have particularly described, both the Person and the Office of a *True Critick,* agreeable to the Definition laid down by me; their Grand Objection, from the Silence of Authors, will fall to the Ground.

I confess to have for a long time born a part in this general Error; from which I should never have acquitted my self, but thro' the Assistance of our Noble *Moderns;* whose most edifying Volumes I turn indefatigably over Night and Day, for the Improvement of my Mind, and the good of my Country: These have with unwearied Pains made many useful Searches into the weak sides of the *Antients,* and given us a comprehensive List of them. Besides, they have proved beyond contradiction,* that the very finest Things delivered of old, have been long since invented, and brought to Light by much later Pens, and that the noblest Discoveries those *Antients* ever made, ** See* Wotton *of Antient and Modern Learning.*

of Art or of Nature, have all been produced by the transcending Genius of the present Age. Which clearly shews, how little Merit those *Ancients* can justly pretend to; and takes off that blind Admiration paid them by Men in a Corner, who have the Unhappiness of conversing too little with *present Things.* Reflecting maturely upon all this, and taking in the whole Compass of Human Nature, I easily concluded, that these *Antients,* highly sensible of their many Imperfections, must needs have endeavoured from some Passages in their Works, to obviate, soften, or divert the Censorious Reader, by *Satyr,* or *Panegyrick* upon the *True Criticks,* in Imitation of their *Masters* the *Moderns.* Now, in the *Common-Places* of both these, † I was plentifully instructed, by a long Course of useful Study in *Prefaces* and *Prologues;* and therefore immediately resolved to try what I could discover of either, by a diligent Perusal of the most Antient Writers, and especially those who treated of the earliest Times. Here I found to my great Surprize, that although they all entered, upon Occasion, into particular Descriptions of the *True Critick,* according as they were governed by their Fears or their Hopes: yet whatever they touch'd of that kind, was with abundance of Caution, adventuring no farther than *Mythology* and *Hieroglyphick.* This, I suppose, *† Satyr, and Panegyrick upon Criticks.*

gave ground to superficial Readers, for urging the Silence of Authors, against the Antiquity of the *True Critick;* tho' the *Types* are so apposite, and the Applications so necessary and natural, that it is not easy to conceive, how any Reader of a *Modern Eye* and *Taste* could over-look them. I shall venture from a great Number to produce a few, which I am very confident, will put this Question beyond Dispute.

IT well deserves considering, that these *Antient Writers* in treating Enigmatically upon the Subject, have generally fixed upon the very *same Hieroglyph,* varying only the Story according to their Affections or their Wit. For first; *Pausanias* is of Opinion,[81] that the Perfection of Writing correct was entirely owing to the Institution of *Criticks;* and, that he can possibly mean no other than the *True Critick,* is, I think, manifest enough from the following Description. He says, *They were a Race of Men, who delighted to nibble at the Superfluities, and Excrescencies of Books; which the Learned at length observing, took Warning of their own Accord, to lop the Luxuriant, the Rotten, the Dead, the Sapless,* and the *Overgrown Branches from their Works.* But now, all this he cunningly shades under the following Allegory; *that*   **Lib——* *the* Nauplians* *in* Argia, *learned the Art of pruning their Vines, by observing, that when an* A S S *had browsed upon one of them, it thrived the better, and bore fairer Fruit.* But *Herodotus*†[82] holding the very same *Hieroglyph,* speaks much plainer, and almost *in terminis.* He hath been   † *Lib.* 4. so bold as to tax the *True Criticks,* of Ignorance and Malice; telling us openly, for I think nothing can be plainer, that *in the Western Part of* Libya, *there were* A S S E S *with* H O R N S: Upon which Relation *Ctesias*‡[83] yet refines, mentioning the very same animal ‡Vide *excerpta* about *India,* adding, *That whereas all other* A S S E S *wanted a* Gall, *ex eo apud* *these horned ones were so redundant in that Part, that their Flesh was* Photium. *not to be eaten because of its extream* Bitterness.

Now, the Reason why those Antient Writers treated this Subject only by Types and Figures, was, because they durst not make open Attacks against a Party so Potent and so Terrible, as the *Criticks* of those Ages were: whose very voice was so Dreadful, that a legion of Authors would tremble, and drop their Pens at the Sound; For so *§ Lib.* 4. *Herodotus* § tells us expresly in another Place, how *a vast Army of* Scythians *was put to flight in a Panick Terror, by the Braying of an* A S S. From hence it is conjectured by certain profound *Philologers,* that the great Awe and Reverence paid to a *True Critick,* by the Writers of *Britain,* have been derived to Us, from those our *Scythian* Ancestors. In short, this Dread was so universal, that in process of Time, those Authors who had a mind to publish their Sentiments more freely, in describing the *True Criticks* of their several Ages, were forced to leave off the use of the former *Hieroglyph,* as too nearly approaching the *Prototype,* and invented other Terms instead thereof that were more cautious and mystical; so *Diodorus** speaking to the same purpose, ventures no farther than to say, That *in the Mountains of* Helicon *there grows a certain* Weed, *which bears a Flower of so damned a Scent, as to poison those who offer to smell it.* Lucretius[84] gives exactly the Same Relation,

       * Lib.

> *Est etiam in magnis Heliconis montibus arbos,*
> *Floris odore hominem tetro consueta necare.* Lib. 6.†

BUT *Ctesias,* whom we lately quoted, hath been a great deal bolder; He had been used with much severity by the *True Criticks* of his own Age, and therefore could not forbear to leave behind him, at least one deep Mark of his Vengeance against the whole Tribe. His Meaning is so near the Surface, that I wonder how it possibly came to be overlook'd by those who deny the Antiquity of the *True Criticks.* For pretending to make a Description of many strange Animals about *India,* he hath set down these remarkable Words. *Amongst the rest,* says he, *there is a* Serpent *that wants* Teeth, *and consequently cannot bite, but if its* Vomit *(to which it is much addicted) happens to fall upon any Thing, a certain Rottenness or Corruption ensues: These* Serpents *are generally found among the Mountains where* Jewels *grow, and they frequently emit a* poisonous Juice *whereof, whoever drinks, that Person's* Brains *flie out of his* Nostrils.

THERE was also among the *Antients* a sort of *Critick,* not distinguisht in *Specie* from the Former, but in Growth or Degree, who seem to have been only the *Tyro's* or *junior* Scholars; yet, because of their differing Employments, they are frequently mentioned as a Sect by themselves. The usual exercise of these younger Students, was to attend constantly at Theatres, and learn to Spy out the *worst Parts* of the Play, whereof they were obliged carefully to take Note, and render a rational Account, to their Tutors. Flesht at these smaller Sports, like young Wolves, they grew up in Time, to be nimble and strong enough for hunting down large Game. For it hath been observed both among Antients and Moderns, that a *True Critick* hath one Quality in common with a *Whore* and an *Alderman,* never to change his

---

† *Near Helicon, and round the Learned Hill,*
  Grow Trees, whose Blossoms with their Odour kill.

title or his Nature; that a *Grey Critick* has been certainly a *Green* one, the Perfections and Acquirements of his Age being only the improved Talents of his Youth; like *Hemp,* which some Naturalists inform us, is bad for *Suffocations,* tho' taken but in the Seed. I esteem the Invention, or at least the Refinement of *Prologues,* to have been owing to these younger Proficients, of whom *Terence*[85] makes frequent and honourable mention, under the Name of *Malevoli.*

NOW, 'tis certain, the Institution of the *True Criticks,* was of absolute Necessity to the Commonwealth of Learning. For all Human Actions seem to be divided like *Themistocles* and his Company; One Man can *Fiddle,* and another can make *a small Town a great City,* and he that cannot do either one or the other, deserves to be kick'd out of the Creation. The avoiding of which Penalty, has doubtless given the first Birth to the Nation of *Criticks,* and withal, an Occasion for their secret Detractors to report; that a *True Critick* is a sort of Mechanick, set up with a Stock and Tools for his Trade, at as little Expence as a *Taylor;* and that there is much Analogy between the Utensils and Abilities of both: That the *Taylor's Hell* is the Type of a Critick's *Common-Place-Book,* and his Wit and Learning held forth by the *Goose:* That it requires at least as many of these, to the making up of one Scholar, as of the others to the Composition of a Man: That the Valour of both is equal, and their *Weapons* near of a Size. Much may be said in answer to these invidious Reflections; and I can positively affirm the first to be a Falshood: For, on the contrary, nothing is more certain, than that it requires greater Layings out, to be free of the *Critick's* Company, than of any other you can name. For, as to be a *true Beggar,* it will cost the richest Candidate every Groat he is worth; so, before one can commence a *True Critick,* it will cost a man all the good Qualities of his Mind; which, perhaps, for a less Purchase, would be thought but an indifferent Bargain.

HAVING thus amply proved the Antiquity of *Criticism,* and described the Primitive State of it; I shall now examine the present Condition of this Empire, and shew how well it agrees with its antient self. A certain Author, whose Works have many Ages since been entirely lost, does in his fifth Book and eighth Chapter, say of *Criticks,* that *their Writings are the Mirrors of Learning.** This I understand in a literal Sense, and suppose our Author must mean, that whoever designs to be a perfect Writer, must inspect into the Books of *Criticks,* and correct his Invention there as in a Mirror. Now, whoever considers, that the *Mirrors* of the Antients were made of

* *A Quotation after the manner of a great Author. Vide* Bently's *Dissertation, &c.*

Brass, and *sine Mercurio,* may presently apply the two Principal Qualifications of a *True Modern Critick,* and consequently, must needs conclude, that these have always been, and must be for ever the same. For, *Brass* is an Emblem of Duration, and when it is skilfully burnished, will cast *Reflections* from its own *Superficies,* without any Assistance of *Mercury* from behind. All the other Talents of a *Critick* will not require a particular Mention, being included, or easily deducible to these. However, I shall conclude with three Maxims, which may serve both as characteristicks to distinguish a *True Modern Critick* from a Pretender, and will be also of admirable Use to those worthy Spirits, who engage in so useful and honourable an Art.

THE first is, That *Criticism,* contrary to all other Faculties of the Intellect, is ever held the truest and best, when it is the very *first* Result of the *Critick*'s Mind: As Fowlers reckon the first aim for the surest, and seldom fail of missing the Mark, if they stay for a Second.

SECONDLY; The *True Criticks* are known by their Talent of swarming about the noblest Writers, to which they are carried meerly by Instinct, as a Rat to the best Cheese, or a Wasp to the fairest Fruit. So, when the *King* is a Horse-back, he is sure to be the *dirtiest* Person of the Company, and they that make their Court best, are such as *bespatter* him most.

LASTLY; A *True Critick,* in the Perusal of a Book, is like a *Dog* at a Feast, whose Thoughts and Stomach are wholly set upon what the Guests *fling away,* and consequently, is apt to *Snarl* most, when there are the fewest *Bones.*

THUS much, I think, is sufficient to serve by way of Address to my Patrons, the *True Modern Criticks,* and may very well atone for my past Silence, as well as That which I am like to observe for the future. I hope I have deserved so well of their whole *Body,* as to meet with generous and tender Usage at their *Hands.* Supported by which Expectation, I go on boldly to pursue those Adventures already so happily begun.

SECTION IV

A TALE *of a* TUB

I have now with much Pains and Study, conducted the Reader to a Period, where he must expect to hear of great Revolutions. For no sooner had Our *Learned Brother,* so often mentioned, got a warm House of his own over his Head, than he began to look big, and to take mightily upon him; insomuch, that unless the Gentle Reader out of his great Candour, will please a little to exalt his Idea, I am afraid he will henceforth hardly know the *Hero* of the Play, when he happens to meet Him; his part, his Dress, and his Mien being so much altered.

HE told his Brothers, he would have them to know, that he was their Elder, and consequently his Father's sole Heir; Nay, a while after, he would not allow them to call Him, Brother, but Mr. *PETER;* and then he must be styl'd, *Father PETER;* and sometimes, *My Lord PETER.* To support this Grandeur, which he soon began to consider, could not be maintained without a Better *Fonde*[86] than what he was born to; After much Thought, he cast about at last, to turn *Projector*[87] and *Virtuoso,* wherein he so well succeeded, that many famous Discoveries, Projects and Machines, which bear great Vogue and Practice at present in the World, are owing entirely to *Lord Peter's* Invention. I will deduce the best Account I have been able to collect of the Chief amongst them, without considering much the Order they came out in; because, I think, Authors are not well agreed as to that Point.

I hope, when this Treatise of mine shall be translated into Foreign Languages, (as I may without Vanity affirm, That the Labour of collecting, the Faithfulness in recounting, and the great Usefulness of the Matter to the Publick, will amply deserve that Justice) that the worthy Members of the several *Academies* abroad, especially those of *France* and *Italy,* will favourably accept these humble Offers, for the Advancement of Universal Knowledge. I do also advertise the most Reverend Fathers the *Eastern* Missionaries, that I have purely for their Sakes, made use of such Words and Phrases, as will best admit an easie Turn into any of the *Oriental* Languages, especially the *Chinese.* And so I proceed with great Content of Mind, upon reflecting, how much Emolument this whole Globe of Earth is like to reap by my Labours.

THE first Undertaking of Lord *Peter,* was to purchase a Large Continent, lately said to have been discovered in *Terra Australis incognita.** This Tract of Land he bought at a very great Penny-worth from the Discoverers themselves, (tho' some pretended to doubt whether they had ever been there) and then retailed it into several Cantons to certain Dealers, who carried over Colonies, but were all Shipwreckt in the Voyage. Upon which, *Lord Peter* sold the said Continent to other Customers *again,* and *again,* and *again,* with the same Success.

THE second Project I shall mention, was his Sovereign Remedy for the

* *That is Purgatory.*

Worms, especially those in the *Spleen.** The Patient was to eat nothing after Supper for three Nights: as soon as he went to Bed, he was carefully
to lye on one Side, and when he grew weary, to turn upon the other: He
must also duly confine his two Eyes to the same Object; and by no means
break Wind at both Ends together, without manifest Occasion.† These
Prescriptions diligently observed, the *Worms* would void insensibly by
Perspiration, ascending thro' the *Brain.*

A third Invention, was the Erecting of a *Whispering-Office,*‡ for the Publick Good and Ease of all such as are Hypochondriacal, or troubled with
the Cholick; as likewise of all Eves-droppers, Physicians, Midwives, small
Politicians, Friends fallen out, Repeating Poets, Lovers Happy or in Despair, Bawds, Privy-Counsellours, Pages, Parasites and Buffoons; In short,
of all such as are in Danger of bursting with too much *Wind.* An *Asse*'s
Head was placed so conveniently, that the Party affected might easily with
his Mouth accost either of the Animal's Ears; which he was to apply close
for a certain Space, and by a fugitive Faculty, peculiar to the Ears of that
Animal, receive immediate Benefit, either by Eructation, or Expiration, or
Evomition.

ANOTHER very beneficial Project of *Lord Peter*'s was an *Office of En-
surance,*§ for Tobacco-Pipes, Martyrs of the Modern Zeal; Volumes of Poetry, Shadows, —————————— and Rivers: That these, nor any of
these shall receive Damage by *Fire.* From whence our *Friendly Societies* may
plainly find themselves, to be only Transcribers from this Original; tho'
the one and the other have been of *great* Benefit to the Undertakers, as well
as of *equal* to the Publick.

LORD *Peter* was also held the Original Author of *Puppets* and *Raree-
Shows;*** the great Usefulness whereof being so generally known, I shall
not enlarge farther upon this Particular.

BUT, another Discovery for which he was much renowned, was his

---

* Penance *and* Absolution *are plaid upon under the Notion of a* Sovereign Remedy for the
Worms, *especially in the Spleen, which by observing* Peters *Prescription would void sensibly by Perspiration ascending thro' the Brain,* &c. W. Wotton.

† *Here the Author ridicules the Penances of the Church of* Rome, *which may be made as easy to the
Sinner as he pleases, provided he will pay for them accordingly.*

‡ *By his* Whispering-Office, *for the Relief of Eves-droppers, Physitians, Bawds, and Privy-
counsellours, he ridicules Auricular Confession, and the Priest who takes it, is described by the Asses Head.*
W. Wotton.

§ *This I take to be the Office of* Indulgences, *the gross Abuses whereof first gave Occasion for the Reformation.*

** *I believe are the Monkeries and ridiculous Processions,* &c. *among the Papists.*

famous Universal *Pickle*.* For having remark'd how your Common *Pickle*†
in use among Huswives, was of no farther Benefit than to preserve dead
Flesh, and certain kinds of Vegetables; *Peter,* with great Cost as well as Art,
had contrived a *Pickle* proper for Houses, Gardens, Towns, Men, Women,
Children, and Cattle; wherein he could preserve them as Sound as Insects
in Amber. Now, this *Pickle* to the Taste, the Smell, and the Sight, appeared
exactly the same, with what is in common Service for Beef, and Butter,
and Herrings, (and has been often that way applied with great Success)
but for its many Sovereign Virtues was a quite different Thing. For *Peter*
would put in a certain Quantity of his *Powder Pimperlim pimp,*‡ after which
it never failed of Success. The Operation was performed by *Spargefaction*[88]
in a proper Time of the Moon. The Patient who was to be *pickled,* if it were
a House, would infallibly be preserved from all Spiders, Rats and Weazels;
If the Party affected were a Dog, he should be exempt from Mange, and
Madness, and Hunger. It also infallibly took away all Scabs and Lice, and
scall'd Heads from Children, never hindring the Patient from any Duty,
either at Bed or Board.

BUT of all *Peter*'s Rarieties, he most valued a certain Set of *Bulls,*§ whose
Race was by great Fortune preserved in a lineal Descent from those that
guarded the *Golden Fleece.* Tho' some who pretended to observe them cu-
riously, doubted the Breed had not been kept entirely chast; because they
had degenerated from their Ancestors in some Qualities and had acquired
others very extraordinary, but a Forein Mixture. The *Bulls* of *Colchos* are
recorded to have *brazen Feet;* But whether it happen'd by ill Pasture and
Running, by an Allay from intervention of other Parents, from stolen Intrigues; Whether a Weakness in their Progenitors had impaired the seminal Virtue; Or by a Decline necessary thro' a long Course of Time, the
Originals of Nature being depraved in these latter sinful Ages of the
World; Whatever was the Cause, 'tis certain that *Lord Peter's Bulls* were ex-
treamely vitiated by the Rust of Time in the Mettal of their Feet, which

---

* *Holy Water, he calls an* Universal Pickle *to preserve Houses, Gardens, Towns, Men, Women, Children and Cattle, wherein he could preserve them as sound as Insects in Amber.* W. Wotton.

† *This is easily understood to be Holy Water, composed of the same Ingredients with many other Pickles.*

‡ *And because Holy Water differs only in Consecration from common Water, therefore he tells us that
his Pickle by the Powder of* Pimperlimpimp *receives new Virtues though it differs not in Sight nor Smell
from the common Pickle, which preserves Beef, and Butter, and Herrings.* W. Wotton.

§ *The Papal* Bulls *are ridicul'd by Name, So that here we are at no loss for the Authors Meaning.*
W. Wotton.

Ibid. *Here the Author has kept the Name, and means the* Popes Bulls, *or rather his Fulminations
and Excommunications, of Heretical Princes, all sign'd with Lead and the Seal of the Fisherman.*

was now sunk into common *Lead.* However the terrible *roaring* peculiar to their Lineage, was preserved; as likewise that Faculty of breathing out *Fire* from their Nostrils; which not-withstanding, many of their Detractors took to be a Feat of Art, and to be nothing so terrible as it appeared; proceeding only from their usual Course of Dyet, which was of *Squibs* and *Crackers.** However, they had two peculiar Marks which extreamly distinguished them from the *Bulls of Jason,* and which I have not met together in the Description of any other Monster, beside that in *Horace;*

> *Varias inducere plumas,*
> and
> *Atrum desinit in piscem.*[89]

For, these had *Fishes Tails,* yet upon Occasion, could *out-fly* any Bird in the Air. *Peter* put these *Bulls* upon several Employs. Sometimes he would set them a *roaring* to fright *Naughty Boys,*† and make them quiet. Sometimes he would send them out upon Errands of great Importance; where it is wonderful to recount, and perhaps the cautious Reader may think much to believe it; An *Appetitus sensibilis,*[90] deriving itself thro' the whole Family, from their Noble Ancestors, Guardians of the *Golden-Fleece;* they continued so extremely fond of *Gold,* that if *Peter* sent them abroad, though it were only upon a Compliment; they would *Roar,* and *Spit,* and *Belch,* and *Piss,* and *Fart,* and *Snivel* out *Fire,* and keep a perpetual Coyl, till you flung them a Bit of *Gold;* but then, *Pulveris exigui jactu,*[91] they would grow calm and quiet as Lambs. In short, whether by secret Connivance, or Encouragement from their Master, or out of their own Liquorish Affection to Gold, or both; it is certain they were no better than a sort of sturdy, swaggering Beggars; and where they could not prevail to get an Alms, would make Women miscarry, and Children fall into Fits; who, to this very Day, usually call Sprites and Hobgoblins by the Name of *Bull-Beggars.* They grew at last so very troublesome to the Neighbourhood, that some Gentlemen of the *North-West,* got a Parcel of right *English Bull-Dogs,* and baited them so terribly, that they felt it ever after.

I must needs mention one more of *Lord Peter*'s Projects, which was very extraordinary, and discovered him to be Master of a high Reach, and pro-

---

* *These are the Fulminations of the Pope threatning Hell and Damnation to those Princes who offend him.*

† *That is Kings who incurr his Displeasure.*

found Invention. Whenever it happened that any Rogue of *Newgate* was condemned to be hang'd, *Peter* would offer him a Pardon for a certain Sum of Money, which when the poor Caitiff had made all Shifts to scrape up and send; *His Lordship* would return a Piece of Paper in this Form.*

> *To all Mayors, Sheriffs, Jaylors, Constables, Bayliffs, Hangmen, &c. Whereas we are informed that A. B. remains in the Hands of you, or any of you, under the Sentence of Death. We will and command you upon Sight hereof, to let the said Prisoner depart to his own Habitation, whether he stands condemned for Murder, Sodomy, Rape, Sacrilege, Incest, Treason, Blasphemy, &c. for which this shall be your sufficient Warrant: And if you fail hereof, G— d—mn You and Yours to all Eternity. And so we bid you heartily Farewel.*

YOUR MOST HUMBLE
MAN'S MAN,
Emperor PETER.

THE Wretches trusting to this, lost their Lives and Money too.

I desire of those whom the *Learned* among Posterity will appoint for Commentators upon this elaborate Treatise; that they will proceed with great Caution upon certain dark points, where-in all who are not *Verè adepti*,[92] may be in Danger to form rash and hasty Conclusions, especially in some mysterious Paragraphs, where certain *Arcana* are joyned for brevity sake, which in the Operation must be divided. And, I am certain, that future Sons of Art, will return large Thanks to my Memory, for so grateful, so useful an *Innuendo.*

IT will be no difficult Part to persuade the Reader, that so many worthy Discoveries met with great Success in the World; tho' I may justly assure him that I have related much the smallest Number; My Design having been only to single out such, as will be of most Benefit for Publick Imitation, or which best served to give some Idea of the Reach and Wit of the Inventor. And therefore it need not be wondred, if by this Time, *Lord Peter* was become exceeding Rich. But alas, he had kept his Brain so long, and so violently upon the Rack, that at last it *shook* it self, and began to *turn round* for a little Ease. In short, what with Pride, Projects, and Knavery, poor *Peter* was grown distracted, and conceived the strangest Imaginations in the World. In the Height of his Fits (as it is usual with those who run made out of Pride) He would call Himself *God Almighty*, and sometimes

---

* *This is a Copy of a General Pardon sign'd* Servus Servorum.

Ibid. *Absolution in* Articulo Mortis, *and the Tax* Cameræ Apostolicæ *are jested upon in Emperor* Peter's *Letter.* W. Wotton.

*Monarch of the Universe.** I have seen him, (says my Author) take three old
high-crown'd Hats,† and clap them all on his Head, three Story high, with a
huge Bunch of *Keys*‡ at his Girdle, and an *Angling Rod* in his Hand. In
which Guise, whoever went to take him by the Hand in the way of Salutation, *Peter* with much Grace, like a well educated Spaniel, would present
them with his *Foot,*§ and if they refused his Civility, then he would raise
it as high as their Chops, and give them a damn'd Kick on the Mouth,
which hath ever since been call'd a *Salute.* Whoever walkt by, without paying him their Compliments, having a wonderful strong Breath, he would
blow their Hats off into the Dirt. Mean time, his Affairs at home went upside down; and his two Brothers had a wretched Time; Where his first
*Boutade*** was, to kick both their *Wives* one Morning out of Doors,†† and
his own too, and in their stead, gave Orders to pick up the first three Strolers could be met with in the Streets. A while after, he nail'd up the Cellar-
Door: and would not allow his Brothers a Drop of *Drink** to their Victuals.
Dining one Day at an Alderman's in the City, *Peter* observed him expatiating after the Manner of his Brethren, in the Praises of his Surloyn of Beef.
Beef, said the Sage Magistrate, *is the King of Meat; Beef comprehends in it the
Quintessence of Partridge, and Quail, and Venison, and Pheasant, and Plum-
pudding and Custard.* When *Peter* came home, he would needs take the Fancy
of cooking up this Doctrine into Use, and apply the Precept in default of
a Surloyn, to his brown Loaf: *Bread,* says he, *Dear Brothers, is the Staff of Life;
in which Bread is contained, inclusivè, the Quintessence of Beef, Mutton, Veal, Venison, Partridge, Plum-pudding, and Custard: And to render all compleat, there is intermingled a due Quantity of Water, whose Crudities are also corrected by Yeast or
Barm, thro' which means it becomes a wholesome fermented Liquor, diffused thro'
the* Mass *of the Bread.* Upon the Strength of these Conclusions, next Day at
Dinner was the brown Loaf served up in all the Formality of a City Feast.

---

* *The Pope is not only allow'd to be the Vicar of* Christ, *but by several Divines is call'd* God upon
Earth, *and other blasphemous Titles.*

† *The Triple Crown.*

‡ *The Keys of the Church.*

Ibid. *The Pope's Universal Monarchy, and his Triple Crown, and Keys, and Fisher's Ring.*
W. Wotton.

§ *Neither does his arrogant way of requiring men to kiss his Slipper, escape Reflexion.* Wotton.

** *This Word properly signifies a sudden Jerk, or Lash of an Horse, when you do not expect it.*

†† *The* Celibacy of the *Romish* Clergy *is struck at in* Peter's *beating his own and Brothers Wives
out of Doors.* W. Wotton.

* *The Pope's refusing the Cup to the Laity, persuading them that the Blood is contain'd in the Bread,
and that the Bread is the real and entire Body of* Christ.

Come Brothers, said *Peter, fall to, and spare not; here is excellent good Mutton,** or *hold, now my Hand is in, I'll help you.* At which word, in much Ceremony, with Fork and Knife, he carves out two good Slices of the Loaf, and presents each on a Plate to his Brothers. The Elder of the two not suddenly entring into *Lord Peter's* Conceit, began with very civil Language to examine the Mystery. *My Lord,* said he, *I doubt, with great Submission, there may be some Mistake. What,* says *Peter, you are pleasant; Come then, let us hear this Jest, your Head is so big with. None in the World, my Lord; but unless I am very much deceived, your Lordship was pleased a while ago, to let fall a Word about Mutton, and I would be glad to see it with all my Heart. How,* said *Peter,* appearing in great Surprise, *I do not comprehend this at all—* Upon which, the younger interposing, to set the Business right; *My Lord,* said he, *My Brother, I suppose is hungry, and longs for the Mutton, your Lordship hath promised us to Dinner. Pray,* said Peter, *take me along with you, either you are both mad, or disposed to be merrier than I approve of; If* You *there, do not like your Piece, I will carve you another, tho' I should take that to be the choice Bit of the whole Shoulder. What then, my Lord,* replied the first, *it seems this is a shoulder of Mutton all this while. Pray Sir,* says *Peter, eat your Vittles*[93] *and leave off your Impertinence, if you please, for I am not disposed to relish it at present:* But the other could not forbear, being over-provoked at the affected Seriousness of *Peter's* Countenance. *By G—, My Lord,* said he, *I can only say, that to my Eyes, and Fingers, and Teeth, and Nose, it seems to be nothing but a Crust of Bread.* Upon which, the second put in his Word: *I never saw a piece of Mutton in my Life, so nearly resembling a Slice from a Twelve-peny Loaf. Look ye, Gentlemen,* cries *Peter* in a Rage, *to convince you, what a couple of blind, positive, ignorant, wilful Puppies you are, I will use but this plain Argument; By G—, it is true, good, natural Mutton as any in* Leaden-Hall *Market; and G—, confound you both eternally, if you offer to believe otherwise.* Such a thundring Proof as this, left no farther Room for Objection: The two Unbelievers began to gather and pocket up their Mistake as hastily as they could. *Why, truly,* said the first, *upon more mature Consideration— Ay,* says the other, interrupting him, *now I have thought better on the Thing, your Lordship seems to have a great deal of Reason. Very well,* said *Peter. Here Boy, fill me a Beer-Glass of Claret. Here's to you both with all my Heart.* The two Brethren much delighted to see him so readily appeas'd returned their most humble Thanks, and said, they would be glad to pledge His Lordship. *That you shall,* said Peter, *I am not a Person to refuse you any Thing that is reasonable; Wine moderately taken, is a*

---

* Transubstantiation. Peter *turns his Bread into Mutton, and according to the Popish Doctrine of Concomitants, his Wine too, which in his way he calls,* Pauming his damn'd Crusts upon the Brothers for Mutton. *W. Wotton.*

Cordial; Here is a Glass apiece for you; 'Tis true natural Juice from the Grape; none of your damn'd Vintners *Brewings.* Having spoke thus, he presented to each of them another large dry Crust, bidding them drink it off, and not be bashful, for it would do them no Hurt. The two Brothers, after having performed the usual Office in such delicate Conjunctures, of staring a sufficient Period at *Lord Peter,* and each other; and finding how Matters were like to go, resolved not to enter on a new Dispute, but let him carry the Point as he pleased; for he was now got into one of his mad Fits, and to Argue or Expostulate further, would only serve to render him a hundred times more untractable.

I have chosen to relate this worthy Matter in all its Circumstances, because it gave a principal Occasion to that great and famous *Rupture,** which happened about the same time among these Brethren, and was never afterwards made up. But, of That, I shall treat at large in another Section.

HOWEVER, it is certain, that *Lord Peter,* even in his lucid Intervals, was very lewdly given in his common Conversation, extream wilful and positive, and would at any time rather argue to the Death, than allow himself to be once in an Error. Besides, he had an abominable Faculty of telling huge palpable *Lies* upon all Occasions; and swearing, not only to the Truth, but cursing the whole Company to Hell, if they pretended to make the least Scruple of believing Him. One time, he swore, he had a *Cow*† at home, which gave as much Milk at a Meal, as would fill three thousand Churches; and what was yet more extraordinary, would never turn Sower. Another time, he was telling of an old *Sign-Post*‡ that belonged to his *Father,* with Nails and Timber enough on it, to build sixteen large Men of War. Talking one Day of *Chinese* Waggons,[94] which were made so light as to sail over Mountains: *Z—nds, said Peter, where's the Wonder of that? By G—, I saw a Large House of Lime and Stone*§ *travel over Sea and Land (granting that it stopt sometimes to bait) above two thousand* German *Leagues.* And that which was the good of it, he would swear desperately all the while, that he never told a

---

* *By this* Rupture *is meant the* Reformation.

† *The ridiculous Multiplying of the Virgin* Mary's Milk *among the Papists, under the Allegory of a* Cow, *which gave as much Milk at a Meal, as would fill three thousand Churches.* W. Wotton.

‡ *By this* Sign-Post *is meant the* Cross *of our Blessed Saviour.*

§ *The Chappel of* Loretto. *He falls here only upon the ridiculous Inventions of Popery: The Church of* Rome *intended by these Things, to gull silly, superstitious People, and rook them of their Money; that the World had been too long in Slavery, our Ancestors gloriously redeem'd us from that Yoke. The Church of* Rome *therefore ought to be expos'd, and he deserves well of Mankind that does expose it.* W. Wotton.

Ibid. *The Chappel of* Loretto, *which travell'd from the* Holy Land *to* Italy.

Lye in his Life; And at every Word; *By G——, Gentlemen, I tell you nothing but the Truth; And the D——l broil them eternally that will not believe me.*

IN short, *Peter* grew so scandalous, that all the Neighbourhood began in plain Words to say, he was no better than a Knave. And his two Brothers long weary of his ill Usage, resolved at last to leave him; but first, they humbly desired a Copy of their Father's *Will*, which had now lain by neglected, time out of Mind. Instead of granting this Request, he called them *damn'd Sons of Whores, Rogues, Traytors,* and the rest of the vile Names he could muster up. However, while he was abroad one Day upon his Projects, the two Youngsters watcht their Opportunity, made a shift to come at the *Will*, and took a *Copia vera,** by which they presently saw how grosly they had been abused; Their Father having left them equal Heirs, and stricly commanded, that whatever they got, should lye in common among them all. Pursuant to which, their next Enterprise was to break open the Cellar-Door, and get a little good *Drink†* to spirit and comfort their Hearts. In copying the *Will*, they had met another Precept against Whoring, Divorce, and separate Maintenance; Upon which, their next Work‡ was to discard their Concubines, and send for their Wives. Whilst all this was in agitation, there enters a Sollicitor from *Newgate,* desiring *Lord Peter* would please to procure a *Pardon* for a *Thief* that was to be *hanged* to morrow. But the two Brothers told him, he was a Coxcomb to seek Pardons from a Fellow, who deserv'd to be hang'd much better than his Client; and discovered all the Method of that Imposture, in the same Form I delivered it a while ago, advising the Sollicitor to put his Friend upon obtaining *a Pardon from the King.§* In the midst of all this Clutter and Revolution, in comes *Peter* with a File of Dragoons** at his Heels, and gathering from all Hands what was in the Wind, He and his Gang, after several Millions of Scurrilities and Curses, not very important here to repeat, by main Force, very fairly kicks them both out of Doors, and would never let them come under his Roof from that Day to this.††

---

* *Translated the Scriptures into the vulgar Tongues.*
† *Administred the Cup to the Laity at the Communion.*
‡ *Allowed the Marriages of Priests.*
§ *Directed Penitents not to trust to Pardons and Absolutions procur'd for Money, but sent them to implore the Mercy of God, from whence alone Remission is to be obtain'd.*
** *By Peter's Dragoons, is meant the Civil Power which those Princes, who were bigotted to the Romish Superstition, employ'd against the Reformers.*
†† *The Pope shuts all who dissent from him out of the Church.*

SECTION V

A DIGRESSION IN THE MODERN KIND

We whom the World is pleased to honor with the Title of *Modern Authors,* should never have been able to compass our great Design of an everlasting Remembrance, and never-dying Fame, if our Endeavours had not been so highly serviceable to the general Good of Mankind. This, *O Universe,* is the Adventurous Attempt of me thy Secretary;

——————*Quemvis perferre laborem*
Suadet, & inducit noctes vigilare serenas.[95]

To this End, I have some Time since, with a World of Pains and Art, dissected the Carcass of *Humane Nature,* and read many useful Lectures upon the several Parts, both *Containing* and *Contained;* till at last it *smelt* so strong, I could preserve it no longer. Upon which, I have been at a great Expence to fit up all the Bones with exact Contexture, and in due Symmetry; so that I am ready to shew a very compleat Anatomy thereof to all curious *Gentlemen and others.* But not to Digress farther in the midst of a Digression, as I have known some Authors inclose Digressions in one another, like a Nest of Boxes; I do affirm, that having carefully cut up *Humane Nature,* I have found a very strange, new, and important Discovery; That the Publick Good of Mankind is performed by two Ways, *Instruction,* and *Diversion.* And I have farther proved in my said several Readings, (which, perhaps, the World may one day see, if I can prevail on any Friend to steal a Copy, or on certain Gentlemen of my Admirers, to be very Importunate) that, as Mankind is now disposed, he receives much greater Advantage by being *Diverted* than *Instructed;* His Epidemical Diseases being *Fastidiosity, Amorphy,* and *Oscitation;*[96] whereas in the present universal Empire of Wit and Learning, there seems but little Matter left for *Instruction.* However, in Compliance with a Lesson of Great Age and Authority, I have attempted carrying the Point in all its Heights; and accordingly throughout this Divine Treatise, have skilfully kneaded up both together with a *Layer* of *Utile* and a *Layer* of *Dulce.*[97]

When I consider how exceedingly our Illustrious *Moderns* have eclipsed the weak glimmering Lights of the *Antients,* and turned them out of the Road of all fashionable Commerce, to a degree, that our choice Town-Wits* of most refined Accomplishments, are in grave Dispute, whether there have been ever any *Antients* or no: In which Point we are like to receive wonderful Satisfaction from the most useful Labours and Lucubrations of that Worthy *Modern,* Dr. *Bently:* I say, when I consider all this, I cannot but bewail, that no famous *Modern* hath ever yet attempted an universal System in a small portable Volume, of all Things that are to be Known, or Believed, or Imagined, or Practised in Life. I am, however, forced to acknowledge, that such an enterprise was thought on some Time ago by a great Philosopher of *O. Brazile.*† The Method he proposed, was by a certain curious *Receipt,* a *Nostrum,*98 which after his untimely Death, I found among his Papers; and do here out of my great Affection to the *Modern Learned,* present them with it, not doubting, it may one Day encourage some worthy Undertaker.

YOU *take fair correct Copies, well bound in Calfs Skin, and Lettered at the Back, of all Modern Bodies of Arts and Sciences whatsoever, and in what Language you please. These you distil in* balneo Mariæ, *infusing* Quintessence of Poppy Q. S. *together with three Pints of* Lethe, *to be had from the Apothecaries. You cleanse away carefully the* Sordes *and* Caput mortuum, *letting all that is volatile evaporate. You preserve only the first Running, which is again to be distilled seventeen times, till what remains will amount to about two Drams. This you keep in a Glass Viol* Hermetically *sealed, for one and twenty Days. Then you begin your Catholick Treatise, taking every Morning fasting, (first shaking the Viol) three Drops of this* Elixir, *snuffing it strongly up your Nose. It will dilate it self about the Brain (where there is any) in fourteen Minutes, and you immediately perceive in your Head an infinite Number of* Abstracts, Summaries, Compendiums, Extracts, Collections, Medulla's, Excerpta quædam's, Florilegia's *and the like, all disposed into great Order, and reducible upon Paper.*

I must needs own, it was by the Assistance of this *Arcanum,* that I, tho' otherwise *impar,* have adventured upon so daring an Attempt; never atchieved or undertaken before, but by a certain Author called *Homer,* in whom, tho' otherwise a Person not without some Abilities, and *for an Antient,* of a tolerable Genius; I have discovered many gross Errors, which are not to be forgiven his very Ashes, if by chance any of them are left. For whereas, we are assured, he design'd his Work for a compleat Body of all

* *The Learned Person here meant by our Author, hath been endeavouring to annihilate so many Antient Writers, that until he is pleas'd to stop his hand it will be dangerous to affirm, whether there have been ever any Antients in the World.*

† *This is an imaginary Island, of Kin to that which is call'd the* Painters Wives Island, *placed in some unknown part of the Ocean, meerly at the Fancy of the Map-maker.*

Knowledge Human, Divine, Political, and Mechanick;* it is manifest, he
hath wholly neglected some, and been very imperfect in the
rest. For, first of all, as eminent a *Cabbalist*[99] as his Disciples
would represent Him, his Account of the *Opus magnum*[100] is
extreamly poor and deficient; he seems to have read but very
superficially, either *Sendivogius, Behmen,* or *Anthroposophia Theomagica.*† He is also quite mistaken about the *Sphæra Pyroplastica,*[101] a neglect not to be attoned for; and (if the Reader will admit so
severe a Censure) *Vix crederem Autorem hunc, unquam audivisse ignis vocem.*[102]
His Failings are not less prominent in several Parts of the *Mechanicks.* For,
having read his Writings with the utmost Application usual among *Modern Wits,* I could never yet discover the least Direction about the Structure
of that useful Instrument a *Save-all.*[103] For want of which, if the *Moderns*
had not lent their Assistance, we might yet have wandred *in the Dark.* But
I have still behind, a Fault far more notorious to tax this Author with; I
mean, his‡ gross Ignorance in the *Common Laws of this Realm,* and in the
Doctrine as well as Discipline of the Church of *England.* A Defect indeed,
for which both he and all the Ancients stand most justly censured by my
worthy and ingenious Friend Mr. *Wotton,* Batchelor of Divinity, in his incomparable Treatise of *Ancient and Modern Learning;* A Book never to be
sufficiently valued, whether we consider the happy Turns and Flowings of
the Author's Wit, the great Usefulness of his sublime Discoveries upon the
Subject of *Flies* and *Spittle,* or the laborious Eloquence of his Stile. And I
cannot forbear doing that Author the Justice of my publick Acknowledgments, for the great *Helps* and *Liftings* I had out of his incomparable Piece,
while I was penning this Treatise.

But, besides these Omissions in *Homer* already mentioned, the curious
Reader will also observe several Defects in that Author's Writings, for
which he is not altogether so accountable. For whereas every Branch of
Knowledge has received such wonderful Acquirements since his Age, especially within these last three Years, or thereabouts; it is almost impossible, he could be so very perfect in Modern Discoveries, as his Advocates
pretend. We freely acknowledge Him to be the Inventor of the *Compass,*
of *Gun-Powder,* and the *Circulation of the Blood:* But, I challenge any of his

* *Homerus omnes
res humanas
Poematis
complexus est.
Xenoph. in
conviv.*

---

† *A Treatise written about fifty Years ago, by a* Welsh *Gentleman of* Cambridge, *his Name, as I remember, was* Vaughan, *as appears by the Answer to it, writ by the Learned Dr.* Henry Moor, *it is a
Piece of the most unintelligible Fustian, that, perhaps, was ever publish'd in any Language.*

‡ *Mr.* Wotton (*to whom our Author never gives any Quarter*) *in his Comparison of Antient and
Modern Learning, Numbers Divinity, Law, &c. among those Parts of Knowledge wherein we excel the
Antients.*

Admirers to shew me in all his Writings, a compleat Account of the *Spleen;* Does he not also leave us wholly to seek in the Art of *Political Wagering?* What can be more defective and unsatisfactory than his long Dissertation upon *Tea?* and as to his Method of *Salivation without Mercury,* so much celebrated of late, it is to my own Knowledge and Experience, a Thing very little to be relied on.

IT was to supply such momentous Defects, that I have been prevailed on after long Sollicitation, to take Pen in Hand; and I dare venture to Promise, the Judicious Reader shall find nothing neglected here, that can be of Use upon any Emergency of Life. I am confident to have included and exhausted all that Human Imagination can *Rise* or *Fall* to. Particularly, I recommend to the Perusal of the Learned, certain Discoveries that are wholly untoucht by others; whereof I shall only mention among a great many more; *My New help of Smatterers,* or the *Art of being Deep-learned, and Shallow-read. A curious Invention about Mouse-Traps. An Universal Rule of Reason, or Every Man his own Carver;* Together with a most useful Engine for *catching of Owls.* All which the judicious Reader will find largely treated on, in the several Parts of this Discourse.

I hold my self obliged to give as much Light as is possible, into the Beauties and Excellencies of what I am writing, because it is become the Fashion and Humor most applauded among the first Authors of this Polite and Learned Age, when they would correct the ill Nature of Critical, or inform the Ignorance of Courteous Readers. Besides, there have been several famous Pieces lately published both in Verse and Prose; wherein, if the Writers had not been pleas'd, out of their great Humanity and Affection to the Publick, to give us a nice Detail of the *Sublime,* and the *Admirable* they contain; it is a thousand to one, whether we should ever have discovered one Grain of either. For my own particular, I cannot deny, that whatever I have said upon this Occasion, had been more proper in a Preface, and more agreeable to the Mode, which usually directs it there. But I here think fit to lay hold on that great and honourable Privilege of being the *Last Writer;* I claim an absolute Authority in Right, as the *freshest Modern,* which gives me a Despotick Power over all Authors before me. In the Strength of which Title, I do utterly disapprove and declare against that pernicious Custom, of making the Preface a Bill of Fare to the Book. For I have always lookt upon it as a high Point of Indiscretion in *Monster-mongers* and other *Retailers of strange Sights;* to hang out a fair large Picture over the Door, drawn after the Life, with a most eloquent Description underneath: This hath saved me many a Threepence, for my Curiosity was fully satisfied, and I never offered to go in, tho' often invited by the urging and attending Orator, with his last *moving* and *standing* Piece of Rhetorick; *Sir, Upon my Word, we are just going to begin.* Such is exactly the Fate, at this Time, of *Prefaces, Epistles, Advertisements, Introductions, Prolegomena's, Apparatus's, To-the-Reader's.* This Expedient was admirable at first; Our Great *Dryden* has long carried it as far as it would go, and with incredible Success. He has often said to me in Confidence, that the World would have never suspected him to be so great a Poet, if he had not assured them so frequently in his Prefaces, that it was impossible they could either doubt or forget it. Perhaps it may be so; However, I much fear, his Instructions have edify'd out of their Place, and taught Men to grow Wiser in certain Points, where he never intended they should; For it is lamentable to behold, with what a lazy Scorn, many of the yawning Readers in our Age, do now a-days twirl over forty or fifty Pages of *Preface* and *Dedication,* (which is the usual *Modern* Stint) as if it were so much *Latin.* Tho' it must be also allowed on the other Hand that a very considerable Number is known to proceed *Criticks* and *Wits,* by reading nothing else. Into which two Factions, I think, all present Readers may justly be divided. Now, for my self, I profess to be of the former Sort; and therefore having the *Modern* Inclination to expatiate upon the Beauty of my own Productions, and display the bright Parts of my Discourse; I thought best to do it in the Body of the Work, where, as it now lies, it makes a very considerable Addition to the Bulk of the Volume, *a Circumstance by no means to be neglected by a skilful Writer.*

HAVING thus paid my due Deference and Acknowledgment to an establish'd Custom of our newest Authors, by *a long Digression unsought for,* and *an universal Censure unprovoked;* By forcing into the Light, with much Pains and Dexterity, my own Excellencies and other Mens Defaults, with great Justice to my self and Candor to them; I now happily resume my Subject, to the Infinite Satisfaction both of the Reader and the Author.

SECTION VI

A TALE *of a* TUB

We left *Lord Peter* in open Rupture with his two Brethren; both forever discarded from his House, and resigned to the wide World, with little or nothing to trust to. Which are Circumstances that render them proper Subjects for the Charity of a Writer's Pen to work on; Scenes of Misery, ever affording the fairest Harvest for great Adventures. And in this, the

World may perceive the Difference between the Integrity of a gener-
ous Author, and that of a common Friend. The latter is observed to
adhere close in Prosperity, but on the Decline of Fortune, to drop sud-
denly off. Whereas, the generous Author, just on the contrary, finds his
Hero on the Dunghil, from thence by gradual Steps, raises Him to a
Throne, and then immediately withdraws, expecting not so much as
Thanks for his Pains: In imitation of which Example, I have placed *Lord
Peter* in a Noble House, given Him a Title to wear, and Money to spend.
There I shall leave Him for some Time; returning where common
Charity directs me, to the Assistance of his two Brothers, at their lowest
Ebb. However, I shall by no means forget my Character of an Historian, to
follow the Truth, step by step, whatever happens, or where-ever it may
lead me.

THE two Exiles so nearly united in Fortune and Interest, took a Lodging together; Where, at their first Leisure, they began to reflect on the
numberless Misfortunes and Vexations of their Life past, and could not
tell, on the sudden, to what Failure in their Conduct they ought to impute
them; When, after some Recollection, they called to Mind the Copy of
their Father's *Will*, which they had so happily recovered. This was immediately produced, and a firm Resolution taken between them, to alter
whatever was already amiss, and reduce all their future Measures to the
strictest Obedience prescribed therein. The main Body of the *Will* (as the
Reader cannot easily have forgot) consisted in certain admirable Rules
about the wearing of their Coats; in the Perusal whereof, the two Brothers
at every Period duly comparing the Doctrine with the Practice, there was
never seen a wider Difference between two Things; horrible downright
Transgressions of every Point. Upon which, they both resolved without
further Delay, to fall immediately upon reducing the Whole, exactly after
their Father's Model.

BUT, here it is good to stop the hasty Reader, ever impatient to see the
End of an Adventure, before We Writers can duly prepare him for it. I am
to record, that these two Brothers began to be distinguished at this Time,
by certain Names. One of them desired to be called *M A R T I N*,* and the
other took the Appellation of *J A C K*.† These two had lived in much
Friendship and Agreement under the Tyranny of their Brother *Peter*, as it
is the Talent of Fellow-Sufferers to do; Men in Misfortune, being like

---

* *Martin Luther.*
† *John Calvin.*

Men in the Dark, to whom all Colours are the same: But when they came forward into the World, and began to display themselves to each other, and to the Light, their Complexions appear'd extreamly different; which the present Posture of their Affairs gave them sudden Opportunity to discover.

BUT, here the severe Reader may justly tax me as a Writer of short Memory, a Deficiency to which a true *Modern* cannot but of Necessity be a little subject. Because, *Memory* being an Employment of the Mind upon things past, is a Faculty, for which the Learned, in our Illustrious Age, have no manner of Occasion, who deal entirely with *Invention,* and strike all Things out of themselves, or at least, by Collision, from each other: Upon which Account we think it highly Reasonable to produce our great Forgetfulness, as an Argument unanswerable for our great Wit. I ought in Method, to have informed the Reader about fifty Pages ago, of a Fancy *Lord Peter* took, and infused into his Brothers, to wear on their Coats what ever Trimmings came up in Fashion; never pulling off any, as they went out of the Mode, but keeping on all together; which amounted in time to a Medley, the most Antick you can possibly conceive; and this to a Degree, that upon the Time of their falling out there was hardly a Thread of the Original Coat to be seen, but an infinite Quantity of *Lace,* and *Ribbands,* and *Fringe,* and *Embroidery,* and *Points;* (I mean, only those *tagg'd with Silver,** for the rest fell off.) Now, this material Circumstance, having been forgot in due Place; as good Fortune hath ordered, comes in very properly here, when the two Brothers are just going to reform their Vestures into the Primitive State, prescribed by their Father's Will.

THEY both unanimously entred upon this great Work, looking sometimes on their Coats, and sometimes on the *Will. Martin* laid the first Hand; at one twitch brought off a large Handful of *Points,* and with a second pull, stript away ten dozen Yards of *Fringe.* But when He had gone thus far, he demurred a while: He knew very well, there yet remained a great deal more to be done; however, the first Heat being over, his Violence began to cool, and he resolved to proceed more moderately in the rest of the Work; having already very narrowly scap'd a swinging Rent in pulling off the *Points,* which being *tagged with Silver* (as we have observed before) the judicious Workman had with much Sagacity, double sown, to preserve them from *falling.* Resolving therefore to rid his Coat of a huge Quantity of *Gold*

---

* *Points tagg'd with Silver, are those Doctrines that promote the Greatness and Wealth of the Church, which have been therefore woven deepest in the Body of Popery.*

Lace; he pickt up the Stitches with much Caution, and diligently gleaned out all the loose Threads as he went, which proved to be a Work of Time. Then he fell about the embroidered *Indian* Figures of Men, Women and Children; against which, as you have heard in its due Place, their Father's Testament was extreamly exact and severe: These, with much Dexterity and Application, were after a while, quite eradicated, or utterly defaced. For the rest, where he observed the Embroidery to be workt so close, as not to be got away without damaging the Cloth, or where it served to hide or strengthen any Flaw in the Body of the Coat, contracted by the perpetual tampering of Workmen upon it; he concluded the wisest Course was to let it remain, resolving in no Case whatsoever, that the Substance of the Stuff should suffer Injury; which he thought the best Method for serving the true Intent and Meaning of his Father's *Will.* And this is the nearest Account I have been able to collect, of *Martin*'s Proceedings upon this great Revolution.

BUT his Brother *Jack,* whose Adventures will be so extraordinary, as to furnish a great Part in the Remainder of this Discourse; entred upon the Matter with other Thoughts, and a quite different Spirit. For, the Memory of *Lord Peter*'s Injuries, produced a Degree of Hatred and Spight, which had a much greater Share of inciting Him, than any Regards after his Father's Commands, since these appeared at best, only Secondary and Subservient to the other. However, for this Meddly of Humor, he made a Shift to find a very plausible Name, honoring it with the Title of *Zeal;* which is, perhaps, the most significant Word that hath been ever yet produced in any Language; As, I think, I have fully proved in my excellent *Analytical* Discourse upon that Subject; wherein I have deduced a *Histori-theo-physi-logical* Account of *Zeal,* shewing how it first proceeded from a *Notion* into a *Word,* and from thence in a hot Summer, ripned into a *tangible Substance.* This Work containing three large Volumes in Folio, I design very shortly to publish by the *Modern* way of *Subscription,* not doubting but the Nobility and Gentry of the Land will give me all possible Encouragement, having already had such a Taste of what I am able to perform.

I record therefore, that Brother *Jack,* brimful of this miraculous Compound, reflecting with Indignation upon *PETER*'s Tyranny, and farther provoked by the Despondency of *Martin;* prefaced his Resolutions to this purpose. *What?* said he; *A Rogue that lock'd up his Drink, turned away our Wives, cheated us of our Fortunes; paumed his damned Crusts upon us for Mutton; and at last kickt us out of Doors; must we be in His Fashions with a Pox? a Rascal, besides, that all the Street cries out against.* Having thus kindled and enflamed himself as high as possible, and by Consequence, in a delicate Temper for beginning a Reformation, he set about the Work immediately, and in three Minutes, made more Dispatch than *Martin* had done in as many Hours. For, (Courteous Reader) you are given to understand, that *Zeal* is never so highly obliged, as when you set it a *Tearing:* and *Jack,* who doated on that Quality in himself, allowed it at this Time its full Swinge. Thus it happened, that stripping down a Parcel of *Gold Lace,* a little too hastily, he rent the *main Body* of his *Coat* from Top to Bottom; and whereas his Talent was not of the happiest in *taking up a Stitch,* he knew no better way, than to dern it again with *Packthred* and a *Scewer.* But the Matter was yet infinitely worse (I record it with Tears) when he proceeded to the *Embroidery:* For, being Clumsy by Nature, and of Temper, Impatient; withal, beholding Millions of Stitches, that required the nicest Hand, and sedatest Constitution, to extricate; in a great Rage, he tore off the whole Piece, Cloth and all, and flung it into the Kennel, and furiously thus continuing his Career; *Ah, Good Brother* Martin, said he, *do as I do, for the Love of God; Strip, Tear, Pull, Rent, Flay off all, that we may appear as unlike the Rogue* Peter, *as it is possible: I would not for a hundred Pounds carry the least Mark about me, that might give Occasion to the Neighbours, of suspecting I was related to such a Rascal.* But *Martin,* who at this Time happened to be extremely flegmatick and sedate, *begged his Brother of all Love, not to damage his Coat by any Means; for he never would get such another: Desired him to consider, that it was not their Business to form their Actions by any Reflection upon* Peter*'s, but by observing the Rules prescribed in their Father's* Will. That *he should remember,* Peter *was still their Brother, whatever Faults or Injuries he had committed; and therefore they should by all means avoid such a Thought, as that of taking Measures for Good and Evil, from no other Rule, than of Opposition to him.* That *it was true, the Testament of their good Father was very exact in what related to the wearing of their* Coats; *yet was it no less penal and strict in prescribing Agreement, and Friendship, and Affection between them. And therefore, if straining a Point were at all dispensable, it would certainly be so, rather to the Advance of Unity, than Increase of Contradiction.*

MARTIN[104] had still proceeded as gravely as he began; and doubtless would have delivered an admirable Lecture of Morality, which might have exceedingly contributed to my Reader's *Repose, both of Body and Mind:* (the true ultimate End of *Ethicks;*) But *Jack* was already gone a Flight-shot beyond his Patience. And as in Scholastick Disputes, nothing serves to rouze the Spleen of him that *Opposes,* so much as a kind of Pedantick affected Calmness in the *Respondent;* Disputants being for the most part like unequal Scales, where the *Gravity* of one Side advances the *Lightness* of the

Other, and causes it to fly up and kick the Beam; So it happened here, that the *Weight* of *Martin*'s Arguments exalted *Jack*'s *Levity*, and made him fly out and spurn against his Brother's Moderation. In short, *Martin*'s *Patience* put *Jack* in a *Rage;* but that which most afflicted him was, to observe his Brother's Coat so well reduced into the State of Innocence; while his own was either wholly rent to his Shirt; or those Places which had scaped his cruel Clutches, were still in *Peter*'s Livery. So that he looked like a drunken *Beau*, half rifled by *Bullies;* Or like a fresh Tenant of *Newgate*, when he has refused the Payment of *Garnish;* Or like a discovered *Shoplifter*, left to the Mercy of *Exchange-Women;* Or like a *Bawd* in her old Velvet-Petticoat, re-sign'd into the secular Hands of the *Mobile*. Like any, or like all of these, a Meddley of *Rags*, and *Lace*, and *Rents*, and *Fringes*, unfortunate *Jack* did now appear: He would have been extremely glad to see his Coat in the Condi-tion of *Martin*'s, but infinitely gladder to find that of *Martin*'s in the same Predicament with his. However, since neither of these was likely to come to pass, he thought fit to lend the whole Business another Turn, and to dress up Necessity into a Virtue. Therefore, after as many of the *Fox*'s Ar-guments,[105] as he could muster up, for bringing *Martin* to *Reason*, as he called it; or, as he meant it, into his own ragged, bobtail'd Condition; and observing he said all to little purpose; what, alas, was left for the forlorn *Jack* to do, but after a Million of Scurrilities against his Brother, to run mad with Spleen, and Spight, and Contradiction. To be short, here began a mortal Breach between these two. *Jack* went immediately to *New Lodg-ings*, and in a few Days it was for certain reported, that he had run out of his Wits. In a short time after, he appeared abroad, and confirmed the Report, by falling into the oddest Whimsies that ever a sick Brain con-ceived.[106]

AND now the little Boys in the Streets began to salute him with sev-eral Names. Sometimes they would call Him, *Jack the Bald;** sometimes, *Jack with a Lanthorn;*† sometimes, *Dutch Jack;*‡ sometimes, *French Hugh;*§ sometimes, *Tom the Beggar;*** and sometimes, *Knocking Jack of the North.*†† And it was under one, or some, or all of these Appellations (which I leave the Learned Reader to determine) that he hath given Rise to the most

---

* *That is* Calvin, *from* Calvus, *Bald.*
† *All those who pretend to Inward Light.*
‡ Jack *of* Leyden, *who gave Rise to the* Anabaptists.
§ *The* Hugonots.
** *The* Gueuses, *by which Name some Protestants in* Flanders *were call'd.*
†† John Knox, *the Reformer of* Scotland.

Illustrious and Epidemick Sect of *Æolists,* who with honourable Commemoration, do still acknowledge the Renowned *J A C K* for their Author
and Founder. Of whose Original, as well as Principles, I am now advancing to gratify the World with a very particular Account.

———*Mellæo contingens cuncta Lepore.*[107]

SECTION VII

A Digression in Praise of Digressions

I have sometimes *heard* of an *Iliad* in a *Nut-Shell;* but it hath been my Fortune to have much oftner *seen* a *Nut-shell* in an *Iliad.* There is no doubt, that
Human Life has received most wonderful Advantages from both; but to
which of the two the World is chiefly indebted, I shall leave among the
Curious, as a Problem worthy of their utmost Enquiry. For the Invention
of the latter, I think the Commonwealth of Learning is chiefly obliged to
the great *Modern* Improvement of *Digressions:* The late Refinements in
Knowledge, running parallel to those of Dyet in our Nation, which among
Men of a judicious Taste, are drest up in various Compounds, consisting
in *Soups* and *Ollio's, Fricassées* and *Ragousts.*

'Tis true, there is a sort of morose, detracting, ill-bred People, who
pretend utterly to disrelish these polite Innovations: And as to the Similitude from Dyet, they allow the Parallel, but are so bold to pronounce the
Example it self, a Corruption and Degeneracy of Taste. They tell us, that
the Fashion of jumbling fifty Things together in a Dish, was at first introduced in Compliance to a depraved and *debauched Appetite,* as well as to a
crazy Constitution; And to see a Man hunting thro' an *Ollio,* after the *Head*
and *Brains* of a *Goose,* a *Wigeon,* or a *Woodcock,* is a Sign, he wants a Stomach
and Digestion for more substantial Victuals. Farther, they affirm, that *Di-*
gressions in a Book, are like *Forein Troops* in a *State,* which argue the Nation
to want a *Heart* and *Hands* of its own, and often, either *subdue* the *Natives,*
or drive them into the most *unfruitful Corners.*

But, after all that can be objected by these supercilious Censors; 'tis
manifest, the Society of Writers would quickly be reduced to a very inconsiderable Number, if Men were put upon making Books, with the fatal
Confinement of delivering nothing beyond what is to the Purpose. 'Tis acknowledged, that were the Case the same among Us, as with the *Greeks*
and *Romans,* when Learning was in its *Cradle,* to be reared and fed, and

cloathed by *Invention;* it would be an easy Task to fill up Volumes upon particular Occasions, without farther exspatiating from the Subject, than by moderate Excursions, helping to advance or clear the main Design. But with *Knowledge,* it has fared as with a numerous Army, encamped in a fruitful Country; which for a few Days maintains it self by the Product of the Soyl it is on; Till Provisions being spent, they send to forrage many a Mile, among Friends or Enemies it matters not. Mean while, the neighbouring Fields trampled and beaten down, become barren and dry, affording no Sustenance but Clouds of Dust.

THE whole Course of Things, being thus entirely changed between *Us* and the *Antients;* and the *Moderns* wisely sensible of it, we of this Age have discovered a shorter, and more prudent Method, to become *Scholars* and *Wits,* without the Fatigue of *Reading* or of *Thinking.* The most accomplisht Way of using Books at present, is twofold: Either first, to serve them as some Men do *Lords,* learn their *Titles* exactly, and then brag of their Acquaintance. Or Secondly, which is indeed the choicer, the profounder, and politer Method, to get a thorough Insight into the *Index,* by which the whole Book is governed and turned, like *Fishes* by the *Tail.* For, to enter the Palace of Learning at the *great Gate,* requires an Expence of Time and Forms; therefore Men of much Haste and little Ceremony, are content to get in by the *Back-Door.* For, the Arts are all in a *flying* March, and therefore more easily subdued by attacking them in the *Rear.* Thus Physicians discover the State of the whole Body, by consulting only what comes from *Behind.* Thus Men catch Knowledge by throwing their *Wit* on the *Posteriors* of a Book, as Boys do Sparrows with flinging *Salt* upon their *Tails.* Thus Human Life is best understood by the wise man's Rule of *Regarding the End.* Thus are the Sciences found like *Hercules's* Oxen, by *tracing them Backwards.* Thus are *old Sciences* unravelled like *old Stockings,* by beginning at the *Foot.*

BESIDES all this, the Army of the Sciences hath been of late with a world of Martial Discipline, drawn into its *close Order,* so that a View, or a Muster may be taken of it with abundance of Expedition. For this great Blessing we are wholly indebted to *Systems* and *Abstracts,* in which the *Modern* Fathers of Learning, like prudent Usurers, spent their Sweat for the Ease of Us their Children. For *Labor* is the Seed of *Idleness,* and it is the peculiar Happiness of our Noble Age to gather the *Fruit.*

Now the Method of growing Wise, Learned, and *Sublime,* having become so regular an Affair, and so established in all its Forms; the Number of Writers must needs have encreased accordingly, and to a Pitch that has made it of absolute Necessity for them to interfere continually with each other. Besides, it is reckoned, that there is not at this present, a sufficient Quantity of new Matter left in Nature, to furnish and adorn any one particular Subject to the Extent of a Volume. This I am told by a very skillful *Computer,* who hath given a full Demonstration of it from Rules of *Arithmetick.*

THIS, perhaps, may be objected against, by those, who maintain the Infinity of Matter, and therefore, will not allow that any *Species* of it can be exhausted. For Answer to which, let us examine the noblest Branch of *Modern* Wit or Invention, planted and cultivated by the present Age, and, which of all others, hath born the most, and the fairest Fruit. For tho' some Remains of it were left us by the *Antients,* yet have not any of those, as I remember, been translated or compiled into Systems for *Modern* Use. Therefore We may affirm, to our own Honor, that it has in some sort, been both invented, and brought to a Perfection by the same Hands. What I mean, is that highly celebrated Talent among the *Modern* Wits, of deducing Similitudes, Allusions, and Applications, very Surprizing, Agreeable, and Apposite, from the *Pudenda* of either Sex, together with *their proper Uses.* And truly, having observed how little Invention bears any Vogue, besides what is derived into these *Channels,* I have sometimes had a Thought, That the happy Genius of our Age and Country, was prophetically held forth by that antient* typical Description of the *Indian* Pygmies; *whose Stature did not exceed above two Foot; Sed quorum pudenda crassa, & ad talos usque pertingentia.*[108] Now, I have been very curious to inspect the late Productions, wherein the Beauties of this kind have most prominently appeared. And altho' this *Vein* hath bled so freely, and all Endeavours have been used in the Power of Human Breath, to dilate, extend, and keep it open: Like the Scythians, *who had a Custom, and an Instrument, to blow up the Privities of their Mares, that they might yield the more Milk;*† Yet I am under an Apprehension, it is near growing dry, and past all Recovery; And that either some new *Fonde* of Wit should, if possible, be provided, or else that we must e'en be content with Repetition here, as well as upon all other Occasions.

* Ctesiæ fragm. apud Photium.

† Herodot. L. 4.

THIS will stand as an uncontestable Argument, that our *Modern* Wits are not to reckon upon the Infinity of Matter, for a constant Supply. What remains therefore, but that our last Recourse must be had to large *Indexes,* and little *Compendiums; Quotations* must be plentifully gathered, and bookt in Alphabet; To this End, tho' Authors need be little consulted, yet *Criticks,* and *Commentators,* and *Lexicons* carefully must. But above all, those judicious Collectors of *bright Parts,* and *Flowers,* and *Observanda's,* are to be nicely dwelt on; by some called the *Sieves* and *Boulters* of Learning; tho' it is left undetermined, whether they dealt in *Pearls* or *Meal;* and consequently, whether we are more to value that which *passed thro',* or what *staid behind.*

BY these Methods, in a few Weeks, there starts up many a Writer, capable of managing the profoundest, and most universal Subjects. For, what tho' his *Head* be empty, provided his *Common-place-Book* be full; And if you will bate him but the Circumstances of *Method,* and *Style,* and *Grammar,* and *Invention;* allow him but the common Priviledges of transcribing from others, and digressing from himself, as often as he shall see Occasion; He will desire no more Ingredients towards fitting up a Treatise, that shall make a very comely Figure on a Bookseller's Shelf, there to be preserved neat and clean, for a long Eternity, adorn'd with the Heraldry of its Title, fairly inscribed on a Label; never to be thumb'd or greas'd by Students, nor bound to everlasting Chains of Darkness in a Library: But when the Fulness of time is come, shall haply undergo the Tryal of Purgatory, in order *to ascend the Sky.*

WITHOUT these Allowances, how is it possible, we *Modern* Wits should ever have an Opportunity to introduce our Collections listed under so many thousand Heads of a different Nature? for want of which, the Learned World would be deprived of infinite Delight, as well as Instruction, and we our selves buried beyond Redress in an inglorious and undistinguisht Oblivion.

FROM such Elements as these, I am alive to behold the Day, wherein the Corporation of Authors can out-vie all its Brethren in the *Guild.* A Happiness derived to us with a great many others, from our *Scythian* Ancestors; among whom, the Number of *Pens* was so infinite, that the *Grecian* Eloquence* had no other way of expressing it, than * *Herodot.* L. 4. by saying, *That in the Regions, far to the* North, *it was hardly possible for a Man to travel, the very Air was so replete with* Feathers.

THE Necessity of this Digression, will easily excuse the Length; and I have chosen for it as proper a Place as I could readily find. If the judicious Reader can assign a fitter, I do here empower him to remove it into any other Corner he please. And so I return with great Alacrity to pursue a more important Concern.

SECTION VIII

A Tale *of a* Tub

The Learned *Æolists,**[109] maintain the Original Cause of all Things to be *Wind,* from which Principle this whole Universe was at first produced, and into which it must at last be resolved; that the same Breath which had kindled, and blew *up* the Flame of Nature, should one Day blow it *out.*

Quod procul à nobis flectat Fortuna gubernans.[110]

THIS is what the *Adepti* understand by their *Anima Mundi;* that is to say, the *Spirit,* or *Breath,* or *Wind* of the World: Or Examine the whole System by the Particulars of Nature, and you will find it not to be disputed. For, whether you please to call the *Forma informans* of Man, by the Name of *Spiritus, Animus, Afflatus,* or *Anima;* What are all these but several Appellations for *Wind?* Which is the ruling *Element* in every Compound, and into which they all resolve upon their Corruption. Farther, what is Life itself, but as it is commonly call'd, the *Breath* of our Nostrils? Whence it is very justly observed by Naturalists, that *Wind* still continues of great Emolument in *certain Mysteries* not to be named, giving Occasion for those happy Epithets of *Turgidus,* and *Inflatus,* apply'd either to the *Emittent,* or *Recipient* Organs.

BY what I have gathered out of antient Records, I find the *Compass* of their Doctrine took in two and thirty Points, wherein it would be tedious to be very particular. However, a few of their most important Precepts, deducible from it, are by no means to be omitted; among which the following Maxim was of much Weight; That since *Wind* had the Master-Share, as well as Operation in every Compound, by Consequence, those Beings must be of chief Excellence, wherein that *Primordium* appears most prominently to abound; and therefore, *Man* is in highest Perfection of all created Things, as having by the great Bounty of Philosophers, been endued with three distinct *Anima's* or *Winds,* to which the Sage *Æolists,* with much Liberality, have added a fourth of equal Necessity, as well as Ornament with the other three; by this *quartum Principium,* taking in the four Corners of the World; which gave Occasion to that Renowned *Cabbalist, Bumbastus,*† of placing the Body of Man, in due position to the four *Cardinal* Points.

* *All Pretenders to Inspiration whatsoever.*

† *This is one of the Names of* Paracelsus; *He was call'd* Christophorus, Theophrastus, Paracelsus, Bumbastus.

IN Consequence of this, their next Principle was, that *Man* brings with him into the World a peculiar Portion or Grain of *Wind*, which may be called a *Quinta essentia*, extracted from the other four. This *Quintessence* is of Catholick Use upon all Emergencies of Life, is improvable into all Arts and Sciences, and may be wonderfully refined, as well as enlarged by certain Methods in Education. This, when *blown* up to its Perfection, ought not to be covetously hoarded up, stifled, or hid under a Bushel, but freely communicated to Mankind. Upon these Reasons, and others of equal Weight, the Wise *Æolists*, affirm the Gift of BELCHING, to be the noblest Act of a Rational Creature. To cultivate which Art, and render it more serviceable to Mankind, they made Use of several Methods. At certain Seasons of the Year, you might behold the Priests amongst them in vast Numbers, with their *Mouths gaping wide against a Storm.** At other times were to be seen several Hundreds link'd together in a circular Chain, with every Man a Pair of Bellows applied to his Neighbour's Breech, by which they blew up each other to the Shape and Size of a *Tun*; and for that Reason, with great Propriety of Speech, did usually call their Bodies, their *Vessels*. When, by these and the like Performances, they were grown sufficiently replete, they would immediately depart, and disembogue for the Publick Good, a plentiful Share of their Acquirements into their Disciples Chaps. For we must here observe, that all Learning was esteemed among them to be compounded from the same Principle. Because, First, it is generally affirmed, or confess'd that Learning *puffeth Men up:* And Secondly, they proved it by the following Syllogism; *Words are but Wind; and Learning is nothing but Words;* Ergo, *Learning is nothing but Wind.* For this Reason, the Philosophers among them, did in their Schools, deliver to their Pupils, all their Doctrines and Opinions by *Eructation*, wherein they had acquired a wonderful Eloquence, and of incredible Variety. But the great Characteristick, by which their chief Sages were best distinguished, was a certain Position of Countenance, which gave undoubted Intelligence to what Degree or Proportion, the Spirit agitated the inward Mass. For, after certain Gripings, the *Wind* and Vapours issuing forth; having first by their Turbulence and Convulsions within, caused an Earthquake in Man's little World; distorted the Mouth, bloated the Cheeks, and gave the Eyes a terrible kind of *Relievo*. At which Junctures, all their *Belches* were received for Sacred, the Sourer the better, and swallowed with infinite Consolation by their meager Devotes. And to render these yet more compleat, because

---

* *This is meant of those Seditious Preachers, who blow up the Seeds of Rebellion, &c.*

the Breath of Man's Life is in his Nostrils, therefore, the choicest, most edifying, and most enlivening *Belches*, were very wisely conveyed thro' that Vehicle, to give them a Tincture as they passed.

THEIR Gods were the four *Winds*, whom they worshipped, as the Spirits that pervade and enliven the Universe, and as those from whom alone all *Inspiration* can properly be said to proceed. However, the Chief of these, to whom they performed the Adoration of *Latria*, was the *Almighty-North*. An antient Deity, whom the Inhabitants of *Megalopolis* in Greece, had likewise in highest Reverence. *Omnium Deorum Boream maxime celebrant.*[111] This God, tho' endued with Ubiquity, was **Pausan.* L.8. yet supposed by the profounder *Æolists*, to possess one peculiar Habitation, or (to speak in Form) a *Cœlum Empyræum*, wherein he was more intimately present. This was situated in a certain Region, well known to the Antient *Greeks*, by them called, Σκοτία, or the *Land of Darkness.*[112] And altho' many Controversies have arisen upon that Matter; yet so much is undisputed, that from a Region of the *like Denomination*, the most refined *Æolists* have borrowed their Original, from whence, in every Age, the zealous among their Priesthood, have brought over their choicest *Inspiration*, fetching it with their own Hands, from the Fountain Head, in certain *Bladders*, and disploding it among the Sectaries in all Nations, who did, and do, and ever will, daily Gasp and Pant after it.

NOW, their Mysteries and Rites were performed in this Manner. 'Tis well known among the Learned, that the Virtuoso's of former Ages, had a Contrivance for carrying and preserving *Winds* in Casks or Barrels, which was of great Assistance upon long Sea Voyages; and the Loss of so useful an Art at present, is very much to be lamented, tho' I know not how, with great Negligence omitted by *Pancirollus.** It was an Invention ascribed to *Æolus* himself, from whom this Sect is denominated, and who in Honour of their Founder's Memory, have to this Day preserved great Numbers of those *Barrels*, whereof they fix one in each of their Temples, first beating out the Top. Into this *Barrel*, upon Solemn Days, the Priest enters; where, having before duly prepared himself by the methods already described, a secret Funnel is also convey'd from his Posteriors, to the Bottom of the Barrel, which admits new Supplies of Inspiration from a *Northern* Chink or Crany. Whereupon, you behold him swell immediately to the Shape and Size of his *Vessel*. In this Posture he disembogues whole Tempests upon his Auditory, as the Spirit from beneath gives him Utterance; which

---

* *An Author who writ* De Artibus Perditis, &c. *of Arts lost, and of Arts invented.*

issuing *ex adytis*, and *penetralibus*,[113] is not performed without much Pain and Gripings. And the *Wind in* breaking forth, deals with his Face, as it does with that of the Sea; first *blackning*, then *wrinkling*, and at last, *bursting it into a Foam.** It is in this Guise, the Sacred *Æolist* delivers his oracular *Belches* to his panting Disciples; Of whom, some are greedily gaping after the sanctified Breath; others are all the while hymning out the Praises of the *Winds*; and gently wafted to and fro by their own Humming, do thus represent the soft Breezes of their Deities appeased.

IT is from this Custom of the Priests, that some Authors maintain these *Æolists*, to have been very antient in the World. Because, the Delivery of their Mysteries, which I have just now mention'd, appears exactly the same with that of other antient Oracles, whose Inspirations were owing to certain subterraneous *Effluviums* of *Wind*, delivered with the *same* Pain to the Priest, and much about the *same* Influence on the People. It is true indeed, that these were frequently managed and directed by *Female* Officers, whose Organs were understood to be better disposed for the Admission of those Oracular *Gusts*, as entring and passing up thro' a Receptacle of greater Capacity, and causing also a Pruriency by the Way, such as with due Management, hath been refined from a Carnal, into a Spiritual Extasie. And to strengthen this profound Conjecture, it is farther insisted, that this Custom of *Female* Priests† is kept up still in certain refined Colleges of our *Modern Æolists*, who are agreed to receive their Inspiration, derived thro' the Receptacle aforesaid, like their Ancestors, the *Sibyls*.

AND, whereas the mind of Man, when he gives the Spur and Bridle to his Thoughts, doth never stop, but natually sallies out into both extreams of High and Low, of Good and Evil; His first Flight of Fancy, commonly transports Him to Idea's of what is most Perfect, finished, and exalted; till having soared out of his own Reach and Sight, not well perceiving how near the Frontiers of Height and Depth, border upon each other; With the same Course and Wing, he falls down plum into the lowest Bottom of things; like one who travels the *East* into the *West*; or like a strait Line drawn by its own Length into a Circle. Whether a Tincture of Malice in our Natures, makes us fond of furnishing every bright Idea with its Reverse; Or, whether Reason reflecting upon the Sum of Things, can, like the Sun, serve only to enlighten one half of the Globe, leaving the other half, by Necessity, under Shade and Darkness: Or, whether Fancy, flying up to

---

* *This is an exact Description of the Changes made in the Face by Enthusiastick Preachers.*
† *Quakers who suffer their Women to preach and pray.*

the imagination of what is Highest and Best, becomes over-shot, and spent, and weary, and suddenly falls like a dead Bird of Paradise, to the Ground. Or, whether after all these *Metaphysical* Conjectures, I have not entirely missed the true Reason; The Proposition, however, which hath stood me in so much Circumstance, is altogether true; That, as the most unciviliz'd Parts of Mankind, have some way or other, climbed up into the Conception of a *God*, or Supream Power, so they have seldom forgot to provide their Fears with certain ghastly Notions, which instead of better, have served them pretty tolerably for a *Devil*. And this Proceeding seems to be natural enough; For it is with Men, whose Imaginations are lifted up very high, after the same Rate, as with those, whose Bodies are so; that, as they are delighted with the Advantage of a nearer Contemplation up-wards, so they are equally terrified with the dismal Prospect of the Precipice below. Thus, in the Choice of a *Devil*, it hath been the usual Method of Mankind, to single out some Being, either in Act, or in Vision, which was in most Antipathy to the God they had framed. Thus also the Sect of *Æolists*, possessed themselves with a dread, and Horror, and Hatred of two Malignant Natures, betwixt whom, and the Deities they adored, perpetual Enmity was established. The first of these, was the *Camelion** sworn Foe to *Inspiration*, who in Scorn, devoured large Influences of their God; without refunding the smallest Blast by *Eructation*. The other was a huge terrible Monster, called *Moulinavent*, who with four strong Arms, waged eternal Battel with all their Divinities, dextrously turning to avoid their Blows, and repay them with Interest.

THUS furnisht, and set out with *Gods*, as well as *Devils*, was the renowned Sect of *Æolists*; which makes at this Day so illustrious a Figure in the World, and whereof, that Polite Nation of *Laplanders*, are beyond all Doubt, a most Authentick Branch; Of whom, I therefore cannot, without Injustice, here omit to make honourable Mention; since they appear to be so closely allied in Point of Interest, as well as Inclinations, with their Brother *Æolists* among Us, as not only to buy their *Winds* by wholesale from the *same* Merchants, but also to retail them after the *same* Rate and Method, and to Customers much alike.

NOW, whether the System here delivered, was wholly compiled by *Jack*, or, as some Writers believe, rather copied from the Original at *Delphos*, with certain Additions and Emendations suited to Times and Circum-

---

* *I do not well understand what the Author aims at here, any more than by the terrible Monster, men-tion'd in the following Lines, called* Moulinavent, *which is the* French *Word for a Windmill.*

stances, I shall not absolutely determine. This I may affirm, that *Jack* gave it at least a new Turn, and formed it into the same Dress and Model, as it lies deduced by me.

I have long sought after this Opportunity, of doing Justice to a Society of Men, for whom I have a peculiar Honour, and whose Opinions, as well as Practices, have been extreamly misrepresented, and traduced by the Malice or Ignorance of their Adversaries. For, I think it one of the greatest, and best of human Actions, to remove Prejudices, and place Things in their truest and fairest Light; which I therefore boldly undertake without any Regards of my own, beside the Conscience, the Honour, and the Thanks.

SECTION IX

A Digression Concerning the Original, the Use and Improvement of Madness in a Commonwealth

Nor shall it any ways detract from the just Reputation of this famous Sect, that its Rise and Institution are owing to such an Author as I have described *Jack* to be: A Person whose Intellectuals were overturned, and his Brain shaken out of its Natural Position; which we commonly suppose to be a Distemper, and call by the Name of *Madness* or *Phrenzy*. For, if we take a Survey of the greatest Actions that have been performed in the World, under the Influence of Single Men; which are, *The Establishment of New Empires by Conquest: The Advance and Progress of New Schemes in Philosophy; and the contriving, as well as the propagating of New Religions:* We shall find the Authors of them all, to have been Persons, whose natural Reason hath admitted great Revolutions from their Dyet, their Education, the Prevalency of some certain Temper, together with the particular Influence of Air and Climate. Besides, there is something Individual in human Minds, that easily kindles at the accidental Approach and Collision of certain Circumstances, which tho' of paltry and mean Appearance, do often flame out into the greatest Emergencies of Life. For great Turns are not always given by strong Hands, but by lucky Adaption, and at proper Seasons; and it is of no import, where the Fire was kindled, if the Vapor has once got up into the Brain. For the *upper Region* of Man, is furnished like the *middle Region* of the Air; The Materials are formed from Causes of the widest Difference, yet produce at last the same Substance and Effect. Mists arise from the Earth, Steams from Dunghils, Exhalations from the Sea, and Smoak from Fire; yet all Clouds are the same in Composition, as well as Consequences: and the Fumes issuing from a Jakes, will furnish as comely and useful a Vapor, as Incense from an Altar. Thus far, I suppose, will easily be granted me; and then it will follow, that as the Face of Nature never produces Rain, but when it is overcast and disturbed, so Human Understanding, seated in the Brain, must be troubled and overspread by Vapours, ascending from the lower Faculties, to water the Invention, and render it fruitful. Now, altho' these Vapours (as it hath been already said) are of as various Original, as those of the Skies, yet the Crop they produce, differs both in Kind and Degree, meerly according to the Soil. I will produce two Instances to prove and Explain what I am now advancing.

A certain Great Prince* raised a mighty Army, filled his Coffers with infinite Treasures, provided an invincible Fleet, and all this, without giving the least Part of his Design to his greatest Ministers, or his nearest Favourites. Immediately the whole World was alarmed; the neighbouring Crowns, in trembling Expectation, towards what Point the Storm would burst; the small Politicians, every where forming profound Conjectures. Some believed he had laid a Scheme for Universal Monarchy: Others, after much Insight, determined the Matter to be a Project for pulling down the *Pope*, and setting up the *Reformed* Religion, which had once been his own. Some, again, of a deeper Sagacity, sent him into *Asia* to subdue the *Turk*, and recover *Palestine*. In the midst of all these Projects and Preparations; a certain *State-Surgeon*,† gathering the Nature of the Disease by these Symptoms, attempted the Cure, at one Blow performed the Operation, broke the Bag, and out flew the *Vapour;* nor did any thing want to render it a compleat Remedy, only, that the Prince unfortunately happened to Die in the Performance. Now, is the Reader exceeding curious to learn, from whence this *Vapour* took its Rise, which had so long set the Nations at a Gaze? What secret Wheel, what hidden Spring could put into Motion so wonderful an Engine? It was afterwards discovered, that the Movement of this whole Machine had been directed by an absent *Female*, whose Eyes had raised a Protuberancy, and before Emission, she was removed into an Enemy's Country. What should an unhappy Prince do in such ticklish Circumstances as these? He tried in vain the Poet's neverfailing Receipt of *Corpora quæque*;[114] For,

---

* *This was* Harry *the Great of* France.[115]

† Ravillac, *who stabb'd* Henry *the Great in his Coach.*

Idque petit corpus mens unde est saucia amore;
Unde feritur, eo tendit, gestitq; coire. Lucr.[116]

HAVING to no purpose used all peaceable Endeavours, the collected part of the *Semen,* raised and enflamed, became adust, converted to Choler, turned head upon the spinal Duct, and ascended to the Brain. The very same Principle that influences a *Bully* to break the Windows of a Whore, who has jilted him, naturally stirs up a Great Prince to raise mighty Armies, and dream of nothing but Sieges, Battles, and Victories.

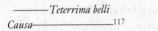

————*Teterrima belli*
Causa————————[117]

THE other Instance*[118] is, what I have read somewhere, in a very antient Author, of a mighty King, who for the space of above thirty Years, amused himself to take and lose Towns; beat Armies, and be beaten; drive Princes out of their Dominions; fright Children from their Bread and Butter; burn, lay waste, plunder, dragoon, massacre Subject and Stranger, Friend and Foe, Male and Female. 'Tis recorded, that the Philosophers of each Country were in grave Dispute, upon Causes Natural, Moral, and Political, to find out where they should assign an original Solution of this *Phænomenon.* At last the *Vapour* or *Spirit,* which animated the Hero's Brain, being in perpetual Circulation, seized upon that Region of the Human Body, so renown'd for furnishing the *Zibeta Occidentalis,*† and gathering there into a Tumor, left the rest of the World for that Time in Peace. Of such mighty Consequence it is, where those Exhalations fix; and of so little, from whence they proceed. The same Spirits which in their superior Progress would conquer a Kingdom, descending upon the *Anus,* conclude in a *Fistula.*

LET us next examine the great Introducers of new Schemes in Philosophy, and search till we can find, from what Faculty of the Soul the Disposition arises in mortal Man, of taking it into his Head, to advance new Systems with such an eager Zeal, in things agreed on all hands impossible to be known: from what Seeds this Dispostion springs, and to what Quality of human Nature these Grand Innovators have been indebted for their

---

* *This is meant of the Present* French *King.*

† Paracelsus, *who was so famous for Chymistry, try'd an Experiment upon human Excrement, to make a Perfume of it, which when he had brought to Perfection, he called* Zibeta Occidentalis, *or* Western-Civet, *the back Parts of Man (according to his Division mention'd by the Author, page [81].) being the* West.

Number of Disciples. Because, it is plain, that several of the chief among them, both *Antient* and *Modern,* were usually mistaken by their Adversaries, and indeed, by all, except their own Followers, to have been Persons Crazed, or out of their Wits, having generally proceeded in the common Course of their Words and Actions, by a Method very different from the vulgar Dictates of *unrefined* Reason: agreeing for the most Part in their several Models, with their present undoubted Successors in the *Academy* of *Modern Bedlam*[119] (whose Merits and Principles I shall farther examine in due Place.) Of this Kind were *Epicurus, Diogenes, Apollonius, Lucretius, Paracelsus, Des Cartes,* and others;[120] who, if they were now in the World, tied fast, and separate from their Followers, would in this our undistinguishing Age, incur manifest Danger of *Phlebotomy,* and *Whips,* and *Chains,* and *dark Chambers,* and *Straw.* For, what Man in the natural State, or Course of Thinking, did ever conceive it in his Power, to reduce the Notions of all Mankind, exactly to the same Length, and Breadth, and Heighth of his own? Yet this is the first humble and civil Design of all Innovators in the Empire of Reason. *Epicurus* modestly hoped, that one Time or other, a certain fortuitous Concourse of all Mens Opinions, after perpetual Justlings, the Sharp with the Smooth, the Light and the Heavy, the Round and the Square, would by certain *Clinamina,*[121] unite in the Notions of *Atoms* and *Void,* as these did in the Originals of all Things. *Cartesius* reckoned to see before he died, the Sentiments of all Philosophers, like so many lesser Stars in his *Romantick* System, rapt and drawn within his own *Vortex.*[122] Now, I would gladly be informed, how it is possible to account for such Imaginations as these in particular Men, without Recourse to my *Phænomenon* of *Vapours,* ascending from the lower Faculties to over-shadow the Brain, and thence distilling into Conceptions, for which the Narrowness of our Mother-Tongue has not yet assigned any other Name, besides that of *Madness* or *Phrenzy.* Let us therefore now conjecture how it comes to pass, that none of these great Prescribers, do ever fail providing themselves and their Notions, with a Number of implicite Disciples. And, I think, the Reason is easie to be assigned: For, there is a peculiar *String* in the Harmony of Human Understanding, which in several individuals is exactly of the same Tuning. This, if you can dexterously screw up to its right Key, and then strike gently upon it; Whenever you have the Good Fortune to light among those of the same Pitch, they will by a secret necessary Sympathy, strike exactly at the same time. And in this one Circumstance, lies all the Skill or Luck of the Matter; for if you chance to jar the String among those who are either above or below your own Height, instead of subscribing to your Doctrine, they will tie you fast, call you Mad, and feed you with Bread and Water. It is therefore a Point of the nicest Conduct to distinguish and adapt this noble Talent, with respect to the Differences of Persons and of Times. *Cicero* understood this very well, when writing to a Friend in *England,* with a Caution, among other Matters, to beware of being cheated by our *Hackney-Coachmen* (who, it seems, in those days, were as arrant Rascals as they are now) has these remarkable Words. *Est quod gaudeas te in ista loca venisse, ubi aliquid sapere viderere.*[*123] For, to speak a bold Truth, it is a fatal Miscarriage, so ill to order Affairs, as to pass for a *Fool* in one Company, when in another you might be treated as a *Philosopher.* Which I desire *some certain Gentlemen of my Acquaintance,* to lay up in their Hearts, as a very seasonable *Innuendo.*

* Epist. ad Fam. Trebatio.

THIS, indeed, was the Fatal Mistake of that worthy Gentleman, my most ingenious Friend, Mr. *Wotton.* A Person, in appearance ordain'd for great Designs, as well as Performances; whether you will consider his *Notions* or his *Looks.* Surely, no Man ever advanced into the Publick, with fitter Qualifications of Body and Mind, for the Propagation of a new Religion. Oh, had those happy Talents misapplied to vain Philosophy, been turned into their proper Channels of *Dreams* and *Visions,* where *Distortion* of Mind and Countenance, are of such Sovereign Use; the base detracting World would not then have dared to report, that something is amiss, that his Brain hath undergone an unlucky Shake; which even his Brother *Modernists* themselves, like Ungrates, do whisper so loud, that it reaches up to the very *Garrat* I am writing in.

LASTLY, Whosoever pleases to look into the Fountains of *Enthusiasm,* from whence, in all Ages, have eternally proceeded such fatning Streams, will find the Spring Head to have been as *troubled* and *muddy* as the Current; Of such great Emolument, is a Tincture of this *Vapour,* which the World calls *Madness,* that without its Help, the World would not only be deprived of those two great Blessings, *Conquests* and *Systems,* but even all Mankind would unhappily be reduced to the same Belief in Things Invisible. Now, the former *Postulatum* being held, that it is of no Import from what Originals this *Vapour* proceeds, but either in what *Angles* it strikes and spreads over the Understanding, or upon what *Species* of Brain it ascends; It will be a very delicate point, to cut the Feather,[124] and divide the several Reasons to a Nice and Curious Reader, how this numerical Difference in the Brain, can produce Effects of so vast a Difference from the same *Vapour,* as to be the sole Point of Individuation between *Alexander the Great,*

Jack of Leyden, and Monsieur *Des Cartes.* The present Argument is the most abstracted that ever I engaged in, it strains my Faculties to their highest Stretch; and I desire the Reader to attend with utmost Perpensity; For, I now proceed to unravel this knotty Point.

THERE is in Mankind a certain† *   *   *   *   *   *   *   *   *   *   *
*   *   *   *   *   *   *   *   *   *   *   *   *   *   *   *   *   *
*   *   *   *   *   *   *   *   *   *   *   *   *   *   *   *   *   *   *Hic multa*
*   *   *   *   *   *   *   *   *   *   *   *   *   *   *   *   *   *   *desiderantur.*[125]
*   *   *   *   *   *   *   *   *   *   *   *   *   *   *   *   *   *
*   *   *   *   *   *   *   *   *   *   *   *   *   *   *   *   *   *
*   *   *   *   *   *   *   *   *   *   *   And this I take to be a clear
Solution of the Matter.

HAVING therefore so narrowly past thro' this intricate Difficulty, the Reader will, I am sure, agree with me in the Conclusion; that if the *Moderns* mean by *Madness,* only a Disturbance or Transposition of the Brain, by Force of certain *Vapours* issuing up from the lower Faculties; Then has this *Madness* been the Parent of all those mighty Revolutions, that have happened in *Empire,* in *Philosophy,* and in *Religion.* For, the Brain, in its natural Position and State of Serenity, disposeth its Owner to pass his Life in the common Forms, without any Thought of subduing Multitudes to his own *Power,* his *Reasons* or his *Visions;* and the more he shapes his Understanding by the Pattern of Human Learning, the less he is inclined to form Parties after his particular Notions; because that instructs him in his private Infirmities, as well as in the stubborn Ignorance of the People. But when a Man's Fancy gets *astride* on his Reason, when Imagination is at Cuffs with the Senses, and common Understanding, as well as common Sense, is Kickt out of Doors; the first Proselyte he makes, is Himself, and when that is once compass'd, the Difficulty is not so great in bringing over others; A strong Delusion always operating from *without,* as vigorously as from *within.* For, Cant and Vision are to the Ear and the Eye, the same that Tickling is to the Touch. Those Entertainments and Pleasures we most value in Life, are such as *Dupe* and play the Wag with the Senses. For, if we take an Examination of what is generally understood by *Happiness,* as it has Respect, either to the Understanding or the Senses, we shall find all its Properties and Adjuncts will herd under this short Definition: That, *it is a*

† *Here is another Defect in the Manuscript, but I think the Author did wisely, and that the Matter which thus strained his Faculties, was not worth a Solution; and it were well if all Metaphysical Cobweb Problems were no otherwise answered.*

perpetual Possession of being well Deceived.[126] And first, with Relation to the Mind or Understanding; 'tis manifest, what mighty Advantages Fiction has over Truth; and the Reason is just at our Elbow; because Imagination can build nobler Scenes, and produce more wonderful Revolutions than Fortune or Nature will be at Expence to furnish. Nor is Mankind so much to blame in his Choice, thus determining him, if we consider that the Debate meerly lies between *Things past,* and *Things conceived;* and so the Question is only this; Whether Things that have Place in the *Imagination,* may not as properly be said to *Exist,* as those that are seated in the *Memory;* which may be justly held in the Affirmative, and very much to the Advantage of the former, since This is acknowledged to be the *Womb* of Things, and the other allowed to be no more than the *Grave.* Again, if we take this Definition of Happiness, and examine it with Reference to the Senses, it will be acknowledged wonderfully adapt. How fade and insipid do all Objects accost us that are not convey'd in the Vehicle of *Delusion?* How shrunk is every Thing, as it appears in the Glass of Nature? So, that if it were not for the Assistance of Artificial *Mediums,* false Lights, refracted Angles, Varnish, and Tinsel; there would be a mighty Level in the Felicity and Enjoyments of Mortal Men. If this were seriously considered by the World, as I have a certain Reason to suspect it hardly will; Men would no longer reckon among their high Points of Wisdom, the Art of exposing weak Sides, and publishing Infirmities; an Employment in my Opinion, neither better nor worse than that of *Unmasking,* which I think, has never been allowed fair Usage, either in the *World* or the *Play-House.*

IN the Proportion that Credulity is a more peaceful Possession of the Mind, than Curiosity, so far preferable is that Wisdom, which converses about the Surface, to that pretended Philosophy which enters into the Depth of Things, and then comes gravely back with Informations and Discoveries, that in the inside they are good for nothing. The two Senses, to which all Objects first address themselves, are the Sight and the Touch; These never examine farther than the Colour, the Shape, the Size, and whatever other Qualities dwell, or are drawn by Art upon the Outward of Bodies; and then comes Reason officiously, with Tools for cutting, and opening, and mangling, and piercing, offering to demonstrate, that they are not of the same consistence quite thro'. Now, I take all this to be the last Degree of perverting Nature; one of whose Eternal Laws it is, to put her best Furniture forward. And therefore, in order to save the Charges of all such expensive Anatomy for the Time to come; I do here think fit to inform the reader, that in such Conclusions as these, Reason is certainly in the Right; and that in most Corporeal Beings, which have fallen under my Cognizance, the *Outside* hath been infinitely preferable to the *In:* Whereof I have been farther convinced from some late Experiments. Last Week I saw a Woman *flay'd*,[127] and you will hardly believe, how much it altered her Person for the worse. Yesterday I ordered the Carcass of a *Beau* to be stript in my Presence; when we were all amazed to find so many unsuspected Faults under one Suit of Cloaths: Then I laid open his *Brain*, his *Heart*, and his *Spleen*;[128] But, I plainly perceived at every Operation, that the farther we proceeded, we found the Defects encrease upon us in Number and Bulk: from all which, I justly formed this Conclusion to my self; That whatever Philosopher or Projector can find out an Art to sodder and patch up the Flaws and Imperfections of Nature, will deserve much better of Mankind, and teach us a more useful Science, than that so much in present Esteem, of widening and exposing them (like him who held *Anatomy* to be the ultimate End of *Physick*.) And he, whose Fortunes and Dispositions have placed him in a convenient Station to enjoy the Fruits of this noble Art; He that can with *Epicurus* content his Ideas with the *Films* and *Images* that fly off upon his Senses from the *Superficies* of Things; Such a Man truly wise, creams off Nature, leaving the Sower and the Dregs, for Philosophy and Reason to lap up. This is the sublime and refined Point of Felicity, called, *the Possession of being well deceived*; The Serene Peaceful State of being a Fool among Knaves.

BUT to return to *Madness*. It is certain, that according to the System I have above deduced; every *Species* thereof proceeds from a Redundancy of *Vapour*; therefore, as some Kinds of *Phrenzy* give double Strength to the Sinews, so there are of other *Species*, which add Vigor, and Life, and Spirit to the Brain: Now, it usually happens, that these active Spirits, getting Possession of the Brain, resemble those that haunt other waste and empty Dwellings, which for want of Business, either vanish, and carry away a Piece of the House, or else stay at home and fling it all out of the Windows. By which are mystically display'd the two principal Branches of *Madness*, and which some Philosophers not considering so well as I, have mistook to be different in their Causes, over-hastily assigning the first to Deficiency, and the other to Redundance.

I think it therefore manifest, from what I have here advanced, that the main Point of Skill and Address, is to furnish Employment for this Redundancy of *Vapour*, and prudently to adjust the Seasons of it; by which means it may certainly become of Cardinal and Catholick Emolument in a Commonwealth. Thus one Man chusing a proper Juncture, leaps into a

Gulph, from thence proceeds a Hero, and is called the Saver of his Country; Another atchieves the same Enterprise, but unluckily timing it, has left the Brand of *Madness*, fixt as a Reproach upon his Memory; Upon so nice a Distinction are we taught to repeat the Name of *Curtius*[129] with Reverence and Love; that of *Empedocles*,[130] with Hatred and Contempt. Thus, also it is usually conceived, that the Elder *Brutus* only personated the *Fool* and *Madman*, for the Good of the Publick: but this was nothing else, than a Redundancy of the same *Vapor*, long misapplied, called by the Latins, *Ingenium par negotiis*:*[131] Or, (to translate it *Tacit. as nearly as I can) a sort of *Phrenzy*, never in its right Element, till you take it up in Business of the State.

Upon all which, and many other Reasons of equal Weight, though not equally curious; I do here gladly embrace an Opportunity I have long sought for, of Recommending it as a very noble Undertaking, to Sir *Edward Seymour*, Sir *Christopher Musgrave*, Sir *John Bowls*, *John How*, Esq;[132] and other Patriots concerned, that they would move for Leave to bring in a Bill, for appointing Commissioners to Inspect into *Bedlam*, and the Parts adjacent; who shall be empowered to *send for Persons, Papers, and Records*: to examine into the Merits and Qualifications of every Student and Professor; to observe with utmost Exactness their several Dispositions and Behaviour; by which means, duly distinguishing and adapting their Talents, they might produce admirable Instruments for the several Offices in a State, *******† *Civil and Military*; proceeding in such Methods as I shall here humbly propose. And, I hope the Gentle Reader will give some Allowance to my great Solicitudes in this important Affair, upon Account of that high Esteem I have ever born that honourable Society, whereof I had some Time the Happiness to be an unworthy Member.

Is any Student tearing his Straw in piece-meal, Swearing and Blaspheming, biting his Grate, foaming at the Mouth, and emptying his Pispot in the Spectator's Faces? Let the Right Worshipful, the *Commissioners of Inspection*, give him a Regiment of Dragoons, and send him into *Flanders* among the *Rest*. Is another eternally talking, sputtering, gaping, bawling, in a Sound without Period or Article? What wonderful Talents are here mislaid! Let him be funished immediately with a green Bag and Papers, and *three Pence*‡ in his Pocket, and away with Him to ‡ *A Lawyer's* *Westminster-Hall*. You will find a Third, gravely taking the Di- *Coach-hire.* mensions of his Kennel; A Person of Foresight and Insight, tho' kept quite

† *Ecclesiastical*. H

in the Dark; for why, like *Moses, Ecce* cornuta erat ejus facies.* He walks duly in one Pace, intreats your Penny with due Gravity and Ceremony; talks much of hard Times, and Taxes, and the *Whore of Babylon;* Bars up the woodden Window of his Cell constantly at eight a Clock: Dreams of *Fire,* and *Shop-lifters,* and *Court-Customers,* and *Priviledg'd Places.* Now, what a Figure would all these Acquirements amount to, if the Owner were sent into the *City* among his Brethren! Behold a Fourth, in much and deep Conversation with himself, biting his Thumbs at proper Junctures; His Countenance chequered with Business and Design; sometimes walking very fast, with his Eyes nailed to a Paper that he holds in his Hands: A great Saver of Time, somewhat thick of Hearing, very short of Sight, but more of Memory. A Man ever in Haste, a great Hatcher and Breeder of Business, and excellent at the Famous Art of *whispering Nothing.* A huge Idolater of Monosyllables and Procrastination; so ready to *Give* his Word to every Body, that he never *keeps* it. One that has forgot the common *Meaning* of Words, but an admirable Retainer of the *Sound.* Extreamly subject to the *Looseness,* for his *Occasions* are perpetually *calling him away.* If you approach his Grate in his familiar Intervals; *Sir,* says he, *Give me a Penny, and I'll sing you a Song:* But *give me the Penny first.* (Hence comes the common Saying, and commoner Practice of parting with Money for a *Song.*) What a compleat System of *Court-Skill* is here described in every Branch of it, and all utterly lost with wrong Application? Accost the Hole of another Kennel, first stopping your Nose, you will behold a surley, gloomy, nasty, slovenly Mortal, raking in his own Dung, and dabling in his Urine. The best Part of his Diet, is the Reversion of his own Ordure, which exspiring into Steams, whirls perpetually about, and at last reinfunds. His Complexion is of a dirty Yellow, with a thin scattered Beard, exactly aggreeable to that of his Dyet upon its first Declination; like other Insects, who having their Birth and Education in an Excrement, from thence borrow their Colour and their Smell. The Student of this Apartment is very sparing of his Words, but somewhat over-liberal of his Breath; He holds his Hand out ready to receive your Penny, and immediately upon Receipt, withdraws to his former Occupations. Now, is it not amazing to think, the Society of *Warwick-Lane,*[133] should have no more Concern, for the Recovery of so useful a Member, who, if one may judge from these Appearances, would become the greatest Ornament to that Illustrious Body? Another Student struts up

---

* Cornutus, *is either Horned or Shining, and by this Term,* Moses *is described in the vulgar* Latin *of the Bible.*

fiercely to your Teeth, puffing with his Lips, half squeezing out his Eyes, and very graciously holds you out his Hand to kiss. The *Keeper* desires you not to be afraid of this Professor, for he will do you no Hurt: To him alone is allowed the Liberty of the Anti-Chamber, and the *Orator* of the Place gives you to understand, that this solemn Person is a *Taylor* run mad with Pride. This considerable Student is adorned with many other Qualities, upon which, at present, I shall not farther enlarge. ———*Hark in your Ear** ——— I am strangely mistaken, if all his Address, his Motions, and his Airs, would not then be very natural, and in their proper Element.

I shall not descend so minutely, as to insist upon the vast Number of *Beaux, Fidlers, Poets,* and *Politicians,* that the World might recover by such a Reformation; But what is more material, besides the clear Gain redounding the Commonwealth, by so large an Acquisition of Persons to employ, whose Talents and Acquirements, if I may be so bold to affirm it, are now buried, or at least misapplied: It would be a mighty Advantage accruing to the Publick from this Enquiry, that all these would very much excel, and arrive at great Perfection in their several Kinds; which, I think, is manifest from what I have already shewn; and shall inforce by this one plain Instance; That even, I my self, the Author of these momentous Truths, am a Person, whose Imaginations are hard-mouth'd, and exceedingly disposed to run away with his *Reason,* which I have observed from long Experience, to be a very light Rider, and easily shook off;[134] upon which Account, my Friends will never trust me alone, without a solemn Promise, to vent my Speculations in this, or the like manner, for the universal Benefit of Human kind; which, perhaps, the gentle, courteous, and candid Reader, brimful of that *Modern* Charity and Tenderness, usually annexed to his *Office,* will be very hardly persuaded to believe.

SECTION X

A TALE *of a* Tub

It is an unanswerable Argument of a very refined Age, the wonderful Civilities that have passed of late Years, between the Nation of *Authors,* and that of *Readers.* There can hardly pop out a *Play,*† a *Pamphlet,* or a *Poem,* without a Preface full of Acknowledgements to the World, for the general Reception and Applause they have given it, which the Lord knows where, or

---

* *I cannot conjecture what the Author means here, or how this Chasm could be fill'd, tho' it is capable of more than one Interpretation.*

† *This is literally true, as we may observe in the Prefaces to most Plays, Poems, &c.*

when, or how, or from whom it received. In due Deference to so laudable a Custom, I do here return my humble Thanks to *His Majesty*, and both Houses of *Parliament*; To the *Lords* of the King's most honourable Privy-Council, to the Reverend the *Judges:* To the *Clergy*, and *Gentry*, and *Yeomantry* of this Land: But in a more especial manner, to my worthy Brethren and Friends at *Will's Coffee-House*, and *Gresham-College*, and *Warwick-Lane*, and *Moor-Fields*, and *Scotland-Yard*, and *Westminster-Hall*, and *Guild-Hall*;[135] In short, to all Inhabitants and Retainers whatsoever, either in Court, or Church, or Camp, or City, or Country; for their generous and universal Acceptance of this Divine Treatise. I accept their Approbation, and good Opinion with extream Gratitude, and to the utmost of my poor Capacity, shall take hold of all Opportunities to return the Obligation.

I am also happy, that Fate has flung me into so blessed an Age for the mutual Felicity of *Booksellers* and *Authors*, whom I may safely affirm to be at this Day the two only satisfied Parties in *England*. Ask an *Author* how his last Piece hath succeeded; *Why, truly he thanks his Stars, the World has been very favourable, and he has not the least Reason to complain: And yet, By G——, He writ it in a Week at Bits and Starts, when he could steal an Hour from his urgent Affairs:* as it is a hundred to one, you may see farther in the Preface, to which he refers you; and for the rest, to the Bookseller. There you go as a Customer, and make the same Question: *He blesses his God, the* Thing *takes wonderfully, he is just Printing a Second Edition, and has but three left in his Shop. You beat down the* Price: *Sir, we shall not differ;* and in hopes of your Custom another Time, lets you have it as reasonable as you please; *And, pray send as many of your Acquaintance as you will, I shall upon your Account furnish them all at the same Rate.*

Now, it is not well enough consider'd, to what Accidents and Occasions the World is indebted for the greatest Part of those noble Writings, which hourly start up to entertain it. If it were not for a *rainy Day, a drunken Vigil, a Fit of the Spleen, a Course of Physick, a sleepy Sunday, an ill Run at Dice, a long Taylor's Bill, a Beggar's Purse, a factious Head, a hot Sun, costive Dyet, Want of Books, and a just Contempt of Learning.* But for these Events, I say, and some Others too long to recite, (especially *a prudent Neglect of taking Brimstone inwardly,*) I doubt, the Number of *Authors*, and of *Writings* would dwindle away to a Degree most woful to behold. To confirm this Opinion, hear the Words of the famous *Troglodyte* Philosopher; *'Tis certain* (said he) *some Grains of Folly are of course annexed, as Part of the Composition of Human Nature, only the Choice is left us, whether we please to wear them* Inlaid *or* Embossed; *And we need not go very far to seek how that is usually determined, when we remember, it is with Human Faculties as with Liquors, the lightest will be ever at the Top.*

THERE is in this famous Island of *Britain* a certain paultry *Scribbler,* very voluminous, whose Character the Reader cannot wholly be a Stranger to. He deals in a pernicious Kind of Writings, called *Second Parts,* and usually passes under the Name of *The Author of the First.* I easily foresee, that as soon as I lay down my Pen, this nimble *Operator* will have stole it, and treat me as inhumanly as he hath already done Dr. *Blackmore, L'Estrange,* and many others who shall here be nameless, I therefore fly for Justice and Relief, into the Hands of that great *Rectifier of Saddles,* and *Lover of Mankind,* Dr. *Bently,* begging he will take this enormous Grievance into his most *Modern* Consideration: And if it should so happen, that the *Furniture of an Ass,* in the Shape of a *Second Part,* must for my Sins be clapt, by a Mistake upon my Back, that he will immediately please, in the Presence of the World, to lighten me of the Burthen, and take it home to *his own House,* till the *true Beast* thinks fit to call for it.

IN the mean time I do here give this publick Notice, that my Resolutions are, to circumscribe within this Discourse the whole Stock of Matter I have been so many Years providing. Since my *Vein* is once opened, I am content to exhaust it all at a Running, for the peculiar Advantage of my dear Country, and for the universal Benefit of Mankind. Therefore hospitably considering the Number of my Guests, they shall have my whole Entertainment at a Meal; And I scorn to set up the *Leavings* in the Cupboard. What the *Guests* cannot eat may be given to the *Poor,* and the *Dogs** under the Table may gnaw the *Bones;* This I understand for a more generous Proceeding, than to turn the Company's Stomachs, by inviting them again to morrow to a scurvy Meal of *Scraps.*

IF the Reader fairly considers the Strength of what I have advanced in the foregoing Section, I am convinced it will produce a wonderful Revolution in his Notions and Opinions; And he will be abundantly better prepared to receive and to relish the concluding Part of this miraculous Treatise. Readers may be divided into three Classes, the *Superficial,* the *Ignorant,* and the *Learned:* And I have with much Felicity fitted my Pen to the Genius and Advantage of each. The *Superficial* Reader will be strangely provoked to *Laughter;* which clears the Breast and the Lungs, is Soverain against the *Spleen,* and the most innocent of all *Diureticks.* The *Ignorant* Reader (between whom and the former, the Distinction is extreamly nice) will find himself disposed to *Stare;* which is an admirable Remedy for ill Eyes, serves to raise and enliven the Spirits, and wonderfully helps

---

* *By Dogs, the Author means common injudicious Criticks, as he explains it himself before in his* Digression upon Criticks, *Page* [57].

Perspiration. But the Reader truly *Learned,* chiefly for whose Benefit I wake, when others sleep, and sleep when others wake, will here find sufficient Matter to employ his Speculations for the rest of his Life. It were much to be wisht, and I do here humbly propose for an Experiment, that every Prince in *Christendom* will take seven of the *deepest Scholars* in his Dominions, and shut them up close for *seven* Years, in *seven* Chambers, with a Command to write *seven* ample Commentaries on this comprehensive Discourse. I shall venture to affirm, that whatever Difference may be found in their several Conjectures, they will be all, without the least Distortion, manifestly deduceable from the Text. Mean time, it is my earnest Request, that so useful an Undertaking may be entered upon (if their Majesties please) with all convenient speed; because I have a strong Inclination, before I leave the World, to taste a Blessing, which we *mysterious* Writers can seldom reach, till we have got into our Graves. Whether it is, that *Fame* being a Fruit grafted on the Body, can hardly grow, and much less ripen, till the *Stock* is in the Earth: Or, whether she be a Bird of Prey, and is lured among the rest, to pursue after the Scent of a *Carcass:* Or, whether she conceives, her Trumpet sounds best and farthest, when she stands on a *Tomb,* by the Advantage of a rising Ground, and the Echo of a hollow Vault.

'Tis true, indeed, the Republick of *dark* Authors, after they once found out this excellent Expedient of *Dying,* have been peculiarly happy in the Variety, as well as Extent of their Reputation. For, *Night* being the universal Mother of Things, wise Philosophers hold all Writings to be *fruitful* in the Proportion they are *dark;* And therefore, the *true* *illuminated** (that is to say, the *Darkest* of all) have met with such   * *A Name of the Rosycrucians.* numberless Commentators, whose *Scholiastick* Midwifry hath deliver'd them of Meanings, that the Authors themselves, perhaps, never conceived, and yet may very justly be allowed the Lawful Parents of them:† The Words of such Writers being like Seed, which, however scattered at random, when they light upon a fruitful Ground, will multiply far beyond either the Hopes or Imagination of the Sower.

AND therefore in order to promote so useful a Work, I will here take Leave to glance a few *Innuendo's,* that may be of great Assistance to those sublime Spirits, who shall be appointed to labor in a universal Comment upon this wonderful Discourse. And First, I have couched a very pro-

† *Nothing is more frequent than for Commentators to force Interpretation, which the Author never meant.*

found Mystery* in the Number of O's multiply'd by *Seven*, and divided by *Nine*. Also, if a devout Brother of the *Rosy Cross* will pray fervently for sixty three Mornings, with a lively Faith, and then transpose certain Letters and Syllables according to Prescription, in the second and fifth Section; they will certainly reveal into a full Receit of the *Opus Magnum*. Lastly, Whoever will be at the Pains to calculate the whole Number of each Letter in this Treatise, and sum up the Difference exactly between the several Numbers, assigning the true natural Cause for every such Difference; the Discoveries in the Product, will plentifully reward his Labour. But then he must beware of *Bythus* and *Sigè*,† and be sure not to forget the Qualities of *Acamoth; A cujus lacrymis humecta prodit Substantia, à risu lucida, à tristitiâ solida, & à timore mobilis,* wherein *Eugenius Philalethes*‡ hath committed an unpardonable Mistake.

‡ *Vid. Anima magica abscondita*

SECTION XI

A TALE *of a* Tub

After so wide a Compass as I have wandered, I do now gladly overtake, and close in with my Subject, and shall henceforth hold on with it an even Pace to the End of my Journey, except some beautiful Prospect appears within sight of my Way; whereof, tho' at present I have neither Warning nor Expectation, yet upon such an Accident, come when it will, I shall beg my Readers Favour and Company, allowing me to conduct him thro' it along with my self. For in *Writing*, it is as in *Travelling*: If a Man is in haste to be at home, (which I acknowledge to be none of my Case, having never

---

* *This is what the* Cabbalists *among the Jews have done with the* Bible, *and pretend to find wonderful Mysteries by it.*

† *I was told by an Eminent Divine, whom I consulted on this Point, that these two Barbarous Words, with that of* Acamoth *and its Qualities, as here set down, are quoted from* Irenæus. *This be discover'd by searching that Antient Writer for another Quotation of our Author, which he has placed in the Title Page, and refers to the Book and Chapter; the Curious were very Inquisitive, whether those Barbarous words,* Basima Eacabasa, &c. *are really in* Irenæus, *and upon enquiry 'twas found they were a sort of Cant or Jargon of certain Hereticks, and therefore very properly prefix'd to such a Book as this of our Author.*

‡ *To the abovementioned Treatise, called* Anthroposophia Theomagica, *there is another annexed, called* Anima Magica Abscondita, *written by the same Author* Vaughan, *under the Name of* Eugenius Philalethes, *but in neither of those Treatises is there any mention of* Acamoth *or its Qualities, so that this is nothing but Amusement, and a Ridicule of dark, unintelligible Writers; only the Words,* A cujus lacrymis, &c. *are as we have said, transcribed from* Irenæus, *tho' I know not from what part. I believe one of the Authors Designs was to set curious Men a hunting thro' Indexes, and enquiring for Books out of the common Road.*

so little Business, as when I am there) if his *Horse* be tired with long Riding, and ill Ways, or be naturally a Jade, I advise him clearly to make the straitest and the commonest Road, be it ever so dirty; But, then surely, we must own such a man to be a scurvy Companion at best; He *spatters* himself and his Fellow-Travellers at every Step: All their Thoughts, and Wishes, and Conversation turn entirely upon the Subject of their Journey's End; and at every Splash, and Plunge, and Stumble, they heartily wish one another at the Devil.

ON the other side, when a Traveller and his *Horse* are in Heart and Plight, when his Purse is full, and the Day before him; he takes the Road only where it is clean or convenient; entertains his Company there as agreeably as he can; but upon the first Occasion, carries them along with him to every delightful Scene in View, whether of Art, of Nature, or of both; and if they chance to refuse out of Stupidity or Weariness; let them jog on by themselves, and be d—n'd; He'll overtake them at the next Town; at which arriving, he Rides furiously thro', the Men, Women, and Children run out to gaze, a hundred *noisy Curs** run *barking* after him, of which, if he honors the boldest with a *Lash of his Whip,* it is rather out of Sport than Revenge: But should some *sourer Mungrel* dare too near an Approach, he receives a *Salute* on the Chaps by an accidental Stroak from the Courser's Heels, (nor is any Ground lost by the Blow) which sends him yelping and limping home.

I now proceed to sum up the singular Adventures of my renowned *Jack;* the State of whose Dispositions and Fortunes, the careful Reader does, no doubt, most exactly remember, as I last parted with them in the Conclusion of a former Section. Therefore, his next Care must be from two of the foregoing, to extract a Scheme of Notions, that may best fit his Understanding for a true Relish of what is to ensue.

JACK had not only calculated the first Revolutions of his Brain so prudently, as to give Rise to that Epidemick Sect of *Æolists,* but succeeding also into a new and strange Variety of Conceptions, the Fruitfulness of his Imagination led him into certain Notions, which, altho' in Appearance very unaccountable, were not without their Mysteries and their Meanings, nor wanted Followers to countenance and improve them. I shall therefore be extreamly careful and exact in recounting such material Passages of this Nature, as I have been able to collect, either from undoubted Tradition, or indefatigable Reading; and shall describe them as

---

* *By these are meant what the Author calls,* The True Criticks, *Page* [57].

graphically as it is possible, and as far as Notions of that Height and Latitude can be brought within the Compass of a Pen. Nor do I at all question,
but they will furnish Plenty of noble Matter for such, whose convert-
ing Imaginations dispose them to reduce all Things into *Types;* who can
make *Shadows,* no thanks to the Sun; and then mold them into Substances,
no thanks to Philosophy; whose peculiar Talent lies in fixing Tropes
and Allegories to the *Letter,* and refining what is Literal into Figure and
Mystery.

JACK had provided a fair Copy of his Father's *Will,* engrossed in Form
upon a large Skin of Parchment; and resolving to act the Part of a most
dutiful Son, he became the fondest[136] Creature of it imaginable. For,
altho', as I have often told the Reader, it consisted wholly in certain plain,
easy Directions about the management and wearing of their Coats, with
Legacies and Penalties, in case of Obedience or Neglect; yet he began to
entertain a Fancy, that the Matter was *deeper* and *darker,* and therefore must
needs have a great deal more of Mystery at the Bottom. *Gentlemen,* said he,
*I will prove this very Skin of Parchment to be Meat, Drink, and Cloth, to be the
Philosopher's Stone, and the Universal Medicine.* In consequence of which Raptures, he resolved to make use of it in the most necessary, as well as the
most paltry Occasions of Life.* He had a Way of working it into any
Shape he pleased; so that it served him for a Night-cap when he went to
Bed, and for an Umbrello in rainy Weather. He would lap a Piece of it
about a sore Toe, or when he had Fits, burn two Inches under his Nose; or
if any Thing lay heavy on his Stomach, scrape off, and swallow as much of
the Powder as would lie on a silver Penny, they were all infallible Remedies. With Analogy to these Refinements, his common Talk and Conversation, ran wholly in the Phrase of his Will,† and he circumscribed the
utmost of his Eloquence within that Compass, not daring to let slip a Syllable without Authority from thence. Once at a strange House, he was
suddenly taken short, upon an urgent Juncture, whereon it may not be allowed too particularly to dilate; and being not able to call to mind, with
that Suddenness, the Occasion required, an Authentick Phrase for demanding the Way to the Backside; he chose rather as the more prudent
Course, to incur the Penalty in such Cases usually annexed. Neither was

* *The Author here lashes those Pretenders to Purity, who place so much Merit in using Scripture
Phrases on all Occasions.*

† *The* Protestant Dissenters *use* Scripture Phrases *in their serious Discourses, and Composures
more than the* Church of England-Men, *accordingly* Jack *is introduced making his common Talk and
Conversation to run wholly in the Phrase of his WILL.* W. Wotton.

it possible for the united Rhetorick of Mankind to prevail with him to make himself clean again: Because having consulted the Will upon this Emergency, he met with a Passage near the Bottom (whether foisted in by the Transcriber, is not known) which seemed to forbid it.*

HE made it a Part of his Religion, never to say Grace to† his Meat, nor could all the World Persuade him, as the common Phrase is, to eat his Victuals *like a Christian.*‡

HE bore a strange kind of Appetite to *Snap-Dragon,*§[137] and to the livid Snuffs of a burning Candle, which he would catch and swallow with an Agility, wonderful to conceive; and by this Procedure, maintained a perpetual Flame in his Belly, which issuing in a glowing Stream from both his Eyes, as well as his Nostrils, and his Mouth; made his Head appear in a dark Night, like the Scull of an Ass, wherein a roguish Boy hath conveyed a Farthing Candle, *to the Terror of His Majesty's Liege Subjects.* Therefore, he made use of no other Expedient to light himself home, but was wont to say, That *a Wise Man was his own Lanthorn.*

HE would shut his Eyes as he walked along the Streets, and if he happened to bounce his Head against a Post, or fall into the Kennel (as he seldom missed either to do one or both) he would tell the gibing Prentices, who looked on, that *he submitted with entire Resignation, as to a Trip, or a Blow of Fate, with whom he found, by long Experience, how vain it was either to wrestle or to cuff; and whoever durst undertake to do either, would be sure to come off with a swinging Fall, or a bloody Nose. It was ordained,* said he, *some few Days before the Creation, that my Nose and this very Post should have a Rencounter; and therefore, Nature thought fit to send us both into the World in the same Age, and to make us Country-men and Fellow-Citizens. Now, had my Eyes been open, it is very likely, the Business might have been a great deal worse; For, how many a confounded Slip is daily got by Man, with all his Foresight about him? Besides, the Eyes of the Understanding see best, when those of the Senses are out of the way; and therefore, blind Men are observed to tread their Steps with much more Caution, and Conduct, and Judgment, than those who rely with too much Confidence, upon the Virtue of the visual Nerve, which every little Accident shakes out of Order, and a Drop, or a Film, can wholly disconcert; like a Lanthorn among a Pack of roaring Bullies, when they*

---

* *I cannot guess the Author's meaning here, which I would be very glad to know, because it seems to be of Importance.*

† *The slovenly way of Receiving the Sacrament among the Fanaticks.*

‡ *This is a common Phrase to express Eating cleanlily, and is meant for an Invective against that undecent Manner among some People in Receiving the Sacrament, so in the Lines before, which is to be understood of the Dissenters refusing to kneel at the Sacrament.*

§ *I cannot well find the Author's meaning here, unless it be the hot, untimely, blind Zeal of Enthusiasts.*

scower the Streets; exposing its Owner, and it self, to outward Kicks and Buffets,
which both might have escaped, if the Vanity of Appearing would have suffered them
to walk in the Dark. But, farther; if we examine the Conduct *of these boasted*
Lights, it will prove yet a great deal worse than their Fortune: *'Tis true, I have broke*
my Nose against this Post, because Fortune either forgot, or did not think it conve-
nient to twitch me by the Elbow, and give me notice to avoid it. But, let not this en-
courage either the present Age or Posterity, to trust their Noses *into the keeping of*
their Eyes, which may prove the fairest Way of losing them for good and all. For, O ye
Eyes, Ye blind Guides; miserable Guardians are Ye of our frail Noses; Ye, I say, who
fasten upon the first Precipice in view, and then tow our wretched willing Bodies
after You, to the very Brink of Destruction: But, alas, that Brink is rotten, our Feet
slip, and we tumble down prone into a Gulph, without one hospitable Shrub in the
Way to break the Fall; a Fall, to which not any Nose of mortal Make is
equal, except that of the Giant Laurcalco,* *who was Lord of the* Silver * *Vide* Don
Bridge. *Most properly, therefore, O Eyes, and with great Justice, may* Quixot.
You be compared to those foolish Lights, which conduct Men thro' Dirt
and Darkness, till they fall into a deep Pit, or a noisom Bog.

THIS I have produced, as a Scantling[138] of *Jack*'s great Eloquence, and
the Force of his Reasoning upon such abstruse Matters.

HE was besides, a Person of great Design and Improvement in Affairs
of *Devotion,* having introduced a new Deity, who hath since met with a vast
Number of Worshippers; by some called *Babel,* by others, *Chaos;* who had
an antient Temple of *Gothick* Structure upon *Salisbury* Plain; famous for its
Shrine, and Celebration by Pilgrims.

WHEN he had some Roguish Trick† to play, he would down with his
Knees, up with his Eyes, and fall to Prayers, tho' in the midst of the Kennel. Then it was that those who understood his Pranks, would be sure
to get far enough out of his Way; And whenever Curiosity attracted
Strangers to Laugh, or to Listen; he would of a sudden, with one Hand out
with his *Gear,* and piss full in their Eyes, and with the other, all to-
bespatter them with Mud.

IN Winter he went always loose and unbuttoned, and clad as thin as
possible, to let *in* the ambient Heat; and in Summer, lapt himself close and
thick to keep it *out.*‡

IN all Revolutions of Government,§ he would make his Court for
the Office of *Hangman* General; and in the Exercise of that Dignity,

---

† *The Villanies and Cruelties committed by Enthusiasts and Phanaticks among us, were all performed*
under the Disguise of Religion and long Prayers.

‡ *They affect Differences in Habit and Behaviour.*

§ *They are severe Persecutors, and all in a Form of Cant and Devotion.*

wherein he was very dextrous, would make use of no other* *Vizard* than a long *Prayer*.

HE had a Tongue so Musculous and Subtil, that he could twist it up into his Nose, and deliver a strange Kind of Speech from thence. He was also the first in these Kingdoms, who began to improve the *Spanish* Accomplishment of *Braying;* and having large Ears, perpetually exposed and arrect, he carried his Art to such a Perfection, that it was a Point of great Difficulty to distinguish either by the View or the Sound, between the *Original* and the *Copy*.

HE was troubled with a Disease, reverse to that called the Stinging of the *Tarantula;* and would run Dog-mad,† at the Noise of *Musick*, especially a *Pair of Bag-Pipes.* But he would cure himself again, by taking two or three Turns in *Westminster-Hall*, or *Billingsgate*, or in a *Boarding-School*, or the *Royal-Exchange*, or a *State Coffee-House.*

HE was a Person that *feared‡* no *Colours*, but mortally *hated* all, and upon that Account, bore a cruel Aversion to *Painters;* insomuch, that in his Paroxysms, as he walked the Streets, he would have his Pockets loaden with Stones, to pelt at the *Signs.*

HAVING from this manner of Living, frequent Occasion to *wash* himself, he would often leap over Head and Ears into the Water, tho' it were in the midst of the Winter, but was always observed to come out again much *dirtier,* if possible, than he went in.

HE was the first that ever found out the Secret of contriving a *Soporiferous* Medicine§ to be convey'd in at the *Ears;* It was a Compound of *Sulphur* and *Balm of Gilead*, with a little *Pilgrim's Salve.*

HE wore a large Plaister of artificial *Causticks* on his Stomach, with the Fervor of which, he could set himself a *groaning*, like the famous *Board*[139] upon Application of a red-hot Iron.

He would stand in the Turning of a Street,** and calling to those who passed by, would cry to One; *Worthy Sir, do me the Honour of a good Slap in the*

---

* Cromwell *and his Confederates went, as they called it,* to seek God, *when they resolved to murther the King.*

† *This is to expose our Dissenters Aversion to Instrumental Musick in Churches.* W. Wotton.

‡ *They quarrel at the most Innocent Decency and Ornament, and defaced the Statues and Paintings on all the Churches in* England.

§ *Fanatick Preaching, composed either of Hell and Damnation, or a fulsome Description of the Joys of Heaven, both in such a dirty, nauseous Style, as to be well resembled to Pilgrims Salve.*

** *The Fanaticks have always had a way of affecting to run into Persecution, and count vast Merit upon every little Hardship they suffer.*

Chaps: To another, *Honest Friend, pray favour me with a handsom Kick on the Arse: Madam, shall I entreat a small Box on the Ear, from your Ladyship's fair Hands? Noble Captain, Lend a reasonable Thwack, for the Love of God, with that Cane of yours, over these poor Shoulders.* And when he had by such earnest Sollicitations, made a shift to procure a Basting sufficient to swell up his Fancy and his Sides, He would return home extremely comforted, and full of terrible Accounts of what he had undergone for the *Publick Good. Observe this Stroak,* (said he, shewing his bare Shoulders) *a plaguy* Janisary *gave it me this very Morning at seven a Clock, as, with much ado, I was driving off the* Great Turk. *Neighbours mine, this broken Head deserves a Plaister; had poor Jack been tender of his Noddle, you would have seen the* Pope, *and the* French *King, long before this time of Day, among your Wives and your Ware-houses. Dear* Christians, *the* Great Mogul *was come as far as* White-Chappel, *and you may thank these poor Sides that he hath not (God bless us) already swallowed up Man, Woman, and Child.*

IT was highly worth observing,* the singular Effects of that Aversion, or Antipathy, which *Jack* and his Brother *Peter* seemed, even to an Affectation, to bear toward each other. *Peter* had lately done *some Rogueries,* that forced him to abscond; and he seldom ventured to stir out before Night, for fear of Bayliffs. Their Lodgings were at the two most distant Parts of the Town from each other; and whenever their Occasions, or Humors called them abroad, they would make Choice of the oddest unlikely Times, and most uncouth Rounds they could invent; that they might be sure to avoid one another: Yet after all this, it was their perpetual Fortune to meet. The Reason of which, is easy enough to apprehend: For, the Phrenzy and the Spleen of both, having the same Foundation, we may look upon them as two Pair of Compasses, equally extended, and the fixed Foot of each, remaining in the same Center; which, tho' moving contrary Ways at first, will be sure to encounter somewhere or other in the Circumference. Besides, it was among the great Misfortunes of *Jack,* to bear a huge Personal Resemblance with his Brother *Peter.* Their Humours and Dispositions were not only the same, but there was a close Analogy in their Shape, their Size and their Mien. Insomuch, as nothing was more frequent than for a Bayliff to seize *Jack* by the Shoulders, and cry, *Mr.* Peter,

---

The Papists and Fanaticks, tho' they appear the most Averse to each other, yet bear a near Resemblance in many things, as has been observed by Learned Men.

Ibid. *The Agreement of our Dissenters and the Papists in that which Bishop* Stillingfleet *called,* The Fanaticism of the Church of *Rome, is ludicrously described for several Pages together by* Jack's Likeness to Peter, *and their being often mistaken for each other, and their frequent Meeting, when they least intended it.* W. Wotton.

You are the King's Prisoner. Or, at other Times, for one of *Peter's* nearest Friends, to accost *Jack* with open Arms, *Dear* Peter, *I am glad to see thee, pray send me one of your best Medicines for the Worms.* This we may suppose, was a mortifying Return of those Pains and Proceedings, *Jack* had laboured in so long; And finding, how directly opposite all his Endeavours had answered to the sole End and Intention, which he had proposed to himself; How could it avoid having terrible Effects upon a Head and Heart so furnished as his? However, the poor Remainders of his *Coat* bore all the Punishment; The orient Sun never entred upon his diurnal Progress, without missing a Piece of it. He hired a Taylor to stitch up the Collar so close, that it was ready to choak him, and squeezed out his Eyes at such a Rate, as one could see nothing but the White. What little was left of the main Substance of the Coat, he rubbed every day for two hours, against a roughcast Wall, in order to grind away the Remnants of *Lace* and *Embroidery*; but at the same time went on with so much Violence, that he proceeded a *Heathen Philosopher.* Yet after all he could do of this kind, the Success continued still to disappoint his Expectation. For, as it is the Nature of Rags, to bear a kind of mock Resemblance to Finery; there being a sort of fluttering Appearance in both, which is not to be distinguished at a Distance, in the Dark, or by short-sighted Eyes: So, in those Junctures, it fared with *Jack* and his Tatters, that they offered to the first View a ridiculous Flanting, which assisting the Resemblance in Person and Air, thwarted all his Projects of Separation, and left so near a Similitude between them, as frequently deceived the very Disciples and Followers of both. * * *

* * * * * * * * * * * * * * * * * *Desunt*
* * * * * * * * * * * * * * * * * *nonnulla*[140]
* * * * * * * * * * * * * * * * * * *
* * * * * * * * * * * * * * * * * * *

THE old *Sclavonian* Proverb said well, That *it is with Men, as with Asses; whoever would keep them fast, may find a very good Hold at their Ears.* Yet, I think, we may affirm, and it hath been verified by repeated Experience, that,

Effugiet tamen hæc sceleratus vincula Proteus.[141]

IT is good therefore, to read the Maxims of our Ancestors, with great Allowances to Times and Persons: For, if we look into Primitive Records, we shall find, that no Revolutions have been so great, or so frequent, as those of human *Ears.* In former Days, there was a curious Invention to catch and keep them; which, I think, we may justly reckon among the *Artes perditæ.*[142] And how can it be otherwise, when in these latter Centuries, the very Species is not only diminished to a very lamentable Degree, but the poor Remainder is also degenerated so far, as to mock our skilfullest *Tenure?* For, if the only slitting of one *Ear* in a Stag, hath been found sufficient to propagate the Defect thro' a whole Forest; Why should we wonder at the greatest Consequences, from so many Loppings and Mutilations, to which the *Ears* of our Fathers and our own, have been of late so much exposed? 'Tis true, indeed, that while this *Island* of ours, was under the *Dominion of Grace,* many Endeavours were made to improve the Growth of *Ears* once more among us. The Proportion of Largeness, was not only lookt upon as an Ornament of the *Outward* Man, but as a Type of Grace in the *Inward.* Besides, it is held by Naturalists, that if there be a Protuberancy of Parts in the *Superiour* Region of the Body, as in the *Ears* and *Nose,* there must be a Parity also in the *Inferior:* And therefore in that truly pious Age, the *Males* in every Assembly, according as they were gifted, appeared very forward in exposing their *Ears* to view, and the Regions about them; because *Hippocrates*[*143] tells us, that *when the Vein behind the Ear happens to be cut, a Man becomes a Eunuch:* And the *Females* were nothing backwarder in beholding * *Lib. de aëre locis & aquis.*

and edifying by them: Whereof those who had already *used the Means,* lookt about them with great Concern, in hopes of conceiving a suitable Offspring by such a Prospect: Others, who stood Candidates for *Benevolence,* found there a plentiful Choice, and were sure to fix upon such as discovered the largest *Ears,* that the Breed might not dwindle between them. Lastly, the devouter Sisters, who lookt upon all extraordinary Dilatations of that Member, as Protrusions of Zeal, or spiritual Excrescencies, were sure to honor every Head they sat upon, as if they had been *Marks of Grace;* but, especially, that of the Preacher, whose *Ears* were usually of the prime Magnitude; which upon that Account, he was very frequent and exact in exposing with all Advantages to the People: in his Rhetorical *Paroxysms,* turning sometimes to *hold forth* the one, and sometimes to *hold forth* the other: From which Custom, the whole Operation of Preaching is to this very Day among their Professors, styled by the Phrase of *Holding forth.*

SUCH was the Progress of the *Saints,* for advancing the Size of that Member; And it is thought, the Success would have been every way answerable, if in Process of time, a cruel King† had not arose, who raised

---

† *This was King* Charles *the Second, who at his Restauration, turned out all the Dissenting Teachers that would not conform.*

a bloody Persecution against all *Ears,* above a certain Standard: Upon which, some were glad to hide their flourishing Sprouts in a black Border, others crept wholly under a Perewig: some were slit, others cropt, and a great Number sliced off to the Stumps. But of this, more hereafter, in my *general History of Ears;* which I design very speedily to bestow upon the Publick.

FROM this brief Survey of the falling State of *Ears,* in the last Age, and the small Care had to advance their antient Growth in the present, it is manifest, how little Reason we can have to rely upon a Hold so short, so weak, and so slippery; and that, whoever desires to catch Mankind fast, must have Recourse to some other Methods. Now, he that will examine Human Nature with Circumspection enough, may discover several *Handles,* whereof the *Six* Senses* afford one apiece, be- side a great Number that are screw'd to the Passions, and some   * *Including Scaliger's.*[144]
few riveted to the Intellect. Among these last, *Curiosity* is one, and of all others, affords the firmest Grasp: *Curiosity,* that Spur in the side, that Bridle in the Mouth, that Ring in the Nose, of a lazy, an impatient, and a grunting Reader. By this *Handle* it is, that an Author should seize upon his Readers; which as soon as he hath once compast, all Resistance and struggling are in vain; and they become his Prisoners as close as he pleases, till Weariness or Dullness force him to let go his Gripe.

AND therefore, I the Author of this miraculous Treatise, having hitherto, beyond Expectation, maintained by the aforesaid *Handle,* a firm Hold upon my gentle Readers; It is with great Reluctance, that I am at length compelled to remit my Grasp; leaving them in the Perusal of what remains, to that natural *Oscitancy* inherent in the Tribe. I can only assure thee, Courteous Reader, for both our Comforts, that my Concern is altogether equal to thine, for my Unhappiness in losing, or mislaying among my Papers the remaining Part of these Memoirs; which consisted of Accidents, Turns, and Adventures, both New, Agreeable, and Surprizing; and therefore, calculated in all due Points, to the delicate Taste of this our noble Age. But, alas, with my utmost Endeavours, I have been able only to retain a few of the Heads. Under which, there was a full Account, how *Peter* got a *Protection* out of the *King's-Bench;* and of a Reconcilement between *Jack* and Him, upon a Design they had in a certain *rainy Night,* to trepan Brother *Martin* into a *Spunging-house,* and there strip him to the Skin. How *Martin,* with much ado, shew'd them both a fair pair of Heels. How a *new Warrant* came out against *Peter:* upon which, how *Jack* left him in the lurch, *stole his Protection, and made use of it*

himself.* How *Jack*'s Tatters came into Fashion in *Court* and *City*; How *he*†
got upon a great Horse, and eat Custard.‡ But the Particulars of all these, with
several others, which have now slid out of my Memory, are lost beyond all
Hopes of Recovery. For which Misfortune, leaving my Readers to condole
with each other, as far as they shall find it to agree with their several Constitutions; but conjuring them by all the Friendship that hath passed between Us, from the Title-Page to this, not to proceed so far as to injure
their Healths, for an Accident past Remedy; I now go on to the Ceremonial Part of an accomplish'd Writer, and therefore, by a Courtly *Modern*,
least of all others to be omitted.

---

* *In the Reign of King* James *the Second, the Presbyterians by the King's Invitation, joined with the Papists, against the Church of* England, *and Address him for Repeal of the Penal-Laws and Test. The King by his Dispensing Power, gave Liberty of Conscience, which both Papists and Presbyterians made use of, but upon the Revolution, the Papists being down of Course, the Presbyterians freely continued their Assemblies, by Virtue of King* James's *Indulgence, before they had a Toleration by Law; this I believe the Author means by* Jack's *stealing* Peter's *Protection, and making use of it himself.*

† *Sir* Humphry Edwyn, *a Presbyterian, was some Years ago Lord-Mayor of* London, *and had the Insolence to go in his Formalities to a Conventicle, with the Ensigns of his Office.*

‡ *Custard is a famous Dish at a Lord-Mayors Feast.*

THE
CONCLUSION

Going too long is a Cause of Abortion as effectual, tho' not so frequent, as *Going too short;* and holds true especially in the *Labors* of the Brain. Well fare the Heart of that Noble *Jesuit,** who first adventur'd to confess in Print, that Books must be suited to their several Seasons, like Dress, and Dyet, and Diversions: And better fare our noble Nation, for refining upon this, among other *French* Modes. I am living fast, to see the Time, when a *Book* that misses its Tide, shall be neglected, as the *Moon* by day, or like *Mackarel* a Week after the Season. No Man hath more nicely observed our Climate, than the Bookseller who bought the Copy of this Work; He knows to a Tittle what Subjects will best go off in a *dry Year,* and which it is proper to expose foremost, when the Weather-glass is fallen to *much Rain.* When he had seen this Treatise, and consulted his *Almanack* upon it; he gave me to understand, that he had maturely considered the two Principal Things, which were the *Bulk,* and the *Subject;* and found, it would never *take,* but after a long Vacation, and then only, in case it should happen to be a hard Year for Turnips. Upon which I desired to know, *considering my urgent Necessities,* what he thought might be acceptable this Month. He lookt *Westward,* and said, *I doubt we shall have a Fit of bad Weather; However, if you could prepare some pretty little Banter (but not in Verse) or a small Treatise upon the ——— it would run like Wild-Fire. But,* if it hold up, *I have already hired an Author to write something against* Dr. Bentley, *which, I am sure, will turn to Account.*

AT length we agreed upon this Expedient; That when a Customer comes for one of these, and desires in Confidence to know the Author; he will tell him very privately, as a Friend, naming which ever of the Wits

* *Pere d' Orleans.*

shall happen to be that Week in the Vogue; and if *Durfy*'s last Play should be in Course, I had as lieve he may be the Person as *Congreve.*[145] This I mention, because I am wonderfully well acquainted with the present Relish of Courteous Readers; and have often observed, with singular Pleasure, that a *Fly* driven from a *Honey-pot,* will immediately, with very good Appetite alight, and finish his Meal on an *Excrement.*

I have one Word to say upon the Subject of *Profound Writers,* who are grown very numerous of late; And, I know very well, the judicious World is resolved to list me in that Number. I conceive therefore, as to the Business of being *Profound,* that it is with *Writers,* as with *Wells;* A Person with good Eyes may see to the Bottom of the deepest, provided any *Water* be there; and, that often, when there is nothing in the World at the Bottom, besides *Dryness* and *Dirt,* tho' it be but a Yard and half under Ground, it shall pass, however, for wondrous *Deep,* upon no wiser a Reason than because it is wondrous *Dark.*

I am now trying an Experiment very frequent among Modern Authors; which is, to *write upon Nothing.*[146] When the Subject is utterly exhausted, to let the Pen still move on; by some called, the Ghost of Wit, delighting to walk after the Death of its Body. And to say the Truth, there seems to be no Part of Knowledge in fewer Hands, than That of Discerning *when to have Done.* By the Time that an Author has writ out a Book, he and his Readers are become old Acquaintance, and grow very loth to part: So that I have sometimes known it to be in Writing, as in Visiting, where the Ceremony of taking Leave, has employ'd more Time than the whole Conversation before. The Conclusion of a Treatise, resembles the Conclusion of Human Life, which hath sometimes been compared to the End of a Feast; where few are satisfied to depart, *ut plenus vitæ conviva.*[147] For Men will sit down after the fullest Meal, tho' it be only to *doze,* or to *sleep* out the rest of the Day. But, in this latter, I differ extreamly from other Writers; and shall be too proud, if by all my Labors, I can have any ways contributed to the *Repose* of Mankind in Times* so turbulent and unquiet as these. Neither, do I think such an Employment so very alien from the Office of a *Wit,* as some would suppose. For among a very Polite Nation in *Greece,*†[148] there were the *same* † *Trezenii* Temples built and consecrated to *Sleep* and the *Muses,* be- *Pausan. I. 2.* tween which two Deities, they believed the strictest Friendship was established.

I have one concluding Favour, to request of my Reader; that he will not

---

* *This was writ before the Peace of* Riswick.

expect to be equally diverted and informed by every Line, or every Page of this Discourse; but give some Allowance to the Author's Spleen, and short Fits or Intervals of Dullness, as well as his own; And lay it seriously to his Conscience, whether, if he were walking the Streets, in dirty Weather, or a rainy Day; he would allow it fair Dealing in Folks at their Ease from a Window, to Critick his Gate, and ridicule his Dress at such a Juncture.

IN my Disposure of Employments of the Brain, I have thought fit to make *Invention* the *Master,* and to give *Method* and *Reason,* the Office of its *Lacquays.* The Cause of this Distribution was, from observing it my peculiar Case, to be often under a Temptation of being *Witty,* upon Occasions, where I could be neither *Wise* nor *Sound,* nor any thing to the Matter in hand. And, I am too much a Servant of the *Modern* Way, to neglect any such Opportunities, whatever Pains or Improprieties I may be at, to introduce them. For, I have observed, that from a laborious Collection of Seven Hundred Thirty Eight *Flowers,* and *shining Hints* of the best *Modern* Authors, digested with great Reading, into my Book of *Common-places;* I have not been able after five Years to draw, hook, or force into common Conversation, any more than a Dozen. Of which Dozen, the one Moiety failed of Success, by being dropt among unsuitable Company; and the other cost me so many Strains, and Traps, and *Ambages*[149] to introduce, that I at length resolved to give it over. Now, this Disappointment, (to discover a Secret) I must own, gave me the first Hint of setting up for an *Author;* and, I have since found among some particular Friends, that it is become a very general Complaint, and has produced the same Effects upon many others. For, I have remarked many a *towardly Word,* to be wholly neglected or despised in *Discourse,* which hath passed very smoothly, with some Consideration and Esteem, after its Preferment and Sanction in *Print.* But now, since by the Liberty of Encouragement of the Press, I am grown absolute Master of the Occasions and Opportunities, to expose the Talents I have acquired; I already discover, that the *Issues* of my *Observanda* begin to grow too large for the *Receipts.* Therefore, I shall here pause awhile, till I find, by feeling the World's Pulse, and my own, that it will be of absolute Necessity for us both, to resume my Pen.

A
FULL AND TRUE ACCOUNT
OF THE
BATTEL
FOUGHT LAST FRIDAY,
BETWEEN THE
ANTIENT AND THE *MODERN*
BOOKS
IN
ST. JAMES'S LIBRARY

THE
BOOKSELLER
TO THE
READER

The following Discourse, as it is unquestionably of the same Author, so it seems to have been written about the same time with the former, I mean, the Year 1697, when the famous Dispute was on Foot, about *Antient and Modern Learning.* The Controversy took its Rise from an Essay of Sir *William Temple's*, upon that Subject; which was answer'd by *W. Wotton*, B.D. with an Appendix by Dr. *Bentley*, endeavouring to destroy the Credit of *Æsop* and *Phalaris*, for Authors, whom Sir *William Temple* had in the Essay before-mentioned, highly commended. In that Appendix, the Doctor falls hard upon a new Edition of *Phalaris*, put out by the Honourable *Charles Boyle* (now *Earl* of *Orrery*) to which, Mr. *Boyle* replyed at large, with great Learning and Wit; and the Doctor, voluminously, rejoyned. In this Dispute, the Town high resented to see a Person of Sir *William Temple's* Character and Merits, roughly used by the two Reverend Gentlemen aforesaid, and without any manner of Provocation. At length, there appearing no End of the Quarrel, our Author tells us, that the BOOKS in St. *James's* Library, looking upon themselves as Parties principally concerned, took up the Controversie, and came to a decisive Battel; But, the Manuscript, by the Injury of Fortune, or Weather, being in several Places imperfect, we cannot learn to which side the Victory fell.

I must warn the Reader, to beware of applying to Persons what is here meant, only of Books in the most literal Sense. So, when *Virgil* is mentioned, we are not to understand the Person of a famous Poet, call'd by that Name, but only certain Sheets of Paper, bound up in Leather, containing in Print, the Works of the said Poet, and so of the rest.

THE
PREFACE
OF THE
AUTHOR

Satyr is a sort of Glass, *wherein Beholders do generally discover every body's Face but their Own; which is the chief Reason for that kind of Reception it meets in the World, and that so very few are offended with it. But if it should happen otherwise, the Danger is not great; and, I have learned from long Experience, never to apprehend Mischief from those Understandings, I have been able to provoke; For, Anger and Fury, though they add Strength to the* Sinews *of the* Body, *yet are found to relax those of the* Mind, *and to render all its Efforts feeble and impotent.*

THERE is a Brain *that will endure but one* Scumming: *Let the Owner gather it with Discretion, and manage his little Stock with Husbandry; but of all things, let him beware of bringing it under the* Lash *of his* Betters; *because, That will make it all bubble up into Impertinence, and he will find no new Supply: Wit, without knowledge, being a Sort of* Cream, *which gathers in a Night to the Top, and by a skilful Hand, may be soon* whipt *into Froth; but once scumm'd away, what appears underneath will be fit for nothing, but to be thrown to the Hogs.*

A FULL AND TRUE

ACCOUNT

OF THE

BATTEL *FOUGHT LAST FRIDAY*,[1] &c.

Whoever examines with due Circumspection into the *Annual Records* of *Time*,* will find it remarked, that *War is the Child of Pride*, and *Pride the Daughter of Riches*; The former of which Assertions may be soon granted; but one cannot so easily subscribe to the latter: For *Pride* is nearly related to Beggary and *Want*, either by Father or Mother, and sometimes by both; And, to speak naturally, it very seldom happens among Men to fall out, when all have enough: Invasions usually travelling from *North* to *South*, that is to say, from Poverty upon Plenty. The most antient and natural Grounds of Quarrels, are *Lust* and *Avarice*; which, tho' we may allow to be Brethren or collateral Branches of *Pride*, are certainly the Issues of *Want*. For, to speak in the Phrase of Writers upon the Politicks, we may observe in the Republick of *Dogs*, (which in its Original seems to be an Institution of the *Many*) that the whole State is ever in the profoundest Peace, after a full Meal; and, that Civil Broils arise among them, when it happens For one great *Bone* to be seized on by some *leading Dog*, who either divides it among the *Few*, and then it falls to an *Oligarchy*, or keeps it to Himself, and then it runs up to a *Tyranny*. The same Reasoning also, holds Place among them, in those Dissensions we behold upon a Turgescency[3] in any of their Females. For, the Right of Possession lying in common (it being impossible to establish a Property in so delicate a Case) Jealousies and Suspicions do so abound, that the whole Commonwealth of that Street, is reduced to a manifest *State of War*, of every *Citizen* against every *Citizen*; till some One of more Courage, Conduct, or Fortune than the rest,

* *Riches produceth Pride; Pride is War's Ground, &c.* Vid. Ephem. de *Mary Clarke*; opt. Edit.[2]

seizes and enjoys the Prize; Upon which, naturally arises Plenty of Heart-burning, and Envy, and Snarling against the *Happy Dog*. Again, if we look upon any of these Republicks engaged in a Forein War, either of Invasion or Defence, we shall find, the same Reasoning will serve, as to the Grounds and Occasions of each; and, that *Poverty*, or *Want*, in some Degree or other, (whether Real, or in Opinion, which makes no Alteration in the Case) has a great Share, as well as *Pride*, on the Part of the Aggressor.

NOW, whoever will please to take this Scheme, and either reduce or adapt it to an Intellectual State, or Commonwealth of Learning, will soon discover the first Ground of Disagreement between the two great Parties at this Time in Arms; and may form just Conclusions upon the Merits of either Cause. But the Issue or Events of this War are not so easie to conjecture at: For, the present Quarrel is so enflamed by the warm Heads of either Faction, and the Pretensions *somewhere or other* so exorbitant, as not to admit the least Overtures of Accommodation: This Quarrel first began (as I have heard it affirmed by an old Dweller in the Neighbourhood) about a small Spot of Ground, *lying* and *being* upon one of the two Tops of the Hill *Parnassus;* the highest and largest of which, had it seems, been time out of Mind, in quiet Possession of certain Tenants, call'd the *Antients;* And the other was held by the *Moderns*. But, these disliking their present Station, sent certain Ambassadors to the *Antients*, complaining of a great Nuisance, how the Height of that Part of *Parnassus*, quite spoiled the Prospect of theirs, especially towards the *East;* and therefore, to avoid a War, offered them the Choice of this Alternative; either that the *Antients* would please to remove themselves and their Effects down to the lower Summity, which the *Moderns* would graciously surrender to them, and advance in their Place; or else, that the said *Antients* will give leave to the *Moderns* to come with Shovels and Mattocks, and level the said Hill, as low as they shall think it convenient. To which, the *Antients* made Answer: How little they expected such a Message as this, from a Colony, whom they had admitted out of their own Free Grace, to so near a Neighbourhood. That, as to their own Seat, they were *Aborigines* of it, and therefore, to talk with them of a Removal or Surrender, was a Language they did not understand. That, if the Height of the Hill, on their side, shortned the Prospect of the *Moderns*, it was a Disadvantage they could not help, but desired them to consider, whether that Injury (if it be any) were not largely recompenced by the *Shade* and *Shelter* it afforded them. That, as to levelling or digging down, it was either Folly or Ignorance to propose it, if they did, or did not know, how that side of the Hill was an entire Rock, which would break their Tools and Hearts; without any Damage to itself. That they would therefore advise the *Moderns,* rather to raise their own side of the Hill, than dream of pulling down that of the *Antients,* to the former of which, they would not only give Licence, but also largely contribute. All this was rejected by the *Moderns,* with much Indignation, who still insisted upon one of the two Expedients; And so this Difference broke out into a long and obstinate War, maintain'd on the one Part, by Resolution, and by the Courage of certain Leaders and Allies; but, on the other, by the greatness of their Number, upon all Defeats, affording continual Recruits. In this Quarrel, whole Rivulets of *Ink* have been exhausted, and the Virulence of both Parties enormously augmented. Now, it must here be understood, that *Ink* is the great missive Weapon, in all Battels of the *Learned,* which, convey'd thro' a sort of Engine, call'd a *Quill,* infinite Numbers of these are darted at the Enemy, but the Valiant on each side, with equal Skill and Violence, as if it were an Engagement of *Porcupines.* This malignant Liquor was compounded by the Engineer, who invented it, of two Ingredients, which are *Gall* and *Copperas,* by its Bitterness and Venom, to *Suit* in some Degree, as well as to *Foment* the Genius of the Combatants. And as the *Grecians,* after an Engagement, when they could not *agree* about the Victory, were wont to set up Trophies on both sides, the beaten Party being content to be at the same Expence, to keep it self in Countenance (A laudable and antient Custom, happily reviv'd of late, in the Art of War) so the *Learned,* after a sharp and bloody Dispute, do on both sides hang out their Trophies too, which-ever comes by the worst. These Trophies have largely inscribed on them the Merits of the Cause; a full impartial Account of such a Battel, and how the Victory fell clearly to the Party that set them up. They are known to the World under several Names; As, *Disputes, Arguments, Rejoynders, Brief Considerations, Answers, Replies, Remarks, Reflexions, Objections, Confutations.* For a very few Days they are fixed up in all Publick Places, either by themselves or their Representa- ^*Their Title-Pages.* tives,* for Passengers to gaze at: From whence the chiefest and largest are removed to certain Magazines, they call, *Libraries,* there to remain in a Quarter purposely assign'd them, and from thenceforth, begin to be called, *Books of Controversie.*

IN these Books, is wonderfully instilled and preserved, the Spirit of each Warrier, while he is alive; and after his Death, his Soul transmigrates there, to inform them. This, at least, is the more common Opinion; But, I believe, it is with Libraries, as with other Cœmeteries, where some Philosophers affirm, that a certain Spirit, which they call *Brutum hominis,* hovers over the Monument, till the Body is corrupted, and turns to *Dust,* or to *Worms,* but then vanishes or dissolves: So, we may say, a restless Spirit haunts over every *Book,* till *Dust* or *Worms* have seized upon it; which to some, may happen in a few Days, but to others, later; And therefore, *Books* of Controversy, being of all others, haunted by the most disorderly Spirits, have always been confined in a separate Lodge from the rest; and for fear of mutual violence against each other, it was thought Prudent by our Ancestors, to bind them to the Peace with strong Iron Chains. Of which Invention, the original Occasion was this: When the Works of *Scotus* first came out, they were carried to a certain great Library, and had Lodgings appointed them; But this Author was no sooner settled, than he went to visit his Master *Aristotle,* and there both concerted together to seize *Plato* by main Force, and turn him out of his antient Station among the *Divines,* where he had peaceably dwelt near Eight Hundred Years. The Attempt succeeded, and the two Usurpers have reigned ever since in his stead: But to maintain Quiet for the future, it was decreed, that all *Polemicks* of the larger Size, should be held fast with a Chain.

By this Expedient, the publick Peace of Libraries, might certainly have been preserved, if a new Species of controversial Books had not arose of late Years, instinct with a most malignant Spirit, from the War above-mentioned, between the *Learned,* about the higher Summity of *Parnassus.*

When these Books were first admitted into the Publick Libraries, I remember to have said upon Occasion, to several Persons concerned, how I was sure, they would create Broyls wherever they came, unless a World of Care were taken: And therefore, I advised, that the Champions of each side should be coupled together, or otherwise mixt, that like the blending of contrary Poysons, their Malignity might be employ'd among themselves. And it seems, I was neither an ill Prophet, nor an ill Counsellor; for it was nothing else but the Neglect of this Caution, which gave Occasion to the terrible Fight that happened on *Friday* last between the *Antient* and *Modern Books* in the *King's Library.* Now, because the Talk of this Battel is so fresh in every body's Mouth, and the Expectation of the Town so great to be informed in the Particulars; I, being possessed of all Qualifications requisite in an *Historian,* and retained by neither Party; have resolved to comply with the urgent *Importunity of my Friends,* by writing down a full impartial Account thereof.

The *Guardian* of the *Regal Library,* a Person of great Valor, but chiefly renowned for his *Humanity,*[*4] had been a fierce Champion for the *Moderns,*

---

* *The Honourable Mr.* Boyle, *in the Preface to his Edition of* Phalaris, *says, he was refus'd a Manuscript by the Library-Keeper,* pro solita Humanitate suâ.

and in an Engagement upon *Parnassus,* had vowed, with his own Hands, to knock down two of the *Antient* Chiefs,[5] who guarded a small Pass on the superior Rock; but endeavouring to climb up, was cruelly obstructed by his own unhappy Weight, and tendency towards his Center; a Quality, to which, those of the *Modern* Party, are extreme subject; For, being light-headed, they have in Speculation, a wonderful Agility, and conceive nothing too high for them to mount; but in reducing to Practice, discover a mighty Pressure about their Posteriors and their Heels. Having thus failed in his Design, the disappointed Champion bore a cruel Rancour to the *Antients,* which he resolved to gratifie, by shewing all Marks of his Favour to the *Books* of their Adversaries, and lodging them in the fairest Apartments; when at the same time, whatever *Book* had the boldness to own it self for an Advocate of the *Antients,* was buried alive in some obscure Corner, and threatned upon the least Displeasure, to be turned out of Doors. Besides, it so happened, that about this time, there was a strange confusion of Place among all the *Books* in the Library; for which several Reasons were assigned. Some imputed it to a great heap of *learned Dust,* which a perverse Wind blew off from a Shelf of *Moderns* into the *Keeper's* Eyes. Others affirmed, He had a Humour to pick the *Worms* out of the *Schoolmen,* and swallow them fresh and fasting; whereof some fell upon his *Spleen,* and some climbed up into his Head, to the great Perturbation of both. And lastly, others maintained, that by walking much in the dark about the Library, he had quite lost the Situation of it out of his Head; And therefore, in replacing his *Books,* he was apt to mistake, and clap *Des-Cartes* next to *Aristotle;* Poor *Plato* had got between *Hobbes* and the *Seven Wise Masters,* and *Virgil* was hemm'd in with *Dryden* on one side, and *Withers*[6] on the other.

MEAN while, those *Books* that were Advocates for the *Moderns,* chose out one from among them, to make a Progress thro' the whole Library, examine the Number and Strength of their Party, and concert their Affairs. This Messenger performed all things very industriously, and brought back with him a List of their Forces, in all Fifty Thousand, consisting chiefly of *light Horse, heavy-armed Foot,* and *Mercenaries;* Whereof the *Foot* were in general but sorrily armed, and worse clad; Their *Horses* large, but extremely out of Case and Heart; However, some few by trading among the *Antients,* had furnisht themselves tolerably enough.

WHILE Things were in this Ferment; *Discord* grew extremely high, hot Words passed on both sides, and ill blood was plentifully bred. Here a solitary *Antient,* squeezed up among a whole Shelf of *Moderns,* offered fairly to dispute the Case, and to prove by manifest Reasons, that the Priority was due to them, from long Possession, and in regard of their Prudence, Antiquity, and above all, their great Merits towards the *Moderns*. But these denied the Premises, and seemed very much to wonder, how the *Antients* could pretend to insist upon their Antiquity, when it was so plain (if they went to that) that the *Moderns* were much more *Antient** of the two. As for any Obligations they owed to the *Antients*, they renounced them all. *'Tis true,* said they, *we are informed, some few of our Party have been so mean to borrow their Subsistence from You; But the rest, infinitely the greater Number (and especially, we* French *and* English*) were so far from stooping to so base an Example, that there never passed, till this very hour, six Words between us. For, our* Horses *are of our own breeding, our* Arms *of our own forging, and our* Cloaths *of our own cutting out and sowing.* Plato was by chance upon the next Shelf, and observing those that spoke to be in the ragged Plight, mentioned a while ago; their *Jades* lean and foundred, their *Weapons* of rotten Wood, their *Armour* rusty, and nothing but Raggs underneath; he laugh'd loud, and in his pleasant way, swore, *by G——, he believ'd them.*

According to the Modern Paradox.

Now, the *Moderns* had not proceeded in their late Negotiation, with Secrecy enough to escape the Notice of the Enemy. For, those Advocates, who had begun the Quarrel, by setting first on Foot the Dispute of Precedency, talkt so loud of coming to a Battel, that *Temple* happened to over-hear them, and gave immediate Intelligence to the *Antients;* who thereupon drew up their scattered Troops together, resolving to act upon the defensive; Upon which, several of the *Moderns* fled over to their Party, and among the rest, *Temple* himself. This *Temple* having been educated and long conversed among the *Antients,* was, of all the *Moderns,* their greatest Favorite, and became their greatest Champion.

Things were at this Crisis, when a material Accident fell out. For, upon the highest Corner of a large Window, there dwelt a certain *Spider,*[7] swollen up to the first Magnitude, by the Destruction of infinite Numbers of *Flies,* whose Spoils lay scattered before the Gates of his Palace, like human Bones before the Cave of some Giant. The Avenues to his Castle were guarded with Turn-pikes, and Palissadoes, all after the *Modern* way of Fortification. After you had passed several Courts, you came to the Center, wherein you might behold the *Constable* himself in his own Lodgings, which had Windows fronting to each Avenue, and Ports to sally out upon all Occasions of Prey or Defence. In this Mansion he had for some Time dwelt in Peace and Plenty, without Danger to his *Person* by *Swallows* from above, or to his *Palace* by *Brooms* from below: When it was the Pleasure of Fortune to conduct thither a wandring *Bee*, to whose Curiosity a broken Pane in the Glass had discovered it self; and in he went, where expatiating a while, he at last happened to alight upon one of the outward Walls of the *Spider*'s Cittadel; which yielding to the unequal Weight, sunk down to the very Foundation. Thrice he endeavoured to force his Passage, and Thrice the Center shook. The *Spider* within, feeling the terrible Convulsion, supposed at first, that *Nature* was approaching to her final Dissolution; or else, that *Beelzebub* with all his Legions, was come to revenge the Death of many thousands of his Subjects, whom his Enemy had slain and devoured. However, he at length valiantly resolved to issue forth, and meet his Fate. Mean while, the *Bee* had acquitted himself of his Toils, and posted securely at some Distance, was employed in cleansing his wings, and disengaging them from the ragged Remnants of the Cobweb. By this Time the *Spider* was adventured out, when beholding the Chasms, and Ruins, and Dilapidations of his Fortress, he was very near at his Wit's end, he stormed and swore like a Mad-man, and swelled till he was ready to burst. At length, casting his Eye upon the *Bee*, and wisely gathering Causes from Events, (for they knew each other by Sight) *A Plague split you*, said he, *for a giddy Son of a Whore; Is it you, with a Vengeance, that have made this Litter here? Could you not look before you, and be d———n'd? Do you think I have nothing else to do (in the Devil's Name) but to Mend and Repair after your Arse? Good Words, Friend*, said the *Bee*, (having now pruned himself, and being disposed to drole) *I'll give you my Hand and Word to come near your Kennel no more; I was never in such a confounded Pickle since I was born. Sirrah*, replied the *Spider, if it were not for breaking an old Custom in our Family, never to stir abroad against an Enemy, I should come and teach you better Manners. I pray, have Patience*, said the *Bee, or you will spend your Substance, and for ought I see, you may stand in need of it all, towards the Repair of your House. Rogue, Rogue*, replied the *Spider, yet, methinks, you should have more Respect to a Person, whom all the World allows to be so much your Betters. By my Troth*, said the *Bee, the Comparison will amount to a very good Jest, and you will do me a Favour, to let me know the Reasons, that all the World is pleased to use in so hopeful a Dispute.* At this, the *Spider* having swelled himself into the Size and Posture of a Disputant, began his Argument in the true Spirit of Controversy, with a Resolution to be heartily scurrilous and angry, to urge *on* his own Reasons, without the least Regard to the Answers or Objections of his Opposite; and fully predetermined in his Mind against all Conviction.

    NOT to disparage my self, said he, *by the Comparison with such a Rascal; What art thou but a Vagabond without House or Home, without Stock or Inheritance? Born to no Possession of your own, but a Pair of Wings, and a Drone-Pipe. Your Livelihood is an universal Plunder upon Nature; a Freebooter over Fields and Gardens; and for the sake of Stealing, will rob a Nettle as readily as a Violet. Whereas I am a domestick Animal, furnist with a Native Stock within my self. This large Castle (to shew my Improvements in the Mathematicks) is all built with my own Hands, and the Materials extracted altogether out of my own Person.*

I am glad, answered the Bee, *to hear you grant at least, that I am come honestly by my Wings and my Voice, for then, it seems, I am obliged to Heaven alone for my Flights and my Musick; and Providence would never have bestowed me two such Gifts, without designing them for the noblest Ends. I visit, indeed, all the Flowers and Blossoms of the Field and the Garden, but whatever I collect from thence, enriches my self, without the least Injury to their Beauty, their Smell, or their Taste. Now, for you and your Skill in Architecture, and other Mathematicks, I have little to say: In that Building of yours, there might, for ought I know, have been Labor and Method enough, but by woful Experience for us both, 'tis too plain, the Materials are nought, and I hope, you will henceforth take Warning, and consider Duration and matter, as well as method and Art. You, boast, indeed, of being obliged to no other Creature, but of drawing, and spinning out all from your self; That is to say, if we may judge of the Liquor in the Vessel by what issues out, You possess a good plentiful Store of Dirt and Poison in your Breast; And, tho' I would by no means, lessen or disparage your genuine Stock of either, yet, I doubt you are somewhat obliged for an Encrease of both, to a little foreign Assistance. Your inherent Portion of Dirt, does not fail of Acquisitions, by Sweepings exhaled from below: and one Insect furnishes you with a share of Poison to destroy another. So that in short, the Question comes all to this; Whether is the nobler Being of the two, That which by a lazy Contemplation of four Inches round; by an overweening Pride, which feeding and engendering on it self, turns all into Excrement and Venom; producing nothing at last, but Fly-bane and a Cobweb; Or That, which, by an universal Range, with long Search, much Study, true Judgment, and Distinction of Things, brings home Honey and Wax.*

THIS Dispute was managed with such Eagerness, Clamor, and Warmth, that the two Parties of *Books* in Arms below, stood Silent a while, waiting in Suspense what would be the Issue; which was not long undetermined: for the *Bee* grown impatient at so much loss of Time, fled strait away to a bed of Roses, without looking for a Reply; and left the *Spider* like an Orator, *collected* in himself, and just prepared to burst out.

IT happened upon this emergency, that *Æsop* broke silence first. He had been of late most barbarously treated by a strange Effect of the *Regent's Humanity,* who had tore off his Title-page, sorely defaced one half of his

Leaves, and chained him fast among a Shelf of *Moderns.* Where soon discovering how high the Quarrel was like to proceed, He tried all his Arts, and turned himself to a thousand Forms: At length in the borrowed Shape of an *Ass,* the *Regent* mistook Him for a *Modern;* by which means, he had Time and Opportunity to escape to the *Antients,* just when the *Spider* and the *Bee* were entring into their Contest; to which He gave His Attention with a world of Pleasure; and when it was ended, swore in the loudest Key, that in all his Life, he had never known two Cases so parallel and adapt to each other, as That in the Window, and this upon the Shelves. The *Disputants,* said he, *have admirably managed the Dispute between them, have taken in the full Strength of all that is to be said on both sides, and exhausted the Substance of every Argument* pro *and* con. *It is but to adjust the Reasonings of both to the present Quarrel, then to compare and apply the Labors and Fruits of each, as the* Bee *has learnedly deduced them; and we shall find the Conclusions fall plain and close upon the* Moderns *and* Us. *For, pray Gentlemen, was ever any thing so* Modern *as the* Spider *in his Air, his Turns, and his Paradoxes? He argues in the Behalf of* You *his* Brethren, *and* Himself, *with many Boastings of his native Stock, and great Genius; that he Spins and Spits wholly from himself, and scorns to own any Obligation or Assistance from without. Then he displays to you his great Skill in Architecture, and Improvement in the Mathematicks. To all this, the* Bee, *as an Advocate, retained by us the* Antients, *thinks fit to Answer; That if one may judge of the grat Genius or Inventions of the* Moderns, *by what they have produced, you will hardly have Countenance to bear you out in boasting of either. Erect your Schemes with as much Method and Skill as you please; yet, if the materials be nothing but Dirt, spun out of your own Entrails (the Guts of* Modern *Brains) the Edifice will conclude at last in a* Cobweb: *The Duration of which, like that of other* Spiders *Webs, may be imputed to their being forgotten, or neglected, or hid in a Corner. For any Thing else of Genuine, that the* Moderns *may pretend to, I cannot recollect; unless it be a large Vein of Wrangling and Satyr, much of a Nature and Substance with the* Spider's *Poison; which, however they pretend to spit wholly out of themselves, is improved by the same Arts, by feeding upon the* Insects *and* Vermin *of the Age. As for* Us, *the* Antients, *We are content with the* Bee, *to pretend to Nothing of our own, beyond our* Wings *and our* Voice: *that is to say, our* Flights *and our* Language; *For the rest, whatever we have got, has been by infinite Labor, and search, and ranging thro' every Corner of Nature: The Difference is, that instead of Dirt and Poison, we have rather chose to fill our Hives with* Honey *and* Wax, *thus furnishing Mankind with the two Noblest of Things, which are* Sweetness *and* Light.

'TIS wonderful to conceive the Tumult arisen among the *Books,* upon the Close of this long Descant of *Æsop;* Both Parties took the Hint, and heightened their Animosities so on a sudden, that they resolved it should come to a Battel. Immediately, the two main Bodies withdrew under their several Ensigns, to the farther Parts of the Library, and there entred into Cabals, and Consults upon the present Emergency. The *Moderns* were in very warm Debates upon the Choice of their *Leaders;* and nothing less than the Fear impending from their Enemies, could have kept them from Mutinies upon this Occasion. The Difference was greatest among the *Horse,* where every private *Trooper* pretended to the chief Command, from *Tasso* and *Milton,* to *Dryden* and *Withers.* The *Light-Horse*[8] were Commanded by *Cowly,* and *Despreaux.* There, came the *Bowmen*[9] under their valiant Leaders, *Des-Cartes, Gassendi,* and *Hobbes,* whose Strength was such, that they could shoot their Arrows beyond the *Atmosphere,* never to fall down again, but turn like that of *Evander,* into *Meteors,* or like the *Canon-ball* into *Stars.* *Paracelsus* brought a *Squadron* of *Stink-Pot-Flingers*[10] from the snowy Mountains of *Rhœtia.* There, came a vast Body of *Dragoons,*[11] of different Nations, under the leading of *Harvey,* their great *Aga:* Part armed with *Scythes,* the Weapons of Death; Part with *Launces* and long *Knives,* all steept in *Poison;* Part shot *Bullets* of a most malignant Nature, and used *white Powder* which infallibly killed without *Report.* There, came several Bodies of *heavy-armed Foot,*[12] all *Mercenaries,* under the Ensigns of *Guiccardine, Davila, Polydore Virgil, Buchanan, Mariana, Cambden,* and others. The *Engineers*[13] were commanded by *Regiomontanus* and *Wilkins.* The rest were a confused Multitude, led by *Scotus, Aquinas,* and *Bellarmine;* of mighty Bulk and Stature, but without either Arms, Courage, or Discipline. In the last Place, came infinite Swarms of *Calones,** a disorderly Rout led by *Lestrange;* Rogues and Ragamuffins, that follow the Camp for nothing but the Plunder; All without *Coats* to cover them.

THE Army of the *Antients* was much fewer in Number; *Homer* led the *Horse,* and *Pindar* the *Light-Horse; Euclid* was chief *Engineer: Plato* and *Aristotle* commanded the *Bowmen, Herodotus* and *Livy* the *Foot, Hippocrates* the *Dragoons.* The *Allies,* led by *Vossius* and *Temple,* brought up the Rear.

ALL things violently tending to a decisive Battel; *Fame,* who much frequented, and had a large Apartment formerly assigned her in the *Regal Library,* fled up strait to *Jupiter,* to whom she delivered a faithful account of all that passed between the two Parties below. (For, among the Gods, she always tells Truth.) *Jove* in great concern, convokes a Council in the *Milky-Way.* The Senate assembled, he declares the Occasion of convening

* *These are Pamphlets, which are not bound or cover'd.*

them; a bloody Battel just impendent between two mighty Armies of *Antient* and *Modern* Creatures, call'd *Books*, wherein the Celestial Interest was but too deeply concerned. *Momus*, the Patron of the *Moderns*, made an Excellent Speech in their Favor, which was answered by *Pallas* the Protectress of the *Antients*. The Assembly was divided in their affections; when *Jupiter* commanded the Book of Fate to be laid before Him. Immediately were brought by *Mercury*, three large Volumes in Folio, containing Memoirs of all Things past, present, and to come. The Clasps were of Silver, double Gilt; the Covers, of Celestial Turky-leather, and the Paper such as here on Earth might almost pass for Vellum. *Jupiter* having silently read the Decree, would communicate the Import to none, but presently shut up the Book.

WITHOUT the Doors of this Assembly, there attended a vast Number of light, nimble Gods, menial Servants to *Jupiter:* These are his ministring Instruments in all Affairs below. They travel in a Caravan, more or less together, and are fastened to each other like a Link of Gally-slaves, by a light Chain, which passes from them to *Jupiter's* great Toe: And yet in receiving or delivering a Message, they may never approach above the lowest Step of his Throne, where he and they whisper to each other thro' a long hollow Trunk. These Deities are call'd by mortal Men, *Accidents*, or *Events;* but the Gods call them, *Second Causes. Jupiter* having delivered his Message to a certain Number of these Divinities, they flew immediately down to the Pinnacle of the Regal Library, and consulting a few Minutes, entered unseen, and disposed the Parties according to their Orders.

MEAN while, *Momus* fearing the worst, and calling to mind an antient Prophecy, which bore no very good Face to his Children the *Moderns;* bent his Flight to the Region of a malignant Deity, call'd *Criticism.* She dwelt on the Top of a snowy Mountain in *Nova Zembla;* there *Momus* found her extended in her Den, upon the Spoils of numberless Volumes half devoured. At her right Hand sat *Ignorance*, her Father and Husband, blind with Age; at her left, *Pride* her Mother, dressing her up in the Scraps of Paper herself had torn. There, was *Opinion* her Sister, light of Foot, hoodwinkt, and headstrong, yet giddy and perpetually turning. About her play'd her Children, *Noise* and *Impudence, Dullness* and *Vanity, Positiveness, Pedantry*, and *Ill-Manners.* The Goddess herself had Claws like a Cat: Her Head, and Ears, and Voice, resembled those of an *Ass;* Her Teeth fallen out before; Her Eyes turned inward, as if she lookt only upon herself: Her Diet was the overflowing of her own *Gall:* Her *Spleen* was so large, as to stand prominent like a Dug of the first Rate, nor wanted Excrescencies in form of Teats, at which a Crew of ugly Monsters were greedily sucking; and, what is wonderful to conceive, the bulk of Spleen encreased faster than the Sucking could diminish it. *Goddess,* said *Momus, can you sit idly here, while our devout Worshippers, the* Moderns, *are this Minute entring into a cruel Battel, and, perhaps, now lying under the Swords of their Enemies; Who then hereafter, will ever sacrifice, or build Altars to our Divinities? Haste therefore to the* British Isle, *and, if possible, prevent their Destruction, while I make Factions among the Gods, and gain them over to our Party.*

MOMUS having thus delivered himself, staid not for an answer, but left the Goddess to her own Resentment; Up she rose in a Rage, and as it is the Form upon such Occasions, began a Soliloquy. *'Tis I* (said she) *who give Wisdom to Infants and Idiots; By Me, Children grow wiser than their Parents. By Me,* Beaux *become Politicians; and* School-boys, *Judges of Philosophy. By Me, Sophisters debate, and conclude upon the Depths of Knowledge; and Coffee-house Wits instinct by Me, can correct an Author's Style, and display his minutest Errors, without understanding a Syllable of his Matter or his Language. By Me, Striplings spend their Judgment, as they do their Estate, before it comes into their Hands. 'Tis I, who have deposed Wit and Knowledge from their Empire over* Poetry, *and advanced my self in their stead. And shall a few* upstart Antients *dare to oppose me?—But, come, my aged Parents, and you, my Children dear, and thou my beauteous Sister; let us ascend my Chariot, and haste to assist our devout* Moderns, *who are now sacrificing to us a* Hecatomb, *as I perceive by that grateful Smell, which from thence reaches my Nostrils.*

The Goddess and her Train having mounted the Chariot, which was drawn by *tame Geese,* flew over infinite Regions, shedding her Influence in due Places, till at length, she arrived at her beloved Island of *Britain;* but in hovering over its *Metropolis,* what Blessings did she not let fall upon her Seminaries of *Gresham* and *Covent-Garden?* And now she reach'd the fatal Plain of St. *James*'s Library, at what time the two Armies were upon the Point to engage; where entring with all her Caravan, unseen, and landing upon a Case of Shelves, now desart, but once inhabited by a colony of *Virtuoso's,* she staid a while to observe the Posture of both Armies.

But here, the tender Cares of a Mother began to fill her Thoughts, and move in her Breast. For, at the Head of a Troop of *Modern Bow-men,* she cast her Eyes upon her Son *Wotton;* to whom the Fates had assigned a very short Thead. *Wotton,* a young Hero, whom an unknown Father of mortal Race, begot by stollen Embraces with this Goddess. He was the Darling of his Mother, above all her Children, and she resolved to go and comfort Him. But first, according to the good old Custom of Deities, she cast about to change her Shape; for fear the Divinity of her Countenance might dazzle his Mortal Sight, and over-charge the rest of his Senses. She therefore gathered up her Person into an *Octavo* Compass: Her Body grew white and arid, and split in pieces with Driness; the thick turned into Pastboard, and the thin into Paper, upon which, her Parents and Children, artfully strowed a Black Juice, or Decoction of Gall and Soot, in Form of Letters; her Head, and Voice, and Spleen, kept their primitive Form, and that which before, was a Cover of Skin, did still continue so. In which Guise, she march'd on towards the *Moderns,* undistinguishable in Shape and Dress from the *Divine Bentley, Wotton*'s dearest Friend. *Brave Wotton,* said the Goddess, *Why do our Troops stand idle here, to spend their present Vigour and Opportunity of the Day? Away, let us haste to the Generals, and advise to give the Onset immediately.* Having spoke thus, she took the ugliest of her Monsters, full glutted from her Spleen, and flung it invisibly into his Mouth; which flying strait up into his Head, squeez'd out his Eye-Balls, gave him a distorted Look, and half over-turned his Brain. Then she privately ordered two of her beloved Children, *Dulness* and *Ill-Manners,* closely to attend his Person in all Encounters. Having thus accoutred him, she vanished in a Mist, and the *Hero* perceived it was the Goddess, his Mother.

THE destined Hour of Fate, being now arrived, the Fight began; whereof, before I dare adventure to make a particular Description, I must, after the Example of other Authors, petition for a hundred Tongues, and Mouths, and Hands, and Pens; which would all be too little to perform so immense a Work. Say, Goddess, that presidest over History; who it was that first advanced in the Field of Battle. *Paracelsus,* at the Head of his *Dragoons,* observing *Galen* in the adverse Wing, darted his Javelin with a mighty Force, which the brave *Antient* received upon his Shield, the Point breaking in the second fold. * * * * * * * * * * * *

* * * * * * * * * * * * * * * * * * * *Hic pauca desunt.*[14]

* * * They bore the wounded *Aga,* on their Shields to his Chariot * * * * * * * * * * * * * * * * * * *

* * * * * * * * * * * * * * * * * * *Desunt nonnulla.*

* * * * * * * * * * * * * * * * * * * *

THEN *Aristotle* observing *Bacon* advance with a furious Mien, drew his Bow to the Head, and left fly his Arrow, which mist the valiant *Modern,* and went hizzing over his Head; but *Des-Cartes* it hit; The Steel Point quickly found a *Defect* in his *Head-piece;* it pierced the Leather and the Past-board, and went in at his right Eye. The Torture of the Pain, whirled the valiant

Bow-man round, till Death, like a Star of superior Influence, drew him into his own *Vortex.* * * * * * * * * * * * * *

* * * * * * * * * * * * * * * * * *   *Ingens hiatus hic*
                                                          in MS.
* * * * * * * * * * * * * * * * *

when *Homer* appeared at the Head of the Cavalry, mounted on a furious Horse, with Difficulty managed by the Rider himself, but which no other Mortal durst approach; He rode among the Enemies Ranks, and bore down all before him. Say, Goddess, whom he slew first, and whom he slew last. First, *Gondibert* advanced against Him, clad in heavy Armour, and mounted on a staid sober Gelding, not so famed for his Speed as his Docility in kneeling, whenever his Rider would mount or alight. He had made a Vow to *Pallas,* that he would never leave the Field, till he had spoiled *Homer** of his Armour; Madman, who had never once   * *Vid. Homer.* seen the Wearer, nor understood his Strength. Him *Homer* overthrew, Horse and Man to the Ground, there to be trampled and choak'd in the Dirt. Then, with a long Spear, he slew *Denham,* a stout *Modern,* who from his Father's† side, derived his Lineage from *Apollo,* but his Mother was of Mortal Race. He fell, and bit the Earth. The Celestial Part *Apollo* took, and made it a Star, but the Terrestrial lay wallowing upon the Ground. Then *Homer* slew *Wesley* with a kick of his Horse's heel; He took *Perrault* by mighty Force out of his Saddle, then hurl'd him at *Fontenelle,* with the same Blow dashing out both their Brains.

ON the left Wing of the Horse, *Virgil* appeared in shining Armor, compleatly fitted to his Body; He was mounted on a dapple grey Steed,[15] the slowness of whose Pace, was an Effect of the highest Mettle and Vigour. He cast his Eye on the adverse Wing, with a desire to find an Object worthy of his valour, when behold, upon a sorrel Gelding[16] of a monstrous Size, appear'd a Foe, issuing from among the thickest of the Enemy's Squadrons; But his Speed was less than his Noise; for his Horse, old and lean, spent the Dregs of his Strength in a high Trot, which tho' it made slow advances, yet caused a loud Clashing of his Armor, terrible to hear. The two Cavaliers had now approached within the Throw of a Lance, when the Stranger desired a Parley, and lifting up the Vizard of his Helmet, a Face hardly appeared from within, which after a pause, was known for that of the renowned *Dryden.* The brave *Antient* suddenly started, as one possess'd with Surprize and Disappointment together: For, the Hel-

† *Sir* John Denham*'s Poems are very Unequal, extremely Good, and very Indifferent, so that his Detractors said, he was not the real Author of* Coopers-Hill.

met was nine times too large for the Head, which appeared situate far in the hinder Part, even like the Lady in a Lobster,[17] or like a Mouse under a Canopy of State, or like a shriveled Beau from within the Pent-house of a modern Perewig: And the voice was suited to the Visage, sounding weak and remote. *Dryden* in a long Harangue soothed up the good *Antient*, called him *Father,* and by a large deduction of Genealogies, made it plainly appear, that they were nearly related. Then he humbly proposed an Exchange of Armor, as a lasting Mark of Hospitality between them. *Virgil* consented (for the Goddess *Diffidence* came unseen, and cast a Mist before his Eyes) tho' his was of Gold, and cost a hundred Beeves,[18] the others but of rusty Iron. However, this glittering Armor became the *Moderns* yet worse than his Own. Then, they agreed to exchange Horses; but when it came to the Trial, *Dryden* was afraid, and utterly unable to mount. * * * * * * * * * * * * * * * * * *Alter hiatus in*
* * * * * * * * * * * * * * * * * * * *MS.*
* * * * * * * * * * * * * * * *

* * * * * * * *Lucan* appeared upon a fiery Horse, of admirable Shape, but head-strong, bearing the Rider where he list, over the Field; he made a mighty Slaughter among the Enemy's Horse; which Destruction to stop, *Blackmore,* a famous *Modern* (but one of the *Mercenaries*) strenuously opposed himself; and darted a Javelin, with a strong Hand, which falling short of its Mark, struck deep in the Earth. Then *Lucan* threw a Lance; but *Æsculapius* came unseen, and turn'd off the Point. *Brave* Modern, *said* Lucan, *I perceive some God protects you, for never did my Arm so deceive me before; But, what Mortal can contend with a God? Therefore, let us Fight no longer, but present Gifts to each other. Lucan* then bestowed the *Modern a Pair of Spurs,* and *Blackmore* gave *Lucan* a Bridle. *Pauca desunt.*
* * * * * * * * * * * * * * * * * * *
* *

Creech; But, the Goddess *Dulness* took a Cloud, formed into the Shape of *Horace,* armed and mounted, and placed it in a flying Posture before Him. Glad was the Cavalier, to begin a Combat with a flying Foe, and pursued the Image, threatning loud; till at last it led him to the peaceful Bower of his Father *Ogleby,* by whom he was disarmed, and assigned to his Repose.

THEN *Pindar* slew ——, and ——, and *Oldham,* and —— and *Afra* the *Amazon* light of foot; Never advancing in a direct Line, but wheeling with incredible Agility and Force, he made a terrible Slaughter among the Enemies *Light-Horse.* Him, when *Cowley* observed, his generous Heart burnt within him, and he advanced against the fierce *Antient*, imitating his Ad-

dress, and Pace, and Career, as well as the Vigour of his Horse, and his own Skill would allow. When the two Cavaliers had approach'd within the Length of three Javelins; first *Cowley* threw a Lance, which miss'd *Pindar,* and passing into the Enemy's Ranks, fell ineffectual to the Ground. Then *Pindar* darted a Javelin, so large and weighty, that scarce a dozen *Cavaliers,* as *Cavaliers* are in our degenerate Days, could raise it from the Ground: yet he threw it with Ease, and it went by an unerring Hand, singing through the Air; Nor could the *Modern* have avoided present Death, if he had not luckily opposed the Shield that had been given Him by *Venus.* And now both Hero's drew their Swords, but the *Modern* was so aghast and disordered, that he knew not where he was; his Shield dropt from his Hands; thrice he fled, and thrice he could not escape; at last he turned, and lifting up his Hands, in the Posture of a Suppliant, *God-like* Pindar, said he, *spare my Life, and possess my Horse with these Arms; besides the Ransom which my Friends will give, when they hear I am alive, and your Prisoner. Dog,* said Pindar, *Let your Ransom stay with your Friends; But your Carcass shall be left for the* Fowls of the Air, *and the* Beasts of the Field. With that, he raised his Sword, and with a mighty Stroak, cleft the wretched *Modern* in twain, the Sword pursuing the Blow; and one half lay panting on the Ground, to be trod in pieces by the Horses Feet, the other half was born by the frighted Steed thro' the field. This *Venus** took, and wash'd it seven times in *Ambrosia,* then struck it thrice with a Sprig of *Amarant;* upon which, the Leather grew round and soft, the Leaves turned into Feathers, and being gilded before, continued gilded still; so it became a *Dove,* and She harness'd it to her Chariot. *
* * * * * * * * * * * * * * * * * * * *
* * * * * * * * * * * * * * * * * *Hiatus valdè*
* * * * * * * * * * * * * * * * * * *deflendus in MS.*
* * * * * * * * * * * * * * * * * *
* * * * * * * * * * * * * * * * * * * *

DAY being far spent, and the numerous Forces of the *Moderns* half inclining to a Retreat, there issued forth from a Squadron of their *heavy armed Foot,* a Captain, whose Name was *Bentley;* in Person, *The Episode of* the most deformed of all the *Moderns;* Tall, but without Shape *Bentley and* or Comeliness; Large, but without Strength or Proportion. His *Wooton.* Armour was patch'd up of a thousand incoherent Pieces; and the Sound of it, as he march'd, was loud and dry, like that made by the Fall of a Sheet of

---

* *I do not approve the Author's Judgment in this, for I think* Cowley's Pindaricks are much preferable to his Mistress.

Lead, which an *Etesian* Wind[19] blows suddenly down from the Roof of some Steeple. His Helmet was of old rusty Iron, but the Vizard was Brass, which tainted by his Breath, corrupted into Copperas, nor wanted Gall from the same Fountain; so, that whenever provoked by Anger or Labour, an atramentous Quality, of most malignant Nature, was seen to distil from his Lips. In his* right Hand he grasp'd a Flail, and (that he might never be unprovided of an *offensive* Weapon) a Vessel full of *Ordure* in his Left: thus, compleatly arm'd, he advanc'd with a slow and heavy Pace, where the *Modern* Chiefs were holding a Consult upon the Sum of Things; who, as he came onwards, laugh'd to behold his crooked Leg, and hump Shoulder, which his Boot and Armour vainly endeavouring to hide were forced to comply with, and expose. The Generals made use of him for his Talent of Railing; which kept within Government, proved frequently of great Service to their Cause, but at other times did more Mischief than Good; For at the least Touch of Offence, and often without any at all, he would, like a wounded Elephant, convert it against his Leaders. Such, at this Juncture, was the Disposition of *Bentley*, grieved to see the Enemy prevail, and dissatisfied with every Body's Conduct but his own. He humbly gave the *Modern* Generals to understand, that he conceived, with great Submission, they were all a Pack of *Rogues*, and *Fools*, and *Sons of Whores*, and d——mn'd *Cowards*, and *confounded Loggerheads*, and *illiterate Whelps*, and *nonsensical Scoundrels;* That if Himself had been constituted General, those *presumptuous Dogs*, the *Antients*, would long before this, have been beaten out of the Field. *You*, said he, *sit here idle, but, when I, or any other valiant* Modern, *kill an Enemy, you are sure to seize the Spoil. But, I will not march one Foot against the Foe, till you all swear to me, that, whomever I take or kill, his Arms I shall quietly possess. Bentley* having spoke thus, *Scaliger* bestowing him a sower Look; *Miscreant* Prater, said he, *Eloquent only in thine own Eyes, Thou railest without Wit, or Truth, or Discretion. The Malignity of thy Temper perverteth Nature; Thy* Learning *makes thee more* Barbarous, *thy Study of* Humanity, *more* Inhuman; *Thy* Converse *amongst Poets more* groveling, miry, *and* dull. *All Arts of* civilizing *others, render thee* rude *and* untractable; Courts *have taught thee* ill Manners, *and* polite Conversation *has finish'd thee a* Pedant. *Besides, a greater Coward burtheneth not the Army. But never despond, I pass my Word, whatever Spoil thou takest, shall certainly be thy own; though, I hope, that vile Carcass will first become a prey to Kites and Worms.*

Vid. Homer.
de Thersite.

---

* *The Person here spoken of, is famous for letting fly at every Body without Distinction, and using mean and foul Scurrilities.*

BENTLEY durst not reply; but half choaked with Spleen and Rage, withdrew, in full Resolution of performing some great Achievment. With him, for his Aid and Companion, he took his beloved *Wotton;*[20] resolving by Policy or Surprize, to attempt some neglected Quarter of the *Antients* Army. They began their March over Carcasses of their slaughtered Friends; then to the Right of their own Forces: then wheeled Northward, till they came to *Aldrovandus*'s Tomb, which they pass'd on the side of the declining Sun. And now they arrived with Fear towards the Enemy's Out-guards; looking about, if haply, they might spy the Quarters of the Wounded, or some straggling Sleepers, unarm'd and remote from the rest. As when two *Mungrel-Curs,* whom *native Greediness,* and *domestick Want,* provoke, and join in Partnership, though fearful, nightly to invade the Folds of some rich Grazier; They, with Tails depress'd, and lolling Tongues, creep soft and slow; mean while, the conscious *Moon,* now in her *Zenith,* on their guilty Heads, darts perpendicular Rays; Nor dare they bark, though much provok'd at her refulgent Visage, whether seen in Puddle by Reflexion, or in Sphear direct; but one surveys the Region round, while t'other scouts the Plain, if haply, to discover at distance from the Flock, some *Carcass* half devoured, the Refuse of gorged Wolves, or ominous Ravens. So march'd this lovely, loving Pair of Friends, nor with less Fear and Circumspection; when, at distance, they might perceive two shining Suits of Armor, hanging upon an Oak, and the Owners not far off in a profound Sleep. The two Friends drew Lots, and the pursuing of this Adventure, fell to *Bentley;* On he went, and in his Van *Confusion* and *Amaze;* while *Horror* and *Affright* brought up the Rear. As he came near; Behold two Hero's of the *Antients* Army, *Phalaris* and *Æsop,* lay fast asleep: *Bentley* would fain have dispatch'd them both, and stealing close, aimed his Flail at *Phalaris*'s Breast. But, then, the Goddess *Affright* interposing, caught the *Modern* in her icy Arms, and dragg'd him from the Danger she foresaw; For both the dormant Hero's happened to turn at the same Instant, tho' soundly Sleeping, and busy in a Dream. For *Phalaris* was just that Minute dreaming, how a most vile *Poetaster* had lampoon'd him, and how he had got him roaring in his *Bull.*[*][21] And *Æsop* dream'd, that as he and the *Antient Chiefs* were lying on the Ground, a *Wild Ass* broke loose, ran about trampling and kicking, and dunging in their Faces. *Bentley* leaving the two Hero's asleep, seized on both their Armors, and withdrew in quest of his Darling *Wotton.*

HE, in the mean time, had wandred long in search of some Enterprize,

---

[*] *This is according to* Homer, *who tells the Dreams of those who were kill'd in their Sleep.*

till at length, he arrived at a small *Rivulet,* that issued from a Fountain hard by, call'd in the Language of mortal Men, *Helicon.* Here he stopt, and, parch'd with thirst, resolved to allay it in this limpid Stream. Thrice, with profane Hands, he essay'd to raise the Water to his Lips, and thrice it slipt all thro' his Fingers. Then he stoop'd prone on his Breast, but e'er his Mouth had kiss'd the liquid Crystal, *Apollo* came, and, in the Channel, held his *Shield* betwixt the *Modern* and the Fountain, so that he drew up nothing but *Mud.* For, altho' no Fountain on Earth can compare with the Clearness of *Helicon,* yet there lies at Bottom, a thick sediment of *Slime* and *Mud;* For, so *Apollo* begg'd of *Jupiter,* as a Punishment to those who durst attempt to taste it with unhallowed Lips, and for a Lesson to all, not to *draw too deep,* or *far from the Spring.*

AT the Fountain Head, *Wotton* discerned two Hero's; The one he could not distinguish, but the other was soon known for *Temple,* General of the *Allies* to the *Antients.* His Back was turned, and he was employ'd in Drinking large Draughts in his Helmet, from the Fountain, where he had withdrawn himself to rest from the Toils of the War. *Wotton,* observing him, with quaking Knees, and trembling Hands, spoke thus to Himself: *Oh, that I could kill this Destroyer of our Army, what Renown should I purchase among the Chiefs! But to issue out against Him, Man for Man, Shield against Shield, and Launce against Launce; what* Modern *of us dare? For, he fights like a* $\quad$ Vid. Homer *God, and* Pallas *or* Apollo *are ever at his Elbow. But, Oh,* Mother! *if what Fame reports, be true, that I am the Son of so great a Goddess, grant me to Hit* Temple *with this Launce, that the Stroak may send Him to Hell, and that I may return in Safety and Triumph, laden with his Spoils.* The first Part of his Prayer, the Gods granted, at the Intercession of His *Mother* and of *Momus;* but the rest, by a perverse Wind sent from *Fate,* was scattered in the Air. Then *Wotton* grasp'd his Launce, and brandishing it thrice over his head, darted it with all his Might, the *Goddess,* his *Mother,* at the same time, adding Strength to his Arm. Away the Launce went hizzing, and reach'd even to the Belt of the averted *Antient,* upon which, lightly grazing, it fell to the Ground. *Temple* neither felt the Weapon touch him, nor heard it fall; And *Wotton,* might have escaped to his Army, with the Honor of having remitted his Launce against so great a Leader, unrevenged; But, *Apollo* enraged, that a Javelin, flung by the Assistance of so foul a *Goddess,* should pollute his Fountain, put on the shape of ——,[22] and softly came to young *Boyle,* who then accompanied *Temple:* He pointed, first to the Launce, then to the distant *Modern* that flung it, and commanded the young Hero to take immediate Revenge. *Boyle,* clad in a suit of Armor which had been *given him*

by all the Gods, immediately advanced against the trembling Foe, who now fled before him. As a young Lion, in the *Libyan Plains,* or *Araby Desart,* sent by his aged Sire to hunt for Prey, or Health, or Exercise; He scours along, wishing to meet some Tiger from the Mountains, or a furious Boar; If Chance, a *Wild Ass,* with Brayings importune, affronts his Ear, the generous Beast, though loathing to distain his Claws with Blood so vile, yet much provok'd at the offensive Noise; which *Echo,* foolish Nymph, like her *ill-judging Sex,* repeats much louder, and with more Delight than *Philomela's* Song: He vindicates the Honor of the Forest, and hunts the noisy, long-ear'd Animal. So *Wotton* fled, so *Boyle* pursued. But *Wotton* heavy-arm'd, and slow of foot, began to slack his Course; when his Lover *Bentley* appeared, returning laden with the Spoils of the two sleeping *Antients.* Boyle observed him well, and soon discovering the Helmet and Shield of *Phalaris,* his Friend, both which he had lately with his own Hands, new polish'd and gilded; Rage sparkled in His Eyes, and leaving his Pursuit after *Wotton,* he furiously rush'd on against this new Approacher. Fain would he be revenged on both; but both now fled different Ways: And as a Woman in a little House, that gets a painful Livelihood by Spinning;* if chance her *Geese* be scattered o'er the Common, she courses round the Plain from side to side, compelling here and there,
the Straglers to the Flock; They cackle loud, and flutter o'er the   *Vid. Homer*
Champain. So *Boyle* pursued, so fled this Pair of Friends: finding
at length, their Flight was vain, they bravely joyn'd, and drew themselves in *Phalanx.* First, *Bentley* threw a Spear with all his Force, hoping to pierce the Enemy's Breast; But *Pallas* came unseen, and in the Air took off the Point, and clap'd on one of *Lead,* which after a dead Bang against the Enemy's Shield, fell blunted to the Ground. Then *Boyle* observing well his Time, took a Launce of wondrous Length and sharpness; and as this Pair of Friends compacted stood close Side to Side, he wheel'd him to the right, and with unusual Force, darted the Weapon. *Bentley* saw his Fate approach, and flanking down his Arms, close to his Ribs, hoping to save his Body; in went the Point, passing through Arm and Side, nor stopt, or spent its Force, till it had also pierc'd the valiant *Wotton,* who going to sustain his dying Friend, shared his Fate. As, when a skilful Cook has truss'd a Brace of *Woodcocks,* He, with Iron Skewer, pierces the tender Sides of both, their Legs and Wings close pinion'd to their Ribs; So was this pair of Friends

---

* *This is also, after the manner of* Homer; *the Woman's getting a painful Livelihood by Spinning, has nothing to do with the Similitude, nor would be excusable without such an Authority.*

transfix'd; till down they fell, joyn'd in their Lives, joyn'd in their Deaths; so closely joyn'd, that *Charon* would mistake them both for one, and waft them over *Styx* for half his Fare. Farewel, beloved, loving Pair; Few Equals have you left behind: And happy and immortal shall you be, if all my Wit and Eloquence can make you.

AND, now *
* *
* * * * * * * * * * * * *   *Desunt cætera.*

A
DISCOURSE
Concerning the
Mechanical Operation
of the
SPIRIT
in a
LETTER
to a
Friend.
A
FRAGMENT

The Bookseller's Advertisement

The following Discourse came into my Hands perfect and entire. But there being several Things in it, which the present Age would not very well bear, I kept it by me some Years, resolving it should never see the Light. At length, by the Advice and Assistance of a judicious Friend, I retrench'd those Parts that might give most Offence, and have now ventured to publish the Remainder; Concerning the Author, I am wholly ignorant; neither can I conjecture, whether it be the same with That of the two foregoing Pieces, the Original having been sent me at a different Time, and in a different Hand. The learned Reader will better determine; to whose Judgment I entirely submit it.

A Discourse

Concerning the

Mechanical Operation of the

Spirit, &c.

For T.H. *Esquire, at his Chambers in the Academy of the* Beaux Esprits *in* New-Holland.[1]

Sir,

It is now a good while since I have had in my Head something, not only very material, but absolutely necessary to my Health, that the World should be informed in. For, to tell you a Secret, I am able to *contain* it no longer. However, I have been perplexed for some time, to resolve what would be the most proper Form to send it abroad in. To which End, I have three Days been coursing thro' *Westminster-Hall*, and St. *Paul's Church-yard*, and *Fleet-street*, to peruse *Titles;* and, I do not find any which holds so general a Vogue, as that of *A Letter to a Friend:* Nothing is more common than to meet with long Epistles address'd to Persons and Places, where, at first thinking, one would be apt to imagine it not altogether so necessary or Convenient; Such as, *a Neighbour at next Door, a mortal Enemy, a perfect Stranger,* or *a Person of Quality in the Clouds;* and these upon Subjects, in appearance, the least proper for Conveyance by the Post; as, *long Schemes in Philosophy; dark and wonderful Mysteries of State; Laborious Dissertations in Criticism and Philosophy, Advice to Parliaments,* and the like.

Now, Sir, to proceed after the Method in present Wear. (For, let me say what I will to the contrary, I am afraid you will publish this *Letter*, as soon as ever it comes to your Hands;) I desire you will be my Witness to the World,

This Discourse is not altogether equal to the two Former, the best Parts of it being omitted; whether the Bookseller's Account be true, that he durst not print the rest, I know not, nor indeed is it easie to determine whether he may be rely'd on, in any thing he says of this, or the former Treatises, only as to the Time they were writ in, which, however, appears more from the Discourses themselves than his Relation.

how careless and sudden a Scribble it has been; That it was but Yesterday, when You and I began accidentally to fall into Discourse on this Matter: That I was not very well, when we parted: That the Post is in such haste, I have had no manner of Time to digest it into Order, or correct the Style; And if any other Modern Excuses, for Haste and Negligence, shall occur to you in Reading, I beg you to insert them, faithfully promising they shall be thankfully acknowledged.

PRAY, Sir, in your next Letter to the *Iroquois Virtuosi,* do me the Favour to present my humble Service to that illustrious Body, and assure them, I shall send an Account of those *Phænomena,* as soon as we can determine them at *Gresham.*

I have not had a Line from the *Literati* of *Tobinambou,*[2] these three last Ordinaries.

AND now, Sir, having dispatch'd what I had to say of Forms, or of Business, let me intreat, you will suffer me to proceed upon my Subject; and to pardon me, if I make no farther Use of the Epistolary Stile, till I come to conclude.

SECTION I

TIS recorded of *Mahomet,* that upon a Visit he was going to pay in *Paradise,* he had an Offer of several Vehicles to conduct him upwards; as fiery Chariots, wing'd Horses, and celestial Sedans; but he refused them all, and would be born to Heaven upon nothing but his *Ass.* Now, this Inclination of *Mahomet,* as singular as it seems, hath been since taken up by a great Number of devout *Christians;* and doubtless, with very good Reason. For, since That *Arabian* is known to have borrowed a Moiety of his Religious System from the *Christian* Faith; it is but just he should pay Reprisals to such as would Challenge them; wherein the good People of *England,* to do them all Right, have not been backward. For, tho' there is not any other Nation in the World, so plentifully provided with Carriages for that Journey, either as to Safety or Ease; yet there are abundance of us, who will not be satisfied with any other Machine, beside this of *Mahomet.*

FOR my own part, I must confess to bear a very singular Respect to this Animal, by whom I take human Nature to be most admirably held forth in all its Qualities as well as Operations: And therefore, whatever in my small Reading, occurs, concerning this our Fellow-Creature, I do never fail to set it down, by way of Common-place; and when I have occasion to write upon Human Reason, Politicks, Eloquence, or Knowledge; I lay my *Memorandums* before me, and insert them with a wonderful Facility of Application. However, among all the Qualifications, ascribed to this distinguish'd Brute, by Antient or Modern Authors; I cannot remember this Talent, of bearing his Rider to Heaven, has been recorded for a Part of his Character, except in the two Examples mentioned already; Therefore, I conceive the Methods of this Art, to be a Point of useful Knowledge in very few Hands, and which the Learned World would gladly be better informed in. This is what I have undertaken to perform in the following Discourse. For, towards the Operation already mentioned, many peculiar Properties are required, both in the *Rider* and the *Ass;* which I shall endeavour to set in as clear a Light as I can.

BUT, because I am resolved, by all means, to avoid giving Offence to any Party whatever; I will leave off discoursing so closely to the *Letter* as I have hitherto done, and go on for the future by way of Allegory, tho' in such a manner, that the judicious Reader, may without much straining, make his Applications as often as he shall think fit. Therefore, if you please from hence forward, instead of the Term, *Ass,* we shall make use of *Gifted,* or *enlightned Teacher;* And the Word *Rider,* we will exchange for that of *Fanatick Auditory,* or any other Denomination of the like Import. Having settled this weighty Point; the great Subject of Enquiry before us, is to examine, by what Methods this *Teacher* arrives at his *Gifts* or *Spirit,* or *Light;* and by what Intercourse between him and his Assembly, it is cultivated and supported.

IN all my Writings, I have had constant Regard to this great End, not to suit and apply them to particular Occasions and Circumstances of Time, of Place, or of Person; but to calculate them for universal Nature, and Mankind in general. And of such Catholick use, I esteem this present Disquisition: For I do not remember any other Temper of Body, or Quality of Mind, wherein all Nations and Ages of the World have so unanimously agreed, as That of a *Fanatick* Strain, or Tincture of *Enthusiasm;* which improved by certain Persons or Societies of Men, and by them practised upon the rest, has been able to produce Revolutions of the greatest Figure in History; as will soon appear to those who know any thing of *Arabia, Persia, India,* or *China,* of *Morocco* and *Peru:* Farther, it has possessed as great a Power in the Kingdom of Knowledge, where it is hard to assign one Art or Science, which has not annexed to it some *Fanatick* Branch: Such are the *Philosopher's Stone; The Grand Elixer; The Planetary Worlds; The Squaring of the Circle; The Summun bonum;* Utopian *Commonwealths;* with some others of less or subordinate Note; which all serve for nothing else, but to employ or amuse this Grain of *Enthusiasm,* dealt into every Composition.*

* Some Writers hold them for the same, others not.

BUT, if this Plant has found a Root in the Fields of *Empire,* and of *Knowledge,* it has fixt deeper, and spread yet farther upon *Holy Ground.*

Wherein, though it hath pass'd under the general Name of *Enthusiasm*, and perhaps arisen from the same Original, yet hath it produced certain Branches of a very different Nature, however often mistaken for each other. The Word in its universal Acceptation, may be defined, *A lifting up of the Soul or its Faculties above Matter.* This Description will hold good in general; but I am only to understand it, as applied to *Religion;* wherein there are three general Ways of ejaculating the Soul, or transporting it beyond the Sphere of Matter. The first, is the immediate Act of God, and is called, *Prophecy* or *Inspiration.* The second, is the immediate Act of the Devil, and is termed *Possession.* The third, is the Product of natural Causes, the effect of strong Imagination, Spleen, violent Anger, Fear, Grief, Pain, and the like. These three have been abundantly treated on by Authors, and therefore shall not employ my Enquiry. But, the fourth Method of *Religious Enthusiasm,* or launching out the Soul, as it is purely an Effect of Artifice and *Mechanick Operation,* has been sparingly handled, or not at all, by any Writer; because tho' it is an Art of great Antiquity, yet having been confined to few Persons, it long wanted those Advancements and Refinements, which it afterwards met with, since it has grown so Epidemick, and fallen into so many cultivating Hands.

It is therefore upon this *Mechanical Operation of the Spirit,* that I mean to treat, as it is at present performed by our *British Workmen.* I shall deliver to the Reader the Result of many judicious Observations upon the Matter; tracing, as near as I can, the whole Course and Method of this *Trade,* producing parallel Instances, and relating certain Discoveries that have luckily fallen in my way.

I have said, that there is one Branch of *Religious Enthusiasm,* which is purely an Effect of Nature; whereas, the Part I mean to handle, is wholly an Effect of Art, which, however, is inclined to work upon certain Natures and Constitutions, more than others. Besides, there is many an Operation, which in its Original, was purely an Artifice, but through a long Succession of Ages, hath grown to be natural. *Hippocrates,* tells us, that among our Ancestors, the *Scythians,* there was a Nation call'd, *Longheads,** which at first began by a Custom among Midwives and Nurses, of molding, and squeezing, and bracing up the Heads of Infants; by which * *Macrocephali.* means, Nature shut out at one Passage, was forc'd to seek another, and finding room above, shot upwards, in the Form of a Sugar-Loaf; and being diverted that way, for some Generations, at last found it out of her self, needing no Assistance from the Nurse's Hand. This was the Original of the *Scythian Long-heads,* and thus did Custom, from being a second Nature proceed to be a first. To all which, there is something very analogous among Us of this Nation, who are the undoubted Posterity of that refined People. For, in the Age of our Fathers, there arose a Generation of Men in this Island, call'd *Round-heads*,[3] whose Race is now spread over three Kingdoms, yet in its Beginning, was meerly an Operation of Art, produced by a pair of Cizars, a Squeeze of the Face, and a black Cap. These Heads, thus formed into a perfect Sphere in all Assemblies, were most exposed to the view of the Female Sort, which did influence their Conceptions so effectually, that Nature, at last, took the Hint, and did it of her self; so that a *Round-head* has been ever since as familiar a Sight among Us, as a *Long-head* among the *Scythians*.

UPON these Examples, and others easy to produce, I desire the curious Reader to distinguish, First between an Effect grown from *Art* into *Nature*, and one that is natural from its Beginning; Secondly, between an Effect wholly natural, and one which has only a natural Foundation, but where the Superstructure is entirely Artificial. For, the first and the last of these, I understand to come within the Districts of my Subject. And having obtained these allowances, they will serve to remove any objections that may be raised hereafter against what I shall advance.

THE Practitioners of this famous Art, proceed in general upon the following Fundamental; That, *the Corruption of the Senses is the Generation of the Spirit*: Because the *Senses* in Men are so many Avenues to the Fort of *Reason*, which in this Operation is wholly block'd up. All Endeavours must be therefore used, either to divert, bind up, stupify, fluster, and amuse the *Senses*, or else to justle them out of their Stations; and while they are either absent, or otherwise employ'd or engaged in a Civil War against each other, the *Spirit* enters and performs its Part.

NOW, the usual Methods of managing the Senses upon such Conjectures, are what I shall be very particular in delivering, as far as it is lawful for me to do; but having had the Honour to be Initiated into the Mysteries of every Society, I desire to be excused from divulging any Rites, wherein the *Profane* must have no Part.

BUT here, before I can proceed farther, a very dangerous Objection must, if possible, be removed: For, it is positively denied by certain Criticks,[4] that the *Spirit* can by any means be introduced into an Assembly of Modern Saints, the Disparity being so great in many material Circumstances, between the Primitive Way of Inspiration, and that which is practised in the present Age. This they pretend to prove from the second Chapter of the *Acts*,[5] where comparing both, it appears; First, that *the Apostles were gathered together with one accord in one place*; by which is meant, an universal Agreement in Opinion, and Form of Worship; a Harmony (say they) so far from being found between any two Conventicles among Us, that it is in vain to expect it between any two Heads in the same. Secondly, the *Spirit* instructed the Apostles in the Gift of speaking several Languages; a Knowledge so remote from our Dealers in this Art, that they neither understand Propriety of Words, or Phrases in their own. Lastly, (say these Objectors) The Modern Artists do utterly exclude all Approaches of the *Spirit,* and bar up its antient Way of entring, by covering themselves so close, and so industriously a top. For, they will needs have it as a Point clearly gained, that the *Cloven Tongues* never sat upon the Apostles Heads, while their Hats were on.

NOW, the Force of these Objections, seems to consist in the different Acceptation of the Word, *Spirit:* which if it be understood for a supernatural Assistance, approaching from without, the Objectors have Reason, and their Assertions may be allowed; But the *Spirit* we treat of here, proceeding entirely from within, the Argument of these Adversaries is wholly eluded. And upon the same Account, our Modern Artificers, find it an Expedient of absolute Necessity, to cover their Heads as close as they can, in order to prevent Perspiration, than which nothing is observed to be a greater Spender of Mechanick Light, as we may, perhaps, farther shew in convenient Place.

TO proceed therefore upon the *Phænomenon* of *Spiritual Mechanism,* It is here to be noted, that in forming and working up the *Spirit,* the Assembly has a considerable Share, as well as the Preacher; The Method of this *Arcanum,* is as follows. They violently strain their Eye balls inward, half closing the Lids; Then, as they sit, they are in a perpetual Motion of *See-saw,* making long Hums at proper Periods, and continuing the Sound at equal Height, chusing their Time in those Intermissions, while the Preacher is at Ebb. Neither is this Practice, in any part of it, so singular or improbable, as not to be traced in distant Regions, from Reading and Observation. For, first, the *Jauguis,*[*][6] or enlightened Saints of *India,* see all their Visions, by help of an acquired straining and pressure of the Eyes. Secondly, the Art of *See-saw* on a Beam, and swinging by Session upon a Cord, in order to raise artificial Extasies, hath been derived to Us, from our *Scythian*[†] Ancestors, where it is practised at this Day, among the Women. Lastly, the whole Proceeding, as I have here related it, is performed by the Natives of *Ireland,* with a considerable Improvement; And it is granted, that this noble Nation, hath of all others, admitted fewer Corruptions, and degenerated least from the Purity of the Old *Tartars.* Now it is usual for a

* *Bernier, Mem. de Mogol.*

† *Guagnini Hist. Sarmat.*

Knot of *Irish*, Men and Women, to abstract themselves from Matter, bind up all their Senses, grow visionary and spiritual, by Influence of a short Pipe of Tobacco, handed round the Company; each preserving the Smoak in his Mouth, till it comes again to his Turn to take in fresh: At the same Time, there is a Consort of a continued gentle Hum, repeated and renewed by Instinct, as Occasion requires, and they move their Bodies up and down, to a Degree, that sometimes their Heads and Points lie parallel to the Horizon. Mean while, you may observe their Eyes turn'd up in the Posture of one, who endeavours to keep himself awake; by which, and many other Symptoms among them, it manifestly appears, that the Reasoning Faculties are all suspended and superseded, that Imagination hath usurped the Seat, scattering a thousand Deliriums over the Brain. Returning from this Digression, I shall describe the Methods, by which the *Spirit* approaches. The Eyes being disposed according to Art, at first, you can see nothing, but after a short pause, a small glimmering Light begins to appear, and dance before you. Then, by frequently moving your Body up and down, you perceive the Vapors to ascend very fast, till you are perfectly dosed and flustred like one who drinks too much in a Morning. Mean while, the Preacher is also at work; He begins a loud Hum, which pierces you quite thro'; This is immediately returned by the Audience, and you find your self prompted to imitate them, by a meer spontaneous Impulse, without knowing what you do. The *Interstitia* are duly filled up by the Preacher, to prevent too long a Pause, under which the *Spirit* would soon faint and grow languid.

THIS is all I am allowed to discover about the Progress of the *Spirit*, with relation to that part, which is born by the *Assembly*; But in the Methods of the Preacher, to which I now proceed, I shall be more large and particular.

SECTION II

You will read it very gravely remarked in the Books of those illustrious and right eloquent Pen-men, the Modern Travellers; that the fundamental Difference in Point of Religion, between the wild *Indians* and Us, lies in this; that We worship *God*, and they worship the *Devil*. But, there are certain Criticks, who will by no means admit of this Distinction; rather believing, that all Nations whatsoever, adore the *true God*, because, they seem to intend their Devotions to some invisible Power, of greatest *Goodness* and *Ability* to help them, which perhaps will take in the brightest

Attributes ascribed to the Divinity. Others, again, inform us, that those Idolaters adore two *Principles;* the *Principle* of *Good,* and That of *Evil:* Which indeed, I am apt to look upon as the most Universal Notion, that Mankind, by the meer Light of Nature, ever entertained of Things Invisible. How this Idea hath been managed by the *Indians* and Us, and with what Advantage to the Understandings of either, may well deserve to be examined. To me, the difference appears little more than this, That They are put oftener upon their Knees by their *Fears,* and We by our *Desires;* That the former set them a *Praying,* and Us a *Cursing.* What I applaud them for, is their Discretion, in limiting their Devotions and their Deities to their several Districts, nor ever suffering the Liturgy of the *white* God, to cross or interfere with that of the *Black.* Not so with Us, who pretending by the Lines and Measures of our Reason, to extend the Dominion of one invisible Power, and contract that of the other, have discovered a gross Ignorance in the Natures of Good and Evil, and most horribly confounded the Frontiers of both. After Men have lifted up the Throne of their Divinity to the *Cœlum Empyræum,* adorned him with all such Qualities and Accomplishments, as themselves seem most to value and possess: After they have sunk their *Principle* of *Evil* to the lowest Center, bound him with Chains, loaded him with Curses, furnish'd him with viler Dispositions than any *Rake-hell* of the Town, accoutred him with Tail, and Horns, and huge Claws, and Sawcer Eyes; I laugh aloud, to see these Reasoners, at the same time, engaged in wise Dispute, about certain Walks and Purlieus, whether they are in the Verge of God or the Devil, seriously debating, whether such and such Influences come into Mens Minds, from above or below, or whether certain Passions and Affections are guided by the Evil Spirit or the Good.

> *Dum fas atque nefas exiguo fine libidinum*
> *Discernunt avidi*——[7]

Thus do Men establish a Fellowship of *Christ* with *Belial,* and such is the Analogy they make between *cloven Tongues,* and *cloven Feet.* Of the like Nature is the Disquisition before us: It hath continued these hundred Years an even Debate, whether the Deportment and the Cant of our *English* Enthusiastick Preachers, were *Possession,* or *Inspiration,* and a World of Argument has been drained on either side, perhaps, to little Purpose. For, I think, it is in *Life* as in *Tragedy,* where, it is held, a Conviction of great Defect, both in Order and Invention, to interpose the Assistance of preternatural Power, without an absolute and last Necessity. However, it is a Sketch of Human Vanity, for every Individual, to imagine the whole Universe is interess'd in his meanest Concern. If he hath got cleanly over a Kennel, some Angel, unseen, descended on purpose to help him by the Hand; if he hath knockt his Head against a Post, it was the Devil, for his Sins, let loose from Hell, on purpose to buffet him. Who, that sees a little paultry Mortal, droning, and dreaming, and drivelling to a Multitude, can think it agreeable to common good Sense, that either Heaven or Hell should be put to the Trouble of Influence or Inspection upon what he is about? Therefore, I am resolved immediately, to weed this Error out of Mankind, by making it clear, that this Mystery, of venting spiritual Gifts is nothing but a *Trade*, acquired by as much Instruction, and mastered by equal Practice and Application as others are. This will best appear, by describing and deducing the whole Process of the Operation, as variously as it hath fallen under my Knowledge or Experience. * * *

* * * * * * * * * * * * * * * * * * * *
* * * * * * * * * * * * * * * * * * * *
* * * * * * * * * * * * * * * * * * * *
* * * * * * * * * * * * * * * * * * * *
* * * * * * * * * * * * * * * * * * * *
* * * * * * * * * * * * * * * * * * * *
* * * * * * * * * * * * * * * * * * * *
* * * * * * * * * * * * * * * * * * * *

Here the whole Scheme of spiritual Mechanism was deduced and explained, with an Appearance of great reading and observation; but it was thought neither safe nor Convenient to Print it.

HERE it may not be amiss, to add a few Words upon the laudable Practice of wearing *quilted Caps;* which is not a Matter of meer Custom, Humor, or Fashion, as some would pretend, but an Institution of great Sagacity and Use; these, when moistned with Sweat, stop all Perspiration, and by reverberating the Heat, prevent the Spirit from evaporating any way, but at the Mouth; even as a skilful Housewife, that covers her Still with a wet Clout, for the same Reason, and finds the same Effect. For, it is the Opinion of Choice *Virtuosi*, that the Brain is only a Crowd of little Animals, but with Teeth and Claws extremely sharp, and therefore, cling together in the Contexture we behold, like the Picture of *Hobbes's Leviathan*,[8] or like Bees in perpendicular swarm upon a Tree, or like a Carrion corrupted into Vermin, still preserving the Shape and Figure of the Mother Animal. That all Invention is formed by the Morsure[9] of two or more of these Animals, upon certain capillary Nerves, which proceed from thence, whereof three Branches spread into the Tongue, and two into the right Hand. They hold also, that these Animals are of a Constitution extremely cold; that their Food is the Air we attract, their Excrement Phlegm; and that what we vulgarly call Rheums, and Colds, and Distillations, is nothing else but an Epidemical Looseness, to which that little Commonwealth is very subject, from the Climate it lyes under. Farther, that nothing less than a violent Heat, can disentangle these Creatures from their hamated[10] Station of Life, or give them Vigor and Humor, to imprint the Marks of their little Teeth. That if the Morsure be Hexagonal, it produces Poetry; the Circular gives Eloquence; If the Bite hath been Conical, the Person, whose Nerve is so affected, shall be disposed to write upon the Politicks; and so of the rest.

I shall now Discourse briefly, by what kind of Practices the Voice is best governed, towards the Composition and Improvement of the *Spirit;* for, without a competent Skill in tuning and toning each Word, and Sylla-ble, and Letter, to their due Cadence, the whole Operation is incompleat, misses entirely of its effect on the Hearers, and puts the Workman himself to continual Pains for new Supplies, without Success. For, it is to be understood, that in the Language of the Spirit, *Cant* and *Droning* supply the Place of *Sense* and *Reason,* in the Language of Men: Because, in Spiri-tual Harangues, the Disposition of the Words according to the Art of Grammar, hath not the least Use, but the Skill and Influence wholly lye in the Choice and Cadence of the Syllables; Even as a discreet *Composer,* who in setting a Song, changes the Words and Order so often, that he is forced to make it *Nonsense,* before he can make it *Musick.* For this Reason, it hath been held by some, that the Art of Canting is ever in greatest Perfection, when managed by *Ignorance:* Which is thought to be enigmatically meant by *Plutarch,* when he tells us, that the best Musical Instruments were made from the Bones of an *Ass.* And the profounder Criticks upon that Passage, are of Opinion, the Word in its genuine Signification, means no other than a *Jaw-bone:* tho' some rather think it to have been the *Os sacrum;* but in so nice a Case, I shall not take upon me to decide: The Curious are at Lib-erty, to *pick* from it whatever they please.

THE first Ingredient, towards the Art of Canting, is a competent Share of *Inward Light;*[11] that is to say, a large Memory, plentifully fraught with Theological Polysyllables, and mysterious Texts from holy Writ, applied and digested by those Methods, and Mechanical Operations already re-lated: the Bearers of this *Light,* resembling *Lanthorns,* compact of Leaves from old *Geneva* Bibles; Which Invention, Sir *Humphry Edwyn,*[12] during his Mayoralty, of happy Memory, highly approved and advanced; affirming, the Scripture to be now fulfilled, where it says, *Thy Word is a Lanthorn to my Feet, and a Light to my Paths.*

Now, the Art of *Canting* consists in skilfully adapting the Voice, to whatever Words the Spirit delivers, that each may strike the Ears of the Audience, with its most significant Cadence. The Force, or Energy of this Eloquence, is not to be found, as among antient Orators, in the Disposition of Words to a Sentence, or the turning of long Periods; but agreeable to the Modern Refinements in Musick, is taken up wholly in dwelling, and dilating upon Syllables and Letters. Thus it is frequent for a single *Vowel* to draw Sighs from a Multitude; and for a whole Assembly of Saints to sob to the Musick of one solitary *Liquid.* But these are Trifles; when even Sounds inarticulate are observed to produce as forcible Effects. A Master Work-man shall *blow his Nose so powerfully,* as to pierce the Hearts of his People, who are disposed to receive the *Excrements* of his Brain with the same Reverence, as the *Issue* of it. Hawking, Spitting, and Belching, the Defects of other Mens Rhetorick, are the Flowers, and Figures, and Ornaments of his. For, the *Spirit* being the same in all, it is of no Import through what Vehicle it is convey'd.

It is a Point of too much Difficulty, to draw the Principles of this famous Art within the Compass of certain adequate Rules. However, perhaps, I may one day, oblige the World with my Critical Essay upon the Art of *Canting, Philosophically, Physically, and Musically considered.*

But, among all Improvements of the *Spirit,* wherein the Voice hath born a Part, there is none to be compared with That of *conveying the Sound thro' the Nose,* which under the Denomination of *Snuffling,** hath passed with so great Applause in the World. The Originals of this Institution are very dark; but having been initiated into the Mystery of it, and Leave being given me to publish it to the World, I shall deliver as direct a Relation as I can.

This Art, like many other famous Inventions, owed its Birth, or at least, Improvement and Perfection, to an Effect of Chance, but was established upon solid Reasons, and hath flourished in this Island ever since, with great Lustre. All agree, that it first appeared upon the Decay and Discouragement of *Bag-pipes,* which having long suffered under the Mortal Hatred of the *Brethren,* tottered for a Time, and at last fell with *Monarchy.* The Story is thus related.

---

* *The* Snuffling *of Men, who have lost their Noses by lewd Courses, is said to have given Rise to that Tone, which our Dissenters did too much Affect.* W. Wooton.

As yet, *Snuffling* was not; when the following Adventure happened to a *Banbury Saint*. Upon a certain Day, while he was far engaged among the Tabernacles of the *Wicked*, he felt the Outward Man put into odd Commotions, and strangely prick'd forward by the Inward: An Effect very usual among the Modern Inspired. For, some think, that the *Spirit* is apt to feed on the *Flesh*, like hungry Wines upon raw Beef. Others rather believe, there is a perpetual Game at *Leap-Frog* between both; and, sometimes, the *Flesh* is uppermost, and sometimes the *Spirit*; adding, that the former, while it is in the State of a *Rider*, wears huge *Rippon* Spurs, and when it comes to the Turn of being *Bearer*, is wonderfully headstrong, and hard-mouth'd. However it came about, the *Saint* felt his *Vessel* full *extended* in every Part (a very natural Effect of strong *Inspiration*;) and the Place and Time falling out so unluckily, that he could not have the Convenience of Evacuating upwards, by Repetition, Prayer, or Lecture; he was forced to open an inferior Vent. In short, he wrestled with the Flesh so long, that he at length subdued it, coming off with honourable Wounds, all *before*. The Surgeon had now cured the Parts, primarily affected; but the Disease driven from its Post, flew up into his Head; And, as a skilful General, valiantly attack'd in his Trenches, and beaten from the Field, by flying Marches withdraws to the Capital City, breaking down the Bridges to prevent Pursuit; So the Disease repell'd from its first Station, fled before the *Rod* of *Hermes*, to the upper Region, there fortifying it self; but, finding the Foe making Attacks at the *Nose*, broke down the *Bridge*, and retir'd to the *Head*-Quarters. Now, the Naturalists observe, that there is in human Noses, an *Idiosyncrasy*, by Virtue of which, the more the Passage is obstructed, the more our Speech delights to go through, as the Musick of a Flagelate is made by the *Stops*. By this Method, the Twang of the Nose, becomes perfectly to resemble the *Snuffle* of a Bag-pipe, and is found to be equally attractive of *British* Ears; whereof the Saint had sudden Experience, by practising his new Faculty with wonderful Success in the Operation of the *Spirit*: For, in a short Time, no Doctrine pass'd for Sound and Orthodox, unless it were delivered thro' the Nose. Strait, every Pastor copy'd after this Original; and those, who could not otherwise arrive to a Perfection, spirited by a noble Zeal, made use of the same Experiment to acquire it. So that, I think, it may be truly affirmed, the *Saints* owe their Empire to the *Snuffling* of one *Animal*, as *Darius* did his, to the *Neighing* of another; and both Stratagems were performed by the same Art; for we read, how the *Persian Beast** acquired his Faculty, by *covering a Mare* the Day   * *Herodot.* Before.

I should now have done, if I were not convinced, that whatever I have yet advanced upon this Subject, is liable to great Exception. For, allowing all I have said to be true, it may still be justly objected, that there is in the Commonwealth of *artificial Enthusiasm,* some real Foundation for Art to work upon in the Temper and Complexion of Individuals, which other Mortals seem to want. Observe, but the Gesture, the Motion, and the Countenance, of some choice Professors, tho' in their most familiar Actions, you will find them of a different Race from the rest of human Creatures. Remark your commonest Pretender to a Light *within,* how dark, and dirty, and gloomy he is *without;* As Lanthorns, which the more Light they bear in their Bodies, cast out so much the more Soot, and Smoak, and fuliginous Matter to adhere to the Sides. Listen, but to their ordinary Talk, and look on the Mouth that delivers it; you will imagine you are hearing some antient Oracle, and your Understanding will be *equally* informed. Upon these, and the like Reasons, certain Objectors pretend to put it beyond all Doubt, that there must be a sort of preternatural *Spirit,* possessing the Heads of the Modern Saints; And some will have it to be the *Heat* of Zeal, working upon the *Dregs* of Ignorance, as other *Spirits* are produced from *Lees,* by the Force of Fire. Some again think, that when our earthly Tabernacles are disordered and desolate, shaken and out of Repair; the *Spirit* delights to dwell within them, as Houses are said to be haunted, when they are forsaken and gone to Decay.

To set this Matter in as fair a Light as possible; I shall here, very briefly, deduce the History of *Fanaticism,*[13] from the most early Ages to the present. And if we are able to fix upon any one material or fundamental Point, wherein the chief Professors have universally agreed, I think we may reasonably lay hold on That, and assign it for the great Seed or Principle of the *Spirit.*

THE most early Traces we meet with, of *Fanaticks,* in antient Story, are among the *Ægyptians,* who instituted those Rites, known in *Greece* by the Names of *Orgya, Panegyres,* and *Dionysia,* whether introduced there by *Orpheus* or *Melampus,* we shall not dispute at present, nor in all likelihood, at any time for the future. These Feasts were celebrated to the Honor of *Osyris,* whom the *Grecians* called *Dionysius,* and is the same with *Bacchus:* Which has betray'd some superficial Readers to imagine, that the whole Business was nothing more than a Set of roaring, scouring Companions, overcharg'd with Wine; but this is a scandalous Mistake foisted on the World, by a sort of Modern Authors, who have too *literal* an Understanding; and, because Antiquity is to be

Diod. Sic. L. 1. Plut. de Iside & Osyride.

traced *backwards,* do therefore, like *Jews,* begin their Books at the wrong End, as if Learning were a sort of *Conjuring.* These are the Men, who pretend to understand a Book, by scouting thro' the *Index,* as if a Traveller should go about to describe a *Palace,* when he had seen nothing but the *Privy;* or like certain Fortune-tellers in *Northern America,* who have a Way of reading a Man's Destiny, by peeping in his *Breech.* For, at the Time of instituting these Mysteries,* there was not one Vine in all *Egypt,* the Natives drinking nothing but *Ale;* which Liquor seems to have been far more antient than Wine, and has the Honor of owing its Invention and Progress, not only to the *Egyptian Osyris,*† but to the *Grecian Bacchus,* who in their famous Expedition, carried the Receipt[14] of it along with them, and gave it to the Nations they visited or subdued. Besides, *Bacchus* himself, was very seldom, or never Drunk: For, it is recorded of him, that he was the first Inventor‡ of the *Mitre,* which he wore continually on his Head (as the whole Company of *Bacchanals* did) to prevent Vapors and the Head-ach, after hard Drinking. And for this Reason (say some) the *Scarlet Whore,* when she makes the Kings of the Earth drunk with her Cup of Abomination, is always sober her self, tho' she never balks the Glass in her Turn, being, it seems, kept upon her Legs by the Virtue of her *Triple Mitre.* Now, these Feasts were instituted in imitation of the famous Expedition *Osyris* made thro' the World, and of the Company that attended him, whereof the *Bacchanalian* Ceremonies were so many Types and Symbols. From which Account, it is manifest, that the Fanatick Rites of these *Bacchanals,* cannot be imputed to Intoxications by Wine, but must needs have had a deeper Foundation. What this was, we may gather large Hints from certain Circumstances in the Course of their Mysteries. For, in the first Place, there was in their Processions, an entire *Mixture and Confusion of Sexes;* they affected to ramble about Hills and Desarts: Their Garlands were of *Ivy* and *Vine,* Emblems of Cleaving and Clinging; or of *Fir,* the Parent of *Turpentine.* It is added, that they imitated *Satyrs,* were attended by *Goats,* and rode upon *Asses,* all Companions of great Skill and Practice in Affairs of Gallantry. They bore for their Ensigns, certain curious Figures, perch'd upon long Poles, made into the Shape and Size of the *Virga genitalis,* with its *Appurtenances,* which were so many Shadows and Emblems of the whole Mystery, as well as Trophies set up by the Female Conquerors. Lastly, in a certain Town of *Attica,* the whole Solemnity stript§ of all its Types, was performed in *puris*

* *Herod.* L.2.

† *Diod. Sic.* L. 1. & 3.

‡ *Id.* L. 4.

See the Particulars in Diod. Sic. *L.* 1. & 3.

§ *Dionysia Brauronia.*

naturalibus, the Votaries, not flying in Coveys, but sorted into Couples. The same may be farther conjectured from the Death of *Orpheus,* one of the Institutors of these Mysteries, who was torn in Pieces by Women, because he refused to *communicate his Orgyes** to them; which others explained, by telling us, he had *castrated* himself upon Grief, for the Loss of his Wife.

* *Vid. Photium in excerptis è Conone.*

OMITTING many others of less Note, the next *Fanaticks* we meet with, of any Eminence, were the numerous Sects of *Hereticks* appearing in the five first Centuries of the *Christian Æra,* from *Simon Magus* and his Followers, to those of *Eutyches.* I have collected their Systems from infinite Reading, and comparing them with those of their Successors in the several Ages since, I find there are certain Bounds set even to the Irregularities of Human Thought, and those a great deal narrower than is commonly apprehended. For, as they all frequently interfere, even in their wildest Ravings; So there is one fundamental Point, wherein they are sure to meet, as Lines in a Center, and that is the *Community of Women:* Great were their Sollicitudes in this Matter, and they never fail'd of certain Articles in their Schemes of Worship, on purpose to establish it.

THE last *Fanaticks* of Note, were those which started up in *Germany,* a little after the *Reformation* of *Luther;* Springing, as *Mushrooms* do at the *End of a Harvest;* Such were *John* of *Leyden, David George, Adam Neuster,* and many others; whose Visions and Revelations, always terminated in *leading about half a dozen Sisters, apiece,* and making That Practice a fundamental Part of their System. For, Human Life is a continual Navigation, and, if we expect our *Vessels* to pass with Safety, thro' the Waves and Tempests of this fluctuating World, it is necessary to make a good Provision of the *Flesh,* as Sea-men lay in store of *Beef* for a long Voyage.

NOW from this brief Survey of some Principal Sects, among the *Fanaticks,* in all Ages (having omitted the *Mahometans* and others, who might also help to confirm the Argument I am about) to which I might add several among our selves, such as the *Family of Love, Sweet Singers of Israel,* and the like: And from reflecting upon that fundamental Point in their Doctrines, about *Women,* wherein they have so unanimously agreed; I am apt to imagine, that the Seed or Principle, which has ever put Men upon *Visions* in Things *Invisible,* is of a Corporeal Nature: For the profounder Chymists inform us, that the Strongest *Spirits* may be extracted from *Human Flesh.* Besides, the Spinal Marrow, being nothing else but a Continuation of the Brain, must needs create a very free Communication between the Superior Faculties and those below: And thus the *Thorn in the Flesh* serves for a

Spur to the *Spirit*. I think, it is agreed among Physicians, that nothing affects the Head so much, as a tentiginous Humor, repelled and elated to the upper Region, found by daily practice, to run frequently up into Madness. A very eminent Member of the Faculty, assured me, that when the *Quakers* first appeared, he seldom was without some Female Patients among them, for the *furor*———.[15] Persons of a visionary Devotion, either Men or Women, are in their Complexion, of all others, the most amorous: For, *Zeal* is frequently kindled from the same Spark with other Fires, and from inflaming Brotherly Love, will proceed to raise That of a Gallant. I f we inspect into the usual Process of modern Courtship, we shall find it to consist in a devout Turn of the Eyes, called *Ogling*; an artificial Form of Canting and Whining by rote, every Interval, for want of other Matter, made up with a Shrug, or a Hum, a Sigh or a Groan; The Style compact of insignificant Words, Incoherences and Repetition. These, I take, to be the most accomplish'd Rules of Address to a Mistress; and where are these performed with more Dexterity, than by the *Saints*? Nay, to bring this Argument yet closer, I have been informed by certain Sanguine Brethren of the first Class, that in the Height and *Orgasmus* of their Spiritual exercise it has been frequent with them * * * * * ; immediately after which, they found the *Spirit* to relax and flag of a sudden with the Nerves, and they were forced to hasten to a Conclusion. This may be farther Strengthened, by observing, with Wonder, how unaccountably all Females are attracted by Visionary or Enthusiastick Preachers, tho' never so comtemptible in their *outward Men*; which is usually supposed to be done upon Considerations, purely Spiritual, without any carnal Regards at all. But I have Reason to think, the *Sex* hath certain Characteristicks, by which they form a truer Judgment of Human Abilities and Performings, than we our selves can possibly do of each other. Let That be as it will, thus much is certain, that however Spiritual Intrigues begin, they generally conclude like all others; they may branch upwards toward Heaven, but the Root is in the Earth. Too intense a Contemplation is not the Business of Flesh and Blood; it must by the necessary Course of Things, in a little Time, let go its Hold, and fall into *Matter*. Lovers, for the sake of Celestial Converse, are but another sort of *Platonicks*, who pretend to see Stars and Heaven in Ladies Eyes, and to look or think no lower; but the same *Pit* is provided for both; and they seem a perfect Moral to the Story of that Philosopher, who, while his Thoughts and Eyes were fixed upon the *Constellations*, found himself seduced by his *lower Parts* into a *Ditch*.[16]

I had somewhat more to say upon this Part of the Subject; but the Post is just going, which forces me in great Haste to conclude,

Sir,

Yours, &c.

*Pray, burn this
Letter as soon
as it comes to
your Hands.*

II

EARLY WRITINGS
ON RELIGION

THE

SENTIMENTS

OF A

CHURCH-OF-ENGLAND MAN,

WITH RESPECT TO

RELIGION *AND* GOVERNMENT

Written in the YEAR 1708.

Whoever hath examined the Conduct and Proceedings of both *Parties*[1] for some Years past, whether in or out of Power, cannot well conceive it possible to go far towards the Extreams of either, without offering some Violence to his Integrity or Understanding. A wise and a good Man may indeed be sometimes induced to comply with a Number, whose Opinion he generally approves, although it be perhaps against his own. But this Liberty should be made use of upon very few Occasions, and those of small Importance, and then only with a View of bringing over his own Side another Time to something of greater and more publick Moment. But, to sacrifice the Innocency of a Friend, the Good of our Country, or our own Conscience, to the Humour, or Passion, or Interest, of a Party; plainly shews that either our Heads or our Hearts are not as they should be: Yet this very Practice is the fundamental Law of each Faction among us; as may be obvious to any who will impartially, and without Engagement, be at the Pains to examine their Actions; which, however, is not so easy a Task: For, it seems a Principle in human Nature, to incline one Way more than another, even in Matters where we are wholly unconcerned. And it is a common Observation, that in reading a History of Facts done a Thousand Years ago; or standing by a Play among those who are perfect Strangers to us; we are apt to find our Hopes and Wishes engaged on a sudden in favour of one Side more than another. No Wonder then, that we are all so ready to interest our selves in the Course of publick Affairs; where the most inconsiderable have some *real* Share, and by the wonderful Importance which every Man is of to himself, a very great *imaginary* one.

And indeed when the two Parties that divide the whole Commonwealth, come once to a Rupture, without any Hopes left of forming a Third with better Principles, to ballance the others; it seems every Man's Duty to chuse one of the two Sides, although he cannot entirely approve of either; and all Pretences to Neutrality are justly exploded[2] by both; being too stale and obvious; only intending the Safety and Ease of a few Individuals, while the Publick is embroiled. This was the Opinion and Practice of the latter *Cato*,[3] whom I esteem to have been the wisest and best of all the *Romans*. But before Things proceed to open Violence, the truest Service a private Man may hope to do his Country, is by unbiassing his Mind as much as possible, and then endeavouring to moderate between the Rival Powers; which must needs be owned a fair Proceeding with the World: Because, it is of all others the least consistent with the common Design of making a Fortune by the *Merit* of an *Opinion.*

I HAVE gone as far as I am able in qualifying my self to be such a Moderator: I believe, I am no *Bigot* in Religion; and I am sure, I am none in Government. I converse in full Freedom with many considerable Men of both Parties; and if not in equal Number, it is purely accidental and personal, as happening to be near the Court, and to have made Acquaintance there, more under one Ministry than another. Then, I am not under the Necessity of declaring my self by the Prospect of an Employment. And lastly, if all this be not sufficient, I industriously conceal my Name; which wholly exempts me from any Hopes and Fears in delivering my Opinion.

IN consequence of this free Use of my Reason, I cannot possibly think so well or so ill of either Party, as they would endeavour to persuade the World of each other, and of themselves. For Instance; I do not charge it upon the Body of the *Whigs,* or the *Tories,* that their several Principles lead them to introduce Presbytery, and the Religion of the Church of *Rome,* or a Commonwealth and arbitrary Power. For, why should any Party be accused of a Principle which they solemnly disown and protest against? But, to this they have a mutual Answer ready; they both assure us, that their Adversaries are not to be believed; that they disown their Principles out of Fear; which are manifest enough when we examine their Practices. To prove this, they will produce Instances, on one Side, either of avowed Presbyterians, or Persons of libertine and atheistical Tenets; and on the other, of professed Papists, or such as are openly in the Interest of the abdicated Family.[4] Now, it is very natural for all subordinate Sects and Denominations in a State, to side with some general Party, and to chuse that which they find to agree with themselves in some general Principle. Thus at the *Restoration,*[5] the Presbyterians, Anabaptists, Independants, and other Sects, did all with very good Reason unite and solder up their several Schemes to join against the *Church;* who, without regard to their Distinctions, treated them all as equal Adversaries. Thus, our present Dissenters do very naturally close in with the Whigs, who profess *Moderation,*[6] declare they abhor all Thoughts of *Persecution,* and think it hard, that those who differ only in a few *Ceremonies* and *Speculations,* should be denied the Privilege and Profit of Serving their Country in the highest Employments of State. Thus, the Atheists, Libertines, Despisers of Religion and Revelation in general; that is to say, all those who usually pass under the Name of *Free-Thinkers,* do properly joyn with the same Body; because they likewise preach up *Moderation,* and are not so over nice to distinguish between an unlimited Liberty of Conscience, and an unlimited Freedom of Opinion. Then, on the other Side, the profest Firmness of the *Tories* for Episcopacy, as an Apostolical Institution: Their Aversion from those Sects who lie under the Reproach of having once destroyed their Constitution, and who they imagine, by too indiscreet a Zeal for Reformation, have defaced the primitive Model of the Church: Next, their Veneration for Monarchical Government in the common Course of Succession, and their Hatred to Republican Schemes. These, I say, are Principles which not only the nonjuring Zealots profess, but even Papists themselves fall readily in with. And every Extreme here mentioned, flings a general Scandal upon the whole Body it pretends to adhere to.

BUT surely no Man whatsoever ought in Justice or good Manners to be charged with Principles he actually disowns, unless his Practices do openly, and without the least Room for Doubt, contradict his Profession: Not upon small Surmises, or because he has the Misfortune to have ill Men sometimes agree with him in a few general Sentiments. However, although the Extreams of *Whig* and *Tory* seem with little Justice to have drawn Religion into their Controversies, wherein they have small Concern; yet they both have borrowed one leading Principle from the Abuse of it; which is, to have built their several Systems of political Faith, not upon Enquiries after Truth, but upon Opposition to each other, upon injurious Appellations, charging their Adversaries with horrid Opinions, and then reproaching them for the want of Charity; *Et neuter falso.*[7]

IN order to remove these Prejudices, I have thought nothing could be more effectual than to describe the Sentiments of a *Church-of-*England *Man* with respect to *Religion* and *Government.* This I shall endeavour to do in such a Manner as may be liable to the least Objection from either Party; and which I am confident would be assented to by great Numbers in both, if they were not misled to those mutual Misrepresentations, by such Motives as they would be ashamed to own.

I SHALL begin with *Religion.*

AND here, although it makes an odd Sound, yet it is necessary to say, that whoever professeth himself a Member of the Church of *England,* ought to believe a God, and his Providence, together with revealed Religion, and the Divinity of *Christ.* For beside those many Thousands, who (to speak in the Phrase of Divines) do practically deny all this by the Immorality of their Lives; there is no small Number, who in their Conversation and Writings directly or by consequence endeavour to overthrow it: Yet all these place themselves in the List of the National Church; although at the same Time (as it is highly reasonable) they are great Sticklers for Liberty of Conscience.

To enter upon Particulars: A *Church-of-*England *Man* hath a true Veneration for the Scheme established among us of Ecclesiastical Government; and although he will not determine whether Episcopacy be of Divine Right, he is sure it is most agreeable to primitive Institution; fittest, of all others for preserving Order and Purity, and under its present Regulations, best calculated for our Civil State: He should therefore think the Abolishment of that Order among us, would prove a mighty Scandal, and Corruption to our Faith, and manifestly dangerous to our Monarchy; nay, he would defend it by Arms against all the Powers on Earth, except our own Legislature; in which Case, he would submit as to a general Calamity, a Dearth, or a Pestilence.

As to Rites and Ceremonies, and Forms of Prayer, he allows there might be some useful Alterations; and more, which in the Prospect of uniting Christians might be very supportable, as Things declared in their own Nature indifferent; to which he therefore would readily comply, if the *Clergy,* or, (although this be not so fair a Method) if the *Legislature* should direct: Yet, at the same Time, he cannot altogether blame the former for their Unwillingness to consent to any Alteration; which, beside the Trouble, and perhaps Disgrace, would certainly never produce the good Effects intended by it. The only Condition that could make it prudent, and just for the Clergy to comply in altering the Ceremonial, or any other indifferent Part, would be a firm Resolution in the Legislature, to interpose by some strict and effectual Laws, to prevent the rising and spreading of new Sects, how plausible soever, for the future; else there must never be an End: And it would be to act like a Man, who should pull down and change the Ornaments of his House, in Compliance to every one who was disposed to find fault as he passed by; which, besides the perpetual Trouble and Expence, would very much damage, and perhaps in Time destroy the Building. Sects, in a State, seem only tolerated, with any Reason, because they are already spread; and because it would not be agreeable with so mild a Government, or so pure a Religion as ours, to use violent Methods against great Numbers of *mistaken* People, while they do not manifestly endanger the Constitution of either. But the greatest Advocates for general Liberty of Conscience, will allow that they ought to be checked in their Beginnings, if they will allow them to be an Evil at all; or, which is the same Thing, if they will only grant, it were better for the Peace of the State, that there should be none. But, while the Clergy consider the natural Temper of Mankind in general, or of our own Country in particular; what Assurances can they have, that any Compliances they shall make, will remove the Evil of Dissention, while the Liberty still continues of professing whatever new Opinions we please? Or, how can it be imagined, that the Body of Dissenting Teachers, who must be all undone by such a Revolution, will not cast about for some new Objections to withhold their Flocks, and draw in fresh Proselytes by some further Innovations or Refinements?

UPON these Reasons, He is for tolerating such different Forms in religious Worship, as are already admitted; but, by no Means, for leaving it in the Power of those who are tolerated, to advance their own Models upon the Ruin of what is already established; which it is natural for all Sects to desire, and which they cannot justify by any consistent Principles, if they do not endeavour; and yet, which they cannot succeed in, without the utmost Danger to the publick Peace.

TO prevent these Inconveniences, He thinks it highly just, that all Rewards of Trust, Profit, or Dignity, which the State leaves in the Disposal of the Administration, should be given only to those, whose Principles direct them to preserve the Constitution in all its Parts. In the late Affair of *Occasional Conformity*,[8] the general Argument of those who were against it, was not, to deny it an Evil in it self, but that the Remedy proposed was violent, untimely, and improper; which is the Bishop of *Salisbury*'s* Opinion, in the Speech he made and published against the Bill:[9] But, however just their Fears, or Complaints might have been upon that Score, he thinks it a little too gross and precipitate to employ their Writers already, in Arguments for repealing the *Sacramental Test*,[10] upon no wiser a Maxim, than that no Man should, on the Account of Conscience, be deprived the Liberty of serving his Country; a Topick, which may be equally applied to admit *Papists, Atheists, Mahometans, Heathens,* and *Jews.* If the Church wants Members of its own, to employ in the Service of the Publick; or be so unhappily contrived, as to exclude from its Communion, such Persons who are likeliest to have great Abilities; it is time it should be altered, and reduced into some more perfect, or, at least, more popular Form: But, in the mean while, it is not altogether improbable, that when those, who dislike

* *Dr.* Burnet.

the Constitution, are so very zealous in their Offers for the Service of their Country, they are not wholly unmindful of their Party, or of themselves.

THE *Dutch*, whose Practice is so often quoted to prove and celebrate the great Advantages of a general Liberty of Conscience, have yet a National Religion, professed by all who bear Office among them: But why should they be a Precedent for us, either in Religion or Government? Our Country differs from theirs, as well in Situation, Soil, and Productions of Nature, as in the Genius and Complexion of Inhabitants. They are a Commonwealth, founded on a sudden, by a desperate Attempt in a desperate Condition, not formed or digested into a regular System, by mature Thought and Reason, but huddled up under the Pressure of sudden Exigences; calculated for no long Duration, and hitherto subsisting by Accident in the Midst of contending Powers, who cannot *yet* agree about sharing it amongst them. These Difficulties do, indeed, preserve them from any great Corruptions, which their crazy Constitution would extreamly subject them to in a long Peace. That Confluence of People, in a persecuting Age, to a Place of Refuge nearest at Hand, put them upon the Necessity of Trade, to which they wisely gave all Ease and Encouragement: And, if we could think fit to imitate them in this last Particular, there would need no more to invite Foreigners among us; who seem to think no farther, than how to secure their Property and Conscience, without projecting any Share in that Government which gives them Protection; or calling it *Persecution,* if it be denied them. But I speak it for the Honour of our Administration; that although our Sects are not so numerous as those in *Holland;* which I presume is not our *Fault;* and I wish may not be our *Misfortune;* we much excel them, and all *Christendom* besides, in our Indulgence to tender Consciences. One single Compliance with the National Form of receiving the Sacrament, is all we require to qualify any Sectary among us for the greatest Employments in the State; after which, he is at Liberty to rejoin his own Assemblies for the rest of his Life.* Besides, I will suppose any of the numerous Sects in *Holland,* to have so far prevailed as to have raised a Civil War, destroyed their Government and Religion, and put their *Administrators* to Death; after which, I will suppose the People to have recovered all again, and to have settled on their old Foundation: Then I would put a Query; whether that Sect, which was the unhappy Instrument of all this Confusion, could reasonably expect to

---

* *When this was written, there was no Law against Occasional Conformity.*

be entrusted for the future with the greatest Employments; or, indeed, to be hardly tolerated among them?

TO go on with the Sentiments of a *Church-of*-England *Man:* He does not see how that mighty Passion for the Church, which some Men pretend, can well consist with those Indignities, and that Contempt they bestow on the Persons of the Clergy. It is a strange Mark whereby to distinguish *High-Church* Men, that they are such, who imagine the Clergy can never be too *low.* He thinks the Maxim these Gentlemen are so fond of; that they are for an *humble* Clergy, is a very good one: And so is He; and for an humble Laity too; since Humility is a Virtue that perhaps equally befits and adorns every Station of Life.

BUT then, if the Scribblers on the other Side freely speak the Sentiments of their Party; a Divine of the Church of *England* cannot look for much better Quarter from thence. You shall observe nothing more frequent in their weekly Papers, than a way of affecting to confound the Terms of *Clergy* and *High-Church;* of applying both indifferently, and then loading the latter with all the Calumny they can invent. They will tell you they honour a Clergyman; but talk, at the same Time, as if there were not Three in the Kingdom, who could fall in with their Definition. After the like Manner, they insult the *Universities,* as poisoned Fountains, and Corrupters of Youth.

NOW, it seems clear to me, that the *Whigs* might easily have procured, and maintained a Majority among the Clergy, and perhaps in the Universities, if they had not too much encouraged, or connived at this Intemperance of Speech, and Virulence of Pen, in the worst and most prostitute of their Party: Among whom there hath been, for some Years past, such a perpetual Clamour against the Ambition, the implacable Temper, and the Covetousness of the *Priesthood:* Such a Cant of *High-Church,* and *Persecution,* and being *Priest-ridden;* so many Reproaches about *narrow Principles,* or *Terms of Communion:* Then such scandalous Reflections on the Universities, for infecting the Youth of the Nation with arbitrary and *Jacobite*[11] Principles; that it was natural for those, who had the Care of Religion and Education, to apprehend some general Design of altering the Constitution of both. And all this was the more extraordinary, because it could not easily be forgot, that whatever Opposition was made to the Usurpations of King *James,* proceeded altogether from the Church of *England,* and chiefly from the *Clergy,* and one of the Universities.[12] For, if it were of any Use to recall Matters of Fact, what is more notorious than that Prince's applying himself first to the Church of *England;* and upon their Refusal to fall in with his Measures, making the like Advances to the *Dissenters* of all Kinds, who readily and almost universally complied with him; affecting, in their numerous Addresses and Pamphlets, the Style of *Our Brethren the Roman Catholicks;* whose Interests they put on the same Foot with their own: And some of *Cromwell*'s Officers took Posts in the Army raised against the Prince of *Orange*. These Proceedings of theirs, they can only extenuate by urging the Provocations they had met from the Church in King *Charles*'s Reign; which, although perhaps excuseable upon the Score of human Infirmity, are not, by any Means, a Plea of Merit, equal to the Constancy and Sufferings of the Bishops and Clergy; or of the Head and Fellows of *Magdalen* College; that furnished the Prince of *Orange*'s Declaration[13] with such powerful Arguments, to justify and promote the Revolution.

THEREFORE a *Church-of-*England *Man* abhors the Humour of the Age, in delighting to fling Scandals upon the Clergy in general; which, besides the Disgrace to the Reformation, and to Religion it self, casts an Ignominy upon the Kingdom, that it doth not deserve. We have no better Materials to compound the Priesthood of, than the Mass of Mankind, which, corrupted as it is, those who receive Orders, must have some Vices to leave behind them, when they enter into the Church; and if a few do still adhere, it is no wonder, but rather a great one that they are no worse. Therefore He cannot think *Ambition,* or *Love of Power,* more justly laid to their Charge, than to other Men; because, that would be to make Religion it self, or at least the best Constitution of Church-Government, answerable for the Errors and Depravity of human Nature.

WITHIN these last two Hundred Years, all Sorts of Temporal Power have been wrested from the Clergy, and much of their Ecclesiastick: The Reason, or Justice of which Proceeding, I shall not examine; but that the Remedies were a little too violent, with respect to their *Possessions,* the Legislature hath lately confessed, by the Remission of their *first Fruits.*[14] Neither do the common Libellers deny this; who in their Invectives only tax the Church with an unsatiable Desire of Power and Wealth, (equally common to all Bodies of Men as well as Individuals) but thank God, that the Laws have deprived them of both. However, it is worth observing the Justice of Parties: The Sects among us are apt to complain, and think it hard Usage to be reproached now, after Fifty Years, for overturning the State, for the Murder of a King, and the Indignity of an Usurpation; yet these very Men, and their Partisans, are continually reproaching the Clergy, and laying to their Charge the Pride, the Avarice, the Luxury, the Ignorance, and Superstition of *Popish* Times, for a Thousand Years past.

HE thinks it a Scandal to Government, that such an unlimited Liberty should be allowed of publishing Books against those Doctrines in Religion, wherein all Christians have agreed; much more to connive at such Tracts as reject all Revelation, and, by their Consequences, often deny the very Being of a God. Surely it is not a sufficient Atonement for the Writers, that they profess much Loyalty to the present Government, and sprinkle, up and down, some Arguments in Favour of the *Dissenters;* that they dispute, as strenuously as they can, for Liberty of Conscience, and inveigh largely against all Ecclesiasticks, under the Name of *High-Church;* and, in short, under the Shelter of some popular Principles in Politicks and Religion, undermine the Foundations of all Piety and Virtue.

As He doth not reckon every *Schism* of that damnable Nature, which some would represent; so He is very far from closing with the new Opinion of those, who would make it no Crime at all; and argue at a wild Rate, that God Almighty is delighted with the Variety of Faith and Worship, as he is with the Varieties of Nature. To such Absurdities are Men carried by the Affectation of *Free-thinking,* and *removing the Prejudices of Education;* under which Head, they have, for some Time, begun to list *Morality* and *Religion.* It is certain, that before the *Rebellion* in 1642, although the Number of *Puritans* (as they were then called) were as great as it is with us; and although they affected to follow Pastors of that Denomination, yet those Pastors had Episcopal Ordination, possessed Preferments in the Church, and were sometimes promoted to Bishopricks themselves. But a Breach, in the general Form of Worship, was, in those Days, reckoned so dangerous and sinful in it self, and so offensive to *Roman Catholicks* at home and abroad; that it was too unpopular to be attempted: Neither, I believe, was the Expedient then found out, of maintaining separate Pastors out of private Purses.

WHEN a *Schism* is once spread in a Nation, there grows, at length, a Dispute which are the Schismaticks. Without entering on the Arguments, used by both Sides among us, to fix the Guilt on each other; it is certain, that in the Sense of the Law, the *Schism* lies on that Side which opposeth it self to the Religion of the State. I leave it among *Divines* to dilate upon the Danger of *Schism,* as a Spiritual Evil; but I would consider it only as a Temporal one. And I think it clear, that any great Separation from the established Worship, although to a new one that is more pure and perfect, may be an Occasion of endangering the publick Peace; because, it will compose a Body always in Reserve, prepared to follow any discontented Heads, upon the plausible Pretexts of advancing *true Religion,* and oppos-

ing Error, Superstition, or Idolatry. For this Reason, *Plato* lays it down as a Maxim, that *Men ought to worship the Gods, according to the Laws of the Country;* and he introduceth *Socrates,* in his last Discourse, utterly disowning the Crime laid to his Charge, of *teaching new Divinities,* or Methods of Worship. Thus the poor *Hugonots* of *France,* were engaged in a Civil War, by the specious Pretences of some who, under the Guise of Religion, sacrificed so many Thousand Lives to their own Ambition, and Revenge. Thus was the whole Body of *Puritans* in *England,* drawn to be the Instruments, or Abettors of all Manner of Villany, by the Artifices of a *few Men,* whose Designs,* from the first, were levelled to destroy the Constitution, both of Religion and Government. And thus, even in *Holland* it self, where it is pretended that the Variety of *Lord *Clarendon's* Hist.
Sects live so amicably together, and in such perfect Obedience to the Magistrate; it is notorious, how a turbulent Party joining with the *Arminians,* did, in the Memory of our Fathers, attempt to destroy the Liberty of that Republick. So that, upon the whole, where *Sects* are tolerated in a State, it is fit they should enjoy a full Liberty of Conscience, and every other Privilege of free-born Subjects, *to which no Power is annexed.* And to preserve their Obedience upon all Emergencies, a Government cannot give them too much Ease, nor trust them with too little *Power.*

THE *Clergy* are usually charged with a *persecuting Spirit,* which they are said to discover by an implacable Hatred against all *Dissenters;* and this appears to be more unreasonable, because they suffer less in their Interests by a *Toleration,* than any of the *Conforming Laity:* For, while the *Church* remains in its present Form, no *Dissenter* can possibly have any Share in its Dignities, Revenues, or Power; whereas, by once receiving the Sacrament, he is rendered capable of the highest Employments in the State. And it is very possible, that a narrow Education, together with a Mixture of human Infirmity, may help to beget, among some of the *Clergy in Possession,* such an Aversion and Contempt for all *Innovators,* as *Physicians* are apt to have for *Empiricks,*[15] or *Lawyers* for *Pettifoggers,* or *Merchants* for *Pedlars.* But, since the Number of Sectaries doth not concern the Clergy, either in Point of Interest, or Conscience, (it being an Evil not in their Power to remedy) it is more fair and reasonable to suppose, their Dislike proceeds from the Dangers they apprehend to the Peace of the Commonwealth; in the Ruin whereof, they must expect to be the first and greatest Sufferers.

To conclude this Section; it must be observed, that there is a very good Word, which hath of late suffered much by both Parties; I mean MODERA-TION; which the one Side very justly disowns, and the other as unjustly pretends to. Beside what passeth every Day in Conversation; any Man who reads the Papers published by Mr. *Lesly*,[16] and others of his Stamp, must needs conclude, that if this Author could make the Nation see his Adversaries, under the Colours he paints them in; we had nothing else to do, but rise as one Man, and destroy such Wretches from the Face of the Earth.[17] On the other Side, how shall we excuse the Advocates for *Moderation;* among whom, I could appeal to an Hundred Papers of universal Approbation, by the Cause they were writ for, which lay such Principles to the whole Body of the *Tories,* as, if they were true, and believed; our next Business should, in Prudence, be to erect Gibbets in every Parish, and hang them out of the Way. But, I suppose it is presumed, the common People understand *Raillery,* or at least *Rhetorick;* and will not take *Hyperboles* in too literal a Sense;[18] which, however, in some Junctures might prove a desperate Experiment. And this is *Moderation,* in the *modern* Sense of the Word; to which, speaking impartially, the Bigots of both Parties are *equally* entituled.

SECTION II

THE SENTIMENTS OF A CHURCH-OF-ENGLAND MAN, WITH RESPECT TO GOVERNMENT

We look upon it as a very just Reproach, although we cannot agree where to fix it; that there should be so much Violence and Hatred in religious Matters, among Men who agree in all Fundamentals, and only differ in some Ceremonies; or, at most, meer speculative Points. Yet is not this frequently the Case between contending Parties in a State? For Instance; do not the Generality of *Whigs* and *Tories* among us, profess to agree in the same *Fundamentals;* their Loyalty to the Queen, their Abjuration of the *Pretender,* the Settlement of the Crown in the *Protestant* Line; and a *Revolution Principle?* Their Affection to the Church Established, with Toleration of *Dissenters?* Nay, sometimes they go farther, and pass over into each other's Principles; the *Whigs* become great Asserters of the Prerogative; and the *Tories,* of the People's Liberty; these crying down almost the whole Set of Bishops, and those defending them; so that the Differences fairly stated, would be much of a Sort with those in Religion among us; and amount to little more than, *who should take Place,* or *go in and out first,* or *kiss the Queen's Hand;* and what are these but a few *Court Ceremonies?* or *who should be in the Ministry?* And what is that to the Body of the Nation, but a meer *specula-*

tive Point? Yet I think it must be allowed, that no religious Sects ever carried their mutual Aversions to greater Heights, than our State Parties have done; who, the more to enflame their Passions, have mixed Religious and Civil Animosities together; borrowing one of their Appellations from the Church, with the Addition of *High* and *Low;* how little soever their Disputes relate to the Term, as it is generally understood.

I NOW proceed to deliver the Sentiments of a *Church-of*-England *Man,* with respect to Government.

HE doth not think the Church of *England* so narrowly calculated, that it cannot fall in with any regular Species of Government; nor does he think any one regular Species of Government, more acceptable to God than another. The three generally received in the *Schools,* have all of them their several Perfections, and are subject to their several Depravations: However, few States are ruined by any Defect in their Institution, but generally by the Corruption of Manners; against which, the best Institution is no long Security, and without which, a very ill one may subsist and flourish: Whereof there are two pregnant Instances now in *Europe.* The first is the *Aristocracy* of *Venice;* which, founded upon the wisest Maxims, and digested by a great Length of Time, hath, in our Age, admitted so many Abuses, through the Degeneracy of the Nobles, that the Period of its Duration seems to approach. The other is the United Republicks of the *States General;* where a Vein of Temperance, Industry, Parsimony, and a publick Spirit, running through the whole Body of the People, hath preserved an infant Commonwealth of an untimely Birth and sickly Constitution, for above an Hundred Years, through so many Dangers and Difficulties, as a much more healthy one could never have struggled against, without those Advantages.

WHERE Security of Person and Property are preserved by Laws, which none but the *Whole* can repeal, there the great Ends of Government are provided for, whether the Administration be in the Hands of *One,* or of *Many.* Where any one *Person,* or *Body* of Men, who do not represent the *Whole,* seize into their Hands the Power in the last Resort; there is properly no longer a Government, but what *Aristotle,* and his Followers, call the *Abuse* and *Corruption* of one. This Distinction excludes arbitrary Power, in whatever Numbers; which, notwithstanding all that *Hobbes, Filmer,*[19] and others have said to its Advantage, I look upon as a greater Evil than *Anarchy* it self; as much as a *Savage* is in a happier State of Life, than a *Slave* at the Oar.

IT is reckoned ill Manners, as well as unreasonable, for Men to quarrel upon Difference in Opinion; because, that is usually supposed to be a Thing, which no Man can help in himself: But this I do not conceive to be an universal infallible Maxim, except in those Cases where the Question is pretty equally disputed among the Learned and the Wise: Where it is otherwise, a Man of tolerable Reason, some Experience, and willing to be instructed, may apprehend he is got into a wrong Opinion, although the whole Course of his Mind, and Inclination, would persuade him to believe it true: He may be convinced that he is in an Error, although he doth not see where it lies; by the bad Effects of it in the common Conduct of his Life; and by observing those Persons, for whose Wisdom, and Goodness he hath the greatest Deference, to be of a contrary Sentiment. According to *Hobbes*'s Comparison of *Reasoning* with *casting up Accounts;* whoever finds a Mistake in the *Sum total,* must allow himself out; although, after repeated Tryals, he may not see in which Article he hath misreckoned. I will instance, in one Opinion, which I look upon every Man obliged in Conscience to quit, or in Prudence to conceal; I mean, that whoever argues in Defence of absolute Power in a single Person, although he offers the old Plausible Plea, that *it is his Opinion, which he cannot help, unless he be convinced,* ought, in all free States, to be treated as the common Enemy of Mankind. Yet this is laid as a heavy Charge upon the *Clergy* of the two Reigns before the *Revolution;* who, under the Terms of *Passive Obedience,* and *Non-Resistance,* are said to have preached up the unlimited Power of the Prince, because they found it a Doctrine that pleased the Court, and made Way for their Preferment. And I believe, there may be Truth enough in this Accusation, to convince us, that human Frailty will too often interpose it self among Persons of the holiest Function. However, it may be offered in Excuse for the Clergy, that in the best Societies there are some ill Members, which a corrupted Court and Ministry will industriously find out, and introduce. Besides, it is manifest that the greater Number of those, who held and preached this Doctrine, were misguided by equivocal Terms, and by perfect Ignorance in the Principles of Government, which they had not made any Part of their Study. The Question originally put, and as I remember to have heard it disputed in publick Schools, was this; *Whether under any Pretence whatsoever, it may be lawful to resist the supreme Magistrate,* which was held in the Negative; and this is certainly the right Opinion. But many of the Clergy and other learned Men, deceived by a dubious Expression, mistook the *Object* to which *Passive Obedience* was due. By the *Supreme Magistrate* is properly understood the Legislative Power, which in all Government must be absolute and unlimited. But the Word *Magistrate* seeming to denote a *single Person,* and to express the *Executive* Power; it came to pass, that the Obedience due to the *Legislature* was, for want of knowing or considering this easy Distinction, misapplied to the *Administration.* Neither is it any Wonder, that the Clergy, or other well-meaning People should often fall into this Error, which deceived *Hobbes* himself so far, as to be the Foundation of all the political Mistakes in his Book;[20] where he perpetually confounds the *Executive* with the *Legislative* Power; though all well-instituted States have ever placed them in different Hands; as may be obvious to those who know any thing of *Athens, Sparta, Thebes,* and other Republicks of *Greece;* as well as the greater ones of *Carthage* and *Rome.*

BESIDES, it is to be considered, that when these Doctrines began to be preached among us, the Kingdom had not quite worn out the Memory of that horrid *Rebellion,* under the Consequences of which it had groaned almost twenty Years. And a *weak Prince,* in Conjunction with a Succession of most prostitute Ministers, began again to dispose the People to new Attempts; which it was, no doubt, the Clergy's Duty to endeavour to prevent; if some of them had not for want of Knowledge in Temporal Affairs; and others perhaps from a worse Principle, proceeded upon a Topick, that strictly followed, would enslave all Mankind.

AMONG other Theological Arguments made use of in those Times, in praise of Monarchy, and Justification of absolute Obedience to a Prince, there seemed to be one of a singular Nature: It was urged, that *Heaven* was governed by a *Monarch,* who had none to controul[21] his Power, but was absolutely obeyed: Then it followed, That earthly Governments were the more perfect, the nearer they imitated the Government in Heaven. All which I look upon as the strongest Argument against *despotick* Power that ever was offered; since no Reason can possibly be assigned, why it is best for the World that God Almighty hath such a Power, which doth not directly prove that no Mortal Man should ever have the like.

BUT although a *Church-of*-England *Man* thinks every Species of Government equally *lawful;* he doth not think them equally *expedient;* or for every Country indifferently. There may be something in the Climate, naturally disposing Men towards one Sort of Obedience; as it is manifest all over *Asia,* where we never read of any Commonwealth, except some small ones on the *Western* Coasts, established by the *Greeks.* There may be a great deal in the Situation of a Country, and in the present *Genius* of the People. It hath been observed, that the temperate Climates usually run into moderate Governments, and the Extreames into despotick Power. It is a Remark of *Hobbes,* that the Youth of *England* are corrupted in their

Principles of Government, by reading the Authors of *Greece* and *Rome*, who writ under Commonwealths. But it might have been more fairly offered for the Honour of Liberty, that while the rest of the known World was over-run with the Arbitrary Government of single Persons; *Arts* and *Sciences* took their Rise, and flourished only in those few small Territories where the People were *free*. And although *Learning* may continue after *Liberty* is lost, as it did in *Rome*, for a while upon the Foundations laid under the Commonwealth, and the particular Patronage of some Emperors; yet it hardly ever began under a *Tyranny* in any Nation: Because *Slavery* is of all Things the greatest Clog and Obstacle to *Speculation*. And indeed, Arbitrary Power is but the first natural Step from *Anarchy* or the *Savage Life*; the adjusting *Power* and *Freedom* being an Effect and Consequence of maturer Thinking: And this is no where so duly regulated as in a limited Monarchy: Because I believe it may pass for a Maxim in State, that *the Administration cannot be placed in too few Hands, nor the Legislature in too many*. Now in this material Point, the Constitution of the *English* Government far exceeds all others at this Time on the Earth; to which the present Establishment of the *Church* doth so happily agree, that I think, whoever is an Enemy to *either*, must of necessity be so to *both*.

HE thinks, as our Monarchy is constituted, an Hereditary Right is much to be preferred before *Election*. Because, the Government here, especially by some late Amendments, is so regularly disposed in all its Parts, that it almost executes it self. And therefore, upon the Death of a Prince among us, the Administration goes on without any Rub, or Interruption. For the same Reasons, we have less to apprehend from the *Weakness*, or *Fury* of our Monarchs, who have such wise Councils to guide the first, and Laws to restrain the other. And therefore, this Hereditary Right should be kept so sacred, as never to break the Succession, unless where the preserving it may endanger the Constitution; which is not from any intrinsick Merit, or unalienable Right in a *particular Family*; but to avoid the Consequences that usually attend the Ambition of Competitors, to which elective Kingdoms are exposed; and which is the only Obstacle to hinder them from arriving at the greatest Perfection that Government can possibly reach. Hence appears the Absurdity of that Distinction between a King *de facto*,[22] and one *de jure*,[23] with respect to us: For every *limited* Monarch is a King *de jure*, because he governs by the Consent of the *Whole*; which is Authority sufficient to abolish all precedent Right. If a King come in by *Conquest*, he is no longer a *limited* Monarch: If he afterwards consent to Limitations, he becomes immediately King *de jure*, for the same Reason.

THE great Advocates for *Succession,* who affirm it ought not to be violated upon any Regard, or Consideration whatsoever, do insist much upon one Argument, that seems to carry but little Weight. They would have it, that a *Crown* is a Prince's Birth-right, and ought, at least, to be as well secured to him, and his Posterity, as the Inheritance of any private Man: In short, that he has the same Title to his Kingdom, which every Individual hath to his Property. Now, the Consequence of this Doctrine must be, that as a Man may find several Ways to waste, mispend, or abuse his Patrimony, without being answerable to the Laws; so a King may, in like Manner, do what he will with *his own;* that is, he may squander and misapply his Revenues, and even alienate the Crown, without being called to an Account by his Subjects. They allow such a Prince to be guilty, indeed, of much Folly and Wickedness; but for these he is *answerable to God,* as every private Man must be, who is guilty of Mismanagement in his own Concerns. Now, the Folly of this Reasoning will best appear, by applying it in a parallel Case: Should any Man argue, that a Physician is supposed to understand his own Art best; that the Law protects and encourages his Profession: And therefore, although he should manifestly prescribe *Poison* to all his Patients, whereof they must immediately die; he cannot be justly punished, but is answerable only to God. Or, should the same be offered in Behalf of a Divine, who would preach against Religion, and moral Duties: In either of these two Cases, every Body would find out the Sophistry; and presently answer, that, although common Men are not exactly skilled in the Composition, or Application of Medicines, or in prescribing the Limits of Duty; yet the Difference between *Poisons* and *Remedies,* is easily known by their Effects, and common Reason soon distinguishes between *Virtue* and *Vice:* And it must be necessary to forbid both these the further Practice of their Professions; because, their Crimes are not purely personal to the Physician, or the Divine, but destructive to the Publick. All which is infinitely stronger, in respect to a Prince; in whose good, or ill Conduct, the Happiness, or Misery of a whole Nation is included; whereas, it is of small Consequence to the Publick, farther than Example, how any private Person manageth his Property.

BUT, granting that the Right of a lineal Successor to a Crown, were upon the same Foot with the Property of a Subject; still it may, at any Time, be transferred by the legislative Power, as other Properties frequently are. The supreme Power in a State can *do no Wrong;* because, whatever that doth, is the Action of all: And when the *Lawyers* apply this

Maxim to the *King,* they must understand it only in that Sense, as he is Administrator of the supreme Power; otherwise, it is not universally true, but may be controuled in several Instances easy to produce.

AND these are the Topicks we must proceed upon, to justify our Exclusion of the young *Pretender* in *France.*[24] That of his suspected Birth,[25] being meerly popular, and therefore not made use of, as I remember, since the Revolution, in any Speech, Vote, or Proclamation, where there was Occasion to mention him.

AS to the *Abdication* of King *James,* which the Advocates on that Side look upon to have been forcible and unjust, and consequently void in it self; I think a Man may observe every Article of the *English* Church, without being in much Pain about it. It is not unlikely that all Doors were laid open for his Departure, and perhaps not without the Privity of the Prince of *Orange;* as reasonably concluding, that the Kingdom might better be settled in his Absence: But, to affirm, he had any Cause to apprehend the same Treatment with his *Father,* is an improbable Scandal flung upon the Nation by a few biggotted *French* Scribblers, or the invidious Assertion of a ruined Party at home, in the Bitterness of their Souls: Not one material Circumstance agreeing with those in 1648; and the greatest Part of the Nation having preserved the utmost Horror for that ignominious *Murder.* But whether his Removal were caused by his own *Fears,* or other Mens *Artifices,* it is manifest to me, that supposing the Throne to be vacant,[26] which was the Foot the Nation went upon; the Body of the People was thereupon left at Liberty, to chuse what Form of Government they pleased, by themselves, or their Representatives.

THE only Difficulty of any Weight against the Proceedings at the Revolution, is an obvious Objection, to which the Writers upon that Subject have not yet given a direct, or sufficient Answer; as if they were in Pain at some Consequences, which they apprehended those of the contrary Opinion might draw from it. I will repeat this Objection, as it was offered me some Time ago, with all its Advantages, by a very pious, learned, and worthy Gentleman* of the Non-juring Party.

THE Force of his Argument turned upon this: that the Laws made by the supreme Power, cannot otherwise than by the supreme Power be annulled: That this consisting in *England* of a King, Lords, and Commons, whereof each have a negative Voice, no Two of them can repeal, or enact a Law without Consent of the Third; much less, may any one of them be

---

* Mr. Nelson, *Author of the Feasts and Fasts, &c.*

entirely excluded from its Part of the Legislature, by a *Vote* of the other Two. That all these Maxims were openly violated at the Revolution; where an Assembly of the *Nobles* and *People,* not summoned by the King's Writ, (which was an essential Part of the Constitution,) and consequently no lawful Meeting; did, meerly upon their own Authority, declare the King to have abdicated, the Throne vacant; and gave the Crown, by a Vote, to a *Nephew,* when there were three Children to inherit; although by the fundamental Laws of the Realm, the next Heir is immediately to succeed. Neither doth it appear, how a Prince's *Abdication* can make any other Sort of Vacancy in the Throne, than would be caused by his Death; since he cannot abdicate for his Children, (who claim their right of Succession by Act of Parliament,) otherwise than by his own Consent, in Form, to a Bill from the two Houses.

AND this is the Difficulty that seems chiefly to stick with the most reasonable of those, who, from a meer Scruple of Conscience, refuse to join with us upon the Revolution Principle; but for the rest, are, I believe, as far from loving arbitrary Government, as any others can be, who are born under a free Constitution, and are allowed to have the least Share of common good Sense.

IN this Objection, there are two Questions included: First, Whether upon the Foot of our Constitution, as it stood in the Reign of the late King *James;* a King of *England* may be deposed? The second is, Whether the People of *England,* convened by their own Authority, after the King had withdrawn himself in the Manner he did, had Power to alter the Succession?

As for the first; it is a Point I shall not presume to determine; and shall therefore only say, that to any Man who holds the Negative, I would demand the Liberty of putting the Case as strongly as I please. I will suppose a Prince limited by Laws like ours, yet running into a Thousand Caprices of Cruelty, like *Nero* or *Caligula.*[27] I will suppose him to murder his Mother and his Wife, to commit Incest, to ravish Matrons, to blow up the Senate, and burn his Metropolis; openly to renounce God and Christ, and worship the Devil: These, and the like Exorbitances are in the Power of a single Person to commit without the Advice of a Ministry, or Assistance of an Army. And if such a King, as I have described, cannot be deposed but by his own Consent in Parliament, I do not well see how he can be *resisted;* or what can be meant by a *limited* Monarchy; or what signifies the People's Consent, in making and repealing Laws, if the Person who administers hath no Tie but Conscience, and is answerable to none but God. I desire no stronger Proof that an Opinion must be false, than to find very great Absurdities annexed to it; and there cannot be greater than in the present Case: For it is not a bare Speculation, that Kings may run into such Enormities as are above-mentioned; the Practice may be proved by Examples, not only drawn from the first *Cæsars,* or later Emperors, but many modern Princes of *Europe;* such as *Peter* the Cruel, *Philip* the Second of *Spain, John Basilovits* of *Muscovy;* and in our own Nation, King *John, Richard* the Third, and *Henry* the Eighth. But there cannot be equal Absurdities supposed in maintaining the contrary Opinion; because it is certain, that Princes have it in their Power to keep a Majority on their Side by any tolerable Administration; till provoked by continual Oppressions, no Man indeed can then answer where the Madness of the People will stop.

As to the second Part of the Objection; whether the People of *England* convened by their own Authority, upon King *James's* precipitate Departure, had Power to alter the Succession?

In answer to this, I think it is manifest from the Practice of the wisest Nations, and who seem to have had the truest Notions of Freedom; that when a Prince was laid aside for Male-Administration, the *Nobles* and *People,* if they thought it necessary for the Publick Weal, did resume the Administration of the supreme Power, (the Power it self having been always in them) and did not only alter the Succession, but often the very Form of Government too; because they believed there was no natural Right in one Man to govern another; but that all was by Institution, Force, or Consent. Thus, the Cities of *Greece,* when they drove out their tyrannical Kings, either chose others from a new Family, or abolished the kingly Government, and became free States. Thus the *Romans,* upon the Expulsion of *Tarquin,* found it inconvenient for them to be subject any longer to the Pride, the Lust, the Cruelty, and arbitrary Will of single Persons; and therefore by general Consent, entirely altered the whole Frame of their Government. Nor do I find the Proceedings of either, in this Point, to have been condemned by any Historian of the succeeding Ages.

But a great deal hath been already said by other Writers, upon this invidious and beaten Subject; therefore I shall let it fall; although the Point be commonly mistaken, especially by the *Lawyers;* who of all other Professions seem least to understand the Nature of Government in general; like Underworkmen, who are expert enough at making a single Wheel in a Clock, but are utterly ignorant how to adjust the several Parts, or to regulate the Movement.

To return therefore from this Digression: It is a *Church-of*-England

Man's Opinion, that the Freedom of a Nation consists in an absolute *un-limited legislative* Power, wherein the whole Body of the People are *fairly* represented; and in an *executive* duly *limited:* Because on this Side likewise, there may be dangerous Degrees, and a very ill Extream. For when two Parties in a State are pretty equal in *Power, Pretensions, Merit,* and *Virtue,* (for these two last are, with relation to Parties and a Court, quite different Things,) it hath been the Opinion of the best Writers upon Government, that a Prince ought not in any sort to be under the Guidance, or Influence of either; because he declines, by this Means, from his Office of presiding over the *Whole,* to be the Head of a *Party;* which, besides the Indignity, renders him answerable for all publick Mismanagements, and the Consequences of them: And in whatever State this happens, there must either be a Weakness in the Prince or Ministry, or else the former is too much restrained by the Nobles, or those who represent the People.

To conclude: A *Church-of-*England *Man* may with Prudence and a good Conscience approve the professed Principles of one Party more than the other, according as he thinks they best promote the Good of Church and State; but he will never be swayed by Passion or Interest to advance an Opinion meerly because it is *That* of the Party he most approves; which one single Principle he looks upon as the Root of all our civil Animosities. To enter into a *Party* as into an Order of *Fryars,* with so resigned an Obedience to Superiors, is very unsuitable both with the civil and religious Liberties, we so zealously assert. Thus the Understandings of a whole Senate are often enslaved by three or four Leaders on each Side; who instead of intending the publick Weal, have their Hearts wholly set upon *Ways and Means* how to get, or to keep Employments. But to speak more at large; how has this Spirit of Faction mingled it self with the Mass of the People, changed their Nature and Manners, and the very Genius of the Nation? Broke all the Laws of Charity, Neighbourhood, Alliance and Hospitality; destroyed all Ties of Friendship, and divided Families against themselves? And no Wonder it should be so, when in order to find out the Character of a Person; instead of enquiring whether he be a Man of Virtue, Honour, Piety, Wit, good Sense, or Learning; the modern Question is only, Whether he be a *Whig* or a *Tory;* under which Terms all good and ill Qualities are included.

Now, because it is a Point of Difficulty to chuse an exact Middle between two ill Extreams; it may be worth enquiring in the present Case, which of these a wise and good Man would rather seem to avoid: Taking therefore their own good and ill Characters with due Abatements and Allowances for Partiality and Passion; I should think that, in order to preserve the Constitution entire in Church and State; whoever hath a true Value for both, would be sure to avoid the Extreams of *Whig* for the Sake of the former, and the Extreams of *Tory* on Account of the latter.

I HAVE now said all that I could think convenient upon so nice a Subject; and find, I have the Ambition common with other Reasoners, to wish at least, that both Parties may think me *in the right*, which would be of some Use to those who have any Virtue left, but are blindly drawn into the Extravagancies of either, upon false Representations, to serve the Ambition or Malice of designing Men, without any Prospect of their own. But if that may not be hoped for; my next Wish should be, that both might think me *in the wrong*; which I would understand, as an ample Justification of my self, and a sure Ground to believe, that I have proceeded at least with Impartiality, and perhaps with Truth.

AN

ARGUMENT

TO PROVE, THAT THE

ABOLISHING OF CHRISTIANITY

IN

ENGLAND,

MAY, AS THINGS NOW STAND,

BE ATTENDED WITH SOME

INCONVENIENCIES, AND PERHAPS, NOT

PRODUCE

THOSE MANY GOOD EFFECTS PROPOSED

THEREBY.

Written in the YEAR 1708.

I am very sensible what a Weakness and Presumption it is, to reason against the general Humour and Disposition of the World. I remember it was with great Justice, and a due Regard to the Freedom both of the Publick and the Press, forbidden upon severe Penalties to write or discourse, or lay Wagers against the *Union*,[1] even before it was confirmed by Parliament: Because that was looked upon as a Design to oppose the Current of the People; which besides the Folly of it, is a manifest Breach of the Fundamental Law, that makes this Majority of Opinion the Voice of God.[2] In like Manner, and for the very same Reasons, it may perhaps be neither safe nor prudent to argue against the Abolishing of Christianity, at a Juncture when all Parties appear so unanimously determined upon the Point; as we cannot but allow from their Actions, their Discourses, and their Writings. However, I know not how, whether from the Affectation of Singularity, or the Perverseness of human Nature; but so it unhappily falls out, that I cannot be entirely of this Opinion. Nay, although I were sure an Order were issued out for my immediate Prosecution by the Attorney-General; I should still confess, that in the present Posture of our Affairs at home or abroad, I do not yet see the absolute Necessity of extirpating the Christian Religion from among us.

THIS perhaps may appear too great a Paradox, even for our wise and paradoxical Age to endure: Therefore I shall handle it with all Tenderness, and with the utmost Deference to that great and profound Majority, which is of another Sentiment.

AND yet the Curious may please to observe, how much the Genius of a Nation is liable to alter in half an Age: I have heard it affirmed for certain by some very old People, that the contrary Opinion was even in their Memories as much in Vogue as the other is now; and, that a Project for the Abolishing of Christianity would then have appeared as singular, and been thought as absurd, as it would be at this Time to write or discourse in its Defence.

THEREFORE I freely own, that all Appearances are against me. The System of the Gospel, after the Fate of other Systems is generally antiquated and exploded;[3] and the Mass or Body of the common People, among whom it seems to have had its latest Credit, are now grown as much ashamed of it as their Betters: Opinions, like Fashions always descending from those of Quality to the middle Sort, and thence to the Vulgar, where at length they are dropt and vanish.

BUT here I would not be mistaken; and must therefore be so bold as to borrow a Distinction from the Writers on the other Side, when they make a Difference between nominal and real *Trinitarians*.[4] I hope, no Reader imagines me so weak to stand up in the Defence of *real* Christianity; such as used in primitive Times (if we may believe the Authors of those Ages) to have an Influence upon Mens Belief and Actions: To offer at the Restoring of that, would indeed be a wild Project; it would be to dig up Foundations; to destroy at one Blow *all* the Wit, and *half* the Learning of the Kingdom; to break the entire Frame and Constitution of Things; to ruin Trade, extinguish Arts and Sciences with the Professors of them; in short, to turn our Courts, Exchanges and Shops into Deserts: And would be full as absurd as the Proposal of *Horace*,[5] where he advises the *Romans*, all in a Body, to leave their City, and seek a new Seat in some remote Part of the World, by Way of Cure for the Corruption of their Manners.

THEREFORE, I think this Caution was in it self altogether unnecessary, (which I have inserted only to prevent all Possibility of cavilling) since every candid Reader will easily understand my Discourse to be intended only in Defence of *nominal* Christianity; the other having been for some Time wholly laid aside by general Consent, as utterly inconsistent with our present Schemes of Wealth and Power.

BUT why we should therefore cast off the Name and Title of Christians, although the general Opinion and Resolution be so violent for it; I confess I cannot (with Submission) apprehend the Consequence necessary. However, since the Undertakers propose such wonderful Advantages to the Nation by this Project; and advance many plausible Objections against the System of Christianity; I shall briefly consider the Strength of both; fairly allow them their greatest Weight, and offer such Answers as I think most reasonable. After which I will beg leave to shew what Inconveniencies may possibly happen by such an Innovation, in the present Posture of our Affairs.

First, ONE great Advantage proposed by the Abolishing of Christianity is, That it would very much enlarge and establish Liberty of Conscience, that great Bulwark of our Nation, and of the *Protestant* Religion, which is still too much limited by *Priest-Craft*, notwithstanding all the good Intentions of the Legislature; as we have lately found by a severe Instance. For it is confidently reported, that two young Gentlemen of great Hopes, bright Wit, and profound Judgment, who upon a thorough Examination of Causes and Effects, and by the meer Force of natural Abilities, without the least Tincture of Learning; having made a Discovery, that there was no God, and generously communicating their Thoughts for the Good of the Publick; were some Time ago, by an unparalleled Severity, and upon I know not what *obsolete* Law, broke *only* for *Blasphemy*.[6] And as it hath been wisely observed; if Persecution once begins, no Man alive knows how far it may reach, or where it will end.

IN Answer to all which, with Deference to wiser Judgments; I think this rather shews the Necessity of a *nominal* Religion among us. Great Wits love to be free with the highest Objects; and if they cannot be allowed a *God* to revile or renounce; they will *speak Evil of Dignities,* abuse the Government, and reflect upon the Ministry; which I am sure, few will deny to be of much more pernicious Consequence; according to the Saying of *Tiberius; Deorum offensa Diis curæ.*[7] As to the particular Fact related, I think it is not fair to argue from one Instance; perhaps another cannot be produced; yet (to the Comfort of all those, who may be apprehensive of Persecution) Blasphemy we know is freely spoke a Million of Times in every Coffee-House and tavern, or where-ever else *good Company* meet. It must be allowed indeed, that to break an *English Free-born* Officer only for Blasphemy, was, to speak the gentlest of such an Action, a very high Strain of absolute Power. Little can be said in Excuse for the General; perhaps he was afraid it might give Offence to the Allies, among whom, for ought I know, it may be the Custom of the Country to believe a God. But if he argued, as some have done, upon a mistaken Principle, that an Officer who is guilty of speaking Blasphemy, may, some Time or other, proceed so far as to raise a Mutiny; the Consequence is, by no Means, to be admitted: For, surely the Commander of an *English* Army is like to be but ill obeyed, whose Soldiers fear and reverence him as little as they do a Deity.

IT is further objected against the Gospel System, that it obliges Men to the Belief of Things too difficult for Free-Thinkers, and such who have shaken off the Prejudices that usually cling to a confined Education. To which I answer, that Men should be cautious how they raise Objections, which reflect upon the Wisdom of the Nation. Is not every Body freely allowed to believe whatever he pleaseth; and to publish his Belief to the World whenever he thinks fit; especially if it serve to strengthen the Party which is in the Right? Would any indifferent Foreigner, who should read the Trumpery lately written by *Asgill, Tindall, Toland, Coward,*[8] and Forty more, imagine the Gospel to be our Rule of Faith, and confirmed by Parliaments? Does any Man either believe, or say he believes, or desire to have it thought that he says he believes one Syllable of the Matter? And is any Man worse received upon that Score; or does he find his Want of *Nominal* Faith a Disadvantage to him, in the Pursuit of any Civil, or Military Employment?[9] What if there be an old dormant Statute or two against him? Are they not now obsolete, to a Degree, that *Empson* and *Dudley*[10] themselves, if they were now alive, would find it impossible to put them in Execution?

IT is likewise urged, that there are, by Computation, in this Kingdom, above ten Thousand Parsons; whose Revenues added to those of my Lords the Bishops, would suffice to maintain, at least, two Hundred young Gentlemen of Wit and Pleasure, and Free-thinking; Enemies to Priest-craft, narrow Principles, Pedantry, and Prejudices; who might be an Ornament to the Court and Town: And then again, so great a Number of able (bodied) Divines might be a Recruit to our Fleet and Armies. This, indeed, appears to be a Consideration of some Weight: But then, on the other Side, several Things deserve to be considered likewise: As, First, Whether it may not be thought necessary, that in certain Tracts of Country, like what we call Parishes, there should be *one* Man at least, of Abilities to read and write. Then, it seems a wrong Computation, that the Revenues of the Church throughout this Island, would be large enough to maintain two Hundred young Gentlemen, or even Half that Number, after the present refined Way of Living; that is, to allow each of them such a Rent, as, in the modern Form of Speech, would make them *easy.* But still, there is in this Project a greater Mischief behind; and we ought to beware of the Woman's Folly, who killed the Hen, that every Morning laid her a Golden Egg. For, pray, what would become of the Race of Men in the next Age, if we had nothing to trust to besides the scrophulous consumptive Productions furnished by our Men of Wit and Pleasure; when having squandered away their Vigour, Health, and Estates; they are forced, by some disagreeable Marriage, to piece up their broken Fortunes, and entail Rottenness and Politeness on their Posterity? Now, here are ten Thousand Persons reduced by the wise Regulations of *Henry* the Eighth,[11] to the Necessity of a low Diet, and moderate Exercise, who are the only great Restorers of our Breed; without which, the Nation would, in an Age or two, become but one great Hospital.

ANOTHER Advantage proposed by the abolishing of Christianity, is, the clear Gain of one Day in Seven, which is now entirely lost, and consequently the Kingdom one Seventh less considerable in Trade, Business, and Pleasure; beside the Loss to the Publick of so many stately Structures now in the Hands of the Clergy; which might be converted into Theatres, Exchanges, Market-houses, common Dormitories, and other publick Edifices.

I HOPE I shall be forgiven a hard Word, if I call this a perfect Cavil. I readily own there hath been an old Custom, Time out of Mind, for People to assemble in the Churches every *Sunday,* and that Shops are still frequently shut; in order, as it is conceived, to preserve the Memory of that antient Practice; but how this can prove a Hindrance to Business, or Pleasure, is hard to imagine. What if the Men of Pleasure are forced, one Day in the Week, to game at home, instead of the *Chocolate-House?* Are not the *Taverns* and *Coffee-Houses* open? Can there be a more convenient Season for taking a Dose of Physick? Are fewer Claps got upon *Sundays* than other Days? Is not that the chief Day for Traders to sum up the Accounts of the Week; and for Lawyers to prepare their Briefs? But I would fain know how it can be pretended, that the Churches are misapplied. Where are more Appointments and Rendezvouzes of Gallantry? Where more Care to appear in the foremost Box with greater Advantage of Dress? Where more Meetings for Business? Where more Bargains driven of all Sorts? And where so many Conveniences, or Incitements to sleep?

THERE is one Advantage, greater than any of the foregoing, proposed by the abolishing of Christianity; that it will utterly extinguish Parties among us, by removing those factious Distinctions of High and Low Church, of *Whig* and *Tory, Presbyterian* and *Church-of-England;* which are now so many grievous Clogs upon publick Proceedings, and dispose Men to prefer the gratifying themselves, or depressing their Adversaries, before the most important Interest of the State.

I CONFESS, if it were certain that so great an Advantage would redound to the Nation by this Expedient, I would submit and be silent: But, will any Man say, that if the Words *Whoring, Drinking, Cheating, Lying, Stealing,* were, by Act of Parliament, ejected out of the *English* Tongue and Dictionaries; we should all awake next Morning chaste and temperate, honest and just, and Lovers of Truth. Is this a fair Consequence? Or if the Physicians would forbid us to pronounce the Words *Pox, Gout, Rheumatism,* and *Stone;* would that Expedient serve like so many *Talismans* to destroy the Diseases themselves? Are Party and Faction rooted in Mens Hearts no deeper than Phrases borrowed from Religion; or founded upon no firmer Principles? And is our Language so poor, that we cannot find other Terms to express them? Are Envy, Pride, Avarice and Ambition, such ill Nomenclators, that they cannot furnish Appellations for their Owners? Will not *Heydukes* and *Mamalukes, Mandarins,* and *Potshaws,* or any other Words formed at Pleasure, serve to distinguish those who are in the *Ministry* from others, who *would be in* it *if they could*? What, for Instance, is easier than to vary the Form of Speech; and instead of the Word *Church,* make it a Question in Politicks, Whether the *Monument* be in Danger? Because Religion was nearest at Hand to furnish a few convenient Phrases; is our Invention so barren, we can find no others? Suppose, for Argument Sake, that the *Tories* favoured *Margarita,* the *Whigs* Mrs. *Tofts,* and the *Trimmers Valentini;** would not *Margaritians, Toftians,* and *Valentinians,* be very tolerable Marks of Distinction? The *Prasini* and *Veneti,* two most virulent Factions in *Italy,* began (if I remember right) by a Distinction of Colours in Ribbonds; which we might do, with as good a Grace, about the Dignity of the *Blue* and the *Green;* and would serve as properly to divide the Court, the Parliament, and the Kingdom between them, as any Terms of Art whatsoever, borrowed from Religion. Therefore, I think there is little Force in this Objection against *Christianity;* or Prospect of so great an Advantage as is proposed in the Abolishing of it.

IT is again objected, as a very absurd, ridiculous Custom, that a Set of Men should be suffered, much less employed, and hired to bawl one Day in Seven, against the Lawfulness of those Methods most in Use towards the Pursuit of Greatness, Riches, and Pleasure; which are the constant Practice of all Men alive on the other Six. But this Objection is, I think, a little unworthy so refined an Age as ours. Let us argue this Matter calmly. I appeal to the Breast of any polite Free-Thinker, whether in the Pursuit of gratifying a predominant Passion, he hath not always felt a wonderful Incitement, by reflecting it was a Thing forbidden: And therefore we see, in order to cultivate this Taste, the Wisdom of the Nation hath taken special Care, that the Ladies should be furnished with prohibited Silks, and the Men with prohibited Wine: And, indeed, it were to be wished, that some other Prohibitions were promoted, in order to improve the Pleasures of the Town; which, for want of such Expedients, begin already, as I am told, to flag and grow languid; giving way daily to cruel Inroads from the Spleen.[12]

IT is likewise proposed, as a great Advantage to the Publick, that if we once discard the System of the Gospel, all Religion will, of Course, be banished for ever; and consequently along with it, those grievous

---

* Italian *Singers then in Vogue.*

Prejudices of Education; which, under the Names of Virtue, Conscience, Honour, Justice, and the like, are so apt to disturb the Peace of human Minds; and the Notions whereof are so hard to be eradicated by right Reason, or Free-thinking, sometimes during the whole Course of our Lives.

HERE, first, I observe how difficult it is to get rid of a Phrase, which the World is once grown fond of, although the Occasion that first produced it, be entirely taken away. For several Years past, if a Man had but an ill-favoured Nose, the Deep-Thinkers of the Age would, some way or other, contrive to impute the Cause to the Prejudice of his Education. From this Fountain are said to be derived all our foolish Notions of Justice, Piety, Love of our Country; all our Opinions of God, or a future State, Heaven, Hell, and the like: And there might formerly, perhaps, have been some Pretence for this Charge. But so effectual Care hath been since taken, to remove those Prejudices by an entire Change in the Methods of Education; that (with Honour I mention it to our polite Innovators) the young Gentlemen, who are now on the Scene, seem to have not the least Tincture left of those Infusions, or String of those Weeds; and, by Consequence, the Reason for abolishing *Nominal* Christianity upon that Pretext, is wholly ceased.

FOR the rest, it may perhaps admit a Controversy, whether the Banishing all Notions of Religion whatsoever, would be convenient for the Vulgar. Not that I am in the least of Opinion with those, who hold Religion to have been the Invention of Politicians, to keep the lower Part of the World in Awe, by the Fear of invisible Powers; unless Mankind were then very different from what it is now: For I look upon the Mass, or Body of our People here in *England*, to be as Free-Thinkers, that is to say, as stanch Unbelievers, as any of the highest Rank. But I conceive some scattered Notions about a superior Power to be of singular Use for the common People, as furnishing excellent Materials to keep Children quiet, when they grow peevish; and providing Topicks of Amusement in a tedious Winter Night.

LASTLY, It is proposed as a singular Advantage, that the Abolishing of Christianity, will very much contribute to the uniting of *Protestants*, by enlarging the Terms of Communion, so as to take in all Sorts of *Dissenters*; who are now shut out of the Pale upon Account of a few Ceremonies, which all Sides confess to be Things indifferent: That this alone will effectually answer the great Ends of a Scheme for Comprehension, by opening a large noble Gate, at which all Bodies may enter; whereas the chaffering with *Dissenters*, and dodging about this or the other Ceremony, is but like opening a few Wickets, and leaving them at jar, by which no more than one can get in at a Time, and that not without stooping and sideling, and squeezing his Body.

To all this I answer, That there is one darling Inclination of Mankind, which usually affects to be a Retainer to Religion, although she be neither its Parent, its Godmother, or its Friend; I mean the Spirit of Opposition, that lived long before Christianity, and can easily subsist without it. Let us, for Instance, examine wherein the Opposition of Sectaries among us consists; we shall find Christianity to have no Share in it at all. Does the Gospel any where prescribe a starched squeezed Countenance, a stiff formal Gait, a Singularity of Manners and Habit, or any affected Modes of Speech, different from the reasonable Part of Mankind? Yet, if Christianity did not lend its Name, to stand in the Gap, and to employ or divert these Humours, they must of Necessity be spent in Contraventions to the Laws of the Land, and Disturbance of the publick Peace. There is a Portion of Enthusiasm assigned to every Nation, which if it hath not proper Objects to work on, will burst out, and set all in a Flame. If the Quiet of a State can be bought by only flinging Men a few Ceremonies to devour, it is a Purchase no wise Man would refuse. Let the Mastiffs amuse themselves about a Sheep-skin stuffed with Hay, provided it will keep them from worrying the Flock. The Institution of Convents abroad, seems in one Point a Strain of great Wisdom; there being few Irregularities in human Passions, that may not have recourse to vent themselves in some of those Orders; which are so many Retreats for the Speculative, the Melancholy, the Proud, the Silent, the Politick and the Morose, to spend themselves, and evaporate the noxious Particles; for each of whom, we in this Island are forced to provide a several Sect of Religion, to keep them quiet. And whenever Christianity shall be abolished, the Legislature must find some other Expedient to employ and entertain them. For what imports it, how large a Gate you open, if there will be always left a Number, who place a Pride and a Merit in refusing to enter?

Having thus considered the most important Objections against Christianity, and the chief Advantages proposed by the Abolishing thereof; I shall now with equal Deference and Submission to wiser Judgments as before, proceed to mention a few Inconveniences that may happen, if the Gospel should be repealed; which perhaps the Projectors may not have sufficiently considered.

And first, I am very sensible how much the Gentlemen of Wit and Pleasure are apt to murmur, and be choqued[13] at the sight of so many daggled-tail Parsons, who happen to fall in their Way, and offend their

Eyes: But at the same Time these wise Reformers do not consider what an Advantage and Felicity it is, for great Wits to be always provided with Objects of Scorn and Contempt, in order to exercise and improve their Talents, and divert their Spleen from falling on each other, or on themselves; especially when all this may be done without the least imaginable *Danger to their Persons.*

AND to urge another Argument of a parallel Nature: If Christianity were once abolished, how would the Free-Thinkers, the strong Reasoners, and the Men of profound Learning be able to find another Subject so calculated in all Points whereon to display their Abilities. What wonderful Productions of Wit should we be deprived of, from those whose Genius, by continual Practice hath been wholly turned upon Raillery and Invectives against Religion; and would therefore never be able to shine or distinguish themselves upon any other Subject. We are daily complaining of the great Decline of Wit among us; and would we take away the greatest, perhaps the only Topick we have left? Who would ever have suspected *Asgill* for a Wit, or *Toland* for a Philosopher, if the inexhaustible Stock of Christianity had not been at hand to provide them with Materials? What other Subject through all Art or Nature could have produced *Tindal* for a profound Author, or furnished him with Readers? It is the wise Choice of the Subject that alone adorns and distinguishes the Writer. For had an hundred such Pens as these been employed on the Side of Religion, they would have immediately sunk into Silence and Oblivion.

NOR do I think it wholly groundless, or my Fears altogether imaginary; that the Abolishing of Christianity may perhaps bring the Church in Danger; or at least put the Senate to the Trouble of another Securing Vote. I desire, I may not be mistaken: I am far from presuming to affirm or think, that the Church is in Danger at present, or as Things now stand; but we know not how soon it may be so, when the Christian Religion is repealed. As plausible as this Project seems, there may a dangerous Design lurk under it. Nothing can be more notorious, than that the *Atheists, Deists, Socinians, Anti-Trinitarians,* and other Subdivisions of Free-Thinkers, are Persons of little Zeal for the present Ecclesiastical Establishment: Their declared Opinion is for repealing the Sacramental Test; they are very indifferent with regard to Ceremonies; nor do they hold the *Jus Divinum*[14] of Episcopacy. Therefore this may be intended as one politick Step towards altering the Constitution of the Church Established, and setting up *Presbytery* in the stead; which I leave to be further considered by those at the Helm.

IN the last Place, I think nothing can be more plain, than that by this

Expedient, we shall run into the Evil we chiefly pretend to avoid; and that the Abolishment of the Christian Religion, will be the readiest Course we can take to introduce Popery. And I am the more inclined to this Opinion, because we know it hath been the constant Practice of the *Jesuits* to send over Emissaries, with Instructions to personate themselves Members of the several prevailing Sects amongst us. So it is recorded, that they have at sundry Times appeared in the Guise of *Presbyterians, Anabaptists, Independents,* and *Quakers,* according as any of these were most in Credit: So, since the Fashion hath been taken up of exploding Religion, the *Popish* Missionaries have not been wanting to mix with the Free-Thinkers; among whom, *Toland,* the great Oracle of the *Anti-Christians,* is an *Irish* Priest, the Son of an *Irish* Priest; and the most learned and ingenious Author of a Book,[15] called the *Rights of the Christian Church,* was, in a proper Juncture, reconciled to the *Romish* Faith; whose true Son, as appears by an Hundred Passages in his Treatise, he still continues. Perhaps I could add some others to the Number; but the Fact is beyond Dispute; and the Reasoning they proceed by, is right: For, supposing Christianity to be extinguished, the People will never be at Ease, till they find out some other Method of Worship; which will as infallibly produce Superstition, as this will end in *Popery.*

AND therefore, if, notwithstanding all I have said, it shall still be thought necessary to have a Bill brought in for repealing Christianity; I would humbly offer an Amendment, that instead of the Word *Christianity,* may be put *Religion* in general; which I conceive, will much better answer all the good Ends proposed by the Projectors of it. For, as long as we leave in Being a God, and his Providence, with all the necessary Consequences, which curious and inquisitive Men will be apt to draw from such Premises; we do not strike at the Root of the Evil, although we should ever so effectually annihilate the present Scheme of the Gospel. For, of what Use is Freedom of Thought, if it will not produce Freedom of Action; which is the sole End, how remote soever, in Appearance, of all Objections against Christianity? And therefore, the Free-Thinkers consider it as a Sort of Edifice, wherein all the Parts have such a mutual Dependance on each other, that if you happen to pull out one single Nail, the whole Fabrick must fall to the Ground. This was happily expressed by him, who had heard of a Text brought for Proof of the Trinity, which in an antient Manuscript was differently read; he thereupon immediately took the Hint, and by a sudden Deduction of a long *Sorites,* most logically concluded: Why, if it be as you say, I may safely whore and drink on, and defy the Parson. From which, and many the like Instances easy to be produced,

I think nothing can be more manifest, than that the Quarrel is not against any particular Points of hard Digestion in the Christian System; but against Religion in general; which, by laying Restraints on human Nature, is supposed the great Enemy to the Freedom of Thought and Action.

UPON the whole; if it shall still be thought for the Benefit of Church and State, that Christianity be abolished; I conceive, however, it may be more convenient to defer the Execution to a Time of Peace; and not venture in this Conjuncture to disoblige our Allies; who, as it falls out, are all Christians; and many of them, by the Prejudices of their Education, so bigotted, as to place a Sort of Pride in the Appellation. If, upon being rejected by them, we are to trust to an Alliance with the *Turk,* we shall find our selves much deceived: For, as he is too remote, and generally engaged in War with the *Persian* Emperor; so his People would be more scandalized at our Infidelity, than our Christian Neighbours. Because, the *Turks* are not only strict Observers of religious Worship; but, what is worse, believe a God; which is more than is required of us, even while we preserve the Name of Christians.

TO conclude: Whatever some may think of the great Advantages to Trade, by this favourite Scheme; I do very much apprehend, that in six Months Time, after the Act is past for the Extirpation of the Gospel, the Bank and *East-India* Stock may fall, at least, One *per Cent.* And, since that is Fifty Times more than ever the Wisdom of our Age thought fit to venture for the *Preservation* of Christianity, there is no Reason we should be at so great a Loss, meerly for the Sake of *destroying* it.

A
PROJECT

FOR THE

Advancement of RELIGION,

AND THE

Reformation of MANNERS

Written in the Year 1709.

TO THE
Counters of BERKELEY.[1]

Madam,

My Intention in prefixing your Ladyship's Name, is not after the common Form, to desire your Protection of the following Papers; which I take to be a very unreasonable Request; since by being inscribed to your Ladyship, although without your Knowledge, and from a concealed Hand, you cannot recommend them without some Suspicion of Partiality. My real Design is, I confess, the very same I have often detested in most Dedications; That of publishing your Praises to the World. Not upon the Subject of your noble Birth, for I know others as noble; or of the Greatness of your Fortune, for I know others far greater; or of that beautiful Race (the Images of their Parents) which calls you Mother: For even this may, perhaps, have been equalled in some other Age, or Country. Besides, none of these Advantages to derive any Accomplishments to the Owners; but serve, at best, only to adorn what they really possess. What I intend, is your Piety, Truth, good Sense, and good Nature, Affability and Charity; wherein I wish your Ladyship had many Equals, or any Superiors; and I wish I could say, I knew them too; for then your Ladyship might have had a Chance to escape this Address. In the mean Time, I think it highly necessary for the Interest of Virtue and Religion, that the whole Kingdom should be informed in some Parts of your Character: For Instance: That the easiest and politest Conversation, joined with the truest Piety, may be observed in your Ladyship, in as great Perfection, as they were ever seen apart in any other Persons. That by your Prudence and Management under several Disadvantages, you have preserved the Lustre of that most noble Family, into which you are grafted, and which the unmeasurable Profusion of Ancestors, for many Generations, had too much eclipsed. Then, how happily you perform every Office of Life, to which Providence hath called you: In the Education of those two incomparable Daughters, whose Conduct is so universally admired; in every Duty of a prudent, complying, affectionate Wife; in that Care which descends to the meanest of your Domesticks; and lastly, in that endless Bounty to the Poor, and Discretion where to distribute it. I insist on my Opinion, that it is of Importance for the Publick to know this, and a great deal more of your Ladyship; yet whoever goes about to inform them, shall, instead of finding Credit, perhaps be censured for a Flatterer. To avoid so usual a Reproach, I declare this to be no Dedication; but meerly an Introduction to a Proposal for the Advancement of Religion and Morals; by tracing, however imperfectly, some few Lineaments in the Character of a Lady, who hath spent all her Life in the Practice and Promotion of both.

———

Among the Schemes offered to the Publick in this projecting Age, I have observed, with some Displeasure, that there have never been any for the Improvement of Religion and Morals: Which, besides the Piety of the Design from the Consequences of such a Reformation in a future Life, would be the best natural Means for advancing the publick Felicity of the State, as well as the present Happiness of every Individual. For, as much as Faith and Morality are declined among us, I am altogether confident, they might, in a short Time, and with no very great Trouble, be raised to as high a Perfection, as Numbers are capable of receiving. Indeed, the Method is so easy and obvious, and some present Opportunities so good; that, in order to have this Project reduced to Practice, there seems to want nothing more than to put those in mind, who by their Honour, Duty, and Interest are chiefly concerned.

BUT, because it is idle to propose Remedies before we are assured of the Disease, or to be in Fear, until we are convinced of the Danger; I shall first shew in general, that the Nation is extreamly corrupted in Religion and Morals; and then, I will offer a short Scheme for the Reformation of both.

AS to the first; I know it is reckoned but a Form of Speech, when Divines complain of the Wickedness of the Age: However, I believe, upon a fair Comparison with other Times and Countries, it would be found an undoubted Truth.

FOR first, to deliver nothing but plain Matter of Fact, without Exaggeration or Satyr: I suppose it will be granted, that hardly One in a Hundred among our People of Quality, or Gentry, appears to act by any Principle of Religion. That great Numbers of them do entirely discard it, and are ready to own their Disbelief of all Revelation in ordinary Discourse. Nor is the Case much better among the Vulgar, especially in great Towns; where the Prophaneness and Ignorance of Handicraftsmen, small Traders, Servants, and the like, are to a Degree very hard to be imagined greater. Then, it is observed abroad, that no Race of Mortals hath so little Sense of Religion as the *English* Soldiers: To confirm which, I have been often told by great Officers in the Army, that in the whole Compass of their Acquaintance, they could not recollect three of their Profession, who seemed to regard, or believe one Syllable of the Gospel: And the same, at least, may be affirmed of the Fleet. The Consequences of all which, upon the Actions of Men, are equally manifest. They never go about, as in former Times, to hide or palliate their Vices; but expose them freely to View, like any other common Occurrences of Life, without the least Reproach from the World, or themselves. For Instance, any Man will tell you, he intends to be drunk this Evening, or was so last Night, with as little Ceremony or Scruple, as he would tell you the Time of the Day. He will let you know he is going to a Wench, or that he has got a Clap; with as much Indifferency as he would a Piece of publick News. He will swear, curse, or blaspheme, without the least Passion or Provocation. And, although all Regard for Reputation be not quite laid aside in the other Sex; it is, however, at so low an Ebb, that very few among them, seem to think Virtue and Conduct of any Necessity for preserving it. If this be not so; how comes it to pass, that Women of tainted Reputations find the same Countenance and Reception in all publick Places, with those of the nicest Virtue, who pay, and receive Visits from them, without any Manner of Scruple? Which Proceeding, as it is not very old among us, so I take it to be of most pernicious Consequence. It looks like a Sort of compounding between Virtue and Vice; as if a Woman were allowed to be vicious, provided she be not profligate: As if there were a certain Point where Gallantry ends, and Infamy begins; or that an Hundred criminal Amours were not as pardonable as Half a Score.

BESIDE those Corruptions already mentioned, it would be endless to ennumerate such as arise from the Excess of Play, or Gaming: The Cheats, the Quarrels, the Oaths and Blasphemies, among the Men: Among the Women, the Neglect of Household Affairs, the unlimited Freedoms, the undecent Passion; and lastly the known Inlet to all Lewdness, when after an ill Run, the *Person* must answer the Defects of the *Purse:* The Rule on such Occasions holding true in Play, as it doth in Law; *Quod non habet in Crumena, luat in Corpore.*[2]

BUT all these are Trifles in Comparison, if we step into other Scenes, and consider the Fraud and Cozenage of trading Men and Shop-Keepers; that insatiable Gulph of Injustice and Oppression: The *Law.* The open Traffick of all Civil and Military Employments (I wish it rested there) without the least Regard to Merit or Qualifications: The corrupt Management of Men in Office: The many detestable Abuses in chusing those, who represent the People; with the Management of Interest and Factions among the Representatives: To which I must be bold to add the Ignorance among some of the lower Clergy; the mean servile Temper of others; the pert pragmatical Demeanour of several young Stagers in Divinity, upon their first producing themselves into the World. With many other Circumstances needless, or rather invidious to mention; which falling in with the Corruptions already related, have, however unjustly, almost rendered the whole Order contemptible.

THIS is a short View of the general Depravities among us, without entering into Particulars, which would be an endless Labour. Now, as universal and deep-rooted as these Corruptions appear to be, I am utterly deceived, if an effectual Remedy might not be applied to most of them; neither am I at present upon a wild speculative Project, but such a one, as may be easily put in Execution.

FOR, while Prerogative of giving all Employments continues in the Crown, either immediately or by Subordination; it is in the Power of the *Prince* to make Piety and Virtue become the Fashion of the Age; if at the same Time he would make them necessary Qualifications for Favour and Preferment.

IT is clear from present Experience, that the bare Example of the best Prince, will not have any mighty Influence where the Age is very corrupt. For, when was there ever a better Prince on the Throne than the present Queen? I do not talk of her Talent for Government, her Love of the People, or any other Qualities that are purely regal; but her Piety, Charity, Temperance, conjugal Love, and whatever other Virtues do best adorn a private Life; wherein without Question or Flattery, she hath no Superior: Yet neither will it be Satyr or peevish Invective to affirm, that Infidelity and Vice are not much diminished since her coming to the Crown; nor will, in Probability, till more effectual Remedies be provided.

THUS human Nature seems to lie under this Disadvantage, that the Example alone of a vicious Prince, will in Time corrupt an Age; but the Example of a good one will not be sufficient to reform it without further Endeavours. Princes must therefore supply this Defect by a vigorous Exercise of that Authority, which the Law hath left them, by making it every Man's Interest and Honour to cultivate Religion and Virtue; by rendering Vice a Disgrace, and the certain Ruin to Preferment or Pretensions: All which they should first attempt in their own Courts and Families. For Instance, might not the Queen's Domesticks of the middle and lower Sort, be obliged upon Penalty of Suspension, or Loss of their Employments, to a constant weekly Attendance on the Service of the Church; to a decent Behaviour in it; to receive the Sacrament four times a Year; to avoid Swearing and irreligious profane Discourses; and to the Appearance at least, of Temperance and Chastity? Might not the Care of all this be committed to the strict Inspection of proper Officers? Might not those of higher Rank, and nearer Access to Her Majesty, receive her own Commands to the same Purpose, and be countenanced or disfavoured according as they obey? Might not the Queen lay her Injunctions on the Bishops and other great Men of undoubted Piety, to make diligent Enquiry, and give Her Notice, whether any Person about Her should happen to be of Libertine Principles or Morals? Might not all those who enter upon any Office in Her Majesty's Family, be obliged to take an Oath parallel with that against *Symony*, which is administered to the Clergy? It is not to be doubted, but that if these or the like Proceedings were duly observed, Morality and Religion would soon become fashionable Court-Virtues; and be taken up as the only Methods to get or keep Employments there; which alone would have a mighty Influence upon many of the Nobility, and principal Gentry.

BUT, if the like Methods were pursued as far as possible, with Regard to those who are in the great Employments of the State; it is hard to conceive how general a Reformation they might in Time produce among us. For if Piety and Virtue were once reckoned Qualifications necessary to Preferment; every Man thus endowed, when put into great Stations, would readily imitate the Queen's Example in the Distribution of all Offices in his Disposal; especially, if any apparent Transgression through Favor or Partiality, would be imputed to him for a Misdemeanour, by which he must certainly forfeit his Favour and Station: And there being such great Numbers in Employment, scattered through every Town and County in this Kingdom; if all these were exemplary in the Conduct of their Lives, Things would soon take a new Face, and Religion receive a mighty Encouragement: Nor would the publick Weal be less advanced; since of nine Offices in ten that are ill executed, the Defect is not in Capacity or Understanding, but in common Honesty. I know no Employment, for which Piety disqualifies any Man; and if it did, I doubt, the Objection would not be very seasonably offered at present: Because, it is perhaps too just a Reflection, that in the Disposal of Places, the Question whether a Person be *fit* for what he is recommended to, is generally the last that is thought on, or regarded.

I HAVE often imagined, that something parallel to the Office of Censors antiently in *Rome*, would be of mighty Use among us; and could be easily limited from running into any Exorbitances. The *Romans* understood Liberty at least as well as we; were as jealous of it, and upon every Occasion as bold Assertors: Yet I do not remember to have read any great Complaints of the Abuses in that Office among them; but many admirable Effects of it are left upon Record. There are several pernicious Vices frequent and notorious among us, that escape or elude the Punishment of any Law we have yet invented, or have had no Law at all against them; such as Atheism, Drunkenness, Fraud, Avarice, and several others; which by this Institution wisely regulated, might be much reformed. Suppose for Instance, that itinerary Commissioners were appointed to inspect every where throughout the Kingdom, into the Conduct (at least) of Men in Office, with respect to their Morals and Religion, as well as their Abilities; to receive the Complaints and Informations that should be offered against them; and make their Report here upon Oath, to the Court or the Ministry; who should reward or punish accordingly. I avoid entering into the Particulars of this or any other Scheme, which coming from a private hand, might be liable to many Defects, but would soon be digested by the Wisdom of the Nation: And surely, six thousand Pounds a Year would not be ill laid out among as many Commissioners duly qualified; who in three Divisions should be personally obliged to take their yearly Circuits for that Purpose.

BUT this is beside my present Design, which was only to shew what Degree of Reformation is in the Power of the Queen, without Interposition of the Legislature; and which Her Majesty is without Question obliged in Conscience to endeavour by Her Authority, as much as She doth by her Practice.

IT will be easily granted, that the Example of this great Town[3] hath a mighty Influence over the whole Kingdom; and it is as manifest, that the Town is equally influenced by the Court and the Ministry, and those, who by their Employments or their Hopes, depend upon them. Now, if under so excellent a Princess, as the present Queen, we would suppose a Family strictly regulated as I have above proposed; a Ministry, where every single Person was of distinguished Piety; if we should suppose all great Offices of State and Law filled after the same Manner, and with such as were equally diligent in chusing Persons, who in their several Subordinations would be obliged to follow the Examples of their Superiors, under the Penalty of Loss of Favour and Place; will not every Body grant, that the Empire of Vice and Irreligion would be soon destroyed in this great Metropolis, and receive a terrible Blow through the whole Island, which hath so great an Intercourse with it, and so much affects to follow its Fashions?

FOR, if Religion were once understood to be the necessary Step to Favour and Preferment; can it be imagined, that any Man would openly offend against it, who had the least Regard for his Reputation or his Fortune? There is no Quality so contrary to any Nature, which Men cannot affect, and put on upon Occasion, in order to serve an Interest, or gratify a prevailing Passion: The proudest Man will personate Humility, the morosest learn to flatter, the laziest will be sedulous and active, where he is in pursuit of what he hath much at Heart: How ready therefore would most Men be to step into the Paths of Virtue and Piety, if they infallibly led to Favour and Fortune?

IF Swearing and Prophaneness, scandalous and avowed Lewdness, excessive Gaming and Intemperance were a little discountenanced in the Army, I cannot readily see what ill Consequences could be apprehended: If Gentlemen of that Profession were at least obliged to some external Decorum in their Conduct; or even if a profligate Life and Character were not a Means of Advancement, and the Appearance of Piety a most infallible Hindrance; it is impossible the Corruptions there should be so universal and exorbitant. I have been assured by several great Officers, that no Troops abroad are so ill disciplined as the *English;* which cannot well be otherwise, while the common Soldiers have perpetually before their Eyes the vicious Example of their Leaders: And it is hardly possible for those to commit any Crime, whereof these are not infinitely more guilty, and with less Temptation.

IT is commonly charged upon the Gentlemen of the Army, that the beastly Vice of Drinking to Excess, hath been lately from their Example restored among us; which for some Years before was almost dropt in *England.* But whoever the Introducers were, they have succeeded to a Miracle; many of the young Nobility and Gentry are already become great Proficients, and are under no manner of Concern to hide their Talent; but are got beyond all Sense of Shame, or Fear of Reproach.

THIS might soon be remedied, if the Queen would think fit to declare, that no young Person of Quality whatsoever, who was notoriously addicted to that or any other Vice should be capable of Her Favour, or even admitted into her Presence; with positive Command to Her Ministers and others in great Office, to treat them in the same Manner; after which, all Men, who had any Regard for their Reputation, or any Prospect of Preferment, would avoid their Commerce. This would quickly make that Vice so scandalous, that those, who could not subdue, would at least endeavour to disguise it.

BY the like Methods, a Stop might be put to that ruinous Practice of deep Gaming: And the Reason why it prevails so much, is because a Treatment *directly opposite* in every Point is made use of to promote it; by which Means the Laws enacted against this Abuse are wholly eluded.

IT cannot be denied, that the want of strict Discipline in the Universities, hath been of pernicious Consequence to the Youth of this Nation, who are there almost left entirely to their own Management; especially those among them of better Quality and Fortune; who, because they are not under a Necessity of making Learning their Maintenance, are easily allowed to pass their Time, and take their Degrees with little or no Improvement: Than which there cannot well be a greater Absurdity. For if no Advancement of Knowledge can be had from those Places, the Time there spent is at best utterly lost, because every ornamental Part of Education is better taught elsewhere: And as for keeping Youths out of Harm's Way, I doubt, where so many of them are got together, at full Liberty of doing what they please, it will not answer the End. But, whatever Abuses, Corruptions, or Deviations from Statutes have crept into the Universities, through Neglect, or Length of Time; they might in a great Degree be reformed by strict Injunctions from Court, (upon each Particular, to the Visitors and Heads of Houses;) besides the peculiar Authority the Queen may have in several Colleges, whereof her Predecessors were the Founders. And among other Regulations, it would be very convenient to prevent the Excess of Drinking, with that scurvy Custom among the Lads, and Parent of the former Vice, the taking of Tobacco, where it is not absolutely necessary in point of Health.

FROM the Universities, the young Nobility, and others of great Fortunes are sent for early up to Town, for fear of contracting any Airs of Pedantry by a College-Education. Many of the younger Gentry retire to the Inns of Court, where they are wholly left to their own Discretion. And the Consequence of this Remisness in Education appears by observing that nine in ten of those, who rise in the Church or the Court, the Law or the Army, are younger Brothers, or new Men, whose narrow Fortunes have forced them upon Industry and Application.

As for the Inns of Court; unless we suppose them to be much degenerated, they must needs be the worst instituted Seminaries in any Christian Country; but whether they may be corrected without Interposition of the Legislature, I have not Skill enough to determine. However it is certain, that all wise Nations have agreed in the Necessity of a strict Education; which consisted among other Things, in the Observance of moral Duties, especially Justice, Temperance, and Chastity, as well as the Knowledge of Arts, and bodily Exercises: But all these, among us, are laughed out of Doors.

WITHOUT the least Intention to offend the Clergy; I cannot but think, that through a mistaken Notion and Practice, they prevent themselves from doing much Service, which otherwise might lie in their Power, to Religion and Virtue: I mean, by affecting so much to converse with each other, and caring so little to mingle with the Laity. They have their particular Clubs, and particular Coffee-Houses, where they generally appear in Clusters: A single Divine dares hardly shrew his Person among Numbers of fine Gentlemen; or if he happen to fall into such Company, he is silent and suspicious; in continual Apprehension, that some pert Man of Pleasure should break an unmannerly Jest, and render him ridiculous. Now, I take this Behaviour of the Clergy, to be just as reasonable, as if the Physicians should agree to spend their Time in visiting one another, or their several Apothecaries, and leave their Patients to shift for themselves. In my humble Opinion, the Clergy's Business lies entirely among the Laity; neither is there, perhaps, a more effectual Way to forward the Salvation of Mens Souls, than for spiritual Persons to make themselves as agreeable as they can, in the Conversations of the World; for which a learned Education gives them great Advantage, if they would please to improve and apply it. It so happens, that the *Men of Pleasure,* who never go to Church, nor amuse themselves to read Books of Devotion, form their Ideas of the Clergy, from a few poor Strolers they often observe in the Streets, or sneaking out of some Person of Quality's House, where they are hired by the Lady at Ten Shillings a Month; while those of better Figure and Parts do seldom appear to correct these Notions. And let some Reasoners think what they please; it is certain, that Men must be brought to esteem and love the Clergy, before they can be persuaded to be in love with Religion. No Man values the best Medicine, if administered by a Physician, whose Person he hates or despises. If the Clergy were as forward to appear in all Companies, as other Gentlemen, and would a little study the Arts of Conversation, to make themselves agreeable, they might be welcome at every Party, where there was the least Regard for Politeness, or good Sense; and consequently prevent a Thousand vicious or prophane Discourses, as well as Actions: Neither would Men of Understanding complain, that a Clergyman was a Constraint upon the Company; because they could not speak Blasphemy, or obscene Jests before him. While the People are so jealous of the Clergy's Ambition, as to abhor all Thoughts of the Return of Ecclesiastick Discipline among them; I do not see any other Method left for Men of that Function to take, in order to reform the World, than by using all honest Arts to make themselves acceptable to the Laity. This, no doubt, is Part of that Wisdom of the Serpent, which the Author of Christianity directs;[4] and is the very Method used by St. *Paul,* who *became all Things to all Men, to the* Jews *a* Jew, *and a* Greek *to the* Greeks.[5]

How to remedy these Inconveniences, may be a Matter of some Difficulty; since the Clergy seem to be of an Opinion, that this Humour of sequestring themselves is a Part of their Duty; nay, as I remember, they have been told so by some of their Bishops in their Pastoral Letters, particularly by *one*[*] among them; who yet, in his own Practice, hath all his Life-time taken a Course directly contrary. But I am deceived, if an awkard Shame, and fear of ill Usage from the Laity, have not a greater Share in this mistaken Conduct, than their own Inclinations: However, if the outward Profession of Religion and Virtue, were once in Practice and Countenance at Court, as well as among all Men in Office, or who have any Hopes or Dependance for Preferment; a good Treatment of the Clergy would be the necessary Consequence of such a Reformation; and they would soon be wise enough to see their own Duty and Interest, in qualifying themselves for Lay-Conversation, when once they were out of Fear of being choqued[6] by Ribaldry, or Prophaneness.

There is one further Circumstance upon this Occasion, which I know not whether it will be very orthodox to mention: The Clergy are the only Set of Men among us, who constantly wear a distinct Habit from others: The Consequence of which (not in Reason, but in Fact) is this, that as long as any scandalous Persons appear in that Dress, it will continue, in some Degree, a general Mark of Contempt. Whoever happens to see a *Scoundrel in a Gown,* reeling home at Midnight, (a Sight neither *frequent* nor *miraculous*) is apt to entertain an ill Idea of the whole Order; and, at the same Time, to be extreamly comforted in his own Vices. Some Remedy might be put to this, if those straggling Gentlemen, who come up to Town to *seek their Fortunes,* were fairly dismissed to the *West Indies;* where there is Work enough, and where some better Provision should be made for them, than I doubt there is at present. Or, what if no Person were allowed to wear the Habit, who had not some Preferment in the Church; or, at least, some temporal Fortune sufficient to keep him out of Contempt?

* *Supposed to be Dr.* Burnet, *Bishop of* Salisbury.

THERE is one Abuse in this Town, which wonderfully contributes to the Promotion of Vice; when such Men are often put into the Commission of the Peace, whose Interest it is, that Virtue should be utterly banished from among us; who maintain, or at least enrich themselves by encouraging the grossest Immoralities; to whom all the *Bawds* of the *Ward* pay Contribution for Shelter and Protection from the Laws. Thus these worthy Magistrates, instead of lessening Enormities, are the Occasion of just twice as much Debauchery as there would be without them. For those infamous Women are forced upon doubling their Work and Industry, to answer double Charges, of paying the Justice, and supporting themselves: Like Thieves who escape the Gallows, and are let out to steal, in order to discharge the Goaler's Fees.

IT is not to be questioned, but the Queen and Ministry might easily redress this abominable Grievance; by enlarging the Number of Justices of the Peace; by endeavouring to chuse Men of virtuous Principles; by admitting none, who have not considerable Fortunes; perhaps by receiving into the Number some of the most eminent Clergy: Then, by forcing all of them, upon severe Penalties, to act when there is Occasion; and not permitting any, who are offered, to refuse the Commission. But in these two last Cases, which are very material, I doubt there would be need of the Legislature.

THE Reformation of the Stage is entirely in the Power of the Queen; and in the Consequences it hath upon the Minds of younger People, doth very well deserve the strictest Care. Beside the undecent and prophane Passages; beside the perpetual turning into Ridicule the very Function of the Priesthood; with other Irregularities in most modern Comedies, which have been often objected to them; it is worth observing the distributive Justice of the Authors, which is constantly applied to the Punishment of Virtue, and the Reward of Vice; directly opposite to the Rules of their best Criticks, as well as to the Practice of Dramatick Poets in all other Ages and Countries. For Example; a Country 'Squire, who is represented with no other Vice but that of being a Clown, and having the provincial Accent upon his Tongue, which is neither a Fault, nor in his Power to remedy, must be condemned to marry a cast Wench, or a cracked Chamber Maid. On the other Side, a Rakehell of the Town, whose Character is set off with no other Accomplishments but excessive Prodigality, Prophaneness, Intemperance, and Lust; is rewarded with the Lady of great Fortune, to repair his own, which his Vices had almost ruined. And as in a Tragedy, the Hero is represented to have obtained many Victories, in order to raise his Character in the Minds of the Spectators; so the Hero of a Comedy is represented to have been victorious in all his Intrigues for the same Reason. I do not remember that our *English* Poets ever suffered a criminal Amour to succeed upon the Stage, until the Reign of King *Charles* the Second. Ever since that Time, the Alderman is made a Cuckold, the deluded Virgin is debauched; and Adultery and Fornication are supposed to be committed behind the Scenes, as Part of the Action. These and many more Corruptions of the Theatre, peculiar to our Age and Nation, need continue no longer than while the Court is content to connive at, or neglect them. Surely a Pension would not be ill employed on some Man of Wit, Learning, and Virtue, who might have Power to strike out every offensive, or unbecoming Passage from Plays already written, as well as those that may be offered to the Stage for the future. By which, and other wise Regulations, the Theatre might become a very innocent and useful Diversion, instead of being a Scandal and Reproach of our Religion and Country.

THE Proposals I have hitherto made, for the Advancement of Religion and Morality, are such, as come within the Reach of the Administration; such as a pious active Prince, with a steddy Resolution, might soon bring to Effect. Neither am I aware of any Objections to be raised against what I have advanced; unless it should be thought, that the making Religion a necessary Step to Interest and Favour, might encrease Hypocrisy among us: And I readily believe it would. But if One in Twenty should be brought over to true Piety by this, or the like Methods, and the other Nineteen be only Hypocrites, the Advantage would still be great. Besides, Hypocrisy is much more eligible than open Infidelity and Vice: It wears the Livery of Religion,[7] it acknowledgeth her Authority, and is cautious of giving Scandal. Nay, a long continued Disguise is too great a Constraint upon human Nature, especially an *English* Disposition. Men would leave off their Vices out of meer Weariness, rather than undergo the Toil and Hazard, and perhaps Expence of practising them perpetually in private. And, I believe, it is often with Religion as it is with Love; which, by much Dissembling, at last grows real.

ALL other Projects to this great End, have proved hitherto ineffectual. Laws against Immorality have not been executed; and Proclamations occasionally issued out to enforce them, are wholly unregarded as Things of Form. Religious Societies, although begun with excellent Intention, and by Persons of true Piety, are said, I know not whether truly or no, to have dwindled into factious Clubs, and grown a Trade to enrich little knavish

Informers of the meanest Rank, such as common Constables, and broken Shop-keepers.

AND that some effectual Attempt should be made towards such a Reformation, is perhaps more necessary, than People commonly apprehend; because the Ruin of a State is generally preceded by an universal Degeneracy of Manners, and Contempt of Religion; which is entirely our Case at present.

Diis te minorem, quod geris, imperas.[8]

NEITHER is this a Matter to be deferred till a more convenient Time of Peace and Leisure: A Reformation in Mens Faith and Morals, is the best natural, as well as religious Means to bring the War to a good Conclusion. Because, if Men in Trust performed their Duty for Conscience Sake, Affairs would not suffer through Fraud, Falshood, and Neglect, as they now perpetually do: And if they believed a God and his Providence, and acted accordingly, they might reasonably hope for his Divine Assistance in so just a Cause as ours.

NOR could the Majesty of the *English* Crown appear, upon any Occasion, in a greater Lustre, either to Foreigners, or Subjects, than by an Administration, which producing such good Effects, would discover so much Power. And Power being the natural Appetite of Princes; a limited Monarch cannot so well gratify it in any Point, as a strict Execution of the Laws.

BESIDES; all Parties would be obliged to close with so good a Work as this, for their own Reputation: Neither is any Expedient more likely to unite them. For, the most violent Partymen I have ever observed, are such as in the Conduct of their Lives have discovered least Sense of Religion, or Morality; and when all such are laid aside, at least those among them who shall be found incorrigible, it will be a Matter, perhaps, of no great Difficulty to reconcile the rest.

THE many Corruptions, at present, in every Branch of Business, are almost inconceivable. I have heard it computed by skilful Persons, that of Six Millions, raised every Year for the Service of the Publick, one Third, at least, is sunk and intercepted through the several Classes and Subordinations of artful Men in Office, before the Remainder is applied to the proper Use. This is an accidental ill Effect of our Freedom: And while such Men are in Trust, who have no Check from within, nor any Views but towards their Interest; there is no other Fence against them, but the

Certainty of being hanged upon the first Discovery, by the arbitrary Will of an unlimited Monarch, or his *Vizier.* Among Us, the only Danger to be apprehended, is the Loss of an Employment; and that Danger is to be eluded a Thousand Ways. Besides, when Fraud is great, it furnisheth Weapons to defend it self: And, at worst, if the Crimes be so flagrant, that a Man is laid aside out of perfect Shame, (which rarely happens) he retires loaded with the Spoils of the Nation; *Et fruitur Diis iratis.*[9] I could name a Commission, where several Persons out of a Sallary of Five Hundred Pounds, without other visible Revenues, have always lived at the Rate of Two Thousand, and laid out Forty or Fifty Thousand upon Purchases of Land, or Annuities. An Hundred other Instances of the same Kind might easily be produced. What Remedy, therefore, can be found against such Grievances in a Constitution like ours, but to bring Religion into Countenance, and encourage those who, from the Hope of future Reward, and Dread of future Punishment, will be moved to act with Justice and Integrity?

THIS is not to be accomplished any other Way, than by introducing Religion, as much as possible, to be the Turn and Fashion of the Age; which only lies in the Power of the Administration; the Prince with utmost Strictness regulating the Court, the Ministry, and other Persons in great Employment; and these, by their Example and Authority, reforming all who have Dependance on them.

IT is certain, that a Reformation, successfully carried on in this great Town, would, in Time, spread it self over the whole Kingdom; since most of the considerable Youth pass here that Season of their Lives, wherein the strongest Impressions are made, in order to improve their Education, or advance their Fortune: And those among them who return into their several Countries, are sure to be followed and imitated, as the greatest Patterns of Wit and good Breeding.

AND if Things were once in this Train; that is, if Virtue and Religion were established as the necessary Titles to Reputation and Peferment; and if Vice and Infidelity were not only loaden with Infamy, but made the infallible Ruin of all Mens Pretensions; our Duty, by becoming our Interest, would take Root in our Natures, and mix with the very Genius of our People; so that it would not be easy for the Example of one wicked Prince, to bring us back to our former Corruptions.

I HAVE confined my self (as it is before observed) to those Methods for the Advancement of Piety, which are in the Power of a Prince limited like ours, by a strict Execution of the Laws already in Force. And this is enough for a Project that comes without any Name, or Recommendation: I doubt, a great deal more than will suddenly be reduced into Practice. Although, if any Disposition should appear towards so good a Work, it is certain, that the Assistance of the legislative Power would be necessary to make it more compleat. I will instance only in a few Particulars.

IN order to reform the Vices of this Town, which, as we have said, hath so mighty an Influence on the whole Kingdom; it would be very instrumental, to have a Law made, that all Taverns, or Ale-houses should be obliged to dismiss their Company by Twelve at Night, and shut up their Doors; and that no Woman should be suffered to enter any Tavern, or Ale-house upon any Pretence whatsoever. It is easy to conceive, what a Number of ill Consequences such a Law would prevent; the Mischiefs of Quarrels and Lewdness, and Thefts, and Midnight Brawls, the Diseases of Intemperance and Venery; and a Thousand other Evils needless to mention. Nor would it be amiss, if the Masters of those publick Houses were obliged, upon the severest Penalties, to give only a proportioned Quantity of Drink to every Company; and when he found his Guests disordered with Excess, to refuse them any more.

I BELIEVE there is hardly a Nation in *Christendom,* where all Kind of Fraud is practised in so unmeasurable a Degree as with us. The Lawyer, the Tradesman, the Mechanick, have found so many Arts to deceive in their several Callings, that they far outgrow the common Prudence of Mankind, which is in no Sort able to fence against them. Neither could the Legislature, in any Thing, more consult the publick Good, than by providing some effectual Remedy against this Evil; which, in several Cases, deserves greater Punishment than many Crimes that are capital among us. The Vintner, who, by mixing Poison with his Wines, destroys more Lives than any malignant Disease: The Lawyer, who persuades you to a Purchase, which he knows is mortgaged for more than the Worth, to the Ruin of you and your Family: The Banquier or Scrivener, who takes all your Fortune to dispose of, when he hath beforehand resolved to break the following Day; do surely deserve the Gallows much better than the Wretch, who is carried thither for stealing a Horse.

IT cannot easily be answered to God or Man, why a Law is not made for limiting the Press; at least so far as to prevent the publishing of such pernicious Books, as under Pretence of *Free-Thinking,* endeavour to overthrow those Tenets in Religion, which have been held inviolable almost in all Ages by every Sect that pretends to be Christian; and cannot therefore with any Colour of Reason he called *Points in Controversy,* or *Matters of*

Speculation, as some would pretend. The Doctrine of the *Trinity,* the *Divinity of Christ,* the *Immortality of the Soul,* and even the Truth of all Revelation are daily exploded,[10] and denied in Books openly printed; although it is to be supposed, that neither Party avow such Principles, or own the supporting of them to be any way necessary to their Service.

IT would be endless to set down every Corruption or Defect, which requires a Remedy from the legislative Power. Senates are like to have little Regard for any Proposals that come from *without Doors:* Although under a due Sense of my own Inabilities, I am fully convinced that the unbiased Thoughts of an honest and wise Man, employed on the Good of his Country, may be better digested, than the Results of a Multitude, where Faction and Interest too often prevail: As a single Guide may direct the Way, better than five Hundred who *have contrary Views,* or *look asquint,* or *shut their Eyes.*

I SHALL mention but one more Particular, which I think a Parliament ought to take under Consideration: Whether it be not a Shame to our Country, and a Scandal to Christianity, that in many Towns, where there is a prodigious Increase in the Number of Houses and Inhabitants, so little Care should be taken for the Building of Churches, that five Parts in six of the People are absolutely hindered from hearing Divine Service? Particularly here in *London,** where a single Minister with one or two sorry Curates, hath the Care sometimes of above twenty thousand Souls incumbent on him. A Neglect of Religion so ignominious in my Opinion, that it can hardly be equalled in any civilized Age or Country.

BUT, to leave these airy Imaginations of introducing new Laws for the Amendment of Mankind: What I principally insist on is the due Execution of the old, which lies wholly in the Crown, and in the Authority derived from thence: I return therefore to my former Assertion; that, if Stations of Power, Trust, Profit, and Honour were constantly made the Rewards of Virtue and Piety; such an Administration must needs have a mighty Influence on the Faith and Morals of the whole Kingdom: And Men of great Abilities would *then* endeavour to excel in the Duties of a religious Life, in order to qualify themselves for publick Service. I may possibly be wrong in some of the Means I prescribe towards this End; but that is no material Objection against the Design it self. Let those, who are at

---

* *This Paragraph is known to have given the first Hint to certain Bishops, particularly to that most excellent Prelate Bishop* Atterbury, *in the Earl of* Oxford's *Ministry, to procure a Fund for building fifty new Churches in* London.

the Helm contrive it better, which perhaps they may easily do. Every Body will agree, that the Disease is manifest, as well as dangerous; that some Remedy is necessary, and that none yet applied hath been effectual; which is a sufficient Excuse for any Man who wishes well to his Country, to offer his Thoughts, when he can have no other end in View but the publick Good. The present Queen is a Prince of as many and great Virtues as ever filled a Throne: How would it brighten Her Character to the present and after Ages, if she would exert Her utmost Authority to instil some Share of those Virtues into Her People, which they are too degenerate to learn only from Her Example. And, be it spoke with all the Veneration possible for so excellent a Sovereign; Her best Endeavours in this weighty Affair, are a most important Part of Her Duty, as well as of Her Interest, and Her Honour.

BUT, it must be confessed, That as Things are now, every Man thinks he hath laid in a sufficient Stock of Merit, and may pretend to any Employment, provided he hath been loud and frequent in declaring himself hearty for the Government. It is true he is a *Man of Pleasure,* and a *Free-Thinker;* that is, in other Words, he is profligate in his Morals, and a despiser of Religion; but in Point of Party, he is one to be *confined* in; he is an Asserter of Liberty and Property; he rattles it out against *Popery,* and *Arbitrary Power,* and *Priest Craft,* and *High-Church.* It is enough: He is a Person fully qualified for any Employment in the Court, or the Navy, the Law, or the Revenue; where he will be sure to leave no Arts untried of Bribery, Fraud, Injustice, Oppression, that he can practice with any Hope of Impunity. No Wonder such Men are true to a Government, where Liberty runs high, where Property, *however attained,* is so well secured, and where the Administration is at least so gentle: It is impossible they could chuse any other Constitution, without changing to their Loss.

FIDELITY, to a present Establishment, is indeed one principal Means to defend it from a foreign Enemy; but without other Qualifications will not prevent Corruptions from within: And States are more often ruined by these than the other.

TO conclude: Whether the Proposals I have offered towards a Reformation, be such as are most prudent and convenient, may probably be a Question; but it is none at all, whether *some* Reformation be absolutely necessary; because the Nature of Things is such, that if Abuses be not remedied, they will certainly encrease, nor ever stop till they end in the Subversion of a Common-Wealth. As there must always of Necessity be some Corruptions; so in a well-instituted State, the executive Power will be always contending against them, by *reducing Things* (as *Machiavel* speaks) *to their first Principles*,[11] never letting Abuses grow inveterate, or multiply so far that it will be hard to find Remedies, and perhaps impossible to apply them. As he that would keep his House in Repair, must attend every little Breach or Flaw, and supply it immediately, else Time alone will bring all to Ruin; how much more the common Accidents of Storms and Rain? He must live in perpetual Danger of his House falling about his Ears; and will find it cheaper to throw it quite down, and build it again from the Ground, perhaps upon a new Foundation, or at least in a new Form, which may neither be so safe nor so convenient as the old.

III

ENGLISH POLITICAL
WRITINGS

FROM *THE EXAMINER*

No. 16. *Thursday, November 23, 1710*

Qui sunt boni cives? qui belli, qui domi de patriâ bene merentes, nisi qui patriæ beneficia meminerunt?[1]

I will employ this present Paper upon a Subject which of late hath very much affected me, which I have considered with a good deal of Application, and made several Enquiries about, among those Persons who I thought were best able to inform me; and if I deliver my Sentiments with some Freedom, I hope it will be forgiven, while I accompany it with that Tenderness which so nice a Point requires.

I SAID in a former Paper (Numb. 13.) that one specious Objection to the late Removals at Court, was the Fear of giving Uneasiness to a General, who hath been long successful abroad: And accordingly, the common Clamour of Tongues and Pens for some Months past, hath run against the Baseness, the Inconstancy and Ingratitude of the whole Kingdom to the Duke of *Marlborough,* in return of the most eminent Services that ever were performed by a Subject to his Country; not to be equalled in History. And then to be sure some bitter Stroak of Detraction against *Alexander* and *Cæsar,* who never did us the least Injury. Besides, the People who read *Plutarch* come upon us with Parallels drawn from the *Greeks* and *Romans,* who ungratefully dealt with I know not how many of their most deserving Generals: While the profounder Politicians, have seen Pamphlets, where *Tacitus* and *Machiavel* have been quoted to shew the Danger of too resplendent a Merit. If a Stranger should hear these furious Out-cries of Ingratitude against our General, without knowing the Particulars, he would be apt to enquire where was his Tomb, or whether he were allowed Christian Burial? Not doubting but we had put him to some ignominious Death. Or, hath he been tried for his Life, and very narrowly escaped? Hath he been accused of high Crimes and Misdemeanours? Has the Prince seized on his Estate, and left him to starve? Hath he been hooted at as he passed the Streets, by an ungrateful Rabble? Have neither Honours, Offices nor Grants, been conferred on him or his Family? Have not he and they been barbarously stript of them all? Have not he and his Forces been ill payed abroad? And doth not the Prince, by a scanty, limited Commission, hinder him from pursuing his own Methods in the Conduct of the War? Hath he no Power at all of disposing Commissions as he pleaseth? Is he not severely used by the Ministry or Parliament, who yearly call him to a strict Account? Has the Senate ever thanked him for good Success; and have they not always publickly censured him for the least Miscarriage? Will the Accusers of the Nation join Issue upon any of these Particulars; or, tell us in what Point our damnable Sin of Ingratitude lies? Why, it is plain and clear; for while he is commanding abroad, the Queen dissolveth her Parliament, and changeth her Ministry at home: In which *universal Calamity,* no less than *two Persons* allied by Marriage² to the General, have lost their Places. Whence came this wonderful Sympathy between the Civil and Military Powers? Will the Troops in *Flanders* refuse to fight, unless they can have *their own* Lord Keeper; *their own* Lord President of the Council; *their own* chief Governor of *Ireland;* and *their own* Parliament? In a Kingdom where the People are free, how came they to be so fond of having their Counsels under the Influence of their Army, or those that lead it? Who in all well-instituted States, had no Commerce with the Civil Power; further than to receive their Orders, and obey them without Reserve.

WHEN a General is not so Popular, either in his Army, or at home, as one might expect from a long Course of Success; it may perhaps be ascribed to his *Wisdom,* or perhaps to his Complection. The Possession of some one *Quality,* or a Defect in *some other,* will extremely damp the Peoples Favour, as well as the Love of the Soldiers. Besides, this is not an Age to produce Favourites of the People, while we live under a Queen who engrosseth all our Love, and all our Veneration; and where, the only Way for a great General or Minister, to acquire any Degree of subordinate Affection from the Publick, must be by all Marks of the most *entire Submission and Respect* to her sacred Person and Commands; otherwise, no pretence of great Services, either in the Field or the Cabinet, will be able to skreen them from universal Hatred.

BUT the late Ministry was closely joined to the General, by Friendship, Interest, Alliance, Inclination and Opinion; which cannot be affirmed of the present; and the Ingratitude of the Nation lieth in the People's *joining as one Man,*[3] to wish, that such a Ministry should be changed. Is it not at the same Time notorious to the whole Kingdom, that nothing but a tender Regard to the General, was able to preserve that Ministry so long, until neither God nor Man could suffer their Continuance? Yet in the highest Ferment of Things, we heard few or no Reflections upon this great Commander; but all seemed Unanimous in wishing he might still be at the Head of the Confederate Forces; only at the same Time, in Case he were resolved to resign, they chose rather to turn their Thoughts somewhere else, than throw up all in Despair. And this I cannot but add, in Defence of the People, with Regard to the Person we are speaking of; that in the high Station he hath been for many Years past, his *real Defects* (as nothing Human is without them) have in a detracting Age been very sparingly mentioned, either in Libels or Conversation; and all his *Successes* very freely and universally applauded.

THERE is an active and a passive Ingratitude: Applying both to this Occasion; We may say, the first is, when a Prince or People returns good Services with Cruelty or ill Usage: The other is, when good Services are not at all, or very meanly rewarded. We have already spoke of the former; let us therefore in the second Place, examine how the Services of our General have been rewarded; and whether upon that Article, either Prince or People have been guilty of Ingratitude?

THOSE are the most valuable Rewards which are given to us from the certain Knowledge of the Donor, that they *fit our Temper best:* I shall therefore say nothing of the Title of *Duke,* or the *Garter,* which the Queen bestowed the General in the beginning of her Reign: But I shall come to *more substantial* Instances,[4] and mention nothing which hath not been given in the Face of the World. The Lands of *Woodstock,* may, I believe, be reckoned worth 40,000 *l.* On the building of *Blenheim* Castle 200,000 *l.* have been already expended, although it be not yet near finished. The Grant of 5000 *l. per Annum,* on the Post Office, is richly worth 100,000 *l.* His Principality in *Germany* may be computed at 30,000 *l.* Pictures, Jewels, and other Gifts from Foreign Princes, 60,000 *l.* The Grant at the *Pall-Mall,* the Rangership, &*c.* for want of more certain Knowledge, may be called 10,000 *l.* His own, and his Dutchess's Employments at five Years Value, reckoning only the known and avowed Salaries, are very low rated at 100,000 *l.* Here is a good deal above half a Million of Money; and I dare say, those who are loudest with the Clamour of Ingratitude, will readily own, that all this is but a Trifle, in Comparison of what is *untold.*

THE Reason of my stating this Account is only to convince the World, that we are not quite so ungrateful either as the *Greeks* or the *Romans.* And in order to adjust this Matter with all Fairness, I shall confine myself to the latter, who were much the more generous of the two. A Victorious General of *Rome* in the Height of that Empire, having *entirely subdued his Enemies,* was rewarded with the larger Triumph; and perhaps a Statue in the *Forum;* a Bull for a Sacrifice; an embroidered Garment to appear in; a Crown of Laurel; a Monumental Trophy with Inscriptions; sometimes five hundred or a thousand Copper Coins were struck on Occasion of the Victory; which, doing Honour to the General, we will place to his Account: And lastly, sometimes, although not very frequently, a Triumphal Arch. These are all the Rewards that I can call to Mind, which a victorious General received after his return from the most glorious Expedition; conquered some great Kingdom; brought the King himself, his Family and Nobles to adorn the Triumph in Chains; and made the Kingdom either a *Roman* Province, or at best, a poor depending State, in humble Alliance to that Empire. Now, of all these Rewards, I find but two which were of real Profit to the General: The *Laurel Crown,* made and sent him at the Charge of the Publick; and the *embroidered Garment;* but I cannot find whether this last were paid for by the Senate or the General: However, we will take the more favourable Opinion; and in all the rest, admit the whole Expence, as if it were ready Money in the General's Pocket. Now according to these Computations on both Sides, we will draw up two fair Accounts; the one of *Roman* Gratitude, and the other of *British* Ingratitude; and set them together in Ballance.

A Bill of ROMAN *Gratitude.*				*A Bill of* BRITISH *Ingratitude.*			
Imprim.	*l.*	*s.*	*d.*	Imprim.	*l.*	*s.*	*d.*
For Frankincense and Earthen Pots to burn it in	4	10	0	Woodstock.	40000	0	0
				Blenheim.	200000	0	0
A Bull for Sacrifice	8	0	0	Post-Office Grant.	100000	0	0
An embroidered Garment	50	0	0	Mildenheim.	30000	0	0
A Crown of Laurel	0	0	2	Pictures, Jewels, &c.	60000	0	0

A Statue	100	0	0	*Pall Mall* }			
A Trophy	80	0	0	*Grant, &c.* }	10000	0	0
A thousand Copper Medals, Value half- pence a Piece }	2	1	8	Employments.	100000	0	0
					540000	0	0
A Triumphal Arch	500	0	0				
A Triumphal Carr, valued as a Modern Coach }	100	0	0				
Casual Charges at the Triumph. }	150	0	0				
	994	11	10				

THIS is an Account of the visible Profits on both Sides; and if the *Roman* General had any *private Perquisites,* they may be easily discounted, and by more probable Computations; and differ yet more upon the Balance; if we consider, that all the Gold and Silver for *Safeguards* and *Contributions;* and all *valuable Prizes* taken in the War, were openly exposed in the Triumph; and then lodged in the Capital for the Publick Service.

So that upon the Whole, we are not yet quite so bad at *worst,* as the *Romans* were at *best.* And I doubt, those who raise this hideous Cry of In- gratitude, may be mightily mistaken in the Consequences they propose from such Complaints. I remember a Saying of *Seneca,*[5] *Multos ingratos in- venimus, plures facimus:* We find many ungrateful Persons in the World, but we *make* more, by setting too high a Rate upon our Pretensions, and un- dervaluing the Rewards we receive. When unreasonable Bills are brought in, they ought to be taxed, or cut off in the Middle. Where there have been long Accounts between two Persons, I have known one of them perpetu- ally making large Demands, and pressing for Payments; who when the Ac- counts were cast up on both Sides, was found to be Debtor for some Hundreds. I am thinking, if a Proclamation were issued out for every Man to send in his *Bill of Merits,* and the lowest Price he set them at, what a pretty Sum it would amount to, and how many such Islands as this must be Sold to pay them. I form my Judgment from the Practice of those who sometimes happen to *pay themselves;* and I dare affirm, would not be so un- just to take a Farthing more than they think is due to their Deserts. I will Instance only in one Article. A Lady* of my Acquaintance, appropriated

* *Supposed to be her late Majesty Queen* Anne.

twenty six Pounds a Year out of her own Allowance, for certain Uses, which her Woman† received, and was to pay to the Lady or her Order, as it was called for. But after eight Years, it appeared upon the strictest Calculation, that the Woman had paid but four Pounds a Year, and sunk two and twenty for her own Pocket: It is but supposing instead of twenty six Pounds, twenty six thousand; and by that you may judge what the Pretensions of *Modern Merit* are, where it happens to be its own Paymaster.

† *The Duchess of* Marlborough.

A SHORT CHARACTER OF
HIS EXCELLENCY
THOMAS EARL OF WHARTON,
LORD LIEUTENANT OF IRELAND

*With an Account of some smaller Facts during his Government,
which will not be put into the Articles of Impeachment.*

London, Aug. 30, 1710.

The Kingdom of *Ireland*, being governed by Deputation from hence, its Annals, since the *English* Establishment, are usually digested under the Heads of the several Governors: But, the Affairs and Events in that Island, for some Years past, have been either so insignificant, or so annexed to those of *England*, that they have not furnished Matter of any great Importance to History. The Share of Honour, which Gentlemen from thence have had by their Conduct and Employments in the Army, turneth all to the Article of this Kingdom; the rest which relateth to Politics, or the Art of Government, is inconsiderable to the last Degree, however it may be represented at Court by those who preside there, and would value themselves upon every Step they make, towards finishing the Slavery of that People, as if it were gaining a mighty Point to the Advantage of *England*.

GENERALLY speaking, the Times which afford most plentiful Matter for Story, are those in which a Man would least chuse to live; such as under the various Events and Revolutions of War, the Intrigues of a ruined Faction, or the Violence of a prevailing one, and lastly the arbitrary, unlawful Acts of oppressing Governors. In the War, *Ireland* hath no Share but in Subordination to us; the same may be said of their Factions, which, at present, are but imperfect Transcripts of ours: But the third Subject for

History, which is arbitrary Power, and Oppression; as it is that by which the People of *Ireland* have for some Time, been distinguished from all her Majesty's* Subjects, so being now at its greatest Height under his Excellency *Thomas* Earl of *Wharton,* a short Account of his Government, may be of some Use or Entertainment to the present Age, although, I hope, it will be incredible to the next: And, because this Account may be judged rather an History of his Excellency, than of his Government, I must here declare that I have not the least View to his Person in any Part of it. I have had the Honour of much Conversation with his Lordship, and am thoroughly convinced how indifferent he is to Applause, and how insensible of Reproach: Which is not a Humour put on to serve a Turn, or keep a Countenance, nor arising from the Consciousness of Innocence, or any Grandeur of Mind, but the meer unaffected Bent of his Nature.

HE is without the Sense of Shame or Glory, as some Men are without the Sense of Smelling; and, therefore, a good Name to him is no more than a precious Ointment would be to these. Whoever, for the Sake of others, were to describe the Nature of a Serpent, a Wolf, a Crocodile or a Fox, must be understood to do it without any personal Love or Hatred for the Animals themselves.

IN the same Manner, his Excellency is one whom I neither personally love nor hate. I see him at Court, at his own House, and sometimes at mine (for I have the Honour of his Visits) and when these Papers are public, it is Odds but he will tell me, as he once did upon a like Occasion, that he is damnably mauled; and then with the easiest Transition in the World, ask about the Weather, or Time of the Day? So that I enter on the Work with more Chearfulness, because I am sure, neither to make him angry, nor any Way hurt his Reputation; a Pitch of Happiness and Security to which his Excellency hath arrived, which no Philosopher before him could reach.

I INTEND to execute this Performance by first giving a Character of his Excellency, and then relating some Facts during his Government, which will serve to confirm it.

I KNOW very well that Mens Characters are best known from their Actions; but these being confined to his Administration in *Ireland,* his Character may, perhaps, take in something more, which the Narrowness of the Time, or the Scene hath not given him Opportunity to exert.

THOMAS, Earl of *Wharton,* Lord Lieutenant of *Ireland,* by the Force of a wonderful Constitution hath some Years passed his Grand Climacteric,[1]

---

* *Queen* ANNE.

without any visible Effects of old Age, either on his Body or his Mind, and in Spight of a continual Prostitution to those Vices which usually wear out both. His Behaviour is in all the Forms of a young Man at five and twenty. Whether he walketh or whistleth, or sweareth, or talketh Bawdy, or calleth Names, he acquitteth himself in each beyond a Templar[2] of three Years standing. With the same Grace, and in the same Style he will rattle his Coachman in the Middle of the Street, where he is Governor of the Kingdom; and, all this is without Consequence, because it is in his Character, and what every Body expecteth. He seemeth to be but an ill Dissembler, and an ill Liar, although they are the two Talents he most practiseth, and most valueth himself upon. The Ends he hath gained by Lying appear to be more owing to the Frequency, than the Art of them: His Lies being sometimes detected in an Hour, often in a Day, and always in a Week. He tells them freely in mixed Companies, although he knows half of those that hear him to be his Enemies, and is sure they will discover them the Moment they leave him. He sweareth solemnly he loveth, and will serve you; and your Back is no sooner turned, but he tells those about him you are a Dog and a Rascal. He goeth constantly to Prayers in the Forms of his Place, and will talk Bawdy and Blasphemy at the Chapel Door. He is a Presbyterian in Politics, and an Atheist in Religion; but he chuseth at present to whore with a Papist. In his Commerce with mankind his general Rule is, to endeavour to impose on their Understanding, for which he hath but one Receipt, a Composition of Lies and Oaths: And this he applieth indifferently, to a Freeholder of forty Shillings, and a Privy-Counsellor; by which the Easy and the Honest are often either deceived or amused, and either Way he gaineth his Point. He will openly take away your Employment To-day, because you are not of his Party; To-morrow he will meet or send for you, as if nothing at all had passed, lay his Hands with much Friendship on your Shoulders, and with the greatest Ease and Familiarity, tell you that the Faction are driving at something in the House; that you must be sure to attend, and to speak to all your Friends to be there, although he knoweth at the same Time, that you and your Friends are against him in the very Point he mentioneth: And however absurd, ridiculous and gross this may appear, he hath often found it successful, some Men having such an aukward Bashfulness, they know not how to refuse on a sudden, and every Man having something to hope or fear, which often hinders them from driving Things to Extremes with Persons of Power, whatever Provocations they may have received. He hath sunk his Fortune by endeavouring to ruin one

Kingdom,* and hath raised it by going far in the Ruin of another.† With a good natural Understanding, a great Fluency in Speaking, and no ill Taste of Wit, he is generally the worst Companion in the World; his Thoughts being wholely taken up between Vice and Politics, so that Bawdy, Prophaneness and Business, fill up his whole Conversation. To gratify himself in the two first he maketh use of suitable Favourites, whose Talents reach no higher than to entertain him with all the Lewdness that passeth in Town. As for Business, he is said to be very dextrous at that Part of it which turneth upon Intrigue, and he seemeth to have transferred those Talents of his Youth for intriguing with Women, into public Affairs. For, as some vain young Fellows, to make a Gallantry appear of Consequence, will chuse to venture their Necks by climbing up a Wall or Window at Midnight to a common Wench, where they might as freely have gone in at the Door, and at Noon-Day; so his Excellency, either to keep himself in Practice, or advance the Fame of his Politics, affects the most obscure, troublesome, and winding Paths, even in the most common Affairs, those which would be brought about as well in the ordinary Forms, or would follow of Course whether he intervened or not.

HE bears the Gallantries of his Lady with the Indifference of a Stoic, and thinks them well recompenced by a Return of Children to support his Family without the Fatigues of being a Father. He has three predominant Passions, which you will seldom find united in the same Man, as arising from different Dispositions of Mind, and naturally thwarting each other: These are Love of Power, Love of Money, and Love of Pleasure; they ride him sometimes by Turns, and sometimes all together: Since he went into *Ireland*, he seemeth most disposed to the second, and hath met with great Success, having gained by his Government, of under two Years, five and forty thousand Pounds by the most favourable Computation, half in the regular Way, and half in the prudential.

HE was never yet known to refuse or keep a Promise; as I remember he told a Lady, but with an Exception to the Promise he then made (which was to get her a Pension) yet he broke even that, and I confess, deceived us both. But here I desire to distinguish between a Promise and a Bargain; for he will be sure to keep the latter when he has the fairest Offer.

THUS much for his Excellency's Character: I shall now proceed to his Actions, only during the Time he was Governor of *Ireland*, which were

* *England.*
† *Ireland.*

transmitted to me by an eminent Person in Business there, who had all Opportunities of being well informed, and whose Employment did not lie at his Excellency's Mercy.

THIS Intelligence being made up of several Facts independent of each other, I shall hardly be able to relate them in due Order of Time, my Correspondent omitting that Circumstance, and transmitting them to me just as he recollected them; so that the Gentlemen of that Kingdom, now in Town, will, I hope, pardon me any Slips I shall make in that or any other Kind, while I keep exactly to the Truth.

THOMAS PROBY, Esq; Chirurgeon-General of *Ireland,* a Person universally esteemed, and whom I have formerly seen here, had built a Country-House, half a Mile from *Dublin,* adjoining to the Phœnix Park. In a Corner of the Park, just under his House, he was much annoyed with a Dog-kennel which belonged to the Government; upon which he applied to *Thomas,* Earl of *Pembroke,* then Lord Lieutenant, and to the Commissioners of the Revenue, for a Lease of about five Acres of that Part of the Park. His Petition was referred to the Lord Treasurer here, and sent back for a Report, which was in his Favour, and the Bargain so hard, that the Lord Treasurer struck off some Part of the Rent. He had a Lease granted him, for which he was to build another Kennel, provide Ice yearly for the Government, and pay a certain Rent; the Land might be worth about thirty Shillings an Acre. His Excellency, soon after his Arrival in *Ireland,* was told of this Lease, and by his absolute Authority commanded Mr. *Proby* to surrender up the Land; which he was forced to do, after all the Expence he had been at, or else, must have expected to lose his Employment; at the same Time he is under an Obligation to pay his Rent, and, I think, he doth it to this Day. There are several Circumstances in this Story which I have forgot, having not been sent to me with the rest; but, I had it from a Gentleman of that Kingdom, who some Time ago was here.

UPON his Excellency's being declared Lord Lieutenant, there came over to make his Court one Dr. *Lloyd,* Fellow of Trinity College, *Dublin,* noted in that Kingdom for being the only Clergyman that declared for taking off the Sacramental Test, as he did openly in their Convocation of which he was a Member. The Merit of this, and some other Principles suitable to it, recommended by *Tom Broderick,* so far ingratiated him with his Excellency, that being provided of a proper Chaplain already, he took him however into a great Degree of Favour: The Doctor attended his Excellency to *Ireland,* and observing a cast Wench in the Family to be in much Confidence with my Lady, he thought by addressing there, to have a short open Passage to Preferment. He met with great Success in his Amour; and walking one Day with his Mistress after my Lord and Lady in the Castle-Garden, my Lady said to his Excellency, "What do you think? we are going to lose poor *Foydy*," a Name of Fondness they usually gave her. "How do you mean?" said my Lord. "Why the Doctor behind us is resolved to take her from us." "Is he, by G—d? why then (G—d d—mn me) he shall have the first Bishoprick that falls."*

THE Doctor, thus encouraged, grew a most violent Lover, returned with his Excellency for *England;* and soon after, the Bishoprick of *Cork* falling void, to shew he meant fair, he married his Damsel publickly here in *London,* and his Excellency as honourably engaged his Credit to get him the Bishoprick; but, the Matter was reckoned so infamous, that both the Archbishops here, especially his Grace of *York,* interposed with the Queen, to hinder so great a Scandal to the Church, and Dr. *Brown,* Provost of *Dublin* College, being then in Town, her Majesty was pleased to nominate him; so that Dr. *Lloyd* was forced to sit down with a moderate Deanery in the Northern Parts of that Kingdom, and the additional Comfort of a sweet Lady, who brought this her first Husband no other Portion, than a Couple of Olive Branches for his Table, though she herself hardly knoweth by what Hand they were planted.

THE Queen reserveth all the great Employments of *Ireland* to be given by herself, though often by the Recommendation of the chief Governor, according to his Credit at Court. The Provostship of *Dublin* College is of this Number, which was now vacant, upon the Promotion of Dr. *Brown;* Dr. *Benjamin Pratt,* a Fellow of that College, and Chaplain to the House of Commons of that Kingdom, as well as domestic Chaplain to the Duke of *Ormond,* was at that Time here, in Attendance upon the Duke. He is a Gentleman of good Birth and Fortune in *Ireland,* and lived here in a very decent Figure: He is a Person of Wit and Learning, hath travelled and conversed in the best Company, and was very much esteemed among us here when I had the Pleasure of his Acquaintance: But, he had the original Sin of being a reputed Tory, and a Dependent on the Duke of *Ormond;* however, he had many Friends among the Bishops and other Nobility to recommend him to the Queen; at the same Time there was another Fellow of that College, one Dr. *Hall,* who had much the Advantage of *Pratt* in Point of Seniority; this Gentleman had very little introduced himself into

---

* *It was confidently reported, as a Conceit of his Excellency, that, talking upon this Subject, he once said with great Pleasure, that he hoped to make his W——e[3] a Bishop.*

the World, but lived retired, although otherwise said to be an excellent Person, and very deserving for his Learning and Sense: He had been recommended from *Ireland* by several Persons, and his Excellency, who had never before seen nor thought of him, after having tried to injure the College by recommending Persons from this Side, at last set up *Hall,* with all imaginable Zeal against *Pratt.* I tell this Story the more fully, because it is affirmed, by his Excellency's Friends, that he never made more Use of his Court Skill, than at this Time, to stop Dr. *Pratt's* Promotion; not only from the Personal Hatred he had to the Man, on Account of his Patron and Principles, but that he might return to *Ireland* with some little Opinion of his Credit at Court; which had mightily suffered by many Disappointments, especially that of his Chaplain Dr *Lloyd.* It would be incredible to relate the man Artifices he used to this End, of which the Doctor had daily intelligence, and would fairly tell his Excellency so at his Levees,[4] who sometimes could not conceal his Surprize, and then would promise with half a dozen Oaths, never to concern himself one Way or other; these were broke every Day, and every Day detected. One Morning, after some Expostulation between the Doctor and his Excellency, and a few additional Oaths, that he would never oppose him more, his Excellency went immediately to the Bishop of *Ely,* and prevailed on him to go to the Queen, from him, and let her Majesty know, that he never could consent, as long as he lived, that Dr. *Pratt* should be Provost, which the Bishop barely complied with, and delivered his Message; although at the same Time he did the Dr. all the good Offices he could. The next Day the Doctor was again with his Excellency, and gave him Thanks for so open a Proceeding; the Affair was now past dissembling, and his Excellency, owned he did not oppose him directly, but confessed he did it collaterally. The Doctor, a little warmed, said, "No, my Lord, you mean directly you did not, but indirectly you did." The Conclusion was, that the Queen named the Doctor to the Place; and, as a further Mortification, just upon the Day of his Excellency's Departure for *Ireland.*

BUT here I must desire the Reader's Pardon, if I cannot digest the following Facts in so good a Manner as I intended; because it is thought expedient, for some Reasons, that the World should be informed of his Excellency's Merits as soon as possible. I will therefore only transcribe the several Passages as they were sent me from *Dublin,* without either correcting the Style, or adding any Remarks of my own. As they are, they may serve for Hints to any Person, who may hereafter have a Mind to write Memoirs of his Excellency's Life.

THE

IMPORTANCE

OF THE

GUARDIAN

CONSIDERED, IN A SECOND

LETTER

TO THE

BAILIFF OF *STOCKBRIDGE*

THE PREFACE

Mr. Steele *in his Letter to the Bailiff of* Stockbridge *has given us leave to* treat him as we think fit, as he is our Brother-Scribler; but not to attack him as an honest Man. *That is to say, he allows us to be his* Criticks, *but not his An-swerers; and he is altogether in the right, for there is in his Letter much to be* Crit-icised, *and little to be* Answered. *The Situation and Importance of* Dunkirk *are pretty well known, Monsieur* Tugghe's *Memorial, published and handed about by the Whigs, is allowed to be a very Trifling Paper: And as to the immediate Demol-ishment of that Town, Mr.* Steele *pretends to offer no other Argument but the Ex-pectations of the People, which is a figurative Speech, naming the tenth Part for the whole: As* Bradshaw[1] *told King* Charles I. *that the People of* England *Expected Justice against him. I have therefore entred very little into the Subject he pretends to Treat, but have considered his Pamphlet partly as a* Critick, *and partly as a* Com-mentator, *which, I think, is* to treat him only as my Brother-Scribler, *accord-ing to the Permission he has graciously allowed me.*

TO THE WORSHIPFUL MR. *JOHN SNOW*,
BAILIFF OF *STOCKBRIDGE*

SIR,

I have just been reading a Twelve-peny Pamphlet about *Dunkirk*, addressed to your Worship from one of your intended Representatives; and I find several Passages in it which want Explanation, especially to You in the Country: For we in Town have a way of Talking and Writing, which is very little understood beyond the Bills of Mortality. I have therefore made bold to send you here a second Letter, by way of Comment upon the former.

In order to this, *You Mr.* Bailiff, *and at the same time the whole Burrough*, may please to take Notice, that *London*-Writers often put Titles to their Papers and Pamphlets which have little or no Reference to the main Design of the Work: So, for Instance, you will observe in reading, that the Letter called, *The Importance of Dunkirk*, is chiefly taken up in shewing you the *Importance* of Mr. *Steele*; wherein it was indeed reasonable your Burrough should be informed, which had chosen him to Represent them.

I would therefore place the *Importance* of this Gentleman before you in a clearer Light than he has given himself the Trouble to do; without running into his early History, because I owe him no Malice.

Mr. *Steele* is Author of two tolerable Plays,[2] (or at least of the greatest part of them) which, added to the Company he kept, and to the continual Conversation and Friendship of Mr. *Addison*,[3] hath given him the Character of a Wit. To take the height of his Learning, you are to suppose a Lad just fit for the University, and sent early from thence into the wide World, where he followed every way of Life that might least improve or preserve the Rudiments he had got. He hath no Invention, nor is Master of a tolerable Style; his chief Talent is Humour, which he sometimes discovers both in Writing and Discourse; for after the first Bottle he is no disagreeable Companion. I never knew him taxed with Ill-nature, which hath made me wonder how Ingratitude came to be his prevailing Vice; and I am apt to think it proceeds more from some unaccountable sort of Instinct, than Premeditation. Being the most imprudent Man alive, he never follows the Advice of his Friends, but is wholly at the mercy of Fools or Knaves, or hurried away by his own Caprice; by which he hath committed more Absurdities in Oeconomy, Friendship, Love, Duty, good Manners, Politicks, Religion and Writing, than ever fell to one Man's share. He was appointed Gazetteer by Mr. *Harley* (then Secretary of State) at the Recommendation of Mr. *Mainwaring*, with a Salary of Three Hundred Pounds; was a Commissioner of Stampt-Paper of equal Profit, and had a Pension of a Hundred Pound *per Annum*, as a Servant to the late Prince *George*.

This Gentleman, whom I have now described to you, began between four and five Years ago to publish a Paper thrice a Week, called the *Tatler*; It came out under the borrowed Name of *Isaac Bickerstaff*, and by Contribution of his ingenious Friends, grew to have a great Reputation, and was equally esteemed by both Parties, because it meddled with neither. But, sometime after *Sacheverell's* Tryal,[4] when Things began to change their Aspect; Mr. *Steele*, whether by the Command of his Superiors, his own Inconstancy, or the Absence of his Assistants, would needs corrupt his Paper with Politicks; published one or two most virulent Libels, and chose for his Subject even that individual Mr. *Harley,* who had made him Gazetteer. But his Finger and Thumb not proving strong enough to stop the general Torrent, there was an universal Change made in the Ministry; and the Two new Secretaries, not thinking it decent to employ a Man in their Office who had acted so infamous a Part; Mr. *Steele,* to avoid being discarded, thought fit to resign his Place of Gazetteer. Upon which occasion I cannot forbear relating a Passage *to You Mr. Bailiff, and the rest of the Burrough,* which discovers a very peculiar Turn of Thought in this Gentleman you have chosen to Represent you. When Mr. *Mainwaring* recommended him to the Employment of Gazetteer, Mr. *Harley* out of an Inclination to encourage Men of Parts, raised that Office from Fifty Pound to Three Hundred Pound a Year; Mr. *Steele* according to form, came to give his new Patron Thanks; but the Secretary, who had rather confer a hundred Favours than receive Acknowledgments for one, said to him in a most obliging manner: Pray Sir, do not thank me, but thank Mr. *Mainwaring.* Soon after Mr. *Steele's* quitting that Employment, he complained to a Gentleman in Office, of the Hardship put upon him in being forced to quit his Place; that he knew Mr. *Harley* was the Cause; that he never had done Mr. *Harley* any Injury, nor received any Obligation from him. The Gentleman amazed at this Discourse, put him in mind of those Libels published in his *Tatlers:* Mr. *Steele* said, he was only the Publisher, for they had been sent him by other Hands. The Gentleman thinking this a very monstrous kind of Excuse, and not allowing it, Mr. *Steele* then said, Well, I have Libelled him, and he has turned me out, and so we are equal. But neither would this be granted: And he was asked whether the Place of Gazetteer were not an Obligation? No, said he, not from Mr. *Harley;* for when I went to thank him, he forbad me, and said, I must only thank Mr. *Mainwaring.*

But I return, Mr. Bailiff, to give you a further Account of this Gentleman's Importance. In less, I think, than Two Years, the Town and He grew weary of the *Tatler:* He was silent for some Months; and then a daily Paper came from him and his Friends under the Name of *Spectator,* with good Success: This being likewise dropt after a certain Period, he hath of late appeared under the Style of *Guardian,* which he hath now likewise quitted for that of *Englishman;* but having chosen other Assistance, or trusting more to himself, his Papers have been very coldly received, which hath made him fly for Relief to the never-failing Source of Faction.

On the . . . . . of *August* last, Mr. *Steele* writes a Letter to *Nestor Ironside,*

Esq; and subscribes it with the Name of *English Tory*. On the 7th the said *Ironside* publishes this Letter in the *Guardian*. How shall I explain this Matter to you, Mr. Bailiff, and your Brethren of the Burrough? You must know then, that Mr. *Steele* and Mr. *Ironside* are the same Persons, because there is a great Relation between *Iron* and *Steel*; and *English Tory* and Mr. *Steele* are the same Persons, because there is no Relation at all between Mr. *Steele* and an *English Tory*; so that to render this Matter clear to the very meanest Capacities, Mr. *English Tory*, the very same Person with Mr. *Steele*, writes a Letter to *Nestor Ironside*, Esq; who is the same Person with *English Tory*, who is the same Person with Mr. *Steele:* And Mr. *Ironside*, who is the same Person with *English Tory*, publishes the Letter written by *English Tory*, who is the same Person with Mr. *Steele*, who is the same Person with Mr. *Ironside*. This Letter written and published by these *Three* Gentlemen who are *One* of your Representatives, complains of a printed Paper in *French* and *English*, lately handed about the Town, and given *gratis* to Passengers in the Streets at Noon-day; the Title whereof is, *A most humble Address or Memorial presented to Her Majesty the Queen of* Great Britain, *by the Deputy of the Magistrates of* Dunkirk. This Deputy, it seems, is called the Sieur *Tugghe*. Now, the Remarks made upon this Memorial by Mr. *English Tory*, in his Letter to Mr. *Ironside*, happening to provoke the *Examiner*, and another Pamphleteer, they both fell hard upon Mr. *Steele*, charging him with Insolence and Ingratitude towards the Queen. But Mr. *Steele* nothing daunted, writes a long Letter *to you Mr. Bailiff, and at the same time to the whole Burrough*, in his own Vindication: But there being several difficult Passages in this Letter, which may want clearing up, I here send you and the Burrough my Annotations upon it.

Mr. *Steele* in order to display his *Importance* to your Burrough, begins his Letter by letting you know *he is no small Man;* because in the Pamphlets he hath sent you down, you will *find him spoken of more than once in Print*. It is indeed a great Thing to be *spoken of in Print*, and must needs make a mighty Sound at *Stockbridge* among the Electors. However, if Mr. *Steele* has really sent you down all the Pamphlets and Papers printed since the Dissolution, you will find he is not the only Person of Importance; I could Instance *Abel Roper*, Mr. *Marten* the Surgeon, Mr. *John Moor* the Apothecary at the Pestle and Mortar, Sir *William Read*, Her Majesty's Oculist, and of later Name and Fame, Mr. *John Smith* the Corncutter, with several others who are *spoken of more than once in Print*. Then he recommends to your Perusal, and sends you a Copy of a printed Paper given *gratis* about the Streets, which is the Memorial of Monsieur *Tugghe* (above-mentioned)

Deputy of the Magistrates of Dunkirk, to desire Her Majesty not to demolish the said Town. He tells you how insolent a Thing it is, that such a Paper should be publickly distributed, and he tells you true; but these Insolences are very frequent among the Whigs: One of their present Topicks for Clamour is *Dunkirk:* Here is a Memorial said to be presented to the Queen by an obscure *Frenchman:* One of your Party gets a Copy, and immediately Prints it by Contribution, and delivers it *gratis* to the People; which answers several Ends. *First,* It is meant to lay an Odium on the Ministry; *Secondly,* If the Town be soon demolished, Mr. *Steele* and his Faction have the Merit, their Arguments and Threatnings have frighted my Lord Treasurer; *Thirdly,* If the Demolishing should be further deferred, the Nation will be fully convinced of his Lordship's Intention to bring over the *Pretender.*

Let us turn over fourteen Pages, which contain the Memorial it self, and which is indeed as idle a one as ever I read; we come now to Mr. *Steele's* Letter under the Name of *English Tory,* to Mr. *Ironside.* In the Preface to this Letter, he hath these Words, *It is certain there is not much danger in delaying the Demolition of* Dunkirk *during the Life of his present most Christian Majesty, who is renowned for the most inviolable Regard to Treaties; but that pious Prince is Aged, and in case of his Decease,* &c. This Preface is in the Words of Mr. *Ironside* a professed Whig, and perhaps you in the Country will wonder to hear a Zealot of your own Party celebrating the *French* King for his Piety and his religious Performance of Treaties. For this I can assure you is not spoken in jest, or to be understood by contrary; There is a wonderful resemblance between that Prince and the Party of Whigs among us. Is he for arbitrary Government? So are they: Hath he persecuted Protestants? So have the Whigs: Did he attempt to restore King *James* and his pretended Son? They did the same. Would he have *Dunkirk* surrendred to him? This is what they desire. Does he call himself the *Most Christian?* The Whigs assume the same Title, though their Leaders deny Christianity: Does he break his Promises? Did they ever keep theirs?

From the 16th to the 38th Page Mr. *Steele's* Pamphlet is taken up with a Copy of his Letter to Mr. *Ironside,* the Remarks of the *Examiner,* and another Author upon that Letter; the Hydrography of some *French* and *English* Ports, and his Answer to Mr. *Tugghe's* Memorial. The Bent of his Discourse is in appearance to shew of what prodigious Consequence to the Welfare of *England,* the Surrendry of *Dunkirk* was. But here, Mr. Bailiff, you must be careful; for all this is said in Raillery; for you may easily remember, that when the Town was first yielded to the Queen, the Whigs declared it was of no Consequence at all, that the *French* could easily repair it after the Demolition, or fortify another a few Miles off, which would be of more Advantage to them. So that what Mr. *Steele* tells you of the prodigious Benefit that will accrue to *England* by destroying this Port, is only suited to present Junctures and Circumstances. For if *Dunkirk* should now be represented as insignificant as when it was first put into Her Majesty's Hands, it would signify nothing whether it were demolished or no, and consequently one principal Topick of Clamour would fall to the Ground.

In Mr. *Steele's* Answer to Monsieur *Tugghe's* Arguments against the Demolishing of *Dunkirk,* I have not observed any thing that so much deserves your peculiar Notice, as the great Eloquence of your new Member, and his wonderful Faculty of varying his Style, which he calls, *proceeding like a Man of great Gravity and Business.* He has Ten Arguments of *Tugghe's* to answer; and because he will not go in the old beaten Road, like a Parson of a Parish, *First, Secondly, Thirdly,* &c. his manner is this,

> In answer to the Sieur's *First.*
> As to the Sieur's *Second.*
> As to his *Third.*
> As to the Sieur's *Fourth.*
> As to Mr. Deputy's *Fifth.*
> As to the Sieur's *Sixth.*
> As to this Agent's *Seventh.*
> As to the Sieur's *Eighth.*
> As to his *Ninth.*
> As to the Memorialist's *Tenth.*

You see every Second Expression is more or less diversified to avoid the Repetition of, *As to the Sieur's,* &c. and there is the Tenth into the Bargain: I could heartily wish Monsieur *Tugghe* had been able to find Ten Arguments more, and thereby given Mr. *Steele* an Opportunity of shewing the utmost Variations our Language would bear in so momentous a Tryal.

Mr. *Steele* tells you, That having now done *with his foreign Enemy Monsieur* Tugghe, *he must face about to his Domestick Foes, who accuse him of Ingratitude and insulting his Prince, while he is eating her Bread.*

To do him Justice, he acquits himself pretty tolerably of this last Charge: For he assures You, he gave up his Stampt-Paper-Office, and Pension as Gentleman-Usher, before he writ that Letter to himself in the

Guardian, so that he had already received his Salary, and spent the Money, and consequently the *Bread was eaten* at least a Week before he would offer to *insult his Prince:* So that the Folly of the Examiner's objecting Ingratitude to him upon this Article, is manifest to all the World.

But he tells you, he has quitted those Employments to render him more useful to his Queen and Country in the Station you have honoured him with. That, no doubt, was the principal Motive; however, I shall venture to add some others. *First,* The *Guardian* apprehended it impossible, that the Ministry would let him keep his Place much longer, after the Part he had acted for above two Years past. *Secondly,* Mr. *Ironside* said publickly, that he was ashamed to be obliged any longer to a Person (meaning Lord *Treasurer*) whom he had used so ill: For it seems, a Man ought not to use his Benefactors ill above two Years and a half. *Thirdly,* The *Sieur Steele* appeals for Protection to you, Mr. Bailiff, from *others* of your *Denomination,* who would have carried him *some where else,*[5] if you had not removed him by your *Habeas Corpus* to St. *Stephen's* Chapel. *Fourthly,* Mr. *English Tory* found, by calculating the Life of a Ministry, that it hath lasted above three Years, and is near expiring; he resolved therefore to *strip off the very Garments spotted with the Flesh,*[6] and be wholly regenerate against the Return of his old Masters.

In order to serve all these Ends, your Burrough hath honoured him (as he expresses it) with chusing him to represent you in Parliament, and it must be owned, he hath equally honoured you. Never was Burrough more happy in suitable Representatives, than you are in Mr. *Steele* and his Collegue, nor were ever Representatives more happy in a suitable Burrough.

When Mr. *Steele* talk'd of *laying before Her Majesty's Ministry, that the Nation has a strict Eye upon their Behaviour with relation to* Dunkirk, Did not you, Mr. Bailiff, and your Brethren of the Burrough presently imagine, he had drawn up a sort of Counter-Memorial to that of Monsieur *Tugghe's,* and presented it in form to my Lord *Treasurer,* or a Secretary of State? I am confident you did; but this comes by not understanding the Town: You are to know then, that Mr. *Steele* publishes every Day a Peny-paper to be read in Coffee-houses, and get him a little Money. This by a Figure of Speech, he calls, *laying Things before the Ministry,* who seem at present a little too busy to regard such Memorials; and, I dare say, never saw his Paper, unless he sent it them by the Peny-Post.

Well, but he tells you, he *cannot offer against the* Examiner *and his other Adversary, Reason and Argument without appearing void of both.* What a singular Situation of the Mind is this! How glad should I be to hear a Man *offer Rea-*

sons and Argument, and yet at the same time appear void of both! But this whole Paragraph is of a peculiar strain; the Consequences so Just and Natural, and such a Propriety in Thinking, as few Authors ever arrived to. *Since it has been the Fashion to run down Men of much greater Consequence than I am; I will not bear the Accusation.* This I suppose is, *to offer Reasons and Arguments, and yet appear void of both.* And in the next Lines; *These Writers shall treat me as they think fit, as I am their Brother-Scribler, but I shall not be so unconcerned when they attack me as an honest Man.* And how does he defend himself ? *I shall therefore inform them that it is not in the Power of a private Man, to hurt the Prerogative,* &c. Well; I shall *treat* him *only as a Brother-Scribler:* And I guess he will hardly be attacked as an honest Man: But if his meaning be that his Honesty ought not to be attacked, because he *has no Power to hurt the Honour and Prerogative of the Crown without being punished;* he will make an admirable Reasoner in the House of Commons.

But all this wise Argumentation was introduced, only to close the Paragraph by haling in a Fact, which he relates to you and your Burrough, in order to quiet the Minds of the People, and express his Duty and Gratitude to the Queen. The Fact is this; That *Her Majesty's Honour is in danger* of being lost *by Her Ministers tolerating Villains without Conscience to abuse the greatest Instruments of Honour and Glory to our Country, the most Wise and Faithful Managers, and the most Pious, disinterested, generous, and self-denying Patriots;* And the Instances he produces, are the Duke of *Marlborough,* the late Earl of *Godolphin,* and about two Thirds of the Bishops.

Mr. Bailiff, I cannot debate this Matter at length, without putting you and the rest of my Countrymen, who will be at the Expence, to Six-pence Charge extraordinary. The Duke and Earl were both removed from their Employments; and I hope you have too great a Respect for the Queen, to think it was done for nothing. The former was *at the Head* of many great Actions; and he has received plentiful Oblations of Praise and Profit: Yet having read all that ever was objected against him by the *Examiner,* I will undertake to prove every Syllable of it true, particularly that famous Attempt to be General for Life. The Earl of *Godolphin* is dead, and his Faults may sojourn with him in the Grave, 'till some Historian shall think fit to revive part of them for Instruction and Warning to Posterity. But it grieved me to the Soul, to see so many good Epithets bestowed by Mr. *Steele* upon the Bishops: Nothing has done more hurt to that Sacred Order for some Years past, than to hear some Prelates extolled by Whigs, Dissenters, Republicans, Socinians, and in short by all who are Enemies to Episcopacy. God, in his Mercy, for ever keep our Prelates from deserving the Praises of such Panegyrists!

Mr. *Steele* is discontented that the Ministry have not *called the* Examiner *to Account as well as the* Flying-Post. I will inform you, Mr. Bailiff, how that Matter stands. The Author of the *Flying-Post*[7] has thrice a Week for above Two Years together, published the most impudent Reflections upon all the present Ministry, upon all their Proceedings, and upon the whole Body of *Tories.* The *Examiner* on the other side, writing in Defence of those whom Her Majesty employs in her greatest Affairs, and of the Cause they are engaged in, hath always borne hard upon the Whigs, and now and then upon some of their Leaders. Now, Sir, we reckon here, that supposing the Persons on both Sides to be of equal Intrinsick Worth, it is more Impudent, Immoral, and Criminal to reflect on a *Majority* in Power, than a *Minority* out of Power. Put the Case, that an odd Rascally Tory in your Borough should presume to abuse your Worship who, in the Language of Mr. *Steele,* is first Minister, and the Majority of your Brethren, for sending Two such Whig-Representatives up to Parliament: And on the other side, that an honest Whig should stand in your Defence, and fall foul on the Tories; would you equally resent the Proceedings of both, and let your Friend and Enemy sit in the Stocks together? Hearken to another Case, Mr. Bailiff; suppose your Worship, during your Annual Administration, should happen to be kick'd and cuff'd by a parcel of Tories, would not the Circumstance of your being a Magistrate, make the Crime the greater, than if the like Insults were committed on an ordinary Tory Shopkeeper, by a Company of honest Whigs? What Bailiff would venture to Arrest Mr. *Steele,* now he has the Honour to be your Representative? and what Bailiff ever scrupled it before?

You must know, Sir, that we have several Ways here of abusing one another, without incurring the Danger of the Law. First, we are careful never to print a Man's Name out at length: but as I do that of Mr. *Steele:*[*] So that although every Body alive knows whom I mean, the Plaintiff can have no Redress in any Court of Justice. Secondly, by putting Cases; Thirdly, by Insinuations; Fourthly, by celebrating the Actions of others, who acted directly contrary to the Persons we would reflect on; Fifthly, by Nicknames, either commonly known or stamp'd for the purpose, which every Body can tell how to apply. Without going on further, it will be enough to inform you, that by some of the ways I have already mentioned, Mr. *Steele* gives you to understand, that the Queen's Honour is blasted by the Actions of Her present Ministers; that Her *Prerogative is disgraced by erecting a dozen Peers, who, by their Votes, turned a Point upon which Your All depended;* That

* The name in the original edition was regularly spelled with a dash, *St——*.

*these Ministers made the Queen lay down Her conquering Arms, and deliver Her
Self up to be vanquish'd; That they made Her Majesty betray Her Allies, by ordering Her Army to face about, and leave them in the Moment of Distress; That the
present Ministers are Men of poor and narrow Conceptions, Self-Interested, and
without Benevolence to Mankind; and were brought into Her Majesty's Favour for
the Sins of the Nation, and only think what they may do, not what they ought to do.*
This is the Character given by Mr. *Steele* of those Persons, whom Her
Majesty has thought fit to place in the highest Stations of the Kingdom,
and to trust them with the Management of Her most weighty Affairs: And
this is the Gentleman who cries out, *Where is Honour? Where is Government?
Where is Prerogative?* Because the *Examiner* has sometimes dealt freely with
those, whom the Queen has thought fit to *Discard*, and the Parliament to
Censure.

But Mr. *Steele* thinks it highly dangerous to the Prince, *that any Man
should be hindered from offering his Thoughts upon public Affairs;* and resolves to
do it, *tho' with the Loss of Her Majesty's Favour.* If a Clergy-man offers to
preach Obedience to the higher Powers, and proves it by Scripture, Mr.
Steele and his Fraternity immediately cry out, What have Parsons to do
with Politicks? I ask, What shadow of a Pretence has he to offer his crude
Thoughts in Matters of State? to Print and Publish them? *to lay them before
the Queen and Ministry?* and to reprove Both for Male-Administration?
How did he acquire these Abilities of directing in the Councils of
Princes? Was it from **Publishing** *Tatlers* and *Spectators,* and Writing now and
then a *Guardian?* Was it from his being a Soldier, Alchymist, Gazetteer,
Commissioner of Stampt Papers, or Gentleman-Usher? No; but he insists
it is every Man's Right to find fault with the Administration in Print,
whenever they please: And therefore you, Mr. Bailiff, and as many of your
Brethren in the Borough as can Write and Read, may publish Pamphlets,
and *lay them before the Queen and Ministry,* to shew your utter dislike of all
their Proceedings; and for this Reason, because you *can certainly see and apprehend with your own Eyes and Understanding, those Dangers which the* Ministers *do not.*

One thing I am extreamly concerned about, that Mr. *Steele* resolves, as
he tells you, when he comes into the House, *to follow no Leaders, but Vote according to the Dictates of his Conscience;* He must, at that rate, be a very useless Member to his Party, unless his Conscience be already cut out and
shaped for their Service, which I am ready to believe it is, if I may have
leave to judge from the whole Tenor of his Life. I would only have his
Friends be cautious, not to reward him too liberally: For, as it was said of

Cranmer, Do the Archbishop an ill Turn, and he is your Friend for ever. So I do affirm of your Member, *Do Mr.* Steele *a good Turn, and he is your Enemy for ever.*

I had like to let slip a very trivial Matter (which I should be sorry to have done). In reading this Pamphlet, I observed several Mistakes, but knew not whether to impute them to the Author or Printer; till turning to the end, I found there was only one *Erratum,* thus set down, *Pag.* 45. *Line* 28. *for* Admonition *read* Advertisement. This (to imitate Mr. *Steele's* Propriety of Speech) is a very *old* Practice among *new* Writers, to make a wilful Mistake, and then put it down as an *Erratum.* The Word is brought in upon this Occasion: To convince all the World that he was not guilty of Ingratitude, by reflecting on the Queen, when he was actually under Sallary, as the *Examiner* affirms; he assures you, he *had resign'd and divested himself of all, before he would presume to write any thing which was so apparently an* ADMONITION *to those employed in Her Majesty's Service.* In case the *Examiner* should find fault with this Word, he might Appeal to the *Erratum;* and having formerly been *Gazetteer,* he conceived he might very safely venture to *Advertise.*

You are to understand, Mr. Bailiff, that in the great Rebellion against King *Charles* I. there was a Distinction found out between the *Personal* and *Political* Capacity of the Prince; by the help of which, those Rebels professed to Fight for the *King,* while the great Guns were discharging against *Charles Stuart.* After the same manner Mr. *Steele* distinguishes between the *Personal* and *Political* Prerogative. He does not care to trust this Jewel *to the Will, and Pleasure, and Passion of Her Majesty.* If I am not mistaken, the Crown-Jewels cannot be alienated by the Prince; but I always thought the Prince could *wear* them during his Reign, else they had as good be in the Hands of the Subject: So, I conceive, Her Majesty may and ought to *wear* the Prerogative; that it is Her's during Life; and She ought to be so much the more careful, neither to soil nor diminish it, for that very Reason, because it is by Law unalienable. But what must we do with this Prerogative, according to the notion of Mr. *Steele?* It must not be trusted with the Queen, because Providence has given Her *Will, Pleasure, and Passion.* Her Ministers must not act by the Authority of it; for then Mr. *Steele* will cry out, What? *Are Majesty and Ministry consolidated? And must there be no Distinction between the one and the other?* He tells you, *The Prerogative attends the Crown;* and therefore, I suppose, must lie in the *Tower* to be shewn for Twelve pence, but never produced, except at a Coronation, or passing an Act. Well; but says he, *A whole Ministry may be Impeached and condemned by the House of Commons, without the Prince's suffering by it.* And what follows? Why, therefore a single Burgess of *Stockbridge,* before he gets into the House, may at any time Revile a whole Ministry in Print, before he knows whether they are guilty of any one Neglect of Duty, or Breach of Trust.

———

I am willing to join Issue with Mr. *Steele* in one Particular; which perhaps may give you some Diversion. He is taxed by the *Examiner* and others, for an insolent Expression, that the *British* Nation *Expects* the immediate Demolition of *Dunkirk.* He says, the Word E X P E C T, was meant to the *Ministry,* and not to the *Queen; but that however, for Argument sake, he will suppose those Words were addressed immediately to the Queen.* Let me then likewise for Argument sake, suppose a very ridiculous Thing, that Mr. *Steele* were admitted to Her Majesty's Sacred Person, to tell his own Story, with his Letter to You, Mr. Bailiff, in his Hand to have recourse to upon Occasion. I think his Speech must be in these Terms.

MADAM,
　　I Richard Steele *Publisher of the* Tatler *and* Spectator, *late* Gazetteer, *Commissioner of Stamp Papers, and Pensioner to Your Majesty, now Burgess Elect of* Stockbridge, *do see and apprehend with my own Eyes and Understanding, the imminent Danger that attends the Delay of the Demolition of* Dunkirk, *which I believe Your Ministers, whose greater Concern it is, do not: For, Madam, the Thing is not done, My Lord* Treasurer *and Lord* Bolingbroke, *my Fellow-Subjects, under whose immediate Direction it is, are careless, and overlook it, or something worse; I mean, they design to sell it to* France, *or make use of it to bring in the* Pretender. *This is clear from their suffering Mr.* Tugghe's *Memorial to be published without punishing the Printer. Your Majesty has told us, that the Equivalent for* Dunkirk *is already in the* French King's *Hands; therefore all Obstacles are removed on the Part of* France; *and I, though a mean Fellow, give Your Majesty to understand in the best Method I can take, and from the Sincerity of my* G R A T E F U L *Heart, that the British Nation* E X P E C T S *the* I M M E D I A T E *Demolition of* Dunkirk; *as you hope to preserve Your Person, Crown, and Dignity, and the Safety and Welfare of the People committed to Your Charge.*

I have contracted such a Habit of treating Princes familiarly, by reading the Pamphlets of Mr. *Steele* and his Fellows, that I am tempted to suppose Her Majesty's Answer to this Speech might be as follows.

　　Mr. Richard Steele, *late Gazetteer, &c. I do not conceive that any of your Titles empower you to be my Director, or to report to me the Expectations of my People. I know their Expectations better than you; they love me, and will trust me. My Ministers were of my own free Choice; I have found them Wise and Faithful; and whoever calls them Fools or Knaves, designs indirectly an Affront to my Self. I am under no Obligations to demolish* Dunkirk, *but to the Most* Christian King; *if you come here as an* Orator *from that Prince to demand it in his Name, where are your Powers? If not, let it suffice you to know, that I have my Reasons for deferring it; and that the Clamours of a* Faction *shall not be a Rule by which I or my Servants are to proceed.*

———

Mr. *Steele* tells you; his *Adversaries are so unjust, they will not take the least Notice of what led him into the Necessity of writing his Letter to the* Guardian. And how is it possible, any Mortal should know all his *Necessities?* Who can guess, whether this *Necessity* were imposed on him by his *Superiours,* or by the Itch of Party, or by the meer want of other Matter to furnish out a *Guardian?*

But Mr. *Steele* has *had a Liberal Education,* and *knows the World as well as the Ministry does,* and *will therefore speak on whether he offends them or no, and though their Cloaths* be ever so *New; when he thinks his Queen and Country is,* (or as a Grammarian would express it, *are*) ill treated.

It would be good to hear Mr. *Steele* explain himself upon this Phrase of *knowing the World;* because it is a Science which maintains abundance of Pretenders. Every idle young Rake, who understands how to pick up a Wench, or bilk a Hackney-Coachman, or can call the Players by their Names, and is acquainted with five or six Faces in the Chocolate-House, will needs pass for a Man that *knows the World.* In the like manner Mr. *Steele* who from some few Sprinklings of rudimental Literature, proceeded a Gentleman of the Horse-Guards, thence by several Degrees to be an Ensign and an Alchymist, where he was wholly conversant with the lower Part of Mankind, thinks he *knows the World* as well as the Prime Minister; and upon the Strength of that Knowledge, will needs direct Her Majesty in the weightiest Matters of Government.

And now, Mr. Bailiff, give me Leave to inform you, that this long Letter of Mr. *Steele* filled with Quotations and a Clutter about *Dunkirk,* was wholly written for the sake of the six last Pages, taken up in vindicating himself directly, and vilifying the Queen and Ministry by Innuendo's. He apprehends, that *some Representations have been given of* him *in your Town, as, that a Man of so small a Fortune as* he *must have secret Views or Supports, which could move him to leave his Employments,* &c. He answers, by owning he *has indeed very particular Views; for he is animated in his Conduct by Justice and Truth, and Benevolence to Mankind.* He has given up his Employments, because he *values no Advantages above the Conveniencies of Life, but as they tend to the Service of the Publick.* It seems, he could not *serve the Publick* as a Pensioner, or

Commissioner of Stamp'd Paper, and therefore gave them up to sit in Parliament out of *Charity to his Country,* and *to contend for Liberty.* He has transcribed the common Places of some canting Moralist *de contemptu mundi, & fuga seculi,*[8] and would put them upon you as Rules derived from his own Practice.

Here is a most miraculous and sudden Reformation, which I believe can hardly be match'd in History or *Legend.* And Mr. *Steele,* not unaware how slow the World was of Belief, has thought fit to anticipate all Objections; he foresees that *prostituted Pens will entertain a Pretender to such Reformations with a Recital of his own Faults and Infirmities, but he is prepared for such Usage, and gives himself up to all nameless Authors, to be treated as they please.*

It is certain, Mr. Bailiff, that no Man breathing can pretend to have arrived at such a sublime pitch of Virtue as Mr. *Steele* without some Tendency in the World, to suspend at least their Belief of the Fact, till Time and Observation shall determine. But I hope few Writers will be so *prostitute* as to trouble themselves with *the Faults and Infirmities of* Mr. *Steele's* past Life, with what he somewhere else calls *the Sins of his Youth,* and in one of his late Paper's confesses to have been *numerous* enough. A shifting scambling Scene of Youth, attended with Poverty and ill Company, may put a Man of no ill Inclinations upon many Extravagancies, which as soon as they are left off, are easily pardoned and forgot. Besides, I think Popish Writers tell us, that the greatest Sinners make the greatest Saints; but so very quick a Sanctification, and carried to so prodigious a Height, will be apt to rouze the Suspicion of Infidels, especially when they consider that this Pretence of his to so Romantick a Virtue, is only advanced by way of Solution to that difficult Problem, *Why has he given up his Employments?* And according to the new Philosophy, they will endeavour to solve it by some easier and shorter way. For Example, the Question is put, Why Mr. *Steele* gives up his Employment and Pension at this Juncture? I must here repeat with some Enlargement what I said before on this Head. These unbelieving Gentlemen will answer, First, That a new Commission was every day expected for the Stamp'd Paper, and he knew his Name would be left out; and therefore his Resignation would be an Appearance of Virtue cheaply bought.

Secondly, He dreaded the Violence of Creditors, against which his Employments were no manner of Security.

Thirdly, being a Person of great Sagacity, he hath some Foresight of a Change from the usual Age of a Ministry, which is now almost expired;

from the little Misunderstandings that have been reported sometimes to happen among the Men in Power; from the Bill of Commerce being rejected, and from some *HORRIBLE EXPECTATIONS,*⁹ wherewith his Party have been deceiving themselves and their Friends *Abroad* for two Years past.

Fourthly, He hopes to come into all the Perquisites of his Predecessor *R I D P A T H*, and be the principal Writer of his Faction, where every thing is printed by Subscription, which will amply make up the Loss of his Place.

But it may be still demanded, Why he affects those exalted Strains of Piety and Resignation? To this I answer, with great probability, That he hath resumed his old Pursuits after the *Philosopher's Stone,* towards which it is held by all *Adepts* for a most essential Ingredient, that a Man must seek it meerly for the Glory of God, and without the least Desire of being rich.

Mr. *Steele* is angry that some of our Friends have been reflected on in a Pamphlet, because they left us in a Point of the greatest Consequence; and upon that Account he runs into their Panegyrick against his Conscience, and the Interest of his Cause, without considering that those Gentlemen have reverted to us again. The Case is thus: He never would have praised them, if they had remained firm, nor should we have railed at them. The one is full as honest, and as natural as the other: However, Mr. *Steele* hopes (I beg you Mr. Bailiff to observe the Consequence) that notwithstanding this Pamphlets reflecting on some Tories who opposed the Treaty of Commerce, *the Ministry will see* Dunkirk *effectually demolished.*

Mr. *Steele* says something in Commendation of the Queen; but stops short, and tells you (if I take his meaning right) that he *shall leave what he has to say on this Topick, till he and Her Majesty are both dead.* Thus, he defers his *Praises* as he does his *Debts,* after the manner of the *Druids,* to be paid in another World. If I have ill interpreted him, it is his own Fault, for studying Cadence instead of Propriety, and filling up Nitches with Words before he has adjusted his Conceptions to them. One part of the Queen's Character is this, *that all the Hours of her Life, are divided between the Exercises of Devotion, and taking Minutes of the Sublime Affairs of Her Government.* Now, if the Business of *Dunkirk* be one of the *Sublime Affairs of Her* Majesty's *Government,* I think we ought to be at ease, or else she *takes Her Minutes* to little Purpose. No, says Mr. *Steele,* the Queen is a *Lady,* and unless a Prince will now and then get drunk with his Ministers, *he cannot learn their Interests or Humours;* but this being by no means proper for a *Lady,* she can know nothing but what they think fit to tell her when they are Sober. And therefore *all the Fellow-Subjects* of these Ministers must watch their Motions and *be very solicitous for what passes beyond the ordinary Rules of Government;* For while we are foolishly *relying upon Her Majesty's Virtues;* These Ministers are *taking the Advantage of encreasing the Power of* France.

There is a very good Maxim, I think it is neither *Whig* nor *Tory,* that the Prince can do no wrong; which I doubt is often applied to very ill Purposes. A Monarch of *Britain* is pleased to create *a Dozen Peers,* and to make a Peace; both these Actions are, (for instance,) within the undisputed Prerogative of the Crown, and are to be reputed and submitted to as the Actions of the Prince: But as a King of *England* is supposed to be guided in Matters of such Importance, by the Advice of those he employs in his Councils; whenever a Parliament thinks fit to complain of such Proceedings, as a publick Grievance, then this Maxim takes Place, that the Prince can do no wrong, and the Advisers are called to Account. But shall this empower such an Individual as Mr. *Steele* in his *Tatling* or *Pamphleteering* Capacity, to fix *the ordinary Rules of Government,* or to affirm that *Her Ministers, upon the Security of Her Majesty's Goodness, are labouring for the Grandeur of* France? What ordinary Rule of Government is transgressed by the Queen's delaying the Demolition of *Dunkirk?* Or what Addition is thereby made to the Grandeur of *France?* Every Taylor in your Corporation is as much a *Fellow-Subject* as Mr. *Steele,* and do you think in your Conscience that every Taylor of *Stockbridge* is fit to direct Her Majesty and Her Ministers in *the sublime Affairs of her Government?*

But He *persists in it, that it is no manner of Diminution of the Wisdom of a Prince, that he is obliged to act by the Information of others.* The Sense is admirable; and the Interpretation is this, that what a Man is forced to *is no diminution of his Wisdom:* But if he would conclude from this Sage Maxim, that, because a Prince *acts by the Information of others,* therefore those Actions may lawfully be traduced in Print by every Fellow-Subject; I hope there is no Man in *England,* so much a *Whig,* as to be of his Opinion.

Mr. *Steele* concludes his Letter to you with a Story about King *William* and his *French Dog-keeper, who gave that Prince a Gun loaden only with Powder, and then pretended to wonder how his Majesty could miss his Aim: Which was no Argument against the King's Reputation for Shooting very finely.* This he would have you apply, by allowing Her Majesty to be a Wise Prince, but deceived by wicked Counsellors, who are in the Interest of *France.* Her Majesty's Aim was Peace, which, I think, She hath not miss'd; and, God be thanked, She hath got it, without any more Expence, either of SHOT or

POWDER. Her *Dog-keepers,* for some Years past, had directed Her *Gun* against Her *Friends,* and at last *loaded* it so deep, that it was in danger to *burst* in Her Hands.

You may please to observe, that Mr. *Steele* calls this *Dog-keeper* a *Minister,* which, with humble Submission, is a gross Impropriety of Speech. The Word is derived from *Latin,* where it properly signifies a *Servant;* but in *English* is never made use of otherwise, than to denominate those who are employ'd in the Service of Church or State: So that the Appellation, as he directs it, is no less absurd, than it would be for you, Mr. Bailiff, to send your 'Prentice for a Pot of Ale, and give him the Title of your *Envoy;* to call a Petty-Constable a *Magistrate,* or the Common Hangman a *Minister* of Justice. I confess, when I was choqued[10] at this Word in reading the Paragraph, a Gentleman offer'd his Conjecture, that it might possibly be intended for a Reflection or a Jest: But if there be any thing further in it, than a want of Understanding our Language, I take it to be only a Refinement upon the old levelling Principle of the Whigs. Thus, in their Opinion, a *Dog-keeper* is as much a *Minister* as any Secretary of State: And thus Mr. *Steele* and my Lord *Treasurer* are both *Fellow-Subjects.* I confess, I have known some *Ministers,* whose Birth, or Qualities, or both, were such that nothing but the Capriciousness of Fortune, and the Iniquity of the Times, could ever have raised them above the Station of *Dog-keepers;* and to whose Administration I should be loath to entrust a Dog I had any Value for: Because, by the Rule of Proportion, they who treated their *Prince* like a *Slave,* would have used their *Fellow-Subjects* like *Dogs;* and how they would treat a *Dog,* I can find no Similitude to express; yet I well remember, they maintained a large Number, whom they taught to *Fawn* upon themselves, and *Bark* at their Mistress. However, while they were in Service, I wish they had only kept Her Majesty's DOGS, and not been trusted with Her GUNS. And thus much by way of Comment upon this worthy Story of King *William* and his *Dog-keeper.*

———

I have now, Mr. Bailiff, explained to you all the difficult Parts in Mr. *Steele's* Letter. As for the Importance of *Dunkirk,* and when it shall be Demolished, or whether it shall be Demolished or not, neither he, nor you, nor I, have any thing to do in the Matter. Let us all say what we please, Her Majesty will think Her self the best *Judge,* and Her Ministers the best *Advisers;* neither hath Mr. *Steele* pretended to prove that any Law Ecclesiastical or Civil, Statute or Common, is broken, by keeping *Dunkirk* undemolished, as long as the Queen shall think best for the Service of Her Self and Her

Kingdoms; and it is not altogether impossible, that there may be some few Reasons of State, which have not been yet communicated to Mr. *Steele.* I am, with Respect to the Borough and Your self,

SIR,

Your most Humble

and most Obedient Servant,

&c.

IV

MISCELLANEOUS PROSE WRITINGS

Mr. *C——ns*'s

DISCOURSE

OF

FREE-THINKING,

PUT INTO PLAIN *ENGLISH*, BY WAY OF

ABSTRACT,

FOR THE

USE OF THE POOR

Our Party having failed, by all their Political Arguments, to re-establish their Power; the wise Leaders have determined, that the last and principle Remedy should be made use of, for opening the Eyes of this blinded Nation; and that a short, but perfect, System of their Divinity, should be publish'd, to which we are all of us ready to subscribe, and which we lay down as a Model, bearing a close Analogy to our Schemes in Religion. Crafty designing Men, that they might keep the World in Awe, have, in their several Forms of Government, placed a Supream Power on Earth, to keep human Kind in fear of being Hanged; and a Supream Power in Heaven, for fear of being Damned. In order to cure Mens Apprehensions of the former, several of our learned Members have writ many profound Treatises in Anarchy; but a brief compleat Body of Atheology seemed yet wanting, till this irrefragable Discourse appeared. However it so happens, that our ablest Brethren, in their elaborate Disquisitions upon this Subject, have written with so much Caution, that ignorant Unbelievers have edified very little by them. I grant that those daring Spirits, who first adventured to write against the direct Rules of the Gospel, the Current of Antiquity, the Religion of the Magistrate, and the Laws of the Land, had some Measures to keep; and particularly when they railed at Religion, were in the right to use little artful Disguises, by which a Jury could only find them guilty of abusing Heathenism or Popery. But the Mystery is now revealed, that there is no such Thing as Mystery or Revelation; and though our Friends are out of Place and Power, yet we may have so much Confidence in the present Ministry to be secure, that those who suffer so many Free Speeches against their Sovereign and themselves to pass unpunished, will never resent our expressing the freest Thoughts against their Religion; but think with Tiberius, That if there be a God, he is able enough to revenge any Injuries done to himself, without expecting the Civil Power to interpose.

By these Reflections I was brought to think, that the most ingenious Author of the Discourse upon Free Thinking, in a Letter to Somebody, Esq; although he hath used less reserve than any of his Predecessors, might yet have been more free and open. I considered, that several Well-willers to Infidelity might be discouraged by a shew of Logick, and multiplicity of Quotations, scattered through his Book, which to Understandings of that Size might carry an appearance of something like Booklearning, and consequently fright them from reading for their Improvement: I could see no Reason why these great Discoveries should be hid from our Youth of Quality, who frequent White's[1] and Tom's; why they should not be adapted to the Capacities *of the* Kit-Cat *and* Hannover *Clubs,*[2] *who might* then *be able to read Lectures on them to their several* Toasts: *And it will be allowed on all Hands, that nothing can sooner help to restore our abdicated Cause, than a firm universal Belief of the Principles laid down by this sublime Author.*

For I am sensible that nothing would more contribute to the continuance of the War, *and the Restoration of the late Ministry, than to have the Doctrines delivered in this Treatise well infused into the People. I have therefore compiled them into the following Abstract, wherein I have adhered to the very Words of our Author, only adding some few Explanations of my own, where the Terms happen to be too learned, and consequently a little beyond the Comprehension of those for whom the Work was principally intended, I mean the Nobility and Gentry of our Party. After which I hope it will be impossible for the Malice of a* Jacobite, High-flying, Priest-ridden Faction, *to misrepresent us. The few Additions I have made, are for no other use than to help the Transition, which could not otherwise be kept in an Abstract; but I have not presumed to advance any thing of my own; which besides would be needless to an Author, who hath so fully handled and demonstrated every Particular. I shall only add, that though this Writer, when he speaks of* Priests, *desires chiefly to be understood to mean the* English *Clergy, yet he includes all* Priests *whatsoever, except the antient and modern* Heathens, *the* Turks, Quakers, *and* Socinians.

THE LETTER

SIR,

I send you this Apology for *Free Thinking,* without the least hopes of doing good, but purely to comply with your Request; for those Truths which no Body can deny, will do no good to those who deny them. The Clergy, who are so impudent to teach the People the Doctrines of Faith, are all either cunning Knaves or mad Fools; for none but artificial designing Men, and crackt-brained Enthusiasts, presume to be Guides to others in matters of Speculation, which all the Doctrines of Christianity are; and whoever has a mind to learn the Christian Religion, naturally chuses such Knaves and Fools to teach them. Now the *Bible,* which contains the Precepts of the Priests Religion, is the most difficult Book in the World to be understood; It requires a thorow Knowledge in Natural, Civil, Ecclesiastical History, Law, Husbandry, Sailing, Physick, Pharmacy, Mathematicks, Metaphysicks, Ethicks, and every thing else that can be named: And every Body who believes it, ought to understand it, and must do so by force of his own *Free Thinking,* without any Guide or Instructor.

How can a Man *think* at all, if he does not think freely? A Man who does not eat and drink freely, does not eat and drink at all. Why may not I be deny'd the liberty of *Free-seeing,* as well as *Free-thinking?* Yet no body pretends that the first is unlawful, for a Cat may look on a King; though you be near-sighted, or have weak or soar Eyes, or are blind, you may be a *Free-seer;* you ought to see for your self, and not trust to a Guide to chuse the Colour of your Stockings, or save you from falling into a Ditch.

In like manner there ought to be no restraint at all on *thinking freely* upon any Proposition, however impious or absurd. There is not the least hurt in the wickedest Thoughts, provided they be free; nor in telling those Thoughts to every Body, and endeavouring to convince the World of them; for all this is included in the Doctrine of *Free-thinking*, as I shall plainly shew you in what follows; and therefore you are all along to understand the Word *Free-thinking* in this Sense.

If you are apt to be afraid of the Devil, *think freely* of him, and you destroy him and his Kingdom. *Free-thinking* has done him more Mischief than all the Clergy in the World ever could do; they *believe in the Devil,* they have an *Interest* in him, and therefore are the great Supports of his Kingdom. The Devil was in the *States General* before they began to be *Free-thinkers.* For *England* and *Holland* were formerly the *Christian* Territories of the Devil; I told you how he left *Holland;* and *Free-thinking* and the *Revolution* banish'd him from *England;* I defy all the Clergy to shew me when they ever had such Success against him. My Meaning is, that to think freely of the Devil, is to think there is no Devil at all; and he that thinks so, the Devil's in him if he be afraid of the Devil.

But within these two or three Years the Devil has come into *England* again, and Dr. *Sacheverell* has given him Commission to appear in the shape of a *Cat,* and carry old Women about upon Broomsticks: And the Devil has now so many *Ministers ordained to his Service,* that they have rendred *Free-thinking* odious, and nothing but the Second Coming of *Christ* can restore it.

The Priests tell me I am to believe the *Bible,* but *Free-thinking* tells me otherwise in many Particulars: The *Bible* says, the *Jews* were a Nation favoured by God; but I who am a *Free-thinker* say, that cannot be, because the *Jews* lived in a *Corner* of the Earth, and *Free-thinking* makes it clear, that those who live in *Corners* cannot be Favourites of God. The *New Testament* all along asserts the Truth of Christianity, but *Free-thinking* denies it; because Christianity was communicated but to a few; and whatever is communicated but to a few, cannot be true; for that is like *Whispering,* and the Proverb says, that there is no Whispering without Lying.

Here is a Society in *London* for propagating *Free-thinking* throughout the World, encouraged and supported by the Queen and many others. You say perhaps, it is for propagating the Gospel. Do you think the Missionaries we send, will tell the Heathens that they must not *think freely?* No surely; why then, 'tis manifest those Missionaries must be *Free-thinkers,* and make the Heathens so too. But why should not the King of *Siam,* whose Religion is Heathenism and Idolatry, send over a parcel of his Priests to convert us to *his Church,* as well as we send Missionaries there? Both Projects are exactly of a Piece, and equally reasonable; and if those Heathen Priests were here, it would be our Duty to hearken to them, and *think freely* whether *they* may not be in the right rather than we. I heartily wish a Detachment of such Divines as Dr. *Atterbury,* Dr. *Smalridge,* Dr. *Swift,* Dr. *Sacheverell,*[3] and some others, were sent every Year to the furthest part of the Heathen World, and that we had a Cargo of their Priests in return, who would spread *Free-thinking* among us; then the War would go on, the late Ministry be restored, and Faction cease, which our Priests inflame by haranguing upon Texts, and falsly call that preaching the Gospel.

I have another Project in my Head which ought to be put in execution, in order to make us *Free-thinkers:* It is a great Hardship and Injustice, that our Priests must not be disturbed while they are prating in their Pulpit. For Example: Why should not *William Penn* the Quaker, or any *Anabaptist, Papist, Muggletonian, Jew* or *Sweet Singer,* have liberty to come into St. *Paul's* Church, in the midst of Divine Service, and endeavour to convert first the Aldermen, then the Preacher, and Singing-Men? Or pray, why might not poor Mr. *Whiston,* who denies the Divinity of Christ, be allow'd to come into the Lower House of Convocation, and convert the Clergy? But alas we are over-run with such false Notions, that if *Penn* or *Whiston* should do their Duty, they would be reckoned Fanaticks, and Disturbers of the Holy Synod, although they have as good a Title to it, as St. *Paul* had to go into the Synagogues of the *Jews;* and their Authority is full as Divine as his.

Christ himself commands us to be *Free-thinkers,* for he bids us search the Scriptures, and take heed what and whom we hear; by which he plainly warns us, not to believe our Bishops and Clergy; for *Jesus Christ,* when he consider'd that all the *Jewish* and *Heathen* Priests, whose Religion he came to abolish, were his Enemies, rightly concluded that those appointed by him to preach his own Gospel, would probably be so too; and could not be secure, that any Sett of Priests, of the Faith he deliver'd, would ever be otherwise; therefore it is fully demonstrated that the Clergy of the Church of *England* are mortal Enemies to Christ, and ought not to be believ'd.

But without the Priviledge of *Free-thinking,* how is it possible to know which is the right *Scripture?* Here are perhaps twenty Sorts of *Scriptures* in the several Parts of the World, and every Sett of Priests contends that their *Scripture* is the true One. The *Indian Bramines* have a Book of Scripture call'd the *Shaster;* the *Persees* their *Zundivastaw;* the *Bonzes* in *China* have theirs, written by the Disciples of *Fo-he,* whom they call *God and Saviour of the World, who was born to teach the way of Salvation, and to give satisfaction for all Men's Sins.* Which you see is directly the same with what our *Priests* pretend of *Christ;* And must we not *think freely* to find out which are in the right, whether the *Bishops* or the *Bonzes?* But the *Talapoins* or *Heathen* Clergy of *Siam* approach yet nearer to the System of our Priests; they have a Book of *Scripture* written by *Sommonocodum,* who, the *Siamese* say, was *born of a Virgin,* and was *the God expected by the Universe;* just as our *Priests* tell us, that *Jesus Christ* was born of the *Virgin Mary,* and was the *Messiah* so long expected. The *Turkish* Priests or *Dervises* have their Scripture, which they call the *Alcoran.* The *Jews* have the *Old Testament* for their Scripture, and the *Christians* have both the Old and the New. Now among all these Scriptures there cannot above one be right; and how is it possible to know which is that, without reading them all, and then *thinking freely,* every one of us for our selves, without following the Advice or Instruction of any Guide, before we venture to chuse? The Parliament ought to be at the Charge of finding a sufficient number of these *Scriptures* for every one of Her Majesty's Subjects, for there are Twenty to One against us, that we may be in the wrong: But a great deal of *Free-thinking* will at last set us all right, and every one will adhere to the *Scripture* he likes best; by which means Religion, Peace, and Wealth, will be for ever secured in Her Majesty's Realms.

And it is the more necessary that the good People of *England* should have liberty to chuse some other *Scripture,* because all *Christian* Priests differ so much about the Copies of theirs, and about the various Readings of the several Manuscripts, which quite destroys the Authority of the Bible: For what Authority can a Book pretend to, where there are various Readings? And for this reason, it is manifest that no Man can know the Opinions of *Aristotle* or *Plato,* or believe the Facts related by *Thucidydes* or *Livy,* or be pleased with the Poetry of *Homer* and *Virgil,* all which Books are utterly useless, upon account of their various Readings. Some Books of *Scripture* are said to be lost, and this utterly destroys the Credit of those that are left: Some we reject, which the *Africans* and *Copticks* receive; and why may we not *think freely,* and reject the rest? Some think the Scriptures wholly inspired, some partly; and some not at all. Now this is just the very Case of the *Bramines, Persees, Bonzes, Talapoins, Dervizes, Rabbi's,* and all *other Priests* who build their Religion upon Books, as our Priests do upon their Bibles; they all equally differ about the Copies, various Readings and Inspirations, of their several Scriptures, and God knows which are in the right; *Free-thinking* alone can determine it.

It would be endless to shew in how many Particulars the Priests of the *Heathen* and *Christian Churches* differ about the Meaning even of those Scriptures which they universally receive as Sacred. But to avoid Prolixity, I shall confine my self to the different Opinions among the Priests of the Church of *England,* and here only give you a Specimen, because even these are too many to be enumerated.

I have found out a Bishop (though indeed his Opinions are condemn'd by all his Brethren) who allows the Scriptures to be so difficult, that God has left them rather as a Trial of our Industry than a Repository of our Faith, and Furniture of *Creeds* and Articles of *Belief;* with several other admirable Schemes of *Free-thinking,* which you may consult at your leisure.

The Doctrine of the *Trinity* is the most fundamental Point of the whole *Christian* Religion. Nothing is more easie to a *Free-thinker,* yet what different Notions of it do the *English* Priests pretend to deduce from Scripture, explaining it by *specifick Unities, eternal Modes of Subsistance,* and the like unintelligible Jargon? Nay, 'tis a Question whether this Doctrine be Fundamental or no; for though Dr. *South* and Bishop *Bull* affirm it, yet Bishop *Taylor* and Dr. *Wallis* deny it. And that excellent *Free-thinking* Prelate, Bishop *Taylor,* observes, that *Athanasius's* Example was followed with too much greediness; by which means it has happened, that the greater number of our Priests are in that Sentiment, and think it necessary to believe the *Trinity,* and Incarnation of *Christ.*

Our Priests likewise dispute several Circumstances about the Resurrection of the Dead, the Nature of our Bodies after the Resurrection, and in what manner they shall be united to our Souls. They also attack one another *very weakly with great Vigour,* about Predestination. And it is certainly true, (for Bishop *Taylor* and Mr. *Whiston* the Socinian say so) that all Churches in Prosperity alter their Doctrines every Age, and are neither satisfy'd with themselves, nor their own Confessions; neither does any Clergymen of Sense believe the Thirty nine Articles.

Our Priests differ about the Eternity of Hell-Torments. The famous Dr. *Henry Moor,* and the most pious and rational of all Priests Doctor *Tillotson,* (both *Free-thinkers*) believe them to be not Eternal. They differ about keeping the Sabbath, the Divine Right of Episcopacy, and the Doctrine of Original Sin; which is the Foundation of the whole Christian Religion; for if Men are not liable to be damned for *Adam's* Sin, the Christian Religion is an Imposture: Yet this is now disputed among them; so is Lay-Baptism; so was formerly the lawfulness of Usury, but now the Priests are common Stock-jobbers, Attorneys and Scriveners. In short there is no end of disputing among Priests, and therefore I conclude, that there ought to be no such Thing in the World as Priests, Teachers, or Guides, for instructing ignorant People in Religion; but that every Man ought to *think freely* for himself.

I will tell you my meaning in all this; the Priests dispute every Point in the Christian Religion, as well as almost every Text in the Bible; and the force of my Argument lies here, that whatever Point is disputed by one or two Divines, however condemned by the Church, not only that particular Point, but the whole Article to which it relates, may lawfully be received or rejected by any *Free Thinker.* For Instance, suppose *Moor* and *Tillotson* deny the Eternity of Hell Torments, a *Free Thinker* may deny all future Punishments whatsoever. The Priests dispute about explaining the *Trinity;* therefore a *Free Thinker* may reject one or two, or the whole three *Persons;* at least he may reject Christianity, because the *Trinity* is the most fundamental Doctrine of that Religion. So I affirm Original Sin, and that Men are now liable to be damned for *Adam's* Sin, to be the Foundation of the whole Christian Religion; but this Point was formerly, and is now disputed, therefore a *Free Thinker* may deny the whole. And I cannot help giving you one further Direction, how I insinuate all along, that the wisest *Free Thinking* Priests, whom you may distinguish by the Epithets I bestow them, were those who differed most from the generality of their Brethren.

But besides, the Conduct of our Priests, in many other Points, makes *Free Thinking* unavoidable; for some of them own, that the Doctrines of the Church are contradictory to one another, as well as to Reason: Which I thus prove; Dr. *Sacheverell* says in his Speech at his Tryal, that by abandoning Passive Obedience we must render our selves the most inconsistent Church in the World: Now 'tis plain, that one Inconsistency could not make the most inconsistent Church in the World; *ergo,* there must have been a great many Inconsistencies and contradictory Doctrines in the Church before. Dr. *South* describes the Incarnation of Christ, as an astonishing Mystery, impossible to be conceived by Mans Reason; *ergo,* it is contradictory to it self, and to Reason, and ought to be exploded[4] by all *Free Thinkers.*

Another Instance of the Priests Conduct, which multiplies *Free Thinkers,* is their acknowledgments of Abuses, Defects, and false Doctrines in the Church; particularly that of eating *Black Pudding,* which is so plainly forbid in the *Old* and *New Testament,* that I wonder those who pretend to believe a Syllable in either, will presume to taste it. Why should I mention the want of Discipline, and of a Side-board at the Altar, with Complaints of other great Abuses and Defects made by some of the Priests, which no Man can *think* on without *Free Thinking,* and consequently rejecting Christianity?

When I see an honest Free Thinking Bishop endeavour to destroy the Power and Privileges of the church, and Dr. *Atterbury* angry with him for it, and calling it *dirty Work,* what can I conclude, by vertue of being a *Free Thinker,* but that Christianity is all a Cheat?

Mr. *Whiston* has publish'd several Tracts, wherein he absolutely denies the Divinity of *Christ:* A Bishop tells him, *Sir, in any Matter where you have the Church's Judgment against you, you should be careful not to break the Peace of the Church, by Writing against it, though you are sure you are in the right.* Now my Opinion is directly contrary; and I affirm, that if Ten thousand Free Thinkers thought differently from the received Doctrine, and from each other, they would be all in Duty bound to publish their Thoughts (provided they were all sure of being in the right) though it broke the Peace of the Church and State, Ten thousand times.

And here I must take leave to tell you, although you cannot but have perceived it from what I have already said, and shall be still more amply convinced by what is to follow; That *Free Thinking* signifies nothing, without *Free Speaking* and *Free Writing.* It is the indispensable Duty of a *Free Thinker,* to endeavour *forcing* all the World to think as he does, and by that means make them *Free Thinkers* too. You are also to understand, that I allow no Man to be a *Free Thinker,* any further than as he differs from the received Doctrines of Religion.

Where a Man falls in, though by perfect Chance, with what is generally believed, he is in that Point a confined and limited Thinker; and you shall see by and by, that I celebrate those for the noblest *Free Thinkers* in every Age, who differed from the Religion of their Countries in the most fundamental Points, and especially in those which bear any Analogy to the chief Fundamentals of Religion among us.

Another Trick of the Priests, is to charge all Men with Atheism, who have more Wit than themselves; which therefore I expect will be my Case for Writing this Discourse: This is what makes them so implacable against Mr. *Gildon*, Dr. *Tindal*, Mr. *Toland*, and my self, and when they call us *Wits* Atheists, it provokes us to be *Free Thinkers*.

Again; The Priests cannot agree when their Scripture was wrote. They differ about the number of Canonical Books, and the various Readings. Now those few among us who understand Latin, are careful to tell this to our Disciples, who presently fall a *Free Thinking*, that the Bible is a Book not to be depended upon in any thing at all.

There is another Thing that mightily spreads *Free Thinking*, which I believe you would hardly guess: The Priests have got a way of late of Writing Books against *Free Thinking*; I mean Treatises in Dialogue, where they introduce *Atheists, Deists, Scepticks* and *Socinians* offering their several Arguments. Now these *Free Thinkers* are too hard for the Priests themselves in their own Books; and how can it be otherwise? For if the Arguments usually offered by *Atheists*, are fairly represented in these Books, they must needs convert every Body that reads them; because *Atheists, Deists, Scepticks* and *Socinians*, have certainly better Arguments to maintain their Opinions, than any the Priests can produce to maintain the contrary.

Mr. *Creech*, a Priest, translated *Lucretius* into *English*, which is a compleat System of Atheism; and several Young Students, who were afterwards Priests, writ Verses in Praise of this Translation. The Arguments against Providence in that Book are so strong, that they have added mightily to the Number of *Free Thinkers*.

What should I mention the pious Cheats of the Priests, who in the *New Testament* translate the Word *Ecclesia* sometimes the *Church*, and sometimes the *Congregation*; and *Episcopus*, sometimes a *Bishop*, and sometimes an *Overseer*? A Priest translating a Book, left out a whole Passage that reflected on the *King*, by which he was an Enemy to *Political Free Thinking*, a most considerable Branch of our System. Another Priest translating a Book of Travels, left out a lying Miracle, out of meer Malice to conceal an Argument for *Free Thinking*. In short, these Frauds are very common in all Books which are published by *Priests*: But however, I love to excuse them whenever I can: And as to this Accusation, they may plead the Authority of the Ancient Fathers of the Church for Forgery, Corruption, and mangling of Authors, with more Reason than for any of their

Articles of Faith. St. *Jerom*, St. *Hilary, Eusebius Vercellensis, Victorinus,* and several others, were all guilty of arrant Forgery and Corruption: For when they translated the Works of several *Free-thinkers,* whom they called *Hereticks,* they omitted all their Heresies or *Free-thinkings,* and had the Impudence to own it to the World.

From these many notorious Instances of the Priests' Conduct, I conclude they are not to be relied on in any one thing relating to Religion, but that every Man must think freely for himself.

But to this it may be objected, that the Bulk of Mankind is as well qualified for *flying* as *thinking,* and if every Man thought it his Duty to *think freely,* and trouble his Neighbour with his Thoughts (which is an essential Part of *Free-thinking,*) it would make wild work in the World. I answer; whoever cannot *think freely,* may let it alone if he pleases, by virtue of his Right to *think freely;* that is to say, if such a Man *freely thinks* that he cannot *think freely,* of which every Man is a sufficient Judge, why then he need not *think freely,* unless he *thinks* fit.

Besides, if the Bulk of Mankind cannot *think freely* in Matters of Speculation, as the Being of a God, the Immortality of the Soul, *&c.* why then, *Free-thinking* is indeed no Duty: But then the *Priests* must allow, that Men are not concerned to believe whether there is a God or no. But still those who are disposed to *think freely,* may *think freely* if they please.

It is again objected, that *Free-thinking* will produce endless Divisions in Opinion, and by consequence disorder Society. To which I answer,

When every single Man comes to have a different Opinion every Day from the whole World, and from himself, by Virtue of *Free-thinking,* and thinks it his Duty to convert every Man to his own *Free-thinking* (as all we *Free-thinkers* do) how can that possibly create so great a Diversity of Opinions, as to have a Sett of Priests agree among themselves to teach the same Opinions in their several Parishes to all who will come to hear them? Besides, if all People were of the same Opinion, the Remedy would be worse than the Disease; I will tell you the Reason some other time.

Besides, difference in Opinion, especially in Matters of great Moment, breeds no Confusion at all. Witness *Papist* and *Protestant, Roundhead* and *Cavalier,* and *Whig* and *Tory* now among us. I observe, the *Turkish* Empire is more at Peace *within it self* than *Christian* Princes are *with one another.* Those noble *Turkish* Virtues of Charity and Toleration, are what contribute chiefly to the flourishing State of that happy Monarchy. There *Christians* and *Jews* are tolerated, and live at ease, if they can hold their Tongues and *think freely,* provided they never set foot within the *Moschs,* nor write against *Mahomet:* A few Plunderings now and then by their *Janisaries* are all they have to fear.

It is objected, that by *Free-thinking,* Men will *think* themselves into *Atheism;* and indeed I have allowed all along, that Atheistical Books convert Men to *Free-thinking.* But suppose that be true; I can bring you two Divines who affirm

Superstition and Enthusiasm to be worse than Atheism, and more mischievous to Society, and in short it is necessary that the Bulk of the People should be Atheists or Superstitious.

It is objected, that Priests ought to be relied on by the People, as Lawyers and Physicians, because it is their Faculty.

I answer, 'Tis true, a Man who is no Lawyer is not suffered to plead for himself; But every Man may be his own Quack if he pleases, and he only ventures his Life; but in the other Case the Priest tells him he must be damned; therefore do not trust the Priest, but *think freely* for your self, and if you happen to think there is no Hell, there certainly is none, and consequently you cannot be damned; I answer further, that wherever there is no *Lawyer, Physician,* or *Priest,* that Country is *Paradise.* Besides, all Priests (except the Orthodox, and those are not ours, nor any that I know) are hired by the Publick to lead Men into Mischief; but *Lawyers* and *Physicians* are not, you hire them your self.

It is objected (by Priests no doubt, but I have forgot their Names) that false Speculations are necessary to be imposed upon Men, in order to assist the Magistrate in keeping the Peace, and that Men ought therefore to be deceived like Children, for their own Good. I answer, that Zeal for imposing Speculations, whether true or false (under which Name of Speculations I include all Opinions of Religion, as the Belief of a God, Providence, Immortality of the Soul, future Rewards and Punishments, *&c.*) has done more hurt than it is possible for Religion to do good. It puts us to the Charge of maintaining Ten thousand Priests in *England,* which is a Burthen upon Society never felt on any other occasion; and a greater Evil to the Publick than if these Ecclesiasticks were only employed in the most innocent Offices of Life, which I take to be *Eating* and *Drinking.* Now if you offer to impose any thing on Mankind besides what relates to moral Duties, as to pay your Debts, not pick Pockets, nor commit Murder, and the like; that is to say, if besides this, you oblige them to believe in God and Jesus Christ, what you add to their Faith will take just so much off from their Morality. By this Argument it is manifest that a perfect moral Man must be a perfect Atheist, every Inch of Religion he gets, loses him an Inch of Morality: For there is a certain *Quantum* belongs to every Man, of which there is nothing to spare. This is clear from the common Practice of all our Priests, they never once Preach to you to love your Neighbour, to be just in your Dealings, or to be Sober and Temperate: The Streets of *London* are full of Common Whores, publickly tolerated in their Wickedness; yet the Priests make no Complaints against this Enormity, either from the Pulpit or the Press: I can affirm, that neither you nor I Sir, have ever heard one Sermon against Whoring since we were Boys. No, the Priests allow all these Vices, and love us the better for them, provided we will promise not to *harangue upon a Text,* nor to sprinkle a little Water in a Child's Face, which they call Baptizing, and would engross it all to themselves.

Besides, the *Priests* engage all the Rogues, Villains and Fools in their Party, in order to make it as large as they can: By this means they seduced *Constantine the Great* over to their Religion, who was the first Christian Emperor, and so horrible a Villain, that the *Heathen* Priests told him they could not expiate his Crimes in their Church; so he was at a loss to know what to do, till an *Ægyptian* Bishop assured him that there was no Villainy so great, but was to be expiated by the Sacraments of the Christian Religion; upon which he became a Christian, and to him that Religion owes its first Settlement.

It is objected, that *Free-thinkers* themselves are the most infamous, wicked and senseless of all Mankind.

I answer, First, We say the same of *Priests* and other Believers. But the Truth is, Men of all Sects are equally good and bad; for no Religion whatsoever contributes in the least to mend Mens Lives.

I answer, Secondly, That *Free-thinkers* use their Understanding, but those who have Religion, do not, therefore the first have more Understanding than the others; Witness *Toland, Tindal, Gildon, Clendon, Coward,* and my self. For, use Legs and have Legs.

I answer, Thirdly, That *Free-thinkers* are the most virtuous Persons in the World; for every *Free-thinker* must certainly differ from the *Priests,* and from Nine hundred ninety nine of a Thousand of those among whom they live; and are therefore Virtuous of course, because every Body hates them.

I answer, Fourthly, That the most virtuous People in all Ages have been *Free-thinkers;* of which I shall produce several Instances.

Socrates was a *Free-thinker;* for he disbelieved the Gods of his Country, and the common *Creeds* about them, and declared his Dislike when he heard Men attribute *Repentance, Anger, and other Passions to the Gods, and talk of Wars and Battles in Heaven, and of the Gods getting Women with Child,* and such like fabulous and blasphemous Stories. I pick out these Particulars, because they are the very same with what the Priests have in their Bibles, where *Repentance* and *Anger* are attributed to God, where it is said, there was *War in Heaven;* and that the *Virgin* Mary *was with Child by the Holy Ghost,* whom the Priests call God; all fabulous and blasphemous Stories. Now, I affirm *Socrates* to have been a true *Christian.* You will ask perhaps how that can be, since he lived Three or four hundred Years before Christ? I answer with *Justin Martyr,* that *Christ* is nothing else but *Reason,* and I hope you do not think *Socrates* lived before *Reason.* Now, this true Christian *Socrates* never made Notions, Speculations, or Mysteries any Part of his Religion, but demonstrated all Men to be Fools who troubled themselves with Enquiries into heavenly Things. Lastly, 'tis plain that *Socrates* was a *Free-thinker,* because he was calumniated for an *Atheist,* as *Free-thinkers* generally are, only because he was an Enemy to all Speculations and Enquiries into heavenly Things. For I argue thus, that if I never trouble my self to think whether there be a God or no, and forbid others to do it, I am a *Free-thinker,* but not an *Atheist.*

Plato was a *Free-thinker,* and his Notions are so like some in the Gospel, that a Heathen charged Christ with borrowing his Doctrine from *Plato.* But *Origen* defends Christ very well against this Charge, by saying he did not understand *Greek,* and therefore could not borrow his Doctrines from *Plato.* However their two Religions agreed so well, that it was common for Christians to turn *Platonists,* and *Platonists* Christians. When the Christians found out this, one of their zealous Priests (worse than any Atheist) forged several Things under *Plato's* Name, but conformable to Christianity, by which the Heathens were fraudulently converted.

Epicurus was the greatest of all *Free-thinkers,* and consequently the most virtuous Man in the World. His Opinions in Religion were the most compleat System of Atheism that ever appeared. Christians ought to have the greatest Veneration for him, because he taught a higher Point of Virtue than Christ; I mean the Virtue of *Friendship,* which in the Sense we usually understand it, is not so much as named in the New Testament.

Plutarch was a *Free-thinker,* notwithstanding his being a *Priest;* but indeed he was a *Heathen Priest.* His *Free-thinking* appears by shewing the Innocence of Atheism (which at worst is only false Reasoning) and the Mischiefs of Superstition; and explains what Superstition is, by calling it a Conceit of immortal Ills after Death, the Opinion of Hell Torments, dreadful Aspects, doleful Groans, and the like. He is likewise very Satyrical upon the publick Forms of Devotion in his own Country (a *Qualification* absolutely necessary to a *Free-thinker*) yet those Forms which he ridicules, are the very same that now pass for *true Worship* in almost all Countries: I am sure some of them do so in ours; such as abject Looks, Distortions, wry Faces, beggarly Tones, Humiliation, and Contrition.

Varro the most Learned among the *Romans* was a *Free-thinker;* for he said, the Heathen Divinity contained many Fables below the Dignity of Immortal Beings; such for Instance as Gods BEGOTTEN and PROCEEDING from other Gods. These two Words I desire you will particularly remark, because they are the very Terms made use of by our Priests in their Doctrine of the *Trinity.* He says likewise, that there are many Things false in Religion, and so say all *Free-thinkers;* but then he adds; *Which the Vulgar ought not to know, but it is Expedient they should believe.* In this last he indeed discovers the whole Secret of a Statesman and Politician, by denying the Vulgar the Priviledge of *Free-thinking,* and here I differ from him. However it is manifest from hence, that the *Trinity* was an Invention of Statesmen and Politicians.

The Grave and Wise *Cato* the Censor will for ever live in that noble *Free-thinking* Saying; I wonder, said he, how one of your Priests can forbear laughing when he sees another. (For Contempt of Priests is another grand Characteristick of a Free-thinker). This shews that *Cato* understood the whole Mystery of the *Roman* Religion, *as by Law Established.* I beg you Sir, not to overlook these last Words, *Religion as by Law Established*. I translate *Haruspex* into the general Word, *Priest*: Thus I apply the Sentence to our *Priests* in *England*, and when Dr. *Smalridge* sees Dr. *Atterbury*, I wonder how either of them can forbear laughing at the Cheat they put upon the People, by making them believe their *Religion as by Law Established*.

Cicero, that consummate Philosopher, and noble Patriot, though he were a *Priest*, and consequently more likely to be a *Knave*; gave the greatest Proofs of his *Free-thinking*. First, He professed the *Sceptick* Philosophy, which doubts of every thing. Then, he wrote two Treatises; in the first, he shews the Weakness of the *Stoicks* Arguments for the Being of the Gods: In the latter, he has destroyed the whole *reveal'd* Religion of the *Greeks* and *Romans* (for why should not theirs be a *reveal'd* Religion as well as that of Christ?) *Cicero* likewise tells us, as his own Opinion, that they who study Philosophy, do not believe there are any Gods: He denies the Immortality of the Soul, and says, there can be nothing after Death.

And because the Priests have the Impudence to quote *Cicero* in their Pulpits and Pamphlets, against *Free-thinking*; I am resolved to disarm them of his Authority. You must know, his Philosophical Works are generally in Dialogues, where People are brought in disputing against one another: Now the Priests when they see an Argument to prove a God, offered perhaps by a *Stoick*, are such Knaves or Blockheads, to quote it as if it were *Cicero*'s own; whereas *Cicero* was so noble a *Free-thinker*, that he believed nothing at all of the Matter, nor ever shews the least Inclination to favour Superstition, or the Belief of God, and the Immortality of the Soul; unless what he throws out sometimes to save himself from Danger, in his Speeches to the *Roman* Mob; whose Religion was, however, much more Innocent and less Absurd, than that of *Popery* at least: And I could say more,—but you understand me.

Seneca was a great *Free-thinker*, and had a noble Notion of the Worship of the Gods, for which our Priests would call any man an Atheist: He laughs at Morning-Devotions, or Worshipping upon Sabbath-Days; he says God has no need of *Ministers* and *Servants*, because he himself *serves* Mankind. This religious Man, like his religious Brethren the *Stoicks*, denies the Immortality of the Soul, and says, all that is feign'd to be so terrible in Hell, is but a Fable: Death puts an end to all our Misery, *&c*. Yet the Priests were anciently so fond of *Seneca*, that they forged a Correspondence of Letters between him and St. *Paul*.

Solomon himself, whose Writings are called the Word of God, was such a *Free Thinker*, that if he were now alive, nothing but his Building of Churches could have kept our Priests from calling him an Atheist. He affirms the Eternity of the World almost in the same manner with *Manilius* the *Heathen* Philosophical Poet (which Opinion entirely overthrows the History of the Creation by *Moses*, and all the *New Testament*): He denies the Immortality of the Soul, assures us that Men die like Beasts, and that both go to one Place.

The Prophets of the *Old Testament* were generally *Free Thinkers:* You must understand, that their way of learning to Prophesie was by *Musick* and *Drinking.* These Prophets writ against the *Established Religion* of the *Jews,* (which those People looked upon as the Institution of God himself) as if they believed it was all a Cheat: That is to say, with as great liberty against the Priests and Prophets of *Israel,* as Dr. *Tindall* did lately against the Priests and Prophets of our *Israel,* who has clearly shewn them and their Religion to be Cheats. To prove this, you may read several Passages in *Isaiah, Ezekiel, Amos, Jeremiah, &c.* wherein you will find such Instances of *Free Thinking,* that if any *Englishman* had talked so in our Days, their Opinions would have been Registred in Dr. *Sacheverell's* Tryal, and in the Representation of the Lower House of Convocation, and produced as so many Proofs of the Prophaneness, Blasphemy, and Atheism of the Nation; there being nothing more Prophane, Blasphemous, or Atheistical in those Representations, than what these Prophets have spoke, whose Writings are yet called by our Priests the *Word of God.* And therefore these Prophets are as much *Atheists* as my self, or as any of my Free-thinking Brethren, whom I lately named to you.

Josephus was a great *Free-thinker:* I wish he had chosen a better Subject to write on, than those ignorant, barbarous, ridiculous Scoundrels the *Jews,* whom God (if we may believe the Priests) thought fit to chuse for his own People. I will give you some Instances of his *Free-thinking.* He says, *Cain* travelled through several Countries, and kept Company with Rakes and profligate Fellows, he corrupted the Simplicities of former Times, *&c.* which plainly supposes Men before *Adam,* and consequently that the Priests' History of the Creation by *Moses,* is an Imposture. He says, the *Israelites* passing through the Red Sea, was no more than *Alexander's* passing at the *Pamphilion* Sea; that as for the appearance of God at Mount *Sinai,* the Reader may believe it as he pleases; that *Moses* persuaded the *Jews,* he had God for his Guide, just as the *Greeks* pretended they had their Laws from *Apollo.* These are noble Strains of *Free Thinking,* which the Priests know not how to solve, but by *thinking* as *freely;* for one of them says, that *Josephus* writ this to make his Work acceptable to the *Heathen,* by striking out every thing that was incredible.

Origen, who was the first Christian that had any Learning, has left a noble Testimony of his *Free Thinking;* for a general Council has determined him to be damn'd; which plainly shews he was a *Free Thinker:* And was no *Saint;* for People were only Sainted because of their want of Learning and excess of Zeal; so that all the Fathers, who are called *Saints* by the Priests, were worse than Atheists.

Minutius Fælix seems to be a true, Modern, Latitudinarian, *Free Thinking* Christian, for he is against Altars, Churches, publick Preaching, and publick Assemblies; and likewise against Priests; for he says, there were several great flourishing Empires before there were any Orders of Priests in the World.

Synesius, who had too much Learning and too little Zeal for a *Saint,* was for some time a great *Free Thinker;* he could not believe the Resurrection till he was made a Bishop, and then pretended to be convinced by a Lying Miracle.

To come to our own Country: My Lord *Bacon* was a great *Free Thinker,* when he tells us, that whatever has the least Relation to Religion, is particularly liable to Suspicion, by which he seems to suspect all the Facts whereon most of the Superstitions (that is to say, what the Priests call the Religions) of the World are grounded. He also prefers Atheism before Superstition.

Mr. *Hobbs* was a Person of great Learning, Virtue and *Free Thinking,* except in his *High-Church* Politicks.

But *Arch Bishop Tillotson* is the Person whom all *English Free Thinkers* own as their Head; and his Virtue is indisputable for this manifest Reason, that Dr. *Hicks,* a Priest, calls him an Atheist; says, he caused several to turn Atheists, and to ridicule the Priesthood and Religion. These must be allowed to be noble effects of *Free Thinking.* This great Prelate assures us, that all the Duties of the Christian Religion, with respect to God, are no other but what natural Light prompts Men to, except the two Sacraments, and praying to God in the Name and Mediation of Christ: As a Priest and Prelate he was obliged to say something of Christianity; but pray observe, Sir, how he brings himself off. He justly affirms that even these things are of less Moment than natural Duties; and because Mothers nursing their Children is a natural Duty, it is of more Moment than the two Sacraments, or than praying to God in the Name and by the Mediation of Christ. This *Free Thinking* Archbishop could not allow a Miracle sufficient to give Credit to a Prophet who taught any thing contrary to our natural Notions: By which it is plain, he rejected at once all the Mysteries of Christianity.

I could name one and twenty more great Men, who were all *Free Thinkers;* but that I fear to be tedious. For, 'tis certain that all Men of Sense depart from the Opinions commonly received; and are consequently more or less Men of Sense, according as they depart more or less from the Opinions commonly received; neither can you name an Enemy to *Free Thinking,* however he be dignify'd or distinguish'd, whether *Archbishop, Bishop, Priest* or *Deacon,* who has not been either a *crack-brain'd Enthusiast,* a *diabolical Villain,* or a most *profound ignorant Brute.*

Thus, Sir, I have endeavour'd to execute your Commands, and you may print this Letter if you please; but I would have you conceal your Name, For my Opinion of Virtue is, that we ought not to venture doing our selves harm, by endeavouring to do good. I am

YOURS, *&c.*

———

I have here given the Publick a brief, but faithful Abstract, of this most excellent Essay; wherein I have all along religiously adhered to our Author's Notions, and generally to his

Words, without any other Addition than that of explaining a few necessary Consequences, for the sake of ignorant Readers; For, to those who have the least degree of Learning, I own they will be wholly useless. I hope I have not, in any single Instance, misrepresented the Thoughts of this admirable Writer. If I have happened to mistake through Inadvertency, I entreat he will condescend to inform me, and point out the Place, upon which I will immediately beg Pardon both of him and the World. The Design of his Piece is to recommend Free-thinking, *and one chief Motive is the Example of many Excellent Men who were of that Sect. He produces as the principal Points of their* Free-thinking; *That they denied the Being of a God, the Torments of Hell, the Immortality of the Soul, the Trinity, Incarnation, the History of the Creation by* Moses, *with many other such* fabulous and blasphemous Stories, *as he judiciously calls them: And he asserts, that whoever denies the most of these, is the compleatest* Free-thinker, *and consequently the wisest and most virtuous Man. The Author, sensible of the Prejudices of the Age, does not directly affirm himself an Atheist; he goes no further than to pronounce that Atheism is the most perfect degree of* Free-thinking; *and leaves the Reader to form the Conclusion. However, he seems to allow, that a Man may be a tolerable* Free-thinker, *tho' he does believe a God; provided he utterly rejects* Providence, Revelation, the Old and New Testament, Future Rewards *and* Punishments, *the* Immortality of the Soul, *and other the like impossible Absurdities. Which Mark of superabundant Caution, sacrificing* Truth *to the* Superstition *of* Priests, *may perhaps be* forgiven, *but ought not to be* imitated *by any who would arrive (even in this Author's Judgment) at the true Perfection of* Free-thinking.

SOME THOUGHTS ON
FREE-THINKING

Discoursing one day with a prelate of the kingdom of Ireland, who is a person of excellent wit and learning, he offered a notion applicable to the subject, we were then upon, which I took to be altogether new and right. He said, that the difference betwixt a mad-man and one in his wits, in what related to speech, consisted in this: That the former spoke out whatever came into his mind, and just in the confused manner as his imagination presented the ideas. The latter only expressed such thoughts, as his judgment directed him to chuse, leaving the rest to die away in his memory. And that if the wisest man would at any time utter his thoughts, in the crude indigested manner, as they come into his head, he would be looked upon as raving mad. And indeed, when we consider our thoughts, as they are the seeds of words and actions, we cannot but agree, that they ought to be kept under the strictest regulation. And that in the great multiplicity of ideas, which ones mind is apt to form, there is nothing more difficult than to select those, which are most proper for the conduct of life: So that I cannot imagine what is meant by the mighty zeal in some people, for asserting the freedom of thinking: Because, if such thinkers keep their thoughts within their own breasts, they can be of no consequence, further than to themselves. If they publish them to the world, they ought to be answerable for the effects their thoughts produce upon others. There are thousands in this kingdom, who, in their thoughts prefer a republick or absolute power of a prince before a limited monarchy; yet, if any of these should publish their opinions, and go about, by writing or discourse, to persuade the people to innovations in government, they would be liable to the severest punishments the law can inflict, and therefore they are usually so wise as to keep their sentiments to themselves. But with respect to religion, the matter is quite otherwise. And the publick, at least here in England, seems to be of opinion with Tiberius, that *Deorum injurias diis curæ.* They leave it to God Almighty to vindicate the injuries done to himself, who is no doubt sufficiently able, by perpetual miracles, to revenge the affronts of impious men. And it should seem, that this is what princes expect from him, though I cannot readily conceive the grounds they go upon: Nor why, since they are God's vice-gerents, they do not think themselves at least equally obliged to preserve their master's honour, as their own. Since this is what they expect from those they depute, and since they never fail to represent the disobedience of their subjects, as offences against God: It is true, the visible reason of this neglect is obvious enough. The consequences of atheistical opinions published to the world, are not so immediate or so sensible, as doctrines of rebellion and sedition, spread in a proper season: However, I cannot but think the same consequences are as natural and probable for the former, though more remote. And whether these have not been in view among our great planters of infidelity in England, I shall hereafter examine.

A

LETTER

TO A

YOUNG LADY,

ON HER

MARRIAGE

Written in the Y E A R *1723.*

MADAM,

The Hurry and Impertinence of receiving and paying Visits on Account of your Marriage, being now over; you are beginning to enter into a Course of Life, where you will want much Advice to divert you from falling into many Errors, Fopperies, and Follies to which your Sex is subject. I have always born an entire Friendship to your Father and Mother; and the Person they have chosen for your Husband hath been for some Years past my particular Favourite. I have long wished you might come together, because I hoped, that from the Goodness of your Disposition, and by following the Council of wise Friends, you might in Time make your self worthy of him. Your Parents were so far in the right, that they did not produce you much into the World; whereby you avoided many wrong Steps which others have taken; and have fewer ill Impressions to be removed: But they failed, as it is generally the Case, in too much neglecting to cultivate your Mind; without which it is impossible to acquire or preserve the Friendship and Esteem of a wise Man, who soon grows weary of acting the Lover, and treating his Wife like a Mistress, but wants a reasonable Companion, and a true Friend through every Stage of his Life. It must be therefore your Business to qualify your self for those Offices; wherein I will not fail to be your Director as long as I shall think you deserve it, by letting you know how you are to act, and what you ought to avoid.

AND beware of despising or neglecting my Instructions, whereon will depend, not only your making a good Figure in the World, but your own real Happiness, as well as that of the Person who ought to be the dearest to you.

I MUST therefore desire you in the first place to be very slow in changing the modest Behaviour of a Virgin: It is usual in young Wives before they have been many Weeks married, to assume a bold, forward Look and manner of Talking; as if they intended to signify in all Companies, that they were no longer Girls, and consequently that their whole Demeanor, before they got a Husband, was all but a Countenance and Constraint upon their Nature: Whereas, I suppose, if the Votes of wise Men were gathered, a very great Majority would be in favour of those Ladies, who after they were entered into that State, rather chose to double their Portion of Modesty and Reservedness.

I MUST likewise warn you strictly against the least Degree of Fondness to your Husband before any Witnesses whatsoever, even before your nearest Relations, or the very Maids of your Chamber. This Proceeding is so extremely odious and disgustful to all who have either good Breeding or good Sense, that they assign two very unamiable Reasons for it; the one is gross Hypocrisy, and the other hath too bad a Name to mention. If there is any Difference to be made, your Husband is the lowest Person in Company, either at home or abroad; and every Gentleman present hath a better Claim to all Marks of Civility and Distinction from you. Conceal your Esteem and Love in your own Breast, and reserve your kind Looks and Language for private Hours; which are so many in the Four and Twenty, that they will afford Time to employ a Passion as exalted as any that was ever described in a *French* Romance.

UPON this Head, I should likewise advise you to differ in Practice from those Ladies who affect abundance of Uneasiness while their Husbands are abroad; start with every knock at the Door, and ring the Bell incessantly for their Servants to let in their Master; will not eat a Bit at Dinner or Supper if the Husband happen to stay out; and receive him at his Return with such a Medley of Chiding and Kindness, and catechizing him where he hath been; that a Shrew from *Billingsgate* would be a more easy and eligible Companion.

OF the same Leaven are those Wives, who when their Husbands are gone a Journey, must have a Letter every Post, upon Pain of Fits and Hystericks; and a Day must be fixed for their Return home without the least Allowance for Business, or Sickness, or Accidents, or Weather: Upon which, I can only say, that in my Observation, those Ladies, who are apt to make the greatest Clutter upon such occasions, would liberally have paid a Messenger for bringing them News, that their Husbands had broken their Necks on the Road.

YOU will perhaps be offended when I advise you to abate a little of that violent Passion for fine Cloaths so predominant in your Sex. It is somewhat hard, that ours, for whose Sake you wear them, are not admitted to be of your Council: I may venture to assure you, that we will make an Abatement at any Time of four Pounds a Yard in a Brocade, if the Ladies will but allow a suitable Addition of Care in the Cleanliness and Sweetness of their Persons: For, the satyrical Part of Mankind will needs believe, that it is not impossible, to be very fine and very filthy; and that the Capacities of a Lady are sometimes apt to fall short in cultivating Cleanliness and Finery together. I shall only add, upon so tender a Subject, what a pleasant Gentleman said concerning a silly Woman of Quality; that nothing could make her supportable but cutting off her Head; for his Ears were offended by her Tongue, and his Nose by her Hair and Teeth.

I AM wholly at a Loss how to advise you in the Choice of Company; which, however, is a Point of as great Importance as any in your Life. If your general Acquaintance be among Ladies who are your Equals or Superiors, provided they have nothing of what is commonly called an ill Reputation, you think you are safe; and this in the Style of the World will pass for good Company. Whereas, I am afraid it will be hard for you to pick out one Female-Acquaintance in this Town, from whom you may not be in manifest Danger of contracting some Foppery, Affectation, Vanity, Folly, or Vice. Your only safe Way of conversing with them, is by a firm Resolution to proceed in your Practice and Behaviour, directly contrary to whatever they shall say or do: And this I take to be a good general Rule, with very few Exceptions. For Instance, In the Doctrines they usually deliver to young-married Women for managing their Husbands; their several Accounts of their own Conduct in that Particular, to recommend it to your Imitation; the Reflections they make upon others of their Sex for acting differently; their Directions how to come off with Victory upon any Dispute or Quarrel you may have with your Husband; the Arts by which you may discover and practice upon his weak Sides; when to work by Flattery and Insinuation; when to melt him with Tears; and when to engage him with a high Hand. In these, and a thousand other Cases, it will be prudent to retain as many of their Lectures in your Memory as you can, and then determine to act in full Opposition to them all.

I HOPE your Husband will interpose his Authority to limit you in the Trade of Visiting: Half a dozen Fools are in all Conscience as many as you should require; and it will be sufficient for you to see them twice a Year: For I think the Fashion does not exact that Visits should be paid to Friends.

I ADVISE that your Company at home should consist of Men rather than Women. To say the Truth, I never yet knew a tolerable Woman to be fond of her own Sex: I confess, when both are mixt and well chosen, and put their best Qualities forward, there may be an Intercourse of Civility and Good-will; which, with the Addition of some Degree of Sense, can make Conversation or any Amusement agreeable. But a Knot of Ladies, got together by themselves, is a very School of Impertinence and Detraction; and it is well if those be the worst.

LET your Men-Acquaintance be of your Husband's Choice, and not recommended to you by any She-companions; because they will certainly fix a Coxcomb upon you; and it will cost you some Time and Pains before you can arrive at the Knowledge of distinguishing such a one from a Man of Sense.

NEVER take a Favourite-Waiting-Maid into your Cabinet-Council, to entertain you with Histories of those Ladies whom she hath formerly served; of their Diversions and their Dresses; to insinuate how great a Fortune you brought, and how little you are allowed to squander; to appeal to her from your Husband, and to be determined by her Judgment, because you are sure it will be always for you; to receive and discard Servants by her Approbation, or Dislike; to engage you by her Insinuations into Misunderstandings with your best Friends; to represent all Things in false Colours, and to be the common Emissary of Scandal.

BUT, the grand Affair of your Life will be to gain and preserve the Friendship and Esteem of your Husband. You are married to a Man of good Education and Learning, of an excellent Understanding, and an exact Taste. It is true, and it is happy for you, that these Qualities in him are adorned with great

Modesty, a most amiable Sweetness of Temper, and an unusual Disposition to Sobriety and Virtue: But neither Good-nature, nor Virtue, will suffer him to esteem you against his Judgment; and although he be not capable of using you ill, yet you will, in Time, grow a Thing indifferent, and perhaps contemptible, unless you can supply the Loss of Youth and Beauty with more durable Qualities. You have but a very few Years to be young and handsome in the Eyes of the World; and as few Months to be so in the Eyes of a Husband, who is not a Fool; for, I hope, you do not still dream of Charms and Raptures; which Marriage ever did, and ever will put a sudden End to. Besides, yours was a Match of Prudence, and common Good-liking, without any Mixture of that ridiculous Passion which hath no Being, but in Play-Books and Romances.

YOU must, therefore, use all Endeavours to attain to some Degree of those Accomplishments, which your Husband most values in other People, and for which he is most valued himself. You must improve your Mind, by closely pursuing such a Method of Study, as I shall direct or approve of. You must get a Collection of History and Travels, which I will recommend to you; and spend some Hours every Day in reading them, and making Extracts from them, if your Memory be weak. You must invite Persons of Knowledge and Understanding to an Acquaintance with you, by whose Conversation you may learn to correct your Taste and Judgment: And when you can bring yourself to comprehend and relish the good Sense of others, you will arrive, in Time, to think rightly yourself, and to become a reasonable and agreeable Companion. This must produce in your Husband a true rational Love and Esteem for you, which old Age will not diminish. He will have a Regard for your Judgment and Opinion, in Matters of the greatest Weight; you will be able to entertain each other, without a third Person to relieve you, by finding Discourse. The Endowments of your Mind will even make your Person more agreeable to him; and when you are alone, your Time will not lie heavy upon your Hands, for want of some trifling Amusement.

As little Respect as I have for the Generality of your Sex, it hath sometimes moved me with Pity, to see the Lady of the House forced to withdraw, immediately after Dinner, and this in Families where there is not much Drinking; as if it were an established Maxim, that Women are incapable of all Conversation. In a Room where both Sexes meet, if the Men are discoursing upon any general Subject, the Ladies never think it their Business to partake in what passes; but, in a separate Club, entertain each other with the Price and Choice of Lace and Silk, and what Dresses they liked, or disapproved at the Church, or the Playhouse. And when you are among yourselves, how naturally, after the first Compliments, do you apply your Hands to each others Lappets, and Ruffles, and Mantuas; as if the whole Business of your Lives, and the publick Concern of the World, depended upon the Cut or Colour of your Petticoats? As Divines say, that some People take more Pains to be damned, than it would cost them to be saved; so your Sex employs more Thought, Memory, and Application to be Fools, than would serve to make them wise and useful. When I reflect on this, I cannot conceive you to be human Creatures, but a Sort of Species hardly a Degree above a Monkey; who hath more diverting Tricks than any of you; is an Animal less mischievous and expensive; might, in Time, be a tolerable Critick in Velvet and Brocade; and, for ought I know, would equally become them.

I WOULD have you look upon finery as a necessary Folly, which all great Ladies did whom I have ever known: I do not desire you to be out of the Fashion, but to be the last and least in it: I expect that your Dress shall be one Degree lower than your Fortune can afford: And, in your own Heart, I would wish you to be an utter Contemner of all Distinctions which a finer Petticoat can give you; because, it will neither make you richer, handsomer, younger, better natured, more virtuous, or wise, than if it hung upon a Peg.

IF you are in Company with Men of Learning; although they happen to discourse of Arts and Sciences out of your Compass, yet you will gather more Advantage by listening to them, than from all the Nonsense and Frippery of your own Sex: But, if they be Men of Breeding as well as Learning, they will seldom engage in any Conversation where you ought not to be a Hearer, and in Time have your Part. If they talk of the Manners and Customs of the several Kingdoms of *Europe;* of Travels into remote Nations; of the State of their own Country; or of the great Men and Actions of *Greece* and *Rome:* If they give their Judgment upon *English* and *French* Writers, either in Verse or Prose; or of the Nature and Limits of Virtue and Vice; it is a Shame for an *English* Lady not to relish such Discourses, not to improve by them, and endeavour by Reading and Information, to have her Share in those Entertainments; rather than turn aside, as it is the usual Custom, and consult with the Woman who sits next her, about a new Cargo of Fans.

IT is a little hard, that not one Gentleman's Daughter in a Thousand, should be brought to read, or understand her own Natural Tongue, or be Judge of the easiest Books that are written in it; as any one may find, who can have the Patience to hear them, when they are disposed to mangle a Play or Novel, where the least Word out of the common Road, is sure to disconcert them; and it is no wonder, when they are not so much as taught to spell in their Childhood, nor can ever attain to it in their whole Lives. I advise you, therefore, to read aloud, more or less, every Day to your Husband, if he will permit you, or to any other Friend, (but not a Female one) who is able to set you right: And as for Spelling, you may compass it in Time, by making Collections from the Books you read.

I KNOW very well, that those who are commonly called learned Women, have lost all Manner of Credit by their impertinent Talkativeness, and Conceit of themselves: But there is an easy Remedy for this; if you once consider, that after all the Pains you may be at, you never can arrive, in Point of Learning, to the Perfection of a School-Boy. But the Reading I would advise you to, is only for Improvement of your own good Sense, which will never fail of being mended by Discretion. It is a wrong Method, and ill Choice of Books, that make those learned Ladies just so much worse for what they have read. And therefore, it shall be my Care to direct you better; a Task for which I take myself to be not ill qualified; because I have spent more Time, and have had more Opportunities than many others, to observe and discover from what Sources the various Follies of Women are derived.

PRAY observe, how insignificant Things are the common Race of Ladies, when they have passed their Youth and Beauty; how contemptible they appear to the Men, and yet more contemptible to the younger Part of their own Sex; and have no Relief but in passing their Afternoons in Visits, where they are never acceptable; and their Evenings at Cards among each other; while the former Part of the Day is spent in Spleen and Envy, or in vain Endeavours to repair by Art and Dress the Ruins of Time: Whereas, I have known Ladies at Sixty, to whom all the polite Part of the Court and Town paid their Addresses; without any further View than that of enjoying the Pleasure of their Conversation.

I AM ignorant of any one Quality that is amiable in a Man, which is not equally so in a Woman: I do not except even Modesty, and Gentleness of Nature. Nor do I know one Vice or Folly, which is not equally detestable in both. There is, indeed, one Infirmity which is generally allowed you, I mean that of Cowardice. Yet there should seem to be something very capricious, that when Women profess their Admiration for a Colonel or a Captain, on Account of his Valour; they should fancy it a very graceful becoming Quality in themselves, to be afraid of their own Shadows; to scream in a Barge, when the Weather is calmest, or in a Coach at the Ring; to run from a Cow at an Hundred Yards Distance; to fall into Fits at the Sight of a Spider, an Ear-wig, or a Frog. At least, if Cowardice be a Sign of Cruelty, (as it is generally granted) I can hardly think it an Accomplishment so desireable, as to be thought worthy of improving by Affectation.

AND as the same Virtues equally become both Sexes; so there is no Quality whereby Women endeavour to distinguish themselves from Men, for which they are not just so much the worse; except that only of Reservedness; which, however, as you generally manage it, is nothing else but Affectation, or Hypocrisy. For, as you cannot too much discountenance those of our Sex, who presume to take unbecoming Liberties before you; so you ought to be wholly unconstrained in the Company of deserving Men, when you have had sufficient Experience of their Discretion.

THERE is never wanting in this Town, a Tribe of bold, swaggering, rattling Ladies, whose Talents pass among Coxcombs for Wit and Humour: Their Excellency lies in rude choquing[1] Expressions, and what they call *running a Man down.* If a Gentleman in their Company, happen to have any Blemish in his Birth, or Person; if any Misfortune hath befallen his Family, or himself, for which he is ashamed; they will be sure to give him broad Hints of it, without any Provocation. I would recommend you to the Acquaintance of a common Prostitute, rather than to that of such Termagants as these. I have often thought that no Man is obliged to suppose such Creatures to be Women; but to treat them like insolent Rascals, disguised in Female Habits, who ought to be stripped, and kicked down Stairs.

I WILL add one Thing, although it be a little out of Place; which is to desire, that you will learn to value and esteem your Husband, for those good Qualities which he really possesseth; and not to fancy others in him, which he certainly hath not. For, although this latter be generally understood for a Mark of Love, yet it is indeed nothing but Affectation, or ill Judgment. It is true, the Person you have chosen wants so very few Accomplishments, that you are in no great Danger of erring on this Side: But my Caution is occasioned by a Lady of your Acquaintance, married to a very valuable Person, whom yet she is so unfortunate as to be always commending for those Perfections, to which he can least pretend.

I CAN give you no Advice upon the Article of Expence; only, I think, you ought to be well informed how much your Husband's Revenue amounts to, and be so good a Computer, as to keep within it, in that Part of the Management which falls to your Share; and not to put yourself in the Number of those politick Ladies, who think they gain a great Point, when they have teazed their Husbands to buy them a new Equipage, a laced Head, or a fine Petticoat; without once considering what long Scores remain unpaid to the Butcher.

I DESIRE you will keep this Letter in your Cabinet, and often examine impartially your whole Conduct by it: And so GOD bless you, and make you a fair Example to your Sex, and a perpetual Comfort to your Husband, and your Parents. I am, with great Truth and Affection,

Madam,
Your most faithful Friend,
And humble Servant.

V

WRITINGS ON IRELAND

THE

STORY

OF THE

INJURED LADY.

WRITTEN BY HERSELF.

IN A LETTER TO HER FRIEND, WITH

HIS ANSWER.

Sir,

Being ruined by the Inconstancy and Unkindness of a Lover,[1] I hope, a true and plain Relation of my Misfortunes may be of Use and Warning to credulous Maids, never to put too much Trust in deceitful Men.

A Gentleman in the Neighbourhood had two Mistresses, another and myself; and he pretended honourable Love to us both. Our three Houses stood pretty near one another; his was parted from mine by a River, and from my Rival's by an old broken Wall. But before I enter into the Particulars of this Gentleman's hard Usage of me, I will give a very just impartial Character of my Rival and myself.

As to her Person she is tall and lean, and very ill-shaped; she hath bad Features, and a worse Complexion; she hath a stinking Breath, and twenty ill Smells about her besides; which are yet more unsufferable by her natural Sluttishness; for she is always lousy, and never without the Itch. As to her other Qualities, she hath no Reputation either for Virtue, Honesty, Truth, or Manners; and it is no Wonder, considering what her Education hath been. Scolding and Cursing are her common Conversation. To sum up all; she is poor and beggarly, and gets a sorry Maintenance by pilfering whereever she comes. As for this Gentleman who is now so fond of her, she still beareth him an invincible Hatred; revileth him to his Face, and raileth at him in all Companies. Her House is frequented by a Company of Rogues and Thieves, and Pickpockets, whom she encourageth to rob his Hen-roosts, steal his Corn and Cattle, and do him all manner of Mischief. She hath been known to come at the Head of these Rascals, and beat her Lover until he was sore from Head to Foot, and then force him to pay for the Trouble she was at. Once, attended with a Crew of Raggamuffins, she broke into his House, turned all Things topsy-turvy, and then set it on Fire. At the same Time she told so many Lies among his Servants, that it set them all by the Ears, and his poor Steward was knocked on the Head;[2] for which I think, and so doth all the Country, that she ought to be answerable.[3] To conclude her Character; she is of a different Religion, being a Presbyterian of the most rank and virulent Kind, and consequently having an inveterate Hatred to the Church; yet, I am sure, I have been always told, that in Marriage there ought to be an Union of Minds as well as of Persons.

I will now give my own Character, and shall do it in few Words, and with Modesty and Truth.

I was reckoned to be as handsome as any in our Neighbourhood, until I became pale and thin with Grief and ill Usage. I am still fair enough, and have, I think, no very ill Feature about me. They that see me now will hardly allow me ever to have had any great Share of Beauty; for besides being so much altered, I go always mobbed and in an Undress, as well out of Neglect, as indeed for want of Cloaths to appear in. I might add to all this, that I was born to a good Estate, although it now turneth to little Account under the Oppressions I endure, and hath been the true Cause of all my Misfortunes.

Some Years ago, this Gentleman taking a Fancy either to my Person or Fortune, made his Addresses to me; which, being then young and foolish, I too readily admitted; he seemed to use me with so much Tenderness, and his Conversation was so very engaging, that all my Constancy and Virtue were too soon overcome; and, to dwell no longer upon a Theme that causeth such bitter Reflections, I must confess with Shame, that I was undone by the common Arts practised upon all easy credulous Virgins, half by Force, and half by Consent, after solemn Vows and Protestations of Marriage. When he had once got Possession, he soon began to play the usual Part of a too fortunate Lover, affecting on all Occasions to shew his Authority, and to act like a Conqueror. First, he found Fault with the Government of my Family, which I grant, was none of the best, consisting of ignorant illiterate Creatures; for at that Time, I knew but little of the World. In compliance to him, therefore, I agreed to fall into his Ways and Methods of Living; I consented that his Steward should govern my House,[4] and have Liberty to employ an Under-Steward,[5] who should receive his Directions. My Lover proceeded further, turning away several old Servants and Tenants, and supplying me with others from his own House. These grew so domineering and unreasonable, that there was no Quiet, and I heard of nothing but perpetual Quarrels, which although I could not possibly help, yet my Lover laid all the Blame and Punishment upon me; and upon every Falling-out, still turned away more of my People, and supplied me in their Stead with a Number of Fellows and Dependents of his own, whom he had no other Way to provide for. Overcome by Love, and to avoid Noise and Contentions, I yielded to all his Usurpations, and finding it in vain to resist, I thought it my best Policy to make my Court to my new Servants, and draw them to my Interests; I fed them from my own Table with the best I had, put my new Tenants on the choice Parts of my Land, and treated them all so kindly, that they began to love me as well as their Master. In process of Time, all my old Servants were gone, and I had not a Creature about me, nor above one or two Tenants but what were of his chusing; yet I had the good Luck by gentle Usage to bring over the greatest Part of them to my Side. When my Lover observed this, he began to alter his Language; and, to those who enquired about me, he would answer, that I was an old Dependent upon his Family, whom he had placed on some Concerns of his own; and he began to use me accordingly, neglecting by Degrees all common Civility in his Behaviour. I shall never forget the Speech[6] he made me one Morning, which he delivered with all the Gravity in the World. He put me in Mind of the vast Obligations I lay under to him, in sending me so many of his People for my own Good, and to teach me Manners: That it had cost him ten Times more than I was worth, to maintain me: That it had been much better for him if I had been damned, or burnt, or sunk to the Bottom of the Sea: That it was but reasonable I should strain myself as far as I was able, to reimburse him some of his Charges: That from henceforward he expected his Word should be a Law to me in all Things: That I must maintain a Parish-watch against Thieves and Robbers,[7] and give Salaries to an Overseer, a Constable, and Others, all of his own chusing, whom he would send from Time to Time to be Spies upon me: That, to enable me the better in supporting these Expences, my Tenants shall be obliged to carry all their Goods cross the River to his Town-market, and pay Toll on both Sides, and then sell them at half Value. But because we were a nasty Sort of People, and that he could not endure to touch any Thing we had a Hand in, and likewise, because he wanted Work to employ his own Folks, therefore we must send all our Goods to his Market just in their Naturals;[8] the Milk immediately from the Cow without making it into Cheese or Butter; the Corn in the Ear; the Grass as it is mowed; the Wool as it cometh from the Sheeps Back; and bring the Fruit upon the Branch, that he might not be obliged to eat it after our filthy Hands: That, if a Tenant carried but a Piece of Bread and Cheese to eat by the Way, or an Inch of Worsted to mend his Stockings, he should forfeit his whole Parcel: And because a Company of Rogues usually plied on the River between us, who often robbed my Tenants of their Goods and Boats, he ordered a Waterman of his to guard them, whose Manner was to be out of the Way until the poor Wretches were plundered; then to overtake the Thieves, and seize all as lawful Prize to his Master and himself. It would be endless to repeat an hundred other Hardships he hath put upon me; but it is a general Rule, that whenever he imagines the smallest Advantage will redound to one of his Foot-boys by any new Oppression of me and my whole Family and Estate, he never disputeth it a Moment. All this hath rendered me so very insignificant and contemptible at Home, that some Servants to whom I pay the greatest Wages, and many Tenants who have the most beneficial Leases, are gone over to live with him; yet I am bound to continue their Wages, and pay their Rents; by which Means one Third Part of my whole Income is spent on his Estate, and above another Third by his Tolls and Markets; and my poor Tenants are so sunk and impoverished, that, instead of maintaining me suitable to my Quality, they can hardly find me Cloaths to keep me warm, or provide the common Necessaries of Life for themselves.

Matters being in this Posture between me and my Lover; I received Intelligence that he had been for some Time making very pressing Overtures of Marriage to my Rival, until there happened some Misunderstandings between them; she gave him ill Words, and threatened to break off all Commerce with him. He, on the other Side, having either acquired Courage by his Triumphs over me, or supposing her as tame a Fool as I, thought at first to carry it with a high Hand; but hearing at the same Time, that she had Thoughts of making some private Proposals to join with me against him, and doubting with very good Reason that I would readily accept them, he seemed very much disconcerted. This I thought was a proper Occasion to shew some great Example of Generosity and Love; and so, without further Consideration, I sent him Word, that hearing there was like to be a Quarrel between him and my Rival; notwithstanding all that had passed, and without binding him to any Conditions in my own Favour, I would stand by him against her and all the World, while I had a Penny in my Purse, or a Petticoat to pawn. This Message was subscribed by all my chief Tenants; and proved so powerful, that my Rival immediately grew more tractable upon it. The Result of which was, that there is now a Treaty of Marriage concluded between them, the Wedding Cloaths are bought, and nothing remaineth but to perform the Ceremony, which is put off for some Days, because they design it to be a publick Wedding. And to reward my Love, Constancy, and Generosity, he hath bestowed on me the Office of being Sempstress to his Grooms and Footmen, which I am forced to accept or starve. Yet, in the Midst of this my Situation, I cannot but have some Pity for this deluded Man, to cast himself away on an infamous Creature, who, whatever she pretendeth, I can prove, would at this very Minute rather be a Whore to a certain Great Man,[9] that shall be nameless, if she might have her Will. For my Part, I think, and so doth all the Country too, that the Man is possessed; at least none of us are able to imagine what he can possibly see in her, unless she hath bewitched him, or given him some Powder.

I am sure, I never sought his Alliance, and you can bear me Witness, that I might have had other Matches; nay, if I were lightly disposed, I could still perhaps have Offers, that some, who hold their Heads higher, would be glad to accept. But alas, I never had any such wicked Thoughts; all I now desire is, only to enjoy a little Quiet, to be free from the Persecutions of this unreasonable Man, and that he will let me manage my own little Fortune to the best Advantage; for which I will undertake to pay him a considerable Pension every Year, much more considerable than what he now gets by his Oppressions; for he must needs find himself a Loser at last, when he hath drained me and my Tenants so dry, that we shall not have a Penny for him or ourselves. There is one Imposition of his, I had almost forgot, which I think unsufferable, and will appeal to you, or any reasonable Person, whether it be so or not. I told you before, that by an old Compact we agreed to have the same Steward, at which Time I consented likewise to regulate my Family and Estate by the same Method with him, which he then shewed me writ down in Form, and I approved of. Now, the Turn he thinks fit to give this Compact[10] of ours is very extraordinary; for he pretends that whatever Orders he shall think fit to prescribe for the future in his Family, he may, if he will, compel mine to observe them, without asking my Advice or hearing my Reasons. So that I must not make a Lease without his Consent, or give any Directions for the well-governing of my Family, but what he countermands whenever he pleaseth. This leaveth me at such Confusion and Uncertainty, that my Servants know not when to obey me, and my Tenants, although many of them be very well inclined, seem quite at a Loss.

But, I am too tedious upon this melancholy Subject, which however, I hope, you will forgive, since the Happiness of my whole Life dependeth upon it. I desire you will think a while, and give your best Advice what Measures I shall take with Prudence, Justice, Courage, and Honour, to protect my Liberty and Fortune against the Hardships and Severities I lie under from that unkind, inconstant Man.

THE ANSWER TO THE INJURED LADY.[11]

MADAM,

I have received your Ladyship's Letter, and carefully considered every Part of it, and shall give you my Opinion how you ought to proceed for your own Security. But first, I must beg Leave to tell your Ladyship, that you were guilty of an unpardonable Weakness the other Day, in making that Offer to your Lover, of standing by him in any Quarrel he might have with your Rival; you know very well, that she began to apprehend he had Designs of using her as he had done you; and common Prudence might have directed you rather to have entered into some Measures with her for joining against him, until he might at least be brought to some reasonable Terms: But your invincible Hatred to that Lady hath carried your Resentments so high, as to be the Cause of your Ruin; yet, if you please to consider, this Aversion of yours began a good while before she became your Rival, and was taken up by you and your Family in a Sort of Compliment to your Lover, who formerly had a great Abhorrence for her. It is true, since that Time you have suffered very much by her Encroachments upon your Estate, but she never pretended to govern or direct you; and now you have drawn a new Enemy upon yourself; for I think you may count upon all the ill Offices she can possibly do you by her Credit with her Husband; whereas, if instead of openly declaring against her without any Provocation, you had but sat still a while, and said nothing, that Gentleman would have lessened his Severity to you out of perfect Fear. This Weakness of yours, you call Generosity; but I doubt there was more in the Matter: In short, Madam, I have good Reasons to think you were betrayed to it by the pernicious Counsels of some about you: For, to my certain Knowledge, several of your Tenants and Servants, to whom you have been very kind, are as arrant Rascals as any in the Country. I cannot but observe what a mighty Difference there is in one Particular between your Ladyship and your Rival. Having yielded up your Person, you thought nothing else worth defending, and therefore you will not now insist upon those very Conditions for which you yielded at first. But your Ladyship cannot be ignorant, that some Years since your Rival did the same Thing, and upon no Conditions at all; nay, this Gentleman kept her as a Miss, and yet made her pay for her very Diet and Lodging. But, it being at a Time when he had no Steward, and his Family out of Order, she stole away, and hath now got the Trick, very well known among Women of the Town, to grant a Man the Favour over Night, and the next Day have the Impudence to deny it to his Face. But, it is too late to reproach you with any former Oversights, which cannot now be rectified. I know the Matters of Fact as you relate them are true and fairly represented. My Advice therefore is this. Get your Tenants together as soon as you conveniently can, and make them agree to the following Resolutions.

First. That your Family and Tenants have no Dependence upon the said Gentleman, further than by the old Agreement, which obligeth you to have the same Steward, and to regulate your Household by such Methods as you shall both agree to.

Secondly. That you will not carry your Goods to the Market of his Town, unless you please, nor be hindered from carrying them any where else.

Thirdly. That the Servants you pay Wages to shall live at Home, or forfeit their Places.

Fourthly. That whatever Lease you make to a Tenant, it shall not be in his Power to break it.

If he will agree to these Articles, I advise you to contribute as largely as you can to all Charges of Parish and County.

I can assure you, several of that Gentleman's ablest Tenants and Servants are against his severe Usage of you, and would be glad of an Occasion to convince the rest of their Error, if you will not be wanting to yourself.

If the Gentleman refuses these just and reasonable Offers, pray let me know it, and, perhaps I may think of something else that will be more effectual.

I am,
Madam,
Your Ladyship's, &c.

A Proposal for
the Universal use
of Irish Manufacture,
in Cloaths and Furniture
of Houses, &c.
Utterly Rejecting and
Renouncing Every Thing
wearable that comes from
England

I t is the peculiar Felicity and Prudence of the People in this Kingdom, that whatever Commodities, or Productions, lie under the greatest Discouragements from *England,* those are what they are sure to be most industrious in cultivating and spreading. *Agriculture,* which hath been the principal Care of all wise Nations, and for the Encouragement whereof there are so many Statute-Laws in *England,* we countenance so well, that the Landlords are every where, by *penal Clauses,*[1] absolutely prohibiting their Tenants from Plowing; not satisfied to confine them within certain Limitations, as it is the Practice of the *English;* one Effect of which, is already seen in the prodigious Dearness of Corn, and the Importation of it from *London,* as the cheaper Market: And, because People are the *Riches of a Country,*[2] and that our *Neighbours* have done, and are doing all that in them lie, to make our Wool a Drug to us, and a Monopoly to them;[3] therefore, the politick Gentlemen of *Ireland* have depopulated vast Tracts of the best Land, for the feeding of Sheep.

I COULD fill a Volume as large as the *History of the wise Men of Goatham,* with a Catalogue only of some *wonderful* Laws and Customs we have observed within thirty Years past. It is true, indeed, our beneficial Traffick of Wool with *France,* hath been our only Support for several Years past; furnishing us all the little Money we have to pay our Rents, and go to Market. But our Merchants assure me, *This Trade hath received a great Damp by the present fluctuating Condition of the Coin in* France; *and that most of their Wine is paid for in Specie, without carrying thither any Commodity from hence.*

HOWEVER, since we are so universally bent upon enlarging our *Flocks,* it may be worth inquiring, what we shall do with our Wool, in case *Barnstable*[4] should be over-stocked, and our *French* Commerce should fail?

I SHOULD wish the Parliament had thought fit to have suspended their Regulation of *Church* Matters, and Enlargements of the *Prerogative,* until a more convenient Time, because they did not appear very pressing, (at least to the Persons *principally concerned*) and, instead of those great Refinements in *Politicks* and *Divinity,* had *amused* Themselves and their Committees, a little, with the *State of the Nation.* For Example: What if the House of Commons had thought fit to make a Resolution, *Nemine Contradicente,* against wearing any Cloath or Stuff in their Families, which were not of the Growth and Manufacture of this Kingdom? What if they had extended it so far, as utterly to exclude all Silks, Velvets, Calicoes, and the whole *Lexicon* of Female Fopperies; and declared, that whoever acted otherwise, should be deemed and reputed *an Enemy to the Nation*? What if they had sent up such a Resolution to be agreed to by the House of Lords; and by their own Practice and Encouragement, spread the Execution of it in their several Countries? What if we should agree to make *burying in Woollen a Fashion*, as our Neighbours have made it a *Law*? What if the Ladies would be content with *Irish* Stuffs for the Furniture of their Houses, for Gowns and Petticoats to themselves and their Daughters? Upon the whole, and to crown all the rest, let a firm Resolution be taken, by *Male* and *Female*, never to appear with one single *Shred* that comes from *England; and let all the People say, AMEN.*

I HOPE, and believe, nothing could please his Majesty better than to hear that his loyal Subjects, of both Sexes, in this Kingdom, celebrated his *Birth-Day* (now approaching) *universally* clad in their own Manufacture. Is there Vertue enough left in this deluded People to save them from the Brink of Ruin? If the Mens Opinions may be taken, the Ladies will look as handsome in Stuffs as Brocades, and, since all will be equal, there may be room enough to employ their Wit and Fancy in chusing and matching of Patterns and Colours. I heard the late Archbishop of *Tuam*[5] mention a pleasant Observation of some Body's; *that* Ireland *would never be happy 'till a Law were made for* burning *every Thing that came from* England, *except their* People *and their* Coals: I must confess, that as to the former, I should not be sorry if they would stay at home; and for the latter, I hope, in a little Time we shall have no Occasion for them.

Non tanti mitra est, non tanti Judicis ostrum.[6]

BUT I should rejoice to see a *Stay-Lace* from *England* be thought *scandalous,* and become a Topick for *Censure* at *Visits* and *Tea Tables.*

IF the unthinking Shopkeepers in this Town, had not been *utterly* destitute of common Sense, they would have made some *Proposal to the Parliament,* with a *Petition* to the Purpose I have mentioned; promising to improve the *Cloaths and Stuffs of the Nation, into all possible Degrees of Fineness and Colours, and engaging not to play the Knave, according to their Custom, by exacting and imposing upon the Nobility and Gentry, either as to the Prices or the Goodness.* For I remember, in *London,* upon a general Mourning, the *rascally Mercers* and *Woollen Drapers,* would, in Four and Twenty Hours, raise their

Cloaths and *Silks* to above a double Price; and if the Mourning continued long, then come whingeing with *Petitions* to the *Court, that they were ready to starve, and their Fineries lay upon their Hands.*

I COULD wish our Shopkeepers would immediately think on this *Proposal,* addressing it to all Persons of Quality, and others; but first be sure to get some Body who can write Sense, to put it into Form.

I THINK it needless to exhort the *Clergy* to follow this good Example, because, *in a little Time, those among them who are so unfortunate to have had their Birth and Education in this Country, will think themselves abundantly happy when they can afford* Irish *Crape, and an* Athlone *Hat;* and as to the others, I *shall not presume* to direct them. I have, indeed, seen the present Archbishop of *Dublin*[7] clad from Head to Foot in our own Manufacture; and yet, under the Rose[8] be it spoken, *his Grace deserves as good a Gown, as if he had not been born among us.*

I HAVE not Courage enough to offer *one Syllable* on this Subject to *their Honours* of the Army: Neither have I sufficiently considered the great Importance of *Scarlet* and *Gold Lace.*

THE Fable, in *Ovid,* of *Arachne* and *Pallas,*[9] is to this Purpose. The Goddess had heard of one *Arachne* a young Virgin, very famous for *Spinning* and *Weaving:* They both met upon a Tryal of Skill; and *Pallas* finding herself almost equalled in her own Art, stung with Rage and Envy, knockt her *Rival* down, turned her into a *Spyder,* enjoining her to *spin* and *weave* for ever, *out of her own Bowels,* and *in a very narrow Compass.* I confess, that from a Boy, I always pitied poor *Arachne,* and could never heartily love the Goddess, on Account of so *cruel and unjust a Sentence;* which, however, is *fully executed* upon *Us* by *England,* with further Additions of *Rigor* and *Severity.* For the greatest Part of *our Bowels and Vitals* is extracted, without allowing us the Liberty of *spinning* and *weaving* them.

THE Scripture tells us, that *Oppression makes a wise Man mad;*[10] therefore, consequently speaking, the Reason why some Men are not *mad,* is because they are not *wise:* However, it were to be wished that *Oppression* would, in Time, teach a little *Wisdom* to *Fools.*

I WAS much delighted with a Person, who hath a great Estate in this Kingdom, upon his Complaints to me, *how grievously POOR England suffers by Impositions from* Ireland. *That we convey our own Wool to* France, *in Spight of all the* Harpies *at the Custom-House. That Mr.* Shutleworth, *and others on the* Cheshire *Coasts, are such Fools to sell us their* Bark *at a good Price, for tanning our own Hydes into Leather; with other Enormities of the like Weight and Kind.* To which I will venture to add more: *That the* Mayorality *of this City is al-*

ways executed by an Inhabitant, *and often by a* Native, *which might as well be done by a* Deputy, *with a moderate Salary, whereby POOR* England *loseth, at least, one thousand Pounds a Year upon the Ballance. That the Governing of this Kingdom costs the Lord Lieutenant three Thousand six Hundred Pounds a Year, so much* net Loss *to POOR* England. *That the People of* Ireland *presume to dig for Coals* in their own Grounds; *and the Farmers in the County of* Wicklow *send their Turf to the very Market of* Dublin, *to the great Discouragement of the Coal Trade at* Mostyn *and* White-haven. *That the Revenues of the* Post-Office *here, so righteously belonging to the* English *Treasury, as arising chiefly from our own Commerce with each other, should be remitted to* London, *clogged with that grievous Burthen of Exchange, and the Pensions paid out of the* Irish *Revenues to* English Favourites, *should lie under the same Disadvantage, to the great Loss of the Grantees. When a* Divine *is sent over to a* Bishoprick *here, with the Hopes of Five and Twenty Hundred Pounds a Year; upon his Arrival, he finds, alas! a dreadful Discount of Ten or Twelve* per Cent. *A* Judge, *or a* Commissioner *of the Revenue, has the same Cause of Complaint.* Lastly, *The Ballad upon* Cotter *is vehemently suspected to be* Irish *Manufacture; and yet is allowed to be sung in our open Streets, under the very* Nose *of the* Government.

THESE are a *few* among the many Hardships we put upon that *POOR* Kingdom of *England;* for which, I am confident, every *honest* Man wisheth a *Remedy:* And, I hear, there is a Project *on Foot* for transporting our best Wheaten *Straw,* by Sea and Land Carriage, to *Dunstable; and obliging us by a Law,* to take off yearly so many *Tun of Straw-Hats,* for the Use of our Women; which will be a *great Encouragement* to the Manufacture of that industrious Town.

I WOULD be glad to learn among the Divines, whether a Law *to bind Men without their own Consent,* be obligatory *in foro Conscientiæ;* because, I find *Scripture, Sanderson* and *Suarez,*[11] are wholly silent in the Matter. The Oracle of *Reason,* the great *Law of Nature,* and general Opinion of *Civilians,*[12] wherever they treat of *limitted Governments,* are, indeed, decisive enough.

IT is wonderful to observe the Biass among our People in favour of *Things, Persons,* and *Wares* of all Kinds that come from *England.* The *Printer* tells his *Hawkers,* that *he has got an excellent new Song just brought from* London. I have somewhat of a Tendency that way my self; and upon hearing a *Coxcomb* from thence displaying himself, with great Volubility, upon the *Park,* the *Play-House,* the *Opera,* the *Gaming Ordinaries,* it was apt to beget in me a Kind of Veneration for his Parts and Accomplishments. It is not many Years, since I remember a *Person* who, by his Style and Literature, seems to have been *Corrector* of a Hedge-Press, in some *Blind-Alley* about *Little-*

Britain,[13] proceed *gradually* to be an *Author*, at least a *Translator** of a lower Rate, although somewhat of a larger Bulk, than any that now *flourishes* in *Grub-street*; and, upon the Strength of this Foundation, came over *here*; *erect* himself up into an *Orator* and *Politician*, and lead a *Kingdom* after him. This, I am told, was the *very Motive* that prevailed on the *Author*† of a Play called, *Love in a Hollow-Tree*, to do us the *Honour* of a Visit; presuming, with very good Reason, *that he was a Writer of a superior Class*. I know *another*, who, for thirty Years past, hath been the *common Standard of Stupidity in England*, where he was never heard a Minute in any *Assembly*, or by any *Party*, with *common Christian Treatment*; yet, upon his Arrival hither, could put on a *Face of Importance and Authority*, talked more than Six, without either *Gracefulness, Propriety*, or *Meaning*; and, at the same Time, be admired and followed as the Pattern of *Eloquence* and *Wisdom*.

NOTHING hath humbled me so much, or shewn a greater Disposition to a *contemptuous* Treatment of *Ireland* in some chief *Governors*, than that high Style of several Speeches from the *Throne*, delivered, as usual, after the *Royal Assent*, in *some Periods* of the last *Reigns*. Such Exaggerations of the prodigious *Condescensions* in the Prince, to pass *those good Laws*, would have but an odd Sound at *Westminster*: Neither do I apprehend, how any *good Law* can pass, wherein the *King's* Interest is not as much concerned as that of the *People*. I remember, after a Speech on the like Occasion, delivered by my Lord *Wharton*,[14] (I think it was his last) he desired Mr. *Addison*[15] to *ask my Opinion of it*: My Answer was, *That his Excellency had very honestly forfeited his Head, on Account of one Paragraph; wherein he asserted, by plain Consequence, a* dispensing Power[16] *in the Queen*. His Lordship owned *it was true*, but *swore* the Words were *put into his Mouth* by direct Orders from Court. From whence it is clear, that some *Ministers* in those Times, were apt, from their *high* Elevation, to look *down* upon this Kingdom, as if it had been one of their *Colonies* of *Out-casts* in *America*. And I observed a little of the same Turn of Spirit in *some great Men*, from whom I expected better; although, to do them Justice, it proved no Point of Difficulty to make them *correct their Idea*, whereof the *whole Nation* quickly found the Benefit. — But that is *forgotten*. How the Style hath since run, I am wholly a Stranger; having never seen a Speech since the last of the Queen.

I WOULD now expostulate a little with our Country Landlords; who, by unmeasurable *screwing* and *racking* their Tenants all over the Kingdom,

---

* Supposed to be *Cæsar's* Commentaries, dedicated to the D[uke] of *Marlborough*.
† L. *G*[*ri*] *mst*[*o*]*n*.

have already reduced the miserable *People* to a *worse Condition* than the *Peasants* in *France,* or the *Vassals* in *Germany*[17] and *Poland;* so that the whole *Species* of what we call *Substantial Farmers,* will, in a very few Years, be utterly at an End. It was pleasant to observe these Gentlemen, *labouring* with all their *Might,* for preventing the *Bishops* from letting their Revenues at a moderate half Value, (whereby the whole *Order* would, in an Age, have been reduced to manifest Beggary) at the very Instant, when they were every where *canting* their own Lands[18] upon short Leases, and sacrificing their *oldest Tenants for a Penny an Acre advance.* I know not how it comes to pass, (and yet, perhaps, I know well enough) that *Slaves* have a natural Disposition to be *Tyrants;* and that when my *Betters* give me a Kick, I am apt to revenge it with six upon my *Footman;* although, perhaps, he may be an honest and diligent Fellow. I have heard *great* Divines affirm, that *nothing is so likely to call down an universal Judgment from Heaven upon a Nation, as universal Oppression;* and whether this be not already verified in Part, *their Worships* the Landlords are *now* at full Leisure to consider. Whoever travels this Country, and observes the *Face* of Nature, or the *Faces,* and Habits, and Dwellings of the *Natives,* will hardly think himself in a Land where either *Law, Religion,* or *common Humanity* is professed.

I CANNOT forbear saying one Word upon a *Thing* they call a *Bank,*[19] which, I hear, is projecting in this Town. I never saw the *Proposals,* nor understand any one Particular of their Scheme: What I wish for, at present, is only a sufficient Provision of *Hemp,* and *Caps,* and *Bells,* to distribute according to the several Degrees of *Honesty* and *Prudence* in *some Persons.* I *hear* only of a monstrous Sum already named; and, if OTHERS do not soon hear of it too, and *hear* it with a *Vengeance,* then am I a Gentleman of less Sagacity than my self, and very few besides, take me to be. And the Jest will be still the better, if it be true, as judicious Persons have assured me, that one Half of this Money will be *real,* and the other Half altogether imaginary. The Matter will be likewise much mended, if the Merchants continue to carry off our Gold, and our Goldsmiths to melt down our heavy Silver.

CAUSES

OF THE

WRETCHED CONDITION

OF

IRELAND

Psalm CXLIV. Part of the 13th and 14th Ver.

That there be no Complaining in our Streets. Happy is the People that is in such a Case.

It is a very melancholy Reflection,[1] that such a Country as ours, which is capable of producing all Things necessary, and most Things convenient for Life, sufficient for the Support of four Times the Number of its Inhabitants, should yet lye under the heaviest Load of Misery and Want, our Streets crouded with Beggars, so many of our lower Sort of Tradesmen, Labourers and Artificers, not able to find Cloaths and Food for their Families.

I THINK it may therefore be of some Use, to lay before you the chief Causes of this wretched Condition we are in, and then it will be easier to assign what Remedies are in our Power towards removing, at least, some Part of these Evils.

FOR it is ever to be lamented, that we lie under many Disadvantages, not by our own Faults, which are peculiar to ourselves, and which no other Nation under Heaven hath any Reason to complain of.

I SHALL, therefore first mention some Causes of our Miseries, which I doubt are not to be remedied, until God shall put it in the Hearts of those who are the stronger, to allow us the common Rights and Privileges of Brethren, Fellow-Subjects, and even of Mankind.

THE first Cause of our Misery is the intolerable Hardships we lie under in every Branch of our Trade, by which we are become as *Hewers of Wood, and Drawers of Water,*[2] to our rigorous Neighbours.

THE second Cause of our miserable State is the Folly, the Vanity, and Ingratitude of those vast Numbers, who think themselves too good to live in the Country which gave them Birth, and still gives them Bread; and rather chuse to pass their Days, and consume their Wealth, and draw out the very Vitals[3] of their Mother Kingdom, among those who heartily despise them.

THESE I have but lightly touched on, because I fear they are not to be redressed, and, besides, I am very sensible how ready some People are to take Offence at the honest Truth; and, for that Reason, I shall omit several other Grievances, under which we are long likely to groan.

I SHALL therefore go on to relate some other Causes of this Nation's Poverty, by which, if they continue much longer, it must infallibly sink to utter Ruin.

THE first is, that monstrous Pride and Vanity in both Sexes, especially the weaker Sex, who, in the Midst of Poverty, are suffered to run into all Kind of Expence and Extravagance in Dress, and particularly priding themselves to wear nothing but what cometh from Abroad, disdaining the Growth or Manufacture of their own Country, in those Articles where they can be better served at Home with half the Expence; and this is grown to such a Height, that they will carry the whole yearly Rent of a good Estate at once on their Body. And, as there is in that Sex a Spirit of Envy, by which they cannot endure to see others in a better Habit than themselves; so those, whose Fortunes can hardly support their Families in the Necessaries of Life, will needs vye with the Richest and Greatest amongst us, to the Ruin of themselves and their Posterity.

NEITHER are the Men less guilty of this pernicious Folly, who, in Imitation of a Gaudiness and Foppery of Dress, introduced of late Years into our neighbouring Kingdom, (as Fools are apt to imitate only the Defects of their Betters) cannot find Materials in their own Country worthy to adorn their Bodies of Clay, while their Minds are naked of every valuable Quality.

THUS our Tradesmen and Shopkeepers, who deal in Home-Goods, are left in a starving Condition, and only those encouraged who ruin the Kingdom by importing among us foreign Vanities.

ANOTHER Cause of our low Condition is our great Luxury, the chief Support of which is the Materials of it brought to the Nation in Exchange for the few valuable Things left us, whereby so many thousand Families want the very Necessaries of Life.

THIRDLY, in most Parts of this Kingdom the Natives are from their Infancy so given up to Idleness and Sloth, that they often chuse to beg or steal, rather than support themselves with their own Labour; they marry without the least View or Thought of being able to make any Provision for their Families; and whereas, in all industrious Nations, Children are looked on as a Help to their Parents, with us, for want of being early trained to work, they are an intolerable Burthen at Home, and a grievous Charge upon the Public, as appeareth from the vast Number of ragged and naked Children in Town and Country, led about by stroling Women, trained up in Ignorance and all Manner of Vice.

LASTLY, A great Cause of this Nation's Misery, is that *Ægyptian* Bondage of cruel, oppressing, covetous Landlords, expecting that all who live under them should *make Bricks without Straw*,[4] who grieve and envy when they see a Tenant of their own in a whole Coat, or able to afford one comfortable Meal in a Month, by which the Spirits of the People are broken, and made for Slavery; the Farmers and Cottagers, almost through the whole Kingdom, being to all Intents and Purposes as real Beggars, as any of those to whom we give our Charity in the Streets. And these cruel Landlords are every Day unpeopling their Kingdom, by forbidding their miserable Tenants to till the Earth, against common Reason and Justice, and contrary to the Practice and Prudence of all other Nations, by which numberless Families have been forced either to leave the Kingdom, or stroll about, and increase the Number of our Thieves and Beggars.

SUCH, and much worse, is our Condition at present, if I had Leisure or Liberty to lay it before you; and, therefore, the next Thing which might be considered is, whether there may be any probable Remedy found, at the least against some Part of these Evils; for most of them are wholely desperate.

BUT this being too large a Subject to be now handled, and the Intent of my Discourse confining me to give some Directions concerning the Poor of this City, I shall keep myself within those Limits. It is indeed in the Power of the Lawgivers to found a School in every Parish of the Kingdom, for teaching the meaner and poorer Sort of Children to speak and read the English Tongue, and to provide a reasonable Maintenance for the Teachers. This would, in Time, abolish that Part of Barbarity and Ignorance, for which our Natives are so despised by all Foreigners; this would bring them to think and act according to the Rules of Reason, by which a Spirit of Industry, and Thrift, and Honesty, would be introduced among them. And, indeed, considering how small a Tax would suffice for such a Work, it is a publick Scandal that such a Thing should never have been endeavoured, or, perhaps, so much as thought on.

TO supply the Want of such a Law, several pious Persons, in many Parts of this Kingdom, have been prevailed on, by the great Endeavours and good Example set them by the Clergy, to erect Charity-Schools in several Parishes, to which very often the richest Parishioners contribute the least. In these Schools, Children are, or ought to be, trained up to read and write, and cast Accompts; and these Children should, if possible, be of honest Parents, gone to Decay through Age, Sickness, or other unavoidable Calamity, by the Hand of God; not the Brood of wicked Strolers; for it is by no means reasonable, that the Charity of well-inclined People should be applied to encourage the Lewdness of those profligate, abandoned Women, who croud our Streets with their borrowed or spurious Issue.

IN those Hospitals which have good Foundations and Rents to support them, whereof, to the Scandal of Christianity, there are very few in this Kingdom; I say, in such Hospitals, the Children maintained, ought to be only of decayed Citizens, and Freemen, and be bred up to good Trades. But in these small Parish Charity Schools which have no Support, but the casual good Will of charitable People, I do altogether disapprove the Custom of putting the Children 'Prentice, except to the very meanest Trades; otherwise the poor honest Citizen who is just able to bring up his Child, and pay a small Sum of Money with him to a good Master, is wholly defeated, and the Bastard Issue, perhaps, of some Beggar, preferred before him. And hence we come to be so over-stocked with 'Prentices and Journeymen, more than our discouraged Country can employ; and, I fear, the greatest Part of our Thieves, Pickpockets, and other Vagabonds are of this Number.

THEREFORE, in order to make these Parish Charity Schools of great and universal Use, I agree with the Opinion of many wise Persons, that a new Turn should be given to this whole Matter.

I THINK there is no Complaint more just than what we find in almost every Family, of the Folly and Ignorance, the Fraud and Knavery, the Idleness and Viciousness, the wasteful squandering Temper of Servants, who are, indeed, become one of the many publick Grievances of the Kingdom; whereof, I believe, there are few Masters that now hear me, who are not convinced by their own Experience. And I am very confident, that more Families, of all Degrees, have been ruined by the Corruptions of Servants, than by all other Causes put together. Neither is this to be wondered at, when we consider from what Nurseries so many of them are received into our Houses. The first is the Tribe of wicked Boys, wherewith most Corners of this Town are pestered, who haunt publick Doors. These, having been born of Beggars, and bred to pilfer as soon as they can go or speak, as Years come on, are employed in the lowest Offices to get themselves Bread, are practised in all Manner of Villainy, and when they are grown up, if they are not entertained in a Gang of Thieves, are forced to seek for a Service. The other Nursery is the barbarous and desert Part of the

Country, from whence such Lads come up hither to seek their Fortunes, who are bred up from the Dunghill in Idleness, Ignorance, Lying, and Thieving. From these two Nurseries, I say, a great Number of our Servants come to us, sufficient to corrupt all the rest. Thus, the whole Race of Servants in this Kingdom have gotten so ill a Reputation, that some Persons from *England,* come over hither into great Stations, are said to have absolutely refused admitting any Servant born among us into their Families. Neither can they be justly blamed; for, although it is not impossible to find an honest Native fit for a good Service, yet the Enquiry is too troublesome, and the Hazard too great for a Stranger to attempt.

IF we consider the many Misfortunes that befal private Families, it will be found that Servants are the Causes and Instruments of them all: Are our Goods embezzled, wasted, and destroyed? Is our House burnt down to the Ground? It is by the Sloth, the Drunkenness or the Villainy of Servants. Are we robbed and murdered in our Beds? It is by Confederacy with our Servants. Are we engaged in Quarrels and Misunderstandings with our Neighbours? These were all begun and inflamed by the false, malicious Tongues of our Servants. Are the Secrets of our Family betrayed, and evil Repute spread of us? Our Servants were the Authors. Do false Accusers rise up against us? (an Evil too frequent in this Country) they have been tampering with our Servants. Do our Children discover Folly, Malice, Pride, Cruelty, Revenge, Undutifulness in their Words and Actions? Are they seduced to Lewdness or scandalous Marriages? It is all by our Servants. Nay, the very Mistakes, Follies, Blunders, and Absurdities of those in our Service, are able to ruffle and discompose the mildest Nature, and are often of such Consequence, as to put whole Families into Confusion.

SINCE therefore not only our domestick Peace and Quiet, and the Welfare of our Children, but even the very Safety of our Lives, Reputations, and Fortunes have so great a Dependence upon the Choice of our Servants, I think it would well become the Wisdom of the Nation to make some Provision in so important an Affair: But, in the mean Time, and perhaps, to better Purpose, it were to be wished, that the Children of both Sexes, entertained in the Parish Charity-Schools, were bred up in such a Manner as would give them a teachable Disposition, and qualify them to learn whatever is required in any Sort of Service. For Instance, they should be taught to read and write, to know somewhat in casting Accompts, to understand the Principles of Religion, to practise Cleanliness, to get a Spirit of Honesty, Industry, and Thrift, and be severely punished for every Neglect in any of these Particulars. For, it is the Misfortune of Mankind, that if they are not used to be taught in their early Childhood, whereby to acquire what I call a teachable Disposition, they cannot, without great Difficulty, learn the easiest Thing in the Course of their Lives, but are always aukward and unhandy; their Minds, as well as Bodies, for want of early Practice, growing stiff and unmanageable, as we observe in the Sort of Gentlemen, who, kept from School by the Indulgence of their Parents but a few Years, are never able to recover the Time they have lost, and grow up in Ignorance and all Manner of Vice, whereof we have too many Examples all over the Nation. But to return to what I was saying: If these Charity-Children were trained up in the Manner I mentioned, and then bound Apprentices in the Families of Gentlemen and Citizens, (for which a late Law[5] giveth great Encouragement) being accustomed from their first Entrance to be always learning some useful Thing, they would learn in a Month more than another, without those Advantages can do in a Year; and, in the mean Time, be very useful in a Family, as far as their Age and Strength would allow. And when such Children come to Years of Discretion, they will probably be a useful Example to their Fellow Servants, at least they will prove a strong Check upon the rest; for, I suppose, every Body will allow, that one good, honest, diligent Servant in a House may prevent Abundance of Mischief in the Family.

THESE are the Reasons for which I urge this Matter so strongly, and I hope those who listen to me will consider them.

I SHALL now say something about that great Number of Poor, who, under the Name of common Beggars, infest our Streets, and fill our Ears with their continual Cries, and craving Importunity. This I shall venture to call an unnecessary Evil, brought upon us for the gross Neglect, and want of proper Management, in those whose Duty it is to prevent it: But, before I proceed farther, let me humbly presume to vindicate the Justice and Mercy of God and his Dealings with Mankind. Upon this Particular He hath not dealt so hardly with his Creatures as some would imagine, when they see so many miserable Objects ready to perish for Want: For it would infallibly be found, upon strict Enquiry, that there is hardly one in twenty of those miserable Objects who do not owe their present Poverty to their own Faults; to their present Sloth and Negligence; to their indiscreet Marriage without the least Prospect of supporting a Family, to their foolish Expensiveness, to their Drunkenness, and other Vices, by which they have squandered their Gettings, and contracted Diseases in their old Age. And, to speak freely, is it any Way reasonable or just, that those who have denied themselves many lawful Satisfactions and Conveniencies of Life, from a Principle of Conscience, as well as Prudence, that they might not be a Burthen to the Public, should be charged with supporting Others, who have brought themselves to less than a Morsel of Bread by their Idleness, Extravagance, and Vice? Yet such and no other, are for the greatest Number not only in those who beg in our Streets, but even of what we call poor decayed House-keepers, whom we are apt to pity as real Objects of Charity, and distinguish them from common Beggars, although, in Truth, they both owe their Undoing to the same Causes; only the former is either too nicely bred to endure walking half naked in the Streets, or too proud to own their Wants. For the Artificer or other Tradesman, who pleadeth he is grown too old to work or look after Business, and therefore expecteth Assistance as a decayed House-keeper; may we not ask him, why he did not take Care, in his Youth and Strength of Days, to make some Provision against old Age, when he saw so many Examples before him of People undone by their Idleness and vicious Extravagance? And to go a little higher; whence cometh it that so many Citizens and Shopkeepers, of the most creditable Trade, who once made a good Figure, go to Decay by their expensive Pride and Vanity, affecting to educate and dress their Children above their Abilities, or the State of Life they ought to expect?

HOWEVER, since the best of us have too many Infirmities to answer for, we ought not to be severe upon those of others; and, therefore, if our Brother, thro' Grief, or Sickness, or other Incapacity, is not in a Condition to preserve his Being, we ought to support him to the best of our Power, without reflecting over seriously on the Causes that brought him to his Misery. But in order to this, and to turn our Charity into its proper Channel, we ought to consider who and where those Objects are, whom it is chiefly incumbent upon us to support.

BY the antient Law of this Realm, still in Force, every Parish is obliged to maintain its own Poor, which although some may think to be not very equal, because many Parishes are very rich, and have few Poor among them, and others the contrary; yet, I think, maybe justly defended: For, as to remote Country Parishes in the desart Parts of the Kingdom, the Necessaries of Life are there so cheap, that the infirm Poor may be provided for with little Burden to the Inhabitants. But in what I am going to say, I shall confine myself only to this City, where we are over-run, not only with our own Poor, but with a far greater Number from every Part of the Nation. Now, I say, this Evil of being encumbered with so many foreign Beggars, who have not the least Title to our Charity, and whom it is impossible for us to support, may be easily remedied, if the Government of this City, in Conjunction with the Clergy and Parish Officers, would think it worth their Care; and I am sure few Things deserve it better. For, if every Parish would take a List of those begging Poor which properly belong to it, and compel each of them to wear a Badge,[6] marked and numbered, so as to be seen and known by all they meet, and confine them to beg within the Limits of their own Parish, severely punishing them when they offend, and driving out all Interlopers from other Parishes, we could then make a Computation of their Numbers; and the Strolers from the Country being driven away, the Remainder would not be too many for the Charity of those who pass by, to maintain; neither would any Beggar, although confined to his own Parish, be hindered from receiving the Charity of the whole Town; because in this Case, those well-disposed Persons who walk the Streets, will give their Charity to such whom they think proper Objects, where-ever they meet them, provided they are found in their own Parishes, and wearing their Badges of Distinction. And, as to those Parishes which border upon the Skirts and Suburbs of the Town, where Country Strolers are used to harbour themselves, they must be forced to go back to their Homes, when they find no Body to relieve them, because they want that Mark which only gives them Licence to beg. Upon this Point, it were to be wished, that inferior Parish Officers had better Encouragement given them, to perform their Duty in driving away all Beggars who do not belong to the Parish, instead of conniving at them, as it is said they do for some small Contribution; for the whole City would save much more by ridding themselves of many hundred Beggars, than they would lose by giving Parish Officers a reasonable Support.

It should seem a strange, unaccountable Thing, that those who have probably been reduced to Want by Riot, Lewdness, and Idleness, although they have Assurance enough to beg Alms publickly from all they meet, should yet be too proud to wear the Parish Badge, which would turn so much to their own Advantage, by ridding them of such great Numbers, who now intercept the greatest Part of what belongeth to them: Yet, it is certain, that there are very many who publickly declare they will never wear those Badges, and many others who either hide or throw them away: But the Remedy for this is very short, easy, and just, by tying them like Vagabonds and sturdy Beggars, and forcibly driving them out of the Town.

Therefore, as soon as this Expedient of wearing Badges shall be put in Practice, I do earnestly exhort all those who hear me, never to give their

Alms to any publick Beggar who doth not fully comply with this Order; by which our Number of Poor will be so reduced, that it will be much easier to provide for the rest. Our Shop-Doors will be no longer crouded with so many Thieves and Pick-pockets, in Beggars Habits, nor our Streets so dangerous to those who are forced to walk in the Night.

THUS I have, with great Freedom delivered my Thoughts upon this Subject, which so nearly concerneth us. It is certainly a bad Scheme, to any Christian Country which God hath blessed with Fruitfulness, and where the People enjoy the just Rights and Privileges of Mankind, that there should be any Beggars at all. But, alas! among us, where the whole Nation itself is almost reduced to Beggary by the Disadvantages we lye under, and the Hardships we are forced to bear; the Laziness, Ignorance, Thoughtlessness, squandering Temper, slavish Nature, and uncleanly Manner of Living in the poor Popish Natives, together with the cruel Oppressions of their Landlords, who delight to see their Vassals in the Dust; I say, that in such a Nation, how can we otherwise expect than to be overrun with Objects of Misery and Want? Therefore, there can be no other Method to free this City from so intolerable a Grievance, than by endeavouring, as far as in us lies, that the Burden may be more equally divided, by contributing to maintain our own Poor, and forcing the Strolers and Vagabonds to return to their several Homes in the Country, there to smite the Conscience of those Oppressors, who first stripped them of all their Substance.

I MIGHT here, if the Time would permit, offer many Arguments to persuade to Works of Charity; but you hear them so often from the Pulpit, that I am willing to hope you may not now want them. Besides, my present Design was only to shew where your Alms would be best bestowed, to the Honour of God, your own Ease and Advantage, the Service of your Country, and the Benefit of the Poor. I desire you will all weigh and consider what I have spoken, and, according to your several Stations and Abilities, endeavour to put it in Practice; and God give you good Success, to whom, with the Son and Holy Ghost, be all Honour, *&c.*

———

The Grace of God, &c.

FROM *THE DRAPIER'S LETTERS*

LETTER I

TO THE *TRADESMEN, SHOP-KEEPERS, FARMERS,* AND *COUNTRY-PEOPLE* IN GENERAL, OF THE KINGDOM OF IRELAND

Brethren, Friends, Countrymen, and *Fellow-Subjects.*

What I intend now to say to you, is, next to your Duty to God, and the Care of your Salvation, of the greatest Concern to your selves, and your Children; your *Bread* and *Cloathing,* and every common Necessary of Life entirely depend upon it. Therefore I do most earnestly exhort you as *Men,* as *Christians,* as *Parents,* and as *Lovers of your Country,* to read this Paper with the utmost Attention, or get it read to you by others; which that you may do at the less Expence, I have ordered the Printer to sell it at the lowest Rate.

IT is a great Fault among you, that when a Person writes with no other Intention than *to do you Good, you will not be at the Pains to read his Advices:* One Copy of this Paper may serve a Dozen of you, which will be less than a Farthing apiece. It is your Folly, that you have no common or general Interest in your View, not even the Wisest among you; neither do you know or enquire, or care who are your Friends, or who are your Enemies.

ABOUT four Years ago, a little Book was written to advise all People to wear the *Manufactures of this our own Dear Country:** It had no other Design, said nothing against the *King* or *Parliament,* or *any* Person whatsoever, yet the POOR PRINTER[1] was prosecuted two Years, with the utmost Violence; and even some WEAVERS themselves, for whose Sake it was written, being upon the JURY, FOUND HIM GUILTY. This would be enough to discourage any Man from endeavouring to do you Good, when you will either neglect him, or fly in his Face for his Pains; and when he must expect only *Danger to himself,* and to be fined and imprisoned, perhaps to his Ruin.

---

* Vide *one of the preceding Pamphlets, entitled,* A Proposal for the Use of Irish *Manufactures.*

HOWEVER, I cannot but warn you once more of the manifest Destruction before your Eyes, if you do not behave your selves as you ought.

I WILL therefore first tell you the *plain Story of the Fact;* and then I will lay before you, how you ought to act in common Prudence, and according to the *Laws of your Country.*

THE *Fact is thus;* It having been many Years since COPPER HALF-PENCE or FARTHINGS were last Coined in this *Kingdom,* they have been for some Time very scarce, and many *Counterfeits* passed about under the Name of RAPS: Several Applications were made to *England,* that we might have Liberty to *Coin New Ones,* as in former Times we did; but they did not succeed. At last one Mr. WOOD, *a mean ordinary Man, a Hard-Ware Dealer,* procured a *Patent* under His MAJESTY'S BROAD SEAL, to coin 108000 *l.* in *Copper* for this *Kingdom;* which Patent however did not oblige any one here to take them, unless they pleased. Now you must know, that the HALF-PENCE and FARTHINGS in *England* pass for very little more than they are worth: And if you should beat them to Pieces, and sell them to the *Brazier,* you would not lose much above a Penny in a Shilling. But Mr. WOOD made his HALF-PENCE of such *Base Metal,* and so much smaller than the *English* ones, that the *Brazier* would hardly give you above a *Penny* of good Money for a *Shilling* of his; so that this sum of 108000 *l.* in good Gold and Silver, must be given for TRASH that will not be worth above *Eight* or *Nine Thousand Pounds* real Value. But this is not the Worst; for Mr. WOOD, when he pleases, may by Stealth send over *another* 108000 *l.* and buy *all our Goods for Eleven Parts in Twelve,* under the Value. For Example, if a *Hatter* sells a Dozen of *Hats* for *Five Shillings* a-piece, which amounts to *Three Pounds,* and receives the Payment in Mr. WOOD's Coin, he really receives only the Value of *Five Shillings.*

PERHAPS you will wonder how such an *ordinary Fellow* as this Mr. WOOD could have so much Interest as to get His MAJESTY'S Broad Seal for so great a Sum of bad Money, to be sent to this poor Country; and that all the *Nobility* and *Gentry* here could not obtain the same Favour, and let us make our own HALF-PENCE, as we used to do. Now I will make that Matter very plain. We are at a great Distance from the *King's Court,* and have no body there to solicit for us, although a great Number of *Lords* and *Squires,* whose Estates are here, and are our Countrymen, spend all their *Lives* and *Fortunes* there. But this same Mr. WOOD was able to attend constantly for his own Interest; he is an ENGLISHMAN and had GREAT FRIENDS, and it seems knew very well *where to give Money,*[2] to those that would speak to OTHERS that could speak to the KING, and would tell a FAIR STORY. And HIS MAJESTY, and perhaps the great Lord or Lords who advised him, might think it was for our *Country's Good;* and so, as the Lawyers express it, the KING was deceived in his Grant; which often happens in *all Reigns.* And I am sure if HIS MAJESTY knew that such a Patent, if it should take Effect according to the Desire of Mr. WOOD, would utterly ruin this Kingdom, which hath given such great Proofs of its *Loyalty;* he would immediately recall it, and perhaps shew his Displeasure to SOME BODY OR OTHER: *But a Word to the Wise is enough.* Most of you must have heard with what Anger our *Honourable House of Commons* received an Account of this WOOD's PATENT. There were several *Fine Speeches* made upon it, and plain Proofs; that it was all a WICKED CHEAT from the *Bottom to the Top;* and several *smart Votes* were printed, which that same WOOD had the Assurance to answer likewise in *Print,* and in so confident a Way, as if he were *a better Man than our whole Parliament* put together.

THIS WOOD, as soon as his *Patent* was passed, or soon after, sends over a great many *Barrels of those* HALF-PENCE, to *Cork* and other *Sea-Port Towns,* and to get them off, offered an *Hundred Pounds* in his *Coin* for *Seventy* or *Eighty* in *Silver:* But the *Collectors* of the KING's Customs very honestly refused to take them, and so did almost every body else. And since the Parliament hath condemned them, and desired the KING that they might be stopped, all the *Kingdom* do abominate them.

BUT WOOD is still working *under hand* to force his HALF-PENCE upon us; and if he can by help of his *Friends* in *England* prevail so far as to get an Order that the *Commissioners* and *Collectors* of the *King*'s Money shall receive them, and that the *Army* is to be paid with them, then he thinks *his Work shall be done.* And this is the Difficulty you will be under in such a *Case:* For the common Soldier when he goes to the *Market* or *Ale-house,* will offer this Money, and if it be refused, perhaps he will *swagger* and *hector,* and *threaten* to *beat* the *Butcher* or *Ale-wife,* or take the Goods by Force, and throw them the bad HALF-PENCE. In this and the like Cases, the *Shop-keeper,* or *Victualler,* or *any other Tradesman* has no more to do, than to demand ten times the Price of his Goods, if it is to be paid in WOOD's Money; for Example, Twenty Pence of that Money for a *Quart of Ale,* and so in all things else, and not part with his Goods till he gets the *Money.*

FOR suppose you go to an *Ale-house* with that base Money, and the *Landlord* gives you a Quart for Four of these HALF-PENCE, what must the *Victualler* do? His *Brewer* will not be paid in that Coin, or if the *Brewer* should be such a Fool, the *Farmers* will not take it from them for their *Bere,** because they are bound by their Leases to pay their Rents in Good and Lawful Money of *England,* which this is not, nor of *Ireland* neither, and the *Squire their Landlord* will never be so bewitched to take such *Trash* for his Land; so that it must certainly stop somewhere or other, and wherever it stops it is the same Thing, and we are all undone.

THE common Weight of these HALF-PENCE[3] is between four and five to an *Ounce;* suppose five, then three Shillings and four Pence will weigh a Pound, and consequently *Twenty Shillings* will weigh *Six Pounds Butter Weight.* Now there are many hundred *Farmers* who pay Two hundred Pounds a Year Rent: Therefore when one of these *Farmers* comes with his Half-Year's Rent, which

---

* *A sort of Barley in* Ireland.

is One hundred Pound, it will be at least Six hundred Pound weight, which is Three Horses Load.

IF a *Squire* has a mind to come to Town to buy Cloaths and Wine and Spices for himself and Family, or perhaps to pass the Winter here; he must bring with him five or six Horses loaden with *Sacks* as the *Farmers* bring their Corn; and when his Lady comes in her Coach to our Shops, it must be followed by a Car loaded with Mr. WOOD's Money. And I hope we shall have the Grace to take it for no more than it is worth.

THEY say SQUIRE CONOLLY[4] has *Sixteen Thousand Pounds a Year;* now if he sends for his *Rent* to Town, *as it is likely he does,* he must have *Two Hundred and Fifty Horses* to bring up his *Half Year's Rent,* and two or three great *Cellars* in his House for Stowage. But what the Bankers will do I cannot tell. For I am assured, that some great Bankers keep by them *Forty Thousand Pounds* in ready Cash to answer all Payments, which Sum in Mr. WOOD's Money, would require Twelve Hundred Horses to carry it.

FOR my own Part, I am already resolved what to do; I have a pretty good Shop of *Irish Stuffs* and *Silks,* and instead of taking Mr. WOOD's bad Copper, I intend to Truck with my Neighbours the *Butchers,* and *Bakers,* and *Brewers,* and the rest, *Goods for Goods,* and the little *Gold* and *Silver* I have, I will keep by me like my *Heart's Blood* till better Times, or until I am just ready to starve, and then I will buy Mr. WOOD's Money, as my Father did the Brass Money in King *James's* Time;[5] who could buy *Ten Pound* of it with a *Guinea,* and I hope to get as much for a *Pistole,* and so purchase *Bread* from those who will be such Fools as to sell it me.

THESE *Half-pence,* if they once pass, will soon be *Counterfeit,* because it may be cheaply done, the *Stuff* is so *Base.* The *Dutch* likewise will probably do the same thing, and send them over to us to pay for our *Goods;* and Mr. WOOD will never be at rest, but coin on: So that in some Years we shall have at least five Times 108000 *l.* of this *Lumber.* Now the current Money of this Kingdom is not reckoned to be above Four Hundred Thousand Pounds in all; and while there is a *Silver* Six-Pence left, these *Blood-suckers* will never be quiet.

WHEN once the *Kingdom* is reduced to such a Condition, I will tell you what must be the End: The *Gentlemen of Estates* will all turn off their *Tenants* for want of Payment; because, as I told you before, the *Tenants* are obliged by their Leases to pay *Sterling,* which is Lawful Current Money of *England;* then they will turn their own *Farmers, as too many of them do already,* run *all* into *Sheep* where they can, keeping only such other *Cattle* as are necessary; then they will be their own *Merchants,* and send their *Wool,* and *Butter,* and *Hides,* and *Linnen* beyond Sea for ready *Money,* and *Wine,* and *Spices,* and *Silks.* They will keep only a few miserable *Cottagers.* The *Farmers* must *Rob* or *Beg,* or leave their *Country.* The *Shopkeepers* in this and every other Town, must *Break* and *Starve:* For it is the *Landed-man* that maintains the *Merchant,* and *Shop-keeper,* and *Handicrafts-Man.*

BUT when the *Squire* turns *Farmer* and *Merchant* himself, all the good Money he gets from abroad, he will hoard up to send for *England,* and keep some poor *Taylor* or *Weaver,* and the like, in his own House, who will be glad to get Bread at any Rate.

I SHOULD never have done, if I were to tell you all the Miseries that we shall undergo, if we be so *Foolish* and *Wicked* as to take this *Cursed Coin.* It would be very hard, if all *Ireland* should be put into *One Scale,* and *this sorry Fellow* WOOD *into the other:* That Mr. WOOD should weigh down *this whole Kingdom,* by which *England* gets above a Million of good Money every Year clear into their *Pockets:* And that is more than the *English* do by *all the World besides.*

BUT your *great Comfort is,* that, as his Majesty's *Patent* doth not oblige you to take this *Money,* so the *Laws* have not given the *Crown* a Power of forcing the *Subjects* to take what *Money* the *King* pleases: For then by the same Reason we might be bound to take *Pebble-stones,* or *Cockle-shells,* or *stamped Leather* for *Current Coin;* if ever we should happen to live under an ill *Prince;* who might likewise by the same Power make a *Guinea* pass for Ten Pounds, a *Shilling* for Twenty Shillings, and so on; by which he would in a short Time get all the *Silver* and *Gold* of the *Kingdom* into his own Hands, and leave us nothing but *Brass* or *Leather,* or what he pleased. Neither is any thing reckoned more *Cruel* or *Oppressive* in the *French Government,* than their common Practice of calling in all their Money after they have sunk it very low, and then coining it a-new at a much higher Value; which however is not the Thousandth Part so wicked as this *abominable Project* of Mr. *Wood.* For the *French* give their Subjects *Silver* for *Silver,* and *Gold* for *Gold;* but this *Fellow* will not so much as give us good *Brass* or *Copper* for our *Gold* and *Silver,* nor even a Twelfth Part of their Worth.

HAVING said this much, I will now go on to tell you the Judgments of some great *Lawyers* in this Matter; whom I fee'd on purpose for your Sakes, and got their *Opinions* under their *Hands,* that I might be sure I went upon good Grounds.

A Famous Law-Book *called the* Mirrour of Justice,[6] *discoursing of the Charters (or Laws) ordained by our* Ancient Kings, *declares the* Law *to be as follows: It was ordained that no* King *of this Realm should* Change, *or* Impair *the* Money, *or make any other* Money *than of* Gold *or* Silver *without the Assent of all the Counties, that is,* as my Lord *Coke* says,* *Without the Assent of* Parliament.

THIS Book is very Ancient, and of great Authority for the Time in which it was wrote, and with that Character is often quoted by that great Lawyer my Lord *Coke.*†[7] By the Laws of *England,* the several Metals are divided into *Lawful* or *true Metal* and *unlawful* or *false Metal;* the Former comprehends *Silver* or *Gold,* the Latter all *Baser Metals:* That the Former is only to pass in Payments, appears

* *2 Inst.* 576.
† *2 Inst.* 576. 7.

by an Act of *Parliament** made the Twentieth Year of *Edward* the *First,* called the *Statute concerning the passing of Pence;* which I give you here as I got it translated into *English;* For some of our *Laws* at that time were, as I am told, writ in *Latin: Whoever in Buying or Selling presumeth to refuse an Half-penny or Farthing of Lawful Money, bearing the Stamp which it ought to have, let him be seized on as a Contemner of the King's Majesty, and cast into Prison.*

BY this *Statute,* no Person is to be reckoned a *Contemner* of the *King's Majesty,* and for that Crime to be *committed to Prison;* but he who refuseth to accept the King's Coin made of *Lawful Metal:* by which as I observed before, *Silver* and *Gold* only are intended.

THAT this is the true *Construction* of the *Act,* appears not only from the plain Meaning of the Words, but from my Lord *Coke's* Observation† upon it. By this Act (says he) it appears, that no Subject can be forced to take in *Buying* or *Selling* or other *Payments,* any Money made but of lawful Metal; that is, of *Silver* or *Gold.*

THE Law of *England* gives the King all Mines of *Gold* and *Silver,* but not the Mines of other *Metals;* the Reason of which *Prerogative* or *Power,* as it is given by my Lord *Coke,‡* is because Money can be made of *Gold* and *Silver,* but not of other Metals.

PURSUANT to this Opinion, *Half-pence* and *Farthings* were anciently made of *Silver,* which is evident from the Act of *Parliament* of *Henry* the IVth. Chap. 4. whereby it is enacted as follows: *Item, for the great Scarcity that is at present within the Realm of England of Half-pence and Farthings of Silver; it is ordained and established, that the Third Part of all the Money of Silver Plate which shall be brought to the Bullion, shall be made in Half-pence and Farthings.* This shews that by the Words *Half-penny* and *Farthing* of Lawful Money in that Statute concerning the *passing of* Pence, is meant a small Coin in *Half-pence* and *Farthings* of *Silver.*

THIS is further manifest from the Statute of the Ninth Year of *Edward* the IIId. Chap. 3. which enacts, *That no sterling Half-penny or Farthing be Molten for to make Vessels, or any other thing by the Gold-smiths, nor others, upon Forfeiture of the Money somolten (or melted.)*

By another Act in this *King's* Reign, *Black Money* was not to be current in *England.* And by an Act made in the Eleventh Year of his Reign, Chap. 5. *Galley Half-pence* were not to pass: What kind of *Coin* these were I do not know; but I presume they were made of *Base Metal.* And these Acts were no New *Laws,* but further Declarations of the old *Laws* relating to the *Coin.*

THUS the *Law* stands in Relation to *Coin.* Nor is there any Example to the contrary, except one in *Davis's Reports;*[8] who tells us, that in the time of

* 2 *Inst.* 577.
† 2 *Inst.* 577.
‡ 2 *Inst.* 577.

Tyrone's Rebellion, *Queen Elizabeth* ordered *Money* of *mixt Metal* to be coined in the Tower of *London*, and sent over hither for Payment of the *Army*; Obliging all People to receive it; and Commanding, that all *Silver Money* should be taken only as *Bullion*, that is, for as much as it weighed. *Davis* tells us several Particulars in this Matter too long here to trouble you with, and that the *Privy Council* of this *Kingdom* obliged a *Merchant* in *England* to receive this *mixt Money* for Goods transmitted hither.

BUT this Proceeding is rejected by all the best Lawyers, as contrary to Law, the *Privy Council* here having no such legal Power. And besides it is to be considered, that the *Queen* was then under great Difficulties by a Rebellion in this *Kingdom* assisted from *Spain*. And, whatever is done in great Exigences and dangerous Times, should never be an Example to proceed by in Seasons of *Peace* and *Quietness*.

I WILL now, my dear Friends, to save you the Trouble, set before you in short, what the *Law* obliges you to do; and what it does not oblige you to.

FIRST, you are obliged to take all Money in Payments which is coined by the *King*, and is of the *English* Standard or Weight; provided it be of *Gold* or *Silver*.

SECONDLY, you are not obliged to take any Money which is not of *Gold* or *Silver*; not only the *Half-pence* or *Farthings* of *England*, but of any other Country. And it is meerly for Convenience, or Ease, that you are content to take them; because the custom of coining *Silver Half-pence* and *Farthings* hath long been left off; I suppose, on Account of their being subject to be lost.

THIRDLY, Much less are we obliged to take those *Vile Half-pence* of that same *Wood*, by which you must lose almost *Eleven*-Pence in every Shilling.

THEREFORE, my Friends, stand to it One and All: Refuse this *Filthy Trash*. It is no Treason to rebel against Mr. *Wood*. His *Majesty* in his Patent obliges no body to take these *Half-pence*: Our *Gracious Prince* hath no such ill Advisers about him; or if he had, yet you see the Laws have not left in the *King's* Power, to force us to take any Coin but what is Lawful, of right Standard, *Gold* and *Silver*. Therefore you have nothing to fear.

AND let me in the next Place apply my self particularly to you who are the poorer Sort of *Tradesmen*: Perhaps you may think you will not be so great Losers as the Rich, if these *Half-pence* should pass; because you seldom see any *Silver*, and your Customers come to your Shops or Stalls with nothing but *Brass*; which you likewise find hard to be got. But you may take my Word, whenever this Money gains Footing among you, you will be utterly undone. If you carry these *Half-pence* to a Shop for *Tobacco* or *Brandy*, or any other Thing you want; the Shop-keeper will advance his Goods accordingly, or else he must break and leave the *Key under the Door*. Do you think I will sell you a Yard of Ten-penny Stuff for Twenty of Mr. *Wood's Half-pence*? No, not under Two Hundred at least; neither will I be at the Trouble of counting, but weigh them in a Lump. I will tell you one Thing further; that if Mr. *Wood*'s Project should take, it will ruin even our Beggars: For when I give a Beggar a Half-penny, it will quench his Thirst, or go a good Way to fill his Belly; but the Twelfth Part of a Half-penny will do him no more Service than if I should give him three Pins out of my Sleeve.

IN short; these *Half-pence* are like the *accursed Thing*,[9] which, as the *Scripture* tells us, the *Children of Israel* were forbidden to touch. They will run about like the *Plague* and destroy every one who lays his Hands upon them. I have heard *Scholars* talk of a Man who told the King that he had invented a Way to torment People by putting them into a *Bull* of Brass with Fire under it: But the *Prince* put the *Projector* first into his own *Brazen Bull*[10] to make the Experiment. This very much resembles the Project of Mr. *Wood;* and the like of this may possibly be Mr. *Wood*'s Fate; that the *Brass* he contrived to torment this *Kingdom* with, may prove his own Torment, and his Destruction at last.

N. B. The Author of this Paper is informed by Persons who have made it their Business to be exact in their Observations on the true Value of these *Half-pence;* that any Person may expect to get a Quart of Two-penny Ale for Thirty Six of them.

I DESIRE that all Families may keep this Paper carefully by them to refresh their Memories whenever they shall have farther Notice of Mr. *Wood*'s Half-pence, or any other the like Imposture.

FROM *THE DRAPIER'S LETTERS*

LETTER IV
TO THE WHOLE PEOPLE OF IRELAND

N. B. *This was the Letter against which the Lord Lieutenant* (Carteret)[1] *and Council, issued a Proclamation, offering three Hundred Pounds to discover the Author; and for which,* Harding *the Printer was tried before one* Whitshed, *then Chief Justice: But the noble Jury would not find the Bill; nor would any Person discover the Author.*

MY DEAR COUNTRYMEN,

Having already written three *Letters,* upon so disagreeable a Subject as Mr. *Wood* and his *Half-pence;* I conceived my Task was at an End: But, I find that Cordials must be frequently applied to weak Constitutions, *Political* as well as *Natural.* A People long used to Hardships, lose by Degrees the very Notions of *Liberty;* they look upon themselves as Creatures at Mercy; and that all Impositions laid on them by a stronger Hand, are, in the Phrase of the *Report, legal* and *obligatory.* Hence proceed that *Poverty* and *Lowness of Spirit,* to which a *Kingdom* may be subject, as well as a *particular Person.* And when *Esau* came fainting from the Field, at the Point to die, it is no Wonder that he sold his *Birth-Right for a Mess of Pottage.*[2]

I THOUGHT I had sufficiently shewn to all who could want Instruction, by what Methods they might safely proceed, whenever this *Coin* should be offered to them: And, I believe, there hath not been, for many Ages, an Example of any Kingdom so firmly united in a Point of great Importance, as this of ours is at present, against that detestable Fraud. But, however, it so happens, that some weak People begin to be alarmed a-new, by Rumours industriously spread. *Wood* prescribes to the News-Mongers in *London,* what they are to write. In one of their Papers published here by some obscure Printer, (and certainly with a bad Design) we are told, that the *Papists in* Ireland *have entered into an Association against his Coin;* although it be notoriously known, that they never once offered to stir in the Matter: So that the two Houses of Parliament, the Privy-Council, the great Number of Corporations, the Lord-Mayor and Aldermen of *Dublin,* the Grand-Juries, and principal Gentlemen of several Counties, are stigmatized in a Lump, under the Name of *Papists.*

THIS Impostor and his Crew, do likewise give out, that, by refusing to receive his Dross for Sterling, we *dispute the King's Prerogative; are grown ripe for Rebellion, and ready to shake off the Dependency of* Ireland *upon the Crown of* England. To Countenance which Reports, he hath published a Paragraph in another News-Paper, to let us know, that *the Lord Lieutenant is ordered to come over immediately to settle his Half-pence.*

I INTREAT you, my dear Countrymen, not to be under the least Concern upon these and the like Rumours; which are no more than the last Howls of a Dog dissected alive, as I hope he hath sufficiently been. These Calumnies are the only Reserve that is left him. For surely, our continued and (almost) unexampled Loyalty, will never be called in Question, for not suffering our selves to be robbed of all that we have, by one obscure *Ironmonger.*

As to disputing the King's *Prerogative,* give me Leave to explain to those who are ignorant, what the Meaning of that Word *Prerogative* is.

THE Kings of these Realms enjoy several Powers, wherein the Laws have not interposed: So, they can make War and Peace without the Consent of Parliament; and this is a very great *Prerogative.* But if the Parliament doth not approve of the War, the King must bear the Charge of it out of his own Purse; and this is as great a Check on the Crown. So the King hath a *Prerogative* to coin Money, without Consent of Parliament: But he cannot compel the Subject to take that Money, except it be Sterling, Gold or Silver; because, herein he is limited by Law. Some Princes have, indeed, extended their *Prerogative* further than the Law allowed them: Wherein, however, the Lawyers of succeeding Ages, as fond as they are of *Precedents,* have never dared to justify them. But, to say the Truth, it is only of late Times that *Prerogative* hath been fixed and ascertained. For, whoever reads the Histories of *England,* will find that some former Kings, and those none of the worst, have, upon several Occasions, ventured to controul[3] the Laws, with very little Ceremony or Scruple, even later than the Days of Queen *Elizabeth.* In her Reign, that pernicious Counsel of sending *base Money* hither, very narrowly failed of losing the Kingdom; being complained of by the Lord Deputy, the Council, and the whole Body of the *English* here: So that soon after her Death, it was recalled by her Successor, and lawful Money paid in Exchange.

HAVING thus given you some Notion of what is meant by the King's *Prerogative,* as far as a *Tradesman* can be thought capable of explaining it, I will only add the Opinion of the great Lord *Bacon;*[4] that, *as God governs the World by the settled Laws of Nature, which he hath made, and never transcends those Laws, but upon high important Occasions: So, among earthly Princes, those are the Wisest and the Best, who govern by the known Laws of the Country, and seldomest make Use of their* Prerogative.

NOW, here you may see that the vile Accusation of *Wood* and his Accomplices, charging us with *disputing the King's Prerogative*, by refusing his Brass, can have no Place; because compelling the Subject to take any Coin, which is not Sterling, is no Part of the King's *Prerogative*; and I am very confident, if it were so, we should be the last of his People to dispute it; as well from that inviolable Loyalty we have always paid to his Majesty, as from the Treatment we might in such a Case justly expect from some, who seem to think, we have neither *common Sense*, nor *common Senses*. But, God be thanked, the best of them are only our *Fellow-Subjects*, and not our *Masters*. One great Merit I am sure we have, which those of *English* Birth can have no Pretence to; that our Ancestors[5] reduced this Kingdom to the Obedience of ENGLAND; for which we have been rewarded with a worse Climate, the Privilege of being governed by Laws to which we do not consent; a ruined Trade, a House of *Peers* without *Jurisdiction*; almost an Incapacity for all Employments, and the Dread of *Wood's* Half-pence.

BUT we are so far from disputing the King's *Prerogative* in coining, that we own he hath Power to give a Patent to any Man, for setting his Royal Image and Superscription upon whatever Materials he pleases; and Liberty to the Patentee to offer them in any Country from *England* to *Japan*; only attended with one small Limitation, that *no body alive is obliged to take them*.

UPON these Considerations, I was ever against all Recourse to *England* for a Remedy against the present impending Evil; especially, when I observed, that the Addresses of both Houses, after long Expectance, produced nothing but a REPORT altogether in Favour of *Wood*; upon which, I made some Observations in a former Letter; and might at least have made as many more: For, it is a Paper of as singular a Nature as I ever beheld.

BUT I mistake; for before this *Report* was made, his Majesty's *most gracious Answer* to the House of Lords was sent over, and printed; wherein there are these Words, *granting the Patent for coining Half-pence and Farthings*, AGREEABLE TO THE PRACTICE OF HIS ROYAL PREDECESSORS, *&c.* That King *Charles* II, and King *James* II, (AND THEY ONLY) did grant Patents for this Purpose, is indisputable, and I have shewn it at large. Their Patents were passed under the great Seal of *Ireland*, by References to *Ireland*; the Copper to be coined in *Ireland*, the Patentee was bound, on Demand, to receive his Coin back in *Ireland*, and pay Silver and Gold in Return. *Wood's* Patent was made under the great Seal of *England*, the Brass coined in *England*, not the least Reference made to *Ireland*; the Sum immense, and the Patentee under no Obligation to receive it again, and give good Money for it: This I only mention, because, in my private Thoughts, I have sometimes made a Query, whether the *Penner* of those Words in his Majesty's *most gracious Answer*, AGREEABLE TO THE PRACTICE OF HIS ROYAL PREDECESSORS, had maturely considered the several Circumstances; which, in my poor Opinion, seem to make a Difference.

LET me now say something concerning the other great Cause of some People's Fear; as *Wood* has taught the *London* News-Writer to express it: That *his Excellency the Lord Lieutenant is coming over to settle Wood's Half-pence.*

WE know very well, that the Lords Lieutenants, for several Years past, have not thought this Kingdom *worthy the Honour of their Residence,* longer than was absolutely necessary for the King's Business; which consequently *wanted no Speed in the Dispatch.* And therefore, it naturally fell into most Mens Thoughts, that a new Governor coming at an *unusual* Time, must portend some *unusual* Business to be done; especially, if the common Report be true; that the Parliament prorogued to I know not when, is, by a new Summons (revoking that Prorogation) to assemble soon after his Arrival: For which extraordinary Proceeding, the Lawyers on t'other Side the Water, have, by great good Fortune, found two *Precedents.*

ALL this being granted, it can never enter into my Head, that so *little a Creature as Wood* could find Credit enough with the King and his Ministers, to have the Lord Lieutenant of *Ireland* sent hither in a Hurry, upon his Errand.

FOR, let us take the whole Matter nakedly, as it lies before us, without the Refinements of some People, with which we have nothing to do. Here is a Patent granted under the great Seal of *England,* upon false Suggestions, to one *William Wood,* for coining Copper Half-pence for *Ireland:* The Parliament here, upon Apprehensions of the worst Consequences from the said Patent, address the King to have it recalled: This is refused, and a Committee of the Privy-Council *report* to his Majesty, that *Wood* has performed the Conditions of his Patent. He then is left to do the best he can with his Half-pence; no Man being obliged to receive them; the People here, being likewise left to themselves, unite as one Man; resolving they will have nothing to do with his Ware. By this plain Account of the Fact, it is manifest, that the King and his Ministry are wholly out of the Case; and the Matter is left to be disputed between him and us. Will any Man therefore attempt to persuade me, that a Lord Lieutenant is to be dispatched over in great Haste, before the ordinary Time, and a Parliament summoned, by anticipating a Prorogation; merely to put an Hundred Thousand Pounds into the Pocket of a *Sharper,* by the Ruin of a most loyal Kingdom?

BUT supposing all this to be true. By what Arguments could a Lord Lieutenant prevail on the same Parliament, which addressed with so much Zeal and Earnestness against this Evil; to pass it into a Law? I am sure their Opinion of *Wood* and his Project is not mended since their last Prorogation: And supposing those *Methods* should be used, which, *Detractors* tell us, have been sometimes put in Practice for *gaining Votes;* it is well known, that in this Kingdom there are few Employments to be given; and if there were more; it is *as well known* to whose Share they must fall.

BUT, because great Numbers of you are altogether ignorant in the Affairs of your Country, I will tell you some Reasons, why there are so few Employments to be disposed of in this Kingdom. All considerable Offices for Life here, are possessed by those, to whom the Reversions were granted; and these have been generally Followers of the Chief Governors, or Persons who had Interest in the Court of *England*. So the Lord *Berkely* of *Stratton*, holds that great Office of *Master of the Rolls*; the Lord *Palmerstown* is *First Remembrancer*, worth near 2000 *l. per Ann*. One *Dodington*, Secretary to the Earl of *Pembroke*, begged the Reversion of *Clerk of the Pells*, worth 2500 *l.* a Year, which he now enjoys by the Death of the Lord *Newtown*. Mr. *Southwell* is Secretary of State, and the Earl of *Burlington* Lord High Treasurer of *Ireland* by Inheritance. These are only a few among many others, which I have been told of, but cannot remember. Nay the Reversion of several Employments during Pleasure are granted the same Way. This among many others, is a Circumstance whereby the Kingdom of *Ireland* is distinguished from all other Nations upon Earth; and makes it so difficult an Affair to get into a Civil Employ, that Mr. *Addison* was forced to purchase an old obscure Place, called *Keeper of the Records in* Bermingham's *Tower*, of Ten Pounds a Year, and to get a Salary of 400 *l.* annexed to it, though all the Records there are not worth Half a Crown, either for Curiosity or Use. And we lately saw a *Favourite Secretary*,* descend to be *Master of the Revels*, which by his *Credit and Extortion* he hath made *Pretty Considerable*. I say nothing of the Under-Treasurership worth about 9000 *l.* a Year; nor the Commissioners of the Revenue, Four of whom generally live in *England*: For I think none of these are granted in Reversion. But the Jest is, that I have known upon Occasion, some of these absent Officers as *Keen* against the Interest of *Ireland*, as if they had never been indebted to Her for a *Single Groat*.

I CONFESS, I have been sometimes tempted to wish that this Project of *Wood* might succeed; because I reflected with some Pleasure what a *Jolly Crew* it would bring over among us of *Lords* and *Squires*, and *Pensioners* of *Both Sexes*, and Officers *Civil* and *Miliary*; where we should live together as merry and sociable as Beggars; only with this one Abatement, that we should neither have *Meat* to feed, nor *Manufactures* to Cloath us; unless we could be content to *Prance* about in *Coats of Mail*; or eat Brass as Ostritches do Iron.

I RETURN from this Digression, to that which gave me the Occasion of making it: And I believe you are now convinced, that if the Parliament of *Ireland* were as *Temptable* as any *other* Assembly, *within a Mile of* Christendom (which God forbid) yet the *Managers* must of Necessity fail for want of *Tools* to work with. But I will yet go one Step further, by Supposing that a Hundred new Employments were erected on Purpose to gratify *Compliers*: Yet still an insuperable Difficulty would remain. For it happens, I know not how, that *Money* is neither *Whig* nor *Tory*, neither of *Town* nor *Country Party*; and it is not improbable, that a Gentleman would rather chuse to live upon his *own Estate*, which brings him

---

* *Mr.* Hopkins, *Secretary to the Duke of* Grafton.

Gold and *Silver,* than with the Addition of an *Employment;* when his *Rents* and *Sallary* must both be paid in *Wood's* Brass, at above Eighty *per Cent.* Discount.

FOR these, and many other Reasons, I am confident you need not be under the least Apprehensions, from the sudden Expectation of the *Lord Lieutenant,* while we continue in our present hearty Disposition; to alter which, there is no suitable Temptation can possibly be offered: And if, as I have often asserted from the best Authority, the *Law* hath not left a *Power* in the *Crown* to force any Money, except Sterling, upon the Subject; much less can the Crown *devolve* such a *Power* upon *another.*

THIS I speak with the utmost Respect to the *Person* and *Dignity* of his Excellency the Lord *Carteret;* whose Character was lately given me, by a Gentleman that hath known him from his first Appearance in the World: That Gentleman describes him as a young Man of great Accomplishments, excellent Learning, Regular in his Life, and of much Spirit and Vivacity. He hath since, as I have heard, been employed abroad; was principal Secretary of State; and is now about the 37th Year of his Age appointed Lord Lieutenant of *Ireland.* From such a Governour this Kingdom may reasonably hope for as much Prosperity, as *under so many Discouragements* it can be capable of receiving.

IT is true indeed, that within the Memory of Man, there have been Governors of so much Dexterity, as to carry Points of terrible Consequence to this Kingdom, by their Power with *those who were in Office;* and by their Arts in managing or deluding others with *Oaths, Affability,* and even with *Dinners.* If *Wood's* Brass had, in those Times, been upon the *Anvil,* it is obvious enough to conceive what Methods would have been taken. *Depending* Persons would have been told in plain Terms, that it was a *Service expected from them, under Pain of the publick Business being put into more complying Hands.* Others would be allured by *Promises.* To the *Country Gentlemen,* besides *good Words, Burgundy* and *Closeting;* it might, perhaps, have been hinted, how *kindly it would be taken to comply with a Royal Patent, although it were not compulsory.* That if any Inconveniences ensued, it might be made up with other *Graces or Favours hereafter.* That *Gentlemen ought to consider, whether it were prudent or safe to disgust* England: They would be desired to *think of some good Bills for encouraging of Trade, and setting the Poor to work: Some further Acts against Popery, and for uniting Protestants.* There would be solemn Engagements, that we should *never be troubled with above Forty Thousand Pounds in his Coin, and all of the best and weightiest Sort; for which we should only give our Manufactures in Exchange, and keep our Gold and Silver at home.* Perhaps, *a seasonable Report of some Invasion would have been spread in the most proper Juncture;* which is a great Smoother of Rubs in publick Proceedings: And we should have been told, that *this was no Time to create Differences, when the Kingdom was in Danger.*

THESE, I say, and the like Methods, would, in corrupt Times, have been taken to let in this Deluge of Brass among us; and, I am confident, would even then have not succeeded; much less under the Administration of so excellent a

Person as the Lord *Carteret;* and in a Country, where the People of all Ranks, Parties, and Denominations, are convinced to a Man, that the utter undoing of themselves and their Posterity for ever, will be dated from the Admission of that execrable Coin: That if it once enters, it can be no more confined to a small or moderate Quantity, than the *Plague* can be confined to a few Families; and that no *Equivalent* can be given by any earthly Power, any more than a dead Carcass can be recovered to Life by a Cordial.

THERE is one comfortable Circumstance in this universal Opposition to Mr. *Wood,* that the People sent over hither from *England,* to *fill up our Vacancies, Ecclesiastical, Civil and Military,* are all on our Side: *Money,* the great *Divider* of the World, hath, by a strange Revolution, been the great *Uniter* of a most *divided* People. Who would leave a Hundred Pounds a Year in *England,* (*a Country of Freedom*) to be paid a Thousand in *Ireland* out of *Wood's* Exchequer? The *Gentleman They* have lately made *Primate,*[6] would never quit his Seat in an *English* House of Lords, and his Preferments at *Oxford* and *Bristol,* worth Twelve Hundred Pounds a Year, for four Times the Denomination here, but not half the Value: Therefore, I expect to hear he will be as good an *Irishman,* at least, upon *this one Article,* as any of his Brethren; or even of *Us,* who have had the *Misfortune* to be born in this Island. For those who, in the common Phrase, do not *come hither to learn the Language,* would never change a better Country for a worse, to receive *Brass* instead of *Gold.*

ANOTHER Slander spread by *Wood* and his Emissaries is, that, by opposing him, we discover an Inclination to *shake off our Dependance upon the Crown of* England. Pray observe, how important a Person is this same *William Wood;* and how the publick Weal of two Kingdoms, is involved in his private Interest. First, all those who refuse to take his Coin *are Papists;* for he tells us, that *none but Papists are associated against him.* Secondly, they *dispute the King's Prerogative.* Thirdly, they *are ripe for Rebellion.* And Fourthly, they are going to *shake off their Dependance upon the Crown of* England; that is to say, *they are going to chuse another King.* For there can be no other Meaning in this Expression, however some may pretend to strain it.

AND this gives me an Opportunity of explaining, to those who are ignorant, another Point, which hath often *swelled in my Breast.* Those who come over hither to us from *England,* and some *weak* People among ourselves, whenever, in Discourse, we make mention of *Liberty* and *Property,* shake their Heads, and tell us, that *Ireland* is a *depending Kingdom;* as if they would seem, by this Phrase, to intend, that the People of *Ireland* is in some State of Slavery or Dependance, different from those of *England:* Whereas, a *depending Kingdom* is a *modern Term of Art;* unknown, as I have heard, to all antient *Civilians,* and *Writers upon Government;* and *Ireland* is, on the contrary, called in some Statutes an *Imperial Crown,* as held only from God; which is as high a Style, as any Kingdom is capable of receiving. Therefore by this Expression, a *depending Kingdom,* there is no more understood, than that by a Statute made here, in the 33d Year of

Henry VIII, *The King and his Successors, are to be Kings Imperial of this Realm, as united and knit to the Imperial Crown of* England. I have looked over all the *English* and *Irish* Statutes, without finding any Law[7] that makes *Ireland depend* upon *England;* any more than *England* doth upon *Ireland.* We have, indeed, obliged ourselves to have *the same King with them;* and consequently they are obliged to have the *same King with us.* For the Law was made by *our own Parliament;* and our Ancestors then were not such *Fools (whatever they were in the preceding Reign)* to bring themselves under I know not what *Dependance,* which is now talked of, without any Ground of *Law, Reason,* or *common Sense.*

Let whoever think otherwise, I *M. B. Drapier,* desire to be excepted. For I declare, next under God, I *depend* only on the King my Sovereign, and on the Laws of my own Country, And I am so far from *depending* upon the People of *England,* that, if they should ever *rebel* against my Sovereign, (which God forbid) I would be ready at the first Command from his Majesty to take Arms against them; as some of *my* Countrymen did against *theirs* at *Preston.*[8] And, if such a Rebellion should prove so successful as to fix the *Pretender* on the Throne of *England;* I would venture to transgress that *Statute* so far, as to lose every Drop of my Blood, to hinder him from being *King* of *Ireland.*

It is true, indeed, that within the Memory of Man, the Parliaments of *England* have *sometimes* assumed the Power[9] of binding this Kingdom, by Laws enacted there; wherein they were, at first, openly opposed (as far as *Truth, Reason,* and *Justice* are capable of *opposing*) by the famous Mr. *Molineaux,*[10] an *English* Gentleman born here; as well as by several of the greatest Patriots, and *best Whigs* in *England;* but the *Love and Torrent* of Power prevailed. Indeed, the Arguments on both Sides were invincible. For in *Reason,* all *Government* without the Consent of the *Governed,* is the *very Definition of Slavery:* But in *Fact, Eleven Men well armed, will certainly subdue one single Man in his Shirt.* But I have done. For those who have used *Power* to cramp *Liberty,* have gone so far as to resent even the *Liberty* of *Complaining;* although a Man upon the Rack, was never known to be refused the Liberty of *roaring* as loud as he thought fit.

And, as we are apt to *sink* too *much* under *unreasonable* Fears, so we are too soon inclined to be *raised* by groundless Hopes, (according to the Nature of all *consumptive* Bodies like ours.) Thus, it hath been given about for several Days past, that *Somebody in England,* empowered a second *Somebody* to write to a third *Somebody* here, to assure us, that we *should no more be troubled with those Half-pence.* And this is reported to have been done by the *same Person,*[*] who was said to have sworn some Months ago, that he would *ram them down our Throats,* (though I doubt they would *stick in our Stomachs*). But which ever of these Reports is true or false, it is no Concern of ours. For, *in this Point,* we have nothing to do with *English Ministers:* And I should be sorry to leave it in their Power to *redress* this Grievance, or to *enforce* it: For the *Report of the Committee* hath given me a *Surfeit.*

[*] *Mr.* Walpole, *now Sir* Robert.

The Remedy is wholly in your own Hands; and therefore I have digressed a little, in order to refresh and continue that *Spirit* so seasonably raised amongst you; and to let you see, that by the Laws of GOD, of NATURE, of NATIONS, and of your own Country, you ARE and OUGHT to be as FREE a People as your Brethren in *England.*

IF the Pamphlets published at *London* by *Wood* and his *Journeymen,* in Defence of his Cause, were Re-printed here, and that our Countrymen could be persuaded to read them, they would convince you of his wicked Design, more than all I shall ever be able to say. In short, I make him a perfect *Saint,* in Comparison of what he appears to be, from the Writings of those whom he *Hires* to justify his *Project.* But he is so far *Master of the Field (let others guess the Reason)* that no *London* Printer dare publish any Paper written in Favour of *Ireland:* And here no Body hath yet been so *bold,* as to publish any Thing in *Favour* of *him.*

THERE was a few Days ago a Pamphlet sent me of near 50 Pages, written in Favour of Mr. *Wood* and his Coinage; printed in *London:* It is not worth answering, because probably it will never be published here: But it gave me an Occasion, to reflect upon an Unhappiness we lie under, that the People of *England* are utterly ignorant of our Case; Which, however, is no Wonder; since it is a Point they do not in the least concern themselves about; farther than, perhaps, as a Subject of Discourse in a Coffee-House, when they have nothing else to talk of. For I have Reason to believe, that no Minister ever gave himself the Trouble of reading any Papers written in our Defence; because I suppose *their Opinions are already determined,* and are formed wholly upon the Reports of *Wood* and his Accomplices; else it would be impossible, that any Man could have the Impudence, to write such a Pamphlet, as I have mentioned.

OUR *Neighbours, whose Understandings are just upon a Level with Ours* (which perhaps are none of the *Brightest*) have a strong Contempt for most Nations, but especially for *Ireland:* They look upon us as a Sort of *Savage Irish,* whom our Ancestors conquered several Hundred Years ago: And if I should describe the *Britons* to you, as they were in *Cæsar*'s Time, when they *painted their Bodies, or cloathed themselves with the Skins of Beasts,* I should act full as reasonably as they do. However, they are so far to be excused, in relation to the present Subject, that, hearing only *one Side of the Cause,* and having neither Opportunity nor Curiosity to examine the *other,* they *believe a Lye,* merely for their Ease; and conclude, because Mr. *Wood* pretends to have *Power,* he hath also *Reason* on his Side.

THEREFORE, to let you see how this Case is represented in *England* by *Wood* and his Adherents, I have thought it proper to extract out of that Pamphlet, a few of those notorious Falshoods, in Point of *Fact* and *Reasoning,* contained therein; the Knowledge whereof, will confirm my Countrymen in their *Own* Right Sentiments, when they will see by comparing both, how much their *Enemies are in the Wrong.*

FIRST, The Writer positively asserts, *That* Wood'*s Half-pence were current* among us for several Months, with the universal Approbation of all People, without one single Gain-sayer; and we all to a Man thought our selves Happy in having them.

SECONDLY, He affirms, *That we were drawn into a Dislike of them, only by some Cunning Evil-designing Men among us, who opposed this Patent of* Wood, *to get another for themselves.*

THIRDLY, That *those who most declared at first against* WOOD's *Patent, were the very Men who intended to get another for their own Advantage.*

FOURTHLY, That *our Parliament and Privy-Council, the Lord Mayor and Alder-men of* Dublin, *the Grand-Juries and Merchants, and in short the whole Kingdom; nay, the very Dogs* (as he expresseth it) *were fond of those Half-pence, till they were inflamed by those few designing Persons aforesaid.*

FIFTHLY, He says directly, *That all those who oppose the Half-pence, were Papists, and Enemies to King* George.

THUS far I am confident the most ignorant among you can safely swear from your own Knowledge, that the Author is a most notorious Lyar in every Article; the direct contrary being so manifest to the whole Kingdom, that if Occasion required, we might get it confirmed *under Five hundred thousand Hands.*

SIXTHLY, He would persuade us, That *if we sell Five Shillings worth of our Goods or Manufactures for Two Shillings and Four-pence worth of Copper, although the Copper were melted down, and that we could get Five Shillings in Gold or Silver for the said Goods; yet to take the said Two Shillings and Four-pence in Copper, would be greatly for our Advantage.*

AND Lastly, He makes us a very fair Offer, as empowered by *Wood,* That *if we will take off Two hundred thousand Pounds in his Half-pence for our Goods, and like-wise pay him Three* per Cent. *Interest for Thirty Years, for an hundred and Twenty thousand Pounds* (at which he computes the Coinage above the intrinsick Value of the Cop-per) *for the Loan of his Coin, he will after that Time give us good Money for what Half-pence will be then left.*

LET me place this Offer in as clear a Light as I can, to shew the unsupport-able Villainy and Impudence of that incorrigible Wretch. First (says he) *I will send Two hundred thousand Pounds of my Coin into your Country: The Copper I compute to be in real Value Eighty thousand Pounds, and I charge you with an hundred and twenty thousand Pounds for the Coinage; so that you see, I lend you an Hundred and twenty thou-sand Pounds for Thirty Years; for which you shall pay me Three* per Cent. *That is to say, Three thousand Six hundred Pounds,* per Ann. *which in Thirty Years will amount to an Hundred and eight thousand Pounds. And when these Thirty Years are expired, return me my Copper, and I will give you Good Money for it.*

THIS is the Proposal made to us by *Wood* in that Pamphlet, written by one of his *Commissioners:* And the Author is supposed to be the same Infamous *Coleby* one of his *Under-Swearers* at the *Committee of Council,* who was tryed for *Robbing the Treasury here,* where he was an Under-Clerk.

BY this Proposal he will first receive Two hundred thousand Pounds, in

Goods or Sterling, for as much Copper as he values at Eighty thousand Pounds; but in Reality not worth Thirty thousand Pounds. Secondly, He will receive for Interest an Hundred and Eight thousand Pounds: And when our Children come Thirty Years hence, to return his Half-pence upon his Executors (for before that Time he will be probably gone *to his own Place*) those Executors will very reasonably reject them as Raps and Counterfeits; which they will be, and Millions of them of his own Coinage.

METHINKS, I am fond of such a *Dealer* as this, who mends every Day upon our Hands, like a *Dutch* Reckoning;[11] where, if you dispute the Unreasonableness and Exorbitance of the Bill, the Landlord shall bring it up every Time with new Additions.

ALTHOUGH these and the like Pamphlets, published by *Wood* in *London,* be altogether unknown here, where no body could read them, without as much *Indignation* as *Contempt* would allow; yet I thought it proper to give you a Specimen how the *Man* employs his Time; where he Rides alone without any Creature to contradict him; while OUR FEW FRIENDS there wonder at our Silence: And the *English* in general, if they think of this Matter at all, impute our Refusal to *Wilfulness* or *Disaffection,* just as *Wood* and his *Hirelings* are pleased to represent.

BUT although our Arguments are not suffered to be printed in *England,* yet the Consequence will be of little Moment. Let *Wood* endeavour to *persuade* the People *There,* that we ought to *Receive* his Coin; and let Me *Convince* our People *Here,* that they ought to *Reject* it under Pain of our utter Undoing. And then let him do his *Best* and his *Worst.*

BEFORE I conclude, I must beg Leave, in all Humility to tell Mr. *Wood,* that he is guilty of great *Indiscretion,* by causing so Honourable a Name as that of Mr. *Walpole*[12] to be mentioned so often, and in such a Manner, upon his Occasion. A short Paper, printed at *Bristol,* and re-printed here, reports Mr. *Wood* to say, that he *wonders at the Impudence and Insolence of the* Irish, *in refusing his Coin,* and *what he will do when Mr.* Walpole *comes to Town.* Where, by the Way, he is mistaken; for it is the *True English People* of *Ireland,* who refuse it; although we take it for granted, that the *Irish* will do so too, whenever they are asked. In another printed Paper of his contriving, it is roundly expressed, that Mr. *Walpole will cram his Brass down our Throats.* Sometimes it is given out, that we must *either take these Half-pence or eat our Brogues.* And, in another News-Letter but of Yesterday, we read, that the same great Man *hath sworn to make us swallow his Coin in Fire-Balls.*

THIS brings to my Mind the known Story of a *Scotch* Man, who receiving Sentence of Death, with all the Circumstances of *Hanging, Beheading, Quartering, Embowelling,* and the like; cried out, *What need all this* COOKERY? And I think we have Reason to ask the same Question: For if we believe *Wood,* here is a *Dinner* getting ready for us, and you see the *Bill of Fare;* and I am sorry the *Drink* was forgot, which might easily be supplied with *Melted Lead* and *Flaming Pitch.*

WHAT vile Words are these to put into the Mouth of a great Counsellor, in high Trust with his Majesty, and looked upon as a prime Minister? If Mr. *Wood* hath no better a Manner of representing his Patrons; when I come to be a *Great Man,* he shall never be suffered to attend at my *Levee.* This is not the Style of a Great Minister; it savours too much of the *Kettle* and the *Furnace;* and came entirely out of *Wood's Forge.*

As for the Threat of making us *eat our Brogues,* we need not be in Pain; for if his Coin should pass, that *Unpolite Covering for the Feet,* would no longer be a *National Reproach;* because, then we should have neither *Shoe* nor *Brogue* left in the Kingdom. But here the Falshood of Mr. *Wood* is fairly detected; for I am confident Mr. *Walpole* never heard of a *Brogue* in his whole Life.

AS to *Swallowing these Half-pence in Fire-balls,* it is a Story equally improbable. For, to execute this *Operation,* the whole Stock of Mr. *Wood's* Coin and Metal must be melted down, and molded into hollow *Balls* with *Wild-fire,* no bigger than a *reasonable* Throat can be able to swallow. Now, the Metal he hath prepared, and already coined, will amount to at least Fifty Millions of Half-pence to be *Swallowed* by a Million and a Half of People; so that allowing Two Half-pence to each *Ball,* there will be about Seventeen *Balls* of *Wild-fire* a-piece, to be swallowed by every Person in the Kingdom: And to administer this Dose, there cannot be conveniently fewer than Fifty thousand *Operators,* allowing one *Operator* to every Thirty; which, considering the *Squeamishness* of some Stomachs, and the *Peevishness* of *Young Children,* is but reasonable. Now, under Correction of better Judgments, I think the Trouble and Charge of such an Experiment, would exceed the Profit; and therefore I take this *Report* to be *spurious;* or, at least, only a new *Scheme* of Mr. *Wood* himself; which, to make it pass the better in *Ireland,* he would Father upon a *Minister of State.*

BUT I will now demonstrate, beyond all Contradiction, that Mr. *Walpole* is against this Project of Mr. *Wood;* and is an entire Friend to *Ireland;* only by this one invincible argument, That he has the Universal Opinion of being a wise Man, an able Minister, and in all his Proceedings, pursuing the *True Interest* of the *King his Master:* And that, as his *Integrity* is above all *Corruption,* so is his *Fortune* above all *Temptation.* I reckon therefore, we are perfectly safe from that *Corner;* and shall never be under the Necessity of Contending with so *Formidable a Power;* but be left to possess our *Brogues* and *Potatoes* in *Peace,* as *Remote from Thunder as we are from Jupiter.* *

---

* *Procul à Jove, procul à fulmine.*

I AM, MY DEAR COUNTRYMEN, YOUR LOVING FELLOW-SUBJECT,

FELLOW-SUFFERER, AND HUMBLE SERVANT,

M. B.

Oct. 13, 1724.

A

Short VIEW

OF THE

State of *IRELAND*

Written in the Year 1727.

I am assured, that it hath, for some Time, been practised as a Method of making Men's Court, when they are asked about the Rate of Lands, the Abilities of Tenants, the State of Trade and Manufacture in this Kingdom, and how their Rents are paid; to answer, that in their Neighbourhood, all Things are in a flourishing Condition, the Rent and Purchase of Land every Day encreasing. And if a Gentleman happen to be a little more sincere in his Representations; besides being looked on as not well affected,[1] he is sure to have a Dozen Contradictors at his Elbow. I think it is no Manner of Secret why these Questions are so *cordially* asked, or so *obligingly* answered.

But since, with regard to the Affairs of this Kingdom, I have been using all Endeavours to subdue my Indignation; to which, indeed, I am not provoked by any personal Interest, being not the Owner of one Spot of Ground in the whole *Island;* I shall only enumerate by Rules generally known, and never contradicted, what are the true Causes of any Countries flourishing and growing rich; and then examine what Effects arise from those Causes in the Kingdom of *Ireland.*

The first Cause of a Kingdom's thriving, is the Fruitfulness of the Soil, to produce the Necessaries and Conveniences of Life; not only sufficient for the Inhabitants, but for Exportation into other Countries.

The Second, is the Industry of the People, in working up all their native Commodities, to the last Degree of Manufacture.

THE Third, is the Conveniency of safe Ports and Havens, to carry out their own Goods, as much manufactured, and bring in those of others, as little manufactured, as the Nature of mutual Commerce will allow.

THE Fourth is, that the Natives should, as much as possible, export and import their Goods in Vessels of their own Timber, made in their own Country.

THE Fifth, is the Priviledge of a free Trade in all foreign Countries, which will permit them; except to those who are in War with their own Prince or State.

THE Sixth, is, by being governed only by Laws made with their own Consent; for otherwise they are not a free People. And therefore, all Appeals for Justice, or Applications for Favour or Preferment, to another Country, are so many grievous Impoverishments.

THE Seventh is, by Improvement of Land, Encouragement of Agriculture, and thereby encreasing the Number of their People; without which, any Country, however blessed by Nature, must continue poor.

THE Eighth, is the Residence of the Prince, or chief Administrator of the Civil Power.

THE Ninth, is the Concourse of Foreigners for Education, Curiosity, or Pleasure; or as to a general Mart of Trade.

THE Tenth, is by disposing all Offices of Honour, Profit, or Trust, only to the Natives, or at least with very few Exceptions; where Strangers have long inhabited the Country, and are supposed to understand, and regard the Interest of it as their own.

THE Eleventh, is when the Rents of Lands, and Profits of Employments, are spent in the Country which produced them, and not in another; the former of which will certainly happen, where the Love of our native Country prevails.

THE Twelfth, is by the publick Revenues being all spent and employed at home; except on the Occasions of a foreign War.

THE Thirteenth is, where the People are not obliged, unless they find it for their own Interest or Conveniency, to receive any Monies, except of their own Coinage by a publick Mint, after the Manner of all civilized Nations.

THE Fourteenth, is a Disposition of the People of a Country to wear their own Manufactures, and import as few Incitements to Luxury, either in Cloaths, Furniture, Food, or Drink, as they possibly can live conveniently without.

THERE are many other Causes of a Nation's thriving, which I cannot at present recollect; but without Advantage from at least some of these, after turning my Thoughts a long Time, I am not able to discover from whence our Wealth proceeds, and therefore would gladly be better informed. In the mean Time, I will here examine what Share falls to *Ireland* of these Causes, or of the Effects and Consequences.

IT is not my Intention to complain, but barely to relate Facts; and the Matter is not of small Importance. For it is allowed, that a Man who lives in a solitary House, far from Help, is not wise in endeavouring to acquire, in the Neighbourhood, the Reputation of being rich; because those who come for Gold, will go off with Pewter and Brass, rather than return empty: And in the common Practice of the World, those who possess most Wealth, make the least parade; which they leave to others, who have nothing else to bear them out, in shewing their Faces on the *Exchange*.

As to the first Cause of a Nation's Riches, being the Fertility of the Soil, as well as Temperature of Climate, we have no Reason to complain; for, although the Quantity of unprofitable Land in this Kingdom, reckoning Bogg, and Rock, and barren Mountain, be double in Proportion to what it is in *England;* yet the native Productions which both Kingdoms deal in, are very near on Equality in Point of Goodness; and might, with the same Encouragement, be as well manufactured. I except Mines and Minerals; in some of which, however, we are only defective in Point of Skill and Industry.

IN the Second, which is the Industry of the People; our Misfortune is not altogether owing to our own Fault, but to a Million of Discouragements.

THE Conveniency of Ports and Havens, which Nature hath bestowed so liberally on this Kingdom, is of no more Use to us, than a beautiful Prospect to a Man shut up in a Dungeon.

As to Shipping of its own, *Ireland* is so utterly unprovided, that of all the excellent Timber cut down within these Fifty or Sixty Years, it can hardly be said, that the Nation hath received the Benefit of one valuable House to dwell in, or one Ship to trade with.

IRELAND is the only Kingdom I ever heard or read of, either in ancient or modern Story, which was denied the Liberty of exporting their native Commodities and Manufactures, wherever they pleased; except to Countries at War with their own Prince or State: Yet this Privilege, by the Superiority of meer Power, is refused us, in the most momentous Parts of Commerce; besides an Act of Navigation,[2] to which we never consented, pinned down upon us, and rigorously executed; and a Thousand other unexampled Circumstances, as grievous, as they are invidious to mention. To go on to the rest.

IT is too well known, that we are forced to obey some Laws we never consented to; which is a Condition I must not call by its true uncontroverted Name, for fear of Lord Chief Justice *Whitshed*'s Ghost,[3] with his *Libertas & natale Solum,** written as a Motto on his Coach, as it stood at the Door of the Court, while he was perjuring himself to betray both. Thus, we are in the Condition of Patients, who have Physick sent them by Doctors at a Distance, Strangers to their Constitution, and the Nature of their Disease: And thus, we are forced to pay five Hundred *per Cent.* to decide our Properties; in all which, we have likewise the Honour to be distinguished from the whole Race of Mankind.

As to Improvement of Land; those few who attempt that, or Planting, through Covetousness, or Want of Skill, generally leave Things worse than they were; neither succeeding in Trees nor Hedges; and by running into the Fancy of Grazing, after the Manner of the *Scythians,*[4] are every Day depopulating the Country.

WE are so far from having a King to reside among us, that even the Viceroy is generally absent four Fifths of his Time in the Government.

NO strangers from other Countries, make this a Part of their Travels; where they can expect to see nothing, but Scenes of Misery and Desolation.

THOSE who have the Misfortune to be born here, have the least Title to any considerable Employment; to which they are seldom preferred, but upon a political Consideration.

ONE third Part of the Rents of *Ireland,* is spent in *England;* which, with the Profit of Employments, Pensions, Appeals, Journeys of Pleasure or Health, Education at the *Inns* of Court, and both Universities, Remittances at Pleasure, the Pay of all Superior Officers in the Army, and other Incidents, will amount to a full half of the Income of the whole Kingdom, all clear Profit to *England.*

WE are denied the Liberty of Coining Gold, Silver, or even Copper. In the Isle of *Man,* they coin their own *Silver;* every petty Prince, Vassal to the *Emperor,* can coin what Money he pleaseth. And in this, as in most of the Articles already mentioned, we are an Exception to all other States or Monarchies that were ever known in the World.

AS to the last, or Fourteenth Article, we take special Care to act

---

* Liberty and my native country.

diametrically contrary to it in the whole Course of our Lives. Both Sexes, but especially the Women, despise and abhor to wear any of their own Manufactures, even those which are better made than in other Countries; particularly a Sort of Silk Plad, through which the Workmen are forced to run a Sort of Gold Thread that it may pass for *Indian*. Even Ale and Potatoes are imported from *England*, as well as Corn: And our foreign Trade is little more than Importation of *French* Wine; for which I am told we pay ready Money.

NOW, if all this be true, upon which I could easily enlarge; I would be glad to know by what secret Method, it is, that we grow a rich and flourishing People, without *Liberty, Trade, Manufactures, Inhabitants, Money*, or the *Privilege of Coining*; without *Industry, Labour*, or *Improvement of Lands*, and with more than half the Rent and Profits of the whole *Kingdom*, annually exported; for which we receive not a single Farthing: And to make up all this, nothing worth mentioning, except the Linnen of the *North*, a Trade casual, corrupted, and at Mercy; and some Butter from *Cork*. If we do flourish, it must be against every Law of Nature and Reason; like the Thorn at *Glassenbury*,[5] that blossoms in the Midst of Winter.

LET the worthy *Commissioners* who come from *England*, ride round the Kingdom, and observe the Face of Nature, or the Faces of the Natives; the Improvement of the Land; the thriving numerous Plantations; the noble Woods; the Abundance and Vicinity of Country-Seats; the commodious Farmers Houses and Barns; the Towns and Villages, where every Body is busy, and thriving with all Kind of Manufactures; the Shops full of Goods, wrought to Perfection, and filled with Customers; the comfortable Diet and Dress, and Dwellings of the People; the vast Numbers of Ships in our Harbours and Docks, and Ship-wrights in our Seaport-Towns; the Roads crouded with Carriers, laden with rich Manufactures; the perpetual Concourse to and fro of pompous Equipages.

WITH what Envy, and Admiration, would those Gentlemen return from so delightful a Progress? What glorious Reports would they make, when they went back to *England*?

BUT my Heart is too heavy to continue this Irony longer; for it is manifest, that whatever Stranger took such a Journey, would be apt to think himself travelling in *Lapland*, or *Ysland*, rather than in a Country so favoured by Nature as ours, both in Fruitfulness of Soil, and Temperature of Climate. The miserable Dress, and Dyet, and Dwelling of the People. The general Desolation in most Parts of the Kingdom. The old Seats of the Nobility and Gentry all in Ruins, and no new ones in their Stead. The

Families of Farmers, who pay great Rents, living in Filth and Nastiness upon Butter-milk and Potatoes, without a Shoe or Stocking to their Feet; or a House so convenient as an *English* Hog-sty, to receive them. These, indeed, may be comfortable Sights to an *English* Spectator; who comes for a short Time, only *to learn the Language,* and returns back to his own Country, whither he finds all our Wealth transmitted.

Nostrâ miserià magnus es.[6]

THERE is not one Argument used to prove the Riches of *Ireland,* which is not a logical Demonstration of its Poverty. The Rise of our Rents is squeezed out of the very Blood, and Vitals, and Cloaths, and Dwellings of the Tenants; who live worse than *English* Beggars. The Lowness of Interest, in all other Countries a Sign of Wealth, is in us a Proof of Misery; there being no Trade to employ any Borrower. Hence, alone, comes the Dearness of Land, since the Savers have no other Way to lay out their Money. Hence the Dearness of Necessaries for Life; because the Tenants cannot afford to pay such extravagant Rates for Land, (which they must take, or go a-begging) without raising the Price of Cattle, and of Corn, although themselves should live upon Chaff. Hence our encrease of Buildings in this City; because Workmen have nothing to do, but employ one another; and one Half of them are infallibly undone. Hence the daily Encrease of *Bankers;* who may be a necessary Evil in a trading Country, but so ruinous in ours; who, for their private Advantage, have sent away all our Silver, and one Third of our Gold; so that within three Years past, the running Cash of the Nation, which was about five Hundred Thousand Pounds, is now less than two; and must daily diminish, unless we have Liberty to coin, as well as that important Kingdom the Isle of *Man;* and the meanest Prince in the *German* Empire,[7] as I before observed.

I HAVE sometimes thought, that this Paradox of the Kingdom growing rich, is chiefly owing to those worthy Gentlemen the BANKERS; who, except some Custom-house Officers, Birds of Passage, oppressive thrifty 'Squires, and a few others who shall be nameless, are the only thriving People among us: And I have often wished, that a Law were enacted to hang up half a Dozen *Bankers* every Year; and thereby interpose at least some short Delay, to the further Ruin of *Ireland.*

YE are idle, ye are idle,[8] answered *Pharoah* to the *Israelites,* when they complained to *his Majesty,* that they were forced to make Bricks without Straw.

ENGLAND enjoys every one of those Advantages for enriching a Nation, which I have above enumerated; and, into the Bargain, a good Million returned to them every Year, without Labour or Hazard, or one Farthing Value received on our Side. But how long we shall be able to continue the Payment, I am not under the least Concern. One Thing I know, that *when the Hen is starved to Death, there will be no more Golden Eggs.*

I THINK it a little unhospitable, and others may call it a subtil Piece of Malice; that, because there may be a Dozen Families in this Town, able to entertain their *English* Friends in a generous Manner at their Tables; their Guests, upon their Return to *England,* shall report, that we wallow in Riches and Luxury.

YET, I confess, I have known an Hospital, where all the Household-Officers grew rich; while the Poor, for whose Sake it was built, were almost starving for want of Food and Raiment.

TO conclude. If *Ireland* be a rich and flourishing Kingdom; its Wealth and Prosperity must be owing to certain Causes, that are yet concealed from the whole Race of Mankind; and the Effects are equally invisible. We need not wonder at Strangers, when they deliver such Paradoxes; but a Native and Inhabitant of this Kingdom, who gives the same Verdict, must be either ignorant to Stupidity; or a Man-pleaser, at the Expence of all Honour, Conscience, and Truth.

A MODEST

PROPOSAL

FOR

PREVENTING THE CHILDREN

OF POOR PEOPLE IN IRELAND,

FROM BEING A BURDEN

TO THEIR PARENTS OR COUNTRY;

AND FOR MAKING THEM

BENEFICIAL TO THE PUBLICK.

Written in the Year 1729.

I t is a melancholly Object[1] to those, who walk through this great Town,[2] or travel in the Country; when they see the *Streets,* the *Roads,* and *Cabbin-doors* crowded with *Beggars* of the Female Sex, followed by three, four, or six Children, *all in Rags,* and importuning every Passenger for an Alms. These *Mothers,* instead of being able to work for their honest Livelyhood, are forced to employ all their Time in stroling to beg Sustenance for their *helpless Infants;* who, as they grow up, either turn *Thieves* for want of Work; or leave their *dear Native Country, to fight for the Pretender*[3] *in* Spain, or sell themselves to the *Barbadoes.*[4]

I THINK it is agreed by all Parties, that this prodigious Number of Children in the Arms, or on the Backs, or at the *Heels* of their *Mothers,* and frequently of their *Fathers,* is *in the present deplorable State of the Kingdom,* a very great additional Grievance; and therefore, whoever could find out a fair, cheap, and easy Method of making these Children sound and useful Members of the Commonwealth, would deserve so well of the Publick, as to have his Statue set up for a Preserver of the Nation.

BUT my Intention is very far from being confined to provide only for the Children of *professed Beggars:* It is of a much greater Extent, and shall take in the whole Number of Infants at a certain Age, who are born of Parents, in effect as little able to support them, as those who demand our Charity in the Streets.

AS to my own Part, having turned my Thoughts for many Years, upon this important Subject, and maturely weighed the several *Schemes of other Projectors,*[5] I have always found them grosly mistaken in their Computation. It is true a Child, *just dropt from its Dam,* may be supported by her Milk, for a Solar Year with little other Nourishment; at most not above the Value of two Shillings; which the Mother may certainly get, or the Value in *Scraps,* by her lawful Occupation of *Begging:* And, it is exactly at one Year old, that I propose to provide for them in such a Manner, as, instead of being a Charge upon their *Parents,* or the *Parish,* or *wanting Food and Raiment* for the rest of their Lives; they shall, on the contrary, contribute to the Feeding, and partly to the Cloathing, of many Thousands.

THERE is likewise another great Advantage in my *Scheme,* that it will prevent those *voluntary Abortions,* and that horrid Practice of *Women murdering their Bastard Children;* alas! too frequent among us; sacrificing the *poor innocent Babes,* I doubt,[6] more to avoid the Expence than the Shame; which would move Tears and Pity in the most Savage and inhuman Breast.

THE Number of Souls in *Ireland* being usually reckoned one Million and a half; of these I calculate there may be about Two hundred Thousand Couple whose Wives are Breeders; from which Number I subtract thirty thousand Couples, who are able to maintain their own Children; although I apprehend there cannot be so many, under *the present Distresses of the Kingdom;* but this being granted, there will remain an Hundred and Seventy Thousand Breeders. I again subtract Fifty Thousand, for those Women who miscarry, or whose Children die by Accident, or Disease, within the Year. There only remain an Hundred and Twenty Thousand Children of poor Parents, annually born: The Question therefore is, How this Number shall be reared, and provided for? Which, as I have already said, under the present Situation of Affairs, is utterly impossible, by all the Methods hitherto proposed: For we can *neither employ them in Handicraft* or *Agriculture;* we neither build Houses, (I mean in the Country) nor cultivate Land: They can very seldom pick up a Livelyhood *by Stealing* until they arrive at six Years old; except where they are of towardly Parts: although, I confess, they learn the Rudiments much earlier; during which Time, they can, however, be properly looked upon only as *Probationers;* as I have been informed by a principal Gentleman in the County of *Cavan,* who protested to me, that he never knew above one or two Instances under the Age of six, even in a Part of the Kingdom *so renowned for the quickest Proficiency in that Art.*

I AM assured by our merchants, that a Boy or a Girl before twelve Years old, is no saleable Commodity; and even when they come to this Age, they will not yield above Three Pounds, or Three Pounds and half a Crown at most, on the Exchange; which cannot turn to Account either to the Parents or the Kingdom; the Charge of Nutriment and Rags, having been at least four Times that Value.

I SHALL now therefore humbly propose my own Thoughts; which I hope will not be liable to the least Objection.

I HAVE been assured by a very knowing *American* of my Acquaintance in *London;* that a young healthy Child, well nursed, is, at a Year old, a most delicious, nourishing, and wholesome Food; whether *Stewed, Roasted, Baked,* or *Boiled;* and, I make no doubt, that it will equally serve in a *Fricasie,* or *Ragoust.*

I DO therefore humbly offer it to *publick Consideration,* that of the Hundred and Twenty Thousand Children, already computed, Twenty thousand may be reserved for Breed; whereof only one Fourth Part to be Males; which is more than we allow to *Sheep, black Cattle,* or *Swine;* and my Reason is, that these Children are seldom the Fruits of Marriage, *a Circumstance not much regarded by our Savages;* therefore, *one Male* will be sufficient to serve *four Females.* That the remaining Hundred thousand, may, at a Year old, be offered in Sale to the *Persons of Quality* and *Fortune,* through the Kingdom; always advising the Mother to let them suck plentifully in the last Month, so as to render them plump, and fat for a good Table. A Child will make two Dishes at an Entertainment for Friends; and when the Family dines alone, the fore or hind Quarter will make a reasonable Dish; and seasoned with a little Pepper or Salt, will be very good Boiled on the fourth Day, especially in *Winter.*

I HAVE reckoned upon a Medium, that a Child just born will weigh Twelve Pounds; and in a solar Year, if tolerably nursed, encreaseth to twenty eight Pounds.

I GRANT this Food will be somewhat dear, and therefore very *proper for Landlords;* who, as they have already devoured most of the Parents, seem to have the best Title to the Children.

INFANTS Flesh will be in Season throughout the Year; but more plentiful in *March,* and a little before and after: For we are told by a grave Author,*[7] an eminent *French* Physician, that *Fish being a prolifick Dyet,* there are more Children born in *Roman Catholick Countries* about Nine Months after *Lent,* than at any other Season: Therefore reckoning a year after *Lent,* the Markets will be more glutted than usual; because the Number of *Popish Infants,* is, at least, three to one in this Kingdom; and therefore it will have one other Collateral Advantage, by lessening the Number of *Papists* among us.

I HAVE already computed the Charge of nursing a Beggar's Child (in which List I reckon all *Cottagers,*[8] *Labourers,* and Four fifths of the *Farmers*) to be about two Shillings *per Annum,* Rags included; and I believe, no Gentleman would repine to give Ten Shillings for the *Carcase of a good fat Child;* which, as I have said, will make four Dishes of excellent nutritive Meat, when he hath only some particular Friend, or his own Family, to dine with him. Thus the Squire will learn to be a good Landlord, and grow popular among his Tenants; the Mother will have Eight Shillings net Profit, and be fit for Work until she produceth another Child.

THOSE who are more thrifty (*as I must confess the Times require*) may flay

* Rabelais.

the Carcase; the Skin of which, artificially dressed, will make admirable *Gloves for Ladies,* and *Summer Boots for fine Gentlemen.*

As to our City of *Dublin;* Shambles may be appointed for this Purpose, in the most convenient Parts of it; and Butchers we may be assured will not be wanting; although I rather recommend buying the Children alive, and dressing them hot from the Knife, as we do *roasting Pigs.*

A VERY worthy Person, *a true Lover of his Country,* and whose Virtues I highly esteem, was lately pleased, in discoursing on this Matter, to offer a Refinement upon my Scheme. He said, that many Gentlemen of this Kingdom, having of late destroyed their Deer; he conceived, that the Want of Venison might be well supplied by the Bodies of young Lads and Maidens, not exceeding fourteen Years of Age, nor under twelve; so great a Number of both Sexes in every County being now ready to starve, for Want of Work and Service: And these to be disposed of by their Parents, if alive, or otherwise by their nearest Relations. But with due Deference to so excellent a Friend, and so deserving a Patriot, I cannot be altogether in his Sentiments. For as to the Males, my *American* Acquaintance assured me from frequent Experience, that their Flesh was generally tough and lean, like that of our School-boys, by continual Exercise, and their Taste disagreeable; and to fatten them would not answer the Charge. Then, as to the Females, it would, I think, with humble Submission, *be a Loss to the Publick,* because they soon would become Breeders themselves: And besides it is not improbable, that some scrupulous People might be apt to censure such a Practice (although indeed very unjustly) as a little bordering upon Cruelty; which, I confess, hath always been with me the strongest Objection against any Project, how well soever intended.

BUT in order to justify my Friend; he confessed, that this Expedient was put into his Head by the famous *Salmanaazor,*[9] a Native of the Island *Formosa,* who came from thence to *London,* above twenty Years ago, and in Conversation told my Friend, that in his Country, when any young Person happened to be put to Death, the Executioner sold the Carcase to *Persons of Quality,* as a prime Dainty; and that, in his Time, the Body of a plump Girl of fifteen, who was crucified for an Attempt to poison the Emperor, was sold to his Imperial *Majesty's prime Minister of State,* and other great *Mandarins* of the Court, *in Joints from the Gibbet,* at Four hundred Crowns. Neither indeed can I deny, that if the same Use were made of several plump young girls in this Town, who, without one single Groat[10] to their Fortunes, cannot stir Abroad without a Chair,[11] and appear at the *Playhouse,* and *Assemblies* in foreign Fineries, which they never will pay for; the Kingdom would not be the worse.

SOME Persons of a desponding Spirit are in great Concern about that vast Number of poor People, who are Aged, Diseased, or Maimed; and I have been desired to employ my Thoughts what Course may be taken, to ease the Nation of so grievous an Incumbrance. But I am not in the least Pain upon that Matter; because it is very well known, that they are every Day *dying,* and *rotting,* by *Cold* and *Famine,* and *Filth,* and *Vermin,* as fast as can be reasonably expected. And as to the younger Labourers, they are now in almost as hopeful a Condition: They cannot get Work, and consequently pine away for Want of Nourishment, to a Degree, that if at any Time they are accidentally hired to common Labour, they have not Strength to perform it; and thus the Country, and themselves, are in a fair Way of being soon delivered from the Evils to come.

I HAVE too long digressed; and therefore shall return to my Subject. I think the Advantages by the Proposal which I have made, are obvious, and many, as well as of the highest Importance.

FOR, *First,* as I have already observed, it would greatly lessen the *Number of Papists,* with whom we are yearly overrun; being the principal Breeders of the Nation, as well as our most dangerous Enemies; and who stay at home on Purpose, with a Design to *deliver the Kingdom to the Pretender;* hoping to take their Advantage by the Absence *of so many good Protestants,* who have chosen rather to leave their Country, than stay at home, and pay Tithes against their Conscience, to an idolatrous *Episcopal Curate.*[12]

SECONDLY, The poorer Tenants will have something valuable of their own, which, by Law, may be made liable to Distress, and help to pay their Landlord's Rent; their Corn and Cattle being already seized, and *Money a Thing unknown.*

THIRDLY, Whereas the Maintenance of an Hundred Thousand Children, from two Years old, and upwards, cannot be computed at less than ten Shillings a Piece *per Annum,* the Nation's Stock will be thereby encreased Fifty Thousand Pounds *per Annum;* besides the Profit of a new Dish, introduced to the Tables of all *Gentlemen of Fortune* in the Kingdom, who have any Refinement in Taste; and the Money will circulate among ourselves, the Goods being entirely of our own Growth and Manufacture.

FOURTHLY, The constant Breeders, besides the Gain of Eight Shillings *Sterling per Annum,* by the Sale of their Children, will be rid of the Charge of maintaining them after the first Year.

FIFTHLY, This Food would likewise bring great *Custom to Taverns,* where the Vintners will certainly be so prudent, as to procure the best Receipts[13] for dressing it to Perfection; and consequently, have their Houses frequented by all the *fine Gentlemen,* who justly value themselves upon their

Knowledge in good Eating; and a skilful Cook, who understands how to oblige his Guests, will contrive to make it as expensive as they please.

SIXTHLY, This would be a great Inducement to Marriage, which all wise Nations have either encouraged by Rewards, or enforced by Laws and Penalties. It would encrease the Care and Tenderness of Mothers towards their Children, when they were sure of a Settlement for Life, to the poor Babes, provided in some Sort by the Publick, to their annual Profit instead of Expence. We should soon see an honest Emulation among the married Women, *which of them could bring the fattest Child to the Market*. Men would become as *fond* of their Wives, during the Time of their Pregnancy, as they are now of their *Mares* in Foal, their *Cows* in Calf, or *Sows* when they are ready to farrow; nor offer to beat or kick them, (as it is too *frequent* a Practice) for fear of a Miscarriage.

MANY other Advantages might be enumerated. For instance, the Addition of some Thousand Carcasses in our Exportation of barrelled Beef: The Propagation of *Swines Flesh*, and Improvement in the Art of making good *Bacon*; so much wanted among us by the great Destruction of *Pigs*, too frequent at our Tables, and are no way comparable in Taste, or Magnificence, to a well-grown fat yearling Child; which, roasted whole, will make a considerable Figure at a *Lord Mayor's Feast*, or any other publick Entertainment. But this, and many others, I omit; being studious of Brevity.

SUPPOSING that one Thousand Families in this City, would be constant Customers for Infants Flesh; besides others who might have it at *merry Meetings*, particularly *Weddings* and *Christenings*; I compute that *Dublin* would take off, annually, about Twenty Thousand Carcasses; and the rest of the Kingdom (where probably they will be sold somewhat cheaper) the remaining Eighty Thousand.

I CAN think of no one Objection, that will possibly be raised against this Proposal; unless it should be urged, that the Number of People will be thereby much lessened in the Kingdom. This I freely own; and it was indeed one principal Design in offering it to the World. I desire the Reader will observe, that I calculate my Remedy *for this one individual Kingdom of* IRELAND, *and for no other that ever was, is, or I think ever can be upon Earth*. Therefore, let no man talk to me of other Expedients:[14] *Of taxing our Absentees at five Shillings a Pound: Of using neither Cloaths, nor Household Furniture except what is of our own Growth and Manufacture: Of utterly rejecting the Materials and Instruments that promote foreign Luxury: Of curing the Expensiveness of Pride, Vanity, Idleness, and Gaming in our Women: Of introducing a Vein of Parsimony, Prudence and Temperance: Of learning to love our Country, wherein we dif-*

fer even from LAPLANDERS, *and the Inhabitants of* TOPINAMBOO:[15] *Of quitting our Animosities, and Factions; nor act any longer like the* Jews, *who were murdering one another at the very Moment their City was taken.*[16] *Of being a little cautious not to sell our Country and Consciences for nothing: Of teaching Landlords to have, at least, one Degree of Mercy towards their Tenants.* Lastly, *Of putting a Spirit of Honesty, Industry, and Skill into our Shop-keepers; who, if a Resolution could now be taken to buy only our native Goods, would immediately unite to cheat and exact upon us in the Price, the Measure, and the Goodness; nor could ever yet be brought to make one fair Proposal of just Dealing, though often and earnestly invited to it.*

THEREFORE I repeat, let no Man talk to me of these and the like Expedients; till he hath, at least, a Glimpse of Hope, that there will ever be some hearty and sincere Attempt to put *them in Practice.*

BUT, as to my self; having been wearied out for many Years with offering vain, idle, visionary Thoughts; and at length utterly despairing of Success, I fortunately fell upon this Proposal; which, as it is wholly new, so it hath something *solid* and *real,* of no Expence, and little Trouble, full in our own Power; and whereby we can incur no Danger in *disobliging* ENGLAND: For, this Kind of Commodity will not bear Exportation; the Flesh being of too tender a Consistence, to admit a long Continuance in Salt; *although, perhaps, I could name a Country, which would be glad to eat up our whole Nation without it.*

AFTER all, I am not so violently bent upon my own Opinion, as to reject any Offer proposed by wise Men, which shall be found equally innocent, cheap, easy, and effectual. But before something of that Kind shall be advanced, in Contradiction to my Scheme, and offering a better; I desire the Author, or Authors, will be pleased maturely to consider two Points. *First,* As Things now stand, how they will be able to find Food and Raiment, for a Hundred Thousand useless Mouths and Backs? And *secondly,* There being a round Million of Creatures in human Figure, throughout this Kingdom; whose whole Subsistence, put into a common Stock, would leave them in Debt two Millions of Pounds *Sterling;* adding those, who are Beggars by Profession, to the Bulk of Farmers, Cottagers, and Labourers, with their Wives and Children, who are Beggars in Effect; I desire those Politicians, who dislike my Overture, and may perhaps be so bold to attempt an Answer, that they will first ask the Parents of these Mortals, Whether they would not, at this Day, think it a great Happiness to have been sold for Food at a Year old, in the Manner I prescribe; and thereby have avoided such a perpetual Scene of Misfortunes, as they have since gone through; by the *Oppression of Landlords;* the Impossibility of paying

Rent, without Money or Trade; the Want of common Sustenance, with neither House nor Cloaths, to cover them from the Inclemencies of Weather; and the most inevitable Prospect of intailing the like, or greater Miseries upon their Breed for ever.

I PROFESS, in the Sincerity of my Heart, that I have not the least personal Interest, in endeavouring to promote this necessary Work; having no other Motive than the *publick Good of my Country, by advancing our Trade, providing for Infants, relieving the Poor, and giving some Pleasure to the Rich.* I have no Children, by which I can propose to get a single Penny; the youngest being nine Years old, and my Wife past Child-bearing.

A Proposal for giving Badges to the Beggars in all the Parishes of Dublin.
By the Dean of St. Patrick's.

It hath been a general Complaint, that the Poor-House, especially since the new Constitution by Act of Parliament,[1] hath been of no Benefit to this City, for the Ease of which it was wholly intended. I had the Honour to be a Member of it many Years before it was new modelled by the Legislature; not from any personal Regard, but meerly as one of the two Deans, who are of Course put into most Commissions that relate to the City; and I have likewise the Honour to have been left out of several Commissions upon the Score of Party, in which my Predecessors, Time out of Mind, have always been Members.

THE first Commission was made up of about fifty Persons, which were the Lord Mayor, Aldermen, and Sheriffs, and some few other Citizens: The Judges, the two Arch-Bishops, the two Deans of the City, and one or two more Gentlemen. And I must confess my Opinion, that the dissolving the old Commission, and establishing a new one of near three Times the Number, have been the great Cause of rendering so good a Design not only useless, but a Grievance instead of a Benefit to the City. In the present Commission all the City-Clergy are included, besides a great Number of 'Squires, not only those who reside in *Dublin,* and the Neighbourhood, but several who live at a great Distance, and cannot possibly have the least Concern for the Advantage of the City.

AT the few General Meetings that I have attended since the new Establishment, I observed very little was done except one or two Acts of extream Justice, which I then thought might as well have been spared: And I have found the Court of Assistants usually taken up in little Brangles about Coachmen, or adjusting Accounts of Meal and Small-Beer; which, however necessary, might sometimes have given Place to Matters of much greater Moment, I mean some Schemes recommended to the General Board, for answering the chief Ends in erecting and establishing such a Poor-House, and endowing it with so considerable a Revenue: And the principal End I take to have been that of maintaining the Poor and Orphans of the City, where the Parishes are not able to do it; and clearing the Streets from all Strollers, Foreigners, and sturdy Beggars, with which, to the universal Complaint and Admiration, *Dublin* is more infested since the Establishment of the Poor-House, than it was ever known to be since its first Erection.

As the whole Fund for supporting this Hospital is raised only from the Inhabitants of the City; so there can be hardly any Thing more absurd than to see it misemployed in maintaining Foreign Beggars and Bastards, or Orphans, whose Country Landlords never contributed one Shilling towards their Support. I would engage, that half this Revenue, if employed with common Care, and no very great Degree of common Honesty, would maintain all the real Objects of Charity in this City, except a small Number of Original Poor in every Parish, who might without being burthensome to the Parishioners find a tolerable Support.

I HAVE for some Years past applied myself to several Lord Mayors, and to the late Arch-Bishop of *Dublin,* for a Remedy to this Evil of Foreign Beggars; and they all appeared ready to receive a very plain Proposal,[2] I mean, that of badging the Original Poor of every Parish, who begged in the Streets; that, the said Beggars should be confined to their own Parishes; that, they should wear their Badges well sown upon one of their Shoulders, always visible, on Pain of being whipt and turned out of Town;[3] or whatever legal Punishment may be thought proper and effectual. But, by the wrong Way of thinking in some Clergymen, and the Indifference of others, this Method was perpetually defeated to their own continual disquiet, which they do not ill deserve; and if the Grievance affected only them, it would be of less Consequence; because the Remedy is in their own Power. But, all Street-walkers, and Shop-keepers, bear an equal Share in this hourly Vexation.

I NEVER heard more than one Objection against this Expedient of badging the Poor, and confining their Walks to their several Parishes. The Objection was this: What shall we do with the Foreign Beggars? Must they be left to starve? I answered, No; but they must be driven or whipt out of Town; and let the next Country Parish do as they please, or rather after the Practice in *England,* send them from one Parish to another, until they reach their own Homes. By the old Laws of *England* still in Force, and I presume by those of *Ireland,* every Parish is bound to maintain its own Poor; and the Matter is of no such Consequence in this Point as some would make it, whether a Country Parish be rich or poor. In the remoter and poorer Parishes of the Kingdom, all Necessaries for Life proper for poor People are comparatively cheaper; I mean Butter-milk, Oatmeal, Potatoes, and other Vegetables; and every Farmer or Cottager, who is not himself a Beggar, can sometimes spare a Sup or a Morsel, not worth the fourth Part of a Farthing, to an indigent Neighbour of his own Parish, who is disabled from Work. A Beggar Native of the Parish is known to the

'Squire, to the Church Minister, to the Popish Priest, or the Conventicle Teachers, as well as to every Farmer: He hath generally some Relations able to live, and contribute something to his Maintenance. None of which Advantages can be reasonably expected on a Removal to Places where he is altogether unknown. If he be not quite maimed, he and his Trull, and Litter of Brats (if he hath any) may get half their Support by doing some Kind of Work in their Power, and thereby be less burthensome to the People. In short, all Necessaries of Life grow in the Country, and not in Cities, and are cheaper where they grow; nor is it equal that Beggars should put us to the Charge of giving them Victuals, and the Carriage too.

BUT, when the Spirit of wandring takes him, attended by his Female, and their Equipage of Children, he becomes a Nuisance to the whole Country: He and his Female are Thieves, and teach the Trade of stealing to their Brood at four Years old; and if his Infirmities be counterfeit, it is dangerous for a single Person unarmed to meet him on the Road. He wanders from one County to another, but still with a View to this Town, whither he arrives at last, and enjoys all the Priviledges of a *Dublin* Beggar.

I DO not wonder that the Country 'Squires should be very willing to send up their Colonies; but why the City should be content to receive them, is beyond my Imagination.

IF the City were obliged by their Charter to maintain a thousand Beggars, they could do it cheaper by eighty per Cent. a hundred Miles off, than in this Town, or any of its Suburbs.

THERE is no Village in *Connaught*, that in Proportion shares so deeply in the Daily encreasing Miseries of *Ireland*, as its Capital City; to which Miseries there hardly remained any Addition, except the perpetual Swarms of Foreign Beggars, who might be banished in a Month without Expence, and with very little Trouble.

As I am personally acquainted with a great Number of Street Beggars, I find some weak Attempts have been made in one or two Parishes to promote the wearing of Badges; and my first Question to those who ask an Alms is, *Where is your Badge?* I have in several Years met with about a Dozen who were ready to produce them, some out of their Pockets, others from under their Coat, and two or three on their Shoulders, only covered with a Sort of Capes which they could lift up or let down upon Occasion. They are too lazy to work; they are not afraid to steal, nor ashamed to beg, and yet are too proud to be seen with a Badge, as many of them have confessed to me, and not a few in very injurious Terms, particularly the Females. They all look upon such an Obligation as a high Indignity done to their

Office. I appeal to all indifferent People whether such Wretches deserve to be relieved. As to my self, I must confess, this absurd Insolence hath so affected me, that for several Years past, I have not disposed of one single Farthing to a Street Beggar, nor intend to do so until I see a better Regulation; and I have endeavoured to persuade all my Brother-walkers to follow my Example, which most of them assure me they do. For, if Beggary be not able to beat out Pride, it cannot deserve Charity. However, as to Persons in Coaches and Chairs, they bear but little of the Persecution we suffer, and are willing to leave it intirely upon us.

To say the Truth, there is not a more undeserving vicious Race of human Kind than the Bulk of those who are reduced to Beggary, even in this beggarly Country. For, as a great Part of our publick Miseries is originally owing to our own Faults (but, what those Faults are I am grown by Experience too wary to mention) so I am confident, that among the meaner People, nineteen in twenty of those who are reduced to a starving Condition, did not become so by what Lawyers call the Work of GOD, either upon their Bodies or Goods; but meerly from their own Idleness, attended with all Manner of Vices, particularly Drunkenness, Thievery, and Cheating.

WHOEVER inquires, as I have frequently done, from those who have asked me an Alms, what was their former Course of Life, will find them to have been Servants in good Families, broken Tradesmen, Labourers, Cottagers, and what they call decayed Housekeepers; but (to use their own Cant) reduced by Losses and Crosses, by which nothing can be understood but Idleness and Vice.

As this is the only Christian Country where People contrary to the old Maxim, are the Poverty and not the Riches of the Nation; so, the Blessing of Increase and Multiply is by us converted into a Curse: And, as Marriage hath been ever countenanced in all free Countries, so we should be less miserable if it were discouraged in ours, as far as can be consistent with Christianity. It is seldom known in *England*, that the Labourer, the lower Mechanick, the Servant, or the Cottager, thinks of marrying until he hath saved up a Stock of Money sufficient to carry on his Business; nor takes a Wife without a suitable Portion; and as seldom fails of making a yearly Addition to that Stock, with a View of providing for his Children. But, in this Kingdom the Case is directly contrary, where many thousand Couples are yearly married, whose whole united Fortunes, bating the Rags on their Backs, would not be sufficient to purchase a Pint of Buttermilk for their Wedding Supper, nor have any Prospect of supporting their *honourable State* but by Service, or Labour, or Thievery. Nay, their *Happiness* is often deferred until they find Credit to borrow, or cunning to steal a Shilling to pay their Popish Priest, or infamous Couple-Beggar.[4] Surely no miraculous Portion of Wisdom would be required to find some kind of Remedy against this destructive Evil, or at least, not to draw the Consequences of it upon our decaying City, the greatest Part whereof must of Course in a few Years become desolate, or in Ruins.

IN all other Nations, that are not absolutely barbarous, Parents think themselves bound by the Law of Nature and Reason to make some Provision for their Children; but the Reasons offered by the Inhabitants of *Ireland* for marrying, is, that they may have Children to maintain them when they grow old and unable to work.

I AM informed that we have been for some Time past extremely obliged to *England* for one very beneficial Branch of Commerce: For, it seems they are grown so Gracious as to transmit us continually Colonies of Beggars, in Return of a Million of Money they receive yearly from hence. That I may give no Offence, I profess to mean real *English* Beggars in the literal Meaning of the Word, as it is usually understood by Protestants. It seems, the Justices of the Peace and Parish Officers in the Western Coasts of *England,* have a good while followed the Trade of exporting hither their supernumerary Beggars, in order to advance the *English* Protestant Interest among us; and, these they are so kind to send over Gratis, and Duty-free. I have had the Honour more than once to attend large Cargoes of them from *Chester* to *Dublin:* And I was then so ignorant as to give my Opinion, that our City should receive them into Bridewell, and after a Month's Residence, having been well whipt twice a Day, fed with Bran and Water, and put to hard Labour, they should be returned honestly back with Thanks as cheap as they came: Or, if that were not approved of, I proposed, that whereas one *English* Man is allowed to be of equal intrinsick Value with twelve born in *Ireland,* we should in Justice return them a Dozen for One, to dispose of as they pleased. But to return.

AS to the native Poor of this City, there would be little or no Damage in confining them to their several Parishes. For Instance; a Beggar of the Parish of St. *Warborough's,* or any other Parish here, if he be an Object of Compassion, hath an equal Chance to receive his Proportion of Alms from every charitable Hand; because the Inhabitants, one or other, walk through every Street in Town, and give their Alms, without considering the Place, wherever they think it may be well disposed of: And, these Helps, added to what they get in Eatables by going from House to House, among the Gentry and Citizens, will, without being very burthensome, be sufficient to keep them alive.

IT is true, the Poor of the Suburb Parishes will not have altogether the same Advantage, because they are not equally in the Road of Business and Passengers: But here it is to be considered, that the Beggars there have not so good a Title to Publick Charity, because most of them are Strollers from the Country, and compose a principal Part of that great Nuisance, which we ought to remove.

I SHOULD be apt to think, that few Things can be more irksome to a City-Minister, than a Number of Beggars which do not belong to his District, whom he hath no Obligation to take Care of, who are no Part of his Flock, and who take the Bread out of the Mouths of those, to whom it properly belongs. When I mention this Abuse to any Minister of a City-Parish, he usually lays the Fault upon the Beadles, who he says are bribed by the Foreign Beggars; and as those Beadles often keep Ale-Houses, they find their Account in such Customers. This Evil might easily be remedyed, if the Parishes would make some small Addition to the Salaries of a Beadle, and be more careful in the Choice of those Officers. But, I conceive there is one effectual Method, in the Power of every Minister to put in Practice; I mean, by making it the Interest of all his own original Poor, to drive out Intruders: For, if the Parish-Beggars were absolutely forbidden by the Minister and Church-Officers, to suffer Strollers to come into the Parish, upon Pain of themselves being not permitted to beg Alms at the Church-Doors, or at the Houses and Shops of the Inhabitants; they would prevent Interlopers more effectually than twenty Beadles.

AND, here I cannot but take Notice of the great Indiscretion in our City-Shopkeepers, who suffer their Doors to be daily besieged by Crowds of Beggars, (as the Gates of a Lord are by Duns,) to the great Disgust and Vexation of many Customers, whom I have frequently observed to go to other Shops, rather than suffer such a Persecution; which might easily be avoided, if no Foreign Beggars were allowed to infest them.

WHEREFORE, I do assert, that the Shopkeepers who are the greatest Complainers of this Grievance, (lamenting that for every Customer, they are worried by fifty Beggars,) do very well deserve what they suffer, when a 'Prentice with a Horse-Whip is able to lash every Beggar from the Shop, who is not of the Parish, and doth not wear the Badge of that Parish on his Shoulder, well fastned and fairly visible; and if this Practice were universal in every House, to all the sturdy Vagrants, we should in a few Weeks clear the Town of all Mendicants, except those who have a proper Title to our Charity: As for the Aged and Infirm, it would be sufficient to give them nothing, and then they must starve or follow their Brethren.

IT was the City that first endowed this Hospital, and those who afterwards contributed, as they were such who generally inhabited here; so they intended what they gave to be for the Use of the City's Poor. The Revenues which have since been raised by Parliament, are wholly paid by the City, without the least Charge upon any other Part of the Kingdom; and therefore nothing could more defeat the original Design, than to misapply those Revenues on strolling Beggars, or Bastards from the Country, which bears no Share in the Charges we are at.

IF some of the Out-Parishes be over-burthened with Poor, the Reason must be, that the greatest Part of those Poor are Strollers from the Country, who nestle themselves where they can find the cheapest Lodgings, and from thence infest every Part of the Town, out of which they ought to be whipped as a most insufferable Nuisance, being nothing else but a profligate Clan of Thieves, Drunkards, Heathens, and Whoremongers, fitter to be rooted out off the Face of the Earth,[5] than suffered to levy a vast annual Tax upon the City, which shares too deep in the publick Miseries brought on us by the Oppressions we lye under from our Neighbours, our Brethren, our Countrymen, our Fellow Protestants, and Fellow Subjects.

SOME Time ago I was appointed one of a Committee to inquire into the State of the Workhouse; where we found that a Charity was bestowed by a great Person for a certain Time, which in its Consequences operated very much to the Detriment of the House: For, when the Time was elapsed, all those who were supported by that Charity, continued on the same Foot with the rest of the Foundation; and being generally a Pack of profligate vagabond Wretches from several Parts of the Kingdom, corrupted all the rest; so partial, or treacherous, or interested, or ignorant, or mistaken, are generally all Recommenders, not only to Employments, but even to Charity it self.

I KNOW it is complained, that the Difficulty of driving Foreign Beggars out of the City is charged upon the *Bellowers* (as they are called) who find their Accounts best in suffering those Vagrants to follow their Trade through every Part of the Town. But, this Abuse might easily be remedyed and very much to the Advantage of the whole City, if better Salaries were given to those who execute that Office in the several Parishes, and would make it their Interest to clear the Town of those Caterpillars, rather than hazard the Loss of an Employment that would give them an honest Livelyhood. But, if that should fail, yet a general Resolution of never giving

Charity to a Street Beggar out of his own Parish, or without a visible Badge, would infallibly force all Vagrants to depart.

THERE is generally a Vagabond Spirit in Beggars, which ought to be discouraged and severely punished. It is owing to the same Causes that drove them into Poverty; I mean, Idleness, Drunkenness, and rash Marriages without the least Prospect of supporting a Family by honest Endeavours; which never came into their Thoughts. It is observed, that hardly one Beggar in twenty looks upon himself to be relieved by receiving Bread or other Food; and they have in this Town been frequently seen to pour out of their Pitcher good Broth that hath been given them, into the Kennel;[6] neither do they much regard Cloaths, unless to sell them; for, their Rags are Part of their Tools with which they work: They want only Ale, Brandy, and other strong Liquors, which cannot be had without Money; and Money, as they conceive, always abounds in the Metropolis.

I HAD some other Thoughts to offer upon this Subject. But, as I am a Desponder in my Nature, and have tolerably well discovered the Disposition of our People, who never will move a Step towards easing themselves from any one single Grievance; it will be thought, that I have already said too much, and to little or no Purpose; which hath often been the Fate, or Fortune of the Writer.

J. SWIFT.

April 22,
1737.

VI

GULLIVER'S TRAVELS

VOLUME III.

Of the AUTHOR's

WORKS.

CONTAINING,

TRAVELS

INTO SEVERAL

Remote Nations of the WORLD.

In Four PARTS, *viz.*

I. A Voyage to LIL-
LIPUT.

II. A Voyage to BROB-
DINGNAG.

III. A Voyage to LA-

PUTA, BALNIBARBI.
LUGGNAGG, GLUBB-
DUBDRIB and JAPAN.

IV. A Voyage to the
COUNTRY of the
HOUYHNHNMS.

By *LEMUEL GULLIVER*, first a Surgeon,
and then a CAPTAIN of several SHIPS.

——— ——— *Retroq;*
Vulgus abhorret ab his.

In this Impression several Errors in the *London* and *Dublin*
Editions are corrected.

DUBLIN:

Printed by and for GEORGE FAULKNER, Printer
and Bookseller, in *Essex-Street,* opposite to the
Bridge. MDCCXXXV.

CAPT: LEMUEL GULLIVER
Splendide Mendax Hor.

ADVERTISEMENT

Mr. Sympson's *Letter to Captain* Gulliver,[1] *prefixed to this Volume, will make a long Advertisement unnecessary. Those Interpolations*[2] *complained of by the Captain, were made by a Person since deceased, on whose Judgment the Publisher relyed to make any Alterations that might be thought necessary. But, this Person, not rightly comprehending the Scheme of the Author, nor able to imitate his plain simple Style, thought fit among many other Alterations and Insertions, to compliment the Memory of her late Majesty, by saying,* That she governed without a Chief Minister. *We are assured, that the Copy sent to the Bookseller in* London, *was a Transcript of the Original, which Original being in the Possession of a very worthy Gentleman in* London, *and a most intimate Friend of the Authors; after he had bought the Book in Sheets, and compared it with the Originals, bound it up with blank Leaves, and made those Corrections, which the Reader will find in our Edition. For, the same Gentleman did us the Favour to let us transcribe his Corrections.*

A Letter from Capt. Gulliver, to his Cousin Sympson[3]

I hope you will be ready to own publickly, whenever you shall be called to it, that by your great and frequent Urgency you prevailed on me to publish a very loose and uncorrect Account of my Travels; with Direction to hire some young Gentlemen of either University to put them in Order, and correct the Style, as my Cousin *Dampier*[4] did by my Advice, in his Book called, *A Voyage round the World*. But I do not remember I gave you Power to consent, that any thing should be omitted, and much less that any thing should be inserted: Therefore, as to the latter, I do here renounce every thing of that Kind; particularly a Paragraph about her Majesty the late Queen *Anne*, of most pious and glorious Memory; although I did reverence and esteem her more than any of human Species. But you, or your Interpolator, ought to have considered, that as it was not my Inclination, so was it not decent to praise any Animal of our Composition before my Master *Houyhnhnm:* And besides, the Fact was altogether false; for to my Knowledge, being in *England* during some Part of her Majesty's Reign, she did govern by a chief Minister; nay, even by two successively; the first whereof was the Lord of *Godolphin,* and the second the Lord of *Oxford;*[5] so that you have made me *say the thing that was not.* Likewise, in the Account of the Academy of Projectors, and several Passages of my Discourse to my Master *Houyhnhnm,* you have either omitted some material Circumstances, or minced or changed them in such a Manner, that I do hardly know mine own Work. When I formerly hinted to you something of this in a Letter, you were pleased to answer, that you were afraid of giving Offence; that People in Power were very watchful over the

Press; and apt not only to interpret, but to punish every thing which looked like an *Inuendo* (as I think you called it.) But pray, how could that which I spoke so many Years ago, and at above five Thousand Leagues distance, in another Reign, be applyed to any of the *Yahoos,* who now are said to govern the Herd; especially, at a time when I little thought on or feared the Unhappiness of living under them. Have not I the most Reason to complain, when I see these very *Yahoos* carried by *Houyhnhnms* in a Vehicle, as if these were Brutes, and those the rational Creatures? And, indeed, to avoid so monstrous and detestable a Sight, was one principal Motive of my Retirement hither.

THUS much I thought proper to tell you in Relation to your self, and to the Trust I reposed in you.

I DO in the next Place complain of my own great Want of Judgment, in being prevailed upon by the Intreaties and false Reasonings of you and some others, very much against mine own Opinion, to suffer my Travels to be published. Pray bring to your Mind how often I desired you to consider, when you insisted on the Motive of *publick Good;* that the *Yahoos* were a Species of Animals utterly incapable of Amendment by Precepts or Examples: And so it hath proved; for instead of seeing a full Stop put to all Abuses and Corruptions, at least in this little Island, as I had Reason to expect: Behold, after above six Months Warning, I cannot learn that my Book hath produced one single Effect according to mine Intentions: I desired you would let me know by a Letter, when Party and Faction were extinguished; Judges learned and upright; Pleaders honest and modest, with some Tincture of common Sense; and *Smithfield*[6] blazing with Pyramids of Law-Books; the young Nobility's Education entirely changed; the Physicians banished; the Female *Yahoos* abounding in Virtue, Honour, Truth and good Sense: Courts and Levees of great Ministers thoroughly weeded and swept; Wit, Merit and Learning rewarded; all Disgracers of the Press in Prose and Verse, condemned to eat nothing but their own Cotten,[7] and quench their Thirst with their own Ink. These, and a Thousand other Reformations, I firmly counted upon by your Encouragement; as indeed they were plainly deducible from the Precepts delivered in my Book. And, it must be owned, that seven Months were a sufficient Time to correct every Vice and Folly to which *Yahoos* are subject; if their Natures had been capable of the least Disposition to Virtue or Wisdom: Yet so far have you been from answering mine Expectation in any of your Letters; that on the contrary, you are loading our Carrier every Week with Libels, and Keys,[8] and Reflections, and Memoirs, and Second Parts; wherein I see myself accused of reflecting upon great States-Folk; of degrading human Nature, (for so they have still the Confidence to stile it) and of abusing the Female Sex. I find likewise, that the Writers of those Bundles are not agreed among themselves; for some of them will not allow me to be Author of mine own Travels; and others make me Author of Books to which I am wholly a Stranger.

I FIND likewise, that your Printer hath been so careless as to confound the Times, and mistake the Dates of my several Voyages and Returns; neither assigning the true Year, or the true Month, or Day of the Month: And I hear the original Manuscript is all destroyed, since the Publication of my Book. Neither have I any Copy left; however, I have sent you some Corrections, which you may insert, if ever there should be a second Edition: And yet I cannot stand to them, but shall leave that Matter to my judicious and candid Readers, to adjust it as they please.

I HEAR some of our Sea-*Yahoos* find Fault with my Sea-Language, as not proper in many Parts, nor now in Use. I cannot help it. In my first Voyages, while I was young, I was instructed by the oldest Mariners, and learned to speak as they did. But I have since found that the Sea-*Yahoos* are apt, like the Land ones, to become new fangled in their Words; which the latter change every Year; insomuch, as I remember upon each Return to mine own Country, their old Dialect was so altered, that I could hardly understand the new. And I observe, when any *Yahoo* comes from *London* out of Curiosity to visit me at mine own House, we neither of us are able to deliver our Conceptions in a Manner intelligible to the other.

If the Censure of *Yahoos* could any Way affect me, I should have great Reason to complain, that some of them are so bold as to think my Book of Travels a meer Fiction out of mine own Brain; and have gone so far as to drop Hints, that the *Houyhnhnms* and *Yahoos* have no more Existence than the Inhabitants of *Utopia*.⁹

INDEED I must confess, that as to the People of *Lilliput*, *Brobdingrag*, (for so the Word should have been spelt, and not erroneously *Brobdingnag*) and *Laputa*; I have never yet heard of any *Yahoo* so presumptuous as to dispute their Being, or the Facts I have related concerning them; because the Truth immediately strikes every Reader with Conviction. And, is there less Probability in my Account of the *Houyhnhnms* or *Yahoos*, when it is manifest as to the latter, there are so many Thousands in this City, who only differ from their Brother Brutes in *Houyhnhnmland*, because they use a Sort of *Jabber*, and do not go naked. I wrote for their Amendment, and not their Approbation. The united Praise of the whole Race would be of less Consequence to me, than the neighing of those two degenerate *Houyhnhnms* I keep in my Stable; because, from these, degenerate as they are, I still improve in some Virtues, without any Mixture of Vice.

Do these miserable Animals presume to think that I am so far degenerated as to defend my Veracity; *Yahoo* as I am, it is well known through all *Houyhnhnmland,* that by the Instructions and Example of my illustrious Master, I was able in the Compass of two Years (although I confess with the utmost Difficulty) to remove that infernal Habit of Lying, Shuffling, Deceiving, and Equivocating, so deeply rooted in the very Souls of all my Species; especially the *Europeans.*

I HAVE other Complaints to make upon this vexatious Occasion; but I forbear troubling myself or you any further. I must freely confess, that since my last Return, some corruptions of my *Yahoo* Nature have revived in me by Conversing with a few of your Species, and particularly those of mine own Family, by an unavoidable Necessity; else I should never have attempted so absurd a Project as that of reforming the *Yahoo* Race in this Kingdom; but, I have now done with all such visionary Schemes for ever.

April 2, 1727.

THE PUBLISHER *TO THE* READER

THE AUTHOR of these Travels, Mr. *Lemuel Gulliver,* is my antient and intimate Friend; there is likewise some Relation between us by the Mother's
Side. About three Years ago Mr. *Gulliver* growing weary of the Concourse
of curious People coming to him at his House in *Redriff,*[10] made a small
Purchase of Land, with a convenient House, near *Newark,* in *Nottinghamshire,* his native Country; where he now lives retired, yet in good Esteem among his Neighbours.

ALTHOUGH Mr. *Gulliver* was born in *Nottinghamshire,* where his Father
dwelt, yet I have heard him say, his Family came from *Oxfordshire;* to confirm which, I have observed in the Church-Yard at *Banbury,*[11] in that
County, several Tombs and Monuments of the *Gullivers.*

BEFORE he quitted *Redriff,* he left the Custody of the following Papers
in my Hands, with the Liberty to dispose of them as I should think fit. I
have carefully perused them three Times: The Style is very plain and
simple; and the only Fault I find is, that the Author, after the Manner of
Travellers, is a little too circumstantial. There is an Air of Truth apparent
through the whole; and indeed the Author was so distinguished for his Veracity, that it became a Sort of Proverb among his Neighbours at *Redriff,*
when any one affirmed a Thing, to say, it was as true as if Mr. *Gulliver* had
spoke it.

BY the Advice of several worthy Persons, to whom, with the Author's
Permission, I communicated these Papers, I now venture to send them
into the World; hoping they may be, at least for some time, a better Entertainment to our young Noblemen, than the common Scribbles of Politicks
and Party.

THIS Volume would have been at least twice as large, if I had not made bold to strike out innumerable Passages relating to the Winds and Tides, as well as to the Variations and Bearings in the several Voyages; together with the minute Descriptions of the Management of the Ship in Storms, in the Style of Sailors: Likewise the Account of the Longitudes and Latitudes; wherein I have Reason to apprehend that Mr. *Gulliver* may be a little dissatisfied: But I was resolved to fit the Work as much as possible to the general Capacity of Readers. However, if my own Ignorance in Sea-Affairs shall have led me to commit some Mistakes, I alone am answerable for them: And if any Traveller hath a Curiosity to see the whole Work at large, as it came from the Hand of the Author, I will be ready to gratify him.

As for any further Particulars relating to the Author, the Reader will receive Satisfaction from the first Pages of the Book.

RICHARD SYMPSON.

The Contents

PART I

CHAPTER I.

The Author giveth some Account of himself and Family; his first Inducements to travel. He is shipwrecked, and swims for his Life; gets safe on shoar in the Country of Lilliput; *is made a Prisoner, and carried up the Country.*

Page 385

CHAPTER II.

The Emperor of Lilliput, *attended by several of the Nobility, comes to see the Author in his Confinement. The Emperor's Person and Habit described. Learned Men appointed to teach the Author their Language. He gains Favour by his mild Disposition. His Pockets are searched, and his Sword and Pistols taken from him.*

Page 393

CHAPTER III.

The Author diverts the Emperor and his Nobility of both Sexes, in a very uncommon Manner. The Diversions of the Court of Lilliput *described. The Author hath his Liberty granted him upon certain Conditions.*

Page 401

CHAPTER IV.

Mildendo, the Metropolis of Lilliput, *described, together with the Emperor's Palace. A Conversation between the Author and a principal Secretary, concerning the Affairs of that Empire: The Author's Offers to serve the Emperor in his Wars.*

Page 408

CHAPTER V.

The Author *by an extraordinary Stratagem prevents an Invasion. A high Title of Honour is conferred upon him. Ambassadors arrive from the Emperor of* Blefuscu, *and sue for Peace. The Empress's Apartment on fire by an Accident; the* Author *instrumental in saving the rest of the Palace.*

Page 412

CHAPTER VI.

Of the Inhabitants of Lilliput; *their Learning, Laws, and Customs. The Manner of Educating their Children. The Author's Way of living in that Country. His Vindication of a great Lady.*

Page 418

CHAPTER VII.

The Author being informed of a Design to accuse him of High Treason, makes his Escape to Blefuscu. *His Reception there.*

Page 426

CHAPTER VIII.

The Author, by a lucky Accident, finds Means to leave Blefuscu; *and after some Difficulties, returns safe to his Native Country.*

Page 433

PART II

CHAPTER I.

A great Storm described. The long Boat sent to fetch Water, the Author goes with it to discover the Country. He is left on Shoar, is seized by one of the Natives, and carried to a Farmer's House. His Reception there, with several Accidents that happened there. A Description of the Inhabitants.

Page 441

CHAPTER II.

A Description of the Farmer's Daughter. The Author carried to a Market-Town, and then to the Metropolis. The Particulars of his Journey.

Page 451

CHAPTER III.

The Author sent for to Court. The Queen buys him of his Master the Farmer, and presents him to the King. He disputes with his Majesty's great Scholars. An Apartment at Court provided for the Author. He is in high Favour with the Queen. He stands up for the Honour of his own Country. His Quarrels with the Queen's Dwarf.

Page 456

CHAPTER IV.

The Country described. A Proposal for correcting modern Maps. The King's Palace, and some Account of the Metropolis. The Author's Way of travelling. The chief Temple described.

Page 464

CHAPTER V.

Several Adventures that happened to the Author. The Execution of a Criminal. The Author shews his Skill in Navigation.

Page 468

CHAPTER VI.

Several Contrivances of the Author to please the King and Queen. He shews his Skill in Musick. The King enquires into the State of Europe, which the Author relates to him. The King's Observations thereon.

Page 476

CHAPTER VII.

The Author's Love of his Country. He makes a Proposal of much Advantage to the King; which is rejected. The King's great Ignorance of Politicks. The Learning of that Country very imperfect and confined. Their Laws, and military Affairs, and Parties in the State.

Page 483

CHAPTER VIII.

The King and Queen make a Progress to the Frontiers. The Author attends them. The Manner in which he leaves the Country very particularly related. He returns to England.

Page 489

PART III

CHAPTER I.

The Author sets out on his Third Voyage. Is taken by Pyrates. The Malice of a Dutchman. His Arrival at an Island. He is received into Laputa.

Page 501

CHAPTER II.

The Humours and Dispositions of the Laputians described. An Account of their Learning. Of the King and his Court. The Author's Reception there. The Inhabitants subject to Fears and Disquietudes. An Account of the Women.

Page 506

CHAPTER III.

A Phænomenon solved by modern Philosophy and Astronomy. The Laputians *great Improvements in the latter. The King's Method of suppressing Insurrections.*

Page 513

CHAPTER IV.

The Author leaves Laputa, *is conveyed to* Balnibarbi, *arrives at the Metropolis. A Description of the Metropolis and the Country adjoining. The Author hospitably received by a great Lord. His Conversation with that Lord.*

Page 519

CHAPTER V.

The Author permitted to see the grand Academy of Lagado. *The Academy largely described. The Arts wherein the Professors employ themselves.*

Page 524

CHAPTER VI.

A further Account of the Academy. The Author proposeth some Improvements, which are honourably received.

Page 531

CHAPTER VII.

The Author leaves Lagado, *arrives at* Maldonada. *No Ship ready. He takes a short Voyage to* Glubbdubdrib. *His Reception by the Governor.*

Page 536

CHAPTER VIII.

A further Account of Glubbdubdrib. *Antient and Modern History corrected.*

Page 540

CHAPTER IX.

The Author's Return to Maldonada. *Sails to the Kingdom of* Luggnagg. *The Author confined. He is sent for to Court. The Manner of his Admittance. The King's great Lenity to his Subjects.*

Page 545

CHAPTER X.

The Luggnuggians *commended. A particular Description of the* Struldbrugs, *with many Conversations between the Author and some eminent Persons upon that Subject.*

Page 548

CHAPTER XI.

The Author leaves Luggnagg *and sails to* Japan. *From thence he returns in a* Dutch *Ship to* Amsterdam, *and from* Amsterdam *to* England.

Page 555

PART IV

CHAPTER I.

The Author sets out as Captain of a Ship. His Men conspire against him, confine him a long Time to his Cabbin, set him on Shore in an unknown Land. He travels up into the Country. The Yahoos, *a strange Sort of Animal, described. The Author meets two* Houyhnhnms.

Page 561

CHAPTER II.

The Author conducted by a Houyhnhnm *to his House. The House described. The Author's Reception. The Food of the* Houyhnhnms. *The Author in Distress for Want of Meat, is at last relieved. His Manner of feeding in that Country.*

Page 567

CHAPTER III.

The Author studious to learn the Language, the Houyhnhnm *his Master assists in teaching him. The Language described. Several* Houyhnhnms *of Quality come out of Curiosity to see the Author. He gives his Master a short Account of his Voyage.*

Page 572

CHAPTER IV.

The Houyhnhnms *Notion of Truth and Falshood. The Author's Discourse disapproved by his Master. The Author gives a more particular Account of himself, and the Accidents of his Voyage.*

Page 577

CHAPTER V.

The Author at his Master's Commands informs him of the State of England. *The Causes of War among the Princes of* Europe. *The Author begins to explain the* English *Constitution.*

Page 582

CHAPTER VI.

A Continuation of the State of England, *under Queen* Anne. *The Character of a first Minister in the Courts of* Europe.

Page 588

CHAPTER VII.

The Author's great Love of his Native Country. His Master's Observations upon the Constitution and Administration of England, *as described by the Author, with parallel Cases and Comparisons. His Master's Observations upon human Nature.*

Page 594

CHAPTER VIII.

The Author relateth several Particulars of the Yahoos. *The great Virtues of the* Houyhnhnms. *The Education and Exercise of their Youth. Their general Assembly.*

Page 600

CHAPTER IX.

A grand Debate at the General Assembly of the Houyhnhnms; *and how it was determined. The Learning of the* Houyhnhnms. *Their Buildings. Their Manner of Burials. The Defectiveness of their Language.*

Page 605

CHAPTER X.

The Author's Oeconomy and happy Life among the Houyhnhnms. *His great Improvement in Virtue, by conversing with them. Their Conversations. The Author hath Notice given him by his Master that he must depart from the Country. He falls into a Swoon for Grief, but submits. He contrives and finishes a Canoo, by the Help of a Fellow-Servant, and puts to Sea at a Venture.*

Page 610

CHAPTER XI.

The Author's dangerous Voyage. He arrives at New-Holland, *hoping to settle there. Is wounded with an Arrow by one of the Natives. Is seized and carried by Force into a* Portugueze *Ship. The great Civilities of the Captain. The Author arrives at* Europe.

Page 616

CHAPTER XII.

The Author's Veracity. His Design in publishing this Work. His Censure of those Travellers who swerve from the Truth. The Author clears himself from any sinister Ends in writing. An Objection answered. The Method of planting Colonies. His Native Country commended. The Right of the Crown to those Countries described by the Author is justified. The Difficulty of conquering them. The Author takes his last Leave of the Reader; proposeth his Manner of Living for the future, gives good Advice, and concludes.

Page 623

PART I

A VOYAGE TO LILLIPUT

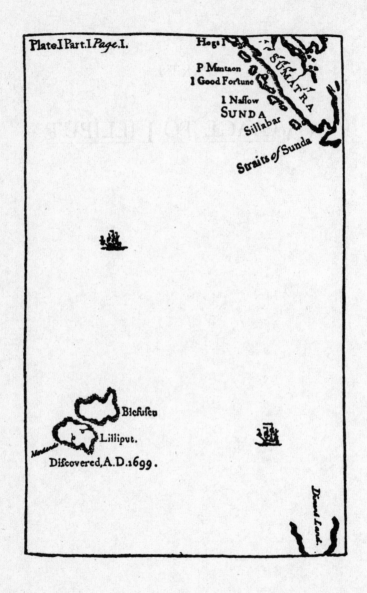

Plate I Part.I *Page.I.*

Hog I

P Mintaon
I Good Fortune

I Naſſow
SUNDA
Sillabar

SUMATRA

Straits *of* Sunda

Blefuſcu

Mildendo Lilliput.

Diſcovered, A.D. 1699.

Dwarf Land

CHAPTER I

The Author giveth some Account of himself and Family; his first Inducements to travel. He is shipwrecked, and swims for his Life; gets safe on shoar in the Country of Lilliput; *is made a Prisoner, and carried up the Country.*

My Father had a small Estate in *Nottinghamshire;* I was the Third of five Sons. He sent me to *Emanuel-College* in *Cambridge,* at Fourteen Years old,[1] where I resided three Years, and applied my self close to my Studies: But the Charge of maintaining me (although I had a very scanty Allowance) being too great for a narrow Fortune; I was bound Apprentice to Mr. *James Bates,* an eminent Surgeon in *London,* with whom I continued four Years; and my Father now and then sending me small Sums of Money, I laid them out in learning Navigation, and other Parts of the Mathematicks, useful to those who intend to travel, as I always believed it would be some time or other my Fortune to do. When I left Mr. *Bates,* I went down to my Father; where, by the Assistance of him and my Uncle *John,* and some other Relations, I got Forty Pounds, and a Promise of Thirty Pounds a Year to maintain me at *Leyden:*[2] There I studied Physick two Years and seven Months, knowing it would be useful in long Voyages.

SOON after my Return from *Leyden,* I was recommended by my good Master Mr. *Bates,* to be Surgeon to the *Swallow,* Captain *Abraham Pannell* Commander; with whom I continued three Years and a half, making a Voyage or two into the *Levant,*[3] and some other Parts. When I came back, I resolved to settle in *London,* to which Mr. *Bates,* my Master, encouraged me; and by him I was recommended to several Patients. I took Part of a small House in the *Old Jury;* and being advised to alter my Condition, I married Mrs.[4] *Mary Burton,* second Daughter to Mr. *Edmond Burton,* Hosier, in *Newgate-Street,* with whom I received four Hundred Pounds for a Portion.[5]

BUT, my good Master *Bates* dying in two Years after, and I having few

Friends, my Business began to fail; for my Conscience would not suffer me to imitate the bad Practice of too many among my Brethren. Having therefore consulted with my Wife, and some of my Acquaintance, I determined to go again to Sea. I was Surgeon successively in two Ships, and made several Voyages, for six Years, to the *East* and *West-Indies;* by which I got some Addition to my Fortune. My Hours of Leisure I spent in reading the best Authors, ancient and modern; being always provided with a good Number of Books; and when I was ashore, in observing the Manners and Dispositions of the People, as well as learning their Language; wherein I had a great Facility by the Strength of my Memory.

THE last of these Voyages not proving very fortunate, I grew weary of the Sea, and intended to stay at home with my Wife and Family. I removed from the *Old Jury* to *Fetter-Lane,* and from thence to *Wapping,* hoping to get Business among the Sailors; but it would not turn to account. After three Years Expectation that things would mend, I accepted an advantageous Offer from Captain *William Prichard,* Master of the *Antelope,* who was making a Voyage to the *South-Sea.* We set sail from *Bristol, May* 4th, 1699, and our Voyage at first was very prosperous.

IT would not be proper for some Reasons, to trouble the Reader with the Particulars of our Adventures in those Seas: Let it suffice to inform him, that in our Passage from thence to the *East-Indies,* we were driven by a violent Storm to the Northwest of *Van Diemen's* Land.[6] By an Observation, we found ourselves in the Latitude of 30 Degrees 2 Minutes South. Twelve of our Crew were dead by immoderate Labour, and ill Food; the rest were in a very weak Condition. On the fifth of *November,* which was the beginning of Summer in those Parts, the Weather being very hazy, the Seamen spyed a Rock, within half a Cable's length[7] of the Ship; but the Wind was so strong, that we were driven directly upon it, and immediately split. Six of the Crew, of whom I was one, having let down the Boat into the Sea, made a Shift to get clear of the Ship, and the Rock. We rowed by my Computation, about three Leagues, till we were able to work no longer, being already spent with Labour while we were in the Ship. We therefore trusted ourselves to the Mercy of the Waves; and in about half an Hour the Boat was overset by a sudden Flurry from the North. What became of my Companions in the Boat, as well as of those who escaped on the Rock, or were left in the Vessel, I cannot tell; but conclude they were all lost. For my own Part, I swam as Fortune directed me, and was pushed forward by Wind and Tide. I often let my Legs drop, and could feel no Bottom: But when I was almost gone, and able to struggle no longer, I found myself within my Depth; and by this Time the Storm was much abated. The Declivity was so small, that I walked near a Mile before I got to the Shore, which I conjectured was about Eight o'Clock in the Evening. I then advanced forward near half a Mile, but could not discover any Sign of Houses or Inhabitants; at least I was in so weak a Condition, that I did not observe them. I was extremely tired, and with that, and the Heat of the Weather, and about half a Pint of Brandy that I drank as I left the Ship, I found my self much inclined to sleep. I lay down on the Grass, which was very short and soft; where I slept sounder than ever I remember to have done in my Life, and as I reckoned, above Nine Hours; for when I awaked, it was just Day-light. I attempted to rise, but was not able to stir: For as I happened to lie on my Back, I found my Arms and Legs were strongly fastened on each Side to the Ground; and my Hair, which was long and thick, tied down in the same Manner. I likewise felt several slender Ligatures across my Body, from my Armpits to my Thighs. I could only look upwards; the Sun began to grow hot, and the Light offended mine Eyes. I heard a confused Noise about me, but in the Posture I lay, could see nothing except the Sky. In a little time I felt something alive moving on my left Leg, which advancing gently forward over my Breast, came almost up to my Chin; when bending mine Eyes downwards as much as I could, I perceived it to be a human Creature not six Inches high, with a Bow and Arrow in his Hands, and a Quiver at his Back. In the mean time, I felt at least Forty more of the same Kind (as I conjectured) following the first. I was in the utmost Astonishment, and roared so loud, that they all ran back in a Fright; and some of them, as I was afterwards told, were hurt with the Falls they got by leaping from my Sides upon the Ground. However, they soon returned; and one of them, who ventured so far as to get a full Sight of my Face, lifting up his Hands and Eyes by way of Admiration, cryed out in a shrill, but distinct Voice, *Hekinah Degul:* The others repeated the same Words several times, but I then knew not what they meant. I lay all this while, as the Reader may believe, in great Uneasiness: At length, struggling to get loose, I had the Fortune to break the Strings, and wrench out the Pegs that fastened my left Arm to the Ground; for, by lifting it up to my Face, I discovered the Methods they had taken to bind me; and, at the same time, with a violent Pull, which gave me excessive Pain, I a little loosened the Strings that tied down my Hair on the left Side; so that I was just able to turn my Head about two Inches. But the Creatures ran off a second time, before I could seize them; whereupon there was a great Shout in a very shrill Accent; and after it ceased, I heard one of them cry aloud, *Tolgo Phonac;* when in an Instant I felt above an Hundred Arrows discharged on my left Hand, which pricked me like so many Needles; and besides, they shot another Flight into the Air, as we do Bombs in *Europe;* whereof many, I suppose, fell on my Body, (though I felt them not) and some on my Face, which I immediately covered with my left Hand. When this Shower of Arrows was over, I fell a groaning with Grief and Pain; and then striving again to get loose, they discharged another Volly larger than the first; and some of them attempted with Spears to stick me in the Sides; but, by good Luck, I had on me a Buff Jerkin,[8] which they could not pierce. I thought it the most prudent Method to lie still; and my Design was to continue so till Night, when my left Hand being already loose, I could easily free myself: And as for the Inhabitants, I had Reason to believe I might be a Match for the greatest Armies they could bring against me, if they were all of the same Size with him that I saw. But Fortune disposed otherwise of me. When the People observed I was quiet, they discharged no more Arrows: But by the Noise increasing, I knew their Numbers were greater; and about four Yards from me, over-against my right Ear, I heard a Knocking for above an Hour, like People at work; when turning my Head that Way, as well as the Pegs and Strings would permit me, I saw a Stage erected about a Foot and a half from the Ground, capable of holding four of the Inhabitants, with two or three Ladders to mount it: From whence one of them, who seemed to be a Person of Quality, made me a long Speech, whereof I understood not one Syllable. But I should have mentioned, that before the principal Person began his Oration, he cryed out three times *Langro Dehul san:* (these Words and the former were afterwards repeated and explained to me.) Where-upon immediately about fifty of the Inhabitants came, and cut the Strings that fastened the left side of my Head, which gave me the Liberty of turning it to the right, and of observing the Person and Gesture of him who was to speak. He appeared to be of a middle Age, and taller than any of the other three who attended him; whereof one was a Page, who held up his Train, and seemed to be somewhat longer than my middle Finger; the other two stood one on each side to support him. He acted every part of an Orator; and I could observe many Periods of Threatnings, and others of Promises, Pity, and Kindness. I answered in a few Words, but in the most submissive Manner, lifting up my left Hand and both mine Eyes to the Sun, as calling him for a Witness; and being almost famished with Hunger, having not eaten a Morsel for some Hours before I left the Ship, I found the Demands of Nature so strong upon me, that I could not for-bear shewing my Impatience (perhaps against the strict Rules of De-cency) by putting my Finger frequently on my Mouth, to signify that I wanted Food. The *Hurgo* (for so they call a great Lord, as I afterwards learnt) understood me very well: He descended from the Stage, and commanded that several Ladders should be applied to my Sides, on which above an hundred of the Inhabitants mounted, and walked towards my Mouth, laden with Baskets full of Meat, which had been provided, and sent thither by the King's Orders upon the first Intelligence he received of me. I observed there was the Flesh of several Animals, but could not distinguish them by the Taste. There were Shoulders, Legs, and Loins shaped like those of Mutton, and very well dressed, but smaller than the Wings of a Lark. I eat them by two or three at a Mouthful; and took three Loaves at a time, about the bigness of Musket Bullets. They supplyed me as fast as they could, shewing a thousand Marks of Wonder and Astonishment at my Bulk and Appetite. I then made another Sign that I wanted Drink. They found by my eating that a small Quantity would not suffice me; and being a most ingenious People, they slung up with great Dexterity one of their largest Hogsheads;[9] then rolled it towards my Hand, and beat out the Top; I drank it off at a Draught, which I might well do, for it hardly held half a Pint, and tasted like a small Wine of *Burgundy,* but much more delicious. They brought me a second Hogshead, which I drank in the same Manner, and made Signs for more, but they had none to give me. When I had performed these Wonders, they shouted for Joy, and danced upon my Breast, repeating several times as they did at first, *Hekinah Degul.* They made me a Sign that I should throw down the two Hogsheads, but first warned the People below to stand out of the Way, crying aloud, *Borach Mivola;* and when they saw the Vessels in the Air, there was an universal Shout of *Hekinah Degul.* I confess I was often tempted, while they were passing backwards and forwards on my Body, to seize Forty or Fifty of the first that came in my Reach, and dash them against the Ground. But the Remembrance of what I had felt, which probably might not be the worst they could do; and the Promise of Honour I made them, for so I interpreted my submissive Behaviour, soon drove out those Imaginations. Besides, I now considered my self as bound by the Laws of Hospitality to a People who had treated me with so much Expence and Magnificence. However, in my Thoughts I could not sufficiently wonder at the Intrepidity of these diminutive Mortals, who durst venture to mount and walk on my Body, while one of my Hands was at Liberty, without trembling at the very Sight of so prodigious a Creature as I must appear to them. After some time, when they observed that I made no more Demands for Meat, there appeared before me a Person of high Rank from his Imperial Majesty. His Excellency having mounted on the Small of my Right Leg, advanced forwards up to my Face, with about a Dozen of his Retinue; And producing his Credentials under the Signet Royal, which he applied close to mine Eyes, spoke about ten Minutes, without any Signs of Anger, but with a kind of determinate Resolution; often pointing forwards, which, as I afterwards found was towards the Capital City, about half a Mile distant, whither it was agreed by his Majesty in Council that I must be conveyed. I answered in few Words, but to no Purpose, and made a Sign with my Hand that was loose, putting it to the other, (but over his Excellency's Head, for Fear of hurting him or his Train) and then to my own Head and Body, to signify that I desired my Liberty. It appeared that he understood me well enough; for he shook his Head by way of Disapprobation, and held his Hand in a Posture to shew that I must be carried as a Prisoner. However, he made other Signs to let me understand that I should have Meat and Drink enough, and very good Treatment. Whereupon I once more thought of attempting to break my Bonds; but again, when I felt the Smart of their Arrows upon my Face and Hands, which were all in Blisters, and many of the Darts still sticking in them; and observing likewise that the Number of my Enemies encreased; I gave Tokens to let them know that they might do with me what they pleased. Upon this, the *Hurgo* and his Train withdrew, with much Civility and chearful Countenances. Soon after I heard a general Shout, with frequent Repetitions of the Words, *Peplom Selan,* and I felt great Numbers of the People on my Left Side relaxing the Cords to such a Degree, that I was able to turn upon my Right, and to ease my self with making Water; which I very plentifully did, to the great Astonishment of the People, who conjecturing by my Motions what I was going to do, immediately opened to the right and left on that Side, to avoid the Torrent which fell with such Noise and Violence from me. But before this, they had dawbed my Face and both my Hands with a sort of Ointment very pleasant to the Smell, which in a few Minutes removed all the Smart of their Arrows. These Circumstances, added to the Refreshment I had received by their Victuals and Drink, which were very nourishing, disposed me to sleep. I slept about eight Hours as I was afterwards assured; and it was no Wonder; for the Physicians, by the Emperor's Order, had mingled a sleeping Potion in the Hogsheads of Wine.

IT seems that upon the first Moment I was discovered sleeping on the Ground after my Landing, the Emperor had early Notice of it by an Express; and determined in Council that I should be tyed in the Manner I have related (which was done in the Night while I slept) that Plenty of Meat and Drink should be sent me, and a Machine prepared to carry me to the Capital City.

THIS Resolution perhaps may appear very bold and dangerous, and I am confident would not be imitated by any Prince in *Europe* on the like Occasion; however, in my Opinion it was extremely Prudent as well as Generous. For supposing these People had endeavoured to kill me with their Spears and Arrows while I was asleep; I should certainly have awaked with the first Sense of Smart, which might so far have rouzed my Rage and Strength, as to enable me to break the Strings wherewith I was tyed; after which, as they were not able to make Resistance, so they could expect no Mercy.

THESE People are most excellent Mathematicians, and arrived to a great Perfection in Mechanicks by the Countenance and Encouragement of the Emperor, who is a renowned Patron of Learning. This Prince hath several Machines fixed on Wheels, for the Carriage of Trees and other great Weights. He often buildeth his largest Men of War, whereof some are Nine Foot long, in the Woods where the Timber grows, and has them carried on these Engines three or four Hundred Yards to the Sea. Five Hundred Carpenters and Engineers were immediately set at work to prepare the greatest Engine they had. It was a Frame of Wood raised three Inches from the Ground, about seven Foot long and four wide, moving upon twenty two Wheels. The Shout I heard, was upon the Arrival of this Engine, which, it seems, set out in four Hours after my Landing. It was brought parallel to me as I lay. But the principal Difficulty was to raise and place me in this Vehicle. Eighty Poles, each of one Foot high, were erected for this Purpose, and very strong Cords of the bigness of Packthread were fastened by Hooks to many Bandages, which the Workmen had girt round my Neck, my Hands, my Body, and my Legs. Nine Hundred of the strongest Men were employed to draw up these Cords by many Pullies fastned on the Poles; and thus in less than three Hours, I was raised and slung into the Engine, and there tyed fast. All this I was told; for while the whole Operation was performing, I lay in a profound Sleep, by the Force of that soporiferous Medicine infused into my Liquor. Fifteen hundred of the Emperor's largest Horses, each about four Inches and a half high, were employed to draw me towards the Metropolis, which, as I said, was half a Mile distant.

ABOUT four Hours after we began our Journey, I awaked by a very ridiculous Accident; for the Carriage being stopt a while to adjust something that was out of Order, two or three of the young Natives had the Curiosity to see how I looked when I was asleep; they climbed up into the Engine, and advancing very softly to my Face, one of them, an Officer in the Guards, put the sharp End of his Half-Pike a good way up into my left

Nostril, which tickled my Nose like a Straw, and made me sneeze violently: Whereupon they stoleoff unperceived; and it was three Weeks before I knew the Cause of my awaking so suddenly. We made a long March the remaining Part of the Day, and rested at Night with Five Hundred Guards on each Side of me, half with Torches, and half with Bows and Arrows, ready to shoot me if I should offer to stir. The next Morning at Sun-rise we continued our March, and arrived within two Hundred Yards of the City-Gates about Noon. The Emperor, and all his Court, came out to meet us; but his great Officers would by no means suffer his Majesty to endanger his Person by mounting on my Body.

AT the Place where the Carriage stopt, there stood an ancient Temple, esteemed to be the largest in the whole Kingdom; which having been polluted some Years before by an unnatural Murder, was, according to the Zeal of those People, looked upon as Prophane, and therefore had been applied to common Use, and all the Ornaments and Furniture carried away. In this Edifice it was determined I should lodge. The great Gate fronting to the North was about four Foot high, and almost two Foot wide, through which I could easily creep. On each Side of the Gate was a small Window not above six Inches from the Ground: Into that on the Left Side, the King's Smiths conveyed fourscore and eleven Chains, like those that hang to a Lady's Watch in *Europe,* and almost as large, which were locked to my Left Leg with six and thirty Padlocks. Over against this Temple, on the other Side of the great Highway, at twenty Foot Distance, there was a Turret at least five Foot high. Here the Emperor ascended with many principal Lords of his Court, to have an Opportunity of viewing me, as I was told, for I could not see them. It was reckoned that above an hundred thousand Inhabitants came out of the Town upon the same Errand; and in spight of my Guards, I believe there could not be fewer than ten thousand, at several Times, who mounted upon my Body by the Help of Ladders. But a Proclamation was soon issued to forbid it, upon Pain of Death. When the Workmen found it was impossible for me to break loose, they cut all the Strings that bound me; whereupon I rose up with as melancholly a Disposition as ever I had in my Life. But the Noise and Astonishment of the People at seeing me rise and walk, are not to be expressed. The Chains that held my left Leg were about two Yards long, and gave me not only the Liberty of walking backwards and forwards in a Semicircle; but being fixed within four Inches of the Gate, allowed me to creep in, and lie at my full Length in the Temple.

CHAPTER II

The Emperor of Lilliput, *attended by several of the Nobility, comes to see the Author in his Confinement. The Emperor's Person and Habit described. Learned Men appointed to teach the Author their Language. He gains Favour by his mild Disposition. His Pockets are searched, and his Sword and Pistols taken from him.*

When I found myself on my Feet, I looked about me, and must confess I never beheld a more entertaining Prospect. The Country round appeared like a continued Garden; and the inclosed Fields, which were generally Forty Foot square, resembled so many Beds of Flowers. These Fields were intermingled with Woods of half a Stang,[10] and the tallest Trees, as I could judge, appeared to be seven Foot high. I viewed the Town on my left Hand, which looked like the painted Scene of a City in a Theatre.

I HAD been for some Hours extremely pressed by the Necessities of Nature; which was no Wonder, it being almost two Days since I had last disburthened myself. I was under great Difficulties between Urgency and Shame. The best Expedient I could think on, was to creep into my House, which I accordingly did; and shutting the Gate after me, I went as far as the Length of my Chain would suffer; and discharged my Body of that uneasy Load. But this was the only Time I was ever guilty of so uncleanly an Action; for which I cannot but hope the candid Reader will give some Allowance, after he hath maturely and impartially considered my Case, and the Distress I was in. From this Time my constant Practice was, as soon as I rose, to perform that Business in open Air, at the full Extent of my Chain; and due Care was taken every Morning before Company came, that the offensive Matter should be carried off in Wheelbarrows, by two Servants appointed for that Purpose. I would not have dwelt so long upon a Circumstance, that perhaps at first Sight may appear not very momentous; if I had not thought it necessary to justify my Character in Point of Cleanliness to the World; which I am told, some of my

Maligners have been pleased, upon this and other Occasions, to call in Question.

WHEN this Adventure was at an End, I came back out of my House, having Occasion for fresh Air. The Emperor was already descended from the Tower, and advancing on Horseback towards me, which had like to have cost him dear; for the Beast, although very well trained, yet wholly unused to such a Sight, which appeared as if a Mountain moved before him, reared up on his hinder Feet: But that Prince, who is an excellent Horseman, kept his Seat, until his Attendants ran in, and held the Bridle, while his Majesty had Time to dismount. When he alighted, he surveyed me round with great Admiration, but kept beyond the Length of my Chains. He ordered his Cooks and Butlers, who were already prepared, to give me Victuals and Drink, which they pushed forward in a sort of Vehicles upon Wheels until I could reach them. I took those Vehicles, and soon emptied them all; twenty of them were filled with Meat, and ten with Liquor; each of the former afforded me two or three good Mouthfuls, and I emptied the Liquor of ten Vessels, which was contained in earthen Vials, into one Vehicle, drinking it off at a Draught; and so I did with the rest. The Empress, and young Princes of the Blood, of both Sexes, attended by many Ladies, sate at some Distance in their Chairs; but upon the Accident that happened to the Emperor's Horse, they alighted, and came near his Person; which I am now going to describe. He is taller by almost the Breadth of my Nail, than any of his Court; which alone is enough to strike an Awe into the Beholders. His Features are strong and masculine, with an *Austrian* Lip,[11] and arched Nose, his Complexion olive, his Countenance erect, his Body and Limbs well proportioned, all his Motions graceful, and his Deportment majestick. He was then past his Prime, being twenty-eight Years and three Quarters old, of which he had reigned about seven,[12] in great Felicity, and generally victorious. For the better Convenience of beholding him, I lay on my Side, so that my Face was parallel to his, and he stood but three Yards off: However, I have had him since many Times in my Hand, and therefore cannot be deceived in the Description. His Dress was very plain and simple, the Fashion of it between the *Asiatick* and the *European;* but he had on his Head a light Helmet of Gold, adorned with Jewels, and a Plume on the Crest. He held his Sword drawn in his Hand, to defend himself, if I should happen to break loose; it was almost three Inches long, the Hilt and Scabbard were Gold enriched with Diamonds. His Voice was shrill, but very clear and articulate, and I could distinctly hear it when I stood up. The Ladies and Courtiers were all most magnificently clad, so that the Spot they stood upon seemed to resemble a Petti-coat spread on the Ground, embroidered with Figures of Gold and Silver. His Imperial Majesty spoke often to me, and I returned Answers, but neither of us could understand a Syllable. There were several of his Priests and Lawyers present (as I conjectured by their Habits) who were commanded to address themselves to me, and I spoke to them in as many Languages as I had the least Smattering of, which were *High* and *Low Dutch, Latin, French, Spanish, Italian,* and *Lingua Franca;* but all to no purpose. After about two Hours the Court retired, and I was left with a strong Guard, to prevent the Impertinence, and probably the Malice of the Rabble, who were very impatient to croud about me as near as they durst; and some of them had the Impudence to shoot their Arrows at me as I sate on the Ground by the Door of my House; whereof one very narrowly missed my left Eye. But the Colonel ordered six of the Ringleaders to be seized, and thought no Punishment so proper as to deliver them bound into my Hands, which some of his Soldiers accordingly did, pushing them forwards with the But-ends of their Pikes into my Reach: I took them all in my right Hand, put five of them into my Coat-pocket; and as to the sixth, I made a Countenance as if I would eat him alive. The poor Man squalled terribly, and the Colonel and his Officers were in much Pain, especially when they saw me take out my Penknife: But I soon put them out of Fear; for, looking mildly, and immediately cutting the Strings he was bound with, I set him gently on the Ground, and away he ran. I treated the rest in the same Manner, taking them one by one out of my Pocket; and I observed, both the Soldiers and People were highly obliged at this Mark of my Clemency, which was represented very much to my Advantage at Court.

TOWARDS Night I got with some Difficulty into my House, where I lay on the Ground, and continued to do so about a Fortnight; during which time the Emperor gave Orders to have a Bed prepared for me. Six Hundred Beds of the common Measure were brought in Carriages, and worked up in my House; an Hundred and Fifty of their Beds sown together made up the Breadth and Length, and these were four double, which however kept me but very indifferently from the Hardness of the Floor, that was of smooth Stone. By the same Computation they provided me with Sheets, Blankets, and Coverlets, tolerable enough for one who had been so long enured to Hardships as I.

As the News of my Arrival spread through the Kingdom, it brought prodigious Numbers of rich, idle, and curious People to see me; so that the Villages were almost emptied, and great Neglect of Tillage and Houshold Affairs must have ensued, if his Imperial Majesty had not provided by several Proclamations and Orders of State against this Inconveniency. He directed that those, who had already beheld me, should return home, and not presume to come within fifty Yards of my House, without Licence from Court; whereby the Secretaries of State got considerable Fees.

IN the mean time, the Emperor held frequent Councils to debate what Course should be taken with me; and I was afterwards assured by a particular Friend, a Person of great Quality, who was as much in the *Secret* as any; that the Court was under many Difficulties concerning me. They apprehended my breaking loose; that my Diet would be very expensive, and might cause a Famine. Sometimes they determined to starve me, or at least to shoot me in the Face and Hands with poisoned Arrows, which would soon dispatch me: But again they considered, that the Stench of so large a Carcase might produce a Plague in the Metropolis, and probably spread through the whole Kingdom. In the midst of these Consultations, several Officers of the Army went to the Door of the great Council-Chamber; and two of them being admitted, gave an Account of my Behaviour to the six Criminals above-mentioned; which made so favourable an Impression in the Breast of his Majesty, and the whole Board, in my Behalf, that an Imperial Commission was issued out, obliging all the Villages nine hundred Yards round the City to deliver in every Morning six Beeves,[13] forty Sheep, and other Victuals for my Sustenance; together with a proportionable Quantity of Bread and Wine, and other Liquors: For the due Payment of which his Majesty gave Assignments upon his Treasury. For this Prince lives chiefly upon his own Demesnes;[14] seldom, except upon great Occasions raising any Subsidies upon his Subjects, who are bound to attend him in his Wars at their own Expence. An Establishment was also made of Six Hundred Persons to be my Domesticks, who had Board-Wages allowed for their Maintenance, and Tents built for them very conveniently on each side of my Door. It was likewise ordered, that three hundred Taylors should make me a Suit of Cloaths after the Fashion of the Country: That, six of his Majesty's greatest Scholars should be employed to instruct me in their Language: And, lastly, that the Emperor's Horses, and those of the Nobility, and Troops of Guards, should be exercised in my Sight, to accustom themselves to me. All these Orders were duly put in Execution; and in about three Weeks I made a great Progress in Learning their Language; during which Time, the Emperor frequently honoured me with his Visits, and was pleased to assist my Masters in teaching me. We began already to converse together in some Sort; and the first Words I learnt, were to express my Desire, that he would please to give me my Liberty; which I every Day repeated on my Knees. His Answer, as I could apprehend, was, that this must be a Work of Time, not to be thought on without the Advice of his Council; and that first I must *Lumos Kelmin pesso desmar lon Emposo;* that is, *Swear a Peace with him and his Kingdom.* However, that I should be used with all Kindness; and he advised me to acquire by my Patience and discreet Behaviour, the good Opinion of himself and his Subjects. He desired I would not take it ill, if he gave Orders to certain proper Officers to search me; for probably I might carry about me several Weapons, which must needs be dangerous Things, if they answered the Bulk of so prodigious a Person. I said, his Majesty should be satisfied, for I was ready to strip my self, and turn up my Pockets before him. This I delivered, part in Words, and part in Signs. He replied, that by the Laws of the Kingdom, I must be searched by two of his Officers: That he knew this could not be done without my Consent and Assistance; that he had so good an Opinion of my Generosity and Justice, as to trust their Persons in my Hands: That whatever they took from me should be returned when I left the Country, or paid for at the Rate which I would set upon them. I took up the two Officers in my Hands, put them first into my Coat-Pockets, and then into every other Pocket about me, except my two Fobs, and another secret Pocket which I had no Mind should be searched, wherein I had some little Necessaries of no Consequence to any but my self. In one of my Fobs there was a Silver Watch, and in the other a small Quantity of Gold in a Purse. These Gentlemen, having Pen, Ink, and Paper about them, made an exact Inventory of every thing they saw; and when they had done, desired I would set them down, that they might deliver it to the Emperor. This Inventory I afterwards translated into *English,* and is Word for Word as follows.

IMPRIMIS,[15] In the right Coat-Pocket of the *Great Man Mountain* (for so I interpret the Words *Quinbus Flestrin*) after the strictest Search, we found only one great Piece of coarse Cloth, large enough to be a Foot-Cloth for your Majesty's chief Room of State. In the left Pocket, we saw a huge Silver Chest, with a Cover of the same Metal, which we, the Searchers, were not able to lift. We desired it should be opened; and one of us stepping into it, found himself up to the mid Leg in a sort of Dust, some part whereof flying up to our Faces, set us both a sneezing for several Times together. In his right Waistcoat-Pocket, we found a prodigious Bundle of white thin Substances, folded one over another, about the Bigness of three Men, tied with a strong Cable, and marked with Black Figures; which we humbly conceive to be Writings; every Letter almost half as large as the Palm of our Hands. In the left there was a sort of Engine, from the Back of which were extended twenty long Poles, resembling the Pallisado's before your Majesty's Court; wherewith we conjecture the *Man Mountain* combs his Head; for we did not always trouble him with Questions, because we found it a great Difficulty to make him understand us. In the large Pocket on the right Side of his middle Cover, (so I translate the Word *Ranfu-Lo,* by which they meant my Breeches) we saw a hollow Pillar of Iron, about the Length of a Man, fastened to a strong piece of Timber, larger than the Pillar; and upon one side of the Pillar were huge Pieces of Iron sticking out, cut into strange Figures; which we know not what to make of. In the left Pocket, another Engine of the same kind. In the smaller Pocket on the right Side, were several round flat Pieces of white and red Metal, of different Bulk: Some of the white, which seemed to be Silver, were so large and heavy, that my Comrade and I could hardly lift them. In the left Pocket were two black Pillars irregularly shaped: we could not, without Difficulty, reach the Top of them as we stood at the Bottom of his Pocket: One of them was covered, and seemed all of a Piece; but at the upper End of the other, there appeared a white round Substance, about twice the bigness of our Heads. Within each of these was inclosed a prodigious Plate of Steel; which, by our Orders, we obliged him to shew us, because we apprehended they might be dangerous Engines. He took them out of their Cases, and told us, that in his own Country his Practice was to shave his Beard with one of these, and to cut his Meat with the other. There were two Pockets which we could not enter: These he called his Fobs; they were two large Slits cut into the Top of his middle Cover, but squeezed close by the Pressure of his Belly. Out of the right Fob hung a great Silver Chain, with a wonderful kind of Engine at the Bottom. We directed him to draw out whatever was at the End of that Chain; which appeared to be a Globe, half Silver, and half of some transparent Metal: For on the transparent Side we saw certain strange Figures circularly drawn, and thought we could touch them, until we found our Fingers stopped with that lucid Substance. He put this Engine to our Ears, which made an incessant Noise like that of a Water-Mill. And we conjecture it is either some unknown Animal, or the God that he worships: But we are more inclined to the latter Opinion, because he assured us (if we understood him right, for he expressed himself very imperfectly) that he seldom did any Thing without consulting it. He called it his Oracle, and said it pointed out the Time for every Action of his Life. From the left Fob he took out a Net almost large enough for a Fisherman, but contrived to open and shut like a Purse, and served him for the same Use: We found therein several massy Pieces of yellow Metal, which if they be real Gold, must be of immense Value.

HAVING thus, in Obedience to your Majesty's Commands, diligently searched all his Pockets; we observed a Girdle about his Waist made of the Hyde of some prodigious Animal; from which, on the left Side, hung a Sword of the Length of five Men; and on the right, a Bag or Pouch divided into two Cells; each Cell capable of holding three of your Majesty's Subjects. In one of these Cells were several Globes or Balls of a most ponderous Metal, about the Bigness of our Heads, and required a strong Hand to lift them: The other Cell contained a Heap of certain black Grains, but of no great Bulk or Weight, for we could hold above fifty of them in the Palms of our Hands.

THIS is an exact Inventory of what we found about the Body of the *Man Mountain;* who used us with great Civility, and due Respect to your Majesty's Commission. Signed and Sealed on the fourth Day of the eighty ninth Moon of your Majesty's auspicious Reign.

CLEFREN FRELOCK, MARSI FRELOCK.

———

WHEN this Inventory was read over to the Emperor, he directed me to deliver up the several Particulars. He first called for my Scymiter, which I took out, Scabbard and all. In the mean time he ordered three thousand of his choicest Troops, who then attended him, to surround me at a Distance, with their Bows and Arrows just ready to discharge: But I did not observe it; for mine Eyes were wholly fixed upon his Majesty. He then desired me to draw my Scymiter, which, although it had got some Rust by the Sea-Water, was in most Parts exceeding bright. I did so, and immediately all the Troops gave a Shout between Terror and Surprize; for the Sun shone clear, and the Reflexion dazzled their Eyes, as I waved the Scymiter to and fro in my Hand. His Majesty, who is a most magnanimous Prince, was less daunted than I could expect; he ordered me to return it into the Scabbard, and cast it on the Ground as gently as I could, about six Foot from the End of my Chain. The next Thing he demanded was one of the hollow Iron Pillars, by which he meant my Pocket-Pistols. I drew it out, and at his Desire, as well as I could, expressed to him the Use of it, and charging it only with Powder, which by the Closeness of my Pouch, happened to escape wetting in the Sea, (an Inconvenience that all prudent Mariners take special Care to provide against) I first cautioned the Emperor not to be afraid; and then I let it off in the Air. The Astonishment here was much greater than at the Sight of my Scymiter. Hundreds fell down as if they had been struck dead; and even the Emperor, although he stood his Ground, could not recover himself in some time. I delivered up both my Pistols in the same Manner as I had done my Scymiter, and then my Pouch of Powder and Bullets; begging him that the former might be kept from Fire; for it would kindle with the smallest Spark, and blow up his Imperial Palace into the Air. I likewise delivered up my Watch, which the Emperor was very curious to see; and commanded two of his tallest Yeomen of the Guards to bear it on a Pole upon their Shoulders, as Dray-men in *England* do a Barrel of Ale. He was amazed at the continual Noise it made, and the Motion of the Minute-hand, which he could easily discern; for their Sight is much more acute than ours: He asked the Opinions of his learned Men about him, which were various and remote, as the Reader may well imagine without my repeating; although indeed I could not very perfectly understand them. I then gave up my Silver and Copper Money, my Purse with nine large Pieces of Gold, and some smaller ones; my Knife and Razor, my Comb and Silver Snuff-Box, my Handkerchief and Journal Book. My Scymiter, Pistols, and Pouch, were conveyed in Carriages to his Majesty's Stores; but the rest of my Goods were returned me.

I HAD, as I before observed, one private Pocket which escaped their Search, wherein there was a Pair of Spectacles (which I sometimes use for the Weakness of mine Eyes) a Pocket Perspective,[16] and several other little Conveniences; which being of no Consequence to the Emperor, I did not think my self bound in Honour to discover; and I apprehended they might be lost or spoiled if I ventured them out of my Possession.

CHAPTER III

The Author diverts the Emperor and his Nobility of both Sexes, in a very uncommon Manner. The Diversions of the Court of Lilliput *described. The Author hath his Liberty granted him upon certain Conditions.*

My Gentleness and good Behaviour had gained so far on the Emperor and his Court, and indeed upon the Army and People in general, that I began to conceive Hopes of getting my Liberty in a short Time. I took all possible Methods to cultivate this favourable Disposition. The Natives came by Degrees to be less apprehensive of any Danger from me. I would sometimes lie down, and let five or six of them dance on my Hand. And at last the Boys and Girls would venture to come and play at Hide and Seek in my Hair. I had now made a good Progress in understanding and speaking their Language. The Emperor had a mind one Day to entertain me with several of the Country Shows; wherein they exceed all Nations I have known, both for Dexterity and Magnificence. I was diverted with none so much as that of the Rope-Dancers,[17] performed upon a slender white Thread, extended about two Foot, and twelve Inches from the Ground. Upon which, I shall desire Liberty, with the Reader's Patience, to enlarge a little.

This Diversion is only practised by those Persons, who are Candidates for great Employments, and high Favour, at Court. They are trained in this Art from their Youth, and are not always of noble birth, or liberal Education. When a great Office is vacant, either by Death or Disgrace, (which often happens) five or six of those Candidates petition the Emperor to entertain his Majesty and the Court with a Dance on the Rope; and whoever jumps the highest without falling, succeeds in the Office. Very often the chief Ministers themselves are commanded to shew their Skill, and to convince the Emperor that they have not lost their Faculty. *Flimnap,* the

Treasurer, is allowed to cut a Caper on the strait Rope, at least an Inch higher than any other Lord in the whole Empire. I have seen him do the Summerset[18] several times together, upon a Trencher fixed on the Rope, which is no thicker than a common Packthread in *England*. My Friend *Reldresal,* principal Secretary for private Affairs, is, in my Opinion, if I am not partial, the second after the Treasurer; the rest of the great Officers are much upon a Par.

THESE Diversions are often attended with fatal Accidents, whereof great Numbers are on Record. I my self have seen two or three Candidates break a Limb. But the Danger is much greater, when the Ministers themselves are commanded to shew their Dexterity: For, by contending to excel themselves and their Fellows, they strain so far, that there is hardly one of them who hath not received a Fall; and some of them two or three. I was assured, that a Year or two before my Arrival, *Flimnap* would have infallibly broke his Neck, if one of the *King's Cushions,*[19] that accidentally lay on the Ground, had not weakened the Force of his Fall.

THERE is likewise another Diversion, which is only shewn before the Emperor and Empress, and first Minister, upon particular Occasions. The Emperor lays on a Table three fine silken Threads of six Inches long. One is Blue, the other Red, and the third Green.[20] These Threads are proposed as Prizes, for those Persons whom the Emperor hath a mind to distinguish by a peculiar Mark of his Favour. The Ceremony is performed in his Majesty's great Chamber of State; where the Candidates are to undergo a Tryal of Dexterity very different from the former; and such as I have not observed the least Resemblance of in any other Country of the old or the new World. The Emperor holds a Stick in his Hands, both Ends parallel to the Horizon, while the Candidates advancing one by one, sometimes leap over the Stick, sometimes creep under it backwards and forwards several times, according as the Stick is advanced or depressed. Sometimes the Emperor holds one End of the Stick, and his first Minister the other; sometimes the Minister has it entirely to himself. Whoever performs his Part with most Agility, and holds out the longest in *leaping* and *creeping,* is rewarded with the Blue-coloured Silk; the Red is given to the next, and the Green to the third, which they all wear girt twice round about the Middle; and you see few great Persons about this Court, who are not adorned with one of these Girdles.

THE Horses of the Army, and those of the Royal Stables, having been daily led before me, were no longer shy, but would come up to my very Feet, without starting. The Riders would leap them over my Hand as I held it on the Ground; and one of the Emperor's Huntsmen, upon a large Courser, took my Foot, Shoe and all; which was indeed a prodigious Leap. I had the good Fortune to divert the Emperor one Day, after a very extraordinary Manner. I desired he would order several Sticks of two Foot high, and the Thickness of an ordinary Cane, to be brought me; whereupon his Majesty commanded the Master of his Woods to give Directions accordingly; and the next Morning six Wood-men arrived with as many Carriages, drawn by eight Horses to each. I took nine of these Sticks, and fixing them firmly in the Ground in a Quadrangular Figure, two Foot and a half square; I took four other Sticks, and tyed them parallel at each Corner, about two Foot from the Ground; then I fastened my Handkerchief to the nine Sticks that stood erect; and extended it on all Sides, till it was as tight as the Top of a Drum; and the four parallel Sticks rising about five Inches higher than the Handkerchief, served as Ledges on each Side. When I had finished my Work, I desired the Emperor to let a Troop of his best Horse, Twenty-four in Number, come and exercise upon this Plain. His Majesty approved of the Proposal, and I took them up one by one in my Hands, ready mounted and armed, with the proper Officers to exercise them. As soon as they got into Order, they divided into two Parties, performed mock Skirmishes, discharged blunt Arrows, drew their Swords, fled and pursued, attacked and retired; and in short discovered the best military Discipline I ever beheld. The parallel Sticks secured them and their Horses from falling over the Stage; and the Emperor was so much delighted, that he ordered this Entertainment to be repeated several Days; and once was pleased to be lifted up, and give the Word of Command; and, with great Difficulty, persuaded even the Empress her self to let me hold her in her close Chair, within two Yards of the Stage, from whence she was able to take a full View of the whole Performance. It was my good Fortune that no ill Accident happened in these Entertainments; only once a fiery Horse that belonged to one of the Captains, pawing with his Hoof struck a Hole in my Handkerchief, and his Foot slipping, he overthrew his Rider and himself; but I immediately relieved them both: For covering the Hole with one Hand, I set down the Troop with the other, in the same Manner as I took them up. The Horse that fell was strained in the left Shoulder, but the Rider got no Hurt; and I repaired my Handkerchief as well as I could: However, I would not trust to the Strength of it any more in such dangerous Enterprizes.

ABOUT two or three Days before I was set at Liberty, as I was entertaining the Court with these Kinds of Feats, there arrived an Express to inform his Majesty, that some of his Subjects riding near the Place where I was first taken up, had seen a great black Substance lying on the Ground, very oddly shaped, extending its Edges round as wide as his Majesty's Bedchamber, and rising up in the Middle as high as a Man: That it was no living Creature, as they at first apprehended; for it lay on the Grass without Motion, and some of them had walked round it several Times: That by mounting upon each others Shoulders, they had got to the Top, which was flat and even; and, stamping upon it, they found it was hollow within: That they humbly conceived it might be something belonging to the *Man-Mountain;* and if his Majesty pleased, they would undertake to bring it with only five Horses. I presently knew what they meant; and was glad at Heart to receive this Intelligence. It seems, upon my first reaching the Shore, after our Shipwreck, I was in such Confusion, that before I came to the Place where I went to sleep, my Hat, which I had fastened with a String to my Head while I was rowing, and had stuck on all the Time I was swimming, fell off after I came to Land; the String, as I conjecture, breaking by some Accident which I never observed, but thought my Hat had been lost at Sea. I intreated his Imperial Majesty to give Orders it might be brought to me as soon as possible, describing to him the Use and the Nature of it: And the next Day the Waggoners arrived with it, but not in a very good Condition; they had bored two Holes in the Brim, within an Inch and a half of the Edge, and fastened two Hooks in the Holes; these Hooks were tied by a long Cord to the Harness, and thus my Hat was dragged along for above half an *English* Mile: But the Ground in that Country being extremely smooth and level, it received less Damage than I expected.

Two Days after this Adventure, the Emperor having ordered that Part of his Army, which quarters in and about his Metropolis, to be in a Readiness, took a fancy of diverting himself in a very singular Manner. He desired I would stand like a *Colossus*,[21] with my Legs as far asunder as I conveniently could. He then commanded his General (who was an old experienced Leader, and a great Patron of mine) to draw up the Troops in close Order, and march them under me; the Foot by Twenty-four in a Breast, and the Horse by Sixteen, with Drums beating, Colours flying, and Pikes advanced. This Body consisted of three Thousand Foot, and a Thousand Horse. His Majesty gave Orders, upon pain of Death, that every Soldier in his March should observe the strictest Decency, with regard to my Person; which, however, could not prevent some of the younger Officers from turning up their Eyes as they passed under me.

And, to confess the Truth, my Breeches were at that Time in so ill a Condition, that they afforded some Opportunities for Laughter and Admiration.

I HAD sent so many Memorials and Petitions for my Liberty, that his Majesty at length mentioned the Matter first in the Cabinet, and then in a full Council; where it was opposed by none, except *Skyresh Bolgolam,* who was pleased, without any Provocation, to be my mortal Enemy. But it was carried against him by the whole Board, and confirmed by the Emperor. That Minister was *Galbet,* or Admiral of the Realm; very much in his Master's Confidence, and a Person well versed in Affairs, but of a morose and sour Complection. However, he was at length persuaded to comply; but prevailed that the Articles and Conditions upon which I should be set free, and to which I must swear, should be drawn up by himself. These Articles were brought to me by *Skyresh Bolgolam* in Person, attended by two under Secretaries, and several Persons of Distinction. After they were read, I was demanded to swear to the Performance of them; first in the Manner of my own Country, and afterwards in the Method prescribed by their Laws; which was to hold my right Foot in my left Hand, to place the middle Finger of my right Hand on the Crown of my Head, and my Thumb on the Tip of my right Ear. But, because the Reader may perhaps be curious to have some Idea of the Style and Manner of Expression peculiar to that People, as well as to know the Articles upon which I recovered my Liberty; I have made a Translation of the whole Instrument, Word for Word, as near as I was able; which I here offer to the Publick.

———

GOLBASTO MOMAREN EVLAME GURDILO SHEFIN MULLY ULLY GUE, most Mighty Emperor of *Lilliput,* Delight and Terror of the Universe, whose Dominions extend five Thousand Blustrugs, (about twelve Miles in Circumference) to the Extremities of the Globe: Monarch of all Monarchs: Taller than the Sons of Men; whose Feet press down to the Center, and whose Head strikes against the Sun: At whose Nod the Princes of the Earth shake their Knees; pleasant as the Spring, comfortable as the Summer, fruitful as Autumn, dreadful as Winter. His most sublime Majesty proposeth to the *Man-Mountain,* lately arrived at our Celestial Dominions, the following Articles, which by a solemn Oath he shall be obliged to perform.

    First, The *Man-Mountain* shall not depart from our Dominions, without our Licence under our Great Seal.

Secondly, He shall not presume to come into our Metropolis, without our express Order; at which time, the Inhabitants shall have two Hours Warning, to keep within their Doors.

Thirdly, The said *Man-Mountain* shall confine his Walks to our principal high Roads; and not offer to walk or lie down in a Meadow, or Field of Corn.

Fourthly, As he walks the said Roads, he shall take the utmost Care not to trample upon the Bodies of any of our loving Subjects, their Horses, or Carriages; nor take any of our said Subjects into his Hands, without their own Consent.

Fifthly, If an Express require extraordinary Dispatch; the *Man-Mountain* shall be obliged to carry in his Pocket the Messenger and Horse, a six Days Journey once in every Moon, and return the said Messenger back (if so required) safe to our Imperial Presence.

Sixthly, He shall be our Ally against our enemies in the Island of *Blefuscu,* and do his utmost to destroy their Fleet, which is now preparing to invade Us.

Seventhly, That the said *Man-Mountain* shall, at his Times of Leisure, be aiding and assisting to our Workmen, in helping to raise certain great Stones, towards covering the Wall of the principal Park, and other our Royal Buildings.

Eighthly, That the said *Man-Mountain* shall, in two Moons Time, deliver in an exact Survey of the Circumference of our Dominions, by a Computation of his own Paces round the Coast.

Lastly, That upon his solemn Oath to observe all the above Articles, the said *Man-Mountain* shall have a daily Allowance of Meat and Drink, sufficient for the Support of 1728 of our Subjects; with free Access to our Royal Person, and other Marks of our Favour. Given at our Palace at *Belfaborac* the Twelfth Day of the Ninety-first Moon of our Reign.

———

I SWORE and subscribed to these Articles with great Chearfulness and Content, although some of them were not so honourable as I could have wished; which proceeded wholly from the Malice of *Skyresh Bolgolam* the High Admiral: Whereupon my Chains were immediately unlocked, and I was at full Liberty: The Emperor himself, in Person, did me the Honour to be by at the whole Ceremony. I made my Acknowledgments, by prostrating myself at his Majesty's Feet: But he commanded me to rise; and after many gracious Expressions, which, to avoid the Censure of Vanity, I shall not repeat; he added, that he hoped I should prove a useful Servant, and well deserve all the Favours he had already conferred upon me, or might do for the future.

THE Reader may please to observe, that in the last Article for the Recovery of my Liberty the Emperor stipulates to allow me a Quantity of Meat and Drink, sufficient for the Support of 1728 *Lilliputians.* Some time after, asking a Friend at Court how they came to fix on that determinate Number; he told me, that his Majesty's Mathematicians, having taken the Height of my Body by the Help of a Quadrant, and finding it to exceed theirs in the Proportion of Twelve to One, they concluded from the Similarity of their Bodies, that mine must contain at least 1728 of theirs, and consequently would require as much Food as was necessary to support that Number of *Lilliputians.* By which, the Reader may conceive an Idea of the Ingenuity of that People, as well as the prudent and exact Oeconomy of so great a Prince.

CHAPTER IV

Mildendo, the Metropolis of Lilliput, described, together with the Emperor's Palace. A Conversation between the Author and a principal Secretary, concerning the Affairs of that Empire: The Author's Offers to serve the Emperor in his Wars.

The first Request I made after I had obtained my Liberty, was, that I might have Licence to see *Mildendo*, the Metropolis; which the Emperor easily granted me, but with a special Charge to do no Hurt, either to the Inhabitants, or their Houses. The People had Notice by Proclamation of my Design to visit the Town. The Wall which encompassed it, is two Foot and an half high, and at least eleven Inches broad, so that a Coach and Horses may be driven very safely round it; and it is flanked with strong Towers at ten Foot Distance. I stept over the great *Western* Gate, and passed very gently, and sideling through the two principal Streets, only in my short Waistcoat, for fear of damaging the Roofs and Eves of the Houses with the Skirts of my Coat. I walked with the utmost Circumspection, to avoid treading on any Stragglers, who might remain in the Streets, although the Orders were very strict, that all people should keep in their Houses, at their own Peril. The Garret Windows and Tops of Houses were so crowded with Spectators, that I thought in all my Travels I had not seen a more populous Place. The City is an exact Square, each Side of the Wall being five Hundred Foot long. The two great Streets which run cross and divide it into four Quarters, are five Foot wide. The Lanes and Alleys which I could not enter, but only viewed them as I passed, are from Twelve to Eighteen Inches. The Town is capable of holding five Hundred Thousand Souls. The Houses are from three to five Stories. The Shops and Markets well provided.

THE Emperor's Palace is in the Center of the City, where the two great Streets meet. It is inclosed by a Wall of two Foot high, and Twenty Foot distant from the Buildings. I had his Majesty's Permission to step over this Wall; and the Space being so wide between that and the Palace, I could easily view it on every Side. The outward Court is a Square of Forty Foot, and includes two other Courts: In the inmost are the Royal Apartments, which I was very desirous to see, but found it extremely difficult; for the great Gates, from one Square into another, were but Eighteen Inches high, and seven Inches wide. Now the Buildings of the outer Court were at least five Foot high; and it was impossible for me to stride over them, without infinite Damage to the Pile, although the Walls were strongly built of hewn Stone, and four Inches thick. At the same time, the Emperor had a great Desire that I should see the Magnificence of his Palace: But this I was not able to do till three Days after, which I spent in cutting down with my Knife some of the largest Trees in the Royal Park, about an Hundred Yards distant from the City. Of these Trees I made two Stools, each about three Foot high, and strong enough to bear my Weight. The People having received Notice a second time, I went again through the City to the Palace, with my two Stools in my Hands. When I came to the Side of the outer Court, I stood upon one Stool, and took the other in my Hand: This I lifted over the Roof, and gently set it down on the Space between the first and second Court, which was eight Foot wide. I then stept over the Buildings very conveniently from one Stool to the other, and drew up the first after me with a hooked Stick. By this Contrivance I got into the inmost Court; and lying down upon my Side, I applied my Face to the Windows of the middle Stories, which were left open on Purpose, and discovered the most splendid Apartments that can be imagined. There I saw the Empress, and the young Princes in their several Lodgings, with their chief Attendants about them. Her Imperial Majesty was pleased to smile very graciously upon me, and gave me out of the Window her Hand to kiss.

But I shall not anticipate the Reader with farther Descriptions of this Kind, because I reserve them for a greater Work, which is now almost ready for the Press; containing a general Description of this Empire, from its first Erection, through a long Series of Princes, with a particular Account of their Wars and Politicks, Laws, Learning, and Religion; their Plants and Animals, their peculiar Manners and Customs, with other Matters very curious and useful; my chief Design at present being only to relate such Events and Transactions as happened to the Publick, or to my self, during a Residence of about nine Months in that Empire.

One Morning, about a Fortnight after I had obtained my Liberty; *Reldresal*, Principal Secretary (as they style him) of private Affairs, came to my House, attended only by one Servant. He ordered his Coach to wait at a Distance, and desired I would give him an Hour's Audience; which I readily consented to, on Account of his Quality, and Personal Merits, as well as of the many good Offices he had done me during my Sollicitations at Court. I offered to lie down, that he might the more conveniently reach my Ear; but he chose rather to let me hold him in my Hand during our Conversation. He began with Compliments on my Liberty; said, he might pretend to some Merit in it; but, however, added, that if it had not been for the present Situation of things at Court, perhaps I might not have obtained it so soon. For, *said he,* as flourishing a Condition as we appear to be in to Foreigners, we labour under two mighty Evils; a violent Faction at home, and the Danger of an Invasion by a most potent Enemy from abroad. As to the first, you are to understand, that for above seventy Moons past, there have been two struggling Parties in this Empire, under the Names of *Tramecksan,* and *Slamecksan,* from the high and low Heels on their Shoes, by which they distinguish themselves.[22]

IT is alledged indeed, that the high Heels are most agreeable to our ancient Constitution: But however this be, his Majesty hath determined to make use of only low Heels in the Administration[23] of the Government, and all Offices in the Gift of the Crown; as you cannot but observe; and particularly, that his Majesty's Imperial Heels are lower at least by a *Drurr* than any of his Court; (*Drurr* is a Measure about the fourteenth Part of an Inch.) The Animosities between these two Parties run so high, that they will neither eat nor drink, nor talk with each other. We compute the *Tramecksan,* or High-Heels, to exceed us in Number; but the Power is wholly on our Side. We apprehend his Imperial Highness, the Heir to the Crown, to have some Tendency towards the High-Heels; at least we can plainly discover one of his Heels higher than the other; which gives him a Hobble in his Gait. Now, in the midst of these intestine Disquiets, we are threatened with an Invasion from the Island of *Blefuscu,* which is the other great Empire of the Universe, almost as large and powerful as this of his Majesty. For as to what we have heard you affirm, that there are other Kingdoms and States in the World, inhabited by human Creatures as large as your self, our Philosophers are in much Doubt; and would rather conjecture that you dropt from the Moon, or one of the Stars; because it is certain, than an hundred Mortals of your Bulk, would, in a short Time, destroy all the Fruits and Cattle of his Majesty's Dominions. Besides, our Histories of six Thousand Moons make no Mention of any other Regions, than the two great Empires of *Lilliput* and *Blefuscu.* Which two mighty Powers have, as I was going to tell you, been engaged in a most obstinate

War for six and thirty Moons past. It began upon the following Occasion. It is allowed on all Hands, that the primitive Way of breaking Eggs before we eat them, was upon the larger End: But his present Majesty's Grandfather, while he was a Boy, going to eat an Egg, and breaking it according to the ancient Practice, happened to cut one of his Fingers. Whereupon the Emperor his Father, published an Edict, commanding all his Subjects, upon great Penalties, to break the smaller End of their Eggs. The People so highly resented this Law, that our Histories tell us, there have been six Rebellions raised on that Account; wherein one Emperor lost his Life, and another his Crown.[24] These civil Commotions were constantly fomented by the Monarchs of *Blefuscu;* and when they were quelled, the Exiles always fled for Refuge to that Empire. It is computed, that eleven Thousand Persons have, at several Times, suffered Death, rather than submit to break their Eggs at the smaller End. Many hundred large Volumes have been published upon this Controversy: But the Books of the *Big-Endians* have been long forbidden, and the whole Party rendred incapable by Law of holding Employments. During the Course of these Troubles, the Emperors of *Blefuscu* did frequently expostulate by their Ambassadors, accusing us of making a Schism in Religion, by offending against a fundamental Doctrine of our great Prophet *Lustrog,* in the fifty-fourth Chapter of the *Brundrecal,* (which is their *Alcoran.*[25]) This, however, is thought to be a meer Strain upon the Text: For the Words are these; *That all true Believers shall break their Eggs at the convenient End:* and which is the convenient End, seems, in my humble Opinion, to be left to every Man's Conscience, or at least in the Power of the chief Magistrate to determine. Now the *Big-Endian* Exiles have found so much Credit in the Emperor of *Blefuscu's* Court; and so much private Assistance and Encouragement from their Party here at home, that a bloody War hath been carried on between the two Empires for six and thirty Moons with various Success; during which Time we have lost Forty Capital Ships, and a much greater Number of smaller Vessels, together with thirty thousand of our best Seamen and Soldiers; and the Damage received by the Enemy is reckoned to be somewhat greater than ours. However, they have now equipped a numerous Fleet, and are just preparing to make a Descent upon us: And his Imperial Majesty, placing great Confidence in your Valour and Strength, hath commanded me to lay this Account of his Affairs before you.

I DESIRED the Secretary to present my humble Duty to the Emperor, and to let him know, that I thought it would not become me, who was a Foreigner, to interfere with Parties; but I was ready, with the Hazard of my Life, to defend his Person and State against all Invaders.

CHAPTER V

The Author *by an extraordinary Stratagem prevents an Invasion. A high Title of Honour is conferred upon him. Ambassadors arrive from the Emperor of* Blefuscu, *and sue for Peace. The Empress's Apartment on fire by an Accident; the* Author *instrumental in saving the rest of the Palace.*

The Empire of *Blefuscu,* is an Island situated to the North North-East Side of *Lilliput,* from whence it is parted only by a Channel of eight Hundred Yards wide. I had not yet seen it, and upon this Notice of an intended Invasion, I avoided appearing on that Side of the Coast, for fear of being discovered by some of the Enemies Ships, who had received no Intelligence of me; all intercourse between the two Empires having been strictly forbidden during the War, upon Pain of Death; and an Embargo laid by our Emperor upon all Vessels whatsoever. I communicated to his Majesty a Project I had formed of seizing the Enemies whole Fleet; which, as our Scouts assured us, lay at Anchor in the Harbour ready to sail with the first fair Wind. I consulted the most experienced Seamen, upon the Depth of the Channel, which they had often plummed; who told me, that in the Middle at high Water it was seventy *Glumgluffs* deep, which is about six Foot of *European* Measure; and the rest of it fifty *Glumgluffs* at most. I walked to the North-East Coast over against *Blefuscu;* where, lying down behind a Hillock, I took out my small Pocket Perspective Glass, and viewed the Enemy's Fleet at Anchor, consisting of about fifty Men of War, and a great Number of Transports: I then came back to my House, and gave Order (for which I had a Warrant) for a great Quantity of the strongest Cable and Bars of Iron. The Cable was about as thick as Packthread, and the Bars of the Length and Size of a Knitting-Needle. I trebled the Cable to make it stronger; and for the same Reason I twisted three of the Iron Bars together, bending the Extremities into a Hook. Having thus fixed fifty Hooks to as many Cables, I went back to the North-East Coast, and putting off my Coat, Shoes, and Stockings, walked into the Sea in my Leathern Jerken, about half an Hour before high Water. I waded with what Haste I cold, and swam in the Middle about thirty Yards until I felt the Ground; I arrived at the Fleet in less than half an Hour. The Enemy was so frighted when they saw me, that they leaped out of their Ships, and swam to Shore; where there could not be fewer than thirty thousand Souls. I then took my Tackling, and fastning a Hook to the Hole at the Prow of each, I tyed all the Cords together at the End. While I was thus employed, the Enemy discharged several Thousand Arrows, many of which stuck in my Hands and Face; and besides the excessive Smart, gave me much Disturbance in my Work. My greatest Apprehension was for mine Eyes, which I should have infallibly lost, if I had not suddenly thought of an Expedient. I kept, among other little Necessaries, a Pair of Spectacles in a private Pocket, which, as I observed before, had escaped the Emperor's Searchers. These I took out, and fastened as strongly as I could upon my Nose; and thus armed went on boldly with my Work in spight of the Enemy's Arrows; many of which struck against the Glasses of my Spectacles, but without any other Effect, further than a little to discompose them. I had now fastened all the Hooks, and taking the Knot in my Hand, began to pull; but not a Ship would stir, for they were all too fast held by their Anchors; so that the boldest Part of my Enterprize remained. I therefore let go the Cord, and leaving the Hooks fixed to the Ships, I resolutely cut with my Knife the Cables that fastened the Anchors; receiving above two hundred Shots in my Face and Hands: Then I took up the knotted End of the Cables to which my Hooks were tyed; and with great Ease drew fifty of the Enemy's largest Men of War after me.[26]

THE *Blefuscudians,* who had not the least Imagination of what I intended, were at first confounded with Astonishment. They had seen me cut the Cables, and thought my Design was only to let the Ships run a-drift, or fall foul on each other: But when they perceived the whole Fleet moving in Order, and saw me pulling at the End; they set up such a Scream of Grief and Dispair, that it is almost impossible to describe or conceive. When I had got out of Danger, I stopt a while to pick out the Arrows that stuck in my Hands and Face, and rubbed on some of the same Ointment that was given me at my first Arrival, as I have formerly mentioned. I then took off my Spectacles, and waiting about an Hour until the Tyde was a little fallen, I waded through the Middle with my Cargo, and arrived safe at the Royal Port of *Lilliput.*

THE Emperor and his whole Court stood on the Shore, expecting the

Issue of this great Adventure. They saw the Ships move forward in a large Half-Moon, but could not discern me, who was up to my Breast in Water. When I advanced to the Middle of the Channel, they were yet more in Pain because I was under Water to my Neck. The Emperor concluded me to be drowned, and that the Enemy's Fleet was approaching in a hostile Manner: But he was soon eased of his Fears; for the Channel growing shallower every Step I made, I came in a short Time within Hearing; and holding up the End of the Cable by which the Fleet was fastened, I cryed in a loud Voice, *Long live the most puissant Emperor of Lilliput!* This great Prince received me at my Landing with all possible Encomiums, and created me a *Nardac* upon the Spot, which is the highest Title of Honour among them.

His Majesty desired I would take some other Opportunity of bringing all the rest of his Enemy's Ships into his Ports. And so unmeasurable is the Ambition of Princes, that he seemed to think of nothing less than reducing the whole Empire of *Blefuscu* into a Province, and governing it by a Viceroy; of destroying the *Big-Endian* Exiles, and compelling that People to break the smaller End of their Eggs; by which he would remain sole Monarch of the whole World. But I endeavoured to divert him from this Design, by many Arguments drawn from the Topicks of Policy as well as Justice: And I plainly protested, that I would never be an Instrument of bringing a free and brave People into Slavery: And when the Matter was debated in Council, the wisest Part of the Ministry were of my Opinion.

This open bold Declaration of mine was so opposite to the Schemes and Politicks of his Imperial Majesty, that he could never forgive me: He mentioned it in a very artful Manner at Council, where, I was told, that some of the wisest appeared, at least by their Silence, to be of my Opinion; but others, who were my secret Enemies, could not forbear some Expressions, which by a Side-wind reflected on me. And from this Time began an Intrigue between his Majesty, and a Junta of Ministers maliciously bent against me, which broke out in less than two Months, and had like to have ended in my utter Destruction. Of so little Weight are the greatest Services to Princes, when put into the Balance with a Refusal to gratify their Passions.

About three Weeks after this Exploit, there arrived a solemn Embassy from *Blefuscu*, with humble Offers of a Peace;[27] which was soon concluded upon Conditions very advantageous to our Emperor; wherewith I shall not trouble the Reader. There were six Ambassadors, with a Train of about five Hundred Persons; and their Entry was very magnificent, suitable to the Grandeur of their Master, and the Importance of their Business. When their Treaty was finished, wherein I did them several good Offices by the Credit I now had, or at least appeared to have at Court; their Excellencies, who were privately told how much I had been their Friend, made me a Visit in Form. They began with many Compliments upon my Valour and Generosity; invited me to that Kingdom in the Emperor their Master's Name; and desired me to shew them some Proofs of my prodigious Strength, of which they had heard so many Wonders; wherein I readily obliged them, but shall not interrupt the Reader with the Particulars.

WHEN I had for some time entertained their Excellencies to their infinite Satisfaction and Surprize, I desired they would do me the Honour to present my most humble Respects to the Emperor their Master, the Renown of whose Virtues had so justly filled the whole World with Admiration, and whose Royal Person I resolved to attend before I returned to my own Country. Accordingly, the next time I had the Honour to see our Emperor, I desired his general Licence to wait on the *Blefuscudian* Monarch, which he was pleased to grant me, as I could plainly perceive, in a very cold Manner; but could not guess the Reason, till I had a Whisper from a certain Person, that *Flimnap* and *Bolgolam* had represented my Intercourse with those Ambassadors, as a Mark of Disaffection, from which I am sure my Heart was wholly free. And this was the first time I began to conceive some imperfect Idea of Courts and Ministers.

IT is to be observed, that these Ambassadors spoke to me by an Interpreter; the Languages of both Empires differing as much from each other as any two in *Europe,* and each Nation priding itself upon the Antiquity, Beauty, and Energy of their own Tongues, with an avowed Contempt for that of their Neighbour: Yet our Emperor standing upon the Advantage he had got by the Seizure of their Fleet, obliged them to deliver their Credentials, and make their Speech in the *Lilliputian* Tongue. And it must be confessed, that from the great Intercourse of Trade and Commerce between both Realms; from the continual Reception of Exiles, which is mutual among them; and from the Custom in each Empire to send their young Nobility and richer Gentry to the other, in order to polish themselves, by seeing the World, and understanding Men and Manners; there are few Persons of Distinction, or Merchants, or Seamen, who dwell in the Maritime Parts, but what can hold Conversation in both Tongues; as I found some Weeks after, when I went to pay my Respects to the Emperor of *Blefuscu,* which in the Midst of great Misfortunes, through the Malice of my Enemies, proved a very happy Adventure to me, as I shall relate in its proper Place.

THE Reader may remember, that when I signed those Articles upon which I recovered my Liberty, there were some which I disliked upon Account of their being too servile, neither could any thing but an extreme Necessity have forced me to submit. But being now a *Nardac*, of the highest Rank in that Empire, such Offices were looked upon as below my Dignity; and the Emperor (to do him Justice) never once mentioned them to me. However, it was not long before I had an Opportunity of doing his Majesty, at least, as I then thought, a most signal Service. I was alarmed at Midnight with the Cries of many Hundred People at my Door; by which being suddenly awaked, I was in some Kind of Terror. I heard the Word *Burglum* repeated incessantly; several of the Emperor's Court making their Way through the Croud, intreated me to come immediately to the Palace, where her Imperial Majesty's Apartment was on fire, by the Carelessness of a Maid of Honour, who fell asleep while she was reading a Romance. I got up in an Instant; and Orders being given to clear the Way before me; and it being likewise a Moonshine Night, I made a shift to get to the Palace without trampling on any of the People. I found they had already applied Ladders to the Walls of the Apartment, and were well provided with Buckets, but the Water was at some Distance. These Buckets were about the Size of a large Thimble, and the poor People supplied me with them as fast as they could; but the Flame was so violent, that they did little Good. I might easily have stifled it with my Coat, which I unfortunately left behind me for haste, and came away only in my Leathern Jerkin. The Case seemed wholly desperate and deplorable; and this magnificent Palace would have infallibly been burnt down to the Ground, if, by a Presence of Mind, unusual to me, I had not suddenly thought of an Expedient. I had the Evening before drank plentifully of a most delicious Wine, called *Glimigrim,* (the *Blefuscudians* call it *Flunec,* but ours is esteemed the better Sort) which is very diuretick. By the luckiest Chance in the World, I had not discharged myself of any Part of it. The Heat I had contracted by coming very near the Flames, and by my labouring to quench them, made the Wine begin to operate by Urine; which I voided in such a Quantity, and applied so well to the proper Places, that in three Minutes the Fire was wholly extinguished;[28] and the rest of that noble Pile, which had cost so many Ages in erecting, preserved from Destruction.

IT was now Day-light, and I returned to my House, without waiting to congratulate with the Emperor; because, although I had done a very eminent Piece of Service, yet I could not tell how his Majesty might resent the Manner by which I had performed it: For, by the fundamental Laws of the Realm, it is Capital in any Person, of what Quality soever, to make water within the Precincts of the Palace. But I was a little comforted by a Message from his Majesty, that he would give Orders to the Grand Justiciary for passing my Pardon in Form; which, however, I could not obtain. And I was privately assured, that the Empress conceiving the greatest Abhorrence of what I had done, removed to the most distant Side of the Court, firmly resolved that those Buildings should never be repaired for her Use; and, in the Presence of her chief Confidents, could not forbear vowing Revenge.

CHAPTER VI

Of the Inhabitants of Lilliput; *their Learning, Laws, and Customs. The Manner of Educating their Children. The Author's Way of living in that Country. His Vindication of a great Lady.*

Although I intend to leave the Description of this Empire to a particular Treatise, yet in the mean time I am content to gratify the curious Reader with some general Ideas.[29] As the common Size of the Natives is somewhat under six Inches, so there is an exact Proportion in all other Animals, as well as Plants and Trees: For Instance, the tallest Horses and Oxen are between four and five Inches in Height, the Sheep an Inch and a half, more or less; their Geese about the Bigness of a Sparrow; and so the several Gradations downwards, till you come to the smallest, which, to my Sight, were almost invisible; but Nature hath adapted the Eyes of the *Lilliputians* to all Objects proper for their View: They see with great Exactness, but at no great Distance. And to show the Sharpness of their Sight towards Objects that are near, I have been much pleased with observing a Cook pulling a Lark, which was not so large as a common Fly; and a young Girl threading an invisible Needle with invisible Silk. Their tallest Trees are about seven Foot high; I mean some of those in the great Royal Park, the Tops whereof I could but just reach with my Fist clinched. The other Vegetables are in the same Proportion: But this I leave to the Reader's Imagination.

I SHALL say but little at present of their Learning, which for many Ages hath flourished in all its Branches among them: But their Manner of Writing is very peculiar; being neither from the Left to the Right, like the *Europeans;* nor from the Right to the Left, like the *Arabians;* nor from up to down, like the *Chinese;* nor from down to up, like the *Cascagians;*[30] but aslant from one Corner of the Paper to the other, like Ladies in *England.*

THEY bury their Dead with their Heads directly downwards; because they hold an Opinion, that in eleven Thousand Moons they are all to rise again; in which Period, the Earth (which they conceive to be flat) will turn upside down, and by this Means they shall, at their Resurrection, be found ready standing on their Feet. The Learned among them confess the Absurdity of this Doctrine; but the Practice still continues, in Compliance to the Vulgar.

THERE are some Laws and Customs in this Empire very peculiar; and if they were not so directly contrary to those of my own dear Country, I should be tempted to say a little in their Justification. It is only to be wished, that they were as well executed. The first I shall mention, relateth to Informers. All Crimes against the State, are punished here with the utmost Severity; but if the Person accused make his Innocence plainly to appear upon his Tryal, the Accuser is immediately put to an ignominious Death; and out of his Goods or Lands, the innocent Person is quadruply recompensed for the Loss of his Time, for the Danger he underwent, for the Hardship of his Imprisonment, and for all the Charges he hath been at in making his Defence. Or, if that Fund be deficient, it is largely supplyed by the Crown. The Emperor doth also confer on him some publick Mark of his Favour; and Proclamation is made of his Innocence through the whole City.

THEY look upon Fraud as a greater Crime than Theft, and therefore seldom fail to punish it with Death: For they alledge, that Care and Vigilance, with a very common Understanding, may preserve a Man's Goods from Thieves; but Honesty hath no Fence against superior Cunning: And since it is necessary that there should be a perpetual Intercourse of buying and selling, and dealing upon Credit; where Fraud is permitted or connived at, or hath no Law to punish it, the honest Dealer is always undone, and the Knave gets the Advantage. I remember when I was once interceeding with the King for a Criminal who had wronged his Master of a great Sum of Money, which he had received by Order, and ran away with; and happening to tell his Majesty, by way of Extenuation, that it was only a Breach of Trust; the Emperor thought it monstrous in me to offer, as a Defence, the greatest Aggravation of the Crime: And truly, I had little to say in Return, farther than the common Answer, that different Nations had different Customs;[31] for, I confess, I was heartily ashamed.

ALTHOUGH we usually call Reward and Punishment, the two Hinges upon which all Government turns; yet I could never observe this Maxim to be put in Practice by any Nation, except that of *Lilliput*. Whoever can there bring sufficient Proof that he hath strictly observed the Laws of his Country for Seventy-three Moons, hath a Claim to certain Privileges, according to his Quality and Condition of Life, with a proportionable Sum of Money out of a Fund appropriated for that Use: He likewise acquires the Title of *Snilpall,* or *Legal,* which is added to his Name, but doth not descend to his Posterity. And these People thought it a prodigious Defect of Policy among us, when I told them that our Laws were enforced only by Penalties, without any Mention of Reward. It is upon this account that the Image of Justice, in their Courts of Judicature, is formed with six Eyes, two before, as many behind, and on each Side one, to signify Circumspection; with a Bag of Gold open in her right Hand, and a Sword sheathed in her left, to shew she is more disposed to reward than to punish.

In chusing Persons for all Employments, they have more Regard to good Morals than to great Abilities: For, since Government is necessary to Mankind, they believe that the common Size of human Understandings, is fitted to some Station or other; and that Providence never intended to make the Management of publick Affairs a Mystery, to be comprehended only by a few Persons of sublime Genius, of which there seldom are three born in an Age: But, they suppose Truth, Justice, Temperance, and the like, to be in every Man's Power; the Practice of which Virtues, assisted by Experience and a good Intention, would qualify any Man for the Service of his Country, except where a Course of Study is required. But they thought the Want of Moral Virtues was so far from being supplied by superior Endowments of the Mind, that Employments could never be put into such dangerous Hands as those of Persons so qualified; and at least, that the Mistakes committed by Ignorance in a virtuous Disposition, would never be of such fatal Consequence to the Publick Weal, as the Practices of a Man, whose Inclinations led him to be corrupt, and had great Abilities to manage, to multiply, and defend his Corruptions.

In like Manner, the Disbelief of a Divine Providence renders a Man uncapable of holding any publick Station: For, since Kings avow themselves to be the Deputies of Providence, the *Lilliputians* think nothing can be more absurd than for a Prince to employ such Men as disown the Authority under which he acteth.

In relating these and the following Laws, I would only be understood to mean the original Institutions, and not the most scandalous Corruptions into which these People are fallen by the degenerate Nature of Man. For as to that infamous Practice of acquiring great Employments by dancing on the Ropes, or Badges of Favour and Distinction by leaping over Sticks, and creeping under them; the Reader is to observe, that they were first introduced by the Grand-father of the Emperor now reigning; and grew to the present Height, by the gradual Increase of Party and Faction.

INGRATITUDE is among them a capital Crime, as we read it to have been in some other Countries: For they reason thus; that whoever makes ill Returns to his Benefactor, must needs be a common Enemy to the rest of Mankind, from whom he hath received no Obligation; and therefore such a Man is not fit to live.

THEIR Notions relating to the Duties of Parents and Children differ extremely from ours.[32] For, since the Conjunction of Male and Female is founded upon the great Law of Nature, in order to propagate and continue the Species; the *Lilliputians* will needs have it, that Men and Women are joined together like other Animals, by the Motives of Concupiscence; and that their Tenderness towards their Young, proceedeth from the like natural Principle: For which Reason they will never allow, that a Child is under any Obligation to his Father for begetting him, or to his Mother for bringing him into the World; which, considering the Miseries of human Life, was neither a Benefit in itself, nor intended so by his Parents, whose Thoughts in their Love-encounters were otherwise employed. Upon these, and the like Reasonings, their Opinion is, that Parents are the last of all others to be trusted with the Education of their own Children: And therefore they have in every Town publick Nurseries, where all Parents, except Cottagers and Labourers, are obliged to send their Infants of both Sexes to be reared and educated when they come to the Age of twenty Moons; at which Time they are supposed to have some Rudiments of Docility. These Schools are of several kinds, suited to different Qualities, and to both Sexes. They have certain Professors well skilled in preparing Children for such a Condition of Life as befits the Rank of their Parents, and their own Capacities as well as Inclinations. I shall first say something of the Male Nurseries, and then of the Female.

THE Nurseries for Males of Noble or Eminent Birth, are provided with grave and learned Professors,[33] and their several Deputies. The Clothes and Food of the Children are plain and simple. They are bred up in the Principles of Honour, Justice, Courage, Modesty, Clemency, Religion, and Love of their Country: They are always employed in some Business, except in the Times of eating and sleeping, which are very short, and two Hours for Diversions, consisting of bodily Exercises. They are dressed by Men until four Years of Age, and then are obliged to dress themselves, although their Quality be ever so great; and the Women Attendants, who are aged proportionably to ours at fifty, perform only the most menial Offices. They are never suffered to converse with Servants, but go together in small or greater Numbers to take their Diversions, and always in the Presence of a Professor, or one of his Deputies; whereby they avoid those early bad Impressions of Folly and Vice to which our Children are subject. Their Parents are suffered to see them only twice a Year; the Visit is not to last above an Hour; they are allowed to kiss the Child at Meeting and Parting; but a Professor, who always standeth by on those Occasions, will not suffer them to whisper, or use any fondling Expressions,[34] or bring any Presents of Toys, Sweet-meats, and the like.

THE Pension from each Family for the Education and Entertainment of a Child, upon Failure of due Payment, is levyed by the Emperor's Officers.

THE Nurseries for Children of ordinary Gentlemen, Merchants, Traders, and Handicrafts, are managed proportionably after the same Manner; only those designed for Trades, are put out Apprentices at seven Years old; whereas those of Persons of Quality continue in their Exercises until Fifteen, which answers to One and Twenty with us: But the Confinement is gradually lessened for the last three Years.

IN the Female Nurseries, the young Girls of Quality are educated much like the Males, only they are dressed by orderly Servants of their own Sex, but always in the Presence of a Professor or Deputy, until they come to dress themselves, which is at five Years old. And if it be found that these Nurses ever presume to entertain the Girls with frightful or foolish Stories, or the common Follies practised by Chamber-Maids among us; they are publickly whipped thrice about the City, imprisoned for a Year, and banished for Life to the most desolate Part of the Country. Thus the young Ladies there are as much ashamed of being Cowards and Fools, as the Men; and despise all personal Ornaments beyond Decency and Cleanliness; neither did I perceive any Difference in their Education, made by their Difference of Sex, only that the Exercises of the Females were not altogether so robust; and that some Rules were given them relating to domestick Life, and a smaller Compass of Learning was enjoyned them: For, their Maxim is, that among People of Quality, a Wife should be always a reasonable and agreeable Companion, because she cannot always be young. When the Girls are twelve Years old, which among them is the marriageable Age, their Parents or Guardians take them home, with great Expressions of Gratitude to the Professors, and seldom without Tears of the young Lady and her Companions.

IN the Nurseries of Females of the meaner Sort, the Children are instructed in all Kinds of Works proper for their Sex, and their several Degrees: Those intended for Apprentices are dismissed at seven Years old, the rest are kept to eleven.

THE meaner Families who have Children at these Nurseries, are obliged, besides their annual Pension, which is as low as possible, to return to the Steward of the Nursery a small Monthly Share of their Gettings, to be a Portion for the Child; and therefore all Parents are limited in their Expences by the Law. For the *Lilliputians* think nothing can be more unjust, than that People, in Subservience to their own Appetites, should bring Children into the World, and leave the Burthen of supporting them on the Publick. As to Persons of Quality, they give Security to appropriate a certain Sum for each Child, suitable to their Condition; and these Funds are always managed with good Husbandry, and the most exact Justice.

THE Cottagers and Labourers keep their Children at home, their Business being only to till and cultivate the Earth; and therefore their Education is of little Consequence to the Publick; but the Old and Diseased among them are supported by Hospitals: For begging is a Trade unknown in this Empire.

AND here it may perhaps divert the curious Reader, to give some Account of my Domestick, and my Manner of living in this Country, during a Residence of nine Months and thirteen Days. Having a Head mechanically turned, and being likewise forced by Necessity, I had made for myself a Table and Chair convenient enough, out of the largest Trees in the Royal Park. Two hundred Sempstresses were employed to make me Shirts, and Linnen for my Bed and Table, all of the strongest and coarsest kind they could get; which, however, they were forced to quilt together in several Folds; for the thickest was some Degrees finer than Lawn. Their Linnen is usually three Inches wide, and three Foot make a Piece. The Sempstresses took my Measure as I lay on the Ground, one standing at my Neck, and another at my Mid-Leg, with a strong Cord extended, that each held by the End, while the third measured the Length of the Cord with a Rule of an Inch long. Then they measured my right Thumb, and desired no more; for by a mathematical Computation, that twice round the Thumb is once round the Wrist, and so on to the Neck and the Waist; and by the Help of my old Shirt, which I displayed on the Ground before them for a Pattern, they fitted me exactly. Three hundred Taylors were employed in the same Manner to make me Clothes; but they had another Contrivance for taking my Measure. I kneeled down, and they raised a Ladder from the Ground to my Neck; upon this Ladder one of them mounted, and let fall a Plum-Line from my Collar to the Floor, which just answered the Length of my Coat; but my Waist and Arms I measured myself. When my Cloaths were finished, which was done in my House, (for the largest of theirs would not have been able to hold them) they looked like the Patch-work made by the Ladies in *England,* only that mine were all of a Colour.

I HAD three hundred Cooks to dress my Victuals, in little convenient Huts built about my House, where they and their Families lived, and prepared me two Dishes a-piece. I took up twenty Waiters in my Hand, and placed them on the Table; an hundred more attended below on the Ground, some with Dishes of Meat, and some with Barrels of Wine, and other Liquors, slung on their Shoulders; all which the Waiters above drew up as I wanted, in a very ingenious Manner, by certain Cords, as we draw the Bucket up a Well in *Europe.* A Dish of their Meat was a good Mouthful, and a Barrel of their Liquor a reasonable Draught. Their Mutton yields to ours, but their Beef is excellent. I have had a Sirloin so large, that I have been forced to make three Bits of it; but this is rare. My Servants were astonished to see me eat it Bones and all, as in our Country we do the Leg of a Lark. Their Geese and Turkeys I usually eat at a Mouthful, and I must confess they far exceed ours. Of their smaller Fowl I could take up twenty or thirty at the End of my Knife.

ONE Day his Imperial Majesty being informed of my Way of living, desired that himself, and his Royal Consort; with the young Princes of the Blood of both Sexes, might have the Happiness (as he was pleased to call it) of dining with me. They came accordingly, and I placed them upon Chairs of State on my Table, just over against me, with their Guards about them. *Flimnap* the Lord High Treasurer attended there likewise, with his white Staff;[35] and I observed he often looked on me with a sour Countenance, which I would not seem to regard, but eat more than usual, in Honour to my dear Country, as well as to fill the Court with Admiration. I have some private Reasons to believe, that this Visit from his Majesty gave *Flimnap* an Opportunity of doing me ill Offices to his Master. That Minister had always been my secret Enemy, although he outwardly caressed me more than was usual to the Moroseness of his Nature. He represented to the Emperor the low Condition of his Treasury; that he was forced to take up Money at great Discount; that Exchequer Bills would not circulate under nine *per Cent.* below Par; that I had cost his Majesty above a Million and a half of *Sprugs,* (their greatest Gold Coin, about the Bigness of a Spangle;) and upon the whole, that it would be adviseable in the Emperor to take the first fair Occasion of dismissing me.

I AM here obliged to vindicate the Reputation of an excellent Lady, who was an innocent Sufferer upon my Account. The Treasurer took a Fancy to be jealous of his Wife, from the Malice of some evil Tongues, who informed him that her Grace had taken a violent Affection for my Person; and the Court-Scandal ran for some Time that she once came privately to my Lodging. This I solemnly declare to be a most infamous Falshood, without any Grounds, farther than that her Grace was pleased to treat me with all innocent Marks of Freedom and Friendship. I own she came often to my House, but always publickly, nor ever without three more in the Coach, who were usually her Sister, and young Daughter, and some particular Acquaintance; but this was common to many other Ladies of the Court. And I still appeal to my Servants round, whether they at any Time saw a Coach at my Door without knowing what Persons were in it. On those Occasions, when a Servant had given me Notice, my Custom was to go immediately to the Door; and after paying my Respects, to take up the Coach and two Horses very carefully in my Hands, (for if there were six Horses, the Postillion always unharnessed four) and place them on a Table, where I had fixed a moveable Rim quite round, of five Inches high, to prevent Accidents. And I have often had four Coaches and Horses at once on my Table full of Company, while I sat in my Chair leaning my Face towards them; and when I was engaged with one Sett, the Coachmen would gently drive the others round my Table. I have passed many an Afternoon very agreeably in these Conversations: But I defy the Treasurer, or his two Informers. (I will name them, and let them make their best of it) *Clustril* and *Drunlo,* to prove that any Person ever came to me *incognito,* except the Secretary *Reldresal,* who was sent by express Command of his Imperial Majesty, as I have before related. I should not have dwelt so long upon this Particular, if it had not been a Point wherein the Reputation of a great Lady is so nearly concerned; to say nothing of my own; although I had the Honour to be a *Nardac,* which the Treasurer himself is not; for all the World knows he is only a *Clumglum,* a Title inferior by one Degree, as that of a Marquess is to a Duke in *England;* yet I allow he preceded me in right of his Post. These false Informations, which I afterwards came to the Knowledge of, by an Accident not proper to mention, made the Treasurer shew his Lady for some Time an ill Countenance, and me a worse: For although he were at last undeceived and reconciled to her, yet I lost all Credit with him; and found my Interest decline very fast with the Emperor himself, who was indeed too much governed by that Favourite.

CHAPTER VII

*The Author being informed of a Design to accuse him of High
Treason, makes his Escape to* Blefuscu. *His Reception there.*

Before I proceed to give an Account of my leaving this Kingdom, it may
be proper to inform the Reader of a private Intrigue which had been for
two Months forming against me.

I HAD been hitherto all my Life a Stranger to Courts, for which I was
unqualified by the Meanness of my Condition. I had indeed heard and
read enough of the Dispositions of great Princes and Ministers; but never
expected to have found such terrible Effects of them in so remote a Country, governed, as I thought, by very different Maxims from those in *Europe*.

WHEN I was just preparing to pay my Attendance on the Emperor of
Blefuscu; a considerable Person at Court (to whom I had been very serviceable at a time when he lay under the highest Displeasure of his Imperial Majesty) came to my House very privately at Night in a close Chair,
and without sending his Name, desired Admittance: The Chair-men were
dismissed; I put the Chair, with his Lordship in it, into my Coat-Pocket;
and giving Orders to a trusty Servant to say I was indisposed and gone to
sleep, I fastened the Door of my House, placed the Chair on the Table, according to my usual Custom, and sat down by it. After the common Salutations were over, observing his Lordship's Countenance full of Concern;
and enquiring into the Reason, he desired I would hear him with Patience,
in a Matter that highly concerned my Honour and my Life. His Speech
was to the following Effect, for I took Notes of it as soon as he left me.

———

YOU are to know, said he, that several Committees of Council have been
lately called in the most private Manner on your Account: And it is but
two Days since his Majesty came to a full Resolution.

YOU are very sensible that *Skyris Bolgolam* (*Galbet*, or High Admiral) hath been your mortal Enemy almost ever since your Arrival. His original Reasons I know not; but his Hatred is much encreased since your great Success against *Blefuscu*, by which his Glory, as Admiral, is obscured. This Lord, in Conjunction with *Flimnap* the High Treasurer, whose Enmity against you is notorious on Account of his Lady; *Limtoc* the General, *Lalcon* the Chamberlain, and *Balmuff* the grand Justiciary, have prepared Articles of Impeachment against you, for Treason, and other capital Crimes.

THIS Preface made me so impatient, being conscious of my own Merits and Innocence, that I was going to interrupt; when he intreated me to be silent; and thus proceeded.

OUT of Gratitude for the Favours you have done me, I procured Information of the whole Proceedings, and a Copy of the Articles, wherein I venture my Head for your Service.

ARTICLES OF IMPEACHMENT[36] AGAINST QUINBUS FLESTRIN, (*THE* MAN·MOUNTAIN.)

ARTICLE I.

Whereas, by a Statute made in the Reign of his Imperial Majesty *Calin Deffar Plune*, it is enacted, That whoever shall make water within the Precincts of the Royal Palace, shall be liable to the Pains and Penalties of High Treason: Notwithstanding, the said *Quinbus Flestrin*, in open Breach of the said Law, under Colour of extinguishing the Fire kindled in the Apartment of his Majesty's most dear Imperial Consort, did maliciously, traitorously, and devilishly, by discharge of his Urine, put out the said Fire kindled in the said Apartment, lying and being within the Precincts of the said Royal Palace; against the Statute in that Case provided, &c. against the Duty, &c.

ARTICLE II.

THAT the said *Quinbus Flestrin* having brought the Imperial Fleet of *Blefuscu* into the Royal Port, and being afterwards commanded by his Imperial Majesty to seize all the other Ships of the said Empire of *Blefuscu*, and reduce that Empire to a Province, to be governed by a Vice-Roy from hence; and to destroy and put to death not only all the *Big-Endian Exiles*, but likewise all the People of that Empire, who would not immediately forsake the *Big-Endian* Heresy: He the said *Flestrin*, like a false Traitor against his most Auspicious, Serene,[37] Imperial Majesty, did petition to be excused from the said Service, upon Pretence of Unwillingness to force the Consciences, or destroy the Liberties and Lives of an innocent People.

ARTICLE III.

THAT, whereas certain Embassadors arrived from the Court of *Blefuscu* to sue for Peace in his Majesty's Court: He the said *Flestrin* did, like a false Traitor, aid, abet, comfort, and divert the said Embassadors; although he knew them to be Servants to a Prince who was lately an open Enemy to his Imperial Majesty, and in open War against his said Majesty.

ARTICLE IV.

THAT the said *Quinbus Flestrin,* contrary to the Duty of a faithful Subject, is now preparing to make a Voyage to the Court and Empire of *Blefuscu,* for which he hath received only verbal Licence from his Imperial Majesty; and under Colour of the said Licence, doth falsely and traitorously intend to take the said Voyage, and thereby to aid, comfort, and abet the Emperor of *Blefuscu,* so late an Enemy, and in open War with his Imperial Majesty aforesaid.

THERE are some other Articles, but these are the most important, of which I have read you an Abstract.

IN the several Debates upon this Impeachment, it must be confessed that his Majesty gave many Marks of his great *Lenity;* often urging the Services you had done him, and endeavouring to extenuate your Crimes. The Treasurer and Admiral insisted that you should be put to the most painful and ignominious Death, by setting Fire on your House at Night; and the General was to attend with Twenty Thousand Men armed with poisoned Arrows, to shoot you on the Face and Hands. Some of your Servants were to have private Orders to strew a poisonous Juice[38] on your Shirts and Sheets, which would soon make you tear your own Flesh, and die in the utmost Torture. The General came into the same Opinion; so that for a long time there was a Majority against you. But his Majesty resolving, if possible, to spare your Life, at last brought off the Chamberlain.

UPON this Incident, *Reldresal,* principal Secretary for private Affairs, who always approved himself your true Friend, was commanded by the Emperor to deliver his Opinion, which he accordingly did; and therein justified the good Thoughts you have of him. He allowed your Crimes to be great; but that still there was room for Mercy, the most commendable Virtue in a Prince, and for which his Majesty was so justly celebrated. He said, the Friendship between you and him was so well known to the World, that perhaps the most honourable Board might think him partial: However, in Obedience to the Command he had received, he would freely offer his Sentiments. That if his Majesty, in Consideration of your Services, and pursuant to his own merciful Disposition, would please to spare your Life, and only give order to put out both your Eyes;[39] he humbly conceived, that by this Expedient, Justice might in some measure be satisfied, and all the World would applaud the *Lenity* of the Emperor, as well as the fair and generous Proceedings of those who have the Honour to be his Counsellors. That the Loss of your Eyes would be no Impediment to your bodily Strength, by which you might still be useful to his Majesty. That Blindness is an Addition to Courage, by concealing Dangers from us; that the Fear you had for your Eyes, was the greatest Difficulty in bringing over the Enemy's Fleet; and it would be sufficient for you to see by the Eyes of the Ministers, since the greatest Princes do no more.[40]

THIS Proposal was received with the utmost Disapprobation by the whole Board. *Bolgolam,* the Admiral, could not preserve his Temper; but rising up in Fury, said, he wondered how the Secretary durst presume to give his Opinion for preserving the Life of a Traytor: That the Services you had performed, were, by all true Reasons of State, the great Aggravation of your Crimes; that you, who were able to extinguish the Fire, by discharge of Urine in her Majesty's Apartment (which he mentioned with Horror) might, at another time, raise an Inundation by the same Means, to drown the whole Palace; and the same Strength which enabled you to bring over the Enemy's Fleet, might serve, upon the first Discontent, to carry it back: That he had good Reasons to think you were a *Big-Endian* in your Heart; and as Treason begins in the Heart before it appears in Overt-Acts; so he accused you as a Traytor on that Account, and therefore insisted you should be put to death.

THE Treasurer was of the same Opinion; he shewed to what Streights his Majesty's Revenue was reduced by the Charge of maintaining you, which would soon grow insupportable: That the Secretary's Expedient of putting out your Eyes, was so far from being a Remedy against this Evil, that it would probably increase it; as it is manifest from the common Practice of blinding some Kind of Fowl, after which they fed the faster, and grew sooner fat: That his sacred Majesty, and the Council, who are your Judges, were in their own Consciences fully convinced of your Guilt; which was a sufficient Argument to condemn you to death, without the *formal Proofs required by the strict Letter of the Law.*

BUT his Imperial Majesty fully determined against capital Punishment, was graciously pleased to say, that since the Council thought the Loss of your Eyes too easy a Censure, some other may be inflicted hereafter. And your Friend the Secretary humbly desiring to be heard again, in Answer to what the Treasurer had objected concerning the great Charge his Majesty was at in maintaining you; said, that his Excellency, who had the sole Disposal of the Emperor's Revenue, might easily provide against this Evil, by gradually lessening your Establishment; by which, for want of sufficient Food, you would grow weak and faint, and lose your Appetite, and consequently decay and consume in a few Months; neither would the Stench of your Carcass be then so dangerous, when it should become more than half diminished; and immediately upon your Death, five or six Thousand of his Majesty's Subjects might, in two or three Days, cut your Flesh from your Bones, take it away by Cart-loads, and bury it in distant Parts to prevent Infection; leaving the Skeleton as a Monument of Admiration to Posterity.

THUS by the great Friendship of the Secretary, the whole Affair was compromised. It was strictly enjoined, that the Project of starving you by Degrees should be kept a Secret; but the Sentence of putting out your Eyes was entered on the Books; none dissenting except *Bolgolam* the Admiral, who being a Creature of the Empress, was perpetually instigated by her Majesty to insist upon your Death; she having born perpetual Malice against you, on Account of that infamous and illegal Method you took to extinguish the Fire in her Apartment.

IN three Days your Friend the Secretary will be directed to come to your House, and read before you the Articles of Impeachment; and then to signify the great *Lenity* and Favour of his Majesty and Council; whereby you are only condemned to the Loss of your Eyes, which his Majesty doth not question you will gratefully and humbly submit to; and Twenty of his Majesty's Surgeons will attend, in order to see the Operation well performed, by discharging very sharp pointed Arrows into the Balls of your Eyes, as you lie on the Ground.

I LEAVE to your Prudence what Measures you will take; and to avoid Suspicion, I must immediately return in as private a Manner as I came.

HIS Lordship did so, and I remained alone, under many Doubts and Perplexities of Mind.

IT was a Custom introduced by this Prince and his Ministry, (very different, as I have been assured, from the Practices of former Times) that after the Court had decreed any cruel Execution, either to gratify the Monarch's Resentment, or the Malice of a Favourite; the Emperor always made a Speech to his whole Council, expressing his *great Lenity and Tenderness, as Qualities known and confessed by all the World*. This Speech was immediately published through the Kingdom; nor did any thing terrify the People so much as those Encomiums on his Majesty's Mercy;[41] because it was observed, that the more these Praises were enlarged and insisted on, the more *inhuman* was the Punishment, and the *Sufferer more innocent*. Yet, as to myself, I must confess, having never been designed for a Courtier, either by my Birth or Education, I was so ill a Judge of Things, that I could not discover the *Lenity* and Favour of this Sentence; but conceived it (perhaps erroneously) rather to be rigorous than gentle. I sometimes thought of standing my Tryal; for although I could not deny the Facts alledged in the several Articles, yet I hoped they would admit of some Extenuations. But having in my Life perused many State-Tryals, which I ever observed to terminate as the Judges thought fit to direct; I durst not rely on so dangerous a Decision, in so critical a Juncture, and against such powerful Enemies. Once I was strongly bent upon Resistance: For while I had Liberty, the whole Strength of that Empire could hardly subdue me, and I might easily with Stones pelt the Metropolis to Pieces: But I soon rejected that Project with Horror, by remembering the Oath I had made to the Emperor, the Favours I received from him, and the high Title of *Nardac* he conferred upon me. Neither had I so soon learned the Gratitude of Courtiers, to persuade myself that his Majesty's *present Severities acquitted me of all past Obligations*.[42]

AT last I fixed upon a Resolution, for which it is probable I may incur some Censure, and not unjustly; for I confess I owe the preserving mine Eyes, and consequently my Liberty, to my own great Rashness and Want of Experience: Because if I had then known the Nature of Princes and Ministers, which I have since observed in many other Courts, and their Methods of treating Criminals less obnoxious than myself; I should with great Alacrity and Readiness have submitted to so *easy* a Punishment. But hurried on by the Precipitancy of Youth; and having his Imperial Majesty's Licence to pay my Attendance upon the Emperor of *Blefuscu;* I took this Opportunity, before the three Days were elapsed, to send a Letter to my Friend the Secretary, signifying my Resolution of setting out that Morning for *Blefuscu,* pursuant to the Leave I had got; and without waiting for an Answer, I sent to that Side of the Island where our Fleet lay. I seized a large Man of War, tied a Cable to the Prow, and lifting up the Anchors, I stript myself, put my Cloaths (together with my Coverlet, which I carryed under my Arm) into the Vessel; and drawing it after me, between wading and swimming, arrived at the Royal Port of *Blefuscu,* where the People had long expected me: They lent me two Guides to direct me to the Capital City, which is of the same Name; I held them in my Hands until I came within two Hundred Yards of the Gate; and desired them to signify my Arrival to one of the Secretaries, and let him know, I there waited his Majesty's Commands. I had an Answer in about an Hour, that his Majesty, attended by the Royal Family, and great Officers of the Court, was coming out to receive me. I advanced a Hundred Yards; the Emperor, and his Train, alighted from their Horses, the Empress and Ladies from their Coaches; and I did not perceive they were in any Fright or Concern. I lay on the Ground to kiss his Majesty's and the Empress's Hand. I told his Majesty, that I was come according to my Promise, and with the Licence of the Emperor my Master, to have the Honour of seeing so mighty a Monarch, and to offer him any Service in my Power, consistent with my Duty to my own Prince; not mentioning a Word of my Disgrace, because I had hitherto no regular Information of it, and might suppose myself wholly ignorant of any such Design; neither could I reasonably conceive that the Emperor would discover the Secret while I was out of his Power: Wherein, however, it soon appeared I was deceived.

I SHALL not trouble the Reader with the particular Account of my Reception at this Court, which was suitable to the Generosity of so great a Prince; nor of the Difficulties I was in for want of a House and Bed, being forced to lie on the Ground, wrapt up in my Coverlet.

CHAPTER VIII

The Author, by a lucky Accident, finds Means to leave Blefuscu; *and, after some Difficulties, returns safe to his Native Country.*

Three Days after my Arrival, walking out of Curiosity to the North-East Coast of the Island; I observed, about half a League off, in the Sea, somewhat that looked like a Boat overturned: I pulled off my Shoes and Stockings, and wading two or three Hundred Yards, I found the Object to approach nearer by Force of the Tide; and then plainly saw it to be a real Boat, which I supposed might, by some Tempest, have been driven from a Ship. Whereupon I returned immediately towards the City, and desired his Imperial Majesty to lend me Twenty of the tallest Vessels he had left after the Loss of his Fleet, and three Thousand Seamen under the Command of his Vice-Admiral. This Fleet sailed round, while I went back the shortest Way to the Coast where I first discovered the Boat; I found the Tide had driven it still nearer; the Seamen were all provided with Cordage, which I had beforehand twisted to a sufficient Strength. When the Ships came up, I stript myself, and waded till I came within an Hundred Yards of the Boat; after which I was forced to swim till I got up to it. The Seamen threw me the End of the Cord, which I fastened to a Hole in the forepart of the Boat, and the other End to a Man of War: But I found all my Labour to little Purpose; for being out of my Depth, I was not able to work. In this Necessity, I was forced to swim behind, and push the Boat forwards as often as I could, with one of my Hands; and the Tide favouring me, I advanced so far, that I could just hold up my Chin and feel the Ground. I rested two or three Minutes, and then gave the Boat another Shove, and so on till the Sea was no higher than my Arm-pits. And now the most laborious Part being over, I took out my other Cables which were stowed in one of the Ships, and fastening them first to the Boat, and then to nine of the Vessels which attended me; the Wind being favourable, the Seamen towed, and I shoved till we arrived within forty Yards of the Shore; and waiting till the Tide was out, I got dry to the Boat, and by the Assistance of two Thousand Men, with Ropes and Engines, I made a shift to turn it on its Bottom, and found it was but little damaged.

I SHALL not trouble the Reader with the Difficulties I was under by the Help of certain Paddles, which cost me ten Days making, to get my Boat to the Royal Port of *Blefuscu;* where a mighty Concourse of People appeared upon my Arrival, full of Wonder at the Sight of so prodigious a Vessel. I told the Emperor, that my good Fortune had thrown this Boat in my Way, to carry me to some Place from whence I might return into my native Country; and begged his Majesty's Orders for getting Materials to fit it up; together with his Licence to depart; which, after some kind of Expostulations, he was pleased to grant.

I DID very much wonder, in all this Time, not to have heard of any Express relating to me from our Emperor to the Court of *Blefuscu.* But I was afterwards given privately to understand, that his Imperial Majesty, never imagining I had the least Notice of his Designs, believed I was only gone to *Blefuscu* in Performance of my Promise, according to the Licence he had given me, which was well known at our Court; and would return in a few Days when that Ceremony was ended. But he was at last in pain at my long absence; and, after consulting with the Treasurer, and the rest of that Cabal; a Person of Quality was dispatched with the Copy of the Articles against me. This Envoy had Instructions to represent to the Monarch of *Blefuscu,* the great *Lenity* of his Master, who was content to punish me no further than with the Loss of mine Eyes: That I had fled from Justice, and if I did not return in two Hours, I should be deprived of my Title of *Nardac,* and declared a Traitor. The Envoy further added; that in order to maintain the Peace and Amity between both Empires, his Master expected, that his Brother of *Blefuscu* would give Orders to have me sent back to *Lilliput,* bound Hand and Foot, to be punished as a Traitor.

THE Emperor of *Blefuscu* having taken three Days to consult, returned an Answer consisting of many Civilities and Excuses. He said, that as for sending me bound, his Brother knew it was impossible; that although I had deprived him of his Fleet, yet he owed great Obligations to me for many good Offices I had done him in making the Peace. That however, both their Majesties would soon be made easy; for I had found a prodigious Vessel on the shore, able to carry me on the Sea, which he had given order to fit up with my own Assistance and Direction; and he hoped in a few Weeks both Empires would be freed from so insupportable an Incumbrance.

WITH this Answer the Envoy returned to *Lilliput,* and the Monarch of *Blefuscu* related to me all that had past; offering me at the same time (but under the strictest Confidence) his gracious Protection, if I would continue in his Service; wherein although I believed him sincere, yet I resolved never more to put any Confidence in Princes or Ministers, where I could possibly avoid it; and therefore, with all due Acknowledgments for his favourable Intentions, I humbly begged to be excused. I told him, that since Fortune, whether good or evil, had thrown a Vessel in my Way; I resolved to venture myself in the Ocean, rather than be an Occasion of Difference between two such mighty Monarchs. Neither did I find the Emperor at all displeased; and I discovered by a certain Accident, that he was very glad of my Resolution, and so were most of his Ministers.

THESE Considerations moved me to hasten my Departure somewhat sooner than I intended; to which the Court, impatient to have me gone, very readily contributed. Five hundred Workmen were employed to make two Sails to my Boat, according to my Directions, by quilting thirteen fold of their strongest Linnen together. I was at the Pains of making Ropes and Cables, by twisting ten, twenty or thirty of the thickest and strongest of theirs. A great Stone that I happened to find, after a long Search by the Sea-shore, served me for an Anchor. I had the Tallow of three hundred Cows for greasing my Boat, and other Uses. I was at incredible Pains in cutting down some of the largest Timber Trees for Oars and Masts, wherein I was, however, much assisted by his Majesty's Ship-Carpenters, who helped me in smoothing them, after I had done the rough Work.

IN about a Month, when all was prepared, I sent to receive his Majesty's Commands, and to take my leave. The Emperor and Royal Family came out of the Palace; I lay down on my Face to kiss his Hand, which he very graciously gave me; so did the Empress, and young Princes of the Blood. His Majesty presented me with fifty Purses of two hundred *Sprugs* a-piece, together with his Picture at full length, which I put immediately into one of my Gloves, to keep it from being hurt. The Ceremonies at my Departure were too many to trouble the Reader with at this time.

I STORED the Boat with the Carcasses of an hundred Oxen, and three hundred Sheep, with Bread and Drink proportionable, and as much Meat ready dressed as four hundred Cooks could provide. I took with me six Cows and two Bulls alive, with as many Yews and Rams, intending to carry them into my own Country, and propagate the Breed. And to feed them on board, I had a good Bundle of Hay, and a Bag of Corn. I would gladly have taken a Dozen of the Natives; but this was a thing the Emperor would by no Means permit; and besides a diligent Search into my Pockets, his Majesty engaged my Honour not to carry away any of his Subjects, although with their own Consent and Desire.

HAVING thus prepared all things as well as I was able; I set sail on the Twenty-fourth Day of *September* 1701, at six in the Morning; and when I had gone about four Leagues to the Northward, the Wind being at South-East; at six in the Evening, I descryed a small Island about half a League to the North West. I advanced forward, and cast Anchor on the Lee-side of the Island, which seemed to be uninhabited. I then took some Refreshment, and went to my Rest. I slept well, and as I conjecture at least six Hours; for I found the Day broke in two Hours after I awaked. It was a clear Night; I eat my Breakfast before the Sun was up; and heaving Anchor, the Wind being favourable, I steered the same Course that I had done the Day before, wherein I was directed by my Pocket-Compass. My Intention was to reach, if possible, one of those Islands, which I had reason to believe lay to the North-East of *Van Diemen's* Land. I discovered nothing all that Day; but upon the next, about three in the Afternoon, when I had by my Computation made Twenty-four Leagues from *Blefuscu,* I descryed a Sail steering to the South-East; my Course was due East. I hailed her, but could get no Answer; yet I found I gained upon her, for the Wind slackened. I made all the Sail I could, and in half an Hour she spyed me, then hung out her Antient,[43] and discharged a Gun. It is not easy to express the Joy I was in upon the unexpected Hope of once more seeing my beloved Country, and the dear Pledges I had left in it. The Ship slackned her Sails, and I came up with her between five and six in the Evening, *September* 26; but my Heart leapt within me to see her *English* Colours. I put my Cows and Sheep into my Coat-Pockets, and got on board with all my little Cargo of Provisions. The Vessel was an *English* Merchant-man, returning from *Japan* by the *North* and *South Seas;* the Captain, Mr. *John Biddel* of *Deptford,* a very civil Man, and an excellent Sailor. We were now in the Latitude of 30 Degrees South; there were about fifty Men in the Ship; and here I met an old Comrade of mine, one *Peter Williams,* who gave me a good Character to the Captain. This Gentleman treated me with Kindness, and desired I would let him know what Place I came from last, and whither I was bound; which I did in few Words; but he thought I was raving, and that the Dangers I underwent had disturbed my Head; whereupon I took my black Cattle and Sheep out of my

Pocket, which, after great Astonishment, clearly convinced him of my Veracity. I then shewed him the Gold given me by the Emperor of *Blefuscu,* together with his Majesty's Picture at full Length, and some other Rarities of that Country. I gave him two Purses of two Hundred *Sprugs* each, and promised, when we arrived in *England,* to make him a Present of a Cow and a Sheep big with Young.

I SHALL not trouble the Reader with a particular Account of this Voyage, which was very prosperous for the most Part. We arrived in the *Downs* on the 13th of *April* 1702. I had only one Misfortune, that the Rats on board carried away one of my Sheep; I found her Bones in a Hole, picked clean from the Flesh. The rest of my Cattle I got safe on Shore, and set them a grazing in a Bowling-Green at *Greenwich,* where the Fineness of the Grass made them feed very heartily, although I had always feared the contrary: Neither could I possibly have preserved them in so long a Voyage, if the Captain had not allowed me some of his best Bisket, which rubbed to Powder, and mingled with Water, was their constant Food. The short Time I continued in *England,* I made a considerable Profit by shewing my Cattle to many Persons of Quality, and others: And before I began my second Voyage, I sold them for six Hundred Pounds. Since my last Return, I find the Breed is considerably increased, especially the Sheep; which I hope will prove much to the Advantage of the Woollen Manufacture, by the Fineness of the Fleeces.

I STAYED but two Months with my Wife and Family; for my insatiable Desire of seeing foreign Countries would suffer me to continue no longer. I left fifteen Hundred Pounds with my Wife and fixed her in a good House at *Redriff.* My remaining Stock I carried with me, Part in Money, and Part in Goods, in Hopes to improve my Fortunes. My eldest Uncle, *John,* had left me an Estate in Land, near *Epping,* of about Thirty Pounds a Year; and I had a long Lease of the *Black-Bull* in *Fetter-Lane,* which yielded me as much more: So that I was not in any Danger of leaving my Family upon the Parish. My Son *Johnny,* named so after his Uncle, was at the Grammar School, and a towardly Child. My Daughter *Betty* (who is now well married, and has Children) was then at her Needle-Work. I took Leave of my Wife, and boy and Girl, with Tears on both Sides; and went on board the *Adventure,* a Merchant-Ship of three Hundred Tons, bound for *Surat,* Captain *John Nicholas* of *Liverpool,* Commander. But my Account of this Voyage must be referred to the second Part of my Travels.

The End of the First Part.

PART II

A VOYAGE TO BROBDINGNAG

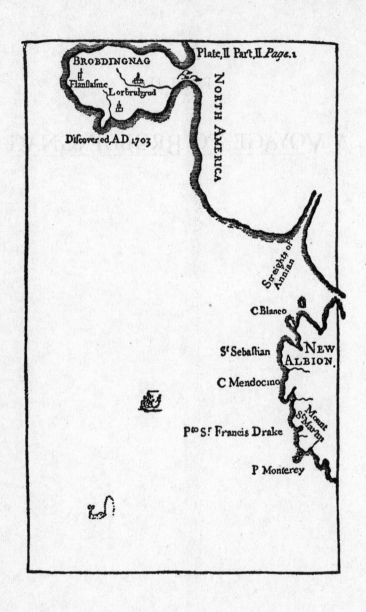

Plate. II Part. II *Page.* 1

BROBDINGNAG

Flanflasnic

Lorbrulgrud

Discovered AD 1703

NORTH AMERICA

Sreights of Anaian

C. Blanco

St Sebastian

C Mendocino

NEW ALBION.

Pto St Francis Drake

Mount St Martin

P Monterey

CHAPTER I

*A great Storm described. The long Boat sent to fetch Water, the
Author goes with it to discover the Country. He is left on Shoar,
is seized by one of the Natives, and carried to a Farmer's House.
His Reception there, with several Accidents that happened there.
A Description of the Inhabitants.*

Having been condemned by Nature and Fortune to an active and restless
Life; in two Months after my Return, I again left my native Country, and
took Shipping in the *Downs* on the 20th Day of *June* 1702, in the *Adventure,*
Capt. *John Nicholas,* a *Cornish* Man, Commander, bound for *Surat.* We had a
very prosperous Gale till we arrived at the *Cape* of *Good-hope,* where we
landed for fresh Water; but discovering a Leak we unshipped our Goods,
and wintered there; for the Captain falling sick of an Ague, we could not
leave the *Cape* till the End of *March.* We then set sail, and had a good Voyage till we passed the *Streights* of *Madagascar;* but having got Northward of
that Island, and to about five Degrees South Latitude, the Winds, which in
those Seas are observed to blow a constant equal Gale between the North
and West, from the Beginning of *December* to the Beginning of *May,* on the
19th of *April* began to blow with much greater Violence, and more West-
erly than usual; continuing so for twenty Days together, during which
time we were driven a little to the East of the *Molucca* Islands, and about
three Degrees Northward of the Line, as our Captain found by an Observation he took the 2d of *May,* at which time the Wind ceased, and it was a
perfect Calm, whereat I was not a little rejoyced. But he being a Man well
experienced in the Navigation of those Seas, bid us all prepare against a
Storm, which accordingly happened the Day following: For a Southern
Wind, called the Southern *Monsoon,* began to set in.

FINDING it was like to overblow, we took in our Sprit-sail, and stood by
to hand the Fore-sail; but making foul Weather, we looked the Guns were
all fast, and handed the Missen. The Ship lay very broad off, so we thought

it better spooning before the Sea, than trying or hulling. We reeft the Foresail and set him, we hawled aft the Fore-sheet; the Helm was hard a Weather. The Ship wore bravely. We belay'd the Foredown-hall; but the Sail was split, and we hawl'd down the Yard, and got the Sail into the Ship, and unbound all the things clear of it. It was a very fierce Storm; the Sea broke strange and dangerous. We hawl'd off upon the Lanniard of the Wipstaff, and helped the Man at Helm. We would not get down our Top-Mast, but let all stand, because she scudded before the Sea very well, and we knew that the Top-Mast being aloft, the Ship was the wholesomer, and made better way through the Sea, seeing we had Sea room. When the Storm was over, we set Fore-sail and Main-sail, and brought the Ship to. Then we set the Missen, Maintop-Sail and the Foretop-Sail. Our Course was East North-east, the Wind was at South-west. We got the Star-board Tacks aboard, we cast off our Weather-braces and Lifts; we set in the Lee-braces, and hawl'd forward by the Weather-bowlings, and hawl'd them tight, and belayed them, and hawl'd over the Missen Tack to Windward, and kept her full and by as near as she would lye.[1]

DURING this Storm, which was followed by a strong Wind West South-west, we were carried by my Computation about five hundred Leagues to the East, so that the oldest Sailor on Board could not tell in what part of the World we were. Our Provisions held out well, our Ship was staunch, and our Crew all in good Health; but we lay in the utmost Distress for Water. We thought it best to hold on the same Course rather than turn more Northerly, which might have brought us to the North-west Parts of great *Tartary*, and into the frozen Sea.[2]

ON the 16*th* Day of *June* 1703, a Boy on the Top-mast discovered Land. On the 17*th* we came in full View of a great Island or Continent, (for we knew not whether) on the Southside whereof was a small Neck of Land jutting out into the Sea, and a Creek too shallow to hold a Ship of above one hundred Tuns. We cast Anchor within a League of this Creek, and our Captain sent a dozen of his Men well armed in the Long Boat, with Vessels for Water if any could be found. I desired his leave to go with them, that I might see the Country, and make what Discoveries I could. When we came to Land we saw no River or Spring, nor any Sign of In-habitants. Our Men therefore wandered on the Shore to find out some fresh Water near the Sea, and I walked alone about a Mile on the other side, where I observed the Country all barren and rocky. I now began to be weary, and seeing nothing to entertain my Curiosity, I returned gently down towards the Creek; and the Sea being full in my View, I saw our Men already got into the Boat, and rowing for Life to the Ship. I was going to hollow after them, although it had been to little purpose, when I observed a huge Creature walking after them in the Sea, as fast as he could: He waded not much deeper than his Knees, and took prodigious strides: But our Men had the start of him half a League, and the Sea thereabouts being full of sharp pointed Rocks, the Monster was not able to overtake the Boat. This I was afterwards told, for I durst not stay to see the Issue of that Adventure; but ran as fast as I could the Way I first went; and then climbed up a steep Hill, which gave me some Prospect of the Country. I found it fully cultivated; but that which first surprized me was the Length of the Grass, which in those Grounds that seemed to be kept for Hay, was above twenty Foot high.

I FELL into a high Road, for so I took it to be, although it served to the Inhabitants only as a foot Path through a Field of Barley. Here I walked on for sometime, but could see little on either Side, it being now near Harvest, and the Corn rising at least forty Foot. I was an Hour walking to the end of this Field; which was fenced in with a Hedge of at least one hundred and twenty Foot high, and the Trees so lofty that I could make no Computation of their Altitude. There was a Stile to pass from this Field into the next: It had four Steps, and a Stone to cross over when you came to the uppermost. It was impossible for me to climb this Stile, because every Step was six Foot high, and the upper Stone above twenty. I was endeavouring to find some Gap in the Hedge; when I discovered one of the Inhabitants in the next Field advancing towards the Stile, of the same Size with him whom I saw in the Sea pursuing our Boat. He appeared as Tall as an ordinary Spire-steeple; and took about ten Yards at every Stride, as near as I could guess. I was struck with the utmost Fear and Astonishment, and ran to hide my self in the Corn, from whence I saw him at the Top of the Stile, looking back into the next Field on the right Hand; and heard him call in a Voice many Degrees louder than a speaking Trumpet; but the Noise was so High in the Air, that at first I certainly thought it was Thunder. Whereupon seven Monsters like himself came towards him with Reaping-Hooks in their Hands, each Hook about the largeness of six Scythes. These People were not so well clad as the first, whose Servants or Labourers they seemed to be. For, upon some Words he spoke, they went to reap the Corn in the Field where I lay. I kept from them at as great a Distance as I could, but was forced to move with extream Difficulty; for the Stalks of the Corn were sometimes not above a Foot distant, so that I could hardly squeeze my Body betwixt them. However, I made a shift to go forward till I came to a part of the Field where the Corn had been laid by the Rain and Wind: Here it was impossible for me to advance a step; for the Stalks were so interwoven that I could not creep through, and the Beards of the fallen Ears so strong and pointed, that they pierced through my Cloaths into my Flesh. At the same time I heard the Reapers not above an hundred Yards behind me. Being quite dispirited with Toil, and wholly overcome by Grief and Despair, I lay down between two Ridges, and heartily wished I might there end my Days. I bemoaned my desolate Widow, and Fatherless Children: I lamented my own Folly and Wilfulness in attempting a second Voyage against the Advice of all my Friends and Relations. In this terrible Agitation of Mind I could not forbear thinking of *Lilliput,* whose Inhabitants looked upon me as the greatest Prodigy that ever appeared in the World; where I was able to draw an Imperial Fleet in my Hand, and perform those other Actions which will be recorded for ever in the Chronicles of that Empire, while Posterity shall hardly believe them, although attested by Millions. I reflected what a Mortification it must prove to me to appear as inconsiderable in this Nation, as one single *Lilliputian* would be among us. But, this I conceived was to be the least of my Misfortunes: For, as human Creatures are observed to be more Savage and cruel in Proportion to their Bulk; what could I expect but to be a Morsel in the Mouth of the first among these enormous Barbarians who should happen to seize me? Undoubtedly Philosophers are in the Right when they tell us, that nothing is great or little otherwise than by Comparison:[3] It might have pleased Fortune to let the *Lilliputians* find some Nation, where the People were as diminutive with respect to them, as they were to me. And who knows but that even this prodigious Race of Mortals might be equally overmatched in some distant Part of the World, whereof we have yet no Discovery?

SCARED and confounded as I was, I could not forbear going on with these Reflections; when one of the Reapers approaching within ten Yards of the Ridge where I lay, made me apprehend that with the next Step I should be squashed to Death under his Foot, or cut in two with his Reaping Hook. And therefore when he was again about to move, I screamed as loud as Fear could make me. Whereupon the huge Creature trod short, and looking round about under him for some time, at last espied me as I lay on the Ground. He considered a while with the Caution of one who endeavours to lay hold on a small dangerous Animal in such a Manner that it shall not be able either to scratch or to bite him; as I my self have sometimes done with a *Weasel* in *England.* At length he ventured to take me up behind by the middle between his Fore-finger and Thumb, and brought me within three Yards of his Eyes, that he might behold my Shape more perfectly. I guessed his Meaning; and my good Fortune gave me so much Presence of Mind, that I resolved not to struggle in the least as he held me in the Air above sixty Foot from the Ground; although he grievously pinched my Sides, for fear I should slip through his Fingers. All I ventured was to raise mine Eyes towards the Sun, and place my Hands together in a supplicating Posture, and to speak some Words in an humble melancholy Tone, suitable to the Condition I then was in. For, I apprehended every Moment that he would dash me against the Ground, as we usually do any little hateful Animal which we have a Mind to destroy. But my good Star would have it, that he appeared pleased with my Voice and Gestures, and began to look upon me as a Curiosity; much wondering to hear me pronounce articulate Words, although he could not understand them. In the mean time I was not able to forbear Groaning and shedding Tears, and turning my Head towards my Sides; letting him know, as well as I could, how cruelly I was hurt by the Pressure of his Thumb and Finger. He seemed to apprehend my Meaning; for, lifting up the Lappet[4] of his Coat, he put me gently into it, and immediately ran along with me to his Master, who was a substantial Farmer, and the same Person I had first seen in the Field.

THE Farmer having (as I supposed by their Talk) received such an Account of me as his Servant could give him, took a piece of a small Straw, about the Size of a walking Staff, and therewith lifted up the Lappets of my Coat; which it seems he thought to be some kind of Covering that Nature had given me. He blew my Hairs aside to take a better View of my Face. He called his Hinds[5] about him, and asked them (as I afterwards learned) whether they had ever seen in the Fields any little Creature that resembled me. He then placed me softly on the Ground upon all four; but I got immediately up, and walked slowly backwards and forwards, to let those People see I had no Intent to run away. They all sate down in a Circle about me, the better to observe my Motions. I pulled off my Hat, and made a low Bow towards the Farmer: I fell on my Knees, and lifted up my Hands and Eyes, and spoke several Words as loud as I could: I took a Purse of Gold out of my Pocket, and humbly presented it to him. He received it on the Palm of his Hand, then applied it close to his Eye, to see what it was, and afterwards turned it several times with the Point of a Pin, (which he took out of his Sleeve,) but could make nothing of it. Whereupon I made a Sign that he should place his Hand on the Ground: I then took the Purse, and opening it, poured all the Gold into his Palm. There were six *Spanish*-Pieces of four Pistoles each, besides twenty or thirty smaller

Coins. I saw him wet the Tip of his little Finger upon his Tongue, and take up one of my largest Pieces, and then another; but he seemed to be wholly ignorant what they were. He made me a Sign to put them again into my Purse, and the Purse again into my Pocket; which after offering to him several times, I thought it best to do.

THE Farmer by this time was convinced I must be a rational Creature. He spoke often to me, but the Sound of his Voice pierced my Ears like that of a Water-Mill; yet his Words were articulate enough. I answered as loud as I could in several Languages; and he often laid his Ear within two Yards of me, but all in vain, for we were wholly unintelligible to each other. He then sent his Servants to their Work, and taking his Handkerchief out of his Pocket, he doubled and spread it on his Hand, which he placed flat on the Ground with the Palm upwards, making me a Sign to step into it, as I could easily do, for it was not above a Foot in thickness. I thought it my part to obey; and for fear of falling, laid my self at full Length upon the Handkerchief, with the Remainder of which he lapped me up to the Head for further Security; and in this Manner carried me home to his House. There he called his Wife, and shewed me to her; but she screamed and ran back as Women in *England* do at the Sight of a Toad or a Spider. However, when she had a while seen my Behaviour, and how well I observed the Signs her Husband made, she was soon reconciled, and by Degrees grew extreamly tender of me.

IT was about twelve at Noon, and a Servant brought in Dinner. It was only one substantial Dish of Meat (fit for the plain Condition of an Husband-Man) in a Dish of about four and twenty Foot Diameter. The Company were the Farmer and his Wife, three Children, and an old Grandmother: When they were sat down, the Farmer placed me at some Distance from him on the Table, which was thirty Foot high from the Floor. I was in a terrible Fright, and kept as far as I could from the Edge, for fear of falling. The Wife minced a bit of Meat, then crumbled some Bread on a Trencher, and placed it before me. I made her a low Bow, took out my Knife and Fork, and fell to eat; which gave them exceeding Delight. The Mistress sent her Maid for a small Dram-cup, which held about two Gallons; and filled it with Drink: I took up the Vessel with much difficulty in both Hands, and in a most respectful Manner drank to her Ladyship's Health, expressing the Words as loud as I could in *English;* which made the Company laugh so heartily, that I was almost deafened with the Noise. This Liquour tasted like a small Cyder, and was not unpleasant. Then the Master made me a Sign to come to his Trencher side; but as I walked on the Table, being in great surprize all the time, as the indulgent

Reader will easily conceive and excuse, I happened to stumble against a Crust, and fell flat on my Face, but received no hurt. I got up immediately, and observing the good People to be in much Concern, I took my Hat (which I held under my Arm out of good Manners) and waving it over my Head, made three Huzza's, to shew I had got no Mischief by the Fall. But advancing forwards toward my Master (as I shall henceforth call him) his youngest Son who sate next him, an arch Boy of about ten Years old, took me up by the Legs, and held me so high in the Air, that I trembled every Limb; but his Father snatched me from him; and at the same time gave him such a Box on the left Ear, as would have felled an *European* Troop of Horse to the Earth; ordering him to be taken from the Table. But, being afraid the Boy might owe me a Spight; and well remembring how mischievous all Children among us naturally are to Sparrows, Rabbits, young Kittens, and Puppy-Dogs; I fell on my Knees, and pointing to the Boy, made my Master understand, as well as I could, that I desired his Son might be pardoned. The Father complied, and the Lad took his Seat again; whereupon I went to him and kissed his Hand, which my Master took, and made him stroak me gently with it.

IN the Midst of Dinner my Mistress's favourite Cat leapt into her Lap. I heard a Noise behind me like that of a Dozen Stocking-Weavers at work; and turning my Head, I found it proceeded from the Purring of this Animal, who seemed to be three Times larger than an Ox, as I computed by the View of her Head, and one of her Paws, while her Mistress was feeding and stroaking her. The Fierceness of this Creature's Countenance altogether discomposed me; although I stood at the further End of the Table, above fifty Foot off; and although my Mistress held her fast for fear she might give a Spring, and seize me in her Talons. But it happened there was no Danger; for the Cat took not the least Notice of me when my Master placed me within three Yards of her. And as I have been always told, and found true by Experience in my Travels, that flying, or discovering Fear before a fierce Animal, is a certain Way to make it pursue or attack you; so I resolved in this dangerous Juncture to shew no Manner of Concern. I walked with Intrepidity five or six Times before the very Head of the Cat, and came within half a Yard of her; whereupon she drew her self back, as if she were more afraid of me: I had less Apprehension concerning the Dogs, whereof three or four came into the Room, as it is usual in Farmers Houses; one of which was a Mastiff equal in Bulk to four Elephants, and a Grey-hound somewhat taller than the Mastiff, but not so large.

WHEN Dinner was almost done, the Nurse came in with a Child of a

Year old in her Arms; who immediately spyed me, and began a Squall that you might have heard from *London-Bridge* to *Chelsea;* after the usual Oratory of Infants, to get me for a Play-thing. The Mother out of pure Indulgence took me up, and put me towards the Child, who presently seized me by the Middle, and got my Head in his Mouth, where I roared so loud that the Urchin was frighted, and let me drop; and I should infallibly have broke my Neck, if the Mother had not held her Apron under me. The Nurse to quiet her Babe made use of a Rattle, which was a Kind of hollow Vessel filled with great Stones, and fastned by a Cable to the Child's Waist: But all in vain, so that she was forced to apply the last Remedy by giving it suck. I must confess no Object ever disgusted me so much as the Sight of her monstrous Breast, which I cannot tell what to compare with, so as to give the curious Reader an Idea of its Bulk, Shape and Colour. It stood prominent six Foot, and could not be less than sixteen in Circumference. The Nipple was about half the Bigness of my Head, and the Hue both of that and the Dug so varified with Spots, Pimples and Freckles, that nothing could appear more nauseous: For I had a near Sight of her, she sitting down the more conveniently to give Suck, and I standing on the Table. This made me reflect upon the fair Skins of our *English* Ladies, who appear so beautiful to us, only because they are of our own Size, and their Defects not to be seen but through a magnifying Glass, where we find by Experiment that the smoothest and whitest Skins look rough and coarse, and ill coloured.

I REMEMBER when I was at *Lilliput,* the Complexions of those diminutive People appeared to me the fairest in the world: And talking upon this Subject with a Person of Learning there, who was an intimate Friend of mine; he said, that my Face appeared much fairer and smoother when he looked on me from the Ground, than it did upon a nearer View when I took him up in my Hand, and brought him close; which he confessed was at first a very shocking Sight. He said, he could discover great Holes in my Skin; that the Stumps of my Beard were ten Times stronger than the Bristles of a Boar; and my Complexion made up of several Colours altogether disagreeable: Although I must beg Leave to say for my self, that I am as fair as most of my Sex and Country, and very little Sunburnt by all my Travels. On the other Side, discoursing of the Ladies in that Emperor's Court, he used to tell me, one had Freckles, another too wide a Mouth, a third too large a Nose; nothing of which I was able to distinguish. I confess this Reflection was obvious enough; which, however, I could not forbear, lest the Reader might think those vast Creatures were actually deformed: For I must do them Justice to say they are a comely Race of People; and particularly the Features of my Master's Countenance, although he were but a Farmer, when I beheld him from the Height of sixty Foot, appeared very well proportioned.

WHEN Dinner was done, my Master went out to his Labourers; and as I could discover by his Voice and Gesture, gave his Wife a strict Charge to take Care of me. I was very much tired and disposed to sleep, which my Mistress perceiving, she put me on her own Bed, and covered me with a clean white Handkerchief, but larger and coarser than the Main Sail of a Man of War.

I SLEPT about two Hours, and dreamed I was at home with my Wife and Children, which aggravated my Sorrows when I awaked and found my self alone in a vast Room, between two and three Hundred Foot wide, and above two Hundred high; lying in a Bed twenty Yards wide. My Mistress was gone about her houshold Affairs, and had locked me in. The Bed was eight Yards from the Floor. Some natural Necessities required me to get down: I durst not presume to call, and if I had, it would have been in vain with such a Voice as mine at so great a Distance from the Room where I lay, to the Kitchen where the Family kept. While I was under these Circumstances, two Rats crept up the Curtains, and ran smelling backwards and forwards on the Bed: One of them came up almost to my Face; whereupon I rose in a Fright, and drew out my Hanger[6] to defend my self. These horrible Animals had the Boldness to attack me on both Sides, and one of them held his Fore-feet at my Collar; but I had the good Fortune to rip up his Belly before he could do me any Mischief. He fell down at my Feet; and the other seeing the Fate of his Comrade, made his Escape, but not without one good Wound on the Back, which I gave him as he fled, and made the Blood run trickling from him. After this Exploit I walked gently to and fro on the Bed, to recover my Breath and Loss of Spirits. These Creatures were of the Size of a large Mastiff, but infinitely more nimble and fierce; so that if I had taken off my Belt before I went to sleep, I must have infallibly been torn to Pieces and devoured. I measured the Tail of the dead Rat, and found it to be two Yards long, wanting an Inch; but it went against my Stomach to drag the Carcass off the Bed, where it lay still bleeding; I observed it had yet some Life, but with a strong Slash cross the Neck, I thoroughly dispatched it.

SOON after, my Mistress came into the Room, who seeing me all bloody, ran and took me up in her Hand. I pointed to the dead *Rat,* smiling and making other Signs to shew I was not hurt; whereat she was extremely rejoyced, calling the Maid to take up the dead *Rat* with a Pair of Tongs, and throw it out of the Window. Then she set me on a Table, where I shewed her my Hanger all bloody, and wiping it on the Lappet of my Coat, returned it to the Scabbard. I was pressed to do more than one Thing, which another could not do for me; and therefore endeavoured to make my Mistress understand that I desired to be set down on the Floor; which after she had done, my Bashfulness would not suffer me to express my self farther than by pointing to the Door, and bowing several Times. The good Woman with much Difficulty at last perceived what I would be at; and taking me up again in her Hand, walked into the Garden where she set me down. I went on one Side about two Hundred Yards; and beckoning to her not to look or to follow me, I hid my self between two Leaves of Sorrel, and there discharged the Necessities of Nature.

I HOPE, the gentle Reader will excuse me for dwelling on these and the like Particulars; which however insignificant they may appear to grovelling vulgar Minds, yet will certainly help a Philosopher to enlarge his Thoughts and Imagination, and apply them to the Benefit of publick as well as private Life; which was my sole Design in presenting this and other Accounts of my Travels to the World; wherein I have been chiefly studious of Truth, without affecting any Ornaments of Learning, or of Style. But the whole Scene of this Voyage made so strong an Impression on my Mind, and is so deeply fixed in my Memory, that in committing it to Paper, I did not omit one material Circumstance: However, upon a strict Review, I blotted out several Passages of less Moment which were in my first Copy, for fear of being censured as tedious and trifling, whereof Travellers are often, perhaps not without Justice, accused.

A Description of the Farmer's Daughter. The Author carried to a Market-Town, and then to the Metropolis. The Particulars of his Journey.

My Mistress had a Daughter of nine Years old, a Child of towardly Parts for her Age, very dextrous at her Needle, and skilful in dressing her Baby.[7] Her Mother and she contrived to fit up the Baby's Cradle for me against Night: The Cradle was put into a small Drawer of a Cabinet, and the Drawer placed upon a hanging Shelf for fear of the *Rats*. This was my Bed all the Time I stayed with those People, although made more convenient by Degrees, as I began to learn their Language, and make my Wants known. This young Girl was so handy, that after I had once or twice pulled off my Cloaths before her, she was able to dress and undress me, although I never gave her that Trouble when she would let me do either my self. She made me seven Shirts, and some other Linnen of as fine Cloth as could be got, which indeed was coarser than Sackcloth; and these she constantly washed for me with her own Hands. She was likewise my School-Mistress to teach me the Language: When I pointed to any thing, she told me the Name of it in her own Tongue, so that in a few Days I was able to call for whatever I had a mind to. She was very good natured, and not above forty Foot high, being little for her Age. She gave me the Name of *Grildrig*, which the Family took up, and afterwards the whole Kingdom. The Word imports what the *Latins* call *Nanunculus*, the *Italians Homunceletino*, and the *English Mannikin*. To her I chiefly owe my Preservation in that Country: We never parted while I was there; I called her my *Glumdalclitch*, or little Nurse: And I should be guilty of great Ingratitude if I omitted this honourable Mention of her Care and Affection towards me, which I heartily wish it lay in my Power to requite as she deserves, instead of being the innocent but unhappy Instrument of her Disgrace, as I have too much Reason to fear.

It now began to be known and talked of in the Neighbourhood, that my Master had found a strange Animal in the Field, about the Bigness of a *Splacknuck*, but exactly shaped in every Part like a human Creature; which it likewise imitated in all its actions; seemed to speak in a little Language of its own, had already learned several Words of theirs, went erect upon two Legs, was tame and gentle, would come when it was called, do whatever it was bid, had the finest Limbs in the World, and a Complexion fairer than a Nobleman's Daughter of three Years old. Another Farmer who lived hard by, and was a particular Friend of my Master, came on a Visit on Purpose to enquire into the Truth of this Story. I was immediately produced, and placed upon a Table; where I walked as I was commanded, drew my Hanger, put it up again, made my Reverence to my Master's Guest, asked him in his own Language how he did, and told him he was welcome; just as my little Nurse had instructed me. This Man, who was old and dim-sighted, put on his Spectacles to behold me better, at which I could not forbear laughing very heartily; for his Eyes appeared like the Full-Moon shining into a Chamber at two Windows. Our People, who discovered the Cause of my Mirth, bore me Company in Laughing; at which the old Fellow was Fool enough to be angry and out of Countenance. He had the Character of a great Miser; and to my Misfortune he well deserved it by the cursed Advice he gave my Master, to shew me as a Sight upon a Market-Day in the next Town, which was half an Hour's Riding, about two and twenty Miles from our House. I guessed there was some Mischief contriving, when I observed my Master and his Friend whispering long together, sometimes pointing at me; and my Fears made me fancy that I overheard and understood some of their Words. But, the next Morning *Glumdalclitch* my little Nurse told me the whole Matter, which she had cunningly picked out from her Mother. The poor Girl laid me on her Bosom, and fell a weeping with Shame and Grief. She apprehended some Mischief would happen to me from rude vulgar Folks, who might squeeze me to Death, or break one of my Limbs by taking me in their Hands. She had also observed how modest I was in my Nature, how nicely I regarded my Honour; and what an Indignity I should conceive it to be exposed for Money as a publick Spectacle to the meanest of the People. She said, her *Papa* and *Mamma* had promised that *Grildrig* should be hers; but now she found they meant to serve her as they did last Year, when they pretended to give her a Lamb; and yet, as soon as it was fat, sold it to a Butcher. For my own Part, I may truly affirm that I was less concerned than my Nurse. I had a strong Hope which never left me, that I should one Day recover my Liberty; and as to the Ignominy of being carried about for a Monster,[8] I considered my self to be a perfect Stranger in the Country; and that such a Misfortune could never be charged upon me as a Reproach if ever I should return to *England;* since the King of *Great Britain* himself, in my Condition, must have undergone the same Distress.[9]

MY Master, pursuant to the Advice of his Friend, carried me in a Box the next Market-Day to the neighbouring Town; and took along with him his little Daughter my Nurse upon a Pillion behind him. The Box was close on every Side, with a little Door for me to go in and out, and a few Gimlet-holes to let in Air. The Girl had been so careful to put the Quilt of her Baby's Bed into it, for me to lye down on. However, I was terribly shaken and discomposed in this Journey, although it were but of half an Hour. For the Horse went about forty Foot at every Step; and trotted so high, that the Agitation was equal to the rising and falling of a Ship in a great Storm, but much more frequent: Our Journey was somewhat further than from *London* to St. *Albans.*[10] My Master alighted an Inn which he used to frequent; and after consulting a while with the Inn-keeper, and making some necessary Preparations, he hired the *Grultrud,* or Cryer, to give Notice through the Town, of a strange Creature to be seen at the Sign of the Green *Eagle,* not so big as a *Splacnuck,* (an Animal in that Country very finely shaped, about six Foot long) and in every Part of the Body resembling an human Creature; could speak several Words, and perform an Hundred diverting Tricks.

I WAS placed upon a Table in the largest Room of the Inn, which might be near three Hundred Foot square. My little Nurse stood on a low Stool close to the Table, to take care of me, and direct what I should do. My Master, to avoid a Croud, would suffer only Thirty People at a Time to see me. I walked about on the Table as the Girl commanded; she asked me Questions as far as she knew my Understanding of the Language reached, and I answered them as loud as I could. I turned about several Times to the Company, paid my humble Respects, said they were welcome; and used some other Speeches I had been taught. I took up a Thimble filled with Liquor, which *Glumdalclitch* had given me for a Cup, and drank their Health. I drew out my Hanger, and flourished with it after the Manner of Fencers in *England.* My Nurse gave me Part of a Straw, which I exercised as a Pike, having learned the Art in my Youth. I was that Day shewn to twelve Sets of Company; and as often forced to go over again with the same Fopperies, till I was half dead with Weariness and Vexation. For, those who had seen me, made such wonderful Reports, that the People were ready to break down the Doors to come in. My Master for his own Interest would not suffer any one to touch me, except my Nurse; and, to prevent Danger, Benches were set round the Table at such a Distance, as put me out of every Body's Reach. However, an unlucky School-Boy aimed a Hazel Nut directly at my Head, which very narrowly missed me; otherwise, it came with so much Violence, that it would have infallibly knocked out my Brains; for it was almost as large as a small Pumpion:[11] But I had the Satisfaction to see the young Rogue well beaten, and turned out of the Room.

MY Master gave publick Notice, that he would shew me again the next Market-Day: And in the mean time, he prepared a more convenient Vehicle for me, which he had Reason enough to do; for I was so tired with my first Journey, and with entertaining Company eight Hours together, that I could hardly stand upon my Legs, or speak a Word. It was at least three Day before I recovered my Strength; and that I might have no rest at home, all the neighbouring Gentlemen from an Hundred Miles round, hearing of my Fame, came to see me at my Master's own House. There could not be fewer than thirty Persons with their Wives and Children; (for the Country is very populous;) and my Master demanded the Rate of a full Room whenever he shewed me at Home, although it were only to a single Family. So that for some time I had but little Ease every Day of the Week, (except *Wednesday,* which is their Sabbath) although I were not carried to the Town.

MY Master finding how profitable I was like to be, resolved to carry me to the most considerable Cities of the Kingdom. Having therefore provided himself with all things necessary for a long Journey, and settled his Affairs at Home; he took Leave of his Wife; and upon the 17*th* of *August* 1703, about two Months after my Arrival, we set out for the Metropolis, situated near the Middle of that Empire, and about three Thousand Miles distance from our House: My Master made his Daughter *Glumdalclitch* ride behind him. She carried me on her Lap in a Box tied about her Waist. The Girl had lined it on all Sides with the softest Cloth she could get, well quilted underneath; furnished it with her Baby's Bed, provided me with Linnen and other Necessaries; and made every thing as convenient as she could. We had no other Company but a Boy of the House, who rode after us with the Luggage.

MY Master's Design was to shew me in all the Towns by the Way, and to step out of the Road for Fifty or an Hundred Miles, to any Village or Person of Quality's House where he might expect Custom. We made easy Journies of not above seven or eight Score Miles a Day: For *Glumdalclitch,* on Purpose to spare me, complained she was tired with the trotting of the Horse. She often took me out of my Box at my own Desire, to give me Air, and shew me the Country; but always held me fast by Leading-strings. We passed over five or six Rivers many Degrees broader and deeper than the *Nile* or the *Ganges;* and there was hardly a Rivulet so small as the *Thames* at *London-Bridge.* We were ten Weeks in our Journey; and I was shewn in Eighteen large Towns, besides many Villages and private Families.

ON the 26th Day of *October,* we arrived at the Metropolis, called in their Language *Lorbrulgrud,* or *Pride of the Universe.* My Master took a Lodging in the principal Street of the City, not far from the Royal Palace; and put out Bills in the usual Form, containing an exact Description of my Person and Parts. He hired a large Room between three and four Hundred Foot wide. He provided a Table sixty Foot in Diameter, upon which I was to act my Part; and pallisadoed it round three Foot from the Edge, and as many high, to prevent my falling over. I was shewn ten Times a Day to the Wonder and Satisfaction of all People. I could now speak the Language tolerably well; and perfectly understood every Word that was spoken to me. Besides, I had learned their Alphabet, and could make a shift to explain a Sentence here and there; for *Glumdalclitch* had been my Instructer while we were at home, and at leisure Hours during our Journey. She carried a little Book in her Pocket, not much larger than a *Sanson's Atlas,*[12] it was a common Treatise for the use of young Girls, giving a short Account of their Religion; out of this she taught me my Letters, and interpreted the Words.

CHAPTER III

The Author sent for to Court. The Queen buys him of his Master the Farmer, and presents him to the King. He disputes with his Majesty's great Scholars. An Apartment at Court provided for the Author. He is in high Favour with the Queen. He stands up for the Honour of his own Country. His Quarrels with the Queen's Dwarf.

The frequent Labours I underwent every Day, made in a few Weeks a very considerable Change in my Health: The more my Master got by me, the more unsatiable he grew. I had quite lost my Stomach, and was almost reduced to a Skeleton. The Farmer observed it; and concluding I soon must die, resolved to make as good a Hand of me as he could. While he was thus reasoning and resolving with himself; a *Slardral,* or Gentleman Usher, came from Court, commanding my Master to bring me immediately thither for the Diversion of the Queen and her Ladies. Some of the latter had already been to see me; and reported strange Things of my Beauty, Behaviour, and good Sense. Her Majesty and those who attended her, were beyond Measure delighted with my Demeanor. I fell on my Knees, and begged the Honour of kissing her Imperial Foot; but this Gracious Princess held out her little Finger towards me (after I was set on a Table) which I embraced in both my Arms, and put the Tip of it, with the utmost Respect, to my Lip. She made me some general Questions about my Country and my Travels, which I answered as distinctly and in as few Words as I could. She asked, whether I would be content to live at Court. I bowed down to the Board of the Table, and humbly answered, that I was my Master's Slave; but if I were at my own Disposal, I should be proud to devote my Life to her Majesty's Service. She then asked my Master whether he were willing to sell me at a good Price. He, who apprehended I could not live a Month, was ready enough to part with me; and demanded a Thousand Pieces of Gold; which were ordered him on the Spot, each Piece being about the Bigness of eight Hundred Moydores:[13] But, allowing for the Proportion of all Things between that Country and *Europe,* and the high Price of Gold among them; was hardly so great a Sum as a Thousand Guineas would be in *England.* I then said to the Queen; since I was now her Majesty's most humble Creature and Vassal, I must beg the Favour, that *Glumdalclitch,* who had always tended me with so much Care and Kindness, and understood to do it so well, might be admitted into her Service, and continue to be my Nurse and Instructor. Her Majesty agreed to my Petition; and easily got the Farmer's Consent, who was glad enough to have his Daughter preferred at Court: And the poor Girl herself was not able to hide her Joy. My late Master withdrew, bidding me farewell, and saying he had left me in a good Service; to which I replyed not a Word, only making him a slight Bow.

THE Queen observed my Coldness; and when the Farmer was gone out of the Apartment, asked me the Reason. I made bold to tell her Majesty, that I owed no other Obligation to my late Master, than his not dashing out the Brains of a poor harmless Creature found by Chance in his Field; which Obligation was amply recompenced by the Gain he had made in shewing me through half the Kingdom, and the Price he had now sold me for. That the Life I had since led, was laborious enough to kill an Animal of ten Times my Strength. That my Health was much impaired by the continual Drudgery of entertaining the Rabble every Hour of the Day; and that if my Master had not thought my Life in Danger, her Majesty perhaps would not have got so cheap a Bargain. But as I was out of all fear of being ill treated under the Protection of so great and good an Empress, the Ornament of Nature, the Darling of the World, the Delight of her Subjects, the Phœnix of the Creation; so, I hoped my late Master's Apprehensions would appear to be groundless; for I already found my Spirits to revive by the Influence of her most August Presence.

THIS was the Sum of my Speech, delivered with great Improprieties and Hesitation; the latter Part was altogether framed in the Style peculiar to that People, whereof I learned some Phrases from *Glumdalclitch,* while she was carrying me to Court.

THE Queen giving great Allowance for my Defectiveness in speaking, was however surprised at so much Wit and good Sense in so diminutive an Animal. She took me in her own Hand, and carried me to the King, who was then retired to his Cabinet. His Majesty, a Prince of much Gravity, and austere Countenance, not well observing my Shape at first View, asked the Queen after a cold Manner, how long it was since she grew fond of a *Splacknuck;* for such it seems he took me to be, as I lay upon my Breast in her Majesty's right Hand. But this Princess, who hath an infinite deal of Wit and Humour, set me gently on my Feet upon the Scrutore; and commanded me to give His Majesty an Account of my self, which I did in a very few Words; and *Glumdalclitch*, who attended at the Cabinet Door, and could not endure I should be out of her Sight, being admitted; confirmed all that had passed from my Arrival at her Father's House.

THE King, although he be as learned a Person as any in his Dominions and had been educated in the Study of Philosophy, and particularly Mathematicks; yet when he observed my Shape exactly, and saw me walk erect, before I began to speak, conceived I might be a piece of Clock-work, (which is in that Country arrived to a very great Perfection) contrived by some ingenious Artist. But, when he heard my Voice, and found what I delivered to be regular and rational, he could not conceal his Astonishment. He was by no means satisfied with the Relation I gave him of the Manner I came into his Kingdom; but thought it a Story concerted between *Glumdalclitch* and her Father, who had taught me a Sett of Words to make me sell at a higher Price. Upon this Imagination he put several other Questions to me, and still received rational Answers, no otherwise defective than by a Foreign Accent, and an imperfect Knowledge in the Language; with some rustick Phrases which I had learned at the Farmer's House, and did not suit the polite Style of a Court.

HIS Majesty sent for three great Scholars who were then in their weekly waiting (according to the Custom in that Country.) These Gentlemen, after they had a while examined my Shape with much Nicety, were of different Opinions concerning me. They all agreed that I could not be produced according to the regular Laws of Nature; because I was not framed with a Capacity of preserving my Life, either by Swiftness, or climbing of Trees, or digging Holes in the Earth. They observed by my Teeth, which they viewed with great Exactness, that I was a carnivorous Animal; yet most Quadrupeds being an Overmatch for me; and Field-Mice, with some others, too nimble, they could not imagine how I should be able to support my self, unless I fed upon Snails and other Insects; which they offered by many learned Arguments to evince that I could not possibly do. One of them seemed to think that I might be an Embrio, or abortive Birth. But this Opinion was rejected by the other two, who observed my Limbs to be perfect and finished; and that I had lived several Years, as it was manifested from my Beard; the Stumps whereof they plainly discovered through a Magnifying-Glass. They would not allow me to be a Dwarf, because my Littleness was beyond all Degrees of Comparison; for the Queen's favourite Dwarf, the smallest ever known in that Kingdom, was near thirty Foot high. After much Debate, they concluded unanimously that I was only *Relplum Scalcath*, which is interpreted literally *Lusus Naturæ*;[14] a Determination exactly agreeable to the Modern Philosophy of *Europe*: whose Professors, disdaining the old Evasion of *occult Causes*, whereby the Followers of *Aristotle* endeavour in vain to disguise their Ignorance; have invented this wonderful Solution of all Difficulties, to the unspeakable Advancement of human Knowledge.

AFTER this decisive Conclusion, I entreated to be heard a Word or two. I applied my self to the King, and assured His Majesty, that I came from a Country which abounded with several Millions of both Sexes, and of my own Stature; where the Animals, Trees, and Houses were all in Proportion; and where by Consequence I might be as able to defend my self, and to find Sustenance, as any of his Majesty's Subjects could so here; which I took for a full Answer to those Gentlemen's Arguments. To this they only replied with a Smile of Contempt; saying, that the Farmer had instructed me very well in my Lesson. The King, who had a much better Understanding, dismissing his learned Men, sent for the Farmer, who by good Fortune was not yet gone out of Town: Having therefore first examined him privately, and then confronted him with me and the young Girl; his Majesty began to think that what we told him might possibly be true. He desired the Queen to order, that a particular Care should be taken of me; and was of Opinion, that *Glumdalclitch* should still continue in her Office of tending me, because he observed we had a great Affection for each other. A convenient Apartment was provided for her at Court; she had a sort of Governess appointed to take care of her Education, a Maid to dress her, and two other Servants for menial Offices; but, the Care of me was wholly appropriated to her self. The Queen commanded her own Cabinet-maker to contrive a Box that might serve me for a Bed-chamber, after the Model that *Glumdalclitch* and I should agree upon. This Man was a most ingenious Artist; and according to my Directions, in three Weeks finished for me a wooden Chamber of sixteen Foot square, and twelve High; with Sash Windows, a Door, and two Closets, like a *London* Bed-chamber. The Board that made the Ceiling was to be lifted up and down by two Hinges, to put in a Bed ready furnished by her Majesty's Upholsterer; which *Glumdalclitch* took out every Day to air, made it with her own Hands, and letting it down at Night, locked up the Roof over me. A Nice Workman, who was famous for little Curiosities, undertook to make me two Chairs, with Backs and Frames, of a Substance not unlike Ivory; and two Tables, with a Cabinet to put my Things in. The Room was quilted on all Sides, as well as the Floor and the Ceiling, to prevent any Accident from the Carelessness of those who carried me; and to break the Force of a Jolt when I went in a Coach. I desired a Lock for my Door to prevent Rats and Mice from coming in: The Smith after several Attempts made the smallest that was ever seen among them; for I have known a larger at the Gate of a Gentleman's House in *England*. I made a shift to keep the Key in a Pocket of my own, fearing *Glumdalclitch* might lose it. The Queen likewise ordered the thinnest Silks that could be gotten, to make me Cloaths; not much thicker than an *English* Blanket, very cumbersome till I was accustomed to them. They were after the Fashion of the Kingdom, partly resembling the *Persian,* and partly the *Chinese;* and are a very grave decent Habit.

THE Queen became so fond of my Company, that she could not dine without me. I had a Table placed upon the same at which her Majesty eat, just at her left Elbow; and a Chair to sit on. *Glumdalclitch* stood upon a Stool on the Floor, near my Table, to assist and take Care of me. I had an entire set of Silver Dishes and Plates, and other Necessaries, which in Proportion to those of the Queen, were not much bigger than what I have seen in a *London* Toy-shop, for the Furniture of a Baby-house:[15] These my little Nurse kept in her Pocket, in a Silver Box, and gave me at Meals as I wanted them; always cleaning them her self. No Person dined with the Queen but the two Princesses Royal; the elder sixteen Years old, and the younger at that time thirteen and a Month. Her Majesty used to put a Bit of Meat upon one of my Dishes, out of which I carved for my self; and her Diversion was to see me eat in Miniature. For the Queen (who had indeed but a weak Stomach) took up at one Mouthful, as much as a dozen *English* Farmers could eat at a Meal, which to me was for some time a very nauseous Sight. She would craunch[16] the Wing of a Lark, Bones and all, between her Teeth, although it were nine Times as large as that of a full grown Turkey; and put a Bit of Bread in her Mouth, as big as two twelve-penny Loaves. She drank out of a golden Cup, above a Hogshead at a Draught. Her Knives were twice as long as a Scythe set strait upon the Handle. The Spoons, Forks, and other Instruments were all in the same Proportion. I remember when *Glumdalclitch* carried me out of Curiosity to see some of the Tables at Court, where ten or a dozen of these enormous Knives and Forks were lifted up together; I thought I had never till then beheld so terrible a Sight.

IT is the Custom, that every *Wednesday,* (which as I have before observed, was their Sabbath) the King and Queen, with the Royal Issue of both Sexes, dine together in the Apartment of his Majesty; to whom I was now become a Favourite; and at these Times my little Chair and Table were placed at his left Hand before one of the Salt-sellers. This Prince took a Pleasure in conversing with me; enquiring into the Manners, Religion, Laws, Government, and Learning of *Europe,* wherein I gave him the best Account I was able. His Apprehension was so clear, and his Judgment so exact, that he made very wise Reflexions and Observations upon all I said. But, I confess, that after I had been a little too copious in talking of my own beloved Country; of our Trade, and Wars by Sea and Land, of our Schisms in Religion, and Parties in the State; the Prejudices of his Education prevailed so far, that he could not forbear taking me up in his right Hand, and stroaking me gently with the other; after an hearty Fit of laughing, asked me whether I were a *Whig* or a *Tory.* Then turning to his first Minister, who waited behind him with a white Staff, near as tall as the Main-mast of the Royal *Sovereign;* he observed, how contemptible a Thing was human Grandeur, which could be mimicked by such diminutive Insects as I: And yet, said he, I dare engage, those Creatures have their Titles and Distinctions of Honour; they contrive little Nests and Burrows, that they call Houses and Cities; they make a Figure in Dress and Equipage; they love, they fight, they dispute, they cheat, they betray. And thus he continued on, while my Colour came and went several Times, with Indignation to hear our noble Country, the Mistress of Arts and Arms, the Scourge of *France,* the Arbitress of *Europe,* the Seat of Virtue, Piety, Honour and Truth, the Pride and Envy of the World, so contemptuously treated.

BUT, as I was not in a Condition to resent Injuries, so, upon mature Thoughts, I began to doubt whether I were injured or no. For, after having been accustomed several Months to the Sight and Converse of this People, and observed every Object upon which I cast mine Eyes, to be of proportionable Magnitude; the Horror I had first conceived from their Bulk and Aspect was so far worn off, that if I had then beheld a Company of *English* Lords and Ladies in their Finery and Birth-day Cloaths,17 acting their several Parts in the most courtly Manner of Strutting, and Bowing and Prating; to say the Truth, I should have been strongly tempted to laugh as much at them as this King and his Grandees did at me. Neither indeed could I forbear smiling at my self, when the Queen used to place me upon her Hand towards a Looking-Glass, by which both our Persons appeared before me in full View together; and there could nothing be more ridiculous than the Comparison: So that I really began to imagine my self dwindled many Degrees below my usual Size.

NOTHING angred and mortified me so much as the Queen's Dwarf,

who being of the lowest Stature that was ever in that Country, (for I verily think he was not full Thirty Foot high) became so insolent at seeing a
Creature so much beneath him, that he would always affect to swagger and
look big as he passed by me in the Queen's Antichamber, while I was
standing on some Table talking with the Lords or Ladies of the Court;
and he seldom failed of a smart Word or two upon my Littleness; against
which I could only revenge my self by calling him *Brother,* challenging him
to wrestle; and such Repartees as are usual in the Mouths of *Court Pages.*
One Day at Dinner, this malicious little Cubb was so nettled with something I had said to him, that raising himself upon the Frame of her
Majesty's Chair, he took me up by the Middle, as I was sitting down, not
thinking any Harm, and let me drop into a large Silver Bowl of Cream;
and then ran away as fast as he could. I fell over Head and Ears, and if I
had not been a good Swimmer, it might have gone very hard with me; for
Glumdalclitch in that Instant happened to be at the other End of the Room;
and the Queen was in such a Fright, that she wanted Presence of Mind to
assist me. But my little Nurse ran to my Relief; and took me out, after
I had swallowed above a Quart of Cream. I was put to Bed; however I
received no other Damage than the Loss of a Suit of Cloaths, which was
utterly spoiled. The Dwarf was soundly whipped, and as a further Punishment, forced to drink up the Bowl of Cream, into which he had thrown
me; neither was he ever restored to Favour: For, soon after the Queen bestowed him to a Lady of high Quality; so that I saw him no more, to my
very great Satisfaction; for I could not tell to what Extremity such a malicious Urchin might have carried his Resentment.

He had before served me a scurvy Trick, which set the Queen a laughing, although at the same time she were heartily vexed, and would have immediately cashiered him, if I had not been so generous as to intercede. Her
Majesty had taken a Marrow-bone upon her Plate; and after knocking out
the Marrow, placed the Bone again in the Dish erect as it stood before; the
Dwarf watching his Opportunity, while *Glumdalclitch* was gone to the Side-
board, mounted the Stool that she stood on to take care of me at Meals;
took me up in both Hands, and squeezing my Legs together, wedged them
into the Marrow-bone above my Waist; where I stuck for some time, and
made a very ridiculous Figure. I believe it was near a Minute before any
one knew what was become of me; for I thought it below me to cry out. But,
as Princes seldom get their Meat hot, my Legs were not scalded, only my
Stockings and Breeches in a sad Condition. The Dwarf at my Entreaty had
no other Punishment than a sound whipping.

I WAS frequently raillied by the Queen upon Account of my Fearfulness; and she used to ask me whether the People of my Country were as great Cowards as my self. The Occasion was this. The Kingdom is much pestered with Flies in Summer; and these odious Insects, each of them as big as a *Dunstable* Lark, hardly gave me any Rest while I sat at Dinner, with their continual Humming and Buzzing about mine Ears. They would sometimes alight upon my Victuals, and leave their loathsome Excrement or Spawn behind, which to me was very visible, although not to the Natives of that Country, whose large Opticks were not so acute as mine in viewing smaller Objects. Sometimes they would fix upon my Nose or Forehead, where they stung me to the Quick, smelling very offensively; and I could easily trace that viscous Matter, which our Naturalists tell us enables those Creatures to walk with their Feet upwards upon a Cieling. I had much ado to defend my self against these detestable Animals, and could not forbear starting when they came on my Face. It was the common Practice of the Dwarf to catch a Number of these Insects in his Hand, as School-boys do among us, and let them out suddenly under my Nose, on Purpose to frighten me, and divert the Queen. My Remedy was to cut them in Pieces with my Knife as they flew in the Air; wherein my Dexterity was much admired.

I REMEMBER one Morning when *Glumdalclitch* had set me in my Box upon a Window, as she usually did in fair Days to give me Air, (for I durst not venture to let the Box be hung on a Nail out of the Window, as we do with Cages in *England*) after I had lifted up one of my Sashes, and sat down at my Table to eat a Piece of Sweet-Cake for my Breakfast; above twenty Wasps, allured by the Smell, came flying into the Room, humming louder than the Drones of as many Bagpipes. Some of them seized my Cake, and carried it piecemeal away; others flew about my Head and Face, confounding me with the Noise, and putting me in the utmost Terror of their Stings. However I had the Courage to rise and draw my Hanger, and attack them in the Air. I dispatched four of them, but the rest got away, and I presently shut my Window. These Insects were as large as Partridges; I took out their stings, found them an Inch and a half long, and as sharp as Needles. I carefully preserved them all, and having since shewn them with some other Curiosities in several Parts of *Europe;* upon my Return to *England* I gave three of them to *Gresham College*,[18] and kept the fourth for my self.

CHAPTER IV

The Country described. A Proposal for correcting modern Maps. The King's Palace, and some Account of the Metropolis. The Author's Way of travelling. The chief Temple described.

I now intend to give the Reader a short Description of this Country, as far as I travelled in it, which was not above two thousand Miles round *Lorbrulgrud* the Metropolis. For, the Queen, whom I always attended, never went further when she accompanied the King in his Progresses; and there staid till his Majesty returned from viewing his Frontiers. The whole Extent of this Prince's Dominions reacheth about six thousand Miles in Length, and from three to five in Breadth. From whence I cannot but conclude, that our Geographers of *Europe* are in a great Error, by supposing nothing but Sea between *Japan* and *California*: For it was ever my Opinion, that there must be a Balance of Earth to counterpoise the great Continent of *Tartary;* and therefore they ought to correct their Maps and Charts, by joining this vast Tract of Land to the North-west Parts of *America;* wherein I shall be ready to lend them my Assistance.

THE Kingdom is a Peninsula, terminated to the North-east by a Ridge of Mountains thirty Miles high which are altogether impassable by Reason of the Volcanoes upon the Tops. Neither do the most Learned know what sort of Mortals inhabit beyond those Mountains, or whether they be inhabited at all. On the three other Sides it is bounded by the Ocean. There is not one Sea-port in the whole Kingdom; and those Parts of the Coasts into which the Rivers issue, are so full of pointed Rocks, and the Sea generally so rough, that there is no venturing with the smallest of their Boats; so that these People are wholly excluded from any Commerce with the rest of the World. But the large Rivers are full of Vessels, and abound with excellent Fish; for they seldom get any from the Sea, because the Sea-fish are of the same Size with those in *Europe,* and consequently not worth catching; whereby it is manifest, that Nature in the Production of Plants and Animals of so extraordinary a Bulk, is wholly confined to this Continent; of which I leave the Reasons to be determined by Philosophers. However, now and then they take a Whale that happens to be dashed against the Rocks, which the common People feed on heartily. These Whales I have known so large that a Man could hardly carry one upon his Shoulders; and sometimes for Curiosity they are brought in Hampers to *Lorbrulgrud:* I saw one of them in a Dish at the King's Table, which passed for a Rarity; but I did not observe he was fond of it; for I think indeed the Bigness disgusted him, although I have seen one somewhat larger in *Greenland.*

THE Country is well inhabited, for it contains fifty one Cities, near an hundred walled Towns, and a great Number of Villages. To satisfy my curious Reader, it may be sufficient to describe *Lorbrulgrud.* This City stands upon almost two equal Parts on each Side the River that passes through. It contains above eighty thousand Houses. It is in Length three *Glonglungs* (which make about fifty four English Miles) and two and a half in Breadth, as I measured it myself in the Royal Map made by the King's Order, which was laid on the Ground on purpose for me, and extended an hundred Feet; I paced the Diameter and Circumference several times Bare-foot, and computing by the Scale, measured it pretty exactly.

THE King's Palace is no regular Edifice, but an Heap of Buildings about seven Miles round: The chief Rooms are generally two hundred and forty Foot high, and broad and long in Proportion. A Coach was allowed to *Glumdalclitch* and me, wherein her Governess frequently took her out to see the Town, or go among the Shops; and I was always of the Party, carried in my Box; although the Girl at my own Desire would often take me out, and hold me in her Hand, that I might more conveniently view the Houses and the People as we passed along the Streets. I reckoned our Coach to be about a Square of *Westminster-Hall,* but not altogether so High; however, I cannot be very exact. One Day the Governess ordered our Coachman to stop at several Shops; where the Beggars watching their Opportunity, crouded to the Sides of the Coach, and gave me the most horrible Spectacles that ever an *European* Eye beheld. There was a Woman with a Cancer in her Breast, swelled to a monstrous Size, full of Holes, in two or three of which I could have easily crept, and covered my whole Body. There was a Fellow with a Wen in his Neck, larger than five Woolpacks; and another with a couple of wooden Legs, each about twenty Foot high. But, the most hateful Sight of all was the Lice crawling on their Cloaths: I could see distinctly the Limbs of these Vermin with my naked

Eye, much better than those of an *European* Louse through a Microscope; and their Snouts with which they rooted like Swine. They were the first I had ever beheld; and I should have been curious enough to dissect one of them, if I had proper Instruments (which I unluckily left behind me in the Ship) although indeed the Sight was so nauseous, that it perfectly turned my Stomach.

BESIDE the large Box in which I was usually carried, the Queen ordered a smaller one to be made for me, of about twelve Foot Square, and ten high, for the Convenience of Travelling; because the other was somewhat too large for *Glumdalclitch's* Lap, and cumbersom in the Coach; it was made by the same Artist, whom I directed in the whole Contrivance. This travelling Closet was an exact Square with a Window in the Middle of three of the Squares, and each Window was latticed with Iron Wire on the outside, to prevent Accidents in long Journeys. On the fourth Side, which had no Window, two strong Staples were fixed, through which the Person that carried me, when I had a Mind to be on Horseback, put in a Leathern Belt, and buckled it about his Waist. This was always the Office of some grave trusty Servant in whom I could confide, whether I attended the King and Queen in their Progresses, or were disposed to see the Gardens, or pay a Visit to some great Lady or Minister of State in the Court, when *Glumdalclitch* happened to be out of Order: For I soon began to be known and esteemed among the greatest Officers, I suppose more upon Account of their Majesty's Favour, than any Merit of my own. In Journeys, when I was weary of the Coach, a Servant on Horseback would buckle my Box, and place it on a Cushion before him; and there I had a full Prospect of the Country on three Sides from my three Windows. I had in this Closet a Field-Bed and a Hammock hung from the Ceiling, two Chairs and a Table, neatly screwed to the Floor, to prevent being tossed about by the Agitation of the Horse or the Coach. And having been long used to Sea-Voyages, those Motions, although sometimes very violent, did not much discompose me.

WHENEVER I had a Mind to see the Town, it was always in my Travelling-Closet; which *Glumdalclitch* held in her Lap in a kind of open Sedan, after the Fashion of the Country, born by four Men, and attended by two others in the Queen's Livery. The People who had often heard of me, were very curious to croud about the Sedan; and the Girl was complaisant enough to make the Bearers stop, and to take me in her Hand that I might be more conveniently seen.

I WAS very desirous to see the chief Temple, and particularly the

Tower belonging to it, which is reckoned the highest in the Kingdom. Accordingly one Day my Nurse carried me thither, but I may truly say I came back disappointed; for, the Height is not above three thousand Foot, reckoning from the Ground to the highest Pinnacle top; which allowing for the Difference between the Size of those People, and us in *Europe,* is no great matter for Admiration, nor at all equal in Proportion, (if I rightly remember) to *Salisbury* Steeple. But, not to detract from a Nation to which during my Life I shall acknowledge myself extremely obliged; it must be allowed, that whatever this famous Tower wants in Height, is amply made up in Beauty and Strength. For the Walls are near an hundred Foot thick, built of hewn Stone, whereof each is about forty Foot square, and adorned on all Sides with Statues of Gods and Emperors cut in Marble larger than the Life, placed in their several Niches. I measured a little Finger which had fallen down from one of these Statues, and lay unperceived among some Rubbish; and found it exactly four Foot and an Inch in Length. *Glumdalclitch* wrapped it up in a Handkerchief, and carried it home in her Pocket to keep among other Trinkets, of which the Girl was very fond, as Children at her Age usually are.

THE King's Kitchen is indeed a noble Building, vaulted at Top, and about six hundred Foot high. The great Oven is not so wide by ten Paces as the Cupola at St. *Paul's*: For I measured the latter on purpose after my Return. But if I should describe the Kitchen-grate, the prodigious Pots and Kettles, the Joints of Meat turning on the Spits, with many other Particulars; perhaps I should be hardly believed; at least a severe Critick would be apt to think I enlarged a little, as Travellers are often suspected to do. To avoid which Censure, I fear I have run too much into the other Extream; and that if this Treatise should happen to be translated into the Language of *Brobdingnag,* (which is the general Name of that Kingdom) and transmitted thither; the King and his People would have Reason to complain; that I had done them an Injury by a false and diminutive Representation.

HIS Majesty seldom keeps above six hundred Horses in his Stables: They are generally from fifty four to sixty Foot high. But, when he goes abroad on solemn Days, he is attended for State by a Militia Guard of five hundred Horse, which indeed I thought was the most splendid Sight that could be ever beheld, till I saw part of his Army in Battalia: whereof I shall find another Occasion to speak.

CHAPTER V

*Several Adventures that happened to the Author. The Execution
of a Criminal. The Author shews his Skill in Navigation.*

I should have lived happy enough in that Country, if my Littleness had
not exposed me to several ridiculous and troublesome Accidents; some of
which I shall venture to relate. *Glumdalclitch* often carried me into the Gardens of the Court in my smaller Box, and would sometimes take me out of
it and hold me in her Hand, or set me down to walk. I remember, before
the Dwarf left the Queen, he followed us one Day into those Gardens; and
my Nurse having set me down, he and I being close together, near some
Dwarf Apple-trees, I must need shew my Wit by a silly Allusion between
him and the Trees, which happens to hold in their Language as it doth in
ours. Whereupon, the malicious Rogue watching his Opportunity, when I
was walking under one of them, shook it directly over my head, by which
a dozen Apples, each of them near as large as a *Bristol* Barrel, came tumbling about my Ears; one of them hit me on my Face, but I received no
other Hurt; and the Dwarf was pardoned at my Desire, because I had
given the Provocation.

ANOTHER Day, *Glumdalclitch* left me on a smooth Grass-plot to divert
my self while she walked at some Distance with her Governess. In the
mean time, there suddenly fell such a violent Shower of Hail, that I
was immediately by the Force of it struck to the Ground: And when I was
down, the Hail-stones gave me such cruel Bangs all over the Body, as if I
had been pelted with Tennis-Balls; however I made a Shift to creep on all
four, and shelter my self by lying flat on my Face on the Lee-side of a Border of Lemmon Thyme; but so bruised from Head to Foot, that I could
not go abroad in ten Days. Neither is this at all to be wondered at; because

Nature in that Country observing the same Proportion through all her Operations, a Hail-stone is near Eighteen Hundred Times as large as one in *Europe;* which I can assert upon Experience, having been so curious to weigh and measure them.

But, a more dangerous Accident happened to me in the same Garden, when my little Nurse, believing she had put me in a secure Place, which I often entreated her to do, that I might enjoy my own Thoughts; and having left my Box at home to avoid the Trouble of carrying it, went to another Part of the Garden with her Governess and some Ladies of her Acquaintance. While she was absent and out of hearing, a small white Spaniel belonging to one of the chief Gardiners, having got by Accident into the Garden, happened to range near the Place where I lay. The Dog following the Scent, came directly up, and taking me in his Mouth, ran strait to his Master, wagging his Tail, and set me gently on the Ground. By good Fortune he had been so well taught, that I was carried between his Teeth without the least Hurt, or even tearing my Cloaths. But, the poor Gardiner, who knew me well, and had a great Kindness for me, was in a terrible Fright. He gently took me up in both his Hands, and asked me how I did; but I was so amazed[19] and out of Breath, that I could not speak a Word. In a few Minutes I came to my self, and he carried me safe to my little Nurse, who by this time had returned to the Place where she left me, and was in cruel Agonies when I did not appear, nor answer when she called; she severely reprimanded the Gardiner on Account of his Dog. But, the Thing was hushed up, and never known at Court; for the Girl was afraid of the Queen's Anger; and truly as to my self, I thought it would not be for my Reputation that such a Story should go about.

This Accident absolutely determined *Glumdalclitch* never to trust me abroad for the future out of her Sight. I had been long afraid of this Resolution; and therefore concealed from her some little unlucky Adventures that happened in those Times when I was left by my self. Once a Kite[20] hovering over the Garden, made a Stoop at me, and if I had not resolutely drawn my Hanger, and run under a thick Espalier, he would have certainly carried me away in his Talons. Another time, walking to the Top of a fresh Mole-hill, I fell to my Neck in the Hole through which that Animal had cast up the Earth; and coined some Lye not worth remembring, to excuse my self for spoiling my Cloaths. I likewise broke my right Shin against the Shell of a Snail, which I happened to stumble over, as I was walking alone, and thinking on poor *England*.

I cannot tell whether I were more pleased or mortified to observe in those solitary Walks, that the smaller Birds did not appear to be at all afraid of me; but would hop about within a Yard Distance, looking for Worms, and other Food, with as much Indifference and Security as if no Creature at all were near them. I remember, a Thrush had the Confidence to snatch out of my Hand with his Bill, a Piece of Cake that *Glumdalclitch* had just given me for my Breakfast. When I attempted to catch any of these Birds, they would boldly turn against me, endeavouring to pick my Fingers, which I durst not venture within their Reach; and then they would hop back unconcerned to hunt for Worms or Snails, as they did before. But, one Day I took a thick Cudgel, and threw it with all my Strength so luckily at a Linnet, that I knocked him down, and seizing him by the Neck with both my Hands, ran with him in Triumph to my Nurse. However, the Bird who had only been stunned, recovering himself, gave me so many Boxes with his Wings on both Sides of my Head and Body, although I held him at Arms Length, and was out of the Reach of his Claws, that I was twenty Times thinking to let him go. But I was soon relieved by one of our Servants, who wrung off the Bird's Neck; and I had him next Day for Dinner by the Queen's Command. This Linnet, as near as I can remember, seemed to be somewhat larger than an *English* Swan.

THE Maids of Honour often invited *Glumdalclitch* to their Apartments, and desired she would bring me along with her, on Purpose to have the Pleasure of seeing and touching me. They would often strip me naked from Top to Toe, and lay me at full Length in their Bosoms; wherewith I was much disgusted; because, to say the Truth, a very offensive Smell came from their Skins; which I do not mention or intend to the Disadvantage of those excellent Ladies, for whom I have all Manner of Respect: But, I conceive, that my Sense was more acute in Proportion to my Littleness; and that those illustrious Persons were no more disagreeable to their Lovers, or to each other, than People of the same Quality are with us in *England*. And, after all, I found their natural Smell was much more supportable than when they used Perfumes, under which I immediately swooned away. I cannot forget, that an intimate Friend of mine in *Lilliput* took the Freedom in a warm Day, when I had used a good deal of Exercise, to complain of a strong Smell about me; although I am as little faulty that way as most of my Sex: But I suppose, his Faculty of Smelling was as nice with regard to me, as mine was to that of this People. Upon this Point, I cannot forbear doing Justice to the Queen my Mistress, and *Glumdalclitch* my Nurse; whose Persons were as sweet as those of any Lady in *England*.

THAT which gave me most Uneasiness among these Maids of Honour, when my Nurse carried me to visit them, was to see them use me without any Manner of Ceremony, like a Creature who had no Sort of Consequence. For, they would strip themselves to the Skin, and put on their Smocks in my Presence, while I was placed on their Toylet[21] directly before their naked Bodies; which, I am sure, to me was very far from being a tempting Sight, or from giving me any other Motions[22] than those of Horror and Disgust. Their Skins appeared so coarse and uneven, so variously coloured when I saw them near, with a Mole here and there as broad as a Trencher, and Hairs hanging from it thicker than Pack-threads; to say nothing further concerning the rest of their Persons. Neither did they at all scruple while I was by, to discharge what they had drunk, to the Quantity of at least two Hogsheads, in a Vessel that held above three Tuns. The handsomest among these Maids of Honour, a pleasant frolicksome Girl of sixteen, would sometimes set me astride upon one of her Nipples; with many other Tricks, wherein the Reader will excuse me for not being over particular. But, I was so much displeased, that I entreated *Glumdalclitch* to contrive some excuse for not seeing that young Lady any more.

ONE Day, a young Gentleman who was Nephew to my Nurse's Governess, came and pressed them both to see an Execution. It was of a Man who had murdered one of that Gentleman's intimate Acquaintance. *Glumdalclitch* was prevailed on to be of the Company, very much against her Inclination, for she was naturally tender hearted: And, as for my self, although I abhorred such Kind of Spectacles; yet my Curiosity tempted me to see something that I thought must be extraordinary. The Malefactor was fixed in a Chair upon a Scaffold erected for the Purpose; and his Head cut off at one Blow with a Sword of about forty Foot long. The Veins and Arteries spouted up such a prodigious Quantity of Blood, and so high in the Air, that the great *Jet d'Eau* at *Versailles*[23] was not equal for the Time it lasted; and the Head when it fell on the Scaffold Floor, gave such a Bounce, as made me start, although I were at least an *English* Mile distant.

THE Queen, who often used to hear me talk of my Sea-Voyages, and took all Occasions to divert me when I was melancholy, asked me whether I understood how to handle a Sail or an Oar; and whether a little Exercise of Rowing might not be convenient for my Health. I answered, that I understood both very well. For although my proper Employment had been to be Surgeon or Doctor to the Ship; yet often upon a Pinch, I was forced to work like a common Mariner. But, I could not see how this could be done in their Country, where the smallest Wherry was equal to a first

Rate Man of War among us; and such a Boat as I could manage, would never live in any of their Rivers: Her Majesty said, if I would contrive a Boat, her own Joyner should make it, and she would provide a Place for me to sail in. The Fellow was an ingenious Workman, and by my Instructions in ten Days finished a Pleasure-Boat with all its Tackling, able conveniently to hold eight *Europeans*. When it was finished, the Queen was so delighted, that she ran with it in her Lap to the King, who ordered it to be put in a Cistern full of Water, with me in it, by way of Tryal; where I could not manage my two Sculls or little Oars for want of Room. But, the Queen had before contrived another Project. She ordered the Joyner to make a wooden Trough of three Hundred Foot long, fifty broad, and eight deep; which being well pitched to prevent leaking, was placed on the Floor along the Wall, in an outer Room of the Palace. It had a Cock near the Bottom, to let out the Water when it began to grow stale; and two Servants could easily fill it in half an Hour. Here I often used to row for my Diversion, as well as that of the Queen and her Ladies, who thought themselves agreeably entertained with my Skill and Agility. Sometimes I would put up my Sail, and then my Business was only to steer, while the Ladies gave me a Gale with their Fans; and when they were weary, some of the Pages would blow my Sail forward with their Breath, while I shewed my Art by steering Starboard or Larboard as I pleased. When I had done, *Glumdalclitch* always carried back my Boat into her Closet, and hung it on a Nail to dry.

IN this Exercise I once met an Accident which had like to have cost me my Life. For, one of the Pages having put my Boat into the Trough; the Governess who attended *Glumdalclitch*, very officiously lifted me up to place me in the Boat; but I happened to slip through her Fingers, and should have infallibly fallen down forty Foot upon the Floor, if by the luckiest Chance in the World, I had not been stop'd by a Corking-pin that stuck in the good Gentlewoman's Stomacher; the Head of the Pin passed between my Shirt and the Waistband of my Breeches; and thus I was held by the Middle in the Air, till *Glumdalclitch* ran to my Relief.

ANOTHER time, one of the Servants, whose Office it was to fill my Trough every third Day with fresh Water; was so careless to let a huge Frog (not perceiving it) slip out of his Pail. The Frog lay concealed till I was put into my Boat, but then seeing a resting Place, climbed up, and made it lean so much on one Side, that I was forced to balance it with all my Weight on the other, to prevent overturning. When the Frog was got in, it hopped at once half the Length of the Boat, and then over my Head, backwards and forwards, dawbing my Face and Cloaths with its odious Slime. The Largeness of its Features made it appear the most deformed Animal that can be conceived. However, I desired *Glumdalclitch* to let me deal with it alone. I banged it a good while with one of my Sculls, and at last forced it to leap out of the Boat.

BUT, the greatest Danger I ever underwent in that Kingdom, was from a Monkey, who belonged to one of the Clerks of the Kitchen. *Glumdalclitch* had locked me up in her Closet, while she went somewhere upon Business, or a Visit. The Weather being very warm, the Closet Window was left open, as well as the Windows and the Door of my bigger Box, in which I usually lived, because of its Largeness and Conveniency. As I sat quietly meditating at my Table, I heard something bounce in at the Closet Window, and skip about from one Side to the other; whereat, although I were much alarmed, yet I ventured to look out, but not stirring from my Seat; and then I saw this frolicksome Animal, frisking and leaping up and down, till at last he came to my Box, which he seemed to view with great Pleasure and Curiosity, peeping in at the Door and every Window. I retreated to the farther Corner of my Room, or Box; but the Monkey looking in at every Side, put me into such a Fright, that I wanted Presence of Mind to conceal my self under the Bed, as I might easily have done. After some time spent in peeping, grinning, and chattering, he at last espyed me; and reaching one of his Paws in at the Door as a Cat does when she plays with a Mouse, although I often shifted Place to avoid him; he at length seized the Lappet of my Coat (which being made of that Country Silk, was very thick and strong) and dragged me out. He took me up in his right Forefoot, and held me as a Nurse doth a Child she is going to suckle; just as I have seen the same Sort of Creature do with a Kitten in *Europe:* And when I offered to struggle, he squeezed me so hard, that I thought it more prudent to submit. I have good Reason to believe that he took me for a young one of his own Species, by his often stroaking my Face very gently with his other Paw. In these Diversions he was interrupted by a Noise at the Closet Door, as if some Body were opening it; whereupon he suddenly leaped up to the Window at which he had come in, and thence upon the Leads and Gutters, walking upon three Legs, and holding me in the fourth, till he clambered up to a Roof that was next to ours. I heard *Glumdalclitch* give a Shriek at the Moment he was carrying me out. The poor Girl was almost distracted: That Quarter of the Palace was all in an Uproar; the Servants ran for Ladders; the Monkey was seen by Hundreds in the Court, sitting upon the Ridge of a Building, holding me like a Baby in one of his Fore-Paws, and feeding me with the other, by cramming into my Mouth some Victuals he had squeezed out of the Bag on one Side of his Chaps, and patting me when I would not eat; whereat many of the Rabble below could not forbear laughing; neither do I think they justly ought to be blamed; for without Question, the Sight was ridiculous enough to every Body but my self. Some of the People threw up Stones, hoping to drive the Monkey down; but this was strictly forbidden, or else very probably my Brains had been dashed out.

THE Ladders were now applied, and mounted by several Men; which the Monkey observing, and finding himself almost encompassed; not being able to make Speed enough with his three Legs, let me drop on a Ridge-Tyle, and made his Escape. Here I sat for some time five Hundred Yards from the Ground, expecting every Moment to be blown down by the Wind, or to fall by my own Giddiness, and come tumbling over and over from the Ridge to the Eves. But an honest Lad, one of my Nurse's Footmen, climbed up, and putting me into his Breeches Pocket, brought me down safe.

I WAS almost choaked with the filthy Stuff the Monkey had crammed down my Throat; but, my dear little Nurse picked it out of my Mouth with a small Needle; and then I fell a vomiting, which gave me great Relief. Yet I was so weak and bruised in the Sides with the Squeezes given me by this odious Animal, that I was forced to keep my Bed a Fortnight. The King, Queen, and all the Court, sent every Day to enquire after my Health; and her Majesty made me several Visits during my Sickness. The Monkey was killed, and an Order made that no such Animal should be kept about the Palace.

WHEN I attended the King after my Recovery, to return him Thanks for his Favours, he was pleased to railly me a good deal upon this Adventure. He asked me what my Thoughts and Speculations were while I lay in the Monkey's Paw; how I liked the Victuals he gave me, his Manner of Feeding; and whether the fresh Air on the Roof had sharpened my Stomach. He desired to know what I would have done upon such an Occasion in my own Country. I told his Majesty, that in *Europe* we had no Monkies, except such as were brought for Curiosities from other Places, and so small, that I could deal with a Dozen of them together, if they presumed to attack me. And as for that monstrous Animal with whom I was so lately engaged, (it was indeed as large as an Elephant) if my Fears had suffered me to think so far as to make Use of my Hanger (looking fiercely, and clapping my Hand upon the Hilt as I spoke) when he poked his Paw into my Chamber, perhaps I should have given him such a Wound, as would have made him glad to withdraw it with more Haste than he put it in. This I delivered in a firm Tone, like a Person who was jealous lest his Courage should be called in Question. However, my Speech produced nothing else besides a loud Laughter; which all the Respect due to his Majesty from those about him, could not make them contain. This made me reflect, how vain an Attempt it is for a Man to endeavour doing himself Honour among those who are out of all Degree of Equality or Comparison with him. And yet I have seen the Moral of my own Behaviour very frequent in *England* since my Return; where a little contemptible Varlet, without the least Title to Birth, Person, Wit, or common Sense, shall presume to look with Importance, and put himself upon a Foot with the greatest Persons of the Kingdom.

I WAS every Day furnishing the Court with some ridiculous Story; and *Glumdalclitch,* although she loved me to Excess, yet was arch enough to inform the Queen, whenever I committed any folly that she thought would be diverting to her Majesty. The Girl who had been out of Order, was carried by her Governess to take the Air about an Hour's Distance, or thirty Miles from Town. They alighted out of the Coach near a small Footpath in a Field; and *Glumdalclitch* setting down my travelling Box, I went out of it to walk. There was a Cow-dung in the Path,[24] and I must needs try my Activity by attempting to leap over it. I took a Run, but unfortunately jumped short, and found my self just in the Middle up to my Knees. I waded through with some Difficulty, and one of the Footmen wiped me as clean as he could with his Handkerchief; for I was filthily bemired, and my Nurse confined me to my Box until we returned home; where the Queen was soon informed of what had passed, and the Footmen spread it about the Court; so that all the Mirth, for some Days, was at my Expence.

CHAPTER VI

Several Contrivances of the Author to please the King and Queen. He shews his Skill in Musick. The King enquires into the State of Europe, which the Author relates to him. The King's Observations thereon.

I used to attend the King's Levee[25] once or twice a Week, and had often seen him under the Barber's Hand, which indeed was at first very terrible to behold. For, the Razor was almost twice as long as an ordinary Scythe. His Majesty, according to the Custom of the Country, was only shaved twice a Week. I once prevailed on the Barber to give me some of the Suds or Lather, out of which I picked Forty or Fifty of the strongest Stumps of Hair. I then took a Piece of fine Wood, and cut it like the Back of a Comb, making several Holes in it at equal Distance, with as small a Needle as I could get from *Glumdalclitch*. I fixed in the Stumps so artificially, scraping and sloping them with my Knife towards the Points, that I made a very tolerable Comb; which was a seasonable Supply, my own being so much broken in the Teeth, that it was almost useless: Neither did I know any Artist in that Country so nice and exact, as would undertake to make me another.

AND this puts me in mind of an Amusement wherein I spent many of my leisure Hours. I desired the Queen's Woman to save for me the Combings of her Majesty's Hair, whereof in time I got a good Quantity; and consulting with my Friend the Cabinetmaker, who had received general Orders to do little Jobbs for me; I directed him to make two Chair-frames, no larger than those I had in my Box, and then to bore little Holes with a fine Awl round those Parts where I designed the Backs and Seats; through these Holes I wove the strongest Hairs I could pick out, just after the Manner of Cane-chairs in *England*. When they were finished, I made a Present of them to her Majesty, who kept them in her Cabinet, and used to shew them for Curiosities; as indeed they were the Wonder of every one who beheld them. The Queen would have had me sit upon one of these Chairs, but I absolutely refused to obey her; protesting I would rather dye a Thousand Deaths than place a dishonourable Part of my Body on those precious Hairs that once adorned her Majesty's Head. Of these Hairs (as I had always a Mechanical Genius) I likewise made a neat little Purse about five Foot long, with her Majesty's Name decyphered in Gold Letters; which I gave to *Glumdalclitch,* by the Queen's Consent. To say the Truth, it was more for Shew than Use, being not of Strength to bear the Weight of the larger coins; and therefore she kept nothing in it, but some little Toys that Girls are fond of.

THE King, who delighted in Musick, had frequent Consorts[26] at Court, to which I was sometimes carried, and set in my Box on a Table to hear them: But, the Noise was so great, that I could hardly distinguish the Tunes. I am confident, that all the Drums and Trumpets of a Royal Army, beating and sounding together just at your Ears, could not equal it. My Practice was to have my Box removed from the Places where the Performers sat, as far as I could; then to shut the Doors and Windows of it, and draw the Window-Curtains; after which I found their Musick not disagreeable.

I HAD learned in my Youth to play a little upon the Spinet; *Glumdalclitch* kept one in her Chamber, and a Master attended twice a Week to teach her: I call it a Spinet, because it somewhat resembled that Instrument, and was play'd upon in the same Manner. A Fancy came into my Head, that I would entertain the King and Queen with an *English* Tune upon this Instrument. But this appeared extremely difficult: For, the Spinet was near sixty Foot long, each Key being almost a Foot wide; so that, with my Arms extended, I could not reach to above five Keys; and to press them down required a good smart stroak with my Fist, which would be too great a Labour, and to no purpose. The Method I contrived was this. I prepared two round Sticks about the Bigness of common Cudgels; they were thicker at one End than the other; and I covered the thicker End with a Piece of a Mouse's Skin, that by rapping on them, I might neither Damage the Tops of the Keys, nor interrupt the Sound. Before the Spinet, a Bench was placed about four Foot below the Keys, and I was put upon the Bench. I ran sideling upon it that way and this, as fast as I could, banging the proper Keys with my two Sticks; and made a shift to play a Jigg to the great Satisfaction of both their Majesties: But, it was the most violent Exercise I ever underwent, and yet I could not strike above sixteen Keys, nor, consequently, play the Bass and Treble together, as other Artists do; which was a great Disadvantage to my Performance.

THE King, who as I before observed, was a Prince of excellent Understanding, would frequently order that I should be brought in my Box, and set upon the Table in his Closet. He would then command me to bring one of my Chairs out of the Box, and sit down within three Yards Distance upon the Top of the Cabinet; which brought me almost to a Level with his Face. In this Manner I had several Conversations with him. I one Day took the Freedom to tell his Majesty, that the Contempt he discovered towards *Europe,* and the rest of the World, did not seem answerable to those excellent Qualities of Mind, that he was Master of. That, Reason did not extend itself with the Bulk of the Body: On the contrary, we observed in our Country, that the tallest Persons were usually least provided with it. That among other Animals, Bees and Ants had the Reputation of more Industry, Art, and Sagacity than many of the larger Kinds. And that, as inconsiderable as he took me to be, I hoped I might live to do his Majesty some signal Service. The King heard me with Attention; and began to conceive a much better Opinion of me than he had ever before. He desired I would give him as exact an Account of the Government of *England* as I possibly could; because, as fond as Princes commonly are of their own Customs (for so he conjectured of other Monarchs by my former Discourses) he should be glad to hear of any thing that might deserve Imitation.

IMAGINE with thy self, courteous Reader, how often I then wished for the Tongue of *Demosthenes* or *Cicero,* that might have enabled me to celebrate the Praise of my own dear native Country in a Style equal to its Merits and Felicity.

I BEGAN my Discourse by informing his Majesty, that our Dominions consisted of two Islands, which composed three mighty Kingdoms under one Sovereign, besides our Plantations in *America.* I dwelt long upon the Fertility of our Soil, and the Temperature of our Climate. I then spoke at large upon the Constitution of an *English* Parliament, partly made up of an illustrious Body called the House of Peers, Persons of the noblest Blood, and of the most ancient and ample Patrimonies. I described that extraordinary Care always taken of their Education in Arts and Arms, to qualify them for being Counsellors born to the King and Kingdom; to have a Share in the Legislature, to be Members of the highest Court of Judicature from whence there could be no Appeal; and to be Champions always ready for the Defence of their Prince and Country by their Valour, Conduct and Fidelity. That these were the Ornament and Bulwark of the

Kingdom; worthy Followers of their most renowned Ancestors, whose Honour had been the Reward of their Virtue; from which their Posterity were never once known to degenerate. To these were joined several holy Persons, as part of that Assembly, under the Title of Bishops; whose peculiar Business it is, to take care of Religion, and of those who instruct the People therein. These were searched and sought out through the whole Nation, by the Prince and wisest Counsellors, among such of the Priesthood, as were most deservedly distinguished by the Sanctity of their Lives, and the Depth of their Erudition; who were indeed the spiritual Fathers of the Clergy and the People.

THAT, the other Part of the Parliament consisted of an Assembly called the House of Commons; who were all principal Gentlemen, *freely* picked and culled out by the People themselves, for their great Abilities, and Love of their Country, to represent the Wisdom of the whole Nation. And, these two Bodies make up the most august Assembly in *Europe;* to whom, in Conjunction with the Prince, the whole Legislature is committed.

I THEN descended to the Courts of Justice, over which the Judges, those venerable Sages and Interpreters of the Law, presided, for determining the disputed Rights and Properties of Men, as well as for the Punishment of Vice, and Protection of Innocence. I mentioned the prudent Management of our Treasury; the Valour and Atchievements of our Forces by Sea and Land. I computed the Number of our People, by reckoning how many Millions there might be of each Religious Sect, or Political Party among us. I did not omit even our Sports and Pastimes, or any other Particular which I thought might redound to the Honour of my Country. And, I finished all with a brief historical Account of Affairs and Events in *England* for about an hundred Years past.

THIS Conversation was not ended under five Audiences, each of several Hours; and the King heard the whole with great Attention; frequently taking Notes of what I spoke, as well as Memorandums of what Questions he intended to ask me.

WHEN I had put an End to these long Discourses, his Majesty in a sixth Audience consulting his Notes, proposed many Doubts, Queries, and Objections, upon every Article.[27] He asked, what Methods were used to cultivate the Minds and Bodies of our young Nobility; and in what kind of Business they commonly spent the first and teachable Part of their Lives. What Course was taken to supply that Assembly, when any noble Family became extinct. What Qualifications were necessary in those who are to be created new Lords: Whether the Humour of the Prince, a Sum of Money to a Court-Lady, or a Prime Minister; or a Design of strengthening a Party opposite to the publick Interest, ever happened to be Motives in those Advancements. What Share of Knowledge these Lords had in the Laws of their Country, and how they came by it, so as to enable them to decide the Properties of their Fellow-Subjects in the last Resort. Whether they were always so free from Avarice, Partialities, or Want, that a Bribe, or some other sinister View, could have no Place among them. Whether those holy Lords I spoke of, were constantly promoted to that Rank upon Account of their Knowledge in religious Matters, and the Sanctity of their Lives, had never been Compliers with the Times, while they were common Priests; or slavish prostitute Chaplains to some Nobleman, whose Opinions they continued servilely to follow after they were admitted into that Assembly.

HE then desired to know, what Arts were practised in electing those whom I called Commoners. Whether, a Stranger with a strong Purse might not influence the vulgar Voters to chuse him before their own Landlord, or the most considerable Gentleman in the Neighbourhood. How it came to pass that People were so violently bent upon getting into this Assembly, which I allowed to be a great Trouble and Expence, often to the Ruin of their Families, without any Salary or Pension: Because this appeared such an exalted Strain of Virtue and publick Spirit, that his Majesty seemed to doubt it might possibly not be always sincere: And he desired to know, whether such zealous Gentlemen could have any Views of refunding themselves for the Charges and Trouble they were at, by sacrificing the publick Good to the Designs of a weak and vicious Prince, in Conjunction with a corrupted Ministry. He multiplied his Questions, and sifted me thoroughly upon every Part of this Head; proposing numberless Enquiries and Objections, which I think it not prudent or convenient to repeat.

UPON what I said in relation to our Courts of Justice, his Majesty desired to be satisfied in several Points: And, this I was the better able to do, having been formerly almost ruined by a long Suit in Chancery, which was decreed for me with Costs. He asked, what Time was usually spent in determining between Right and Wrong; and what Degree of Expence. Whether Advocates and Orators had Liberty to plead in Causes manifestly known to be unjust, vexatious, or oppressive. Whether Party in Religion or Politicks were observed to be of any Weight in the Scale of Justice. Whether those pleading Orators were Persons educated in the general Knowledge of Equity; or only in provincial, national, and other local Customs. Whether they or their Judges had any Part in penning those Laws, which they assumed the Liberty of interpreting and glossing upon at their Pleasure. Whether they had ever at different Times pleaded for and against the same Cause, and cited Precedents to prove contrary Opinions. Whether they were a rich or a poor Corporation. Whether they received any pecuniary Reward for pleading or delivering their Opinions. And particularly whether they were ever admitted as Members in the lower Senate.

HE fell next upon the Management of our Treasury; and said, he thought my Memory had failed me, because I computed our Taxes at about five or six Millions a Year; and when I came to mention the Issues, he found they sometimes amounted to more than double; for, the Notes he had taken were very particular in this Point; because he hoped, as he told me, that the Knowledge of our Conduct might be useful to him; and he could not be deceived in his Calculations. But, if what I told him were true, he was still at a Loss how a Kingdom could run out of its Estate like a private Person. He asked me, who were our Creditors? and, where we found Money to pay them? He wondered to hear me talk of such charge-able and extensive Wars; that, certainly we must be a quarrelsome People, or live among very bad Neighbours; and that our Generals must needs be richer than our Kings. He asked, what Business we had out of our own Is-lands, unless upon the Score of Trade or Treaty, or to defend the Coasts with our Fleet. Above all, he was amazed to hear me talk of a mercenary standing Army in the Midst of Peace, and among a free People. He said, if we were governed by our own Consent in the Persons of our Representa-tives, he could not imagine of whom we were afraid, or against whom we were to fight; and would hear my Opinion, whether a private Man's House might not better be defended by himself, his Children, and Family; than by half a Dozen Rascals picked up at a Venture in the Streets, for small Wages, who might get an Hundred Times more by cutting their Throats.

HE laughed at my odd Kind of Arithmetick (as he was pleased to call it) in reckoning the Numbers of our People by a Computation drawn from the several Sects among us in Religion and Politicks. He said, he knew no Reason, why those who entertain Opinions prejudicial to the Publick, should be obliged to change, or should not be obliged to conceal them. And, as it was Tyranny in any Government to require the first, so it was Weakness not to enforce the second: For, a Man may be allowed to keep Poisons in his Closet, but not to vend them about as Cordials.

HE observed, that among the Diversions of our Nobility and Gentry, I had mentioned Gaming. He desired to know at what Age this Entertainment was usually taken up, and when it was laid down. How much of their Time it employed; whether it ever went so high as to affect their Fortunes. Whether mean vicious People, by their Dexterity in that Art, might not arrive at great Riches, and sometimes keep our very Nobles in Dependance, as well as habituate them to vile Companions; wholly take them from the Improvement of their Minds, and force them by the Losses they received, to learn and practice that infamous Dexterity upon others.

HE was perfectly astonished with the historical Account I gave him of our Affairs during the last Century; protesting it was only an Heap of Conspiracies, Rebellions, Murders, Massacres, Revolutions, Banishments; the very worst Effects that Avarice, Faction, Hypocrisy, Perfidiousness, Cruelty, Rage, Madness, Hatred, Envy, Lust, Malice, and Ambition could produce.

HIS Majesty in another Audience, was at the Pains to recapitulate the Sum of all I had spoken; compared the Questions he made, with the Answers I had given; then taking me into his Hands, and stroaking me gently, delivered himself in these Words, which I shall never forget, nor the Manner he spoke them in. My little Friend *Grildrig*, you have made a most admirable Panegyrick upon your Country. You have clearly proved that Ignorance, Idleness, and Vice are the proper Ingredients for qualifying a Legislator. That Laws are best explained, interpreted, and applied by those whose Interest and Abilities lie in perverting, confounding, and eluding them. I observe among you some Lines of an Institution, which in its Original might have been tolerable; but these half erased, and the rest wholly blurred and blotted by Corruptions. It doth not appear from all you have said, how any one Perfection is required towards the Procurement of any one Station among you; much less that Men are ennobled on Account of their Virtue, that Priests are advanced for their Piety or Learning, Soldiers for their Conduct or Valour, Judges for their Integrity, Senators for the Love of their Country, or Counsellors for their Wisdom. As for yourself (continued the King) who have spent the greatest Part of your Life in travelling; I am well disposed to hope you may hitherto have escaped many Vices of your Country. But, by what I have gathered from your own Relation, and the Answers I have with much Pains wringed and extorted from you; I cannot but conclude the Bulk of your Natives, to be the most pernicious Race of little odious Vermin that Nature ever suffered to crawl upon the Surface of the Earth.[28]

CHAPTER VII

The Author's Love of his Country. He makes a Proposal of much Advantage to the King; which is rejected. The King's great Ignorance in Politicks. The Learning of that Country very imperfect and confined. Their Laws, and military Affairs, and Parties in the State.

Nothing but an extreme Love of Truth could have hindered me from concealing this Part of my Story. It was in vain to discover my Resentments, which were always turned into Ridicule: And I was forced to rest with Patience, while my noble and most beloved Country was so injuriously treated. I am heartily sorry as any of my Readers can possibly be, that such an Occasion was given: But this Prince happened to be so curious and inquisitive upon every Particular, that it could not consist either with Gratitude or good Manners to refuse giving him what Satisfaction I was able. Yet thus much I may be allowed to say in my own Vindication; that I artfully eluded many of his Questions; and gave to every Point a more favourable turn by many Degrees than the strictness of Truth would allow. For, I have always born that laudable Partiality to my own Country, which *Dionysius Halicarnassensis*[29] with so much Justice recommends to an Historian. I would hide the Frailties and Deformities of my Political Mother, and place her Virtues and Beauties in the most advantageous Light. This was my sincere Endeavour in those many Discourses I had with that Monarch, although it unfortunately failed of Success.

But, great Allowances should be given to a King who lives wholly secluded from the rest of the World, and must therefore be altogether unacquainted with the Manners and Customs that most prevail in other Nations: The want of which Knowledge will ever produce many *Prejudices*,[30] and a certain *Narrowness of Thinking;* from which we and the politer Countries of *Europe* are wholly exempted. And it would be hard indeed, if so remote a Prince's Notions of Virtue and Vice were to be offered as a Standard for all Mankind.

To confirm what I have now said, and further to shew the miserable Effects of a *confined Education;* I shall here insert a Passage which will hardly obtain Belief. In hopes to ingratiate my self farther into his Majesty's Favour, I told him of an Invention discovered between three and four hundred Years ago, to make a certain Powder; into an heap of which the smallest Spark of Fire falling, would kindle the whole in a Moment, although it were as big as a Mountain; and make it all fly up in the Air together, with a Noise and Agitation greater than Thunder. That, a proper Quantity of this Powder rammed into an hollow Tube of Brass or Iron, according to its Bigness, would drive a Ball of Iron or Lead with such Violence and Speed, as nothing was able to sustain its Force. That, the largest Balls thus discharged, would not only Destroy whole Ranks of an Army at once; but batter the strongest Walls to the Ground; sink down Ships with a thousand Men in each, to the Bottom of the Sea; and when linked together by a Chain, would cut through Masts and Rigging; divide Hundreds of Bodies in the Middle, and lay all Waste before them. That we often put this Powder into large hollow Balls of Iron, and discharged them by an Engine into some City we were besieging; which would rip up the Pavement, tear the Houses to Pieces, burst and throw Splinters on every Side, dashing out the Brains of all who came near. That I knew the Ingredients very well, which were Cheap, and common; I understood the Manner of compounding them, and could direct his Workmen how to make those Tubes of a Size proportionable to all other Things in his Majesty's Kingdom; and the largest need not be above two hundred Foot long; twenty or thirty of which Tubes, charged with the proper Quantity of Powder and Balls, would batter down the Walls of the strongest Town in his Dominions in a few Hours; or destroy the whole Metropolis, if ever it should pretend to dispute his absolute Commands. This I humbly offered to his Majesty, as a small Tribute of Acknowledgment in return of so many Marks that I had received of his Royal Favour and Protection.

THE King was struck with Horror at the Description I had given of those terrible Engines, and the Proposal I had made. He was amazed how so impotent and groveling an Insect as I (these were his Expressions) could entertain such inhuman Ideas, and in so familiar a Manner as to appear wholly unmoved at all the Scenes of Blood and Desolation, which I had painted as the common Effects of those destructive Machines; whereof he said, some evil Genius, Enemy to Mankind, must have been the first Contriver. As for himself, he protested, that although few Things delighted him so much as new Discoveries in Art or in Nature; yet he would rather lose Half his Kingdom than be privy to such a Secret; which he commanded me, as I valued my Life, never to mention any more.

A STRANGE Effect of *narrow Principles* and *short Views!* that a Prince possessed of every Quality which procures Veneration, Love and Esteem; of strong Parts, great Wisdom and profound Learning; endued with admirable Talents for Government, and almost adored by his Subjects; should form a *nice unnecessary Scruple,* whereof in *Europe* we can have no Conception, let slip an Opportunity put into his Hands, that would have made him absolute Master of the Lives, the Liberties, and the Fortunes of his People. Neither do I say this with the least Intention to detract from the many Virtues of that excellent King; whose Character I am sensible will on this Account be very much lessened in the Opinion of an *English* Reader: But, I take this Defect among them to have risen from their Ignorance; by not having hitherto reduced *Politicks* into a *Science,* as the more acute Wits of *Europe* have done. For, I remember very well, in a Discourse one Day with the King; when I happened to say, there were several thousand Books among us written upon the *Art of Government;* it gave him (directly contrary to my Intention) a very mean Opinion of our Understandings. He professed both to abominate and despise all *Mystery, Refinement,* and *Intrigue,* either in a Prince or a Minister. He could not tell what I meant by *Secrets of State,* where an Enemy or some Rival Nation were not in the Case. He confined the Knowledge of governing within very *narrow Bounds;* to common Sense and Reason, to Justice and Lenity, to the Speedy Determination of Civil and criminal Causes; with some other obvious Topicks which are not worth considering. And, he gave it for his Opinion; that whoever could make two Ears of Corn, or two Blades of Grass to grow upon a Spot of Ground where only one grew before; would deserve better of Mankind, and do more essential Service to his Country, than the whole Race of Politicians put together.

THE Learning of this People is very defective; consisting only in Morality, History, Poetry and Mathematicks; wherein they must be allowed to excel. But, the last of these is wholly applied to what may be useful in Life; to the Improvement of Agriculture and all mechanical Arts; so that among us it would be little esteemed. And as to Ideas, Entities, Abstractions and Transcendentals, I could never drive the least Conception into their Heads.

No Law of that Country must exceed in Words the Number of Letters in their Alphabet; which consists only of two and twenty. But indeed, few of them extend even to that Length. They are expressed in the most plain and simple Terms, wherein those People are not Mercurial enough to discover above one Interpretation. And, to write a Comment upon any Law, is a capital Crime. As to the Decision of civil Causes, or Proceedings against Criminals, their Precedents are so few, that they have little Reason to boast of any extraordinary Skill in either.

THEY have had the Art of Printing, as well as the *Chinese,* Time out of Mind. But their Libraries are not very large; for that of the King's, which is reckoned the largest, doth not amount to above a thousand Volumes; placed in a Gallery of twelve hundred Foot long; from whence I had Liberty to borrow what Books I pleased. The Queen's Joyner had contrived in one of *Glumdalclitch's* Rooms a Kind of wooden Machine five and twenty Foot high, formed like a standing Ladder; the Steps were each fifty Foot long: It was indeed a moveable Pair of Stairs, the lowest End placed at ten Foot Distance from the Wall of the Chamber. The Book I had a Mind to read was put up leaning against the Wall. I first mounted to the upper Step of the Ladder, and turning my Face towards the Book, began at the Top of the Page, and so walking to the Right and Left about eight or ten Paces according to the Length of the Lines, till I had gotten a little below the Level of mine Eyes; and then descending gradually till I came to the Bottom: After which I mounted again, and began the other Page in the same Manner, and so turned over the Leaf, which I could easily do with both my Hands, for it was as thick and stiff as a Paste-board, and in the largest Folio's not above eighteen or twenty Foot long.

THEIR Stile is clear, masculine, and smooth, but not Florid; for they avoid nothing more than multiplying unnecessary Words, or using various Expressions. I have perused many of their Books, especially those in History and Morality. Among the latter I was much diverted with a little old Treatise, which always lay in *Glumdalclitch's* Bedchamber, and belonged to her Governess, a grave elderly Gentlewoman, who dealt in Writings of Morality and Devotion. The Book treats of the Weakness of Human kind; and is in little Esteem except among Women and the vulgar. However, I was curious to see what an Author of that Country could say upon such a Subject. This Writer went through all the usual Topicks of *European* Moralists; shewing how diminutive, contemptible, and helpless an Animal was Man in his own Nature; how unable to defend himself from the Inclemencies of the Air, or the Fury of wild Beasts: How much he was excelled by one Creature in Strength, by another in Speed, by a third in Foresight, by a fourth in Industry. He added, that Nature was degenerated in these latter declining Ages of the World, and could now produce only small abortive Births in Comparison of those in ancient Times. He said, it was very reasonable to think, not only that the Species of Men were originally much larger, but also that there must have been Giants in former Ages; which, as it is asserted by History and Tradition, so it hath been confirmed by huge Bones and Sculls casually dug up in several Parts of the Kingdom, far exceeding the common dwindled Race of Man in our Days. He argued, that the very Laws of Nature absolutely required we should have been made in the Beginning, of a Size more large and robust, not so liable to Destruction from every little Accident of a Tile falling from an House, or a Stone cast from the Hand of a Boy, or of being drowned in a little Brook. From this Way of Reasoning the Author drew several moral Applications useful in the Conduct of Life, but needless here to repeat. For my own Part, I could not avoid reflecting, how universally this Talent was spread of drawing Lectures in Morality, or indeed rather Matter of Discontent and repining, from the Quarrels we raise with Nature. And, I believe upon a strict Enquiry, those Quarrels might be shewn as ill-grounded among us, as they are among that People.

As to their military Affairs; they boast that the King's Army consists of an hundred and seventy six thousand Foot, and thirty two thousand Horse: If that may be called an Army which is made up of Tradesmen in the several Cities, and Farmers in the Country, whose Commanders are only the Nobility and Gentry, without Pay or Reward. They are indeed perfect enough in their Exercises; and under very good Discipline, wherein I saw no great merit: For, how should it be otherwise, where every Farmer is under the Command of his own Landlord, and every Citizen under that of the principal Men in his own City, chosen after the Manner of *Venice* by *Ballot*?[31]

I HAVE often seen the Militia of *Lorbrulgrud* drawn out to Exercise in a great Field near the City, of twenty Miles Square. They were in all not above twenty five thousand Foot, and six thousand Horse; but it was impossible for me to compute their Number, considering the Space of Ground they took up. A *Cavalier* mounted on a large Steed might be about Ninety Foot high. I have seen this whole Body of Horse upon the Word of Command draw their Swords at once, and brandish them in the Air. Imagination can Figure nothing so Grand, so surprising and so astonishing. It looked as if ten thousand Flashes of Lightning were darting at the same time from every Quarter of the Sky.

I WAS curious to know how this Prince, to whose Dominions there is no Access from any other Country, came to think of Armies, or to teach his

People the Practice of military Discipline. But I was soon informed, both by Conversation, and Reading their Histories. For, in the Course of many Ages they have been troubled with the same Disease, to which the whole Race of Mankind is Subject; the Nobility often contending for Power, the People for Liberty, and the King for absolute Dominion. All which, however happily tempered by the Laws of that Kingdom, have been sometimes violated by each of the three Parties; and have more than once occasioned Civil Wars, the last whereof was happily put an End to by this Prince's Grandfather in a general Composition; and the Militia then settled with common Consent hath been ever since kept in the strictest Duty.

CHAPTER VIII

The King and Queen make a Progress to the Frontiers. The Author attends them. The Manner in which he leaves the Country very particularly related. He returns to England.

I had always a strong Impulse that I should some time recover my Liberty, although it were impossible to conjecture by what Means, or to form any Project with the least Hope of succeeding. The Ship in which I sailed was the first ever known to be driven within Sight of that Coast; and the King had given strict Orders, that if at any Time another appeared, it should be taken ashore, and with all its Crew and Passengers brought in a Tumbril to *Lorbrulgrud.* He was strongly bent to get me a Woman of my own Size, by whom I might propagate the Breed: But I think I should rather have died than undergone the Disgrace of leaving a Posterity to be kept in Cages like tame Canary Birds; and perhaps in time sold about the Kingdom to Persons of Quality for Curiosities. I was indeed treated with much Kindness; I was the Favourite of a great King and Queen, and the Delight of the whole Court; but it was upon such a Foot as ill became the Dignity of human Kind. I could never forget those domestick Pledges I had left behind me. I wanted to be among People with whom I could converse upon even Terms; and walk about the Streets and Fields without Fear of being trod to Death like a Frog or young Puppy. But, my Deliverance came sooner than I expected, and in a Manner not very common: The whole Story and Circumstances of which I shall faithfully relate.

I HAD now been two Years in this Country; and, about the Beginning of the third, *Glumdalclitch* and I attended the King and Queen in Progress to the South Coast of the Kingdom. I was carried as usual in my Travelling-Box, which, as I have already described, was a very convenient Closet of twelve Foot wide. I had ordered a Hammock to be fixed by silken Ropes from the four Corners at the Top; to break the Jolts, when a Servant carried me before him on Horseback, as I sometimes desired; and would often sleep in my Hammock while we were upon the Road. On the Roof of my Closet, set not directly over the Middle of the Hammock, I ordered the Joyner to cut out a Hole of a Foot square to give me Air in hot Weather as I slept; which Hole I shut at pleasure with a Board that drew backwards and forwards through a Groove.

WHEN we came to our Journey's End, the King thought proper to pass a few Days at a Palace he hath near *Flanflasnic*, a City within eighteen *English* Miles of the Sea-side. *Glumdalclitch* and I were much fatigued: I had gotten a small Cold; but the poor Girl was so ill as to be confined to her Chamber. I longed to see the Ocean, which must be the only scene of my Escape, if ever it should happen. I pretended to be worse than I really was; and desired leave to take the fresh Air of the Sea, with a Page whom I was very fond of, and who had sometimes been trusted with me. I shall never forget with what Unwillingness *Glumdalclitch* consented; nor the strict Charge she gave the Page to be careful of me; bursting at the same time into a Flood of Tears, as if she had some Foreboding of what was to happen. The Boy took me out in my Box about Half an Hour's Walk from the Palace, towards the Rocks on the Sea-shore. I ordered him to set me down; and lifting up one of my Sashes, cast many a wistful melancholy Look towards the Sea. I found myself not very well; and told the Page that I had a Mind to take a Nap in my Hammock, which I hoped would do me good. I got in, and the Boy shut the Window close down, to keep out the Cold. I soon fell asleep: And all I can conjecture is, that while I slept, the Page thinking no Danger could happen, went among the Rocks to look for Birds Eggs; having before observed him from my Window searching about, and picking up one or two in the Clefts. Be that as it will; I found my self suddenly awaked with a violent Pull upon the Ring which was fastned at the Top of my Box, for the Conveniency of Carriage. I felt the Box raised very high in the Air, and then born forward with prodigious Speed. The first Jolt had like to have shaken me out of my Hammock; but afterwards the Motion was easy enough. I called out several times as loud as I could raise my Voice, but all to no purpose. I looked towards my Windows, and could see nothing but the Clouds and Sky. I heard a Noise just over my Head like the clapping of Wings; and then began to perceive the woful Condition I was in; that some Eagle had got the Ring of my Box in his Beak, with an Intent to let it fall on a Rock, like a Tortoise in a Shell, and then pick out my Body and devour it. For the Sagacity and Smell of this Bird enable him to discover his Quarry at a great Distance, although better concealed than I could be within a two Inch Board.

IN a little time I observed the Noise and flutter of Wings to encrease very fast; and my Box was tossed up and down like a Sign-post in a windy Day. I heard several Bangs or Buffets, as I thought, given to the Eagle (for such I am certain it must have been that held the Ring of my Box in his Beak) and then all on a sudden felt my self falling perpendicularly down for above a Minute; but with such incredible Swiftness that I almost lost my Breath. My Fall was stopped by a terrible Squash, that sounded louder to mine Ears than the Cataract of *Niagara;* after which I was quite in the Dark for another Minute, and then my Box began to rise so high that I could see Light from the Tops of my Windows. I now perceived that I was fallen into the Sea. My Box, by the Weight of my Body, the Goods that were in, and the broad Plates of Iron fixed for Strength at the four Corners of the Top and Bottom, floated about five Foot deep in Water. I did then, and do now suppose, that the Eagle which flew away with my Box was pursued by two or three others, and forced to let me drop while he was defending himself against the Rest, who hoped to share in the Prey. The Plates of Iron fastned at the Bottom of the Box, (for those were the strongest) preserved the Balance while it fell; and hindred it from being broken on the Surface of the Water. Every Joint of it was well grooved, and the Door did not move on Hinges, but up and down like a Sash; which kept my Closet so tight that very little Water came in. I got with much Difficulty out of my Hammock, having first ventured to draw back the Slip board on the Roof already mentioned, contrived on purpose to let in Air; for want of which I found my self almost stifled.

How often did I then wish my self with my dear *Glumdalclitch,* from whom one single Hour had so far divided me! And I may say with Truth, that in the midst of my own Misfortune, I could not forbear lamenting any poor Nurse, the Grief she would suffer for my Loss, the Displeasure of the Queen, and the Ruin of her Fortune. Perhaps many Travellers have not been under greater Difficulties and Distress than I was at this Juncture; expecting every Moment to see my Box dashed in Pieces, or at least overset by the first violent Blast, or a rising Wave. A Breach in one single Pane of Glass would have been immediate Death: Nor could any thing have preserved the Windows but the strong Lattice Wires placed on the outside against Accidents in Travelling. I saw the Water ooze in at several Crannies, although the Leaks were not considerable; and I endeavoured to stop them as well as I could. I was not able to lift up the Roof of my

Closet, which otherwise I certainly should have done, and sat on the Top of it, where I might at least preserve myself from being shut up, as I may call it, in the Hold. Or, if I escaped these Dangers for a Day or two, what could I expect but a miserable Death of Cold and Hunger! I was four Hours under these Circumstances, expecting and indeed wishing every Moment to be my last.

I HAVE already told the Reader, that there were two strong Staples fixed upon the Side of my Box which had no Window, and into which the Servant, who used to carry me on Horseback, would put a Leathern Belt, and buckle it about his Waist. Being in this disconsolate State, I heard, or at least thought I heard some kind of grating Noise on that Side of my Box where the Staples were fixed; and soon after I began to fancy that the Box was pulled, or towed along in the Sea; for I now and then felt a sort of tugging, which made the Waves rise near the Tops of my Windows, leaving me almost in the Dark. This gave me some faint Hopes of Relief, although I were not able to imagine how it could be brought about. I ventured to unscrew one of my Chairs, which were always fastned to the Floor; and having made a hard shift to screw it down again directly under the Slipping-board that I had lately opened; I mounted on the Chair, and putting my Mouth as near as I could to the Hole, I called for Help in a loud Voice, and in all the Languages I understood. I then fastned my Handkerchief to a Stick I usually carried, and thrusting it up the Hole, waved it several times in the Air; that if any Boat or Ship were near, the Seamen might conjecture some unhappy Mortal to be shut up in the Box.

I FOUND no Effect from all I could do, but plainly perceived my Closet to be moved along; and in the Space of an Hour, or better, that Side of the Box where the Staples were, and had no Window, struck against something that was hard. I apprehended it to be a Rock, and found my self tossed more than ever. I plainly heard a Noise upon the Cover of my Closet, like that of a Cable, and the grating of it as it passed through the Ring. I then found my self hoisted up by Degrees at least three Foot higher than I was before. Whereupon, I again thrust up my Stick and Handkerchief, calling for Help till I was almost hoarse. In return to which, I heard a great Shout repeated three times, giving me such Transports of Joy as are not to be conceived but by those who feel them. I now heard a trampling over my Head; and somebody calling through the Hole with a loud Voice in the *English* Tongue: *If there be any Body below, let them speak.* I answered, I was an *Englishman*, drawn by ill Fortune into the greatest Calamity that ever any Creature underwent; and begged, by all that was moving, to be delivered out of the Dungeon I was in. The Voice replied, I was safe, for my Box was fastned to their Ship; and the Carpenter should immediately come, and saw an Hole in the Cover, large enough to pull me out. I answered, that was needless, and would take up too much Time; for there was no more to be done, but let one of the Crew put his Finger into the Ring, and take the Box out of the Sea into the Ship, and so into the Captain's Cabbin. Some of them upon hearing me talk so wildly, thought I was mad; others laughed; for indeed it never came into my Head, that I was now got among People of my own Stature and Strength. The Carpenter came, and in a few Minutes sawed a Passage about four Foot square; then let down a small Ladder, upon which I mounted, and from thence was taken into the Ship in a very weak Condition.

THE Sailors were all in Amazement, and asked me a thousand Questions, which I had no Inclination to answer. I was equally confounded at the Sight of so many Pigmies; for such I took them to be, after having so long accustomed mine Eyes to the monstrous Objects I had left. But the Captain, Mr. *Thomas Wilcocks*, an honest worthy *Shropshire* Man, observing I was ready to faint, took me into his Cabbin, gave me a Cordial to comfort me, and made me *turn in* upon his own Bed; advising me to take a little Rest, of which I had great need. Before I went to sleep I gave him to understand, that I had some valuable Furniture in my Box too good to be lost; a fine Hammock, an handsome Field-Bed, two Chairs, a Table and a Cabinet: That my Closet was hung on all Sides, or rather quilted with Silk and Cotton: That if he would let one of the Crew bring my Closet into his Cabbin, I would open it before him, and shew him my Goods. The Captain hearing me utter these Absurdities, concluded I was raving: However, (I suppose to pacify me) he promised to give Order as I desired; and going upon Deck, sent some of his Men down into my Closet, from whence (as I afterwards found) they drew up all my Goods, and stripped off the Quilting; but the Chairs, Cabinet and Bed-sted being screwed to the Floor, were much damanged by the Ignorance of the Seamen, who tore them up by Force. Then they knocked off some of the Boards for the Use of the Ship; and when they had got all they had a Mind for, let the Hulk drop into the Sea, which by Reason of many Breaches made in the Bottom and Sides, sunk *to rights*. And indeed I was glad not to have been a Spectator of the Havock they made; because I am confident it would have sensibly touched me, by bringing former Passages into my Mind, which I had rather forget.

I SLEPT some Hours, but perpetually disturbed with Dreams of the Place I had left, and the Dangers I had escaped. However, upon waking I found my self much recovered. It was now about eight a Clock at Night, and the Captain ordered Supper immediately, thinking I had already fasted too long. He entertained me with great Kindness, observing me not to look wildly, or talk inconsistently; and when we were left alone, desired I would give him a Relation of my Travels, and by what Accident I came to be set adrift in that monstrous wooden Chest. He said, that about twelve a Clock at Noon, as he was looking through his Glass, he spied it at a Distance, and thought it was a Sail, which he had a Mind to make; being not much out of his Course, in hopes of buying some Biscuit, his own beginning to fall short. That, upon coming nearer, and finding his Error, he sent out his Long-boat to discover what I was; that his Men came back in a Fright, swearing they had seen a swimming House. That he laughed at their Folly, and went himself in the Boat, ordering his Men to take a strong Cable along with them. That the Weather being calm, he rowed round me several times, observed my Windows, and the Wire Lattices that defended them. That he discovered two Staples upon one Side, which was all of Boards, without any Passage for Light. He then commanded his Men to row up to that Side; and fastning a Cable to one of the Staples, ordered his Men to tow my Chest (as he called it) towards the Ship. When it was there, he gave Directions to fasten another Cable to the Ring fixed in the Cover, and to raise up my Chest with Pullies, which all the Sailors were not able to do above two or three Foot. He said, they saw my Stick and Handkerchief thrust out of the Hole, and concluded, that some unhappy Man must be shut up in the Cavity. I asked whether he or the Crew had seen any prodigious Birds in the Air about the Time he first discovered me: To which he answered, that discoursing this Matter with the Sailors while I was asleep, one of them said he had *observed* three Eagles flying towards the North; but remarked nothing of their being larger than the usual Size; which I suppose must be imputed to the great Height they were at: And he could not guess the Reason of my Question. I then asked the Captain how far he reckoned we might be from Land; he said, by the best Computation he could make, we were at least an hundred Leagues. I assured him, that he must be mistaken by almost half; for I had not left the Country from whence I came, above two Hours before I dropt into the Sea. Whereupon he began again to think that my Brain was disturbed, of which he gave me a Hint, and advised me to go to Bed in a Cabin he had provided. I assured him I was well refreshed with his good Entertainment and Company, and as much in my Senses as ever I was in my Life. He then grew serious, and desired to ask me freely whether I were not troubled in Mind by the Consciousness of some enormous Crime, for which I was punished at the

Command of some Prince, by exposing me in that Chest; as great Criminals in other Countries have been forced to Sea in a leaky Vessel without Provisions: For, although he should be sorry to have taken so ill a Man into his Ship, yet he would engage his Word to set me safe on Shore in the first Port where we arrived. He added, that his Suspicions were much increased by some very absurd Speeches I had delivered at first to the Sailors, and afterwards to himself, in relation to my Closet or Chest, as well as by my odd Looks and Behaviour while I was at Supper.

I BEGGED his Patience to hear me tell my Story; which I faithfully did from the last Time I left *England,* to the Moment he first discovered me. And, as Truth always forceth its Way into rational Minds; so, this honest worthy Gentleman, who had some Tincture of Learning, and very good Sense, was immediately convinced of my Candor and Veracity. But, further to confirm all I had said, I entreated him to give Order that my Cabinet should be brought, of which I kept the Key in my Pocket, (for he had already informed me how the Seamen disposed of my Closet) I opened it in his Presence, and shewed him the small Collection of Rarities I made in the Country from whence I had been so strangely delivered. There was the Comb I had contrived out of the Stumps of the King's Beard; and another of the same Materials, but fixed into a paring of her Majesty's Thumbnail, which served for the Back. There was a Collection of Needles and Pins from a Foot to half a Yard long. Four Wasp-Stings, like Joyners Tacks: Some Combings of the Queen's Hair: A Gold Ring which one Day she made me a Present of in a most obliging Manner, taking it from her little Finger, and throwing it over my Head like a Collar. I desired the Captain would please to accept this Ring in Return of his Civilities; which he absolutely refused. I shewed him a Corn that I had cut off with my own Hand from a Maid of Honour's Toe; it was about the Bigness of a *Kentish* Pippin, and grown so hard, that when I returned to *England,* I got it hollowed into a Cup and set in Silver. Lastly, I desired him to see the Breeches I had then on, which were made of a Mouse's Skin.

I COULD force nothing on him but a Footman's Tooth, which I observed him to examine with great Curiosity, and found he had a Fancy for it. He received it with abundance of Thanks, more than such a Trifle could deserve. It was drawn by an unskilful Surgeon in a Mistake from one of *Glumdalclitch's* Men, who was afflicted with the Tooth-ach; but it was as sound as any in his Head. I got it cleaned, and put it into my Cabinet. It was about a Foot long, and four Inches in Diameter.

THE Captain was very well satisfied with this plain Relation I had given him; and said, he hoped when we returned to *England,* I would oblige the World by putting it in Paper, and making it publick. My Answer was, that I thought we were already overstocked with Books of Travels: That nothing could now pass which was not extraordinary; wherein I doubted, some Authors less consulted Truth than their own Vanity or Interest, or the Diversion of ignorant Readers. That my Story could contain little besides common Events, without those ornamental Descriptions of strange Plants, Trees, Birds, and other Animals; or the barbarous Customs and Idolatry of savage People, with which most Writers abound. However, I thanked him for his good Opinion, and promised to take the Matter into my Thoughts.

HE said, he wondered at one Thing very much; which was, to hear me speak so loud; asking me whether the King or Queen of that Country were thick of Hearing. I told him it was what I had been used to for above two Years past; and that I admired as much at the Voices of him and his Men, who seemed to me only to whisper, and yet I could hear them well enough. But, when I spoke in that Country, it was like a Man talking in the Street to another looking out from the Top of a Steeple, unless when I was placed on a Table, or held in any Person's Hand. I told him, I had likewise observed another Thing; that when I first got into the Ship, and the Sailors stood all about me, I thought they were the most little contemptible Creatures I had ever beheld. For, indeed, while I was in that Prince's Country, I could never endure to look in a Glass after mine Eyes had been accustomed to such prodigious Objects; because the Comparison gave me so despicable a Conceit of my self. The Captain said, that while we were at Supper, he observed me to look at every thing with a Sort of Wonder; and that I often seemed hardly able to contain my Laughter; which he knew not well how to take, but imputed it to some Disorder in my Brain. I answered, it was very true; and I wondered how I could forbear, when I saw his Dishes of the Size of a Silver Three-pence, a Leg of Pork hardly a Mouthful, a Cup not so big as a Nutshell: And so I went on, describing the rest of his Houshold-stuff and Provisions after the same Manner. For although the Queen had ordered a little Equipage of all Things necessary for me while I was in her Service; yet my Ideas were wholly taken up with what I saw on every Side of me; and I winked at my own Littleness, as People do at their own Faults. The Captain understood my Raillery very well, and merrily replied with the old *English* Proverb, that he doubted, mine Eyes were bigger than my Belly; for he did not observe my Stomach so good, although I had fasted all Day: And continuing in his Mirth, protested he would have gladly given an Hundred Pounds to have seen my Closet in the Eagle's Bill, and afterwards in its Fall from so great an Height into the Sea; which would certainly have been a most astonishing Object, worthy to have the Description of it transmitted to future Ages: And the Comparison of *Phaeton*[32] was so obvious, that he could not forbear applying it, although I did not much admire the Conceit.

THE Captain having been at *Tonquin*,[33] was in his Return to *England* driven North Eastward to the Latitude of 44 Degrees, and of Longitude 143. But meeting a Trade Wind two Days after I came on board him, we sailed Southward a long Time, and coasting *New-Holland*,[34] kept our Course West-south-west, and then South-south-west till we doubled the *Cape of Good-hope.* Our Voyage was very prosperous, but I shall not trouble the Reader with a Journal of it. The Captain called in at one or two Ports, and sent in his Long-boat for Provisions and fresh Water; but I never went out of the Ship till we came into the *Downs,* which was on the 3d Day of *June* 1706, about nine Months after my Escape. I offered to leave my Goods in Security for Payment of my Freight; but the Captain protested he would not receive one Farthing. We took kind Leave of each other; and I made him promise he would come to see me at my House in *Redriff.* I hired a Horse and Guide for five Shillings, which I borrowed of the Captain.

AS I was on the Road; observing the Littleness of the Houses, the Trees, the Cattle and the People, I began to think my self in *Lilliput.* I was afraid of trampling on every Traveller I met; and often called aloud to have them stand out of the Way; so that I had like to have gotten one or two broken Heads for my Impertinence.

WHEN I came to my own House, for which I was forced to enquire, one of the Servants opening the Door, I bent down to go in (like a Goose under a Gate) for fear of striking my Head. My Wife ran out to embrace me, but I stooped lower than her Knees, thinking she could otherwise never be able to reach my Mouth. My Daughter kneeled to ask my Blessing, but I could not see her till she arose; having been so long used to stand with my Head and Eyes erect to above Sixty Foot; and then I went to take her up with one Hand, by the Waist. I looked down upon the Servants, and one or two Friends who were in the House, as if they had been Pigmies, and I a Giant. I told my wife, she had been too thrifty; for I found she had starved herself and her Daughter to nothing. In short, I behaved my self so unaccountably, that they were all of the Captain's Opinion when he first saw me; and concluded I had lost my Wits. This I mention as an Instance of the great Power of Habit and Prejudice.

IN a little Time I and my Family and Friends came to a right Understanding: But my Wife protested I should never go to Sea any more; although my evil Destiny so ordered, that she had not Power to hinder me; as the Reader may know hereafter. In the mean Time, I here conclude the second Part of my unfortunate Voyages.

The End of the Second Part.

PART III

A VOYAGE TO LAPUTA, BALNIBARBI, LUGGNAGG, GLUBBDUBDRIB, AND JAPAN

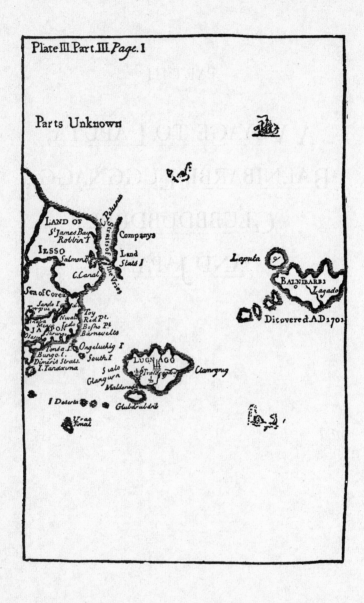

Plate III.Part.III.*Page.*1

Parts Unknown

Land of
St James Bay
Robbin I.
IESSO
Salmon
C.Canal

Companys

Land
Stats I.

Laputa

BALNIBARBI
Lagado

Discovered A.D.1703

Sea of Corea
Sando I.
Thevos
Inaba
Mens
JA
Naso
Nivato
Jedo
Barings

Try
Red Pt.
Bosho Pt.
Barnevelts

Tonda I.
Bungo I.
Dimeris Strats.
I.Tanaxima

Ongeluckig I.
South.I.

Glangura
Maldonada

LUGNAGG
S.alo
Tralaregdub

Clamryng

I Deserta

Glubdubdrib

Vran
Xmal

CHAPTER I

*The Author sets out on his Third Voyage. Is taken by Pyrates.
The Malice of a* Dutchman. *His Arrival at an Island. He is
received into* Laputa.

I had not been at home above ten Days, when Captain *William Robinson,* a
Cornish Man, Commander of the *Hopewell,* a stout Ship of three Hundred
Tuns, came to my House. I had formerly been Surgeon of another Ship
where he was Master, and a fourth Part Owner, in a Voyage to the *Levant.*
He had always treated me more like a Brother than an inferior Officer; and
hearing of my Arrival made me a Visit, as I apprehended only out of
Friendship, for nothing passed more than what is usual after long Absence.
But repeating his Visits often, expressing his Joy to find me in good
Health, asking whether I were now settled for Life, adding that he intended a Voyage to the *East-Indies,* in two Months, at last he plainly invited
me, although with some Apologies, to be Surgeon of the Ship. That I
should have another Surgeon under me, besides our two Mates; that my
Sallary should be double to the usual Pay; and that having experienced
my Knowledge in Sea-Affairs to be at least equal to his, he would enter
into any Engagement to follow my Advice, as much as if I had Share in the
Command.

He said so many other obliging things, and I knew him to be so honest
a Man, that I could not reject his Proposal; the Thirst I had of seeing the
World, notwithstanding my past Misfortunes, continuing as violent as
ever. The only Difficulty that remained, was to persuade my Wife, whose
Consent however I at last obtained, by the Prospect of Advantage she proposed to her Children.

We set out the 5th Day of *August,* 1706, and arrived at Fort St. *George,*[1]
the 11th of *April* 1707. We stayed there three Weeks to refresh our Crew,

many of whom were sick. From thence we went to *Tonquin,* where the Captain resolved to continue some time; because many of the Goods he intended to buy were not ready, nor could he expect to be dispatched in several Months. Therefore in hopes to defray some of the Charges he must be at, he bought a Sloop, loaded it with several Sorts of Goods, wherewith the *Tonquinese* usually trade to the neighbouring Islands; and putting Fourteen Men on Board, whereof three were of the Country, he appointed me Master of the Sloop, and gave me Power to traffick, while he transacted his Affairs at *Tonquin.*

WE had not sailed above three Days, when a great Storm arising, we were driven five Days to the North-North-East, and then to the East; after which we had fair Weather, but still with a pretty strong Gale from the West. Upon the tenth Day we were chased by two Pyrates, who soon overtook us; for my Sloop was so deep loaden, that she sailed very slow; neither were we in a Condition to defend our selves.

WE were boarded about the same Time by both the Pyrates, who entered furiously at the Head of their Men; but finding us all prostrate upon our Faces, (for so I gave Order,) they pinioned us with strong Ropes, and setting a Guard upon us, went to search the Sloop.

I OBSERVED among them a *Dutchman,* who seemed to be of some Authority, although he were not Commander of either Ship. He knew us by our Countenances to be *Englishmen,* and jabbering to us in his own Language, swore we should be tyed Back to Back, and thrown into the Sea. I spoke *Dutch* tolerably well; I told him who we were, and begged him in Consideration of our being Christians and Protestants, of neighbouring Countries, in strict Alliance, that he would move the Captains to take some Pity on us. This inflamed his Rage; he repeated his Threatnings, and turning to his Companions, spoke with great Vehemence, in the *Japanese* Language, as I suppose; often using the Word *Christianos.*

THE largest of the two Pyrate Ships was commanded by a *Japanese* Captain, who spoke a little *Dutch,* but very imperfectly. He came up to me, and after several Questions, which I answered in great Humility, he said we should not die. I made the Captain a very low Bow, and then turning to the *Dutchman,* said, I was sorry to find more Mercy in a Heathen, than in a Brother Christian. But I had soon Reason to repent those foolish Words; for that malicious Reprobate, having often endeavoured in vain to persuade both the Captains that I might be thrown into the Sea, (which they would not yield to after the Promise made me, that I should not die) however prevailed so far as to have a Punishment inflicted on me, worse in all human Appearance than Death it self. My Men were sent by an equal Division into both the Pyrate-Ships, and my Sloop new manned. As to my self, it was determined that I should be set a-drift, in a small Canoe, with Paddles and a Sail, and four Days Provisions; which last the *Japanese* Captain was so kind to double out of his own Stores, and would permit no Man to search me. I got down into the Canoe, while the *Dutchman* standing upon the Deck, loaded me with all the Curses and injurious Terms his Language could afford.

About an Hour before we saw the Pyrates, I had taken an Observation, and found we were in the Latitude of 46 N. and of Longitude 183. When I was at some Distance from the Pyrates, I discovered by my Pocket-Glass several Islands to the South-East. I set up my Sail, the Wind being fair, with a Design to reach the nearest of those Islands, which I made a Shift to do in about three Hours. It was all rocky; however I got many Birds Eggs; and striking Fire, I kindled some Heath and dry Sea-weed, by which I roasted my Eggs. I eat no other Supper, being resolved to spare my Provisions as much as I could. I passed the Night under the Shelter of a Rock, strowing some Heath under me, and slept pretty well.

The next Day I sailed to another Island, and thence to a third and fourth, sometimes using my Sail, and sometimes my Paddles. But not to trouble the Reader with a particular Account of my Distresses; let it suffice, that on the 5th Day, I arrived at the last Island in my Sight, which lay South-South-East to the former.

This Island was at a greater Distance than I expected, and I did not reach it in less than five Hours. I encompassed it almost round before I could find a convenient Place to land in, which was a small Creek, about three Times the Wideness of my Canoe. I found the Island to be all rocky, only a little intermingled with Tufts of Grass, and sweet smelling Herbs. I took out my small Provisions, and after having refreshed myself, I secured the Remainder in a Cave, whereof there were great Numbers. I gathered Plenty of Eggs upon the Rocks, and got a Quantity of dry Sea-weed, and parched Grass, which I designed to kindle the next Day, and roast my Eggs as well as I could. (For I had about me my Flint, Steel, Match, and Burning-glass.) I lay all Night in the Cave where I had lodged my Provisions. My Bed was the same dry Grass and Sea-weed which I intended for Fewel. I slept very little; for the Disquiets of my Mind prevailed over my Wearyness, and kept me awake. I considered how impossible it was to preserve my Life, in so desolate a Place; and how miserable my End must be. Yet I found my self so listless and desponding, that I had not the Heart to rise; and before I could get Spirits enough to creep out of my Cave, the Day was far advanced. I walked a while among the Rocks, the Sky was perfectly clear, and the Sun so hot, that I was forced to turn my Face from it: When all on a Sudden it became obscured, as I thought, in a Manner very different from what happens by the Interposition of a Cloud. I turned back, and perceived a vast Opake Body between me and the Sun, moving forwards towards the Island: It seemed to be about two Miles high, and hid the Sun six or seven Minutes, but I did not observe the Air to be much colder, or the Sky more darkned, than if I had stood under the Shade of a Mountain. As it approached nearer over the Place where I was, it appeared to be a firm Substance, the Bottom flat, smooth, and shining very bright from the Reflexion of the Sea below. I stood upon a Height about two Hundred Yards from the Shoar, and saw this vast Body descending almost to a Parallel with me, at less than an *English* Mile Distance. I took out my Pocket-Perspective, and could plainly discover Numbers of People moving up and down the Sides of it, which appeared to be sloping, but what those People were doing, I was not able to distinguish.

THE natural Love of Life gave me some inward Motions of Joy; and I was ready to entertain a Hope, that this Adventure might some Way or other help to deliver me from the desolate Place and Condition I was in. But, at the same Time, the Reader can hardly conceive my Astonishment, to behold an Island in the Air, inhabited by Men, who were able (as it should seem) to raise, or sink, or put it into a progressive Motion, as they pleased. But not being, at that Time, in a Disposition to philosophise upon this Phænomenon, I rather chose to observe what Course the Island would take; because it seemed for a while to stand still. Yet soon after it advanced nearer; and I could see the Sides of it, encompassed with several Gradations of Galleries and Stairs, at certain Intervals, to descend from one to the other. In the lowest Gallery, I beheld some People fishing with long Angling Rods, and others looking on. I waved my Cap, (for my Hat was long since worn out,) and my Handkerchief towards the Island; and upon its nearer Approach, I called and shouted with the utmost Strength of my Voice; and then looking circumspectly, I beheld a Crowd gathered to that Side which was most in my View. I found by their pointing towards me and to each other, that they plainly discovered me, although they made no Return to my Shouting: But I could see four or five Men running in great Haste up the Stairs to the Top of the Island, who then disappeared. I happened rightly to conjecture, that these were sent for Orders to some Person in Authority upon this Occasion.

THE Number of People increased; and in less than Half an Hour, the Island was moved and raised in such a Manner, that the lowest Gallery appeared in a Parallel of less than an Hundred Yards Distance from the Height where I stood. I then put my self into the most supplicating Postures, and spoke in the humblest Accent, but received no Answer. Those who stood nearest over-against me, seemed to be Persons of Distinction, as I supposed by their Habit. They conferred earnestly with each other, looking often upon me. At length one of them called out in a clear, polite, smooth Dialect, not unlike in Sound to the *Italian;* and therefore I returned an Answer in that Language, hoping at least that the Cadence might be more agreeable to his Ears. Although neither of us understood the other, yet my Meaning was easily known, for the People saw the Distress I was in.

THEY made Signs for me to come down from the Rock, and go towards the Shoar, which I accordingly did; and the flying Island being raised to a convenient Height, the Verge directly over me, a Chain was let down from the lowest Gallery, with a Seat fastned to the Bottom, to which I fixed my self, and was drawn up by Pullies.

CHAPTER II

The Humours and Dispositions of the Laputians *described. An Account of their Learning. Of the King and his Court. The Author's Reception there. The Inhabitants subject to Fears and Disquietudes. An Account of the Women.*

At my alighting I was surrounded by a Crowd of People, but those who stood nearest seemed to be of better Quality. They beheld me with all the Marks and Circumstances of Wonder; neither indeed was I much in their Debt; having never till then seen a Race of Mortals so singular in their Shapes, Habits, and Countenances. Their Heads were all reclined either to the Right, or the Left; one of their Eyes turned inward, and the other directly up to the Zenith. Their outward Garments were adorned with the Figures of Suns, Moons, and Stars, interwoven with those of Fiddles, Flutes, Harps, Trumpets, Guittars, Harpsicords, and many more Instruments of Musick, unknown to us in *Europe.* I observed here and there many in the Habit of Servants, with a blown Bladder fastned like a Flail to the End of a short Stick, which they carried in their Hands. In each Bladder was a small Quantity of dried Pease, or little Pebbles, (as I was afterwards informed.) With these Bladders they now and then flapped the Mouths and Ears of those who stood near them, of which Practice I could not then conceive the Meaning. It seems, the Minds of these People are so taken up with intense Speculations, that they neither can speak, nor attend to the Discourses of others, without being rouzed by some external Taction[2] upon the Organs of Speech and Hearing; for which Reason, those Persons who are able to afford it, always keep a *Flapper,* (the Original is *Climenole*) in their Family, as one of their Domesticks; nor ever walk abroad or make Visits without him. And the Business of this Officer is, when two or more Persons are in Company, gently to strike with his Bladder the Mouth of him who is to speak, and the Right Ear of him or them to whom the Speaker addresseth himself. This *Flapper* is likewise employed diligently to attend his Master in his Walks, and upon Occasion to give him a soft Flap on his Eyes; because he is always so wrapped up in Cogitation, that he is in manifest Danger of falling down every Precipice, and bouncing his Head against every Post; and in the Streets, of jostling others, or being jostled himself into the Kennel.[3]

IT was necessary to give the Reader this Information, without which he would be at the same Loss with me, to understand the Proceedings of these People, as they conducted me up the Stairs, to the Top of the Island, and from thence to the Royal Palace. While we were ascending, they forgot several Times what they were about, and left me to my self, till their Memories were again rouzed by their *Flappers;* for they appeared altogether unmoved by the Sight of my foreign Habit and Countenance, and by the shouts of the Vulgar, whose Thoughts and Minds were more disengaged.

AT last we entered the Palace, and proceeded into the Chamber of Presence; where I saw the King seated on his Throne, attended on each Side by Persons of prime Quality. Before the Throne, was a large Table filled with Globes and Spheres, and Mathematical Instruments of all Kinds. His Majesty took not the least Notice of us, although our Entrance were not without sufficient Noise, by the Concourse of all Persons belonging to the Court. But, he was then deep in a Problem, and we attended at least an Hour, before he could solve it. There stood by him on each Side, a young Page, with Flaps in their Hands; and when they saw he was at Leisure, one of them gently struck his Mouth, and the other his Right Ear; at which he started like one awaked on the sudden, and looking towards me, and the Company I was in, recollected the Occasion of our coming, whereof he had been informed before. He spoke some Words; whereupon immediately a young Man with a Flap came up to my Side, and flapt me gently on the Right Ear; but I made Signs as well as I could, that I had no Occasion for such an Instrument; which as I afterwards found, gave his Majesty and the whole Court a very mean Opinion of my Understanding. The King, as far as I could conjecture, asked me several Questions, and I addressed my self to him in all the Languages I had. When it was found, that I could neither understand nor be understood, I was conducted by his Order to an Apartment in his Palace, (this Prince being distinguished above all his Predecessors for his Hospitality to Strangers,[4]) where two Servants were appointed to attend me. My Dinner was brought, and four Persons of Quality, whom I remembered to have seen very near the King's Person, did me the Honour to dine with me. We had two Courses, of three Dishes each. In the first Course, there was a Shoulder of Mutton, cut into an Æquilateral Triangle; a Piece of Beef into a Rhomboides; and a Pudding into a Cycloid. The second Course was two Ducks, trussed up into the Form of Fiddles; Sausages and Puddings resembling Flutes and Haut-boys, and a Breast of Veal in the Shape of a Harp. The Servants cut our Bread into Cones, Cylinders, Parallelograms, and several other Mathematical Figures.

WHILE we were at Dinner, I made bold to ask the Names of several Things in their Language; and those noble Persons, by the Assistance of their *Flappers,* delighted to give me Answers, hoping to raise my Admiration of their great Abilities, if I could be brought to converse with them. I was soon able to call for Bread, and Drink, or whatever else I wanted.

AFTER Dinner my Company withdrew, and a Person was sent to me by the King's Order, attended by a *Flapper.* He brought with him Pen, Ink, and Paper, and three or four Books; giving me to understand by Signs, that he was sent to teach me the Language. We sat together four Hours, in which Time I wrote down a great Number of Words in Columns, with the Translations over against them. I likewise made a Shift to learn several short Sentences. For my Tutor would order one of my Servants to fetch something, to turn about, to make a Bow, to sit, or stand, or walk, and the like. Then I took down the Sentence in Writing. He shewed me also in one of his Books, the Figures of the Sun, Moon, and Stars, the Zodiack, the Tropics, and Polar Circles, together with the Denominations of many Figures of Planes and Solids. He gave me the Names and Descriptions of all the Musical Instruments, and the general Terms of Art in playing on each of them. After he had left me, I placed all my Words with their Interpretations in alphabetical Order. And thus in a few Days, by the Help of a very faithful Memory, I got some Insight into their Language.

THE Word, which I interpret the *Flying* or *Floating Island,* is in the Original *Laputa;* whereof I could never learn the true Etymology. *Lap* in the old obsolete Language signifieth *High,* and *Untuh* a *Governor;* from which they say by Corruption was derived *Laputa* from *Lapuntuh.* But I do not approve of this Derivation, which seems to be a little strained. I ventured to offer to the Learned among them a Conjecture of my own, that *Laputa* was *quasi Lap outed; Lap* signifying properly the dancing of the Sun Beams in the Sea; and *outed* a Wing, which however I shall not obtrude, but submit to the judicious Reader.

THOSE to whom the King had entrusted me, observing how ill I was clad, ordered a Taylor to come next Morning, and take my Measure for a Suit of Cloths. This Operator did his Office after a different Manner from those of his Trade in *Europe*. He first took my Altitude by a Quadrant, and then with Rule and Compasses, described the Dimensions and Out-Lines of my whole Body; all which he entred upon Paper, and in six Days brought my Cloths very ill made, and quite out of Shape, by happening to mistake a Figure in the Calculation. But my Comfort was, that I observed such Accidents very frequent, and little regarded.

During my Confinement for want of Cloaths, and by an Indisposition that held me some Days longer, I much enlarged my Dictionary; and when I went next to Court, was able to understand many Things the King spoke, and to return him some Kind of Answers. His Majesty had given Orders, that the Island should move North-East and by East, to the vertical Point over *Lagado*, the Metropolis of the whole Kingdom, below upon the firm Earth. It was about Ninety Leagues distant, and our Voyage lasted four Days and an Half. I was not in the least sensible of the progressive Motion made in the Air by the Island. On the second Morning, about Eleven o'Clock, the King himself in Person, attended by his Nobility, Courtiers, and Officers, having prepared all their Musical Instruments, played on them for three Hours without Intermission; so that I was quite stunned with the Noise; neither could I possibly guess the Meaning, till my Tutor informed me. He said, that the People of their Island had their Ears adapted to hear the Musick of the Spheres, which always played at certain Periods; and the Court was now prepared to bear their Part in whatever Instrument they most excelled.

In our Journey towards *Lagado* the Capital City, his Majesty ordered that the Island should stop over certain Towns and Villages, from whence he might receive the Petitions of his Subjects. And to this Purpose, several Packthreads were let down with small Weights at the Bottom. On these Packthreads the People strung their Petitions, which mounted up directly like the Scraps of Paper fastned by School-boys at the End of the String that holds their Kite. Sometimes we received Wine and Victuals from below, which were drawn up by Pullies.

The Knowledge I had in Mathematicks gave me great Assistance in acquiring their Phraseology, which depended much upon that Science and Musick; and in the latter I was not unskilled. Their Ideas are perpetually conversant in Lines and Figures. If they would, for Example, praise the Beauty of a Woman, or any other Animal, they describe it by Rhombs, Circles, Parallelograms, Ellipses, and other Geometrical Terms; or else by

Words of Art drawn from Musick, needless here to repeat. I observed in the King's Kitchen all Sorts of Mathematical and Musical Instruments, after the Figures of which they cut up the Joynts that were served to his Majesty's Table.

THEIR Houses are very ill built, the Walls bevil, without one right Angle in any Apartment; and this Defect ariseth from the Contempt they bear for practical Geometry; which they despise as vulgar and mechanick, those Instructions they give being too refined for the Intellectuals of their Workmen; which occasions perpetual Mistakes. And although they are dextrous enough upon a Piece of Paper in the Management of the Rule, the Pencil, and the Divider, yet in the common Actions and Behaviour of Life, I have not seen a more clumsy, awkward, and unhandy People, nor so slow and perplexed in their Conceptions upon all other Subjects, except those of Mathematicks and Musick. They are very bad Reasoners, and vehemently given to Opposition, unless when they happen to be of the right Opinion, which is seldom their Case. Imagination, Fancy, and Invention, they are wholly Strangers to, nor have any Words in their Language by which those Ideas can be expressed; the whole Compass of their Thoughts and Mind, being shut up within the two forementioned Sciences.

MOST of them, and especially those who deal in the Astronomical Part, have great Faith in judicial Astrology, although they are ashamed to own it publickly. But, what I chiefly admired, and thought altogether unaccountable, was the strong Disposition I observed in them towards News and Politicks; perpetually enquiring into publick Affairs, giving their Judgments in Matters of State; and passionately disputing every Inch of a Party Opinion. I have indeed observed the same Disposition among most of the Mathematicians[5] I have known in *Europe;* although I could never discover the least Analogy between the two Sciences; unless those People suppose, that because the smallest Circle hath as many Degrees as the largest, therefore the Regulation and Management of the World require no more Abilities than the handling and turning of a Globe. But, I rather take this Quality to spring from a very common Infirmity of human Nature, inclining us to be more curious and conceited in Matters where we have least Concern, and for which we are least adapted either by Study or Nature.

THESE People are under continual Disquietudes,[6] never enjoying a Minute's Peace of Mind; and their Disturbances proceed from Causes which very little affect the rest of Mortals. Their Apprehensions arise from several Changes they dread in the Celestial Bodies. For Instance;

that the Earth by the continual Approaches of the Sun towards it, must in Course of Time be absorbed or swallowed up. That the Face of the Sun will by Degrees be encrusted with its own Effluvia, and give no more Light to the World. That, the Earth very narrowly escaped a Brush from the Tail of the last Comet, which would have infallibly reduced it to Ashes; and that the next, which they have calculated for One and Thirty Years hence, will probably destroy us. For, if in its Perihelion it should approach within a certain Degree of the Sun, (as by their Calculations they have Reason to dread) it will conceive a Degree of Heat ten Thousand Times more intense than that of red hot glowing Iron; and in its Absence from the Sun, carry a blazing Tail Ten Hundred Thousand and Fourteen Miles long; through which if the Earth should pass at the Distance of one Hundred Thousand Miles from the *Nucleus,* or main Body of the Comet, it must in its Passage be set on Fire, and reduced to Ashes. That the Sun daily spending its Rays without any Nutriment to supply them, will at last be wholly consumed and annihilated; which must be attended with the Destruction of this Earth, and of all the Planets that receive their Light from it.

THEY are so perpetually alarmed with the Apprehensions of these and the like impending Dangers, that they can neither sleep quietly in their Beds, nor have any Relish for the common Pleasures or Amusements of Life. When they meet an Acquaintance in the Morning, the first Question is about the Sun's Health; how he looked at his Setting and Rising, and what Hopes they have to avoid the Stroak of the approaching Comet. This Conversation they are apt to run into with the same Temper that Boys discover, in delighting to hear terrible Stories of Sprites and Hobgoblins, which they greedily listen to, and dare not go to Bed for fear.

THE Women of the Island have Abundance of Vivacity; they contemn their Husbands, and are exceedingly fond of Strangers, whereof there is always a considerable Number from the Continent below, attending at Court, either upon Affairs of the several Towns and Corporations, or their own particular Occasions; but are much despised, because they want the same Endowments. Among these the Ladies chuse their Gallants: But the Vexation is, that they act with too much Ease and Security; for the Husband is always so rapt in Speculation, that the Mistress and Lover may proceed to the greatest Familiarities before his Face, if he be but provided with Paper and Implements, and without his *Flapper* at his Side.

THE Wives and Daughters lament their Confinement to the Island, although I think it the most delicious Spot of Ground in the World; and although they live here in the greatest Plenty and Magnificence, and are allowed to do whatever they please: They long to see the World, and take the Diversions of the Metropolis, which they are not allowed to do without a particular Licence from the King; and this is not easy to be obtained, because the People of Quality have found by frequent Experience, how hard it is to persuade their Women to return from below. I was told, that a great Court Lady, who had several Children, is married to the prime Minister, the richest Subject in the Kingdom, a very graceful Person, extremely fond of her, and lives in the finest Palace of the Island; went down to *Lagado,* on the Pretence of Health, there hid her self for several Months, till the King sent a Warrant to search for her; and she was found in an obscure Eating-House all in Rags, having pawned her Cloths to maintain an old deformed Footman, who beat her every Day, and in whose Company she was taken much against her Will. And although her Husband received her with all possible Kindness, and without the least Reproach; she soon after contrived to steal down again with all her Jewels, to the same Gallant, and hath not been heard of since.

THIS may perhaps pass with the Reader rather for an *European* or *English* Story,[7] than for one of a Country so remote. But he may please to consider, that the Caprices of Womankind are not limited by any Climate or Nation; and that they are much more uniform than can be easily imagined.

IN about a Month's Time I had made a tolerable Proficiency in their Language, and was able to answer most of the King's Questions, when I had the Honour to attend him. His Majesty discovered not the least Curiosity to enquire into the Laws, Government, History, Religion, or Manners of the Countries where I had been; but confined his Questions to the State of Mathematicks, and received the Account I gave him, with great Contempt and Indifference, though often rouzed by his *Flapper* on each Side.

CHAPTER III

A Phænomenon solved by modern Philosophy and Astronomy. The Laputians *great Improvements in the latter. The King's Method of suppressing Insurrections.*

I desired Leave of this Prince to see the Curiosities of the Island; which he was graciously pleased to grant, and ordered my Tutor to attend me. I chiefly wanted to know to what Cause in Art or in Nature, it owed its several Motions; whereof I will now give a philosophical Account to the Reader.

THE flying or floating Island is exactly circular; its Diameter 7837 Yards, or about four Miles and an Half, and consequently contains ten Thousand Acres. It is three Hundred Yards thick. The Bottom, or under Surface, which appears to those who view it from below, is one even regular Plate of Adamant, shooting up to the Height of about two Hundred Yards. Above it lye the several Minerals in their usual Order; and over all is a Coat of rich Mould ten or twelve Foot deep. The Declivity of the upper Surface, from the Circumference to the Center, is the natural Cause why all the Dews and Rains which fall upon the Island, are conveyed in small Rivulets towards the Middle, where they are emptied into four large Basons, each of about Half a Mile in Circuit, and two Hundred Yards distant from the Center. From these Basons the Water is continually exhaled by the Sun in the Day-time, which effectually prevents their overflowing. Besides, as it is in the Power of the Monarch to raise the Island above the Region of Clouds and Vapours, he can prevent the falling of Dews and Rains whenever he pleases. For the highest Clouds cannot rise above two Miles, as Naturalists agree, at least they were never known to do so in that Country.

AT the Center of the Island there is a Chasm about fifty Yards in Diameter, from whence the Astronomers descend into a large Dome, which is therefore called *Flandona Gagnole*, or the *Astronomers Cave*; situated at the Depth of an Hundred Yards beneath the upper Surface of the Adamant. In this Cave are Twenty Lamps continually burning, which from the Reflection of the Adamant cast a strong Light into every Part. The Place is stored with great Variety of Sextants, Quadrants, Telescopes, Astrolabes, and other Astronomical Instruments. But the greatest Curiosity, upon which the Fate of the Island depends, is a Load-stone of a prodigious Size, in Shape resembling a Weaver's Shuttle. It is in Length six Yards, and in the thickest Part at least three Yards over. This Magnet is sustained by a very strong Axle of Adamant, passing through its Middle, upon which it plays, and is poized so exactly that the weakest Hand can turn it. It is hooped round with an hollow Cylinder of Adamant, four Foot deep, as many thick, and twelve Yards in Diameter, placed horizontally, and supported by Eight Adamantine Feet, each Six Yards high. In the Middle of the Concave Side there is a Groove Twelve Inches deep, in which the Extremities of the Axle are lodged, and turned round as there is Occasion.

THIS Stone cannot be moved from its Place by any Force, because the Hoop and its Feet are one continued Piece with that Body of Adamant which constitutes the Bottom of the Island.

BY Means of this Load-stone, the Island is made to rise and fall, and move from one Place to another. For, with respect to that Part of the Earth over which the Monarch presides, the Stone is endued at one of its Sides with an attractive Power, and at the other with a repulsive. Upon placing the Magnet erect with its attracting End towards the Earth, the Island descends; but when the repelling Extremity points downwards, the Island mounts directly upwards. When the Position of the Stone is oblique, the Motion of the Island is so too. For in this Magnet the Forces always act in Lines parallel to its Direction.

BY this oblique Motion the Island is conveyed to different Parts of the Monarch's Dominions. To explain the Manner of its Progress, let *A B* represent a Line drawn cross the Dominions of *Balnibarbi*; let the Line *c d* represent the Load-stone, of which let *d* be the repelling End, and *c* the attracting End, the Island being over *C*; let the Stone be placed in the Position *c d* with its repelling End downwards; then the Island will be driven upwards obliquely towards *D*. When it is arrived at *D*, let the Stone be turned upon its Axle till its attracting End points towards *E*, and then the Island will be carried obliquely towards *E*; where if the Stone be again turned upon its Axle till it stands in the Position *E F*, with its repelling

Plate IIII. Part.III.

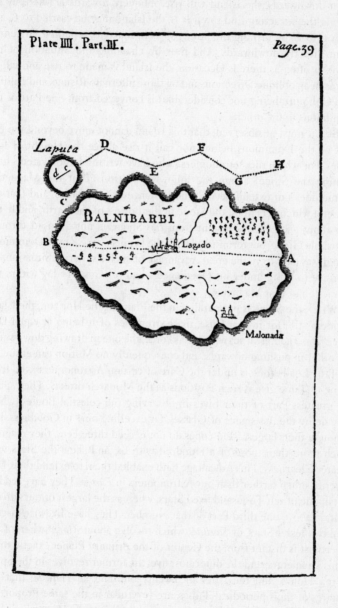

Point downwards, the Island will rise obliquely towards *F,* where by directing the attracting End towards *G,* the Island may be carried to *G,* and from *G* to *H,* by turning the Stone, so as to make its repelling Extremity point directly downwards. And thus by changing the Situation of the Stone as often as there is Occasion, the Island is made to rise and fall by Turns in an oblique Direction; and by those alternate Risings and Fallings (the Obliquity being not considerable) is conveyed from one Part of the Dominions to the other.

BUT it must be observed, that this Island cannot move beyond the Extent of the Dominions below; nor can it rise above the Height of four Miles. For which the Astronomers (who have written large Systems concerning the Stone) assign the following Reason: That the Magnetick Virtue does not extend beyond the Distance of four Miles, and that the Mineral which acts upon the Stone in the Bowels of the Earth, and in the Sea about six Leagues distant from the Shoar, is not diffused through the whole Globe, but terminated with the Limits of the King's Dominions: And it was easy from the great Advantage of such a superior Situation, for a Prince to bring under his Obedience whatever Country lay within the Attraction of that Magnet.

WHEN the Stone is put parallel to the Plane of the Horizon, the Island standeth still; for in that Case, the Extremities of it being at equal Distance from the Earth, act with equal Force, the one in drawing downwards, the other in pushing upwards; and consequently no Motion can ensue.

THIS Load-stone is under the Care of certain Astronomers, who from Time to Time give it such Positions as the Monarch directs. They spend the greatest Part of their Lives in observing the celestial Bodies, which they do by the Assistance of Glasses, far excelling ours in Goodness. For, although their largest Telescopes do not exceed three Feet, they magnify much more than those of a Hundred with us, and shew the Stars with greater Clearness. This Advantage hath enabled them to extend their Discoveries much farther than our Astronomers in *Europe.* They have made a Catalogue of ten Thousand fixed Stars, whereas the largest of ours do not contain above one third Part of that Number. They have likewise discovered two lesser Stars, or *Satellites,* which revolve about *Mars;*[8] whereof the innermost is distant from the Center of the primary Planet exactly three of his Diameters, and the outermost five; the former revolves in the Space of ten Hours, and the latter in Twenty-one and an Half; so that the Squares of their periodical Times, are very near in the same Proportion with the Cubes of their Distance from the Center of *Mars;* which evidently shews them to be governed by the same Law of Gravitation, that influences the other heavenly Bodies.

THEY have observed Ninety-three different Comets, and settled their Periods with great Exactness. If this be true, (and they affirm it with great Confidence) it is much to be wished that their Observations were made publick; whereby the Theory of Comets, which at present is very lame and defective, might be brought to the same Perfection with other Parts of Astronomy.

THE King would be the most absolute Prince in the Universe, if he could but prevail on a Ministry to join with him; but these having their Estates below on the Continent, and considering that the Office of a Favourite hath a very uncertain Tenure, would never consent to the enslaving their Country.

IF any Town should engage in Rebellion or Mutiny, fall into violent Factions, or refuse to pay the usual Tribute; the King hath two Methods of reducing them to Obedience. The first and the mildest Course is by keeping the Island hovering over such a Town, and the Lands about it; whereby he can deprive them of the Benefit of the Sun and the Rain, and consequently afflict the Inhabitants with Dearth and Diseases. And if the Crime deserve it, they are at the same time pelted from above with great Stones, against which they have no Defence, but by creeping into Cellars or Caves, while the Roofs of their Houses are beaten to Pieces. But if they still continue obstinate, or offer to raise Insurrections; he proceeds to the last Remedy, by letting the Island drop directly upon their Heads, which makes a universal Destruction both of Houses and Men. However, this is an Extremity to which the Prince is seldom driven, neither indeed is he willing to put it in Execution; nor dare his Ministers advise him to an Action, which as it would render them odious to the People, so it would be a great Damage to their own Estates that lie all below; for the Island is the King's Demesn.

BUT there is still indeed a more weighty Reason, why the Kings of this Country have been always averse from executing so terrible an Action, unless upon the utmost Necessity. For if the Town intended to be destroyed should have in it any tall Rocks, as it generally falls out in the larger Cities; a Situation probably chosen at first with a View to prevent such a Catastrophe: Or if it abound in high Spires or Pillars of Stone, a sudden Fall might endanger the Bottom or under Surface of the Island, which although it consist as I have said, of one entire Adamant two hundred Yards thick, might happen to crack by too great a Choque, or burst by approaching too near the Fires from the Houses below; as the Backs both of Iron and Stone will often do in our Chimneys. Of all this the People are well apprized, and understand how far to carry their Obstinacy, where their Liberty or Property is concerned. And the King, when he is highest provoked, and most determined to press a City to Rubbish, orders the Island to descend with great Gentleness, out of a Pretence of Tenderness to his People, but indeed for fear of breaking the Adamantine Bottom; in which Case it is the Opinion of all their Philosophers, that the Load-stone could no longer hold it up, and the whole Mass would fall to the Ground.[9]

BY a fundamental Law of this Realm, neither the King nor either of his two elder Sons, are permitted to leave the Island; nor the Queen till she is past Child-bearing.[10]

CHAPTER IV

The Author leaves Laputa, *is conveyed to* Balnibarbi, *arrives at the Metropolis. A Description of the Metropolis and the Country adjoining. The Author hospitably received by a great Lord. His Conversation with that Lord.*

Although I cannot say that I was ill treated in this Island, yet I must confess I thought my self too much neglected, not without some Degree of Contempt. For neither Prince nor People appeared to be curious in any Part of Knowledge, except Mathematicks and Musick, wherein I was far their inferior, and upon that Account very little regarded.

ON the other Side, after having seen all the Curiosities of the Island, I was very desirous to leave it, being heartily weary of those People. They were indeed excellent in two Sciences for which I have great Esteem, and wherein I am not unversed; but at the same time so abstracted and involved in Speculation, that I never met with such disagreeable Companions. I conversed only with Women, Tradesmen, *Flappers,* and Court-Pages, during two Months of my Abode there; by which at last I rendered my self extremely contemptible; yet these were the only People from whom I could ever receive a reasonable Answer.

I HAD obtained by hard Study a good Degree of Knowledge in their Language: I was weary of being confined to an Island where I received so little Countenance; and resolved to leave it with the first Opportunity.

THERE was a great Lord at Court, nearly related to the King, and for that Reason alone used with respect. He was universally reckoned the most ignorant and stupid Person among them. He had performed many eminent Services for the Crown, had great natural and acquired Parts, adorned with Integrity and Honour; but so ill an Ear for Musick, that his Detractors reported he had been often known to beat Time in the wrong Place; neither could his Tutors without extreme Difficulty teach him to demonstrate the most easy Proposition in the Mathematicks. He was pleased to shew me many Marks of Favour, often did me the Honour of a Visit, desired to be informed in the Affairs of *Europe,* the Laws and Customs, the Manners and Learning of the several Countries where I had travelled. He listened to me with great Attention, and made very wise Observations on all I spoke. He had two *Flappers* attending him for State, but never made use of them except at Court, and in Visits of Ceremony; and would always command them to withdraw when we were alone together.

I INTREATED this illustrious Person to intercede in my Behalf with his Majesty for Leave to depart; which he accordingly did, as he was pleased to tell me, with Regret: For, indeed he had made me several Offers very advantageous, which however I refused with Expressions of the highest Acknowledgment.

ON the 16th Day of *February,* I took Leave of his Majesty and the Court. The King made me a Present to the Value of about two Hundred Pounds *English;* and my Protector his Kinsman as much more, together with a Letter of Recommendation to a Friend of his in *Lagado,* the Metropolis: The Island being then hovering over a Mountain about two Miles from it, I was let down from the lowest Gallery, in the same Manner as I had been taken up.

THE Continent, as far as it is subject to the Monarch of the *Flying Island,* passeth under the general Name of *Balnibarbi;* and the Metropolis, as I said before, is called *Lagado.* I felt some little Satisfaction in finding my self on firm Ground. I walked to the City without any Concern, being clad like one of the Natives, and sufficiently instructed to converse with them. I soon found out the Person's House to whom I was recommended; presented my Letter from his Friend the Grandee in the Island, and was received with much Kindness. This great Lord, whose Name was *Munodi,* ordered me an Apartment in his own House, where I continued during my Stay, and was entertained in a most hospitable Manner.

THE next Morning after my Arrival he took me in his Chariot to see the Town, which is about half the Bigness of *London;* but the Houses very strangely built, and most of them out of Repair. The People in the Streets walked fast, looked wild, their Eyes fixed, and were generally in Rags. We passed through one of the Town Gates, and went about three Miles into the Country, where I saw many Labourers working with several Sorts of Tools in the Ground, but was not able to conjecture what they were about; neither did I observe any Expectation either of Corn or Grass, although the Soil appeared to be excellent. I could not forbear admiring at these odd Appearances both in Town and Country; and I made bold to desire my Conductor, that he would be pleased to explain to me what could be meant by so many busy Heads, Hands and Faces, both in the Streets and the Fields, because I did not discover any good Effects they produced; but on the contrary, I never knew a Soil so unhappily cultivated, Houses so ill contrived and so ruinous, or a People whose Countenances and Habit expressed so much Misery and Want.

THIS Lord *Munodi* was a Person of the first Rank, and had been some Years Governor of *Lagado;* but by a Cabal of Ministers was discharged for Insufficiency. However the King treated him with Tenderness, as a well-meaning Man, but of a low contemptible Understanding.

WHEN I gave that free Censure of the Country and its Inhabitants, he made no further Answer than by telling me, that I had not been long enough among them to form a Judgment; and that the different Nations of the World had different Customs; with other common Topicks to the same Purpose. But when we returned to his Palace, he asked me how I liked the Building, what Absurdities I observed, and what Quarrel I had with the Dress and Looks of his Domesticks. This he might safely do; because every Thing about him was magnificent, regular and polite. I answered, that his Excellency's Prudence, Quality, and Fortune, had exempted him from those Defects which Folly and Beggary had produced in others. He said, if I would go with him to his Country House about Twenty Miles distant, where his Estate lay, there would be more Leisure for this Kind of Conversation. I told his Excellency, that I was entirely at his Disposal; and accordingly we set out next Morning.

DURING our Journey, he made me observe the several Methods used by Farmers in managing their Lands; which to me were wholly unaccountable: For except in some very few Places, I could not discover one Ear of Corn, or Blade of Grass. But, in three Hours travelling, the Scene was wholly altered; we came into a most beautiful Country; Farmers Houses at small Distances, neatly built, the Fields enclosed, containing Vineyards, Corngrounds and Meadows. Neither do I remember to have seen a more delightful Prospect. His Excellency observed my Countenance to clear up; he told me with a Sigh, that there his Estate began, and would continue the same till we should come to his House. That his Countrymen ridiculed and despised him for managing his Affairs no better, and for setting so ill an Example to the Kingdom; which however was followed by very few, such as were old and wilful, and weak like himself.

WE came at length to the House, which was indeed a noble Structure, built according to the best Rules of ancient Architecture. The Fountains, Gardens, Walks, Avenues, and Groves were all disposed with exact Judgment and Taste. I gave due Praises to every Thing I saw, whereof his Excellency took not the least Notice till after Supper; when, there being no third Companion, he told me with a very melancholy Air, that he doubted he must throw down his Houses in Town and Country, to rebuild them after the present Mode; destroy all his Plantations, and cast others into such a Form as modern Usage required; and give the same Directions to all his Tenants, unless he would submit to incur the Censure of Pride, Singularity, Affectation, Ignorance, Caprice; and perhaps encrease his Majesty's Displeasure.

THAT the Admiration I appeared to be under, would cease or diminish when he had informed me of some Particulars, which probably I never heard of at Court, the People there being too much taken up in their own Speculations, to have Regard to what passed here below.

THE Sum of his Discourse was to this Effect. That about Forty Years ago, certain Persons went up to *Laputa,* either upon Business or Diversion; and after five Months Continuance, came back with a very little Smattering in Mathematicks, but full of Volatile Spirits acquired in that Airy Region. That these Persons upon their Return, began to dislike the Management of every Thing below; and fell into Schemes of putting all Arts, Sciences, Languages, and Mechanicks upon a new Foot. To this End they procured a Royal Patent for erecting an Academy of PROJECTORS in *Lagado:* And the Humour prevailed so strongly among the People, that there is not a Town of any Consequence in the Kingdom without such an Academy. In these Colleges, the Professors contrive new Rules and Methods of Agriculture and Building, and new Instruments and Tools for all Trades and Manufactures, whereby, as they undertake, one Man shall do the Work of Ten; a Palace may be built in a Week, of Materials so durable as to last for ever without repairing. All the Fruits of the Earth shall come to Maturity at whatever Season we think fit to chuse, and increase an Hundred Fold more than they do at present; with innumerable other happy Proposals. The only Inconvenience is, that none of these Projects are yet brought to Perfection; and in the mean time, the whole Country lies miserably waste, the Houses in Ruins, and the People without Food or Cloaths. By all which, instead of being discouraged, they are Fifty Times more violently bent upon prosecuting their Schemes, driven equally on by Hope and Despair: That, as for himself, being not of an enterprizing Spirit, he was content to go on in the old Forms; to live in the Houses his

Ancestors had built, and act as they did in every Part of Life without Innovation. That, some few other Persons of Quality and Gentry had done the same; but were looked on with an Eye of Contempt and ill Will, as Enemies to Art, ignorant, and ill Commonwealthsmen, preferring their own Ease and Sloth before the general Improvement of their Country.

His Lordship added, that he would not by any further Particulars prevent the Pleasure I should certainly take in viewing the grand Academy, whither he was resolved I should go. He only desired me to observe a ruined Building upon the Side of a Mountain about three Miles distant, of which he gave me this Account. That he had a very convenient Mill within Half a Mile of his House, turned by a Current from a large River, and sufficient for his own Family as well as a great Number of his Tenants. That, about seven Years ago,[11] a Club of those Projectors came to him with Proposals to destroy this Mill, and build another on the Side of that Mountain, on the long Ridge whereof a long Canal must be cut for a Repository of Water, to be conveyed up by Pipes and Engines to supply the Mill: Because the Wind and Air upon a Height agitated the Water, and thereby made it fitter for Motion: And because the Water descending down a Declivity would turn the Mill with half the Current of a River whose Course is more upon a Level. He said, that being then not very well with the Court, and pressed by many of his Friends, he complyed with the Proposal; and after employing an Hundred Men for two Years, the Work miscarryed, the Projectors went off, laying the Blame intirely upon him; railing at him ever since, and putting others upon the same Experiment, with equal Assurance of Success, as well as equal Disappointment.

In a few Days we came back to Town; and his Excellency, considering the bad Character he had in the Academy, would not go with me himself, but recommended me to a Friend of his to bear me Company thither. My Lord was pleased to represent me as a great Admirer of Projects, and a Person of much Curiosity and easy Belief; which indeed was not without Truth; for I had my self been a Sort of Projector in my younger Days.

CHAPTER V

The Author permitted to see the grand Academy of Lagado.[12] *The Academy largely described. The Arts wherein the Professors employ themselves.*

This Academy is not an entire single Building, but a Continuation of several Houses on both Sides of a Street; which growing waste, was purchased and applyed to that Use.

I WAS received very kindly by the Warden, and went for many Days to the Academy. Every Room hath in it one or more Projectors; and I believe I could not be in fewer than five Hundred Rooms.

THE first Man I saw was of a meagre Aspect, with sooty Hands and Face, his Hair and Beard long, ragged and singed in several Places. His Clothes, Shirt, and Skin were all of the same Colour. He had been Eight Years upon a Project for extracting Sun-Beams out of Cucumbers, which were to be put into Vials hermetically sealed, and let out to warm the Air in raw inclement Summers. He told me, he did not doubt in Eight Years more, that he should be able to supply the Governors Gardens with Sunshine at a reasonable Rate; but he complained that his Stock was low, and intreated me to give him something as an Encouragement to Ingenuity, especially since this had been a very dear Season for Cucumbers. I made him a small Present, for my Lord had furnished me with Money on purpose, because he knew their Practice of begging from all who go to see them.

I WENT into another Chamber, but was ready to hasten back, being almost overcome with a horrible Stink. My Conductor pressed me forward, conjuring me in a Whisper to give no Offence, which would be highly resented; and therefore I durst not so much as stop my Nose. The Projector of this Cell was the most ancient Student of the Academy. His Face and Beard were of a pale Yellow; his Hands and Clothes dawbed over with

Filth. When I was presented to him, he gave me a very close Embrace, (a Compliment I could well have excused.) His Employment from his first coming into the Academy, was an Operation to reduce human Excrement to its original Food, by separating the several Parts, removing the Tincture which it receives from the Gall, making the Odour exhale, and scumming off the Saliva. He had a weekly Allowance from the Society, of a Vessel filled with human Ordure, about the Bigness of a *Bristol* Barrel.

I SAW another at work to calcine Ice into Gunpowder; who likewise shewed me a Treatise he had written concerning the Malleability of Fire, which he intended to publish.

THERE was a most ingenious Architect who had contrived a new Method for building Houses, by beginning at the Roof, and working downwards to the Foundation; which he justified to me by the like Practice of those two prudent Insects the Bee and the Spider.

THERE was a Man born blind, who had several Apprentices in his own Condition: Their Employment was to mix Colours for Painters, which their Master taught them to distinguish by feeling and smelling. It was indeed my Misfortune to find them at that Time not very perfect in their Lessons; and the Professor himself happened to be generally mistaken: This Artist is much encouraged and esteemed by the whole Fraternity.

IN another Apartment I was highly pleased with a Projector, who had found a Device of plowing the Ground with Hogs, to save the Charges of Plows, Cattle, and Labour. The Method is this: In an Acre of Ground you bury at six Inches Distance, and eight deep, a Quantity of Acorns, Dates, Chesnuts, and other Maste[13] or Vegetables whereof these Animals are fondest; then you drive six Hundred or more of them into the Field, where in a few Days they will root up the whole Ground in search of their Food, and make it fit for sowing, at the same time manuring it with their Dung. It is true, upon Experiment they found the Charge and Trouble very great, and they had little or no Crop. However, it is not doubted that this Invention may be capable of great Improvement.

I WENT into another Room, where the Walls and Ceiling were all hung round with Cobwebs, except a narrow Passage for the Artist to go in and out. At my Entrance he called aloud to me not to disturb his Webs. He lamented the fatal Mistake the World had been so long in of using Silk-Worms, while we had such plenty of domestick Insects, who infinitely excelled the former, because they understood how to weave as well as spin. And he proposed farther, that by employing Spiders, the Charge of dying Silks would be wholly saved; whereof I was fully convinced when he shewed me a vast Number of Flies most beautifully coloured, wherewith he fed his Spiders; assuring us, that the Webs would take a Tincture from them; and as he had them of all Hues, he hoped to fit every Body's Fancy, as soon as he could find proper Food for the Flies, of certain Gums, Oyls, and other glutinous Matter, to give a Strength and Consistence to the Threads.

THERE was an Astronomer who had undertaken to place a Sun-Dial upon the great Weather-Cock on the Town-House, by adjusting the annual and diurnal Motions of the Earth and Sun, so as to answer and coincide with all accidental Turnings of the Wind.

I WAS complaining of a small Fit of the Cholick; upon which my Conductor led me into a Room, where a great Physician resided, who was famous for curing that Disease by contrary Operations from the same Instrument. He had a large Pair of Bellows, with a long slender Muzzle of Ivory. This he conveyed eight Inches up the Anus, and drawing in the Wind, he affirmed he could make the Guts as lank as a dried Bladder. But when the Disease was more stubborn and violent, he let in the Muzzle while the Bellows was full of Wind, which he discharged into the Body of the Patient; then withdrew the Instrument to replenish it, clapping his Thumb strongly against the Orifice of the Fundament; and this being repeated three or four Times, the adventitious Wind would rush out, bringing the noxious along with it (like Water put into a Pump) and the Patient recovers. I saw him try both Experiments upon a Dog, but could not discern any Effect from the former. After the latter, the Animal was ready to burst, and made so violent a Discharge, as was very offensive to me and my Companions. The Dog died on the Spot, and we left the Doctor endeavouring to recover him by the same Operation.

I VISITED many other Apartments, but shall not trouble my Reader with all the Curiosities I observed, being studious of Brevity.

I HAD hitherto seen only one Side of the Academy, the other being appropriated to the Advancers of speculative Learning; of whom I shall say something when I have mentioned one illustrious Person more, who is called among them *the universal Artist.* He told us, he had been Thirty Years employing his Thoughts for the Improvement of human Life. He had two large Rooms full of wonderful Curiosities, and Fifty Men at work. Some were condensing Air into a dry tangible Substance, by extracting the Nitre, and letting the aqueous or fluid Particles percolate: Others softening Marble for Pillows and Pin-cushions; others petrifying the Hoofs of a living Horse to preserve them from foundring. The Artist himself was at that Time busy upon two great Designs: The first, to sow Land with Chaff, wherein he affirmed the true seminal Virtue to be contained, as he demonstrated by several Experiments which I was not skilful enough to comprehend. The other was, by a certain Composition of Gums, Minerals, and Vegetables outwardly applied, to prevent the Growth of Wool upon two young Lambs; and he hoped in a reasonable Time to propagate the Breed of naked Sheep all over the Kingdom.

WE crossed a Walk to the other Part of the Academy, where, as I have already said, the Projectors in speculative Learning resided.

THE first Professor I saw was in a very large Room, with Forty Pupils about him. After Salutation, observing me to look earnestly upon a Frame, which took up the greatest Part of both the Length and Breadth of the Room; he said, perhaps I might wonder to see him employed in a Project for improving speculative Knowledge by practical and mechanical Operations. But the World would soon be sensible of its Usefulness; and he flattered himself, that a more noble exalted Thought never sprang in any other Man's Head. Every one knew how laborious the usual Method is of attaining to Arts and Sciences; whereas by his Contrivance, the most ignorant Person at a reasonable Charge, and with a little bodily Labour, may write Books in Philosophy, Poetry, Politicks, Law, Mathematicks and Theology, without the least Assistance from Genius or Study. He then led me to the Frame, about the Sides whereof all his Pupils stood in Ranks. It was Twenty Foot square, placed in the Middle of the Room. The Superficies was composed of several Bits of Wood, about the Bigness of a Dye, but some larger than others. They were all linked together by slender Wires. These Bits of Wood were covered on every Square with Paper pasted on them; and on these Papers were written all the Words of their Language in their several Moods, Tenses, and Declensions, but without any Order. The Professor then desired me to observe, for he was going to set his Engine at work. The Pupils at his Command took each of them hold of an Iron Handle, whereof there were Forty fixed round the Edges of the Frame; and giving them a sudden Turn, the whole Disposition of the Words was entirely changed. He then commanded Six and Thirty of the Lads to read the several Lines softly as they appeared upon the Frame; and where they found three or four Words together that might make Part of a Sentence, they dictated to the four remaining Boys who were Scribes. This Work was repeated three or four Times, and at every Turn the Engine was so contrived, that the Words shifted into new Places, as the square Bits of Wood moved upside down.

Plate.V.Part.III.

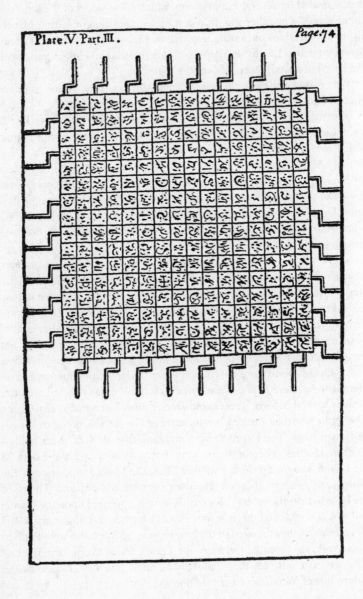

Six Hours a-Day the young Students were employed in this Labour; and the Professor shewed me several Volumes in large Folio already collected, of broken Sentences, which he intended to piece together; and out of those rich Materials to give the World a compleat Body of all Arts and Sciences; which however might be still improved, and much expedited, if the Publick would raise a Fund for making and employing five Hundred such Frames in *Lagado*, and oblige the Managers to contribute in common their several Collections.

He assured me, that this Invention had employed all his Thoughts from his Youth; that he had emptied the whole Vocabulary into his Frame, and made the strictest Computation of the general Proportion there is in Books between the Numbers of Particles, Nouns, and Verbs, and other Parts of Speech.

I MADE my humblest Acknowledgments to this illustrious Person for his great Communicativeness; and promised if ever I had the good Fortune to return to my native Country, that I would do him Justice, as the sole Inventer of this wonderful Machine; the Form and Contrivance of which I desired Leave to delineate upon Paper as in the Figure here annexed. I told him, although it were the Custom of our Learned in *Europe* to steal Inventions from each other, who had thereby at least this Advantage, that it became a Controversy which was the right Owner; yet I would take such Caution, that he should have the Honour entire without a Rival.

We next went to the School of Languages, where three Professors sat in Consultation upon improving that of their own Country.

The first Project was to shorten Discourse by cutting Polysyllables into one, and leaving out Verbs and Participles; because in Reality all things imaginable are but Nouns.

The other, was a Scheme for entirely abolishing all Words whatsoever: And this urged as a great Advantage in Point of Health as well as Brevity. For, it is plain, that every Word we speak is in some Degree a Diminution of our Lungs by Corrosion; and consequently contributes to the shortning of our Lives. An expedient was therefore offered, that since Words are only Names for *Things*,[14] it would be more convenient for all Men to carry about them, such *Things* as were necessary to express the particular Business they are to discourse on. And this Invention would certainly have taken Place, to the great Ease as well as Health of the Subject, if the Women in Conjunction with the Vulgar and Illiterate had not threatned to raise a Rebellion, unless they might be allowed the Liberty to speak with their Tongues, after the Manner of their Forefathers: Such constant irreconcileable Enemies to Science are the common People. However, many of the most Learned and Wise adhere to the new Scheme of expressing themselves by *Things*; which hath only this Inconvenience attending it; that if a Man's Business be very great, and of various Kinds, he must be obliged in Proportion to carry a greater Bundle of *Things* upon his Back, unless he can afford one or two strong Servants to attend him. I have often beheld two of those Sages almost sinking under the Weight of their Packs, like Pedlars among us; who when they met in the Streets would lay down their Loads, open their Sacks, and hold Conversation for an Hour together; then put up their Implements, help each other to re-sume their Burthens, and take their Leave.

BUT, for short Conversations a Man may carry Implements in his Pockets and under his Arms, enough to supply him, and in his House he cannot be at a Loss; therefore the Room where Company meet who prac-tice this Art, is full of all *Things* ready at Hand, requisite to furnish Mat-ter for this Kind of artificial Converse.

ANOTHER great Advantage proposed by this Invention, was, that it would serve as an universal Language to be understood in all civilized Nations, whose Goods and Utensils are generally of the same Kind, or nearly resembling, so that their Uses might easily be comprehended. And thus, Embassadors would be qualified to treat with foreign Princes or Ministers of State, to whose Tongues they were utter Strangers.

I WAS at the Mathematical School, where the Master taught his Pupils after a Method scarce imaginable to us in *Europe*. The Proposition and Demonstration were fairly written on a thin Wafer, with Ink composed of a Cephalick Tincture.[15] This the Student was to swallow upon a fasting Stomach, and for three Days following eat nothing but Bread and Water. As the Wafer digested, the Tincture mounted to his Brain, bearing the Proposition along with it. But the Success hath not hitherto been answer-able, partly by some Error in the *Quantum*[16] or Composition, and partly by the Perverseness of Lads; to whom this Bolus is so nauseous, that they generally steal aside, and discharge it upwards before it can operate; nei-ther have they been yet persuaded to use so long an Abstinence as the Pre-scription requires.

CHAPTER VI

A further Account of the Academy. The Author proposeth some Improvements, which are honourably received.

In the School of political Projectors I was but ill entertained; the Professors appearing in my Judgment wholly out of their Senses; which is a Scene that never fails to make me melancholy. These unhappy People were proposing Schemes for persuading Monarchs to chuse Favourites upon the Score of their Wisdom, Capacity and Virtue; of teaching Ministers to consult the publick Good; of rewarding Merit, great Abilities, and eminent Services; of instructing Princes to know their true Interest, by placing it on the same Foundation with that of their People: Of chusing for Employments Persons qualified to exercise them; with many other wild impossible Chimæras, that never entered before into the Heart of Man to conceive; and confirmed in me the old Observation, that there is nothing so extravagant and irrational which some Philosophers have not maintained for Truth.

But, however I shall so far do Justice to this Part of the Academy, as to acknowledge that all of them were not so visionary. There was a most ingenious Doctor who seemed to be perfectly versed in the whole Nature and System of Government. This illustrious Person had very usefully employed his Studies in finding out effectual Remedies for all Diseases and Corruptions, to which the several Kinds of publick Administration are subject by the Vices or Infirmities of those who govern, as well as by the Licentiousness of those who are to obey. For Instance: Whereas all Writers and Reasoners have agreed, that there is a strict universal Resemblance between the natural and the political Body; can there be any thing more evident, than that the Health of both must be preserved, and the Diseases cured by the same Prescriptions? It is allowed, that Senates and great Councils are often troubled with redundant, ebullient, and other peccant Humours;[17] with many Diseases of the Head, and more of the Heart; with strong Convulsions, with grievous Contractions of the Nerves and Sinews in both Hands, but especially the Right: With Spleen, Flatus, Vertigoes and Deliriums; with scrophulous Tumours full of fœtid purulent Matter; with sower frothy Ructations; with Canine Appetites and Crudeness of Digestion; besides many others needless to mention. This Doctor therefore proposed, that upon the meeting of a Senate, certain Physicians should attend at the three first Days of their sitting, and at the Close of each Day's Debate, feel the Pulses of every Senator; after which having maturely considered, and consulted upon the Nature of the several Maladies, and the Methods of Cure; they should on the fourth Day return to the Senate-House, attended by their Apothecaries stored with proper Medicines; and before the Members sat, administer to each of them Lenitives, Aperitives, Abstersives, Corrosives, Restringents, Palliatives, Laxatives, Cephalalgicks, Ictericks, Apophlegmaticks, Acousticks,[18] as their several Cases required; and according as these Medicines should operate, repeat, alter, or omit them at the next Meeting.

THIS Project could not be of any great Expence to the Publick; and might in my poor Opinion, be of much Use for the Dispatch of Business in those Countries where Senates have any Share in the legislative Power; beget Unanimity, shorten Debates, open a few Mouths which are now closed, and close many more which are now open; curb the Petulancy of the Young, and correct the Positiveness of the Old; rouze the Stupid, and damp the Pert.

AGAIN; Because it is a general Complaint that the Favourites of Princes are troubled with short and weak Memories; the same Doctor proposed, that whoever attended a first Minister, after having told his Business with the utmost Brevity, and in the plainest Words; should at his Departure give the said Minister a Tweak by the Nose, or a Kick in the Belly, or tread on his Corns, or lug him thrice by both Ears, or run a Pin into his Breech, or pinch his Arm black and blue; to prevent Forgetfulness: And at every Levee Day repeat the same Operation, till the Business were done or absolutely refused.

HE likewise directed, that every Senator in the great Council of a Nation, after he had delivered his Opinion, and argued in the Defence of it, should be obliged to give his Vote directly contrary; because if that were done, the Result would infallibly terminate in the Good of the Publick.

WHEN Parties in a State are violent, he offered a wonderful Contrivance to reconcile them. The Method is this. You take an Hundred Leaders of each Party; you dispose them into Couples of such whose Heads are nearest of a Size; then let two nice Operators saw off the *Occiput*[19] of each Couple at the same Time, in such a Manner that the Brain may be equally divided. Let the *Occiputs* thus cut off be interchanged, applying each to the Head of his opposite Party-man. It seems indeed to be a Work that requireth some Exactness; but the Professor assured us, that if it were dextrously performed, the Cure would be infallible. For he argued thus; that the two half Brains being left to debate the Matter between themselves within the Space of one Scull, would soon come to a good Understanding, and produce that Moderation as well as Regularity of Thinking, so much to be wished for in the Heads of those, who imagine they came into the World only to watch and govern its Motion: And as to the Difference of Brains in Quantity or Quality, among those who are Directors in Faction; the Doctor assured us from his own Knowledge, that it was a perfect Trifle.

I HEARD a very warm Debate between two Professors, about the most commodious and effectual Ways and Means of raising Money without grieving the Subject. The first affirmed, the justest Method would be to lay a certain Tax upon Vices and Folly; and the Sum fixed upon every Man, to be rated after the fairest Manner by a Jury of his Neighbours. The second was of an Opinion directly contrary; to tax those Qualities of Body and Mind for which Men chiefly value themselves; the Rate to be more or less according to the Degrees of excelling; the Decision whereof should be left entirely to their own Breast. The highest Tax was upon Men, who are the greatest Favourites of the other Sex; and the Assessments according to the Number and Natures of the Favours they have received; for which they are allowed to be their own Vouchers. Wit, Valour, and Politeness were likewise proposed to be largely taxed, and collected in the same Manner, by every Person giving his own Word for the Quantum of what he possessed. But, as to Honour, Justice, Wisdom and Learning, they should not be taxed at all; because, they are Qualifications of so singular a Kind, that no Man will either allow them in his Neighbour, or value them in himself.

THE Women were proposed to be taxed according to their Beauty and Skill in Dressing; wherein they had the same Privilege with the Men, to be determined by their own Judgment. But Constancy, Chastity, good Sense, and good Nature were not rated, because they would not bear the Charge of Collecting.

TO keep Senators in the Interest of the Crown, it was proposed that the

Members should raffle for Employments; every Man first taking an Oath, and giving Security that he would vote for the Court, whether he won or no; after which the Losers had in their Turn the Liberty of raffling upon the next Vacancy. Thus, Hope and Expectation would be kept alive; none would complain of broken Promises, but impute their Disappointments wholly to Fortune, whose Shoulders are broader and stronger than those of a Ministry.

ANOTHER Professor shewed me a large Paper of Instructions for discovering Plots and Conspiracies against the Government. He advised great Statesmen to examine into the Dyet of all suspected Persons; their Times of eating; upon which Side they lay in Bed; with which Hand they wiped their Posteriors; to take a strict View of their Excrements, and from the Colour, the Odour, the Taste, the Consistence, the Crudeness, or Maturity of Digestion, form a Judgment of their Thoughts and Designs: Because Men are never so serious, thoughtful, and intent, as when they are at Stool; which he found by frequent Experiment: For in such Conjunctures, when he used merely as a Trial to consider which was the best Way of murdering the King, his Ordure would have a Tincture of Green; but quite different when he thought only of raising an Insurrection, or burning the Metropolis.

THE whole Discourse was written with great Acuteness, containing many Observations both curious and useful for Politicians, but as I conceived not altogether compleat. This I ventured to tell the Author, and offered if he pleased to supply him with some Additions. He received my Proposition with more Compliance than is usual among Writers, especially those of the Projecting Species; professing he would be glad to receive farther Information.

I TOLD him, that in the Kingdom of *Tribnia*,[20] by the Natives called *Langden*,[21] where I had long sojourned, the Bulk of the People consisted wholly of Discoverers, Witnesses, Informers, Accusers, Prosecutors, Evidences, Swearers; together with their several subservient and subaltern Instruments; all under the Colours, the Conduct, and pay of Ministers and their Deputies. The Plots in that Kingdom[22] are usually the Workmanship of those Persons who desire to raise their own Characters of profound Politicians; to restore new Vigour to a crazy Administration; to stifle or divert general Discontents; to fill their Coffers with Forfeitures; and raise or sink the Opinion of publick Credit, as either shall best answer their private Advantage. It is first agreed and settled among them, what suspected Persons shall be accused of a Plot: Then, effectual Care is taken to secure all their Letters and other Papers, and put the Owners in Chains. These Papers are delivered to a Set of Artists very dextrous in finding out the mysterious Meanings of Words, Syllables and Letters. For Instance, they can decypher a Close-stool to signify a Privy-Council; a Flock of Geese, a Senate; a lame Dog, an Invader; the Plague, a standing Army; a Buzard, a Minister; the Gout, a High Priest; a Gibbet, a Secretary of State; a Chamber pot, a Committee of Grandees; a Sieve a Court Lady; a Broom, a Revolution; a Mouse-trap, an Employment; a bottomless Pit, the Treasury; a Sink, a C——t; a Cap and Bells, a Favourite; a broken Reed, a Court of Justice; an empty Tun, a General; a running Sore, the Administration.

WHEN this Method fails, they have two others more effectual; which the Learned among them call Acrosticks, and Anagrams. *First,* they can decypher all initial Letters into political Meanings: Thus, *N,* shall signify a Plot; *B,* a Regiment of Horse; *L,* a Fleet at Sea. Or, *secondly,* by transposing the Letters of the Alphabet, in any suspected Paper, they can lay open the deepest Designs of a discontented Party. So for Example, if I should say in a Letter to a Friend, *Our Brother* Tom *has just got the Piles;* a Man of Skill in this Art would discover how the same Letters which compose that Sentence, may be analysed into the following Words; *Resist,* ——— *a Plot is brought home* ——— *The Tour.* And this is the Anagrammatick Method.

THE Professor made me great Acknowledgments for communicating these Observations, and promised to make honourable mention of me in his Treatise.

I SAW nothing in this Country that could invite me to a longer Contiunance; and began to think of returning home to *England.*

CHAPTER VII

The Author leaves Lagado, *arrives at* Maldonada. *No Ship ready. He takes a short Voyage to* Glubbdubdrib. *His Reception by the Governor.*

The Continent of which this Kingdom is a part, extends itself, as I have Reason to believe, Eastward to that unknown Tract of *America,* Westward of *California,* and North to the Pacifick Ocean, which is not above an hundred and fifty Miles from *Lagado;* where there is a good Port and much Commerce with the great Island of *Luggnagg,* situated to the North-West about 29 Degrees North Latitude, and 140 Longitude. This Island of *Luggnagg* stands South Eastwards of *Japan,* about an hundred Leagues distant. There is a strict Alliance between the *Japanese* Emperor and the King of *Luggnagg,* which affords frequent Opportunities of sailing from one Island to the other. I determined therefore to direct my Course this Way, in order to my Return to *Europe.* I hired two Mules with a Guide to shew me the Way, and carry my small Baggage. I took leave of my noble Protector, who had shewn me so much Favour, and made me a generous Present at my Departure.

My Journey was without any Accident or Adventure worth relating. When I arrived at the Port of *Maldonada,* (for so it is called) there was no Ship in the Harbour bound for *Luggnagg,* nor like to be in some Time. The Town is about as large as *Portsmouth.* I soon fell into some Acquaintance, and was very hospitably received. A Gentleman of Distinction said to me, that since the Ships bound for *Luggnagg* could not be ready in less than a Month, it might be no disagreeable Amusement for me to take a Trip to the little Island of *Glubbdubdrib,* about five Leagues off to the South-West. He offered himself and a Friend to accompany me, and that I should be provided with a small convenient Barque for the Voyage.

GLUBBDUBDRIB, as nearly as I can interpret the Word, signifies the Island of *Sorcerers* or *Magicians.* It is about one third as large as the Isle of *Wight,* and extreamly fruitful: It is governed by the Head of a certain Tribe, who are all Magicians. This Tribe marries only among each other; and the eldest in Succession is Prince or Governor. He hath a noble Palace, and a Park of about three thousand Acres, surrounded by a Wall of hewn Stone twenty Foot high. In this Park are several small Inclosures for Cattle, Corn and Gardening.

THE Governor and his Family are served and attended by Domesticks of a Kind somewhat unusual. By his Skill in Necromancy, he hath Power of calling whom he pleaseth from the Dead, and commanding their Service for twenty four Hours, but no longer; nor can he call the same Persons up again in less than three Months, except upon very extraordinary Occasions.

WHEN we arrived at the Island, which was about Eleven in the Morning, one of the Gentlemen who accompanied me, went to the Governor, and desired Admittance for a Stranger, who came on purpose to have the Honour of attending on his Highness. This was immediately granted, and we all three entered the Gate of the Palace between two Rows of Guards, armed and dressed after a very antick Manner, and something in their Countenances that made my Flesh creep with a Horror I cannot express. We passed through several Apartments between Servants of the same Sort, ranked on each Side as before, till we came to the Chamber of Presence, where after three profound Obeysances, and a few general Questions, we were permitted to sit on three Stools near the lowest Step of his Highness's Throne. He understood the Language of *Balnibarbi,* although it were different from that of his Island. He desired me to give him some Account of my Travels; and to let me see that I should be treated without Ceremony, he dismissed all his Attendants with a Turn of his Finger, at which to my great Astonishment they vanished in an Instant, like Visions in a Dream, when we awake on a sudden. I could not recover myself in some Time, till the Governor assured me that I should receive no Hurt; and observing my two Companions to be under no Concern, who had been often entertained in the same Manner, I began to take Courage; and related to his Highness a short History of my several Adventures, yet not without some Hesitation, and frequently looking behind me to the Place where I had seen those domestick Spectres. I had the Honour to dine with the Governor, where a new Set of Ghosts served up the Meat, and waited at Table. I now observed myself to be less terrified than I had been in the

Morning. I stayed till Sun-set, but humbly desired his Highness to excuse me for not accepting his Invitation of lodging in the Palace. My two Friends and I lay at a private House in the Town adjoining, which is the Capital of this little Island; and the next Morning we returned to pay our Duty to the Governor, as he was pleased to command us.

AFTER this Manner we continued in the Island for ten Days, most Part of every Day with the Governor, and at Night in our Lodging. I soon grew so familiarized to the Sight of Spirits, that after the third or fourth Time they gave me no Emotion at all; or if I had any Apprehensions left, my Curiosity prevailed over them. For his Highness the Governor ordered me to call up whatever Persons I would chuse to name, and in whatever Numbers among all the Dead from the Beginning of the World to the present Time, and command them to answer any Questions I should think fit to ask; with this Condition, that my Questions must be confined within the Compass of the Times they lived in. And one Thing I might depend upon, that they would certainly tell me Truth; for Lying was a Talent of no Use in the lower World.

I MADE my humble Acknowledgments to his Highness for so great a Favour. We were in a Chamber, from whence there was a fair Prospect into the Park. And because my first Inclination was to be entertained with Scenes of Pomp and Magnificence, I desired to see *Alexander* the Great, at the Head of his Army just after the Battle of *Arbela;* which upon a Motion of the Governor's Finger immediately appeared in a large Field under the Window, where we stood. *Alexander* was called up into the Room: It was with great Difficulty that I understood his *Greek,* and had but little of my own. He assured me upon his Honour that he was not poisoned, but dyed of a Fever by excessive Drinking.

NEXT I saw *Hannibal* passing the *Alps,* who told me he had not a Drop of Vinegar in his Camp.[23]

I SAW *Cæsar* and *Pompey* at the Head of their Troops just ready to engage. I saw the former in his last great Triumph. I desired that the Senate of *Rome* might appear before me in one large Chamber, and a modern Representative, in Counterview, in another. The first seemed to be an Assembly of Heroes and Demy-Gods; the other a Knot of Pedlars, Pickpockets, Highwaymen and Bullies.

THE Governor at my Request gave the Sign for *Cæsar* and *Brutus*[24] to advance towards us. I was struck with a profound Veneration at the Sight of *Brutus;* and could easily discover the most consummate Virtue, the greatest Intrepidity, and Firmness of Mind, the truest Love of his Country, and general Benevolence for Mankind in every Lineament of his Countenance. I observed with much Pleasure, that these two Persons were in good Intelligence with each other; and *Cæsar* freely confessed to me, that the greatest Actions of his own Life were not equal by many Degrees to the Glory of taking it away. I had the Honour to have much Conversation with *Brutus;* and was told that his Ancestor *Junius,*[25] *Socrates,*[26] *Epaminondas,*[27] *Cato* the Younger,[28] Sir *Thomas More*[29] and himself, were perpetually together: A *Sextumvirate*[30] to which all the Ages of the World cannot add a Seventh.

IT would be tedious to trouble the Reader with relating what vast Numbers of illustrious Persons were called up, to gratify that insatiable Desire I had to see the World in every Period of Antiquity placed before me. I chiefly fed mine Eyes with beholding the Destroyers of Tyrants and Usurpers, and the Restorers of Liberty to oppressed and injured Nations. But it is impossible to express the Satisfaction I received in my own Mind, after such a Manner as to make it a suitable Entertainment to the Reader.

CHAPTER VIII

A further Account of Glubbdubdrib. *Antient and Modern History corrected.*

Having a Desire to see those Antients, who were most renowned for Wit and Learning, I set apart one Day on purpose. I proposed that *Homer* and *Aristotle* might appear at the Head of all their Commentators; but these were so numerous, that some Hundreds were forced to attend in the Court and outward Rooms of the Palace. I knew and could distinguish those two Heroes at first Sight, not only from the Croud, but from each other. *Homer*[31] was the taller and comelier Person of the two, walked very erect for one of his Age, and his Eyes were the most quick and piercing I ever beheld. *Aristotle* stooped much, and made use of a Staff. His Visage was meager, his Hair lank and thin, and his Voice hollow. I soon discovered, that both of them were perfect Strangers to the rest of the Company, and had never seen or heard of them before. And I had a Whisper from a Ghost, who shall be nameless, that these Commentators always kept in the most distant Quarters from their Principals in the lower World, through a Consciousness of Shame and Guilt, because they had so horribly misrepresented the Meaning of those Authors to Posterity. I introduced *Didymus* and *Eustathius*[32] to *Homer,* and prevailed on him to treat them better than perhaps they deserved; for he soon found they wanted a Genius to enter into the Spirit of a Poet. But *Aristotle* was out of all Patience with the Account I gave him of *Scotus*[33] and *Ramus,*[34] as I presented them to him; and he asked them whether the rest of the Tribe were as great Dunces as themselves.

I THEN desired the Governor to call up *Descartes*[35] and *Gassendi,*[36] with whom I prevailed to explain their Systems to *Aristotle.* This great Philosopher freely acknowledged his own Mistakes in Natural Philosophy, because he proceeded in many things upon Conjecture, as all Men must do; and he found, that *Gassendi,* who had made the Doctrine of *Epicurus* as palatable as he could, and the *Vortices* of *Descartes,* were equally exploded. He predicted the same Fate to *Attraction,*[37] whereof the present Learned are such zealous Asserters. He said, that new Systems of Nature were but new Fashions, which would vary in every Age; and even those who pretend to demonstrate them from Mathematical Principles, would flourish but a short Period of Time, and be out of Vogue when that was determined.

I SPENT five Days in conversing with many others of the antient Learned. I saw most of the first *Roman* Emperors. I prevailed on the Governor to call up *Eliogabalus's*[38] Cooks to dress us a Dinner; but they could not shew us much of their Skill, for want of Materials. A *Helot*[39] of *Agesilaus*[40] made us a Dish of *Spartan* Broth, but I was not able to get down a second *Spoonful.*

THE two Gentlemen who conducted me to the Island were pressed by their private Affairs to return in three Days, which I employed in seeing some of the modern Dead, who had made the greatest Figure for two or three Hundred Years past in our own and other Countries of *Europe;* and having been always a great Admirer of old illustrious Families,[41] I desired the Governor would call up a Dozen or two of Kings with their Ancestors in order, for eight or nine Generations. But my Disappointment was grievous and unexpected. For, instead of a long Train with Royal Diadems, I saw in one Family two Fidlers, three spruce Courtiers, and an *Italian* Prelate. In another, a Barber, an Abbot, and two Cardinals. I have too great a Veneration for crowned Heads to dwell any longer on so nice a Subject: But as to Counts, Marquesses, Dukes, Earls, and the like, I was not so scrupulous. And I confess it was not without some Pleasure that I found my self able to trace the particular Features, by which certain Families are distinguished up to their Originals. I could plainly discover from whence one Family derives a long Chin; why a second hath abounded with Knaves for two Generations, and Fools for two more; why a third happened to be crack-brained, and a fourth to be Sharpers. Whence it came, what *Polydore Virgil*[42] says of a certain great House, *Nec Vir fortis, nec Fæmina Casta.*[43] How Cruelty, Falshood, and Cowardice grew to be Characteristicks by which certain Families are distinguished as much as by their Coat of Arms. Who first brought the Pox[44] into a noble House, which hath lineally descended in scrophulous Tumours to their Posterity. Neither could I wonder at all this, when I saw such an Interruption of Lineages by Pages, Lacqueys, Valets, Coachmen, Gamesters, Fidlers, Players, Captains, and Pick-pockets.

I WAS chiefly disgusted with modern History. For having strictly examined all the Persons of greatest Name in the Courts of Princes for an Hundred Years past, I found how the World had been misled by prostitute Writers, to ascribe the greatest Exploits in War to Cowards, the wisest Counsel to Fools, Sincerity to Flatterers, *Roman* Virtue to Betrayers of their Country, Piety to Atheists, Chastity to Sodomites, Truth to Informers. How many innocent and excellent Persons had been condemned to Death or Banishment, by the practising of great Ministers upon the Corruption of Judges, and the Malice of Factions. How many Villains had been exalted to the highest Places of Trust, Power, Dignity, and Profit: How great a Share in the Motions and Events of Courts, Councils, and Senates might be challenged by Bawds, Whores, Pimps, Parasites, and Buffooons: How low an Opinion I had of human Wisdom and Integrity, when I was truly informed of the Springs and Motives of great Enterprizes and Revolutions in the World, and of the contemptible Accidents to which they owed their Success.

HERE I discovered the Roquery and Ignorance of those who pretend to write *Anecdotes,* or secret History; who send so many Kings to their Graves with a Cup of Poison; will repeat the Discourse between a Prince and chief Minister, where no Witness was by; unlock the Thoughts and Cabinets of Embassadors and Secretaries of State; and have the perpetual Misfortune to be mistaken. Here I discovered the true Causes of many great Events that have surprized the World: How a Whore can govern the Backstairs, the Back-stairs a Council, and the Council a Senate. A general confessed in my Presence, that he got a Victory purely by the Force of Cowardice and ill Conduct: And an Admiral, that for want of proper Intelligence, he beat the Enemy to whom he intended to betray the Fleet. Three Kings protested to me, that in their whole Reigns they did never once prefer any Person of Merit, unless by Mistake or Treachery of some Minister in whom they confided: Neither would they do it if they were to live again; they confided: Neither would they do it if they were to live again; and they shewed with great Strength of Reason, that the Royal Throne could not be supported without Corruption; because, that positive, confident, restive Temper, which Virtue infused into Man, was a perpetual Clog to publick Business.

I HAD the Curiosity to enquire in a particular Manner, by what Method great Numbers had procured to themselves high Titles of Honour, and prodigious Estates; and I confined my Enquiry to a very modern Period: However, without grating upon present Times, because I would be sure to give no Offence even to Foreigners, (for I hope the Reader need not be told that I do not in the least intend my own Country in what I say upon this Occasion) a great Number of Persons concerned were called up, and upon a very slight Examination, discovered such a Scene of Infamy, that I cannot reflect upon it without some Seriousness. Perjury, Oppression, Subornation, Fraud, Pandarism, and the like *Infirmities* were amongst the most excusable Arts they had to mention; and for these I gave, as it was reasonable, due Allowance. But when some confessed, they owed their Greatness and Wealth to Sodomy or Incest; others to the prostituting of their own Wives and Daughters; others to the betraying their Country or their Prince; some to poisoning, more to the perverting of Justice in order to destroy the Innocent: I hope I may be pardoned if these discoveries inclined me a little to abate of that profound Veneration which I am naturally apt to pay to Persons of high Rank, who ought to be treated with the utmost Respect due to their sublime Dignity, by us their Inferiors.

I HAD often read of some great Services done to Princes and States, and desired to see the Persons by whom those Services were performed. Upon Enquiry I was told, that their Names were to be found on no Record, except a few of them whom History hath represented as the vilest Rogues and Traitors. As to the rest, I had never once heard of them. They all appeared with dejected Looks, and in the meanest Habit; most of them telling me they died in Poverty and Disgrace, and the rest on a Scaffold or a Gibbet.

AMONG others there was one Person whose Case appeared a little singular. He had a Youth about Eighteen Years old standing by his Side. He told me, he had for many Years been Commander of a Ship; and in the Sea Fight at *Actium*,[45] had the good Fortune to break through the Enemy's great Line of Battle, sink three of their Capital Ships, and take a fourth, which was the sole Cause of *Antony's* Flight, and of the Victory that ensued: That the Youth standing by him, his only Son, was killed in the Action. He added, that upon the Confidence of some Merit, the War being at an End, he went to *Rome,* and solicited at the Court of *Augustus* to be preferred to a greater Ship, whose Commander had been killed; but without any regard to his Pretensions, it was given to a Boy who had never seen the Sea, the Son of a *Libertina,* who waited on one of the Emperor's Mistresses. Returning back to his own Vessel, he was charged with Neglect of Duty, and the Ship given to a favourite Page of *Publicola* the Vice-Admiral; whereupon he retired to a poor Farm, at a great Distance from *Rome*, and there ended his Life. I was so curious to know the Truth of this Story, that I desired *Agrippa* might be called, who was Admiral in that Fight. He appeared, and confirmed the whole Account, but with much more Advantage to the Captain, whose Modesty had extenuated or concealed a great Part of his Merit.

I WAS surprized to find Corruption grown so high and so quick in that Empire, by the Force of Luxury so lately introduced; which made me less wonder at many parallel Cases in other Countries, where Vices of all Kinds have reigned so much longer, and where the whole Praise as well as Pillage hath been engrossed by the chief Commander, who perhaps had the least Title to either.

As every Person called up made exactly the same Appearance he had done in the World, it gave me melancholy Reflections to observe how much the Race of human Kind was degenerate among us, within these Hundred Years past. How the Pox under all its Consequences and Denominations had altered every Lineament of an *English* Countenance; shortened the Size of Bodies, unbraced the Nerves, relaxed the Sinews and Muscles, introduced a sallow Complexion, and rendered the Flesh loose and *rancid*.

I DESCENDED so low as to desire that some *English* Yeomen of the old Stamp, might be summoned to appear; once so famous for the Simplicity of their Manners, Dyet and Dress; for Justice in their Dealings; for their true Spirit of Liberty; for their Valour and Love of their Country. Neither could I be wholly unmoved after comparing the Living with the Dead, when I considered how all these pure native Virtues were prostituted for a Piece of Money by their Grand-children; who in selling their Votes, and managing at Elections[46] have acquired every Vice and Corruption that can possibly be learned in a Court.

CHAPTER IX

The Author's Return to Maldonada. *Sails to the Kingdom of* Luggnagg. *The Author confined. He is sent for to Court. The Manner of his Admittance. The King's great Lenity to his Subjects.*

The Day of our Departure being come, I took leave of his Highness the Governor of *Glubbdubdribb,* and returned with my two Companions to *Maldonada,* where after a Fortnight's waiting, a Ship was ready to sail for *Luggnagg.* The two Gentlemen and some others were so generous and kind as to furnish me with Provisions, and see me on Board. I was a Month in this Voyage. We had one violent Storm, and were under a Necessity of steering Westward to get into the Trade-Wind, which holds for above sixty Leagues. On the 21st of *April,* 1708, we sailed in the River of *Clumegnig,* which is a Seaport Town, at the South-East Point of *Luggnagg.* We cast Anchor within a League of the Town, and made a Signal for a Pilot. Two of them came on Board in less than half an Hour, by whom we were guided between certain Shoals and Rocks, which are very dangerous in the Passage, to a large Basin, where a Fleet may ride in Safety within a Cable's Length of the Town-Wall.

SOME of our Sailors, whether out of Treachery or Inadvertence, had informed the Pilots that I was a Stranger and a great Traveller, whereof these gave Notice to a Custom-House Officer, by whom I was examined very strictly upon my landing. This Officer spoke to me in the Language of *Balnibarbi,* which by the Force of much Commerce is generally understood in that Town, especially by Seamen, and those employed in the Customs. I gave him a short Account of some Particulars, and made my Story as plausible and consistents as I could; but I thought it necessary to disguise my Country, and call my self a *Hollander;* because my Intentions were for *Japan,* and I knew the *Dutch* were the only *Europeans* permitted to enter into that Kingdom.[47] I therefore told the Officer, that having been shipwrecked on the Coast of *Balnibarbi,* and cast on a Rock, I was received up into *Laputa,* or the flying Island (of which he had often heard) and was now endeavouring to get to *Japan,* from whence I might find a Convenience of returning to my own Country. The Officer said, I must be confined till he could receive Orders from Court, for which he would write immediately, and hoped to receive an Answer in a Fortnight. I was carried to a convenient Lodging, with a Centry placed at the Door; however I had the Liberty of a large Garden, and was treated with Humanity enough, being maintained all the Time at the King's Charge. I was visited by several Persons, chiefly out of Curiosity, because it was reported I came from Countries very remote, of which they had never heard.

I HIRED a young Man who came in the same Ship to be an Interpreter; he was a Native of *Luggnagg,* but had lived some Years at *Maldonada,* and was a perfect Master of both Languages. By his Assistance I was able to hold a Conversation with those that came to visit me; but this consisted only of their Questions and my Answers.

THE Dispatch came from Court about the Time we expected. It contained a Warrant for conducting me and my Retinue to *Traldragdubh* or *Trildrogdrib,* (for it is pronounced both Ways as near as I can remember) by a Party of Ten Horse. All my Retinue was that poor Lad for an Interpreter, whom I persuaded into my Service. At my humble Request we had each of us a Mule to ride on. A Messenger was dispatched half a Day's Journey before us, to give the King Notice of my Approach, and to desire that his Majesty would please to appoint a Day and Hour, when it would be his gracious Pleasure that I might have the Honour to *lick the Dust before his Footstool.*[48] This is the Court Style, and I found it to be more than Matter of Form: For upon my Admittance two Days after my Arrival, I was commanded to crawl upon my Belly, and lick the Floor as I advanced; but on account of my being a Stranger, Care was taken to have it so clean that the Dust was not offensive. However, this was a peculiar Grace, not allowed to any but Persons of the highest Rank, when they desire an Admittance: Nay, sometimes the Floor is strewed with Dust on purpose, when the Person to be admitted happens to have powerful Enemies at Court: And I have seen a great Lord with his Mouth so crammed, that when he had crept to the proper Distance from the Throne, he was not able to speak a Word. Neither is there any Remedy, because it is capital for those who receive an Audience to spit or wipe their Mouths in his Majesty's Presence. There is indeed another Custom, which I cannot altogether approve of. When the King hath a Mind to put any of his Nobles to

Death in a gentle indulgent Manner; he commands to have the Floor strowed with a certain brown Powder, of a deadly Composition, which being licked up infallibly kills him in twenty-four Hours. But in Justice to this Prince's great Clemency,[49] and the Care he hath of his Subjects Lives, (wherein it were much to be wished that the Monarchs of *Europe* would imitate him) it must be mentioned for his Honour, that strict Orders are given to have the infected Parts of the Floor well washed after every such Execution; which if his Domesticks neglect, they are in Danger of incurring his Royal Displeasure. I my self heard him give Directions, that one of his Pages should be whipt, whose Turn it was to give Notice about washing the Floor after an Execution, but maliciously had omitted it; by which Neglect a young Lord of great Hopes coming to an Audience, was unfortunately poisoned, although the King at that Time had no Design against his Life. But this good Prince was so gracious, as to forgive the Page his Whipping, upon Promise that he would do so no more, without special Orders.

To return from this Digression; when I had crept within four Yards of the Throne, I raised my self gently upon my Knees, and then striking my Forehead seven Times against the Ground, I pronounced the following Words, as they had been taught me the Night before, *Ickpling Gloffthrobb Squutserumm blhiop Mlashnalt Zwin tnodbalkguffh Slhiophad Gurdlubh Asht.* This is the Compliment established by the Laws of the Land for all Persons admitted to the King's Presence. It may be rendered into *English* thus: *May your cœlestial Majesty out-live the Sun, eleven Moons and an half.* To this the King returned some Answer, which although I could not understand, yet I replied as I had been directed; *Fluft drin Yalerick Dwuldum prastrad mirplush,* which properly signifies, *My Tongue is in the Mouth of my Friend;* and by this Expression was meant that I desired leave to bring my Interpreter; whereupon the young Man already mentioned was accordingly introduced; by whose Intervention I answered as many Questions as his Majesty could put in above an Hour. I spoke in the *Balnibarbian* Tongue, and my Interpreter delivered my Meaning in that of *Luggnagg.*

THE King was much delighted with my Company, and ordered his *Bliffmarklub* or High Chamberlain to appoint a Lodging in the Court for me and my Interpreter, with a daily Allowance for my Table, and a large Purse of Gold for my common Expences.

I STAYED three Months in this Country out of perfect Obedience to his Majesty, who was pleased highly to favour me, and made me very honourable Offers. But I thought it more consistent with Prudence and Justice to pass the Remainder of my Days with my Wife and Family.

The Luggnuggians *commended. A particular Description of the* Struldbrugs, *with many Conversations between the Author and some eminent Persons upon that Subject.*

The *Luggnuggians* are a polite and generous People, and although they are not without some Share of that Pride which is peculiar to all *Eastern* Countries, yet they shew themselves courteous to Strangers, especially such who are countenanced by the Court. I had many Acquaintance among Persons of the best Fashion, and being always attended by my Interpreter, the Conversation we had was not disagreeable.

One Day in much good Company, I was asked by a Person of Quality, whether I had seen any of their *Struldbrugs* or *Immortals*.[50] I said I had not; and desired he would explain to me what he meant by such an Appellation, applyed to a mortal Creature. He told me, that sometimes, although very rarely, a Child happened to be born in a Family with a red circular Spot in the Forehead, directly over the left Eye-brow, which was an infallible Mark that it should never dye. The Spot, as he described it, was about the Compass of a Silver Threepence, but in the Course of Time grew larger, and changed its Colour; for at Twelve Years old it became green, so continued till Five and Twenty, then turned to a deep blue; at Five and Forty it grew coal black, and as large as an *English* Shilling; but never admitted any farther Alteration. He said these Births were so rare, that he did not believe there could be above Eleven Hundred *Struldbrugs* of both Sexes in the whole Kingdom, of which he computed about Fifty in the Metropolis, and among the rest a young Girl born about three Years ago. That, these Productions were not peculiar to any Family, but a meer Effect of Chance; and the Children of the *Struldbruggs* themselves, were equally mortal with the rest of the People.

I FREELY own myself to have been struck with inexpressible Delight upon hearing this Account: And the Person who gave it me happening to understand the *Balnibarbian* Language, which I spoke very well, I could not forbear breaking out into Expressions perhaps a little too extravagant. I cryed out as in a Rapture; Happy Nation, where every Child hath at least a Chance for being immortal! Happy People who enjoy so many living Examples of antient Virtue, and have Masters ready to instruct them in the Wisdom of all former Ages! But, happiest beyond all Comparison are those excellent *Struldbruggs,* who being born exempt from that universal Calamity of human Nature, have their Minds free and disingaged, without the Weight and Depression of Spirits caused by the continual Apprehension of Death. I discovered my Admiration that I had not observed any of these illustrious Persons at Court; the black Spot on the Forehead, being so remarkable a Distinction, that I could not have easily overlooked it: And it was impossible that his Majesty, a most judicious Prince, should not provide himself with a good Number of such wise and able Counsellors. Yet perhaps the Virtue of those Reverend Sages was too strict for the corrupt and libertine Manners of a Court. And we often find by Experience, that young Men are too opinionative and volatile to be guided by the sober Dictates of their Seniors. However, since the King was pleased to allow me Access to his Royal Person, I was resolved upon the very first Occasion to deliver my Opinion to him on this Matter freely, and at large by the Help of my Interpreter; and whether he would please to take my Advice or no, yet in one Thing I was determined, that his Majesty having frequently offered me an Establishment in this Country, I would with great Thankfulness accept the Favour, and pass my Life here in the Conversation of those superiour Beings the *Struldbruggs,* if they would please to admit me.

THE Gentleman to whom I addressed my Discourse, because (as I have already observed) he spoke the Language of *Balnibarbi,* said to me with a Sort of a Smile, which usually ariseth from Pity to the Ignorant, that he was glad of any Occasion to keep me among them, and desired my Permission to explain to the Company what I had spoke. He did so; and they talked together for some time in their own Language, whereof I understood not a Syllable, neither could I observe by their Countenances what Impression my Discourse had made on them. After a short Silence, the same Person told me, that his Friends and mine (so he thought fit to express himself) were very much pleased with the judicious Remarks I had made on the great Happiness and Advantages of immortal Life; and they were desirous to know in a particular Manner, what Scheme of Living I should have formed to myself, if it had fallen to my Lot to have been born a *Struldbrugg.*

I ANSWERED, it was easy to be eloquent on so copious and delightful a Subject, especially to me who have been often apt to amuse myself with Visions of what I should do if I were a King, a General, or a great Lord: And upon this very Case I had frequently run over the whole System how I should employ myself, and pass the Time if I were sure to live for ever.

THAT, if it had been my good Fortune to come into the World a *Struldbrugg;* as soon as I could discover my own Happiness by understanding the Difference between Life and Death, I would first resolve by all Arts and Methods whatsoever to procure myself Riches: in the Pursuit of which, by Thrift and Management, I might reasonably expect in about two Hundred Years, to be the wealthiest Man in the Kingdom. In the second Place, I would from my earliest Youth apply myself to the Study of Arts and Sciences, by which I should arrive in time to excel all others in Learning. Lastly, I would carefully record every Action and Event of Consequence that happened in the Publick, impartially draw the Characters of the several Successions of Princes, and great Ministers of State; with my own Observations on every Point. I would exactly set down the several Changes in Customs, Language, Fashion of Dress, Dyet and Diversions. By all which Acquirements, I should be a living Treasury of Knowledge and Wisdom, and certainly become the Oracle of the Nation.

I WOULD never marry after Threescore, but live in an hospitable Manner, yet still on the saving Side. I would entertain myself in forming and directing the Minds of hopeful young Men, by convincing them from my own Remembrance, Experience and Observation, fortified by numerous Examples, of the Usefulness of Virtue in publick and private Life. But, my choise and constant Companions should be a Sett of my own immortal Brotherhood, among whom I would elect a Dozen from the most ancient down to my own Contemporaries. Where any of these wanted Fortunes, I would provide them with convenient Lodges round my own Estate, and have some of them always at my Table, only mingling a few of the most valuable among you Mortals, whom Length of Time would harden me to lose with little or no Reluctance, and treat your Posterity after the same Manner; just as a Man diverts himself with the annual Succession of Pinks and Tulips in his Garden, without regretting the Loss of those which withered the preceding Year.

THESE *Struldbruggs* and I would mutually communicate our Observations and Memorials through the Course of Time; remark the several Gradations by which Corruption steals into the World, and oppose it in every Step, by giving perpetual Warning and Instruction to Mankind; which, added to the strong Influence of our own Example, would probably prevent that continual Degeneracy of human Nature, so justly complained of in all Ages.

ADD to all this, the Pleasure of seeing the various Revolutions of States and Empires; the Changes in the lower and upper World; antient Cities in Ruins, and obscure Villages become the Seats of Kings. Famous Rivers lessening into shallow Brooks; the Ocean leaving one Coast dry, and overwhelming another: The Discovery of many Countries yet unknown. Barbarity overrunning the politest Nations, and the most barbarous becoming civilized. I should then see the Discovery of the *Longitude*, the *perpetual Motion*, the *universal Medicine*, and many other great Inventions brought to the utmost Perfection.

WHAT wonderful Discoveries should we make in Astronomy, by outliving and confirming our own Predictions; by observing the Progress and Returns of Comets, with the Changes of Motion in the Sun, Moon and Stars.

I ENLARGED upon many other Topicks, which the natural Desire of endless Life and sublunary Happiness could easily furnish me with. When I had ended, and the Sum of my Discourse had been interpreted as before, to the rest of the Company, there was a good Deal of Talk among them in the Language of the Country, not without some Laughter at my Expence. At last the same Gentleman who had been my Interpreter, said, he was desired by the rest to set me right in a few Mistakes, which I had fallen into through the common Imbecility of human Nature, and upon that Allowance was less answerable for them. That, this Breed of *Struldbruggs* was peculiar to their Country, for there were no such People either in *Balnibarbi* or *Japan*, where he had the Honour to be Embassador from his Majesty, and found the Natives in both those Kingdoms very hard to believe that the Fact was possible; and it appeared from my Astonishment when he first mentioned the Matter to me, that I received it as a Thing wholly new, and scarcely to be credited. That in the two Kingdoms abovementioned, where during his Residence he had conversed very much, he observed long Life to be the universal Desire and Wish of Mankind. That, whoever had one Foot in the Grave, was sure to hold back the other as strongly as he could. That the oldest had still Hopes of living one Day longer, and looked on Death as the greatest Evil, from which Nature always prompted him to retreat; only in this Island of *Luggnagg*, the Appetite for living was not so eager, from the continual Example of the *Struldbruggs* before their Eyes.

THAT the System of Living contrived by me was unreasonable and unjust, because it supposed a Perpetuity of Youth, Health, and Vigour, which no Man could be so foolish to hope, however extravagant he might be in his Wishes. That, the Question therefore was not whether a Man would chuse to be always in the Prime of Youth, attended with Prosperity and Health; but how he would pass a perpetual Life under all the usual Disadvantages which old Age brings along with it. For although few Men will avow their Desires of being immortal upon such hard Conditions, yet in the two Kingdoms beforementioned of *Balnibarbi* and *Japan,* he observed that every Man desired to put off Death for sometime longer, let it approach ever so late; and he rarely heard of any Man who died willingly, except he were incited by the Extremity of Grief or Torture. And he appealed to me whether in those Countries I had travelled as well as my own, I had not observed the same general Disposition.

AFTER this Preface, he gave me a particular Account of the *Struldbruggs* among them. He said they commonly acted like Mortals, till about Thirty Years old, after which by Degrees they grew melancholy and dejected, increasing in both till they came to Fourscore. This he learned from their own Confession; for otherwise there not being above two or three of that Species born in an Age, they were too few to form a general Observation by. When they came to Fourscore Years, which is reckoned the Extremity of living in this Country, they had not only all the Follies and Infirmities of other old Men, but many more which arose from the dreadful Prospect of never dying. They were not only opinionative, peevish, covetous, morose, vain, talkative; but uncapable of Friendship, and dead to all natural Affection, which never descended below their Grand-children. Envy and impotent Desires, are their prevailing Passions. But those Objects against which their Envy seems principally directed, are the Vices of the younger Sort, and the Deaths of the old. By reflecting on the former, they find themselves cut off from all Possibility of Pleasure; and whenever they see a Funeral, they lament and repine that others are gone to an Harbour of Rest, to which they themselves never can hope to arrive. They have no Remembrance of any thing but what they learned and observed in their Youth and middle Age, and even that is very imperfect: And for the Truth or Particulars of any Fact, it is safer to depend on common Traditions than upon their best Recollections. The least miserable among them, appear to be those who turn to Dotage, and entirely lose their Memories; these meet with more Pity and Assistance, because they want many bad Qualities which abound in others.

IF a *Struldbrugg* happen to marry one of his own Kind, the Marriage is dissolved of Course by the Courtesy of the Kingdom, as soon as the younger of the two comes to be Fourscore. For the Law thinks it a reasonable Indulgence, that those who are condemned without any Fault of their own to a perpetual Continuance in the World, should not have their Misery doubled by the Load of a Wife.

AS soon as they have compleated the Term of Eighty Years, they are looked on as dead in Law; their Heirs immediately succeed to their Estates, only a small Pittance is reserved for their Support; and the poor ones are maintained at the publick Charge. After that Period they are held incapable of any Employment of Trust or Profit; they cannot purchase Lands, or take Leases, neither are they allowed to be Witnesses in any Cause, either Civil or Criminal, not even for the Decision of Meers[51] and Bounds.

AT Ninety they lose their Teeth and Hair; they have at that Age no Distinction of Taste, but eat and drink whatever they can get, without Relish or Appetite. The Diseases they were subject to, still continue without encreasing or diminishing. In talking they forget the common Appellation of Things, and the Names of Persons, even of those who are their nearest Friends and Relations. For the same Reason they never can amuse themselves with reading, because their Memory will not serve to carry them from the Beginning of a Sentence to the End; and by this Defect they are deprived of the only Entertainment whereof they might otherwise be capable.

THE Language of this Country being always upon the Flux, the *Struldbruggs* of one Age do not understand those of another; neither are they able after two Hundred Years to hold any Conversation (farther than by a few general Words) with their Neighbours the Mortals; and thus they lye under the Disadvantage of living like Foreigners in their own Country.

THIS was the Account given me of the *Struldbruggs,* as near as I can remember. I afterwards saw five or six of different Ages, the youngest not above two Hundred Years old, who were brought to me at several Times by some of my Friends; but although they were told that I was a great Traveller, and had seen all the World, they had not the least Curiosity to ask me a Question; only desired I would give them *Slumskudask,* or a Token of Remembrance; which is a modest Way of begging, to avoid the

Law that strictly forbids it, because they are provided for by the Publick, although indeed with a very scanty Allowance.

THEY are despised and hated by all Sorts of People: When one of them is born, it is reckoned ominous, and their Birth is recorded very particularly; so that you may know their Age by consulting the Registry, which however hath not been kept above a Thousand Years past, or at least hath been destroyed by Time or publick Disturbances. But the usual Way of computing how old they are, is, by asking them what Kings or great Persons they can remember, and then consulting History; for infallibly the last Prince in their Mind did not begin his Reign after they were Fourscore Years old.

THEY were the most mortifying Sight I ever beheld; and the Women more horrible than the Men. Besides the usual Deformities in extreme old Age, they acquired an additional Ghastliness in Proportion to their Number of Years, which is not to be described; and among half a Dozen I soon distinguished which was the eldest, although there were not above a Century or two between them.

THE Reader will easily believe, that from what I had heard and seen, my keen Appetite for Perpetuity of Life was much abated. I grew heartily ashamed of the pleasing Visions I had formed; and thought no Tyrant could invent a Death into which I would not run with Pleasure from such a Life. The King heard of all that had passed between me and my Friends upon this Occasion, and raillied me very pleasantly; wishing I would send a Couple of *Struldbruggs* to my own Country, to arm our People against the Fear of Death; but this it seems is forbidden by the fundamental Laws of the Kingdom; or else I should have been well content with the Trouble and Expence of transporting them.

I COULD not but agree, that the Laws of this Kingdom relating to the *Struldbruggs,* were founded upon the strongest Reasons, and such as any other Country would be under the Necessity of enacting in the like Circumstances. Otherwise, as Avarice is the necessary Consequent of old Age, those Immortals would in time become Proprietors of the whole Nation, and engross the Civil Power; which, for want of Abilities to manage, must end in the Ruin of the Publick.

CHAPTER XI

The Author leaves Luggnagg *and sails to* Japan. *From thence he returns in a* Dutch *Ship to* Amsterdam, *and from* Amsterdam *to* England.

I thought this Account of the *Struldbruggs* might be some Entertainment to the Reader, because it seems to be a little out of the common Way; at least, I do not remember to have met the like in any Book of Travels that hath come to my Hands: And if I am deceived, my Excuse must be, that it is necessary for Travellers, who describe the same Country, very often to agree in dwelling on the same Particulars, without deserving the Censure of having borrowed or transcribed from those who wrote before them.

THERE is indeed a perpetual Commerce between this Kingdom and the great Empire of *Japan;* and it is very probable that the *Japanese* Authors may have given some Account of the *Struldbruggs;* but my Stay in *Japan* was so short, and I was so entirely a Stranger to the Language, that I was not qualified to make any Enquiries. But I hope the *Dutch* upon this Notice will be curious and able enough to supply my Defects.

HIS Majesty having often pressed me to accept some Employment in his Court, and finding me absolutely determined to return to my Native Country; was pleased to give me his Licence to depart; and honoured me with a Letter of Recommendation under his own Hand to the Emperor of *Japan.* He likewise presented me with four Hundred forty-four large Pieces of Gold (this Nation delighting in even Numbers) and a red Diamond which I sold in *England* for Eleven Hundred Pounds.

ON the 6th Day of *May,* 1709, I took a solemn Leave of his Majesty, and all my Friends. This Prince was so gracious as to order a Guard to conduct me to *Glanguenstald,* which is a Royal Port to the *South-West* Part of the Island. In six Days I found a Vessel ready to carry me to *Japan;* and spent fifteen Days in the Voyage. We landed at a small Port-Town called *Xamoschi*, situated on the *South-East* Part of *Japan*. The Town lies on the *Western* Part, where there is a narrow Streight, leading *Northward* into a long Arm of the Sea, upon the *North-West* Part of which *Yedo*[52] the Metropolis stands. At landing I shewed the Custom-House Officers my Letter from the King of *Luggnagg* to his Imperial Majesty: They knew the Seal perfectly well; it was as broad as the Palm of my Hand. The Impression was, *A King lifting up a lame Beggar from the Earth*. The Magistrates of the Town hearing of my Letter, received me as a publick Minister; they provided me with Carriages and Servants, and bore my Charges to *Yedo*, where I was admitted to an Audience, and delivered my Letter; which was opened with great Ceremony, and explained to the Emperor by an Interpreter, who gave me Notice of his Majesty's Order, that I should signify my Request; and whatever it were, it should be granted for the sake of his Royal Brother of *Luggnagg*. This Interpreter was a Person employed to transact Affairs with the *Hollanders:* He soon conjectured by my Countenance that I was an *European*, and therefore repeated his Majesty's Commands in *Low-Dutch*, which he spoke perfectly well. I answered, (as I had before determined) that I was a *Dutch* Merchant, shipwrecked in a very remote Country, from whence I travelled by Sea and Land to *Luggnagg*, and then took Shipping for *Japan*, where I knew my Countrymen often traded, and with some of these I hoped to get an Opportunity of returning into *Europe:* I therefore most humbly entreated his Royal Favour to give Order, that I should be conducted in Safety to *Nangasac*. To this I added another Petition, that for the sake of my Patron the King of *Luggnagg*, his Majesty would condescend to excuse my performing the Ceremony imposed on my Countrymen, of *trampling upon the Crucifix;*[53] because I had been thrown into his Kingdom by my Misfortunes, without any Intention of trading. When this latter Petition was interpreted to the Emperor, he seemed a little surprised; and said, he believed I was the first of my Countrymen who ever made any Scruple in this Point; and that he began to doubt whether I were a real *Hollander* or no; but rather suspected I must be a CHRISTIAN. However, for the Reasons I had offered, but chiefly to gratify the King of *Luggnagg*, by an uncommon Mark of his Favour, he would comply with the *singularity* of my Humour; but the Affair must be managed with Dexterity, and his Officers should be commanded to let me pass as it were by Forgetfulness. For he assured me, that if the Secret should be discovered by my Countrymen, the *Dutch*, they would cut my Throat in the Voyage. I returned my Thanks by the Interpreter for so unusual a

Favour; and some Troops being at that Time on their March to *Nangasac*, the Commanding Officer had Orders to convey me safe thither, with particular Instructions about the Business of the *Crucifix*.

ON the 9th Day of *June*, 1709, I arrived at *Nangasac*, after a very long and troublesome Journey. I soon fell into Company of some *Dutch* Sailors belonging to the *Amboyna*[54] of *Amsterdam*, a stout Ship of 450 Tuns. I had lived long in *Holland*, pursuing my Studies at *Leyden*, and I spoke *Dutch* well: The Seamen soon knew from whence I came last; they were curious to enquire into my Voyages and Course of Life. I made up a Story as short and probable as I could, but concealed the greatest Part. I knew many Persons in *Holland*; I was able to invent Names for my Parents, whom I pretended to be obscure People in the Province of *Guelderland*. I would have given the Captain (one *Theodorus Vangrult*) what he pleased to ask for my Voyage to *Holland*; but, understanding I was a Surgeon, he was contented to take half the usual Rate, on Condition that I would serve him in the Way of my Calling. Before we took Shipping, I was often asked by some of the Crew, whether I had performed the Ceremony abovementioned? I evaded the Question by general Answers, that I had satisfied the Emperor and Court in all Particulars. However, a malicious Rogue of a Skipper[55] went to an Officer, and pointing to me, told him, I had not yet *trampled on the Crucifix:* But the other, who had received Instructions to let me pass, gave the Rascal twenty Strokes on the Shoulders with a Bamboo; after which I was no more troubled with such Questions.

NOTHING happened worth mentioning in this Voyage. We sailed with a fair Wind to the *Cape of Good Hope*, where we staid only to take in fresh Water. On the 6th of *April* we arrived safe at *Amsterdam*, having lost only three Men by Sickness in the Voyage, and a fourth who fell from the Foremast into the Sea, not far from the Coast to *Guinea*. From *Amsterdam* I soon after set sail for *England* in a small Vessel belonging to that City.

ON the 10th of *April*, 1710, we put in at the *Downs*. I landed the next Morning, and saw once more my Native Country after an Absence of five Years and six Months compleat. I went strait to *Redriff*, whither I arrived the same Day at two in the Afternoon, and found my Wife and Family in good Health.

The End of the Third Part.

PART IV

A Voyage to the Country
of the Houyhnhnms[1]

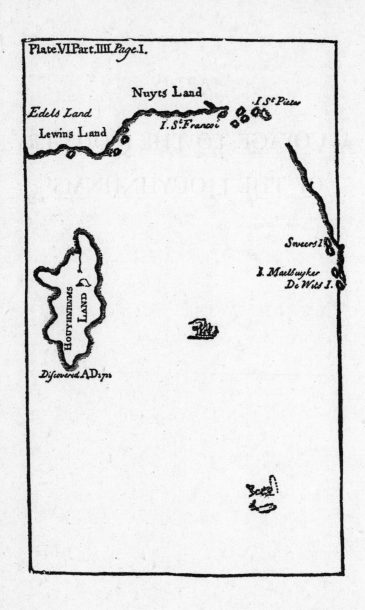

CHAPTER I

The Author sets out as Captain of a Ship. His Men conspire against him, confine him a long Time to his Cabbin, set him on Shore in an unknown Land. He travels up into the Country. The Yahoos,[2] *a strange Sort of Animal, described. The Author meets two* Houyhnhnms.

I continued at home with my Wife and Children about five Months in a very happy Condition, if I could have learned the Lesson of knowing when I was well. I left my poor Wife big with Child, and accepted an advantageous Offer made me to be Captain of the *Adventure*, a stout Merchant-man of 350 Tuns: For I understood Navigation well, and being grown weary of a Surgeon's Employment at Sea, which however I could exercise upon Occasion, I took a skilful young Man of that Calling, one *Robert Purefoy*, into my Ship. We set sail from *Portsmouth* upon the 7th Day of *September*, 1710; on the 14th we met with Captain *Pocock* of *Bristol*, at *Tenariff*, who was going to the Bay of *Campeachy*, to cut Logwood. On the 16th he was parted from us by a Storm: I heard since my Return, that his Ship foundered, and none escaped, but one Cabbin-Boy. He was an honest Man, and a good Sailor, but a little too positive in his own Opinions, which was the Cause of his Destruction, as it hath been of several others. For if he had followed my Advice, he might at this Time have been safe at home with his Family as well as my self.

I HAD several Men died in my Ship of Calentures,[3] so that I was forced to get Recruits out of *Barbadoes*, and the *Leeward Islands*, where I touched by the Direction of the Merchants who employed me; which I had soon too much Cause to repent; for I found afterwards that most of them had been Buccaneers. I had fifty Hands on Board; and my Orders were, that I should trade with the *Indians* in the *South-Sea*, and make what Discoveries I could. These Rogues whom I had picked up, debauched my other Men, and they all formed a Conspiracy to seize the Ship and secure me; which they did one Morning, rushing into my Cabbin, and binding me Hand and Foot, threatening to throw me overboard, if I offered to stir. I told them, I was their Prisoner, and would submit. This they made me swear to do, and then unbound me, only fastening one of my Legs with a Chain near my Bed; and placed a Centry at my Door with his Piece charged, who was commanded to shoot me dead if I attempted my Liberty. They sent me down Victuals and Drink, and took the Government of the Ship to themselves. Their Design was to turn Pirates, and plunder the *Spaniards,* which they could not do, till they got more Men. But first they resolved to sell the Goods in the Ship, and then go to *Madagascar* for Recruits, several among them having died since my Confinement. They sailed many Weeks, and traded with the *Indians;* but I knew not what Course they took, being kept close Prisoner in my Cabbin, and expecting nothing less than to be murdered, as they often threatened me.

UPON the 9th Day of *May,* 1711, one *James Welch* came down to my Cabbin; and said he had Orders from the Captain to set me ashore. I expostulated with him, but in vain; neither would he so much as tell me who their new Captain was. They forced me into the Long-boat, letting me put on my best Suit of Cloaths, which were as good as new, and a small Bundle of Linnen, but no Arms except my Hanger; and they were so civil as not to search my Pockets, into which I conveyed what Money I had, with some other little Necessaries. They rowed about a League; and then set me down down on a Strand. I desired them to tell me what Country it was: They all swore, they knew no more than my self, but said, that the Captain (as they called him) was resolved, after they had sold the Lading, to get rid of me in the first Place where they discovered Land. They pushed off immediately, advising me to make haste, for fear of being overtaken by the Tide; and bade me farewell.

IN this desolate Condition I advanced forward, and soon got upon firm Ground, where I sat down on a Bank to rest my self, and consider what I had best to do. When I was a little refreshed, I went up into the Country, resolving to deliver my self to the first Savages I should meet; and purchase my Life from them by some Bracelets, Glass Rings, and other Toys, which Sailors usually provide themselves with in those Voyages, and whereof I had some about me: The Land was divided by long Rows of Trees, not regularly planted, but naturally growing; there was great Plenty of Grass, and several Fields of Oats. I walked very circumspectly for fear of being surprised, or suddenly shot with an Arrow from behind, or on either Side. I fell into a beaten Road, where I saw many Tracks of human Feet, and some of Cows, but most of Horses. At last I beheld several Animals in a Field, and one or two of the same Kind sitting in Trees. Their Shape was very singular, and deformed, which a little discomposed me, so that I lay down behind a Thicket to observe them better. Some of them coming forward near the Place where I lay, gave me an Opportunity of distinctly marking their Form. Their Heads and Breasts were covered with a thick Hair, some frizzled and others lank; they had Beards like Goats, and a Long Ridge of Hair down their Backs, and the fore Parts of their Legs and Feet; but the rest of their Bodies were bare, so that I might see their Skins, which were of a brown Buff Colour. They had no Tails, nor any Hair at all on their Buttocks, except about the *Anus;* which, I presume Nature had placed there to defend them as they sat on the Ground; for this Posture they used, as well as lying down, and often stood on their hind Feet. They climbed high Trees, as nimbly as a Squirrel, for they had strong extended Claws before and behind, terminating in sharp Points, and hooked. They would often spring, and bound, and leap with prodigious Agility. The Females were not so large as the Males; they had long lank Hair on their Heads, and only a Sort of Down on the rest of their Bodies, except about the *Anus,* and *Pudenda.* Their Dugs⁴ hung between their fore Feet, and often reached almost to the Ground as they walked. The Hair of both Sexes was of several Colours, brown, red, black and yellow. Upon the whole, I never beheld in all my Travels so disagreeable an Animal, or one against which I naturally conceived so strong an Antipathy. So that thinking I had seen enough, full of Contempt and Aversion, I got up and pursued the beaten Road, hoping it might direct me to the Cabbin of some *Indian.* I had not gone far when I met one of these Creatures full in my Way, and coming up directly to me. The ugly Monster, when he saw me, distorted several Ways every Feature of his Visage, and stared as at an Object he had never seen before; then approaching nearer, lifted up his fore Paw, whether out of Curiosity or Mischief, I could not tell: But I drew my Hanger, and gave him a good Blow with the flat Side of it; for I durst not strike him with the Edge, fearing the Inhabitants might be provoked against me, if they should come to know, that I had killed or maimed any of their Cattle.⁵ When the Beast felt the Smart, he drew back, and roared so loud, that a Herd of at least forty came flocking about me from the next Field, howling and making odious Faces; but I ran to the Body of a Tree, and leaning my Back against it, kept them off, by waving my Hanger. Several of this cursed Brood getting hold of the Branches behind, leaped up into the Tree, from whence they began to discharge their Excrements on my Head: However, I escaped pretty well, by sticking close to the Stem of the Tree, but was almost stifled with the Filth, which fell about me on every Side.

IN the Midst of this Distress, I observed them all to run away on a sudden as fast as they could; at which I ventured to leave the Tree, and pursue the Road, wondering what it was that could put them into this Fright. But looking on my Left-Hand, I saw a Horse walking softly in the Field; which my Persecutors having sooner discovered, was the Cause of their Flight. The Horse started a little when he came near me, but soon recovering himself, looked full in my Face with manifest Tokens of Wonder: He viewed my Hands and Feet, walking round me several times. I would have pursued my Journey, but he placed himself directly in the Way, yet looking with a very mild Aspect, never offering the least Violence. We stood gazing at each other for some time; at last I took the Boldness, to reach my Hand towards his Neck, with a Design to stroak it; using the common Style and Whistle of Jockies when they are going to handle a strange Horse. But, this Animal seeming to receive my Civilities with Disdain, shook his Head, and bent his Brows, softly raising up his Left Fore-Foot to remove my Hand. Then he neighed three or four times, but in so different a Cadence, that I almost began to think he was speaking to himself in some Language of his own.

WHILE He and I were thus employed, another Horse came up; who applying himself to the first in a very formal Manner, they gently struck each others Right Hoof before, neighing several times by Turns, and varying the Sound, which seemed to be almost articulate. They went some Paces off, as if it were to confer together, walking Side by Side, backward and forward, like Persons deliberating upon some Affair of Weight; but often turning their Eyes towards me, as it were to watch that I might not escape. I was amazed to see such Actions and Behaviour in Brute Beasts; and concluded with myself, that if the Inhabitants of this Country were endued with a proportionable Degree of Reason, they must needs be the wisest People upon Earth. This Thought gave me so much Comfort, that I resolved to go forward until I could discover some House or Village, or meet with any of the Natives; leaving the two Horses to discourse together as they pleased. But the first, who was a Dapple-Grey, observing me to steal off, neighed after me in so expressive a Tone, that I fancied myself to understand what he meant; whereupon I turned back, and came near him, to expect his farther Commands; but concealing my Fear as much as I could; for I began to be in some Pain, how this Adventure might terminate: and the Reader will easily believe I did not much like my present Situation.

THE two Horses came up close to me, looking with great Earnestness upon my Face and Hands. The grey Steed rubbed my Hat all round with his Right Fore-hoof, and discomposed it so much, that I was forced to adjust it better, by taking it off, and settling it again; whereat both he and his Companion (who was a brown Bay) appeared to be much surprized; the latter felt the Lappet of my Coat, and finding it to hang loose about me, they both looked with new Signs of Wonder. He stroked my Right Hand, seeming to admire the Softness, and Colour; but he squeezed it so hard between his Hoof and his Pastern, that I was forced to roar; after which they both touched me with all possible Tenderness. They were under great Perplexity about my Shoes and Stockings, which they felt very often, neighing to each other, and using various Gestures, not unlike those of a Philosopher, when he would attempt to solve some new and difficult Phænomenon.

UPON the whole, the Behaviour of these Animals was so orderly and rational, so acute and judicious, that I at last concluded, they must needs be Magicians, who had thus metamorphosed themselves upon some Design; and seeing a Stranger in the Way, were resolved to divert themselves with him; or perhaps were really amazed at the Sight of a Man so very different in Habit, Feature and Complexion from those who might probably live in so remote a Climate. Upon the Strength of this Reasoning, I ventured to address them in the following Manner: Gentlemen, if you be Conjurers, as I have good Cause to believe, you can understand any Language; therefore I make bold to let your Worships know, that I am a poor distressed *Englishman,* driven by his Misfortunes upon your Coast; and I entreat one of you, to let me ride upon his Back, as if he were a real Horse, to some House or Village, where I can be relieved. In return of which Favour, I will make you a Present of this Knife and Bracelet, (taking them out of my Pocket.) The two Creatures stood silent while I spoke, seeming to listen with great Attention; and when I had ended, they neighed frequently towards each other, as if they were engaged in serious Conversation. I plainly observed, that their Language expressed the Passions very well, and the Words might with little Pains be resolved into an Alphabet more easily than the *Chinese.*

I COULD frequently distinguish the Word *Yahoo,* which was repeated by each of them several times; and although it were impossible for me to conjecture what it meant, yet while the two Horses were busy in Conversation, I endeavoured to practice this Word upon my Tongue; and as soon as they were silent, I boldly pronounced *Yahoo* in a loud Voice, imitating, at the same time, as near as I could, the Neighing of a Horse; at which they were both visibly surprized, and the Grey repeated the same Word twice, as if he meant to teach me the right Accent, wherein I spoke after him as well as I could, and found myself perceivably to improve every time, although very far from any Degree of Perfection. Then the Bay tried me with a second Word, much harder to be pronounced; but reducing it to the *English Orthography,* may be spelt thus, *Houyhnhnm.* I did not succeed in this so well as the former, but after two or three farther Trials, I had better Fortune; and they both appeared amazed at my Capacity.

AFTER some farther Discourse, which I then conjectured might relate to me, the two Friends took their Leaves, with the same Compliment of striking each other's Hoof; and the Grey made me Signs that I should walk before him; wherein I thought it prudent to comply, till I could find a better Director. When I offered to slacken my Pace, he would cry *Hhuun, Hhuun;* I guessed his Meaning, and gave him to understand, as well as I could, that I was weary, and not able to walk faster; upon which, he would stand a while to let me rest.

CHAPTER II

The Author conducted by a Houyhnhnm *to his House. The House described. The Author's Reception. The Food of the* Houyhnhnms. *The Author in Distress for want of Meat, is at last relieved. His Manner of feeding in that Country.*

Having travelled about three Miles, we came to a long Kind of Building, made of Timber, stuck in the Ground, and wattled a-cross; the Roof was low, and covered with Straw. I now began to be a little comforted; and took out some Toys, which Travellers usually carry for Presents to the Savage *Indians* of *America* and other Parts, in hopes the People of the House would be thereby encouraged to receive me kindly. The Horse made me a Sign to go in first; it was a large Room with a smooth Clay Floor, and a Rack and Manger extending the whole Length on one Side. There were three Nags, and two Mares, not eating, but some of them sitting down upon their Hams, which I very much wondered at; but wondered more to see the rest employed in domestick Business: The last seemed but ordinary Cattle; however this confirmed my first Opinion, that a People who could so far civilize brute Animals, must needs excel in Wisdom all the Nations of the World. The Grey came in just after, and thereby prevented any ill Treatment, which the others might have given me. He neighed to them several times in a Style of Authority, and received Answers.

BEYOND this Room there were three others, reaching the Length of the House, to which you passed through three Doors, opposite to each other, in the Manner of a Vista: We went through the second Room towards the third; here the Grey walked in first, beckoning me to attend: I waited in the second Room, and got ready my Presents, for the Master and Mistress of the House: They were two Knives, three Bracelets of false Pearl, a small Looking Glass and a Bead Necklace. The Horse neighed three or four Times, and I waited to hear some Answers in a human Voice, but I heard no other Returns than in the same Dialect, only one or two a little shriller than his. I began to think that this House must belong to some Person of great Note among them, because there appeared so much ceremony before I could gain Admittance. But, that a Man of Quality should be served all by Horses, was beyond my Comprehension. I feared my Brain was disturbed by my Sufferings and Misfortunes: I roused my self, and looked about me in the Room where I was left alone; this was furnished as the first, only after a more elegant Manner. I rubbed mine Eyes often, but the same Objects still occurred. I pinched my Arms and Sides, to awake my self, hoping I might be in a Dream. I then absolutely concluded, that all these Appearances could be nothing else but Necromancy and Magick. But I had no Time to pursue these Reflections; for the Grey Horse came to the Door, and made me a Sign to follow him into the third Room; where I saw a very comely Mare, together with a Colt and Fole, sitting on their Haunches, upon Mats of Straw, not unartfully made, and perfectly neat and clean.

THE Mare soon after my Entrance, rose from her Mat, and coming up close, after having nicely observed my Hands and Face, gave me a most contemptuous Look; then turning to the Horse, I heard the Word *Yahoo* often repeated betwixt them; the meaning of which Word I could not then comprehend, although it were the first I had learned to pronounce; but I was soon better informed, to my everlasting Mortification: For the Horse beckoning to me with his Head, and repeating the Word *Hhuun, Hhuun,* as he did upon the Road, which I understood was to attend him, led me out into a kind of Court, where was another Building at some Distance from the House. Here we entered, and I saw three of those detestable Creatures, which I first met after my landing, feeding upon Roots, and the Flesh of some Animals, which I afterwards found to be that of Asses and Dogs, and now and then a Cow dead by Accident or Disease. They were all tied by the Neck with strong Wyths, fastened to a Beam; they held their Food between the Claws of their fore Feet, and tore it with their Teeth.

THE Master Horse ordered a Sorrel Nag, one of his Servants, to untie the largest of these Animals, and take him into the Yard. The Beast and I were brought close together; and our Countenances diligently compared, both by Master and Servant, who thereupon repeated several Times the Word *Yahoo.* My Horror and Astonishment are not to be described, when I observed, in this abominable Animal, a perfect human Figure; the Face of it indeed was flat and broad, the Nose depressed, the Lips large, and the Mouth wide: But these Differences are common to all savage Nations, where the Lineaments of the Countenance are distorted by the Natives suffering their Infants to lie grovelling on the Earth, or by carrying them on their Backs, nuzzling with the Face against the Mother's Shoulders. The Fore-feet of the *Yahoo* differed from my Hands in nothing else, but the Length of the Nails, the Coarseness and Brownness of the Palms, and the Hairiness on the Backs. There was the same Resemblance between our Feet, with the same Differences, which I knew very well, although the Horses did not, because of my Shoes and Stockings; the same in every Part of our Bodies, except as to Hairiness and Colour, which I have already described.

THE great Difficulty that seemed to stick with the two Horses, was, to see the rest of my Body so very different from that of a *Yahoo,* for which I was obliged to my Cloaths, whereof they had no Conception: The Sorrel Nag offered me a Root, which he held (after their Manner, as we shall describe in its proper Place) between his Hoof and Pastern; I took it in my Hand, and having smelt it, returned it to him again as civilly as I could. He brought out of the *Yahoo*'s Kennel a Piece of Ass's Flesh, but it smelt so offensively that I turned from it with loathing; he then threw it to the *Yahoo,* by whom it was greedily devoured. He afterwards shewed me a Wisp of Hay, and a Fettlock full of Oats; but I shook my Head, to signify, that neither of these were Food for me. And indeed, I now apprehended, that I must absolutely starve, if I did not get to some of my own Species: For as to those filthy *Yahoos,* although there were few greater Lovers of Mankind, at that time, than myself; yet I confess I never saw any sensitive Being so detestable on all Accounts; and the more I came near them, the more hateful they grew, while I stayed in that Country. This the Master Horse observed by my Behaviour, and therefore sent the *Yahoo* back to his Kennel. He then put his Forehoof to his Mouth, at which I was much surprized, although he did it with Ease, and with a Motion that appear'd perfectly natural; and made other Signs to know what I would eat; but I could not return him such an Answer as he was able to apprehend; and if he had understood me I did not see how it was possible to contrive any way for finding myself Nourishment. While we were thus engaged, I observed a Cow passing by; whereupon I pointed to her, and expressed a Desire to let me go and milk her. This had its Effect; for he led me back into the House, and ordered a Mare-servant to open a Room, where a good Store of Milk lay in Earthen and Wooden Vessels, after a very orderly and cleanly Manner. She gave me a large Bowl full, of which I drank very heartily, and found myself well refreshed.

ABOUT Noon I saw coming towards the House a Kind of Vehicle, drawn like a Sledge by four *Yahoos*. There was in it an old Steed,[6] who seemed to be of Quality; he alighted with his Hind-feet forward, having by Accident got a Hurt in his Left Fore-foot. He came to dine with our Horse, who received him with great Civility. They dined in the best Room, and had Oats boiled in Milk for the second Course, which the old Horse eat warm, but the rest cold. Their Mangers were placed circular in the Middle of the Room, and divided into several Partitions, round which they sat on their Haunches upon Bosses of Straw. In the Middle was a large Rack with Angles answering to every Partition of the Manger. So that each Horse and Mare eat their own Hay, and their own Mash of Oats and Milk, with much Decency and Regularity. The Behaviour of the young Colt and Fole appeared very modest; and that of the Master and Mistress extremely chearful and complaisant[7] to their Guest. The Grey ordered me to stand by him; and much Discourse passed between him and his Friend concerning me, as I found by the Stranger's often looking on me, and the frequent Repetition of the Word *Yahoo*.

I HAPPENED to wear my Gloves; which the Master Grey observing, seemed perplexed; discovering Signs of Wonder what I had done to my Fore-feet; he put his Hoof three or four times to them, as if he would signify, that I should reduce them to their former Shape, which I presently did, pulling off both my Gloves, and putting them into my Pocket. This occasioned farther Talk, and I saw the Company was pleased with my Behaviour, whereof I soon found the good Effects. I was ordered to speak the few Words I understood; and while they were at Dinner, the Master taught me the Names for Oats, Milk, Fire, Water, and some others; which I could readily pronounce after him; having from my Youth a great Facility in learning Languages.

WHEN Dinner was done, the Master Horse took me aside, and by Signs and Words made me understand the Concern he was in, that I had nothing to eat. Oats in their Tongue are called *Hlunnh*. This Word I pronounced two or three times; for although I had refused them at first, yet upon second Thoughts, I considered that I could contrive to make of them a Kind of Bread, which might be sufficient with Milk to keep me alive, till I could make my Escape to some other Country, and to Creatures of my own Species. The Horse immediately ordered a white Mare-servant of his Family to bring me a good Quantity of Oats in a Sort of wooden Tray. These I heated before the Fire as well as I could, and rubbed them till the Husks came off, which I made a shift to winnow from the Grain; I ground and beat them between two Stones, then took Water, and made them into a Paste or Cake, which I toasted at the Fire, and eat warm with Milk. It was at first a very insipid Diet, although common enough in many Parts of *Europe,* but grew tolerable by Time; and having been often reduced to hard Fare in my Life, this was not the first Experiment I had made how easily Nature is satisfied. And I cannot but observe, that I never had one Hour's Sickness, while I staid in this Island. It is true, I sometimes made a shift to catch a Rabbet, or Bird, by Springes made of *Yahoos* Hairs; and I often gathered wholesome Herbs, which I boiled, or eat as Salades with my Bread; and now and then, for a Rarity, I made a little Butter, and drank the Whey. I was at first at a great Loss for Salt; but Custom soon reconciled the Want of it; and I am confident that the frequent Use of Salt among us is an Effect of Luxury, and was first introduced only as a Provocative to Drink; except where it is necessary for preserving of Flesh in long Voyages, or in Places remote from great Markets. For we observe no Animal to be fond of it but Man: And as to myself, when I left this Country, it was a great while before I could endure the Taste of it in any thing that I eat.

THIS is enough to say upon the Subject of my Dyet, wherewith other Travellers fill their Books, as if the Readers were personally concerned, whether we fare well or ill. However, it was necessary to mention this Matter, lest the World should think it impossible that I could find Sustenance for three Years in such a Country, and among such Inhabitants.

WHEN it grew towards Evening, the Master Horse ordered a Place for me to lodge in; it was but Six Yards from the House, and separated from the Stable of the *Yahoos.* Here I got some Straw, and covering myself with my own Cloaths, slept very sound. But I was in a short time better accommodated, as the Reader shall know hereafter, when I come to treat more particularly about my Way of living.

CHAPTER III

The Author studious to learn the Language, the Houyhnhnm *his Master assists in teaching him. The Language described. Several* Houyhnhnms *of Quality come out of Curiosity to see the Author. He gives his Master a short Account of his Voyage.*

My principal Endeavour was to learn the Language, which my Master (for so I shall henceforth call him) and his Children, and every Servant of his House were desirous to teach me. For they looked upon it as a Prodigy, that a brute Animal should discover such Marks of a rational Creature. I pointed to every thing, and enquired the Name of it, which I wrote down in my *Journal Book* when I was alone, and corrected my bad Accent, by desiring those of the Family to pronounce it often. In this Employment, a Sorrel Nag, one of the under Servants, was very ready to assist me.

In speaking, they pronounce through the Nose and Throat, and their Language approaches nearest to the *High Dutch* or *German*,[8] of any I know in *Europe*; but is much more graceful and significant. The Emperor *Charles* V. made almost the same Observation when he said, That if he were to speak to his Horse, it should be in *High Dutch*.

The Curiosity and Impatience of my Master were so great, that he spent many Hours of his Leisure to instruct me. He was convinced (as he afterwards told me) that I must be a *Yahoo*, but my Teachableness, Civility and Cleanliness astonished him; which were Qualities altogether so opposite to those Animals. He was most perplexed about my Cloaths, reasoning sometimes with himself, whether they were a Part of my Body; for I never pulled them off till the Family were asleep, and got them on before they waked in the Morning. My Master was eager to learn from whence I came; how I acquired those Appearances of Reason, which I discovered[9] in all my Actions; and to know my Story from my own Mouth, which he hoped he should soon do by the great Proficiency I made in learning and pronouncing their Words and Sentences. To help my Memory, I formed all I learned into the *English* Alphabet, and writ the Words down with the Translations. This last, after some time, I ventured to do in my Master's Presence. It cost me much Trouble to explain to him what I was doing; for the Inhabitants have not the least Idea of Books or Literature.[10]

IN about ten Weeks time I was able to understand most of his Questions; and in three Months could give him some tolerable Answers. He was extremely curious to know from what Part of the Country I came, and how I was taught to imitate a rational Creature; because the *Yahoos,* (whom he saw I exactly resembled in my Head, Hands and Face, that were only visible,) with some Appearance of Cunning, and the strongest Disposition to Mischief, were observed to be the most unteachable of all Brutes. I answered; that I came over the Sea, from a far Place, with many others of my own Kind, in a great hollow Vessel made of the Bodies of Trees: That, my Companions forced me to land on this Coast, and then left me to shift for myself. It was with some Difficulty, and by the Help of many Signs, that I brought him to understand me. He replied, That I must needs be mistaken, or that I *said the thing which was not.* (For they have no Word in their Language to express Lying or Falshood.) He knew it was impossible that there could be a Country beyond the Sea,[11] or that a Parcel of Brutes could move a wooden Vessel whither they pleased upon Water. He was sure no *Houyhnhnm* alive could make such a Vessel, or would trust *Yahoos* to manage it.

THE Word *Houyhnhnm,* in their Tongue, signifies a *Horse;* and in its Etymology, *the Perfection of Nature.*[12] I told my Master, that I was at a Loss for Expression, but would improve as fast as I could; and hoped in a short time I should be able to tell him Wonders: He was pleased to direct his own Mare, his Colt and Fole, and the Servants of the Family to take all Opportunities of instructing me; and every Day for two or three Hours, he was at the same Pains himself: Several Horses and Mares of Quality in the Neighbourhood came often to our House, upon the Report spread of a wonderful *Yahoo,* that could speak like a *Houyhnhnm,* and seemed in his Words and Actions to discover some Glimmerings of Reason. These delighted to converse with me; they put many Questions, and received such Answers, as I was able to return. By all which Advantages, I made so great a Progress, that in five Months from my Arrival, I understood whatever was spoke, and could express myself tolerably well.

THE *Houyhnhnms* who came to visit my Master, out of a Design of seeing and talking with me, could hardly believe me to be a right *Yahoo*, because my Body had a different Covering from others of my Kind. They were astonished to observe me without the usual Hair or Skin, except on my Head, Face and Hands: But I discovered that Secret to my Master, upon an Accident, which happened about a Fortnight before.

I HAVE already told the Reader, that every Night when the Family were gone to Bed, it was my Custom to strip and cover myself with my Cloaths: It happened one Morning early, that my Master sent for me, by the Sorrel Nag, who was his Valet; when he came, I was fast asleep, my Cloaths fallen off on one Side, and my Shirt above my Waste. I awaked at the Noise he made, and observed him to deliver his Message in some Disorder; after which he went to my Master, and in a great Fright gave him a very confused Account of what he had seen: This I presently discovered; for going as soon as I was dressed, to pay my Attendance upon his Honour, he asked me the Meaning of what his Servant had reported; that I was not the same Thing when I slept as I appeared to be at other times; that his Valet assured him, some Part of me was white, some yellow, at least not so white, and some brown.

I HAD hitherto concealed the Secret of my Dress, in order to distinguish myself as much as possible, from that cursed Race of *Yahoos;* but now I found it in vain to do so any longer. Besides, I considered that my Cloaths and Shoes would soon wear out, which already were in a declining Condition, and must be supplied by some Contrivance from the Hides of *Yahoos,* or other Brutes; whereby the whole Secret would be known. I therefore told my Master, that in the Country from whence I came, those of my Kind always covered their Bodies with the Hairs of certain Animals prepared by Art, as well for Decency, as to avoid Inclemencies of Air both hot and cold; of which, as to my own Person I would give him immediate Conviction, if he pleased to command me; only desiring his Excuse, if I did not expose those Parts that Nature taught us to conceal. He said, my Discourse was all very strange, but especially the last Part; for he could not understand why Nature should teach us to conceal what Nature had given. That neither himself nor Family were ashamed of any Parts of their Bodies; but however I might do as I pleased. Whereupon I first unbuttoned my Coat, and pulled it off. I did the same with my Wastecoat; I drew off my Shoes, Stockings and Breeches. I let my Shirt down to my Waste, and drew up the Bottom, fastening it like a Girdle about my Middle to hide my Nakedness.

MY Master observed the whole Performance with great Signs of Curiosity and Admiration. He took up all my Cloaths in his Pastern, one Piece after another, and examined them diligently; he then stroaked my Body very gently, and looked round me several Times; after which he said, it was plain I must be a perfect *Yahoo;* but that I differed very much from the rest of my Species, in the Whiteness, and Smoothness of my Skin, my want of Hair in several Parts of my Body, the Shape and Shortness of my Claws behind and before, and my Affectation of walking continually on my two hinder Feet. He desired to see no more; and gave me leave to put on my Cloaths again, for I was shuddering with Cold.

I EXPRESSED my Uneasiness at his giving me so often the Appellation of *Yahoo,* an odious Animal, for which I had so utter an Hatred and Contempt. I begged he would forbear applying that Word to me, and take the same Order in his Family, and among his Friends whom he suffered to see me. I requested likewise, that the Secret of my having a false Covering to my Body might be known to none but himself, at least as long as my present Cloathing should last: For as to what the Sorrel Nag his Valet had observed, his Honour might command him to conceal it.

ALL this my Master very graciously consented[13] to; and thus the Secret was kept till my Cloaths began to wear out, which I was forced to supply by several Contrivances, that shall hereafter be mentioned. In the mean Time, he desired I would go on with my utmost Diligence to learn their Language, because he was more astonished at my Capacity for Speech and Reason, than at the Figure of my Body, whether it were covered or no; adding, that he waited with some Impatience to hear the Wonders which I promised to tell him.

FROM thenceforward he doubled the Pains he had been at to instruct me; he brought me into all Company, and made them treat me with Civility, because, as he told them privately, this would put me into good Humour, and make me more diverting.

EVERY Day when I waited on him, beside the Trouble he was at in teaching, he would ask me several Questions concerning my self, which I answered as well as I could; and by those Means he had already received some general Ideas, although very imperfect. It would be tedious to relate the several Steps, by which I advanced to a more regular Conversation: But the first Account I gave of my self in any Order and Length, was to this Purpose:

THAT, I came from a very far Country, as I already had attempted to tell him, with about fifty more of my own Species; that we travelled upon the Seas, in a great hollow Vessel made of Wood, and larger than his Honour's House. I described the Ship to him in the best Terms I could; and explained by the Help of my Handkerchief displayed, how it was driven forward by the Wind. That, upon a Quarrel among us, I was set on Shoar on this Coast, where I walked forward without knowing whither, till he delivered me from the Persecution of those execrable *Yahoos*. He asked me, Who made the Ship, and how it was possible that the *Houynhnhnms* of my Country would leave it to the Management of Brutes? My Answer was, that I durst proceed no farther in my Relation, unless he would give me his Word and Honour that he would not be offended; and then I would tell him the Wonders I had so often promised. He agreed; and I went on by assuring him, that the Ship was made by Creatures like myself, who in all the Countries I had travelled, as well as in my own, were the only governing, rational Animals; and that upon my Arrival hither, I was as much astonished to see the *Houyhnhnms* act like rational Beings, as he or his Friends could be in finding some Marks of Reason in a Creature he was pleased to call a *Yahoo*,[14] to which I owned my Resemblance in every Part, but could not account for their degenerate and brutal Nature. I said farther, That if good Fortune ever restored me to my native Country, to relate my Travels hither, as I resolved to do; every Body would believe that I *said the Thing which was not;* that I invented the Story out of my own Head: And with all possible Respect to Himself, his Family, and Friends, and under his Promise of not being offended, our Countrymen would hardly think it probable, that a *Houyhnhnm* should be the presiding Creature of a Nation, and a *Yahoo* the Brute.

CHAPTER IV

The Houyhnhnms *Notion of Truth and Falshood. The Author's Discourse disapproved by his Master. The Author gives a more particular Account of himself, and the Accidents of his Voyage.*

My Master heard me with great Appearances of Uneasiness in his Countenance; because *Doubting* or *not believing,* are so little known in this Country, that the Inhabitants cannot tell how to behave themselves under such Circumstances. And I remember in frequent Discourses with my Master concerning the Nature of Manhood, in other Parts of the World; having Occasion to talk of *Lying,* and *false Representation,* it was with much Difficulty that he comprehended what I meant; although he had otherwise a most acute Judgment. For he argued thus; That the Use of Speech was to make us understand one another, and to receive Information of Facts; now if any one *said the Thing which was not,* these Ends were defeated; because I cannot properly be said to understand him; and I am so far from receiving Information, that he leaves me worse than in Ignorance; for I am led to believe a Thing *Black* when it is *White,* and *Short* when it is *Long.* And these were all the Notions he had concerning that Faculty of *Lying,* so perfectly well understood, and so universally practised among human Creatures.

To return from this Digression; when I asserted that the *Yahoos* were the only governing Animals in my Country, which my Master said was altogether past his Conception, he desired to know, whether we had *Houyhnhnms* among us, and what was their Employment: I told him, we had great Numbers; that in Summer they grazed in the Fields, and in Winter were kept in Houses, with Hay and Oats, where *Yahoo*-Servants were employed to rub their Skins smooth, comb their Manes, pick their Feet, serve them with Food, and make their Beds. I understand you well, said my Master; it is now very plain from all you have spoken, that whatever Share of Reason the *Yahoos* pretend to, the *Houyhnhnms* are your Masters; I heartily wish our *Yahoos* would be so tractable. I begged his Honour would please to excuse me from proceeding any farther, because I was very certain that the Account he expected from me would be highly displeasing. But he insisted in commanding me to let him know the best and the worst: I told him he should be obeyed. I owned, that the *Houyhnhnms* among us, whom we called *Horses*, were the most generous and comely Animal we had; that they excelled in Strength and Swiftness; and when they belonged to Persons of Quality, employed in Travelling, Racing, and drawing Chariots, they were treated with much Kindness and Care, till they fell into Diseases, or became foundered in the Feet; but then they were sold, and used to all kind of Drudgery till they died; after which their Skins were stripped and sold for what they were worth, and their Bodies left to be devoured by Dogs and Birds of Prey. But the common Race of Horses had not so good Fortune, being kept by Farmers and Carriers, and other mean People, who put them to greater Labour, and feed them worse. I described as well as I could, our Way of Riding; the Shape and Use of a Bridle, a Saddle, a Spur, and a Whip; of Harness and Wheels. I added, that we fastened Plates of a certain hard Substance called *Iron* at the Bottom of their Feet, to preserve their Hoofs from being broken by the Stony Ways on which we often travelled.

MY Master, after some Expressions of great Indignation, wondered how we dared to venture upon a *Houyhnhnm*'s Back; for he was sure, that the weakest Servant in his House would be able to shake off the strongest *Yahoo;* or by lying down, and rolling upon his Back, squeeze the Brute to Death. I answered, That our Horses were trained up from three or four Years old to the several Uses we intended them for; That if any of them proved intolerably vicious, they were employed for Carriages; that they were severely beaten while they were young for any mischievous Tricks: That the Males, designed for the common Use of Riding or Draught, were generally *castrated* about two Years after their Birth, to take down their Spirits, and make them more tame and gentle: That they were indeed sensible of Rewards and Punishments; but his Honour would please to consider, that they had not the least Tincture of Reason any more than the *Yahoos* in this Country.

IT put me to the Pains of many Circumlocutions to give my Master a right Idea of what I spoke; for their Language doth not abound in Variety of Words, because their Wants and Passions are fewer than among us. But it is impossible to express his noble Resentment at our savage Treatment of the *Houyhnhnm* Race;[15] particularly after I had explained the Manner and Use of *Castrating* Horses among us, to hinder them from propagating their Kind, and to render them more servile. He said, if it were possible there could be any Country where *Yahoos* alone were endued with Reason, they certainly must be the governing Animal, because Reason will in Time always prevail against Brutal Strength. But, considering the Frame of our Bodies, and especially of mine, he thought no Creature of equal Bulk was so ill-contrived, for employing that Reason in the common Offices of Life; whereupon he desired to know whether those among whom I lived, resembled me or the *Yahoos* of his Country. I assured him, that I was as well shaped as most of my Age; but the younger and the Females were much more soft and tender, and the Skins of the latter generally as white as Milk. He said, I differed indeed from other *Yahoos,* being much more cleanly, and not altogether so deformed; but in point of real Advantage, he thought I differed for the worse. That my Nails were of no Use either to my fore or hinder Feet: As to my fore Feet, he could not properly call them by that Name, for he never observed me to walk upon them; that they were too soft to bear the Ground; that I generally went with them uncovered, neither was the Covering I sometimes wore on them, of the same Shape, or so strong as that on my Feet behind. That I could not walk with any Security; for if either of my hinder Feet slipped, I must inevitably fall. He then began to find fault with other Parts of my Body; the Flatness of my Face, the Prominence of my Nose, mine Eyes placed directly in Front, so that I could not look on either Side without turning my Head: That I was not able to feed my self, without lifting one of my fore Feet to my Mouth; And therefore Nature had placed those Joints to answer that Necessity. He knew not what could be the Use of those several Clefts and Divisions in my Feet behind; that these were too soft to bear the Hardness and Sharpness of Stones without a Covering made from the Skin of some other Brute; that my whole Body wanted a Fence against Heat and Cold, which I was forced to put on and off every Day with Tediousness and Trouble. And lastly, that he observed every Animal in this Country naturally to abhor the *Yahoos,* whom the Weaker avoided, and the Stronger drove from them. So that supposing us to have the Gift of Reason, he could not see how it were possible to cure that natural Antipathy which every Creature discovered against us; nor consequently, how we could tame and render them serviceable. However, he would (as he said) debate the Matter no farther, because he was more desirous to know my own Story, the Country, where I was born, and the several Actions and Events of my Life before I came hither.

I ASSURED him, how extreamly desirous I was that he should be satisfied in every Point; but I doubted much, whether it would be possible for me to explain my self on several Subjects whereof his Honour could have no Conception, because I saw nothing in his Country to which I could resemble them. That however, I would do my best, and strive to express my self by Similitudes, humbly desiring his Assistance when I wanted proper Words; which he was pleased to promise me.

I SAID, my Birth was of honest Parents, in an Island called *England,* which was remote from this Country, as many Days Journey as the strongest of his Honour's Servants could travel in the Annual Course of the Sun. That I was bred a Surgeon, whose Trade it is to cure Wounds and Hurts in the Body, got by Accident or Violence. That my Country was governed by a Female Man, whom we called a *Queen.* That I left it to get Riches, whereby I might maintain my self and Family when I should return. That in my last Voyage, I was Commander of the Ship and had about fifty *Yahoos* under me, many of which died at Sea, and I was forced to supply them by others picked out from several Nations. That our Ship was twice in Danger of being sunk; the first Time by a great Storm, and the second, by striking against a Rock. Here my Master interposed, by asking me, How I could persuade Strangers out of different Countries to venture with me, after the Losses I had sustained, and the Hazards I had run. I said, they were Fellows of desperate Fortunes, forced to fly from the Places of their Birth, on Account of their Poverty or their Crimes. Some were undone by Law-suits; others spent all they had in Drinking, Whoring and Gaming; others fled for Treason; many for Murder, Theft, Poysoning, Robbery, Perjury, Forgery, Coining false Money; for committing Rapes or Sodomy; for flying from their Colours,[16] or deserting to the Enemy; and most of them had broken Prison. None of these durst return to their native Countries for fear of being hanged, or of starving in a Jail; and therefore were under a Necessity of seeking a Livelihood in other Places.

DURING this Discourse, my Master was pleased often to interrupt me. I had made Use of many Circumlocutions in describing to him the Nature of the several Crimes, for which most of our Crew had been forced to fly their Country. This Labour took up several Days Conversation before he was able to comprehend me. He was wholly at a Loss to know what could be the Use or Necessity of practising those Vices. To clear up which I endeavoured to give him some Ideas of the Desire of Power and Riches; of the terrible Effects of Lust, Intemperance, Malice, and Envy. All this I was forced to define and describe by putting of Cases, and making Suppositions. After which, like one whose Imagination was struck with something never seen or heard of before, he would lift up his Eyes with Amazement and Indignation. Power, Government, War, Law, Punishment, and a Thousand other Things had no Terms, wherein that Language could express them; which made the Difficulty almost insuperable to give my Master any Conception of what I meant: But being of an excellent Understanding, much improved by Contemplation and Converse, he at last arrived at a competent Knowledge of what human Nature in our Parts of the World is capable to perform; and desired I would give him some particular Account of that Land, which we call *Europe*, especially, of my own Country.

CHAPTER V

The Author at his Master's Commands informs him of the State
of England. The Causes of War among the Princes of Europe.
The Author begins to explain the English Constitution.

The Reader may please observe, that the following Extract of many Conversations I had with my Master, contains a Summary of the most material Points, which were discoursed at several times for above two Years; his Honour often desiring fuller Satisfaction as I farther improved in the *Houyhnhnm* Tongue. I laid before him, as well as I could, the whole State of *Europe;* I discoursed of Trade and Manufactures, of Arts and Sciences; and the Answers I gave to all the Questions he made, as they arose upon several Subjects, were a Fund of Conversation not to be exhausted. But I shall here only set down the Substance of what passed between us concerning my own Country, reducing it into Order as well as I can, without any Regard to Time or other Circumstances, while I strictly adhere to Truth. My only Concern is, that I shall hardly be able to do Justice to my Master's Arguments and Expressions, which must needs suffer by my Want of Capacity, as well as by a Translation into our barbarous *English.*

IN Obedience therefore to his Honour's Commands, I related to him the *Revolution*[17] under the Prince of *Orange;* the long War with *France* entered into by the said Prince, and renewed by his Successor the present Queen; wherein the greatest Powers of *Christendom* were engaged, and which still continued: I computed at his Request, that about a Million of *Yahoos* might have been killed in the whole Progress of it; and perhaps a Hundred or more Cities taken, and five times as many Ships burnt or sunk.

HE asked me what were the usual Causes or Motives that made one Country go to War with another. I answered, they were innumerable; but I should only mention a few of the chief. Sometimes the Ambition of

Princes, who never think they have Land or People enough to govern: Sometimes the Corruption of Ministers, who engage their Master in a War in order to stifle or divert the Clamour of the Subjects against their evil Administration. Difference in Opinions[18] hath cost many Millions of Lives: For Instance, whether *Flesh* be *Bread,* or *Bread* be *Flesh:* Whether the Juice of a certain *Berry* be *Blood* or *Wine:* Whether *Whistling* be a Vice or a Virtue: Whether it be better to *kiss a Post,* or throw it into the Fire: What is the best Colour for a *Coat,* whether *Black, White, Red* or *Grey;* and whether it should be *long* or *short, narrow* or *wide, dirty* or *clean;* with many more.[19] Neither are any Wars so furious and bloody, or of so long Continuance, as those occasioned by Difference in Opinion, especially if it be in things indifferent.

SOMETIMES the Quarrel between two Princes is to decide which of them shall dispossess a Third of his Dominions, where neither of them pretend to any Right. Sometimes one Prince quarrelleth with another, for fear the other should quarrel with him. Sometimes a War is entered upon, because the Enemy is too *strong,* and sometimes because he is too *weak.* Sometimes our Neighbours *want* the *Things* which we *have,* or *have* the Things which we want; and we both fight, till they take ours or give us theirs. It is a very justifiable Cause of War to invade a Country after the People have been wasted by Famine, destroyed by Pestilence, or embroiled by Factions amongst themselves. It is justifiable to enter into a War against our nearest Ally, when one of his Towns lies convenient for us, or a Territory of Land, that would render our Dominions round and compact. If a Prince send Forces into a Nation, where the People are poor and ignorant, he may lawfully put half of them to Death, and make Slaves of the rest, in order to civilize and reduce them from their barbarous Way of Living. It is a very kingly, honourable, and frequent Practice, when one Prince desires the Assistance of another to secure him against an Invasion, that the Assistant, when he hath driven out the Invader, should seize on the Dominions himself, and kill, imprison or banish the Prince he came to relieve. Allyance by Blood or Marriage, is a sufficient Cause of War between Princes; and the nearer the Kindred is, the greater is their Disposition to quarrel: *Poor* Nations are *hungry,* and *rich* Nations are *proud;* and Pride and Hunger will ever be at Variance. For these Reasons, the Trade of a *Soldier* is held the most honourable of all others: Because a *Soldier* is a *Yahoo* hired to kill in cold Blood as many of his own Species, who have never offended him, as possibly he can.

THERE is likewise a Kind of beggarly Princes in *Europe,* not able to

584 · *Gulliver's Travels*

make War by themselves, who hire out their Troops to richer Nations for so much a Day to each Man; of which they keep three Fourths to themselves, and it is the best Part of their Maintenance; such are those in many *Northern* Parts[20] of *Europe*.

WHAT you have told me, (said my Master) upon the Subject of War, doth indeed discover most admirably the Effects of that Reason you pretend to: However, it is happy that the *Shame* is greater than the *Danger;* and that Nature hath left you utterly uncapable of doing much Mischief: For your Mouths lying flat with your Faces, you can hardly bite each other to any Purpose, unless by Consent. Then, as to the Claws upon your Feet before and behind, they are so short and tender, that one of our *Yahoos* would drive a Dozen of yours before him. And therefore in recounting the Numbers of those who have been killed in Battle, I cannot but think that you have *said the Thing which is not.*

I COULD not forbear shaking my Head and smiling a little at his Ignorance. And, being no Stranger to the Art of War, I gave him a Description of Cannons, Culverins, Muskets, Carabines, Pistols, Bullets, Powder, Swords, Bayonets, Sieges, Retreats, Attacks, Undermines, Countermines, Bombardments, Seafights; Ships sunk with a Thousand Men; twenty Thousand killed on each Side; dying Groans, Limbs flying in the Air: Smoak, Noise, Confusion, trampling to Death under Horses Feet: Flight, Pursuit, Victory; Fields strewed with Carcases left for Food to Dogs, and Wolves, and Birds of Prey; Plundering, Stripping, Ravishing, Burning and Destroying. And, to set forth the Valour of my own dear Countrymen, I assured him, that I had seen them blow up a Hundred Enemies at once in a Siege, and as many in a Ship; and beheld the dead Bodies drop down in Pieces from the Clouds, to the great Diversion of all the Spectators.

I WAS going on to more Particulars, when my Master commanded me Silence. He said, whoever understood the Nature of *Yahoos* might easily believe it possible for so vile an Animal, to be capable of every Action I had named, if their Strength and Cunning equalled their Malice. But, as my Discourse had increased his Abhorrence of the whole Species, so he found it gave him a Disturbance in his Mind, to which he was wholly a Stranger before. He thought his Ears being used to such abominable Words, might by Degrees admit them with less Detestation. That, although he hated the *Yahoos* of this Country, yet he no more blamed them for their odious Qualities, than he did a *Gnnayh* (a Bird of Prey) for its Cruelty, or a sharp Stone for cutting his Hoof. But, when a Creature pretending to Reason, could be capable of such Enormities, he dreaded lest the Corruption of that Faculty might be worse than Brutality itself. He seemed therefore confident, that instead of Reason, we were only possessed of some Quality fitted to increase our natural Vices; as the Reflection from a troubled Stream returns the Image of an ill-shapen Body, not only *larger,* but more *distorted.*

HE added, That he had heard too much upon the Subject of War, both in this, and some former Discourses. There was another Point which a little perplexed him at present. I had said, that some of our Crew left their Country on Account of being ruined by *Law:* That I had already explained the Meaning of the Word; but he was at a Loss how it should come to pass, that the *Law* which was intended for *every* Man's Preservation, should be any Man's Ruin. Therefore he desired to be farther satisfied what I meant by *Law,* and the Dispensers thereof, according to the present Practice in my own Country: Because he thought, Nature and Reason were sufficient Guides[21] for a reasonable Animal, as we pretended to be, in shewing us what we ought to do, and what to avoid.

I ASSURED his Honour, that *Law* was a Science wherein I had not much conversed, further than by employing Advocates, in vain, upon some Injustices that had been done me. However, I would give him all the Satisfaction I was able.

I SAID there was a Society of Men among us, bred up from their Youth in the Art of proving by Words multiplied for the Purpose, that *White* is *Black,* and *Black* is *White,* according as they are paid. To this Society all the rest of the People are Slaves.

FOR Example. If my Neighbour hath a mind to my *Cow,* he hires a Lawyer to prove that he ought to have my *Cow* from me. I must then hire another to defend my Right; it being against all Rules of *Law* that any Man should be allowed to speak for himself. Now in this Case, I who am the true Owner lie under two great Disadvantages. First, my Lawyer being practiced almost from his Cradle in defending Falshood; is quite out of his Element when he would be an Advocate for Justice, which as an Office unnatural, he always attempts with great Awkwardness, if not with Ill-will. The second Disadvantage is, that my Lawyer must proceed with great Caution: Or else he will be reprimanded by the Judges, and abhorred by his Brethren, as one who would lessen the Practice of the Law. And therefore I have but two Methods to preserve my *Cow.* The first is, to gain over my Adversary's Lawyer with a double Fee; who will then betray his Client, by insinuating that he hath Justice on his Side. The second Way is for my Lawyer to make my Cause appear as unjust as he can; by allowing the *Cow* to belong to my Adversary; and this if it be skilfully done, will certainly bespeak the Favour of the Bench.

NOW, your Honour is to know, that these Judges are Persons appointed to decide all Controversies of Property, as well as for the Tryal of Criminals; and picked out from the most dextrous Lawyers who are grown old or lazy: And having been byassed all their Lives against Truth and Equity, are under such a fatal Necessity of favouring Fraud, Perjury and Oppression; that I have known some of them to have refused a large Bribe from the Side where Justice lay, rather than injure the *Faculty*,[22] by doing any thing unbecoming their Nature or their Office.

IT is Maxim among these Lawyers, that whatever hath been done before, may legally be done again: And therefore they take special Care to record all the Decisions formerly made against common Justice and the general Reason of Mankind. These, under the Name of *Precedents*, they produce as Authorities to justify the most iniquitous Opinions; and the Judges never fail of decreeing accordingly.

IN pleading, they studiously avoid entering into the *Merits* of the Cause; but are loud, violent and tedious in dwelling upon all *Circumstances* which are not to the Purpose. For Instance, in the Case already mentioned: They never desire to know what Claim or Title my Adversary hath to my *Cow*; but whether the said *Cow* were Red or Black; her Horns long or short; whether the Field I graze her in be round or square; whether she were milked at home or abroad; what Diseases she is subject to, and the like. After which they consult *Precedents*, adjourn the Cause, from Time to Time, and in Ten, Twenty, or Thirty Years come to an Issue.

IT is likewise to be observed, that this Society hath a peculiar Cant and Jargon of their own, that no other Mortal can understand, and wherein all their Laws are written, which they take special Care to multiply; whereby they have wholly confounded the very Essence of Truth and Falshood, of Right and Wrong; so that it will take Thirty Years to decide whether the Field, left me by my Ancestors for six Generations, belong to me, or to a Stranger three Hundred Miles off.

IN the Tryal of Persons accused for Crimes against the State, the Method is much more short and commendable: The Judge first sends to sound the Disposition of those in Power; after which he can easily hang or save the Criminal, strictly preserving all the Forms of Law.

HERE my Master interposing, said it was a Pity, that Creatures endowed with such prodigious Abilities of Mind as these Lawyers, by the Description I gave of them must certainly be, were not rather encouraged to be Instructors of others in Wisdom and Knowledge. In Answer to which, I assured his Honour, that in all Points out of their own Trade, they were usually the most ignorant and stupid Generation among us, the most despicable in common Conversation, avowed Enemies to all Knowledge and Learning; and equally disposed to pervert the general Reason of Mankind, in every other Subject of Discourse, as in that of their own Profession.

CHAPTER VI

A Continuation of the State of England, *under Queen* Anne. *The Character of a first Minister in the Courts of* Europe.

My Master was yet wholly at a Loss to understand what Motives could incite this Race of Lawyers to perplex, disquiet, and weary themselves by engaging in a Confederacy of Injustice, merely for the Sake of injuring their Fellow-Animals; neither could he comprehend what I meant in saying they did it for *Hire.* Whereupon I was at much Pains to describe to him the Use of *Money,* the Materials it was made of, and the Value of the Metals: That when a *Yahoo* had got a great Store of this precious Substance, he was able to purchase whatever he had a mind to; the finest Cloathing, the noblest Houses, great Tracts of Land, the most costly Meats and Drinks; and have his Choice of the most beautiful Females. Therefore since *Money* alone, was able to perform all these Feats, our *Yahoos* thought, they could never have enough of it to spend or to save, as they found themselves inclined from their natural Bent either to Profusion or Avarice. That, the rich Man enjoyed the Fruit of the poor Man's Labour, and the latter were a Thousand to One in Proportion to the former. That the Bulk of our People was forced to live miserably, by labouring every Day for small Wages to make a few live plentifully. I enlarged myself much on these and many other Particulars to the same Purpose: But his Honour was still to seek:[23] For he went upon a Supposition that all Animals had a Title to their Share in the Productions of the Earth; and especially those who presided over the rest. Therefore he desired I would let him know, what these costly Meats were, and how any of us happened to want them. Whereupon I enumerated as many Sorts as came into my Head, with the various Methods of dressing them, which could not be done without sending Vessels by

Sea to every Part of the World, as well for Liquors to drink, as for Sauces, and innumerable other Conveniencies. I assured him, that this whole Globe of Earth must be at least three Times gone round, before one of our better Female *Yahoos* could get her Breakfast, or a Cup to put it in. He said, That must needs be a miserable Country which cannot furnish Food for its own Inhabitants. But what he chiefly wondered at, was how such vast Tracts of Ground as I described, should be wholly without *Fresh water,* and the People put to the Necessity of sending over the Sea for Drink. I replied, that *England* (the dear Place of my Nativity) was computed to produce three Times the Quantity of Food, more than its Inhabitants are able to consume, as well as Liquors extracted from Grain, or pressed out of the Fruit of certain Trees, which made excellent Drink; and the same Proportion in every other Convenience of Life. But, in order to feed the Luxury and Intemperance of the Males, and the Vanity of the Females, we sent away the greatest Part of our necessary Things to other Countries, from whence in Return we brought the Materials of Diseases, Folly, and Vice, to spend among ourselves. Hence it follows of Necessity, that vast Numbers of our People are compelled to seek their Livelihood by Begging, Robbing, Stealing, Cheating, Pimping, Forswearing, Flattering, Suborning, Forging, Gaming, Lying, Fawning, Hectoring, Voting, Scribling, Stargazing, Poysoning, Whoring, Canting, Libelling, Free-thinking, and the like Occupations: Every one of which Terms, I was at much Pains to make him understand.

THAT, *Wine* was not imported among us from foreign Countries, to supply the Want of Water or other Drinks, but because it was a Sort of Liquid which made us merry, by putting us out of our Senses; diverted all melancholy Thoughts, begat wild extravagant Imaginations in the Brain, raised our Hopes, and banished our Fears; suspended every Office of Reason for a Time, and deprived us of the Use of our Limbs, untill we fell into a profound Sleep; although it must be confessed, that we always awaked sick and dispirited; and that the Use of this Liquor filled us with Diseases, which made our Lives uncomfortable and short.

BUT beside all this, the Bulk of our People supported themselves by furnishing the Necessities or Conveniencies of Life to the Rich, and to each other. For Instance, when I am at home and dressed as I ought to be, I carry on my Body the Workmanship of an Hundred Tradesmen; the Building and Furniture of my House employ as many more; and five Times the Number to adorn my Wife.[24]

I WAS going on to tell him of another Sort of People, who get their Livelihood by attending the Sick; having upon some Occasions informed his Honour that many of my Crew had died of Diseases. But here it was with the utmost Difficulty, that I brought him to apprehend what I meant. He could easily conceive, that a *Houyhnhnm* grew weak and heavy a few Days before his Death; or by some Accident might hurt a Limb. But that Nature, who worketh all things to Perfection, should suffer any Pains to breed in our Bodies, he thought impossible; and desired to know the Reason of so unaccountable an Evil. I told him, we fed on a Thousand Things which operated contrary to each other; that we eat when we were not hungry, and drank without the Provocation of Thirst: That we sat whole Nights drinking strong Liquors without eating a Bit; which disposed us to Sloth, enflamed our Bodies, and precipitated or prevented Digestion. That, prostitute Female *Yahoos* acquired a certain Malady, which bred Rottenness in the Bones of those, who fell into their Embraces: That this and many other Diseases, were propagated from Father to Son; so that great Numbers come into the World with complicated Maladies upon them: That, it would be endless to give him a Catalogue of all Diseases incident to human Bodies; for they could not be fewer than five or six Hundred, spread over every Limb, and Joynt: In short, every Part, external and intestine, having Diseases appropriated to each. To remedy which, there was a Sort of People bred up among us, in the Profession or Pretence of curing the Sick. And because I had some Skill in the Faculty, I would in Gratitude to his Honour, let him know the whole Mystery and Method by which they proceed.

THEIR Fundamental is, that all Diseases arise from *Repletion;* from whence they conclude, that a great *Evacuation* of the Body is necessary, either through the natural Passage, or upwards at the Mouth. Their next Business is, from Herbs, Minerals, Gums, Oyls, Shells, Salts, Juices, Seaweed, Excrements, Barks of Trees, Serpents, Toads, Frogs, Spiders, dead Mens Flesh and Bones, Birds, Beasts and Fishes, to form a Composition for Smell and Taste the most abominable, nauseous and detestable, that they can possibly contrive, which the Stomach immediately rejects with Loathing: And this they call a *Vomit.* Or else from the same Store-house, with some other poysonous Additions, they command us to take in at the Orifice *above* or *below,* (just as the Physician then happens to be disposed) a Medicine equally annoying and disgustful to the Bowels; which relaxing the Belly, drives down all before it: And this they call a *Purge,* or a *Clyster.*[25] For Nature (as the Physicians alledge) having intended the superior anterior Orifice only for the *Intromission* of Solids and Liquids, and the inferior Posterior for Ejection; these Artists ingeniously considering that in all

Diseases Nature is forced out of her Seat; therefore to replace her in it, the Body must be treated in a Manner directly contrary, by interchanging the Use of each Orifice; forcing Solids and Liquids in at the *Anus,* and making Evacuations at the Mouth.

BUT, besides real Diseases, we are subject to many that are only imaginary, for which the Physicians have invented imaginary Cures; these have their several Names, and so have the Drugs that are proper for them; and with these our Female *Yahoos* are always infested.

ONE great Excellency in this Tribe is their Skill at *Prognosticks,* wherein they seldom fail; their Predictions in real Diseases, when they rise to any Degree of Malignity, generally portending *Death,* which is always in their Power, when Recovery is not: And therefore, upon any unexpected Signs of Amendment, after they have pronounced their Sentence, rather than be accused as false Prophets, they know how to approve their Sagacity to the World by a seasonable Dose.

THEY are likewise of special Use to Husbands and Wives, who are grown weary of their Mates; to eldest Sons, to great Ministers of State, and often to Princes.

I HAD formerly upon Occasion discoursed with my Master upon the Nature of *Government* in general, and particularly of our own *excellent Constitution,* deservedly the Wonder and Envy of the whole World. But having here accidentally mentioned a *Minister of State;* he commanded me some Time after to inform him, what Species of *Yahoo* I particularly meant by that Appellation.

I TOLD him, that a *First* or *Chief Minister of State,* whom I intended to describe, was a Creature wholly exempt from Joy and Grief, Love and Hatred, Pity and Anger; at least makes use of no other Passions but a violent Desire of Wealth, Power, and Titles: That he applies his Words to all Uses, except to the Indication of his Mind; That he never tells a *Truth,* but with an Intent that you should take it for a *Lye;* nor a *Lye,* but with a Design that you should take it for a *Truth;* That those he speaks worst of behind their Backs, are in the surest way to Preferment; and whenever he begins to praise you to others or to your self, you are from that Day forlorn. The worst Mark you can receive is a *Promise,* especially when it is confirmed with an Oath; after which every wise Man retires, and gives over all Hopes.

THERE are three Methods by which a Man may rise to be Chief Minister; The first is, by knowing how with Prudence to dispose of a Wife, a Daughter, or a Sister: The second, by betraying or undermining his Predecessor: And the third is, by a *furious Zeal* in publick Assemblies against the Corruptions of the Court. But a wise Prince would rather chuse to employ those who practise the last of these Methods; because such Zealots prove always the most obsequious and subservient to the Will and Passions of their Master. That, these *Ministers* having all Employments at their Disposal, preserve themselves in Power by bribing the Majority of a Senate or great Council; and at last by an Expedient called an *Act of Indemnity*[26] (whereof I described the Nature to him) they secure themselves from After-reckonings, and retire from the Publick, laden with the Spoils of the Nation.

THE Palace of a *Chief Minister,* is a Seminary to breed up others in his own Trade: The Pages, Lacquies, and Porter, by imitating their Master, become *Ministers of State* in their several Districts, and learn to excel in the three principal *Ingredients,* of *Insolence, Lying,* and *Bribery.* Accordingly, they have a *Subaltern* Court paid to them by Persons of the best Rank; and sometimes by the Force of Dexterity and Impudence, arrive through several Gradations to be Successors to their Lord.

HE is usually governed by a decayed Wench, or favourite Footman, who are the Tunnels through which all Graces are conveyed, and may properly be called, *in the last Resort,* the Governors of the Kingdom.

ONE Day, my Master, having heard me mention the *Nobility* of my Country, was pleased to make me a Compliment which I could not pretend to deserve: That, he was sure, I must have been born of some Noble Family, because I far exceeded in Shape, Colour, and Cleanliness, all the *Yahoos* of his Nation, although I seemed to fail in Strength, and Agility, which must be imputed to my different Way of Living from those other Brutes; and besides, I was not only endowed with the Faculty of Speech, but likewise with some Rudiments of Reason, to a Degree, that with all his Acquaintance I passed for a Prodigy.

HE made me observe, that among the *Houyhnhnms,* the *White,* the *Sorrel,* and the *Iron-grey,* were not so exactly shaped as the *Bay,* the *Dapple-grey,* and the *Black;* nor born with equal Talents of Mind, or a Capacity to improve them; and therefore continued always in the Condition of Servants, without ever aspiring to match out of their own Race, which in that Country would be reckoned monstrous and unnatural.[27]

I MADE his Honour my most humble Acknowledgements for the good Opinion he was pleased to conceive of me; but assured him at the same Time, that my Birth was of the lower Sort, having been born of plain, honest Parents, who were just able to give me a tolerable Education: That,

Nobility among us was altogether a different Thing from the Idea he had of it; That, our young *Noblemen* are bred from their Childhood in Idleness and Luxury; that, as soon as Years will permit, they consume their Vigour, and contract odious Diseases among lewd Females; and when their Fortunes are almost ruined, they marry some Woman of mean Birth, disagreeable Person, and unsound Constitution, merely for the sake of Money, whom they hate and despise. That, the Productions of such Marriages are generally scrophulous, rickety or deformed Children; by which Means the Family seldom continues above three Generations, unless the Wife take Care to provide a healthy Father among her Neighbours, or Domesticks, in order to improve and continue the Breed. That, a weak diseased Body, a meager Countenance, and sallow Complexion, are the true Marks of *noble Blood;* and a healthy robust Appearance is so disgraceful in a Man of Quality, that the World concludes his real Father to have been a Groom or a Coachman. The Imperfections of his Mind run parallel with those of his Body; being a Composition of Spleen, Dulness, Ignorance, Caprice, Sensuality and Pride.

WITHOUT the Consent of this illustrious Body, no Law can be enacted, repealed, or altered: And these Nobles have likewise the Decision of all our Possessions without Appeal.

The Author's great Love of his Native Country. His Master's Observations upon the Constitution and Administration of En-gland, as described by the Author, with parallel Cases and Comparisons. His Master's Observations upon human Nature.

The Reader may be disposed to wonder how I could prevail on my self to give so free a Representation of my own Species, among a Race of Mortals who were already too apt to conceive the vilest Opinion of Human Kind, from that entire Congruity betwixt me and their *Yahoos*. But I must freely confess, that the many Virtues of those excellent *Quadrupeds* placed in opposite View to human Corruptions, had so far opened mine Eyes, and enlarged my Understanding, that I began to view the Actions and Passions of Man in a very different Light; and to think the Honour of my own Kind not worth managing;[28] which, besides, it was impossible for me to do before a Person of so acute a Judgment as my Master, who daily convinced me of a thousand Faults in my self, whereof I had not the least Perception before, and which with us would never be numbered even among human Infirmities. I had likewise learned from his Example an utter Detestation of all Falsehood or Disguise; and *Truth* appeared so amiable to me, that I determined upon sacrificing every thing to it.

Let me deal so candidly with the Reader, as to confess, that there was yet a much stronger Motive for the Freedom I took in my Representation of Things. I had not been a Year in this Country, before I contracted such a Love and Veneration for the Inhabitants, that I entered on a firm Resolution never to return to human Kind, but to pass the rest of my Life among these admirable *Houyhnhnms* in the Contemplation and Practice of every Virtue; where I could have no Example or Incitement to Vice. But it was decreed by Fortune, my perpetual Enemy, that so great a Felicity should not fall to my Share. However, it is now some Comfort to reflect, that in what I said of my Countrymen, I *extenuated* their Faults as much as I durst before so strict an Examiner; and upon every Article, gave as *favourable* a Turn as the Matter would bear. For, indeed, who is there alive that will not be swayed by his Byass and Partiality to the Place of his Birth?

I HAVE related the Substance of several Conversations I had with my Master, during the greatest Part of the Time I had the Honour to be in his Service; but have indeed for Brevity sake omitted much more than is here set down.

WHEN I had answered all his Questions, and his Curiosity seemed to be fully satisfied; he sent for me on Morning early, and commanding me to sit down at some Distance, (an Honour which he had never before conferred upon me) He said, he had been very seriously considering my whole Story, as far as it related both to my self and my Country: That, he looked upon us as a Sort of Animals to whose Share, by what Accident he could not conjecture, some small Pittance of *Reason* had fallen, whereof we made no other Use than by its Assistance to aggravate our *natural* Corruptions, and to acquire new ones which Nature had not given us. That, we disarmed our selves of the few Abilities she had bestowed; had been very successful in multiplying our original Wants, and seemed to spend our whole Lives in vain Endeavours to supply them by our own Inventions. That, as to my self, it was manifest I had neither the Strength or Agility of a common *Yahoo;* that I walked infirmly on my hinder Feet; had found out a Contrivance to make my Claws of no Use or Defence, and to remove the Hair from my Chin, which was intended as a Shelter from the Sun and the Weather. Lastly, That I could neither run with Speed, nor climb Trees like my *Brethren* (as he called them) the *Yahoos* in this Country.

THAT, our Institutions of *Government* and *Law* were plainly owing to our gross Defects in *Reason,* and by consequence, in *Virtue;* because *Reason* alone is sufficient to govern a *Rational* Creature; which was therefore a Character we had no Pretence to challenge, even from the Account I had given of my own People; although he manifestly perceived, that in order to favour them, I had concealed many Particulars, and often *said the Thing which was not.*

HE was the more confirmed in this Opinion, because he observed, that as I agreed in every Feature of my Body with other *Yahoos,* except where it was to my real Disadvantage in point of Strength, Speed and Activity, the Shortness of my Claws, and some other Particulars where Nature had no Part; so, from the Representation I had given him of our Lives, our Manners, and our Actions, he found as near a Resemblance in the Disposition of our Minds. He said, the *Yahoos* were known to hate one another more than they did any different Species of Animals; and the Reason usually assigned, was, the Odiousness of their own Shapes, which all could see in the rest, but not in themselves. He had therefore begun to think it not unwise in us to *cover* our Bodies, and by that Invention, conceal many of our Deformities from each other, which would else be hardly supportable. But, he now found he had been mistaken; and that the Dissentions of those Brutes in his Country were owing to the same Cause with ours, as I had described them. For, if (said he) you throw among five *Yahoos* as much Food as would be sufficient for fifty, they will, instead of eating peaceably, fall together by the Ears, each single one impatient to *have all to it self;* and therefore a Servant was usually employed to stand by while they were feeding abroad, and those kept at home were tied at a Distance from each other. That, if a Cow died of Age or Accident, before a *Houyhnhnm* could secure it for his own *Yahoos,* those in the Neighbourhood would come in Herds to seize it, and then would ensue such a Battle as I had described, with terrible Wounds made by their Claws on both Sides, although they seldom were able to kill one another, for want of such convenient Instruments of Death as we had invented. At other Times the like Battles have been fought between the *Yahoos* of several Neighbourhoods without any visible Cause: Those of one District watching all Opportunities to surprise the next before they are prepared. But if they find their Project hath miscarried, they return home, and for want of Enemies, engage in what I call a *Civil War* among themselves.

THAT, in some Fields of his Country, there are certain *shining Stones* of several Colours, whereof the *Yahoos* are violently fond; and when Part of these *Stones* are fixed in the Earth, as it sometimes happeneth, they will dig with their Claws for whole Days to get them out, and carry them away, and hide them by Heaps in their Kennels; but still looking round with great Caution, for fear their Comrades should find out their Treasure. My Master said, he could never discover the Reason of this unnatural Appetite, or how these *Stones* could be of any Use to a *Yahoo;* but now he believed it might proceed from the same Principle of *Avarice,* which I had ascribed to Mankind. That he had once, by way of Experiment, privately removed a Heap of these *Stones* from the Place where one of his *Yahoos* had buried it: Whereupon, the sordid Animal missing his Treasure, by his loud lamenting brought the whole Herd to the Place, there miserably howled, then fell to biting and tearing the rest; began to pine away, would neither eat nor sleep, nor work, till he ordered a Servant privately to convey the *Stones* into the same Hole, and hide them as before; which when his *Yahoo* had found, he presently recovered his Spirits and good Humour; but took Care to remove them to a better hiding Place; and hath ever since been a very serviceable Brute.

My Master farther assured me, which I also observed my self; That in the Fields where these *shining Stones* abound, the fiercest and most frequent Battles are fought, occasioned by perpetual Inroads of the neighbouring *Yahoos.*

He said, it was common when two *Yahoos* discovered such a *Stone* in a Field, and were contending which of them should be the Proprietor, a third would take the Advantage, and carry it away from them both; which my Master would needs contend to have some Resemblance with our *Suits at Law;* wherein I thought it for our Credit not to undeceive him; since the Decision he mentioned was much more equitable than many Decrees among us: Because the Plaintiff and Defendant there lost nothing beside the *Stone* they contended for; whereas our *Courts of Equity,* would never have dismissed the Cause while either of them had any thing left.

My Master continuing his Discourse, said, There was nothing that rendered the *Yahoos* more odious, than their undistinguishing Appetite to devour every thing that came in their Way, whether Herbs, Roots, Berries, corrupted Flesh of Animals, or all mingled together: And it was peculiar in their Temper, that they were fonder of what they could get by Rapine or Stealth at a greater Distance, than much better Food provided for them at home. If their Prey held out, they would eat till they were ready to burst, after which Nature had pointed out to them a certain *Root* that gave them a general Evacuation.

There was also another Kind of *Root* very *juicy,* but something rare and difficult to be found, which the *Yahoos* sought for with much Eagerness, and would suck it with great Delight: It produced the same Effects that Wine hath upon us. It would make them sometimes hug, and sometimes tear one another; they would howl and grin, and chatter, and reel, and tumble, and then fall asleep in the Mud.

I did indeed observe, that the *Yahoos* were the only Animals in this Country subject to any Diseases; which however, were much fewer than Horses have among us, and contracted not by any ill Treatment they meet with, but by the Nastiness and Greediness of that sordid Brute. Neither has their Language any more than a general Appellation for those Maladies; which is borrowed from the Name of the Beast, and called *Hnea Yahoo,* or the *Yahoo's-Evil;* and the Cure prescribed is a Mixture of *their own*

Dung and *Urine*, forcibly put down the *Yahoo's* Throat. This I have since often known to have been taken with Success: And do here freely recommend it to my Countrymen, for the publick Good, as an admirable Specifick against all Diseases produced by Repletion.

As to Learning, Government, Arts, Manufactures, and the like; my Master confessed he could find little or no Resemblance between the *Yahoos* of that Country and those in ours. For, he only meant to observe what Parity there was in our Natures. He had heard indeed some curious *Houyhnhnms* observe, that in most Herds there was a Sort of ruling *Yahoo*, (as among us there is generally some leading or principal Stag in a Park) who was always more *deformed* in Body, and *mischievous in Disposition*, than any of the rest. That, this *Leader* had usually a Favourite as *like himself* as he could get, whose Employment was to *lick his Master's Feet and Posteriors, and drive the Female* Yahoos *to his Kennel;* for which he was now and then rewarded with a Piece of Ass's Flesh. This *Favourite* is hated by the whole Herd; and therefore to protect himself, keeps always *near the Person of his Leader.* He usually continues in Office till a worse can be found; but the very Moment he is discarded, his Successor, at the Head of all the *Yahoos* in that District, Young and Old, Male and Female, come in a Body, and discharge their Excrements upon him from Head to Foot. But how far this might be applicable to our *Courts* and *Favourites*, and *Ministers of State*, my Master said I could best determine.

I DURST make no Return to this malicious Insinuation, which debased human Understanding below the Sagacity of a common *Hound*, who hath Judgment enough to distinguish and follow the Cry of the *ablest Dog in the Pack*, without being ever mistaken.

MY Master told me, there were some Qualities remarkable in the *Yahoos*, which he had not observed me to mention, or at least very slightly, in the Accounts I had given him of human Kind. He said, those Animals, like other Brutes, had their Females in common; but in this they differed, that the She- *Yahoo* would admit the Male, while she was pregnant; and that the Hees would quarrel and fight with the Females as fiercely as with each other. Both which Practices were such Degrees of infamous Brutality, that no other sensitive Creature ever arrived at.

ANOTHTER Thing he wondered at in the *Yahoos*, was their strange Disposition to Nastiness and Dirt; whereas there appears to be a natural Love of Cleanliness in all other Animals. As to the two former Accusations, I was glad to let them pass without any Reply, because I had not a Word to offer upon them in Defence of my Species, which otherwise I certainly had done from my own Inclinations. But I could have easily vindicated human Kind from the Imputation of Singularity upon the last Article, if there had been any *Swine* in that Country, (as unluckily for me there were not) which although it may be a *sweeter Quadruped* than a *Yahoo*, cannot I humbly conceive in Justice pretend to more Cleanliness; and so his Honour himself must have owned, if he had seen their filthy Way of feeding, and their Custom of wallowing and sleeping in the Mud.

MY Master likewise mentioned another Quality, which his Servants had discovered in several *Yahoos*, and to him was wholly unaccountable. He said, a Fancy would sometimes take a *Yahoo*, to retire into a Corner, to lie down and howl, and groan, and spurn away all that came near him, although he were young and fat, and wanted neither Food nor Water; nor did the Servants imagine what could possibly ail him. And the only Remedy they found was to set him to hard Work, after which he would infallibly come to himself. To this I was silent out of Partiality to my own Kind; yet here I could plainly discover the true Seeds of *Spleen*,[29] which only seizeth on the *Lazy*, the *Luxurious*, and the *Rich*; who, if they were forced to undergo the *same Regimen*, I would undertake for the Cure.

HIS Honour had farther observed, that a Female *Yahoo* would often stand behind a Bank or a Bush, to gaze on the young Males passing by, and then appear, and hide, using many antick Gestures and Grimaces; at which time it was observed, that she had a most *offensive Smell*; and when any of the Males advanced, would slowly retire, looking often back, and with a counterfeit Shew of Fear, run off into some convenient Place where she knew the Male would follow her.

AT other times, if a Female Stranger came among them, three or four of her own Sex would get about her, and stare and chatter, and grin, and smell her all over; and then turn off with Gestures that seemed to express Contempt and Disdain.

PERHAPS my Master might refine a little in these Speculations, which he had drawn from what he observed himself, or had been told him by others: However, I could not reflect without some Amazement, and much Sorrow, that the Rudiments of *Lewdness, Coquetry, Censure,* and *Scandal,* should have Place by Instinct in Womankind.

I EXPECTED every Moment, that my Master would accuse the *Yahoos* of those unnatural Appetites in both Sexes, so common among us. But Nature it seems hath not been so expert a Schoolmistress; and these politer Pleasures are entirely the Productions of Art and Reason, on our Side of the Globe.

CHAPTER VIII

The Author relateth several Particulars of the Yahoos. *The great Virtues of the* Houyhnhnms. *The Education and Exercise of their Youth. Their general Assembly.*

As I ought to have understood human Nature much better than I supposed it possible for my Master to do, so it was easy to apply the Character he gave of the *Yahoos* to myself and my Countrymen; and I believed I could yet make farther Discoveries from my own Observation. I therefore often begged his Honour to let me go among the Herds of *Yahoos* in the Neighbourhood; to which he always very graciously consented, being perfectly convinced that the Hatred I bore those Brutes would never suffer me to be corrupted by them; and his Honour ordered one of his Servants, a strong Sorrel Nag, very honest and good-natured, to be my Guard; without whose Protection I durst not undertake such Adventures. For I have already told the Reader how much I was pestered by those odious Animals upon my first Arrival. I afterwards failed very narrowly three or four times of falling into their Clutches, when I happened to stray at any Distance without my Hanger. And I have Reason to believe, they had some Imagination that I was of their own Species, which I often assisted myself, by stripping up my Sleeves, and shewing my naked Arms and Breast in their Sight, when my Protector was with me: At which times they would approach as near as they durst, and imitate my Actions after the Manner of Monkeys, but ever with great Signs of Hatred; as a tame *Jack Daw* with Cap and Stockings, is always persecuted by the wild ones, when he happens to be got among them.

THEY are prodigiously nimble from their Infancy; however, I once caught a young Male of three Years old, and endeavoured by all Marks of Tenderness to make it quiet; but the little Imp fell a squalling, and scratching, and biting with such Violence, that I was forced to let it go; and it was high time, for a whole Troop of old ones came about us at the Noise; but finding the Cub was safe, (for away it ran) and my Sorrel Nag being by, they durst not venture near us. I observed the young Animal's Flesh to smell very rank, and the Stink was somewhat between a *Weasel* and a *Fox*, but much more disagreeable. I forgot another Circumstance, (and perhaps I might have the Reader's Pardon, if it were wholly omitted) that while I held the odious Vermin in my Hands, it voided its filthy Excrements of a yellow liquid Substance, all over my Cloaths; but by good Fortune there was a small Brook hard by, where I washed myself as clean as I could; although I durst not come into my Master's Presence, until I were sufficiently aired.

BY what I could discover, the *Yahoos* appear to be the most unteachable of all Animals, their Capacities never reaching higher than to draw or carry Burthens. Yet I am of Opinion, this Defect ariseth chiefly from a perverse, restive Disposition. For they are cunning, malicious, treacherous and revengeful. They are strong and hardy, but of a cowardly Spirit, and by Consequence insolent, abject, and cruel. It is observed, that the *Redhaired* of both Sexes are more libidinous and michievous than the rest, whom yet they much exceed in Strength and Activity.

THE *Houyhnhnms* keep the *Yahoos* for present Use in Huts not far from the House; but the rest are sent abroad to certain Fields, where they dig up Roots, eat several Kinds of Herbs, and search about for Carrion, or sometimes catch *Weasels* and *Luhimuhs* (a Sort of *wild Rat*) which they greedily devour. Nature hath taught them to dig deep Holes with their Nails on the Side of a rising Ground, wherein they lie by themselves; only the Kennels of the Females are larger, sufficient to hold two or three Cubs.

THEY swim from their Infancy like Frogs, and are able to continue long under Water, where they often take Fish, which the Females carry home to their Young. And upon this Occasion, I hope the Reader will pardon my relating an odd Adventure.

BEING one Day abroad with my Protector the Sorrel Nag, and the Weather exceeding hot, I entreated him to let me bathe in a River that was near. He consented, and I immediately stripped myself stark naked, and went down softly into the stream. It happened that a young Female *Yahoo*[30] standing behind a Bank, saw the whole Proceeding; and inflamed by Desire, as the Nag and I conjectured, came running with all Speed, and leaped into the Water within five Yards of the Place where I bathed. I was never in my Life so terribly frighted; the Nag was grazing at some Distance, not suspecting any Harm: She embraced me after a most fulsome Manner; I roared as loud as I could, and the Nag came galloping towards me, whereupon she quitted her Grasp, with the utmost Reluctancy, and leaped upon the opposite Bank, where she stood gazing and howling all the time I was putting on my Cloaths.

THIS was Matter of Diversion to my Master and his Family, as well as of Mortification to my self. For now I could no longer deny, that I was a real *Yahoo*, in every Limb and Feature, since the Females had a natural Propensity to me as one of their own Species: Neither was the Hair of this Brute of a Red Colour, (which might have been some Excuse for an Appetite a little irregular) but black as a Sloe, and her Countenance did not make an Appearance altogether so hideous as the rest of the Kind; for, I think, she could not be above Eleven Years old.

HAVING already lived three Years in this Country, the Reader I suppose will expect, that I should, like other Travellers, give him some Account of the Manners and Customs of its Inhabitants, which it was indeed my principal Study to learn.

As these noble *Houyhnhnms* are endowed by Nature with a general Disposition to all Virtues, and have no Conceptions or Ideas of what is evil in a rational Creature; so their grand Maxim is, to cultivate *Reason*, and to be wholly governed by it. Neither is *Reason* among them a Point problematical as with us, where Men can argue with Plausibility on both Sides of a Question; but strikes you with immediate Conviction; as it must needs do where it is not mingled, obscured, or discoloured by Passion and Interest. I remember it was with extreme Difficulty that I could bring my Master to understand the Meaning of the Word *Opinion*, or how a Point could be disputable; because *Reason* taught us to affirm or deny only where we are certain; and beyond our Knowledge we cannot do either. So that Controversies, Wranglings, Disputes, and Positiveness in false or dubious Propositions, are Evils unknown among the *Houyhnhnms*. In the like Manner when I used to explain to him our several Systems of *Natural Philosophy*, he would laugh that a Creature pretending to *Reason*, should value itself upon the Knowledge of other Peoples Conjectures, and in Things, where that Knowledge, if it were certain, could be of no Use. Wherein he agreed entirely with the Sentiments of *Socrates*,[31] as *Plato* delivers them; which I mention as the highest Honour I can do that Prince of Philosophers. I have often since reflected what Destruction such a Doctrine would make in the Libraries of *Europe*; and how many Paths to Fame would be then shut up in the Learned World.

FRIENDSHIP and *Benevolence* are the two principal Virtues among the *Houyhnhnms;* and these not confined to particular Objects, but universal to the whole Race. For, a Stranger from the remotest Part, is equally treated with the nearest Neighbour, and where-ever he goes, looks upon himself as at home. They preserve *Decency* and *Civility* in the highest Degrees, but are altogether ignorant of *Ceremony.* They have no Fondness[32] for their Colts or Foles; but the Care they take in educating them proceedeth entirely from the Dictates of *Reason.* And, I observed my Master to shew the same Affection to his Neighbour's Issue that he had for his own. They will have it that *Nature* teaches them to love the whole Species, and it is *Reason* only that maketh a Distinction of Persons, where there is a superior Degree of Virtue.

WHEN the Matron *Houyhnhnms* have produced one of each Sex, they no longer accompany with their Consorts, except they lose one of their Issue by some Casualty, which very seldom happens: But in such a Case they meet again; or when the like Accident befalls a Person, whose Wife is past bearing, some other Couple bestows on him one of their own Colts,[33] and then go together a second Time, until the Mother be pregnant. This Caution is necessary to prevent the Country from being over-burthened with Numbers. But the Race of inferior *Houyhnhnms* bred up to be Servants is not so strictly limited upon this Article; these are allowed to produce three of each Sex, to be Domesticks in the Noble Families.

IN their Marriages they are exactly careful to chuse such Colours as will not make any disagreeable Mixture in the Breed.[34] *Strength* is chiefly valued in the Male, and *Comeliness* in the Female; not upon the Account of *Love,* but to preserve the Race from degenerating: For, where a Female happens to excel in *Strength,* a Consort is chosen with regard to *Comeliness.* Courtship, Love, Presents, Joyntures, Settlements, have no Place in their Thoughts; or Terms whereby to express them in their Language. The young Couple meet and are joined, merely because it is the Determination of their Parents and Friends: It is what they see done every Day; and they look upon it as one of the necessary Actions in a reasonable Being. But the Violation of Marriage, or any other Unchastity, was never heard of: And the married Pair pass their Lives with the same Friendship, and mutual Benevolence that they bear to all others of the same Species, who come in their Way; without Jealousy, Fondness, Quarrelling, or Discontent.

IN educating the Youth of both Sexes, their Method is admirable, and highly deserveth our Imitation. These are not suffered to taste a Grain of *Oats,* except upon certain Days, till Eighteen Years old; nor *Milk,* but very rarely; and in Summer they graze two Hours in the Morning, and as many in the Evening, which their Parents likewise observe; but the Servants are not allowed above half that Time; and a great Part of their Grass is brought home, which they eat at the most convenient Hours, when they can be best spared from Work.

TEMPERANCE, *Industry, Exercise* and *Cleanliness,* are the Lessons equally enjoyned to the young ones of both Sexes: And my Master thought it monstrous in us to give the Females a different Kind of Education from the Males, except in some Articles of Domestick Management; whereby, as he truly observed, one Half of our Natives were good for nothing but bringing Children into the World: And to trust the Care of their Children to such useless Animals, he said was yet a greater Instance of Brutality.

BUT the *Houyhnhnms* train up their Youth to Strength, Speed, and Hardiness, by exercising them in running Races up and down steep Hills, or over hard stony Grounds; and when they are all in a Sweat, they are ordered to leap over Head and Ears into a Pond or a River. Four times a Year the Youth of certain Districts meet to shew their Proficiency in Running, and Leaping, and other Feats of Strength or Agility; where the Victor is rewarded with a Song made in his or her Praise. On this Festival the Servants drive a Herd of *Yahoos* into the Field, laden with Hay, and Oats, and Milk for a Repast to the *Houyhnhnms;* after which, these Brutes are immediately driven back again, for fear of being noisome to the Assembly.

EVERY fourth Year, at the *Vernal Equinox,* there is a Representative Council of the whole Nation, which meets in a Plain about twenty Miles from our House, and continueth about five or six Days. Here they inquire into the State and Condition of the several Districts; whether they abound or be deficient in Hay or Oats, or Cows or *Yahoos?* And where-ever there is any Want (which is but seldom) it is immediately supplied by unanimous Consent and Contribution. Here likewise the Regulation of Children is settled: As for instance, if a *Houyhnhnm* hath two Males, he changeth one of them with another who hath two Females: And when a Child hath been lost by any Casualty, where the Mother is past Breeding, it is determined what Family shall breed another to supply the Loss.

CHAPTER IX

A grand Debate at the General Assembly of the Houyhnhnms; *and how it was determined. The Learning of the* Houyhnhnms. *Their Buildings. Their Manner of Burials. The Defectiveness of their Language.*

One of these Grand Assemblies was held in my time, about three Months before my Departure, whither my Master went as the Representative of our District. In this Council was resumed their old Debate, and indeed, the only Debate that ever happened in their Country; whereof my Master after his Return gave me a very particular Account.

THE Question to be debated was, Whether the *Yahoos* should be exterminated from the Face of the Earth.[35] One of the *Members* for the Affirmative offered several Arguments of great Strength and Weight; alledging, That, as the *Yahoos* were the most filthy, noisome, and deformed Animal which Nature ever produced, so they were the most restive and indocible, mischievous and malicious: They would privately suck the Teats of the *Houyhnhnms* Cows; kills and devour their Cats, trample down their Oats and Grass, if they were not continually watched; and commit a Thousand other Extravagancies. He took Notice of a general Tradition, that *Yahoos* had not been always in their Country: But, that many Ages ago, two of these Brutes appeared together upon a Mountain; whether produced by the Heat of the Sun upon corrupted Mud and Slime, or from the Ooze and Froth of the Sea, was never known.[36] That these *Yahoos* engendered, and their Brood in a short time grew so numerous as to over-run and infest the whole Nation. That the *Houyhnhnms* to get rid of this Evil, made a general Hunting, and at last inclosed the whole Herd; and destroying the Older, every *Houyhnhnm* kept two young Ones in a Kennel, and brought them to such a Degree of Tameness, as an Animal so savage by Nature can be capable of acquiring; using them for Draught and Carriage. That, there seemed to be much Truth in this Tradition, and that those Creatures could not be *Ylnhniamshy* (or *Aborigines* of the Land) because of the violent Hatred the *Houyhnhnms* as well as all other Animals, bore them; which although their evil Disposition sufficiently deserved, could never have arrived at so high a Degree, if they had been *Aborigines*, or else they would have long since been rooted out. That, the Inhabitants taking a Fancy to use the Service of the *Yahoos*, had very imprudently neglected to cultivate the Breed of *Asses*, which were a comely Animal, easily kept, more tame and orderly, without any offensive Smell, strong enough for Labour, although they yield to the other in Agility of Body; and if their Braying be no agreeable Sound, it is far preferable to the horrible Howlings of the *Yahoos*.

SEVERAL others declared their Sentiments to the same Purpose; when my Master proposed an Expedient to the Assembly, whereof he had indeed borrowed the Hint from me. He approved of the Tradition, mentioned by the *Honourable Member*, who spoke before; and affirmed, that the two *Yahoos* said to be first seen among them, had been driven thither over the Sea; that coming to Land, and being forsaken by their Companions, they retired to the Mountains, and degenerating by Degrees, became in Process of Time, much more savage than those of their own Species in the Country from whence these two Originals came. The Reason of his Assertion was, that he had now in his Possession, a certain wonderful *Yahoo*, (meaning myself) which most of them had heard of, and many of them had seen. He then related to them, how he first found me; that, my Body was all covered with an artificial Composure of the Skins and hairs of other Animals: That, I spoke in a Language of my own, and had thoroughly learned theirs: That, I had related to him the Accidents which brought me thither: That, when he saw me without my Covering, I was an exact *Yahoo* in every Part, only of a whiter Colour, less hairy, and with shorter Claws. He added, how I had endeavoured to persuade him, that in my own and other Countries the *Yahoos* acted as the governing, rational Animal, and held the *Houyhnhnms* in Servitude: That, he observed in me all the Qualities of a *Yahoo*, only a little more civilized by some Tincture of Reason; which however was in a Degree as far inferior to the *Houyhnhnm* Race, as the *Yahoos* of their Country were to me: That, among other things, I mentioned a Custom we had of *castrating Houyhnhnms* when they were young, in order to render them tame; that the Operation was easy and safe; that it was no Shame to learn Wisdom from Brutes, as Industry is taught by the Ant, and Building by the Swallow. (For so I translate the Word *Lyhannh*, although it be a much larger Fowl) That, this Invention[37] might be practiced upon the younger *Yahoos* here, which, besides rendering them tractable and fitter for Use, would in an Age put an End to the whole Species without destroying Life. That, in the mean time the *Houyhnhnms* should be *exhorted* to cultivate the Breed of Asses, which, as they are in all respects more valuable Brutes; so they have this Advantage, to be fit for Service at five Years old, which the others are not till Twelve.

THIS was all my Master thought fit to tell me at that Time, of what passed in the Grand Council. But he was pleased to conceal one Particular, which related personally to myself, whereof I soon felt the unhappy Effect, as the Reader will know in its proper Place, and from whence I date all the succeeding Misfortunes of my Life.

THE *Houyhnhnms* have no Letters, and consequently, their Knowledge is all traditional. But there happening few Events of any Moment among a People so well united, naturally disposed to every Virtue, wholly governed by Reason, and cut off from all Commerce with other Nations: the historical Part is easily preserved without burthening their Memories. I have already observed, that they are subject to no Diseases, and therefore can have no Need of Physicians. However, they have excellent Medicines composed of Herbs, to cure accidental Bruises and Cuts in the Pastern or Frog of the Foot by sharp Stones, as well as other Maims and Hurts in the several Parts of the Body.

THEY calculate the Year by the Revolution of the Sun and the Moon, but use no Subdivisions into Weeks. They are well enough acquainted with the Motions of those two Luminaries, and understand the Nature of *Eclipses;* and this is the utmost Progress of their *Astronomy.*

IN *Poetry* they must be allowed to excel all other Mortals; wherein the Justness of their Similes, and the Minuteness, as well as Exactness of their Descriptions, are indeed inimitable. Their Versus abound very much in both of these; and usually contain either some exalted Notions of Friendship and Benevolence, or the Praises of those who were Victors in Races, and other bodily Exercises. Their Buildings, although very rude and simple, are not inconvenient, but well contrived to defend them from all Injuries of Cold and Heat. They have a Kind of Tree, which at Forty Years old loosens in the Root, and falls with the first Storm; it grows very strait, and being pointed like Stakes with a sharp Stone, (for the *Houyhnhnms* know not the Use of Iron) they stick them erect in the Ground about ten Inches asunder, and then weave in Oat-straw, or sometimes Wattles betwixt them. The Roof is made after the same Manner, and so are the Doors.

THE *Houyhnhnms* use the hollow Part between the Pastern and the

Hoof of their Fore-feet, as we do our Hands, and this with greater Dexterity, than I could at first imagine. I have seen a white Mare of our Family thread a Needle (which I lent her on Purpose) with that Joynt. They milk their Cows, reap their Oats, and do all the Work which requires Hands, in the same Manner. They have a kind of hard Flints, which by grinding against other Stones, they form into Instruments, that serve instead of Wedges, Axes, and Hammers. With Tools made of these Flints, they likewise cut their Hay, and reap their Oats, which there groweth naturally in several Fields: The *Yahoos* draw home the Sheaves in Carriages, and the Servants tread them in certain covered Hutts, to get out the Grain, which is kept in Stores. They make a rude Kind of earthen and wooden Vessels, and bake the former in the Sun.

IF they can avoid Casualties, they die only of old Age, and are buried in the obscurest Places that can be found, their Friends and Relations expressing neither Joy nor Grief at their Departure; nor does the dying Person discover the least Regret that he is leaving the World, any more than if he were upon returning home from a Visit to one of his Neighbours: I remember, my Master having once made an Appointment with a Friend and his Family to come to his House upon some Affair of Importance; on the Day fixed, the Mistress and her two Children came very late; she made two Excuses, first for her Husband, who, as she said, happened that very Morning to *Lhnuwnh*. The Word is strongly expressive in their Language, but not easily rendered into *English*; it signifies, *to retire to his first Mother*. Her Excuse for not coming sooner, was, that her Husband dying late in the Morning, she was a good while consulting her Servants about a convenient Place where his Body should be laid; and I observed she behaved herself at our House, as chearfully as the rest: she died about three Months after.

THEY live generally to Seventy or Seventy-five Years, very seldom to Fourscore: Some Weeks before their Death they feel a gradual Decay, but without Pain. During this time they are much visited by their Friends, because they cannot go abroad with their usual Ease and Satisfaction. However, about ten Days before their Death, which they seldom fail in computing, they return the Visits that have been made them by those who are nearest in the Neighbourhood, being carried in a convenient Sledge drawn by *Yahoos*; which Vehicle they use, not only upon this Occasion, but when they grow old, upon long Journeys, or when they are lamed by any Accident. And therefore when the dying *Houyhnhnms* return those Visits, they take a solemn Leave of their Friends, as if they were going to some remote Part of the Country, where they designed to pass the rest of their Lives.

I KNOW not whether it may be worth observing, that the *Houyhnhnms* have no Word in their Language to express any thing that is *evil*, except what they borrow from the Deformities or ill Qualities of the *Yahoos*. Thus they denote the Folly of a Servant, an Omission of a Child, a Stone that cuts their Feet, a Continuance of foul or unseasonable Weather, and the like, by adding to each the Epithet of *Yahoo*. For Instance, *Hhnm Yahoo, Whnaholm Yahoo, Ynlhmnawihlma Yahoo,* and an ill contrived House, *Ynholmhnmrohlnw Yahoo.*

I COULD with great Pleasure enlarge farther upon the Manners and Virtues of this excellent People; but intending in a short time to publish a Volume by itself expressly upon that Subject, I refer the Reader thither. And in the mean time, proceed to relate my own sad Catastrophe.

CHAPTER X

The Author's Oeconomy and happy Life among the Houy-hnhnms. *His great Improvement in Virtue, by conversing with them. Their Conversations. The Author hath Notice given him by his Master that he must depart from the Country. He falls into a Swoon for Grief, but submits. He contrives and finishes a Canoo, by the Help of a Fellow-Servant, and puts to Sea at a Venture.*

I had settled my little Oeconomy to my own Heart's Content. My Master had ordered a Room to be made for me after their Manner, about six Yards from the House; the Sides and Floors of which I plaistered with Clay, and covered with Rush-mats of my own contriving: I had beaten Hemp, which there grows wild, and made of it a Sort of Ticking: This I filled with the Feathers of several Birds I had taken with Springes made of *Yahoos* Hairs; and were excellent Food. I had worked two Chairs with my Knife, the Sorrel Nag helping me in the grosser and more laborious Part. When my Cloaths were worn to Rags, I made my self others with the Skins of Rabbets, and of a certain beautiful Animal about the same Size, called *Nnuh-noh*, the Skin of which is covered with a fine Down. Of these I likewise made very tolerable Stockings. I soaled my Shoes with Wood which I cut from a Tree, and fitted to the upper Leather, and when this was worn out, I supplied it with the Skins of *Yahoos*, dried in the Sun. I often got Honey out of hollow Trees, which I mingled with Water, or eat it with my Bread. No Man could more verify the Truth of these two Maxims, *That, Nature is very easily satisfied;* and, *That, Necessity is the Mother of Invention.* I enjoyed perfect Health of Body, and Tranquility of Mind; I did not feel the Treachery or Inconstancy of a Friend, nor the Injuries of a secret or open Enemy. I had no Occasion of bribing, flattering or pimping, to procure the Favour of any great Man, or of his Minion. I wanted no Fence against Fraud or Oppression: Here was neither Physician to destroy my Body, nor Lawyer to ruin my Fortune: No Informer to watch my Words and Actions, or forge Accusations against me for Hire: Here were no Gibers, Censurers, Backbiters, Pickpockets, Highwaymen, House-breakers, Attorneys, Bawds, Buffoons, Gamesters, Politicans, Wits, Spleneticks, tedious Talkers, Controvertists, Ravishers, Murderers, Robbers, Virtuoso's; no Leaders or Followers of Party and Faction; no Encouragers to Vice, by Seducement or Examples: No Dungeon, Axes, Gibbtes, Whipping-posts, or Pillories; No cheating Shopkeepers or Mechanicks: No Pride, Vanity or Affectation: No Fops, Bullies, Drunkards, strolling Whores, or Poxes: No ranting, lewd, expensive Wives: No stupid, proud Pedants: No importunate, over-bearing, quarrelsome, noisy, roaring, empty, conceited, swearing Companions: No Scoundrels raised from the Dust upon the Merit of their Vices; or Nobility thrown into it on account of their Virtues: No Lords, Fidlers, Judges or Dancing-masters.

I HAD the Favour of being admitted to several *Houyhnhnms,* who came to visit or dine with my Master; where his Honour graciously suffered me to wait in the Room, and listen to their Discourse. Both he and his Company would often descend to ask me Questions, and receive my Answers. I had also sometimes the Honour of attending my Master in his Visits to others. I never presumed to speak, except in answer to a Question; and then I did it with inward Regret, because it was a Loss of so much Time for improving my self: But I was infinitely delighted with the Station of an humble Auditor in such Conversations, where nothing passed but what was useful, expressed in the fewest and most significant Words: Where (as I have already said) the greatest *Decency* was observed, without the least Degree of Ceremony; where no Person spoke without being pleased himself, and pleasing his Companions: Where there was no Interruption, Tediousness, Heat, or Difference of Sentiments. They have a Notion, That when People are met together, a short Silence doth much improve Conversation: This I found to be true; for during those little Intermissions of Talk, new Ideas would arise in their Minds, which very much enlivened the Discourse. Their Subjects are generally on Friendship and Benevolence; on Order and Oeconomy; sometimes upon the visible Operations of Nature, or ancient Traditions; upon the Bounds and Limits of Virtue; upon the unerring Rules of Reason; or upon some Determinations, to be taken at the next great Assembly; and often upon the various Excellencies of *Poetry.* I may add, without Vanity, that my Presence often gave them sufficient Matter for Discourse, because it afforded my Master an Occasion of letting his Friends into the History of me and my Country, upon which they were all pleased to discant in a Manner not very advantageous to human Kind; and for that Reason I shall not repeat what they said: Only I may be allowed to observe, That his Honour, to my great Admiration, appeared to understand the Nature of *Yahoos* much better than my self. He went through all our Vices and Follies, and discovered many which I had never mentioned to him; by only supposing what Qualities a *Yahoo* of their Country, with a small Proportion of Reason, might be capable of exerting: And concluded, with too much Probability, how vile as well as miserable such a Creature must be.

I FREELY confess, that all the little Knowledge I have of any Value, was acquired by the Lectures I received from my Master, and from hearing the Discourses of him and his Friends; to which I should be prouder to listen, than to dictate to the greatest and wisest Assembly in *Europe*. I admired the Strength, Comeliness and Speed of the Inhabitants; and such a Constellation of Virtues in such amiable Persons produced in me the highest Veneration. At first, indeed, I did not feel that natural Awe which the *Yahoos* and all other Animals bear towards them; but it grew upon me by Degrees, much sooner than I imagined, and was mingled with a respectful Love and Gratitude, that they would condescend to distinguish me from the rest of my Species.

WHEN I thought of my Family, my Friends, my Countrymen, or human Race in general, I considered them as they really were, *Yahoos* in Shape and Disposition, perhaps a little more civilized, and qualified with the Gift of Speech; but making no other Use of Reason, than to improve and multiply those Vices, whereof their Brethren in this Country had only the Share that Nature allotted them. When I happened to behold the Reflection of my own Form in a Lake or Fountain, I turned away my Face in Horror and detestation of my self; and could better endure the Sight of a common *Yahoo,* than of my own Person. By conversing with the *Houyhnhnms,* and looking upon them with Delight, I fell to imitate their Gait and Gesture, which is now grown into a Habit; and my Friends often tell me in a blunt Way, that *I trot like a Horse;* which, however, I take for a great Compliment: Neither shall I disown, that in speaking I am apt to fall into the Voice and manner of the *Houyhnhnms,* and hear my self ridiculed on that Account without the least Mortification.

IN the Midst of this Happiness, when I looked upon my self to be fully settled for Life, my Master sent for me one Morning a little earlier than his usual Hour. I observed by his Countenance that he was in some Perplexity, and at a Loss how to begin what he had to speak. After a short Silence, he told me, he did not know how I would take what he was going to say: That, in the last general Assembly, when the Affair of the *Yahoos* was entered upon, the Representatives had taken Offence at his keeping a *Yahoo* (meaning my self) in his Family more like a *Houyhnhnm* than a Brute Animal. That, he was known frequently to converse with me, as if he could receive some Advantage or Pleasure in my Company: That, such a Practice was not agreeable to Reason or Nature, nor a thing ever heard of before among them. The Assembly did therefore *exhort* him, either to employ me like the rest of my Species, or command me to swim back to the Place from whence I came. That, the first of these Expedients was utterly rejected by all the *Houyhnhnms,* who had ever seen me at his House or their own: For, they alledged, That because I had some Rudiments of Reason, added to the natural Pravity[38] of those Animals, it was to be feared, I might be able to seduce them into the woody and mountainous Parts of the Country, and bring them in Troops by Night to destroy the *Houyhnhnms* Cattle, as being naturally of the ravenous Kind, and averse from Labour.

My Master added, That he was daily pressed by the *Houyhnhnms* of the Neighbourhood to have the Assembly's *Exhortation* executed, which he could not put off much longer. He doubted,[39] it would be impossible for me to swim to another Country; and therefore wished I would contrive some Sort of Vehicle resembling those I had described to him, that might carry me on the Sea; in which Work I should have the Assistance of his own Servants, as well as those of his Neighbours. He concluded, that for his own Part he could have been content to keep me in his Service as long as I lived; because he found I had cured myself of some bad Habits and Dispositions, by endeavouring, as far as my inferior Nature was capable, to imitate the *Houyhnhnms.*

I SHOULD here observe to the Reader, that a Decree of the general Assembly in this County, is expressed by the Word *Hnhloayn,* which signifies an *Exhortation;* as near as I can render it: For they have no Conception how a rational Creature can be *compelled,* but only advised, or *exhorted;* because no Person can disobey Reason, without giving up his Claim to be a rational Creature.

I WAS struck with the utmost Grief and Despair at my Master's Discourse; and being unable to support the Agonies I was under, I fell into a Swoon at his Feet: When I came to myself, he told me, that he concluded I had been dead. (For these People are subject to no such Imbecillities of Nature) I answered, in a faint Voice, that Death would have been too great an Happiness; that although I could not blame the Assembly's *Exhortation,* or the Urgency of his Friends; yet in my weak and corrupt Judgment, I thought it might consist with Reason to have been less rigorous. That, I could not swim a League, and probably the nearest Land to theirs might be distant above an Hundred: That, many Materials, necessary for making a small Vessel to carry me off, were wholly wanting in this Country, which however, I would attempt in Obedience and Gratitude to his Honour, although I concluded the thing to be impossible, and therefore looked on myself as already devoted to Destruction. That, the certain Prospect of an unnatural Death, was the least of my Evils: For, supposing I should escape with Life by some strange Adventure, how could I think with Temper, of passing my Days among *Yahoos,* and relapsing into my old Corruptions, for want of Examples to lead and keep me within the Paths of Virtue. That, I knew too well upon what solid Reasons all the Determinations of the wise *Houyhnhnms* were founded, not to be shaken by Arguments of mine, a miserable *Yahoo;* and therefore after presenting him with my humble Thanks for the Offer of his Servants Assistance in making a Vessel, and desiring a reasonable Time for so difficult a Work, I told him, I would endeavour to preserve a wretched Being; and, if ever I returned to *England,* was not without Hopes of being useful to my own Species, by celebrating the Praises of the renowned *Houyhnhnms,* and proposing their Virtues to the Imitation of Mankind.

My Master in a few Words made me a very gracious Reply, allowed me the Space of two *Months* to finish my Boat; and ordered the Sorrel Nag, my Fellow-Servant, (for so at this Distance I may presume to call him) to follow my Instructions, because I told my Master, that his Help would be sufficient, and I knew he had a Tenderness for me.

In his Company my first Business was to go to that Part of the Coast, where my rebellious Crew had ordered me to be set on Shore. I got upon a Height, and looking on every Side into the Sea, fancied I saw a small Island, towards the *North-East:* I took out my Pocket-glass, and could then clearly distinguish it about five Leagues off, as I computed; but it appeared to the Sorrel Nag to be only a blue Cloud: For, as he had no Conception of any Country beside his own, so he could not be as expert in distinguishing remote Objects at Sea, as we who so much converse in that Element.

After I had discovered this Island, I considered no farther; but resolved, it should, if possible, be the first Place of my Banishment, leaving the Consequence to Fortune.

I returned home, and consulting with the Sorrel Nag, we went into a Copse at some Distance, where I with my Knife, and he with a sharp Flint fastened very artificially, after their Manner, to a wooden Handle, cut down several Oak Wattles[40] about the Thickness of a Walking-staff, and some larger Pieces. But I shall not trouble the Reader with a particular Description of my own Mechanicks: Let it suffice to say, that in six Weeks time, with the Help of the Sorrel Nag, who performed the Parts that required most Labour, I finished a Sort of *Indian* Canoo, but much larger, covering it with the Skins of *Yahoos,* well stitched together, with hempen Threads of my own making. My Sail was likewise composed of the Skins of the same Animal; but I made use of the youngest I could get, the older being too tough and thick; and I likewise provided myself with four Paddles. I laid in a Stock of boiled Flesh, of Rabbets and Fowls; and took with me two Vessels, one filled with Milk, and the other with Water.

I TRIED my Canoo in a large Pond near my Master's House, and then corrected in it what was amiss; stopping all the Chinks with *Yahoos* Tallow, till I found it stanch, and able to bear me, and my Freight. And when it was as compleat as I could possibly make it, I had it drawn on a Carriage very gently by *Yahoos,* to the Sea-side, under the Conduct of the Sorrel Nag, and another Servant.

WHEN all was Ready, and the Day came for my Departure, I took Leave of my Master and Lady, and the whole Family, mine Eyes flowing with Tears, and my Heart quite sunk with Grief. But his Honour, out of Curiosity, and perhaps (if I may speak it without Vanity) partly out of Kindness, was determined to see me in my Canoo; and got several of his neighbouring Friends to accompany him. I was forced to wait above an Hour for the Tide, and then observing the Wind very fortunately bearing towards the Island, to which I intended to steer my Course, I took a second Leave of my Master: But as I was going to prostrate myself to kiss his Hoof, he did me the Honour to raise it gently to my Mouth. I am not ignorant how much I have been censured for mentioning this last Particular. Detractors are pleased to think it improbable, that so illustrious a Person should descend to give so great a Mark of Distinction to a Creature so inferior as I. Neither have I forgot, how apt some Travellers are to boast of extraordinary Favours they have received. But, if these Censurers were better acquainted with the noble and courteous Disposition of the *Houyhnhnms,* they would soon change their Opinion.

I PAID my Respects to the rest of the *Houyhnhnms* in his Honour's Company; then getting into my Canoo, I pushed off from Shore.

CHAPTER XI

The Author's dangerous Voyage. He arrives at New-Holland,[41]
hoping to settle there. Is wounded with an Arrow by one of the
Natives. Is seized and carried by Force into a Portugueze
Ship. The great Civilities of the Captain. The Author arrives
at England.

I began this desperate Voyage on *February* 15, 171 , at 9 o'Clock in the
Morning. The Wind was very favourable; however, I made use at first only
of my Paddles; but considering I should soon be weary, and that the Wind
might probably chop about, I ventured to set up my little Sail; and thus,
with the Help of the Tide, I went at the Rate of a League and a Half an
Hour, as near as I could guess. My Master and his Friends continued on
the Shoar, till I was almost out of Sight; and I often heard the Sorrel Nag
(who always loved me) crying out, *Hnuy illa nyha maiah Yahoo,* Take Care of
thy self, gentle *Yahoo.*

MY Design was, if possible, to discover some small Island uninhabited,
yet sufficient by my Labour to furnish me with Necessaries of Life, which
I would have thought a greater Happiness than to be first Minister in the
politest Court of *Europe;* so horrible was the Idea I conceived of returning
to live in the Society and under the Government of *Yahoos.* For in such a
Solitude as I desired, I could at least enjoy my own Thoughts, and reflect
with Delight on the Virtues of those inimitable *Houyhnhnms,* without any
Opportunity of degenerating into the Vices and Corruptions of my own
Species.

THE Reader may remember what I related when my Crew conspired
against me, and confined me to my Cabbin. How I continued there several
Weeks, without knowing what Course we took; and when I was put ashore
in the Long-boat, how the Sailors told me with Oaths, whether true or
false, that they knew not in what Part of the World we were. However, I
did then believe us to be about ten Degrees *Southward* of the *Cape of Good*

Hope, or about 45 Degrees *Southern* Latitude, as I gathered from some general Words I overheard among them, being I supposed to the *South-East* in their intended Voyage to *Madagascar.* And although this were but little better than Conjecture, yet I resolved to steer my Course *Eastward,* hoping to reach the *South-West* Coast of *New-Holland,* and perhaps some such Island as I desired, lying *Westward* of it. The Wind was full *West,* and by six in the Evening I computed I had gone *Eastward* at least eighteen Leagues; when I spied a very small Island about half a League off, which I soon reached. It was nothing but a Rock with one Creek, naturally arched by the Force of Tempests. Here I put in my Canoo, and climbing a Part of the Rock, I could plainly discover Land to the *East,* extending from *South* to *North.* I lay all Night in my Canoo; and repeating my Voyage early in the Morning, I arrived in seven Hours to the *South-East* Point of *New-Holland.* This confirmed me in the Opinion I have long entertained, that the *Maps* and *Charts* place this Country at least three Degrees more to the *East* than it really is; which Thought I communicated many Years ago to my worthy Friend Mr. *Herman Moll,*[42] and gave him my Reasons for it, although he hath rather chosen to follow other Authors.

I SAW no Inhabitants in the Place where I landed; and being unarmed, I was afraid of venturing far into the Country. I found some Shell-Fish on the Shore, and eat them raw, not daring to kindle a Fire, for fear of being discovered by the Natives. I continued three Days feeding on Oysters and Limpits, to save my own Provisions; and I fortunately found a Brook of excellent Water, which gave me great Relief.

ON the fourth Day, venturing out early a little too far, I saw twenty or thirty Natives upon a Height, not above five hundred Yards from me. They were stark naked, Men, Women and Children round a Fire, as I could discover by the Smoke. One of them spied me, and gave Notice to the rest; five of them advanced towards me, leaving the Women and Children at the Fire. I made what haste I could to the Shore, and getting into my Canoo, shoved off: The Savages observing me retreat, ran after me; and before I could get far enough into the Sea, discharged an Arrow, which wounded me deeply on the Inside of my left Knee (I shall carry the Mark to my Grave.) I apprehended the Arrow might be poisoned; and paddling out of the Reach of their Darts (being a calm Day) I made a shift to suck the Wound, and dress it as well as I could.

I WAS at a Loss what to do, for I durst not return to the same Landing-place, but stood to the *North,* and was forced to paddle; for the Wind, although very gentle, was against me, blowing *North-West.* As I was looking about for a secure Landing-place, I saw a Sail to the *North North-East*, which appearing every Minute more visible, I was in some Doubt, whether I should wait for them or no; but at last my Detestation of the *Yahoo* Race prevailed; and turning my Canoo, I sailed and paddled together to the *South*, and got into the same Creek from whence I set out in the Morning; choosing rather to trust my self among these *Barbarians*, than live with *European Yahoos*. I drew up my Canoo as close as I could to the Shore, and hid my self behind a Stone by the little Brook, which, as I have already said, was excellent Water.

THE Ship came within half a League of this Creek, and sent out her Long-Boat with Vessels to take in fresh Water (for the Place it seems was very well known) but I did not observe it until the Boat was almost on Shore; and it was too late to seek another Hiding-Place. The Seamen at their landing observed my Canoo, and rummaging it all over, easily conjectured that the Owner could not be far off. Four of them well armed searched every Cranny and Lurking-hole, till at last they found me flat on my Face behind the Stone. They gazed a while in Admiration at my strange uncouth Dress; my Coat made of Skins, my wooden-soaled Shoes, and my furred Stockings; from whence, however, they concluded I was not a Native of the Place, who all go naked. One of the Seamen in *Portugueze* bid me rise, and asked who I was. I understood that Language very well, and getting upon my Feet, said, I was a poor *Yahoo*, banished from the *Houyhnhnms*, and desired they would please to let me depart. They admired to hear me answer them in their own Tongue, and saw by my Complection I must be an Eurpoean; but were at a Loss to know what I meant by *Yahoos* and *Houyhnhnms*, and at the same Time fell a laughing at my strange Tone in speaking, which resembled the Neighing of a Horse. I trembled all the while betwixt Fear and Hatred: I again desired Leave to depart, and was gently moving to my Canoo; but they laid hold on me, desiring to know what Country I was of? whence I came? with many other Questions. I told them, I was born in *England*, from whence I came about five Years ago, and then their Country and ours were at Peace. I therefore hoped they would not treat me as an Enemy, since I meant them no Harm, but was a poor *Yahoo*, seeking some desolate Place where to pass the Remainder of his unfortunate Life.

WHEN they began to talk, I thought I never heard or saw any thing so unnatural; for it appeared to me as monstrous as if a Dog or Cow should speak in *England*, or a *Yahoo* in *Houyhnhnm-Land*. The honest Portuguese were equally amazed at my strange Dress, and the odd Manner of delivering my Words, which however they understood very well. They spoke to me with great Humanity, and said they were sure their Captain would carry me *gratis* to *Lisbon,* from whence I might return to my own Country; that two of the Seamen would go back to the Ship, to inform the Captain of what they had seen, and receive his Orders; in the mean Time, unless I would give my solemn Oath not to fly, they would secure me by Force. I thought it best to comply with their Proposal. They were very curious to know my Story, but I gave them very little Satisfaction; and they all conjectured, that my Mixfortunes had impaired my Reason. In two Hours the Boat, which went loaden with Vessels of Water, returned with the Captain's Commands to fetch me on Board. I fell on my Knees to preserve my Liberty; but all was in vain, and the Men having tied me with Cords, heaved me into the Boat, from whence I was taken into the Ship, and from thence into the Captain's Cabbin.

His Name was *Pedro de Mendez;* he was a very courteous and generous Person; he entreated me to give some Account of my self, and desired to know what I would eat or drink; said, I should be used as well as himself, and spoke so many obliging Things, that I wondered to find such Civilities from a *Yahoo.* However, I remained silent and sullen; I was ready to faint at the very Smell of him and his Men. At last I desired something to eat out of my own Canoo; but he ordered me a Chicken and some excellent Wine, and then directed that I should be put to Bed in a very clean Cabbin. I would not undress my self, but lay on the Bed-cloaths; and in half an Hour stole out, when I thought the Crew was at Dinner; and getting to the Side of the Ship, was going to leap into the Sea, and swim for my Life, rather than continue among *Yahoos.* But one of the Seamen prevented me, and having informed the Captain, I was chained to my Cabbin.

After Dinner *Don Pedro* came to me, and desired to know my Reason for so desperate an Attempt; assured me he only meant to do me all the Service he was able; and spoke so very movingly, that at last I descended to treat him like an Animal which had some little Portion of Reason. I gave him a very short Relation of my Voyage; of the Conspiracy against me by my own Men; of the Country where they set me on Shore, and of my five Years Residence there. All which he looked upon as if it were a Dream or a Vision; whereat I took great Offence: For I had quite forgot the Faculty of Lying, so peculiar to *Yahoos* in all Countries where they preside, and consequently the Disposition of suspecting Truth in others of their own Species. I asked him, Whether it were the Custom of his Country to *say the Thing that was not?* I assured him I had almost forgot what he meant by

Falshood; and if I had lived a thousand Years in *Houyhnhnmland*, I should never have heard a Lie from the meanest Servant. That I was altogether indifferent whether he believed me or no; but however, in return for his Favours, I would give so much Allowance to the Corruption of his Nature, as to answer any Objection he would please to make; and he might easily discover the Truth.

THE Captain, a wise Man, after many Endeavours to catch me tripping in some Part of my Story, at last began to have a better Opinion of my Veracity. But he added, that since I professed so inviolable an Attachment to Truth, I must give him my Word of Honour to bear him Company in this Voyage without attempting any thing against my Life; or else he would continue me a Prisoner till we arrived at *Lisbon.* I gave him the Promise he required; but at the same time protested that I would suffer the greatest Hardships rather than return to live among *Yahoos.*

OUR Voyage passed without any considerable Accident. In Gratitude to the Captain I sometimes sate with him at his earnest Request, and strove to conceal my Antipathy against human Kind, although it often broke out; which he suffered to pass without Observation. But the greatest Part of the Day, I confined myself to my Cabbin, to avoid seeing any of the Crew. The Captain had often intreated me to strip myself of my savage Dress, and offered to lend me the best Suit of Cloaths he had. This I would not be prevailed on to accept, abhorring to cover myself with any thing that had been on the Back of a *Yahoo.* I only desired he would lend me two clean Shirts, which having been washed since he wore them, I believed would not so much defile me. These I changed every second Day, and washed them myself.

WE arrived at *Lisbon, Nov.* 5, 1715. At our landing, the Captain forced me to cover myself with his Cloak, to prevent the Rabble from crouding about me. I was conveyed to his own House; and at my earnest Request, he led me up to the highest Room backwards.[43] I conjured him to conceal from all Persons what I had told him of the *Houyhnhnms;* because the least Hint of such a Story would not only draw Numbers of People to see me, but probably put me in Danger of being imprisoned, or burnt by the *Inquisition.*[44] The Captain persuaded me to accept a Suit of Cloaths newly made; but I would not suffer the Taylor to take my Measure; however, Don *Pedro* being almost of my Size, they fitted me well enough. He accoutred me with other Necessaries all new, which I aired for Twenty-four Hours before I would use them.

THE Captain had no Wife, nor above three Servants, none of which

were suffered to attend at Meals; and his whole Deportment was so obliging, added to very good *human* Understanding, that I really began to tolerate his Company. He gained so far upon me, that I ventured to look out of
the back Window. By Degrees I was brought into another Room, from
whence I peeped into the Street, but drew my Head back in a Fright. In a
Week's Time he seduced me down to the Door. I found my Terror gradually lessened, but my Hatred and Contempt seemed to increase. I was at
last bold enough to walk the Street in his Company, but kept my Nose
well stopped with Rue, or sometimes with Tobacco.[45]

IN ten Days, Don *Pedro,* to whom I had given some Account of my domestick Affairs, put it upon me as a Point of Honour and Conscience, that
I ought to return to my native Country, and live at home with my Wife
and Children. He told me, there was an *English* Ship in the Port just ready
to sail, and he would furnish me with all things necessary. It would be tedious to repeat his Arguments, and my Contradictions. He said, it was altogether impossible to find such a solitary Island as I had desired to live in;
but I might command in my own House, and pass my time in a Manner as
recluse as I pleased.

I COMPLIED at last, finding I could not do better. I left *Lisbon* the 24th
Day of *November,* in an *English* Merchant-man, but who was the Master I
never inquired. Don *Pedro* accompanied me to the Ship, and lent me
Twenty Pounds. He took kind Leave of me, and embraced me at parting;
which I bore as well as I could. During this last Voyage I had no Commerce with the Master, or any of his Men; but pretending I was sick kept
close in my Cabbin. On the Fifth of *December,* 1715, we cast Anchor in the
Downs about Nine in the Morning, and at Three in the Afternoon I got
safe to my House at *Redriff.*

MY Wife and Family received me with great Surprize and Joy, because
they concluded me certainly dead; but I must freely confess, the Sight of
them filled me only with Hatred, Disgust and Contempt; and the more, by
reflecting on the near Alliance I had to them. For, although since my unfortunate Exile from the *Houyhnhnm* Country, I had compelled myself to
tolerate the Sight of *Yahoos,* and to converse with Don *Pedro de Mendez;* yet
my Memory and Imaginations were perpetually filled with the Virtues
and Ideas of those exalted *Houyhnhnms.* And when I began to consider, that
by copulating with one of the *Yahoo*-Species, I had become a Parent of
more; it struck me with the utmost Shame, Confusion and Horror.

As soon as I entered the House, my Wife took me in her Arms, and
kissed me; at which, having not been used to the Touch of that odious

Animal for so many Years, I fell in a Swoon for almost an Hour. At the Time I am writing, it is five Years since my last Return to *England:* During the first Year I could not endure my Wife or Children in my Presence, the very Smell of them was intolerable; much less could I suffer them to eat in the same Room. To this Hour they dare not presume to touch my Bread, or drink out of the same Cup; neither was I ever able to let one of them take me by the Hand. The first Money I laid out was to buy two young Stone-Horses,[46] which I keep in a good Stable, and next to them the Groom is my greatest Favourite; for I feel my Spirits revive by the Smell he contracts in the Stable. My Horses understand me tolerably well; I converse with them at least four Hours every Day. They are Strangers to Bridle or Saddle; they live in great Amity with me, and Friendship to each other.

The Author's Veracity. His Design in publishing this Work. His Censure of those Travellers who swerve from the Truth. The Author clears himself from any sinister Ends in writing. An Objection answered. The Method of planting Colonies. His Native Country commended. The Right of the Crown to those Countries described by the Author, is justified. The Difficulty of conquering them. The Author takes his last Leave of the Reader; proposeth his Manner of Living for the future; gives good Advice, and concludeth.

Thus, gentle Reader, I have given thee a faithful History of my Travels for Sixteen Years, and above Seven Months; wherein I have not been so studious of Ornament as of Truth. I could perhaps like others have astonished thee with strange improbable Tales; but I rather chose to relate plain Matter of Fact in the simplest Manner and Style; because my principal Design was to inform, and not to amuse thee.

IT is easy for us who travel into remote Countries, which are seldom visited by *Englishmen* or other *Europeans,* to form Descriptions of wonderful Animals both at Sea and Land. Whereas, a Traveller's chief Aim should be to make Men wiser and better, and to improve their Minds by the bad, as well as good Example of what they deliver concerning foreign Places.

I COULD heartily wish a Law were enacted, that every Traveller, before he were permitted to publish his Voyages, should be obliged to make Oath before the *Lord High Chancellor,* that all he intended to print was absolutely true to the best of his Knowledge; for then the World would no longer be deceived as it usually is, while some Writers, to make their Works pass the better upon the Publick, impose the grossest Falsities on the unwary Reader. I have perused several Books of Travels with great Delight in my younger Days; but, having since gone over most Parts of the Globe, and been able to contradict many fabulous Accounts from my own Observation; it hath given me a great Disgust against this Part of Reading, and some Indignation to see the Credulity of Mankind so impudently abused. Therfore since my Acquaintance were pleased to think my poor Endeavours might not be unacceptable to my Country; I imposed on myself as a Maxim, never to be swerved from, that I would *strictly adhere to Truth;* neither indeed can I be ever under the least Temptation to vary from it, while I retain in my Mind the Lectures and Example of my noble Master, and the other illustrious *Houyhnhnms,* of whom I had so long the Honour to be an humble Hearer.

——*Nec si miserum Fortuna Sinonem
Finxit, vanum etiam, mendacemque improba finget.*[47]

I KNOW very well, how little Reputation is to be got by Writings which require neither Genius nor Learning, nor indeed any other Talent, except a good Memory, or an exact *Journal.* I know likewise, that Writers of Travels, like *Dictionary*-Makers, are sunk into Oblivion by the Weight and Bulk of those who come last, and therefore lie uppermost. And it is highly probable, that such Travellers who shall hereafter visit the Countries described in this Work of mine, may be detecting my Errors, (if there be any) and adding many new Discoveries of their own, jostle me out of Vogue, and stand in my Place; making the World forget that ever I was an Author. This indeed would be too great a Mortification if I wrote for Fame: But, as my sole Intention was the PUBLICK GOOD, I cannot be altogether disappointed. For, who can read of the Virtues I have mentioned in the glorious *Houyhnhnms,* without being ashamed of his own Vices, when he considers himself as the reasoning, governing Animal of his Country? I shall say nothing of those remote Nations where *Yahoos* preside; amongst which the least corrupted are the *Brobdingnagians,* whose wise Maxims in Morality and Government, it would be our Happiness to observe. But I forbear descanting further, and rather leave the judicious Reader to his own Remarks and Applications.

I AM not a little pleased that this Work of mine can possibly meet with no Censurers: For what Objections can be made against a Writer who relates only plain Facts that happened in such distant Countries, where we have not the least Interest with respect either to Trade or Negotiations? I have carefully avoided every Fault with which common Writers of Travels are often too justly charged. Besides, I meddle not the least with any

Party, but write without Passion, Prejudice, or Ill-will against any Man or Number of Men whatsoever. I write for the noblest End, to inform and instruct Mankind, over whom I may, without Breach of Modesty, pretend to some Superiority, from the Advantages I received by conversing so long among the most accomplished *Houyhnhnms.* I write without any View towards Profit or Praise. I never suffer a Word to pass that may look like Reflection, or possibly give the least Offence even to those who are most ready to take it. So that, I hope, I may with Justice pronounce myself an Author perfectly blameless; against whom the Tribes of Answerers, Considerers, Observers, Reflectors, Detectors, Remarkers, will never be able to find Matter for exercising their Talents.

I CONFESS, it was whispered to me, that I was bound in Duty as a Subject of *England,* to have given in a Memorial to a Secretary of State, at my first coming over; because, whatever Lands are discovered by a Subject, belong to the Crown. But I doubt, whether our Conquests in the Countries I treat of, would be as easy as those of *Ferdinando Cortez*[48] over the naked *Americans.* The *Lilliputians* I think, are hardly worth the Charge of a Fleet and Army to reduce them; and I question whether it might be prudent or safe to attempt the *Brobdingnagians:* Or, whether an *English* Army would be much at their Ease with the Flying Island over their Heads. The *Houyhnhnms,* indeed, appear not to be so well prepared for War, a Science to which they are perfect Strangers, and especially against missive Weapons. However, supposing myself to be a Minister of State, I could never give my Advice for invading them. Their Prudence, Unanimity, Unacquaintedness with Fear, and their Love of their Country would amply supply all Defects in the military Art. Imagine twenty Thousand of them breaking into the Midst of an *European* Army, confounding the Ranks, overturning the Carriages, battering the Warriors Faces into Mummy,[49] by terrible Yerks[50] from their hinder Hoofs: For they would well deserve the Character given to *Augustus; Recalcitrat undique tutus.*[51] But instead of Proposals for conquering that magnanimous Nation, I rather wish they were in a Capacity or Disposition to send a sufficient Number of their Inhabitants for civilizing *Europe;* by teaching us the first Principles of Honour, Justice, Truth, Temperance, publick Spirit, Fortitude, Chastity, Friendship, Benevolence, and Fidelity. The *Names* of all which Virtues are still retained among us in most Languages, and are to be met with in modern as well as ancient Authors; which I am able to assert from my own small Reading.

BUT, I had another Reason which made me less forward to enlarge his Majesty's Dominions by my Discoveries: To say the Truth, I had conceived a few Scruples with relation to the distributive Justice of Princes upon those Occasions. For Instance, A Crew of Pyrates are driven by a Storm they know not whither; at length a Boy discovers Land from the Top-mast; they go on Shore to rob and plunder; they see an harmless People, are entertained with Kindness, they give the Country a new Name, they take formal Possession of it for the King, they set up a rotten Plank or a Stone for a Memorial, they murder two or three Dozen of the Natives, bring away a Couple more by Force for a Sample, return home, and get their Pardon. Here commences a new Dominion acquired with a Title by *Divine Right.* Ships are sent with the first Opportunity; the Natives driven out or destroyed, their Princes tortured to discover their Gold; a free Licence given to all Acts of Inhumanity and Lust; the Earth reeking with the Blood of its Inhabitants: And this execrable Crew of Butchers employed in so pious an Expedition, is a *modern Colony* sent to convert and civilize an idolatrous and barbarous People.

BUT this Description, I confess, doth by no means affect the *British* Nation, who may be an Example to the whole World for their Wisdom, Care, and Justice in planting Colonies; their liberal Endowments for the Advancement of Religion and Learning; their Choice of devout and able Pastors to propagate *Christianity;* their Caution in stocking their Provinces with People of sober Lives and Conversations from this the Mother Kingdom; their strict Regard to the Distribution of Justice, in supplying the Civil Administration through all their Colonies with Officers of the greatest Abilities, utter Strangers to Corruption: And to crown all, by sending the most vigilant and virtuous Governors, who have no other Views than the Happiness of the People over whom they preside, and the Honour of the King their Master.

BUT, as those Countries which I have described do not appear to have a Desire of being conquered, and enslaved, murdered or driven out by Colonies; nor abound either in Gold, Silver, Sugar or Tobacco; I did humbly conceive they were by no Means proper Objects of our Zeal, our Valour, or our Interest. However, if those whom it more concerns, think fit to be of another Opinion, I am ready to depose, when I shall be lawfully called, That no *European* did ever visit these Countries before me. I mean, if the Inhabitants ought to be believed.[52]

BUT, as to the Formality of taking Possession in my Sovereign's Name, it never came once into my Thoughts; and if it had, yet as my Affairs then stood, I should perhaps in point of Prudence and Self-Preservation, have put it off to a better Opportunity.

HAVING thus answered the *only* Objection that can be raised against me as a Traveller; I here take a final Leave of my Courteous Readers, and return to enjoy my own Speculations in my little Garden at *Redriff;* to apply those excellent Lessons of Virtue which I learned among the *Houyhnhnms;* to instruct the *Yahoos* of my own Family as far as I shall find them docible Animals; to behold my Figure often in a Glass, and thus if possible habituate my self by Time to tolerate the Sight of a human Creature: To lament the Brutality of *Houyhnhnms* in my own Country, but always treat their Persons with Respect, for the Sake of my noble Master, his Family, his Friends, and the whole *Houyhnhnm* Race, whom these of ours have the Honour to resemble in all their Lineaments, however their Intellectuals came to degenerate.

I BEGAN last Week to permit my Wife to sit at Dinner with me, at the farthest End of a long Table; and to answer (but with the utmost Brevity) the few Questions I asked her. Yet the Smell of a *Yahoo* continuing very offensive, I always keep my Nose well stopt with Rue, Lavender, or Tobacco-Leaves. And although it be hard for a Man late in Life to remove old Habits; I am not altogether out of Hopes in some Time to suffer a Neighbour *Yahoo* in my Company, without the Apprehensions I am yet under of his Teeth or his Claws.

MY Reconcilement to the *Yahoo*-kind in general might not be so difficult, if they would be content with those Vices and Follies only which Nature hath entitled them to. I am not in the least provoked at the Sight of a Lawyer, a Pickpocket, a Colonel, a Fool, a Lord, a Gamester, a Politician, a Whoremunger, a Physician, an Evidence, a Suborner, an Attorney, a Traytor, or the like: This is all according to the due Course of Things: but, when I behold a Lump of Deformity, and Diseases both in Body and Mind, smiten with *Pride,* it immediately breaks all the Measures of my Patience; neither shall I be ever able to comprehend how such an Animal and such a Vice could tally together. The wise and virtuous *Houyhnhnms,* who abound in all Excellencies that can adorn a rational Creature, have no Name for this Vice in their Language, which hath no Terms to express any thing that is evil, except those whereby they describe the detestable Qualities of their *Yahoos;* among which they were not able to distinguish this of Pride, for want of thoroughly understanding Human Nature, as it sheweth it self in other Countries, where that Animal presides. But I, who had more Experience, could plainly observe some Rudiments of it among the wild *Yahoos.*

BUT the *Houyhnhnms,* who live under the Government of Reason, are no more proud of the good Qualities they possess, than I should be for not wanting a Leg or an Arm, which no Man in his Wits would boast of, although he must be miserable without them. I dwell the longer upon this Subject from the Desire I have to make the Society of an *English Yahoo* by any Means not insupportable; and therefore I here intreat those who have any Tincture of this absurd Vice, that they will not presume to appear in my Sight.

VII

PERSONAL WRITINGS

OF
MEAN AND GREAT
FIGURES

MADE BY SEVERAL PERSONS

OF THOSE WHO HAVE MADE GREAT FIGURES IN SOME PARTICULAR ACTION OR CIRCUMSTANCE OF THEIR LIVES

Alexander the great, after his Victory, [at the Streights of Mount Taurus] when he entered the Tent where the Queen and the Princess of Persia fell at his feet.

Socrates, the whole last Day of his Life, and particularly from the Time he took the Poison to the Moment he expired.

Cicero when he was recalled from his Banishment. The People, through every place he passed meeting him with Shouts of Joy and Congratulation, and all Rome coming out to receive him.

Regulus when he went out of Rome attended by his Friends to the Gates, and returned to Carthage according to his Word of Honor, although he knew he must be put to a cruell Death, for advising the Romans to pursue their War with that Commonwealth.

Scipio the Elder when he dismissed a beautifull Captive Lady, presented to him after a great Victory, turning his Head aside, to preserve his own Virtue.

The same Scipio, when he and Hannibal met before the Battle; if the Fact be true.

Cincinnatus when the Messengers, sent by the Senate to make him Dictator, found him at the Plow.

Epaminondas when the Persian Ambassador came to his House and found him in the midst of Poverty.

The Earl of Strafford the Day that he made his own Defence at his Tryall.

King Charles the Martyr during his whole Tryall, and at his Death.

The Black Prince when he waited at Supper on the King of France, whom he had conquered and taken Prisoner the same Day.

Virgil, when at Rome the whole Audience rose up, out of Veneration, as he entered the Theatre.

Mahomet the great when he cut off his beloved Mistress's head on a Stage erected for that purpose: to convince his Soldiers who taxed him for preferring his Love to his Glory.

Cromwell, when he quelled a mutiny in Hyde-Park.

Harry the Great of France, when he entered Paris, and sate at Cards the same Night with some great Ladyes, who were his mortal Enemyes.

Robert Harley Earl of Oxford, at His Tryall.

Cato of Utica, when he provided for the Safety of his Friends and had determined to dy.

Sir Tho More during his Imprisonment, and at his Execution.

The Earl of Oxford when he was stabbed by Guiscard.

Marius when the Soldier sent to kill him in the Dungeon was struck with so much aw and Veneration that his sword fell from his Hand.

Douglas when the ship he commanded was on Fire, and he lay down to dy in it, because it should not be said that one of his Family ever quitted their Post.

Sr Jerom Bows.

OF THOSE WHO HAVE MADE A MEAN CONTEMPTIBLE FIGURE IN SOME ACTION OR CIRCUMSTANCE OF THEIR LIFE

Antony at Actium when he fled after Cleopatra.

Pompey when he was killed on the seashore in Ægypt.

Nero and Vitellius when they were put to Death.

Lepidus when he was compelled to lay down his Share in the Triumvirate.

Cromwell the Day he refused the Kingship out of Fear.

Perseus K. of Macedon when he was led in Triumph.

Richard the 2d of Engd after he was deposed.

The present K. of Poland, when the K. of Sweden forced him to give up his Kingdom, and when he took it again upon the King of Sweden's Defeat by the Muscovites.

King James 2d of England, when the Pr of Orange sent to him at Midnight to leave London.

King Wm 3rd of England, when he sent to beg the House of Commons to continue his Dutch Guards, and was refused.

The late Queen Ann of Engld, when she sent Whitworth to Muscovy on an Ambassy of Humiliation, for an Insult committed here on that Prince's Ambassador.

The Lord Chancellor Bacon, when he was convicted of Bribery.

The late Duke of Marlborough when he was forced after his own Disgrace, to carry his Dutchesses Gold Key to the Queen.

The old Earl of Pembroke when a Scotch Lord gave him a Lash with a Whip at Newmarket in presence of all the Nobility, and he bore it with Patience.

King Charles 2d of Engd when he entered into the Second Dutch War, and in many other Actions during his whole Reign.

Philip the 2d of Spayn after the Defeat of the Armada.

The Emperor Charles the fifth, when he resigned his Crown, and nobody would believe his Reasons.

K. Charles 1st. of England, when in Gallantry to his Queen, he thought to surprize her with a Present of a Diamond Buckle, which he pushed down her Back, and tore her Flesh with the Tongue; upon which she drew it out, and flung it on the ground.

Fairfax, the Parliament Generall, at the Time of King Charles' Tryall.

Julius Cæsar when Antony offered to put a Diadem on his Head, and the People shouted for Joy to see him Decline it; which he never offered to do till he saw their Dislike in their Countenances.

Coriolanus when he withdrew His Army from Rome at the Intreaty of his Mother.

Hannibal at Antiochus's Court.

Beau Fielding, at fifty years old, when in a Quarrel upon the Stage he was run into his Breast, which he opened and shewed to the Ladyes, that he might move their Love and Pity; but they all fell a laughing.

The Count de Bussy Rabutin when he was recalled to Court after 20 Years banishment into the Country, and affected to make the same Figure he did in his Youth.

The Earl of Sunderland when he turned Papist in the Time of K. James 2d, and underwent all the Forms of a Heterick converted.

Pope [Clement VII] when he was taken Prisoner at Rome by the Emperor Charles the fifth's Forces.

Queen Mary of Scotland when she suffered Bothwell to ravish her, and pleaded that as her Excuse for marrying Him.

K. John of England, when he gave up his Kingdom to the Pope, to be held as a Fief from the See of Rome.

FAMILY OF SWIFT

The Family of the Swifts was antient in Yorkshire, from them descended; a noted Person who passed under the name of Cavaliero Swift, a Man of Wit and humor. He was made an Irish peer by King James or K Charles 1. with the Title of Baron Carlingford, but never was in that Kingdom. Many traditionall pleasant Storyes are related of him, which the Family planted in Ireland hath received from their parents. [Another of the same *crossed out*] This Lord dyed without Issue male, and his heiress whether of the first or second Descent was married to Robt Fielding Esqr commonly called handsom Fielding, she brought him a considerable Estate [but *crossed out*] in York-shire, which he squandred away, but had no Children: The Earl of Eglington married another Coheiress of the same family, as he hath often told me.

Another of the same family was / Sr Edwd. Swift, well known in the times of the great Rebellion and usurpation, but I am ignorant whether he left heirs or no.

Of the other branch whereof the greatest part settled in Ireland The Founder was William Swift Prebendary of Canterbury, towards the last years of Qu. Elisab. and during the reign of K. James 1st. He was a Divine of some distinction. There is a Sermon of his extant and the Title is to be seen in the Catalogue of the Bodleyan Library, but I never could get a Copy, and I suppose it would now be of little value.

This William married the Heiress of Philpot, I suppose a Yorkshire Gentleman, by whom he got a very considerable estate, which however she kept in her own power, I know not by what artifice. [*Added in the mar-*

gin: She was a capricious ill-natured and passionate woman, of which I have been told severall instances] and it hath been a continuall tradition in the family that she absolutely disinherited her onely son Thomas for no greater crime than that of robbing an orchard when he / was a boy. And thus much is certain that Thomas never enjoyed more than one hundred pounds a year which was all at Goodrich in Herefordshire, [*added in margin:* except—*above* and *crossed out*—a Church or Chaptr Lease, which was not renewed] whereof not above one half is now in the possession of a great-great-grandson.

His original picture is now in the hands of Godwin Swift of Dublin Esqr his great Grandson as well as that of his wife's [*added in margin:* who seems to have a good deal of the Shrew in her Countenance] whose [of *erased*] arms as an heiress are joined with his own, and by the last he seems to have been a person somewhat fantastick. For there he gives as his device a Dolphin (in those days called a Swift) twisted about an Anchor, with this motto, Festine lente.[1]

There is likewise a Seal with the same coat of arms, (but not joynd with the wifes) which the sd William commonly made use of, and this is also now in the Possession of Godwin Swift above mentioned.

His eldest son Thomas[2] seems to [be *erased*] have been a Clergy-man before his Fathers death. He was Vicar of Goodri[*dge*]ch in Herefordshire, within a mile or two of Ross, he had likewise another Church-living with about one hundred pounds a year in Land (part whereof was by Church Leases)

[*N.B. The phrase in brackets crossed out and three and a half lines in the margin thoroughly obliterated.*]

as I have already mentioned. He built a house on his own Land in the Village of Goodri[*dge*]ch, which by the Architecture, denotes the builder to have been somewhat whimsical and singular, and very much towards a Projector. The house is above an hundred years old and still in good repair, inhabited by a Tenant of the femal line, but the Landlord a young Gentleman lives upon his own estate in Ireland. [*Another passage entirely obliterated in the margin.*]

This Thomas was more [*later:* much] distinguished by his courage, as well as his loyalty to K. Charles the 1st, and the Sufferings he underwent for that Prince, more than any person of his condition in England. Some Historians / of those times relate severall particulars [*in margin:* See a book called Mercurius Rusticus, and another in Folio called the Lives of those who suffered persecution for K. Ch. 1.] of what he acted, and what hardships he underwent for the Person and cause of that blessed Martyred Prince, He was plundred by the roundheads six and thirty times [*in margin:* Some say above 50]. He engaged his small estate, and gatherd all the money he could get, quilted it in his wastcoat, got off to [*some erasures*] a town held for the King, where [he was askt *erased*] being asked by the Governr who knew him well, that he could do for his Majesty, Mr Swift said he would give the King his Coat, and stripping it off presented it to the Governor, who observing it to be worth little, Mr Swift said, then take my wastcoat, he bid [him *erased and in margin* the Governor] weigh it in his hand, who ordering it to be unripped found it lined with three hundred broad pieces of gold, which as it proved a seasonable relief, must be allowed an extraordinary supply from a private Clergy-man with ten Children of a small Estate, so often plundred and soon after turned out of / his livings in the Church.

At another time being inform'd that three hundred horse of the Rebel Party intended in a week to pass over a certain river upon an attempt against the Cavaliers, Mr Swift having a head mechanically turned [with some knowledge in the Mathematicks *crossed out*] he contrived certain pieces of Iron with three Spikes, whereof one must allways be with the point upwards: he placed them over night in the ford where he received notice that the Rebels would pass early the next morning, which they accordingly did, and lost two hundred of their men, who were drowned or trod to death by the falling of their horses, or / torn by the Spikes.

His Sons, whereof [fore *erased*] four were settled in Ireld (driven thither by their sufferings, and by the death of their father) [had *erased*] related many other passages [from *erased*] which they learned either from their father himself, or from what had been told [related to *erased*] them by the most credible Persons of Herefordshire and some neighboring Countyes, and which some of those Sons often told to their children many of which are still remembered, but many more forgot.

He was deprived of both his Church livings [sooner than most others *erased and in margin:* sooner than most other Loyall Clergymen [for *crossed out*] upon account of his superior zeal for the King's Cause] and his estate sequestred. His Preferments [at least that of Goodridge *added above the line*] were given to a fanatical Saint, who scrupled not / however to conform upon the Restoration, and lived many years, I think till after the Revolution, I have seen many Persons at Goodridge, who knew and told me his name, which I cannot now remembr.

[*Added later in the margin:* The Lord Treasurer Oxford told [him *erased*] the Dean that he had among his Father's (Sr Edward Harley's) Papers severall Letters from Mr Thomas Swift writ in those Times, which he promised to give to the Grandson whose life I am writing, but nevr going to his House in Herefordshire while he was Treasurer, and the Queen's death happening in three days after his removal, the Dean went to Ireld, and the Earl being Tryed for his life, and dying while the Dean was in Ireld, he could never get them.]

Mr Thomas Swift dyed in the year 1658, and in the [*number obliterated*] year of his Age, His body lyes under the Altar at Goodri[*dge*]ch with a short inscription. He dyed about two Years before the return of King Charles the Second, who by the reccommendations of some Prelates had promised if ever God should restore him, that he would promote Mr Swift in the Church, and otherways reward his family for [what they had suffered *erased*] his extraordinary Services / and zeal, and persecutions in the royal cause. But Mr Swifts merit dyed with himself.

He left ten Sons and three or four Daughters, most of which lived to be Men and Women. His eldest Son, Godwin Swift of the Inner Temple Esqr (so styled by Guillim) [*in margin:* The Herald; in whose book The Family is described at large.] was I think called to the barr before the Restoration. He marryed a relation of the old Marchioness of Ormond, and upon that account as well as his fathers loyalty, the old D of Ormonde made him his attorney generall in the Palatinate of Tippe[*rar*]y. He had four wives, one of which to the great offence of his family was coheiress to Admiral Deane who was one of the Regicides. [who *erased*] Godwin left severall children who have all estates. He was an / ill pleader, but [perhaps a little too *added above the line*] dextrous in the subtil parts of the Law.

The second Son of Mr Thomas Swift was called by the same Name, was bred at Oxford, and took Oders. He marryed the eldest Daughter of Sr Wm D'avenant, but dyed young and left onely one son, who was also called Thomas, and is now Rectr of Puttenham in Surry. His widow lived long, was extremely poor, and in part supported by the famous Dr South who had been her husband's intimate friend.

The rest of his Sons, as far as I [*erasure*] can call to mind were Mr Dryden Swift (called so after the name of his mother, who was a near relation to Mr Dryden the Poet,[3] / William, Adam, and Jonathan [*erased and inserted above the line before Adam*] who all lived and dyed in Ireland. But none of them left male issue except Jonathan, who besides a Daughter left one Son born seven Months after his fathers death, of whose life I intend to write a few memorials.

J.S. D.D., and D of St P——[4] was the onely son of Jonathan Swift, who was the seventh or eighth son of [that eminent Person *erased*] Mr Thomas Swift above mentioned, so eminent for his Loyalty and his sufferings.

His Father dyed young, about two years after his marriage. He had some employments, and agencyes. [had *erased*] his death was much lamented on account of his reputation for integrity with a tolerable good / understanding.

He married Mrs Abigail Erich of Leicester-shire, descended from the most antient family of [the *added above the line*] Ericks, who derive their Lineage from Erick the Forester, a great Commander, who raised an army to oppose the Invasion of William the Conqueror, by whom he was vanquished, but [was *erased*] afterwards employed to command that Prince's forces, and in his old age retired to his house in Leicestershire where his family hath continued ever since, but declining every age, and are now in the condition of very private Gentlemen.

This marriage was on both sides very indiscreet, for his wife brought [Mr Swift *erased*] her husband little or no fortune, and his death / happening so suddenly before he could make a sufficient establishment for his family: And his son (not then born) hath often been heard to say that he felt the consequences of that marriage not onely through the whole course of his education, but during the greatest part of his life.

He was born in Dublin on St Andrews day, [*a date? completely obliterated in the margin*] and when he was a year old, an event happened to him that seems very unusuall; for his Nurse who was a woman of Whitehaven, [having absolute *crossed out*] being under an absolute necessity of seeing one of her relations, who was then extremely sick, and from whom she expected a Legacy; and being at the same time extremely fond of the infant, she stole him on shipboard unknown to his Mother and Uncle, and carryed him with / her to Whitehaven, where he continued for almost [two *erased*] three years. For when the matter was discovered, His Mother sent orders by all means not to hazard a second voyage, till he could be better able to bear it. The nurse was so carefull of him that before he returnd he had learnt to spell, and by the time that he was three years old he could read any chapter in the Bible.

After his return to Ireld, [when *erased*] he was sent at six years old to the School of Kilkenny, from whence at fourteen he was admitted into the University at Dublin, where by the ill Treatment of his nearest Relations, he was so discouraged and sunk in his Spirits, that he too much neglected his [Studyes *erased*] Academical Studyes, for [*in the margin:* some parts of] which he had no great relish by Nature, and turned himself to reading

History and Poetry. / So that when the time came for taking his degree of Batchlor, although he had lived with great Regularity and due Observance of the Statutes, he was stopped of his Degree, for Dullness and Insufficiency, and at last hardly admitted in a manner little to his Credit, which is called in that Colle[d]ge *Speciali gratia*, [which *erased and in the margin:* And this descreditable mark] as I am told, stands upon record in their Colle[d]ge Registry.

The Troubles[5] then breaking out, he went to his Mother, who lived in Leicester, and after continuing there some Months, he was received [into the *erased*] by Sr Wm Temple,[6] whose Father had been a great Friend to the Family, and who was now retired to his House called Moorpark near Farnham in Surrey, where he continued for about two years. For he happened before / twenty years old, by a Surfeit of fruit to contract a giddyness and coldness of Stomach, that almost brought him to his Grave, and this disorder [continued *erased*] pursued him with Intermissions of two or thre years to the end of his Life. Upon this Occasion he returned to Ireld by advice of Physicians, who weakly imagined that his native air might be of some use to recover his Health. But growing worse, he soon went back to Sr Wm Temple; with whom growing into some confidence, he was often trusted with matters of great Importance. King William had a high esteem for Sr Wm Temple by a long acquaintance, while that Gentlmn was Ambassador and Mediator of a Generall peace at Nimeguen. The King soon after his Expedition to England, visited his old Friend often at Sheen, and took his advice / in affairs of greatest consequence. But Sr W. T. weary of living so near London, and resolving to retire to a more private Scene, bought an Estate near Farnham in Surrey of about 100 ll a year, [*added later in the line*] where Mr Swift [*and in the margin*] accompanied him.

About that time a Bill was brought in to the H. of Commons for Triennial Parlmts, against which the King who was a stranger to our Constitution, was very averse, by the Advice of some [very *erased*] weak People, who persuaded the Earl of Portland that K.Ch. 1st lost his [life and *erased*] Crown and Life by consenting to pass such a bill. The Earl who was a weak man, came down to Moorpark by His Majesty's orders to have Sr Wm Temple's advice, who said much to show him the Mistake. But he continued still to advise the King against passing the Bill. Whereupon Mr Swift was sent to Kensington with the whole Account of that matter, in writing, to convince the King and the Earl how ill they were informed. He told the Earl to whom he was referred by His Majesty, (and gave it in writing) that the Ruin of K. Charles the 1st was not owing to his passing the Triennial bill, which did not hinder him from dissolving any Parlmt, but to the passing another bill, which put it out of his / power to dissolve the Parliamnt then in being, without the consent of the House. Mr Swift who was well versed in English History although he were then under [three and *erased*] twenty [one *added above the line*] years old, gave the King a short account of the Matter, but a more large one to the Earl of Portland; but all in vain: For the King by ill advisers was prevayled upon [*above the line:* to refuse passing the Bill]. This was the first time that Mr Swift had ever any converse with [a King *erased*] Courts, and he told his friends [that *erased*] it was the first incident that helped to cure him of vanity. The Consequence of this wrong Step in His Majesty was very unhappy; For it put that Prince under a necessity of introducing those People called Whigs into power and Employments, in order to pacify them. For, although it be held a part of the Kings Prerogative to refuse passing Bills, Yet the Learned in the Law, think otherwise, from that Expression used at the Coronation wherein the Prince obligeth himself to consent to all Laws *quas vulgus elegerit.*[7]

Mr Swift lived with him some time, but resolving to settle himself in some way of [life *erased*] living, was inclined to take orders. However, although his fortune was very small, he had a scruple of entring into the Church meerly for support, and Sr Wm Temple then being Master of the Rolls in Ireland offered him an Employ of about 120 ll a year in that office, whereupon Mr Swift told him, that since he had now an opportunity of living without being driven into the Church for a maintenance, he was resolved to [go to *above the line*] Ireld and take holy Orders. He was recommended to the Lord Capel, then Ld Deputy, who gave him a Prebend in the North, worth about 100 ll a year, of which / growing weary in a few months, he returned to England; resigned his Living in favor of a Friend, and continued to Sr W Temple's house till the Death of that great Man, who besides a Legacy [of a 100 ll *erased*] left him the care and trust and Advantage of publishing his posthumous Writings.

Upon this Event Mr Swift removed to London, and applyed by Petition to King William, upon the Claym of a Promise his Majesty had mad[*e*] to Sr W T that he would give Mr Swift a Prebend of Canterbury or Westminster. The Earl of Rumney who professed much friendship for him, promised to second his Petition, but, as he was an old vitious [rake *erased*] illiterate Rake without any sense of Truth or Honor, said not a word to the King: And Mr Swift after long attendance in vain; thought it better to comply with an Invitation given him by the E. of Berkeley to attend him to Ireland as his Chaplain and private Secretary; His Lordship having been appointed one of the Lords Justices of that Kingdom. / He attended his Lordship; who landed near Waterford, and Mr. Swift acted as Secretary [till *erased*] the whole Journy to Dublin. But another Person had so far insinuated himself into the Earls favor, by telling him, that the Post of (private *erased*) Secretary was not proper for a Clergyman, nor would be of any advantage to one who aimed onely at Church-preferments, that his Lordship after a poor Apology gave that Office to the other.

In some Months, the Deanry of Derry fell vacant; and it was [my Lord's *erased, and in the margin* this *erassd, then added:* the Earl of Berkeley's] turn to dispose of it. Yet things were so ordered that the Secretary having received a Bribe, the Deanry was disposed of to another, and Mr Swift was put off with some other Church-livings not worth above a third part of that rich Deanry, and at this present time, not a sixth. The Excuse [was *erased*] pretended was his being too young, although he / were then 30 years old.

ON THE

DEATH

OF

MRS. JOHNSON,[1] [STELLA.]

This day, being Sunday, January 28th, 1727–8, about eight o'clock at night, a servant brought me a note, with an account of the death of the truest, most virtuous, and valuable friend, that I, or perhaps any other person ever was blessed with. She expired about six in the evening of this day; and, as soon as I am left alone, which is about eleven at night, I resolve, for my own satisfaction, to say something of her life and character.

She was born at Richmond in Surrey on the thirteenth day of March, in the year 1681. Her father was a younger brother of a good family in Nottinghamshire, her mother of a lower degree; and indeed she had little to boast of her birth. I knew her from six years old, and had some share in her education, by directing what books she should read, and perpetually instructing her in the principles of honour and virtue; from which she never swerved in any one action or moment of her life. She was sickly from her childhood until about the age of fifteen: But then grew into perfect health, and was looked upon as one of the most beautiful, graceful, and agreeable young women in London, only a little too fat. Her hair was blacker than a raven, and every feature of her face in perfection. She lived generally in the country, with a family, where she contracted an intimate friendship with another lady* of more advanced years. I was then (to my mortification) settled in Ireland; and, about a year after, going to visit my friends in England, I found she was a little uneasy upon the death of a person on whom she had some dependance. Her fortune, at that time, was in

* Mrs. Dingley.

all not above fifteen hundred pounds, the interest of which was but a scanty maintenance, in so dear a country, for one of her spirit. Upon this consideration, and indeed very much for my own satisfaction, who had few friends or acquaintance in Ireland, I prevailed with her and her dear friend and companion, the other lady, to draw what money they had into Ireland, a great part of their fortune being in annuities upon funds. Money was then at ten *per cent.* in Ireland, besides the advantage of turning it, and all necessaries of life at half the price. They complied with my advice, and soon after came over; but, I happening to continue some time longer in England, they were much discouraged to live in Dublin, where they were wholly strangers. She was at that time about nineteen years old, and her person was soon distinguished. But the adventure looked so like a frolic, the censure held, for some time, as if there were a secret history in such a removal; which, however, soon blew off by her excellent conduct. She came over with her friend on the ———— in the year 170–; and they both lived together until this day, when death removed her from us. For some years past, she had been visited with continual ill-health; and several times, within these two years, her life was despaired of. But, for this twelve-month past, she never had a day's health; and, properly speaking, she hath been dying six months, but kept alive, almost against nature, by the generous kindness of two physicians, and the care of her friends. Thus far I writ the same night between eleven and twelve.

Never was any of her sex born with better gifts of the mind, or more improved them by reading and conversation. Yet her memory was not of the best, and was impaired in the latter years of her life. But I cannot call to mind that I ever once heard her make a wrong judgment of persons, books, or affairs. Her advice was always the best, and with the greatest freedom, mixt with the greatest decency. She had a gracefulness some-what more than human in every motion, word, and action. Never was so happy a conjunction of civility, freedom, easiness and sincerity. There seemed to be a combination among all that knew her, to treat her with a dignity much beyond her rank: Yet people of all sorts were never more easy than in her company. Mr. Addison, when he was in Ireland, being in-troduced to her, immediately found her out; and, if he had not soon after left the kingdom, assured me he would have used all endeavours to culti-vate her friendship. A rude or conceited coxcomb passed his time very ill, upon the least breach of respect; for in such a case she had no mercy, but was sure to expose him to the contempt of the standers-by; yet in such a manner as he was ashamed to complain, and durst not resent. All of us, who had the happiness of her friendship, agreed unanimously, that, in an afternoon or evening's conversation, she never failed before we parted of delivering the best thing that was said in the company. Some of us have written down several of her sayings, or what the French call *Bon Mots*, wherein she excelled almost beyond belief. She never mistook the understanding of others; nor ever said a severe word, but where a much severer was deserved.

Her servants loved and almost adored her at the same time. She would, upon occasions, treat them with freedom, yet her demeanour was so awful, that they durst not fail in the least point of respect. She chid them seldom, but it was with severity, which had an effect upon them for a long time after.

January 29th, My Head achs, and I can write no more.

January 30th, Tuesday.

This is the night of the funeral, which my sickness will not suffer me to attend. It is now nine at night, and I am removed into another apartment, that I may not see the light in the church, which is just over against the window of my bedchamber.

With all the softness of temper that became a lady, she had the personal courage of a hero. She and her friend having removed their lodgings to a new house, which stood solitary, a parcel of rogues, armed, attempted the house, where there was only one boy: She was then about four and twenty: And, having been warned to apprehend some such attempt, she learned the management of a pistol; and the other women and servants being half-dead with fear, she stole softly to her dining-room window, put on a black hood, to prevent being seen, primed the pistol fresh, gently lifted up the sash; and, taking aim with the utmost presence of mind, discharged the pistol loaden with the bullets, into the body of one villain, who stood the fairest mark. The fellow, mortally wounded, was carried off by the rest, and died the next morning, but his companions could not be found. The Duke of Ormond hath often drank her health to me upon that account, and had always an high esteem of her. She was indeed under some apprehensions of going in a boat, after some danger she had narrowly escaped by water, but she was reasoned thoroughly out of it. She was never known to cry out, or discover any fear, in a coach or on horseback, or any uneasiness by those sudden accidents with which most of her sex, either by weakness or affectation, appear so much disordered.

She never had the least absence of mind in conversation, nor given to interruption, or appeared eager to put in her word by waiting impatiently until another had done. She spoke in a most agreeable voice, in the plainest words, never hesitating, except out of modesty before new faces, where she was somewhat reserved; nor, among her nearest friends, ever spoke much at a time. She was but little versed in the common topics of female chat; scandal, censure, and detraction, never came out of her mouth: Yet, among a few friends, in private conversation, she made little ceremony in discovering her contempt of a coxcomb, and describing all his follies to the life; but the follies of her own sex she was rather inclined to extenuate or to pity.

When she was once convinced by open facts of any breach of truth or honour, in a person of high station, especially in the church, she could not conceal her indignation, nor hear them named without shewing her displeasure in her countenance; particularly one or two of the latter sort, whom she had known and esteemed, but detested above all mankind, when it was manifest that they had sacrificed those two precious virtues to their ambition, and would much sooner have forgiven them the common immoralities of the laity.

Her frequent fits of sickness, in most parts of her life, had prevented her from making that progress in reading which she would otherwise have done. She was well versed in the Greek and Roman story, and was not unskilled in that of France and England. She spoke French perfectly, but forgot much of it by neglect and sickness. She had read carefully all the best books of travels, which serve to open and enlarge the mind. She understood the Platonic and Epicurean philosophy, and judged very well of the defects of the latter. She made very judicious abstracts of the best books she had read. She understood the nature of government, and could point out all the errors of Hobbes, both in that and religion. She had a good insight into physic, and knew somewhat of anatomy; in both which she was instructed in her younger days by an eminent physician, who had her long under his care, and bore the highest esteem for her person and understanding. She had a true taste of wit and good sense, both in poetry and prose, and was a perfect good critic of style: Neither was it easy to find a more proper or impartial judge, whose advice an author might better rely on, if he intended to send a thing into the world, provided it was on a subject that came within the compass of her knowledge. Yet, perhaps, she was sometimes too severe, which is a safe and pardonable error. She preserved her wit, judgment, and vivacity to the last, but often used to complain of her memory.

Her fortune, with some accession, could not, as I have heard say, amount to much more than two thousand pounds, whereof a great part fell with her life, having been placed upon annuities in England, and one in Ireland. In a person so extraordinary, perhaps it may be pardonable to mention some particulars, although of little moment, further than to set forth her character. Some presents of gold-pieces being often made to her while she was a girl, by her mother and other friends, on promise to keep them, she grew into such a spirit of thrift, that, in about three years, they amounted to above two hundred pounds. She used to shew them with boasting; but her mother, apprehending she would be cheated of them, prevailed, in some months, and with great importunities, to have them put out to interest: When the girl lost the pleasure of seeing and counting her gold, which she never failed of doing many times in a day, and despaired of heaping up such another treasure, her humour took quite the contrary turn: She grew careless and squandering of every new acquisition, and so continued until about two and twenty; when, by advice of some friends, and the fright of paying large bills of tradesmen, who enticed her into their debt, she began to reflect upon her own folly, and was never at rest until she had discharged all her shop-bills, and refunded herself a considerable sum she had run out. After which, by the addition of a few years, and a superior understanding, she became, and continued all her life a most prudent œconomist; yet still with a strong bent to the liberal side, wherein she gratified herself by avoiding all expence in cloaths, (which she ever despised) beyond what was merely decent. And, although her frequent returns of sickness were very chargeable, except fees to physicians, of which she met with several so generous, that she could force nothing on them, (and indeed she must otherwise have been undone;) yet she never was without a considerable sum of ready money. Insomuch that, upon her death, when her nearest friends thought her very bare, her executors found in her strong box about a hundred and fifty pounds in gold. She lamented the narrowness of her fortune in nothing so much, as that it did not enable her to entertain her friends so often, and in so hospitable a manner as she desired. Yet they were always welcome; and, while she was in health to direct, were treated with neatness and elegance: So that the revenues of her and her companion, passed for much more considerable than they really were. They lived always in lodgings, their domesticks consisting of two maids and one man. She kept an account of all the family-expences, from her arrival in Ireland to some months before her death; and she would often repine, when looking back upon the annals of her household bills, that every thing necessary for life was double the price, while interest of money was sunk almost to one half; so that the addition made to her fortune was indeed grown absolutely necessary.

[I since writ as I found time.]

But her charity to the poor was a duty not to be diminished, and therefore became a tax upon those tradesmen who furnish the fopperies of other ladies. She bought cloaths as seldom as possible, and those as plain and cheap as consisted with the situation she was in; and wore no lace for many years. Either her judgment or fortune was extraordinary, in the choice of those on whom she bestowed her charity; for it went further in doing good, than double the sum from any other hand. And I have heard her say, she always met with gratitude from the poor: Which must be owing to her skill in distinguishing proper objects, as well as her gracious manner in relieving them.

But she had another quality that much delighted her, although it may be thought a kind of check upon her bounty; however, it was a pleasure she could not resist: I mean that of making agreeable presents, wherein I never knew her equal, although it be an affair of as delicate a nature as most in the course of life. She used to define a present, That it was a gift to a friend of something he wanted or was fond of, and which could not be easily gotten for money. I am confident, during my acquaintance with her, she hath, in these, and some other kinds of liberality, disposed of to the value of several hundred pounds. As to presents made to herself, she received them with great unwillingness, but especially from those to whom she had ever given any; being on all occasions the most disinterested mortal I ever knew or heard of.

From her own disposition, at least as much as from the frequent want of health, she seldom made any visits; but her own lodgings, from before twenty years old, were frequented by many persons of the graver sort, who all respected her highly, upon her good sense, good manners, and conversation. Among these were the late Primate Lindsay, Bishop Lloyd, Bishop Ashe, Bishop Brown, Bishop Stearn, Bishop Pulleyn, with some others of later date; and indeed the greatest number of her acquaintance was among the clergy. Honour, truth, liberality, good-nature, and modesty, were the virtues she chiefly possessed, and most valued in her acquaintance; and where she found them, would be ready to allow for some defects, nor valued them less, although they did not shine in learning or in wit; but would never give the least allowance for any failures in the former, even to those who made the greatest figure in either of the two latter. She had no use of any person's liberality, yet her detestation of covetous people made her uneasy if such a one was in her company; upon which occasion she would say many things very entertaining and humorous.

She never interrupted any person who spoke; she laught at no mistakes they made, but helped them out with modesty; and if a good thing were spoken, but neglected, she would not let it fall, but set it in the best light to those who were present. She listened to all that was said, and had never the least distraction, or absence of thought.

It was not safe nor prudent, in her presence, to offend in the least word against modesty; for she then gave full employment to her wit, her contempt and resentment, under which even stupidity and brutality were forced to sink into confusion; and the guilty person, but her future avoiding him like a bear or a satyr, was never in a way to transgress a second time.

It happened one single coxcomb, of the pert kind, was in her company, among several other ladies; and, in his flippant way, began to deliver some double meanings; the rest flapt their fans, and used the other common expedients practised in such cases, of appearing not to mind or comprehend what was said. Her behaviour was very different, and perhaps may be censured. She said thus to the man: 'Sir, all these ladies and I understand your meaning very well, having, in spite of our care, too often met with those of your sex who wanted manners and good sense. But, believe me, neither virtuous, nor even vicious women love such kind of conversation. However, I will leave you, and report your behaviour: And, whatever visit I make, I shall first enquire at the door whether you are in the house, that I may be sure to avoid you.' I know not whether a majority of the ladies would approve of such a proceeding; but I believe the practice of it would soon put an end to that corrupt conversation, the worst effect of dulness, ignorance, impudence, and vulgarity, and the highest affront to the modesty and understanding of the female sex.

By returning very few visits, she had not much company of her own sex, except those whom she most loved for their easiness, or esteemed for their good sense; and those, not insisting on ceremony, came often to her. But she rather chose men for her companions, the usual topics of ladies discourse being such as she had little knowledge of, and less relish. Yet no man was upon the rack to entertain her, for she easily descended to any thing that was innocent and diverting. News, politics, censure, family-management, or town-talk, she always diverted to something else; but these indeed seldom happened, for she chose her company better: And therefore many, who mistook her and themselves, having solicited her acquaintance, and finding themselves disappointed after a few visits, dropt off; and she was never known to enquire into the reason, or ask what was become of them.

She was never positive in arguing, and she usually treated those who were so, in a manner which well enough gratified that unhappy disposition; yet in such a sort as made it very contemptible, and at the same time did some hurt to the owners. Whether this proceeded from her easiness in general, or from her indifference to certain persons, or from her despair of mending them, or from the same practice which she much liked in Mr. Addison, I cannot determine; but when she saw any of the company very warm in a wrong opinion, she was more inclined to confirm them in it, than oppose them. The excuse she commonly gave when her friends asked the reason, was, That it prevented noise, and saved time. Yet I have known her very angry with some whom she much esteemed for sometimes falling into that infirmity.

She loved Ireland much better than the generality of those who owe both their birth and riches to it; and, having brought over all the fortune she had in money, left the reversion of the best part of it, one thousand pounds, to Dr. Stephens's Hospital. She detested the tyranny and injustice of England, in their treatment of this kingdom. She had indeed reason to love a country, where she had the esteem and friendship of all who knew her, and the universal good report of all who ever heard of her, without one exception, if I am told the truth by those who keep general conversation. Which character is the more extraordinary, in falling to a person of so much knowledge, wit, and vivacity, qualities that are used to create envy, and consequently censure; and must be rather imputed to her great modesty, gentle behaviour, and inoffensiveness, than to her superior virtues.

Although her knowledge, from books and company, was much more extensive than usually falls to the share of her sex; yet she was so far from making a parade of it, that her female visitants, on their first acquaintance, who expected to discover it, by what they call hard words and deep discourse, would be sometimes disappointed, and say, they found she was like other women. But wise men, through all her modesty, whatever they discoursed on, could easily observe that she understood them very well, by the judgment shewn in her observations, as well as in her questions.

THOUGHTS

ON

Various Subjects

We have just Religion enough to make us *hate*, but not enough to make us *love* one another.

REFLECT on Things past, as Wars, Negotiations, Factions, and the like; we enter so little into those Interests, that we wonder how Men could possibly be so busy, and concerned for Things so transitory: Look on the present Times, we find the same Humour, yet wonder not at all.

A WISE Man endeavours, by considering all Circumstances, to make Conjectures, and form Conclusions: But the smallest Accident intervening, (and in the Course of Affairs it is impossible to foresee all) doth often produce such Turns and Changes, that at last he is just as much in doubt of Events, as the most ignorant and unexperienced Person.

POSITIVENESS is a good Quality for Preachers and Orators; because whoever would obtrude his Thoughts and Reasons upon a Multitude, will convince others the more, as he appears convinced himself.

HOW is it possible to expect that Mankind will take *Advice*, when they will not so much as take *Warning*?

I FORGET whether Advice be among the lost Things which, *Ariosto* says, are to be found in the Moon: That and Time ought to have been there.

NO Preacher is listened to, but Time; which gives us the same Train and Turn of Thought, that elder People have tried in vain to put into our Heads before.

WHEN we desire or sollicit any Thing; our Minds run wholly on the good Side, or Circumstances of it; when it is obtained, our Minds run only on the bad ones.

IN a *Glass-House,* the Workmen often fling in a small Quantity of fresh Coals, which seems to disturb the Fire, but very much enlivens it. This may allude to a gentle stirring of the Passions, that the Mind may not languish.

RELIGION seems to have grown an Infant with Age, and requires Miracles to nurse it, as it had in its Infancy.

ALL Fits of Pleasure are ballanced by an equal Degree of Pain, or Languor; it is like spending this Year, Part of the next Year's Revenue.

THE latter Part of a wise Man's Life is taken up in curing the Follies, Prejudices, and false Opinions he had contracted in the former.

IF a Writer would know how to behave himself with relation to Posterity; let him consider in old Books, what he finds, that he is glad to know; and what Omissions he most laments.

WHATEVER the Poets pretend, it is plain they give Immortality to none but themselves: It is *Homer* and *Virgil* we reverence and admire, not *Achilles* or *Æneas.* With Historians it is quite the contrary; our Thoughts are taken up with the Actions, Persons, and Events we read; and we little regard the Authors.

WHEN a true Genius appears in the World, you may know him by this infallible Sign; that the Dunces are all in Confederacy against him.

MEN, who possess all the Advantages of Life, are in a State where there are many Accidents to disorder and discompose, but few to please them.

IT is unwise to punish Cowards with Ignominy; for if they had regarded that, they would not have been Cowards: Death is their proper Punishment, because they fear it most.

THE greatest Inventions were produced in the Times of Ignorance; as the Use of the *Compass, Gunpowder,* and *Printing;* and by the dullest Nation, as the *Germans.*

ONE Argument to prove that the common Relations of *Ghosts* and *Spectres* are generally false; may be drawn from the Opinion held, that Spirits are never seen by more than one Person at a Time: That is to say, it seldom happens that above one Person in a Company is possest with any high Degree of Spleen or Melancholy.

I AM apt to think, that in the Day of Judgment there will be small Allowance given to the Wise for their want of Morals, or to the Ignorant for their want of Faith; because, both are without Excuse. This renders the Advantages equal of Ignorance and Knowledge. But some Scruples in the Wise, and some Vices in the Ignorant, will perhaps be forgiven upon the Strength of Temptation to each.

THE Value of several Circumstances in History, lessens very much by distance of Time; although some minute Circumstances are very valuable; and it requires great Judgment in a Writer to distinguish.

IT is grown a Word of Course for Writers to say, this *critical Age,* as Divines say, this *sinful Age.*

IT is pleasant to observe, how free the present Age is in laying Taxes on the next. *Future Ages shall talk of this: This shall be famous to all Posterity.* Whereas, their Time and Thoughts will be taken up about present Things, as ours are now.

THE *Camelion,* who is said to feed upon nothing but Air, hath of all Animals the nimblest Tongue.

WHEN a Man is made a spiritual Peer, he loses his Sirname; when a temporal, his Christian Name.

IT is in Disputes as in Armies; where the weaker Side sets up false Lights, and makes a great Noise, that the Enemy may believe them to be more numerous and strong than they really are.

SOME Men, under the Notions of weeding out Prejudices; eradicate Religion, Virtue, and common Honesty.

IN all well-instituted Commonwealths, Care hath been taken to limit Mens Possessions; which is done for many Reasons; and among the rest, for one that perhaps is not often considered: Because when Bounds are set to Mens Desires, after they have acquired as much as the Laws will permit them, their private Interest is at an End; and they have nothing to do, but to take care of the Publick.

THERE are but three Ways for a Man to revenge himself of a censorious World: To despise it; to return the like; or to endeavour to live so as to avoid it. The first of these is usually pretended; the last is almost impossible; the universal Practice is for the second.

Herodotus tells us, that in cold Countries Beasts very seldom have Horns; but in hot they have very large ones. This might bear a pleasant Application.

I NEVER heard a finer Piece of Satyr against *Lawyers,* than that of *Astrologers;* when they pretend by Rules of Art to foretell in what Time a Suit will end, and whether to the Advantage of the Plaintiff or Defendant: Thus making the Matter depend entirely upon the Influence of the Stars, without the least regard to the Merits of the Cause.

THAT Expression in *Apocrypha* about *Tobit,* and his Dog following him, I have often heard ridiculed; yet *Homer* has the same Words of *Telemachus* more than once; and *Virgil* says something like it of *Evander.* And I take the Book of *Tobit* to be partly poetical.

I HAVE known some Men possessed of good Qualities, which were very serviceable to others, but useless to themselves; like a Sun-Dial on the Front of a House, to inform the Neighbours and Passengers, but not the Owner within.

IF a Man would register all his Opinions upon Love, Politicks, Religion, Learning, and the like; beginning from his Youth, and so go on to old Age: What a Bundle of Inconsistencies and Contradictions would appear at last?

WHAT they *do* in Heaven we are ignorant of; what they do *not* we are told expresly; that they neither marry, nor are given in Marriage.

WHEN a Man observes the Choice of Ladies now-a-days, in the dispensing of their Favours; can he forbear paying some Veneration to the Memory of those Mares mentioned by *Xenophon;* who, while their Manes were on; that is, while they were in their Beauty, would never admit the Embraces of an Ass. *De re equestri.*

IT is a miserable Thing to live in Suspence; it is the Life of a Spider. *Vive quidem, pende tamen, improba, dixit.*

THE Stoical Scheme of supplying our Wants, by lopping off our Desires; is like cutting off our Feet when we want Shoes.

PHYSICIANS ought not to give their Judgment of Religion, for the same Reason that Butchers are not admitted to be Jurors upon Life and Death.

THE Reason why so few Marriages are happy, is, because young Ladies spend their Time in making *Nets,* and not in making *Cages.*

IF a Man will observe as he walks the Streets, I believe he will find the merriest Countenances in Mourning-Coaches.

NOTHING more unqualifies a Man to act with Prudence, than a Misfortune that is attended with Shame and Guilt.

THE Power of Fortune is confest only by the Miserable; for the Happy impute all their Success to Prudence or Merit.

AMBITION often puts Men upon doing the meanest Offices; so climbing is performed in the same Posture with Creeping.

ILL Company is like a Dog, who fouls those most whom he loves best.

CENSURE is the Tax a Man pays to the Publick for being eminent.

THOUGHTS

ON

RELIGION

I am in all opinions to believe according to my own impartial reason; which I am bound to inform and improve, as far as my capacity and opportunities will permit.

It may be prudent in me to act sometimes by other men's reason, but I can think only by my own.

If another man's reason fully convinceth me, it becomes my own reason.

To say a man is bound to believe, is neither truth nor sense.

You may force men, by interest or punishment, to say or swear they believe, and to act as if they believed: You can go no further.

Every man, as a member of the commonwealth, ought to be content with the possession of his own opinion in private, without perplexing his neighbour or disturbing the public.

Violent zeal for truth hath an hundred to one odds to be either petulancy, ambition, or pride.

There is a degree of corruption where some nations, as bad as the world is, will proceed to an amendment; until which time particular men should be quiet.

To remove opinions fundamental in religion is impossible, and the attempt wicked, whether those opinions be true or false; unless your avowed design be to abolish that religion altogether. So, for instance, in the famous doctrine of Christ's divinity, which hath been universally received by all bodies of Christians, since the condemnation of Arianism under Constantine and his successors: Wherefore the proceedings of the Socinians are both vain and unwarrantable; because they will be never able to advance their own opinion, or meat any other success than breeding doubts and disturbances in the world. *Qui ratione sua disturbant mœnia mundi.*

The want of belief is a defect that ought to be concealed when it cannot be overcome.

The Christian religion, in the most early times, was proposed to the Jews and Heathens, without the article of Christ's divinity; which, I remember, Erasmus accounts for, by it's being too strong a meat for babes. Perhaps, if it were now softened by the Chinese missionaries, the conversion of those infidels would be less difficult: And we find by the Alcoran, it is the great stumbling block of the Mahometans. But, in a country already Christian, to bring so fundamental a point of faith into debate, can have no consequences that are not pernicious to morals and public peace.

I have been often offended to find St. Paul's allegories, and other figures of Grecian eloquence, converted by divines into articles of faith.

God's mercy is over all his works, but divines of all sorts lessen that mercy too much.

I look upon myself, in the capacity of a clergyman, to be one appointed by providence for defending a post assigned me, and for gaining over as many enemies as I can. Although I think my cause is just, yet one great motion is my submitting to the pleasure of Providence, and to the laws of my country.

I am not answerable to God for the doubts that arise in my own breast, since they are the consequence of that reason which he hath planted in me, if I take care to conceal those doubts from others, if I use my best endeavours to subdue them, and if they have no influence on the conduct of my life.

I believe that thousands of men would be orthodox enough in certain points, if divines had not been too curious, or too narrow, in reducing orthodoxy within the compass of subtleties, niceties, and distinctions, with little warrant from Scripture, and less from reason or good policy.

I never saw, heard, nor read, that the clergy were beloved in any nation where Christianity was the religion of the country. Nothing can render them popular but some degree of persecution.

Those fine gentlemen who affect the humour of railing at the clergy, are, I think, bound in honour to turn parsons themselves, and shew us better examples.

Miserable mortals! can we contribute to the *honour and Glory of God?* I could wish that expression were struck out of our Prayer-books.

Liberty of conscience, properly speaking, is no more than the liberty of possessing our own thoughts and opinions, which every man enjoys without fear for the magistrate: But how far he shall publicly act in pursuance of those opinions, is to be regulated by the laws of the country. Perhaps, in my own thoughts, I prefer a well-instituted commonwealth before a monarchy; and I know several others of the same opinion. Now, if, upon this pretence, I should insist upon liberty of conscience, form conventicles of republicans, and print books, preferring that government, and condemning what is established, the magistrate would, with great justice, hang me and my disciples. It is the same case in religion, although not so avowed, where liberty of conscience, under the present acceptation, equally produces revolutions, or at least convulsions and disturbances in a state; which politicians would see well enough, if their eyes were not blinded by faction, and of which these kingdoms, as well as France, Sweden, and other countries, are flaming instances. Cromwell's notion upon this article, was natural and right; when, upon the surrender of a town in Ireland, the Popish governor insisted upon an article for liberty of conscience, Cromwell said, he meddled with no man's conscience; but, if by liberty of the Mass, he had express orders from the parliament of England against admitting any such liberty at all.

It is impossible that any thing so natural, so necessary, and so universal as death, should ever have been designed by providence as an evil to mankind.

Although reason were intended by providence to govern our passions, yet it seems that, in two points of the greatest moment to the being and continuance of the world, God hath intended our passions to prevail over reason. The first is, the propagation of our species, since no wise man ever married from the dictates of reason. The other is, the love of life, which, from the dictates of reason, every man would despise, and wish it at an end, or that it never had a beginning.

FURTHER THOUGHTS ON RELIGION

The Scripture-system of man's creation, is what Christians are bound to believe, and seems most agreeable of all others to probability and reason. Adam was formed from a piece of clay, and Eve from one of his ribs. The text mentioneth nothing of his Maker's intending him for, except to rule over the beasts of the field and birds of the air. As to Eve, it doth not appear that her husband was her monarch, only she was to be his help meet, and placed in some degree of subjection. However, before his fall, the beasts were his most obedient subjects, whom he governed by absolute power. After his eating the forbidden fruit, the course of nature was changed, the animals began to reject his government; some were able to escape by flight, and others were too fierce to be attacked. The Scripture mentioneth no particular acts of royalty in Adam[1] over his posterity, who were cotemporary with him, or of any monarch until after the flood; whereof the first was Nimrod, the mighty hunter, who, as Milton expresseth it, made men, and not beasts, his prey. For men were easier caught by promises, and subdued by the folly or treachery of their own species. Whereas the brutes prevailed only by their courage or strength, which, among them, are peculiar to certain kinds. Lions, bears, elephants, and some other animals, are strong or valiant, and their species never degenerates in their native soil, except they happen to be enslaved or destroyed by human fraud: But men degenerate every day, merely by the folly, the perverseness, the avarice, the tyranny, the pride, the treachery, or inhumanity of their own kind.

VIII

PARODIES, HOAXES, AND SOTTISIERS, ETC.

A

MEDITATION

UPON A

BROOM-STICK:

ACCORDING TO

THE STYLE AND MANNER OF THE

HONOURABLE ROBERT BOYLE'S

MEDITATIONS

Written in the YEAR 1703.

This single Stick, which you now behold ingloriously lying in that neglected Corner, I once knew in a flourishing State in a Forest: It was full of Sap, full of Leaves, and full of Boughs: But now, in vain does the busy Art of Man pretend to vye with Nature, by tying that withered Bundle of Twigs to its sapless Trunk: It is now at best but the Reverse of what it was; a Tree turned upside down, the Branches on the Earth, and the Root in the Air: It is now handled by every dirty Wench, condemned to do her Drugery; and by a capricious Kind of Fate, destined to make other Things clean, and be nasty it self. At length, worn to the Stumps in the Service of the Maids, it is either thrown out of Doors, or condemned to its last Use of kindling a Fire. When I beheld this, I sighed, and said within my self SURELY MORTAL MAN IS A BROOMSTICK; Nature sent him into the World strong and lusty, in a thriving Condition, wearing his own Hair on his Head, the proper Branches of this reasoning Vegetable; till the Axe of Intemperance has lopped off his Green Boughs, and left him a withered Trunk: He then flies to Art, and puts on a *Perriwig;* valuing himself upon an unnatural Bundle of Hairs, all covered with Powder, that never grew on his Head: But now, should this our *Broom-stick* pretend to enter the Scene, proud of those *Birchen* Spoils it never bore, and all covered with Dust, though the Sweepings of the finest Lady's Chamber; we should be apt to ridicule and despise its Vanity. Partial Judges that we are of our own Excellencies, and other Mens Defaults!

BUT a *Broom-stick,* perhaps you will say, is an Emblem of a Tree standing on its Head; and pray what is Man but a topsy-turvy Creature? His Animal Faculties perpetually mounted on his Rational; his Head where his Heels should be, groveling on the Earth. And yet, with all his Faults, he sets up to be a universal Reformer and Correcter of Abuses; a Remover of Grievances; rakes into every Slut's Corner of Nature, bringing hidden Corruptions to the Light, and raiseth a mighty Dust where there was none before; sharing deeply all the while in the very same Pollutions he pretends to sweep away. His last Days are spent in Slavery to Women, and generally the least deserving; till worn to the Stumps, like his Brother *Bezom,*[1] he is either kicked out of Doors, or made use of to kindle Flames for others to warm themselves by.

FROM

THE BICKERSTAFF PAPERS

PREDICTIONS FOR THE YEAR 1708

Wherein the Month, and Day of the Month, are set down, the Persons named, and the great Actions and Events of next Year particularly related as they will come to pass.

Written to prevent the People of England from being farther imposed on by vulgar Almanack-Makers.

BY ISAAC BICKERSTAFF,* Esq;

Having long considered the gross Abuse of Astrology in this Kingdom; upon debating the Matter with my self, I could not possibly lay the Fault upon the Art, but upon those gross Impostors, who set up to be the Artists. I know, several learned Men have contended, that the whole is a Cheat; that it is absurd and ridiculous to imagine, the Stars can have any Influence at all upon human Actions, Thoughts, or Inclinations: And whoever hath not bent his Studies that Way, may be excused for thinking so, when he sees in how wretched a Manner this noble Art is treated, by a few mean illiterate Traders between us and the Stars; who import a yearly Stock of Nonsense, Lies, Folly, and Impertinence, which they offer to the World as genuine from the Planets; although they descend from no greater a Height than their own Brains.

I INTEND, in a short Time, to publish a large and rational Defence of this Art; and, therefore, shall say no more in its Justification at present, than that it hath been in all Ages defended by many learned Men; and among the rest, by *Socrates* himself; whom I look upon as undoubtedly the wisest of uninspired Mortals: To which if we add, that those who have condemned this Art, although otherwise learned, having been such as either did not apply their Studies this Way; or at least did not succeed in

---

* *It is said, that the Author, when he had writ the following Paper, and being at a Loss what Name to prefix to it; passing through* Long-Acre, *observed a Sign over a House where a Locksmith dwelt, and found the Name* Bickerstaff *written under it: Which being a Name somewhat uncommon, he chose to call himself Isaac Bickerstaff. This Name was sometime afterward made Use of by Sir* Richard Steele, *and Mr.* Addison, *in the* TATLERS; *in which Papers, as well as many of the* SPECTATORS, *it is well known, that the Author had a considerable Part.*

their Applications; their Testimony will not be of much Weight to its Disadvantage, since they are liable to the common Objection of condemning what they did not understand.

NOR am I at all offended, or think it an Injury to the Art, when I see the common Dealers in it, the *Students in Astrology,* the *Philomaths,* and the rest of that Tribe, treated by wise Men with the utmost Scorn and Contempt: But I rather wonder, when I observe Gentlemen in the Country, rich enough to serve the Nation in Parliament, poring in *Partrige's* Almanack, to find out the Events of the Year at Home and Abroad; not daring to propose a Hunting-Match, until *Gadbury,*[1] or he, hath fixed the Weather.

I WILL allow either of the Two I have mentioned, or any other of the Fraternity, to be not only Astrologers, but Conjurers too; if I do not produce an Hundred Instances in all their Almanacks, to convince any reasonable Man, that they do not so much as understand Grammar and Syntax; that they are not able to spell any Word out of the usual Road; nor even in their Prefaces to write common Sense, or intelligible *English.* Then, for their Observations and Predictions, they are such as will equally suit any Age, or Country in the World. *This Month a certain great Person will be threatned with Death, or Sickness.* This the News-Paper will tell them; for there we find at the End of the Year, that no Month passes without the Death of some Person of Note; and it would be hard, if it should be otherwise, when there are at least two Thousand Persons of Note in this Kingdom, many of them old; and the Almanack-maker has the Liberty of chusing the sickliest Season of the Year, where he may fix his Prediction. Again, *This Month an eminent Clergyman will be preferred;* of which there may be some Hundreds, Half of them with one Foot in the Grave. Then, *Such a Planet in such a House shews great Machinations, Plots and Conspiracies, that may in Time be brought to Light:* After which, if we hear of any Discovery, the Astrologer gets the Honour; if not, his Prediction still stands good. And at last, *God preserve King* William *from all his open and secret Enemies, Amen.* When if the King should happen to have died, the Astrologer plainly foretold it; otherwise, it passeth but for the pious Ejaculation of a loyal Subject: Although it unluckily happened in some of their Almanacks, that poor King *William* was prayed for many Months after he was dead; because, it fell out that he died about the Beginning of the Year.

To mention no more of their impertinent Predictions: What have we to do with their Advertisements about *Pills, and Drinks for the Venereal Disease,* or their mutual quarrels in Verse and Prose of *Whig* and *Tory?* wherewith the Stars have little to do.

HAVING long observed and lamented these, and a hundred other Abuses of this Art, too tedious to repeat; I resolved to proceed in a new Way; which I doubt not will be to the general Satisfaction of the Kingdom. I can this Year produce but a Specimen of what I design for the future; having employed most Part of my Time in adjusting and correcting the Calculations I made for some Years past; because I would offer nothing to the World of which I am not as fully satisfied, as that I am now alive. For these two last Years I have not failed in above one or two Particulars, and those of no very great Moment. I exactly foretold the Miscarriage at *Toulon,* with all its Particulars; and the Loss of Admiral *Shovel;* although I was mistaken as to the Day, placing that Accident about thirty six Hours sooner than it happened; but upon reviewing my Schemes, I quickly found the Cause of that Error. I likewise foretold the Battle at *Almanza* to the very Day and Hour, with the Loss on both Sides, and the Consequences thereof. All which I shewed to some Friends many Months before they happened; that is, I gave them Papers sealed up, to open at such a Time, after which they were at liberty to read them; and there they found my Predictions true in every Article, except one or two, very minute.

As for the few following Predictions I now offer the World, I forbore to publish them, till I had perused the several Almanacks for the Year we are now entered upon: I found them all in the usual Strain, and I beg the Reader will compare their Manner with mine: And here I make bold to tell the World, that I lay the whole Credit of my Art upon the Truth of these Predictions; and I will be content that *Partrige,* and the rest of his Clan, may hoot me for a Cheat and Impostor, if I fail in any single Particular of Moment. I believe any Man, who reads this Paper, will look upon me to be at least a Person of as much Honesty and Understanding, as a common Maker of Almanacks. I do not lurk in the Dark; I am not wholly unknown in the World: I have set my Name at length, to be a Mark of Infamy to Mankind, if they shall find I deceive them.

IN one Point I must desire to be forgiven; that I talk more sparingly of Home-Affairs. As it would be Imprudence to discover Secrets of State, so it might be dangerous to my Person: But in smaller Matters, and such as are not of publick Consequence, I shall be very free: And the Truth of my Conjectures will as much appear from these as the other. As for the most signal Events abroad in *France, Flanders, Italy* and *Spain,* I shall make no Scruple to predict them in plain Terms: Some of them are of Importance, and I hope, I shall seldom mistake the Day they will happen: Therefore, I think good to inform the Reader, that I all along make use of the *Old Stile*[2] observed in *England;* which I desire he will compare with that of the News-Papers, at the Time they relate the Actions I mention.

I MUST add one Word more: I know it hath been the Opinion of several learned Persons, who think well enough of the true Art of Astrology, That the Stars do only *incline,* and do not force the Actions or Wills of Men: And therefore, however I may proceed by right Rules, yet I cannot in Prudence so confidently assure that the Events will follow exactly as I predict them.

I HOPE, I have maturely considered this Objection, which in some Cases is of no little Weight. For Example: A Man may, by the Influence of an over-ruling Planet, be disposed or inclined to Lust, Rage, or Avarice; and yet by the Force of Reason overcome that evil Influence. And this was the Case of *Socrates:* But the great Events of the World usually depending upon Numbers of Men, it cannot be expected they should all unite to cross their Inclinations, from pursuing a general Design, wherein they unanimously agree. Besides, the Influence of the Stars reacheth to many Actions and Events, which are not any way in the Power of Reason; as Sickness, Death, and what we commonly call Accidents; with many more needless to repeat.

BUT now it is Time to proceed to my Predictions; which I have begun to calculate from the Time that the *Sun* enters into *Aries.* And this I take to be properly the Beginning of the natural Year. I pursue them to the Time that he enters *Libra,* or somewhat more, which is the busy Period of the Year. The Remainder I have not yet adjusted upon Account of several Impediments needless here to mention. Besides, I must remind the Reader again, that this is but a Specimen of what I design in succeeding Years to treat more at large, if I may have Liberty and Encouragement.

MY first Prediction is but a Trifle; yet I will mention it, to shew how ignorant those sottish Pretenders to Astrology are in their own Concerns: It relates to *Partrige* the Almanack-Maker; I have consulted the Star of his Nativity by my own Rules; and find he will infallibly die upon the 29th of *March* next, about eleven at Night, of a raging Fever: Therefore I advise him to consider of it, and settle his Affairs in Time.

THE Month of *APRIL* will be observable for the Death of many great Persons. On the 4th will die the Cardinal *de Noailles,* Archbishop of *Paris:* On the 11th the young Prince of *Asturias,* Son to the Duke of *Anjou:* On the 14th a great Peer of this Realm will die at his Country-House: On the 19th an old *Layman* of great Fame for Learning: And on the 23rd an eminent Goldsmith in *Lombard Street.* I could mention others, both at home and abroad, if I did not consider such Events of very little Use or Instruction to the Reader, or to the World.

As to publick Affairs: On the 7th of this Month, there will be an Insurrection in *Dauphine,* occasioned by the Oppressions of the People; which will not be quieted in some Months.

ON the 15th will be a violent Storm on the South-East Coast of *France;* which will destroy many of their Ships, and some in the very Harbour.

THE 19th will be famous for the Revolt of a whole Province or Kingdom, excepting one City; by which the Affairs of a certain Prince in the Alliance will take a better Face.

MAY, Against common Conjectures, will be no very busy Month in *Europe;* but very signal for the Death of the *Dauphine,* which will happen on the 7th, after a short Fit of Sickness, and grievous Torments with the Strangury. He dies less lamented by the Court than the Kingdom.

ON the 9th a *Mareschal* of *France* will break his Leg by a Fall from his Horse. I have not been able to discover whether he will then die or not.

ON the 11th will begin a most important Siege, which the Eyes of all *Europe* will be upon: I cannot be more particular; for in relating Affairs that so nearly concern the *Confederates,* and consequently this Kingdom; I am forced to confine my self, for several Reasons very obvious to the Reader.

ON the 15th News will arrive of a very *surprizing Event,* than which nothing could be more unexpected.

ON the 19th, three Noble Ladies of this Kingdom, will, against all Expectation, prove with Child, to the great Joy of their Husbands.

ON the 23d, a famous Buffoon of the Play-House will die a ridiculous Death, suitable to his Vocation.

JUNE. This Month will be distinguished at home, by the utter dispersing of those ridiculous deluded Enthusiasts, commonly called the *Prophets;*[3] occasioned chiefly by seeing the Time come, when many of their Prophecies were to be fulfilled; and then finding themselves deceived by contrary Events. It is indeed to be admired how any Deceiver can be so weak to foretel Things near at hand; when a very few Months must of Necessity discover the Imposture to all the World: In this Point less prudent than common Almanack-Makers, who are so wise to wander in Generals, talk dubiously, and leave to the Reader the Business of interpreting.

ON the 1st of this Month a *French* General will be killed by a random Shot of a Cannon-Ball.

ON the 6th a Fire will break out in the Suburbs of *Paris,* which will destroy above a thousand Houses; and seems to be the Foreboding of what will happen, to the Surprize of all *Europe,* about the End of the following Month.

ON the 10th a great Battle will be fought, which will begin at four of the Clock in the Afternoon, and last till nine at Night with great Obstinacy, but no very decisive Event. I shall not name the Place, for the Reasons aforesaid; but the Commanders on each left Wing will be killed. —— I see Bonfires and hear the Noise of Guns for a Victory.

ON the 14th there will be a false Report of the *French* King's Death.

ON the 20th Cardinal *Portocarero* will die of a Dissentery, with great Suspicion of Poison; but the Report of his Intention to revolt to King *Charles* will prove false.

JULY. The 6th of this Month a *certain General* will, by a glorious Action, recover the Reputation he lost by former Misfortunes.

ON the 12th a *great Commander* will die a Prisoner in the Hands of his Enemies.

ON the 14th a shameful Discovery will be made of a *French* Jesuit giving Poison to a great Foreign General; and when he is put to the Torture, will make wonderful Discoveries.

IN short, this will prove a Month of great Action, if I might have Liberty to relate the Particulars.

AT home, the Death of an old famous Senator will happen on the 15th at his Country-House, worn with Age and Diseases.

BUT that which will make this Month memorable to all Posterity, is the Death of the *French* King *Lewis* the Fourteenth, after a Week's Sickness at *Marli;* which will happen on the 29th, about six a-Clock in the Evening. It seems to be an Effect of the Gout in his Stomach, followed by a Flux. And in three Days after Monsieur *Chamillard* will follow his Master, dying suddenly of an Apoplexy.

IN this Month likewise an *Ambassador* will die in *London;* but I cannot assign the Day.

AUGUST. The affairs of *France* will seem to suffer no Change for a while under the Duke of *Burgundy*'s Administration. But the Genius that animated the whole Machine being gone, will be the Cause of mighty Turns and Revolutions in the following Year. The new King makes yet little Change either in the Army or the Ministry; but the Libels against his Grandfather, that fly about his very Court, give him Uneasiness.

I SEE an Express in mighty Haste, with Joy and Wonder in his Looks, arriving by the Break of Day, on the 26th of this Month, having travelled in three Days a prodigious Journey by Land and Sea. In the Evening I hear Bells and Guns, and see the Blazing of a Thousand Bonfires.

A YOUNG Admiral, of noble Birth, does likewise this Month gain immortal Honour, by a great Atchievement.

THE Affairs of *Poland* are this Month entirely settled: *Augustus* resigns his Pretensions, which he had again taken up for some Time: *Stanislaus* is peaceably possessed of the Throne; and the King of *Sweden* declares for the Emperor.

I CANNOT omit one particular Accident here at home; that near the End of this Month, much Mischief will be done at *Bartholomew* Fair, by the Fall of a Booth.

SEPTEMBER. This Month begins with a very surprizing Fit of frosty Weather, which will last near twelve Days.

THE Pope having long languished last Month; the Swellings in his Legs breaking, and the Flesh mortifying, will die on the 11th Instant: And in three Weeks Time, after a mighty Contest, be succeeded by a Cardinal of the *Imperial* Faction, but Native of *Tuscany,* who is now about Sixty-One Years old.

THE *French* Army acts now wholly on the Defensive, strongly fortified in their Trenches; and the young *French* King sends Overtures for a Treaty of Peace, by the Duke of *Mantua;* which, because it is a Matter of State that concerns us here at home, I shall speak no farther of it.

I SHALL add but one Prediction more, and that in mystical Terms, which shall be included in a Verse out of *Virgil.*

> Alter erit jam Tethys, & altera quœ vehat Argo,
> Dilectos Heroas.[4]

UPON the 25th Day of this Month, the fulfilling of this Prediction will be manifest to every Body.

THIS is the farthest I have proceeded in my Calculations for the present Year. I do not pretend, that these are all the great Events which will happen in this Period; but that those I have set down will infallibly come to pass. It may, perhaps, still be objected, why I have not spoke more particularly of Affairs at home; or of the Success of our Armies abroad, which I might, and could very largely have done. But those in Power have wisely discouraged Men from meddling in publick Concerns; and I was resolved, by no Means, to give the least Offence. This I will venture to say; that it will be a glorious Campaign for the Allies; wherein the *English*

Forces, both by Sea and Land, will have their full Share of Honour: That Her Majesty Queen ANNE will continue in Health and Prosperity: And that no ill Accident will arrive to any in the chief Ministry.

As to the particular Events I have mentioned, the Readers may judge by the fulfilling of them, whether I am of the Level with common Astrologers; who, with an old paultry Cant, and a few Pot-hooks for Planets to amuse the Vulgar, have, in my Opinion, too long been suffered to abuse the World. But an honest Physician ought not to be despised, because there are such Things as Mountebanks. I hope, I have some Share of Reputation, which I would not willingly forfeit for a Frolick, or Humour: And I believe no Gentleman, who reads this Paper, will look upon it to be of the same Cast, or Mold, with the common Scribbles that are every Day hawked about. My Fortune hath placed me above the little Regard of writing for a few Pence, which I neither value nor want: Therefore, let not wise Men too hastily condemn this Essay, intended for a good Design, to cultivate and improve an antient Art, long in Disgrace by having fallen into mean unskilful Hands. A little Time will determine whether I have deceived others, or my self; and I think it is no very unreasonable Request, that Men would please to suspend their Judgments till then. I was once of the Opinion with those who despise all Predictions from the Stars, till in the Year 1686, a Man of Quality shewed me, written in his *Album*, that the most learned Astronomer Captain *Hally*, assured him, he would never believe any thing of the Stars Influence, if there were not a great Revolution in *England* in the Year 1688. Since that Time I began to have other Thoughts; and after Eighteen Years diligent Study and Application, I think I have no Reason to repent of my Pains. I shall detain the Reader no longer than to let him know, that the Account I design to give of next Year's Events, shall take in the principal Affairs that happen in *Europe:* And if I be denied the Liberty of offering it to my own Country, I shall appeal to the learned World, by publishing it in *Latin,* and giving Order to have it printed in *Holland.*

THE ACCOMPLISHMENT OF THE FIRST OF MR. *BICKERSTAFF*'S PREDICTIONS. BEING AN ACCOUNT OF THE DEATH OF MR. *PARTRIGE,* THE ALMANACK-MAKER, UPON THE 29TH INST.

In a Letter to a Person of Honour.

Written in the Year 1708.

My LORD,

In Obedience to your Lordship's Commands, as well as to satisfy my own Curiosity, I have for some Days past enquired constantly after *Partrige* the Almanack-maker; of whom it was foretold in Mr. *Bickerstaff*'s Predictions, published about a Month ago, that he should die the 29th Instant, about Eleven at Night, of a raging Fever. I had some Sort of Knowledge of him when I was employed in the Revenue; because he used every Year to present me with his Almanack, as he did other Gentlemen upon the score of some little Gratuity we gave him. I saw him accidentally once or twice about ten Days before he died; and observed he began very much to droop and languish, although I hear his Friends did not seem to apprehend him in any Danger. About two or three Days ago he grew ill; was confined first to his Chamber, and in a few Hours after to his Bed; where Dr. *Case* and Mrs. *Kirleus** were sent for to visit, and to prescribe to him. Upon this Intelligence I sent thrice every Day one Servant or other to enquire after his Health; and Yesterday about four in the Afternoon, Word was brought me that he was past Hopes: Upon which I prevailed with my self to go and see him; partly out of Commiseration, and, I confess, partly out of Curiosity. He knew me very well, seemed surprized at my Condescension, and made me Compliments upon it as well as he could in the Condition he was. The People about him said, he had been for some Hours delirious; but when I saw him, he had his Understanding as well as ever I knew, and spoke strong and hearty, without any seeming Uneasiness or Constraint. After I had told him I was sorry to see him in those melancholly Circumstances, and said some other Civilities, suitable to the Occasion; I desired him to tell me freely and ingenu-

---

* *Two famous Quacks at that Time in* London.

ously whether the Predictions Mr. *Bickerstaff* had published relating to his Death, had not too much affected and worked on his Imagination. He confessed he had often had it in his Head, but never with much Apprehension till about a Fortnight before; since which Time it had the perpetual Possession of his Mind and Thoughts; and he did verily believe was the true natural Cause of his present Distemper: For, said he, I am thoroughly persuaded, and I think I have very good Reasons, that Mr. *Bickerstaff* spoke altogether by guess, and knew no more what will happen this Year than I did my self. I told him his Discourse surprized me; and I would be glad he were in a State of Health to be able to tell me what Reason he had to be convinced of Mr. *Bickerstaff*'s Ignorance. He replied, I am a poor ignorant Fellow, bred to a mean Trade; yet I have Sense enough to know, that all Pretences of foretelling by Astrology are Deceits; for this manifest Reason, because the Wise and Learned, who can only judge whether there be any Truth in this Science, do all unanimously agree to laugh at and despise it; and none but the poor ignorant Vulgar give it any Credit, and that only upon the Word of such silly Wretches as I and my Fellows, who can hardly write or read. I then ask him, why he had not calculated his own Nativity, to see whether it agreed with *Bickerstaff*'s Predictions? At which he shook his Head, and said, O! Sir, this is no Time for jesting, but for repenting those Fooleries, as I do now from the very Bottom of my Heart. By what I can gather from you, said I, the Observations and Predictions you printed with your Almanacks were meer Impositions upon the People. He replied, if it were otherwise, I should have the less to answer for. We have a common Form for all those Things: As to foretelling the Weather, we never meddle with that, but leave it to the Printer, who takes it out of any old Almanack as he thinks fit: The rest was my own Invention to make my Almanack sell; having a Wife to maintain, and no other Way to get my Bread; for mending old Shoes is a poor Livelihood: And (added he, sighing) I wish I may not have done more Mischief by my Physick than my Astrology; although I had some good Receipts from my Grandmother, and my own Compositions were such, as I thought could at least do no Hurt.

I HAD some other Discourse with him, which now I cannot call to Mind; and I fear I have already tired your Lordship. I shall only add one Circumstance, That on his Death-Bed he declared himself a Nonconformist,[1] and had a fanatick Preacher to be his spiritual Guide. After half an Hour's Conversation, I took my Leave, being almost stifled by the Closeness of the Room. I imagined he could not hold out long; and therefore withdrew to a little Coffee-House hard by, leaving a Servant at the House with Orders to come immediately, and tell me, as near as he could, the Minute when *Partrige* should expire, which was not above two Hours after; when looking upon my Watch, I found it to be above five Minutes after Seven: By which it is clear, that Mr. *Bickerstaff* was mistaken almost four Hours in his Calculation. In the other Circumstances he was exact enough. But whether he hath not been the Cause of this poor Man's Death, as well as the Predictor, may be very reasonably disputed. However, it must be confessed, the Matter is odd enough, whether we should endeavour to account for it by Chance or the Effect of Imagination: For my own Part, although I believe no Man hath less Faith in these Matters; yet I shall wait with some Impatience, and not without Expectation, the fulfilling of Mr. *Bickerstaff*'s second Prediction; that the Cardinal *de Noailles* is to die upon the 4th of *April;* and if that should be verified as exactly as this poor *Partrige;* I must own, I should be wholly surprized, and at a Loss; and should infallibly expect the Accomplishment of all the rest.

A VINDICATION OF *ISAAC BICKERSTAFF*, ESQ; AGAINST WHAT IS OBJECTED TO HIM BY MR. *PARTRIGE*, IN HIS ALMANACK FOR THE PRESENT YEAR 1709.

BY THE SAID ISAAC BICKERSTAFF, *Esq;*

Written in the Year 1709.

Mr. *Partrige* hath been lately pleased to treat me after a very rough Manner, in *that which is called,* His Almanack for the present Year: Such Usage is very undecent from *one Gentleman to another,* and doth not at all contribute to the Discovery of Truth; which ought to be the great End in all Disputes of the *Learned.* To call a Man *Fool* and *Villain,* and *impudent Fellow,* only for differing from him in a Point meerly speculative, is, in my humble Opinion, a very improper Stile for a Person of *his Education.* I appeal to the *learned World,* whether in my last Year's Predictions, I gave him the least Provocation for such unworthy Treatment. Philosophers have differed in all Ages, but the discreetest among them have always differed as became Philosophers. Scurrility and Passion, in a Controversy among *Scholars,* is just so much of nothing to the Purpose; and, at best, a tacit Confession of a weak Cause: My Concern is not so much for my own Reputation, as that of the *Republick of Letters,* which Mr. *Partrige* hath endeavoured to wound through my Sides. If Men of publick Spirit must be superciliously treated for their ingenuous Attempts; how will true useful Knowledge be ever advanced? I wish Mr. *Partrige* knew the Thoughts which *foreign Universities* have conceived of his ungenerous Proceedings with me; but I am too tender of his Reputation to publish them to the World. That Spirit of Envy and Pride, which blasts so many rising Genius's in our Nation, is yet unknown among *Professors* abroad: The Necessity of justifying my self, will excuse my Vanity, when I tell the Reader, that I have near an Hundred *honorary* Letters from several Parts of *Europe,* (some as far as *Muscovy*) in Praise of my Performance. Besides several others, which, as I have been credibly informed, were opened in the Post-Office, and never sent me.* It is true, the *Inquisition* in *Portugal* was pleased to burn my Predictions, and condemn the Author and Readers of them; but, I hope, at the same Time, it will be considered in how deplorable a State *Learning* lies at present in that Kingdom: And with the profoundest Veneration for *crowned Heads,* I will presume to add; that it a little concerned *his Majesty of Portugal,* to interpose his Authority in Behalf of a *Scholar* and a *Gentleman,* the Subject of a Nation with which he is now in so strict an Alliance. But, the other Kingdoms and states of *Europe* have treated me with more Candour and Generosity. If I had leave to print the *Latin* Letters transmitted to me from foreign Parts, they would fill a Volume, and be a full Defence against all that Mr. *Partrige,* or his Accomplices of the *Portugal Inquisition,* will be ever able to object; who, by the way, are the only Enemies my Predictions have ever met with at home or abroad. But, I hope, I know better what is due to the Honour of a *learned Correspondence,* in so tender a Point. Yet, some of those illustrious Persons will, perhaps, excuse me for transcribing a Passage or two in my own Vindication. The most learned Monsieur *Leibnitz* thus addresseth to me his third Letter:† *Illustrissimo Bickerstaffio Astrologiæ Instauratori,* &c. Monsieur *le Clerc* quoting my Predictions in a Treatise he published last Year, is pleased to say, *Ità nuperime Bickerstaffius magnum illud Angliæ sidus.* Another great Professor writing of me, has these Words: *Bickerstaffius, nobilis Anglus, Astrologorum hujusce Seculi facilè Princeps.* Signior *Magliabecchi,* the *Great Duke's* famous Library-keeper, spends almost his whole Letter in Compliments and Praises. It is true, the renowned *Professor* of Astronomy at *Utrecht,* seems to differ from me in one Article; but it is after the modest Manner that becomes a Philosopher; as, *Pace tanti viri dixerim:* And, *Page* 55, he seems to lay the Error upon the Printer, (as indeed it ought) and says, *vel forsan error Typographi, cum alioquin Bickerstaffius vir doctissimus,* &c.[1]

IF Mr. *Partrige* had followed these Examples in the Controversy between us, he might have spared me the Trouble of justifying my self in so publick a Manner. I believe few Men are readier to own their Errors than I, or more thankful to those who will please to inform him of them. But it seems this Gentleman, instead of encouraging the Progress of his own Art, is pleased to look upon all Attempts of that Kind, as an Invasion of his

---

* *This is Fact, as the Author was assured by Sir* Paul Methuen, *then Ambassador to that Crown.*

† *The Quotations here inserted, are in Imitation of Dr.* Bentley, *in some Part of the famous Controversy between him and* Charles Boyle, *Esq; afterwards Earl of* Orrery.

Province. He hath been indeed so wise, to make no Objection against the Truth of my Predictions, except in one single Point, relating to himself: and to demonstrate how much Men are blinded by their own Partiality; I do solemnly assure the Reader, that he is the *only* Person from whom I ever heard that Objection offered; which Consideration alone, I think, will take off all its Weight.

WITH my utmost Endeavours, I have not been able to trace above two Objections ever made against the Truth of my last Year's Prophecies: The first is of a *French* Man, who was pleased to publish to the World, that *the Cardinal* de Noailles *was still alive, notwithstanding the pretended Prophecy of Monsieur* Biquerstaffe: But how far a *French* Man, a *Papist*, and an *Enemy* is to be believed, in his own Cause, against an *English Protestant*, who is *true to the Government*, I shall leave to the candid and impartial Reader.

THE other Objection, is the unhappy Occasion of this Discourse; and relates to an Article in my Predictions, which foretold the Death of Mr. *Partrige* to happen on *March* 29, 1708. This he is pleased to contradict absolutely in the Almanack he hath published for the present Year; and in that ungentlemanly Manner, (pardon the Expression) as I have above related. In that Work, he very roundly asserts, That he *is not only now alive, but was likewise alive upon that very 29th of* March, *when I had foretold he should die*. This is the Subject of the present Controversy between us; which I design to handle with all Brevity, Perspicuity, and Calmness: In this Dispute, I am sensible, the Eyes not only of *England*, but of all *Europe*, will be upon us: and the *Learned* in every Country will, I doubt not, take Part on that side where they find most Appearance of Reason and Truth.

WITHOUT entering into Criticisms of *Chronology* about the Hour of his Death; I shall only prove, that Mr. *Partrige* is not alive. And my first Argument is thus: Above a Thousand Gentlemen having bought his Almanacks for this Year, meerly to find what he said against me; at every Line they read, they would lift up their Eyes, and cry out, betwixt Rage and Laughter, *They were sure no Man* alive *ever writ such damned Stuff as this*. Neither did I ever hear that Opinion disputed: So that Mr. *Partrige* lies under a *Dilemma*, either of disowning his Almanack, or allowing himself to be *no Man alive*. But now, if an *uninformed* Carcass walks still about, and is pleased to call it self *Partrige*, Mr. *Bickerstaff* does not think himself any way answerable for that. Neither had the said Carcass any Right to beat the poor Boy, who happened to pass by it in the Street, crying, *A full and true Account of Dr.* Partrige's *Death*, &c.

SECONDLY, Mr. *Partrige* pretends to tell Fortunes, and recover stolen

Goods; which all the Parish says he must do by conversing with the Devil, and other evil Spirits: And no wise Man will ever allow he could converse personally with either till after he was dead.

THIRDLY, I will plainly prove him to be dead, out of his own Almanack for this Year, and from the very Passage which he produceth to make us think him alive. He there says, *He is not only* now *alive, but was also alive upon that very 29th of* March, *which I foretold* he *should die on:* By this, he declares his Opinion, that a Man may be alive *now,* who was not alive a Twelve-month ago. And, indeed, there lies the Sophistry of his Argument. He dares not assert, he was alive ever since the 29th of *March,* but that he *is now alive, and was so on that Day:* I grant the latter, for he did not die till Night, as appears by the printed Account of his Death, in a *Letter to a Lord;* and whether he be since revived, I leave the World to judge. This, indeed, is perfect cavilling, and I am ashamed to dwell any longer upon it.

FOURTHLY, I will appeal to Mr. *Partrige* himself, whether it be probable I could have been so indiscreet, to begin my Predictions with the *only* Fals-hood that ever was pretended to be in them; and this is an Affair at Home, where I had so many Opportunities to be exact; and must have given such Advantages against me to a Person of Mr. *Partrige's* Wit and Learning, who, if he could possibly have raised one single Objection more against the Truth of my Prophecies, would hardly have spared me.

AND here I must take Occasion to reprove the abovementioned Writer of the Relation of Mr. *Partrige's* Death, in a *Letter to a Lord;* who was pleased to tax me with a Mistake of *four whole Hours* in my Calculation of that Event. I must confess, this Censure, pronounced with an Air of Certainty, in a Matter that so nearly concerned me, and by a *grave judicious Author,* moved me not a little. But although I was at that Time out of Town, yet several of my Friends, whose Curiosity had led them to be exactly in-formed, (for as to my own Part, having no doubt at all in the Matter, I never once thought of it,) assured me I computed to something under half an Hour; which (I speak my private Opinion) is an Error of no very great Magnitude, that Men should raise Clamour about it. I shall only say, it would not be amiss, if that Author would henceforth be more tender of other Mens Reputation as well as his own. It is well there were no more Mistakes of that Kind; if there had, I presume he would have told me of them with as little Ceremony.

THERE is one Objection against Mr. *Partrige's* Death, which I have sometimes met with, although indeed very slightly offered; That he still continues to write Almanacks. But this is no more than what is common to all of that Profession; *Gadbury, Poor Robin, Dove, Wing,* and several others, do yearly publish their Almanacks, although several of them have been dead since before the *Revolution.* Now the natural Reason of this I take to be, that whereas it is the Privilege of other Authors, *to live after their Deaths;* Almanack-makers are alone excluded; because their Dissertations treating only upon the Minutes as they pass, become useless as those go off. In consideration of which, *Time,* whose *Registers* they are, gives them a Lease in Reversion, to continue their Works after their Death.

I SHOULD not have given the Publick or my self the Trouble of this Vindication, if my Name had not been made use of by several Persons, to whom I never lent it; one of which, a few Days ago, was pleased to father on me a new Set of Predictions. But I think these are Things too serious to be trifled with. It grieved me to the Heart, when I saw my Labours, which had cost me so much Thought and Waching, bawled about by common Hawkers, which I only intended for the weighty Consideration of the gravest Persons. This prejudiced the World so much at first, that several of my Friends had the Assurance to ask me, Whether I were in jest? To which I only answered coldly, *That the Event will shew.* But it is the Talent of our Age and Nation, to turn Things of the greatest Importance into Ridicule. When the End of the Year had *verified all my Predictions;* out comes Mr. *Partrige's* Almanack, disputing the Point of his Death; so that I am employed, like the General who was forced to kill his Enemies twice over, whom a *Necromancer* had raised to Life. If Mr. *Partrige* hath practised the same Experiment upon himself, and be again alive; long may he continue so; but that doth not in the least contradict my Veracity: For I think I have clearly proved, by *invincible Demonstration,* that he died at farthest within half an Hour of the Time I foretold; and not four Hours sooner, as the above-mentioned Author, in his Letter to a Lord, hath maliciously suggested, with Design to blast my Credit, by charging me with so gross a Mistake.

A FAMOUS PREDICTION OF *MERLIN,* THE *BRITISH* WIZARD, WRITTEN ABOVE A THOUSAND YEARS AGO, AND RELATING TO THE YEAR 1709.

WITH EXPLANATORY NOTES. BY T. N. *Philomath.*

Written in the Year 1709.

Last Year was published a Paper of Predictions, pretended to be written by one *Isaac Bickerstaff,* Esq; but the true Design of it was to ridicule the Art of Astrology, and expose its Professors as ignorant, or Impostors. Against this Imputation, Dr. *Partrige* hath learnedly vindicated himself in his Almanack for that Year.

FOR a farther Defence of this famous Art, I have thought fit to present the World with the following Prophecy. The Original is said to be of the famous *Merlin,* who lived about a thousand Years ago; And the following Translation is two hundred Years old; for it seems to be written near the End of *Henry* the Seventh's Reign. I found it in an old Edition of *Merlin's* Prophecies; imprinted at *London* by *Johan Haukyns,* in the Year 1530. *Page* 39. I set it down Word for Word in the old Orthography [see p. 684], and shall take leave to subjoin a few explanatory Notes.

EXPLANATORY NOTES.

Seven and Ten. This Line describes the Year when these Events shall happen. Seven and Ten make Seventeen, which I explain seventeen Hundred, and this Number added to Nine makes the Year we are now in; for it must be understood of the Natural Year, which begins the First of *January.*

Tamys Ryvere twys, &c. The River *Thames* frozen twice in one Year, so as Men to walk on it, is a very signal Accident; which perhaps hath not fallen out for several Hundred Years before; and is the Reason why some Astrologers have thought that this Prophecy could never be fulfilled; because they imagined such a Thing could never happen in our Climate.

SEUEN and TEN addyd to NINE,
Of Fraunce hir Woe thys is the Sygne,
Tamys Ryuere twys y-frozen,
Walke sans wetyng Shoes ne Hosen.
Then cometh foorthe, Ich understonde,
From Toune of Stoffe to fattyn Londe,
An herdie Chiftan, woe the Morne
To Fraunce, that evere he was borne.
Then shall the Fyshe beweyle his Bosse;
Nor shall grin Berrys make up the Losse.
Yonge Symnele shall again miscartye:
And Norways Pryd again shall martey.
And from the Tree where Blosums fele,
Ripe Fruit shall come, and all is wele.
Reaums shall daunce Honde in Honde,
And it shall be merye in old Inglonde.
Then old Inglonde shall be no more,
And no Man shall be sorie therefore.
Geryon shall have three Hedes agayne,
Till Hapsburge makyth them but twayne.

From Toune of Stoffe, &c. This is a plain Designation of the Duke of *Marlborough.* One Kind of stuff used to fatten Land is called *Marle,* and every Body knows, that *Borough* is a Name for a Town; and this Way of Expression is after the usual dark Manner of old Astrological Predictions.

Then shall the Fyshe, &c. By the *Fish* is understood the *Dauphin* of *France,* as the Kings eldest Sons are called: It is here said, he shall lament the Loss of the Duke of *Burgundy,* called the *Bosse,* which is an old *English* Word for *Hump-shoulder,* or *Crook-back,* as that Duke is known to be: And the Prophecy seems to mean, that he should be overcome, or slain. By the *Grin Berrys,* in the next Line, is meant the young Duke of *Berry,* the *Dauphin's* third Son, who shall not have Valour or Fortune enough to supply the Loss of his eldest Brother.

Yonge Symnele, &c. By *Symnele* is meant the pretended Prince of *Wales;* who, if he offers to attempt any Thing against *England,* shall miscarry as he did before.[1] *Lambert Symnel* is the Name of a young Man noted in our Histories for personating the Son (as I remember) of *Edward* the Fourth.

And Norways Pryd, &c. I cannot guess who is meant by *Norways Pride,** perhaps the Reader may, as well as the Sense of the two following Lines.

Reaums shall, &c. *Reaums,* or as the Word is now, *Realms,* is the old Name for *Kingdoms:* And this is a very plain Prediction of our happy *Union,* with the Felicities that shall attend it. It is added, that *Old England* shall be no more, and yet no Man shall be sorry for it.[2] And, indeed, properly speaking, *England* is now no more; for the whole Island is one Kingdom, under the Name of *Britain.*

Geryon shall, &c. This Prediction, though somewhat obscure, is wonderfully adapt. *Geryon* is said to have been a King of *Spain,* whom *Hercules* slew. It was a Fiction of the Poets, that he had three Heads, which the Author says he shall have again. That is, *Spain* shall have three Kings; which is now wonderfully verified: For, besides the King of *Portugal,* which properly is Part of *Spain,* there are now two Rivals for *Spain; Charles* and *Philip.* But *Charles* being descended from the Count of *Hapsburgh,* Founder of the *Austrian* Family, shall soon make those Heads but two; by overturning *Philip,* and driving him out of *Spain.*

SOME of these Predictions are already fulfilled; and it is highly probable the rest may be in due Time: And, I think, I have not forced the Words, by my Explication, into any other Sense than what they will naturally bear.

---

* *Queen* Anne. *The Prophecy means, that she should marry a second Time, and have Children that would live.*

If this be granted, I am sure it must be also allowed, that the Author (who-ever he were) was a Person of extraordinary Sagacity; and that Astrology brought to such Perfection as this, is, by no Means, an Art to be despised; whatever Mr. *Bickerstaff*, or other merry Gentlemen are pleased to think. As to the Tradition of these Lines, having been writ in the Original by *Merlin;* I confess, I lay not much Weight upon it: But it is enough to justify their Authority, that the Book from whence I have transcribed them, was printed 170 Years ago, as appears by the Title-Page. For the Satisfaction of any Gentleman, who may be either doubtful of the Truth, or curious to be informed; I shall give Order to have the very Book sent to the Printer of this Paper, with Directions to let any Body see it that pleases; because I believe it is pretty scarce.

From A Compleat
COLLECTION
of genteel and
Ingenious Conversation,
according
To the most polite Mode and
Method, now used at court, and in
the best Companies of *England*.

THE MEN.	THE LADIES.
LORD SPARKISH	
LORD SMART	LADY SMART
SIR JOHN LINGER	MISS NOTABLE
MR. NEVEROUT	LADY ANSWERALL
COLONEL ATWIT	

SECOND CONVERSATION

[*Lord* Smart, *and the former Company at three a Clock, coming to dine.*]

[*After Salutations.*]

LORD SM. I'm sorry I was not at home this Morning, when you all did us the Honour to call here. But I went to the Levee To-Day.

LORD SP. O, my Lord; I'm sure the Loss was ours.

LADY SM. Gentlemen, and Ladies, you are come into a sad dirty House, I am sorry for it, but we have had our Hands in Mortar.

LORD SP. O, Madam, your Ladyship is pleased to say so, but I never saw any Thing so clean and so fine. I profess it is a perfect Paradise.

LADY SM. My Lord, your Lordship is always very obliging.

LORD SP. Pray, Madam, whose Picture is that?

LADY SM. Why, my Lord, it was drawn for me.

LORD SP. I'll swear, the Painter did not flatter your Ladyship.

COL. My Lord, the Day is finely cleared up.

LORD SM. Ay, Colonel, 'tis a Pity that fair Weather should ever do any harm. [*to* Neverout.] Why, *Tom,* you are high in the Mode.

NEV. My Lord, it is better to be out of the World, than out of the Fashion.

LORD SM. But, *Tom,* I hear, you and Miss are always quarrelling: I fear, it is your Fault, for I can assure you, she is very good humoured.

NEV. Ay, my Lord, so is the Devil when he's pleas'd.

LORD SM. Miss, what do you think of my Friend *Tom*?

MISS. My Lord, I think he is not the wisest Man in the World; and truly, he's sometimes very rude.

LORD SP. That may be true; but yet, he that hangs *Tom* for a fool, may find a Knave in the Halter.

MISS. Well, however, I wish he were hang'd, if it were only to try.

NEV. Well, Miss, if I must be hanged, I won't go far to chuse my Gallows: It shall be about your fair Neck.

MISS. I'll see your Nose Cheese first, and the Dogs eating it. But, my Lord, Mr. *Neverout*'s Wit begins to run low, for I vow he said this before. Pray, Colonel, give him a Pinch, and I'll do as much for you.

LORD SP. My Lady *Smart*, your Ladyship has a very fine Scarf.

LADY SM. Yes, my Lord, it will make a flaming Figure in a Country Church.

[*Footman comes in.*]

FOOTMAN. Madam, Dinner's upon the Table.

COL. Faith, I'm glad of it; my Belly began to cry Cupboard.

NEV. I wish I may never hear worse News.

MISS. What; Mr. *Neverout*, you are in great haste; I believe your Belly thinks your Throat's cut.

NEV. No, faith Miss, three Meals a Day, and a good Supper at night, will serve my Turn.

MISS. To say the Truth, I'm hungry.

NEV. And I'm angry, so let us both go fight.

[*They go in to Dinner, and after the usual Compliments, take their Seats.*]

LORD SM. Ladies and Gentlemen, will you eat any Oysters before Dinner.

COL. With all my Heart. [*Takes an Oyster.*] He was a bold Man that first eat an Oyster.

LADY SM. They say, Oysters are a cruel Meat; because we eat them alive: then, they are an uncharitable Meat; for we leave nothing to the Poor. And, they are an ungodly Meat, because we never say Grace to them.

NEV. Faith, that's as well said, as if I had said it my self.

LADY SM. Well, we are all well set, if we be but as well serv'd. Come, Colonel, handle your Arms: Shall I help you to some Beef?

COL. If your Ladyship pleases; and pray don't cut like a Mother-in-law, but send me a large Slice; for I love to lay a good Foundation: I vow 'tis a noble Sirloyn.

NEV. Ay, here's Cut and come again.

MISS. But pray, why is it called a Sirloyn?

LORD SP. Why, you must know, that our King *James* I. who loved good Eating, being invited to Dinner by one of his Nobles, and seeing a large Loyn of Beef at his Table; he drew out his Sword, and in a Frolick Knighted it. Few People know the Secret of this.

LADY SM. Beef is Man's Meat, my Lord.

LORD SM. But, my Lord, I say, Beef is the King of Meat.

MISS. Pray, what have I done, that I must not have a Plate?

LADY SM. [*To* Lady *Answerall.*] What will your Ladyship please to eat?

LADY ANSW. Pray, Madam, help your self.

COL. They say Eating and Scratching wants but a Beginning. If you will give me Leave, I'll help my self to a Slice of this Shoulder of Veal.

LADY SM. Colonel, you can't do a kinder Thing. Well, you are all heartily welcome, as I may say.

COL. They say there are thirty and two good Bits in a Shoulder of Veal.

LADY SM. Ay, Colonel; thirty bad Bits, and two good ones; you see I understand you; but, I hope you have got one of the two good ones?

NEV. Colonel, I'll be of your Mess.

COL. Then, pray *Tom,* carve for your self: They say, two Hands in a Dish, and one in a Purse. Hah, said I well, *Tom?*

NEV. Colonel, you spoke like an Oracle.

[*Miss to Lady* Answerall.]

MISS. Madam, will your Ladyship help me to some Fish?

LORD SM. [*To* Neverout.] *Tom,* they say Fish should swim thrice.

NEV. How is that, my Lord?

LORD SM. Why, *Tom,* first it should swim in the Sea; (do you mind me?) then it should swim in Butter; and at last Sirrah, it should swim in good Claret. I think I have made it out.

[*Footman to Lord* Smart.]

FOOTMAN. My Lord, Sir *John Linger* is coming up.

LORD SM. God so! I invited him to Dinner with me to-Day, and forgot it. Well, desire him to walk in.

[*Sir* John Linger *comes in.*]

SIR JOHN. What, are you at it? Why, then I'll be gone.

LADY SM. Sir *John,* I beg you will set down; come, the more, the merrier.

SIR JOHN. Ay; but the fewer the better Cheer.

LADY SM. Well, I am the worst in the World at making Apologies. It was my Lord's Fault. I doubt you must kiss the Hare's Foot.

SIR JOHN. I see you are fast by the Teeth.

COL. Faith, Sir *John*, we are killing that would kill us.

LORD SP. You see, Sir *John*, we are upon a Business of Life and Death. Come, will you do as we do. You are come in Pudden Time.

SIR JOHN. Ay, this you would be doing if I were dead. What, you keep Court Hours I see. I'll be going, and get a Bit of Meat at my Inn.

LADY SM. Why, we won't eat you, Sir *John*.

SIR JOHN. It is my own Fault; but, I was kept by a Fellow, who bought some *Derbyshire* Oxen from me.

NEV. You see, Sir *John*, we stayed for you, as one Horse does for another.

LADY SM. My Lord, will you help Sir *John* to some Beef. Lady *Answerall*, pray eat, you see your Dinner. I am sure, if we had known we should have such good Company, we should have been better provided; but, you must take the Will for the Deed. I'm afraid you are invited to your Loss.

COL. And, pray, Sir *John*, how do you like the Town? You have been absent a long Time.

SIR JOHN. Why, I find little *London* stands just where it did when I left it last.

NEV. What do you think of *Hanover-Square*, why, Sir *John*, *London* is gone out of Town since you saw it.

LADY SM. Sir *John*, I can only say, you are heartily welcome; and I wish I had something better for you.

COL. Here's no Salt; Cuckolds will run away with the Meat.

LORD SM. Pray edge a little, to make more Room for Sir *John*. Sir *John* fall to, you know half an Hour is soon lost at Dinner.

SIR JOHN. I protest, I can't eat a Bit; for I took Share of a Beef-Stake, and two Mugs of Ale with my Chapman, besides a Tankard of *March* Beer as soon as I got out of Bed.

LADY ANSW. Not fresh and fasting, I hope.

SIR JOHN. Yes faith, Madam, I always wash my Kettle before I put the Meat in it.

LADY SM. Poh! Sir *John*, you have seen nine Houses since you eat last: come, you have kept a Corner of your Stomach for a Bit of Venison-Pasty.

SIR JOHN. Well, I'll try what I can do when it comes up.

LADY ANSW. Come, Sir *John*, you may go further, and fare worse.

MISS. [*To* Neverout.] Pray, Mr. *Neverout*, will you please to send me a Piece of Tongue?

NEV. By no Means, Madam; one Tongue's enough for a Woman.

COL. Miss, here's a Tongue that never told a Lye.

MISS. That was because it could not speak. Why, Colonel, I never told a Lye in my Life.

NEV. I appeal to all the Company, whether that be not the greatest Lye that ever was told.

COL. [*To* Neverout.] Prethee, *Tom*, send me the two Legs, and Rump, and Liver, of that Pigeon; for you must know, I love what no Body else loves.

NEV. But what if any of the Ladies should long. Well, here take it, and the Devil do you good with it.

LADY ANSW. Well; this eating and drinking takes away a Body's Stomach.

NEV. I'm sure I have lost mine.

MISS. What! the Bottom of it, I suppose.

NEV. No really, Miss, I have quite lost it.

MISS. I should be sorry a poor Body had found it.

LADY SM. But, Sir *John*, we hear you are marryed since we saw you last. What; you have stolen a Wedding, it seems.

SIR JOHN. Well, one can't do a foolish Thing once in one's Life, but one must hear of it a hundred Times.

COL. And pray, Sir *John*, how does your Lady unknown?

SIR JOHN. My Wife's well, Colonel; and at your Service in a civil Way. Ha, ha. [*He laughs.*]

MISS. Pray, Sir *John*, is your Lady tall, or short?

SIR JOHN. Why, Miss, I thank God, she's a little Evil.

LORD SP. Come, give me a Glass of Claret.

[*Footman fills him a Bumper.*]

Why do you fill so much?

NEV. My Lord, he fills as he loves you.

LADY SM. Miss, shall I send you some Cucumber?

MISS. Madam, I dare not touch it; for they say, Cucumbers are cold in the third Degree.

LADY SM. Mr. *Neverout*, do you love Pudden?

NEV. Madam, I'm like all Fools; I love every Thing that is good: But the Proof of the Pudden, is in the eating.

COL. Sir *John,* I hear you are a great Walker, when you are at home.

SIR JOHN. No, Faith, Colonel, I always love to walk with a Horse in my Hand. But I have had devilish bad Luck in Horse-Flesh, of late.

LADY SM. Why then, Sir *John,* you must kiss a Parson's Wife.

LADY SM. They say, Sir *John,* that your Lady has a great deal of Wit.

SIR JOHN. Madam, she can make a Pudden; and has just Wit enough to know her Husband's Breeches from another Man's.

LADY SM. My Lord *Sparkish,* I have some excellent Cyder, will you please to taste it.

LORD SP. My Lord, I should like it well enough, if it were not so treacherous.

LORD SM. Pray, my Lord, how is it treacherous?

LORD SP. Because it smiles in my Face, and cuts my Throat.

[*Here a loud Laugh.*]

MISS. Odd so, Madam, your Knives are very sharp, for I have cut my Finger.

LADY SM. I'm sorry for it, pray which Finger?

MISS. Why, this Finger, (God bless the Mark) no, 'tis this: I vow, I can't find which it is.

NEV. Ay, the Fox had a Wound, and he could not tell where, &c. Bring some Water to throw in her Face.

MISS. Pray, Mr. *Neverout,* did you ever draw a Sword in Anger? I warrant, you would faint at the Sight of your own Blood.

LADY SM. Mr. *Neverout,* shall I send you some Veal?

NEV. No, Madam, I don't love it.

MISS. Then pray for them that do. I desire your Ladyship will send me a Bit.

LORD SM. *Tom,* my Service to you.

NEV. My Lord; this Moment, I did my self the Honour to drink to your Lordship.

LORD SM. Why then, that's *Hartfordshire* Kindness.

LORD SP. Why then, Colonel, my humble Service to you.

NEV. Pray, my Lord, don't make a Bridge of my Nose.

LORD SP. Well, a Glass of this Wine is as comfortable, as Matrimony to an old Maid.

COL. Sir *John,* I design one of these Days, to come and beat up your Quarters in *Derbyshire.*

SIR JOHN. Faith, Colonel, come and welcome; and stay away, and heartily welcome. But you were born within the Sound of *Bow* Bell, and don't Care to stir so far from *London.*

MISS. Pray, Colonel, send me some Fritters.

[*Colonel takes them out with his Hand.*]

COL. Here, Miss, they say, Fingers were made before Forks, and Hands before Knives.

LADY SM. Methinks, this Pudden is too much boyl'd.

LADY ANSW. O, Madam, they say a Pudden is Poison, when it's too much boyl'd.

NEV. Miss, shall I help you to a Pigeon? Here's a Pigeon so finely roasted, it cries, Come eat me.

MISS. No, Sir, I thank you.

NEV. Why then, you may chuse.

MISS. I have chosen already.

NEV. Well; you may be worse offered, before you are twice married.

[*The Colonel fills a large Plate of Soupe.*]

LORD SM. Why, Colonel, you don't mean to eat all that Soupe?

COL. O, my Lord, this is my sick Dish; when I am well, I have a Bigger.

MISS. [*To Colonel.*] Sup *Simon;* good Broth.

NEV. This seems to be a good Pullet.

MISS. I warrant, Mr. *Neverout,* knows what's good for himself.

LORD SP. *Tom,* I shan't take your Word for it, help me to a Wing.

[Neverout *tries to cut off a Wing.*]

NEV. I'gad, I can't hit the Joynt.

LORD SP. Why then, think of a Cuckold.

NEV. O, now I have nickt it.

[*Gives it Lord* Sparkish.]

LORD SP. Why, a Man may eat this, though his Wife lay a Dying.

COL. Pray, Friend, give me a Glass of Small-Beer, if it be good.

LORD SM. Why, Colonel, they say, there is no such Thing as good Small-Beer, good brown Bread, or a good old Woman.

LADY SM. [*To Lady* Answerall.] Madam, I beg your Ladyship's Pardon, I did not see you when I was cutting that Bit.

LADY ANSW. O, Madam, after you is good Manners.

LADY SM. Lord, here's a Hair in the Sawce.

LORD SP. Then, Madam, set the Hounds after it.

NEV. Pray, Colonel, help me, however, to some of that same Sawce.

COL. Come, I think you are more Sawce than Pig.

LORD SM. Sir *John,* chear up, my Service to you: Well, what do you think of the World to come?

SIR JOHN. Truly, my Lord, I think of it as little as I can.

LADY SM. [*Putting a Skewer on a Plate.*] Here, take this Skewer, and carry it down to the Cook, to dress it for her own Dinner.

NEV. I beg your Ladyship's Pardon; but this Small-Beer is dead.

LADY SM. Why then, let it be bury'd.

COL. This is admirable black Pudden; Miss, shall I carve you some? I am the worst Carver in the World; I should never make a good Chaplain. I can just carve Pudden, and that's all.

MISS. No, thank ye, Colonel; for they say, those that eat black Pudden, will dream of the Devil.

LORD SM. O, here comes the Venison Pasty: Here, take the Soupe away.

[*He cuts it up, and tastes the Venison.*]

S'buds, this Venison is musty.

[Neverout *eats a Piece, and burns his Mouth.*]

LORD SM. What's the Matter, *Tom?* You have Tears in your Eyes, I think. What dost cry for, Man?

NEV. My Lord, I was just thinking of my poor Grandmother; she dyed just this very Day seven Years.

[*Miss takes a Bit, and burns her Mouth.*]

NEV. And pray, Miss, why do you cry too?

MISS. Because you were not hanged the Day your Grandmother dyed.

LORD SM. I'd have given forty Pounds, Miss, to have said that.

COL. I'gad, I think, the more I eat, the hungryer I am.

LORD SP. Why, Colonel, they say, one Shoulder of Mutton drives down another.

NEV. I'gad, if I were to fast for my Life, I would take a good Breakfast in the Morning, a good Dinner at Noon, and a good Supper at Night.

LORD SP. My Lord, this Venison is plaguily pepper'd. Your Cook has a heavy Hand.

LORD SM. My Lord, I hope you are Pepper Proof. Come, here's a Health to the Founders.

LADY SM. Ay, and to the Confounders too.

LORD SM. Lady *Answerall,* does not your Ladyship love Venison?

LADY ANSW. No, my Lord, I can't endure it in my Sight; therefore please send me a good Piece of Meat and Crust.

LORD SP. [*Drinks to* Neverout.] Come, *Tom,* not always to my Friends, but once to you.

NEV. [*Drinks to Lady* Smart.] Come, Madam, here's a Health to our Friends, and hang the rest of our Kin.

LADY SM. [*To Lady* Answerall.] Madam, will your Ladyship have any of this Hare?

LADY ANSW. No, Madam; they say 'tis melancholy Meat.

LADY SM. Then, Madam, shall I send you the Brains: I beg your Lady-ship's Pardon, for they say, 'tis not good Manners to offer Brains.

LADY ANSW. No, Madam, for perhaps it will make me Hare-brain'd.

NEV. Miss, I must tell you one Thing.

MISS. [*With a Glass in her Hand.*] Hold your Tongue, Mr. *Neverout;* don't speak in my Tip.

COL. Well, he was an ingenious Man that first found out eating and drinking.

LORD SP. Of all Vittels, Drink digests the quickest. Give me a Glass of Wine.

NEV. My Lord, your Wine is too strong.

LORD SM. Ay, *Tom,* as much as you are too good.

MISS. This Almond Pudden was pure good; but it is grown quite cold.

NEV. So much the better Miss; cold Pudden will settle your Love.

MISS. Pray, Mr. *Neverout,* are you going to take a Voyage?

NEV. Why, do you ask, Miss?

MISS. Because, you have laid in so much Beef.

SIR JOHN. You two have eat up the whole Pudden betwixt you.

MISS. Sir *John,* here's a little Bit left, will you please to have it?

SIR JOHN. No, thankee, I don't love to make a Fool of my Mouth.

COL. [*Calling to the Butler.*] *John,* is your Small-Beer good?

BUTLER. An please your Honour, my Lord and Lady like it; I think it is good.

COL. Why then, *John,* d'ye see, if you are sure your Small-Beer is good, d'ye mark? Then give me a Glass of Wine. [*All laugh.*]

LADY SM. Sir *John,* how does your Neighbour *Gatherall* of the Park? I hear he has lately made a Purchase.

SIR JOHN. Oh; *Dick Gatherall* knows how to butter his Bread, as well as any Man in *Derbyshire.*

LADY SM. Why he used to go very fine, when he was here in Town.

SIR JOHN. Ay, and it became him, as a Saddle becomes a Sow.

COL. I knew his Lady; and, I think, she's a very good Woman.

SIR JOHN. Faith, she has more Goodness in her little Finger, than he has in his whole Body.

[*Colonel tasting the Wine.*]

LORD SM. Well, Colonel how do you like the Wine?

COL. This wine should be eaten; 'tis too good to be drank.

LORD SM. I'm very glad you like it; and, pray don't spare it.

COL. No, my Lord; I'll never starve in a Cook's Shop.

LADY SM. And, pray Sir *John*, what do you say to my Wine?

SIR JOHN. I'll take another Glass first: Second Thoughts are best.

LORD SP. Pray, Lady *Smart*, you sit near that Ham, will you please to send me a Bit?

LADY SM. With all my Heart. [*She sends him a Piece.*] Pray, my Lord, how do you like it?

LORD SP. I think it is a Limb of *Lot's* Wife. [*He eats it with Mustard.*] I'gad, my Lord, your Mustard is very uncivil.

LADY SM. Why uncivil, my Lord?

LORD SP. Because, it takes me by the Nose, I'gad.

LADY SM. Mr. *Neverout*, I find you are a very good Carver.

COL. Oh Madam, that's no Wonder; for you must know, *Tom Neverout* carves a-Sundays.

[*Mr.* Neverout *overturns the Saltcellar.*]

LADY SM. Mr. *Neverout*, you have overturn'd the Salt; and that's a Sign of Anger. I'm afraid Miss and you will fall out.

LADY ANSW. No, no; throw a little of it into the Fire, and all will be well.

NEV. O Madam, the falling *out* of Lovers, you know——

MISS. Lovers! very fine! fall *out* with him! I wonder when we were *in*.

SIR JOHN. For my Part, I believe the young Gentlewoman is his Sweet-Heart; there's such fooling and fidling betwixt them. I am sure, they say in our Country, that shiddle come sh——'s the Beginning of Love.

MISS. Nay, I love Mr. *Neverout*, as the Devil loves holy Water. I love him like Pye, I'd rather the Devil wou'd have him than I.

NEV. Miss, I'll tell you one thing.

MISS. Come, here's t'ye to stop your Mouth.

NEV. I'd rather you would stop it with a Kiss.

MISS. A Kiss; marry come up my dirty Couzin: Are you no sicker? Lord! I wonder what Fool it was, that first invented kissing?

NEV. Well, I'm very dry.

MISS. Then you are the better to burn, and the worse to fry.

LADY ANSW. God bless you, Colonel, you have a good Stroak with you.

COL. O Madam, formerly I could eat all, but now I leave nothing; I eat but one Meal a-Day.

MISS. What? I suppose, Colonel, that's from Morning till Night.

NEV. Faith, Miss, and well was his Want.

LORD SM. Pray, Lady *Answerall*, taste this Bit of Venison.

LADY ANSW. I hope, your Lordship, will set me a good Example.

LORD SM. Here's a Glass of Cyder fill'd. Miss, you must drink it.

MISS. Indeed, my Lord, I can't.

NEV. Come Miss; better Belly burst than good Liquor be lost.

MISS. Pish, well, in Life there was never any Thing so teazing; I had rather shed it in my Shoes: I wish it were in your Guts, for my Share.

LORD SM. Mr. *Neverout*, you ha'n't tasted my Cyder yet.

NEV. No, my Lord. I have been just eating Soupe; and they say, if one drinks in one's Porridge, one will cough in one's Grave.

LORD SM. Come, take Miss's Glass, she wish't it was in your Guts; let her have her Wish for once; Ladies can't abide to have their Inclinations cross't.

LADY SM. [*To Sir* John.] I think, Sir *John*, you have not tasted the Venison yet.

SIR JOHN. I seldom eat it, Madam: However, please to send me a little of the Crust.

LORD SP. Why, Sir *John*, you had as good eat the Devil, as the Broth he's boyl'd in.

NEV. I have dined as well as my Lord-Mayor.

MISS. I thought I could have eaten this Wing of a Chicken; but, I find, my Eye's bigger than my Belly.

LORD SM. Indeed, Lady *Answerall*, you have eaten nothing.

LADY ANSW. Pray, my Lord, see all the Bones on my Plate. They say, a Carpenter's known by his Chips.

NEV. Miss, will you reach me that Glass of Jelly?

MISS. [*Giving it to him.*] You see, 'tis but ask and have.

NEV. Miss, I would have a bigger Glass.

MISS. What, you don't know your own Mind; you are neither well full nor fasting. I think that is enough.

NEV. Ay, one of the enough's: I am sure it is little enough.

MISS. Yes, but you know sweet Things are bad for the Teeth.

NEV. [*To Lady* Answerall.] Madam, I don't like this Part of the Veal you sent me.

LADY ANSW. Well, Mr. *Neverout,* I find you are a true *English*-Man, you never know when you are well.

COL. Well, I have made my whole Dinner of Beef.

LADY ANS. Why, Colonel, a Belly full is a Belly full, if it be but of Wheat-Straw.

COL. Well, after all, Kitchen Physick is the best Physick.

LORD SM. And the best Doctors in the World, are Doctor *Diet,* Doctor *Quiet,* and Doctor *Merryman.*

LORD SP. What do you think of a little House well filled?

SIR JOHN. And a little Land well till'd?

COL. Ay, and a little Wife well will'd?

NEV. My Lady *Smart,* pray help me to some of the Breast of that Goose.

LORD SM. *Tom,* I have heard, that Goose upon Goose is false Heraldry.

MISS. What! will you never have done stuffing?

LORD SM. This Goose is quite raw. Well; God sends Meat, but the Devil sends Cooks.

NEV. Miss, can you tell which is the white Goose, or the grey Goose the Gander?

MISS. They say, a Fool will ask more Questions, than twenty wise Men can answer.

COL. Indeed, Miss, *Tom Neverout* has posed you.

MISS. Why, Colonel, every Dog has his Day. But, I believe, I shall never see a Goose again, without thinking on Mr. *Neverout.*

LORD SM. Well said Miss; I'faith Girl, thou hast brought thy self off cleverly. *Tom,* what say you to that?

COL. Faith, *Tom* is nonplust; he looks plaguily down in the Mouth.

MISS. Why, my Lord, you see he's the provokingest Creature in Life: I believe, there is not such another in the varsal World.

LADY ANSW. Oh Miss, the World's a wide Place.

NEV. Well, Miss, I'll give you Leave to call me any Thing, so you don't call me Spade.

LORD SM. Well, but after all, *Tom,* can you tell me what's *Latin* for a Goose?

NEV. O my Lord, I know that; Why, Brandy is *Latin* for a Goose; and *Tace* is *Latin* for a Caudle.

MISS. Is that Manners, to shew your Learning before Ladies? Methinks you are grown very brisk of a sudden. I think, the Man's glad he's alive.

SIR JOHN. The Devil take your Wit, if this be Wit: for it spoils Company. Pray, Mr. Butler, bring me a Dram after my Goose; 'tis very good for the Wholesoms.

LORD SM. Come, bring me the Loaf; I sometimes love to cut my own Bread.

MISS. I suppose, my Lord, you lay longest a Bed to-Day.

LORD SM. Miss, if I had said so, I should have told a Fib: I warrant you lay a Bed 'till the Cows came home. But, Miss, shall I cut you a little Crust, now my Hand is in?

MISS. If you please, my Lord; a Bit of under Crust.

NEV. [*Whispering Miss.*] I find you love to lie under.

MISS. [*Aloud; pushing him from her.*] What does the Man mean? Sir, I don't understand you at all.

NEV. Come, all Quarrels laid aside: Here, Miss, may you live a thousand Years. [*He drinks to her.*]

MISS. Pray Sir, don't stint me.

LORD SM. Sir *John,* will you taste my *October?* I think it is very good; but, I believe, not equal to yours in *Derbyshire.*

SIR JOHN. My Lord, I beg your Pardon; but, they say, the Devil made Askers.

LORD SM. [*To the Butler.*] Here, bring up the great Tankard full of *October,* for Sir *John.*

COL. [*Drinking to Miss.*] Miss, your Health; may you live all the Days of your Life.

LADY ANSW. Well, Miss, you'll certainly be soon marryed: Here's two Bachelors drinking to you at once.

LADY SM. Indeed, Miss, I believe you were wrapt in your Mother's Smock, you are so well beloved.

MISS. Where's my Knife, sure I han't eaten it? O, here it is.

SIR JOHN. No, Miss, but your Maidenhead hangs in your Light.

MISS. Pray, Sir *John,* is that a *Derbyshire* Compliment? Here, Mr. *Neverout,* will you take this Piece of Rabbit, that you bid me carve for you?

NEV. I don't know.

MISS. Why, why, take it, or let it alone.

NEV. I will.

MISS. What will you?

NEV. Why, take it, or let it alone.

MISS. Well, you're a provoking Creature.

SIR JOHN. [*Talking with a Glass of Wine in his Hand.*] I remember a Farmer in our Country——

LORD SM. [*Interrupting him.*] Pray, Sir *John*, did you ever hear of Parson *Palmer*?

SIR JOHN. No, my Lord, what of him?

LORD SM. Why, he used to preach over his Liquor.

SIR JOHN. I beg your Pardon. Here's your Lordship's Health; I'd drink it up, if it were a Mile to the Bottom.

LADY SM. Mr. *Neverout*, have you been at the new Play?

NEV. Yes, Madam, I went the first Night.

LADY SM. Well, and how did it take?

NEV. Why, Madam, the Poet is *damn'd*.

SIR JOHN. God forgive you; that's very uncharitable; you ought not to judge so rashly of any Christian.

NEV. [*Whispers Lady* Smart.] Was ever such a Dunce? How well he knows the Town! see how he stares like a stuck Pig! Well, but Sir *John*, are you acquainted with any of our fine Ladies yet? Any of our famous Toasts?

SIR JOHN. No, damn your Fireships; I have a Wife of my own.

LADY SM. Pray, my Lady *Answerall*, how do you like these preserved Oranges?

LADY ANSW. Indeed, Madam, the only Fault I find, is, that they are too good.

LADY SM. O, Madam, I have heard 'em say, that too good, is stark nought.

[*Miss drinking Part of a Glass of Wine.*]

NEV. Pray, let me drink your Snuff.

MISS. No, indeed, you shan't drink after me; for you'll know my Thoughts.

NEV. I know them already; you are thinking of a good Husband. Besides, I can tell your Meaning, by your Mumping.

LADY SM. Pray, my Lord, did you not order the Butler to bring up a Tankard of our *October* to Sir *John*? I believe, they stay to brew it.

[*The Butler brings the Tankard to Sir* John.]

SIR JOHN. Won't your Lordship please to drink first?

LORD SM. No, Sir *John*, 'tis in a very good Hand: I'll pledge you.

COL. [*To Lord* Smart.] My Lord, I love *October* as well as Sir *John*; and I hope, you won't make Fish of one, and Flesh of another.

LORD SM. Colonel, you're heartily welcome: Come, Sir *John*, take it by Word of Mouth, and then give it the Colonel.

[*Sir* John *drinks.*]

LORD SM. Well, Sir *John,* how do you like it?

SIR JOHN. Not as well as my own in *Derbyshire.* 'Tis plaguy small.

LADY SM. I never taste Malt Liquor; but they say, 'tis well Hopp'd.

SIR JOHN. Hopp'd! Why, if it had hopp'd a little further, it would have hopp'd into the River. O, my Lord; my Ale is Meat, Drink, and Cloth. It will make a Cat speak, and a wise Man dumb.

LADY SM. I was told, ours was very strong.

SIR JOHN. Ay, Madam, strong of the Water: I believe, the Brewer forgot the Malt, or the River was too near him. Faith, it is meer Whip-belly-vengeance: He that drinks most, has the worst Share.

COL. I believe, Sir *John,* Ale is as plenty as Water, at your House.

SIR JOHN. Why, Faith, at *Christmas* we have many Comers and Goers; and they must not be sent away without a Cup of good *Christmas* Ale, for fear they should p—ss behind the Door.

LADY SM. I hear, Sir *John,* has the nicest Garden in *England;* they say, 'tis kept so clean, that you can't find a Place where to spit.

SIR JOHN. O, Madam, you are pleased to say so.

LADY SM. But, Sir *John,* your Ale is terrible strong and heady in *Derbyshire;* and will soon make one drunk and sick, what do you then?

SIR JOHN. Why, indeed, it is apt to Fox one; but our Way is, to take a Hair of the same Dog next Morning. I take a new laid Egg for Breakfast; and Faith, one should drink as much after an Egg, as after an Ox.

LORD SM. *Tom Neverout,* will you taste a Glass of the *October?*

NEV. No, Faith, my Lord, I like your Wine; and I won't put a Churl upon a Gentleman: Your Honour's Claret is good enough for me.

LADY SM. What? is this Pigeon left for Manners? Colonel, shall I send you the Legs and Rump?

COL. Madam, I could not eat a Bit more, if the House was full.

LORD SM. [*Carving a Partridge.*] Well, one may ride to *Rumford* upon this Knife, it is so blunt.

LADY ANSW. My Lord, I beg your Pardon; but they say, an ill Workman never had good Tools.

LORD SM. Will your Lordship have a Wing of it?

LORD SP. No, my Lord, I love the Wing of an Ox a great deal better.

LORD SM. I'm always cold after eating.

COL. My Lord, they say, that's a Sign of long Life.

LORD SM. Ay, I believe I shall live 'till all my Friends are weary of me.

COL. Pray, does any Body here hate Cheese? I would be glad of a Bit.

LORD SM. An odd kind of Fellow dined with me t'other Day; and when the Cheese came upon the Table, he pretended to faint. So, some Body said, pray take away the Cheese: No, said I, pray take away the Fool: Said I well? [*Here a long and loud laugh.*]

COL. Faith, my Lord, you served the Coxcomb right enough: And therefore, I wish we had a Bit of your Lordship's *Oxfordshire* Cheese.

LORD SM. Come, hang saving, bring us a halfporth of Cheese.

LADY ANSW. They say, Cheese digests every Thing but itself.

[*Footman brings in a great whole Cheese.*]

LORD SP. Ay, this would look handsome if any Body should come in.

SIR JOHN. Well, I'm weily brosten, as they sayn in *Lancashire*.

LADY SM. Oh, Sir *John*, I wou'd I had something to brost you withal.

LORD SM. Come, they say, 'tis merry in Hall, when Beards wag all.

LADY SM. Miss, shall I help you to some Cheese? Or, will you carve for your self?

NEV. I'll hold fifty Pound, Miss won't cut the Cheese.

MISS. Pray, why so, Mr. *Neverout?*

NEV. O, there is a Reason, and you know it well enough.

MISS. I can't, for my Life, understand what the Gentleman means.

LORD SM. Pray, *Tom,* change the Discourse, in troth you are too bad.

[*Colonel whispers* Neverout.]

COL. Smoak Miss, you have made her fret like Gum taffety.

LADY SM. Well; but Miss (hold your Tongue, Mr. *Neverout*) shall I cut you a Bit of Cheese?

MISS. No really, Madam, I have dined this half Hour.

LADY SM. What? quick at Meat, quick at work, they say.

[*Sir* John *nods.*]

LORD SM. What, you are sleepy Sir *John.* Do you sleep after Dinner?

SIR JOHN. Yes, Faith, I sometimes take a Nap after my Pipe; for when the Belly's full, the Bones will be at rest.

LORD SM. Come, Colonel, help your self, and your Friends will love you the better.

[*To Lady* Answerall.]

Madam, your Ladyship eats nothing.

LADY ANSW. Lord, Madam, I have fed like a Farmer; I shall grow as fat as a Porpoise: I swear, my Jaws are weary with chawing.

COL. I have a Mind to eat a Piece of that Sturgeon, but I fear it will make me sick.

NEV. A rare Soldier indeed; let it alone, and I warrant, it won't hurt you.

COL. Well, but it would vex a Dog to see a Pudden creep.

[*Sir* John *rises.*]

LORD SM. Sir *John*, what are you doing?

SIR JOHN. Swolks, I must be going, by'r Lady; I have earnest Business; I must do, as the Beggars do, go away when I have got enough.

LORD SM. Well, but stay 'till this Bottle's out: You know, the Man was hanged that left his Liquor behind him; besides, a Cup in the Pate, is a Mile in the Gate; and, a Spur in the Head, is worth two in the Heel.

SIR JOHN. Come then, one Brimmer to all your Healths.

[*The Footman gives him a Glass half full.*]

Pray, Friend, what was the rest of this Glass made for? An Inch at the Top, Friend, is worth two at the Bottom.

[*He gets a Brimmer, and drinks it off.*]

Well; there's no Deceit in a Brimmer; and there's no false Latin in this, your Wine is excellent good, so I thank you for the next; for, I am sure of this. Madam, has your Ladyship any Commands in *Derbyshire*? I must go fifteen Miles To-Night.

LADY SM. None, Sir *John*, but to take Care of yourself; and my most humble Service to your Lady unknown.

SIR JOHN. Well, Madam, I can but love and thank you.

LADY SM. Here, bring Water to wash; though really you have all eaten so little, that you have no Need to wash your Mouths.

LORD SM. But prithee, Sir *John*, stay a while longer.

SIR JOHN. No, my Lord, I am to smoak a Pipe with a Friend, before I leave the Town.

COL. Why, Sir *John*, had not you better set out To-morrow?

SIR JOHN. Colonel, you forget, To-morrow is *Sunday*.

COL. Now, I always love to begin a Journey on Sundays, because I shall have the Prayers of the Church; to preserve all that Travel by Land or by Water.

SIR JOHN. Well, Colonel, thou art a mad Fellow to make a Priest of.

NEV. Fye, Sir *John*, do you take Tobacco? How can you make a Chimney of your Mouth?

SIR JOHN. [*To* Neverout.] What? you don't smoak, I warrant you, but you smock. (Ladies, I beg your Pardon.) Colonel, do you never smoke?

COL. No, Sir *John*, but I take a Pipe sometimes.

SIR JOHN. I'Faith, one of your finical *London* Blades dined with me last Year in *Derbyshire:* So, after Dinner, I took a Pipe: So, my Gentleman turn'd away his Head: So, said I, what Sir, do you never smoak? So, he answered as you do, Colonel, no; but I sometimes take a Pipe: So, he took a Pipe in his Hand, and fiddled with it, 'till he broke it: So, said I, pray, Sir, can you make a Pipe? So, he said, no: So, said I, why then, Sir, if you can't make a Pipe, you should not break a Pipe. So, we all laught.

LORD SM. Well, but Sir *John*, they say, that the Corruption of Pipes, is the Generation of Stoppers.

SIR JOHN. Colonel, I hear you go sometimes to *Derbyshire*, I wish you would come and foul a Plate with me.

COL. I hope, you'll give me a Soldier's Bottle.

SIR JOHN. Come, and try.

SIR JOHN. Mr. *Neverout*, you are a Town-Wit, can you tell me what Kind of Herb is Tobacco?

NEV. Why, an *Indian* Herb, Sir *John*.

SIR JOHN. No, 'tis a Pot-Herb; and so here's t'ye in a Pot of my Lord's *October*.

LADY SM. I hear, Sir *John*, since you are married, you have forsworn the Town.

SIR JOHN. No, Madam, I never forswore any Thing but building of Churches.

LADY SM. Well, but Sir *John*, when may we hope to see you again in *London*?

SIR JOHN. Why, Madam, not 'till the Ducks have eat up the Dirt, as the Children say.

NEV. Come, Sir *John*, I foresee it will rain terribly.

LORD SM. Come, Sir *John*, do nothing rashly, let us drink first.

LORD SP. Nay, I know Sir *John* will go, though he was sure it would rain Cats and Dogs. But, pray stay, Sir *John*, you'll be Time enough to go to Bed by Candle-light.

LORD SM. Why, Sir *John*, if you must needs go, while you stay, make good Use of your Time. Here's my Service to you. A Health to our Friends in *Derbyshire*.

SIR JOHN. Not a Drop more.

COL. Why, Sir *John,* you used to love a Glass of good Wine in former Times.

SIR JOHN. Why, so I do still, Colonel; but a Man may love his House very well, without riding on the Ridge; besides, I must be with my Wife on *Tuesday,* or there will be the Devil and all to pay.

COL. Well, if you go To-Day, I wish you may be wet to the Skin.

SIR JOHN. Ay, but they say, the Prayers of the Wicked won't prevail.

[*Sir* John *takes his Leave, and goes away.*]

LORD SM. Well, Miss, how do you like Sir *John?*

MISS. Why, I think, he's a little upon the Silly, or so; I believe he has not all the Wit in the World; but I don't pretend to be a Judge.

NEV. Faith, I believe he was bred at *Hogsnorton,* where the Pigs play upon the Organs.

LORD SP. Why, *Tom,* I thought you and he had been Hand and Glove.

NEV. Faith, he shall have a clean Threshold for me, I never darkned his Door in my Life, neither in Town, nor Country; but, he's a queer old Duke, by my Conscience; and yet, after all, I take him to be more Knave than Fool.

LORD SM. Well, come, a Man's a Man, if he has but a Hose on his Head.

COL. I was once with him, and some other Company, over a Bottle; and I'gad, he fell asleep, and snored so loud, that we thought he was driving his Hogs to Market.

NEV. Why, what? You can have no more of a Cat, than her Skin. You can't make a Silk Purse out of a Sow's Ear.

LORD SP. Well, since he's gone, the Devil go with him, and Sixpence; and there's Money and Company too.

NEV. Pray, Miss, let me ask you a Question?

MISS. Well, but don't ask Questions with a dirty Face. I warrant, what you have to say, will keep cold.

COL. Come, my Lord, against you are disposed. Here's to all that love and honour you.

LORD SP. Ay, that was always *Dick Nimble's* Health, I'm sure you know, he is dead.

COL. Dead! Well, my Lord, you love to be a Messenger of ill News, I'm heartily sorry; but, my Lord, we must all dye.

NEV. I knew him very well; but pray, how came he to dye?

MISS. There's a Question! You talk like a Poticary. Why, he dyed, because he could live no longer.

NEV. Well; rest his Soul; we must live by the Living, and not by the Dead.

LORD SP. You know his House was burnt down to the Ground.

COL. Yes, it was in the News. Why; Fire and Water are good Servants, but they are very bad Masters.

LORD SM. Here, take away, and set down a Bottle of Burgundy. Ladies, you'll stay and drink a Glass of Wine before you go to your Tea.

[*All's taken away, and the Wine set down.*]

[*Miss gives* Neverout *a smart Pinch.*]

NEV. Lord, Miss, what d'ye mean? D'ye think I have no feeling?

MISS. I'm forced to pinch, for the Times are hard.

NEV. [*Giving Miss a Pinch.*] Take that, Miss: What's Sawce for a Goose, is Sawce for a Gander.

MISS. [*screaming.*] Well, Mr. *Neverout*, if I live, that shall neither go to Heaven nor Hell with you.

NEV. [*takes Miss's Hand.*] Come, Miss, let us lay all Quarrels aside, and be Friends.

MISS. Don't be mauming and gauming a Body so. Can't you keep your filthy Hands to your self?

NEV. Pray, Miss, where did you get that Pick-Tooth Case?

MISS. I came honestly by it.

NEV. I'm sure it was mine, for I lost just such a one. Nay, I don't tell you a Lye.

MISS. No, if you Lye, 'tis much.

NEV. Well, I'm sure 'tis mine.

MISS. What, you think every Thing is yours; but a little the King has.

NEV. Colonel, you have seen my fine Pick-Tooth Case: Don't you think this is the very same?

COL. Indeed, Miss, it is very like it.

MISS. Ay, what he says, you'll swear.

NEV. Well; but I'll prove it to be mine.

MISS. Ay, do if you can.

NEV. Why; what's yours is mine, and what's mine is my own.

MISS. Well, run on 'till you're weary, no Body holds you.

[Neverout *gapes.*]

COL. What, Mr. *Neverout*, do you gape for Preferment?

NEV. Faith, I may gape long enough before it falls into my Mouth.

LADY SM. Mr. *Neverout,* I hear you live high.

NEV. Yes, Faith, Madam, live high, and lodge in a Garret.

COL. But, Miss, I forgot to tell you, that Mr. *Neverout* got the devilishest Fall in the Park To-Day.

MISS. I hope he did not hurt the Ground. But, how was it Mr. *Neverout?* I wish I had been there to laugh.

NEV. Why, Madam, it was a Place where a Cuckold had been bury'd, and one of his Horns sticking out, I happened to stumble against it. That was all.

LADY SM. Ladies, let us leave the Gentlemen to themselves; I think it is Time to go to our Tea.

LADY ANSW. and MISS. My Lords, and Gentlemen, your most humble Servant.

LORD SM. Well, Ladies, we'll wait on you an Hour hence.

[*The Gentlemen alone.*]

LORD SM. Come, John, bring us a fresh Bottle.

COL. Ay, my Lord; and pray let him carry off the dead Men, (as we say in the Army.) [*Meaning the empty Bottles.*]

LORD SP. Mr. *Neverout,* pray is not that Bottle full?

NEV. Yes, my Lord, full of Emptiness.

LORD SM. And, d'ye hear, *John,* bring clean Glasses.

COL I'll keep mine, for I think the Wine is the best Liquor to wash Glasses in.

THE LAST

SPEECH

AND

DYING WORDS

OF

EBENEZOR ELLISTON, *WHO WAS*

EXECUTED

THE SECOND DAY OF MAY, 1722

Published at his Desire, for the Common Good.

N. B. *About the Time that this Speech was written, the Town was much pestered with* Street-Robbers; *who, in a barbarous Manner would seize on Gentlemen, and take them into remote Corners, and after they had robbed them, would leave them bound and gagged. It is remarkable, that this Speech had so good an Effect, that there have been very few Robberies of that kind committed since.*

I am now going to suffer the just Punishment for my Crimes prescribed by the Law of God and my Country. I know it is the constant Custom, that those who come to this Place should have Speeches made for them, and cryed about in their own Hearing, as they are carried to Execution; and truly they are such Speeches that although our Fraternity be an ignorant illiterate People, they would make a Man ashamed to have such Nonsense and false *English* charged upon him even when he is going to the Gallows: They contain a pretended Account of our Birth and Family; of the Fact for which we are to die; of our sincere Repentance; and a Declaration of our Religion. I cannot expect to avoid the same Treatment with my Predecessors. However, having had an Education one or two Degrees better than those of my Rank and Profession; I have been considering ever since my Commitment, what it might be proper for me to deliver upon this Occasion.

AND First, I cannot say from the Bottom of my Heart, that I am truly sorry for the Offence I have given to God and the World; but I am very much so, for the bad Success of my Villanies in bringing me to this untimely End. For it is plainly evident, that after having some time ago obtained a Pardon from the Crown, I again took up my old Trade; my evil Habits were so rooted in me, and I was grown so unfit for any other kind of Employment. And therefore although in Compliance with my Friends, I resolve to go to the Gallows after the usual Manner, Kneeling, with a Book in my Hand, and my Eyes lift up; yet I shall feel no more Devotion in my Heart than I have observed in some of my Comrades, who have been drunk among common Whores the very Night before their Execution.[1] I can say further from my own Knowledge, that two of my Fraternity after they had been hanged, and wonderfully came to Life, and made their Escapes, as it sometimes happens; proved afterwards the wickedest Rogues I ever knew, and so continued until they were hanged again for good and all; and yet they had the Impudence at both Times they went to the Gallows, to smite their Breasts, and lift up their Eyes to Heaven all the Way.

SECONDLY, From the Knowledge I have of my own wicked Dispositions and that of my Comrades, I give it as my Opinion, that nothing can be more unfortunate to the Publick, than the Mercy of the Government in ever pardoning or transporting us; unless when we betray one another, as we never fail to do, if we are sure to be well paid; and then a Pardon may do good; by the same Rule, *That it is better to have but one Fox in a Farm than three or four.* But we generally make a Shift to return after being transported, and are ten times greater Rogues than before, and much more cunning. Besides, I know it by Experience, that some Hopes we have of finding Mercy, when we are tried, or after we are condemned, is always a great Encouragement to us.

THIRDLY, Nothing is more dangerous to idle young Fellows than the Company of those odious common Whores we frequent, and of which this Town is full: These Wretches put us upon all Mischief to feed their Lusts and Extravagancies: They are ten times more bloody and cruel than Men; their Advice is always not to spare if we are pursued; they get drunk with us, and are common to us all; and yet, if they can get any Thing by it, are sure to be our Betrayers.

NOW, as I am a dying Man, something I have done which may be of good Use to the Publick. I have left with an honest Man (and indeed the only honest Man I was ever acquainted with) the Names of all my wicked Brethren, the present Places of their Abode, with a short Account of the chief Crimes they have committed; in many of which I have been their Accomplice, and heard the rest from their own Mouths: I have likewise set down the Names of those we call our Setters, of the wicked Houses we frequent, and of those who receive and buy our stolen Goods. I have solemnly charged this honest Man, and have received his Promise upon Oath, that whenever he hears of any Rogue to be tryed for robbing, or House-breaking, he will look into his List, and if he finds the Name there of the Thief concerned, to send the whole Paper to the Government. Of this I here give my Companions fair and publick Warning, and hope they will take it.

IN the Paper abovementioned, which I left with my Friend, I have also set down the Names of several Gentlemen who have been robbed in *Dublin* Streets for three Years past: I have told the Circumstances of those Robberies; and shewn plainly that nothing but the Want of common Courage was the Cause of their Misfortunes. I have therefore desired my Friend, that whenever any Gentleman happens to be robbed in the Streets, he will get that Relation printed and published with the first Letters of those Gentlemens Names, who by their own Want of Bravery are likely to be the Cause of all the Mischief of that Kind, which may happen for the future.

I CANNOT leave the World without a short Description of that Kind of Life, which I have led for some Years past; and is exactly the same with the rest of our wicked Brethren.

ALTHOUGH we are generally so corrupted from our Childhood, as to have no Sense of Goodness; yet something heavy always hangs about us, I know not what it is, that we are never easy till we are half drunk among our Whores and Companions; nor sleep sound, unless we drink longer than we can stand. If we go abroad in the Day, a wise Man would easily find us to be Rogues by our Faces; we have such a suspicious, fearful, and constrained Countenance; often turning back, and slinking through narrow Lanes and Allies. I have never failed of knowing a Brother Thief by his Looks, though I never saw him before. Every Man among us keeps his particular Whore, who is however common to us all, when we have a mind to change. When we have got a Booty, if it be in Money, we divide it equally among our Companions, and soon squander it away on our Vices in those Houses that receive us; for the Master and Mistress, and the very Tapster, go Snacks;[2] and besides make us pay treble Reckonings. If our Plunder be Plate, Watches, Rings, Snuff-Boxes, and the like; we have Customers in all Quarters of the Town to take them off. I have seen a Tankard worth Fifteen Pounds sold to a Fellow in————Street for Twenty Shillings; and a Gold Watch for Thirty. I have set down his Name, and that of several others in the Paper already mentioned. We have Setters watching in Corners, and by dead Walls, to give us Notice when a Gentleman goes by; especially if he be any thing in Drink. I believe in my Conscience, that if an Account were made of a Thousand Pounds in stolen Goods; considering the low Rates we sell them at, the Bribes we must give for Concealment, the Extortions of Ale-house Reckonings, and other necessary Charges, there would not remain Fifty Pounds clear to be divided among the Robbers. And out of this we must find Cloaths for our Whores, besides treating them from Morning to Night; who, in Requital, reward us with nothing but Treachery and the Pox. For when our Money is gone, they are every Moment threatning to inform against us, if we will not go out to look for more. If any Thing in this World be like Hell, as I have heard it described by our Clergy; the truest Picture of it must be in the Back-Room of one of our Ale-houses at Midnight; where a Crew of Robbers and their Whores are met together after a Booty, and are beginning to grow drunk; from which Time, until they are past their Senses, is such a continued horrible Noise of Cursing, Blasphemy, Lewdness, Scurrility, and brutish Behaviour; such Roaring and Confusion, such a Clatter of Mugs and Pots at each other's Heads; that *Bedlam*, in Comparison, is a sober and orderly Place: At last they all tumble from their Stools and Benches, and sleep away the rest of the Night; and generally the Landlord or his Wife, or some other Whore who has a stronger Head than the rest, picks their Pockets before they wake. The Misfortune is, that we can never be easy till we are drunk; and our Drunkenness constantly exposes us to be more easily betrayed and taken.

THIS is a short Picture of the Life I have led; which is more miserable than that of the poorest Labourer who works for four Pence a Day; and yet Custom is so strong, that I am confident, if I could make my Escape at the Foot of the Gallows, I should be following the same Course this very Evening. So that upon the whole, we ought to be looked upon as the common Enemies of Mankind; whose Interest it is to root us out like Wolves, and other mischievous Vermin,[3] against which no fair Play is required.

IF I have done Service to Men in what I have said, I shall hope I have done Service to GOD; and that will be better than a silly Speech made for me full of Whining and Canting, which I utterly despise, and have never been used to; yet such a one I expect to have my Ears tormented with, as I am passing along the Streets.

GOOD People fare ye well; bad as I am, I leave many worse behind me. I hope you shall see me die like a Man, the Death of a Dog.

E. E.

DIRECTIONS

TO

SERVANTS

IN GENERAL; AND IN PARTICULAR TO

THE BUTLER,	PORTER,
COOK,	DAIRY-MAID,
FOOTMAN,	CHAMBER-MAID,
COACHMAN,	NURSE,
GROOM,	LAUNDRESS,
HOUSE-STEWARD,	HOUSE-KEEPER,
AND	TUTORESS, OR
LAND-STEWARD,	GOVERNESS.

BY THE REVEREND DR. SWIFT, D.S.P.D.

THE PUBLISHER'S PREFACE

The following Treatise of Directions to Servants *was began some Years ago by the Author, who had not Leisure to finish and put it into proper Order, being engaged in many other Works of greater Use to his Country, as may be seen by most of his Writings. But, as the Author's Design was to expose the Villanies and Frauds of Servants to their Masters and Mistresses, we shall make no Apology for its Publication; but give it our Readers in the same Manner as we find it, in the Original, which may be seen in the Printer's Custody. The few Tautologies that occur in the Characters left unfinished, will make the Reader look upon the Whole as a rough Draught with several Outlines only drawn: However, that there may appear no Daubing or Patch-Work by other Hands, it is thought most adviseable to give it in the Author's own Words.*

It is imagined, that he intended to make a large Volume of this Work; but as Time and Health would not permit him, the Reader may draw from what is here exhibited, Means to detect the many Vices and Faults, which People in that Kind of low Life are subject to.

If Gentlemen would seriously consider this Work, which is written for their Instruction, (although ironically) it would make them better (Economists, and preserve their Estates and Families from Ruin.

It may be seen by some scattered Papers (wherein were given Hints for a Dedication and Preface, and a List of all Degrees of Servants) that the Author intended to have gone through all their Characters.

This is all that need be said as to this Treatise, which can only be looked upon as a Fragment.

Dublin, Nov. 8, 1745   G.F.

RULES THAT CONCERN
ALL SERVANTS IN GENERAL

When your Master or Lady call a Servant by Name, if that Servant be not in the Way, none of you are to answer, for then there will be no End of your Drudgery: And Masters themselves allow, that if a Servant comes when he is called, it is sufficient.

When you have done a Fault, be always pert and insolent, and behave your self as if you were the injured Person; this will immediately put your Master or Lady off their Mettle.

If you see your Master wronged by any of your Fellow-servants, be sure to conceal it, for fear of being called a Telltale: However, there is one Exception, in case of a favourite Servant, who is justly hated by the whole Family; who therefore are bound in Prudence to lay all the Faults they can upon the Favourite.

The Cook, the Butler, the Groom, the Market-man, and every other Servant, who is concerned in the Expences of the Family, should act as if his Master's whole Estate ought to be applied to that Servant's particular Business. For Instance, if the Cook computes his Master's Estate to be a thousand Pounds a Year, he reasonably concludes that a thousand Pounds a Year will afford Meat enough, and therefore, he need not be saving; the Butler makes the same Judgment; so may the Groom and the Coachman; and thus every Branch of Expence will be filled to your Master's Honour.

When you are chid before Company, (which with Submission to our Masters and Ladies is an unmannerly Practice) it often happens that some Stranger will have the Good-nature to drop a Word in your Excuse; in such a Case, you have a good Title to justify your self, and may rightly conclude, that whenever he chides you afterwards on other Occasions, he may be in the wrong; in which Opinion you will be the better confirmed by stating the Case to your Fellow-servants in your own Way, who will certainly decide in your Favour: Therefore, as I have said before, whenever you are chidden, complain as if you were injured.

It often happens that Servants sent on Messages, are apt to stay out somewhat longer than the Message requires, perhaps two, four, six, or eight Hours, or some such Trifle; for the Temptation to be sure was great, and Flesh and Blood cannot always resist: When you return, the Master storms, the Lady scolds, stripping, cudgelling, and turning off, is the Word. But here you ought to be provided with a Set of Excuses, enough to serve on all Occasions: For Instance, your Uncle came fourscore Miles to Town this Morning, on purpose to see you, and goes back by Break of Day To-morrow: A Brother-Servant, that borrowed Money of you when he was out of Place, was running away to *Ireland:* You were taking Leave of an old Fellow-servant, who was shipping for *Barbados:* Your Father sent a Cow for you to sell, and you could not find a Chapman till Nine at Night: You were taking Leave of a dear Cousin who is to be hanged next *Saturday:* You wrencht your Foot against a Stone, and were forced to stay three Hours in a Shop, before you could stir a Step: Some Nastiness was thrown on you out of a Garret Window, and you were ashamed to come Home before you were cleaned, and the Smell went off: You were pressed for the Sea-service, and carried before a Justice of Peace, who kept you three Hours before he examined you, and you got off with much a-do: A Bailiff by Mistake seized you for a Debtor, and kept you the whole Evening in a Spunging-house:[1] You were told your Master had gone to a Tavern, and come to some Mischance, and your Grief was so great that you inquired for his Honour in a hundred Taverns between *Pall-mall* and *Temple-bar.*

Take all Tradesmens Parts against your Master, and when you are sent to buy any Thing, never offer to cheapen it, but generously pay the full Demand. This is highly for your Master's Honour; and may be some Shillings in your Pocket; and you are to consider, if your Master hath paid too much, he can better afford the Loss than a poor Tradesman.

Never submit to stir a Finger in any Business but that for which you were particularly hired. For Example, if the Groom be drunk or absent, and the Butler be ordered to shut the Stable Door, the Answer is ready, An please your Honour, I don't understand Horses; If a Corner of the Hanging wants a single Nail to fasten it, and the Footman be directed to tack it up, he may say, he doth not understand that Sort of Work, but his Honour may send for the Upholsterer.

Masters and Ladies are usually quarrelling with the Servants for not shutting the Doors after them: But neither Masters nor Ladies consider, that those Doors must be open before they can be shut, and that the Labour is double to open and shut the Doors; therefore the best, the shortest, and easiest Way is to do neither. But if you are so often teized to shut the Door, that you cannot easily forget it, then give the Door such a Clap as you go out, as will shake the whole Room, and make every Thing rattle in it, to put your Master and Lady in Mind that you observe their Directions.

If you find yourself to grow into Favour with your Master or Lady, take some Opportunity, in a very mild Way, to give them Warning;[2] and when they ask the Reason, and seem loth to part with you, answer That you would rather live with them, than any Body else, but a poor Servant is not to be blamed if he strives to better himself; that Service is no Inheritance, that your Work is great, and your Wages very small: Upon which, if your Master hath any Generosity, he will add five or ten Shillings a Quarter rather than let you go: But, if you are baulked, and have no Mind to go off, get some Fellow-servant to tell your Master, that he hath prevailed upon you to stay.

Whatever good Bits you can pilfer in the Day, save them to junket with your Fellow-servants at Night, and take in the Butler, provided he will give you Drink.

Write your own Name and your Sweet-heart's with the Smoak of a Candle on the Roof of the Kitchen, or the Servants Hall, to shew your Learning.

If you are a young sightly Fellow, whenever you whisper your Mistress at the Table, run your Nose full in her Cheek, or if your Breath be good, breathe full in her Face; this I know to have had very good Consequences in some Families.

Never come till you have been called three or four Times; for none but Dogs will come at the first Whistle; And when the Master calls [*Who's there?*] no Servant is bound to come; for [*Who's there*] is no Body's Name.

When you have broken all your earthen Drinking Vessels below Stairs (which is usually done in a Week) the Copper Pot will do as well; it can boil Milk, heat Porridge, hold Small-Beer, or in Case of Necessity serve for a Jordan;[3] therefore apply it indifferently to all these Uses; but never wash or scour it, for Fear of taking off the Tin.

Although you are allowed Knives for the Servants Hall, at Meals, yet you ought to spare them, and make Use only of your Master's.

Let it be a constant Rule, that no Chair, Stool, or Table in the Servants

Hall, or the Kitchen, shall have above three Legs, which hath been the antient, and constant Practice in all the Families I ever knew, and is said to be founded upon two Reasons; first, to shew that Servants are ever in a tottering Condition; secondly, it was thought a Point of Humility, that the Servants Chairs and Tables should have at least one Leg fewer than those of their Masters. I grant there hath been an Exception to this Rule, with regard to the Cook, who by old Custom was allowed an easy Chair to sleep in after Dinner; and yet I have seldom seen them with above three Legs. Now this epidemical Lameness of Servants Chairs is by Philosophers imputed to two Causes, which are observed to make the greatest Revolutions in States and Empires; I mean, Love and War. A Stool, a Chair, or a Table, is the first Weapon taken up in a general Romping or Skirmish; and after a Peace, the Chairs, if they be not very strong, are apt to suffer in the Conduct of an Amour; the Cook being usually fat and heavy, and the Butler a little in Drink.

I could never endure to see Maid-Servants so ungenteel as to walk the Streets with their Pettycoats pinned up; it is a foolish Excuse to alledge, their Pettycoats will be dirty, when they have so easy a Remedy as to walk three or four Times down a clean Pair of Stairs after they come home.

When you stop to tattle with some crony Servant in the same Street, leave your own Street-Door open, that you may get in without knocking, when you come back; otherwise your Mistress may know you are gone out, and you will be chidden.

I do most earnestly exhort you all to Unanimity and Concord. But mistake me not: You may quarrel with each other as much as you please, only bear in Mind that you have a common Enemy, which is your Master and Lady, and you have a common Cause to defend. Believe an old Practitioner; whoever out of Malice to a Fellow-servant, carries a Tale to his Master, shall be ruined by a general Confederacy against him.

The general Place of Rendezvous for all Servants, both in Winter and Summer, is the Kitchen; there the grand Affairs of the Family ought to be consulted; whether they concern the Stable, the Dairy, the Pantry, the Laundry, the Cellar, the Nursery, the Dining-room, or my Lady's Chamber: There, as in your own proper Element, you can laugh, and squall, and romp, in full Security.

When any Servant comes home drunk, and cannot appear, you must all join in telling your Master, that he is gone to Bed very sick; upon which your Lady will be so good-natured, as to order some comfortable Thing for the poor Man, or Maid.

When your Master and Lady go abroad together, to Dinner, or on a Visit for the Evening, you need leave only one Servant in the House, unless you have a Black-guard-boy to answer at the Door, and attend the Children, if there be any. Who is to stay at home is to be determined by short and long Cuts, and the Stayer at home may be comforted by a Visit from a Sweet-heart, without Danger of being caught together. These Opportunities must never be missed, because they come but sometimes; and all is safe enough while there is a Servant in the House.

When your Master or Lady comes home, and wants a Servant who happens to be abroad, your Answer must be, that he is but just that Minute stept out, being sent for by a Cousin who is dying.

If your Master calls you by Name, and you happen to answer at the fourth Call, you need not hurry yourself; and if you be chidden for staying, you may lawfully say, you came no sooner, because you did not know what you were called for.

When you are chidden for a Fault, as you go out of the Room, and down Stairs, mutter loud enough to be plainly heard; this will make him believe you are innocent.

Whoever comes to visit your Master or Lady when they are abroad, never burthen your Memory with the Persons Name, for indeed you have too many other Things to remember. Besides, it is a Porter's Business, and your Master's Fault that he doth not keep one; and who can remember Names? and you will certainly mistake them, and you can neither write nor read.

If it be possible, never tell a Lye to your Master or Lady, unless you have some Hopes that they cannot find it out in less than half an Hour. When a Servant is turned off, all his Faults must be told, although most of them were never known by his Master or Lady; and all Mischiefs done by others, charged to him. [Instance them.] And when they ask any of you, why you never acquainted them before? The Answer is, Sir, or Madam, really I was afraid it would make you angry; and besides perhaps you might think it was Malice in me. Where there are little Masters and Misses in a House, they are usually great Impediments to the Diversions of the Servants; the only Remedy is to bribe them with Goody Goodyes, that they may not tell Tales to Papa and Mamma.

I advise you of the Servants, whose Master lives in the Country, and who expect Vales,[4] always to stand Rank and File when a Stranger is taking his Leave; so that he must of Necessity pass between you; and he must have more Confidence, or less Money than usual, if any of you let him escape, and, according as he behaves himself, remember to treat him the next Time he comes.

If you are sent with ready Money to buy any Thing at a Shop, and happen at that Time to be out of Pocket (which is very usual) sink the Money and take up the Goods on your Master's Account. This is for the Honour of your Master and yourself; for he becomes a Man of Credit at your Recommendation.

When your Lady sends for you up to her Chamber, to give you any Orders, be sure to stand at the Door, and keep it open, fiddling with the Lock all the while she is talking to you, and keep the Button in your Hand for fear you should forget to shut the Door after you.

If your Master or Lady happen once in their Lives to accuse you wrongfully, you are a happy Servant, for you have nothing more to do, than for every Fault you commit, while you are in their Service, to put them in Mind of that false Accusation, and protest yourself equally innocent in the present Case.

When you have a Mind to leave your Master, and are too bashful to break the Matter for fear of offending him, your best way is to grow rude and saucy of a sudden, and beyond your usual Behaviour, till he find it necessary to turn you off; and when you are gone, to revenge yourself, give him and his Lady such a Character to all your Brother-servants, who are out of Place, that none will venture to offer their Service.

Some nice Ladies who are afraid of catching Cold, having observed that the Maids and Fellows below Stairs often forget to shut the Door after them, as they come in or go out into the back Yards, have contrived that a Pulley and Rope with a large Piece of Lead at the End, should be so fixt as to make the Door shut of itself, and require a strong Hand to open it; which is an immense Toil to Servants, whose Business may force them to go in and out fifty Times in a Morning: But Ingenuity can do much, for prudent Servants have found out an effectual Remedy against this insupportable Grievance, by tying up the Pulley in such a Manner, that the Weight of the Load will have no Effect; however, as to my own Part, I would rather chuse to keep the Door always open, by laying a heavy Stone at the Bottom of it.

The Servants Candlesticks are generally broken, for nothing can last for ever: But, you may find out many Expedients: You may conveniently stick your Candle in a Bottle, or with a Lump of Butter against the Wainscot, in a Powder-horn, or in an old Shoe, or in a cleft Stick, or in the Barrel of a Pistol, or upon its own Grease on a Table, in a Coffee Cup or a

Drinking Glass, a Horn Can, a Tea Pot, a twisted Napkin, a Mustard Pot, an Ink-horn, a Marrowbone, a Piece of Dough, or you may cut a Hole in a Loaf, and stick it there.

When you invite the neighbouring Servants to junket with you at home in an Evening, teach them a particular way of tapping or scraping at the Kitchen Window, which you may hear, but not your Master or Lady, whom you must take Care not to disturb or frighten at such unseasonable Hours.

Lay all Faults on a Lap-dog, a favourite Cat, a Monkey, a Parrot, a Magpye, a Child, or on the Servant who was last turned off: By this Rule you will excuse yourself, do no Hurt to any Body else, and save your Master or Lady from the Trouble and Vexation of chiding.

When you want proper Instruments for any Work you are about, use all Expedients you can invent, rather than leave your Work undone. For Instance, if the Poker be out of the Way or broken, stir up the Fire with the Tongs; if the Tongs are not at Hand, use the Muzzle of the Bellows, the wrong End of the Fire-Shovel, the Handle of the Fire-Brush, the End of a Mop, or your Master's Cane. If you want Paper to singe a Fowl, tear the first Book you see about the House. Wipe your Shoes for want of a Clout,[5] with the Bottom of a Curtain, or a Damask Napkin. Strip your Livery Lace for Garters. If the Butler wants a Jordan, in case of need, he may use the great Silver Cup.

There are several Ways of putting out Candles, and you ought to be instructed in them all: You may run the Candle End against the Wainscot, which puts the Snuff out immediately: You may lay it on the Floor, and tread the Snuff out with your Foot; You may hold it upside down until it is choaked with its own Grease; or cram it into the Socket of the Candle-stick: You may whirl it round in your Hand till it goes out: When you go to Bed, after you have made Water, you may dip your Candle End into the Chamber-Pot: You may spit on your Finger and Thumb, and pinch the Snuff until it goes out: The Cook may run the Candle's Nose into the Meal Tub, or the Groom into a Vessel of Oats, or a Lock of Hay, or a Heap of Litter: The House-maid may put out her Candle by running it against a Looking-glass, which nothing cleans so well as Candle Snuff: But the quickest and best of all Methods, is to blow it out with your Breath, which leaves the Candle clear and readier to be lighted.

There is nothing so pernicious in a Family as a Tell-tale, against whom it must be the principal Business of you all to unite: Whatever Office he serves in, take all Opportunities to spoil the Business he is about, and to cross him in every Thing. For Instance, if the Butler be the Tell-tale, break his Glasses whenever he leaves the Pantry open; or lock the Cat or the Mastiff in it, who will do as well: Mislay a Fork or a Spoon, so as he may never find it. If it be the Cook, whenever she turns her Back, throw a Lump of Soot or a Handful of Salt in the Pot, or smoking Coals into the Dripping-Pan, or daub the roast Meat with the Back of the Chimney, or hide the Key of the Jack. If a Footman be suspected, let the Cook daub the Back of his new Livery; or when he is going up with a Dish of Soup, let her follow him softly with a Ladle-full, and drible it all the Way up Stairs to the Dining-room, and then let the House-maid make such a Noise, that her Lady may hear it. The Waiting-maid is very likely to be guilty of this Fault, in hopes to ingratiate herself. In this Case, the Laundress must be sure to tear her Smocks in the washing, and yet wash them but half; and, when she complains, tell all the House that she sweats so much, and her Flesh is so nasty, that she fouls a Smock more in one Hour, than the Kitchen-maid doth in a week.

CHAPTER I

Directions to the Butler

In my Directions to Servants, I find from my long Observation, that you, Butler, are the principal Party concerned.

Your Business being of the greatest Variety, and requiring the greatest Exactness, I shall, as well as I can recollect, run through the several Branches of your Office, and order my Instructions accordingly.

In waiting at the Side-board, take all possible Care to save your own Trouble, and your Master's Drink and Glasses: Therefore, first, since those who dine at the same Table are supposed to be Friends, let them all drink out of the same Glass without washing; which will save you much Pains, as well as the Hazard of breaking them. Give no Person any Liquor till he has called for it thrice at least; by which means, some out of Modesty, and others out of Forgetfulness, will call the seldomer, and thus your Master's Liquor be saved.

If any one desires a Glass of Bottled-Ale; first shake the Bottle, to see whether any thing be in it, then taste it, to know what Liquor it is, that you may not be mistaken; and lastly, wipe the Mouth of the Bottle with the Palm of your Hand, to shew your Cleanliness.

Be more careful to have the Cork in the Belly of the Bottle than in the Mouth; and, if the Cork be musty, or white Fryers in your Liquor, your Master will save the more.

If an humble Companion, a Chaplain, a Tutor, or a dependent Cousin happen to be at Table, whom you find to be little regarded by the Master, and the Company, which no Body is readier to discover and observe than we Servants, it must be the Business of you and the Footman, to follow the Example of your Betters, by treating him many Degrees worse than any of the rest; and you cannot please your Master better, or at least your Lady.

If any one calls for Small-beer towards the end of Dinner, do not give yourself the Pains of going down to the Cellar, but gather the Droppings and Leavings out of the several Cups, and Glasses, and Salvers into one; but turn your Back to the Company, for Fear of being observed: On the contrary, if any one calls for Ale towards the end of Dinner, fill the largest Tankard top-full, by which you will have the greatest Part left to oblige your Fellow-servants without the Sin of stealing from your Master.

There is likewise an honest Perquisite by which you have a Chance of getting every Day the best Part of a Bottle of Wine to your self; for you are not to suppose that Gentlefolks will value the Remainder of a Bottle; therefore, always set a fresh one before them after Dinner, although there hath not been above a Glass drank of the other.

Take special Care that your Bottles be not musty before you fill them, in order to which, blow strongly into the Mouth of every Bottle, and then if you smell nothing but your own Breath, immediately fill it.

If you are sent down in haste to draw any Drink, and find it will not run, do not be at the Trouble of opening a Vent, but blow strongly into the Fosset, and you will find it immediately pour into your Mouth; or take out the Vent, but do not stay to put it in again, for fear your Master should want you.

If you are curious to taste some of your Master's choice Bottles, empty as many of them just below the Neck as will make the Quantity you want; but then take Care to fill them up again with clean Water, that you may not lessen your Master's Liquor.

There is an excellent Invention found out of late Years in the Management of Ale and Small-beer at the Side-board: For Instance, a Gentleman calls for a Glass of Ale, and drinks but half; another calls for Small-beer: You immediately teem out the Remainder of the Ale into the Tankard, and fill the Glass with Small-beer, and so backwards and forwards as long as Dinner lasts; by which you answer three great Ends: First, you save your self the Trouble of washing, and consequently the Danger of breaking your Glasses: Secondly, you are sure not to be mistaken in giving Gentlemen the Liquor they call for: And lastly, by this Method you are certain that nothing is lost.

Because Butlers often forget to bring up their Ale and Beer Time enough, be sure you remember to have up yours two Hours before Dinner; and place them in the sunny Part of the Room, to let People see that you have not been negligent.

Some Butlers have a Way of decanting (as they call it) bottled Ale, by which they lose a good Part of the Bottom: Let your Method be to turn the Bottle directly upside down, which will make the Liquor appear double the Quantity; by this means, you will be sure not to lose one Drop, and the Froth will conceal the Muddiness.

Clean your Plate, wipe your Knives, and rub the foul Table, with the Napkins and Table-cloth used that Day; for, it is but one washing, besides you save wearing out the coarse Rubbers; in Reward of which good Husbandry, my Judgment is, that you may lawfully make use of the finest Damask Napkins to be Night-caps for yourself.

When you clean your Plate, leave the Whiteing plainly to be seen in all the Chinks, for fear your Lady should believe you had not cleaned it.

There is nothing wherein the Skill of a Butler more appears, than the Management of Candles, whereof, although some Part may fall to the Share of other Servants, yet you being the principal Person concerned, I shall direct my Instructions upon this Article to you only, leaving your Fellow-Servants to apply them upon Occasion.

First, to avoid burning Day-light, and to save your Master's Candles, never bring them up until Half an Hour after it be dark, although they be called for ever so often.

Let your sockets be full of Grease to the Brim, with the old Snuff at the Top, then stick on your fresh Candles. It is true, this may endanger their falling, but the Candles will appear so much the longer and handsomer before Company. At other Times, for Variety, put your Candles loose in the Sockets, to shew they are clean to the Bottom.

When your Candle is too big for the Socket, melt it to a right Size in the Fire; and to hide the Smut, wrap it in Paper half way up.

You cannot but observe the great Extravagance of late Years among the Gentry upon the Article of Candles, which a good Butler ought by all means to discourage, both to save his own Pains and his Master's Money: This may be contrived several Ways: As when you are ordered to put Candles into the Sconces.

Sconces are great Wasters of Candles, and you, who are always to consider the Advantage of your Master, should do your utmost to discourage them: Therefore, your Business must be to press the Candle with both your Hands into the Socket, so as to make it lean in such a manner, that the Grease may drop all upon the Floor, if some Lady's Head-dress or Gentleman's Perriwig be not ready to intercept it: You may likewise stick the Candle so loose that it will fall upon the Glass of the Sconce, and break it into Shatters; this will save your Master many a fair Penny in the Year, both in Candles, and to the Glass-man, and yourself much Labour, for the Sconces spoiled cannot be used.

Never let the Candles burn too low, but give them as a lawful Perquisite to your Friend the Cook, to increase her Kitchen-stuff; or if this be not allowed in your House, give them in Charity to the poor Neighbours, who often run on your Errands.

When you cut Bread for a Toast, do not stand idly watching it, but lay it on the Coals, and mind your other Business; then come back, and if you find it toasted quite through, scrape off the burned Side, and serve it up.

When you dress up your Side-board, set the best Glasses as near the Edge of the Table as you can; by which Means they will cast a double Lustre, and make a much finer Figure; and the Consequence can be at worst but the breaking of half a Dozen, which is a Trifle in your Master's Pocket.

Wash the Glasses with your own Water, to save your Master's Salt.

When any Salt is spilt on the Table, do not let it be lost, but when Dinner is done, fold up the Table-cloth with the Salt in it, then shake the Salt out into the Salt-cellar, to serve next Day: But the shortest and surest Way is, when you remove the Cloth, to wrap the Knives, Forks, Spoons, Salt-cellars, broken Bread, and Scraps of Meat altogether in the Tablecloth, by which you will be sure to lose nothing, unless you think it better to shake them out of the Window among the Beggars, that they may with more Convenience eat the Scraps.

Leave the Dregs of Ale, Wine, and other Liquors, in the Bottles: To rince them is but Loss of Time, since all will be done at once in a general washing; and you will have a better Excuse for breaking them.

If your Master hath many musty, or very foul and crusted Bottles, I advise you in Point of Conscience, that those may be the first you truck at the next Ale-house for Ale or Brandy.

When a Message is sent to your Master, be kind to your Brother-servant who brings it; give him the best Liquor in your Keeping, for your Master's Honour; and with the first Opportunity he will do the same to you.

After Supper, if it be dark, carry your Plate and China together in the same Basket, to save Candle-light; for you know your Pantry well enough to put them up in the Dark.

When Company is expected at Dinner, or in Evenings, be sure to be Abroad, that nothing may be got which is under your Key, by which your Master will save his Liquor, and not wear out his Plate.

I come now to a most important Part of your Oeconomy, the Bottling of a Hogshead of Wine, wherein I recommend three Virtues, Cleanliness, Frugality, and brotherly Love. Let your Corks be of the longest Kind you can get; which will save some Wine in the Neck of every Bottle: As to your Bottles, chuse the smallest you can find, which will increase the Number of Dozens, and please your Master; for a Bottle of Wine is always a Bottle of Wine, whether it hold more or less; and if your Master hath his proper Number of Dozens, he cannot complain.

Every Bottle must be first rinced with Wine, for fear of any Moisture left in the Washing; some out of mistaken Thrift will rince a Dozen Bottles with the same Wine; but I would advise you, for more Caution, to change the Wine at every second Bottle; a Jill may be enough. Have Bottles ready by to save it; and it will be a good Perquisite, either to sell or drink with the Cook.

Never draw your Hogshead too low; nor tilt it for fear of disturbing the Liquor. When it begins to run slow, and before the Wine grows cloudy, shake the Hogshead, and carry a Glass of it to your Master, who will praise your Discretion, and give you all the rest as a Perquisite of your Place: You may tilt the Hogshead the next Day, and in a Fortnight get a Dozen or two of good clear Wine, to dispose of as you please.

In bottling Wine, fill your Mouth full of Corks, together with a large Plug of Tobacco, which will give to the Wine the true Taste of the Weed, so delightful to all good Judges in drinking.

When you are ordered to decant a suspicious Bottle, if a Pint be out, give your Hand a dextrous Shake, and shew it in a Glass, that it begins to be muddy.

When a Hogshead of Wine or any other Liquor is to be bottled off, wash your Bottles immediately before you begin; but, be sure not to drain them, by which good Management your Master will save some Gallons in every Hogshead.

This is the Time that in Honour to your Master, you ought to shew your Kindness to your Fellow-servants, and especially to the Cook. What signifies a few Flaggons out of a whole Hogshead? But make them be drunk in your Presence; for fear they should be given to other Folks, and so your Master be wronged: But, advise them if they get drunk to go to Bed, and leave Word they are sick, which last Caution I would have all the Servants observe, both Male and Female.

If your Master finds the Hogshead to fall short of his Expectation, what is plainer, than that the Vessel leaked: That, the Wine-Cooper had not filled it in proper Time: That the Merchant cheated him with a Hogshead below the common Measure?

When you are to get Water on for Tea after Dinner (which in many

Families is Part of your Office) to save Firing, and to make more Haste, pour it into the Tea-kettle, from the Pot where Cabbage or Fish have been boiling, which will make it much wholsomer, by curing the acid corroding Quality of the Tea.

Be saving of your Candles, and let those in the Sconces, the Hall, the Stairs, and in the Lanthorn, burn down into the Sockets, until they go out of themselves, for which your Master and Lady will commend your Thriftiness, as soon as they shall smell the Snuffs.

If a Gentleman leaves his Snuff-box or Pick-tooth-case on the Table after Dinner, and goes away, look upon it as part of your Vails; for so it is allowed by all Servants, and you do no Wrong to your Master or Lady.

If you serve a Country 'Squire, when Gentlemen and Ladies come to dine at your House, never fail to make their Servants drunk, and especially the Coachman, for the Honour of your Master; to which, in all your Actions, you must have a special Regard, as being the best Judge: For the Honour of every Family is deposited in the Hands of the Cook, the Butler, and the Groom, as I shall hereafter demonstrate.

Snuff the Candles at Supper as they stand on the Table, which is much the securest Way; because, if the burning Snuff happens to get out of the Snuffers, you have a Chance that it may fall into a Dish of Soup, Sackposset, Rice-milk, or the like, where it will be immediately extinguished with very little Stink.

When you have snuffed the Candle, always leave the Snuffers open, for then the Snuff will of itself burn away to Ashes, and cannot fall out and dirty the Table, when you snuff the Candles again.

That the Salt may lie smooth in the Salt-cellar, press it down with your moist Palm.

When a Gentleman is going away after dining with your Master, be sure to stand full in his View, and follow him to the Door, and as you have Opportunity look full in his Face, perhaps it may bring you a Shilling; but, if the Gentleman hath lain there a Night, get the Cook, the House-maid, the Stable-men, the Scullion, and the Gardener, to accompany you, and to stand in his Way to the Hall in a Line on each Side him: If the Gentleman performs handsomely, it will do him Honour, and cost your Master nothing.

You need not wipe your Knife to cut Bread for the Table, because, in cutting a Slice or two it will wipe itself.

Put your Finger into every Bottle, to feel whether it be full, which is the surest Way; for Feeling hath no Fellow.

When you go down to the Cellar to draw Ale or Small-beer, take care to observe directly the following Method. Hold the Vessel between the Finger and Thumb of your right Hand, with the Palm upwards, then hold the Candle between your Fingers, but a little leaning towards the Mouth of the Vessel, then take out the Spiggot with your Left-hand, and clap the Point of it in your Mouth, and keep your Left-hand to watch Accidents; when the Vessel is full withdraw the Spiggot from your Mouth, well wetted with Spittle, which being of a slimy Consistence will make it stick faster in the Fosset: If any Tallow drops into the Vessel you may easily (if you think of it) remove it with a Spoon, or rather with your Finger.

Always lock up a Cat in the Closet where you keep your *China* Plates, for fear the Mice may steal in and break them.

A good Butler always breaks off the Point of his Bottle-screw in two Days, by trying which is harder, the Point of the Screw, or the Neck of the Bottle: In this Case, to supply the Want of a Screw, after the Stump hath torn the Cork in Pieces, make use of a Silver Fork, and when the Scraps of the Cork are almost drawn out, flirt the Mouth of the Bottle into the Cistern, three or four times, until you quite clear it.

If a Gentleman dines often with your Master, and gives you nothing when he goes away, you may use several Methods to shew him some Marks of your Displeasure, and quicken his Memory: If he calls for Bread or Drink you may pretend not to hear, or send it to another who called after him: If he asks for Wine, let him stay awhile, and then send him Small-beer; give him always foul Glasses; send him a Spoon when he wants a Knife; wink at the Footman to leave him without a Plate: By these, and the like Expedients, you may probably be a better Man by half a Crown before he leaves the House, provided you watch an Opportunity of standing by when he is going.

If your Lady loves Play, your Fortune is fixed for ever: Moderate Gaming will be a Perquisite of ten shillings a Week; and in such a Family I would rather chuse to be Butler than Chaplain, or even rather than be Steward: It is all ready Money and got without Labour, unless your Lady happens to be one of those, who either obligeth you to find Wax-Candles, or forceth you to divide it with some favourite Servants; but at worst, the old Cards are your own; and, if the Gamesters play deep or grow peevish, they will change the Cards so often, that the old ones will be a considerable Advantage by selling them to Coffee-Houses, or Families who love Play, but cannot afford better than Cards at secondhand: When you attend at this Service, be sure to leave new Packs within the Reach of the

Gamesters, which, those who have ill Luck will readily take to change their Fortune; and now and then an old Pack mingled with the rest will easily pass. Be sure to be very officious on Play-nights, and ready with your Candles to light out your Company, and have Salvers of Wine at Hand to give them when they call; but manage so with the Cook, that there be no Supper, because it will be so much saved in your Master's Family; and, because a Supper will considerably lessen your Gains.

Next to Cards there is nothing so profitable to you as Bottles, in which Perquisite you have no Competitors, except the Footmen, who are apt to steal and vend them for Pots of Beer: But you are bound to prevent any such Abuses in your Master's Family: The Footmen are not to answer for what are broken at a general Bottling; and those may be as many as your Discretion will make them.

The Profit of Glasses is so very inconsiderable, that it is hardly worth mentioning: It consists only in a small Present made by the Glassman, and about four Shillings in the Pound added to the Prices for your Trouble and Skill in chusing them. If your Master hath a large Stock of Glasses, and you or your Fellow-servants happen to break any of them without your Master's Knowledge, keep it a Secret till there are not enough left to serve the Table, then tell your Master that the Glasses are gone; this will be but one Vexation to him, which is much better than fretting once or twice a Week; and it is the Office of a good Servant to discompose his Master and his Lady as seldom as he can; and here the Cat and Dog will be of great Use to take the Blame from you. *Note,* That Bottles missing are supposed to be half stolen by Stragglers and other Servants, and the other half broken by Accident, and at a general Washing.

Whet the Backs of your Knives until they are as sharp as the Edge, which will have this Advantage, that when Gentlemen find them blunt on one Side, they may try the other; and to shew you spare no Pains in sharpening the Knives, whet them so long, till you wear out a good Part of the Iron, and even the Bottom of the Silver Handle. This doth Credit to your Master, for it shews good House-keeping, and the Goldsmith may one Day make you a Present.

Your Lady, when she finds the Small-beer or Ale dead, will blame you for not remembering to put the Peg into the Vent-hole. This is a great Mistake, nothing being plainer, than that the Peg keeps the Air in the Vessel, which spoils the Drink, and therefore ought to be let out; but if she insisteth upon it, to prevent the Trouble of pulling out the Vent, and putting it in a Dozen Times a Day, which is not to be born by a good Servant, leave the Spiggot half out at Night, and you will find with only the Loss of two or three Quarts of Liquor, the Vessel will run freely.

When you prepare your Candles, wrap them up in a Piece of brown Paper, and so stick them in the Socket: Let the Paper come half way up the Candle, which looks handsome, if any Body should come in.

Do all in the Dark (as clean Glasses, &c.) to save your Master's Candles.

CHAPTER II

Directions to the Cook

Although I am not ignorant that it hath been a long Time since the Custom began among People of Quality to keep Men cooks, and generally of the *French* Nation;[6] yet because my Treatise is chiefly calculated for the general Run of Knights, Squires, and Gentlemen both in Town and Country, I shall therefore apply to you Mrs. Cook, as a Woman: However, a great Part of what I intend, may serve for either Sex; and your Part naturally follows the former, because the Butler and you are joined in Interest. Your Vails are generally equal, and paid when others are disappointed. You can junket together at Nights upon your own Prog, when the rest of the House are abed; and have it in your Power to make every Fellow-servant your Friend. You can give a good Bit or a good Sup to the little Masters and Misses, and gain their Affections. A Quarrel between you is very dangerous to you both, and will probably end in one of you being turned off; in which fatal Case, perhaps, it will not be so easy in some Time to cotton with another. And now Mrs. Cook, I proceed to give you my Instructions, which I desire you will get some Fellow-servant in the Family to read to you constantly one Night in every Week upon your going to Bed, whether you serve in Town or Country; for my Lessons shall be fitted to both.

If your Lady forgets at Supper that there is any cold Meat in the House, do not you be so officious as to put her in Mind; it is plain she did not want it; and if she recollects it the next Day, say she gave you no Orders, and it is spent; therefore, for fear of telling a Lye, dispose of it with the Butler, or any other Crony, before you go to Bed.

Never send up a Leg of a Fowl at Supper, while there is a Cat or Dog in the House, that can be accused for running away with it: But, if there happen to be neither, you must lay it upon the Rats, or a strange Grey-hound.

It is ill Housewifry to foul your Kitchen Rubbers with wiping the Bottoms of the Dishes you send up, since the Table-cloath will do as well, and is changed every Meal.

Never clean your Spits after they have been used; for the Grease left upon them by Meat, is the best Thing to preserve them from Rust; and when you make use of them again, the same Grease will keep the Inside of the Meat moist.

If you live in a rich Family, roasting and boiling are below the Dignity of your Office, and which it becomes you to be ignorant of; therefore leave that Work wholly to the Kitchen Wench, for fear of disgracing the Family you live in.

If you be employed in Marketing, buy your Meat as cheap as you can: but when you bring in your Accounts, be tender of your Master's Honour; and set down the highest Rate; which besides is but Justice; for no body can afford to sell at the same Rate that he buys; and I am confident that you may alway safely swear that you gave no more than what the Butcher and Poulterer asked. If your Lady orders you to set up a Piece of Meat for Supper, you are not to understand that you must set it up *all*; therefore you may give half to yourself and the Butler.

Good Cooks cannot abide what they very justly call fidling Work, where Abundance of Time is spent and little done: Such, for Instance, is the dressing small Birds, requiring a world of Cookery and Clutter; and a second or third Spit; which by the way is absolutely needless; for it would be a very ridiculous Thing indeed, if a Spit which is strong enough to turn a Sirloyn of Beef, should not be able to turn a Lark. However, if your Lady be nice, and is afraid that a large Spit will tear them, place them hand-somely in the Dripping-pan, where the Fat of roasted Mutton or Beef falling on the Birds, will serve to baste them; and so save both Time and Butter: for what Cook of any Spirit would lose her Time in picking Larks, Wheatears, and other small Birds; therefore, if you cannot get the Maids, or the young Misses to assist you, e'en make short Work, and either singe or flay them; there is no great Loss in the Skins, and the Flesh is just the same.

If you are employed in Market, do not accept a Treat of a Beef-stake and Pot of Ale from the Butcher, which I think in Conscience is no better than wronging your Master; but do you always take that Perquisite in Money, if you do not go in Trust; or in Poundage when you pay the Bills.

The Kitchen Bellows being usually out of Order with stirring the Fire with the Muzzle to save Tongs and Poker; borrow the Bellows out of your Lady's Bed-chamber, which being least used, are commonly the best in the House: and if you happen to damage or grease them, you have a Chance to keep them entirely for your own Use.

Let a Blackguard Boy be always about the House to send on your Errands, and go to Market for you in rainy Days; which will save your Cloaths, and make you appear more creditable to your Mistress.

If your Mistress allows you the Kitchen-stuff, in return of her Generosity, take care to boil and roast your Meat sufficient. If she keeps it for her own Profit, do her Justice; and rather than let a good Fire be wanting, enliven it now and then with the Dripping and the Butter that happens to turn to Oil.

Send up your Meat well stuck with Scewers, to make it look round and plump; and an Iron Scewer, rightly employed now and then, will make it look handsomer.

When you roast a long Joint of Meat, be careful only about the Middle, and leave the two extreme Parts raw; which may serve another Time, and will also save Firing.

When you scour your Plates and Dishes, bend the Brim inward, so as to make them hold the more.

Always keep a large Fire in the Kitchen when there is a small Dinner, or the Family dines abroad; that the Neighbours seeing the Smoak, may commend your Master's Housekeeping: But, when much Company is invited, then be as sparing as possible of your Coals; because a great deal of the Meat being half raw will be saved, and serve for next Day.

Boil your Meat constantly in Pump Water, because you must sometimes want River or Pipe Water, and then your Mistress observing your Meat of a different Colour, will chide you when you are not in Fault.

When you have Plenty of Fowl in the Larder, leave the Door open, in Pity to the poor Cat, if she be a good Mouser.

If you find it necessary to go to market in a wet Day, take out your Mistress's Riding-hood and Cloak to save your Cloaths.

Get three or four Char-women constantly to attend you in the Kitchen, whom you pay at small Charges, only with the broken Meat, a few Coals, and all the Cinders.

To keep troublesome Servants out of the Kitchen, always leave the Winder sticking on the Jack to fall on their Heads.

If a Lump of Soot falls into the Soup, and you cannot conveniently get it out, scum it well, and it will give the Soup a high *French* Taste.

If you melt your Butter to Oil, be under no Concern, but send it up; for Oil is a genteeler Sauce than Butter.

Scrape the Bottoms of your Pots and Kettles with a Silver Spoon, for fear of giving them a Taste of Copper.

When you send up Butter for Sauce, be so thrifty as to let it be half Water; which is also much wholesomer.

Never make use of a Spoon in any thing that you can do with your Hands, for fear of wearing out your Master's Plate.

When you find that you cannot get Dinner ready at the Time appointed, put the Clock back, and then it may be ready to a Minute.

Let a red hot Coal now and then fall into the Dripping-pan, that the Smoak of the Dripping may ascend, and give the roast Meat a high Taste.

You are to look upon your Kitchen as your Dressing-room; but, you are not to wash your Hands till you have gone to the Necessary-house, and spitted your Meat, trussed your Pullets, pickt your Sallad, nor indeed till after you have sent up the second Course; for your Hands will be ten times fouled with the many Things you are forced to handle; but when your Work is over, one Washing will serve for all.

There is but one Part of your Dressing that I would admit while the Victuals are boiling, roasting, or stewing, I mean the combing your Head, which loseth no Time, because you can stand over your Cookery, and watch it with one Hand, while you are using your Comb with the other.

If some of the Combings happen to be sent up with the Victuals, you may safely lay the Fault upon any of the Footmen that hath vexed you: As those Gentlemen are sometimes apt to be malicious if you refuse them a Sop in the Pan, or a Slice from the Spit; much more when you discharge a Ladle-full of hot Porridge on their Legs, or send them up to their Masters with a Dish-clout pinned at their Tails.

In roasting and boiling, order the Kitchen-maid to bring none but the large Coals, and save the small ones for the Fires above Stairs; the first are properest for dressing Meat, and when they are out, if you happen to miscarry in any Dish, you may fairly lay the Fault upon want of Coals: Besides, the Cinder-pickers will be sure to speak ill of your Master's Housekeeping, where they do not find Plenty of large Cinders mixed with fresh large Coals: Thus you may dress your Meat with Credit, do an Act of Charity, raise the Honour of your Master, and sometimes get Share of a Pot of Ale for your Bounty to the Cinder-women.

As soon as you have sent up the second Course, you have nothing to do in a great Family until Supper: Therefore, scour your Hands and Face, put on your Hood and Scarfe, and take your Pleasure among your Cronies, till Nine or Ten at Night——But dine first.

Let there be always a strict Friendship between you and the Butler, for it is both your Interests to be united: The Butler often wants a comfortable Tit-bit, and you much oftener a cool Cup of good Liquor. However, be cautious of him, for he is sometimes an inconstant Lover, because he hath great Advantage to allure the Maids with a Glass of Sack,[7] or White Wine and Sugar.

When you roast a Breast of Veal, remember your Sweetheart the Butler loves a Sweet-bread; therefore set it aside till Evening: You can say, the Cat or the Dog has run away with it, or you found it tainted, or fly-blown; and besides, it looks as well on the Table without the Sweet-bread as with it.

When you make the Company wait long for Dinner, and the Meat be overdone, (which is generally the Case) you may lawfully lay the Fault on your Lady, who hurried you so to send up Dinner, that you were forced to send it up too much boiled and roasted.

When you are in haste to take down your Dishes, tip them in such a manner, that a Dozen will fall together upon the Dresser, just ready for your Hand.

To save Time and Trouble, cut your Apples and Onions with the same Knife, for well-bred Gentry love the Taste of an Onion in every thing they eat.

Lump three or four Pounds of Butter together with your Hands, then dash it against the Wall just over the Dresser, so as to have it ready to pull by Pieces as you have occasion for it.

If you have a Silver Saucepan for the Kitchen Use, let me advise you to batter it well, and keep it always black; make room for the Saucepan by wriggling it on the Coals, &c.: This will be for your Master's Honour, because it shews there has been constant good Housekeeping: And in the same manner, if you are allowed a large Silver Spoon for the Kitchen, have the Bole of it be worn out with continual scraping and stirring, and often say merrily, This Spoon owes my Master no Service.

When you send up a Mess of Broth, Water-gruel, or the like, to your Master in a Morning, do not forget with your Thumb and two Fingers to put Salt on the Side of the Plate; for if you make use of a Spoon, or the End of a Knife, there may be Danger that the Salt would fall, and that would be a Sign of ill Luck. Only remember to lick your Thumb and Fingers clean, before you offer to touch the Salt.

If your Butter, when it is melted, tastes of Brass, it is your Master's Fault, who will not allow you a Silver Sauce-pan; besides, the less of it will go further, and new tinning is very chargeable: If you have a Silver Sauce-pan, and the Butter smells of Smoak, lay the Fault upon the Coals.

If your Dinner miscarries in almost every Dish, how could you help it: You were teized by the Footmen coming into the Kitchen; and, to prove it true, take Occasion to be angry, and throw a Ladle-full of Broth on one or two of their Liveries; besides, *Friday* and *Childermas-day* are two cross Days in the Week, and it is impossible to have good Luck on either of them; therefore on those two Days you have a lawful Excuse.

CHAPTER III

Directions to the Footman

Your Employment being of a mixt Nature, extends to a great Variety of Business, and you stand in a fair way of being the Favourite of your Master or Mistress, or of the young Masters and Misses; you are the fine Gentleman of the Family, with whom all the Maids are in Love. You are sometimes a Pattern of Dress to your Master, and sometimes he is so to you. You wait at Table in all Companies, and consequently have the Opportunity to see and know the World, and to understand Men and Manners; I confess your Vails are but few, unless you are sent with a Present, or attend the Tea in the Country; but you are called Mr. in the Neighbourhood, and sometimes pick up a Fortune, perhaps your Master's Daughter; and I have known many of your Tribe to have good Commands in the Army. In Town you have a Seat reserved for you in the Play-house, where you have an Opportunity of becoming Wits and Criticks: You have no profest Enemy except the Rabble, and my Lady's Waiting-woman, who are sometimes apt to call you Skipkennel. I have a true Veneration for your Office, because I had once the Honour to be one of your Order, which I foolishly left by demeaning myself with accepting an Employment in the Custom-house.—But that you, my Brethren, may come to better Fortunes, I shall here deliver my Instructions, which have been the Fruits of much Thought and Observation, as well as of seven Years Experience.

In order to learn the Secrets of other Families, tell your Brethren those of your Master's; thus you will grow a favourite both at home and abroad, and regarded as a Person of Importance.

Never be seen in the Streets with a Basket or Bundle in your Hands, and carry nothing but what you can hide in your Pocket, otherwise you will disgrace your Calling: To prevent which, always retain a Blackguard Boy to carry your Loads; and if you want Farthings, pay him with a good Slice of Bread or Scrap of Meat.

Let a Shoe-boy clean your own Shoes first, for fear of fouling the Chambers, and then let him clean your Master's; keep him on purpose for that Use and to run of Errands, and pay him with Scraps. When you are sent on an Errand, be sure to hedge in some Business of your own, either to see your Sweet-heart, or drink a Pot of Ale with some Brother-Servant, which is so much Time clear gained.

There is a great Controversy about the most convenient and genteel Way of holding your Plate at Meals; some stick it between the Frame and the Back of the Chair, which is an excellent Expedient, where the Make of the Chair will allow it: Others, for fear the Plate should fall, grasp it so firmly, that their Thumb reacheth to the Middle of the Hollow; which however, if your Thumb be dry, is no secure Method; and therefore in that Case, I advise your wetting the Bowl of it with your Tongue: As to that absurd Practice of letting the Back of the Plate lye leaning on the Hollow of your Hand, which some Ladies recommend, it is universally exploded,[8] being liable to so many Accidents. Others again, are so refined, that they hold their Plate directly under the left Arm-pit, which is the best Situation for keeping it warm; but this may be dangerous in the Article of taking away a Dish, where your Plate may happen to fall upon some of the Company's Heads. I confess myself to have objected against all these Ways, which I have frequently tried; and therefore I recommend a Fourth, which is to stick your Plate up to the Rim inclusive, in the left Side between your Waistcoat and your Shirt: This will keep it at least as warm as under your Arm-pit, or Ockster, (as the *Scots* call it) this will hide it so, as Strangers may take you for a better Servant, too good to hold a Plate; this will secure it from falling; and thus disposed, it lies ready for you to whip it out in a Moment, ready warmed, to any Guest within your Reach, who may want it. And lastly, there is another Convenience in this Method, that if any Time during your waiting, you find yourselves going to cough or sneeze, you can immediately snatch out your Plate, and hold the hollow Part close to your Nose or Mouth, and, thus prevent spirting any Moisture from either, upon the Dishes or the Ladies Head-dress: You see Gentlemen and Ladies observe a like Practice on such an Occasion, with a Hat or a Handkerchief; yet a Plate is less fouled and sooner cleaned than either of these; for, when your Cough or Sneeze is over, it is but returning your Plate to the same Position, and your Shirt will clean it in the Passage.

Take off the largest Dishes, and set them on with one Hand, to shew the Ladies your Vigour and Strength of Back; but always do it between two Ladies, that if the Dish happens to slip, the Soup or Sauce may fall on their Cloaths, and not daub the Floor: By this Practice, two of our Brethren, my worthy Friends, got considerable Fortunes.

Learn all the new-fashion Words, and Oaths, and Songs, and Scraps of Plays that your Memory can hold. Thus, you will become the Delight of nine Ladies in ten, and the Envy of ninety nine Beaux in a hundred.

Take Care, that at certain Periods, during Dinner especially, when Persons of Quality are there, you and your Brethren be all out of the Room together, by which you will give yourselves some Ease from the Fatigue of waiting, and at the same Time leave the Company to converse more freely, without being constrained by your Presence.

When you are sent on a Message, deliver it in your own Words, altho' it be to a Duke or a Dutchess, and not in the Words of your Master or Lady; for how can they understand what belongs to a Message as well as you, who have been bred to the Employment: But never deliver the Answer till it is called for, and then adorn it with your own Style.

When Dinner is done, carry down a great Heap of Plates to the Kitchen, and when you come to the Head of the Stairs, trundle them all before you: There is not a more agreeable Sight or Sound, especially if they be Silver; besides the Trouble they save you, and there they will lie ready near the Kitchen Door, for the Scullion to wash them.

If you are bringing up a Joint of Meat in a Dish, and it falls out of your Hand, before you get into the Dining Room, with the Meat on the Ground, and the Sauce spilled, take up the Meat gently, wipe it with the Lap of your Coat, then put it again into the Dish, and serve it up; and when your Lady misses the Sauce, tell her, it is to be sent up in a Plate by itself.

When you carry up a Dish of Meat, dip your Fingers in the Sauce, or lick it with your Tongue, to try whether it be good, and fit for your Master's Table.

You are the best Judge of what Acquaintance your Lady ought to have, and therefore, if she sends you on a Message of Compliment or Business to a Family you do not like, deliver the Answer in such a Manner, as may breed a Quarrel between them not to be reconciled: Or, if a Footman comes from the same Family on the like Errand, turn the Answer she orders you to deliver, in such a Manner, as the other Family may take it for an Affront.

When you are in Lodgings, and no Shoe-boy to be got, clean your Master's Shoes with the Bottom of the Curtains, a clean Napkin, or your Landlady's Apron.

Ever wear your Hat in the House, but when your Master calls; and as soon as you come into his Presence, pull it off to shew your Manners.

Never clean your Shoes on the Scraper, but in the Entry, or at the Foot of the Stairs, by which you will have the Credit of being at home, almost a Minute sooner, and the Scraper will last the longer.

Never ask Leave to go abroad, for then it will be always known that you are absent, and you will be thought an idle rambling Fellow; whereas, if you go out, and no body observes, you have a Chance of coming home without being missed, and you need not tell your Fellow-servants where you are gone, for they will be sure to say, you were in the House but two Minutes ago, which is the Duty of all Servants.

Snuff the Candles with your Fingers, and throw the Snuff on the Floor, then tread it out to prevent stinking: This Method will very much save the Snuffers from wearing out. You ought also to snuff them close to the Tallow, which will make them run, and so encrease the Perquisite of the Cook's Kitchen-Stuff; for she is the Person you ought in Prudence to be well with.

While Grace is saying after Meat, do you and your Brethren take the Chairs from behind the Company, so that when they go to sit again, they may fall backwards, which will make them all merry; but be you so discreet as to hold your Laughter till you get to the Kitchen, and then divert your Fellow-servants.

When you know your Master is most busy in Company, come in and pretend to settle about the Room; and if he chides, say, you thought he rung the Bell. This will divert him from plodding on Business too much, or spending himself in Talk, or racking his Thoughts, all which are hurtful to his Constitution.

If you are ordered to break the Claw of a Crab or a Lobster, clap it between the Sides of the Dining Room Door between the Hinges: Thus you can do it gradually without mashing the Meat, which is often the Case by using the Street-Door-Key, or the Pestle.

When you take a foul Plate from any of the Guests, and observe the foul Knife and Fork lying on the Plate, shew your Dexterity, take up the Plate, and throw off the Knife and Fork on the Table, without shaking off the Bones or broken Meat that are left: Then the Guest, who hath more Time than you, will wipe the Fork and Knife already used.

When you carry a Glass of Liquor to any Person who hath called for it, do not bob him on the Shoulder, or cry Sir, or Madam, here's the Glass, that would be unmannerly, as if you had a Mind to force it down one's Throat; but stand at the Person's right Shoulder, and wait his Time; and if he strikes it down with his Elbow by Forgetfulness, that was his Fault and not yours.

When your Mistress sends you for a Hackney Coach in a wet Day, come back in the Coach to save your Cloaths and the Trouble of walking; it is better the Bottom of her Petty-coats should be daggled with your dirty Shoes, than your Livery be spoiled, and yourself get a Cold.

There is no Indignity so great to one of your Station, as that of lighting your Master in the Streets with a Lanthorn; and therefore, it is very honest Policy to try all Arts how to evade it: Besides, it shews your Master to be either poor or covetous, which are the two worst Qualities you can meet with in any Service. When I was under these Circumstances, I made use of several wise Expedients, which I here recommend to you: Sometimes I took a Candle so long, that it reached to the very Top of the Lanthorn, and burned it: But, my Master after a good Beating, ordered me to paste the Top with Paper. I then used a middling Candle, but stuck it so loose in the Socket, that it leaned towards one Side, and burned a whole Quarter of the Horn. Then I used a Bit of Candle of half an Inch, which sunk in the Socket, and melted the Solder, and forced my Master to walk half the Way in the Dark. Then he made me stick two Inches of Candle in the Place where the Socket was; after which, I pretended to stumble, put out the Candle, and broke all the Tin Part to Pieces: At last, he was forced to make use of a Lanthorn-boy out of perfect good Husbandry.

It is much to be lamented, that Gentlemen of our Employment have but two Hands to carry Plates, Dishes, Bottles, and the like out of the Room at Meals; and the Misfortune is still the greater, because one of those Hands is required to open the Door, while you are encumbered with your Load: Therefore, I advise, that the Door may be always left at jarr, so as to open it with your Foot, and then you may carry out Plates and Dishes from your Belly up to your Chin, besides a good Quantity of Things under your Arms, which will save you many a weary Step; but take Care that none of the Burthen falls until you are out of the Room, and if possible, out of Hearing.

If you are sent to the Post-Office with a Letter in a cold rainy Night, step to the Ale-house, and take a Pot, until it is supposed you have done your Errand; but take the next fair Opportunity to put the Letter in carefully, as becomes an honest Servant.

If you are ordered to make Coffee for the Ladies after Dinner, and the Pot happens to boil over, while you are running up for a Spoon to stir it, or are thinking of something else, or struggling with the Chamber-maid for a Kiss, wipe the Sides of the Pot clean with a Dishclout, carry up your Coffee boldly, and when your Lady finds it too weak, and examines you whether it hath not run over, deny the Fact absolutely, swear you put in more Coffee than ordinary, that you never stirred an Inch from it, that you strove to make it better than usual, because your Mistress had Ladies with her, that the Servants in the Kitchen will justify what you say: Upon this, you will find that the other Ladies will pronounce your Coffee to be very good, and your Mistress will confess that her Mouth is out of Taste, and she will for the future suspect herself, and be more cautious in finding Fault. This I would have you do from a Principle of Conscience, for Coffee is very unwholesome; and out of Affection to your Lady, you ought to give it her as weak as possible: And upon this Argument, when you have a Mind to treat any of the Maids with a Dish of fresh Coffee, you may, and ought to subtract a third Part of the Powder, on account of your Lady's Health, and getting her Maids Good-will.

If your Master sends you with a small trifling Present to one of his Friends, be as careful of it as you would be of a Diamond Ring: Therefore, if the Present be only Half a Dozen Pippins, send up the Servant who received the Message to say, that you were ordered to deliver them with your own Hands. This will shew your Exactness and Care to prevent Accidents or Mistakes; and the Gentleman or Lady cannot do less than give you a Shilling: So when your Master receives the like Present, teach the Messenger who brings it to do the same, and give your Master Hints that may stir up his Generosity; for Brother Servants should assist one another, since it is all for your Master's Honour, which is the chief Point to be consulted by every good Servant, and of which he is the best Judge.

When you step but a few Doors off to tattle with a Wench, or take a running Pot of Ale, or to see a Brother Footman going to be hanged, leave the Street Door open, that you may not be forced to knock, and your Master discover you are gone out; for a Quarter of an Hour's Time can do his Service no Injury.

When you take away the remaining Pieces of Bread after Dinner, put them on foul Plates, and press them down with other Plates over them, so as no body can touch them; and so, they will be a good Perquisite to the Blackguard Boy in ordinary.

When you are forced to clean your Master's Shoes with your own Hand, use the Edge of the sharpest Case Knife, and dry them with the Toes an Inch from the Fire, because wet Shoes are dangerous; and besides, by these Arts you will get them the sooner for yourself.

In some Families the Master often sends to the Tavern for a Bottle of Wine, and you are the Messenger: I advise you, therefore, to take the smallest Bottle you can find; but however, make the Drawer give you a full Quart, then you will get a good Sup for yourself, and your Bottle will be filled. As for a Cork to stop it, you need be at no Trouble, for the Thumb will do as well, or a Bit of dirty chewed Paper.

In all Disputes with Chairmen and Coachmen, for demanding too much, when your Master sends you down to chaffer with them, take Pity of the poor Fellows, and tell your Master that they will not take a Farthing less: It is more for your Interest to get Share of a Pot of Ale, than to save a Shilling for your Master, to whom it is a Trifle.

When you attend your Lady in a dark Night, if she useth her Coach, do not walk by the Coach Side, so as to tire and dirt yourself, but get up into your proper Place, behind it, and so hold the Flambeau sloping forward over the Coach Roof, and when it wants snuffing, dash it against the Corners.

When you leave your Lady at Church on *Sundays,* you have two Hours safe to spend with your Companions at the Ale-house, or over a Beef-Stake and a Pot of Beer at Home with the Cook, and the Maids; and, indeed, poor Servants have so few Opportunities to be happy, that they ought not to lose any.

Never wear Socks when you wait at Meals, on the Account of your own Health, as well as of them who sit at Table; because as most Ladies like the Smell of young Mens Toes, so it is a sovereign Remedy against the Vapours.

Chuse a Service, if you can, where your Livery Colours are least tawdry and distinguishing: Green and Yellow immediately betray your Office, and so do all Kinds of Lace, except Silver, which will hardly fall to your Share, unless with a Duke, or some Prodigal just come to his Estate. The Colours you ought to wish for, are Blue, or Filemot, turned up with Red; which with a borrowed Sword, a borrowed Air, your Master's Linen, and a natural and improved Confidence, will give you what Title you please, where you are not known.

When you carry Dishes or other Things out of the Room at Meals, fill both your Hands as full as possible; for, although you may sometimes spill, and sometimes let fall, yet you will find at the Year's End, you have made great Dispatch, and saved abundance of Time.

If your Master or Mistress happens to walk the Streets, keep on one Side, and as much on the Level with them as you can, which People observing, will either think you do not belong to them, or that you are one of their Companions; but, if either of them happen to turn back and speak to you, so that you are under the Necessity to take off your Hat, use but your Thumb and one Finger, and scratch your Head with the rest.

In Winter Time light the Dining-Room Fire but two Minutes before Dinner is served up, that your Master may see, how saving you are of his Coals.

When you are ordered to stir up the Fire, clean away the Ashes from between the Bars with the Fire-Brush.

When you are ordered to call a Coach, although it be Midnight, go no further than the Door, for Fear of being out of the Way when you are wanted; and there stand bawling, Coach, Coach, for half an Hour.

Although you Gentlemen in Livery have the Misfortune to be treated scurvily by all Mankind, yet you make a Shift to keep up your Spirits, and sometimes arrive at considerable Fortunes. I was an intimate Friend to one of our Brethren, who was Footman to a Court-Lady: She had an honourable Employment, was Sister to an Earl, and the Widow of a Man of Quality. She observed something so polite in my Friend, the Gracefulness with which he tript before her Chair, and put his Hair under his Hat, that she made him many Advances; and one Day taking the Air in her Coach with *Tom* behind it, the Coachman mistook the Way, and stopt at a priviledged Chapel, where the Couple were marryed, and *Tom* came home in the Chariot by his Lady's Side: But he unfortunately taught her to drink Brandy, of which she died, after having pawned all her Plate to purchase it, and *Tom* is now a Journeyman Malster.

Boucher, the famous Gamester, was another of our Fraternity, and when

he was worth 50,000*l*. he dunned[9] the Duke of *B——m* for an Arrear of
Wages in his Service: And I could instance many more, particularly another, whose Son had one of the chief Employments at Court; and is sufficient to give you the following Advice, which is to be pert and sawcy to
all Mankind, especially to the Chaplain, the Waiting-woman, and the better Sort of Servants in a Person of Quality's Family, and value not now and
then a Kicking, or a Caning; for your Insolence will at last turn to good
Account; and from wearing a Livery, you may probably soon carry a Pair
of Colours.

When you wait behind a Chair at Meals, keep constantly wriggling the
Back of the Chair, that the Person behind whom you stand, may know you
are ready to attend him.

When you carry a Parcel of *China* Plates, if they chance to fall, as it is
a frequent Misfortune, your Excuse must be, that a Dog ran across you in
the Hall; that the Chamber-maid accidentally pushed the Door against
you; that a Mop stood across the Entry, and tript you up; that your Sleeve
stuck against the Key, or Button of the Lock.

When your Master and Lady are talking together in their Bed-
chamber, and you have some Suspicion that you or your Fellow-servants
are concerned in what they say, listen at the Door for the publick Good of
all the Servants, and join all to take proper Measures for preventing any
Innovations that may hurt the Community.

Be not proud in Prosperity: You have heard that Fortune turns on a
Wheel; if you have a good Place, you are at the Top of the Wheel. Remember how often you have been stripped, and kicked out of Doors, your
Wages all taken up beforehand, and spent in translated red-heeled Shoes,
second-hand Toupees, and repaired Lace Ruffles, besides a swinging Debt
to the Ale-wife and the Brandy-shop. The neighbouring Tapster, who before would beckon you over to a savoury Bit of Ox-cheek in the Morning,
give it you gratis, and only score you up for the Liquor, immediately after
you were packt off in Disgrace, carried a Petition to your Master, to be
paid out of your Wages, whereof not a Farthing was due, and then pursued
you with Bailiffs into every blind Cellar. Remember how soon you grew
shabby, thread-bare and out-at-heels; was forced to borrow an old Livery
Coat, to make your Appearance while you were looking for a Place; and
sneak to every House where you have an old Acquaintance to steal you a
Scrap, to keep Life and Soul together; and upon the whole, were in the
lowest Station of Human Life, which, as the old Ballad says, is that of a
Skipkennel turned out of Place:[10] I say, remember all this now in your

flourishing Condition. Pay your Contributions duly to your late Brothers the Cadets, who are left to the wide World: Take one of them as your Dependant, to send on your Lady's Messages when you have a Mind to go to the Ale-house; slip him out privately now and then a Slice of Bread, and a Bit of cold Meat, your Master can afford it; and if he be not yet put upon the Establishment for a Lodging, let him lye in the Stable, or the Coach-house, or under the Back-stairs, and recommend him to all the Gentlemen who frequent your House, as an excellent Servant.

To grow old in the Office of a Footman, is the highest of all Indignities: Therefore, when you find Years coming on, without Hopes of a Place at Court, a Command in the Army, a Succession to the Stewardship, an Employment in the Revenue (which two last you cannot obtain without Reading and Writing) or running away with your Master's Niece or Daughter; I directly advise you to go upon the Road, which is the only Post of Honour left you: There you will meet many of your old Comrades, and live a short Life and a merry one, and make a Figure at your Exit, wherein I will give you some Instructions.

The last Advice I shall give you, relates to your Behaviour when you are going to be hanged; which, either for robbing your Master, for House-breaking, or going upon the High-way, or in a drunken Quarrel, by killing the first Man you meet, may very probably be your Lot, and is owing to one of these three Qualities; either a Love of good Fellowship, a Generosity of Mind, or too much Vivacity of Spirits. Your good Behaviour on this Article, will concern your whole Community: At your Tryal deny the Fact with all Solemnity of Imprecations: A hundred of your Brethren, if they can be admitted, will attend about the Bar, and be ready upon Demand to give you a good Character before the Court: Let nothing prevail on you to confess, but the Promise of a Pardon for discovering your Comrades: But, I suppose all this to be in vain, for if you escape now, your Fate will be the same another Day. Get a Speech to be written by the best Author of *Newgate:* Some of your kind Wenches will provide you with a *Holland* Shirt, and white Cap crowned with a crimson or black Ribbon: Take Leave chearfully of all your Friends in *Newgate:* Mount the Cart with Courage: Fall on your Knees: Lift up your Eyes: Hold a Book in your Hands although you cannot read a Word: Deny the Fact at the Gallows: Kiss and forgive the Hangman, and so Farewel: You shall be buried in Pomp, at the Charge of the Fraternity: The Surgeon shall not touch a Limb of you; and your Fame shall continue until a Successor of equal Renown succeeds in your Place.

CHAPTER IV

Directions to the Coachman

You are strictly bound to nothing, but to step into the Box, and carry your Master or Lady.

Let your Horses be so well trained, that when you attend your Lady at a Visit, they will wait until you slip into a neighbouring Ale-house, to take a Pot with a Friend.

When you are in no Humour to drive, tell your Master that the Horses have got a Cold; that they want Shoeing; that Rain does them Hurt, and roughens their Coat, and rots the Harness. This may likewise be applied to the Groom.

If your Master dines with a Country Friend, drink as much as you can get; because it is allowed, that a good Coachman never drives so well as when he is drunk, and then shew your Skill, by driving to an Inch by a Precipice; and say you never drive so well as when drunk.

If you find any Gentleman fond of one of your Horses, and willing to give you a Consideration beside the Price; perswade your Master to sell him, because he is so vicious that you cannot undertake to drive with him, and is foundered into the Bargain.

Get a Blackguard-boy to watch your Coach at the Church Door on *Sundays,* that you and your Brother-Coachmen may be merry together at the Ale-house, while your Master and Lady are at Church.

Take Care that your Wheels be good; and get a new Set bought as often as you can, whether you are allowed the old as your Perquisite or not: In one Case it will turn to your honest Profit, and in the other it will be a just Punishment on your Master's Covetousness; and probably the Coach-maker will consider you too.

CHAPTER V

Directions to the Groom

You are the Servant upon whom the Care of your Master's Honour in all Journies entirely depends: Your Breast is the sole Repository of it. If he travels the Country, and lodgeth at Inns, every Dram of Brandy, every Pot of Ale extraordinary that you drink, raiseth his Character; and therefore, his Reputation ought to be dear to you; and, I hope, you will not stint yourself in either. The Smith, the Sadler's Journeyman, the Cook at the Inn, the Ostler and the Boot-catcher, ought all by your Means to partake of your Master's Generosity: Thus, his Fame will reach from one County to another; and what is a Gallon of Ale, or a Pint of Brandy in his Worship's Pocket? And, although he should be in the Number of those who value their Credit less than their Purse, yet your Care of the former ought to be so much the greater. His Horse wanted two Removes; your Horse wanted Nails; his Allowance of Oats and Beans was greater than the Journey required; a third Part may be retrenched, and turned into Ale or Brandy; and thus his Honour may be preserved by your Discretion, and less Expence to him; or, if he travels with no other Servant, the Matter is easily made up in the Bill between you and the Tapster.

Therefore, as soon as you alight at the Inn, deliver your Horses to the Stable-boy, and let him gallop them to the next Pond; then call for a Pot of Ale, for it is very fit that a Christian should drink before a Beast. Leave your Master to the Care of the Servants in the Inn, and your Horses to those in the Stable: Thus both he and they are left in the properest Hands; but you are to provide for yourself; therefore get your Supper, drink freely, and go to Bed without troubling your Master, who is in better Hands than yours. The Ostler is an honest Fellow, loves Horses in his Heart, and would not wrong the dumb Creatures for the World. Be tender of your Master, and order the Servants not to wake him too early. Get your Breakfast before he is up, that he may not wait for you; make the Ostler tell him the Roads are very good, and the Miles short; but advise him to stay a little longer until the Weather clears up, for he is afraid there will be Rain, and he will be Time enough after Dinner.

Let your Master mount before you, out of Good-manners. As he is leaving the Inn, drop a good Word in Favour of the Ostler, what Care he took of the Cattle; and add, that you never saw civiller Servants. Let your Master ride on before, and do you stay until the Landlord hath given you a Dram; then gallop after him thro' the Town or Village with full Speed, for fear he should want you, and to shew your Horsemanship.

If you are a Piece of a Farrier, as every good Groom ought to be, get Sack, Brandy, or Strong-beer to rub your Horses Heels every Night, and be not sparing, for (if any be spent) what is left, you know how to dispose of it.

Consider your Master's Health, and rather than let him take long Journies, say the Cattle are weak, and fallen in their Flesh with hard Riding; tell him of a very good Inn five Miles nearer than he intended to go; or leave one of his Horses Fore Shoes loose in the Morning; or contrive that the Saddle may pinch the Beast in his Withers; or keep him without Corn all Night and Morning, so that he may tire on the Road; or wedge a thin Plate of Iron between the Hoof and the Shoe, to make him halt; and all this in perfect Tenderness to your Master.

When you are going to be hired, and the Gentleman asks you, Whether you are apt to be drunk? Own freely, that you love a Cup of good Ale; but that it is your Way, drunk or sober, never to neglect your Horses.

When your Master hath a Mind to ride out for the Air, or for Pleasure, if any private Business of your own makes it inconvenient for you to attend him; give him to understand, that the Horses want bleeding or purging; that his own Pad hath got a Surfeit; or, that the Saddle wants stuffing; and his Bridle is gone to be mended: This you may honestly do, because it will be no Injury to the Horses or your Master; and at the same time shews the great Care you have of the poor dumb Creatures.

If there be a particular Inn in the Town whither you are going, and where you are well acquainted with the Ostler or Tapster, and the People of the House; find Fault with the other Inns, and recommend your Master thither; it may probably be a Pot and a Dram or two more in your Way, and to your Master's Honour.

If your Master sends you to buy Hay, deal with those who will be the most liberal to you; for Service being no Inheritance, you ought not to let slip any lawful and customary Perquisite. If your Master buys it himself, he wrongs you; and to teach him his Duty, be sure to find fault with that Hay as long as it lasts; and, if the Horses thrive with it, the Fault is yours.

Hay and Oats in the Management of a skilful Groom, will make excellent Ale as well as Brandy; but this I only hint.

When your Master dines, or lies at a Gentleman's House in the Country, altho' there be no Groom, or he be gone abroad, or that the Horses have been quite neglected; be sure to employ one of the Servants to hold the Horse when your Master mounts. This I would have you do, when your Master only alights, to call in for a few Minutes: For Brother-servants must always befriend one another, and this also concerns your Master's Honour; because he cannot do less than give a Piece of Money to him who holds his Horse.

In long Journeys, ask your Master Leave to give Ale to the Horses; carry two Quarts full to the Stable, pour Half a Pint into a Bowl, and if they will not drink it, you and the Ostler must do the best you can; perhaps they may be in a better Humour at the next Inn, for I would have you never fail to make the Experiment.

When you go to air your Horses in the Park, or the Fields, give them to a Horse-boy, or one of the Blackguards, who being lighter than you, may be trusted to run Races with less Damage to the Horses, and teach them to leap over Hedges and Ditches, while you are drinking a friendly Pot with your Brother Grooms: But sometimes you and they may run Races yourselves for the Honour of your Horses, and of your Masters.

Never stint your Horses at home in Hay and Oats, but fill the Rack to the Top, and the Manger to the Brim: For you would take it ill to be stinted yourself, although perhaps, they may not have the Stomach to eat; consider, they have no Tongues to ask. If the Hay be thrown down, there is no Loss, for it will make Litter and save Straw.

When your Master is leaving a Gentleman's House in the Country, where he hath lain a Night; then consider his Honour: Let him know how many Servants there are of both Sexes, who expect Vails; and give them their Cue to attend in two Lines as he leaves the House; but, desire him not to trust the Money with the Butler, for fear he should cheat the rest: This will force your Master to be more generous; and then you may take Occasion to tell your Master, that Squire such a one, whom you lived with last, always gave so much apiece to the common Servants, and so much to the House-keeper, and the rest, naming at least double to what he intended to give; but, be sure to tell the Servants what a good Office you did them: This will gain you Love, and your Master Honour.

You may venture to be drunk much oftener than the Coachman, whatever he pretends to alledge in his own Behalf, because you hazard no Body's Neck but your own; for, the Horse will probably take so much Care of himself, as to come off with only a Strain or a Shoulder-slip.

When you carry your Master's Riding-Coat in a Journey, wrap your own in it, and buckle them up close with a Strap, but turn you Master's In-side out, to preserve the Outside from Wet and Dirt; thus, when it begins to rain, your Master's Coat will be first ready to be given him; and, if it get more Hurt than yours, he can afford it better, for your Livery must always serve its Year's Apprenticeship.

When you come to your Inn with the Horses wet and dirty after hard Riding, and are very hot, make the Ostler immediately plunge them into Water up to their Bellies, and allow them to drink as much as they please; but, be sure to gallop them full-speed a Mile at least, to dry their Skins and warm the Water in their Bellies. The Ostler understands his Business, leave all to his Discretion, while you get a Pot of Ale and some Brandy at the Kitchen Fire to comfort your heart.

If your Horse drop a Fore-Shoe, be so careful to alight and take it up: Then ride with all the Speed you can (the Shoe in your Hand that every Traveller may observe your Care) to the next Smith on the Road, make him put it on immediately, that your Master may not wait for you, and that the poor Horse may be as short a Time as possible without a Shoe.

When your Master lies at a Gentleman's House, if you find the Hay and Oats are good, complain aloud of their Badness; this will get you the Name of a diligent Servant; and be sure to cram the Horses with as much Oats as they can eat, while you are there, and you may give them so much the less for some Days at the Inns, and turn the Oats into Ale. When you leave the Gentleman's House, tell your Master what a covetous Huncks[11] that Gentleman was, that you got nothing but Buttermilk or Water to drink; this will make your Master out of Pity allow you a Pot of Ale the more at the next Inn: But, if you happen to get drunk in a Gentleman's House, your Master cannot be angry, because it cost him nothing; and so you ought to tell him as well as you can in your present Condition, and let him know it is both for his and the Gentleman's Honour to make a Friend's Servant welcome.

A Master ought always to love his Groom, to put him into a handsome Livery, and to allow him a Silver-laced Hat. When you are in this Equipage, all the Honours he receives on the Road are owing to you alone: That he is not turned out of the Way by every Carrier, is caused by the Ci-vility he receives at second Hand from the Respect paid to your Livery.

You may now and then lend your Master's Pad to a Brother Servant, or your favourite Maid, for a short Jaunt, or hire him for a Day, because the Horse is spoiled for want of Exercise: And if your Master happens to want his Horse, or hath a Mind to see the Stable, curse that Rogue the Helper who is gone out with the Key.

When you want to spend an Hour or two with your Companions at the Ale-House, and that you stand in need of a reasonable Excuse for your Stay, go out of the Stable Door, or the back Way, with an old Bridle, Girth, or Stirrup Leather in your Pocket, and on your Return, come home by the Street Door with the same Bridle, Girth, or Stirrup Leather dangling in your Hand, as if you came from the Saddler's, where you were getting the same mended; (if you are not missed all is well), but, if you are met by your Master, you will have the Reputation of a careful Servant. This I have known practised with good Success.

CHAPTER VI

Directions to the House Steward, *and* Land Steward

Lord *Peterborough*'s Steward that pulled down his House, sold the Materials, and charged my Lord with Repairs. Take Money for Forbearance from Tenants. Renew Leases and get by them, and sell Woods. Lend my Lord his own Money. (*Gilblas*[12] said much of this, to whom I refer.)

CHAPTER VII

Directions to the Porter

If your Master be a Minister of State, let him be at Home to none but his Pimp, or Chief Flatterer, or one of his Pensionary Writers, or his hired Spy, and Informer, or his Printer in ordinary, or his City Sollicitor, or a Land-Jobber, or his Inventor of new Funds, or a Stock-Jobber.

CHAPTER VIII

Directions to the Chamber-Maid

The Nature of your Employment differs according to the Quality, the Pride, or the Wealth of the Lady you serve; and this Treatise is to be applied to all Sorts of Families; so, that I find myself under great Difficulty to adjust the Business for which you are hired. In a Family where there is a tolerable Estate, you differ from the House-Maid, and in that View I give my Directions. Your particular Province is your Lady's Chamber, where you make the Bed, and put Things in Order; and if you live in the Country, you take Care of Rooms where Ladies lie who come into the House, which brings in all the Vails that fall to your Share. Your usual Lover, as I take it, is the Coachman; but, if you are under Twenty, and tolerably handsome, perhaps a Footman may cast his Eyes on you.

Get your favourite Footman to help you in making your Lady's Bed; and, if you serve a young Couple, the Footman and you, as you are turning up the Bed-Cloaths, will make the prettiest Observations in the World; which, whispered about, will be very entertaining to the whole Family, and get among the Neighbourhood.

Do not carry down the necessary Vessels for the Fellows to see, but empty them out of the Window, for your Lady's Credit. It is highly improper for Men Servants to know that fine Ladies have Occasion for such Utensils; and do not scour the Chamber pot, because the Smell is wholesome.

If you happen to break any China with the Top of the Whisk on the Mantle-tree or the Cabinet, gather up the Fragments, put them together as well as you can, and place them behind the rest, so that when your Lady comes to discover them, you may safely say they were broke long ago, before you came to the Service. This will save your Lady many an Hour's Vexation.

It sometimes happens that a Looking-Glass is broken by the same Means, while you are looking another Way, as you sweep the Chamber, the long End of the Brush strikes against the Glass, and breaks it to Shivers. This is the extremest of all Misfortunes, and all Remedy desperate in Appearance, because it is impossible to be concealed. Such a fatal Accident once happened in a great Family where I had the Honour to be a

Footman; and I will relate the Particulars, to shew the Ingenuity of the poor Chamber-maid on so sudden and dreadful an Emergency, which perhaps may help to sharpen your Invention, if your evil Star should ever give you the like Occasion. The poor Girl had broken a large Japan Glass of great Value, with a Stroke of her Brush: She had not considered long, when by a prodigious Presence of Mind, she locked the Door, stole into the Yard, brought a Stone of three Pound Weight into the Chamber, laid it on the Hearth just under the Looking-Glass, then broke a Pane in the Sash Window that looked into the same Yard, so shut the Door, and went about her other Affairs. Two Hours after, the Lady goes into the Chamber, sees the Glass broken, the Stone lying under, and a whole Pane in the Window destroyed; from all which Circumstances, she concluded just as the Maid could have wished, that some idle Straggler in the Neighbourhood, or perhaps one of the Out-Servants, had through Malice, Accident, or Carelessness, flung in the Stone and done the Mischief. Thus far all Things went well, and the Girl concluded herself out of Danger: But, it was her ill Fortune, that a few Hours after in came the Parson of the Parish, and the Lady (naturally) told him the Accident, which you may believe had much discomposed her; but the Minister, who happened to understand Mathematicks, after examining the Situation of the Yard, the Window, and the Chimney, soon convinced the Lady, that the Stone could never reach the Looking-Glass without taking three Turns in its Flight from the Hand that threw it; and the Maid being proved to have swept the Room the same Morning, was strictly examined, but constantly denied that she was guilty upon her Salvation, offering to take her Oath upon the Bible, before his Reverence, that she was innocent as the Child unborn; yet the poor Wench was turned off, which I take to have been hard Treatment, considering her Ingenuity: However, this may be a Direction to you in the like Case, to contrive a Story that will better hang together. For Instance, you might say, that while you were at Work with the Mop, or Brush, a Flash of Lightning came suddenly in at the Window, which almost blinded you; that you immediately heard the ringing of broken Glass on the Hearth; that, as soon as you recovered your Eyes, you saw the Looking-Glass all broken to Pieces: Or, you may alledge, that observing the Glass a little covered with Dust, and going very gently to wipe it, you suppose the Moisture of the Air had dissolved the Glue or Cement, which made it fall to the Ground: Or, as soon as the Mischief is done, you may cut the Cords that fastened the Glass to the Wainscot, and so let it fall flat on the Ground; run out in a Fright, tell your Lady, curse the Upholster;

and declare how narrowly you escaped, that it did not fall upon your Head. I offer these Expedients, from a Desire I have to defend the Innocent; for Innocent you certainly must be, if you did not break the Glass on purpose, which I would by no Means excuse, except upon great Provocations.

Oil the Tongs, Poker, and Fire-shovel up to the Top, not only to keep them from rusting, but likewise to prevent meddling People from wasting your Master's Coals with stirring the Fire.

When you are in haste, sweep the Dust into a Corner of the Room, but leave your Brush upon it, that it may not be seen, for that would disgrace you.

Never wash your Hands, or put on a clean Apron, until you have made your Lady's Bed, for fear of rumpling your Apron, or fouling your Hands again.

When you bar the Window-shuts of your Lady's Bed-chamber at Nights, leave open the Sashes, to let in the fresh Air, and sweeten the Room against Morning.

In the Time when you leave the Windows open for Air, leave Books, or something else on the Window-seat, that they may get Air too.

When you sweep your Lady's Room, never stay to pick up foul Smocks, Handkerchiefs, Pinners, Pin-cushions, Teaspoons, Ribbons, Slippers, or whatever lieth in your Way; but sweep all into a Corner, and then you may take them up in a Lump, and save Time.

Making Beds in hot Weather is a very laborious Work, and you will be apt to sweat; therefore, when you find the Drops running down from your Forehead, wipe them off with a Corner of the Sheet, that they may not be seen on the Bed.

When your Lady sends you to wash a *China*-cup, and it happen to fall, bring it up, and swear you did but just touch it with your Hand, when it broke into *three Halves:* And here I must inform you, as well as your fellow Servants, that you ought never to be without an Excuse; it doth no Harm to your Master, and it lessens your Fault: As in this Instance; I do not commend you for breaking the Cup; it is certain you did not break it on purpose, and the Thing is possible, that it might break in your Hand.

You are sometimes desirous to see a Funeral, a Quarrel, a Man going to be hanged, a Wedding, a Bawd carted, or the like: As they pass by in the Street, you lift up the Sash suddenly; there by Misfortune it sticks: This was no Fault of yours; young Women are curious by Nature; you have no Remedy, but to cut the Cord; and lay the Fault upon the Carpenter, unless no Body saw you, and then you are as innocent as any Servant in the House.

Wear your Lady's Smock when she has thrown it off; it will do you Credit, save your own Linen, and be not a Pin the worse.

When you put a clean Pillow-case on your Lady's Pillow, be sure to fasten it well with three corking Pins, that it may not fall off in the Night.

When you spread Bread and Butter for Tea, be sure that all the Holes in the Loaf be left full of Butter, to keep the Bread moist against Dinner; and let the Mark of your Thumb be seen only upon one End of every Slice, to shew your Cleanliness.

When you are ordered to open or lock any Door, Trunk, or Cabinet, and miss the proper Key, or cannot distinguish it in the Bunch; try the first Key that you can thrust in, and turn it with all your Strength until you open the Lock, or break the Key; for your Lady will reckon you a Fool to come back and do nothing.

CHAPTER IX

Directions to the Waiting Maid

Two Accidents have happened to lessen the Comforts and Profits of your Employment; First, that execrable Custom got among Ladies, of trucking their old Cloaths for *China,* or turning them to cover easy Chairs, or making them into patch-work for Screens, Stools, Cushions, and the like. The Second is, the Invention of small Chests and Trunks, with Lock and Key, wherein they keep the Tea and Sugar, without which it is impossible for a Waiting-maid to live: For, by this means, you are forced to buy brown Sugar, and pour Water upon the Leaves, when they have lost all their Spirit and Taste: I cannot contrive any perfect Remedy against either of these two Evils. As to the former, I think there should be a general Confederacy of all the Servants in every Family, for the publick Good, to drive those *China* Hucksters from the Doors; and as to the latter, there is no other Method to relieve your selves, but by a false Key, which is a Point both difficult and dangerous to compass; but, as to the Circumstance of Honesty in procuring one, I am under no Doubt, when your Mistress gives you so just a Provocation, by refusing you an ancient and legal Perquisite. The Mistress of the Tea-shop may now and then give you half an Ounce, but that will be only a Drop in the Bucket: Therefore, I fear you must be forced, like the rest of your Sisters, to run in Trust, and pay for it out of your Wages, as far as they will go, which you can easily make up other ways, if your Lady be handsome, or her Daughters have good Fortunes.

If you are in a great Family, and my Lady's Woman, my Lord may probably like you, although you are not half so handsome as his own Lady. In this Case, take Care to get as much out of him as you can; and never allow him the smallest Liberty, not the squeezing of your Hand, unless he puts a Guinea into it; so, by degrees, make him pay accordingly for every new Attempt, doubling upon him in proportion to the Concessions you allow, and always struggling, and threatning to cry out, or tell your Lady, although you receive his Money: Five Guineas for handling your Breast is a cheap Pennyworth, although you seem to resist with all your Might; but never allow him the last Favour under a hundred Guineas, or a Settlement of twenty Pounds a Year for Life.

In such a Family, if you are handsome, you will have the Choice of three Lovers; the Chaplain, the Steward, and my Lord's Gentleman. I would first advise you to chuse the Steward; but, if you happen to be young with Child by my Lord, you must take up with the Chaplain. I like my Lord's Gentleman the least of the three; for he is usually vain and sawcy from the Time he throws off his Livery; and, if he misseth a Pair of Colours, or a Tide-waiter's Place, he hath no Remedy but the Highway.

I must caution you particularly against my Lord's eldest Son: If you are dextrous enough, it is odds that you may draw him in to marry you, and make you a Lady: If he be a common Rake, or a Fool, (and he must be one or the other) but, if the former, avoid him like *Satan,* for he stands in less Awe of a Mother, than my Lord doth of a Wife; and, after ten thousand Promises, you will get nothing from him, but a big Belly, or a Clap, and probably both together.

When your Lady is ill, and after a very bad Night, is getting a little Nap in the Morning, if a Footman comes with a Message to enquire how she doth, do not let the Compliment be lost, but shake her gently until she wakes; then deliver the Message, receive her Answer, and leave her to sleep.

If you are so happy as to wait on a young Lady with a great Fortune, you must be an ill Manager if you cannot get five or six hundred Pounds for disposing of her. Put her often in Mind, that she is rich enough to make any Man happy; that there is no real Happiness but in Love; that she hath

Liberty to chuse wherever she pleaseth, and not by the Direction of Parents, who never give Allowances for an innocent Passion; that there are a World of handsome, fine, sweet young Gentlemen in Town, who would be glad to die at her Feet; that the Conversation of two Lovers is a Heaven upon Earth; that Love like Death equals all Conditions; that if she should cast her Eyes upon a young Fellow below her in Birth and Estate, his marrying her, would make him a Gentleman; that you saw Yesterday on the *Mall,* the prettiest Ensign; and, that if you had forty thousand Pounds it should be at his Service. Take care that every Body should know what Lady you live with; how great a Favourite you are; and, that she always takes your Advice. Go often to St. *James's* Park, the fine Fellows will soon discover you, and contrive to slip a Letter into your Sleeve or your Bosom: Pull it out in a Fury, and throw it on the Ground, unless you find at least two Guineas along with it; but in that Case, seem not to find it, and to think he was only playing the Wag with you: When you come home, drop the Letter carelessly in your Lady's Chamber; she finds it, is angry; protest you knew nothing of it, only you remember, that a Gentleman in the Park struggled to kiss you, and you believe it was he that put the Letter in your Sleeve or Pettycoat; and, indeed, he was as pretty a Man as ever she saw: That she may burn the Letter if she pleaseth. If your Lady be wise, she will burn some other Paper before you, and read the Letter when you are gone down. You must follow this Practice as often as you safely can; but, let him who pays you best with every Letter, be the handsomest Man. If a Footman presumes to bring a Letter to the House, to be delivered to you, for your Lady, although it come from your best Customer, throw it at his Head; call him impudent Rogue and Villain, and shut the Door in his Face; run up to your Lady, and as a Proof of your Fidelity, tell her what you have done.

I could enlarge very much upon this Subject, but I trust to your own Discretion.

If you serve a Lady who is a little disposed to Gallantries, you will find it a Point of great Prudence how to manage: Three Things are necessary. First, how to please your Lady; Secondly, how to prevent Suspicion in the Husband, or among the Family; and lastly, but principally, how to make it most for your own Advantage. To give you full Directions in this important Affair, would require a large Volume. All Assignations at home are dangerous, both to your Lady and your self; and therefore contrive as much as possible, to have them in a third Place; especially if your Lady, as it is a hundred odds, entertains more Lovers than one, each of whom is often more jealous than a thousand Husbands; and, very unlucky Rencounters may often happen under the best Management. I need not warn you to employ your good Offices chiefly in favour of those, whom you find most liberal; yet, if your Lady should happen to cast an Eye upon a handsome Footman, you should be generous enough to bear with her Humour, which is no Singularity, but a very natural Appetite: It is still the safest of all home Intrigues, and was formerly the least suspected, until of late Years it hath grown more common. The great danger is, lest this Kind of Gentry, dealing too often in bad Ware, may happen not to be sound; and then, your Lady and you are in a very bad Way, although not altogether desperate.

But, to say the Truth, I confess it is a great Presumption in me, to offer you any Instructions in the Conduct of your Lady's Amours, wherein your whole Sisterhood is already so expert, and deeply learned; although it be much more difficult to compass, than that Assistance which my Brother Footmen give their Masters, on the like Occasion; and therefore, I leave this Affair to be treated by some abler Pen.

When you lock up a Silk Mantua, or laced Head in a Trunk or Chest, leave a Piece out, that when you open the Trunk again, you may know where to find it.

CHAPTER X

Directions to the House-Maid

If your Master and Lady go into the Country for a Week or more, never wash the Bed-chamber or Dining-room, until just the Hour before you expect them to return: Thus, the Rooms will be perfectly clean to receive them, and you will not be at the Trouble to wash them so soon again.

I am very much offended with those Ladies, who are so proud and lazy, that they will not be at the Pains of stepping into the Garden to pluck a Rose, but keep an odious Implement sometimes in the Bed-chamber itself, or at least in a dark Closet adjoining, which they make Use of to ease their worst Necessities; and, you are the usual Carriers away of the Pan, which maketh not only the Chamber, but even their Cloaths offensive, to all who come near. Now, to cure them of this odious Practice, let me advise you, on whom this Office lies, to convey away this Utensil, that you will do it openly, down the great Stairs, and in the Presence of the Footmen; and, if any Body knocks, to open the Street-door, while you have the Vessel filled in your Hands: This, if any Thing can, will make your Lady take the Pains of evacuating her Person in the proper Place, rather than expose her Filthiness to all the Men Servants in the House.

Leave a Pail of dirty Water with the Mop in it, a Coal-box, a Bottle, a Broom, a Chamber-pot, and such other unsightly Things, either in a blind Entry, or upon the darkest Part of the Back-stairs, that they may not be seen; and, if People break their Shins by trampling on them, it is their own Fault.

Never empty the Chamber-pots until they are quite full: If that happens in the Night, empty them into the Street; if, in the Morning, into the Garden; for it would be an endless Work to go a dozen Times from the Garret and upper Rooms, down to the Back-sides; but, never wash them in any other Liquor except their own: What cleanly Girl would be dabbling in other Folks Urine? And besides, the Smell of Stale, as I observed before, is admirable against the Vapours; which, a hundred to one, may be your Lady's Case.

Brush down the Cobwebs with a Broom that is wet and dirty, which will make them stick the faster to it, and bring them down more effectually.

When you rid up the Parlour Hearth in a Morning, throw the last Night's Ashes into a Sieve; and what falls through, as you carry it down, will serve instead of Sand for the Room and the Stairs.

When you have scoured the Brasses and Irons in the Parlour Chimney, lay the foul wet Clout upon the next Chair, that your Lady may see you have not neglected your Work: Observe the same Rule, when you clean the Brass Locks, only with this addition, to leave the Marks of your Fingers on the Doors, to shew you have not forgot.

Leave your Lady's Chamber-pot in the Bed-chamber Window, all Day to air.

Bring up none but large Coals to the Dining-room and your Lady's Chamber; they make the best Fires, and, if you find them too big, it is easy to break them on the Marble Hearth.

When you go to Bed, be sure take care of Fire; and therefore blow the Candle out with your Breath, and then thrust it under your Bed. *Note.* The Smell of the Snuff is very good against Vapours.

Persuade the Footman who got you with Child, to marry you before you are six Months gone; and, if your Lady asks you, why you would take a Fellow who was not worth a Groat? Let your Answer be, That Service is no Inheritance.

When your Lady's Bed is made, put the Chamber-pot under it, but in such a manner, as to thrust the Valance along with it, that it may be full in Sight, and ready for your lady when she hath Occasion to use it.

Lock up a Cat or a Dog in some Room or Closet, so as to make such a Noise all over the House, as may frighten away the Thieves, if any should attempt to break or steal in.

When you wash any of the Rooms towards the Street, over Night, throw the foul Water out of the Street Door; but, be sure not to look before you, for fear those on whom the Water lights, might think you uncivil, and that you did it on purpose. If he who suffers, breaks the Windows in revenge, and your Lady chides you, and gives positive Orders that you should carry the Payl down, and empty it in the Sink, you have an easy Remedy. When you wash an upper Room, carry down the Payl so as to let the Water dribble on the Stairs all the way down to the Kitchen; by which, not only your Load will be lighter, but you will convince your Lady, that it is better to throw the Water out of the Windows, or down the Street-Door Steps: Besides, this latter Practice will be very diverting to you and the Family in a frosty Night, to see a hundred People falling on their Noses or Back-sides before your Door, when the Water is frozen.

Polish and brighten the Marble Hearths and Chimney-pieces with a Clout dipt in Grease; nothing makes them shine so well; and, it is the Business of the Ladies to take Care of their Pettycoats.

If your Lady be so nice that she will have the Room scoured with Free-stone, be sure to leave the Marks of the Freestone six Inches deep round the Bottom of the Wainscot, that your Lady may see your Obedience to her Orders.

CHAPTER XI

Directions to the Dairy-Maid

Fatigue of making Butter; Put scalding Water in your Churn, although in Summer, and churn close to the Kitchen Fire, and with Cream of a Week old. Keep Cream for your Sweet-heart.

CHAPTER XII

Directions to the Childrens-Maid

If a Child be sick, give it whatever it wants to eat or drink, although particularly forbid by the Doctor: For what we long for in Sickness, will do us good; and throw the Physick out of the Window; the Child will love you the better; but bid it not tell. Do the same to your Lady when she longs for any thing in Sickness, and engage it will do her good.

If your Mistress comes to the Nursery, and offers to whip a Child, snatch it out of her Hands in a Rage, and tell her she is the cruellest Mother you ever saw: She will chide, but love you the better. Tell the Children Stories of Spirits, when they offer to cry, &c.

Be sure to wean the Children, &c.

CHAPTER XIII

Directions to the Nurse

If you happen to let the Child fall, and lame it, be sure never confess it; and, if it dies, all is safe.

Contrive to be with Child, as soon as you can, while you are giving Suck, that you may be ready for another Service, when the Child you nurse dies, or is weaned.

CHAPTER XIV

Directions to the Laundress

If you singe the Linnen with the Iron, rub the Place with Flour, Chalk, or white Powder; and if nothing will do, wash it so long, till it be either not to be seen, or torn to Rags. Always wash your own Linnen first.

About tearing Linnen in washing.

When your Linnen is pinned on the Line, or on a Hedge, and it rains, whip it off, although you tear it, &c. But the Place for hanging them, is on young Fruit Trees, especially in Blossom; the Linnen cannot be torn, and the Trees give them a fine Smell.

CHAPTER XV

Directions to the House-Keeper

You must always have a favourite Footman whom you can depend upon; and order him to be very watchful when the Second Course is taken off, that it be brought safely to your Office, that you and the Steward may have a Tit-bit together.

CHAPTER XVI

Directions to the Tutoress, *or* Governess

Say the Children have sore Eyes; Miss *Betty* won't take to her Book, &c.

Make the Misses read *French* and *English* Novels, and *French* Romances, and all the Comedies writ in King *Charles* II. and King *William*'s Reigns, to soften their Nature, and make them tender-hearted, &c.

IX

POEMS

VERSES WROTE IN
A LADY'S IVORY TABLE-BOOK
(1698, 1711)

Peruse my Leaves thro' ev'ry Part,
And think thou seest my owners Heart,
Scrawl'd o'er with Trifles thus, and quite
As hard, as sensless, and as light:
Expos'd to every Coxcomb's Eyes,
But hid with Caution from the Wise.
Here you may read (*Dear Charming Saint*)
Beneath (*A new Receit for Paint*[1])
Here in Beau-spelling (*tru tel deth*)
There in her own (*far an el breth*[2])   10
Here (*lovely Nymph pronounce my doom*)
There (*A safe way to use Perfume*)
Here, a Page fill'd with Billet Doux;[3]
On t'other side (*laid out for Shoes*)
(*Madam, I dye without your Grace*)
(Item, *for half a Yard of Lace*.)
Who that had Wit would place it here,
For every peeping Fop to Jear.
To think that your Brains Issue is
Expos'd to th' Excrement of his,   20
In power of Spittle and a Clout
When e're he please to blot it out;
And then to heighten the Disgrace
Clap his own Nonsense in the place.
Whoe're expects to hold his part
In such a Book and such a Heart,
If he be Wealthy and a Fool
Is in all Points the fittest Tool,
Of whom it may be justly said,
He's a Gold Pencil tipt with Lead.   30

To Their Excellencies
the Lords Justices of Ireland.
The Humble Petition of Frances Harris,
Who must Starve,
and Die a Maid if it miscarries.
(1701, 1711)

Humbly Sheweth.

That I went to warm my self in Lady *Betty*'s[1] Chamber, because I was cold,
And I had in a Purse, seven Pound, four Shillings and six Pence, besides
   Farthings, in Money, and Gold;
So because I had been buying things for my *Lady* last Night,
I was resolved to tell[2] my Money, to see if it was right:
Now you must know, because my Trunk has a very bad Lock,
Therefore all the Money, I have, which, *God* knows, is a very small Stock,
I keep in a Pocket ty'd about my Middle, next my Smock.
So when I went to put up my Purse, as *God* would have it, my Smock was
   unript,
And, instead of putting it into my Pocket, down it slipt:
Then the Bell rung, and I went down to put my *Lady* to Bed,   10
And, *God* knows, I thought my Money was as safe as my Maidenhead.
So when I came up again, I found my Pocket feel very light,
But when I search'd, and miss'd my Purse, *Lord!* I thought I should have
   sunk outright:
Lord! Madam, says *Mary,* how d'ye do? Indeed, says I, never worse;
But pray, *Mary,* can you tell what I have done with my Purse!
Lord help me, said *Mary,* I never stirr'd out of this Place!
Nay, said I, I had it in Lady *Betty*'s Chamber, that's a plain Case.
So *Mary* got me to Bed, and cover'd me up warm,
However, she stole away my Garters, that I might do my self no Harm:
So I tumbl'd and toss'd all Night, as you may very well think,   20
But hardly ever set my Eyes together, or slept a Wink.
So I was a-dream'd, methought, that we went and search'd the Folks
   round,

And in a Corner of Mrs. *Dukes*'s Box, ty'd in a Rag, the Money was found.
So next Morning we told *Whittle,* and he fell a Swearing;
Then my Dame *Wadgar* came, and she, you know, is thick of Hearing;
Dame, said I, as loud as I could bawl, do you know what a Loss I have
　　　had?
Nay, said she, my Lord *Collway*'s Folks are all very sad,
For my Lord *Dromedary*[3] comes a *Tuesday* without fail;
Pugh! said I, but that's not the Business that I ail.
Says *Cary,* says he, I have been a Servant this Five and Twenty Years,
　　　come Spring,　　　　　　　　　　　　　　　　　　　　　　30
And in all the Places I liv'd, I never heard of such a Thing.
Yes, says the *Steward,* I remember when I was at my Lady *Shrewsbury*'s,
Such a thing as this happen'd, just about the time of *Goosberries.*
So I went to the Party suspected, and I found her full of Grief;
(Now you must know, of all Things in the World, I hate a Thief.)
However, I was resolv'd to bring the Discourse slily about,
Mrs. *Dukes,* said I, here's an ugly Accident has happen'd out;
'Tis not that I value the Money three Skips of a Louse;
But the Thing I stand upon, is the Credit of the House;
'Tis true, seven Pound, four Shillings, and six Pence, makes a great Hole
　　　in my Wages,　　　　　　　　　　　　　　　　　　　　　40
Besides, as they say, Service is no Inheritance in these Ages.
Now, Mrs. *Dukes,* you know, and every Body understands,
That tho' 'tis hard to judge, yet Money can't go without Hands.
The *Devil* take me, said she, (blessing her self,) if I ever saw't!
So she roar'd like a *Bedlam,*[4] as tho' I had call'd her all to naught;
So you know, what could I say to her any more,
I e'en left her, and came away as wise as I was before.
Well: But then they would have had me gone to the Cunning Man;[5]
No, said I, 'tis the same Thing, the *Chaplain*[6] will be here anon.
So the *Chaplain* came in; now the Servants say, he is my Sweet-heart,　50
Because he's always in my Chamber, and I always take his Part;
So, as the *Devil* would have it, before I was aware, out I blunder'd,
Parson, said I, can you cast a *Nativity,*[7] when a Body's plunder'd?
(Now you must know, he hates to be call'd *Parson,* like the *Devil.*)
Truly, says he, Mrs. *Nab,* it might become you to be more civil:
If your Money be gone, as a Learned *Divine* says, d'ye see,
You are no *Text* for my Handling, so take that from me:
I was never taken for a *Conjurer* before, I'd have you to know.

Lord, said I, don't be angry, I'm sure I never thought you so;
You know, I honour the Cloth, I design to be a *Parson*'s Wife,   60
I never took one in *Your Coat* for a *Conjurer* in all my Life.
With that, he twisted his Girdle at me like a Rope, as who should say,
Now you may go hang your self for me, and so went away.
Well; I thought I should have swoon'd; *Lord*, said I, what shall I do?
I have lost my *Money*, and shall lose my *True-Love* too.
Then my *Lord* call'd me; *Harry*, said my *Lord*, don't cry,
I'll give something towards thy Loss; and says my *Lady*, so will I.
Oh but, said I, what if after all my Chaplain won't *come to?*
For that, he said, (an't please your *Excellencies*) I must Petition You.

The Premises tenderly consider'd, I desire your *Excellencies*
      Protection,   70
And that I may have a Share in next *Sunday*'s Collection:
And over and above, that I may have your *Excellencies* Letter,
With an Order for the *Chaplain* aforesaid; or instead of Him, a Better:
And then your poor *Petitioner*, both Night and Day,
Or the *Chaplain*, (for 'tis his *Trade*) as in Duty bound, shall ever *Pray*.

BAUCIS AND PHILEMON. IMITATED, FROM THE EIGHTH BOOK OF OVID

(1706, 1709)

In antient Times, as Story tells,
The Saints would often leave their Cells.
And strole about, but hide their Quality,
To try good People's Hospitality.

    IT happen'd on a Winter Night,
As Authors of the Legend write;
Two Brother Hermits, Saints by Trade,
Taking their *Tour* in Masquerade;
Disguis'd in tatter'd Habits, went
To a small Village down in *Kent*;   10
Where, in the Strolers Canting Strain,
They beg'd from Door to Door in vain;

Try'd ev'ry Tone might Pity win,
But not a Soul would let them in.

   OUR wand'ring Saints in woful State,
Treated at this ungodly Rate,
Having thro' all the Village pass'd,
To a small Cottage came at last;
Where dwelt a good old honest Yeoman,
Call'd, in the Neighborhood, *Philemon.*   20
Who kindly did the Saints invite
In his Poor Hut to pass the Night;
And then the Hospitable Sire
Bid *Goody*[1] *Baucis* mend the Fire;
While He from out of Chimney took
A Flitch of Bacon off the Hook;
And freely from the fattest Side
Cut out large Slices to be fry'd:
Then stept aside to fetch 'em Drink,
Fill'd a large Jug up to the Brink;   30
And saw it fairly twice go round;
Yet (what is wonderful) they found,
'Twas still replenished to the Top,
As if they ne'er had toucht a Drop.
The good old Couple was amaz'd,
And often on each other gaz'd;
For both were frighted to the Heart,
And just began to cry;—What ar't!
Then softly turn'd aside to view,
Whether the Lights were burning blue.[2]   40
The gentle *Pilgrims* soon aware on't,
Told 'em their Calling, and their Errant:
Good Folks, you need not be afraid,
We are but *Saints,* the Hermits said;
No Hurt shall come to You, or Yours;
But, for that Pack of churlish Boors,
Not fit to live on Christian Ground,
They and their Houses shall be drown'd:[3]
Whilst you shall see your Cottage rise,
And grow a Church before your Eyes.   50

THEY scarce had Spoke; when, fair and soft,
The Roof began to mount aloft;
Aloft rose ev'ry Beam and Rafter,
The heavy Wall climb'd slowly after.

THE Chimney widen'd, and grew higher,
Became a Steeple with a Spire.

THE Kettle to the Top was hoist,
And there stood fast'ned to a Joist:
But with the Upside down, to shew
Its Inclinations for below;   60
In vain; for a Superior Force
Apply'd at Bottom, stops its Course,
Doom'd ever in Suspence to dwell,
'Tis now no Kettle, but a Bell.

A wooden Jack,[4] which had almost
Lost, by Disuse, the Art to Roast,
A sudden Alteration feels,
Increas'd by new Intestine Wheels:
And, what exalts the Wonder more,
The Number made the Motion slow'r: 70
The Flyer, tho't had Leaden Feet,
Turn'd round so quick, you scarce cou'd see't;
But slacken'd by some secret Power,
Now hardly moves an Inch an Hour.
The Jack and Chimney near ally'd,
Had never left each other's Side;
The Chimney to a Steeple grown,
The Jack wou'd not be left alone,
But up against the Steeple rear'd,
Became a Clock, and still adher'd: 80
And still its Love to Houshold Cares
By a shrill Voice at Noon declares,
Warning the Cook-maid, not to burn
That Roast-meat which it cannot turn.

THE Groaning Chair began to crawl
Like an huge Snail along the Wall;
There stuck aloft, in Publick View,
And with small Change, a Pulpit grew.

THE Porringers,[5] that in a Row
Hung high, and made a glitt'ring Show,   90
To a less Noble Substance chang'd,
Were now but Leathern Buckets rang'd.

THE Ballads pasted on the Wall,
Of *Joan* of *France,* and *English Moll,*
Fair *Rosamond,* and *Robin Hood,*
The *Little Children in the Wood:*[6]
Now seem'd to look abundance better,
Improv'd in Picture, Size, and Letter;
And high in Order plac'd, describe
The Heraldry of ev'ry Tribe.   100

A Bedstead of the Antique Mode,
Compact of Timber many a Load,
Such as our Ancestors did use,
Was Metamorphos'd into Pews;
Which still their antient Nature keep;
By lodging Folks dispos'd to Sleep.

THE Cottage by such Feats as these,
Grown to a Church by just Degrees,
The Hermits then desir'd their Host
To ask for what he fancy'd most: 110
Philemon, having paus'd a while,
Return'd 'em Thanks in homely Stile;
Then said; my House is grown so Fine,
Methinks, I still wou'd call it mine:
I'm Old, and fain wou'd live at Ease,
Make me the *Parson,* if you please.

HE spoke, and presently he feels,
His Grazier's Coat fall down his Heels;

He sees, yet hardly can believe,
About each Arm a Pudding-sleeve;   120
His Wastcoat to a Cassock grew,
And both assum'd a Sable Hue;
But being Old, continu'd just
As Thread-bare, and as full of Dust.
His Talk was now of *Tythes* and *Dues,*
Cou'd smoak his Pipe, and read the News;
Knew how to preach old Sermons next,
Vampt[7] in the Preface and the Text;
At Christnings well could act his Part,
And had the Service all by Heart;   130
Wish'd Women might have Children fast,
And thought whose *Sow* had *farrow'd* last:
Against *Dissenters* wou'd repine,
And stood up firm for *Right Divine:*[8]
Found his Head fill'd with many a System,
But Classick Authors—he ne'er miss'd 'em.

THUS having furbish'd up a Parson,
Dame *Baucis* next, they play'd their Farce on:
Instead of Home-spun Coifs[9] were seen,
Good Pinners[10] edg'd with Colberteen:[11]   140
Her Petticoat transform'd apace,
Became Black Sattin, Flounc'd with Lace.
Plain *Goody* would no longer down,
'Twas *Madam,* in her Grogram[12] Gown.
Philemon was in great Surprize,
And hardly could believe his Eyes,
Amaz'd to see Her look so Prim,
And she admir'd as much at Him.

THUS, happy in their Change of Life,
Were several Years this Man and Wife,   150
When on a Day, which prov'd their last,
Discoursing on old Stories past,
They went by chance, amidst their Talk,
To the Church-yard, to take a walk;
When *Baucis* hastily cry'd out;

My Dear, I see your Forehead sprout:
Sprout, quoth the Man, What's this you tell us?
I hope you don't believe me Jealous:
But yet, methinks, I feel it true;
And re'ly, Yours is budding too—   160
Nay,—now I cannot stir my Foot:
It feels as if 'twere taking Root.

   DESCRIPTION would but tire my Muse:
In short, they both were turn'd to *Yews.*
Old Good-man *Dobson* of the Green
Remembers he the Trees has seen;
He'll talk of them from Noon till Night,
And goes with Folks to shew the Sight:
On *Sundays,* after Ev'ning Prayer,
He gathers all the Parish there;   170
Points out the Place of either *Yew;*
Here *Baucis,* there *Philemon* grew.
Till once, a Parson of our Town,
To mend his Barn, cut *Baucis* down;
At which, 'tis hard to be believ'd,
How much the other Tree was griev'd,
Grew Scrubby, dy'd a-top, was stunted:
So, the next Parson stub'd and burnt it.

A Description of the Morning

April, 1709

Now hardly here and there an Hackney-Coach[1]
Appearing, show'd the Ruddy Morns Approach.
Now *Betty*[2] from her Masters Bed had flown,
And softly stole to discompose her own.
The Slipshod Prentice from his Masters Door,
Had par'd[3] the Dirt, and Sprinkled[4] around the Floor.
Now *Moll* had whirl'd her Mop with dext'rous Airs,
Prepar'd to Scrub the Entry and the Stairs.
The Youth with Broomy Stumps began to trace
The Kennel-Edge,[5] where Wheels had worn the Place.   10

The Smallcoal-Man[6] was heard with Cadence deep,
'Till drown'd in Shriller Notes of Chimney-Sweep,
Duns[7] at his Lordships Gate began to meet,
And Brickdust[8] *Moll* had Scream'd through half the Street.
The Turnkey now his Flock returning sees,
Duly let out a Nights to Steal for Fees.[9]
The watchful Bailiffs take their silent Stands,
And School-Boys lag with Satchels in their Hands.[10]

A DESCRIPTION OF A CITY SHOWER

October, 1710

Careful Observers may fortel the Hour
(By sure Prognosticks) when to dread a Show'r:
While Rain depends,[1] the pensive Cat gives o'er
Her Frolicks, and pursues her Tail no more.
Returning Home at Night, you'll find the Sink[2]
Strike your offended Sense with double Stink.
If you be wise, then go not far to Dine,
You'll spend in Coach-hire more than save in Wine.
A coming Show'r your shooting Corns presage,
Old Aches throb, your hollow Tooth will rage.   10
Sauntring in Coffee-house is *Dulman* seen;
He damns the Climate, and complains of Spleen.[3]

  MEAN while the South rising with dabbled[4] Wings,
A Sable Cloud a-thwart the Welkin[5] flings,
That swill'd more Liquor than it could contain,
And like a Drunkard gives it up again.
Brisk *Susan*[6] whips her Linen from the Rope,
While the first drizzling Show'r is born aslope,[7]
Such is that Sprinkling which some careless Quean[8]
Flirts[9] on you from her Mop, but not so clean.   20
You fly, invoke the Gods; then turning, stop
To rail; she singing, still whirls on her Mop.
Not yet, the Dust had shun'd th' unequal Strife,
But aided by the Wind, fought still for Life;
And wafted with its Foe by violent Gust,
'Twas doubtful which was Rain, and which was Dust.

Ah! where must needy Poet seek for Aid,
When Dust and Rain at once his Coat invade;
His only Coat, where Dust confus'd with Rain,
Roughen the Nap, and leave a mingled Stain.   30

    NOW in contiguous Drops the Flood comes down,
Threat'ning with Deluge this *Devoted*[10] Town.
To Shops in Crouds the dagged[11] Females fly,
Pretend to cheapen Goods, but nothing buy.
The Templer[12] spruce, while ev'ry Spout's a-broach,[13]
Stays till 'tis fair, yet seems to call a Coach.
The tuck'd-up Sempstress walks with hasty Strides,
While Streams run down her oil'd Umbrella's Sides.
Here various Kinds by various Fortunes led,
Commence Acquaintance underneath a Shed.   40
Triumphant Tories,[14] and desponding Whigs,
Forget their Fewds, and join to save their Wigs.
Box'd in a Chair[15] the Beau impatient sits,
While Spouts run clatt'ring o'er the Roof by Fits;
And ever and anon with frightful Din
The Leather sounds, he trembles from within.
So when *Troy* Chair-men bore the Wooden Steed,
Pregnant with *Greeks,* impatient to be freed,
(Those Bully *Greeks,* who, as the Moderns do,
Instead of paying Chair-men, run them thro'.)   50
Laoco'n struck the Outside with his Spear,
And each imprison'd Hero quak'd for Fear.[16]

    NOW from all Parts the swelling Kennels flow,
And bear their Trophies with them as they go:
Filth of all Hues and Odours seem to tell
What Street they sail'd from, by their Sight and Smell.
They, as each Torrent drives, with rapid Force
From *Smithfield,*[17] or St. *Pulchre's*[18] shape their Course,
And in huge Confluent join at *Snow-Hill* Ridge,
Fall from the *Conduit* prone to *Holborn-Bridge.*   60
Sweepings from Butchers Stalls, Dung, Guts, and Blood,
Drown'd Puppies, stinking Sprats,[19] all drench'd in Mud,
Dead Cats and Turnip-Tops come tumbling down the
    Flood.[20]

CADENUS AND VANESSA

(1713?, 1726)

The *Shepherds* and the *Nymphs* were seen
Pleading before the *Cyprian* Queen.[1]
The Council for the Fair began,
Accusing that false Creature, *Man.*

   The Brief with weighty Crimes was charg'd,
On which the Pleader much enlarg'd;
That *Cupid* now has lost his Art,
Or blunts the Point of ev'ry Dart;
His Altar now no longer smokes,
His Mother's Aid no Youth invokes: 10
This tempts Free-thinkers[2] to refine,
And bring in doubt their Pow'r divine;
Now Love is dwindled to Intrigue,
And Marriage grown a Money-League.
Which Crimes aforesaid (with her Leave)
Were (as he humbly did conceive)
Against our Sov'reign Lady's Peace,
Against the Statutes in that Case,
Against her Dignity and Crown:
Then pray'd an Answer, and sat down.   20

   The *Nymphs* with Scorn beheld their Foes:
When the Defendant's Council rose,
And, what no Lawyer ever lack'd,
With Impudence own'd all the Fact.
But, what the gentlest Heart would vex,
Laid all the Fault on t'other Sex.
That modern Love is no such Thing
As what those antient Poets sing;
A Fire celestial, chaste, refin'd,
Conceiv'd and kindled in the Mind,   30
Which having found an equal Flame,
Unites, and both become the same,

In different Breasts together burn,
Together both to Ashes turn.
But Women now feel no such Fire,
And only know the gross Desire;
Their Passions move in lower Spheres,
Where-e'er Caprice or Folly steers.
A Dog, a Parrot, or an Ape,
Or some worse Brute in human Shape,   40
Engross the Fancies of the Fair,
The few soft Moments they can spare,
From Visits to receive and pay,
From Scandal, Politicks, and Play,
From Fans, and Flounces, and Brocades,
From Equipage and Park-Parades,
From all the thousand Female Toys,[3]
From every Trifle that employs
The out or inside of their Heads,
Between their Toylets[4] and their Beds.   50

   In a dull Stream, which moving slow
You hardly see the Current flow,
If a small Breeze obstructs the Course,
It whirls about for Want of Force,
And in its narrow Circle gathers
Nothing but Chaff, and Straws, and Feathers:
The Current of a Female Mind
Stops thus, and turns with ev'ry Wind;
Thus whirling round, together draws
Fools, Fops, and Rakes, for Chaff and Straws.   60
Hence we conclude, no Women's Hearts
Are won by Virtue, Wit, and Parts;
Nor are the Men of Sense to blame,
For breasts incapable of Flame;
The Fault must on the *Nymphs* be plac'd,
Grown so corrupted in their Taste.

   The Pleader having spoke his best,
Had Witness ready to attest,
Who fairly could on Oath depose,

When Questions on the Fact arose,   70
That ev'ry Article was true;
Nor further those Deponents knew:
Therefore he humbly would insist,
The Bill might be with Costs dismist.

    The Cause appear'd of so much Weight,
That *Venus,* from the Judgment-Seat,
Desir'd them not to talk so loud,
Else she must interpose a Cloud:
For if the Heav'nly Folk should know
These Pleadings in the Courts below,   80
That Mortals here disdain to love;
She ne'er could shew her Face above.
For Gods, their Betters, are too wise
To value that which Men despise.
And then, said she, my Son and I
Must strole in Air 'twixt Earth and Sky;
Or else, shut out from Heaven and Earth,
Fly to the Sea,⁵ my Place of Birth;
There live with daggl'd *Mermaids* pent,
And keep on Fish perpetual *Lent.*   90

    But since the Case appear'd so nice,
She thought it best to take Advice.
The *Muses,* by their King's Permission,
Tho' Foes to Love, attend the Session,
And on the Right Hand took their Places
In Order; on the Left, the *Graces:*
To whom she might her Doubts propose
On all Emergencies that rose.
The *Muses* oft were seen to frown;
The *Graces* half asham'd look'd down;   100
And 'twas observ'd, there were but few⎫
Of either Sex, among the Crew,   ⎬
Whom she or her Assessors knew.   ⎭
The Goddess soon began to see
Things were not ripe for a Decree,
And said she must consult her Books,

The *Lovers Fleta's, Bractons, Cokes.*[6]
First to a dapper Clerk she beckon'd,
To turn to *Ovid,*[7] Book the Second;
She then referr'd them to a Place   110
In *Virgil* (*vide Dido's*[8] Case:)
As for *Tibullus's*[9] Reports,
They never pass'd for Law in Courts;
For *Cowley's* Briefs, and Pleas of *Waller,*[10]
Still their Authority was smaller.

There was on both Sides much to say:
She'd hear the Cause another Day,
And so she did, and then a Third,
She heard it—there she kept her Word;
But with Rejoinders and Replies,   120
Long Bills, and Answers, stuff'd with Lies,
Demur, Imparlance, and Essoign,
The Parties ne'er could Issue join:
For Sixteen Years the Cause was spun,
And then stood where it first begun.

Now, gentle *Clio,*[11] sing or say,
What *Venus* meant by this Delay.
The Goddess much perplex'd in Mind,
To see her Empire thus declin'd,
When first this grand Debate arose   130
Above her Wisdom to compose,
Conceiv'd a Project in her Head,
To work her Ends; which if it sped,
Wou'd shew the Merits of the Cause,
Far better than consulting Laws.

In a glad Hour *Lucina's*[12] Aid
Produc'd on Earth a wond'rous Maid,
On whom the Queen of Love was bent
To try a new Experiment:
She threw her Law-books on the Shelf,   140
And thus debated with herself.

———

Since Men alledge they ne'er can find
Those Beauties in a Female Mind,
Which raise a Flame that will endure
For ever, uncorrupt and pure;
If 'tis with Reason they complain,
This Infant shall restore my Reign.
I'll search where ev'ry Virtue dwells,
From Courts inclusive, down to Cells,
What Preachers talk, or Sages write,   150
These I will gather and unite,
And represent them to Mankind
Collected in that Infant's Mind.

This said, she plucks in Heav'ns high Bow'rs
A Sprig of *Amaranthine* Flow'rs,
In Nectar thrice infuses Bays,
Three times refin'd in *Titan*'s Rays:
Then calls the *Graces* to her Aid,
And sprinkles thrice the new-born Maid.
From whence the tender Skin assumes   160
A Sweetness above all Perfumes;
From whence a Cleanliness remains,
Incapable of outward Stains;
From whence that Decency of Mind,
So lovely in the Female Kind,
Where not one careless Thought intrudes,
Less modest than the Speech of Prudes;
Where never Blush was call'd in Aid,
That spurious Virtue in a Maid,
A Virtue but at second-hand;   170
They blush because they understand.

The *Graces* next wou'd act their Part,
And shew'd but little of their Art;
Their Work was half already done,
The Child with native Beauty shone,
The outward Form no Help requir'd:
Each breathing on her thrice, inspir'd
That gentle, soft, engaging Air,

Which in old Times adorn'd the Fair;
And said, "*Vanessa* be the Name,   180
"By which thou shalt be known to Fame:
"*Vanessa,* by the Gods enroll'd:
"Her Name on Earth—shall not be told.

    But still the Work was not compleat,
When *Venus* thought on a Deceit:
Drawn by her Doves, away she flies,
And finds out *Pallas*[13] in the Skies:
Dear *Pallas,* I have been this Morn
To see a lovely Infant born:
A Boy in yonder Isle below,   190
So like my own, without his Bow,
By Beauty cou'd your Heart be won,
You'd swear it is *Apollo*'s Son;
But it shall ne'er be said, a Child
So hopeful, has by me been spoil'd;
I have enough besides to spare,
And give him wholly to your Care.

    Wisdom's above suspecting Wiles:
The Queen of Learning gravely smiles,
Down from *Olympus* comes with Joy,   200
Mistakes *Vanessa* for a Boy;
Then sows within her tender Mind
Seeds long unknown to Womankind,
For manly Bosoms chiefly fit,
The Seeds of Knowledge, Judgment, Wit.
Her Soul was suddenly endu'd
With Justice, Truth and Fortitude;
With Honour, which no Breath can Stain,
Which Malice must attack in vain;
With open Heart and bounteous Hand: 210
But *Pallas* here was at a Stand;
She knew in our degen'rate Days
Bare Virtue could not live on Praise,
That Meat must be with Money bought;
She therefore, upon second Thought,

Infus'd, yet as it were by Stealth,
Some small Regard for State and Wealth:
Of which, as she grew up, there stay'd
A Tincture in the prudent Maid:
She manag'd her Estate with Care,   220
Yet like'd three Footmen to her Chair.
But lest he shou'd neglect his Studies
Like a young Heir, the thrifty Goddess
(For fear young Master shou'd be spoil'd,)
Wou'd use him like a younger Child;
And, after long computing, found
'Twou'd come to just Five Thousand Pound.

    The Queen of Love was pleas'd, and proud,
To see *Vanessa* thus endow'd;
She doubted not but such a Dame   230
Thro' ev'ry Breast wou'd dart a Flame;
That ev'ry rich and lordly Swain
With Pride wou'd drag about her Chain;
That Scholars wou'd forsake their Books
To study bright *Vanessa*'s Looks:
As she advanc'd, that Womankind
Wou'd by her Model form their Mind,
And all their Conduct wou'd be try'd
By her, as an unerring Guide.
Offending Daughters oft wou'd hear   240
Vanessa's Praise rung in their Ear:
Miss *Betty,* when she does a Fault,
Lets fall her Knife, or spills the Salt,
Will thus be by her Mother chid,
" 'Tis what *Vanessa* never did.
Thus by the Nymphs and Swains ador'd,
My Pow'r shall be again restor'd,
And happy Lovers bless my Reign——
So *Venus* hop'd, but hop'd in vain.

    For when in time the *Martial Maid*   250
Found out the Trick that *Venus* play'd,
She shakes her Helm, she knits her Brows,

And fir'd with Indignation vows,
To-morrow, ere the setting Sun,
She'd all undo, that she had done.

But in the Poets we may find,
A wholesome Law, Time out of mind,
Had been confirm'd by Fate's Decree;
That Gods, of whatso'er Degree,
Resume not what themselves have giv'n,   260
Or any Brother-God in Heav'n:
Which keeps the Peace among the Gods,
Or they must always be at Odds.
And *Pallas*, if she broke the Laws,
Must yield her Foe the stronger Cause;
A Shame to one so much ador'd
For Wisdom, at *Jove*'s Council-Board.
Besides, she fear'd the Queen of Love
Wou'd meet with better Friends above.
And tho' she must with Grief reflect,   270
To see a Mortal Virgin deck'd
With Graces, hitherto unknown
To Female Breasts, except her own;
Yet she wou'd act as best became
A Goddess of unspotted Fame:
She knew, by Augury Divine,
Venus wou'd fail in her Design:
She study'd well the Point, and found
Her Foe's Conclusions were not sound,
From Premisses erroneous brought,   280
And therefore the Deductions nought,
And must have contrary Effects
To what her treach'rous Foe expects.

In proper Season *Pallas* meets
The Queen of Love, whom thus she greets,
(For Gods, we are by *Homer* told,
Can in Celestial Language scold)
Perfidious Goddess! but in vain
You form'd this Project in your Brain,

A Project for thy Talents fit,   290
With much Deceit and little Wit;
Thou hast, as thou shalt quickly see,
Deceiv'd thy self, instead of me;
For how can Heav'nly Wisdom prove
An Instrument to earthly Love?
Know'st thou not yet that Men commence
Thy Votaries, for Want of Sense?
Nor shall *Vanessa* be the Theme
To manage thy abortive Scheme;
She'll prove the greatest of thy Foes: 300
And yet I scorn to interpose,
But using neither Skill, nor Force,
Leave all Things to their Nat'ral Course.

    The Goddess thus pronounc'd her Doom:
When, lo! *Vanessa* in her Bloom,
Advanc'd like *Atalanta*'s[14] Star,
But rarely seen, and seen from far:
In a new World with Caution stept,
Watch'd all the Company she kept,
Well knowing from the Books she read   310
What dangerous Paths young Virgins tread;
Wou'd seldom at the Park appear,
Nor saw the Play-House twice a Year;
Yet not incurious, was inclin'd
To know the Converse of Mankind.

    First issu'd from Perfumers Shops
A Croud of fashionable Fops;
They ask'd her, how she lik'd the Play,
Then told the Tattle of the Day,
A Duel fought last Night at Two,   320
About a Lady——You know who;
Mention'd a new *Italian*,[15] come
Either from *Muscovy* or *Rome*;
Gave Hints of who and who's together;[16]
Then fell to talking of the Weather:
Last Night was so extremely fine,

The Ladies Walk'd till after Nine.
Then in soft Voice and Speech absurd,
With Nonsense ev'ry second Word,
With Fustian from exploded[17] Plays,   330
They celebrate her Beauty's Praise,
Run o'er their Cant of stupid Lies,
And tell the Murders of her Eyes.

    With silent Scorn *Vanessa* sat,
Scarce list'ning to their idle Chat;
Further than sometimes by a Frown,
When they grew pert, to pull them down.
At last she spitefully was bent
To try their Wisdom's full Extent;
And said, she valu'd nothing less   340
Than Titles, Figure, Shape, and Dress;
That, Merit should be chiefly plac'd
In Judgment, Knowledge, Wit, and Taste;
And these, she offer'd to dispute,
Alone distinguish'd Man from Brute:
That, present Times have no Pretence
To Virtue, in the Noblest Sense,
By *Greeks* and *Romans* understood,
To perish for our Country's Good.
She nam'd the antient Heroes round,   350
Explain'd for what they were renown'd;
Then spoke with Censure, or Applause,
Of foreign Customs, Rites, and Laws;
Thro' Nature, and thro' Art she rang'd,
And gracefully her Subject chang'd:
In vain: her Hearers had no Share
In all she spoke, except to stare.
Their Judgment was upon the Whole,
—That Lady is the dullest Soul—
Then tipt their Forehead in a Jeer,   360
As who should say—she wants it here;
She may be handsome, young and rich,
But none will burn her for a Witch.

—

A Party next of glitt'ring Dames,
From round the Purlieus of *St. James*,[18]
Came early, out of pure Good-will,
To see the Girl in Deshabille.[19]
Their Clamour 'lighting from their Chairs,
Grew louder, all the Way up Stairs;
At Entrance loudest, where they found   370
The Room with Volumes litter'd round
Vanessa held *Montaigne*,[20] and read,
Whilst Mrs. *Susan* comb'd her Head:
They call'd for Tea and Chocolate,
And fell into their usual Chat,
Discoursing with important Face,
On Ribbons, Fans, and Gloves and Lace;
Shew'd Patterns just from *India* brought,
And gravely ask'd her what she thought,
Whether the Red or Green were best,   380
And what they cost? *Vanessa* guess'd,
As came into her Fancy first,
Nam'd half the Rates, and lik'd the worst.
To Scandal next——What aukward Thing
Was that, last *Sunday* in the Ring?[21]
——I'm sorry *Mopsa* breaks so fast;
I said her Face would never last.
Corinna with that youthful Air,
Is thirty, and a Bit to spare.
Her Fondness for a certain Earl   390
Began, when I was but a Girl.
Phyllis, who but a Month ago
Was marry'd to the *Tunbridge*[22] Beau,
I saw coquetting t'other Night
In publick with that odious Knight.

They railly'd next *Vanessa*'s Dress;
That Gown was made for Old Queen *Bess*.
Dear Madam, Let me see your Head:
Don't you intend to put on Red?
A Pettycoat without a Hoop!   400
Sure, you are not asham'd to stoop;

With handsome Garters at your Knees,
No matter what a Fellow sees.

    Fill'd with Disdain, with Rage inflam'd,
Both of her self and Sex asham'd,
The Nymph stood silent out of spight,
Nor wou'd vouchsafe to set them right.
Away the fair Detractors went,
And gave, by turns, their Censures Vent.
She's not so handsome, in my Eyes: **410**
For Wit, I wonder where it lies.
She's fair and clean, and that's the most;
But why proclaim her for a Toast?
A Baby Face, no Life, no Airs,
But what she learnt at Country Fairs;
Scarce knows what Diff'rence is between
Rich *Flanders* Lace, and Colberteen.
I'll undertake my little *Nancy*
In Flounces has a better Fancy.
With all her Wit, I wou'd not ask   **420**
Her Judgment, how to buy a Mask.
We begg'd her but to patch her Face,
She never hit one proper Place;
Which every Girl at five Years old
Can do as soon as she is told.
I own, that out-of-fashion Stuff
Becomes the *Creature* well enough.
The Girl might pass, if we cou'd get her
To know the World a little better.
(*To know the World!* a modern Phrase,   **430**
For Visits, Ombre, Balls and Plays.)

    Thus, to the World's perpetual Shame,
The *Queen of Beauty* lost her Aim.
Too late with Grief she understood,
Pallas had done more Harm than Good;
For great Examples are but vain,
Where Ignorance begets Disdain.
Both Sexes, arm'd with Guilt and Spite,

Against *Vanessa*'s Pow'r unite;
To copy her, few Nymphs aspir'd;   **440**
Her Virtues fewer Swains admir'd:
So Stars beyond a certain Height
Give Mortals neither Heat nor Light.

    Yet some of either Sex, endow'd
With Gifts superior to the Crowd,
With Virtue, Knowledge, Taste and Wit,
She condescended to admit:
With pleasing Arts she could reduce
Mens Talents to their proper Use;
And with Address each Genius held   **450**
To that wherein it most excell'd;
Thus making others Wisdom known,
Cou'd please them, and improve her own.
A modest Youth said something new,
She plac'd it in the strongest View.
All humble Worth she strove to raise;
Would not be prais'd, yet lov'd to praise.
The Learned met with free Approach,
Although they came not in a Coach.
Some Clergy too she wou'd allow,   **460**
Nor quarrell'd at their aukward Bow.
But this was for *Cadenus'* sake;
A Gownman of a diff'rent Make.
Whom *Pallas*, once *Vanessa*'s Tutor,
Had fix'd on for her Coadjutor.

    But *Cupid*, full of Mischief, longs
To vindicate his Mothers' Wrongs.
On *Pallas* all Attempts are vain;
One way he knows to give her Pain:
Vows, on *Vanessa*'s Heart to take   **470**
Due Vengeance, for her Patron's sake.
Those early Seeds by *Venus* sown,
In spight of *Pallas*, now were grown;
And *Cupid* hop'd they wou'd improve
By Time, and ripen into Love.

The Boy made use of all his Craft,
In vain discharging many a Shaft,
Pointed at Col'nels, Lords, and Beaux;
Cadenus warded off the Blows: 480
For placing still some Book betwixt,
The Darts were in the Cover fix'd,
Or often blunted and recoil'd,
On *Plutarch*'s Morals[23] struck, were spoil'd.

 The Queen of Wisdom cou'd foresee,
But not prevent the Fates decree;
And human Caution tries in vain
To break that Adamantine Chain.
Vanessa, tho' by *Pallas* taught,
By *Love* invulnerable thought,
Searching in Books for Wisdom's Aid,   490
Was, in the very Search, betray'd.

 Cupid, tho' all his Darts were lost,
Yet still resolv'd to spare no Cost;
He could not answer to his Fame
The Triumphs of that stubborn Dame,
A Nymph so hard to be subdu'd,
Who neither was Coquette nor Prude.
I find, says he, she wants a Doctor,
Both to adore her and instruct her;
I'll give her what she most admires,   500
Among those venerable Sires.
Cadenus is a Subject fit,
Grown old in Politicks and Wit;
Caress'd by Ministers of State,
Of half Mankind the Dread and Hate.
Whate'er Vexations Love attend,
She need no Rivals apprehend.
Her Sex, with universal Voice,
Must laugh at her capricious Choice.

 Cadenus many things had writ;   510
Vanessa much esteem'd his Wit,

And call'd for his Poetick Works;
Mean time the Boy in secret lurks,
And while the Book was in her Hand,
The Urchin from his private Stand
Took Aim, and shot with all his Strength
A Dart of such prodigious Length,
It pierc'd the feeble Volume thro',
And deep transfix'd her Bosom too.
Some Lines, more moving than the rest,   520
Stuck to the Point that pierc'd her Breast;
And, born directly to the Heart,
With Pains unknown increas'd her Smart.

    Vanessa, not in Years a Score,
Dreams of a Gown of forty-four;[24]
Imaginary Charms can find,
In Eyes with Reading almost blind;
Cadenus now no more appears
Declin'd in Health, advanc'd in Years.
She fancies Musick in his Tongue,   530
Nor further looks, but thinks him young.
What Mariner is not afraid,
To venture in a Ship decay'd?
What Planter will attempt to yoke
A Sapling with a falling Oak?
As Years increase, she brighter shines,
Cadenus with each Day declines,
And he must fall a Prey to Time,
While she continues in her Prime.

    Cadenus, common Forms apart,   540
In every Scene had kept his Heart;
Had sigh'd and languish'd, vow'd, and writ,
For Pastime, or to shew his Wit;
But Time, and Books, and State Affairs
Had spoil'd his fashionable Airs;
He now cou'd praise, esteem, approve,
But understood not what was Love.
His Conduct might have made him styl'd

A Father, and the Nymph his Child.
That innocent Delight he took   550
To see the Virgin mind her Book,
Was but the Master's secret Joy
In School to hear the finest Boy.
Her Knowledge with her Fancy grew;
She hourly press'd for something new;
Ideas came into her Mind
So fast, his Lessons lagg'd behind:
She reason'd, without plodding long,
Nor ever gave her Judgment wrong.
But now a sudden Change was wrought,   560
She minds no longer what he taught.
Cadenus was amaz'd to find
Such Marks of a distracted Mind;
For tho' she seem'd to listen more
To all he spoke, than e'er before;
He found her Thoughts would absent range,
Yet guess'd not whence could spring the Change.
And first he modestly conjectures
His Pupil might be tir'd with Lectures;
Which help'd to mortify his Pride,   570
Yet gave him not the Heart to chide;
But in a mild dejected Strain,
At last he ventur'd to complain:
Said, she shou'd be no longer teiz'd;
Might have her Freedom when she pleas'd:
Was now convinc'd he acted wrong,
To hide her from the World so long;
And in dull Studies to engage
One of her tender Sex and Age.
That ev'ry Nymph with Envy own'd,   580
How she might shine in the *Grand-Monde*,
And ev'ry Shepherd was undone
To see her cloister'd like a Nun.
This was a visionary Scheme,
He wak'd, and found it but a Dream;
A Project far above his Skill,
For Nature must be Nature still.

If he was bolder than became
A Scholar to a Courtly Dame,
She might excuse a Man of Letters;   590
Thus Tutors often treat their Betters.
And since his Talk offensive grew,
He came to take his last Adieu.

    Vanessa, fill'd with just Disdain,
Wou'd still her Dignity maintain,
Instructed from her early Years
To scorn the Art of Female Tears.

    Had he employ'd his Time so long,
To teach her what was Right or Wrong,
Yet cou'd such Notions entertain,   600
That all his Lectures were in vain?
She own'd the wand'ring of her Thoughts,
But he must answer for her Faults.
She well remember'd to her Cost,
That all his Lessons were not lost.
Two Maxims she could still produce,
And sad Experience taught their Use:
That Virtue, pleas'd by being shown,
Knows nothing which it dare not own;
Can make us without Fear disclose   610
Our inmost Secrets to our Foes:
That common Forms were not design'd
Directors to a noble Mind.
Now, said the Nymph, I'll let you see
My Actions with your Rules agree,
That I can vulgar Forms despise,
And have no Secrets to disguise.
I knew by what you said and writ,
How dang'rous Things were Men of Wit,
You caution'd me against their Charms,   620
But never gave me equal Arms:
Your Lessons found the weakest Part,
Aim'd at the Head, but reach'd the Heart.
                    ——

    Cadenus felt within him rise
Shame, Disappointment, Guilt, Surprize.
He knew not how to reconcile
Such Language, with her usual Style:
And yet her Words were so exprest,
He cou'd not hope she spoke in Jest.
His Thoughts had wholly been confin'd   630
To form and cultivate her Mind.
He hardly knew, 'till he was told,
Whether the Nymph were Young or Old;
Had met her in a publick Place,
Without distinguishing her Face.
Much less could his declining Age
Vanessa's earliest Thoughts engage.
And if her Youth Indifference met,
His Person must Contempt beget.
Or grant her Passion be sincere,   640
How shall his Innocence be clear?
Appearances were all so strong,
The World must think him in the Wrong;
Wou'd say, He made a treach'rous Use
Of Wit, to flatter and seduce:
The Town wou'd swear he had betray'd,
By Magick Spells, the harmless Maid;
And ev'ry Beau wou'd have his Jokes,
That Scholars were like other Folks:
That when Platonick Flights were over,   650
The Tutor turn'd a mortal Lover.
So tender of the Young and Fair?
It shew'd a true Paternal Care—
Five thousand Guineas in her Purse?
The Doctor might have fancy'd worse.—

    Hardly at length he Silence broke,
and faulter'd ev'ry Word he spoke;
Interpreting her Complaisance,[25]
Just as a Man *sans Consequence*.[26]
She railly'd well,[27] he always knew,   660
Her Manner now was something new;

And what she spoke was in an Air,
As serious as a Tragick Play'r.
But those who aim at Ridicule
Shou'd fix upon some certain Rule,
Which fairly hints they are in jest,
Else he must enter his Protest:
For, let a Man be ne'er so wise,
He may be caught with sober Lies;
A Science which he never taught,   670
And, to be free, was dearly bought:
For, take it in its proper Light,
'Tis just what Coxcombs call, *a Bite*.[28]

    But not to dwell on Things minute,
Vanessa finish'd the Dispute,
Brought weighty Arguments to prove
That Reason was her Guide in Love.
She thought he had himself describ'd,
His Doctrines when she first imbib'd;
What he had planted, now was grown;   680
His Virtues she might call her own;
As he approves, as he dislikes,
Love or Contempt, her Fancy strikes.
Self-Love, in Nature rooted fast,
Attends us first, and leave us last:
Why she likes him, admire not at her,
She loves herself, and that's the Matter.
How was her Tutor wont to praise
The Genius's of ancient Days!
(Those Authors he so oft had nam'd   690
For Learning, Wit, and Wisdom fam'd;)
Was struck with Love, Esteem, and Awe,
For Persons whom he never saw.
Suppose *Cadenus* flourish'd then,
He must adore such God-like Men.[29]
If one short Volume cou'd comprise
All that was witty, learn'd, and wise,
How wou'd it be esteem'd, and read,
Altho' the Writer long were dead?

If such an Author were alive,   700
How all wou'd for his Friendship strive;
And come in Crowds to see his Face:
And this she takes to be her Case.
Cadenus answers every End,
The Book, the Author, and the Friend.
The utmost her Desires will reach,
Is but to learn what he can teach;
His Converse is a System, fit
Alone to fill up all her Wit;
While ev'ry Passion of her Mind   710
In him is center'd and confin'd.

   Love can with Speech inspire a Mute,
And taught *Vanessa* to dispute.
This Topick, never touch'd before,
Display'd her Eloquence the more:
Her Knowledge, with such Pains acquir'd,
By this new Passion grew inspir'd.
Thro' this she made all Objects pass,
Which gave a Tincture o'er the Mass:
As Rivers, tho' they bend and twine,   720
Still to the Sea their Course incline;
Or, as Philosophers, who find
Some fav'rite System to their Mind,
In ev'ry Point to make it fit,
Will force all Nature to submit.

   Cadenus, who cou'd ne'er suspect
His Lessons wou'd have such Effect,
Or be so artfully apply'd,
Insensibly came on her Side;
It was an unforeseen Event,   730
Things took a Turn he never meant.
Whoe'er excels in what we prize,
Appears a Hero to our Eyes;
Each Girl when pleas'd with what is taught,
Will have the Teacher in her Thought.
When Miss delights in her Spinnet,

A Fidler may a Fortune get;
A Blockhead with melodious Voice
In Boarding-Schools can have his Choice;
And oft' the Dancing-Master's Art   740
Climbs from the Toe to touch the Heart.
In Learning let a Nymph delight,
The Pedant gets a Mistress by't.
Cadenus, to his Grief and Shame,
Cou'd scarce oppose *Vanessa*'s Flame;
But tho' her Arguments were strong,
At least, cou'd hardly wish them wrong.
Howe'er it came, he cou'd not tell,
But, sure, she never talk'd so well.
His Pride began to interpose,   750
Preferr'd before a Crowd of Beaux,
So bright a Nymph to come unsought,
Such Wonder by his Merit wrought;
'Tis Merit must with her prevail,
He never knew her Judgment fail,
She noted all she ever read,
And had a most discerning Head.

    'Tis an old Maxim in the Schools,
That Vanity's the Food of Fools;
Yet now and then your Men of Wit   760
Will condescend to take a Bit.

    So when *Cadenus* could not hide,
He chose to justify his Pride;
Constr'ing the Passion she had shown,
Much to her Praise, more to his Own.
Nature in him had Merit plac'd,
In her, a most judicious Taste.
Love, hitherto a transient Guest,
Ne'er held Possession of his Breast;
So, long attending at the Gate,   770
Disdain'd to enter in so late.
Love, why do we one Passion call?
When 'tis a Compound of them all;

Where hot and cold, where sharp and sweet,
In all their Equipages meet;[30]
Where Pleasures mix'd with Pains appear,
Sorrow with Joy, and Hope with Fear.
Wherein his Dignity and Age
Forbid *Cadenus* to engage.
But Friendship in its greatest Height,   780
A constant, rational Delight,
On Virtue's Basis fix'd to last,
When Love's Allurements long are past;
Which gently warms, but cannot burn;
He gladly offers in return:
His Want of Passion will redeem,
With Gratitude, Respect, Esteem:
With that Devotion we bestow,
When Goddesses appear below.

    While thus *Cadenus* entertains   790
Vanessa in exalted Strains,
The Nymph in sober Words intreats
A Truce with all sublime Conceits.
For why such Raptures, Flights, and Fancies,
To her, who durst not read Romances;
In lofty Style to make Replies,
Which he had taught her to despise.
But when her Tutor will affect
Devotion, Duty, and Respect,
He fairly abdicates his Throne,   800
The Government is now her own;
He has a Forfeiture incurr'd,
She vows to take him at his Word,
And hopes he will not think it strange
If both shou'd now their Stations change.
The Nymph will have her Turn, to be
The Tutor; and the Pupil, he:
Tho' she already can discern,
Her Scholar is not apt to learn;
Or wants Capacity to reach   810
The Science she designs to teach:

Wherein his Genius was below
The Skill of ev'ry common Beau;
Who, tho' he cannot spell, is wise
Enough to read a Lady's Eyes;
And will each accidental Glance
Interpret for a kind Advance.

But what Success *Vanessa* met,
Is to the World a Secret yet:
Whether the Nymph, to please her Swain,   820
Talks in a high Romantick Strain;
Or whether he at last descends
To like with less Seraphick Ends;
Or, to compound the Business, whether
They temper Love and Books together;
Must never to Mankind be told,
Nor shall the conscious Muse unfold.

Mean time the mournful *Queen of Love*
Led but a weary Life above.
She ventures now to leave the Skies,   830
Grown by *Vanessa*'s Conduct wise.
For tho' by one perverse Event
Pallas had cross'd her first Intent,
Tho' her Design was not obtain'd,
Yet had she much Experience gain'd;
And, by the Project vainly try'd,
Cou'd better now the *Cause* decide.

She gave due Notice, that both Parties,
Coram Regina prox' die Martis,[31]
Should at their Peril without fail   840
Come and appear, and save their Bail.
All met, and Silence thrice proclaim'd,
One Lawyer to each Side was nam'd.
The Judge discover'd in her Face
Resentments for her late Disgrace;
And, full of Anger, Shame, and Grief,
Directed them to mind their Brief;

Nor spend their Time to shew their Reading;
She'd have a summary Proceeding.
She gather'd, under ev'ry Head,   850
The Sum of what each Lawyer said;
Gave her own Reasons last; and then
Decreed the Cause against the *Men*.

   But, in a weighty Case like this,
To shew she did not judge amiss,
Which evil Tongues might else report,
She made a Speech in open Court;
Wherein she grievously complains,
"How she was cheated by the Swains:
On whose Petition (humbly shewing   860
That Women were not worth the wooing,
And that unless the Sex would mend,
The Race of Lovers soon must end:)
"She was at Lord knows what Expence,
"To form a Nymph of Wit and Sense;
"A Model for her Sex design'd,
"Who never cou'd one Lover find.
"She saw her Favour was misplac'd;
"The Fellows had a wretched Taste;
"She needs must tell them to their Face,   870
"They were a senseless, stupid Race:
"And were she to begin agen,
"She'd study to reform the *Men;*
"Or add some Grains of Folly more
"To *Women* than they had before,
"To put them on an equal Foot;
"And this, or nothing else, wou'd do't.
"This might their mutual Fancy strike,
"Since ev'ry Being loves its *Like.*

   "But now, repenting what was done,   880
"She left all Business to her Son:
"She puts the World in his Possession,
"And let him use it at Discretion.

      —

The Cry'r was order'd to dismiss
The Court, so made his last *O yes!*
The Goddess wou'd no longer wait;
But rising from her Chair of State,
Left all below at Six and Sev'n,
Harness'd her Doves, and flew to Heav'n.

THE AUTHOR UPON HIMSELF

*A few of the first Lines were wanting in the Copy
sent us by a Friend of the Author's from* London.

(1714, 1735)

* * * * * * * * * * * * * * * * *
  * * * * * * * * * * * * * * * *
  * * * * * * * * * * * * * * *
  * * * * * * * * * * * * * * *

By an —— —— ——[1] pursu'd,
A Crazy Prelate, and a Royal Prude.[2]
By dull Divines, who look with envious Eyes,
On ev'ry Genius that attempts to rise;
And pausing o'er a Pipe, with doubtful Nod,
Give Hints, that Poets ne'er believe in God.
So, Clowns on Scholars as on Wizards look,
And take a Folio for a conj'ring Book.

S——[3] had the Sin of Wit no venial Crime;
Nay, 'twas affirm'd, he sometimes dealt in Rhime:
Humour, and Mirth, had Place in all he writ:
He reconcil'd Divinity and Wit.
He mov'd, and bow'd, and talk't with too much Grace;
Nor shew'd the Parson in his Gait or Face;
Despis'd luxurious Wines, and costly Meat;
Yet, still was at the Tables of the Great.
Frequented Lords; *saw those that saw the Queen;*
At *Child*'s or *Truby*'s[4] never once had been;
Where Town and Country Vicars flock in Tribes,

10

Secur'd by Numbers from the Lay-men's Gibes;   20
And deal in Vices of the graver Sort,
Tobacco, Censure, Coffee, Pride, and Port.

    BUT, after sage Monitions from his Friends,
His Talents to employ for nobler Ends;
To better Judgments willing to submit,
He turns to Pol[it]icks his dang'rous Wit,

    AND now, the publick Int'rest to support,
By *Harley S—* invited comes to Court.
In Favour grows with Ministers of State;
Admitted private, when Superiors wait: 30
And, *Harley,* not asham'd his Choice to own,
Takes him to *Windsor* in his Coach, alone
At *Windsor S—* no sooner can appear,
But, *St. John* comes and whispers in his Ear;
The Waiters stand in Ranks; the Yeomen cry,
Make Room; as if a Duke were passing by.

    NOW *Finch*[5] alarms the Lords; he hears for certain,
This dang'rous Priest is got behind the Curtain:
Finch, fam'd for tedious Elocution, proves
That *S—* oils many a Spring which *Harley* moves.   40
W—[6] and *Ayslaby,* to clear the Doubt,
Inform the Commons, that the Secret's out:
"A *certain* Doctor is observ'd of late,
"To haunt a *certain* Minister of State:
"From whence, with half an Eye we may discover,
"The Peace is made, and *Perkin*[7] must come over.
York is from *Lambeth* sent, to shew the Queen
A dang'rous Treatise[8] writ against the Spleen;
Which by the Style, the Matter, and the Drift,
'Tis thought could be the Work of none but *S—*   50
Poor *York!* the harmless Tool of others Hate;
He sues for Pardon, and repents too late.

    Now, — — — her Vengeance vows
On *S—*'s Reproaches for her — —[9]

From her red Locks her Mouth with Venom fills:
And thence into the Royal Ear instills.
The Qu— incens'd, his Services forgot,
Leaves him a Victim to the vengeful *Scot;*
Now, through the Realm a Proclamation spread,
To fix a Price on his devoted Head.   60
While innocent, he scorns ignoble Flight;
His watchful Friends preserve him by a Sleight.

   By *Harley's* Favour once again he shines;
Is now caress't by Candidate Divines;
Who change Opinions with the changing Scene:
Lord! how were they mistaken in the Dean!
Now, *Delawere* again familiar grows;
And, in *S - - - - t's* Ear thrusts half his powder'd Nose.
The *Scottish* Nation, whom he durst offend,
Again apply that *S*— would be their Friend.   70

   By Faction tir'd, with Grief he waits a while,
His great contending Friends to reconcile.
Performs what Friendship, Justice, Truth require:
What could he more, but decently retire?

MARY THE COOK-MAID'S LETTER
TO DR. SHERIDAN
(1718, 1732)

Well; if ever I saw such another Man since my Mother bound my Head,
You a Gentleman! marry come up, I wonder where you were bred?
I am sure such Words does not become a Man of your Cloth,
I would not give such Language to a Dog, faith and troth.
Yes; you call'd my Master a Knave: Fie Mr. *Sheridan,* 'tis a Shame
For a Parson, who shou'd know better Things, to come out with such a
     Name.
Knave in your Teeth, Mr. *Sheridan,* 'tis both a Shame and a Sin,
And the Dean my Master is an honester Man than you and all your kin:
He has more Goodness in his little Finger, than you have in your whole
     Body,

My Master is a parsonable Man, and not a spindle-shank'd hoddy
   doddy.   10
And now whereby I find you would fain make an Excuse,
Because my Master one Day in anger call'd you Goose.
Which, and I am sure I have been his Servant four Years since *October*,
And he never call'd me worse than Sweet-heart drunk or sober:
Not that I know his Reverence was ever concern'd to my knowledge,
Tho' you and your Come-rogues keep him out so late in your Colledge.

  You say you will eat Grass on his Grave: a Christian eat Grass!
Whereby you now confess your self to be a Goose or an Ass:
But that's as much as to say, that my Master should die before ye,
Well, well, that's as God pleases, and I don't believe that's a true Story, 20
And so say I told you so, and you may go tell my Master; what care I?
And I don't care who knows it, 'tis all one to *Mary*.
Every body knows, that I love to tell Truth and shame the Devil,
I am but a poor Servant, but I think Gentle folks should be civil.
Besides, you found fault with our Vittles one Day that you was here,
I remember it was upon a *Tuesday*, of all Days in the Year.
And *Saunders* the Man says, you are always jesting and mocking,
Mary said he, (one Day, as I was mending my Master's Stocking,)
My Master is so fond of that Minister that keeps the School;
I thought my Master a wise Man, but that Man makes him a Fool. 30
Saunders said I, I would rather than a Quart of Ale,
He would come into our Kitchen, and I would pin a Dish-clout to his Tail.
And now I must go, and get *Saunders* to direct this Letter,
For I write but a sad Scrawl, but my Sister *Marget* she writes better.
Well, but I must run and make the Bed before my Master comes from
   Pray'rs,
And see now, it strikes ten, and I hear him coming up Stairs:
Whereof I cou'd say more to your Verses, if I could write written hand,
And so I remain in a civil way, your Servant to command

                 Mary.

On Stella's Birth-day

(1719, 1728)

Stella this Day is thirty four,[1]
(We won't dispute a Year or more)

However Stella, be not troubled,
Although thy Size and Years are doubled,
Since first I saw Thee at Sixteen[2]
The brightest Virgin of the Green,
So little is thy Form declin'd
Made up so largly in thy Mind.
Oh, would it please the Gods to split
Thy Beauty, Size, and Years, and Wit,   10
No Age could furnish out a Pair
Of Nymphs so gracefull, Wise and fair
With half the Lustre of Your Eyes,
With half thy Wit, thy Years and Size:
And then before it grew too late,
How should I beg of gentle Fate,
(That either Nymph might have her Swain,)
To split my Worship too in twain.

PHILLIS, OR THE PROGRESS OF LOVE
(1719, 1728)

Desponding Phillis was endu'd
With ev'ry Talent of a Prude,
She trembled when a Man drew near;
Salute her, and she turn'd her Ear:
If o'er against her you were plac't
She durst not look above your Wast;
She'd rather take you to her Bed
Than let you see her dress her Head;
In Church you heard her thrô the Crowd
Repeat the Absolution loud;   10
In Church, secure behind her Fan
She durst behold that Monster, Man:
There practic'd how to place her Head,
And bit her Lips to make them red:
Or on the Matt devoutly kneeling
Would lift her Eyes up to the Ceeling,
And heave her Bosom unaware

For neighb'ring Beaux to see it bare.
   At length a lucky Lover came,
And found Admittance from the Dame.   20
Suppose all Partyes now agreed,
The Writings drawn, the Lawyer fee'd,
The Vicar and the Ring bespoke:
Guess how could such a Match be broke.
See then what Mortals place their Bliss in!
Next morn betimes the Bride was missing,
The Mother scream'd, the Father chid,
Where can this idle Wench be hid?
No news of Phil. The Bridegroom came,
And thought his Bride had sculk't for shame,   30
Because her Father us'd to say
The Girl had such a Bashfull way.
   Now, John the Butler must be sent
To learn the Way that Phillis went;
The Groom was wisht to saddle Crop,
For John must neither light nor stop;
But find her where so'er she fled,
And bring her back, alive or dead.
See here again the Dev'l to do;
For truly John was missing too: 40
The Horse and Pillion both were gone
Phillis, it seems, was fled with John.
Old Madam who went up to find
What Papers Phil had left behind,
A Letter on the Toylet sees
To my much honor'd Father; These:
('Tis always done, Romances tell us,
When Daughters run away with Fellows)
Fill'd with the choicest common-places,
By others us'd in the like Cases.   50
That, long ago a Fortune-teller
Exactly said what now befell her,
And in a Glass had made her see
A serving-Man of low Degree:
It was her Fate; must be forgiven;
For Marriages are made in Heaven:

His Pardon begg'd, but to be plain,
She'd do't if 'twere to do again.
Thank God, 'twas neither Shame nor Sin,
For John was come of honest Kin: 60
Love never thinks of Rich and Poor,
She'd beg with John from Door to Door:
Forgive her, if it be a Crime,
She'll never do't another Time,
She ne'r before in all her Life
Once disobey'd him, Maid nor Wife.
One Argument she summ'd up all in,
The Thing was done and past recalling:
And therefore hop'd she would recover
His Favor, when his Passion's over.   70
She valued not what others thought her;
And was—His most obedient Daughter.

   Fair Maidens all attend the Muse
Who now the wandring Pair pursues:
Away they rode in homely Sort
Their Journy long, their Money short;
The loving Couple well bemir'd,
The Horse and both the Riders tir'd:
Their Vittells bad, their Lodging worse,
Phil cry'd, and John began to curse;   80
Phil wish't, that she had strained a Limb
When first she ventur'd out with him.
John wish't, that he had broke a Leg
When first for her he quitted Peg.

   But what Adventures more befell 'um
The Muse has now not time to tell 'um.
How Jonny wheadled, threatned, fawnd,
Till Phillis all her Trinkets pawn'd:
How oft she broke her marriage Vows
In kindness to maintain her Spouse;   90
Till Swains unwholsome spoyld the Trade,
For now the Surgeon must be paid;
To whom those Perquisites are gone
In Christian Justice due to John.

   When Food and Rayment now grew scarce

Fate put a Period to the Farce;
And with exact Poetick Justice:
For John is Landlord, Phillis Hostess;
They keep at Stains the old blue Boar,
Are Cat and Dog, and Rogue and Whore.   100

THE PROGRESS OF BEAUTY
(1719, 1728)

When first Diana[1] leaves her Bed
Vapors and Steams her Looks disgrace,
A frouzy dirty colour'd red
Sits on her cloudy wrinckled Face.

But by degrees when mounted high
Her artificiall Face appears
Down from her Window in the Sky,
Her Spots are gone, her Visage clears.

'Twixt earthly Femals and the Moon
All Parallells exactly run;   10
If Celia[2] should appear too soon
Alas, the Nymph would be undone.

To see her from her Pillow rise
All reeking in a cloudy Steam,
Crackt Lips, foul Teeth, and gummy Eyes,
Poor Strephon, how would he blaspheme!

The Soot or Powder which was wont
To make her Hair look black as Jet,
Falls from her Tresses on her Front
A mingled Mass of Dirt and Sweat.   20

Three Colours, Black, and Red, and White,
So graceful in their proper Place,
Remove them to a diff'rent Light
They form a frightfull hideous Face,

———

For instance; when the Lilly slipps
Into the Precincts of the Rose,
And takes Possession of the Lips,
Leaving the Purple to the Nose.

So Celia went entire to bed,
All her Complexions safe and sound,   30
But when she rose, the black and red
Though still in Sight, had chang'd their Ground.

The Black, which would not be confin'd
A more inferior Station seeks
Leaving the fiery red behind,
And mingles in her muddy Cheeks.

The Paint by Perspiration cracks,
And falls in Rivulets of Sweat,
On either Side you see the Tracks,
While at her Chin the Conflu'ents met.   40

A Skillfull Houswife thus her Thumb
With Spittle while she spins, anoints
And thus the brown Meanders come
In trickling Streams betwixt her Joynts.

But Celia can with ease reduce
By help of Pencil, Paint and Brush
Each Colour to it's Place and Use,
And teach her Cheeks again to blush.

She knows her Early self no more,
But fill'd with Admiration, stands,   50
As other Painters oft adore
The Workmanship of their own Hands.

Thus after four important Hours
Celia's the Wonder of her Sex;
Say, which among the Heav'nly Pow'rs
Could cause such wonderfull Effects.

—

Venus, indulgent to her Kind
Gave Women all their Hearts could wish
When first she taught them where to find
White Lead, and Lusitanian³ Dish.   60

Love with White lead cements his Wings,
White lead was sent us to repair
Two brightest, brittlest earthly Things
A Lady's Face, and China ware.

She ventures now to lift the Sash,
The Window is her proper Sphear;
Ah Lovely Nymph be not too rash,
Nor let the Beaux approach too near.

Take Pattern by your Sister Star,
Delude at once and Bless our Sight,   70
When you are seen, be seen from far,
And chiefly chuse to shine by Night.

In the Pell-mell when passing by,
Keep up the Glasses of your Chair,
Then each transported Fop will cry,
G—d d—m me Jack, she's wondrous fair.

But, Art no longer can prevayl
When the Materialls all are gone,
The best Mechanick Hand must fayl
Where Nothing's left to work upon.   80

Matter, as wise Logicians say,
Cannot without a Form subsist,
And Form, say I, as well as They,
Must fayl if Matter brings no Grist.

And this is fair Diana's Case
For, all Astrologers maintain
Each Night a Bit drops off her Face
When Mortals say she's in her Wain.

———

While Partridge wisely shews the Cause
Efficient of the Moon's Decay,   90
That Cancer[4] with his pois'nous Claws
Attacks her in the milky Way:

But Gadbury in Art profound
From her pale Cheeks pretends to show
That Swain Endymion[5] is not sound,
Or else, that Mercury's[6] her Foe.

But, let the Cause be what it will,
In half a Month she looks so thin
That Flamstead[7] can with all his skill
See but her Forehead and her Chin.   100

Yet as she wasts, she grows discreet,
Till Midnight never shows her Head;
So rotting Celia stroles the Street
When sober Folks are all a-bed.

For sure if this be Luna's Fate,
Poor Celia, but of mortall Race
In vain expects a longer Date
To the Materialls of Her Face.

When Mercury her Tresses mows
To think of Oyl and Soot, is vain,   110
No Painting can restore a Nose,
Nor will her Teeth return again

Two Balls of Glass may serve for Eyes,
White Lead can plaister up a Cleft,
But these alas, are poor Supplyes
If neither Cheeks, nor Lips be left.

Ye Pow'rs who over Love preside,
Since mortal Beautyes drop so soon,
If you would have us well supply'd,
Send us new Nymphs with each new Moon.   120

THE PROGRESS OF POETRY
(1720, 1728)

The Farmer's Goose, who in the Stubble,
Has fed without Restraint, or Trouble;
Grown fat with Corn and Sitting still,
Can scarce get o'er the Barn-Door Sill:
And hardly waddles forth, to cool
Her Belly in the neighb'ring Pool:
Nor loudly cackles at the Door;
For Cackling shews the Goose is poor.

    But when she must be turn'd to graze,
And round the barren Common strays,   10
Hard Exercise, and harder Fare
Soon make my Dame grow lank and spare:
Her Body light, she tries her Wings,
And scorns the Ground, and upward springs,
While all the Parish, as she flies,
Hear Sounds harmonious from the Skies.

    Such is the Poet, fresh in Pay,
(The third Night's Profits of his Play;[1])
His Morning-Draughts 'till Noon can swill,
Among his Brethren of the Quill: 20
With good Roast Beef his Belly full,
Grown lazy, foggy, fat, and dull:
Deep sunk in Plenty, and Delight,
What Poet e'er could take his Flight?
Or stuff'd with Phlegm up to the Throat
What Poet e'er could sing a Note?
Nor *Pegasus* could bear the Load,
Along the high celestial Road;
The Steed, oppress'd, would break his Girth,
To raise the Lumber from the Earth.   30

    But, view him in another Scene,
When all his Drink is *Hippocrene,*

His Money spent, his Patrons fail,
His Credit out for Cheese and Ale;
His Two-Year's Coat so smooth and bare,
Through ev'ry Thread it lets in Air;
With hungry Meals his Body pin'd,
His Guts and Belly full of Wind;
And, like a Jockey for a Race,
His Flesh brought down to Flying-Case: **40**
Now his exalted Spirit loaths
Incumbrances of Food and Cloaths;
And up he rises like a Vapour,
Supported high on Wings of Paper;
He singing flies, and flying sings,
While from below all *Grub-street*[2] rings.

TO STELLA, VISITING ME IN MY SICKNESS
(1720, 1728)

Pallas[1] observing *Stella*'s Wit
Was more than for her Sex was fit;
And that her Beauty, soon or late,
Might breed Confusion in the State,
In high Concern for human Kind,
Fixt *Honour* in her Infant Mind.

But, (not in Wranglings to engage
With such a stupid vicious Age,)
If Honour I would here define,
It answers Faith in Things divine.   **10**
As nat'ral Life the Body warms,
And, Scholars teach, the Soul informs;
So Honour animates the Whole,
And is the Spirit of the Soul.

Those num'rous Virtues which the Tribe
Of tedious Moralists describe,
And by such various Titles call,
True Honour comprehends them all.

Let Melancholy rule supreme,
Choler preside, or Blood, or Phlegm,   20
It makes no Diff'rence in the Case,
Nor is Complexion Honour's Place.

   But, lest we should for Honour take
The drunken Quarrels of a Rake,
Or think it seated in a Scar,
Or on a proud triumphal Car,
Or in the Payment of a Debt
We lose with Sharpers at Piquet;
Or, when a Whore in her Vocation,
Keeps punctual to an Assignation;   30
Or that on which his Lordship swears,
When vulgar Knaves would lose their Ears:
Let *Stella's* fair Example preach
A Lesson she alone can teach.

   In Points of Honour to be try'd,
All Passions must be laid aside:
Ask no Advice, but think alone,
Suppose the Question not your own:
How shall I act? is not the Case,
But how would *Brutus* in my Place?   40
In such a Cause would *Cato* bleed?
And how would *Socrates*[2] proceed?

   Drive all Objections from your Mind,
Else you relapse to Human Kind:
Ambition, Avarice, and Lust,
And factious Rage, and Breach of Trust,
And Flatt'ry tipt with nauseous Fleer,[3]
And guilty Shame, and servile Fear,
Envy, and Cruelty, and Pride,
Will in your tainted Heart preside.   50

   Heroes and Heroins of old,
By Honour only were enroll'd
Among their Brethren of the Skies,

To which (though late) shall *Stella* rise.
Ten thousand Oaths upon Record,
Are not so sacred as her Word:
The World shall in its Atoms end,
E'er *Stella* can deceive a Friend.
By Honour seated in her Breast,
She still determines what is best: 60
What Indignation in her Mind
Against Enslavers of Mankind!
Base Kings and Ministers of State,
Eternal Objects of her Hate.

   She thinks that Nature ne'er design'd
Courage to Man alone confin'd:
Can Cowardice her Sex adorn,
Which most exposes ours to Scorn?
She wonders where the Charm appears
In *Florimel's* affected Fears: 70
For *Stella* never learn'd the Art,
At proper Times to scream and start;
Nor calls up all the House at Night,
And swears she saw a Thing in White.
Doll never flies to cut her Lace,
Or throw cold Water in her Face,
Because she heard a sudden Drum,
Or found an Earwig in a Plum.

   Her Hearers are amaz'd from whence
Proceeds that Fund of Wit and Sense;   80
Which though her Modesty would shroud,
Breaks like the Sun behind a Cloud,
While Gracefulness its Art conceals,
And yet through ev'ry Motion steals.

   Say, *Stella,* was *Prometheus* blind,
And forming you, mistook your Kind?
No: 'Twas for you alone he stole
The Fire that forms a manly Soul;
Then to compleat it ev'ry way,

He molded it with Female Clay: 90
To that you owe the nobler Flame.
To this, the Beauty of your Frame.

   How would Ingratitude delight?
And, how would Censure glut her Spight?
If I should *Stella*'s Kindness hide
In Silence, or forget with Pride.
When on my sickly Couch I lay,
Impatient both of Night and Day,
Lamenting in unmanly Strains,
Call'd ev'ry Pow'r to ease my Pains,   100
Then *Stella* ran to my Relief
With chearful Face, and inward Grief;
And, though by Heaven's severe Decree
She suffers hourly more than me,
No cruel Master could require
From Slaves employ'd for daily Hire
What *Stella* by her Friendship warm'd,
With Vigour and Delight perform'd.

   My sinking Spirits now supplies
With Cordials in her Hands, and Eyes.   110
Now, with a soft and silent Tread,
Unheard she moves about my Bed.
I see her taste each nauseous Draught,
And so obligingly am caught:
I bless the Hand from whence they came,
Nor dare distort my Face for shame.

   Best Pattern of true Friends, beware;
You pay too dearly for your Care;
If, while your Tenderness secures
My Life, it must endanger yours.   120
For such a Fool was never found,
Who pull'd a Palace to the Ground,
Only to have the Ruins made
Materials for an House decay'd.

To Stella, Who Collected and Transcribed his Poems
(1720?, 1728)

As when a lofty Pile is rais'd,
We never hear the Workmen prais'd,
Who bring the Lime, or place the Stones;
But all admire *Inigo Jones:*
So if this Pile of scatter'd Rhymes
Should be approv'd in After-times,
If it both pleases and endures,
The Merit and the Praise are yours.

 Thou *Stella,* wert no longer young,
When first for thee my Harp I strung: 10
Without one Word of *Cupid*'s Darts,
Of killing Eyes, or bleeding Hearts:
With Friendship and Esteem possesst,
I ne'er admitted Love a Guest.[1]

 In all the Habitudes of Life,
The Friend, the Mistress, and the Wife,
Variety we still Pursue,
In Pleasure seek for something new:
Or else, comparing with the rest,
Take Comfort, that our own is best: 20
(The best we value by the worst,
As Tradesmen shew their Trash at first:)
But his Pursuits are at an End,
Whom *Stella* chuses for a *Friend.*

 A Poet, starving in a Garret,
Conning old Topicks like a Parrot,
Invokes his Mistress and his Muse,
And stays at home for want of Shoes:
Should but his Muse descending drop

A Slice of Bread, and Mutton-Chop,   30
Or kindly when his Credit's out,
Surprize him with a Pint of Stout,
Or patch his broken Stocking Soals,
Or send him in a Peck of Coals;
Exalted in his mighty Mind
He flies, and leave the Stars behind,
Counts all his Labours amply paid,
Adores her for the timely Aid.

    Or should a Porter make Enquiries
For *Chloe, Sylvia, Phillis, Iris;*   40
Be told the Lodging, Lane, and Sign,
The Bow'rs that hold those Nymphs divine;
Fair *Chloe* would perhaps be found
With Footmen tippling under Ground,
The charming *Silvia* beating Flax,
Her Shoulders mark'd with bloody Tracks;[2]
Bright *Phillis* mending ragged Smocks,
And radiant *Iris* in the Pox.

    These are the Goddesses enroll'd
In *Curll*'s[3] Collections, new and old,   50
Whose Scoundrel Fathers would not know 'em,
If they should meet 'em in a Poem.

    True Poets can depress and raise;
Are Lords of Infamy and Praise:
They are not scurrilous in Satire,
Nor will in Panygyrick flatter.
Unjustly Poets we asperse;
Truth shines the brighter, clad in Verse;
And all the Fictions they pursue
Do but insinuate what is true.   60

    Now should my Praises owe their Truth
To Beauty, Dress, or Paint, or Youth,
What Stoicks call *without our Power,*
They could not be insur'd an Hour;

'Twere grafting on an annual Stock
That must our Expectation mock,
And making one luxuriant Shoot
Die the next Year for want of Root:
Before I could my Verses bring.
Perhaps you're quite another Thing.   70

So *Mævius*,[4] when he drain'd his Skull
To celebrate some Suburb[5] Trull;
His Similes in Order set,
And ev'ry Crambo[6] he could get;
Had gone through all the Common-Places
Worn out by Wits who rhyme on Faces;
Before he could his Poem close,
The lovely Nymph had lost her Nose.

Your Virtues safely I commend,
They on no Accidents depend: 80
Let Malice look with all her Eyes,
She dares not say the Poet lyes.

Stella, when you these Lines transcribe,
Lest you should take them for a Bribe,
Resolv'd to mortify your Pride,
I'll here expose your weaker Side.

Your Spirits kindle to a Flame,
Mov'd with the lightest Touch of Blame,
And when a Friend in Kindness tries
To shew you where your Error lies,   90
Conviction does but more incense;
Perverseness in your whole Defence:
Truth, Judgment, Wit, give Place to Spite,
Regardless both of Wrong and Right.
Your Virtues, all suspended, wait
Till time hath open'd Reason's Gate:
And what is worse, your Passion bends
Its Force against your nearest Friends;

Which Manners, Decency, and Pride,
Have taught you from the World to hide: 100
In vain; for see, your Friend hath brought
To publick Light your only Fau't;
And yet a Fault we often find
Mix'd in a noble generous Mind;
And may compare to *Ætna*'s Fire,
Which, tho' with Trembling, all admire;
The Heat that makes the Summit glow,
Enriching all the Vales below.
Those who in warmer Climes complain
From *Phœbus* Rays they suffer Pain,   110
Must own, that Pain is largely paid
By gen'rous Wines beneath a Shade.

Yet when I find your Passions rise,
And Anger sparkling in your Eyes,
I grieve those Spirits should be spent,
For nobler Ends by Nature meant.
One Passion, with a diff'rent Turn,
Makes Wit inflame, or Anger burn;
So the Sun's Heat, with different Powers,
Ripens the Grape, the Liquor sours.   120
Thus *Ajax*,[7] when with Rage possesst
By *Pallas* breath'd into his Breast,
His Valour would no more employ;
Which might alone have conquer'd *Troy*;
But blinded by Resentment, seeks
For Vengeance on his Friends the *Greeks*.

You think this Turbulence of Blood
From stagnating preserves the Flood;
Which thus fermenting, by Degrees
Exalts the Spirits, sinks the Lees.   130

Stella, for once you reason wrong;
For should this Ferment last too long,
By Time subsiding, you may find
Nothing but Acid left behind.

From Passion you may then be freed,
When Peevishness and Spleen succeed.

Say, *Stella*, when you copy next,
Will you keep strictly to the Text?
Dare you let these Reproaches stand,
And to your Failing set your Hand?   140
Or if these Lines your Anger fire,
Shall they in baser Flames expire?
Whene'er they burn, if burn they must,
They'll prove my Accusation just.

VERSES TO VANESSA
(1720, 1814)

. . . . Your Friend sent me the verses he promised, w^ch
I here transcribe.

Nymph, would you learn the onely Art
To keep a worthy Lover's heart
First, to adorn your Person well,
In utmost Cleanlyness excell
And thô you must the Fashions take,
Observe them but for fashions sake.
    The strongest Reason will submit
To Virtue,—Honor, Sense, and Wit.
To such a Nymph the Wise and Good
Cannot be faithless if they wou'd: 10
For Vices all have diff'rent Ends,
But Virtue still to Virtue tends.
And when your Lover is not true,
Tis Virtue fails in Him or You:
And either he deserves Disdain,
Or You without a Cause complain.
But here Vanessa cannot err,
Nor are these Rules applyd to Her:
For who could such a Nymph forsake
Except a Blockhead or a Rake   20

> Or how could she her Heart bestow
> Except where Wit and Virtue grew

In my Opinion these Lines are too grave, and therefore may fit you who I fear are in the Spleen, but that is not fit either for your self or the Person you tend, to whom you ought to read—diverting Things. Here is an Epigram that concerns you not.

> Dorinda dreams of Dress a bed
>   'Tis all her Thought and Art,
> Her Lace hath got within her Head
>   Her Stays stick to her Heart.

Aug. 12th 1720

. . . . We live here in a very dull Town, every valuable Creature absent, and Cad—says he is weary of it, and would rather drink his Coffee on the barrennest highest mountain in Wales, than be King here

> A Fig for Partridges and Quails
> Ye Daintyes, I know nothing of ye,
> But on the highest mount in Wales
> Would chuse in Peace to drink my Coffee.

STELLA'S BIRTH-DAY
(1721, 1728)

> All Travellers at first incline
> Where'e'er they see the fairest Sign,
> And if they find the Chambers neat,
> And like the Liquor and the Meat
> Will call again and recommend
> The Angel-Inn to ev'ry Friend:
> And though the Painting grows decayd
> The House will never loose it's Trade;
> Nay, though the treach'rous Rascal Thomas
> Hangs a new Angel two doors from us   10
> As fine as Dawbers Hands can make it
> In hopes that Strangers may mistake it,
> They think it both a Shame and Sin
> To quit the true old Angel-Inn.
>   Now, this is Stella's Case in Fact;

An Angel's Face, a little crack't;
(Could Poets or could Painters fix
How Angels look at thirty six[1])
This drew us in at first to find
In such a Form an Angel's Mind   20
And ev'ry Virtue now supplyes
The fainting Rays of Stella's Eyes:
See, at her Levee crowding Swains
Whom Stella freely entertains
With Breeding, Humor, Wit, and Sense,
And puts them to so small Expence,
Their Minds so plentifully fills,
And makes such reasonable Bills
So little gets for what she gives
We really wonder how she lives;   30
And, had her Stock been less, no doubt
She must have long ago run out.

    Then, who can think we'll quit the Place
When Doll hangs out a newer Face
Nail'd to her Window full in Sight
All Christian People to invite;
Or stop and light at Cloe's Head
With Scraps and Leavings to be fed.

    Then Cloe, still go on to prate
Of thirty six, and thirty eight;   40
Pursue thy Trade of Scandall picking,
Thy Hints that Stella is no Chickin,
Your Innuendo's when you tell us
That Stella loves to talk with Fellows
But let me warn thee to believe
A Truth for which thy Soul should grieve,
That, should you live to see the Day
When Stella's Locks must all be grey
When Age must print a furrow'd Trace
On ev'ry Feature of her Face;   50
Though you and all your senceless Tribe
Could Art or Time or Nature bribe
To make you look like Beauty's Queen
And hold for ever at fifteen.

No Bloom of Youth can ever blind
The Cracks and Wrinckles of your Mind,
All Men of Sense will pass your Dore
And crowd to Stella's at fourscore.

TO STELLA ON HER BIRTH-DAY

(1722, 1766)

While, Stella to your lasting Praise
The Muse her ann'all Tribute pays,
While I assign my self a Task
Which you expect, but scorn to ask;
If I perform this Task with Pain
Let me of partiall Fate complain;
You, every Year the Debt enlarge,
I grow less equall to the Charge:
In you, each Virtue brighter shines,
But my Poetick Vein declines.   10
My Harp will soon in vain be strung,
And all Your Virtues left unsung:
For, none among the upstart Race
Of Poets dare assume my Place;
Your Worth will be to them unknown,
They must have Stella's of their own;
And thus, my Stock of Wit decay'd;
I dying leave the Debt unpay'd,
Unless Delany[1] as my Heir,
Will answer for the whole Arrear.   20

A SATIRICAL ELEGY ON THE DEATH
OF A LATE FAMOUS GENERAL

(1722, 1764)

His Grace! impossible! what dead!
Of old age too, and in his bed!
And could that Mighty Warrior fall?

And so inglorious, after all!
Well, since he's gone, no matter how,
The last loud trump[1] must wake him now:
And, trust me, as the noise grows stronger,
He'd wish to sleep a little longer.
And could he be indeed so old
As by the news-papers we're told?   10
Threescore, I think, is pretty high;
'Twas time in conscience he should die.
This world he cumber'd long enough;
He burnt his candle to the snuff;
And that's the reason, some folks think,
He left behind *so great a s---k.*
Behold his funeral appears,
Nor widow's sighs, nor orphan's tears,
Wont at such times each heart to pierce,
Attend the progress of his herse.   20
But what of that, his friends may say,
He had those honours in his day.
True to his profit and his pride,
He made them weep before he dy'd.

    Come hither, all ye empty things,
Ye bubbles rais'd by breath of Kings;
Who float upon the tide of state,
Come hither, and behold your fate.
Let pride be taught by this rebuke,
How very mean a thing's a Duke;   30
From all his ill-got honours flung,
Turn'd to that dirt from whence he sprung.

THE PROGRESS OF MARRIAGE
(1722, 1765)

    Ætatis suæ[1] fifty two
A rich Divine began to woo
A handsome young imperious *Girl*
Nearly related to an Earl.

Her Parents and her Friends consent,
The Couple to the Temple went:
They first invite the Cyprian Queen,[2]
'Twas answerd, she would not be seen.
The Graces next, and all the Muses
Were bid in form, but sent Excuses: 10
Juno[3] attended at the Porch
With farthing Candle for a Torch,
While Mistress Iris[4] held her Train,
The faded Bow distilling Rain.
Then Hebe[5] came and took her Place
But showed no more than half her Face
Whate'er these dire fore-bodings meant,
In Mirth the wedding-day was spent.
The *Wedding-day*, you take me right,
I promise nothing for the Night: 20
The Bridegroom dresst, to make a Figure,
Assumes an artificiall Vigor;
A flourisht Night-cap on, to grace
His ruddy, wrinckled, smirking Face,
Like the faint red upon a Pippin
Half wither'd by a Winters keeping. .
    And, thus set out this happy Pair,
The Swain is rich, the Nymph is fair;
But, which I gladly would forget,
The Swain is old, the Nymph Coquette.   30
Both from the Goal together start;
Scarce run a Step before they part;
No common Ligament that binds
The various Textures of their Minds,
Their Thoughts, and Actions, Hopes, and Fears,
Less corresponding than their Years.
Her Spouse desires his Coffee soon,
She rises to her Tea at noon.
While He goes out to cheapen Books,
She at the Glass consults her Looks   40
While Betty's[6] buzzing at her Ear,
Lord, what a Dress these Parsons wear,
So odd a Choice, how could she make,

Wish't him a Coll'nell for her Sake.
Then on her fingers Ends she counts
Exact to what his Age amounts,
The Dean, she heard her Uncle say
Is fifty, if he be a Day;
His ruddy Cheeks àre no Disguise;
You see the Crows feet round his Eyes.   50
At one she rambles to the Shops
To cheapen Tea, and talk with Fops.
Or calls a Councel of her Maids
And Tradesmen, to compare Brocades.
Her weighty Morning Bus'ness o'er
Sits down to Dinner just at four;
Minds nothing that is done or said,
Her ev'ning *Work* so fills her Head;
The *Dean*, who us'd to dine at one,
Is maukish, and his Stomach gone;   60
In threed-bare Goun, would scarce a louse hold,
Looks like the Chaplain of the Houshold,
Beholds her from the Chaplain's Place
In French brocades and Flanders Lace;
He wonders what employs her Brain;
But never asks, or asks in vain;
His Mind is full of other Cares,
And in the sneaking Parsons Airs
Computes, that half a Parish Dues
Will hardly find his Wife in Shoes.   70
Canst thou imagine, dull Divine,
'Twill gain her Love to make her fine?
Hath she no other wants beside?
You raise Desire as well as Pride,
Enticing Coxcombs to adore,
And teach her to despise thee more
If in her Coach she'll condescend
To place him at the hinder End
Her Hoop is hoist above his Nose,
His odious Goun would soil her Cloaths,   80
And drops him at the Church, to pray
While she drives on to see the Play.

He like an orderly Divine
Comes home a quarter after nine,
And meets her hasting to the Ball,
Her Chairmen push him from the Wall:
He enters in, and walks up Stairs,
And calls the Family to Prayrs,
Then goes alone to take his Rest
In bed, where he can spare her best.   90
At five the Footmen make a Din,
Her Ladyship is just come in,
The Masquerade began at two,
She stole away with much ado,
And shall be chid this afternoon
for leaving company so soon;
She'll say, and she may truly say't
She can't abide to stay out late.

  But now, though scarce a twelvemonth marry'd,
His Lady has twelve times miscarry'd,   100
The Cause, alas, is quickly guesst,
The Town has whisper'd round the Jest:
Think on some Remedy in time
You find His Rev'rence past his Prime,
Already dwindled to a Lath;
No other way but try the Bath:[7]
  For Venus rising from the Ocean
Infus'd a strong prolifick Potion,
That mixt with Achelous Spring,
The *horned* Floud, as Poets sing:[8]   110
Who with an English Beauty smitten
Ran under Ground from Greece to Brittain,
The genial Virtue with him brought,
And gave the Nymph a plenteous Draught;
Then fled, and left his Horn behind
For Husbands past their Youth to find;
The Nymph who still with Passion burnd,
Was to a boiling Fountain turn'd,
Where Childless wives crowd ev'ry morn
To drink in Achilous' Horn.   120

And here the Father often gains
That Title by another Pains.
    Hither, though much against his Grain,
The *Dean* has carry'd Lady Jane
He for a while would not consent,
But vow'd his Money all was spent;
His Money spent! a clownish Reason?
And, must my Lady slip her Season?
The Doctor with a double Fee
Was *brib'd* to make the *Dean* agree   130
    Here, all Diversions of the Place
Are *proper* in my Lady's Case
With which she patiently complyes,
Merely because her Friends advise;
His Money and her Time employs
In musick, Raffling-rooms, and Toys,
Or in the *cross-bath*[9] seeks an Heir
Since others oft have found one there;
Where if the Dean by chance appears
It shames his Cassock and his Years   140
He keeps his Distance in the Gallery
Till banisht by some Coxcombs Raillery;
For, it would his Character Expose
To bath among the Belles and Beaux.

    So have I seen within a Pen
Young Ducklings, fostered by a Hen;
But when let out, they run and muddle
As Instinct leads them, in a Puddle;
The sober Hen not born to swim
With mournful Note clocks round the Brim.   150
    The Dean with all his best Endeavour
Gets not an Heir, but gets a Feaver;
A Victim to the last Essays
Of Vigor in declining Days.
He dyes, and leaves his mourning Mate
(What could he less,) his whole Estate.

    The Widow goes through all her Forms;
New Lovers now will come in Swarms.

Oh, may I see her soon dispensing
Her Favors to some broken Ensign[10]   160
Him let her Marry for his Face,
And only Coat of tarnish't Lace;
To turn her Naked out of Doors,
And spend her Joynture on his Whores:
But for a parting Present leave her
A rooted Pox to last for ever.

STELLA'S BIRTH-DAY.
A GREAT BOTTLE OF WINE, LONG BURIED,
BEING THAT DAY DUG UP.
(1723, 1728)

Resolv'd my annual Verse to pay
By Duty bound, on *Stella*'s Day;
Furnish'd with Paper, Pens, and Ink,
I gravely sat me down to think:
I bit my Nails, and scratch'd my Head,
But found my Wit and Fancy fled:
Or, if with more than usual Pain,
A Thought came slowly from my Brain,
It cost me Lord knows how much Time
To shape it into Sense and Rhyme;   10
And, what was yet a greater Curse,
Long-thinking made my Fancy worse.

Forsaken by th'inspiring Nine,[1]
I waited at *Apollo*'s Shrine;
I told him what the World would say
If *Stella* were unsung to Day;
How I should hide my Head for Shame,
When both the *Jacks* and *Robin* came;
How *Ford* would frown, how *Jim* would leer,
How *Sh--n* the Rogue would sneer,   20
And swear it does not always follow,
That *Semel'n anno ridet Apollo.*[2]

I have assur'd them twenty times,
That *Phœbus* help'd me in my Rhymes,
Phœbus inspir'd me from above,
And he and I were Hand in Glove.
But finding me so dull and dry since,
They'll call it all poetick Licence:
And when I brag of Aid divine,
Think *Eusden*'s[3] Right as good as mine.   30

    Nor do I ask for *Stella*'s sake;
'Tis my own Credit lies at Stake.
And *Stella* will be sung, while I
Can only be a Stander-by.
    Apollo having thought a little,
Return'd this Answer to a Tittle.

    Though you should live like old *Methusalem,*
I furnish Hints, and you should use all 'em,
You yearly sing as she grows old,
You'd leave her Virtues half untold,   40
But to say truth, such Dulness reigns
Through the whole set of *Ir--sh* D---ns;[4]
I'm daily stunn'd with such a Medley,
D---n *W*--, *D---n D--l,* and D---n *S---;*[5]
That, let what D--n soever come,
My Orders are, I'm not at Home;
And if your Voice had not been loud,
You must have pass'd among the Crowd.

    But, now, your Danger to prevent,
You must apply to Mrs. *Brent,**   50
For she, as Priestess, knows the Rites
Wherein the God of *Earth* delights.
First, nine Ways looking, let her stand
With an old Poker in her Hand;
Let her describe a Circle round

* *The House-Keeper.*

In *Saunder*'s* Cellar on the Ground:
A Spade let prudent *Archy*† hold,
And with Discretion dig the Mould:
Let *Stella* look with watchful Eye,
Rebecca, Ford, and *Grattons* by.   60

Behold the BOTTLE, where it lies
With Neck elated tow'rds the Skies!
The God of Winds and God of Fire
Did to it's wond'rous Birth conspire;
And *Bacchus* for the Poet's Use
Pour'd in a strong inspiring Juice:
See! as you raise it from its Tomb,
It drags behind a spacious Womb,
And in the spacious Womb contains
A Sov'reign Medicine for the Brains.   70

You'll find it soon if Fate consents;
If not, a thousand Mrs. *Brents*,
Ten thousand *Archy*'s arm'd with Spades
May dig in vain in *Pluto*'s Shades.

From thence a plenteous Draught infuse,
And boldly then invoke the Muse:
(But first let *Robert* on his Knees
With Caution drain it from the Lees)
The Muse will at your Call appear,
With *Stella*'s Praise to crown the Year.   80

* *The Butler.*
† *The Footman.*

STELLA AT WOOD-PARK, A HOUSE OF CHARLES FORD, ESQ; EIGHT MILES FROM DUBLIN

——*Cuicunqu; nocere volebat*
Vestimenta dabat pretiosa.

(1723, 1735)

Don *Carlos*[1] in a merry Spight,
Did *Stella* to his House invite:
He entertain'd her half a Year
With gen'rous Wines and costly Chear.
Don *Carlos* made her chief Director,
That she might o'er the Servants hector.
In half a Week the Dame grew nice,
Got all things at the highest Price.
Now at the Table-Head she sits,
Presented with the nicest Bits: 10
She look'd on Partridges with scorn,
Except they tasted of the Corn:
A Haunch of Ven'son made her sweat,
Unless it had the right *Fumette.*
Don *Carlos* earnestly would beg,
Dear Madam, try this Pigeon's Leg;
Was happy when he could prevail
To make her only touch a Quail.
Through Candle-Light she view'd the Wine,
To see that ev'ry Glass was fine.   20
At last grown prouder than the D——l,
With feeding high, and Treatment civil,
Don *Carlos* now began to find
His Malice work as he design'd:
The Winter-Sky began to frown,
Poor *Stella* must pack off to Town.
From purling Streams and Fountains bubbling,

To *Liffy*'s stinking Tide in *Dublin:*
From wholsome Exercise and Air
To sossing² in an easy Chair;   30
From Stomach sharp and hearty feeding,
To piddle like a Lady breeding:
From ruling there the Houshold singly,
To be directed here by *Dingly:*³
From ev'ry Day a lordly Banquet,
To half a Joint, and God be thank it:
From ev'ry Meal *Pontack*⁴ in plenty,
To half a Pint one Day in twenty.
From *Ford* attending at her Call,
To visits of —— ——⁵   40
From *Ford,* who thinks of nothing mean,
To the poor Doings of the D—n.
From growing Riches with good Chear,
To running out by starving here.

  BUT now arrives the dismal Day;
She must return to *Ormond Key:*⁶
The Coachman stopt, she lookt, and swore
The Rascal had mistook the Door:
At coming in you saw her stoop;
The Entry brusht against her Hoop: 50
Each Moment rising in her Airs,
She curst the narrow winding Stairs:
Began a Thousand Faults to spy;
The Ceiling hardly six Foot high;
The smutty Wainscot full of Cracks,
And half the Chairs with broken Backs:
Her Quarter's out at *Lady-Day,*⁷
She vows she will no longer stay,
In Lodgings, like a poor *Grizette,*
While there are Lodgings to be lett.   60

  HOWE'ER, to keep her Spirits up,
She sent for Company to sup;
When all the while you might remark,
She strove in vain to ape *Wood-Park.*

Two Bottles call'd for, (half her Store;
The Cupboard could contain but four;)
A Supper worthy of her self,
Five *Nothings* in five Plates of *Delph*.

THUS, for a Week the Farce went on;
When; all her County-Savings gone,   70
She fell into her former Scene.
Small Beer, a Herring, and the D——n.

THUS, far in jest. Though now I fear
You think my jesting too severe:
But Poets when a Hint is new
Regard not whether false or true:
Yet Raillery gives no Offence,
Where Truth has not the least Pretence;
Nor can be more securely plac't
Than on a Nymph of *Stella*'s Taste.   80
I must confess, your Wine and Vittle
I was too hard upon *a little*;
Your Table neat, your Linnen fine;
And, though in Miniature, you shine,
Yet, when you sigh to leave *Wood-Park*,
The Scene, the Welcome, and the Spark,
To languish in this odious Town,
And pull your haughty Stomach down;
We think you quite mistake the Case;
The Virtue lies not in the Place: 90
For though my Raillery were true,
A Cottage is *Wood-Park* with you.

To Stella

[Written on the Day of her Birth, but not on the Subject,
when I was sick in bed.]

(1724, 1765)

Tormented with incessant pains,
Can I devise poetic strains?
Time was, when I could yearly pay
My verse on Stella's native day:
But now, unable grown to write,
I grieve she ever saw the light.
Ungrateful; since to her I owe
That I these pains can undergo.
She tends me, like an humble slave;
And, when indecently I rave,   10
When out my brutish passions break,
With gall in ev'ry word I speak,
She, with soft speech, my anguish chears,
Or melts my passions down with tears:
Although 'tis easy to descry
She wants assistance more than I;
Yet seems to feel my pains alone,
And is a Stoic in her own.
When, among scholars, can we find
So soft, and yet so firm a mind?   20
All accidents of life conspire
To raise up Stella's virtue higher;
Or else, to introduce the rest
Which had been latent in her breast.
Her firmness who could e'er have known,
Had she not evils of her own?
Her kindness who could ever guess,
Had not her friends been in distress?
Whatever base returns you find
From me, Dear Stella, still be kind.   30
In your own heart you'll reap the fruit,

Tho' I continue still a brute.
But when I once am out of pain,
I promise to be good again:
Meantime your other juster friends
Shall for my follies make amends:
So may we long continue thus,
Admiring you, you pitying us.

PROMETHEUS, A POEM

(1724)

When first the *'Squire,* and *Tinker Wood*
Gravely consulting *Ireland*'s Good,
Together mingl'd in a Mass
Smith's *Dust,* and *Copper, Lead* and *Brass,*
The Mixture thus by Chymick Art,
United close in ev'ry Part.
In Fillets roll'd, or cut in Pieces,
Appear'd like one continu'd Spec'es,
And by the forming Engine struck,
On all the same IMPRESSION stuck.   10

   So to confound, this *hated Coin*
All *Parties* and *Religions* joyn;
Whigs, Tories, Trimmers, Hannoverians,
Quakers, Conformists, Presbyterians,
Scotch, Irish, English, French unite,
With *equal Int'rest, equal Spight,*
Together mingled in a Lump,
Do all in *One Opinion* jump;
And ev'ry one begins to find,
The same IMPRESSION on his Mind;   20
A strange Event! whom *Gold* incites,
To Blood and Quarrels, *Brass* unites:
So Goldsmiths say, the coursest Stuff,
Will serve for *Sodder* well enuff.
So, by the *Kettles* loud Allarm,

The *Bees* are gather'd to a *Swarm:*
So by the *Brazen* Trumpets Bluster,
Troops of all Tongues and Nations Muster:
And so the *Harp* of *Ireland* brings,
Whole Crouds about its *Brazen* Strings.   30

    There is a *Chain* let down from *Jove,*
But fasten'd to his Throne above;
So strong, that from the lower End,
They say, all human Things depend:
This *Chain,* as Antient Poets hold,
When *Jove* was Young, was made of *Gold.*
Prometheus once this *Chain* purloin'd,
Dissolv'd, and into *Money* Coin'd;
Then whips me on a *Chain* of *Brass,*
(*Venus*¹ was Brib'd to let it pass.)   40

    Now while this *Brazen Chain* prevail'd,
Jove saw that all *Devotion* fail'd;
No *Temple,* to his *Godship* rais'd,
No *Sacrifice* on *Altars* blaz'd;
In short such *dire Confusions* follow'd,
Earth must have been in *Chaos* swallow'd.
Jove stood amaz'd, but looking round,
With much ado, the *Cheat* he found;
'Twas plain he cou'd no longer hold
The *World* in any *Chain* but *Gold;*   50
And to the *God of Wealth* his *Brother,*
Sent *Mercury* to get another.

    Prometheus on a Rock is laid,

Ty'd with the *Chain* himself had made;

On Icy *Caucasus* to shiver,

While *Vultures* eat his growing Liver:

Ye Pow'rs of *Grub-street* make me able,

Discreetly to apply this *Fable*.
Say, who is to be understood,
By that old Thief *Prometheus?* WOOD   60
For *Jove,* it is not hard to guess him,
I mean *His M——, God bless him.*
This *Thief* and *Black-Smith* was so bold,
He strove to steal that *Chain* of *Gold,*
Which links the *Subject* to the *King:*
And change it for a *Brazen String.*
But sure if nothing else must pass,
Between the *K——* and US but *Brass,*
Altho' the *Chain* will never crack,
Yet *Our Devotion* may *Grow Slack.*   70

But *Jove* will soon convert I hope,
This *Brazen Chain* into a *Rope;*
With which *Prometheus* shall be ty'd,
And high in Air for ever ride;
Where, if we find his *Liver* grows,
For want of *Vultures,* we have *Crows.*

STELLA'S BIRTH-DAY
(1725, 1728)

As when a beauteous Nymph decays
We say, she's past her Dancing Days;[1]
So, Poets lose their Feet by Time,
And can no longer dance in Rhyme.
Your Annual Bard had rather chose
To celebrate your Birth in Prose;
Yet, merry Folks who want by chance
A Pair to make a Country Dance,
Call the Old Housekeeper, and get her
To fill a Place, for want of better;   10
While *S----n*[2] is off the hooks,
And Friend *D----y*[3] at his Books,
That *Stella* may avoid Disgrace
Once more the D--n[4] supplies their Place.

———

Beauty and Wit, too sad a Truth,
Have always been confin'd to Youth;
The God of Wit, and Beauty's Queen,[5]
He Twenty one, and She Fifteen:
No Poet ever sweetly sung,
Unless he were like *Phœbus,* young;   20
Nor ever Nymph inspir'd to Rhyme,
Unless, like *Venus,* in her Prime.
At Fifty six, if this be true,
Am I a Poet fit for you?
Or at the Age of Forty three,
Are you a Subject fit for me?
Adieu bright Wit, and radiant Eyes;
You must be grave, and I be wise.
Our Fate in vain we would oppose,
But I'll be still your Friend in Prose: 30
Esteem and Friendship to express,
Will not require Poetick Dress;
And if the Muse deny her Aid
To have them *sung,* they may be *said.*

But, *Stella* say, what evil Tongue
Reports you are no longer young?
That *Time* sits with his Scythe to mow
Where erst sate *Cupid* with his Bow;
That half your Locks are turn'd to Grey;
I'll ne'er believe a Word they say.   40
'Tis true, but let it not be known,
My Eyes are somewhat dimmish grown;
For Nature, always in the Right,
To your Decays adapts my Sight,
And Wrinkles undistinguish'd pass,
For I'm asham'd to use a Glass;
And till I see them with these Eyes,
Whoever says you have them, lyes.

No Length of Time can make you quit
Honour and Virtue, Sense and Wit,   50

Thus you may still be young to me,
While I can better *hear* than *see;*
Oh, ne'er may Fortune shew her Spight,
To make me *deaf,* and mend my *Sight.*

ON WOOD THE IRON-MONGER

(1725, 1735)

Salmoneus, as the *Grecian* Tale is,
Was a mad Copper-Smith of *Elis:*[1]
Up at his Forge by Morning-peep,
No Creature in the Lane could sleep.
Among a Crew of royst'ring Fellows
Would sit whole Ev'nings at the Ale-house:
His Wife and Children wanted Bread,
While he went always drunk to Bed.
This vap'ring Scab must needs devise
To ape the Thunder of the Skies;   10
With *Brass* two fiery Steeds he shod,
To make a Clatt'ring as they trod.
Of polish't *Brass,* his flaming Car,
Like Light'ning dazzled from a-far:
And up he mounts into the Box,
And HE must thunder, with a Pox.
Then, furious he begins his March;
Drives rattling o'er a brazen Arch:
With Squibs and Crackers arm'd, to throw
Among the trembling Croud below.   20
All ran to Pray'rs, both Priests and Laity,
To pacify this angry Deity;
When *Jove,* in pity to the Town,
With real Thunder knock't him down.
Then what a huge Delight were all in,
To see the wicked Varlet sprawling;
They search't his Pockets on the Place,
And found his Copper all was base;
They laught at such an *Irish* Blunder,
To take the Noise of Brass for Thunder!   30

THE Moral of this Tale is proper,
Apply'd to *Wood*'s adult'rate Copper;
Which, as he scatter'd, we like Dolts,
Mistook at first for Thunder-Bolts;
Before the *Drapier* shot a Letter,
(Nor *Jove* himself could do it better)
Which lighting on th' Impostor's Crown,
Like real Thunder knock't him down.

A RECEIPT[1] TO RESTORE STELLA'S YOUTH
(1725, 1735)

The *Scottish* Hinds too poor to house
In frosty Nights their starving Cows,
While not a Blade of Grass, or Hay,
Appears from *Michaelmas* to *May*;
Must let their Cattle range in vain
For Food, along the barren Plain;
Meager and lank with fasting grown,
And nothing left but Skin and Bone;
Expos'd to Want, and Wind, and Weather,
They just keep Life and Soul together,   10
'Till Summer Show'rs and Ev'ning Dew,
Again the verdant Glebe renew;
And as the Vegetables rise,
The famish't Cow her Want supplies;
Without an Ounce of last Year's Flesh,
Whate'er she gains is young and fresh;
Grows plump and round, and full of Mettle,
As rising from *Medea*'s Kettle;[2]
With Youth and Beauty to enchant
Europa's counterfeit Gallant.   20
    WHY, *Stella,* should you knit your Brow,
If I compare you to the Cow?
'Tis just the Case: For you have fasted
So long till all your Flesh is wasted,
And must against the warmer Days
Be sent to *Quilca*[3] down to graze;

Where Mirth, and Exercise, and Air,
Will soon your Appetite repair.
The Nutriment will from within
Round all your Body plump your Skin;   30
Will agitate the lazy Flood,
And fill your Veins with sprightly Blood:
Nor Flesh nor Blood will be the same,
Nor ought of *Stella,* but the Name;
For, what was ever understood
By human Kind, but Flesh and Blood?
And if your Flesh and Blood be new,
You'll be no more your former *You;*
But for a blooming Nymph will pass,
Just Fifteen, coming Summer's Grass: 40
Your jetty Locks with Garlands crown'd,
While all the Squires from nine Miles round,
Attended by a Brace of Curs,
With Jocky Boots, and Silver Spurs;
No less than Justices o' *Quorum,*[4]
Their Cow-boys bearing Cloaks before 'um,
Shall leave deciding broken Pates,
To kiss your Steps at *Quilca* Gates;
But, lest you should my Skill disgrace,
Come back before you're out of Case;   50
For if to *Michaelmas* you stay,
The new-born Flesh will melt away;
The Squires in Scorn will fly the House
For better Game, and look for Grouse:
But here, before the Frost can marr it,
We'll make it firm with Beef and Claret.

STELLA'S BIRTH-DAY

(1727, 1728)

This Day, whate'er the Fates decree,
Shall still be kept with Joy by me:
This Day then, let us not be told,
That you are sick, and I grown old,

Nor think on our approaching Ills,
And talk of Spectacles and Pills;
To morrow will be Time enough
To hear such mortifying Stuff.
Yet, since from Reason may be brought
A better and more pleasing Thought,   10
Which can in spite of all Decays,
Support a few remaining Days:
From not the gravest of Divines,
Accept for once some serious Lines.

    Although we now can form no more
Long Schemes of Life, as heretofore;
Yet you, while Time is running fast,
Can look with Joy on what is past.

    Were future Happiness and Pain,
A mere Contrivance of the Brain,   20
As Atheists argue, to entice,
And fit their Proselytes for Vice;
(The only Comfort they propose,
To have Companions in their Woes.)
Grant this the Case, yet sure 'tis hard,
That Virtue, stil'd its own Reward,
And by all Sages understood
To be the chief of human Good,
Should acting, die, nor leave behind
Some lasting Pleasure in the Mind,   30
Which by Remembrance will assuage,
Grief, Sickness, Poverty, and Age;
And strongly shoot a radiant Dart,
To shine through Life's declining Part.

    Say, *Stella,* feel you no Content,
Reflecting on a Life well spent?
Your skilful Hand employ'd to save
Despairing Wretches from the Grave;
And then supporting with your Store,
Those whom you dragg'd from Death before: 40

(So Providence on Mortals waits,
Preserving what it first creates)
Your gen'rous Boldness to defend
An innocent and absent Friend;
That Courage which can make you just,
To Merit humbled in the Dust:
The Detestation you express
For Vice in all its glitt'ring Dress:
That Patience under tort'ring Pain,
Where stubborn Stoicks would complain.   50

   Must these like empty Shadows pass,
Or Forms reflected from a Glass?
Or mere Chimæra's in the Mind,
That fly and leave no Marks behind?
Does not the Body thrive and grow
By Food of twenty Years ago?
And, had it not been still supply'd,
It must a thousand Times have dy'd.
Then, who with Reason can maintain,
That no Effects of Food remain?   60
And, is not Virtue in Mankind
The Nutriment that feeds the Mind?
Upheld by each good Action past,
And still continued by the last:
Then, who with Reason can pretend,
That all Effects of Virtue end?

   Believe me *Stella*, when you show
That true Contempt for Things below,
Nor prize your Life for other Ends
Than merely to oblige your Friends;   70
Your former Actions claim their Part,
And join to fortify your Heart.
For Virtue in her daily Race,
Like *Janus*, bears a double Face;
Looks back with Joy where she has gone,
And therefore goes with Courage on.
She at your sickly Couch will wait,
And guide you to a better State.

———

O then, whatever Heav'n intends,
Take Pity on your pitying Friends;   80
Nor let your Ills affect your Mind,
To fancy they can be unkind.
Me, surely me, you ought to spare,
Who gladly would your Suff'rings share;
Or give my Scrap of Life to you,
And think it far beneath your Due;
You, to whose Care so oft I owe,
That I'm alive to tell you so.

CLEVER TOM CLINCH
GOING TO BE HANGED
(1726?, 1735)

As clever *Tom Clinch*, while the Rabble was bawling,
Rode stately through *Holbourn*,[1] to die in his Calling;
He stopt at the *George* for a Bottle of Sack,[2]
And promis'd to pay for it when he'd come back.
His Waistcoat and Stockings, and Breeches were white,
His Cap had a new Cherry Ribbon to ty't.
The Maids to the Doors and the Balconies ran,
And said, lack-a-day! he's a proper young Man.
But, as from the Windows the Ladies he spy'd,
Like a Beau in the Box, he bow'd low on each Side;   10
And when his last Speech the loud Hawkers did cry,
He swore from his Cart, it was all a damn'd Lye.
The Hangman for Pardon fell down on his Knee;
Tom gave him a Kick in the Guts for his Fee.
Then said, I must speak to the People a little,
But I'll see you all damn'd before I will *whittle*.[3]
My honest Friend *Wild*,[4] may he long hold his Place,
He lengthen'd my Life with a whole Year of Grace.
Take Courage, dear Comrades, and be not afraid,
Nor slip this Occasion to follow your Trade.   20
My Conscience is clear, and my Spirits are calm,
And thus I go off without Pray'r-Book or Psalm.

Then follow the Practice of clever *Tom Clinch*,
Who hung like a Hero, and never would flinch.

HOLYHEAD.[1] SEPT. 25. 1727

(1727, 1882)

Lo here I sit at holy head
With muddy ale and mouldy bread
All Christian vittals stink of fish
I'm where my enemyes would wish
Convict of lyes is every sign,
The Inn has not one drop of wine
I'm fasnd both by wind and tide
I see the ship at anchor ride
The Captain swears the sea's too rough
He has not passengers enough.   10
And thus the Dean is forc't to stay
Till others come to help the pay
In Dublin they'd be glad to see
A packet[2] though it brings in me.
They cannot say the winds are cross
Your Politicians at a loss
For want of matter swears and fretts,
Are forced to read the old gazettes.
I never was in hast before
To reach that slavish hateful shore   20
Before, I always found the wind
To me was most malicious kind
But now, the danger of a friend
On whom my fears and hopes depend
Absent from whom all Clymes are curst
With whom I'm happy in the worst
With rage impatient makes me wait
A passage to the land I hate.
Else, rather on this bleaky shore
Where loudest winds incessant roar   30
Where neither herb nor tree will thrive,
Where nature hardly seems alive.[3]

I'd go in freedom to my grave,
Than Rule yon Isle and be a Slave.

IREL.ᵈ

(1727, 1882)

Remove me from this land of slaves
Where all are fools, and all are knaves
Where every knave & fool is bought
Yet kindly sells himself for nought
Where Whig and Tory fiercely fight
Who's in the wrong, who in the right
And when their country lyse at stake
They only fight for fighting sake,
While English sharpers take the pay,
And then stand by to see fair play,
Mean time the whig is always winner
And for his courage gets—a dinner.
His Excellency[1] too perhaps
Spits in his mouth and stroaks his Chaps[2]
The humble whelp gives ev'ry vote.
To put the question strains his throat.
His Excellency's condescension
Will serve instead of place or pension
When to the window he's trepan'd[3]
When my Lᵈ shakes him by the hand
Or in the presence of beholders,
His arms upon the booby's shoulders
You quickly see the gudgeon bite,
He tells his brothʳ fools at night
How well the Governor's inclind.
So just, so gentle and so kind
He heard I kept a pack of hounds,
And longd to hunt upon my grounds
He sd our Ladyes were so fair
The land had nothing to compair.
But that indeed which pleasd me most
He calld my Dol a perfect toast.

He whisprd publick things at last,
Askt me how our elections past.
Some augmentation⁴ Sʳ You know
Would make at least a handsom show
New Kings a compliment expect
I shall not offer to direct
There are some prating folks in town,
But Sʳ we must support the Crown.   40
Our Letters say a Jesuite boasts
Of some Invasion on your coasts
The King is ready when you will
To pass another Pop-ry bill
And for dissenters he intends
To use them as his truest friends
I think they justly ought to share
In all employmᵗˢ we can spare.⁵
Next for encouragemᵗ of spinning,
A duty might be layd on linnen   50
An act for laying down the Plough,
England will send you corn enough.
Anothʳ act that absentees
For licences shall pay no fees.
If Englands friendship you would keep
Feed nothing in your lands but sheep
But make an act secure and full
To hang up all who smuggle wool.
And then he kindly give me hints
That all our wives should go in Chints.⁶   60
To morrow I shall tell you more,
For I'm to dine with him at four
    This was the Speech, and here's the jest
His arguments convinc't the rest.
Away he runs with zealous hotness
Exceeding all the fools of Totness.
To move that all the Nation round
Should pay a guinea in the pound
Yet should this Blockhead beg a Place
Either from Excellence or grace   70
Tis pre engged and In his room
Townshends cast Page or Walpole's⁷ groom

DIRECTIONS FOR A BIRTH-DAY SONG
(1729, 1765)

To form a just and finish'd piece,
Take twenty Gods of Rome or Greece,
Whose Godships are in chief request,
And fit your present Subject best,
And should it be your Hero's case
To have both male & female Race,
Your bus'ness must be to provide
A score of Goddesses beside.

    Some call their Monarchs Sons of Saturn,
For which they bring a modern Pattern,   10
Because they might have heard of one
Who often long'd to eat his Son:
But this I think will not go down,
For here the Father kept his Crown,

    Why then appoint him Son of Jove,
Who met his Mother in a grove;
To this we freely shall consent,
Well knowing what the Poets meant:
And in their Sense, 'twixt me and you,
It may be literally true.   20

    Next, as the Laws of Song require,
He must be greater than his Sire:
For Jove, as every School-boy knows,
Was able Saturn to depose;
And sure no Christian Poet breathing
Should be more scrup'lous than a Heathen.
Or if to Blasphemy it tends,
That's but a trifle among Friends.

    Your Hero now another Mars is,
Makes mighty Armys turn their Arses.   30
Behold his glitt'ring Faulchion[1] mow
Whole Squadrons with a single blow:
While Victory, with Wings outspread,
Flyes like an Eagle or'e his head;
His milk-white Steed upon it's haunches,

Or pawing into dead mens paunches.
As Overton[2] has drawn his Sire
Still seen o'r'e many an Alehouse fire.
Then from his Arm hoarse thunder rolls
As loud as fifty mustard bowls;   40
For thunder still his arm supplyes,
And lightning always in his Eyes:
They both are cheap enough in Conscience,
And serve to eccho ratling Nonsense;
The rumbling words march fierce along,
Made trebly dreadfull in your Song.

    Sweet Poet, hir'd for birth-day Rimes,
To sing of Wars choose peaceful times.
What tho for fifteen years and more
Janus hath lock'd his Temple-door?   50
Tho not a Coffee-house we read in
Hath mention'd arms on this side Sweden;
Nor London Journals, nor the Post-men,
Tho fond of warlike Lyes as most men;
Thou still with Battles stuff thy head full
For must a Hero not be dreadfull?

    Dismissing Mars, it next must follow
Your Conqu'rer is become Apollo:
That he's Apollo, is as plain, as
That Robin Walpole is Mecaenas:[3]   60
But that he struts, and that he squints,
You'd know him by Apollo's Prints
    But that he squints, and that he struts,
    You'd know him by Apollo's Cuts.
Old Phœbus is but half as bright,
For yours can shine both day and night,
The first perhaps may once an Age
Inspire you with poetick Rage;
Your Phœbus royal, every day
Not only can inspire, but pay.   70

    Then make this new Apollo sit
Sole Patron, Judge, and God of Wit.
"How from his Altitude he stoops,
"To raise up Virtue when she droops,

"On Learning how his Bounty flows,
"And with what Justice he bestows.
"Fair Isis, and ye Banks of Cam,
"Be witness if I tell a Flam:
"What Prodigys in Arts we drain
"From both your Streams in George's Reign! 80
"As from the flowry Bed of Nile—
But here's enough to shew your Style.

  Broad Innuendos, such as this,
If well apply'd, can hardly miss:
For when you bring your Song in print,
He'll get it read, and take the hint,
(It must be read before 'tis warbled
The paper gilt, & Cover marbled)
And will be so much more your Debter
Because he never knew a letter. 90
And as he hears his Wit and Sence,
To which he never made pretence,
Set out in Hyperbolick Strains,
A Guinea shall reward your pains.
For Patrons never pay so well,
As when they scarce have learn'd to spell.

  Next call him Neptune with his Trident,
He rules the Sea, you see him ride in't;
And if provok'd, he soundly ferks his
Rebellious Waves with rods like Xerxes. 100
He would have seiz'd the Spanish Plate,
Had not the Fleet gone out too late,
And in their very Ports besiege,
But that he would not disoblige,
And made the Rascals pay him dearly
For those affronts they give him yearly.

  'Tis not deny'd that when we write,
Our Ink is black, our Paper white;
And when we scrawl our Paper o'r'e,
We blacken what was white before. 110
I think this Practice only fit
For dealers in Satyrick Wit:
But you some white-lead ink must get,

And write on paper black as Jet:
Your Int'rest lyes to learn the knack
Of whitening what before was black.

    Thus your Encomiums, to be strong,
Must be apply'd directly wrong:
A Tyrant for his Mercy praise,
And crown a Royal Dunce with Bays: 120
A squinting Monkey load with charms;
And paint a Coward fierce in arms.
Is he to Avarice inclin'd?
Extol him for his generous mind:
And when we starve for want of Corn,
Come out with Amalthea's Horn.
For Princes love you should descant
On Virtues which they know they want.

    One Compliment I had forgot,
But Songsters must omit it not.   130
(I freely grant the Thought is old)
Why then, your Hero must be told,
In him such Virtues lye inherent,
To qualify him God's Vicegerent,
That with no Title to inherit,
He must have been a King by Merit.
Yet be the Fancy old or new,
'Tis partly false, and partly true,
And take it right, it means no more
Than George and William[4] claim'd before.   140

    Should some obscure inferior fellow
As Julius, or the Youth of Pella,[5]
When all your list of Gods is out,
Presume to shew his mortal snout,
And as a Deity intrude,
Because he had the world subdu'd:
Oh! let him not debase your Thoughts,
Or name him, but to tell his Faults.

    Of Gods I only quote the best,
But you may hook in all the rest.   150
    Now Birth-day Bard, with joy proceed
To praise your Empress, and her Breed.

First, of the first. To vouch your Lyes
Bring all the Females of the Skyes:
The Graces and their Mistress Venus
Must venture down to entertain us.
With bended knees when they adore her
What Dowdys they appear before her!
Nor shall we think you talk at random,
For Venus might be her great Grandam.   160
Six thousand years hath liv'd the Goddess,
Your Heroine hardly fifty odd is.
Besides you Songsters oft have shewn,
That she hath Graces of her own:
Three Graces by Lucina brought her,
Just three; and every Grace a Daughter.
Here many a King his heart and Crown
Shall at their snowy feet lay down:
In Royal Robes they come by dozens
To court their English German Cousins,   170
Besides a pair of princely Babyes,
That five years hence will both be Hebes.

　　Now see her seated on her Throne
With genuin lustre all her own.
Poor Cynthia[6] never shone so bright,
Her Splendor is but borrow'd light;
And only with her Brother linkt
Can shine, without him is extinct.
But Carolina[7] shines the clearer
With neither Spouse nor Brother near her,   180
And darts her Beams or'e both our Isles,
Tho George is gone a thousand miles.
Thus Berecynthia[8] takes her place,
Attended by her heavenly Race,
And sees a Son in every God
Unaw'd by Jove's all-shaking Nod.

　　Now sing his little Highness Freddy,[9]
Who struts like any King already.
With so much beauty, shew me any maid
That could refuse this charming Ganymede,   190
Where Majesty with Sweetness vyes,

And like his Father early wise.
Then cut him out a world of work,
To conquer Spain, and quell the Turk.
Foretell his Empire crown'd with Bays,
And golden Times, and Halcyon days,
But swear his Line shall rule the Nation
For ever—till the Conflagration.

    But now it comes into my mind,
We left a little Duke behind;   200
A Cupid in his face and size,
And only wants to want his eyes.
Make some provision for the Yonker,[10]
Find him a Kingdom out to conquer;
Prepare a Fleet to waft him o'r'e,
Make Gulliver his Commodore,
Into whose pocket valiant Willy put,
Will soon subdue the Realm of Lilliput.

    A skilfull Critick justly blames
Hard, tough, cramp, gutt'rall, harsh, stiff Names.
The Sense can ne're be too jejune,   210
But smooth your words to fit the tune,
Hanover may do well enough;
But George, and Brunswick are too rough.
Hesse Darmstedt makes too rough a sound,
And Guelph the strongest ear will wound.
In vain are all attempts from Germany
To find out proper words for Harmony:
And yet I must except the Rhine,
Because it clinks to Caroline.   220
Hail Queen of Britain, Queen of Rhymes,
Be sung ten hundred thousand times.
Too happy were the Poets Crew,
If their own happyness they knew.
Three Syllables did never meet
So soft, so sliding, and so sweet.
Nine other tuneful words like that
Would prove ev'n Homer's Numbers flat.
Behold three beauteous Vowels stand
With Bridegroom liquids hand in hand,   230

In Concord here for ever fixt,
No jarring consonant betwixt.
    May Caroline continue long,
For ever fair and young—in Song.
What tho the royal Carcase must
Squeez'd in a Coffin turn to dust;
Those Elements her name compose,
Like Atoms are exempt from blows.
    Tho Caroline may fill your gaps
Yet still you must consult the Maps,   240
Find Rivers with harmonious names,
Sabrina, Medway, and the Thames.
Britannia long will wear like Steel
But Albion's cliffs are out at heel,
And Patience can endure no more
To hear the Belgick Lyon roar.
Give up the phrase of haughty Gaul,
But proud Iberia soundly maul,
Restore the Ships by Philip taken,
And make him crouch to save his bacon.   250
    Nassau,[11] who got the name of glorious
Because he never was victorious,
A hanger on has always been,
For old acquaintance bring him in.
    To Walpole you might lend a Line,
But much I fear he's in decline;
And if you chance to come too late
When he goes out, you share his fate,
And bear the new Successor's frown;
Or whom you once sung up, sing down.   260
    Reject with scorn that stupid Notion
To praise your Hero for Devotion:
Nor entertain a thought so odd,
That Princes should believe in God:
But follow the securest rule,
And turn it all to ridicule:
'Tis grown the choicest Wit at Court,
And gives the Maids of Honor Sport.
For since they talk'd with Doctor Clark,[12]

They now can venture in the dark. 270
That sound Divine the Truth has spoke all
And pawn'd his word Hell is not local.
This will not give them half the trouble
Of Bargains sold, or meanings double.
    Supposing now your Song is done,
To Minheer Hendel[13] next you run,
Who artfully will pare and prune
Your words to some Italian Tune.
Then print it in the largest letter,
With Capitals, the more the better. 280
    Present it boldly on your knee,
And take a Guinea for your Fee.

A Dialogue between an eminent Lawyer[1] and Dr. Swift Dean of St. Patrick's, being an allusion to the first Satire of the second book of Horace

Sunt quibus in satyra, &c.

(1 7 2 9 , 1 7 5 5)

Since there are persons who complain
There's too much satire in my vein,
That I am often found exceeding
The rules of raillery and breeding,
With too much freedom treat my betters,
Not sparing even men of letters,
You, who are skill'd in lawyer's lore,
What's your advice? shall I give o're,
Nor ever fools or knaves expose
Either in verse or hum'rous prose, 10
And, to avoid all future ill,
In my 'scritore[2] lock up my quill?
    Since you are pleas'd to condescend
To ask the judgment of a friend,

Your case consider'd, I must think
You shou'd withdraw from pen and ink,
Forbear your poetry and jokes,
And live like other christian fokes;
Or, if the MUSES must inspire
Your fancy with their pleasing fire,   20
Take subjects safer for your wit
Than those on which you lately writ,
Commend the times, your thoughts correct
And follow the prevailing sect,
Assert that HYDE[3] in writing story
Shews all the malice of a TORY,
While BURNET[4] in his deathless page
Discovers freedom without rage;
To WOOLSTON[5] recommend our youth
For learning, probity and truth,   30
That noble genius, who unbinds
The chains which fetter free-born minds,
Redeems us from the slavish fears
Which lasted near two thousand years,
He can alone the priesthood humble,
Make gilded spires and altars tumble.

    MUST I commend against my conscience
Such stupid blasphemy and nonsense?
To such a subject tune my lyre
And sing like one of MILTON's choir,   40
Where DEVILS to a vale retreat
And call the laws of wisdom fate,
Lament upon their hapless fall
That force free virtue shou'd enthrall?
Or, shall the charms of wealth and power
Make me pollute the MUSES' bower?

    As from the tripod of APOLLO
Hear from my desk the words that follow;
Some by philosophers misled,
Must honour you alive and dead,   50
And such as know what *Greece* has writ
Must taste your irony and wit,
While most that are or would be great,
Must dread your pen, your person hate,

And you on DRAPIER's *Hill* must lye,
And there without a mitre dye.

TRAULUS

The First Part. In a Dialogue between Tom and Robin.
(1730)

TOM.

Say, *Robin,* what can *Traulus* mean
By bell'wing thus against the D—?
Why does he call him paultry Scribler,
Papist, and *Jacobite,* and *Lib'ller?*
Yet cannot prove a single Fact.

ROBIN.

Forgive him, *Tom,* his Head is crackt.

TOM.

What Mischief can the D— have done him,
That *Traulus* calls for Vengeance on him?
Why must he sputter, spaul and slaver it
In vain, against the People's Fav'rite?   10
Revile that Nation-saving Paper,
Which gave the D— the Name of *Draper?*

ROBIN.

Why *Tom,* I think the Case is plain,
Party and Spleen have turn'd his Brain,

TOM.

Such Friendship never Man profest,
The D— was never so carest:
For *Traulus* long his Rancour nurst,
Till, God knows why, at last it burst.

That clumsy outside of a Porter,
How could it thus conceal a Courtier?   20

ROBIN.

I own, Appearances are bad;
But still insist the Man is mad.

TOM.

Yet many a Wretch in *Bedlam*, knows,
How to distinguish Friends from Foes;
And tho' perhaps among the Rout,
He wildly flings his Filth about,
He still has Gratitude and Sap'ence,
To spare the Folks that gave him Ha'pence
Nor, in their Eyes at Random pisses,
But turns aside like mad *Ulysses:*   30
While *Traulus* all his Ordure scatters.
To foul the Man he chiefly flatters.
Whence come these inconsistent Fits?

ROBIN.

Why *Tom,* the Man has lost his Wits!

TOM.

Agreed. And yet, when *Towzer* snaps
At People's Heels with frothy Chaps;
Hang's down his Head, and drops his Tail,
To say he's mad will not avail:
The Neighbours all cry, *Shoot him dead,*
Hang, Drown, or knock him on the Head.   40
So, *Traulus* when he first harangu'd,
I wonder why he was not hang'd:
For of the two, without Dispute,
Towzer's the less offensive Brute.

ROBIN.

Tom, you mistake the Matter quite;
Your barking Curs will seldom bite:

And, though you hear him Stut-tut-tut-ter,
He barks as fast as he can utter.
He prates in Spight of all Impediment
While none believes that what he said he meant: 50
Puts in his Finger and his Thumb,
To grope for Words, and out they come.
He calls you Rogue; There's nothing in it,
He fawns upon you in a Minute.
Begs leave to rail, but d—n his Blood,
He only meant it for your Good.
His Friendship was exactly tim'd,
He shot before your Foes were prim'd:
By this Contrivance Mr. D—
By G— I'll bring you off as clean.—   60
Then let him use you e'er so rough,
'Twas all for Love, and that's enough.
For let him sputter thro' a S - ss - n,
It never makes the least Impression.
What e'er he speaks for Madness goes,
With no Effect on Friends or Foes.

TOM.

The scrubest Cur in all the Pack
Can set the Mastiffs on your Back.
I own, his Madness is a Jest,
If that were all. But he's possess't: 70
Incarnate with a thousand Imps,
To work whose Ends, his Madness pimps.
Who o'er each String and Wire preside,
Fill ev'ry Pipe, each Motion guide.
Directing ev'ry Vice we find
In Scripture, to the Dev'l assign'd.
Sent from the Dark infernal Region
In him they lodge, and make him *Legion*.[1]
Of *Brethren* he's *a false Accuser,*
A Sland'rer, Traytor and Seducer;   80
A fawning, base, trepaning Lyar,
The Marks peculiar of his Sire.

Or, grant him but a Drone at best:
A Drone can raise a Hornet's Nest:
The D— hath felt their Stings before;
And, must their Malice ne'er give o'er?
Still swarm and buzz about his Nose?
But *Ireland*'s Friends ne'er wanted Foes.
A Patriot is a dang'rous Post
When wanted by his Country most;   90
Perversely comes in evil Times,
Where Virtues are imputed Crimes,
His Guilt is clear the Proofs are pregnant,
A Traytor to the Vices regnant.

What Spirit since the World began,
Could *always* bear to *Strive with Man?*
Which God pronounc'd he never wou'd,
And soon convinc'd them by a Flood.
Yet still the D— on Freedom raves,
His Spirit always strives with Slaves.   100
'Tis Time at last to spare his Ink,
And let them rot, or hang, or stink.

Traulus

The Second Part.

Traulus of amphibious Breed,
Motly Fruit of Mungril Seed:
By the *Dam* from Lordlings sprung,
By the *Sire* exhal'd from Dung:
Think on ev'ry Vice in both,
Look on him and see their Growth.

VIEW him on the Mother's Side,
Fill'd with Falshood, Spleen and Pride;
Positive and over-bearing,
Changing still, and still adhering,   10
Spightful, peevish, rude, untoward;
Fierce in Tongue, in Heart a Coward:

When his Friends he most is hard on,
Cringing comes to beg their Pardon;
Reputation ever tearing,
Ever dearest Friendship swearing;
Judgement weak, and Passion strong,
Always various, always wrong:
Provocation never waits,
Where he loves, or where he hates.   20
Talks whate'er comes in his Head,
Wishes it were all unsaid.

    LET me now the Vices trace,
From his *Father*'s scoundrel Race,
Who cou'd give the Looby such Airs?
Were they Masons, were they Butchers?
Herald lend the Muse an answer;
From his *Atavus*[2] and Grandsire;
This was dext'rous at his Trowel,
That was bred to kill a Cow well: 30
Hence the greazy clumsy Mien,
In his Dress and Figure seen:
Hence that mean and sordid Soul,
Like his Body, rank and foul:
Hence that wild suspicious Peep,
Like a Rogue that steals a Sheep:
Hence he learnt the Butcher's Guile,
How to cut a Throat and smile:
Like a Butcher doom'd for Life,
In his Mouth to wear his Knife.   40
Hence he draws his daliy Food,
From his Tenants vital Blood.

    LASTLY, let his Gifts be try'd,
Borrow'd from the Mason Side:
Some perhaps may think him able
In the State to build a *Babel*:
Cou'd we place him in a Station,
To destroy the old *Foundation*,
True indeed, I should be gladder,
Cou'd he learn to mount a Ladder.[3]   50

———

MAY he at his latter End
Mount alive, and dead descend.

IN him, tell me which prevail,
Female Vices most, or Male,
What produc'd them, can you tell?
Human Race, or *Imps* of *Hell*.

THE LADY'S DRESSING ROOM
(1730, 1732)

Five Hours, (and who can do it less in?)
By haughty *Celia* spent in Dressing;
The Goddess from her Chamber issues,
Array'd in Lace, Brocades and Tissues.

  Strephon, who found the Room was void,
And *Betty* otherwise employ'd;
Stole in, and took a strict Survey,
Of all the Litter as it lay;
Whereof, to make the Matter clear,
An Inventory follows here.   10

  And first a dirty Smock appear'd,
Beneath the Arm-pits well besmear'd.
Strephon, the Rogue, display'd it wide,
And turn'd it round on every Side.
On such a Point few Words are best,
And *Strephon* bids us guess the rest;
But swears how damnably the Men lie,
In calling *Celia* sweet and cleanly.
Now listen while he next produces,
The various Combs for various Uses,   20
Fill'd up with Dirt so closely fixt,
No Brush could force a way betwixt,
A Paste of Composition rare,

Sweat, Dandriff, Powder, Lead and Hair;
A Forehead Cloth with Oyl upon't
To smooth the Wrinkles on her Front;
Here Allum Flower[1] to stop the Steams,
Exhal'd from sour unsavoury Streams,
There Night-gloves made of *Tripsy*'s Hide,
Bequeath'd by *Tripsy*[2] when she dy'd,   30
With Puppy Water,[3] Beauty's Help
Distill'd from *Tripsy*'s darling Whelp;
Here Gallypots[4] and Vials plac'd,
Some fill'd with Washes, some with Paste,
Some with Pomatum, Paints and Slops,
And Ointments good for scabby Chops.
Hard by a filthy Bason stands,
Fowl'd with the Scouring of her Hands;
The Bason takes whatever comes
The Scrapings of her Teeth and Gums,   40
A nasty Compound of all Hues,
For here she spits, and here she spues.
But oh! it turn'd poor *Strephon*'s Bowels,
When he beheld and smelt the Towels,
Begumm'd,[5] bematter'd, and beslim'd
With Dirt, and Sweat, and Ear-Wax grim'd.
No Object *Strephon*'s Eye escapes,
Here Pettycoats in frowzy[6] Heaps;
Nor be the Handkerchiefs forgot
All varnish'd o'er with Snuff and Snot.   50
The Stockings, why shou'd I expose,
Stain'd with the Marks of stinking Toes;
Or greasy Coifs and Pinners reeking,
Which *Celia* slept at least a Week in?
A Pair of Tweezers next he found
To pluck her Brows in Arches round,
Or, Hairs that sink the Forehead low,
Or on her Chin like Bristles grow.

    The Virtues we must not let pass,
Of *Celia*'s magnifying Glass.   60
When frighted *Strephon* cast his Eye on't

It shew'd the Visage of a Gyant.
A Glass that can to Sight disclose,
The smallest Worm in *Celia*'s Nose,
And faithfully direct her Nail
To squeeze it out from Head to Tail;
For catch it nicely by the Head,
It must come out alive or dead.

    Why *Strephon* will you tell the rest?
And must you needs describe the Chest?   70
That careless Wench! no Creature warn her
To move it out from yonder Corner;
But leave it standing full in Sight
For you to exercise your Spight.
In vain, the Workmen shew'd his Wit
With Rings and Hinges counterfeit
To make it seem in this Disguise,
A Cabinet to vulgar Eyes;
For *Strephon* ventur'd to look in,
Resolv'd to go thro' thick and thin;   80
He lifts the Lid, there needs no more,
He smelt it all the Time before.
As from within *Pandora*'s Box,[7]
When *Epimetheus* op'd the Locks,
A sudden universal Crew
Of humane Evils upwards flew;
He still was comforted to find
That *Hope* at last remain'd behind;
So *Strephon* lifting up the Lid,
To view what in the Chest was hid.   90
The Vapours flew from out the Vent,
But *Strephon* cautious never meant
The Bottom of the Pan to grope,
And fowl his Hands in Search of *Hope*.
O never may such vile Machine
Be once in *Celia*'s Chamber seen!
O may she better learn to keep
"Those Secrets of the hoary deep![8]

—

As Mutton Cutlets, Prime of Meat,
Which tho' with Art you salt and beat,   100
As Laws of Cookery require,
And toast them at the clearest Fire;
If from adown the hopeful Chops
The Fat upon a Cinder drops,
To stinking Smoak it turns the Flame
Pois'ning the Flesh from whence it came;
And up exhales a greasy Stench,
For which you curse the careless Wench;
So Things, which must not be exprest,
When plumpt into the reeking Chest;   110
Send up an excremental Smell
To taint the Parts from whence they fell.
The Pettycoats and Gown perfume,
Which waft a Stink round every Room.

Thus finishing his grand Survey,
Disgusted *Strephon* stole away
Repeating in his amorous Fits,
Oh! *Celia, Celia, Celia* shits!

But Vengeance, Goddess never sleeping
Soon punish'd Strephon for his Peeping;   120
His foul Imagination links
Each Dame he sees with all her Stinks:
And, if unsav'ry Odours fly,
Conceives a Lady standing by;
All Women his Description fits,
And both Idea's jump like Wits:
By vicious Fancy coupled fast,
And still appearing in Contrast.
I pity wretched *Strephon* blind
To all the Charms of Female Kind;   130
Should I the Queen of Love[9] refuse,
Because she rose from stinking Ooze?
To him that looks behind the Scene,
Satira's but some pocky Quean.[10]
When *Celia* in her Glory shows,

If *Strephon* would but stop his Nose;
(Who now so impiously blasphemes
Her Ointments, Daubs, and Paints and Creams,
Her Washes, Slops, and every Clout,
With which he makes so foul a Rout;)   140
He soon would learn to think like me,
And bless his ravisht Sight to see
Such Order from Confusion sprung,
Such gaudy Tulips rais'd from Dung.[11]

A Beautiful Young Nymph Going to Bed
(1731?, 1734)

Corinna, Pride of *Drury-Lane*,[1]
For whom no Shepherd sighs in vain;
Never did *Covent Garden* boast
So bright a batter'd, strolling Toast;[2]
No drunken Rake to pick her up,
No Cellar where on Tick[3] to sup;
Returning at the Midnight Hour;
Four Stories climbing to her Bow'r;
Then, seated on a three-legg'd Chair,
Takes off her artificial Hair: 10
Now, picking out a Crystal Eye,
She wipes it clean, and lays it by.
Her Eye-Brows from a Mouse's Hyde,
Stuck on with Art on either Side,
Pulls off with Care, and first displays 'em,
Then in a Play-Book smoothly lays 'em.
Now dextrously her Plumpers[4] draws,
That serve to fill her hollow Jaws.
Untwists a Wire; and from her Gums
A Set of Teeth completely comes.   20
Pulls out the Rags contriv'd to prop
Her flabby Dugs and down they drop.
Proceeding on, the lovely Goddess
Unlaces next her Steel-Rib'd Bodice;

Which by the Operator's Skill,
Press down the Lumps, the Hollows fill,
Up goes her Hand, and off she slips
The Bolsters that supply her Hips.
With gentlest Touch, she next explores
Her Shankers,[5] Issues,[6] running Sores,   30
Effects of many a sad Disaster;
And then to each applies a Plaister.
But must, before she goes to Bed,
Rub off the Dawbs of White and Red;[7]
And smooth the Furrows in her Front,
With greasy Paper stuck upon't.
She takes a *Bolus*[8] e'er she sleeps;
And then between two Blankets creeps.
With Pains of Love tormented lies;
Or if she chance to close her Eyes,   40
Of *Bridewell* and the *Compter*[9] dreams,
And feels the Lash, and faintly screams;
Or, by a faithless Bully drawn,
At some Hedge-Tavern[10] lies in Pawn;
Or to *Jamaica* seems transported,[11]
Alone, and by no Planter courted;*
Or, near *Fleet-Ditch*'s oozy Brinks,
Surrounded with a Hundred Stinks,
Belated, seems on watch to lye,
And snap some Cully[13] passing by;   50
Or, struck with Fear, her Fancy runs
On Watchmen, Constables and Duns,[14]
From whom she meets with frequent Rubs;[15]
But, never from Religious Clubs;[16]
Whose Favour she is sure to find,
Because she pays 'em all in Kind.
    CORINNA wakes. A dreadful Sight!
Behold the Ruins of the Night!
A wicked Rat her Plaister stole,
Half eat, and dragg'd it to his Hole.   60
The Crystal Eye, alas, was miss't;

---

* —*Et longam incomitata videtur Ire viam*—[12]

And *Puss* had on her Plumpers p---st.
A Pigeon pick'd her Issue-Peas;[17]
And *Shock* [18] her Tresses fill'd with Fleas.
    THE Nymph, tho' in this mangled Plight,
Must ev'ry Morn her Limbs unite.
But how shall I describe her Arts
To recollect the scatter'd Parts?
Or shew the Anguish, Toil, and Pain,
Of gath'ring up herself again?   70
The bashful Muse will never bear
In such a Scene to interfere.
Corinna in the Morning dizen'd,
Who sees, will spew; who smells, be poison'd.

STREPHON AND CHLOE
(1731, 1734)

Of *Chloe* all the Town has rung;
By ev'ry size of Poets sung:
So beautiful a Nymph appears
But once in Twenty Thousand Years.
By Nature form'd with nicest Care,
And, faultless to a single Hair.
Her graceful Mein, her Shape, and Face,
Confest her of no mortal Race:
And then, so nice, and so genteel;
Such Cleanliness from Head to Heel: 10
No Humours gross, or frowzy Steams,
No noisom Whiffs, or sweaty Streams,
Before, behind, above, below,
Could from her taintless Body flow.
Would so discreetly Things dispose,
None ever saw her pluck a Rose.
Her dearest Comrades never caught her
Squat on her Hams, to make Maid's Water.
You'd swear, that so divine a Creature
Felt no Necessities of Nature.   20

In Summer had she walkt the Town,
Her Arm-pits would not stain her Gown:
At Country Dances, not a Nose
Could in the Dog-Days smell her Toes.
Her Milk-white Hands, both Palms and Backs,
Like Iv'ry dry, and soft as Wax.
Her Hands the softest ever felt,
Tho' cold would burn, tho' dry would melt.*

    DEAR *Venus* hide this wond'rous Maid,
Nor let her loose to spoil your Trade.   30
While she engrosseth ev'ry Swain,
You but o'er half the World can reign.
Think what a Case all Men are now in,
What ogling, sighing, toasting, vowing!
What powder'd Wigs! What Flames and Darts!
What Hampers full of bleeding Hearts!
What Sword-knots! What Poetic Strains!
What Billet-doux, and clouded Cains!

    BUT, *Strephon* sigh'd so loud and strong,
He blew a Settlement along: 40
And, bravely drove his Rivals down
With Coach and Six, and House in Town.
The bashful Nymph no more withstands,
Because her dear Papa commands.
The charming Couple now unites;
Proceed we to the Marriage Rites.

    IMPRIMIS, at the Temple Porch
Stood *Hymen* with a flaming Torch.
The smiling *Cyprian* Goddess brings
Her infant Loves with purple Wings;   50
And Pigeons billing, Sparrows treading,
Fair Emblems of a fruitful Wedding.
The Muses next in Order follow,
Conducted by their Squire, *Apollo:*
Then *Mercury* with Silver Tongue,
And *Hebe,* Goddess ever young.
    Behold the Bridegroom and his Bride,

---

* *Tho' deep, yet clear,* &c. DENHAM.

Walk Hand in Hand, and Side by Side;
She by the tender Graces drest,
But, he by *Mars,* in Scarlet Vest.   60
The Nymph was cover'd with her *Flammeum,**
And *Phœbus* sung th' *Epithalamium.*
And, last to make the Matter sure,
Dame *Juno* brought a Priest demure.
Luna† was absent on Pretence
Her Time was not till Nine Months hence.
   THE Rites perform'd, the Parson paid,
In State return'd the grand Parade;
With loud Huzza's from all the Boys,
That now the Pair must *crown their Joys.*   70
   BUT, still the hardest Part remains.
Strephon had long perplex'd his Brains,
How with so high a Nymph he might
Demean himself the Wedding-Night:
For, as he view'd his Person round,
Meer mortal Flesh was all he found:
His Hand, his Neck, his Mouth, and Feet
Were duly washt to keep 'em sweet;
(With other Parts that shall be nameless,
The Ladies else might think me shameless.)   80
The Weather and his Love were hot;
And should he struggle; I know what—
Why let it go, if I must tell it—
He'll sweat, and then the Nymph may smell it.
While she a Goddess dy'd in Grain
Was unsusceptible of Stain:
And, *Venus*-like, her fragrant Skin
Exhal'd *Ambrosia* from within:
Can such a Deity endure
A mortal human Touch impure?   90
How did the humbled Swain detest
His prickled Beard, and hairy Breast!

* A Veil which the *Roman* Brides covered themselves with, when they were going to be married.
  † *Diana,* Goddess of Midwives.

His Night-Cap border'd round with Lace
Could give no Softness to his Face.

    YET, if the Goddess could be kind,
What endless Raptures must he find!
And Goddesses have now and then
Come down to visit mortal Men:
To visit and to court them too;
A certain Goddess,[1] God knows who,   100
(As in a Book he heard it read)
Took Col'nel *Peleus* to her Bed.
But, what if he should lose his Life
By vent'ring *on* his heav'nly Wife?
For *Strephon* could remember well,
That, once he heard a School-boy tell,
How *Semele* of mortal Race,
By Thunder dy'd in *Jove*'s Embrace;
And what if daring *Strephon* dies
By Lightning shot from *Chloe*'s Eyes?   110

    WHILE these Reflections fill'd his Head,
The Bride was put in Form to Bed;
He follow'd, stript, and in he crept,
But, awfully his Distance kept.

    Now, *Ponder well ye Parents dear*,
Forbid your Daughters guzzling Beer;
And make them ev'ry Afternoon
Forbear their Tea, or drink it soon;
That, e'er to Bed they venture up,
They may discharge it ev'ry Sup;   120
If not, they must in evil Plight
Be often forc'd to rise at Night,
Keep them to wholesome Food confin'd
Nor let them taste what causes Wind;
('Tis this the Sage of *Samos* means,
Forbidding his Disciples Beans)*[1]
O, think what Evils must ensue;
Miss *Moll* the Jade will burn it blue:
And when she once has got the Art,

---

* A well known Precept of *Pythagoras*, not to eat Beans.

She cannot help it for her Heart;   130
But, out it flies, even when she meets
Her Bridegroom in the Wedding-Sheets.
Carminative * and *Diuretick,* †
Will damp all Passion Sympathetick;
And, Love such Nicety requires,
One *Blast* will put out all his Fires.
Since Husbands get behind the Scene,
The Wife should study to be clean;
Nor give the smallest Room to guess
The Time when Wants of Nature press;   140
    BUT, after Marriage, practise more
Decorum than she did before;
To keep her Spouse deluded still,
And make him fancy what she will.
    IN Bed we left the married Pair;
'Tis Time to shew how Things went there.
Strephon, who had been often told,
That Fortune still assists the bold,
Resolv'd to make his first Attack:
But, *Chloe* drove him fiercely back.   150
How could a Nymph so chaste as *Chloe,*
With Constitution cold and snowy,
Permit a brutish Man to touch her?
Ev'n Lambs by Instinct fly the Butcher.
Resistance on the Wedding-Night
Is what our Maidens claim by Right:
And, *Chloe,* 'tis by all agreed,
Was Maid in Thought, and Word, and Deed,
Yet, some assign a diff'rent Reason;
That *Strephon* chose no proper Season.   160
    SAY, fair ones, must I make a Pause?
Or freely tell the secret Cause.
    TWELVE Cups of Tea, (with Grief I speak)
Had now constrain'd the Nymph to leak.
This Point must needs be settled first;

* Medicines to break Wind.
† Medicines to provoke Urine.

The Bride must either void or burst.
Then, see the dire Effect of Pease,
Think what can give the Colick Ease,
The Nymph opprest before, behind,
As Ships are toss't by Waves and Wind,   170
Steals out her Hand by Nature led,
And brings a Vessel into Bed:
Fair Utensil, as smooth and white
As *Chloe*'s Skin, almost as bright.
    STREPHON who heard the fuming Rill
As from a mossy Cliff distill;
Cry'd out, ye Gods, what Sound is this?
Can *Chloe,* heav'nly *Chloe*—?
But, when he smelt a noysom Steam
Which oft attends that luke-warm Stream;   180
(*Salerno** both together joins
As sov'reign Med'cines for the Loins)
And, though contriv'd, we may suppose
To slip his Ears, yet struck his Nose:
He found her, while the Scent increas'd,
As *mortal* as himself at least.
But, soon with like Occasions prest,
He boldly sent his Hand in quest,
(Inspir'd with Courage from his Bride,)
To reach the Pot on t'other Side.   190
And as he fill'd the reeking Vase,
Let fly a Rouzer in her Face.
    THE little *Cupids* hov'ring round,
(As Pictures prove) with Garlands crown'd,
Abasht at what they saw and heard,
Flew off, nor evermore appear'd.
    ADIEU to ravishing Delights,
High Raptures, and romantick Flights;
To Goddesses so heav'nly sweet,
Expiring Shepherds at their Feet;   200
To silver Meads, and shady Bow'rs,
Drest up with *Amaranthine* Flow'rs.

* Vide Schol. *Salern. Rules of Health, written by the School of* Salernum. *Mingere cum bumbis res est saluberrima lumbis.*

How great a Change! how quickly made!
They learn to call a Spade, a Spade.
They soon from all Constraint are freed;
Can see each other *do their Need*.
On Box of Cedar sits the Wife,
And makes it warm for *Dearest Life*.
And, by the beastly way of Thinking,
Find great Society in Stinking.   210
Now *Strephon* daily entertains
His *Chloe* in the homeli'st Strains;
And, *Chloe* more experienc'd grown,
With Int'rest pays him back his own.
No Maid at Court is less asham'd,
Howe'er for selling Bargains fam'd,
Than she, to name her Parts behind,
Or when a-bed, to let out Wind.

     FAIR *Decency*, celestial Maid,
Descend from Heav'n to Beauty's Aid;   220
Though Beauty may beget Desire,
'Tis thou must fan the Lover's Fire;
For, Beauty, like supreme Dominion,
Is best supported by Opinion;
If Decency brings no Supplies,
Opinion falls, and Beauty dies.

     To see some radiant Nymph appear
In all her glitt'ring Birth-day Gear,
You think some Goddess from the Sky
Descended, ready cut and dry: 230
But, e'er you sell your self to Laughter,
Consider well what may come after;
For fine Ideas vanish fast,
While all the gross and filthy last.

     O *Strephon*, e'er that fatal Day
When *Chloe* stole your Heart away,
Had you but through a Cranny spy'd
On House of Ease your future Bride,
In all the Postures of her Face,
Which Nature gives in such a Case;   240
Distortions, Groanings, Strainings, Heavings;

'Twere better you had lickt her Leavings,
Than from Experience find too late
Your Goddess grown a filthy Mate.
Your Fancy then had always dwelt
On what you saw, and what you smelt;
Would still the same Ideas give ye,
As when you spy'd her on the Privy.
And, spight of *Chloe*'s Charms divine,
Your Heart had been as whole as mine.   250

AUTHORITIES both old and recent
Direct that Women must be decent;
And, from the Spouse each Blemish hide
More than from all the World beside.

UNJUSTLY all our Nymphs complain,
Their Empire holds so short a Reign;
Is after Marriage lost so soon,
It hardly holds the Honey-moon:
For, if they keep not what they caught,
It is entirely their own Fault.   260
They take Possession of the Crown,
And then throw all their Weapons down;
Though by the Politicians Scheme
Whoe'er arrives at Pow'r supreme,
Those Arts by which at first they gain it,
They still must practise to maintain it.

WHAT various Ways our Females take,
To pass for Wits before a Rake!
And in the fruitless Search pursue
All other Methods but the true.   270

SOME try to learn polite Behaviour,
By reading Books against their Saviour;
Some call it witty to reflect
On ev'ry natural Defect;
Some shew they never want explaining,
To comprehend a double Meaning.
But, sure a Tell-tale out of School
Is of all Wits the greatest Fool;
Whose rank Imagination fills,
Her Heart, and from her Lips distills;   280

You'd think she utter'd from behind,
Or at her Mouth was breaking Wind.
 WHY is a handsome Wife ador'd
By ev'ry Coxcomb, but her Lord?
From yonder Puppet-Man inquire,
Who wisely hides his Wood and Wire;
Shews *Sheba*'s Queen completely drest,
And *Solomon* in Royal Vest;
But, view them litter'd on the Floor,
Or strung on Pegs behind the Door;   290
Punch is exactly of a Piece
With *Lorraine*'s Duke, and Prince of *Greece*.
 A PRUDENT Builder should forecast
How long the Stuff is like to last;
And, carefully observe the Ground,
To build on some Foundation sound;
What House, when its Materials crumble,
Must not inevitably tumble?
What Edifice can long endure,
Rais'd on a Basis unsecure?   300
Rash Mortals, e'er you take a Wife,
Contrive your Pile to last for Life;
Since Beauty scarce endures a Day,
And Youth so swiftly glides away;
Why will you make yourself a Bubble
To build on Sand with Hay and Stubble?
 ON Sense and Wit your Passion found,
By Decency cemented round;
Let Prudence with Good Nature strive,
To keep Esteem and Love alive.   310
Then come old Age whene'er it will,
Your Friendship shall continue still:
And thus a mutual gentle Fire,
Shall never but with Life expire.

CASSINUS AND PETER

A Tragical Elegy

(1731, 1734)

Two College Sophs of *Cambridge* Growth,
Both special Wits, and Lovers both,
Conferring as they us'd to meet,
On Love and Books in Rapture sweet;
(Muse, find me to fix my Metre,
Cassinus this, and t'other *Peter*)
Friend *Peter* to *Cassinus* goes,
To chat a while, and warm his Nose:
But, such a Sight was never seen,
The Lad lay swallow'd up in Spleen;   10
He seem'd as just crept out of Bed;
One greasy Stocking round his Head,
The t'other he sat down to darn
With Threads of diff'rent colour'd Yarn.
His Breeches torn exposing wide
A ragged Shirt, and tawny Hyde.
Scorcht were his Shins, his Legs were bare,
But, well embrown'd with Dirt and Hair.
A Rug was o'er his Shoulders thrown;
A Rug; for Night-gown he had none.   20
His Jordan[1] stood in Manner fitting
Between his Legs, to spew or spit in.
His antient Pipe in Sable dy'd,
And half unsmoakt, lay by his Side,
    HIM thus accoutred *Peter* found,
With Eyes in Smoak and Weeping drown'd:
The Leavings of his last Night's Pot
On Embers plac'd, to drink it hot.
    WHY *Cassy,* thou wilt doze thy Pate:
What makes thee lie a-bed so late?   30
The Finch, the Linnet and the Thrush,
Their Mattins chant in ev'ry Bush:

And, I have heard thee oft salute
Aurora with thy early Flute.
Heaven send thou hast not got the Hypps.
How? Not a Word come from thy lips?
    THEN gave him some familiar Thumps,
A College Joke to cure the Dumps.
    THE Swain at last, with Grief opprest,
Cry'd, *Cælia!* thrice, and sigh'd the rest.   40
    DEAR *Cassy,* though to ask I dread,
Yet, ask I must. Is *Cælia* dead?
    HOW happy I, were that the worst?
But I was fated to be curs'd.
    COME, tell us, has she play'd the Whore?
    OH *Peter,* wou'd it were no more!
    WHY, Plague confound her sandy Locks:
Say, has the small or greater Pox
Sunk down her Nose, or seam'd her Face?
Be easy, 'tis common Case.   50
    OH *Peter*! Beauty's but a Varnish,
Which Time and Accidents will tarnish:
But, *Cælia* has contriv'd to blast
Those Beauties that might ever last.
Nor can Imagination guess,
Nor Eloquence Divine express,
How that ungrateful charming Maid,
My purest Passion has betray'd.
Conceive the most invenom'd Dart,
To pierce an injur'd Lover's Heart.   60
    WHY, hang her, though she seem'd so coy,
I know she loves the Barber's Boy.
    FRIEND *Peter,* this I could excuse;
For, ev'ry Nymph has Leave to chuse;
Nor, have I Reason to complain:
She loves a more deserving Swain.
But, oh! how ill hast thou divin'd
A Crime that shocks all human Kind;
A Deed unknown to Female Race,
At which the Sun should hide his Face.   70
Advice in vain you would apply—

Then, leave me to despair and dye.
Yet, kind *Arcadians,* on my Urn
These Elegies and Sonnets burn,
And on the Marble grave these Rhimes,
A Monument to after-Times:
"Here *Cassy* lies, by *Cælia* slain,
"And dying, never told his Pain.

    VAIN empty World farewel. But hark,
The loud *Cerberian*[2] triple Bark.   80
And there——behold *Alecto*[3] stand,
A Whip of Scorpions in her Hand.
Lo, *Charon*[4] from his leaky Wherry,
Beck'ning to waft me o'er the Ferry.
I come, I come,—*Medusa,*[5] see,
Her Serpents hiss direct at me.
Begone; unhand me, hellish Fry;
Avaunt—ye cannot say 'twas I.*

    DEAR *Cassy,* thou must purge and bleed;
I fear thou wilt be mad indeed.   90
But now, by Friendship's sacred Laws,
I here conjure thee, tell the Cause;
And *Cælia*'s horrid Fact relate;
Thy Friend would gladly share thy Fate.

    TO force it out my Heart must rend;
Yet, when conjur'd by such a Friend—
Think, *Peter,* how my Soul is rack'd.
These Eyes, these Eyes beheld the Fact.
Now, bend thine Ear; since out it must:
But, when thou seest me laid in Dust,   100
The Secret thou shalt ne'er impart;
Not to the Nymph that keeps thy Heart;
(How would her Virgin Soul bemoan
A Crime to all her Sex unknown!)
Nor whisper to the tattling Reeds,
The blackest of all Female Deeds.
Nor blab it on the lonely Rocks,
Where Echo sits, and list'ning mocks.
Nor let the Zephyr's treach'rous Gale

* See *Mackbeth.*

Through *Cambridge* waft the direful Tale.   110
Nor to the chatt'ring feather'd Race,
Discover *Cælia*'s foul Disgrace.
But, if you fail, my Spectre dread
Attending nightly round your Bed;
And yet, I dare confide in you;
So, take my Secret, and adieu.
    NOR wonder how I lost my Wits;
Oh! *Cælia, Cælia Cælia* sh—.

TO MR. GAY[1] ON HIS BEING STEWARD
TO THE DUKE OF QUEENSBERRY.
(1731, 1735)

How could you, *Gay,* disgrace the Muses Train.
To serve a tasteless C—t[2] twelve Years in vain?
Fain would I think, our *Female Friend*[3] sincere,
Till *B*—,[4] the Poet's Foe, possess't her Ear.
Did Female Virtue e'er so high ascend,
To lose an Inch of Favour for a Friend?

    SAY, had the Court no better place to chuse
For thee, than make a dry Nurse of thy Muse?
How cheaply had thy Liberty been sold,
To squire a Royal Girl of two Year old!   10
In Leading strings her Infant-Steps to guide;
Or, with her Go-Cart amble Side by Side.[5]

    BUT princely *Douglas,* and his glorious Dame,[6]
Advanc'd thy Fortune, and preserv'd thy Fame.
Nor, will your nobler Gifts be misapply'd,
When o'er your Patron's Treasure you preside,
The World shall own, his Choice was wise and just,
For, Sons of *Phæbus*[7] never break their Trust.

    NOT Love of Beauty less the Heart inflames
Of Guardian Eunuchs to the *Sultan* Dames,   20
Their Passions not more impotent and cold,

Than those of Poets to the *Lust* of Gold.
With *Pæan*'s purest Fire his Favourites glow;
The Dregs will serve to ripen Ore below;
His meanest Work: For, had he thought it fit,
That, Wealth should be the Appenage of Wit,
The God of *Light* could ne'er have been so *blind*,
To deal it to the worst of Human-kind.

BUT let me now, for I can do it well,
Your Conduct in this new Employ foretell.   30

AND first: To make my Observation right,
I place a ST * * * AN[8] full before my Sight.
A bloated *M—r*[9] in all his Geer,
With shameless Visage, and perfidious Leer,
Two Rows of Teeth arm each devouring Jaw;
And, *Ostrich*-like, his all-digesting Maw.
My Fancy drags this *Monster* to my View,
To show the World his chief Reverse in you.
Of loud un-meaning Sounds, a rapid Flood
Rolls from his Mouth in plenteous Streams of Mud;   40
With these, the Court and Senate-house he plies,
Made up of Noise, and Impudence, and Lies.

NOW, let me show how *B*— and you agree.
You serve a *potent Prince*, as well as He.
The *Ducal* Coffers, trusted to your Charge,
Your honest Care may fill; perhaps enlarge.
His Vassals easy, and the Owner blest;
They pay a Trifle, and enjoy the rest.
Not so a Nation's Revenues are paid:
The Servants Faults are on the Master laid.   50
The People with a Sigh their Taxes bring;
And cursing *B*—, forget to bless— —.[10]

NEXT, hearken GAY, to what thy Charge requires,
With *Servants, Tenants,* and the neighb'ring *Squires.*
Let all Domesticks feel your gentle Sway;
Nor bribe, insult, nor flatter, nor betray.

Let due Reward to Merit be allow'd;
Nor, with your *KINDRED half the Palace crowd.*
Nor, think your self secure in doing wrong,
By *telling Noses with a Party strong.*   60

   BE rich; but of your Wealth make no Parade;
At least, *before your Master's Debts are paid.*
Nor, *in a Palace* [11] *built with Charge immense,*
Presume to treat him at his own Expence.
Each Farmer in the Neighbourhood can count
To what your lawful Perquisites amount.
The Tenants poor, the Hardness of the Times,
Are ill excuses for a Servant's Crimes:
With Int'rest, and a *Præmium* paid beside,
The Master's pressing Wants must be supply'd;   70
With hasty Zeal, behold, the Steward come,
By his own Credit to advance the Sum;
Who, while *th' unrighteous Mammon* is his Friend, [12]
May well conclude his Pow'r will never end.
A faithful Treas'rer! What could he do more?
He lends my Lord, what was my Lord's before.

   THE Law so strictly guards the Monarch's Health,
That no Physician dare prescribes by Stealth:
The Council sit; approve the Doctor's Skill;
And give Advice before he gives the Pill.   80
But, the *State-Emp'ric* acts a safer Part;
And while he *poisons, wins* the Royal Heart.

   BUT, how can I describe the rav'nous Breed?
Then, let me now by Negatives proceed.

   SUPPOSE your Lord a trusty Servant send,
On weighty Bus'ness, to some neighb'ring Friend:
Presume not, *Gay,* unless you serve a Drone,
To countermand his Orders by your own.

   SHOULD some *imperious Neighbour* sink the Boats,
And drain the *Fish-ponds;* while your *Master* doats;   90

Shall he upon the *Ducal* Rights intrench,
Because he brib'd you with a Brace of Tench?

NOR, from your Lord his bad Condition hide;
To feed his Luxury, or sooth his Pride.
Nor, at an under Rate his *Timber* sell;
And, with an Oath, assure him; *all is well.*
Or *swear it rotten; and with humble Airs,*
Request it of him to compleat your Stairs.
Nor, when a Mortgage lies on half his Lands,
Come with a Purse of Guineas in your Hands.   100

HAVE *Peter Waters*[13] always in your Mind;
That Rogue of *genuine ministerial* Kind:
Can half the Peerage by his Arts bewitch;
Starve twenty Lords to make one Scoundrel rich:
And, when he gravely has undone a Score,
Is humbly pray'd to ruin Twenty more.

A DEXT'ROUS Steward, when his Tricks are found,
Hush-money sends to all the Neighbours round:
His Master, unsuspicious of his Pranks,
Pays all the Cost, and gives the Villain Thanks.   110
And, should a Friend attempt to set him right,
His Lordship would impute it all to Spight:
Would love his Fav'rite better than before;
And trust his Honesty just so much more.
Thus Families, like R—ms,[14] with equal Fate,
May sink by *premier Ministers of State.*

SOME, when an Heir succeeds; go boldly on,
And, as they robb'd the *Father,* rob the *Son.*
A Knave, who deep embroils his Lord's Affairs,
Will soon grow *necessary* to his Heirs.   120
His Policy consists in *setting Traps,*
In finding *Ways and Means,* and *stopping Gaps:*
He knows a Thousand Tricks, whene'er he please,
Though not to cure, yet palliate each Disease.
In either Case, an equal Chance is run:

For, keep, or turn him out, my Lord's undone.
You want a Hand to clear a filthy Sink;
No cleanly Workman can endure the Stink.
A strong Dilemma in a desp'rate Case!
To act with Infamy, or quit the Place.   130

    A BUNGLER thus, who scarce the Nail can hit,
With driving wrong, will make the Pannel split:
Nor, dares an abler Workman undertake
To drive a second, lest the whole should break.

    IN ev'ry Court the Parallel will hold;
And Kings, like private Folks, are bought and sold:
The ruling Rogue, who dreads to be cashier'd;
Contrives, as he is *hated,* to be *fear'd:*
Confounds Accounts, perplexes all Affairs;
For, *Vengeance* more *embroils,* than *Skill repairs.*   140
So, Robbers (and their Ends are just the same)
To 'scape Enquiries, *leave the House in Flame.*

    I KNEW a *brazen* Minister of State,
Who bore for twice ten Years the publick Hate.
In every Mouth the Question most in Vogue
Was, *When will* THEY *turn out this odious Rogue?*
A Juncture happen'd in his highest Pride:
While HE went robbing on; *old Master* dy'd.
We thought, there now remain'd no room to doubt:
His Work is done, the Minister must out.   150
The Court *invited* more than One, or Two;
Will you, Sir *Sp—r?*[15] or, will *you,* or *you?*
But, not a Soul his Office durst accept:
The subtle Knave had all the Plunder swept.
And, such was then the Temper of the Times,
He ow'd his Preservation to his Crimes.
The Candidates observ'd his dirty Paws,
Nor found it difficult to guess the Cause:
But when they smelt such foul Corruptions round him;
Away they fled, and left him as they found him.   160

—

THUS, when a greedy Sloven once has thrown
His *Snot* into the *Mess; 'tis all his own.*

VERSES ON THE DEATH OF DR. SWIFT, D.S.P.D.[1] OCCASIONED BY READING A MAXIM IN ROCHEFOUCAULT.
(1731, 1733)

Dans l'adversité de nos meilleurs amis nous trouvons quelque chose, qui ne nous
    deplaist pas.
In the Adversity of our best Friends, we find something that doth not displease us.

As *Rochefoucault* his Maxims drew
From Nature, I believe 'em true:
They argue no corrupted Mind
In him; the Fault is in Mankind.

THIS Maxim more than all the rest
Is thought too base for human Breast;
"In all Distresses of our Friends
"We first consult our private Ends,
"While Nature kindly bent to ease us,
"Points out some Circumstance to please us.   10

IF this perhaps your Patience move
Let Reason and Experience prove.

WE all behold with envious Eyes,
Our *Equal* rais'd above our *Size;*
Who wou'd not at a crowded Show,
Stand high himself, keep others low?
I love my Friend as well as you,
But would not have him stop my View;
Then let him have the higher Post;
I ask but for an Inch at most.   20

———

IF in a Battle you should find,
One, whom you love of all Mankind,
Had some heroick Action done,
A Champion kill'd, or Trophy won;
Rather than thus be over-topt,
Would you not wish his Lawrels cropt?

DEAR honest *Ned* is in the Gout,
Lies rackt with Pain, and you without:
How patiently you hear him groan!
How glad the Case is not your own!   30

WHAT Poet would not grieve to see,
His Brethren write as well as he?
But rather than they should excel,
He'd wish his Rivals all in Hell.

HER End when Emulation misses,
She turns to Envy, Stings and Hisses:
The strongest Friendship yields to Pride,
Unless the Odds be on our Side.

VAIN human Kind! Fantastick Race!
Thy various Follies, who can trace?   40
Self-love, Ambition, Envy, Pride,
Their Empire in our Hearts divide:
Give others Riches, Power, and Station,
'Tis all on me an Usurpation.
I have no Title to aspire;
Yet, when you sink, I seem the higher.
In POPE, I cannot read a Line,
But with a Sigh, I wish it mine:
When he can in one Couplet fix
More Sense than I can do in Six: 50
It gives me such a jealous Fit,
I cry, Pox take him, and his Wit.

WHY must I be outdone by GAY,
In my own hum'rous biting Way?

ARBUTHNOT is no more my Friend,
Who dares to Irony pretend;
Which I was born to introduce,
Refin'd it first, and shew'd its Use.

ST. JOHN, as well as PULTNEY knows,
That I had some repute for Prose;   60
And till they drove me out of Date,
Could maul a Minister of State:
If they have mortify'd my Pride,
And made me throw my Pen aside;
If with such Talents Heav'n hath blest 'em
Have I not Reason to detest 'em?[2]

To all my Foes, dear Fortune, send
Thy Gifts, but never to my Friend:
I tamely can endure the first,
But, this with Envy makes me burst.   70

THUS much may serve by way of Proem,
Proceed we therefore to our Poem.

THE Time is not remote, when I
Must by the Course of Nature dye:
When I foresee my special Friends,
Will try to find their private Ends:
Tho' it is hardly understood,
Which way my Death can do them good;
Yet, thus methinks, I hear 'em speak;
See, how the Dean begins to break: 80
Poor Gentleman, he droops apace,
You plainly find it in his Face:
That old Vertigo in his Head,
Will never leave him, till he's dead:
Besides, his Memory decays,
He recollects not what he says;
He cannot call his Friends to Mind;
Forgets the Place where last he din'd:

Plyes you with Stories o'er and o'er,
He told them fifty Times before.   90
How does he fancy we can sit,
To hear his out-of-fashion'd Wit?
But he takes up with younger Fokes,
Who for his Wine will bear his Jokes:
Faith, he must make his Stories shorter,
Or change his Comrades once a Quarter:
In half the Time, he talks them round;
There must another Sett be found.

    FOR Poetry, he's past his Prime,
He takes an Hour to find a Rhime: 100
His Fire is out, his Wit decay'd,
His Fancy sunk, his Muse a Jade.
I'd have him throw away his Pen;
But there's no talking to some Men.

    AND, then their Tenderness appears,
By adding largely to my Years:
"He's older than he would be reckon'd,
"And well remembers *Charles* the Second.

    "HE hardly drinks a Pint of Wine;
"And that, I doubt, is no good Sign.   110
"His Stomach too begins to fail:
"Last Year we thought him strong and hale;
"But now, he's quite another Thing;
"I wish he may hold out till Spring.

    THEN hug themselves, and reason thus;
"It is not yet so bad with us."

    IN such a Case they talk in Tropes,
And, by their Fears express their Hopes:
Some great Misfortune to portend,
No Enemy can match a Friend;   120
With all the Kindness they profess,
The Merit of a lucky Guess,

(When daily Howd'y's come of Course,
And Servants answer; *Worse and Worse*)
Wou'd please 'em better than to tell,
That, GOD be prais'd, the Dean is well.
Then he who prophecy'd the best,
Approves his Foresight to the rest:
"You know, I always fear'd the worst,
"And often told you so at first:"   130
He'd rather chuse that I should dye,
Than his Prediction prove a Lye.
Not one foretels I shall recover;
But, all agree, to give me over.

    YET shou'd some Neighbour feel a Pain,
Just in the Parts, where I complain;
How many a Message would he send?
What hearty Prayers that I should mend?
Enquire what Regimen I kept;
What gave me Ease, and how I slept?   140
And more lament, when I was dead,
Than all the Sniv'llers round my Bed.

    MY good Companions, never fear,
For though you may mistake a Year;
Though your Prognosticks run too fast,
They must be verify'd at last.

    "BEHOLD the fatal Day arrive!
"How is the Dean? He's just alive.
"Now the departing Prayer is read:
"He hardly breathes. The Dean is dead.   150
"Before the Passing-Bell begun,
"The News thro' half the Town has run.
"O, may we all for Death prepare!
"What has he left? And who's his Heir?
"I know no more than what the News is,
" 'Tis all bequeath'd to publick Uses.
"To publick Use! A perfect Whim!
"What had the Publick done for him!

"Meer Envy, Avarice, and Pride!
"He gave it all:—But first he dy'd.   160
"And had the Dean, in all the Nation,
"No worthy Friend, no poor Relation?
"So ready to do Strangers good,
"Forgetting his own Flesh and Blood?

   NOW Grub-Street Wits are all employ'd;
With Elegies, the Town is cloy'd:
Some Paragraph in ev'ry Paper,
To *curse* the *Dean,* or *bless* the *Drapier.**

   THE Doctors tender of their Fame,
Wisely on me lay all the Blame: 170
"We must confess his Case was nice;
"But he would never take Advice:
"Had he been rul'd, for ought appears,
"He might have liv'd these Twenty Years:
"For when we open'd him we found,
"That all his vital Parts were sound.

   FROM *Dublin* soon to *London* spread,
'Tis told at Court, the Dean is dead.†
   KIND Lady *Suffolk* in the Spleen,‡
Runs laughing up to tell the Queen.   180
The Queen, so Gracious, Mild, and Good,
Cries, "Is he gone? 'Tis time he shou'd.
"He's dead you say; why let him rot;

---

   * *The Author imagines, that the Scriblers of the prevailing Party, which he always opposed, will libel him after his Death; but that others will remember him with Gratitude, who consider the Service he had done to* Ireland, *under the Name of* M. B. *Drapier, by utterly defeating the destructive Project of* Wood's *Half-pence, in five Letters to the People of* Ireland, *at that Time read universally, and convincing every Reader.*

   † *The Dean supposeth himself to dye in* Ireland.

   ‡ *Mrs.* Howard, *afterwards Countess of* Suffolk, *then of the Bed-chamber to the Queen, professed much Friendship for the Dean. The Queen then Princess, sent a dozen times to the Dean (then in London) with her Command to attend her; which at last he did, by Advice of all his Friends. She often sent for him afterwards, and always treated him very Graciously. He taxed her with a Present worth Ten Pounds, which she promised before he should return to* Ireland, *but on his taking Leave, the Medals were not ready.*

"I'm glad the Medals were forgot.*
"I promis'd them, I own; but when?
"I only was the Princess then;
"But now as Consort of the King,
"You know 'tis quite a different Thing.

Now, *Chartres* at Sir *Robert*'s Levee,†
Tells, with a Sneer, the Tidings heavy: 190
"Why, is he dead without his Shoes?²³
(Cries *Bob*) "I'm Sorry for the News;‡
Oh, were the Wrench but living still,
And in his Place my good Friend *Will,*§
Or, had a Mitre on his Head
Provided *Bolingbroke* were dead.**

Now *Curl* his Shop from Rubbish drains;††
Three genuine Tomes of *Swift*'s Remains.

* *The Medals were to be sent to the Dean in four Months, but she forgot them, or thought them too dear. The Dean, being in* Ireland, *sent Mrs.* Howard *a Piece of* Indian *Plad made in that Kingdom: which the Queen seeing took from her, and wore it herself, and sent to the Dean for as much as would cloath herself and Children, desiring he would send the Charge of it. He did the former. It cost thirty-five Pounds, but he said he would have nothing except the Medals. He was the Summer following in* England, *was treated as usual, and she being then Queen, the Dean was promised a Settlement in* England, *but returned as he went, and, instead of Favour or Medals, hath been ever since under her Majesty's Displeasure.*

† Chartres *is a most infamous, vile Scoundrel, grown from a Foot-Boy, or worse, to a prodigious Fortune both in* England *and* Scotland: *He had a Way of insinuating himself into all Ministers under every Change, either as Pimp, Flatterer, or Informer. He was Tryed at Seventy for a Rape, and came off by sacrificing a great Part of his Fortune (he is since dead, but this Poem still preserves the Scene and Time it was writ in.)*

‡ Sir Robert Walpole, *Chief Minister of State, treated the Dean in 1726, with great Distinction, invited him to Dinner at* Chelsea, *with the Dean's Friends chosen on Purpose; appointed an Hour to talk with him of* Ireland, *to which Kingdom and People the Dean found him no great Friend; for he defended* Wood's *Project of Half-pence, &c. The Dean would see him no more; and upon his next Year's return to* England, *Sir* Robert *on an accidental Meeting, only made a civil Compliment, and never invited him again.*

§ *Mr.* William Pultney, *from being Mr.* Walpole's *intimate Friend, detesting his Administration, opposed his Measures, and joined with my* Lord Bolingbroke, *to represent his Conduct in an excellent Paper, called the* Craftsman, *which is still continued.*

** Henry St. John, *Lord Viscount* Bolingbroke, *Secretary of State to* Queen Anne *of blessed Memory. He is reckoned the most Universal Genius in* Europe; Walpole *dreading his Abilities, treated him most injuriously, working with King* George, *who forgot his Promise of restoring the said Lord, upon the restless Importunity of* Walpole.

†† Curl *hath been the most infamous Bookseller of any Age or Country: His Character in Part may be found in Mr.* POPE's *Dunciad. He published three Volumes all charged on the Dean, who never writ three Pages of them: He hath used many of the Dean's Friends in almost as vile a Manner.*

And then to make them pass the glibber,
Revis'd by *Tibbalds, Moore and Cibber.**   200
He'll treat me as he does my Betters.
Publish my Will, my Life, my Letters.†
Revive the Libels born to dye;
Which POPE must bear, as well as I.

   Here shift the Scene, to represent
How those I love, my Death lament.
Poor POPE will grieve a Month; and GAY
A Week; and ARBUTHNOTT a Day.

   ST. JOHN himself will scarce forbear,
To bite his Pen, and drop a Tear.   210
The rest will give a Shrug and cry,
I'm sorry; but we all must dye.
Indifference clad in Wisdom's Guise,
All Fortitude of Mind supplies;
For how can stony Bowels melt,
In those who never Pity felt;
When *We* are lash'd, *They* kiss the Rod;
Resigning to the Will of God.

   THE Fools, my Juniors by a Year,
Are tortur'd with Suspence and Fear.   220
Who wisely thought my Age a Screen,
When Death approach'd, to stand between:
The Screen remov'd, their Hearts are trembling,
They mourn for me without dissembling.

   My female Friends, whose tender Hearts
Have better learn'd to act their Parts.

* *Three stupid Verse Writers in* London, *the last to the Shame of the Court, and the highest Disgrace to Wit and Learning, was made Laureat.* Moore, *commonly called* Jemmy Moore, *Son of* Arthur Moore, *whose Father was Jaylor of* Monaghan *in* Ireland. *See the Character of* Jemmy Moore, *and* Tibbalds, Theobald *in the Dunciad.*

† Curl *is notoriously infamous for publishing the Lives, Letters, and last Wills and Testaments of the Nobility and Ministers of State, as well as of all the Rogues, who are hanged at* Tyburn. *He hath been in Custody of the House of Lords for publishing or forgiving the Letters of many Peers; which made the Lords enter a Resolution in their Journal Book, that no Life or Writings of any Lord should be published without the Consent of the next Heir at Law, or Licence from their House.*

Receive the News in *doleful Dumps,*
"The Dean is dead, (*and what is Trumps?*)
"Then Lord have Mercy on his Soul.
"(Ladies I'll venture for the *Vole.*⁴)   230
"Six Deans they say must bear the Pall.
"(I wish I knew what *King* to call.)
"Madam, your Husband will attend
"The Funeral of so good a Friend.
"No Madam, 'tis a shocking Sight,
"And he's engag'd To-morrow Night!
"My Lady *Club* wou'd take it ill,
"If he shou'd fail her at *Quadrill.*
"He lov'd the Dean. (*I lead a Heart.*)
"But dearest Friends, they say, must part.   240
"His Time was come, he ran his Race;
"We hope he's in a better Place.

    WHY do we grieve that Friends should dye?
No Loss more easy to supply.
One Year is past; a different Scene;
No further mention of the Dean;
Who now, alas, no more is mist,
Than if he never did exist.
Where's now this Fav'rite of *Apollo?*
Departed; *and his Works must follow:*   250
Must undergo the common Fate;
His Kind of Wit is out of Date.
Some Country Squire to *Lintot* * goes,
Enquires for SWIFT in Verse and Prose:
Says *Lintot,* "I have heard the Name:
"He dy'd a Year ago." The same.
He searcheth all his Shop in vain;
"Sir you may find them in *Duck-lane:* †
"I sent them with a Load of Books,
"Last *Monday* to the Pastry-cooks.   260

---

* Bernard Lintot, *a Bookseller in* London. *Vide Mr.* Pope's *Dunciad.*
† *A Place in* London *where old Books are sold.*

"To fancy they cou'd live a Year!
"I find you're but a Stranger here.
"The Dean was famous in his Time;
"And had a Kind of Knack at Rhyme:
"His way of Writing now is past;
"The Town hath got a better Taste:
"I keep no antiquated Stuff;
"But, spick and span I have enough.
"Pray, do but give me leave to shew 'em;
"Here's *Colley Cibber*'s Birth-day Poem.   270
"This Ode you never yet have seen,
"By *Stephen Duck,* upon the Queen.
"Then, here's a Letter finely penn'd
"Against the *Craftsman* and his Friend;
"It clearly shews that all Reflection
"On Ministers, is disaffection.
"Next, here's Sir *Robert*'s Vindication,*
"And Mr. *Henly*'s last Oration:†
"The Hawkers have not got 'em yet,
"Your Honour please to buy a Set?   280

      "HERE'S *Wolston*'s Tracts, the twelfth Edition;‡
" 'Tis read by ev'ry Politician:
"The Country Members, when in Town,
"To all their Boroughs send them down:
"You never met a Thing so smart;
"The Courtiers have them all by Heart:
"Those Maids of Honour (who can read)
"Are taught to use them for their Creed.
"The Rev'rend Author's good Intention,
"Hath been rewarded with a Pension: 290

* Walpole *hires a Set of Party Scriblers, who do nothing else but write in his Defence.*

† Henly *is a Clergyman who wanting both Merit and Luck to get Preferment, or even to keep his Curacy in the Established Church, formed a new Conventicle, which he calls an Oratory. There, at set Times, he delivereth strange Speeches compiled by himself and his Associates, who share the Profit with him: Every Hearer pays a Shilling each Day for Admittance. He is an absolute Dunce, but generally reputed crazy.*

‡ Wolston *was a Clergyman, but for want of Bread, hath in several Treatises, in the most blasphemous Manner, attempted to turn* Our Saviour *and his Miracles into Ridicule. He is much caressed by many great Courtiers, and by all the Infidels, and his Books read generally by the Court Ladies.*

"He doth an Honour to his Gown,
"By bravely running *Priest-craft* down:
"He shews, as sure as GOD's in *Gloc'ster,*
"That *Jesus* was a Grand Impostor:
"That all his Miracles were Cheats,
"Perform'd as Juglers do their Feats:
"The Church had never such a Writer:
"A Shame, he hath not got a Mitre!

    SUPPOSE me dead; and then suppose
A Club assembled at the *Rose;*   300
Where from Discourse of this and that,
I grow the Subject of their Chat:
And, while they toss my Name about,
With Favour some, and some without;
One quite indiff'rent in the Cause,
My Character impartial draws:

    "THE Dean, if we believe Report,
"Was never ill receiv'd at Court:
"As for his Works in Verse and Prose,
"I own my self no Judge of those: 310
"Nor, can I tell what Criticks thought 'em;
"But, this I know, all People bought 'em;
"As with a moral View design'd
"To cure the Vices of Mankind:
"His Vein, ironically grave,
"Expos'd the Fool, and lash'd the Knave:
"To steal a Hint was never known,
"But what he writ was all his own.[5]

    "HE never thought an Honour done him,
"Because a Duke was proud to own him: 320
"Would rather slip aside, and chuse
"To talk with Wits in dirty Shoes:
"Despis'd the Fools with Stars and Garters,
"So often seen caressing *Chartres:**

---

* *See the Notes before on* Chartres.

"He never courted Men in Station,
"*Nor Persons had in Admiration;*
"Of no Man's Greatness was afraid,
"Because he sought for no Man's Aid.
"Though trusted long in great Affairs,
"He gave himself no haughty Airs: 330
"Without regarding private Ends,
"Spent all his Credit for his Friends:
"And only chose the Wise and Good;
"No Flatt'rers; no Allies in Blood;
"But succour'd Virtue in Distress,
"And seldom fail'd of good Success;
"As Numbers in their Hearts must own,
"Who, but for him, had been unknown.

   "WITH Princes kept a due Decorum,
"But never stood in Awe before 'em: 340
"He follow'd *David*'s Lesson[6] just,
"*In Princes never put thy Trust.*
"And, would you make him truly sower;
"Provoke him with *a slave in Power:*
"The *Irish* Senate, if you nam'd,
"With what Impatience he declaim'd!
"Fair LIBERTY was all his Cry;
"For her he stood prepar'd to die;
"For her he boldly stood alone;[7]
"For her he oft expos'd his own.   350
"Two Kingdoms, just as Faction led,*
"Had set a Price upon his Head;
"But, not a Tray'tor cou'd be found,
"To sell him for Six Hundred Pound.

———

* *In the Year* 1713, *the late Queen was prevailed with by an Address of the House of Lords in* England, *to publish a Proclamation, promising Three Hundred Pounds to whatever Person would discover the Author of a Pamphlet called,* The Publick Spirit of the Whiggs; *and in* Ireland, *in the Year* 1724, *my Lord* Carteret *at his first coming into the Government, was prevailed on to issue a Proclamation for promising the like Reward of Three Hundred Pounds, to any Person who could discover the Author of a Pamphlet called,* The Drapier's Fourth Letter, *&c. writ against the destructive Project of coining Half-pence for* Ireland; *but in neither Kingdoms was the Dean discovered.*

"Had he but spar'd his Tongue and Pen,
"He might have rose like other Men:
"But, Power was never in his Thought;
"And, Wealth he valu'd not a Groat:
"Ingratitude he often found,
"And pity'd those who meant the Wound: 360
"But, kept the Tenor of his Mind,
"To merit well of human Kind:
"Nor made a Sacrifice of those
"Who still were true, to please his Foes.
"He labour'd many a fruitless Hour*
"To reconcile his Friends in Power;
"Saw Mischief by a Faction brewing,
"While they pursu'd each others Ruin.
"But, finding vain was all his Care,
"He left the Court in meer Despair.   370

"And, oh! how short are human Schemes!
"Here ended all our golden Dreams.
"What St. John's Skill in State Affairs,
"What Ormond's *Valour,* Oxford's Cares,
"To save their sinking Country lent,
"Was all destroy'd by one Event.
"Too soon that precious Life was ended,†
"One which alone, our Weal depended.
"When up a dangerous Faction starts,‡

* *Queen* ANNE'*s Ministry fell to Variance from the first Year after their Ministry began:* Harcourt *the Chancellor,* and *Lord* Bolingbroke *the Secretary, were discontented with the Treasurer* Oxford, *for his too much Mildness to the Whig Party; this Quarrel grew higher every Day till the Queen's Death: The Dean, who was the only Person that endeavoured to reconcile them, found it impossible; and thereupon retired to the Country about ten Weeks before that fatal Event: Upon which he returned to his Deanry in* Dublin, *where for many Years he was worryed by the new People in Power, and had Hundreds of Libels writ against him in* England.

† *In the Height of the Quarrel between the Ministers, the Queen died.*

‡ *Upon Queen* ANNE'*s Death the Whig Faction was restored to Power, which they exercised with the utmost Rage and Revenge; impeached and banished the Chief Leaders of the Church Party, and stripped all their Adherents of what Employments they had, after which* England *was never known to make so mean a Figure in Europe. The greatest Preferments in the Church in both Kingdoms were given to the most ignorant Men, Fanaticks were publickly caressed,* Ireland *utterly ruined and enslaved, only great Ministers heaping up Millions, and so Affairs continue until this present third Day of May,* 1732, *and are likely to go on in the same Manner.*

"With Wrath and Vengeance in their Hearts: 380
"*By solemn League and Cov'nant bound,*
"To ruin, slaughter, and confound;
"To turn Religion to a Fable,
"And make the Government a *Babel:*
"Pervert the Law, disgrace the Gown,
"Corrupt the Senate, rob the Crown;
"To sacrifice old *England*'s Glory,
"And make her infamous in Story.
"When such a Tempest shook the Land,
"How could unguarded Virtue stand?   390

      "WITH Horror, Grief, Despair the Dean
"Beheld the dire destructive Scene:
"His Friends in Exile, or the Tower,
"Himself within the Frown of Power;*
"Pursu'd by base envenom'd Pens,
"Far to the Land of Slaves and Fens;†
"A servile Race in Folly nurs'd,
"Who truckle most, when treated worst.

      "BY Innocence and Resolution,
"He bore continual Persecution;   400
"While Numbers to Preferment rose;
"Whose Merits were, to be his Foes.
"When, *ev'n his own familiar Friends*
"Intent upon their private Ends;
"Like Renegadoes now he feels,
"*Against him lifting up their Heels.*

      "THE Dean did by his Pen defeat
"An infamous destructive Cheat.‡

---

* *Upon the Queen's Death, the Dean returned to live in* Dublin, *at his Deanry-House: Numberless Libels were writ against him in* England, *as a Jacobite; he was insulted in the Street, and at Nights was forced to be attended by his Servants armed.*

    † *The Land of Slaves and Fens, is* Ireland.

    ‡ *One* Wood, *a Hardware-man from* England, *had a Patent for coining Copper Half-pence in* Ireland, *to the Sum of* 108,000 l. *which in the Consequence, must leave that Kingdom without Gold or Silver (See* Drapier's *Letters.)*

"Taught Fools their Int'rest how to know;
"And gave them Arms to ward the Blow.   **410**
"Envy hath own'd it was his doing,
"To save that helpless Land from Ruin,
"While they who at the Steerage stood,
"And reapt the Profit, sought his Blood.

"To save them from their evil Fate,
"In him was held a Crime of State.
"A wicked Monster on the Bench,*
"Whose Fury Blood could never quench;
"As vile and profligate a Villain,
"As modern *Scroggs,* or old *Tressilian;*†   **420**
"Who long all Justice had discarded,
"*Nor fear'd he GOD, nor Man regarded;*
"Vow'd on the Dean his Rage to vent,
"And make him of his Zeal repent;
"But Heav'n his Innocence defends,
"The grateful People stand his Friends:
"Not Strains of Law, nor Judges Frown,
"Nor Topicks brought to please the Crown,
"Nor Witness hir'd, nor Jury pick'd,
"Prevail to bring him in convict.   **430**

"IN Exile with a steady Heart,‡
"He spent his Life's declining Part;

---

* *One* Whitshed *was then Chief Justice: He had some Years before prosecuted a Printer for a Pamphlet writ by the Dean, to perswade the People of* Ireland *to wear their own Manufactures.* Whitshed *sent the Jury down eleven Times, and kept them nine Hours, until they were forced to bring in a special Verdict. He sat as Judge afterwards on the Tryal of the Printer of the* Drapier's Fourth Letter; *but the Jury, against all he could say or swear, threw out the Bill: All the Kingdom took the* Drapier's *Part, except the Courtiers, or those who expected Places. The* Drapier *was celebrated in many Poems and Pamphlets: His Sign was set up in most Streets of* Dublin *(where many of them still continue) and in several Country Towns.*

† Scroggs *was Chief Justice under King* Charles *the Second: His Judgment always varied in State Tryals, according to Directions from Court.* Tressilian *was a wicked Judge, hanged above three hundred Years ago.*

‡ *In* Ireland, *which he had Reason to call a Place of Exile; to which Country nothing could have driven him, but the Queen's Death, who had determined to fix him in* England, *in Spight of the Dutchess of* Somerset, *&c.*

"Where, Folly, Pride, and Faction sway,
"Remote from ST. JOHN, POPE, and GAY.*

"HIS Friendship there to few confin'd,†
"Were always of the midling Kind:
"No Fools of Rank, a mungril Breed,
"Who fain would pass for Lords indeed:
"Where Titles give no Right or Power,‡
"And Peerage is a wither'd Flower,   440
"He would have held it a Disgrace,
"If such a Wretch had known his Face.
"On Rural Squires, that Kingdom's Bane,
"He vented oft his Wrath in vain:
"Biennial Squires, to Market brought;§
"Who sell their Souls and Votes for Naught;
"The Nation stript go joyful back,
"To rob the Church, their Tenants rack,
"Go Snacks with Thieves and Rapparees,**
"And, keep the Peace, to pick up Fees: 450
"In every Jobb to have a Share,
"A Jayl or Barrack†† to repair;
"And turn the Tax for publick Roads
"Commodious to their own Abodes.

"PERHAPS I may allow, the Dean
"Had too much Satyr in his Vein;
"And seem'd determin'd not to starve it,
"Because no Age could more deserve it.

* Henry St. John, *Lord Viscount* Bolingbroke, *mentioned before.*

    † *In* Ireland *the Dean was not acquainted with one single Lord Spiritual or Temporal. He only conversed with private Gentlemen of the Clergy or Laity, and but a small Number of either.*

    ‡ *The Peers of* Ireland *lost a great Part of their Jurisdiction by one single Act, and tamely submitted to this infamous Mark of Slavery without the least Resentment, or Remonstrance.*

    § *The Parliament (as they call it) in* Ireland *meet but once in two Years; and, after giving five Times more than they can afford, return Home to reimburse themselves by all Country Jobs and Oppressions, of which some few only are here mentioned.*

    ** *The Highway-Men in* Ireland *are, since the late Wars there, usually called Rapparees, which was a Name given to those* Irish *Soldiers who in small Parties used, at that Time, to plunder the Protestants.*

    †† *The Army in* Ireland *is lodged in Barracks, the building and repairing whereof, and other Charges, have cost a prodigious Sum to that unhappy Kingdom.*

"Yet, Malice never was his Aim;
"He lash'd the Vice but spar'd the Name.   **460**
"No Individual could resent,
"Where Thousands equally were meant.
"His Satyr points at no Defect,
"But what all Mortals may correct;
"For he abhorr'd that senseless Tribe,
"Who call it Humour when they jibe:
"He spar'd a Hump or crooked Nose,
"Whose Owners set not up for Beaux.
"True genuine Dulness mov'd his Pity,
"Unless it offer'd to be witty.   **470**
"Those, who their Ignorance confess'd,
"He ne'er offended with a Jest;
"But laugh'd to hear an Idiot quote,
"A Verse from *Horace*, learn'd by Rote.

   "HE knew an hundred pleasant Stories,
"With all the Turns of *Whigs* and *Tories:*
"Was chearful to his dying Day,
"And Friends would let him have his Way.

   "HE gave the little Wealth he had,
"To build a House for Fools and Mad:[8]   **480**
"And shew'd by one satyric Touch,
"No Nation wanted it so much:
"That Kingdom he hath left his Debtor,
"I wish it soon may have a Better.

AN EPISTLE TO A LADY,[1]

Who desired the Author to make Verses on Her, in the Heroick Stile.
(1732?, 1733)

After venting all my Spight,
Tell me, what have I to write?
Ev'ry Error I could find
Thro' the Mazes of your Mind,

Have my busy Muse employ'd,
Till the Company was cloy'd.
Are you positive and fretful?
Heedless, ignorant, forgetful?
Those, and twenty Follies more,
I have often told before.   10

    HEARKEN, what my *Lady* says---:
Have I nothing then to praise?
Ill it fits you to be witty,
Where a Fault shou'd move your Pity.
If you think me too conceited,
Or, to Passion quickly heated:
If my wand'ring Head be less
Set on Reading, than on Dress:
If I always seem too dull t'ye;
I can solve the Diffi---culty.   20

    YOU wou'd teach me to be wise;
Truth and Honour how to prize;
How to shine in Conversation,
And, with Credit fill my Station;
How to relish Notions high;
How to live, and how to die.

    BUT it was decreed by Fate---;
Mr. DEAN, You come too late:
Well I know, you can discern,
I am now too old to learn: 30
Follies, from my Youth instill'd,
Have my Soul entirely fill'd:
In my Head and Heart they center;
Nor will let your Lessons enter.

    BRED a Fondling, and an Heiress;
Drest like any Lady May'ress;
Cocker'd² by the Servants round,
Was too good to touch the Ground:
Thought the Life of ev'ry Lady

Shou'd be one continu'd Play-Day: 40
Balls, and Masquerades, and Shows,
Visits, Plays, and Powder'd Beaux.

THUS you have my Case at large,
And may now perform your Charge.
Those Materials I have furnish'd,
When, by you refin'd and burnish'd,
Must, that all the World may know 'em,
Be reduc'd into a Poem.
But, I beg, suspend a While,
That same paultry *Burlesque* Stile: 50
Drop, for once, your constant Rule,
Turning all to Ridicule:
Teaching others how to ape ye;
Court, nor Parli'ment, can 'scape ye;
Treat the Publick, and your Friends,
Both alike; while neither mends.

SING my Praise in Strain sublime:
Treat me not with Doggrel Rhime.
'Tis but just, you shou'd produce,
With each Fault, each Fault's Excuse: 60
Not to publish ev'ry Trifle,
And my few Perfections stifle.
With some Gifts, at least endow me,
Which my very Foes allow me.
Am I spightful, proud, unjust?
Did I ever break my Trust?
Which, of all our modern Dames
Censures less, or less defames?
In Good Manners, am I faulty?
Can you call me rude, or haughty?   70
Did I e'er my Mite withold
From the Impotent and Old?
When did ever I omit
Due Regard for Men of Wit?
When have I Esteem express'd
For a Coxcomb gaily dress'd?

Do I, like the Female Tribe,
Think it Wit to fleer, and gibe?
Who, with less designing Ends,
Kindlier entertains her Friends?   80

    THINK not Cards my chief Diversion,
'Tis a wrong, unjust Aspersion:
Never know I any Good in 'um,
But, to doze my Head, like *Lodanum.*[3]
We, by Play, as Men by Drinking,
Pass our Nights, to drive out thinking.
From my Ailments give me Leisure,
I shall read and think with Pleasure:
Conversation learn to relish,
And with Books my Mind embellish.   90

    NOW, methinks, I hear you cry;
Mr. DEAN, you must reply.

    MADAM, I allow 'tis true;
All these Praises are your Due.
You, like some acute Philosopher,
Ev'ry Fault have drawn a Gloss over:
Placing in the strongest Light,
All your Virtues to my Sight.

    THO' you lead a blameless Life,
Are an humble, prudent Wife;   100
Answer all domestick Ends,
What is this to us your Friends?
Tho' your Children by a Nod
Stand in Awe without a Rod:
Tho' by your obliging Sway
Servants love you, and obey:
Tho' you treat us with a Smile,
Clear your Looks, and smooth your Stile:
Load our Plates from ev'ry Dish;
This is not the Thing we wish.   110
Col'nel ...... may be your Debtor;

We expect Employment better.
You must learn, if you would gain us,
With good sense to entertain us.

SCHOLARS, when good Sense describing,
Call it *Tasting*, and *Imbibing*:
Metaphorick Meat and Drink,
Is to understand, and think:
We may *carve* for others thus;
And let others carve for us.   120
To discourse, and to attend,
Is to *help* yourself, and Friend.
Conversation is but *carving*,
Carve for all, yourself is starving.
Give no more to ev'ry Guest,
Than he's able to digest:
Give him always of the Prime,
And, but little at a Time.
Carve to all but just enuff,
Let them neither starve, nor stuff: 130
And, that you may have your Due,
Let your Neighbours *carve* for you.

To conclude this long Essay;
Pardon, if I disobey:
Nor, against my nat'ral Vein,
Treat you in Heroick Strain.
I, as all the Parish knows,
Hardly can be grave in Prose:
Still to lash, and lashing Smile,
Ill befits a lofty Stile.   140
From the Planet of my Birth,
I encounter Vice with Mirth.
Wicked Ministers of State
I can easier scorn than hate:
And I find it answers right:
Scorn torments them more than Spight.
All the Vices of a Court,
Do but serve to make me Sport.

Shou'd a Monkey wear a Crown,
Must I tremble at his Frown? 150
Could I not, thro' all his Ermin,
Spy the strutting chatt'ring Vermin?
Safely write a smart Lampoon,
To expose the brisk Baboon?

WHEN my Muse officious ventures
On the Nation's Representers;
Teaching by what *Golden* Rules
Into Knaves they turn their Fools:
How the Helm is rul'd by———[4]
At whose Oars, like Slaves, they all pull: 160
Let the Vessel split on Shelves,
With the Freight enrich themselves:
Safe within my little Wherry,
All their Madness makes me merry:
Like the Watermen of *Thames,*
I row by, and call them Names.
Like the ever-laughing Sage,
In a Jest I spend my Rage:[5]
(Tho' it must be understood,
I would hang them if I cou'd:) 170
If I can but fill my Nitch,
I attempt no higher Pitch.
Leave to D'ANVERS and his Mate,[6]
Maxims wise, to rule the State.
POULTNEY deep, accomplish'd ST. JOHNS,
Scourge the Villains with a Vengeance.
Let me, tho' the Smell be Noisom,
Strip their Bums; let CALEB hoyse 'em;
Then, apply ALECTO's Whip,
Till they wriggle, howl, and skip. 180

DEUCE is in you, Mr. DEAN;
What can all this Passion mean?
Mention Courts, you'll ne'er be quiet;
On Corruptions running Riot.
End, as it befits your Station;

Come to use, and Application:
Nor with Senates keep a Fuss,
I submit; and answer thus.

　　IF the Machinations brewing,
To compleat the Publick Ruin,　　　　　　　　　　　190
Never once cou'd have the Pow'r
To affect me half an Hour;
If I laugh at Whig and Tory;
I conclude a *Fortiori,*
All your Eloquence will scarce
Drive me from my fav'rite Farce.
This I must insist on. For, as
It is well observ'd by HORACE,*
Ridicule has greater Pow'r
To reform the World, than Sour.　　　　　　　　　　200
Horses thus, let Jockeys judge else,
Switches better guide than Cudgels.
Bastings heavy, dry, obtuse,
Only Dulness can produce,
While a little gentle Jerking
Sets the Spirits all a working.

　　THUS, I find it by Experiment,
Scolding moves you less than Merriment.
I may storm and rage in vain;
It but stupifies your Brain.　　　　　　　　　　　210
But, with Raillery to nettle,
Set your Thoughts upon their Mettle:
Gives Imagination Scope,
Never lets your Mind elope:
Drives out Brangling, and Contention,
Brings in Reason and Invention.
For your Sake, as well as mine,
I the lofty Stile decline.
I Shou'd make a Figure scurvy,
And your Head turn Topsy-turvy.　　　　　　　　220

* —Ridiculum Acri,
　Fortius & Melius, &c.[7]

———

I, WHO love to have a Fling,
Both at Senate-House, and——
That they might some better Way tread,
To avoid the publick Hatred;
Thought no Method more commodious,
Than to shew their Vices odious:
Which I chose to make appear,
Not by Anger, but a Sneer:
As my Method of Reforming,
Is by Laughing, not by Storming.   230
(For my Friends have always thought
Tenderness my greatest Fault.)
Wou'd you have me change my Stile,
On your Faults no longer smile?
But, to patch up all our Quarrels,
Quote you Texts from *Plutarch's Morals*;
Or from *Solomon* produce
Maxims teaching Wisdom's Use.

    IF I treat you like——[8]
You have cheap enough compounded.   240
Can you put in higher Claims,
Than the Owners of *St. J—s*?[9]
You are not so great a Grievance
As the Hirelings of *St. St—s*.[10]
You are of a lower Class
Than my Friend Sir *R— Br—s*.[11]
None of these have Mercy found:
I have laugh'd, and lash'd them round.

    HAVE you seen a *Rocket* fly?
You would swear it pierc'd the Sky;   250
It but reach'd the middle Air,
Bursting into Pieces there:
Thousand Sparkles falling down
Light on many a Coxcomb's Crown.
See, what Mirth the Sport creates;
Sindges Hair, but breaks no Pates.

———

THUS, Shou'd I attempt to climb,
Treat you in a Stile sublime,
Such a Rocket is my Muse,
Shou'd I lofty Numbers chuse,   260
E'er I reach'd *Parnassus* Top
I shou'd burst, and bursting drop.
All my *Fire* would fall in Scraps,
Give your Head some gentle Raps;
Only make it smart a while:
Then cou'd I forbear to smile,
When I found the tingling Pain,
Entring warm your frigid Brain
Make you able upon Sight,
To decide of Wrong and Right?   270
Talk with Sense, whate'er you please on,
Learn to relish *Truth* and *Reason.*

THUS we both should gain our Prize:
I to laugh, and you grow wise.

ON POETRY: A RAPSODY

(1733?)

All Human Race wou'd fain be *Wits,*
And Millions miss, for one that hits.
Young's universal Passion,[1] *Pride,*
Was never known to spread so wide.
Say *Britain,* cou'd you ever boast,——
Three *Poets* in an Age at most?
Our chilling Climate hardly bears
A *Sprig* of Bays in Fifty Years:
While ev'ry Fool his Claim alledges,
As if it grew in common Hedges.   10
What Reason can there be assign'd
For this Perverseness in the Mind?
Brutes find out where their Talents lie:
A *Bear* will not attempt to fly:

A founder'd *Horse* will oft debate,
Before he tries a five-barr'd Gate:
A *Dog* by Instinct turns aside,
Who sees the Ditch too deep and wide.
But *Man* we find the only Creature,
Who, led by *Folly,* fights with *Nature;*   20
Who, when *she* loudly cries, *Forbear,*
With Obstinacy fixes there;
And, where his *Genius* least inclines,
Absurdly bends his whole Designs.

   Not *Empire* to the Rising-Sun,
By Valour, Conduct, Fortune won;
Nor highest *Wisdom* in Debates
For framing Laws to govern States;
Nor Skill in Sciences profound,
So large to grasp the Circle round;   30
Such heavenly Influence require,
As how to strike the *Muses Lyre.*

   Not Beggar's Brat, on Bulk begot;
Nor Bastard of a Pedlar *Scot;*
Nor Boy brought up to cleaning Shoes,
The Spawn of *Bridewell,* or the Stews;
Nor Infants dropt, the spurious Pledges
Of *Gipsies* littering under Hedges,
Are so disqualified by Fate
To rise in *Church,* or *Law,* or *State,*   40
As he, whom *Phebus* in his Ire
Hath *blasted* with poetick Fire.

   What hope of Custom in the *Fair,*
While not a Soul demands your Ware?
Where you have nothing to produce
For private Life, or publick Use?
Court, City, Country want you not;
You cannot bribe, betray, or plot.
For Poets, Law makes no Provision:
The Wealthy have you in Derision.   50

Of State-Affairs you cannot smatter,
Are awkward when you try to flatter.
Your Portion, taking *Britain* round,
Was just one annual Hundred Pound.*
Now not so much as in Remainder
Since *Cibber* brought in an Attainder;
For ever fixt by Right Divine,
(A Monarch's Right) on *Grubstreet* Line.
Poor starv'ling Bard, how small thy Gains!
How unproportion'd to thy Pains!   60

        And here a *Simile* comes Pat in:
Tho' *Chickens* take a Month to fatten,
The Guests in less than half an Hour
Will more than half a Score devour.
So, after toiling twenty Days,
To earn a Stock of Pence and Praise,
Thy Labours, grown the Critick's Prey,
Are swallow'd o'er a Dish of Tea;
Gone, to be never heard of more,
Gone, where the *Chickens* went before.   70

        How shall a new Attempter learn
Of diff'rent Spirits to discern,
And how distinguish, which is which,
The Poet's Vein, or scribling Itch?
Then hear an old experienc'd Sinner
Instructing thus a young Beginner.

        Consult yourself, and if you find
A powerful Impulse urge your Mind,
Impartial judge within your Breast
What Subject you can manage best;   80
Whether your Genius most inclines
To Satire, Praise, or hum'rous Lines;
To Elegies in mournful Tone,
Or Prologue sent from Hand unknown.

* Paid to the Poet Laureat, which Place was given to one *Cibber*, a Player.

Then rising with *Aurora*'s Light,
The Muse invok'd, sit down to write;
Blot out, correct, insert, refine,
Enlarge, diminish, interline;
Be mindful, when Invention fails,
To scratch your Head, and bite your Nails.   90

    Your Poem finish'd, next your Care
Is needful, to transcribe it fair.
In modern Wit all printed Trash, is
Set off with num'rous *Breaks*———and *Dashes*—

    To Statesmen wou'd you give a Wipe,
You print it in *Italick Type.*
When Letters are in vulgar Shapes,
'Tis ten to one the Wit escapes;
But when in *Capitals* exprest,
The dullest Reader smoaks the Jest: 100
Or else perhaps he may invent
A better than the Poet meant,
As learned Commentators view
In *Homer* more than *Homer* knew.

    Your Poem in its modish Dress,
Correctly fitted for the Press,
Convey by Penny-Post to *Lintot,*
But let no Friend alive look into't.
If *Lintot* thinks 'twill quit the Cost,
You need not fear your Labour lost: 110
And, how agreeably surpriz'd
Are you to see it advertiz'd!
The Hawker shews you one in Print,
As fresh as Farthings from the Mint:
The Product of your Toil and Sweating;
A Bastard of your own begetting.

    Be sure at *Will*'s[2] the following Day,
Lie Snug, and hear what Criticks say.
And if you find the general Vogue

Pronounces you a stupid Rogue; 120
Damns all your Thoughts as low and little,
Sit still, and swallow down your Spittle.
Be silent as a Politician,
For talking may beget Suspicion:
Or praise the Judgment of the Town,
And help yourself to run it down.
Give up your fond paternal Pride,
Nor argue on the weaker Side;
For Poems read without a Name
We justly praise, or justly blame: 130
And Criticks have no partial Views,
Except they know whom they abuse.
And since you ne'er provok'd their Spight,
Depend upon't their Judgment's right:
But if you blab, you are undone;
Consider what a Risk you run.
You lose your Credit all at once;
The Town will mark you for a Dunce:
The vilest Doggrel *Grubstreet* sends,
Will pass for yours with Foes and Friends. 140
And you must bear the whole Disgrace,
'Till some fresh Blockhead takes your Place.

Your Secret kept, your Poem sunk,
And sent in Quires to line a Trunk;
If still you be dispos'd to rhime,
Go try your Hand a second Time.
Again you fail, yet Safe's the Word,
Take Courage, and attempt a Third.
But first with Care imploy your Thoughts,
Where Criticks mark'd your former Faults. 150
The trivial Turns, the borrow'd Wit,
The *Similes* that nothing fit;
The *Cant* which ev'ry Fool repeats,
Town-Jests, and Coffee-house Conceits;
Descriptions tedious, flat and dry,
And introduc'd the Lord knows why;
Or where we find your Fury set

Against the harmless Alphabet;
On A's and B's your Malice vent,
While Readers wonder whom you meant.   160
A publick, or a private *Robber;*
A *Statesman,* or a South-Sea *Jobber.*
A *Prelate* who no God believes;
A——,³ or Den of Thieves.
A Pick-purse at the Bar, or Bench;
A Duchess, or a Suburb-Wench.
Or oft when Epithets you link,
In gaping Lines to fill a Chink;
Like stepping Stones to save a Stride,
In Streets where Kennels⁴ are too wide: 170
Or like a Heel-piece to support
A Cripple with one Foot too short:
Or like a Bridge that joins a Marish
To Moorlands of a diff'rent Parish.
So have I seen ill-coupled Hounds,
Drag diff'rent Ways in miry Grounds.
So Geographers in *Afric*-Maps
With Savage-Pictures fill their Gaps;
And o'er unhabitable Downs
Place Elephants for want of Towns.   180

    But tho' you miss your third Essay,
You need not throw your Pen away.
Lay now aside all Thoughts of Fame,
To spring more profitable Game.
From Party-Merit seek Support;
The vilest Verse thrives best at Court.
A Pamphlet in Sir *Rob*'s Defence
Will never fail to bring in Pence;
Nor be concern'd about the Sale,
He pays his Workmen on the Nail.   190

    A Prince the Moment he is crown'd,
Inherits ev'ry Virtue round,
As Emblems of the sov'reign Pow'r,
Like other Bawbles of the Tow'r.

Is gen'rous, valiant, just and wise,
And so continues 'till he dies.
His humble *Senate* this professes,
In all their *Speeches, Votes, Addresses.*
But once you fix him in a Tomb,
His Virtues fade, his Vices bloom;   200
And each Perfection wrong imputed
Is Folly, at his Death confuted.
The Loads of Poems in his Praise,
Ascending make one Funeral-Blaze.
As soon as you can hear his Knell,
This God on Earth turns *Devil* in Hell.
And lo, his Ministers of State,
Transform'd to Imps, his Levee wait.
Where, in this Scene of endless Woe,
They ply their former Arts below.   210
And as they sail in *Charon*'s Boat,
Contrive to bribe the Judge's Vote.
To *Cerberus* they give a Sop,
His triple-barking Mouth to Stop:
Or in the Iv'ry Gate of Dreams,
Project * * * and * * * * * * * * ;5
Or hire their Party-Pamphleteers,
To set *Elysium* by the Ears.

  Then *Poet,* if you mean to thrive,
Employ your Muse on Kings alive;   220
With Prudence gath'ring up a Cluster
Of all the Virtues you can muster:
Which form'd into a Garland sweet,
Lay humbly at your Monarch's Feet;
Who, as the Odours reach his Throne,
Will smile, and think 'em all his own:
For *Law* and *Gospel* both determine
All Virtues lodge in royal Ermine.
(I mean the Oracles of Both,
Who shall depose it upon Oath.)   230
Your Garland in the following Reign,
Change but their Names will do again.

———

But if you think this Trade too base,
(Which seldom is the Dunce's Case)
Put on the Critick's Brow, and sit
At *Wills* the puny Judge of Wit.
A Nod, a Shrug, a scornful Smile,
With Caution us'd, may serve a-while.
Proceed no further in your Part,
Before you learn the Terms of Art: 240
(For you may easy be too far gone,
In all our modern Criticks Jargon.)
Then talk with more authentick Face,
Of *Unities, in Time and Place.*
Get Scraps of *Horace* from your Friends,
And have them at your Fingers Ends.
Learn *Aristotle*'s Rules by Rote,
And at all Hazards boldly quote:
Judicious *Rymer* oft review:
Wise *Dennis,* and profound *Bossu.*   250
Read all the *Prefaces* of *Dryden,*⁶
For these our Criticks much confide in,
(Tho' meerly writ at first for filling
To raise the Volume's Price, a Shilling.)

A forward Critick often dupes us
With sham Quotations *Peri Hupsous:**
And if we have not read *Longinus,*
Will magisterially out-shine us.
Then, lest with *Greek* he over-run ye,
Procure the Book for Love or Money,   260
Translated from *Boileau*'s Translation,†⁷
And quote *Quotation* on *Quotation.*

At *Wills* you hear a Poem read,
Where *Battus* from the Table-head,
Reclining on his Elbow-chair,

* A famous Treatise of *Longinus.*
† By Mr. *Welsted.*

Gives Judgment with decisive Air.
To whom the Tribe of circling Wits,
As to an Oracle submits.
He gives Directions to the Town,
To cry it up, or run it down.   270
(Like *Courtiers,* when they send a Note,
Instructing *Members* how to Vote.)
He sets the Stamp of Bad and Good,
Tho' not a Word be understood.
Your Lesson learnt, you'll be secure
To get the Name of *Conoisseur.*
And when your Merits once are known,
Procure Disciples of your own.

   Our Poets (you can never want 'em,
Spread thro' *Augusta Trinobantum*[8])   280
Computing by their Pecks of Coals,
Amount to just Nine thousand Souls.
These o'er their proper Districts govern,
Of Wit and Humour, Judges sov'reign.
In ev'ry Street a City-bard
Rules, like an Alderman his Ward.
His indisputed Rights extend
Thro' all the Lane, from End to End.
The Neighbours round admire his *Shrewdness,*
For songs of *Loyalty* and *Lewdness.*   290
Out-done by none in Rhyming well,
Altho' he never learnt to spell.

   Two bordering Wits contend for Glory;
And one is *Whig,* and one is *Tory.*
And this, for Epicks claims the Bays,
And that, for Elegiack Lays.
Some famed for Numbers soft and smooth,
By Lovers spoke in *Punch*'s Booth.
And some as justly Fame extols
For lofty Lines in *Smithfield* Drols.   300
Bavius in *Wapping* gains Renown,
And *Mœvius* reigns o'er *Kentish-Town:*
Tigellius plac'd in *Phœbus*' Car,

From *Ludgate* shines to *Temple-bar.*
Harmonius *Cibber* entertains
The Court with annual Birth-day Strains;[9]
Whence *Gay* was banish'd in Disgrace,
Where *Pope* will never show his Face;
Where *Y-------*[10] must torture his Invention,
To flatter *Knaves,* or lose his *Pension.*   310

    But these are not a thousandth Part
Of jobbers in the Poets Art,
Attending each his proper Station,
And all in due Subordination;
Thro' ev'ry Alley to be found,
In Garrets high, or under Ground:
And when they join their *Pericranies,*[11]
Out skips a *Book of Miscellanies.*
Hobbes[12] clearly proves that ev'ry Creature
Lives in a State of War by Nature.   320
The Greater for the Smallest watch,
But meddle seldom with their Match.
A Whale of moderate Size will draw
A Shole of Herrings down his Maw.
A Fox with Geese his Belly crams;
A Wolf destroys a thousand Lambs.
But search among the rhiming Race,
The Brave are worried by the Base.
If, on *Parnassus'* Top you sit,
You rarely bite, are always bit: 330
Each Poet of inferior Size
On you shall rail and criticize;
And strive to tear you Limb from Limb,
While others do as much for him.

    The Vermin only teaze and pinch
Their Foes superior by an Inch.
So, Nat'ralists observe, a Flea
Hath smaller Fleas that on him prey,
And these have smaller Fleas to bite 'em,
And so proceed *ad infinitum:*   340
Thus ev'ry Poet in his Kind,

Is bit by him that comes behind;
Who, tho' too little to be seen,
Can teaze, and gall, and give the Spleen;
Call Dunces, Fools, and Sons of Whores,
Lay *Grubstreet* at each others Doors:
Extol the *Greek* and *Roman* Masters,
And curse our modern Poetasters.
Complain, as many an ancient Bard did,
How Genius is no more rewarded;   350
How wrong a Taste prevails among us;
How much our Ancestors out-sung us;
Can personate an awkward Scorn
For those who are not Poets born:
And all their Brother Dunces lash,
Who crowd the Press with hourly Trash.

O, *Grubstreet!* how do I bemoan thee,
Whose graceless Children scorn to own thee!
Their filial Piety forgot,
Deny their Country like a SCOT: 360
Tho' by their Idiom and Grimace
They soon betray their native Place:
Yet *thou* hast greater Cause to be
Asham'd of them, than they of thee.
Degenerate from their ancient Brood,
Since first the Court allow'd them Food.

Remains a Difficulty still,
To purchase Fame by writing ill:
From *Flecknoe*[13] down to *Howard*'s Time,
How few have reach'd the *low Sublime*?   370
For when our high-born *Howard* dy'd,
Blackmore alone his Place supply'd:
And least a Chasm should intervene,
When Death had finish'd *Blackmore*'s Reign,
The *leaden Crown* devolv'd to thee,
Great Poet* of the *Hollow-Tree.*

* Lord *G—*.

But, oh, how unsecure thy Throne!
A thousand Bards thy Right disown:
They plot to turn in factious Zeal,
Duncenia to a Common-weal;   380
And with rebellious Arms pretend
An equal Priv'lege to *descend*.

    In Bulk there are not more Degrees,
From *Elephants* to *Mites* in Cheese,
Than what a curious Eye may trace
In Creatures of the rhiming Race.
From bad to worse, and worse they fall,
But, who can reach the Worst of all?
For, tho' in Nature Depth and Height
Are equally held infinite,   390
In Poetry the Height we know;
'Tis only infinite below.
For Instance: When you rashly think,*
No Rhymer can like *Welsted* sink.
His Merits ballanc'd you shall find,
That *Feilding* leaves him far behind.
Concannen, more aspiring Bard,
Climbs downwards, deeper by a Yard:
Smart JEMMY MOOR with Vigor drops,
The Rest pursue as thick as Hops: 400
With Heads to Points the Gulph they enter,
Linkt perpendicular to the Centre:
And as their Heels elated rise,
Their Heads attempt the nether Skies.

    O, what Indignity and Shame
To prostitute the Muse's Name,
By flatt'ring—whom Heaven design'd
The Plagues and Scourges of Mankind.
Bred up in Ignorance and Sloth,
And ev'ry Vice that nurses both.   410

———

* *Vide* The Treatise on the *Profound,* and Mr. *Pope's Dunciad.*

Fair *Britain* in thy Monarch blest,
Whose Virtues bear the strictest Test;
Whom never *Faction* cou'd bespatter,
Nor *Minister,* nor *Poet* flatter.
What Justice in rewarding Merit?
What Magnanimity of Spirit?
What Lineaments divine we trace
Thro' all the Features of his Face;
Tho' Peace with Olive bind his Hands,
Confest the conqu'ring Hero stands.   420
Hydaspes, Indus, and the *Ganges,*
Dread from his Hand impending Changes.
From him the *Tartar,* and *Chinese,*
Short by the Knees intreat for Peace.
The *Consort* of his Throne and Bed,
A perfect Goddess born and bred.
Appointed sov'reign Judge to sit
On Learning, Eloquence and Wit.
Our eldest Hope, divine *Iülus,*
(Late, very late, O, may he rule us.)   430
What early Manhood has he shown,
Before his downy Beard was grown!
Then think, what Wonders will be done
By going on as he begun;
An Heir for *Britain* to secure
As long as Sun and Moon endure.

The Remnant of the royal Blood,
Comes pouring on me like a Flood.
Bright Goddesses, in Number five;
Duke *William,* sweetest Prince alive.   440

Now sing the *Minister* of *State,*
Who shines alone, without a Mate.
Observe with what majestick Port
This *Atlas* stands to prop the Court:
Intent the Publick Debts to pay,
Like prudent *Fabius** by *Delay.*

---

* *Unus Homo nobis* Cunctando *restituit rem.*[14]

Thou great Vicegerent of the King,
Thy Praises ev'ry Muse shall sing.
In all Affairs thou sole Director,
Of Wit and Learning chief Protector;   450
Tho' small the Time thou hast to spare,
The Church is thy peculiar Care.
Of pious Prelates what a Stock
You chuse to rule the Sable-flock.
You raise the Honour of the Peerage,
Proud to attend you at the Steerage.
You dignify the noble Race,
Content yourself with humbler Place.
Now Learning, Valour, Virtue, Sense,
To Titles give the sole Pretence.   460
St. George beheld thee with Delight,
Vouchsafe to be an azure Knight,
When on thy Breast and Sides *Herculean*,
He fixt the *Star* and *String Cerulean*.

    Say, Poet, in what other Nation,
Shone ever such a Constellation.
Attend ye *Popes*, and *Youngs*, and *Gays*,
And tune your Harps, and strow your Bays.
Your Panegyricks here provide,
You cannot err on Flatt'ry's Side.   470
Above the Stars exalt your Stile,
You still are low ten thousand Mile.
On *Lewis*[15] all his Bards bestow'd,
Of Incense many a thousand Load;
But *Europe* mortify'd his Pride,
And swore the fawning Rascals ly'd:
Yet what the World refus'd to *Lewis*,
Apply'd to--------[16] exactly true is:
Exactly true! Invidious Poet!
'Tis fifty thousand Times below it.   480

    Translate me now some Lines, if you can,
From *Virgil, Martial, Ovid, Lucan;*
They could all Pow'r in Heaven divide,
And do no Wrong to either Side:

They'll teach you how to split a Hair,
Give--------[17] and *Jove* an equal Share.*
Yet, why should we be lac'd so straight;
I'll give my   *   *   *   *   *[18] Butter-weight.
And Reason good; for many a Year
-----[19] never intermeddl'd here: 490
Nor, tho' his Priests be duly paid,
Did ever we *desire* his Aid:
We now can better do without him,
Since *Woolston* gave us Arms to rout him.
*   *   *   *   *   *Cætera desiderantur*[20] *   *   *   *   *

THE YAHOO'S OVERTHROW;

or, The Kevan Bayl's New Ballad,
upon Serjeant Kite's insulting the Dean. To the Tune of Derry down.

(1734, 1765)

Jolly boys of St. Kevans, St. Patrick's, Donore,
And Smithfield, I'll tell you, if not told before,
Bow B---th, that booby, and S---l[1] in grain,
Hath insulted us all by insulting the Dean.
    Knock him down, down, down, knock him down.

The Dean and his merits we ev'ry one know,
But this skip of a Lawyer, where the De'el did he grow?
How greater's his merit at four Courts of House,
Than the barking of Towzer, or leap of a louse?
    Knock him down, &c.   10

That he came from the Temple, his morals do show,
But where his deep law is, few mortals yet know:
His rhet'ric, bombast, silly jests, are by far
More like lampooning than pleading at bar.
    Knock him down, &c.

* *Divisum Imperium cum* Jove Cæsar *habet.*[21]

This pedlar, at speaking and making of laws,
Hath met with returns of all sorts but applause;
Has, with noise and odd gestures, been prating some years,
What honester folks never durst for their ears.
        Knock him down, &c.   20

Of all sizes and sorts, the Fanatical crew
Are his Brother Protestants, good men and true;
Red hat, and blue bonnet, and turbant's² the same,
What the De'el is't to him whence the Devil they came?
        Knock him down, &c.

Hobbes, Tindal, and Woolston, and Collins, and Nayler,
And Muggleton, Toland, and Bradley the taylor,³
Are Christians alike; and it may be averr'd,
He's a Christian as good as the rest of the herd.
        Knock him down, &c.   30

He only the rights of the clergy debates,
Their rights! their importance! We'll set on new rates
On their tythes at half-nothing, their priesthood at less:
What's next to be voted with ease you may guess.
        Knock him down, &c.

At length his Old Master (I need not him name)
To this damnable Speaker had long ow'd a shame;
When his speech came abroad, he paid him off clean,
By leaving him under the pen of the Dean.
        Knock him down, &c.   40

He kindled, as if the whole Satire had been
The oppression of Virtue, not wages of Sin:
He began as he bragg'd, with a rant and a roar;
He bragg'd how he bounc'd, and he swore how he swore.
        Knock him down, &c.

Tho' he cring'd to his Deanship in very low strains,
To others he boasted of knocking out brains,

And slitting of noses, and cropping of ears,
While his own ass's Zaggs were more fit for the shears.
    Knock him down, &c.   50

On this Worrier of Deans whene'er we can hit,
We'll show him the way how to crop and to slit;
We'll teach him some better address to afford
To the Dean of all Deans, tho' he wears not a sword.
    Knock him down, &c.

We'll colt him thro' Kevan, St. Patrick's, Donore,
And Smithfield, as Rap was ne'er colted before;
We'll oil him with kennel, and powd'r him with grains,
A modus right fit for insulters of Deans.
    Knock him down, &c.   60

And, when this is over, we'll make him amends,
To the Dean he shall go; they shall kiss, and be friends:
But how? Why, the Dean shall to him disclose
A face for to kiss, without eyes, ears, or nose.
    Knock him down, &c.

If you say this is hard, on a man that is reckon'd
That serjeant at law, whom we call Kite the Second,
You mistake; for a Slave, who will coax his superiors,
May be proud to be licking a great man's posteriors.
    Knock him down, &c.   70

What care we how high runs his passion or pride?
Tho' his soul he despises, he values his hide:
Then fear not his tongue, his sword, or his knife;
He'll take his revenge on his innocent wife.
   Knock him down, down, down,—keep him down.

A CHARACTER, PANEGYRIC, AND DESCRIPTION OF THE LEGION CLUB

(1736)

As I strole the City, oft I
Spy a Building¹ large and lofty,
Not a Bow-shot from the College,
Half the Globe from Sense and Knowledge.
By the prudent Architect
Plac'd against the Church direct;
Making good my Grandames Jest,
Near the Church—you know the rest.²

TELL us, what this Pile contains?
Many a Head that holds no Brains.   10
These Demoniacs let me dub
With the Name of *Legion Club*.
Such Assemblies, you might swear,
Meet when Butchers bait a Bear;
Such a Noise, and such haranguing,
When a Brother Thief is hanging.
Such a Rout and such a Rabble
Run to hear Jackpudding³ gabble;
Such a Croud their Ordure throws
On a far less Villain's Nose.   20

COULD I from the Building's Top
Hear the rattling Thunder drop,
While the Devil upon the Roof,
If the Devil be Thunder Proof,
Should with Poker fiery-red
Crack the Stones, and melt the Lead;
Drive them down on every Scull,
While the Den of Thieves is full,
Quite destroy that Harpies Nest,
How might then our Isle be blest?   30

For Divines allow, that God
Sometimes makes the Devil his Rod:
And the Gospel will inform us,
He can punish Sins enormous.

YET should *Swift* endow the Schools
For his Lunatics and Fools,
With a Rood or two of Land,
I allow the Pile may stand.
You perhaps will ask me, why so?
But it is with this Proviso,   40
Since the House is like to last,
Let a royal Grant be pass'd,
That the Club have Right to dwell
Each within his proper Cell;
With a Passage left to creep in,
And a Hole above for peeping.

LET them, when they once get in
Sell the Nation for a Pin;
While they sit a picking Straws
Let them rave of making Laws;   50
While they never hold their Tongue,
Let them dabble in their Dung;
Let them form a grand Committee,
How to plague and starve the City;
Let them stare and storm and frown,
When they see a Clergy-Gown,
Let them, 'ere they crack a Louse,
Call for th'Orders of the House;
Let them with their gosling Quills,
Scribble senseless Heads of Bills;   60
We may, while they strain their Throats,
Wipe our A—s with their V—.

LET Sir *T*—,[4] that rampant Ass,
Stuff his Guts with Flax and Grass;
But before the Priest he fleeces
Tear the Bible all to Pieces.

At the Parsons, *Tom,* Halloo Boy,
Worthy Offspring of a Shoeboy,
Footman, Traytor, vile Seducer,
Perjur'd Rebel, brib'd Accuser;   70
Lay thy paltry Priviledge aside,
Sprung from Papists and a Regicide;
Fall a Working like a Mole,
Raise the Dirt about your Hole.

COME, assist me, Muse obedient,
Let us try some new Expedient;
Shift the Scene for half an Hour,
Time and Place are in thy Power.
Thither, gentle Muse, conduct me,
I shall ask, and you instruct me.   80

SEE, the Muse unbars the Gate;
Hark, the Monkeys, how they prate!

ALL ye Gods, who rule the Soul
Styx, through Hell whose Waters roll!
Let me be allow'd to tell
What I heard in yonder Hell.

NEAR the Door an entrance gapes,
Crouded round with antic Shapes;
Poverty, and *Grief,* and *Care,*
Causeless *Joy,* and true *Despair;*   90
Discord periwigg'd with Snakes,
See the dreadful Strides she takes.

BY this odious Crew beset,
I began to rage and fret
And resolv'd to break their Pates,
'Ere we enter'd at the Gates;
Had not *Clio*[5] in the Nick,
Whisper'd me, let down your Stick;
What, said I, is this the Mad-House?
These, she answer'd, are but Shadows,   100

Phantoms, bodiless and vain,
Empty Visions of the Brain.

IN the Porch *Briareus* stands,
Shews a Bribe in all his Hands:
Briareus the Secretary,
But we Mortals call him *Cary*.
When the Rogues their Country fleece,
They may hope for Pence a Piece.

CLIO, who had been so wise
To put on a Fool's Disguise,   110
To bespeak some Approbation,
And be thought a near Relation;
When she saw three hundred Brutes,
All involv'd in wild Disputes;
Roaring till their Lungs were spent,
P-l-ge of P-l-m-nt,
Now a new Misfortune feels,
Dreading to be laid by th' Heels.
Never durst a Muse before
Enter that Infernal Door;   120
Clio stifled with the Smell,
Into Spleen and Vapours fell;
By the *Stygian* Steams that flew,
From the dire infectious Crew.
Not the Stench of Lake *Avernus,*
Could have more offended her Nose;
Had she flown but o'er the Top,
She would feel her Pinions drop,
And by Exhalations dire,
Though a Goddess must expire.   130
In a Fright she crept away,
Bravely I resolved to stay.

WHEN I saw the Keeper frown,
Tipping him with Half a Crown;
Now, said I, we are alone,
Name your Heroes one, by one.

—

WHO is that Hell-featur'd Brawler,
Is it Satan? No 'tis *W*—.[6]
In what Figure can a Bard dress
Jack, the Grandson of Sir *Hardress*?   140
Honest Keeper, drive him further,
In his Looks are Hell and Murther;
See the Scowling Visage drop,
Just as when he murther'd *T*—.[7]

KEEPER, shew me where to fix
On the Puppy Pair of *Dicks,*[8]
By their lanthorn Jaws and Leathern,
You might swear they both are Brethren:
Dick Fitz-Baker, Dick the Player,
Old Acquaintance, are you there?   150
Dear Companions hug and kiss,
Toast *old Glorious*[9] in your Piss.
Tye them Keeper in a Tether,
Let them stare and stink together;
Both are apt to be unruly,
Lash them daily, lash them duly,
Though 'tis hopeless to reclaim them,
Scorpion Rods perhaps may tame them.

KEEPER, yon old Dotard smoke,
Sweetly snoring in his Cloak.   160
Who is he? 'Tis hum-drum *W*—,
Half encompass'd by his Kin:
There observe the Tribe of *B*—*m,*
For he never fails to bring 'em;
While he sleeps the whole Debate,
They submissive round him wait;
Yet would gladly see the Hunks
In his Grave, and search his Trunks.
See they gently twitch his Coat,
Just to yawn, and give his Vote;   170
Always firm in his Vocation,
For the Court against the Nation.

———

THOSE are *A—s, Jack* and *Bob,*
First in every wicked Jobb,
Son and Brother to a Queer,
Brainsick Brute, they call a Peer.
We must give them better Quarter,
For their Ancestor trod Mortar;
And at *Hoath* to boast his Fame,
On a Chimney cut his Name.   **180**

THERE sit *C—s, D—,* and *H—,*
How they swagger from their Garrison.
Such a Triplet could you tell
Where to find on this Side Hell?
H—, and *D—,* and *C—,*
Souse them in their own Ex-crements.
Every Mischief in their Hearts,
If they fail 'tis Want of Parts.

BLESS us, *Morgan!* Art thou there Man?
Bless mine Eyes! Art thou the Chairman?   **190**
Chairman to yon damn'd Committee!
Yet I look on thee with Pity.
Dreadful Sight! What learned *Morgan*
Metamorphos'd to a Gorgan!
For thy horrid Looks, I own,
Half convert me to a Stone.
Hast thou been so long at School,
Now to turn a factious Tool!
Alma Mater was thy Mother,
Every young Divine thy Brother.   **200**
Thou a disobedient Varlet,
Treat thy Mother like a Harlot!
Thou, ungrateful to thy Teachers,
Who are all grown reverend Preachers!
Morgan! Would it not surprise one?
Turn thy Nourishment to Poison!
When you walk among your Books,
They reproach you with their Looks;

Bind them fast, or from the Shelves
They'll come down to right themselves: 210
Homer, Plutarch, Virgil, Flaccus,
All in Arms prepare to back us:
Soon repent, or put to Slaughter
Every *Greek* and *Roman* Author.
While you in your Faction's Phrase
Send the Clergy all to graze;
And to make your Project pass,
Leave them not a Blade of Grass.

How I want thee, humorous *Hogart?*[10]   220
Thou I hear, a pleasant Rogue art;
Were but you and I acquainted,
Every Monster should be painted;
You should try your graving Tools
On this odious Group of Fools;
Draw the Beasts as I describe 'em,
Form their Features, while I gibe them;
Draw them like, for I assure you,
You will need no *Car'catura;*
Draw them so that we may trace
All the Soul in every Face.   230
Keeper, I must now retire,
You have done what I desire:
But I feel my Spirits spent,
With the Noise, the Sight, the Scent.

PRAY be patient, you shall find
Half the best are still behind:
You have hardly seen a Score,
I can shew two hundred more.
Keeper, I have seen enough,
Taking then a Pinch of Snuff;   240
I concluded, looking round 'em,
May their God, the Devil-confound 'em.

VERSES MADE FOR WOMEN
WHO CRY APPLES, &c.
(1746)

APPLES.

Come buy my fine Wares,
Plumbs, Apples, and Pears,
A hundred a Penny,
In Conscience too many,
Come, will you have any;
My Children are seven,
I wish them in Heaven,
My Husband's a Sot,
With his Pipe and his Pot,
Not a Farthing will gain 'em,   10
And I must maintain 'em.

ASPARAGUS.

Ripe 'Sparagrass,
Fit for Lad or Lass,
To make their Water pass:
  O, 'tis pretty Picking
  With a tender Chicken.

ONYONS.

Come, follow me by the Smell,
Here's delicate Onyons to sell,
I promise to use you well.
They make the Blood warmer,
You'll feed like a Farmer:
For this is ev'ry Cook's Opinion,
No sav'ry Dish without an Onyon;
But lest your Kissing should be spoyl'd,
Your Onyons must be th'roughly boyl'd;
   Or else you may spare   10
   Your Mistress a Share,
The Secret will never be known;

She cannot discover
The Breath of her Lover,
But think it as sweet as her own.

OYSTERS.

Charming Oysters I cry,
My Masters come buy,
So plump and so fresh,
So sweet is their Flesh,
  No *Colchester* Oyster,
  Is sweeter and moyster,
  Your Stomach they settle,
  And rouse up your Mettle,
  They'll make you a Dad
  Of a Lass or a Lad;   10
  And, Madam your Wife
  They'll please to the Life;
Be she barren, be she old,
Be she Slut, or be she Scold,
Eat my Oysters, and lye near her,
She'll be fruitful, never fear her.

HERRINGS.

Be not sparing,
Leave off swearing
Buy my Herring
Fresh from *Malahide,*
Better ne'er was try'd.
Come eat 'em with pure fresh Butter and Mustard,
Their Bellies are soft, and as white as a Custard.
Come, Six-pence a Dozen to get me some Bread,
Or, like my own Herrings, I soon shall be dead.

ORANGES.

Come, buy my fine Oranges, Sauce for your Veal,
And charming when squeez'd in a Pot of brown Ale.
Well roasted, with Sugar and Wine in a Cup,
They'll make a sweet Bishop when Gentlefolks sup.

X

SELECTED

CORRESPONDENCE

SO, as I told you just now in the letter I sent half an hour ago, I dined with
Mr. Harley to-day, who presented me to the attorney-general sir Simon Harcourt, with much compliment on all sides, &c. Harley told me he had shown
my memorial[1] to the queen, and seconded it very heartily; and he desires me
to dine with him again on Sunday, when he promises to settle it with her
majesty, before she names a governor;[2] and I protest I am in hopes it will be
done, all but the forms, by that time; for he loves the church: this is a popular
thing, and he would not have a governor share in it; and, besides, I am told by
all hands, he has a mind to gain me over. But in the letter I writ last post
(yesterday) to the archbishop,[3] I did not tell him a syllable of what Mr. Harley
said to me last night, because he charged me to keep it secret; so I would not
tell it to you, but that before this goes, I hope the secret will be over. I am now
writing my poetical *Description of a Shower in London,* and will send it to the
Tatler. This is the last sheet of a whole quire I have written since I came to
town. Pray, now it comes into my head, will you, when you go to Mrs. Walls,
contrive to know whether Mrs. Wesley be in town, and still at her brother's, and
how she is in health, and whether she stays in town. I writ to her from Chester,
to know what I should do with her note; and I believe the poor woman is afraid
to write to me: so I must go to my business, &c.

11. To-day at last I dined with lord Montrath, and carried lord Mountjoy
and sir Andrew Fountain with me; and was looking over them at ombre till
eleven this evening like a fool: they played running ombre[4] half crowns; and sir
Andrew Fountain won eight guineas of Mr. Coote: so I am come home late, and
will say but little to MD[5] this night. I have gotten half a bushel of coals, and
Patrick,[6] the extravagant whelp, had a fire ready for me; but I pickt off the coals
before I went to-bed. It is a sign London is now an empty place, when it will
not furnish me with matter for above five or six lines in a day. Did you smoak[7]
in my last how I told you the very day and the place you were playing at
ombre? But I interlined and altered a little, after I had received a letter from
Mr. Manley, that said you were at it in his house, while he was writing to me;
but without his help I guess'd within one day. Your town is certainly much
more sociable than ours. I have not seen your mother yet, &c.

12. I dined to-day with Dr. Garth[8] and Mr. Addison,[9] at the Devil tavern, by

Temple-bar, and Garth treated; and 'tis well I dine every day, else I should be longer making out my letters: for we are yet in a very dull state, only enquiring every day after new elections, where the Tories carry it among the new members six to one. Mr. Addison's election has passed easy and undisputed; and I believe, if he had a mind to be chosen king, he would hardly be refused. An odd accident has happened at Colchester: one captain Lavallin coming from Flanders or Spain, found his wife with child by a clerk of Doctors Commons,[10] whose trade, you know, it is to prevent fornications: and this clerk was the very same fellow that made the discovery of Dyet's counterfeiting the stamp paper. Lavallin has been this fortnight hunting after the clerk to kill him; but the fellow was constantly employed at the Treasury about the discovery he made: the wife had made a shift to patch up the business, alledging that the clerk had told her her husband was dead, and other excuses; but t'other day somebody told Lavallin his wife had intrigues before he married her: upon which he goes down in a rage, shoots his wife through the head, then falls on his sword; and, to make the matter sure, at the same time discharges a pistol through his own head, and died on the spot, his wife surviving him about two hours; but in what circumstances of mind and body is terrible to imagine. I have finished my poem on the *Shower*, all but the beginning, and am going on with my *Tatler*. They have fixt about fifty things on me since I came: I have printed but three. One advantage I get by writing to you daily, or rather you get, is, that I shall remember not to write the same things twice; and yet I fear I have done it often already: but I'll mind and confine myself to the accidents of the day; and so get you gone to ombre, and be good girls, and save your money, and be rich against Presto[11] comes, and write to me now and then: I am thinking it would be a pretty thing to hear sometimes from sawcy MD; but don't hurt your eyes, Stella, I charge you.

13. O Lord, here's but a trifle of my letter written yet; what shall Presto do for prittle prattle to entertain MD? The talk now grows fresher of the duke of Ormond for Ireland, though Mr. Addison says he hears it will be in commission, and lord Gallaway one. These letters of mine are a sort of journal, where matters open by degrees; and, as I tell true or false, you will find by the event whether my intelligence be good; but I don't care two-pence whether it be or no.—At night. To-day I was all about St. Paul's, and up at the top like a fool, with sir Andrew Fountain and two more; and spent seven shillings for my dinner like a puppy: this is the second time he has served me so; but I'll never do it again, though all mankind should persuade me, unconsidering puppies! There's a young fellow here in town we are all fond of, and about a year or two come from the university, one Harrison,[12] a little pretty fellow, with a great deal of wit, good sense, and good nature; has written some mighty pretty things; that in your 6th *Miscellanea*, about the *Sprig of an Orange*, is his: he has nothing to live on but being governor to one of the duke of Queensbury's sons

for forty pounds a year. The fine fellows are always inviting him to the tavern, and make him pay his club. Henley[13] is a great crony of his: they are often at the tavern at six or seven shillings reckoning, and always makes the poor lad pay his full share. A colonel and a lord were at him and me the same way to-night: I absolutely refused, and made Harrison lag behind, and persuaded him not to go to them. I tell you this, because I find all rich fellows have that humour of using all people without any consideration of their fortunes; but I'll see them rot before they shall serve me so. Lord Halifax is always teazing me to go down to his country house, which will cost me a guinea to his servants, and twelve shillings coach hire; and he shall be hanged first. Is not this a plaguy silly story? But I am vext at the heart; for I love the young fellow, and am resolved to stir up people to do something for him: he is a Whig, and I'll put him upon some of my cast Whigs; for I have done with them, and they have, I hope, done with this kingdom for our time. They were sure of the four members for London above all places, and they have lost three in the four. Sir Richard Onslow, we hear, has lost for Surry; and they are overthrown in most places. Lookee, gentlewomen, if I write long letters, I must write you news and stuff, unless I send you my verses; and some I dare not; and those on the *Shower in London* I have sent to the *Tatler,* and you may see them in Ireland. I fancy you'll smoak me in the *Tatler* I am going to write; for I believe I have told you the hint. I had a letter sent me to-night from sir Matthew Dudley, and found it on my table when I came in. Because it is extraordinary I will transcribe it from beginning to end. It is as follows [Is the Devil in you? Oct. 13, 1710.] I would have answered every particular passage in it, only I wanted time. Here's enough for to-night, such as it is, &c.

14. Is that tobacco at the top of the paper, or what? I don't remember I slobbered. Lord, I dreamt of Stella, &c. so confusedly last night, and that we saw dean Bolton and Sterne go into a shop; and she bid me call them to her, and they proved to be two parsons I know not; and I walked without till she was shifting, and such stuff, mixt with much melancholy and uneasiness, and things not as they should be, and I know not how: and it is now an ugly gloomy morning.—At night. Mr. Addison and I dined with Ned Southwell, and walkt in the Park; and at the Coffee-house I found a letter from the bishop of Clogher, and a pacquet from MD. I opened the bishop's letter; but put up MD's, and visited a lady just come to town, and am now got into bed, and going to open your little letter: and God send I may find MD well, and happy, and merry, and that they love Presto as they do fires. Oh, I won't open it yet! yes I will! no I won't; I am going; I can't stay till I turn over.[14] What shall I do? My fingers itch; and I now have it in my left hand; and now I'll open it this very moment.—I have just got it, and am cracking the seal, and can't imagine what's in it; I fear only some letter from a bishop, and it comes too late: I shall employ nobody's credit but my own. Well, I see though—Pshaw, 'tis from sir Andrew Fountain: What, an-

other! I fancy that is from Mrs. Barton; she told me she would write to me; but she writes a better hand than this: I wish you would inquire; it must be at Dawson's office at the Castle. I fear this is from Patty Rolt, by the scrawl. Well, I'll read MD's letter. Ah, no; it is from poor lady Berkeley, to invite me to Berkeley-castle this winter; and now it grieves my heart: she says she hopes my Lord is in a fair way of recovery; poor lady.[15] Well, now I go to MD's letter: faith, 'tis all right; I hoped it was wrong. Your letter, N. 3, that I have now received, is dated Sept. 26, and Manley's letter, that I had five days ago, was dated Oct. 3, that's a fortnight difference: I doubt it has lain in Steele's office, and he forgot. Well, there's an end of that: he is turned out of his place; and you must desire those who send me pacquets, to inclose them in a paper directed to Mr. Addison, at St. James's Coffee-house: not common letters, but pacquets: the bishop of Clogher may mention it to the archbishop when he sees him. As for your letter, it makes me mad: slidikins,[16] I have been the best boy in Christendom, and you come with your two eggs a penny.—Well; but stay, I'll look over my book; adad, I think there was a *chasm* between my N. 2 and N. 3. Faith, I won't promise to write to you every week; but I'll write every night, and when it is full I will send it; that will be once in ten days, and that will be often enough: and if you begin to take up the way of writing to Presto, only because it is Tuesday, a Monday bedad, it will grow a task; but write when you have a mind.—No, no, no, no, no, no, no, no—Agad, agad, agad, agad, agad, agad; no, poor Stellakins. Slids, I would the horse were in your—chamber. Have not I ordered Parvisol to obey your directions about him? And han't I said in my former letters, that you may pickle him, and boil him, if you will? What do you trouble me about your horses for? Have I any thing to do with them?—Revolutions a hindrance to me in my business; Revolutions—to me in my business? If it were not for the revolutions, I could do nothing at all; and now I have all hopes possible, though one is certain of nothing; but to-morrow I am to have an answer, and am promised an effectual one. I suppose I have said enough in this and a former letter how I stand with new people; ten times better than ever I did with the old; forty times more caressed. I am to dine to-morrow at Mr. Harley's; and if he continues as he has begun, no man has been ever better treated by another. What you say about Stella's mother, I have spoken enough to it already. I believe she is not in town; for I have not yet seen her. My lampoon[17] is cried up to the skies; but nobody suspects me for it, except sir Andrew Fountain: at least they say nothing of it to me. Did not I tell you of a great man who received me very coldly? That's he; but say nothing; 'twas only a little revenge: I'll remember to bring it over. The bishop of Clogher has smoaked my *Tatler*[18] about shortening of words, &c. But God so! &c.

15. I will write plainer if I can remember it; for Stella must not spoil her eyes, and Dingley can't read my hand very well; and I am afraid my letters are too long: then you must suppose one to be two, and read them at twice. I dined

to-day with Mr. Harley: Mr. Prior[19] dined with us. He has left my memorial with the queen, who has consented to give the First-Fruits and Twentieth Parts, and will, we hope, declare it to-morrow in the cabinet. But I beg you to tell it to no person alive; for so I am ordered, till in publick: and I hope to get something of greater value. After dinner came in lord Peterborow:[20] we renewed our acquaintance, and he grew mightily fond of me. They began to talk of a paper of verses called *Sid Hamet*. Mr. Harley repeated part, and then pulled them out, and gave them to a gentleman at the table to read, though they had all read them often: lord Peterborow would let nobody read them but himself: so he did; and Mr. Harley bobbed me[21] at every line to take notice of the beauties. Prior rallied lord Peterborow for author of them; and lord Peterborow said, he knew them to be his; and Prior then turned it upon me, and I on him. I am not guessed at all in town to be the author; yet so it is: but that is a secret only to you. Ten to one whether you see them in Ireland; yet here they run prodigiously. Harley presented me to lord president of Scotland, and Mr. Benson, lord of the treasury. Prior and I came away at nine, and sat at the Smyrna[22] till eleven, receiving acquaintance.

16. This morning early I went in a chair,[23] and Patrick before it, to Mr. Harley, to give him another copy of my memorial, as he desired; but he was full of business, going to the queen, and I could not see him; but he desired I would send up the paper, and excused himself upon his hurry. I was a little baulkt; but they tell me it is nothing. I shall judge by next visit. I tipt his porter with half a crown; and so I am well there for a time at least. I dined at Stratford's in the city, and had Burgundy and Tockay: came back afoot like a scoundrel; then went to Mr. Addison and supt with lord Mountjoy, which made me sick all night. I forgot that I bought six pound of chocolate for Stella, and a little wooden box: and I have a great piece of Brazil tobacco for Dingley, and a bottle of palsy water for Stella: all which, with the two handkerchiefs that Mr. Sterne has bought, and you must pay him for, will be put in the box directed to Mrs. Curry's, and set by Dr. Hawkshaw, whom I have not seen; but Sterne has undertaken it. The chocolate is a present, madam, for Stella. Don't read this, you little rogue, with your little eyes; but give it to Dingley, pray now; and I'll write as plain as the skies: and let Dingley write Stella's part, and Stella dictate to her, when she apprehends her eyes, &c.

17. This letter should have gone this post, if I had not been taken up with business, and two nights being late out; so it must stay till Thursday. I dined to-day with your Mr. Sterne, by invitation, and drank Irish wine; but, before we parted, there came in the prince of puppies, colonel Edgworth; so I went away. This day came out the *Tatler* made up wholly of my *Shower*, and a preface to it. They say 'tis the best thing I ever writ, and I think so too. I suppose the bishop of Clogher will shew it you. Pray tell me how you like it. Tooke is going on with my *Miscellany*.[24] I'd give a penny the letter to the bishop of Kilaloe was in

it: 'twould do him honour. Could not you contrive to say you hear they are printing my *Things* together; and that you wish the bookseller had that letter among the rest: but don't say any thing of it as from me. I forgot whether it was good or no; but only having heard it much commended, perhaps it may deserve it. Well, I have to-morrow to finish this letter in, and then I'll send it next day. I am so vext that you should write your third to me, when you had but my second, and I had written five, which now I hope you have all: and so I tell you, you are sawcy, little, pretty, dear rogues, &c.

18. To-day I dined, by invitation, with Stratford and others, at a young merchant's in the city, with Hermitage and Tockay, and staid till nine, and am now come home. And that dog Patrick is abroad, and drinking, and I can't get my night-gown. I have a mind to turn that puppy away: he has been drunk ten times in three weeks. But I han't time to say more; so good night, &c.

19. I am come home from dining in the city with Mr. Addison, at a merchant's; and just now, at the Coffee-house, we have notice that the duke of Ormond was this day declared lord lieutenant, at Hampton-court, in council. I have not seen Mr. Harley since; but hope the affair is done about First-Fruits. I will see him, if possible, to-morrow morning; but this goes to-night. I have sent a box to Mr. Sterne, to send to you by some friend: I have directed it for Mr. Curry, at his house; so you have warning when it comes, as I hope it will soon. The handkerchiefs will be put in some friend's pocket, not to pay custom. And so here ends my sixth, sent when I had but three of MD's: now I am beforehand, and will keep so; and God Almighty bless dearest MD, &c.

FROM *JOURNAL TO STELLA*, LETTER XXXII

[*TUESDAY*]   *London, October 9, 1711.*

I WAS forced to lie down at twelve to-day, and mend my night's sleep: I slept till after two, and then sent for a bit of mutton and pot of ale from the next cook's shop, and had no stomach. I went out at four, and called to see Biddy Floyd,[1] which I had not done these three months: she is something marked, but has recovered her complexion quite, and looks very well. Then I sat the evening with Mrs. Vanhomrigh, and drank coffee, and ate an egg. I likewise took a new new lodging to-day, not liking a ground floor, nor the ill smell, and other circumstances. I lodge, or shall lodge, by Leicester-Fields, and pay ten shillings a week; that won't hold out long, faith. I shall lie here but one night more. It rained terribly till one o'clock to-day. I lie, for I shall lie here two nights, till Thursday, and then remove. Did I tell you that my friend Mrs. Barton has a brother drowned, that went on the expedition with Jack Hill? He was a lieutenant-colonel, and a coxcomb; and she keeps her chamber in form, and the servants say, she receives no messages.—Answer MD's letter, Presto, d'ye hear?

No, says Presto, I won't yet, I'm busy: you're a saucy rogue. Who talks?

10. It cost me two shillings in coach-hire to dine in the city with a printer. I have sent, and caused to be sent, three pamphlets out in a fortnight, I will ply the rogues warm, and whenever any thing of theirs makes a noise, it shall have an answer. I have instructed an under-spur-leather to write so, that it is taken for mine. A rogue that writes a news-paper called *The Protestant Post-boy,* has reflected on me in one of his papers; but the secretary has taken him up, and he shall have a squeeze extraordinary. He says, that an ambitious Tantivy,[2] missing of his towering hopes of preferment in Ireland, is come over to vent his spleen on the late ministry, &c. I'll *Tantivy* him with a vengeance. I sat the evening at home, and am very busy, and can hardly find time to write, unless it were to MD. I am in furious haste.

11. I dined to-day with lord treasurer.[3] Thursdays are now his days when his choice company comes, but we are too much multiplied. George Granville[4] sent his excuses upon being ill; I hear he apprehends the apoplexy, which would grieve me much. Lord treasurer calls Prior nothing but *Monsieur Baudrier,* which was the feigned name of the Frenchman that writ his journey to Paris. They pretend to suspect me; so I talk freely of it, and put them out of their play. Lord treasurer calls me now Dr. Martin, because *Martin*[5] is a sort of swallow, and so is a *Swift.* When he and I came last Monday from Windsor, we were reading all the signs on the road. He is a pure trifler; tell the bishop of Clogher so. I made him make two lines in verse for the *Bell and Dragon,* and they were rare bad ones. I suppose Dilly is with you by this time: what could his reason be of leaving London, and not owning it? 'Twas plaguy silly. I believe his natural inconstancy made him weary; I think he is the king of inconstancy. I stayed with lord treasurer till ten; we had five lords and three commoners. Go to ombre, sirrahs.

SWIFT TO ALEXANDER POPE

Sep. 29. 1725

SIR,—

... But I am now returning to the noble Scene of Dublin in to the Grande Monde, for fearing of burying my parts to Signalise my self among Curates and Vicars, and correct all Corruption crept in relating to the weight of Bread and Butter through those Dominions where I govern.[1] I have employd my time (besides ditching) in finishing correcting, amending, and Transcribing my Travells, in four parts Compleat newly Augmented, and intended for the press when the world shall deserve them, or rather when a Printer shall be found brave enough to venture his Eares,[2] I like your Schemes of our meeting after Distresses and dispertions but the chief end I propose to my self in all my

labors is to vex the world rather then divert it, and if I could compass that de-
signe without hurting my own person or Fortune I would be the most Indefatigable writer you have ever seen without reading[3] I am exceedingly pleased
that you have done with Translations Lord Treasurer Oxford often lamented
that a rascaly World should lay you under a Necessity of Misemploying your
Genius for so long a time. But since you will now be so much better employd
when you think of the World give it one lash the more at my Request. I have
ever hated all Nations professions and Communityes and all my love is towards
individualls for instance I hate the tribe of Lawyers, but I love Councellor such
a one, Judge such a one for so with Physicians (I will not Speak of my own
Trade) Soldiers, English, Scotch, French; and the rest but principally I hate
and detest that animal called man, although I hartily love John, Peter, Thomas
and so forth. this is the system upon which I have governed my self many years
(but do not tell) and so I shall go on till I have done with them I have got Materials Towards a Treatis proving the falsity of that Definition *animal rationale*;
and to show it should be only *rationis capax*.[4] Upon this great foundation of
Misanthropy (though not Timons manner[5]) The whole building of my Travells is erected: And I never will have peace of mind till all honest men are of
my Opinion: by Consequence you are to embrace it immediatly and procure
that all who deserve my Esteem may do so too. The matter is so clear that it
will admit little dispute. nay I will hold a hundred pounds that you and I agree
in the Point.

I did not know your Odyssey[6] was finished being yet in the Country, which
I shall leave in three days I shall thank you kindly for the Present but shall like
it three fourths the less from the mixture you mention of another hand, however I am glad you saved yourself so much drudgery—I have been long told by
Mr Ford of your great Atchivements in building and planting and especially of
your Subterranean Passage to your Garden whereby you turned a blunder into
a beauty which is a Piece of Ars Poetica

I have almost done with Harridans and shall soon become old enough to
fall in love with Girls of Fourteen. The Lady whom you describe to live at
Court,[7] to be deaf and no party Woman, I take to be Mythology but know not
how to moralize it. She cannot be Mercy, for mercy is neither deaf nor lives at
Court Justice is blind and perhaps deaf but neither is she a Court Lady. Fortune is both blind and deaf and a Court Lady, but then she is a most Damnable
party Woman, and will never make me easy as you promise. It must be riches
which Answers all your description; I am glad she visites you but my voice is so
weak that I doubt she will never hear me.

Mr Lewis sent me an Account of Dr Arbuthnett's Illness which is a very
sensible Affliction to me, who by living so long out of the World have lost that
hardness of Heart contracted by years and generall Conversation. I am daily
loosing Friends, and neither seeking nor getting others. O, if the World had but

a dozen Arbuthnetts[8] in it I would burn my Travells but however he is not without Fault. There is a passage in Bede highly commending the Piety and learning of the Irish in that Age, where after abundance of praises he overthrows them all by lamenting that, Alas, they kept Easter at a wrong time of the Year.[9] So our Doctor has every Quality and virtue that can make a man amiable or usefull, but alas he hath a sort of Slouch in his Walk. I pray god protect him for he is an excellent Christian tho not a Catholick and as fit a man either to dy or Live as ever I knew. . . .

SWIFT TO ALEXANDER POPE

Dublin Novr 26, 1725

SIR,— . . . Drown the World,[1] I am not content with despising it, but I would anger it if I could with safety. I wish there were an Hospital built for it's despisers, where one might act with safety and it need not be a large Building, only I would have it well endowed. . . . I desire you and all my Friends will take a special care that my Affection to the World may not be imputed to my Age, for I have Credible witnesses ready to depose that it hath never varyed from the Twenty First to the f—ty eighth year of my Life,[2] (pray fill that Blank Charitably) I tell you after all that I do not hate Mankind, it is vous autres[3] who hate them because you would have them reasonable Animals, and are Angry for being disappointed. I have always rejected that Definition and made another of my own. I am no more angry with——[4] Then I was with the Kite that last week flew away with one of my Chickins and yet I was pleas'd when one of my Servants Shot him two days after, This I say, because you are so hardy as to tell me of your Intentions to write Maxims in Opposition to Rochfoucault[5] who is my Favorite because I found my whole character in him, however I will read him again because it is possible I may have since undergone some alterations—

SWIFT TO CHARLES WOGAN

[July–2 Aug. 1732]

SIR,

I received your Packet[1] at least two Months ago, and took all this Time not only to consider it maturely myself, but to show it to the few judicious Friends I have in this Kingdom. We all agreed that the Writer was a Scholar, a Man of Genius and of Honour. We guessed him to have been born in this Country from some Passages, but not from the Style, which we were surprized to find so correct in an Exile, a Soldier, and a Native of *Ireland*. The History of yourself, although part of it be employed in your Praise and Importance, we did not dislike, because your Intention was to be wholly unknown, which Circumstance exempts you from any Charge of Vanity. However, altho' I am utterly ignorant of present Persons and Things, I have made a Shift, by talking in general with some Persons, to find out your Name, your Employments, and some of your Actions, with the Addition of such a Character as would give full Credit to more than you have said (I mean of yourself) in the dedicatory Epistle.

You will pardon a natural Curiosity on this Occasion, especially when I began with so little that I did not so much as untie the Strings of the Bag for five Days after I received it, concluding it must come from some *Irish* Fryar in *Spain,* filled with monastick Speculations, of which I have seen some in my Life, little expecting a History, a Dedication, a poetical Translation of the Penitential Psalms, Latin Poems, and the like, and all from a Soldier. In these Kingdoms you would be a most unfashionable military Man, among Troops where the least Pretension to Learning, or Piety, or common Morals, would endanger the Owner to be cashiered. Although I have no great Regard for your Trade, from the Judgment I make of those who profess it in these Kingdoms, yet I cannot but highly esteem those Gentlemen of *Ireland,*[2] who, with all the Disadvantages of being Exiles and Strangers, have been able to distinguish themselves by their Valour and Conduct in so many Parts of *Europe.* I think above all other Nations, which ought to make the *English* ashamed of the Reproaches they cast on the Ignorance, the Dulness, and the Want of Courage, in the *Irish* Natives; those Defects, wherever they happen, arising only from the Poverty and Slavery they suffer from their inhuman Neighbours, and the base corrupt Spirits of too many of the chief Gentry, *&c.* By such Events as these, the very *Grecians* are grown slavish, ignorant, and superstitious. I do assert that from several Experiments in travelling over both Kingdoms, I have found the poor Cottagers here, who could speak our Language, to have much better natural Taste for good Sense, Humour, and Raillery, than ever I observed among People of the like Sort in *England.* But the Millions of Oppressions they lye under, the Tyranny of their Landlords, the ridiculous Zeal of their Priests, and the general Misery of the whole Nation, have been enough to damp the best Spirits under the Sun.

I return to your Packet. Two or three poetical Friends of mine have read your Poems with very good Approbation, yet we all agree some Corrections may be wanting, and at the same Time we are at a Loss how to venture on such a Work. One Gentleman of your own Country, Name, and Family, who could do it best, is a little too lazy; but, however, something shall be done, and submitted to you. I have been only a Man of Rhimes, and that upon Trifles, never having written serious Couplets in my Life; yet never any without a moral View. However, as an Admirer of *Milton,* I will read yours as a Critick, and make Objections where I find any Thing that should be changed. Your Directions about publishing the Epistle and the Poetry will be a Point of some Difficulty. They cannot be printed here with the least Profit to the Author's Friends in Distress. *Dublin* Booksellers have not the least Notion of paying for a Copy. Sometimes Things are printed here by Subscription, but they go on so heavily, that few or none make it turn to Account. In *London* it is otherwise, but even there the Authors must be in Vogue, or, if not known, be discovered by the Style; or the Work must be something that hits the Taste of the Publick, or what is recommended by the presiding Men of Genius.

When *Milton* first published his famous Poem, the first Edition was very long going off; few either read, liked, or understood it, and it gained Ground merely by its Merit. Nothing but an uncertain State of my Health, caused by a Disposition to Giddiness (which, although less violent, is more constant) could have prevented my passing this Summer into *England* to see my Friends, who hourly have expected me: In that Case I could have managed this Affair myself, and would have readily consented that my Name should have stood at Length before your Epistle, and by the Caprice of the World, that Circumstance might have been of Use to make the Thing known, and consequently better answer the charitable Part of your Design by inciting People's Curiosity. And in such a Case, I would have writ a short Acknowledgment of your Letter, and published it in the next Page after your Epistle; but giving you no Name, nor confessing my Conjecture of it. This Scheme I am still upon, as soon as my Health permits me to return to *England*.

As I am conjectured to have generally dealt in Raillery and Satyr, both in Prose and Verse, if that Conjecture be right, although such an Opinion hath been an absolute Bar to my Rising in the World, yet that very World must suppose that I followed what I thought to be my Talent, and charitable People will suppose I had a Design to laugh the Follies of Mankind out of Countenance, and as often to lash the Vices out of Practice. And then it will be natural to conclude, that I have some Partiality for such Kind of Writing, and favour it in others. I think you acknowledge, that in some Time of your Life, you turned to the rallying Part, but I find at present your Genius runs wholly into the grave and sublime, and therefore I find you less indulgent to my Way by your Dislike of the *Beggar's Opera,* in the Persons particularly of *Polly Peachum* and *Macheath;* whereas we think it a very severe satyr upon the most pernicious Villainies of Mankind. And so you are in Danger of quarrelling with the Sentiments of Mr. *Pope,* Mr. *Gay* the Author, Dr. *Arbuthnot,* myself, Dr. *Young,* and all the Brethren whom we own. Dr. *Young* is the gravest among us, and yet his Satyrs have many Mixtures of sharp Raillery. At the same Time you judge very truly, that the Taste of *England* is infamously corrupted by *Sholes* of Wretches who write for their Bread; and therefore I had reason to put Mr. *Pope* on writing the Poem, called the *Dunciad,* and to hale those Scoundrels out of their Obscurity by telling their Names at length, their Works, their Adventures, sometimes their

Lodgings, and their Lineage; not with *A—'s and B—'s* according to the old Way, which would be unknown in a few Years.

As to your Blank-verse, it hath too often fallen into the same vile Hands of late. One *Thomson,* a *Scots*-Man, has succeeded the best in that Way, in four Poems he has writ on the four Seasons. yet I am not over-fond of them, because they are all Description, and nothing is doing, whereas *Milton* engages me in Actions of the highest Importance, *modo me Romae, modo ponit Athenis.*[3] And yours on the seven Psalms, *&c.* have some Advantages that Way.

You see *Pope, Gay,* and I, use all our Endeavours to make folks Merry and wise, and profess to have no Enemies, except Knaves and Fools. I confess myself to be exempted from them in one Article, which was engaging with a Ministry to prevent if possible, the Evils that have over-run the Nation, and my foolish Zeal in endeavouring to save this wretched Island. Wherein though I succeeded absolutely in one important Article, yet even there I lost all Hope of Favour from those in Power here, and disobliged the Court of *England,* and have in twenty years drawn above one thousand scurrilous Libels on myself, without any other Recompence than the Love of the *Irish* Vulgar, and two or three Dozen Sign-Posts of the *Drapier* in this City, beside those that are scattered in Country Towns, and even these are half worn out. So that, whatever little Genius God hath given me, I may justly pretend to have been the worst Manager of it to my own Advantage of any Man upon Earth.

Aug. 2] What I have above written hath long lain by me, that I might consider further: But I have been partly out of Order, and partly plagued by a Lawsuit of ten Years standing, and I doubt very ill closed up, although it concerns two Thirds of my little Fortune. Think whether such Periods of Life are proper to encourage poetical and philosophical Speculations. I shall not therefore tire you any longer, but, with great Acknowledgment for the Distinction you please to shew me, desire to be always thought, with great Truth and a most particular Esteem, Sir, | Your most obedient | and obliged Servant, | J. Swift.

We have sometimes Editions printed here of Books from *England,* which I know not whether you are in a Way of getting. I will name some below, and if you approve of any, I shall willingly increase your Library; they are small, consequently more portable in your Marches, and, which is more important, the Present will be cheaper for me.

Dr. YOUNG's Satyrs	GAY's Fables
Mr. GAY's Works	Art of Politicks, and
Mr. POPE's Works	some other Trifles in
POPE's DUNCIAD	Verse, *&c.*

SWIFT TO WILLIAM PULTENEY[1]

Dublin May 12, 1735

SIR,

Mr. *Stopford*[2] landed yesterday, and sent me the letter which you were pleased to honour me with. I have not yet seen him, for he called when I was not at home. The reason why I ventured to recommend him to your protection, was your being his old patron, to whom he is obliged for all the preferment he got in the Church. He is one of the most deserving gentlemen in the country, and hath a tolerable provision, much more than persons of so much merit can in these times pretend to, in either kingdom. I love the duke of *Dorset* very well, having known him from his youth, and he hath treated me with great civility since he came into this government. It is true, his original principles, as well as his instructions from your side the water, make him act the usual part in managing this nation, for which he must be excused: yet I wish he would a little more consider, that people here might have some small share in employments civil and ecclesiastic, wherein my lord *Carteret* acted a more popular part. The folks here, whom they call a parliament, will imitate yours in every thing, after the same manner as a monkey doth a human creature. If my health were not so bad, although my years be many, I fear I might outlive liberty in *England*. It hath continued longer than in any other monarchy, and must end as all others have done which were established by the *Goths*, and is now falling in the same manner that the rest have done. It is very natural for every king to desire unlimited power; it is as proper an object to their appetites, as a wench to an abandoned young fellow, or wine to a drunkard. But what puzzles me is, to know how a man of birth, title, and fortune, can find his account in making himself and his posterity slaves. They are paid for it; the court will restore what their luxury has destroyed; I have nothing to object. But let me suppose a chief minister;[3] from a scanty fortune, almost eaten up with debts, acquiring by all methods a monstrous overgrown estate, why he will still go on to endeavour making his master absolute, and thereby in the power of seizing all his possessions at his pleasure, and hanging or banishing him into the bargain. Therefore, if I were such a minister, I would act like a prudent gamester, and cut, as the sharper calls it, before luck began to change. What if such a minister, when he had got two or three millions, would pretend conviction, seem to dread attempts upon liberty, and bring over all his forces to the contrary side? As to the lust of absolute power, I despair it can never be cooled, unless princes had capacity to read the history of the *Roman* emperors; how many of them were murdered by their own army, and the same may be said of the *Ottomans* by their janissaries; and many other examples are easy to be found. If I were such a minister I would go farther, and endeavour to be king myself. Such feats have happened among the petty tyrants of old *Greece,* and the worst that happened was only their being murdered for their pains.

I believe in my conscience that you have some mercenary end in all your endeavours to preserve the liberty of your country at the expence of your quiet, and of making all the villains in *England* your enemies. For you almost stand alone, and therefore are sure, if you succeed, to engross the whole glory of recovering a desperate constitution, given over by all its other physicians. May God work a miracle, by changing the hearts of an abandoned people, whose hearts are waxen gross, whose ears are dull of hearing, and whose eyes have been closed; and may he continue you as his chief instrument, by whom this miracle is to be wrought.

I send this letter in a packet to Mr. *Pope,* and by a private hand.[4] I pray God protect you against all your enemies; I mean those of your country, for you can have no other; and as you will never be weary of well doing, so may God give you long life and health the better to support you.

You are pleased to mention some volumes of what are called my works. I have looked on them very little. It is a great mortification to me, although I should not have been dissatisfied if such a thing had been done in *England* by booksellers agreeing among themselves. I never got a farthing by anything I writ, except one about eight year ago, and that was by Mr. *Pope*'s prudent management for me. Here the printers and booksellers have no property in their copies. The printer applied to my friends, and got many things from *England.* The man was civil and humble, but I had no dealings with him, and therefore he consulted some friends, who were readier to direct him than I desired they should. I saw one poem on you and a great Minister, and was not sorry to find it there.[5]

I fear you are tired; I cannot help it, nor could avoid the convenience of writing, when I might be in no danger of post-officers. I am, Sir, with the truest respect and esteem, | Your most obedient and obliged humble servant, | J. Swift.

I desire to present my most humble respects to Mrs. *Pulteney.*

NOTES

The annotation in this selection of Swift's writings is limited to basic explanation: the date and, where particularly relevant as in the case of Swift's prose polemic, the occasion of a work are given; important names and unfamiliar words are glossed. Words that are defined in standard dictionaries such as the *Concise Oxford Dictionary* are not usually explained here. Some allusions and analogues are identified but full annotation has not been attempted. This compilation of notes is, of course, indebted to the cumulative factual findings of previous editors and annotators of Swift.

ABBREVIATIONS

Boccalini: *Advertisements From Parnassus. Written Originally in Italian. By the Famous Trajano Boccalini. Newly Done into English, and adapted to the Present Times ... By N. N. Esq* (London: Printed for Richard Smith, 1704).

Burton: Robert Burton, *The Anatomy of Melancholy,* ed. by Thomas C. Faulkner, Nicolas K. Kiessling, Rhonda L. Blair, intro. by J. B. Bamborough, 6 vols. (Oxford: Clarendon Press, 1989–2000). Reference is by partition, section, member, subsection, and page number.

Corr: *The Correspondence of Jonathan Swift,* ed. by Harold Williams, 5 vols. (Oxford: Clarendon Press, 1963–65).

Ehrenpreis: Irvin Ehrenpreis, *Swift: The Man, His Works, and the Age,* 3 vols. (London: Methuen, 1962–83).

Poems: *The Poems of Jonathan Swift,* ed. by Harold Williams, 2nd ed., 3 vols. (Oxford: Clarendon Press, 1958).

PW: *The Prose Writings of Jonathan Swift*, ed. by Herbert Davis and others, 16 vols. (Oxford: Basil Blackwell, 1939–74).

Rogers: *Jonathan Swift: The Complete Poems*, ed. by Pat Rogers (Harmondsworth: Penguin, 1983).

Turner: *Jonathan Swift: Gulliver's Travels*, ed. by Paul Turner (Oxford and New York: Oxford University Press, 1986 [Oxford World's Classics 1998]).

English translations of classical quotations normally follow the versions in the Loeb editions. Biblical references are to The King James Authorized Version.

A TALE OF A TUB, THE BATTEL OF THE BOOKS, AND A DISCOURSE CONCERNING THE MECHANICAL OPERATION OF THE SPIRIT

Composition c. 1696–97. First published in 1704. Enlarged fifth edition with the Apology and Notes published in 1710. The satire on "abuses" in religion is directed against Roman Catholicism ("Popery"), Protestant Dissent, and sectarian Enthusiasm, and is conducted principally in sections II, IV, VI, VIII, XI, which form a continuous narrative, and in the *Mechanical Operation of the Spirit*. The satire has a contextual location in contemporary religious polemic, especially in anti-popery, anti-Puritan satire, anti-Quaker propaganda, and in Church-of-England responses to anticlericalism and atheism. The narrative of the three brothers and their coats is disrupted by digressions in which "Modernist" corruptions in contemporary letters and learning are satirized. In the Digressions and in the *Battel of the Books* Swift is intervening on the side of the "Antients" in an old controversy concerning the claims of Ancient and Modern culture. This richly intertextual satiric volume has attracted voluminous scholarly commentary. Only some essential annotation can be provided here. The standard scholarly edition with extensive notes is *A Tale of a Tub To which is added The Battle of the Books and the Mechanical Operation of the Spirit*, ed. by A. C. Guthkelch and D. Nichol Smith, 2nd ed. (Oxford, 1958 [1973]).

A Tale of a Tub (p. 3)

Title page: *Tale of a Tub:* The title has the proverbial meaning of an idle or foolish story. It also means a diversionary discourse, as tubs were thrown out to whales by seamen in order to divert them from the ship (Preface, p. 24). The analogy of a discourse to such a tub was common. Tub also signifies a sectarian Tub preacher so the title suggests that this is a tale of fanaticism (the *Mechanical Operation of the Spirit* concludes with a "History of *Fanaticism*" [p. 156]).

    Title page: Diu … desideratum: much desired for a long time.

    Title page: Basima … Iren. Lib. I. C. *18:* On this heretical quotation see Swift's notes at pp. 19, 101. The Church Father Irenaeus' *Adversus Haereses* [*Against Here-*

sies] is an important model for Swift's satire on religious individualism and heterodoxy.

Title page: *Lucretius citation:* "I love to pluck new flowers, and to seek an illustrious chaplet for my head from fields whence before this the Muses have crowned the brows of none." Lucretius, *De Rerum Natura*, I.928–30.

1. *Grub-street:* abode of hack writers, the street was located near Moorfields, in the modern Barbican area.

2. *Terra Australis incognita:* unknown southern land. The continent supposed to lie in the Great Southern Ocean, later identified with Australia.

3. two or three Treatises: William King, *Some Remarks on the Tale of a Tub* (1704); William Wotton, *Observations upon the Tale of a Tub* (1705).

4. a late Discourse: Francis Gastrell, *The Principles of Deism Truly represented and set in a clear Light, in Two Dialogues between a Sceptick and a Deist* (1708).

5. Notion of Prejudices: The allusion is to anticlerical writers. The putative hack author of the *Tale* thinks "it one of the greatest, and best of human Actions, to remove Prejudices" (p. 86).

6. *Nondum … Hostis:* "You have never yet lacked for a foreign enemy." Lucan, *De Bello Civili*, I.23.

7. *Letter of Enthusiasm:* Anthony Ashley Cooper, third Earl of Shaftesbury, *A Letter Concerning Enthusiasm* (1708).

8. *Dryden, L'Estrange:* John Dryden (1631–1700), poet, dramatist, and critic, was a Roman Catholic convert; Sir Roger L'Estrange (1616–1704), Tory journalist and pamphleteer and licenser of the press.

9. one of his Prefaces … *Soul in Patience:* Swift refers to Dryden's "Discourse concerning the Original and Progress of Satire" (1693).

10. the *Earl of Orrery*'s Remarks: Charles Boyle (1674–1731) was an aristocratic undergraduate of Christ Church, Oxford, who was the editor of the Christ Church production *The Epistles of Phalaris* (1695). His "Remarks," entitled *Dr. Bentley's Dissertation on the Epistles of Phalaris and the Fables of Aesop, Examined by the Honourable Charles Boyle, Esq.* (1698), was ghost-written by the brilliant High Church controversialist Francis Atterbury.

11. One of which: William King's *Some Remarks on the Tale of a Tub*. Swift became friendly with this Tory satirist.

12. The other Answer: William Wotton's *Observations*. Wotton (1666–1727) was a classical scholar and a "Modern" in the cultural controversy over the respective merits of ancient and modern authors.

13. Annotation: Swift assimilated William Wotton's annotation into the *Tale*, transforming the hostile critic into an appreciative explicator of the work. Selective quotations from the *Observations* appear as notes signed "W. Wotton."

14. Sir *W. T.:* Sir William Temple (1628–99), statesman, diplomat, and author,

adviser to William III, Swift's first patron. Temple's *Essay upon the Ancient and Modern Learning* (1690) had been attacked by Wotton and precipitated this English outbreak of the Ancients and Moderns controversy, for which see *The Battel of the Books*, "The Bookseller to the Reader" (p. 117).

15. *Porsenna's* Case ... *juravimus:* The Etruscan king Porsenna was told by a captured would-be assassin that "three hundred of us have sworn to attempt the same deed." Lucius Annaeus Florus, *Epitome of Roman History*, I.10.6.

16. Antagonist: Richard Bentley (1662–1742), classical scholar and a "Modern" in the Ancients and Moderns controversy.

17. Banter ... *Alsatia* Phrase: The cant word is associated with a Whitefriars precinct that was a sanctuary for debtors and criminals. Thomas Shadwell's *The Squire of Alsatia* was a very popular play in this period.

18. *mutatis mutandis:* necessary changes being made.

19. *Min-ellius,* or *Farnaby:* classicists and pedagogues.

20. *Optat ... piger:* The lazy ox longs for the horse's trappings. Horace, *Epistles,* I.xiv.43.

21. these *Impedimenta Literarum:* this literary baggage.

22. a Prostitute Bookseller: Edmund Curll.

23. SOMMERS: Baron John Somers (1651–1716), lawyer and leading Whig politician, Lord Chancellor (1697). Member of the Whig Kit Cat Club and prominent patron of writers.

24. *a* late Reign: King William III (died in 1702).

25. Moloch: A false god in the Old Testament to whom burning human sacrifices were made, see Jeremiah 32:35.

26. *the* Memorial of them ... no more to be found: The hack author unable to find the works of his contemporaries is possibly another parody of Dryden. In the "Discourse of Satire," Dryden appeals to Posterity and pronounces the ephemerality of his literary enemies. Like the hack author here, Dryden seemingly echoes biblical passages such as Psalms 9:6, Ecclesiastes 9:5, and Deuteronomy 32:26 (see *The Works of John Dryden*, ed. by H. T. Swedenberg Jr., et al., 20 vols., 4.9).

27. Jakes: lavatory.

28. *a large Folio, well bound:* The folio first edition of Dryden's *Virgil* was sold unbound, with directions to binders on how to assemble the parts.

29. Friend of Your Governor: Sir William Temple.

30. *Elogies:* favorable characterizations.

31. Mignature: miniature.

32. Hobbes's Leviathan ... *Schemes ... given to Rotation:* The absolutism of Thomas Hobbes's *Leviathan* (1651) oversets other political schemes, including republican ones advanced by the Rota Club and in James Harrington's *The Commonwealth of Oceana* (1656).

33. *the* Leviathan *from whence the terrible Wits ... borrow their Weapons:* Contempo-

rary anticlerical radicals took inspiration from Parts III and IV of Hobbes's *Leviathan,* which were provocatively Erastian and anticlerical.

34. Spleen: depression, bad temper, hypochondriacal melancholy—a fashionable condition.

35. *Hors'd for Discipline:* raised up on a man's back in order to be flogged.

36. Monarch *of this Island:* James I and VI, who by the union of the crowns was king of England and Scotland.

37. Roses ... Thistles: The English Order of the Garter had roses around the collar; the Scottish Order of the Thistle had thistles.

38. *from beyond the* Tweed: from Scotland.

39. Pork: referring to the common story of the host who served the same pork meal but differently flavored in each course.

40. Attick *Commonwealth: The Constitution of the Athenians* is no longer attributed to Xenophon.

41. Splendida bilis: gleaming choler. Horace, *Satires,* II.iii.141.

42. Covent-Garden: theater and red-light district.

43. White Hall: royal palace in London, center of government.

44. Inns *of* Court: London's legal center.

45. City: London's financial and commercial center.

46. Scandalum Magnatum: defamation against high-ranking persons.

47. Bar of the House: House of Commons as a legal court.

48. Socrates ... *Contemplation:* The Athenian philosopher appears in this way in Aristophanes' comedy *Clouds,* 218.

49. Senes ... recedant: so that when old they may retire into secure ease. Horace, *Satires,* I.i.31.

50. Sylva Caledonia: the Caledonian (or Scottish) forest.

51. *human Ears:* Mutilation or loss of ears was a punishment for sedition. Puritan pamphleteers such as Alexander Leighton, William Prynne, John Bastwick, and Henry Burton, among others, suffered this punishment during Charles I's reign.

52. Corporeum ... : Lucretius, *De Rerum Natura,* 4.526–27. The English translation given in the footnote is from Thomas Creech's translation of Lucretius (1682).

53. perorare *with a Song:* deliver the final part of a speech, in this case to conclude the gallows speech with a psalm.

54. Meum *and* Tuum: mine and yours.

55. Gresham: The Royal Society, the main scientific society, met at Gresham College until 1710.

56. *Briguing and Caballing:* intriguing or conspiring.

57. Prodigals: refers to the parable of the prodigal son, Luke 15:11–32.

58. Sack-Posset: alcoholic drink containing white wine and milk.

59. Exantlation: drawing out.

60. Tom Thumb ... *Dr.* Faustus ... *Whittington* and his Cat: Like "The *Wise Men of Goatham*" mentioned a few lines later, these were all subjects of chapbooks.

61. *Writer now living:* John Dryden (d. 1700). Dryden's Roman Catholic allegorical poem of 1687 is listed with these chapbook titles and identified with Roman Catholic "dunces." Duns Scotus and Robert Bellarmine were Roman Catholic theologians.

62. *Tommy Potts:* A romantic ballad entitled *The Lovers' Quarrel: or Cupid's Triumph. Being The pleasant History of fair Rosamond of Scotland ... whose Love was obtained by the Valour of Tommy Pots.* Dryden had written an epilogue to a stage version of the Fair Rosamond legend (Frank H. Ellis, "Notes on *A Tale of a Tub*," *Swift Studies,* 1 [1986], 10).

63. (note) *Lambin:* Denys Lambin (1516–72), French scholar. Swift has Wotton corrected on a basic point of the religious allegory.

64. *Bulks:* stalls or part of the framework jutting out from shops.

65. *bilkt:* cheated.

66. *Levee* sub dio: royal morning reception in the open air.

67. Jupiter Capitolinus: the Temple of Jupiter on the Roman Capitol. It was said that the Roman Capitol was saved from invading Gauls when the cries of geese awakened its defenders, hence the feeding of the sacred geese there.

68. Deus ... Gentium: God of lesser nations.

69. ex traduce: by traduction, a form of spiritual transmission.

70. *totidem verbis:* in so many words.

71. we may find them ... *syllabis:* we may find them included or in so many syllables.

72. *totidem literis:* in so many letters.

73. Jure Paterno: by paternal law.

74. altum silentium: deep silence.

75. aliquo ... adhærere: in some way adhere to the essence.

76. *duo ... genera:* there are two kinds.

77. *conceditur ... negatur:* conceded but, if the same is affirmed of the nuncupatory (the oral), denied.

78. cum grano Salis: with a grain of salt.

79. Multa ... sequerentur: much absurdity would follow.

80. Momus ... Hybris ... Zoilus ... Tigellius: The mythological Momus is patron of the Moderns in the *Battel of the Books;* Hybris is the personification of Pride; Zoilus of Amphipolis was a fourth-century critic notorious for his criticism of Homer; Tigellius was a critic of Horace.

81. Pausanias *is of Opinion:* Pausanias, *Description of Greece,* II (Corinth). xxxviii.3.

82. Herodotus: IV.191.

83. Ctesias: Greek physician and historian of the fourth century BCE.

84. Lucretius, *De Rerum Natura*, 6.786–87. The verse translation in the note is from Creech.

85. Terence: Roman comic dramatist of the second century BCE.

86. Fonde: foundation.

87. Projector: planner or promoter of a scheme or enterprise.

88. Spargefaction: action of sprinkling.

89. Varias ... piscem: "to spread feathers of many a hue" and "ends below in a black and ugly fish." Part of a description of a ridiculous monster at the beginning of Horace, *Ars Poetica*, 2–4.

90. Appetitus sensibilis: the natural appetite or bodily desire (as opposed to intellect or reason).

91. Pulveris ... jactu: by the tossing of a little dust. Virgil, *Georgics,* IV.87.

92. Verè adepti: truly adepts.

93. Vittles: victuals.

94. Chinese *Waggons:* John Milton, *Paradise Lost,* III.438–39: "where Chineses drive / With sails and wind their cany wagons light."

95. Quemvis ... serenas: persuades me to undergo any labor, and entices me to spend the tranquil nights in wakefulness. Lucretius, *De Rerum Natura,* 1.141–42.

96. Fastidiosity, Amorphy, *and* Oscitation: Fastidiousness, shapelessness, and yawning.

97. Utile ... Dulce: profit and pleasure.

98. Receipt, *a* Nostrum: prescription. An alchemical prescription follows.

99. Cabbalist: mystic philosopher. Occult or esoteric authors and works are named.

100. Opus magnum: great work.

101. Sphæra Pyroplastica: sphere of fire.

102. Vix ... vocem: I can scarcely believe that this author ever heard of fire.

103. Save-all: a candle holder that saves the candle ends so that they too can be burned.

104. MARTIN: Swift's representation of Martin's moderation has an analogue in Francis Atterbury's defense of Martin Luther's spirit of moderation in Anglican Oxford's paper war against popery in 1687 (see Atterbury's *An Answer to Some Considerations on the Spirit of Martin Luther and The Original of the Reformation; Lately Printed at Oxford* [Oxford, 1687]). Swift's satire in the *Tale* sides with Atterbury and the Tory wits in contemporary controversies in religion and learning.

105. Fox's *Arguments:* In Aesop's fable the fox having lost its tail wants other foxes to cut off their tails.

106. *sick Brain conceived:* The pathologizing of Protestant Dissenters and the Radical Reformation was a standard line in contemporary Anglican polemic. One important resource for Swift's satire was the account of "Religious Melan-

choly" in Burton's *The Anatomy of Melancholy* (see Pt. 3. Sect. 4. Memb. 1. Subs. 1. and ff.). The violence of Swift's satire on Dissent, which pained a Whig cleric like William Wotton, is consonant with the virulent invective of High Church Tory pamphleteers and recalled for the Whig and Deist Charles Gildon the kind of extremism parodied by Daniel Defoe in *The Shortest Way with the Dissenters*. Gildon wrote in his "The Epistle Nuncupatory, To the Author of *A Tale of a Tub*" that Swift had "*certainly discover'd the* Shortest way with CONTROVERSY" ("The Epistle Nuncupatory, To the Author of *A Tale of a Tub*" in *The Golden Spy* [London, 1709]).

107. Mellœo ... Lepore: Inaccurately recalls Lucretius, *De Rerum Natura,* 1.934: "touch all with the Muse's grace."

108. Sed ... pertingentia: But whose genitals were thick, reaching all the way to their ankles.

109. Aeolists: This account of an imaginary religious sect is a violent satire on sectarian Enthusiasm, and especially of the Quakers.

110. Quod ... gubernans: But may pilot fortune steer [violent earthquakes] far from us. Lucretius, *De Rerum Natura,* 5.107.

111. Omnium ... celebrant: They honour Boreas [the North Wind] more than all other gods. Pausanias, *Description of Greece,* VIII (Arcadia). 36.6.

112. Land of Darkness: Scotia means darkness as well as Scotland.

113. ex adytis, *and* penetralibus: brings forth from the inner shrine. Virgil, *Aeneid,* II.297.

114. Corpora quæque: any body. Lucretius, *De Rerum Natura,* 4.1065. Lucretius recommends that the lover cast the collected liquid into any body; promiscuity is recommended as a way to avoid the snares of love.

115. (note): *Harry* the Great: Henri IV of France.

116. Idque ... coire: the body seeks that which has wounded the mind with love; he tends to the source of the blow, and desires to unite in coition. Lucretius, *De Rerum Natura,* 4.1048, 1055.

117. Teterrima ... Causa: [Cunt] the most dreadful cause of war. Horace, *Satires,* I.III.107–8, "Cunnus" in the first four editions was deleted in the fifth edition.

118. *Instance:* Louis XIV.

119. Bedlam: asylum for the insane in London.

120. Epicurus ... *and others:* all regarded as atheistic materialists.

121. Clinamina: the theory of swerving in Lucretius's explanation for the motion of atoms in his materialist Epicurean system. See Lucretius, *De Rerum Natura,* 2.292.

122. Vortex: Descartes's theory of vortices.

123. Est ... viderere: You may well congratulate yourself on having reached those regions where you pass as a man of some knowledge. Cicero, *Letters to His Friends,* VII.10.1. There is a warning to look out for cheating charioteers in Britain in Cicero, *Letters to His Friends,* VII.6.2.

124. *to cut the Feather:* to make a fine distinction.

125. Hic multa desiderantur: here much is lacking.

126. being well Deceived: Among the analogues for this definition, see John Wilmot, Earl of Rochester's poem "A Letter from Artemiza in the Towne to Chloe in the Countrey," l.115: "The perfect Joy of being well deceaved" (*The Works of John Wilmot Earl of Rochester,* ed. by Harold Love [Oxford, 1999], p. 66).

127. *Last Week I saw a Woman* flay'd: On this London spectacle see Ned Ward, *The London Spy* (1698–1700), ed. by Paul Hyland from the Fourth Edition of 1709 (East Lansing, 1993), Part VI.102.110. Compare also Burton, *The Anatomy of Melancholy,* Part 3. Sect. 2. Memb. 5. Subs. 3, p. 226, citing Chrysostom on a woman's beauty as a superficial skin that when taken off reveals *"all loathsomeness under it."* See Prem Nath, "The Background of Swift's Flayed Woman," *Forum for Modern Language Studies,* 20 (1984), 363–66.

128. Beau *to be stript … his* Brain, *his* Heart, *and his* Spleen: Compare the account of "A Beau" in *The London Spy,* Part XVI, p. 295: "His body's but a poor stuffing of a rich case, like bran in a lady's pincushion, that when the outside is stripped off, there remains nothing that's valuable. His Head is a fool's egg.… His brains are the yolk, which conceit has addled."

129. Curtius: Marcus Curtius leaped into a chasm in the Forum to save Rome.

130. Empedocles: He threw himself into the crater of Mount Etna.

131. Ingenium … negotiis: a character equal to the business. Tacitus, *Annals,* VI.39 and XVI.18.

132. Seymour … Musgrave … Bowls … How: leading Tory politicians. John Bolles, MP for Lincoln, 1690–1702, was reputed to be mad and was placed by the Tory House of Commons in the chair of the committee on the Bill for the Act of Settlement in 1701, thus showing the Tory Commons' contempt for this legislature endorsed by William III, which further altered the hereditary succession to the crown.

133. *Society of* Warwick-Lane: the Royal College of Physicians.

134. *a very light Rider, and easily shook off:* The horse-rider figure for imagination and reason was commonplace. Samuel Wesley, one of the satirized Moderns in *The Battel of the Books* (p. 133), used the horse-rider image; see his *An Epistle to a Friend Concerning Poetry* (London, 1700), p. 2, ll.53–54: "Those *Headstrong Coursers* scowr along the Plains, / The *Rider's* down, if once he lose the *Reins.*"

135. Will's Coffee-House … Guild-Hall: Will's was a popular resort of writers; the Royal Society met at Gresham College; Moor-Fields was the location of Bedlam; Scotland Yard housed soldiers; Westminster Hall held the law courts; Guild-Hall was where the Lord Mayor and aldermen of London met.

136. *fondest:* doting; excessively or foolishly affectionate.

137. Snap-Dragon: a game in which raisins are snatched from burning brandy and eaten while on fire.

138. *Scantling:* specimen.

139. groaning, *like the famous* Board: "groaning" boards were exhibited in London.

140. Desunt nonnulla: much is missing.

141. Effugiet … Proteus: Nevertheless the scoundrel Proteus will escape from all these fetters. Horace, *Satires,* II.iii.71.

142. Artes perditæ: lost arts.

143. Hippocrates: Greek physician and aphorist.

144. *Scaliger's:* In *The Anatomy of Melancholy,* Part 1. Sect. 1. Memb. 2. Subs. 6., Burton adds to the five senses Scaliger's sixth sense of titillation.

145. Durfy, Congreve: Thomas Durfey (1653–1723) and William Congreve (1670–1729), playwrights. Durfey was a target of Swift's satire, but Swift was on friendly terms with Congreve, who had been educated, like Swift, at Kilkenny school and Trinity College, Dublin.

146. write upon Nothing: For an example see Rochester's poem "Upon Nothinge" in *The Works of John Wilmot Earl of Rochester,* pp. 46–48.

147. ut … conviva: like a banqueter fed full of life. Lucretius, *De Rerum Natura,* 3.938.

148. *a very Polite Nation in* Greece: The reference is to the Troezenians in Pausanias, *Description of Greece,* II (Corinth), xxxi.3: "Not far from the Muses' Hall is an old altar…. Upon it they sacrifice to the Muses and to Sleep, saying that Sleep is the god that is dearest to the Muses."

149. Ambages: circumlocutions; roundabout modes of speech.

The Battel of the Books (p. 115)

1. A Full and True Account of the Battel Fought last Friday: While mock-epic in character, *The Battel of the Books* is in the form of a journalistic report of a quarrel in the royal library at St. James's palace that began on Mount Parnassus. A principal model for this journalistic prose satire is Boccalini's *Advertisements from Parnassus* (first translated into English in 1656; Swift refers in the *Tale* [p. 18] to the English adaptation of 1704). Advertisement LXXXVI, for example, concerns the defense of Parnassus by Apollo's Literati against the Ignorant who have taken up arms against literature and learning. Virgil is the "Generalissimo of the *Latin Heroicks.*" A self-important Dryden is deflated by being given "the Command of a flying Camp of *English Lyricks*" (Boccalini, Advertisement LXXXVI, pp. 85–86). In the *Battel* Swift sides with his patron Sir William Temple and the Tory wits of Christ Church, Oxford, against William Wotton and Richard Bentley in a recent English outbreak of the Ancients and Moderns controversy. Bentley's textual scholarship had demonstrated that the *Epistles of Phalaris,* praised by Temple and edited by Charles Boyle as an admirable Ancient work, was in fact spurious, a later modern forgery. Francis Atterbury's rejoinder, *Dr. Bentley's Dissertation … examin'd by the Honourable Charles Boyle Esq.,* and Swift's mock-heroic satire were brilliant triumphs of wit over the pedantry of truth.

2. Mary Clarke; *opt. Edit.:* A sheet almanac printed by Mary Clark. Swift's scholarly citation of such a work mocks pedantry.

3. *Turgescency:* swelling or swollen condition.

4. *The* Guardian *of the* Regal Library ... Humanity: Richard Bentley, Keeper of the Royal Library. In his edition of Phalaris's *Epistles,* Boyle complains that Bentley refused him access to a manuscript referring sarcastically in Latin to Bentley's distinguishing "courtesy" ("Humanitate"). In response, Bentley interpreted Boyle as referring to his singular "humanity." Swift's satiric allusion to Bentley's discourtesy and later to the disorganization of the library, which led Bentley to refuse the public access to it, has an analogue in the 1704 Tory adaptation of Boccalini (Advertisement XCI, pp. 130–31).

5. *two of the* Antient *Chiefs:* Phalaris and Aesop.

6. Dryden, Withers: Dryden, who translated Virgil, is here linked (as he was in other anti-Dryden satire of the time) with George Withers, a republican with a reputation as a bad poet.

7. Spider: The antithesis between the spider and the bee was proverbial. Among the many analogues for Swift's spider-bee passage, see Burton, "Democritus to the Reader," pp. 11–14; Boccalini, Advertisement CI, pp. 160–61; John Dunton, *A Voyage Round the World: or, A Pocket Library* (London, 1691), p. 7.

8. Light-Horse: poets.

9. Bowmen: philosophers.

10. Stink-Pot-Flingers: chemists.

11. Dragoons: physicians.

12. heavy-armed Foot: historians.

13. Engineers: mathematicians.

14. Hic pauca desunt, (etc.): Latin formulae indicating a gap or hiatus in the manuscript.

15. *dapple grey Steed:* valued as the best kind of horse; the sorrel ranked below it.

16. *sorrel Gelding:* Dryden, a Jacobite, appropriately rides a "sorrel" horse. Jacobites toasted "Sorrel," the horse that threw King William III, leading to his death.

17. *Lady in a Lobster:* the hard structure in the lobster's stomach. The "Lobsters" were also a regiment in Cromwell's army. Dryden had written *Heroic Stanzas* on the death of Cromwell in 1659.

18. *Beeves:* mature cattle.

19. Etesian *Wind:* annual winds in the Mediterranean.

20. BENTLEY ... *took his beloved* Wotton: The night advance of the two lovers parodies *Aeneid,* IX.314–449.

21. Phalaris ... *in his* Bull: Phalaris, the Sicilian Tyrant, roasted his victims in a brazen bull invented by Perillus, who was the first to be put to death in the torture device.

22. *the shape of* ————: Francis Atterbury.

A Discourse Concerning the Mechanical Operation of the Spirit (p. 141)

1. New-Holland: Australia. The Dutch had sailed along the coast of western Australia.
2. Iroquois ... Gresham ... Tobinambou: Native Americans; the Royal Society met at Gresham College; Indian tribe of Brazil.
3. Round-heads: The Puritans, the Parliamentarians in the Civil War.
4. *by certain Criticks:* principally, the Anglican antagonists of the Protestant sects and Enthusiasm.
5. Acts: Acts 2:1–4. At the Pentecost the Holy Spirit appeared to the Apostles with these signs.
6. Jauguis: yogis.
7. Dum ... avidi: furious with desire, they distinguish right and wrong only by the narrow bounds their passions draw. Horace, *Odes,* I.xviii.10–11.
8. *Picture of* Hobbes's Leviathan: The engraved title page of the first edition of *Leviathan* (1651) shows a king whose body is made up of tiny people.
9. *Morsure:* biting.
10. *hamated:* hooked.
11. Inward Light: the doctrine of the Inner Light.
12. *Sir* Humphry Edwyn: a Dissenting Lord Mayor of London whose "occasional conformity" to the Church of England in order to qualify for public office created a public scandal. In 1697 he attended his meeting-house wearing the insignia of his public office, prompting Tory demands that non-Anglicans be prevented from qualifying themselves by such token communion in the Church of England.
13. *History of* Fanaticism: The polemical point of the satire is to link the Quakers and modern Enthusiasts with heretical antiquity and disreputable aspects of the Radical Reformation. The imputation of carnal lust had long been a theme in anti-puritan satire and was prominent in the contemporary Anglican offensive against Quakerism and Enthusiasm.
14. *Receipt:* recipe.
15. furor————: furor [uterinus]: frenzy of the uterus; nymphomania.
16. *that Philosopher* ... lower Parts *into a* Ditch: Swift adapts the well-known and oft-applied story of the philosopher Thales, who fell into a ditch while observing the stars. For Thales falling into the ditch, see Diogenes Laertius, I.i.34. For the carnal application of "ditch," see Proverbs 23:27; 22:14.

THE SENTIMENTS OF A CHURCH-OF-ENGLAND MAN (P. 163)

First printed in 1711.

1. *both* Parties: Whig and Tory parties.
2. *exploded:* hissed or driven offstage, rejected, or held in contempt. "Explode" is really "ex-plaud," the opposite of applaud (from the Latin *explaudere*).

3. *latter* Cato: Marcus Porcius Cato (95–46 BCE). Defender of the Roman republic against Julius Caesar.

4. *abdicated Family:* the Stuart dynasty in the Catholic male line. James II was held to have "abdicated" in 1688, and his son James Francis Edward Stuart, the "Old Pretender," was excluded in the Act of Settlement (1701).

5. Restoration: restoration of Charles II in 1660.

6. Moderation: a Whig shibboleth.

7. Et neuter falso: and to be neither is mistaken.

8. Occasional Conformity: High Churchmen and Tories wanted to outlaw the practice by which Dissenters, in order to qualify themselves for public office under the Corporation Act (1661) and Test Acts (1673, 1678), took an occasional token communion in the Church of England. Three High Church Tory attempts to pass an Occasional Conformity bill were defeated between 1702 and 1704. But an Occasional Conformity Act was passed under Queen Anne's Tory government in 1711. The Act was repealed by the Whigs in 1719.

9. *Bishop of* Salisbury's ... *Speech* ... *Bill:* Gilbert Burnet (1643–1715), a leading Whig, opposed the Occasional Conformity Bill. His famous speech in the House of Lords in 1703 was published as *The Bishop of Salisbury's Speech in the House of Lords, upon the Bill against Occasional Conformity* (1704).

10. Sacramental Test: the requirement under the Test Acts that public officeholders take the Sacrament according to the Rites of the Church of England. The Sacramental Test was designed to exclude non-Anglicans from political power.

11. Jacobite: supporters of the exiled House of Stuart (from Latin *Jacobus,* James).

12. *whatever Opposition ... one of the Universities:* James II attempted a toleration of Roman Catholics and Protestant Dissenters by edict, issuing Declarations of Indulgence in 1687 and 1688. James received addresses of thanks from nonconformist groups but opposition from his erstwhile Tory Anglican supporters. Seven bishops refused to promulgate his Second Declaration and were sent to the Tower, but were found not guilty at their trial. James also attempted to force a Catholic president and fellows on Magdalen College at Oxford.

13. *Prince of* Orange's *Declaration:* William of Orange's *Declaration of Reasons for Invading* focused on Anglican Tory grievances, especially James's use of the dispensing power to override the Test Acts and break Anglican hegemony, and his proceedings against Magdalen College.

14. first Fruits: a tax on the Church of England clergy remitted by Queen Anne. Swift sought a similar remission for the clergy of the Church of Ireland.

15. Empiricks: quack doctors.

16. Mr. Lesly: Charles Leslie (1650–1722). Jacobite and high-profile High

Church pamphleteer. Swift knew of his pamphlets, which were "violent against Presbyterians and Low Churchmen" (Corr, I.43).

17. *destroy such Wretches from the Face of the Earth:* Genesis 6:7.

18. Hyperboles *in too literal a Sense:* Daniel Defoe's ironic parody of the language of High Church extremists in *The Shortest Way with the Dissenters* (1702) had been taken literally by some High Churchmen and Dissenters as nothing less than a call to destroy Dissenters from the face of the earth.

19. Hobbes, Filmer: Thomas Hobbes (1588–1679) and Robert Filmer (1588–1653), English absolutist thinkers.

20. Hobbes ... *his Book: Leviathan* (1651).

21. *controul:* overrule.

22. de facto: in fact.

23. de jure: by right.

24. *young* Pretender *in* France: James Francis Edward Stuart, son of James II and *de jure* King James III to the Jacobites, was twenty in 1708.

25. *suspected Birth:* Williamite propagandists had alleged that James II's son was supposititious, brought into the Queen's bed in a warming pan.

26. *Throne to be vacant:* After James II had fled to France, the Convention parliament in 1689 transferred the crown to William and Mary on this ground.

27. Nero *or* Caligula: Nero (AD 54–68) and Caligula (AD 37–41), Roman emperors infamous for cruelty.

AN ARGUMENT AGAINST ABOLISHING CHRISTIANITY (P. 187)

This *Argument* for nominal or token Christianity in an anti-Christian world was first printed in Swift's *Miscellanies in Prose and Verse* (1711), placed between two nonironic works of Anglican orthodoxy: *The Sentiments of a Church-of-England Man* and *A Project for the Advancement of Religion*. There are echoes and parallels between the three works.

1. *the* Union: The Union of England and Scotland in 1707.

2. *this Majority of Opinion the Voice of God:* regarded as a Whig shibboleth. Compare the Whig John Toland's *Anglia Libera, or the Limitation and Succession of the Crown of England* (London, 1701), p. 26: *"the Voice of the People is the Voice of God."*

3. *exploded:* hissed or driven offstage, rejected, or held in contempt.

4. *Writers on the other Side ... nominal and real* Trinitarians: Swift refers to Socinian or anti-Trinitarian writers and such works as *A Discourse Concerning the Nominal and Real Trinitarians* (1695). John Toland's notorious *Christianity not Mysterious* (1696), appropriating a distinction from John Locke, distinguished "the *Nominal* from the *Real Essence* of a thing" (p. 83). Toland's book was said to have revived "*Socinian*" principles with an "Antichristian" design (Boccalini, Advertisement XCI, 113). Socinianism (which denies the divinity of Christ) was a principal heresy troubling orthodox clergymen in the decades after the Revolution of 1688–89. It was excepted from toleration in the

religious settlement of 1689, and was being attacked in High Church pamphlet literature in 1708 (when the *Argument* was written) and in 1711. Contemporary Socinian polemicists, while denying the Trinity, expressed willingness for the sake of peace to keep or pay lip service to the nominal terms of Trinitarian worship.

5. *Proposal of* Horace: Horace, *The Epodes,* Epode XVI.

6. obsolete *Law* … Blasphemy: The "Act for the more effectual Suppression of Blaphemy and Profaneness" (1698) proscribed public discourse on the Trinity and prescribed as punishment for a second conviction the deprivation of civil rights and a three-year prison term. Socinians were persecuted for blasphemy in the seventeenth century.

7. Tiberius … curæ: "offense to the gods is the concern of the gods," Tacitus, *Annals,* I.73.

8. Asgill … Coward: John Asgill (1659–1738), Matthew Tindal (1657–1733), John Toland (1670–1722), and William Coward (1656/7–1725) were high-profile heterodox writers. Asgill, a Whig lawyer and MP, was notorious for a pamphlet in 1700 denying the necessity of death as Christ's Crucifixion had redeemed mankind from original sin. Accused of blasphemy, he was expelled from the Irish House of Commons. Tindal, a Deist and anticlerical Whig, was infamous for *The Rights of the Christian Church asserted* (1706), an anticlerical Erastian work. Swift wrote an unpublished answer to it (PW, II.67–107). Toland, a Deist and republican publicist, was the provocative anticlerical author of *Christianity not Mysterious* (1696). Coward, a physician, was notorious for writings attacking the notion of an immaterial and immortal soul, writings that were burned by the public hangman.

9. *Want of* Nominal Faith … *Employment:* The Corporation Act (1661) and the Test Acts (1673, 1678) were designed to protect Anglican hegemony by requiring communion in the Church of England as a qualification for public office. The implication is that the law is disregarded or that only lip service is paid to it. Swift strongly supported the Sacramental Test.

10. Empson and Dudley: unpopular civil servants of Henry VII who revived obsolete statutes.

11. *wise Regulations of* Henry *the Eighth:* Swift regarded Henry VIII as a tyrant who robbed the Church (see PW, V.247–51; IX.220).

12. *Spleen:* a fashionable neurosis of the time; hypochondriacal melancholy.

13. *choqued:* shocked.

14. Jus Divinum: Divine Right.

15. *Author of a Book:* Matthew Tindal.

A PROJECT FOR THE ADVANCEMENT OF RELIGION (P. 201)

First printed in 1709. The Second Earl of Berkeley recommended that this work be shown to Queen Anne in order to promote piety.

1. *Countess of* Berkeley: The Countess of Berkeley (d. 1719) was the sister of Swift's patron, the Second Earl of Berkeley, and wife of the nonjuror Robert Nelson, with whom Swift was friendly.
2. Quod … Corpore: Because he does not have anything in the purse, he pays the debt in the body.
3. *this great Town:* London.
4. *Wisdom of the Serpent … directs:* Matthew 10:16.
5. *St.* Paul … *Greeks:* I Corinthians 9:19–22.
6. *choqued:* shocked.
7. *Livery of Religion:* Swift's argument for public religious conformity irrespective of private belief and even if it means hypocrisy might be compared with some of his *Thoughts on Religion*, with the defense of nominal Christianity in the *Argument Against Abolishing Christianity*, and with the declared preference for appearances to corrupt reality expressed in *A Tale of a Tub* and in the scatological poems.
8. Diis … imperas: Because you hold yourselves as people lower than the gods, you rule over an empire (Horace, *Odes,* III.vi.5).
9. Et … iratis: He enjoys angry Gods.
10. *exploded:* hissed offstage; rejected.
11. reducing Things … Principles: Machiavelli, *Discourses,* III.i.

THE EXAMINER, 23 NOVEMBER 1710 (P. 223)

Swift wrote a series of thirty-three essays for *The Examiner,* the ministerial paper of the new Tory government. The subject of this essay is John Churchill, First Duke of Marlborough (1650–1722), Queen Anne's victorious commander-in-chief of the army in the war with France and hero of the pro-war Whig party.

1. Motto: Cicero, *Pro Cnaeo Plancio,* 80: "What is patriotism, what is service to one's country in war and peace, if it is not a recollection of benefits received from that country?"
2. two Persons *allied by Marriage:* Sidney, First Earl of Godolphin (1645–1712), father-in-law to Marlborough's daughter, Henrietta; Charles Spencer, Third Earl of Sunderland (1674–1722), husband of Marlborough's daughter, Anne.
3. *the People's* joining as one Man: The general election of October 1710 returned a Tory majority.
4. more substantial *Instances:* Swift lists grants and gifts to Marlborough made in recognition of his victories.
5. *a Saying of* Seneca: Seneca, *De Beneficiis,* I.i.4.

A SHORT CHARACTER OF THOMAS EARL OF WHARTON (P. 229)

First printed in December 1710. Thomas, First Earl of Wharton (1648–1715), was a Whig leader and magnate. Lord Lieutenant of Ireland between 1708 and 1710, he resigned on August 30, 1710, the date Swift gives for this satiric pamphlet.

1. *Grand Climacteric:* the 63rd year; the product of two mystical numbers, 7 and 9, and regarded as a critical stage in life. On 7, 9, and 63 as mystical numbers see *A Tale of a Tub,* Section X (p. 101).
2. *a Templar:* law student of the Temple in London.
3. (note): W———e: whore.
4. *Levees:* receptions.

THE IMPORTANCE OF THE GUARDIAN CONSIDERED (P. 237)

First printed end of October 1713. Swift's pamphlet is a Tory reply to the Whig writer and politician Richard Steele (1672–1729), who was editor and principal writer of *The Guardian* (12 March–1 October, 1713), the periodical successor to the *Tatler* (1709–11) and the *Spectator* (1711–12). The *Guardian*'s sequel was *The Englishman.* In *The Guardian* of 7 August 1713, and in later pieces such as *The Importance of Dunkirk Considered* (September 1713), a pamphlet in the form of a letter to John Snow of Stockbridge, Steele expressed alarm that the port and fortifications of Dunkirk had not been demolished as required by the peace treaty with France of 1713. Steele made much of a memorial on behalf of the citizens of Dunkirk against the demolition, asserted his right as a private man to criticize the government, and insinuated that the Tory administration was covertly Jacobite.

1. *Bradshaw:* John Bradshaw presided at the trial of Charles I; one of the regicides.
2. *two tolerable Plays: The Funeral* (1701) and *The Tender Husband* (1705).
3. *Mr.* Addison: Joseph Addison (1672–1719), Whig writer and politician.
4. *Sacheverell's Tryal:* The show trial of the High Church clergyman Henry Sacheverell for preaching an inflammatory sermon in November 1709, "The Perils of False Brethren, Both in Church and State," ended in March 1710. The trial precipitated a surge in popular support for the "Church" or Tory party against the Whig government.
5. some where else: debtors' prison. As an MP attending the House of Commons (which met in St. Stephen's chapel in Westminster), Steele could not be arrested for debt.
6. strip off ... the Flesh: Jude 23.
7. *Author of the* Flying-Post: George Ridpath.
8. de contemptu ... seculi: concerning scorn of the world and fleeing the times.
9. HORRIBLE EXPECTATIONS: Queen Anne's death.
10. *choqued:* shocked.

MR. C———NS'S DISCOURSE OF FREE-THINKING (P. 259)

First printed in 1713. Anthony Collins (1676–1729), Deist and Whig, was a friend and correspondent of John Locke. In his anticlerical *Discourse of Freethinking* (1713), Collins argues for free inquiry and the right of private judgment in matters of religion, claiming great men from Socrates to Archbishop Tillotson as "free-thinkers." Swift's damaging "Abstract" reduces Collins's text to absurdity and identifies the Whig party with this freethinker's "Atheology."

1. *White's*: White's Chocolate-House was notorious as a gambling club.
2. *Kit-Cat* and *Hannover* Clubs: Whig clubs.
3. Atterbury ... Sacheverell: Swift is in the company of high-profile High Church Tory clergymen.
4. *exploded:* clapped or hissed off the stage, rejected.

SOME THOUGHTS ON FREE-THINKING (P. 277)

First printed in 1767.

A LETTER TO A YOUNG LADY, ON HER MARRIAGE (P. 279)

First printed in 1727. The "young lady" has been identified as Deborah Staunton, who married John Rochfort on 19 January 1723 (PW, IX.xxvii). The essay, of importance as an expression of Swift's views on women and marriage, is contextualized in George P. Mayhew, *Rage or Raillery: The Swift Manuscripts at The Huntington Library* (San Marino, 1967), pp. 37–68.

1. *choquing:* shocking.

THE STORY OF THE INJURED LADY (P. 291)

Written in 1707; first printed in 1746. Swift's first pamphlet on Ireland. In this political allegory the injured lady is Ireland, the lover is England, and the rival mistress is Scotland. The pamphlet bitterly opposes the proposed Union of England and Scotland (1707) as a betrayal of Ireland, especially of Irish Anglicanism. Unpublished in Swift's lifetime, the pamphlet exhibits Swift's Irish patriotism and his intense animus against Presbyterian Scotland.

1. *ruined by the Inconstancy and Unkindness:* England's treatment of Ireland as a colony rather than an independent kingdom under the same crown. The allegory identifies political and economic grievances associated with the Williamite Whig government in Ireland and England.
2. *Steward was knocked on the Head:* Charles I, beheaded in 1649.
3. *she ought to be answerable:* For Swift the "cursed Hellish Vilany, Treachery, Treasons of the Scots were the chief Grounds and Causes of that execrable Rebellion" (Swift's marginalia in a copy of Clarendon's *History of the Rebellion* [1707], PW, V.295).
4. *his Steward should govern my House:* Ireland subject to the English crown.
5. *Under-Steward:* viceroy of Ireland.
6. *the Speech:* The speech of Lord Capel, King William III's Lord Deputy of Ireland, at the opening of the Dublin parliament in 1695 adopted a peremptory

tone in demanding Irish acquiescence. Swift wrote that since "Lord *Capel's* Government" Ireland was a "*Betrayed* Kingdom" (PW, II.283).

7. *Parish-watch against Thieves and Robbers:* An Irish "Act for the better suppressing tories, robbers, and rapparees" (1695).

8. *send all our Goods ... in their Naturals:* alludes to Acts of Parliament in Ireland and England destructive to the Irish wool manufacturing industry.

9. *certain Great Man:* the exiled James Francis Edward Stuart, son of the deposed James II, and "Pretender" to the crown. There would be Jacobite Risings in Scotland in 1708, 1715, and 1745. Hostility to the Union fueled Scots Jacobitism.

10. *the Turn he thinks fit to give this Compact:* England is depriving Ireland of its constitutional rights under the crown.

11. *The Answer to the Injured Lady:* Whereas *The Story of the Injured Lady* focuses on English turpitude and oppression, the "Answer" concentrates on Irish responsibility for the country's plight.

A PROPOSAL FOR THE UNIVERSAL USE OF IRISH MANUFACTURE (P. 299)

Printed in 1720. Swift's first pamphlet on Ireland since becoming Dean of St. Patrick's in 1713 and his first political intervention since the Hanoverian accession to the throne (in 1714) appeared anonymously. The Hanoverian Whig establishment regarded the work as seditious and proceeded against the printer, Edward Waters. The proceedings were eventually dropped.

1. penal Clauses: laws against tillage in favor of pasturage.

2. *People are the* Riches of a Country: an economic commonplace of the time.

3. *our Wool a Drug to us, and a Monopoly to them:* Under the Irish Woollens Act (1699) the export of Irish woollen products was prohibited and Irish raw wool could only be exported to England.

4. Barnstable: seaport in Devon.

5. *Archbishop of* Tuam: Rev. John Vesey (1638–1716).

6. Non ... ostrum: A miter is not worth so much, a judge's purple robe is not worth so much.

7. Archbishop of Dublin: Rev. William King.

8. *under the Rose: sub rosa;* in strictest confidence.

9. *Fable, in* Ovid, *of* Arachne *and* Pallas: Ovid, *Metamorphoses,* VI.Iff. The spider who extracts and spins out of its own entrails is the type of the "Modern" in the *Battel of the Books.* Ireland is in a worse condition than the spider in either Ovid's or Swift's fable.

10. Oppression makes a wise Man mad: Ecclesiastes 7:7.

11. Sanderson *and* Suarez: Robert Sanderson (1587–1663), Bishop of Lincoln; Francisco Suárez (1548–1627), Spanish Jesuit and theologian. Both were casuists.

12. Civilians: writers on civil law.

13. Little-Britain: an area of London connected with the book trade.

14. *Lord* Wharton: Thomas, First Earl of Wharton (1648–1715), a leading Whig and Lord Lieutenant of Ireland, 1708–10.

15. Addison: Joseph Addison (1672–1719), writer and Whig politician. A sometime friend of Swift's who was secretary to Wharton when he was Lord Lieutenant of Ireland.

16. a *dispensing Power:* A power claimed by the crown to overrule statutes. James II's use of such a power was a cause of the Revolution that deposed him in 1688–89.

17. Germany: Swift's *Proposal,* with its comparison of the miserable Irish to vassals in Germany, was published during the Hanoverian King George I's sixtieth-birthday celebrations.

18. canting *their own Lands:* leasing lands.

19. Bank: Swift opposed proposals for an Irish bank.

CAUSES OF THE WRETCHED CONDITION OF IRELAND (P. 307)

Composed after 1715. It could belong to the 1720s or 1730s. First printed in 1762. The sermon is a compendium of Swift's views (for example, on economic subjection to England, absentees, exploitative landlords, Irish luxury and foreign imports, charity schools, badging of beggars, and servants) treated in his other Irish tracts and satires.

1. *melancholy Reflection:* Compare the opening of *A Modest Proposal.*

2. Hewers of Wood, and Drawers of Water: Joshua 9:21, 23. The English applied the words to the Irish, regarding them in the way that Saul's children had treated the Gibeonites. Swift parodies the oppressors' biblical language elsewhere (e.g., PW, II.120; XIII.81). In 1715 the Irish Jacobite cleric Charles Leslie wrote that the Hanoverian monarchy supported by the army "shall make you hewers of wood and drawers of water" (*The Church of England's Advice to her Children, and to all Kings, Princes, and Potentates* [1715], in *A Collection of Scarce and Valuable Tracts* [known as the *Somers Tracts*], ed. by Walter Scott, 2nd ed., Vol. XIII [London, 1815], p. 699).

3. draw out the very Vitals: The image is used for England's cruel exploitation of Ireland in *A Proposal for the Universal Use of Irish Manufacture* (p. 303).

4. make Bricks without Straw: Exodus 5:6–18.

5. *a late Law:* law passed by the Irish Parliament in 1715.

6. *wear a Badge:* Badging of Dublin beggars was ordered in 1724. Swift was an advocate of badges for beggars according to the parish to which they belonged as a way of regulating the mendicant population; see *A Proposal for Giving Badges to the Beggars* (1737).

To the Tradesmen, Shop-Keepers, Farmers, and Country-People in General, of the Kingdom of Ireland [*Drapier's Letters* I] (p. 318)

First printed in March 1724. The first of seven pamphlets written during 1724 and 1725 in which Swift, in the guise of a Dublin draper ("M. B. Drapier"), opposes a patent granted to the English ironmonger William Wood (1671–1730) to manufacture copper coinage for Ireland. The initials *M. B.* may stand for the tyrannicide "Marcus Brutus." King George I, who signed the patent on 12 July 1722, is Caesar in the *Drapier's Letters* (PW, X.21). *The Drapier's Letters* powerfully articulated Irish grievance. Swift's participation in the Irish resistance earned the Dean of St. Patrick's a popular reputation as an Irish patriot and a continuing presence in Irish political consciousness.

1. *Poor Printer:* The Tory printer Edward Waters prosecuted for printing *A Proposal for the Universal Use of Irish Manufacture.*
2. where to give Money: King George I's German mistress, the Duchess of Kendal, was reported to have sold the patent for the Irish coinage to Wood for 10,000 pounds.
3. *Weight of these Half-Pence:* Swift's satiric fantasy in *The Drapier's Letters* of the copper coins being transported by horse and cart may recall the historical case of the inconvenience of copper currency in seventeenth-century Sweden, where people carried copper on their backs and in carts as the equivalent for the gold and silver the country lacked.
4. *Conolly:* William Connolly (?1660–1729), Speaker of the Irish House of Commons and a Lord Justice of Ireland.
5. *Brass Money in King James's Time:* James II authorized the use of a debased coinage during the Revolutionary War in Ireland 1689–91. Copper and brass coins were to pass as pieces of higher value with the promise to redeem them at face value in gold and silver later.
6. *Mirrour of Justice:* an antiquarian collection compiled in the reign of Edward I by Andrew Horne, quoted by Lord Coke.
7. *Lord* Coke: Sir Edward Coke (1552–1634), an authority on the royal prerogative. Quotations are from *The Second Part of the Institutes Of the Lawes of England* (1642).
8. Davis's Reports: The reference is to a legal collection published in 1615 by Sir John Davies (1569–1626), an Attorney General for Ireland.
9. accursed Thing: See Joshua 6:18–19.
10. Brazen Bull: Phalaris, a tyrant of Sicily, made the inventor of the brazen bull, Perillus, its first victim. See *The Battel of the Books,* p. 137.

To the whole People of Ireland [*Drapier's Letters* IV] (p. 326)

First printed on 22 October 1724. The pamphlet provocatively takes the controversy over Wood's patent into the radical territory of Ireland's relation to England, advancing a natural-rights case for Irish legislative independence. The English Whig establishment was alarmed. A proclamation was issued against it, the printer was prosecuted, and a reward of 300 pounds offered for the identity of the author. Swift was not betrayed although he was widely reputed to be the author. A Scriptural passage (1 Samuel 14:45) had popular currency: "And the people said ... Shall Jonathan die, who hath wrought this great salvation in Israel? God forbid ... So the people rescued Jonathan, that he died not."

1. *Carteret:* John, Second Baron Carteret (1690–1763), Lord Lieutenant of Ireland, 1724–30.
2. Birth-Right for a Mess of Pottage: Genesis 25:29–34.
3. *controul:* overrule.
4. Bacon: Francis Bacon (1561–1626), Lord Chancellor under James I.
5. *our Ancestors:* Despite its radical rhetorical appeal to the "whole people," the pamphlet is addressed to the ethnically English, Protestant, and propertied people of Ireland.
6. Gentleman They *have lately made* Primate: Hugh Boulter (1672–1742), Archbishop of Armagh in 1724, an English Whig appointment hated by Swift.
7. *without finding any Law:* In fact, the Declaratory Act of 1720 declared Ireland to be a dependent kingdom.
8. Preston: A Jacobite army capitulated at Preston in northern England in November 1715.
9. *assumed the Power:* Refers to the Declaratory Act of George I's reign but also to the treatment of Irish Anglicans and the Protestant Dublin parliament as a conquered people under William III's government. Poyning's Law (1494), revived in 1692 by Henry, Viscount Sidney, William III's viceroy in Ireland, a Revolution Whig hated by Swift, meant Irish legislation had to be approved in England. English economic legislation, such as the Navigation Acts (1660–63), the Cattle Act (1667), and the Woollen Act (1699), discriminated against Ireland.
10. Molineaux: William Molyneux (1656–98) in his *The Case of Ireland's Being Bound by Acts of Parliament in England, Stated* (1698).
11. a Dutch Reckoning: A bill which just gives the total amount not listing individual items.
12. Walpole: Robert Walpole (1676–1745), Whig statesman. "Prime Minister" from 1721–42.

A SHORT VIEW OF THE STATE OF IRELAND (P. 338)

First printed in 1728.

1. *not well affected:* not well disposed or not loyal to the Hanoverian Whig government.
2. *Act of Navigation:* Under the Navigation Acts (1660–63), Ireland was ex-

cluded from the export trade to the colonies; commerce was restricted to English shipping from English ports.

3. Whitshed's *Ghost:* William Whitshed (d. 1727), Whig lawyer and Chief Justice of the King's Bench in Ireland. Presided at the prosecution of Edward Waters for *A Proposal for the Universal Use of Irish Manufacture* (1720) and of John Harding for the fourth *Drapier's Letter* (1724).

4. Scythians: an ancient, barbaric, and nomadic tribe inhabiting Scythia, a region north of the Black Sea. The Irish were traditionally linked with this savage people, as in Edmund Spenser's anti-Irish, English colonialist treatise *A View of the State of Ireland* (completed by 1598, first published 1633).

5. Glassenbury: Glastonbury. The Glastonbury thorn, an early-flowering variety of hawthorn, was said to have sprung up at Glastonbury from the staff of Joseph of Arimathea and to blossom at Christmas.

6. Nostrâ … es: Our country's misery is great.

7. German *Empire:* a "not well affected" reflection, as is the reference to the "Pharoah" as "his Majesty."

8. YE are idle, ye are idle: Exodus 5:17.

A MODEST PROPOSAL (P. 345)

First printed in 1729. This famous satire exploits an old imputation that is succinctly described by the Irish Catholic Jacobite exile Charles Wogan in a letter to Swift of February 27, 1732/3: "Our English ancestors dispatched into Ireland, and their descendants, have taken effectual care to fasten this bugbear upon their mother country, and represent the Irish as monsters and cannibals, in order to justify their own more barbarous oppressions upon that people" (*The Works of Jonathan Swift,* ed. by Walter Scott, Vol. XVIII [Edinburgh, 1814], p. 26). Swift's satire imputes cannibalism to the oppressors as well as to the Irish poor.

1. *melancholly Object:* Begging is a sign of "Melancholy" country in Burton, "Democritus to the Reader," p. 81.

2. *great Town:* Dublin.

3. fight for the Pretender in *Spain:* Irish supporters of the exiled Stuart claimant served in the armies of France and Spain. In a letter to Charles Wogan of July–August 2, 1732, Swift expressed esteem for the Jacobite diaspora (p. 954). Wogan replied: "Nothing can be more distinguishing, in regard of an unhappy people, than [Swift's] character of those abroad, nor more just than his remarks upon the genius and sufferings of those at home" (*The Works of Jonathan Swift,* ed. by Walter Scott, XVIII.11).

4. Barbadoes: Slave and indentured labor were used on the sugar plantations.

5. Projectors: planners or promoters of a scheme or enterprise.

6. *doubt:* think or believe.

7. *grave Author:* Rabelais (c. 1494–1553). French monk, physician, and satirist.

8. Cottagers: tenant farmers.

9. Salmanaazor: George Psalmanazar, a famous imposter who pretended to be a Formosan.

10. *Groat:* proverbially a negligibly small sum of money; fourpence.

11. *Chair:* sedan chair, a vehicle carried by men, a contemporary form of transport.

12. Tithes ... Episcopal Curate: a tax supporting the clergy of the established episcopal Church of Ireland, one of whom was Swift.

13. *Receipts:* recipes.

14. *other Expedients:* serious proposals advanced by Swift in his other Irish writings.

15. TOPINAMBOO: in Brazil. The Tupinamba were a Brazilian warrior tribe reputed to practice cannibalism.

16. like the *Jews* ... City was taken: Titus captured Jerusalem in AD 70. The account of the conflict in the "History of the Jewish Wars" by Flavius Josephus (AD 37–c. 100) was known to Swift.

A PROPOSAL FOR GIVING BADGES TO THE BEGGARS (P. 355)

First printed in 1737. Swift's last pamphlet on Ireland. Unusually, Swift signed this work. The original title page of the pamphlet identified the work as by the "Dean of St. Patrick's" and had an image of the Dean with "M. B. Drapier" printed underneath. Swift not only acknowledged the work, he invoked his full authority for it as Dean and Irish patriot. Swift's punitive severity toward vagabond beggars was not untypical of contemporary cultural attitudes and had a long history. Swift's references to them as "Swarms of Foreign Beggars" and as "Thieves, Drunkards, Heathens, and Whoremongers, fitter to be rooted out off the Face of the Earth" whose poverty is the consequence of "Idleness" is prefigured for instance in Burton's *The Anatomy of Melancholy.* Among the enormities in the body politic "fit to bee rooted out" the "first is idlenesse by reason of which, wee have many swarmes of rogues and beggers, theeves, drunkards, and discontented persons" (Burton, "Democritus to the Reader," pp. 75–76.) Swift was personally charitable to individual "deserving" beggars; see Ehrenpreis, III.812–17.

1. *Poor-House ... Act of Parliament:* A Dublin workhouse for the poor established in 1704 became a hospital for foundlings after 1730.

2. *plain Proposal:* Swift wrote a brief proposal, "Upon Giving Badges to the Poor," in 1726 (PW, XIII.172–73).

3. *whipt and turned out of Town:* Laws prescribing that beggars be whipped and removed date back to the reigns of Henry VIII and Elizabeth I.

4. Couple-Beggar: Priest who performed irregular marriages.

5. rooted out off the Face of the Earth: Genesis 6:7.

6. Kennel: gutter or drain.

GULLIVER'S TRAVELS (P. 365)

First edition 1726. The present text is based on Vol. III of Swift's *Works*, published by George Faulkner in Dublin in 1735, a revised text. Swift's correspondence indicates that *Gulliver's Travels* was composed between 1721 and 1725 (Corr, II.381; III.87). Part III was written after Part IV (Corr, III.5). The book was a publishing sensation in 1726. On 17 November 1726, the poet and dramatist John Gay informed Swift that "From the highest to the lowest it is universally read, from the Cabinet-council to the Nursery" (Corr, III.182). A radical (in the sense of fundamental) satire on humankind in the vehicle of a mock travel book, *Gulliver's Travels* has generated a vast corpus of critical commentary.

Title page: Retroq . . . ab his: the people shrink back from it. Lucretius, *De Rerum Natura*, 4.19–20.

1735 Frontispiece portrait: Splendide Mendax: Gloriously False. Horace, *Odes*, III.xi.35. The phrase in Horace is positive. The caption presents Gulliver as a magnificent liar for noble ends.

1. *Advertisement: Mr. Sympson's* Letter to . . . *Gulliver:* Actually, Captain Gulliver to his Cousin Sympson.
2. Interpolations: Swift complained of changes and interpolations made to the first edition of 1726 published by Benjamin Motte.
3. *A Letter from Capt. Gulliver to his Cousin Sympson:* first printed in the 1735 edition.
4. Dampier: William Dampier (1652–1715), buccaneer, privateer, explorer, and author. His writings are among the voyage books parodied in *Gulliver's Travels.*
5. Godolphin . . . Oxford: successive Lord Treasurers of England during Queen Anne's reign.
6. Smithfield: an open area northwest of St. Paul's, site of the Bartholomew Fair. Heretics or martyrs were burned there in the sixteenth century.
7. *Cotten:* Paper was made of cotton rags.
8. *Keys:* commentaries or explanatory notes.
9. Utopia: Utopia means no place, with a pun on good place, Eu-topia; an allusion to Sir Thomas More's *Utopia* (1516), one of Swift's sources for *Gulliver's Travels.* More's Utopians, like Swift's Houyhnhnms, live according to reason and nature.
10. Redriff: Rotherhithe.
11. Banbury: Banbury in Oxfordshire was associated with Puritan fanaticism. Compare the reference to "a *Banbury Saint*" in the *Mechanical Operation of the Spirit* (p. 155). Gullivers are buried in the churchyard there (see Turner, p. 291).

Part I (p. 383)

1. *at Fourteen Years old:* Swift entered Trinity College Dublin at fourteen.

2. Leyden: in the Netherlands. The university was famous for teaching medicine ("Physick").

3. Levant: the Near East.

4. *Mrs.:* a title used for married and single women.

5. *Portion:* dowry.

6. Van Diemen's *Land:* the island of Tasmania, but also a name for all of Australia.

7. *Cable's length:* 200 yards or 600 feet, a nautical measure.

8. *Buff Jerkin:* leather jacket.

9. *Hogsheads:* large casks or barrels.

10. *Stang:* a rood or quarter of an acre.

11. Austrian *Lip:* a thick underlip.

12. *reigned about seven:* George I had reigned seven years when Swift began composition of *Gulliver's Travels* in 1721.

13. *Beeves:* mature cattle.

14. *Demesnes:* sovereign's territory or domain.

15. *IMPRIMIS:* first of all.

16. *Perspective:* telescope.

17. *Rope-Dancers:* a popular contemporary entertainment.

18. *Summerset:* somersault.

19. King's Cushions: In the fifth *Drapier's Letter* (1724), an eastern king is said to put an unjust judge to death and stuff the hide into a cushion. Swift wonders "what Number of such Cushions" the king had (PW, X.92).

20. *One is Blue ... Green:* The colors correspond with the British Order of the Garter (blue), Order of the Bath (red), and Order of the Thistle (green).

21. Colossus: the statue that stood astride the harbor entrance at Rhodes, one of the Seven Wonders of the Ancient World.

22. *high and low Heels ... distinguish themselves:* The topical application is to the High Church Tory party and Low Church Whig party.

23. *his Majesty hath determined ... low Heels in the Administration:* The Tory party was proscribed from office under George I (1714–27), a proscription continued under George II despite Tory (and Swift's) hopes that George II would show favor to the Tories.

24. *one Emperor lost his Life, and another his Crown:* Charles I was executed in 1649 and James II was deposed in 1689. The entire passage suggests the conflict between Catholic and Protestant since the Reformation.

25. Alcoran: Koran.

26. *Men of War after me:* Gulliver's naval victory reflects contemporary Tory support for naval defence rather than continental land war.

27. *Offers of a Peace:* The passage can be read as generally alluding to the Peace of Utrecht (1713). The Tory architects of the Peace were regarded as traitors by King George I's Whig government.

28. *Urine ... Fire ... extinguished:* Compare the exploits of Gargantua in Rabelais, *Gargantua and Pantagruel,* tr. by J. M. Cohen (Harmondsworth, 1955), I.17.74.

29. *Although I ... general Ideas:* The account of original Lilliput draws on a range of sources, including voyage literature accounts of remote peoples, and social models and institutions advanced in works such as Plato's *Republic* and Plutarch's *Life of Lycurgus.*

30. Cascagians: a Swiftian invention.

31. *different Nations ... different Customs ... ashamed:* Swift's satire rejects cultural relativism insisting on certain universal truths about human nature and societies.

32. *Their Notions ... differ extremely from ours:* Education in Lilliput, as in Houyhnhnmland, is modeled on that of ancient Sparta, described, for example, in Plutarch's *Life of Lycurgus,* xvi.

33. *Professors:* teachers.

34. *not suffer them ... use any fondling Expressions:* One of Swift's hopes in "When I come to be old" (1699) was "Not to be fond of Children, or let them come near me hardly" (PW, I.xxxvii). In Part IV the Houyhnhnms "have no Fondness for their Colts or Foles" (p. 603).

35. *white Staff:* the symbol of the office of Lord High Treasurer.

36. Articles of Impeachment: A topical application of the satire was the Hanoverian Whig regime's impeachment of the Tory leaders Oxford, Bolingbroke, and Ormonde in 1715. Bolingbroke and Ormonde fled to France just as Gulliver departs for Blefuscu. The impeachment is represented as grossly unjust and tyrannical.

37. *Serene:* The German dynasty was often described as the serene House of Hanover.

38. *poisonous Juice:* Hercules died in this way.

39. *to put out both your Eyes:* a court custom of a remote people reported in Jan Huygen Van Linschoten, *Discours of Voyages into [the] Easte & West Indies* (1598), 14. Other analogues include the fate of Zedekiah in Jeremiah 52:11; Samson in Judges 16:21; and the blinding of King Lear.

40. *it would be sufficient ... Princes do no more:* Compare Boccalini, Advertisement I.3: *"For Politicians affirm, Men look much better into their Affairs, when they see with other folks Eyes, than while they make use of their own."*

41. *Encomiums on his Majesty's Mercy:* King George proclaimed his mercy and lenity in his treatment of Jacobite prisoners who surrendered after the 1715 Rebellion, many of whom were executed or transported.

42. *Once I was ... Resistance ... past Obligations:* Gulliver performs the subject's duty of passive obedience and nonresistance to the sovereign though the satire encourages sympathy for the subject who might revolt against such a monarch.

43. *Antient:* ensign.

Part II (p. 439)

1. *Finding it was like to overblow ... she would lye:* The whole paragraph parodies nautical jargon and is in fact hijacked from Samuel Sturmy's *Mariner's Magazine* (1669). The passage Swift stole on how to manage a ship in all weathers is quoted in W. A. Eddy, *Gulliver's Travels: A Critical Study* (1923), pp. 143–44.

2. Tartary ... *frozen Sea:* Siberia and the Arctic Ocean.

3. *Philosophers ... by Comparison:* Swift's friend George Berkeley (1685–1753) was one of these philosophers, especially in his *Essay Towards a New Theory of Vision* (1709).

4. *Lappet:* lapel.

5. *Hinds:* laborers.

6. *Hanger:* short sword.

7. *Baby:* doll.

8. *Monster:* freak.

9. *King of* Great Britain ... *Distress:* The reader is invited to regard the Hanoverian king as a freak.

10. London *to* St. Albans: 20 miles.

11. *Pumpion:* pumpkin.

12. Sanson's Atlas: Nicolas Sanson (1600–67), French cartographer, founder of the Sanson firm. He produced a pocket atlas in four parts (1656–1705). Sanson's cartographic material was incorporated into large-scale atlases.

13. *Moydores:* Portuguese gold coins.

14. Lusus Naturae: frolic or freak of nature.

15. *Baby-house:* dollhouse.

16. *craunch:* crunch.

17. *Birth-day Cloaths:* fine clothes worn on royal birthdays.

18. Gresham College: location of the Royal Society and its collections.

19. *amazed:* dazed.

20. *Kite:* large bird of prey.

21. *Toylet:* dressing table.

22. *Motions:* emotions.

23. Jet d'Eau *at* Versailles: famous water fountain at Louis XIV's palace.

24. *Cow-dung in the Path:* Gulliver's humiliation recalls *Iliad,* XXIII.774–84, where Ajax slips on cow dung and falls flat on his face in it and is laughed at (see Turner, p. 318).

25. *Levee:* morning reception.

26. *Consorts:* concerts.

27. *When I had put an End ... upon every Article:* The King's critique of Gulliver's polity is a combination of traditional satiric themes and contemporary Opposition politics. The attack on a degenerate nobility, corrupt, unfree elections, the legal system, the management of the treasury, and mercenary

standing armies were prominent features of Jacobite propaganda against the Hanoverian Whig state.

28. *Surface of the Earth:* The King's sentiments on humankind and his horror when Gulliver tells him of gunpowder war might be compared with Apollo's reaction to human wickedness and the art of war in Boccalini, Advertisement XLVI.176: "Since Men were grown so wretchedly Foolish and Wicked … He desired … to rid the World of such Vermin … That a second Deluge might at once sweep 'em off the Face of the Earth."

29. Dionysius Halicarnassensis: A Greek writer (flourishing c. 25 BCE) who lived in and eulogized Rome.

30. Prejudices: Opposition to "prejudices" was an anticlerical Whig shibboleth. In "Thoughts on Various Subjects," Swift wrote: "SOME Men, under the Notions of weeding out Prejudices; eradicate Religion, Virtue, and common Honesty" (p. 653). See also the Apology to *A Tale of a Tub* (p. 5).

31. *Manner of* Venice *by* Ballot: The Venetian secret ballot was being recommended as a means of ensuring free elections in the crypto-Jacobite Tory press; see Nathaniel Mist's *The Weekly Journal or Saturday Post,* no. 175 (7 April 1722), 1047.

32. Phaeton: In Greek myth, son of Helios (the sun) who attempted to drive the chariot of the sun, nearly burned up the earth, was struck down by Zeus, and fell into the river Eridanus. The story exemplifies pride before a fall.

33. Tonquin: Northern Vietnam.

34. New-Holland: Australia.

Part III (p. 499)

1. *Fort* St. George: Madras in southeast India.

2. *Taction:* touch.

3. *Kennel:* gutter.

4. *Strangers:* foreigners, alluding to George I's patronage of Hanoverians in England.

5. *Mathematicians:* one of a number of hostile allusions to Isaac Newton, a strong Whig and anti-Jacobite who, as Warden of the Mint, certified the quality of William Wood's copper coinage.

6. *These People are under continual Disquietudes:* The paragraph parodies the views of contemporary astronomers and mathematicians.

7. English *Story:* alluding to the infidelity of prime minister Walpole's first wife, Catherine Shorter, and to a contemporary divorce case involving John Dormer, his wife, and a footman (Turner, p. 329).

8. *two lesser Stars, or* Satellites … *about* Mars: Two satellites were indeed discovered in 1877.

9. *Ground:* In Swift's friend Charles Ford's interleaved copy of the first edition there is a manuscript passage that was intended to be added here before the

final sentence. The passage alludes to the successful Irish resistance to the attempt by George I's Whig government to impose on Ireland the copper coinage manufactured by William Wood. The coded account of popular rebellion in which the citizens threaten to kill the King would have appeared militantly Jacobitical to the Whig authorities and was unpublished in Swift's lifetime. It reads as follows:

About three Years before my Arrival among them, while the King was in his Progress over his Dominions there happened an extraordinary Accident which had like to have put a Period to the Fate of that Monarchy, at least as it is now instituted. Lindalino the second City in the Kingdom was the first his Majesty visited in his Progress. Three Days after his Departure, the Inhabitants who had often complained of great Oppressions, shut the Town Gates, seized on the Governor, and with incredible Speed and Labour erected four large Towers, one at every Corner of the City (which is an exact Square) equal in Height to a strong pointed Rock that stands directly in the Center of the City. Upon the Top of each Tower, as well as upon the Rock, they fixed a great Loadstone, and in case their Design should fail, they had provided a vast Quantity of the most combustible Fewel, hoping to burst therewith the adamantine Bottom of the Island, if the Loadstone Project should miscarry.

It was eight Months before the King had perfect Notice that the Lindalinians were in Rebellion. He then commanded that the Island should be wafted over the City. The People were unanimous, and had laid in Store of Provisions, and a great River runs through the middle of the Town. The King hovered over them several Days to deprive them of the Sun and the Rain. He ordered many Packthreads to be let down, yet not a Person offered to send up a Petition, but instead thereof, very bold Demands, the Redress of all their Grievances, great Immunitys, the Choice of their own Governor, and other the like Exorbitances. Upon which his Majesty commanded all the Inhabitants of the Island to cast great Stones from the lower gallery into the Town; but the Citizens had provided against this Mischief by conveying their Persons and Effects into the four Towers, and other strong Buildings, and Vaults under Ground.

The King being now determined to reduce this proud People, ordered that the Island should descend gently within fourty Yards of the Top of the Towers and Rock. This was accordingly done; but the Officers employed in that Work found the Descent much speedier than usual, and by turning the Loadstone could not without great Difficulty keep it in a firm position, but found the Island inclining to fall. They sent the King immediate Intelligence of this astonishing Event and begged his Majesty's Permission to raise the Island higher; the King consented, a general Council was called, and the Officers of the Loadstone ordered to attend. One of the oldest and expertest among them obtained leave to try an Experiment. He took a strong Line of an Hundred Yards, and the Island being raised over the Town above the attracting Power they had felt, He fastened a Piece of Adamant to the End of his Line which had in it a Mixture of Iron mineral, of the same Nature with that whereof the Bottom or lower Surface of the Island is composed, and from the lower Gallery let it down slowly towards the

Top of the Towers. The Adamant was not descended four Yards, before the Officer felt it drawn so strongly downwards, that he could hardly pull it back. He then threw down several small Pieces of Adamant, and observed that they were all violently attracted by the Top of the Tower. The same Experiment was made on the other three Towers, and on the Rock with the same Effect.

This Incident broke entirely the King's Measures and (to dwell no longer on other Circumstances) he was forced to give the Town their own Conditions.

I was assured by a great Minister, that if the Island had descended so near the Town, as not to be able to raise it self, the Citizens were determined to fix it for ever, to kill the King and all his Servants, and entirely change the Government.

10. *By a fundamental Law ... Child-bearing:* alludes to the Whig repeal of the provision in the Act of Settlement (1701) forbidding the king to leave England without parliamentary approval. There is also an oblique innuendo about princesses in the House of Hanover (both George I and his son were alleged to be illegitimate in contemporary anti-Hanoverian libels). See Swift's "Directions for a Birth-Day Song," ll.15–20, where there is innuendo about the sexual intrigues of Sophia Dorothea, mother of George II.

11. *about seven Years ago:* i.e., 1701. Possibly a political allusion to the Act of Settlement in that year, which had diverted the hereditary succession of the crown from the House of Stuart to the remote (but Protestant) House of Hanover. It may also allude to the South Sea Bubble (1720) speculation and crash or to contemporary entrepreneurial projects involving water and mills, for which see Pat Rogers, "Gulliver and the Engineers," *Modern Language Review,* 70 (1975), 260–70.

12. Academy of *Lagado:* The satire alludes to the Royal Society of London and the Dublin Philosophical Society and actual experiments by Swift's contemporaries and to projects reported in the popular press of the period.

13. Maste: nuts used for pig feed.

14. *Words are only Names for* Things: Thomas Sprat's *History of the Royal Society* (1667) reports that the Royal Society resolved to return to the use of a plain style of "primitive purity, and shortness, when men deliver'd so many *things,* almost in an equal number of *words*" (*The History of the Royal Society,* ed. by Jackson I. Cope and Harold Whitmore Jones (London, 1959), 2.XX.113).

15. *Cephalick Tincture:* medicine for the head.

16. Quantum: quantity.

17. *peccant Humours:* In the old humoral theory of medicine, health depended on a balance of four humors: blood, black bile, phlegm, and choler. A morbid or "peccant" humor caused disease.

18. *Flatus:* wind; *Ructations:* belches; *Lenitives:* painkillers; *Aperitives:* laxatives; *Abstersives:* purgatives; *Restringents:* drugs that inhibit bowel movement; *Cephalalgicks:* medicines for the head; *Ictericks:* jaundice cures; *Apophlegmaticks:* purges for phlegm; *Acousticks:* deafness cures.

19. Occiput: back of the head.

20. Tribnia: anagram of Britain.

21. Langden: anagram of England.

22. *The Plots in that Kingdom:* Swift alludes to the arrest and trial of Bishop Atterbury for Jacobite plotting in 1722. The line taken in the contemporary Jacobite press was that the "Atterbury Plot" was a Whig fabrication.

23. *not a Drop of Vinegar in his Camp:* alludes to the story (in Livy, XXI.xxxvii.2–3) that Hannibal was able to cut through rocks obstructing his way in the Alps by heating them and pouring on vinegar to soften them (Turner, p. 342).

24. Caesar *and* Brutus: Marcus Junius Brutus: tyrannicide, one of the conspirators who assassinated Julius Caesar in 44 BCE.

25. Junius: Lucius Junius Brutus: led an uprising against the Tarquins and liberated Rome.

26. Socrates: Athenian philosopher (469–399 BCE).

27. Epaminondas: Theban commander (c. 420–362 BCE).

28. Cato *the Younger:* Marcus Porcius Cato (95–46 BCE), defender of the Roman Republic against Caesar; a man of austere integrity.

29. *Sir* Thomas More: Sir Thomas More (1478–1535), martyr for the English Roman Catholic Church and author of *Utopia* (1516). He was executed for refusing to acknowledge Henry VIII as head of the English Church. The only modern representative in the "Sextumvirate."

30. Sextumvirate: group of six.

31. Homer ... *Eyes ... beheld:* Homer was traditionally thought to be blind.

32. Didymus *and* Eustathius: wrote commentaries on Homer.

33. Scotus: Duns Scotus (c. 1265–c. 1308), scholastic commentator on Aristotle (the word *dunce* derives from his name).

34. Ramus: Pierre la Ramée (1515–72), an anti-Aristotelian.

35. Descartes: René Descartes (1596–1650), French philosopher and mathematician, advanced a theory of "vortices" of material particles; killed by Aristotle in Swift's *Battel of the Books.*

36. Gassendi: Pierre Gassendi (1592–1655), French philosopher and mathematician who revived the atomic physics of Epicurus.

37. Attraction: Newton's theory of gravitation.

38. Eliogabalus: Heliogabalus, Roman emperor (218–22) notorious for luxury.

39. Helot: Spartan serf.

40. Agesilaus: King of Sparta (c. 444–361 BCE).

41. *old illustrious Families:* Swift's satire on the degenerate aristocracy has a family resemblance to the satiric exposure of the true geneology of ancient families and the baseness of the nobility compiled in Burton's *The Anatomy of Melancholy,* Part 2. Sect. 3. Memb. 2. Subs. 1, pp. 136–42.

42. Polydore Virgil: Polydore Virgil (1470–1555), an Italian who became an archdeacon in England, the author of a massive history of England.

43. Nec ... Casta: Not a man was brave, not a woman chaste.

44. *Pox:* syphilis.

45. Actium: sea battle in 31 BCE in which Octavian (later Augustus) defeated Antony and Cleopatra. "Antony at Actium when he fled after Cleopatra" is one of the contemptible figures in "Of Mean and Great Figures."

46. *managing at Elections:* corrupt influence, bribery.

47. Japan ... *and I knew the* Dutch ... *that Kingdom:* As an anti-Christian measure Japan closed its ports in 1638 to all Europeans except the Dutch.

48. lick the Dust before his Footstool: Among the analogues for this image of prostration see Isaiah 49:23; Psalms 72:9; John Trenchard and Thomas Gordon, *Cato's Letters,* ed. by Ronald Hamowy (Indianapolis, 1995), no. 105 (1 December 1722), p. 742: "introduced into the presence of Dionysius ... according to the custom of the court ... fell upon his face, and kissed the oppressor's feet."

49. *great Clemency:* The despot's euphemistic clemency is another satiric glance at George I.

50. Struldbrugs *or* Immortals: An important antecedent for Swift's satire on the desire for long life is Juvenal, *Satires,* X.188–288.

51. *Meers:* boundaries or landmarks indicating a boundary.

52. Yedo: Tokyo.

53. trampling upon the Crucifix: Compare Charles Leslie, *Cassandra,* no. II (London, 1704), Appendix, no. V, p. 91: "The *Test* in *Japan* for a *Christian,* is the Trampling upon the *Cross.* This is thought a Sufficient Indication, that he who do's it is no *Christian.* By this the *Dutch* Secure that *Trade* to Themselves."

54. Amboyna: Ambon in Indonesia. Infamous for Swift's contemporaries as the site of a Dutch atrocity in 1623 in which Englishmen were tortured and killed.

55. *Skipper:* cabin boy.

Part IV (p. 559)

1. Houyhnhnms: Probably pronounced "whinnims," suggesting the whinny of a horse. The mythic Houyhnhnms are horses, not humans; however, the homonymous similarity between "Houyhnhnm" and "human" and the fact that the order of the Houyhnhnms is modeled on classical utopias enables readers to understand them as pre-Christian "Ancients" or utopians. The Houyhnhnm is Swift's image of the rational animal humans claim to be but are not.

2. *Yahoos,* a strange Sort of Animal: In the fable the Yahoos are a different species from the Houyhnhnms, who regard them as savage animals or beasts of burden. They are not human but they are humanoid. The satire works to conflate human and Yahoo. Several sources for the Yahoos have been proposed: accounts of the people of "savage nations" in voyage literature; ac-

counts of simians in voyage literature; accounts of the "savage Irish" in Swift's and in English colonialist writings; reports of cattle-slaughtering Irish houghers in 1711 (the year Gulliver enters Houyhnhnmland); classical accounts of the helots of ancient Sparta, a serf class with pariah status who were terrorized and periodically slaughtered. The Yahoos have also been seen to embody Christian symbols of original sin.

3. *Calentures:* Tropical fever.

4. *Dugs:* breasts.

5. *the Inhabitants ... any of their Cattle:* In some Irish counties in 1711, bands of houghers were destroying the cattle of pastoralists (*Journal to Stella,* II.525). Gulliver fears he will be regarded as a hougher and, indeed, it is as a potential hougher who might lead Yahoos in raids on Houyhnhnm cattle that Gulliver will be deported from Houyhnhnmland.

6. *an old Steed:* Burton, "Democritus to the Reader," p. 54: "To see horses ride in a Coach, men draw it," a sign of the world turned upside-down.

7. *complaisant:* courteous.

8. *High Dutch or German:* "German" is one of the languages praised for permanence in Swift's *A Proposal for Correcting, Improving and Ascertaining the English Tongue* (1712; PW, IV.9). Emperor Charles V is supposed to have said that he would speak to his God in Spanish, his mistress in Italian, and his horse in German.

9. *discovered:* revealed, displayed, or disclosed.

10. *not the least Idea of Books or Literature:* Ancient Sparta is said to have had no written literature but did have an oral tradition of poetry and song (Plutarch, *Life of Lycurgus,* XXI). Socrates (with whose opinions the Houyhnhnms are elsewhere said to agree) preferred oral poetry over written literature (Plato, *Phaedrus,* 274d–278b).

11. *He knew it was impossible ... Country beyond the Sea:* This Houyhnhnm "limitation" was the utopian aspiration of ancient Sparta's lawgiver Lycurgus. Ancient Sparta was said to be isolated from other countries and thus free from the corrupting luxury associated with foreign contact.

12. *The Word Houyhnhnm ... Perfection of Nature:* A naturalistic argument against the venerable belief that "Man is the most perfect and most noble Creature in the Universe" is advanced in *The Circe of Signior Giovanni Battista Gelli.* Tom Brown's 1702 version of the sixteenth-century Florentine's work, especially the seventh dialogue concerning horse versus man, was one of Swift's possible sources for Part IV. See Benjamin Boyce, *Tom Brown of Facetious Memory* (Cambridge Mass., 1939), pp. 84–85.

13. *my Master very graciously consented:* The Houyhnhnm, it seems, is being corrupted by Gulliver. The Houyhnhnms have no word for lying but Gulliver's Houyhnhnm master is willing to suppress the truth for Gulliver's sake.

14. *I was as much astonished ... act like rational Beings ... call a* Yahoo: Logic texts of

the seventeenth century defined man as a rational animal and often contrasted the horse as an irrational animal. Swift's satiric fable strikingly inverts the familiar definition; see R. S. Crane, "The Houyhnhnms, the Yahoos, and the History of Ideas," in *Reason and the Imagination: Studies in the History of Ideas, 1600–1800,* ed. by J. A. Mazzeo (New York, 1962). Compare Swift's letter to Pope of September 29, 1725: "I have got Materials Towards a Treatis proving the falsity of that Definition *animal rationale....*"

15. Houyhnhnm *Race:* "Race" is used in the sense of species or division of living creatures.

16. *flying from their Colours:* military desertion.

17. *the* Revolution: the Revolution of 1688–89.

18. *Difference in Opinions:* Swift's satire on religious controversy, war, and the profession of soldier might be compared with the violent satiric denunciation of religious madness, war, and its causes compiled in Burton, "Democritus to the Reader," pp. 39–49. The sequence of subjects in Swift's satire in Chapters V and VI—war, law, money—is the sequence in Burton, pp. 39–51.

19. Flesh *be* Bread ... *with many more:* Compare the satire on Roman Catholicism (and doctrines such as transubstantiation), Calvinism, schism, and iconoclasm in *A Tale of a Tub.*

20. *many* Northern *Parts:* A manuscript variant in Charles Ford's hand reads: "Germany and other," which more explicitly points to George I as a beggarly prince who relies on mercenaries.

21. *Nature and Reason were sufficient Guides:* as they are for More's Utopians.

22. Faculty: profession.

23. *was still to seek:* was still to discover or understand.

24. *I carry on my Body ... Wife:* Compare Burton on luxury: " 'tis an ordinary thing ... to weare a whole Mannor on his backe" (Burton, Part 3. Sect. 2. Memb. 2. Subs. 3, p. 101).

25. Clyster: enema.

26. Act of Indemnity: The Act of Indemnity and Oblivion (1660) pardoned all who had fought against the king in the civil war or worked for the republican government, excepting some named individuals. As Tory Examiner, Swift was scathing about a 1708 Act of Indemnity that protected Whig ministers from prosecution (PW, III.140).

27. *He made me observe ... unnatural:* The hierarchical distinction among the Houyhnhnms invites analogies with caste systems such as those in Plato's *Republic* or in Lycurgan Sparta. However, the color hierarchy of the Houyhnhnms follows contemporary equine authorities in which the white and sorrel are ranked below the bay and black. The dapple grey was valued as the best kind of horse. See Richard Nash, "Of Sorrels, Bays, And Dapple Greys," *Swift Studies,* 15 (2000), 110–115.

28. *managing:* treating with care or tact.

29. Spleen: a fashionable neurosis, hypochondriacal melancholy.

30. *a young Female* Yahoo: The female Yahoo's lust for Gulliver indicates that biological kinship between human and yahoo is an objective fact. The episode also activates scenarios of sexual contact between Europeans and natives.

31. *Sentiments of* Socrates: Compare Burton, *The Anatomy of Melancholy,* Part 1. Sect. 2. Memb. 4. Subs. 7, p. 364: "What is most of our Philosophy, but a Labyrinth of opinions, idle questions, propositions, Metaphysicall tearmes; *Socrates* therefore held all philosophers, cavillers and madmen ... because they commonly sought after such things, [which can be neither perceived nor understood by us], or put case they did understand, yet they were altogether unprofitable.... [We] are neither wiser as he followes it, nor modester, nor better, nor richer, nor stronger for the knowledge of it." Turner (p. 362) cites analogues in Plato and Xenophon.

32. *Fondness:* doting, foolish affection.

33. *other Couple bestows ... one of their own Colts:* The wife-sharing for eugenic purposes practiced in ancient Sparta (Plutarch, *Lycurgus,* XV, 6–8) and adopted in Plato's *Republic* is modified in More's *Utopia* and in Swift's Houyhnhnmland into the practice of bestowing children. It is the Yahoos who have "their Females in common" (p. 598).

34. *In their Marriages ... Breed:* The practice of eugenics, education system, and indeed the entire social organization and institutions of Houyhnhnmland, seem to have a principal model in ancient Sparta under the laws of the legendary Lycurgus as mediated by approving classical and later writers in the humanist tradition.

35. *exterminated from the Face of the Earth:* Compare Genesis 6:7, the periodic massacres of helots in ancient Sparta (Plutarch, *Lycurgus,* XXVIII, 1–4), and Swift's punitive extremism in works such as *A Proposal for Giving Badges to the Beggars.*

36. *many Ages ago ... was never known:* The two Brutes upon a mountain suggest a Yahoo Adam and Eve though the "Ancient" Houyhnhnms entertain a Lucretian theory of creation from the earth (see Lucretius, *De Rerum Natura,* 5. 791–98; Turner, p. 364).

37. *this Invention:* The Houyhnhnms will do to the humanoid Yahoos what humans do to horses. Proposals to castrate Irish criminals rather than inflict immediate capital punishment were being advanced in the 1720s; see, for example, *Some Reasons Humbly offer'd, why the Castration of Persons found Guilty of Robbery and Theft, May be the best Method of Punishment for those Crimes* (Dublin, 1725).

38. *Pravity:* depravity.

39. *doubted:* feared.

40. *Wattles:* rods and twigs.

41. New-Holland: Australia.

42. Herman Moll: Dutch cartographer in London.

43. *backwards:* at the back of the house.

44. Inquisition: Swift's *Predictions for the Year 1708* was burned by the Inquisition of Portugal (see *A Vindication of Isaac Bickerstaff*, p. 679). Gulliver's story might be understood by an Inquisition as blasphemy against Genesis 1:27, 28, where it is said that "God created man in his *own* image" and with "dominion" over all living things on earth.

45. *Rue … Tobacco:* Regarded as herbal cures for melancholy affliction in Burton, *The Anatomy of Melancholy,* Part 2. Sect. 4. Memb. 1. Subs. 3, p. 218.

46. Stone-Horses: stallions.

47. Nec … finget: Nor, if Fortune has made Sinon for misery, will she also in her spite make him false and a liar (Virgil, *Aeneid,* II.79–80). The Greek Sinon tells an untrue story persuading the Trojans to take the wooden horse within the walls of their city and this leads to the destruction of Troy. Similarly perhaps, Gulliver is a "magnificent liar" and his Greek-model horses would, if their principles were introduced, destroy modern Troy (London).

48. Cortez: Hernán Cortés (1485–1547), Spanish conquistador who conquered Mexico.

49. *Mummy:* pulp. Gulliver's fantasy of the terror Houyhnhnms could unleash on a European army returns the terror the Spanish with their horses caused the South Americans.

50. *Yerks:* kicks.

51. Recalcitrat … tutus: He kicks back, at every point on his guard (Horace, *Satires,* 2.1.20).

52. *ought to be believed:* In the first edition of 1726 a passage follows in which Gulliver suspects that the two Yahoos who appeared on the mountain in Houyhnhnmland (see p. 606) were English. The passage reads:

believed; unless a Dispute may arise about the two *Yahoos,* said to have been seen many Ages ago on a Mountain in *Houyhnhnmland,* from whence the Opinion is, that the Race of those Brutes hath descended; and these, for any thing I know, may have been *English,* which indeed I was apt to suspect from the Lineaments of their Posterity's Countenances, although very much defaced. But, how far that will go to make out a Title, I leave to the Learned in Colony-Law. But

OF MEAN AND GREAT FIGURES (P. 631)

First printed in 1765.

FAMILY OF SWIFT (P. 635)

First printed in 1765.

1. *Festine lente:* hasten slowly.

2. *His eldest son Thomas:* Swift's royalist grandfather, Thomas Swift (1595–1658).

3. *Mr Dryden the Poet:* Swift and John Dryden were second cousins, once removed.

4. *J.S. D.D., and D of St P—:* Jonathan Swift, Doctor of Divinity, and Dean of St. Patrick's.

5. *The Troubles:* the revolutionary war between Jacobite and Williamite armies in Ireland.

6. *Sr Wm Temple:* Sir William Temple (1628–99). Diplomat and statesman, friend and adviser of William III, and Swift's first patron. Swift worked for Temple at Moor Park in Surrey during the decade 1689–99, editing his memoirs and letters for publication.

7. quas vulgus elegerit: which the public has chosen.

ON THE DEATH OF MRS. JOHNSON [STELLA] (P. 643)

First printed in 1765.

1. *Mrs. Johnson:* Esther Johnson (1681–1728). Swift's "truest, most virtuous, and valuable friend," to whom he gave the poetical name Stella. Some believe she and Swift secretly married. He met her when he joined Sir William Temple's household in 1689 and had a role in her education. She moved to Dublin after Temple's death with her companion Rebecca Dingley and lived in Ireland for the rest of her life.

THOUGHTS ON VARIOUS SUBJECTS (P. 651)

First printed in 1711.

THOUGHTS ON RELIGION (P. 655)

First printed in 1765.

1. *royalty in Adam:* Swift is alluding to that strand of royalist absolutist thinking, identified with the patriarchalist political philosophy of Sir Robert Filmer (1588–1653) and contemporary polemicists such as Charles Leslie (1650–1722), which located an absolute monarchical power of dominion in Adam.

A MEDITATION UPON A BROOM-STICK (P. 661)

First printed in 1710. Robert Boyle (1627–91) was a natural philosopher and Fellow of the Royal Society. Swift is parodying Boyle's *Occasional Reflections upon Several Subjects* (1665). An anecdote from Swift's friend Lady Betty Germain relates that Swift solemnly read this spoof to the Countess of Berkeley as one of Boyle's serious "Meditations."

1. Bezom: A broom made of bound twigs.

The Bickerstaff Papers: Swift's hoax killing of the leading London astrologer and almanac maker John Partridge (1644–1715) was a brilliantly executed April Fools' Day joke. In the first pamphlet, *Predictions for the Year 1708,* "Bickerstaff" predicts that Partridge will die on March 29. Just before April Fools' Day Swift published the *Accomplishment* of the prediction. When Partridge in his almanac for 1709 insisted he was alive and had been alive on March 29, Swift answered the dead man with a *Vindication of Isaac Bickerstaff.* The motives for Swift's satire on Partridge include the folly and imposture of astrology, as Swift saw it, and the fact that Partridge was a stridently anticlerical Whig whose annual almanac, *Merlinus Liberatus,* was his political vehicle.

PREDICTIONS FOR THE YEAR 1708 (P. 667)

First printed in 1708.
1. Gadbury: John Gadbury (1627–1704), prominent astrologer and a Tory predecessor of Partridge.
2. Old Stile: In Swift's lifetime England used the Julian calendar, which after 1700 was eleven days behind the Gregorian calendar used on the continent. New Year was 25 March, not 1 January, in the Julian calendar.
3. *the* Prophets: A group of French Protestant refugees, the "French Prophets" gained notoriety at the end of 1706. Suspected of Socinianism, three members of the enthusiastic sect were pilloried. See Ehrenpreis, II.198.
4. Alter ... Heroas: Virgil, *Eclogues,* Eclogue IV.34–35: "A second Tiphys will then arise, and a second Argo to carry chosen heroes." Swift substitutes Tethys, a goddess, for Virgil's Tiphys, the pilot of the Argo.

THE ACCOMPLISHMENT OF THE FIRST OF MR. BICKERSTAFF'S PREDICTIONS (P. 675)

First printed in 1708.
1. *Nonconformist:* A Protestant Dissenter from the Church of England.

A VINDICATION OF ISAAC BICKERSTAFF (P. 678)

First printed in 1709.
1. (Latin lines): Most illustrious Bickerstaff restorer of Astrology; Thus most recently Bickerstaff that great star of England; Bickerstaff, famous Englishman, easily first among astrologers of the present age; With respect to the great man; or perhaps rather the printer's error since otherwise Bickerstaff the most learned man.

A FAMOUS PREDICTION OF MERLIN ... WITH EXPLANATORY NOTES. BY T. N. PHILOMATH. (P. 683)

First printed in 1709. The archaic language and typography of this pretended prophecy deceived Samuel Johnson, among others. On this hoax, see Ehrenpreis, II.344–45. The prophecy is Partridgeian in its whiggish speculation.

1. *the pretended Prince ... miscarry as he did before:* A Jacobite invasion and rising in Scotland in 1708 had failed.
2. *our happy* Union ... *no Man shall be sorry for it:* T. N. Philomath's view was not shared by Swift, who opposed the Union and wanted it dissolved.

FROM A COMPLEAT COLLECTION (P. 687)

First published in 1738. A lifelong project of Swift's, this satiric compendium of polite conversation derives, it would appear, from recorded conversations and from collections of proverbs. Swift is here the anthologist of contemporary clichés, platitudes, proverbs, slang, and word abuses. In *The Battel of the Books* the satirized Modern Richard Bentley is a product of this culture of politeness: "Courts *have taught thee* ill Manners, *and* polite Conversation *has finish'd thee a* Pedant" (p. 136). This mechanical operation of conversation takes place in the house of Lord and Lady Smart in a fashionable part of London. The "Second" of the "Three Dialogues" is reproduced here. For extensive annotation of the dense texture of proverbs and colloquialisms in this work, see *Swift's Polite Conversation*, with Introduction, Notes and Extensive Commentary by Eric Partridge (London, 1963).

THE LAST SPEECH AND DYING WORDS OF EBENEZOR ELLISTON (P. 711)

First printed at the time of Elliston's execution in 1722. Published in Swift's *Works* of 1735. It was customary for a condemned felon on the scaffold to deliver an address to the crowd. Printed "Last Dying Speeches" were a popular genre. The condemned were expected to repent their crimes and to acknowledge the justice and necessity of the punishment meted to them by the State. Swift's mock scaffold speech indicts the recidivist criminal and the government that should have hanged him long ago. The "Speech" contains off-the-page menaces for the criminal fraternity by claiming Elliston has informed on others.

1. *among common Whores the very Night before their Execution:* for Swift a flagitious sign of the reprobate. Compare his comment on the Republican martyr Sir Henry Vane: "His lady *conceived* of him the night before his execution" (marginalia in Burnet's *History of His Own Times,* PW, V.270).
2. *go Snacks:* share the proceeds.
3. *root us out like ... Vermin:* an example of Swift's rhetoric of extermination. Robbers here share the fate projected for Yahoos in Part IV of *Gulliver's Travels* and for vagabond beggars in *A Proposal for Giving Badges to the Beggars.*

DIRECTIONS TO SERVANTS (P. 717)

First published posthumously in 1745. The unfinished *Directions to Servants* exhibits in quotidian detail and on an encyclopedic scale the follies and iniquities of servants, which Swift had denounced generally in works such as his sermon on the *Causes of the Wretched Condition of Ireland*. The satiric compendium presents a master's nightmare of household subversion and anarchy where the turpitude of servants is manic. What Swift in a letter to John Gay and the Duchess of Queensberry of 28 August 1731 called his "whole duty of servants" was a satiric project upon which he worked for many years. An extract from this work begins the surrealist André Breton's famous *Anthologie de l'humour noir* [*Anthology of Black Humour*].

1. *Spunging-house:* the bailiff's house, where debtors were held.
2. *give them Warning:* notice of resignation.
3. *Jordan:* chamberpot.
4. *Vales:* tips.
5. *Clout:* cloth.
6. *Men cooks … French Nation:* Whig grandees were notorious for employing French cooks, a luxurious sign of their hegemony. Tories were linked with English fare. The fanatically Whig Modest Proposer is *au fait* with French dishes.
7. *Sack:* white wine from Spain or the Canaries.
8. *exploded:* hissed offstage; rejected.
9. *dunned:* importuned for payment of a debt.
10. *Skipkennel turned out of Place:* a lackey out of a position.
11. *Huncks:* miser.
12. Gilblas: Alain-René Lesage's picaresque masterpiece *Gil Blas* (1715–35).

POEMS (P. 769)

Many of Swift's poems are highly allusive and parodic, and densely textured with topical references and names. For extensive annotation and detailed textual and contextual commentary on Swift's poems consult the excellent *Jonathan Swift: The Complete Poems*, ed. by Pat Rogers (Harmondsworth: Penguin, 1983).

Verses wrote in a Lady's Ivory Table-Book (p. 771)

(Title): Table-Book: In this context a memoranda book composed of tablets rather than paper pages; penciled entries can be wiped away by the "power of Spittle" and a cloth or rag ("Clout").

1. Receit for Paint: receipt for cosmetics.
2. far an el breth: for an ill breath (bad breath).
3. Billet Doux: love letters.

To Their Excellencies the Lords Justices of Ireland. The Humble Petition of Frances Harris (p. 772)

(Title): The Lords Justices were the Earl of Berkeley and the Earl of Galway. Swift was Berkeley's chaplain. Frances Harris was a waiting-woman. Swift refers to several other members of Berkeley's household in the poem. The poem deploys proverbial expressions and demotic speech.

1. *Lady* Betty's: Lady Elizabeth Berkeley, daughter of the earl.
2. *to tell:* count.
3. Dromedary: Earl of Drogheda, a replacement for Berkeley and Galway.
4. *a* Bedlam: mad person.
5. *Cunning Man:* fortune-teller.
6. Chaplain: Swift.
7. *cast a* Nativity: make an astrological prediction; draw up a horoscope.

Baucis and Philemon (p. 774)

The poem is based on the story in Ovid, *Metamorphoses,* VIII.626–724.

1. Goody: a contraction of "goodwife."
2. *burning blue:* Candles were believed to burn blue when evil spirits were present.
3. *Not fit to live … shall be drown'd:* a village pump version of the Flood that will destroy humankind from the face of the earth; see Genesis 6:7; 7:4.
4. *Jack:* a device for turning the roasting spit.
5. *Porringers:* small basins.
6. Joan of France … Little Children in the Wood: folk legends and subjects of chapbooks.
7. *Vampt:* revamped or reworked.
8. *stood up firm for* Right Divine: The stereotypical High Church lower clergyman was hostile to Dissent and an adherent of divine hereditary right monarchy.
9. *Coifs:* close-fitting caps.
10. *Pinners:* coifs with flaps.
11. *Colberteen:* lacework.
12. *Grogram:* grosgrain; fabric mainly of silk.

A Description of the Morning (p. 779)

1. *Hackney-Coach:* a hire coach drawn by two horses, seating six. Parodies the sun's chariot in classical dawn sequences.
2. Betty: maid. Parodies Aurora, goddess of the dawn.
3. *par'd:* cleaned.
4. *Sprinkled:* sprinkled sawdust.
5. *Kennel-Edge:* edge of gutter.
6. *Smallcoal-Man:* coal man.
7. *Duns:* debt collectors.
8. *Brickdust:* powdered brick used for scouring. Referring to Moll's tanned complexion or to her vending powdered brick.
9. Fees: Prisoners paid for food and privileges in jail.
10. Among several parallels for this line, see Charles Cotton's poem, "Morning Quatrains," ll. 65–66: "The slick-fac'd School-boy Sachel takes, / And with slow pace small riddance makes." See *Poems of Charles Cotton,* ed. by John Buxton (London, 1958), p. 4.

A Description of a City Shower (p. 780)

1. *depends:* impends
2. *Sink:* lavatory receptacle or sewer.
3. *Spleen:* depressive condition; hypochondriacal melancholy.
4. *dabbled:* muddy.
5. *Welkin:* archaic word for "sky."
6. Susan: maid.
7. *aslope:* aslant.
8. *Quean:* impudent, immodest, ill-behaved woman; strumpet.
9. *Flirts:* flicks.
10. Devoted: doomed, but punning on "devout."
11. *dagged:* wet with the rain shower.
12. *Templer:* law student.
13. *a-broach:* overflowing.
14. *Triumphant Tories:* The Tories had defeated the Whigs in the 1710 election.
15. *Chair:* covered sedan chair.
16. (ll. 47–52): Virgil, *Aeneid,* II.40–56.
17. Smithfield: open area to the northwest of St. Paul's. Sheep and cattle pens were located in West Smithfield.
18. Pulchre's: St. Sepulchre's Church on Snow Hill.
19. *Sprats:* small fish.
20. (ll. 61–63): Swift is trashing the triplet and the twelve-syllable alexandrine. A note in Faulkner's edition of 1735 reads: "These three last lines were intended against that licentious Manner of modern Poets, in making three Rhimes together, which they call *Triplets;* and the last of the three, was two or sometimes more Syllables longer, called an *Alexandrian.* These *Triplets* and *Alexandrians* were brought in by DRYDEN, and other Poets in the Reign of CHARLES II. They were the mere Effect of Haste, Idleness, and want of Money; and have been wholly avoided by the best Poets, since these Verses were written." Swift's final alexandrine parodies such a line as this from Dryden's *Georgics:* "And cakes of rustling Ice come rolling down the Flood" (*Georgics,* I.418). Swift did not wholly avoid triplets in his own poetry.

Cadenus and Vanessa (p. 782)

(Title): *Cadenus* is an anagram of *Decanus* (Dean). Vanessa, now a popular name for girls, was invented by Swift, constructed from Esther Vanhomrigh: "Van" from Vanhomrigh and "essa" from Esther. Esther (or Hester) Vanhomrigh (1688–1723) was of Dutch descent. An intimate friend and correspondent of Swift, she followed Swift to Dublin from London. The poem is Swift's version of their relationship. The poem was not intended for publication. When manuscript copies of it embarrassingly began circulating in public, Swift described the poem as "only a cavalier business" and "a private humorsome thing" (Corr, III.130). Unauthorized editions were printed in 1726. It is Swift's longest poem.

1. (ll. 1–2): The poem's setting is the Court of Love presided over by Venus ("the *Cyprian* Queen"). Standard contemporary legal jargon is deployed throughout the poem.
2. *Free-thinkers:* anticlerical and deistic rejectors of authority in matters of religious belief.
3. *Toys:* trifles.
4. Toylets: dressing tables.
5. *Sea:* Venus emerged from the sea.
6. Fleta's, Bractons, Cokes: venerable legal authorities. Fleta, a commentary on the English law; Henry de Bracton and Edward Coke were authors of works on English law.
7. Ovid; author of the *Amores* (*Love Poems*) and *Ars Amatoria* (*Art of Love*).
8. Dido's *Case:* story of Dido and Aeneas in the *Aeneid*.
9. Tibullus: Roman elegiac poet whose books of poems, in which women are celebrated, have a love theme.
10. Cowley … Waller: Abraham Cowley (1618–67) and Edmund Waller (1606–87), famous and influential seventeenth-century love poets.
11. Clio: muse of history.
12. Lucina: Juno in her aspect as goddess of childbirth.
13. Pallas: The Greek goddess Athene, identified by the Romans with Minerva, goddess of wisdom.
14. Atalanta: In Greek mythology she refused to marry any man who could not defeat her in a foot race. Defeated suitors were killed.
15. *a new* Italian: a new singer for the Italian opera.
16. Compare Rochester's "A Letter from Artemiza in the Towne to Chloe in the Countrey," ll.34–35: "What change has happen'd of Intrigues, and whether / The Old ones last, and who, and who's togeather" (*The Works of John Wilmot Earl of Rochester*, ed. by Harold Love [Oxford, 1999], p. 64).
17. *exploded:* rejected, hissed offstage.
18. St. James: a fashionable area near St. James's palace.
19. *Deshabille:* negligent undress; partly dressed.
20. Montaigne: A favorite French author of Swift's.
21. *the Ring:* In Hyde Park, a fashionable place to promenade.
22. Tunbridge: the wells at Tunbridge had long been a popular resort. See Rochester's "Tunbridge Wells" in *Works*, pp. 49–54.
23. Plutarch's *Morals: Moralia*.
24. (ll. 524–25): Swift was some twenty years older than Vanessa. Swift's relations with women often took this tutor-pupil character.
25. *Complaisance:* courtesy.
26. sans Consequence: as if from a man with indifference or in an unassuming way.
27. *railly'd well:* good-humored ridicule.
28. a Bite: a deception or hoax; a lie told in a serious manner designed as a hu-

morous trick or practical joke. See Corr, I.40, where Swift describes this fashionable mode of humor.

29. *such God-like Men:* another echo of Rochester; compare "A Satyre against Reason and Mankind," l. 220: "If upon Earth there dwell such God-like men" (*Works,* p. 63).

30. *In all their Equipages meet:* In all their array and order.

31. Coram ... Martis: "Before the queen, on *Tuesday* next" (footnote in Faulkner's edition of 1735).

The Author upon Himself (p. 806)

The poem attacks the people Swift believed had opposed his preferment to a bishopric.

1. (l. 1): The missing words are found in the uncanceled state of the poem: "an old red-pate, murdering hag,"; see Rogers, p. 163, and notes, pp. 670–71. The reference is to the Duchess of Somerset, a courtier. Swift insinuates that she had her husband murdered by her new lover; see ll. 53–54.

2. *A Crazy Prelate, and a Royal Prude:* John Sharp, Archbishop of York, and Queen Anne.

3. S——: Swift.

4. Child's or Truby's: coffeehouse and tavern frequented by the clergy.

5. Finch: the earl of Nottingham.

6. W———: Walpole.

7. Perkin: the Pretender.

8. *Treatise: A Tale of a Tub.*

9. (ll. 53–54): See Rogers, p. 164: "Now Madam Königsmark her vengeance vows / On Swift's reproaches for her murdered spouse."

Mary the Cook-Maid's Letter to Dr. Sheridan (p. 808)

The poem is a fine example of raillery directed at Swift's friend and literary collaborator, Dr. Thomas Sheridan (1687–1738), clergyman and schoolmaster. Written in the character of Swift's cook, the poem displays conversational, colloquial vigor and deploys puns and brogue. The cook's garrulity is conveyed in long lines, a technique used in "The Humble Petition of Frances Harris."

On Stella's Birth-day (1719) (p. 809)

(Title): Stella: Esther Johnson (1681–1728). The first of a series of poems Swift addressed to his intimate and dearest friend on her birthday, 13 March.

1. thirty four: She was thirty-eight in 1719.

2. (ll. 4–5): In the cavalier mathematical gallantry of the poem she is now only thirty-two.

Phillis, or The Progress of Love (p. 810)

The "Progress" piece was popular in literature and art of the period. "Progress" often had a negative meaning, recording, as here, the stages of decline.

The Progress of Beauty (p. 813)

1. *Diana:* the moon goddess.
2. *Celia:* a conventional name in pastoral and love poetry.
3. *Lusitanian:* Portuguese. Ancient Lusitania corresponds with modern Portugal.
4. *Cancer:* the zodiac sign of Cancer (the Crab).
5. *Endymion:* the most beautiful of men and loved by the moon goddess.
6. Mercury was used in the treatment of syphilis. The effects of the disease (and the treatment) are listed at ll. 109–12.
7. *Flamstead:* John Flamsteed (1646–1719), a famous contemporary astronomer and Astronomer Royal.

The Progress of Poetry (p. 817)

1. *Profits of his Play:* Playwrights received the takings, less expenses, of the third night's performance of their play.
2. Grub-street: symbolically the abode of hack authors. The street was near Moorfields, in the Barbican area.

To Stella, Visiting me in my Sickness (p. 818)

1. Pallas: Athene, identified by the Romans with Minerva, the goddess of wisdom.
2. Brutus … Cato … Socrates: Both Lucius Junius Brutus and Marcus Brutus, as well as Cato the Younger and Socrates are celebrated in *Gulliver's Travels* as exemplars of virtue or wisdom. Socrates and Cato appear as "Great Figures" in "Of Mean and Great Figures."
3. *Fleer:* mocking look or speech, sneer.

To Stella, Who Collected and Transcribed his Poems (p. 822)

1. The claim is also made in *Cadenus and Vanessa*, ll. 768–69.
2. (ll. 45–46): punishments for prostitutes and disorderly women in places of detention.
3. Curll: Edmund Curll, notorious publisher who pirated works by Swift.
4. Maevius: the archetypal poetaster; see Virgil, *Eclogues,* III.90.
5. *Suburb:* unfashionable outlying part of the city.
6. *Crambo:* a game that involves finding rhymes.
7. Ajax: Ajax was resentful because the armor of the dead Achilles was given to Odysseus and not to him.

Stella's Birth-day (1721) (p. 827)

1. *thirty six:* It was her fortieth birthday in 1721.

To Stella on her Birth-day (1722) (p. 829)

1. *Delany:* Patrick Delany (c. 1685–1768), churchman and close friend of Swift's. Delany did write verses to Stella.

A Satirical Elegy on the Death of a late Famous General (p. 829)
(Title): The Duke of Marlborough died on June 16, 1722. The Whigs ensured he had a lavish funeral. The poem, a bitter inversion of a funeral elegy, reflects Swift's and contemporary Tory hostility.
1. *loud trump:* I Corinthians 15:52.

The Progress of Marriage (p. 830)
The marriage satirized was that between Swift's acquaintance Dean Pratt and Lady Philippa Hamilton.
1. *Aetatis suae:* at the age of fifty-two.
2. *Cyprian Queen:* Venus.
3. *Juno:* goddess of women.
4. *Iris:* goddess of the rainbow.
5. *Hebe:* handmaiden of the gods; associated with perpetual youth.
6. *Betty:* maidservant.
7. *Bath:* the waters at Bath, a popular resort.
8. (ll. 109–10): Ovid, *Metamorphoses,* IX.80–88. The jokes about horns refer to procreation and the cuckold's horns.
9. *cross-bath:* the Cross Bath, near the Roman Baths. James II's queen, Mary of Modena, conceived after visiting the Cross Bath.
10. *Ensign:* lowest-ranking officer.

Stella's Birth-Day. A great Bottle of Wine, long buried, being that Day dug up. (p. 835)
The names in the poem refer to Swift's friends and servants.
1. *Nine:* the muses.
2. *Semel'n ... Apollo:* the proverb in English is "Once a year Apollo laughs."
3. Eusden: Laurence Eusden, poet laureate.
4. *Ir- -sh D- -ns:* Irish Deans.
5. (missing names): Dean White, Dean Daniel, Dean Smedley.

Stella at Wood-Park, A House of Charles Ford (p. 838)
(Title): Charles Ford (1682–1741), born in Dublin, inherited the estate of Wood-park. However, he spent much of his time as an absentee in London. A close friend and correspondent of Swift and Swift's trusted literary assistant, especially in the publication of *Gulliver's Travels.* Ford's political sympathies were Jacobite Tory. For Swift's anti-Hanoverian poem to Ford on his birthday, see *Poems,* I.309–315.
The Latin epigraph is from Horace, *Epistles,* I.xviii.31–32: ... if he wished to hurt someone, would give him expensive clothes."
1. *Don* Carlos: Ford's nickname.
2. *sossing:* lounging.
3. Dingly: Rebecca Dingley, Stella's companion.
4. Pontack: a sweet wine that seems to have been a favorite of Stella and Ford; see *Corr,* III.5.

5. (missing words): Archdeacon Wall.
6. Ormond Key: "Where both the Ladies lodged." Note in Faulkner's 1735 edition.
7. Lady-Day: 25 March.

Prometheus, A Poem (p. 842)

A broadside poem attacking William Wood, ironmonger and entrepreneur, who had been granted a patent to manufacture copper coins for Ireland. There is extensive wordplay on iron and brass. The poem calls for Wood to be hanged and satirizes the corrupt Hanoverian court and Walpole's government.

1. Venus: The Duchess of Kendal.

Stella's Birth-day (p. 844)

1. *past her Dancing Days:* proverbial.
2. (missing name): Sheridan.
3. (missing name): Delany.
4. (missing word): Dean.
5. *God of wit, and Beauty's Queen:* i.e., Apollo and Venus.

On Wood the Iron-monger (p. 846)

1. Elis: In Greek mythology, the King of Elis impiously attempted to emulate Zeus. He drove a chariot through Elis, imitating thunder with brass and lightning by brandishing a torch. See, for example, Virgil, *Aeneid,* VI.585–94.

A Receipt to Restore Stella's Youth (p. 847)

1. (Title): *Receipt:* recipe.
2. Medea's *Kettle:* The cauldron of the sorceress Medea, who could restore youth.
3. Quilca: Thomas Sheridan's house in County Cavan. Swift and Stella made visits there.
4. *Justices o'* Quorum: justices of the peace.

Stella's Birth-day (p. 848)

Swift's last birthday poem for Stella.

Clever Tom Clinch going to be hanged (p. 851)

1. Holbourn: the route from Newgate prison to the place of execution at Tyburn.
2. *Sack:* white wine.
3. whittle: "A Cant Word for confessing at the Gallows." Note in Faulkner's edition of 1735.
4. Wild: Jonathan Wild, a notorious entrepreneurial criminal, receiver of stolen goods and thief-taker.

Holyhead. Sept. 25. 1727 (p. 852)

1. (Title): Holyhead, in Wales. Swift, anxious about Stella's health (l. 23), is waiting for a boat to ferry him across to Ireland.
2. *packet:* the packet boat, the regular boat mail service.

3. (ll. 29–32): The lines might recall the death landscape and pathetic fallacy used by another Anglican dean meditating the death of a loved one; see John Donne's "A nocturnall upon S. Lucies day, Being the shortest day," ll.3–8.

Irel.ª(p. 853)

The poem expresses Swift's animus against pro-English and pro-Dissenting Whig political measures in Ireland.

1. *His Excellency:* the Lord Lieutenant.
2. *Chaps:* jaw.
3. *trepan'd:* to lure or inveigle into a place.
4. *augmentation:* vote to increase funds for the crown or to augment the standing army.
5. (ll. 43–48): Swift opposes anti-Catholic legislation designed to suppress Jacobitism and is hostile to perceived Hanoverian Whig overtures to the Dissenters.
6. *Chints:* chintz; imported calicoes.
7. *Townshend and Walpole:* Whig leaders detested by Swift.

Directions for a Birth-day Song (p. 855)

A sardonic, openly anti-Hanoverian political satire modeled on the satiric "Instructions-to-a-Painter" genre.

1. *Faulchion:* sword.
2. *Overton:* Henry Overton was a print seller.
3. *Mecaenas:* Councillor of Augustus and an enlightened literary patron.
4. *George and William:* George I and William III.
5. *Julius, or the youth of Pella:* Julius Caesar and Alexander the Great.
6. *Cynthia:* the moon.
7. *Carolina:* Queen Caroline.
8. *Berecynthia:* wife of Saturn.
9. *Freddy:* Frederick, Prince of Wales.
10. *Yonker:* young man.
11. *Nassau:* William III.
12. *Doctor Clark:* Samuel Clarke, heterodox clergyman and philosopher.
13. *Minheer Hendel:* the composer George Frederick Handel.

A Dialogue between an eminent Lawyer and Dr. Swift (p. 862)

1. (Title): *Lawyer:* Robert Lindsay.
2. *'scritore:* writing desk.
3. *HYDE:* Edward Hyde, Earl of Clarendon. His *History of the Rebellion* was one of Swift's favorite books. (See PW, V.295–320 for Swift's marginalia in his copy. Swift had read the book four times.)
4. *BURNET:* Whig historian. (See PW, V.266–94 for Swift's hostile marginalia in a copy of Burnet's *History of His Own Times.)*
5. *WOOLSTON:* Thomas Woolston; freethinker tried for blasphemy.

Traulus (p. 864)

A violent personal satire on Viscount Joshua Allen, a Whig whose father was made a viscount for services to the Hanoverian monarchy. Allen had opposed an award to Swift by the Corporation of Dublin and had sought to prosecute the printer of Swift's "A Libel on Dr. Delany."

(First Part): Tom might be Tom Mullinix, a mad Tory beggar. Robin may be Robert Leslie, son of Charles Leslie, and like his father, a Jacobite.

1. Legion: Luke 8:30.
2. Atavus: ancestor.
3. *mount a Ladder:* to be hanged on the gallows.

The Lady's Dressing Room (p. 869)

The first of the "excremental" or "scatological" group of poems.

1. *Allum Flower:* allum powder.
2. Tripsy: Celia's lapdog.
3. *Puppy Water:* a cosmetic derived from the innards of a puppy.
4. *Gallypots:* small pots.
5. *Begumm'd:* stained.
6. *frowzy:* ill-smelling, unkempt.
7. Pandora's *Box:* Epimetheus opened a box given to Pandora by Jove from which issued all the evils afflicting the world. Hope alone remained in the box.
8. *"Those Secrets of the hoary deep!":* Milton, *Paradise Lost,* II.890–91.
9. *Queen of Love:* Venus, who rose from the sea.
10. *pocky Quean:* Compare Burton, Pt. 3. Sect. 2. Memb. 5. Sub. 3, pp. 218–19: "*Aretines Lucretia,* a notable queane, confesseth; ... O Antonia *thou seest what I am without, but within God knowes, a puddle of iniquity, a sinke of sin, a pocky queane.* Let him now that so dotes, meditate on this."
11. (ll. 141–44): An ironic allusion to *Paradise Lost,* III.708–13.

A Beautiful Young Nymph Going to Bed (p. 873)

This poem, *Strephon and Chloe,* and *Cassinus and Peter* were first published together in a pamphlet.

1. Drury-Lane: street in Covent Garden, a theater and red-light area.
2. *Toast:* a lady whose health is proposed and drunk to by a company.
3. *Tick:* credit.
4. *Plumpers:* something placed in the mouth to fill out the cheeks.
5. *Shankers:* chancres.
6. *Issues:* discharges or incisions causing a discharge.
7. *White and Red:* cosmetics.
8. Bolus: a medicine of round shape to be swallowed, larger than a pill.
9. Bridewell ... Compter: prisons for vagrants and prostitutes.
10. *Hedge-Tavern:* rough, poor inn.

11. *transported:* Transportation was a punishment for convicted prostitutes.
12. (Swift's note): She seems to be left lonely, ever wending her way. Virgil, *Aeneid,* IV.467–78.
13. *Cully:* dupe.
14. *Duns:* importuning creditors.
15. *Rubs:* hindrances; unpleasant encounters.
16. *Religious Clubs:* Dissenting conventicles or perhaps groups of religious reformers.
17. *Issue-Peas:* globular bodies inserted in a surgical issue to keep it running.
18. Shock: lapdog.

Strephon and Chloe (p. 875)
This satiric marriage poem deploys proverbial and other stock expressions and contains many allusions to and echoes of classical and English poems. Ovid's *Metamorphoses* and Pope's *The Rape of the Lock* are important allusive presences.
  1. *A certain Goddess:* the goddess Thetis, who was married to a mortal, Peleus. Their son was Achilles.

Cassinus and Peter (p. 884)
  1. *Jordan:* chamberpot.
  2. Cerberian: Cerberus was the three-headed watchdog of Hades.
  3. Alecto: one of the Furies.
  4. Charon: the ferryman who conveys the dead across the underworld river Styx to Hades.
  5. Medusa: a Gorgon who had serpents for hair.

To Mr. Gay (p. 887)
  1. (Title): John Gay (1685–1732), poet and playwright. A member of the Scriblerus Club with Swift, Pope, and Arbuthnot. The poem alludes to the parable of the Unjust Steward (Luke 16:1–13). The poem reflects contemporary Opposition politics in its attack on a corrupt Walpolean regime.
  2. *C—t:* court.
  3. Female Friend: Henrietta Howard, Countess of Suffolk, a courtier, and friend to the Scriblerians.
  4. B—: Bob (Robert Walpole).
  5. (ll. 7–12): Gay had been offered the position of gentleman-usher to Princess Louisa, a child.
  6. *princely* Douglas, *and his glorious Dame:* The Duke and Duchess of Queensberry were Gay's patrons.
  7. *Sons of* Phœbus: poets. Compare John Denham, "On Mr Abraham Cowley" (1667, l.10: "*Phoebus,* the Poets God").
  8. (missing word): STATESMAN.
  9. (missing word): *Minister.*

10. (missing words): the King.
11. Palace: Walpole's mansion in Norfolk.
12. unrighteous Mammon: Luke 16:9,11.
13. Peter Waters: Peter Walters, financial adviser to members of the nobility. Identified with Walpole as a corrupt steward.
14. *R—ms:* Realms.
15. Sp—r: Sir Spencer Compton.

Verses on the Death of Dr. Swift, D.S.P.D. Occasioned By reading a Maxim in Rochefoucault. (p. 892)

A famous poem which has generated a large corpus of commentary and the interpretation of the concluding apologia, especially the degree to which it is ironic, has proved controversial. The poem can be seen to have inaugurated an obituary genre in English poetry. For extensive annotation and guide to the critical commentary and to the poem's complex textual history see Rogers, pp. 846–57. The poem is rich in biblical, literary, and proverbial echoes.

1. (Title): *D.S.P.D.:* Dean of St. Patrick's, Dublin. The maxim in the epigraph is from the first edition of la Rochefoucauld's *Réflexions: ou Sentences et Maximes Morales* (1665), no. xcix.
2. (ll. 47–66): Self-regarding coterie compliment to his high-profile friends Alexander Pope, John Gay, John Arbuthnot, Henry St. John, Lord Bolingbroke, and William Pulteney.
3. *without his Shoes:* Walpole wishes Swift had been hanged (to die in one's shoes meant to be hanged).
4. Vole: to win all the tricks in the fashionable card games of quadrille and ombre.
5. (ll. 317–18): John Denham, "On Mr Abraham Cowley" (1667), ll. 29–30: "To him no Author was unknown, / Yet what he wrote was all his own."
6. David's *Lesson:* Psalm 146:3.
7. *Fair LIBERTY ... stood alone:* Compare John Denham, *Cooper's Hill,* ll. 325–26: "Fair liberty pursu'd, and meant a Prey / To lawless power, here turn'd, and stood at bay."
8. *He gave ... Mad:* refers to Swift's bequest for a mental institution to be built in Dublin. St. Patrick's hospital opened in 1757.

An Epistle to a Lady (p. 908)

1. *Lady:* Lady Acheson of Market Hill.
2. *Cocker'd:* brought up indulgently, coddled.
3. Lodanum: laudanum.
4. (missing name): Walpole.
5. (ll. 163–68): Compare White Kennett's contemporary anecdote (published in 1728) about the author of *The Anatomy of Melancholy,* Robert Burton ("Democritus Junior"): "*Yet I have heard that nothing at last could make him laugh,*

but going down to the Bridge-foot in Oxford, *and hearing the Barge-men scold and storm and swear at one another, at which he would set his Hands to his Sides, and laugh most profusely,"* quoted in Nicolas K. Kiessling, *The Legacy of Democritus Junior Robert Burton* (Oxford, 1990), p. 99.

6. *D'ANVERS and his Mate:* the reference is to the Opposition journal, *The Craftsman.*

7. *Ridiculum . . . Sc.:* Jesting often cuts hard knots better and more forcefully than gravity. Horace, *Satires,* I.x.14–15.

8. (missing words): a crown'd Head.

9. (missing name): St. James.

10. (missing name): St. Stephens

11. (missing name): Robert Brass, i.e., Robert Walpole.

On Poetry: A Rapsody (p. 916)

An outspoken satire on the literary and political culture of the Hanoverian regime and on members of the ruling dynasty.

1. (l. 3): Edward Young's *The Universal Passion* (1725–28).

2. *Will's:* The coffeehouse was the resort of writers and wits.

3. (missing word): Parliament.

4. *Kennels:* gutters.

5. (missing words): Excise and South-Sea Schemes.

6. (ll. 249–51): Swift satirizes the critics Thomas Rymer and John Dennis, and John Dryden in *A Tale of a Tub.* René le Bossu was a French critic of epic poetry.

7. *Boileau's Translation:* Leonard Welsted published a translation of Longinus; Swift implies it is a translation of Boileau's French translation of the Greek.

8. Augusta Trinobantum: ancient name for London.

9. (ll. 297–306): Swift conflates ancient and modern poetasters and charts their low London locale. A world in which Gay and Pope will not be found.

10. (missing name): Young.

11. Pericranies: skulls, brains.

12. Hobbes: *Leviathan,* I.13.

13. (ll. 369ff): Swift's satire on the poetasters of Grub Street is reminiscent, of course, of the satire on dunces and dulness in Dryden's *MacFlecknoe* and Pope's *The Dunciad.*

14. (Latin in note): One man alone restored our state by delaying. Cicero, *De Officiis.* I.xxiv.84.

15. Lewis: Louis XIV.

16. (missing name): George.

17. (missing name): George.

18. (missing word): monarch.

19. (missing name): Christ.

20. Caetera desiderantur: The rest is missing.
21. (Latin in note): Caesar divided sovereignty with Jove.

The Yahoo's Overthrow (p. 930)

The target of this violent and rowdy satire is Richard Bettesworth, an Irish MP who physically threatened Swift in revenge for Swift's satiric insults.

1. *B---th:* Bettesworth. *S---l:* scoundrel.
2. *hat … turbant's:* refer to the Cardinal's red hat, the Scots Presbyterian's blue bonnet, and the turban of the Turk or infidel.
3. *Hobbes … Bradley:* high-profile anticlerical, heretical, or sectarian figures.

A Character, Panegyric, and Description of the Legion Club (p. 933)

One of Swift's last major works. The Legion Club is the Irish House of Commons, which was attempting to deprive the clergy of their tithes. The title alludes to Luke 8:30: "And Jesus asked him, saying, What is thy name? And he said, Legion: because many devils were entered into him." For the contemporary Irish politicians referred to in the poem, see the annotation in Poems, III.827–39 and Rogers, pp. 891–95.

1. *Building:* Parliament House.
2. *you know the rest:* "and far from God."
3. *Jackpudding:* buffoon, especially one assisting a mountebank.
4. *T—:* Sir Thomas Prendergast, son of the informer who revealed the Jacobite assassination plot against William III in 1696. William III rewarded Prendergast's father, but Swift's violent invective against him at ll. 68–70 seems to regret the fact that he betrayed the plot.
5. Clio: muse of history.
6. *W—:* John Waller, M.P.
7. *T—:* Roger Throp, a clergyman.
8. *Pair of* Dicks: Richard Tighe and Richard Bettesworth, Whig targets of Swift's satire.
9. old Glorious: William III.
10. Hogart: William Hogarth, artist and engraver.

Selected Correspondence (p. 943)

From Journal to Stella, *[Letter VI, 10–19 October 1710] (p. 945)*

Swift's letters known as the *Journal to Stella* belong to the period between September 1710 and June 1713. They were addressed to Esther Johnson and her older companion Rebecca Dingley and are a vivid record of Swift's literary, political, and social activity in London. Swift was in London, commissioned by the Irish Bishops, to solicit on behalf of the clergy of the Church of Ireland for a remission of the First Fruits and Twentieth Parts, financial imposts on the clergy paid to the crown. This embassy had been thwarted under the Whigs (who wanted the Sacramental Test removed in Ireland as the price for this remission) but achieved success under Queen Anne's new Tory government. Swift began writing for the Tory government led by Robert Harley in 1710. Esther Johnson, "Stella," as Swift would later call her, was Swift's lifelong and intimate friend (see his "On the Death of Mrs. Johnson"), and the letters were principally meant for her.

1. *my memorial:* for the remission of the First Fruits and Twentieth Parts.
2. *governor:* a Lord Lieutenant of Ireland.
3. *archbishop:* Archbishop William King.
4. *ombre:* fashionable card game.
5. *MD:* My Dear or My Dears.
6. *Patrick:* Swift's servant.
7. *smoak:* detect.
8. *Dr. Garth:* Samuel Garth (1661–1719), poet and physician, author of the mock-epic satire *The Dispensary* (1699).
9. *Mr. Addison:* Joseph Addison (1672–1719), Whig politician and author, contributed to *The Tatler* and co-edited *The Spectator* with Richard Steele, wrote *The Freeholder* (1715–16). His tragedy *Cato* (1713) was a popular success.
10. *Doctors Commons:* the College of Advocates near St. Paul's, members pleaded in the ecclesiastical courts.
11. *Presto:* Swift's nickname in the correspondence.
12. *Harrison:* William Harrison (1685–1713), a minor author whom Swift befriended and sought to help.
13. *Henley:* Anthony Henley, Whig MP and wit.
14. *till I turn over:* i.e., to the next page.
15. *a fair way of recovery; poor lady:* Charles, second Earl of Berkeley had died on September 24.
16. *slidikins:* like "Stellakins" a few lines further on, an example of Swift's "little language" used in the correspondence.
17. *My lampoon:* Swift's satiric poem on the former Lord Treasurer, Sidney Godolphin, *The Virtues of Sid Hamet the Magician's Rod*.
18. Tatler *about shortening of words:* The Tatler, no. 230 (28 September 1710).
19. *Mr. Prior:* Matthew Prior (1664–1721), poet and diplomat.
20. *lord Peterborow:* Charles Mordaunt, third Earl of Peterborough (1658–1735), General and mercurial personality, became a friend of Swift, Pope, Gay, and Arbuthnot.
21. *bobbed me:* urged attention by nudging and nodding or bowing.
22. *Smyrna:* a coffeehouse in Pall Mall.
23. *chair:* sedan chair, a form of transport.
24. *my* Miscellany: *Miscellanies in Prose and Verse,* published in 1711.

From **Journal to Stella** *[extract from Letter XXXII, 9–11 October 1711] (p. 950)*

1. *Biddy Floyd:* Swift addressed a poem to her; see Poems, I.117–18, "To Mrs. Biddy Floyd" (1709).
2. *Tantivy:* nickname for High Church Tories.
3. *lord treasurer:* Robert Harley, Earl of Oxford.
4. *George Granville:* George Granville (1667–1735), Baron Lansdowne (1711), poet, dramatist, Tory politician, and Jacobite.
5. Martin: alluding also surely to the Anglican brother in *A Tale of a Tub.*

Swift to Alexander Pope [29 September 1725] (p. 951)

1. *Dominions where I govern:* the Liberties surrounding St. Patrick's Cathedral.
2. *venture his Eares:* Loss of ears was a punishment for sedition. Cf. The hack author's "History of Ears" in *A Tale of a Tub.*
3. *without reading:* without troubling to read.
4. rationis capax: capable of reason.
5. *Timons manner:* Timon the misanthrope, an Athenian of the fifth century BCE. The reclusive Gulliver in his garden at Redriff is a misanthrope in Timon's manner.
6. *Odyssey:* Pope's *The Odyssey of Homer.*
7. *The Lady ... at Court:* The reference is to Mrs. Howard, a courtier.
8. *if the World had but a dozen Arbuthnets:* Swift's friend the physician, Tory satirist, and member of the Scriblerus Club John Arbuthnot. The line recalls Genesis 18:32 where God will spare Sodom if ten righteous men can be found.
9. *Bede:* The Venerable Bede was much preoccupied with this question. But see Bede, *Historiae Ecclesiasticae,* Liber III, Cap. III.

Swift to Alexander Pope [26 November 1725] (p. 953)

1. *Drown the World:* recalling the Flood that destroys the world in Genesis 6:17; 7:4.
2. *f—ty eighth year of my Life:* Swift was fifty-eight, as Captain Gulliver is said to be on the frontispiece to the first edition of *Gulliver's Travels* in 1726.
3. *vous autres:* you others.
4. *angry with——:* Probably Walpole is meant.
5. *Rochfoucault:* See *Verses on the Death of Dr Swift,* ll. 1–2.

Swift to Charles Wogan [July–2 August 1732] (p. 953)

Charles Wogan (1684–1754), a Roman Catholic, Jacobite soldier, and exile. Descended from an old, well-known Irish family, Wogan was an officer in Dillon's regiment in the French service. He took part in the Jacobite Rising of 1715, was captured and charged with high treason, but escaped to France. He was instrumental in finding a wife for "James III" (the "Old Pretender"). In 1719, he rescued James's bride, Maria Clementina Sobieska, from a castle at Innsbruck where she was held by the Austrians. He went into the Spanish service and was closely associated with the Duke of Ormonde, the leader of the Irish Jacobites in the service of Spain. Wogan was a colonel in the Spanish army and held the Jacobite rank of brigadier. His regiment took part in the capture of Oran in 1732. Sending wine to Swift from the Continent, Wogan wrote that he could offer nothing else "but some heads of the Saracens of Oran, which I shall be ordered to cut off, because they will not become Christians" (Corr, IV.114). He eventually became governor of La Mancha. He was active in the Jacobite rebellion of 1745, leading Irish officers from Spain to France, but was unable to cross to Scotland to join the uprising. Wogan and Swift were united in outrage at the condition of their native country.

1. *Packet:* It included a narrative of his exploits, a paraphrase of the Psalms in Miltonic verse, poems, and literary criticism.
2. *esteem those Gentlemen of* Ireland: the Irish Jacobite diaspora.
3. modo ... Athenis: now he places me in Rome, now in Athens.

Swift to William Pulteney [12 May 1735] (p. 957)

1. Pulteney: William Pulteney (1684–1764), Opposition Whig statesman and orator.
2. Stopford: Tory churchman and Provost of Tuam (1730) esteemed by Swift.
3. *a chief minister:* Robert Walpole.
4. *a private hand:* A high-profile Tory writer, Swift's correspondence was opened by the Whig postal authorities during the Hanoverian period.
5. *was not sorry to find it there:* "On Mr. P——y being put out of the Council," in Poems, II.537.

FURTHER READING

BIBLIOGRAPHICAL AIDS

Landa, Louis A., and Tobin, James Edward. *Jonathan Swift: A List of Critical Studies Published from 1895 to 1945.* 1945. Reprint, New York: Octagon Books, 1975.

Rodino, Richard H. *Swift Studies, 1965–1980: An Annotated Bibliography.* New York: Garland, 1984.

Stathis, James J. *A Bibliography of Swift Studies 1945–1965.* Nashville, Tenn.: Vanderbilt University Press, 1967.

Teerink, H., and Scouten, Arthur H. *A Bibliography of the Writings of Jonathan Swift.* 2d ed. Philadelphia: University of Pennsylvania Press, 1963.

Vieth, David M. *Swift's Poetry 1900–1980: An Annotated Bibliography of Studies.* New York: Garland, 1982.

Williams, Harold. *Dean Swift's Library.* Cambridge: Cambridge University Press, 1932.

MODERN EDITIONS

Correspondence. Edited by Harold Williams. 5 vols. Oxford: Clarendon Press, 1963–65.

Poems. Edited by Harold Williams. 2d ed. 3 vols. Oxford: Clarendon Press, 1958.

Complete Poems. Edited by Pat Rogers. Harmondsworth, England: Penguin; New Haven, Conn.: Yale University Press, 1983.

Prose Works. Edited by Herbert Davis et al. 16 vols. Oxford: Blackwell, 1939–74. Vol. 14, index by Irvin Ehrenpreis et al.; vols. 15–16, *Journal to Stella,* ed. Harold Williams.

INDIVIDUAL WORKS

Directions to Servants. Edited by Claude Rawson. London: Penguin, 1995.

A Discourse of the Contests and Dissentions Between the Nobles and the Commons in Athens and Rome. Edited by Frank H. Ellis. Oxford: Clarendon Press, 1967.

The Drapier's Letters. Edited by Herbert Davis. Oxford: Clarendon Press, 1935.

Gulliver's Travels. Edited by Paul Turner. Oxford and New York: Oxford University Press, 1986 [1998].

The Intelligencer. Edited by James Woolley. Oxford: Clarendon Press, 1992.

Journal to Stella. Edited by Harold Williams. 2 vols. Oxford: Clarendon Press. Reprinted as vols. 15 and 16 of *Prose Works.*

Memoirs of Martinus Scriblerus (with Pope et al.). Edited by Charles Kerby-Miller. New Haven, Conn.: Yale University Press, 1950.

Swift vs. Mainwaring: The Examiner and the Medley. Edited by Frank H. Ellis. Oxford: Clarendon Press, 1985.

A Tale of a Tub. Edited by A. C. Guthkelch and D. Nichol Smith. 2d ed. Oxford: Clarendon Press, 1958.

BIOGRAPHY AND CRITICISM

General

Douglas, Aileen; Kelly, Patrick; and Ross, Ian C., eds. *Locating Swift: Essays from Dublin on the 250th Anniversary of the Death of Jonathan Swift, 1669–1745.* Dublin: Four Courts Press, 1998.

Ehrenpreis, Irvin. *The Personality of Jonathan Swift.* London: Methuen, 1958.

————. *Swift: The Man, His Works, and the Age.* Vol. 1, *Mr. Swift and His Contemporaries.* London: Methuen, 1962. Vol. 2, *Dr. Swift.* London: Methuen, 1967. Vol. 3, *Dean Swift.* London: Methuen, 1983.

Elliott, Robert C. *The Power of Satire.* Princeton, N.J.: Princeton University Press, 1960.

————. *The Literary Persona.* Chicago: University of Chicago Press, 1982.

Fabricant, Carole. *Swift's Landscape.* Baltimore: Johns Hopkins University Press, 1982; Notre Dame: University of Notre Dame Press, 1995.

Johnson, Samuel. "Swift." In *Lives of the English Poets.*

Leavis, F. R. "The Irony of Swift." In *The Common Pursuit.* London: Chatto, 1952; Harmondsworth, England: Penguin, 1962.

Levine, Joseph M. *Dr. Woodward's Shield: History, Science, and Satire in Augustan England.* Berkeley: University of California Press, 1977.

Orrery, John Boyle, Earl of. *Remarks on the Life & Writings of Dr. Jonathan Swift* (*1751*), ed. João Fróes. Newark, Del.: University of Delaware Press, 2000.

Price, Martin. *Swift's Rhetorical Art.* New Haven: Yale University Press, 1953; Carbondale: Southern Illinois University Press Arcturus paperback, 1973.

————. *To the Palace of Wisdom: Studies in Order and Energy from Dryden to Blake.* Garden City, N.Y.: Doubleday, 1964.

Quintana, Ricardo. *The Mind and Art of Jonathan Swift.* 1936. Reprint, Gloucester, Mass.: Peter Smith, 1965.

———. *Swift: An Introduction.* London: Oxford University Press, 1955.

———. *Two Augustans: John Locke, Jonathan Swift.* Madison: University of Wisconsin Press, 1978.

Rawson, Claude. *Gulliver and the Gentle Reader: Studies in Swift and Our Time.* London: Routledge, 1973; paperback, New Jersey: Humanities Press, 1991.

———. *Order from Confusion Sprung: Studies in Eighteenth-Century Literature from Swift to Cowper.* London: Allen and Unwin, 1985; paperback, New Jersey: Humanities Press, 1992.

———. *Satire and Sentiment 1660–1830.* Cambridge: Cambridge University Press, 1994; paperback, New Haven: Yale University Press, 2000.

———. *God, Gulliver and Genocide: Barbarism and the European Imagination, 1492–1945.* Oxford: Oxford University Press, 2001.

Rawson, Claude, ed. *The Character of Swift's Satire: A Revised Focus.* Newark, Del.: University of Delaware Press, 1983.

———. *English Satire and the Satiric Tradition.* Oxford: Blackwell, 1984.

———. *Jonathan Swift: A Collection of Critical Essays.* Englewood Cliffs, N.J.: Prentice Hall, 1994.

Rogers, Pat. *Grub Street: Studies in a Subculture.* London: Methuen, 1972. Abridged as *Hacks and Dunces: Pope, Swift, and Grub Street.* London: Methuen, 1980.

Rosenheim, Edward W. *Swift and the Satirist's Art.* Chicago: University of Chicago Press, 1963.

Schakel, Peter J., ed. *Critical Approaches to Teaching Swift.* New York: AMS Press, 1992.

Williams, Kathleen, ed. *Swift: The Critical Heritage.* London: Routledge, 1970.

A Tale of a Tub

Harth, Phillip. *Swift and Anglican Rationalism: The Religious Background of* A Tale of a Tub. Chicago: University of Chicago Press, 1961.

Levine, Joseph M. *The Battle of the Books: History and Literature in the Augustan Age.* Ithaca, N.Y.: Cornell University Press, 1991.

Paulson, Ronald. *Theme and Structure in Swift's* Tale of a Tub. New Haven: Yale University Press, 1960.

Starkman, Miriam K. *Swift's Satire on Learning in* A Tale of a Tub. Princeton, N.J.: Princeton University Press, 1950. Reprint, New York: Octagon Books, 1968.

Political and Ecclesiastical Writings

Beckett, J. C. *Confrontations: Studies in Irish History.* London: Faber and Faber, 1972.

Cook, Richard I. *Jonathan Swift as a Tory Pamphleteer.* Seattle: University of Washington Press, 1967.

Downie, J. A. *Jonathan Swift: Political Writer.* London: Routledge, 1984.

Ferguson, Oliver W. *Jonathan Swift and Ireland.* Urbana: University of Illinois Press, 1962.

Goldgar, Bertrand A. *The Curse of Party: Swift's Relations with Addison and Steele.* Lincoln: University of Nebraska Press, 1961.

———. *Walpole and the Wits: The Relation of Politics to Literature, 1722–1742.* Lincoln: University of Nebraska Press, 1976.

Higgins, Ian. *Swift's Politics: A Study in Disaffection.* Cambridge: Cambridge University Press, 1994.

Landa, Louis A. *Essays in Eighteenth-Century Literature.* Princeton, N.J.: Princeton University Press, 1980.

———. *Swift and the Church of Ireland.* Oxford: Clarendon Press, 1954.

Lock, F. P. *Swift's Tory Politics.* London: Duckworth, and Newark, Del.: University of Delaware Press, 1983.

Mahony, Robert. *Jonathan Swift: The Irish Identity.* New Haven: Yale University Press, 1995.

Molyneux, William. *The Case of Ireland Stated* (1698). Introduction and afterword by J. G. Simms and Denis Donoghue. Dublin: Cadenus Press, 1977.

Poems

Barnett, Louise K. *Swift's Poetic Worlds.* Newark, Del.: University of Delaware Press, 1982.

England, A. B. *Energy and Order in the Poetry of Swift.* Lewisburg, Penn.: Bucknell University Press, 1980.

Jaffe, Nora Crow. *The Poet Swift.* Hanover, N.H.: University Press of New England, 1977.

Johnson, Maurice. *The Sin of Wit: Jonathan Swift as a Poet.* Syracuse, N.Y.: Syracuse University Press, 1950.

Schakel, Peter J. *The Poetry of Jonathan Swift.* Madison: University of Wisconsin Press, 1978.

Vieth, David M., ed. *Essential Articles for the Study of Swift's Poetry.* Hamden, Conn.: Archon, 1984.

Woolley, James D. *Swift's Later Poems: Studies in Circumstances and Texts.* New York: Garland, 1988.

Gulliver's Travels

Brady, Frank, ed. *Twentieth-Century Interpretations of* Gulliver's Travels. Englewood Cliffs, N.J.: Prentice Hall, 1968.

Case, Arthur E. *Four Essays on* Gulliver's Travels. Princeton, N.J.: Princeton University Press, 1945.

Crane, R. S. "The Houyhnhnms, the Yahoos, and the History of Ideas." In *Reason and the Imagination,* ed. by J. A. Mazzeo. New York: Columbia University Press, 1962. Reprinted in Crane's *The Idea of the Humanities and Other Essays,* 2 vols. Chicago: University of Chicago Press, 1967.

Eddy, W. A. *Gulliver's Travels: A Critical Study.* Princeton, N.J.: Princeton University Press, 1923.

Elliott, Robert C. *The Power of Satire: Magic, Ritual, Art.* Princeton, N.J.: Princeton University Press, 1960.

———. *The Shape of Utopia.* Chicago: University of Chicago Press, 1970.

Foster, Milton P., ed. *A Casebook on Gulliver among the Houyhnhnms.* New York: Crowell, 1961.

Gravil, Richard, ed. Gulliver's Travels: *A Casebook.* London: Macmillan, 1974.

Mezciems, Jenny. "'Tis not to divert the Reader: Moral and Literary Determinants in Some Early Travel Narratives." *Prose Studies* 5 (1982): 1–19. Also in *The Art of Travel: Essays on Travel Writing,* edited by Philip Dodd. London: Frank Cass, 1982.

———. "The Unity of Swift's Voyage to Laputa: Structure as Meaning in Utopian Fiction." *Modern Language Review* 72 (1977): 1–21.

———. "Utopia and 'the Thing which is not' ": More, Swift, and other Lying Idealists." *University of Toronto Quarterly* 52 (1982): 40–62.

Orwell, George. "Politics vs. Literature: An Examination of *Gulliver's Travels*" (1946). In *Collected Essays, Journalism, and Letters of George Orwell,* edited by Sonia Orwell and Ian Angus, vol. 4. London: Secker and Warburg, 1968.

INDEX OF SHORT TITLES

Italics indicate a poem.

Accomplishment of the First of Mr. Bickerstaff's Predictions	675
Advancement of Religion	201
Argument Against Abolishing Christianity	187
Author upon Himself	806
Battle of the Books	115
Baucis and Philemon	774
Beautiful Young Nymph Going to Bed	873
[Bickerstaff Papers]	665
Cadenus and Vanessa	782
Cassinus and Peter, a Tragical Elegy	884
Causes of the Wretched Condition of Ireland	307
Character, Panegyric and Description of the Legion Club	933
Clever Tom Clinch going to be hanged	851
Compleat Collection of genteel and Ingenious Conversation	687
Description of a City Shower	780
Description of the Morning	779
Dialogue between an eminent Lawyer and Dr. Swift Dean of St. Patrick's	862
Directions for a Birth-day Song	855
Directions to Servants	717
[Drapier's Letters]	318

Examiner, 23 November 1710   223

Family of Swift   635
Famous Prediction of Merlin, the British Wizard   683

Gulliver's Travels   365

Holyhead. September 25, 1727   852
Humble Petition of Frances Harris   772

Importance of the Guardian Considered   237
Irel.ᵈ   855

[*Journal to Stella*] VI, 10 October 1710   945
[*Journal to Stella*] XXXII 9 October 1711   950

Lady's Dressing Room   869
Last Speech and Dying Words of Ebenezor Elliston   711
Letter from Swift to Alexander Pope, 29 September 1725   951
Letter from Swift to Alexander Pope, 26 November 1725   953
Letter from Swift to Charles Wogan, July–2 August 1732   953
Letter from Swift to William Pulteney, 12 May 1735   957
Letter to the Shop-keepers, Tradesmen, Farmers, and
    -Common-People   318
Letter to the Whole People of Ireland   338
Letter to a Young Lady, on her Marriage   279

Mary the Cook-Maid's Letter   808
Mechanical Operation of the Spirit   141
Meditation upon a Broom-Stick   661
Modest Proposal   345
Mr. C——ns's Discourse of Free-Thinking   259

Of Mean and Great Figures   631
On Poetry: A Rapsody   916
On the Death of Mrs. Johnson   643
On Wood the Iron-monger   846

Phillis, or The Progress of Love   810
Progress of Beauty   813

INDEX OF FIRST LINES

Ætatis suæ fifty two   830
After venting all my Spight   908
All Human Race wou'd fain be *Wits*   916
All Travellers at first incline   827
As clever *Tom Clinch*, while the Rabble was bawling   851
As I strole the City, oft I   933
As *Rochefoucault* his Maxims drew   892
As when a beauteous Nymph decays   844
As when a lofty Pile is rais'd   822

By an ___ ___ ___ pursu'd   806

Careful Observers may fortel the Hour   780
Come buy my fine Wares   940
Corrina, Pride of *Drury-Lane*   873

Desponding Phillis was endu'd   810
Don *Carlos* in a merry Spight   838

Five Hours, (and who can do it less in?)   869

His Grace! impossible! what dead!   829
How could you, *Gay*, disgrace the Muses Train   887

In antient Times, as Story tells   774

Jolly boys of St. Kevans, St. Patrick's, Donore   930

Lo here I sit at holy head   852

Now hardly here and there an Hackney-Coach   779
Nymph, would you learn the onely Art   826

Of *Chloe* all the Town has rung   875

Pallas observing *Stella*'s Wit   818
Peruse my Leaves thro' ev'ry Part   771

Remove me from this land of slaves   853
Resolv'd my annual Verse to pay   835

Salmoneus, as the *Grecian* Tale is   846
Say, *Robin,* what can *Traulus* mean   864
Since there are persons who complain   862
Stella this Day is thirty four   809
Strephon, who found the Room was void   869

That I went to warm my self in Lady *Betty*'s Chamber,
    because I was cold   772
The Farmer's Goose, who in the Stubble   817
The *Scottish* Hinds too poor to house   847
The *Shepherds* and the *Nymphs* were seen   782
This Day, whate'er the Fates decree   848
To form a just and finish'd piece   855
Tormented with incessant pains   841
Two College Sophs of *Cambridge* Growth   884

Well; if ever I saw such another Man since my Mother
    bound my Head   808
When first Diana leaves her Bed   813
When first the 'Squire, and *Tinker Wood*   842
While, Stella to your lasting Praise   829